CLASSICAL AND MEDIEVAL LITERATURE CRITICISM

Guide to Gale Literary Criticism Series

For criticism on	Consult these Gale series
Authors now living or who died after December 31, 1959	*CONTEMPORARY LITERARY CRITICISM (CLC)*
Authors who died between 1900 and 1959	*TWENTIETH-CENTURY LITERARY CRITICISM (TCLC)*
Authors who died between 1800 and 1899	*NINETEENTH-CENTURY LITERATURE CRITICISM (NCLC)*
Authors who died between 1400 and 1799	*LITERATURE CRITICISM FROM 1400 TO 1800 (LC)* *SHAKESPEAREAN CRITICISM (SC)*
Authors who died before 1400	*CLASSICAL AND MEDIEVAL LITERATURE CRITICISM (CMLC)*
Authors of books for children and young adults	*CHILDREN'S LITERATURE REVIEW (CLR)*
Dramatists	*DRAMA CRITICISM (DC)*
Poets	*POETRY CRITICISM (PC)*
Short story writers	*SHORT STORY CRITICISM (SSC)*
Black writers of the past two hundred years	*BLACK LITERATURE CRITICISM (BLC)*
Hispanic writers of the late nineteenth and twentieth centuries	*HISPANIC LITERATURE CRITICISM (HLC)*
Native North American writers and orators of the eighteenth, nineteenth, and twentieth centuries	*NATIVE NORTH AMERICAN LITERATURE (NNAL)*
Major authors from the Renaissance to the present	*WORLD LITERATURE CRITICISM, 1500 TO THE PRESENT (WLC)*

ISSN 0896-0011

Volume 35

CLASSICAL AND MEDIEVAL LITERATURE CRITICISM

Excerpts from Criticism of the Works of World
Authors from Classical Antiquity through the
Fourteenth Century, from the First Appraisals
to Current Evaluations

Jelena O. Krstović
Editor

GALE GROUP

Detroit
San Francisco
London
Boston
Woodbridge, CT

STAFF

Jelena Krstović, *Editor*
Elisabeth Gellert, *Associate Editor*
Lynn Spampinato, *Managing Editor*

Maria Franklin, *Permissions Manager*
Kimberly F. Smilay, *Permissions Specialist*
Kelly A. Quin, *Permissions Associate*
Erin Bealmear, Sandy Gore, *Permissions Assistants*

Victoria B. Cariappa, *Research Manager*
Patricia T. Ballard, Wendy Festerling, Tracie A. Richardson, Corrine Stocker, *Research Associates*
Phyllis Blackman, *Research Assistant*

Dorothy Maki, *Manufacturing Manager*
Stacy Melson, *Buyer*

Pamela A. Reed, *Imaging Coordinator*
Randy Bassett, *Image Database Supervisor*
Robert Duncan, Michael Logusz, *Imaging Specialists*
Christine O'Bryan, *Graphic Specialist*

This book is printed on acid-free paper that meets the minimum requirements of American National Standard for Information Sciences—Permanence Paper for Printed Library materials, ANSI Z39.48-1984.

Library of Congress Catalog Card Number 88-658021
ISBN 0-7876-3257-0
ISSN 0896-0011
Printed in the United States of America

10 9 8 7 6 5 4 3 2 1

Contents

Preface vii

Acknowledgments xi

Basil of Caesarea 1
Greek patriarch and theologian

Bevis of Hampton 139
Medieval romance

Hypatia 204
Greek mathematician and philosopher

Martial 246
Roman poet

Literary Criticism Series Cumulative Author Index 421

Literary Criticism Series Cumulative Topic Index 495

CMLC Cumulative Nationality Index 505

CMLC Cumulative Title Index 507

CMLC Cumulative Critic Index 535

Preface

Since its inception in 1988, *Classical and Medieval Literature Criticism* has been a valuable resource for students and librarians seeking critical commentary on the writers and works of these periods in world history. Major reviewing sources have assessed *CMLC* as "useful" and "extremely convenient," noting that it "adds to our understanding of the rich legacy left by the ancient period and the Middle Ages," and praising its "general excellence in the presentation of an inherently interesting subject." No other single reference source has surveyed the critical reaction to classical and medieval literature as thoroughly as *CMLC*.

Scope of the Series

CMLC is designed to serve as an introduction for students and advanced readers of the works and authors of antiquity through the fourteenth century. The great poets, prose writers, dramatists, and philosophers of this period form the basis of most humanities curricula, so that virtually every student will encounter many of these works during the course of a high school and college education. By organizing and reprinting an enormous amount of commentary written on classical and medieval authors and works, *CMLC* helps students develop valuable insight into literary history, promotes a better understanding of the texts, and sparks ideas for papers and assignments. Each entry in *CMLC* presents a comprehensive survey of an author's career, an individual work of literature, or a literary topic, and provides the user with a multiplicity of interpretations and assessments. Such variety allows students to pursue their own interests; furthermore, it fosters an awareness that literature is dynamic and responsive to many different opinions.

CMLC continues the survey of criticism of world literature begun by Gale's *Contemporary Literary Criticism (CLC)*, *Twentieth-Century Literary Criticism (TCLC)*, *Nineteenth-Century Literature Criticism (NCLC)*, *Literature Criticism from 1400 to 1800 (LC)*, and *Shakespearean Criticism (SC)*. For additional information about these and Gale's other criticism series, users should consult the Guide to Gale Literary Criticism Series preceding the title page in this volume.

Coverage

Each volume of *CMLC* is carefully compiled to present:

- criticism of authors, works, and topics which represent a variety of genres, time periods, and nationalities

- both major and lesser-known writers and works of the period (such as non-Western authors and literature, increasingly read by today's students)

- 4-6 authors, works, or topics per volume

- individual entries that survey the critical response to each author, work, or topic, including early criticism, later criticism (to represent any rise or decline in reputation), and current retrospective analyses. The length of each author, work, or topic entry also indicates relative importance, reflecting the amount of critical attention the author, work, or topic has received from critics writing in English, and from foreign criticism in translation.

An author may appear more than once in the series if his or her writings have been the subject of a substantial amount of criticism; in these instances, specific works or groups of works by the author will be covered in separate entries. For example, Homer will be represented by three entries, one devoted to the *Iliad,* one to the *Odyssey,* and one to the Homeric Hymns.

Starting with Volume 10, *CMLC* will also occasionally include entries devoted to literary topics. For example, *CMLC*-10 focuses on Arthurian Legend and includes general criticism on that subject as well as individual entries on writers or works central to that topic—Chrétien de Troyes, Gottfried von Strassburg, Layamon, and the Alliterative *Morte Arthure*. Presocratic Philosophy is the focus of *CMLC*-22, which includes general criticism as well as essays on Greek philosophers Anaximander, Heraclitus, Parmenides, and Pythagoras.

Organization of the Book

An author entry consists of the following elements: author heading, biographical and critical introduction, principal works, principal English translations or editions, excerpts of criticism (each preceded by a bibliographic citation and an annotation), and a bibliography of further reading.

• The **Author Heading** consists of the author's most commonly used name, followed by birth and death dates. If the entry is devoted to a work, the heading will consist of the most common form of the title in English translation (if applicable), and the original date of composition. Located at the beginning of the introduction are any name or title variations.

• A **Portrait** of the author is included when available. Many entries also feature illustrations of materials pertinent to the author or work, including manuscript pages, book illustrations, and representations of people, places, and events important to a study of the author or work.

• The **Biographical and Critical Introduction** contains background information that concisely introduces the reader to the author, work, or topic.

• The list of **Principal Works** and **English Translations** or **Editions** is chronological by date of first publication and is included as an aid to the student seeking translated versions or editions of these works for study. The list will focus primarily on twentieth-century translations, selecting those works most commonly considered the best by critics.

• **Criticism** is arranged chronologically in each entry to provide a useful perspective on changes in critical evaluation over the years. All titles by the author featured in the critical entry are printed in boldface type to enable the user to ascertain without difficulty the works being discussed. Also for purposes of easier identification, the critic's name and the publication date of the essay are given at the beginning of each piece of criticism. Anonymous criticism is preceded by the title of the journal in which it appeared. Publication information (such as publisher names and book prices) and parenthetical numerical references (such as footnotes or page and line references to specific editions of works) have been deleted at the editors' discretion to provide smoother reading of the text. Many critical entries in *CMLC* also contain translations to aid the users. Footnotes that appear with previously published pieces of criticism are reprinted at the end of each essay or excerpt. In the case of excerpted criticism, only those footnotes that pertain to the excerpted text are included.

• A complete **Bibliographic Citation** provides original publication information for each piece of criticism.

• Critical excerpts are also prefaced by **Annotations** providing the reader with information about both the critic and the criticism, the scope of the excerpt, the growth of critical controversy, or changes in critical trends regarding an author or work. In some cases, these notes include cross-references to excerpts by critics who discuss each other's commentary. Dates in parentheses within the annotation refer to a book publication date when they follow a book title, and to an essay date when they follow a critic's name.

• An annotated bibliography of **Further Reading** appears at the end of each entry and lists additional secondary sources on the author or work. In some cases it includes essays for which the editors could not obtain reprint rights. When applicable, the Further Reading is followed by references to additional entries on the author in other literary reference series published by Gale.

Topic Entries are subdivided into several thematic rubrics in which criticism appears in order of descending scope.

Cumulative Indexes

Each volume of *CMLC* includes a cumulative **author index** listing all authors who have appeared in Gale's Literary Criticism Series, along with cross references to such biographical series as *Contemporary Authors* and *Dictionary of Literary Biography*. For readers' convenience, a complete list of Gale titles included appears on the page prior to the author index. Useful for locating an author within the various series, this index is particularly valuable for those authors who are identified with a certain period but who, because of their death date, are placed in another, or for those authors whose careers span two periods. For example, Geoffrey Chaucer, who is usually considered a medieval author, is found in *Literature Criticism from 1400 to 1800* because he died after 1399.

Beginning with the tenth volume, *CMLC* includes a cumulative index listing all topic entries that have appeared in the Gale Literary Criticism Series *Classical and Medieval Literature Criticism, Contemporary Literary Criticism, Literature Criticism from 1400 to 1800, Nineteenth-Century Literature Criticism,* and *Twentieth-Century Literary Criticism.*

Beginning with the second volume, *CMLC* also includes a cumulative nationality index. Authors and/or works are grouped by nationality, and the volume in which criticism on them may be found is indicated.

Title Index

Each volume of *CMLC* also includes an index listing the titles of all literary works discussed in the series. Foreign language titles that have been translated are followed by the titles of the translations—for example, *Slovo o polku Igorove (The Song of Igor's Campaign).* Page numbers following these translated titles refer to all pages on which any form of the title, either foreign language or translated, appears. Titles of novels, dramas, nonfiction books, and poetry, short story, or essay collections are printed in italics, while those of all individual poems, short stories, and essays are printed in roman type within quotation marks. In cases where the same title is used by different authors, the author's name or surname is given in parentheses after the title, e.g. *Collected Poems* (Horace) and *Collected Poems* (Sappho).

Critic Index

An index to critics, which cumulates with the second volume, is another useful feature of *CMLC.* Under each critic's name are listed the authors and/or works on whom the critic has written and the volume and page number where criticism may be found.

A Note to the Reader

When writing papers, students who quote directly from any volume in the Literary Criticism Series may use the following general forms to footnote reprinted criticism. The first example pertains to material drawn from a periodical, the second to material reprinted from books.

Rollo May, "The Therapist and the Journey into Hell," *Michigan Quarterly Review,* XXV, No. 4 (Fall 1986), 629-41; excerpted and reprinted in *Classical and Medieval Literature Criticism,* Vol. 3, ed. Jelena O. Krstovic (Detroit: Gale Research, 1989), pp. 154-58.

Dana Ferrin Sutton, *Self and Society in Aristophanes* (University of Press of America, 1980); excerpted and reprinted in *Classical and Medieval Literature Criticism,* Vol. 4, ed. Jelena O. Krstovic (Detroit: Gale Research, 1990), pp. 162-69.

Suggestions Are Welcome

Readers who wish to make suggestions for future volumes, or who have other comments regarding the series, are cordially invited to write or call the editors (1-800-347-GALE; Fax: (248) 699-8049).

Acknowledgments

The editors wish to thank the copyright holders of the excerpted criticism included in this volume and the permissions managers of many book and magazine publishing companies for assisting us in securing reproduction rights. We are also grateful to the staffs of the Detroit Public Library, the Library of Congress, the University of Detroit Mercy Library, Wayne State University Purdy/Kresge Library Complex, and the University of Michigan Libraries for making their resources available to us. Following is a list of the copyright holders who have granted us permission to reproduce material in this volume of **CMLC 35**. Every effort has been made to trace copyright, but if omissions have been made, please let us know.

COPYRIGHTED MATERIAL IN *CMLC*, VOLUME 35, WERE REPRODUCED FROM THE FOLLOWING PERIODICALS:

Arethusa, v. 18, Fall, 1985. (c) 1985 by Arethusa. Reproduced by permission of The Johns Hopkins University Press.–*The Classical Bulletin,* v. 48, December, 1971. Copyright (c) 1971 *The Classical Bulletin.* All rights reserved. Reproduced by permission of Ares Publishers, Inc., conveyed through Copyright Clearance Center, Inc. conveyed through Copyright Clearance Center, Inc.–*The Classical Journal,*. v. 65, May, 1970; v. 83, Dec/Jan, 1988. Both reproduced by permission.–*Hypatia,* v. 4, Spring, 1989. Reproduced by permission *Phoenix,* v. XIX, Autumn, 1965. Reproduced by permission.–*Ramus,* v. 22, 1993. Reproduced by permission.

COPYRIGHTED MATERIAL IN *CMLC*, VOLUME 35, WERE REPRODUCED FROM THE FOLLOWING BOOKS:

Alic, Margaret. From *Hypatia's Heritage*. The Women's Press, 1986. Copyright (c) Margaret Alic 1986. Reproduced by permission.–Anderson, William S. From *Essays on Roman Satire*. Princeton University Press, 1982. Copyright (c) 1982 by Princeton University Press. Reproduced by permission.–Barnes, Geraldine. From *Counsel And Strategy In Middle English Romance*. D.S. Brewer, 1993. (c) Geraldine Barnes 1993. Reproduced by permission.–Crane, Susan. From *Insular Romance*. University of California, 1986. (c) 1986 by The Regents of the University of California. Reproduced by permission of the publisher and the author.–Dzielska, Maria. From *Hypatia of Alexandria*. Harvard University Press, 1995. Copyright (c) 1995 by the President and Fellows of Harvard College. All rights reserved. Reproduced by permission of Harvard University Press.–Fedwick, Paul Jonathan. From *The Church And The Charisma Of Leadership In Basil Of Caesarea*. Pontifical Institute of Mediaeval Studies, 1979. (c) 1979 Pontifical Institute of Mediaeval Studies. Reproduced by permission.–Kay, N.M. From the introduction to *Martial Book XI*. (c) 1985 by N.M. Kay. All rights reserved. Reproduced by permission of Gerald Duckworth and Co. Ltd.–Lessing, Gotthold Ephraim. From *The Classical Heritage*. Edited by J.P. Sullivan. Garland Publishing, Inc., 1993. (c) 1993 J.P. Sullivan. All rights reserved. Reproduced by permission.–Mehl, Dieter. From *The Middle English Romances of the Thirteenth and Fourteenth Centuries*. Routledge & Kegan Paul, 1968. (c) Dieter Mehl 1968. Reproduced by permission.–Osborn, Eric. From *Ethical Patterns in Early Christian Thought*. Cambridge University Press, 1976. (c) Cambridge University Press 1976. Reproduced by permission of Cambridge University Press and the author.–Osen, Lynn M. From *Women in Mathematics*. The MIT Press, 1974. Copyright (c) 1974 by The Massachusetts Institute of Technology. All rights reserved. Reproduced by permission of The MIT Press, Cambridge, M.–Rousseau, Philip. From *Basil of Caesarea*. University of California Press, 1994. (c) 1994 by The Regents of the University of California. Reproduced by permission of the publisher and the author.–Sheldon-Williams, I.P. From *The Cambridge History of Later Greek and Early Medieval Philosophy*. Edited by A.H. Armstrong. Cambridge University Press, 1967. (c) Cambridge University Press 1967. Reproduced by permission of Cambridge University Press and the author–Spector, Shelia A. *From Studies In 'The Bovo Buch,' And 'Bevis Of Hampton.'* 1976. (c) Copyright Shelia Spector 1976. Reproduced by permission of the author.–Sullivan, J.P. From *Martial: the unexpected classic*. Cambridge University Press, 1991. (c) Cambridge University Press 1991. Reproduced by permission of Cambridge University Press and the author.–Swann, Bruce W. From *Martial's Catullus*. Georg Olms Verlag, 1994. (c) Georg Olms AG, Hildesheim 1994. Reproduced by permission.–Waithe, Mary Ellen. From *Hypatia's Daughters*. Indiana University Press, 1996. (c) 1996 by Hypatia, Inc. All rights reserved. Reproduced by permission.

PHOTOGRAPHS AND ILLUSTRATIONS APPEARING IN *CMLC*, VOLUME 35, WERE RECEIVED FROM THE FOLLOWING SOURCES:

Title page from Martial is, dated 1547. The Department of Rare Books and Special Collections, The University of Michigan Library. Reproduced by permission.
Hypatia (left profile, bust), conte crayon drawing. Corbis-Bettmann. Reproduced by permission.

Basil of Caesarea

c. 330-379

(Also known as St. Basil and Basil the Great.) Greek patriarch and theologian.

INTRODUCTION

Revered as a saint in both the Eastern and Western Christian churches, Basil possessed an extraordinary range of natural talents and an indomitable spirit, all of which he devoted to the cause of unifying the fourth-century church in Asia Minor. As Bishop of Caesarea, he demonstrated a remarkable ability for administration, establishing a monastic tradition that survives to the present as well as developing a program of social assistance to the lay community that became a model for the early church. An ardent proponent of Nicene orthodoxy, Basil was in the forefront of the struggle against Arianism, working closely with the other Cappadocian fathers—his friend Gregory of Nazianzus and his brother Gregory of Nyssa—to establish a doctrine of the Trinity that would be accepted by all Christians. His writings on the Holy Spirit are among his most important contributions to the theology of the church. Together with Gregory of Nazianzus and John Chrysostom, Basil is regarded as one of the three supreme figures of Eastern Orthodoxy.

Biographical Information

Basil was born in Caesarea (in modern Turkey) around 330 into a family noted for its Christian piety. His father was a wealthy landowner and a teacher. Basil's grandmother, known as Macrina the Elder, and his mother, Emmelia, were members of the nobility and extremely devout; by precept and example, these women wielded a strong influence on Basil and his nine siblings. After receiving his early education at the family's home near Neocaesarea, Basil studied in Caesarea (c. 345-47), Constantinople (c. 348-50), and Athens (c. 350-55). In school at Caesarea he met Gregory of Nazianzus, and they became lifelong friends and confidants. Basil returned home around 355 and spent a brief period as a teacher, but within a year or so his sister Macrina had persuaded him to abandon this profession and convert to monasticism. In 356-57, after being baptized into the Christian faith, he toured monastic settlements in Egypt, Syria, Palestine, and Mesopotamia, then retired to relative seclusion on his family's lands at Annesi in Pontus, where he established, with his brother Gregory of Nyssa, a monastic community. Eusebius, Bishop of Caesarea, ordained Basil as a priest in 364, and from 365 until

370, Basil divided his time between scholarly and administrative work. In 368 a disastrous famine struck Caesarea, and he spearheaded efforts to relieve the residents, selling off part of his inheritance to cover the cost of assisting them.

When Eusebius died in 370, Basil became Bishop of Caesarea and henceforth worked tirelessly to rid the church of heterodoxies and end the factionalism that threatened its survival. He openly defied the Arian emperor Valens and other powerful opponents, established important connections with Western bishops, and consolidated his authority in the East by appointing orthodox adherents to important positions in his diocese. During this period he also supervised the foundation of a new town in a suburb of Caesarea, where a church, a hospital, and guest quarters for travelers ministered to the needs of his communicants. Basil died on January 1, 379, at the age of forty-nine. Two years after his death, the Council of Constantinople proclaimed the con-substantiality of the Trinity, thus bringing to a close a period of vehement sectarianism and, in effect, validating Basil's long struggle against Arianism.

Major Works

The chronology of composition dates provided here generally follows that of Prudentius Maran, an early eighteenth-century French scholar, and the editor—with Julien Garnier—of Basil's complete works; it also takes into account adjusted dates proposed by twentieth-century commentators.

The collected letters of Basil, perhaps his most famous literary effort, number more than 360, yielding a wealth of information about his career and about social, cultural, and economic life in Cappadocia in the mid-fourth century. (They have not been arranged in chronological order, and the authenticity of a few of them is doubtful; the collection also contains epistles by some of his correspondents.) Written over the period c. 356-78, the letters are addressed to persons of every rank and stature: congregants, monks, and students as well as provincial governors, Eastern and Western bishops, military officers, and magistrates. They treat a broad range of topics—from theological controversies and ecclesiastical politics to education and the proper commemoration of saints and martyrs. The style of the letters is vigorous and frequently colloquial, though Basil's deft use of classical allusions demonstrates his wit and learning. As many commentators have pointed out, the tone of the letters varies; it is civil and kindly in those to friends and other persons who shared his views, but often harsh and critical in epistles to people who differed with him.

Basil's ascetical treatises, written and revised over an extended period (c. 361 to 376), constitute a second significant corpus. These treatises include the *Morals and Obligations,* an anthology of more than 1,500 verses from the New Testament intended to serve as a practical and spiritual guide to all Christians—lay persons as well as monks. This work was originally prefaced by Basil's essay "On the Judgment of God," in which he attacks factionalism within the church; he subsequently added a second preface, entitled "On the Faith," that constitutes a concise statement of his religious beliefs. Basil's recommendations for the regulation of monastic communities were compiled in a work known as the "great" *Asceticon;* this includes the so-called *Short* and *Long Rules,* and a series of questions and answers known as the *Examination of the Brothers.* Basil advocates here a life devoted to God through service to other members of the community as well as to the poor and the sick, and he sets forth times for liturgical prayers, manual labor, and contemplation. Although it requires obedience, the *Asceticon* does not encourage either extreme austerity or self-denial. Basil's *Rules* had a profound influence on St. Benedict (c. 480-547), the patriarch of Western monasticism.

Basil's doctrinal writings comprise a third category of his literary heritage. Of these, *Against Eunomius* (c. 364) and *On the Holy Spirit* (c. 375-76) are generally considered the most important. Written to defend orthodoxy against Eunomius's advocacy of extreme Arianism—the belief that God was of a different, higher order of existence than Christ, and that the Holy Spirit was not divine—*Against Eunomius* consists of five books, of which the first three are by Basil and the last two by another author, perhaps Didymus of Alexandria. Here Basil asserts the *homoousianism* (one substance) of the Son and the Holy Spirit with the Father, thus contributing significantly to the defense of orthodox Christianity. He continued to avow Trinitarianism in *On the Holy Spirit.* Though he does not affirm the equal divinity of the Holy Spirit in this work, he posits an innovative, extra-scriptural authority in support of his argument, claiming that the consubstantiality of the Trinity is traditionally part of the esoteric instruction given to baptized communicants.

Basil's sermons form a fourth subdivision of his work. Among the ones that survive are some delivered while he was a priest; others are from his tenure as Bishop of Caesarea. They deal with a variety of subjects—including personal morality and the veneration of relics—and were generally addressed to converts who were undergoing indoctrination before becoming full members of the church. Among the most famous of these sermons are the nine *Homilies on the Six Days of Creation* (c. 378), in which Basil draws on both Scripture and the scientific writings of Aristotle and the Stoics, though he places much greater reliance on biblical truth and revelation than on natural philosophy. He depicts the universe as a hierarchy whose parts are bound together in harmonious sympathy, and he discusses the order of elements, time and motion, and both the temporal and non-temporal worlds. This series of sermons has traditionally been much admired for its rhetorical grace.

Another of Basil's treatises that was highly regarded for many centuries is the "Address to Young Men on the Profitable Use of Pagan Literature" (perhaps c. 364, though some modern scholars have suggested that it was written in the last years of his life). Here he recommends that before embarking on the much more significant study of Scripture, students should read selectively from the classics of Greek literature in order to develop their intellects—as indeed he himself had done. A further example of his instructional work is the *Philokalia*, a collection of passages from Origen's theological writings that Basil compiled with his friend Gregory of Nazianzus while they were in seclusion at Annesi (c. 358-61) but that remained unpublished until after his death.

Critical Reception

Basil and his writings have had an indelible influence on Christian thought and practice. In addition, his ascetic treatises formed the basis of Eastern monasticism and profoundly affected the development of religious communities in Western Europe. Scholars have long been grateful for the evidence, in both his formal and informal compositions, of doctrinal controversies and ecclesiastical disputes in the fourth-century church. In the 1800s, commentators called attention to the rich and lively narrative of his era that Basil provided in his voluminous correspondence, and many of them rated these letters as his most important literary work. Throughout the twentieth century, critics have shown keen interest in what his writings reveal about Basil's many-sided role as Bishop of Caesarea: administering the organization of an extensive diocese; overseeing the foundation of charitable institutions; supervising the instruction of members of his congregation; counseling people in distress; dealing with secular authorities; resolving political issues within the church; and, above all, championing the principle of religious orthodoxy. Over the past few decades, commentators have become increasingly concerned with Basil's indebtedness to Greek culture and learning. They have looked closely at his letters, the *Homilies on Creation*, and the "Address to Young Men," attempting to determine the extent to which he employed classical authors in his own writings; several have concluded that despite his official, rather disdainful attitude toward Hellenic philosophers, he relied heavily on their work. Indeed, some late twentieth-century scholars have sharply criticized what they see as Basil's condescending attitude toward pagan writers in the "Address to Young Men." Basil's various compositions on the Trinity have also become a critical focal point in recent decades. Many commentators judge *On the Holy Spirit* to be Basil's most significant doctrinal treatise, especially in terms of the line of argument he developed there. Most recently, scholars have turned to an examination of Basil's concept of what it means to be a Christian and a member of the church. They have found that love of God and all humanity, the limitations of human understanding, and the need for steadfast faith are basic, recurring themes that appear throughout his pastoral, ascetic, and doctrinal compositions.

PRINCIPAL WORKS

Epistolae [*Letters*] (correspondence) c. 356-78

Philokalia (anthology of Origen's writings, compiled with Gregory of Nazianzus) c. 358-61

"De judicio Dei" ["On the Judgment of God"] (essay) c. 361-75

Moralia [*Morals and Obligations*] (ascetic treatise) c. 361-76

Regulae brevius tractatae [*Short Rules*] (ascetic treatise) c. 361-76

Regulae fusius tractatae [*Long Rules*] (ascetic treatise) c. 361-76

Homiliae variae [*Diverse Homilies*] (sermons) c. 364-78

"Ad adulescentes de legendis libris Gentilium" ["Address to Young Men on the Profitable Use of Pagan Literature"] (essay) c. 364

Contra Eunomium [*Against Eunomius*] (theological treatise) c. 364

Interrogationes fratrum [*Examination of the Brothers*] (ascetic treatise) c. 365-69

Homiliae in psalmos [*Homilies on the Psalms*] (sermons) c. 368-77

"De fide" ["On the Faith"] (essay) c. 375-76

De spiritu sancto [*On the Holy Spirit*] (theological treatise) c. 375-76

Hexaemeron homiliae [*Homilies on the Six Days of Creation*] (sermons) c. 378

PRINCIPAL ENGLISH TRANSLATIONS

Letters and Select Works of St. Basil (translated by Blomfield Jackson) 1895

**"Address to Young Men on the Right Use of Greek Literature" (Frederick Morgan Padelford) 1902

Ascetic Works of St. Basil (W. K. L. Clarke) 1925

***St. Basil's Letters* 4 vols. (Roy J. Deferrari) 1926-34

Ascetical Works (Monica Wagner) 1950

Letters (Agnes Clare Way) 1951-55

Exigetic Homilies (Agnes Clare Way) 1963

Saint Basil on the Value of Greek Literature (Nigel G. Wilson) 1975

*Includes *On the Holy Spirit*, the *Hexaemeron*, and the *Letters*.

**Vol. XV of Yale Studies in English, *Essays on the Study and Use of Poetry by Plutarch and Basil the Great*, edited by Albert S. Cook.

***Vol. 4 also contains "Address to Young Men on Reading Greek Literature," translated by R. J. Deferrari and M. R. P. McGuire.

CRITICISM

North American Review (essay date 1860)

SOURCE: "The Letters and Times of Basil of Caesarea, ART. IV," *The North American Review,* Vol. XC, No. 187, January-April, 1860, pp. 365-95.

[*In the following, essay, the reviewer characterizes the collected letters of Basil as the most authentic surviving account of the late fourth-century Eastern church. The critic also discusses important aspects of Basil's life, including the period of his seclusion in Pontus and his tenure as Bishop of Caesarea. The abbreviation "Ep." used throughout stands for "epistle."*]

The elder Pitt is said, in the later years of his life, to have deplored his elevation to the peerage, since he perceived that it had withdrawn him from the sphere of popular sympathy and affection, and thus forfeited the great element of his political and social power. The good and eminent men of early Christian times have had equal reason to lament that accession of historical dignity which has been attended with a like forfeiture of real and living power in the Church. The canonization which has made them titular "fathers" and "saints," while it has exalted them to a niche in the history of the Church, where they have been objects of distant and awful veneration, we had almost said of worship, has effectually eliminated them from all living contact with the heart, the memory, the thought and life of the Church.

It has fared especially hard with Basil in this particular. Though his birth and nurture were aristocratic, he was thoroughly, during his life, in spirit and in labors, a man of the people; and he says in a letter to Diodorus, that the highest aim of Christian authorship is "to leave behind one discourses which might be useful to the brotherhood." If we may accept his own declaration, he had no thought of posthumous fame as an author. He states in the same letter, which was written not long before his death, that his infirm health, and the scanty leisure allowed him by the active duties of his office, forbade the attempt to write. He lived heartily and laboriously in and for his own age, and is represented to later times principally by popular, and, as it would seem, extemporaneous homilies and expositions of Scripture, and by his extensive correspondence. But for the titles of "Father," "Saint," "Archbishop," and "the Great,"—for by all these orders and decorations ecclesiastical tradition has raised him to the highest rank of the spiritual peerage (prefixes and affixes, by the way, being alike unknown to his own time and to the two centuries following),—his fame in the Church would have been the natural, healthful, and influential memory of a good man, an eloquent preacher, a laborious pastor, a bold and somewhat sharp asserter of the faith of the Church, but at the same time an earnest advocate of her peace and unity.

By far the most important works which Basil has left to posterity are his letters. He was unrivalled among the great men of the fourth century in this description of writing. Athanasius surpassed him in dialectic and controversial skill and power. Chrysostom was, probably, his superior in eloquence. But neither the letters of Athanasius nor those of Chrysostom (though both of them wrote many which are in all respects worthy of their character and fame) will bear a comparison with those of Basil, either in the easy and captivating grace of their composition, or the variety and importance of their contents. What Voltaire said of the Provincial Letters of Pascal may with truth be affirmed of the letters of Basil,—"they abound in examples of every kind of eloquence." There is scarcely a question pertaining to the doctrine, government, worship, and life of the Church, agitated in that remarkable period,— when all the elements of historical Christianity were in a state of profound and universal fermentation, when the Church was in conflict with heathenism from without and dissent from within, when the imperial power acted at one time as a genial sunshine, stimulating even to an unhealthy luxuriance all the germs of her life, and at another as a sweeping tempest of hostility and persecution,—which is not handled in a profound and masterly way in the course of these letters; and yet they are thrown off with the ease and vivacity which marks the true epistolary genius; they are characterized by the high-bred urbanity and polish of a man who had received the best and most refining culture of his age from school, court, and travel, and they are pervaded withal by a warm, earnest, and elevated piety. In respect to historical materials, they are to the age of Basil what the letters of Cicero are to his,[1] and they derive an especial and inestimable value from the fact that they are an unstudied, actual, and therefore truthful aspect, of an age in relation to which the spirit of historical falsification has shown an almost unparalleled activity and boldness, stimulated as it has been by the powerful interests of a system, which for many centuries had the whole literature of the Church in its irresponsible keeping.

Basil, we say, was an epistolary genius. This kind of writing, to possess its true charm and power, requires a peculiar turn, talent, or temperament. Basil evidently possessed it. In a letter of Athanasius, you have before you in full panoply the theologian and controversialist. Chrysostom cannot lay aside the grave and stately tone of the orator and preacher. But Basil in his letters is a friend talking with a friend, who glides into the discussion of graver topics without losing his colloquial tone. A letter of Athanasius is a controversial tract; a letter of Chrysostom is a sermon; but a letter of Basil is a conversation,—written only because the absence of the person addressed forbids the use of the living voice. He was born to be a letter-writer. Friendship and friendly correspondence was a need of his nature. "Many and great," he says, in a letter to Ambrose, "are the gifts of our Master; such as we cannot measure for their greatness or count for their multitude. But to those who have a just appreciation of his favors, this must appear one of the greatest, that we who are at so great a distance asunder in space are permitted to meet and talk together in our letters." "Thus," he says again to the same person, "we may be near in spirit, though in our earthly residence utterly remote." If such words were addressed only to the princely Bishop of Milan, they might lie open to the suspicion of flattery. But he thus replies to a letter from Pæonius, an humble brother, whose name has come down to our times merely from its association with his own: "How much delight your letter gave me you may conjecture from the nature of its contents";—and concludes as follows: "Since you have begun to write, fail not to continue to do so. You will give more pleasure by sending me letters, than those who send much gold to the covetous." To Phalerius he returns his thanks for a present of fish, and adds: "I am yet more obliged to you for the letter which accompanied the present. Wherefore let me have more letters, and never mind the fish."[2]

The collection which bears the name of Basil contains three hundred and sixty-five letters. A few of them are, beyond all reasonable doubt, spurious, and a few more, by other hands, have probably crept into the collection. They appear to have been written during a period extending from A.D. 357 to 378, while the imperial throne was successively occupied by Constantius, Julian, Jovian, and Valens, the first of whom was an active supporter of Arianism; the second, a bitter and unrelenting persecutor of Christianity in every form; the third, during his very short reign, a professor and friend of the established faith; and the fourth, a zealous and persecuting patron of Arianism. It would be difficult to select a period of the same length during which the Church passed through so many sudden changes, and underwent such violent agitations, both in her dominant type of doctrine and in her relations to the state and the world.

The great advantage we possess for friendly intercourse, and, in fact, for every work and aim of civilized human existence, in the cheap, sure, and rapid conveyance of letters, is vividly brought to mind in almost every page of the correspondence before us. We write what we have to say to a friend, attach a cheap stamp to it, and commit it to the post, assured that it will be conveyed with all possible security and despatch to its destination, though across continents and seas, and through countries under different, perhaps hostile governments. It seldom occurs to us how very recent are the facilities which habitual enjoyment has made so necessary. They are, in fact, in anything like their present perfection, a peculiarity of our own time. It is less than a century since the mail was first carried in coaches running at regular intervals. The first mail-coach left London for Bristol on the 2d of August, 1784. The mails had been previously conveyed by carts with a single horse, or by boys on horseback. The following proclamation of Charles I. dates but little more than two centuries back (1635): "Whereas, to this time, there hath been no certain intercourse between the kingdoms of England and Scotland, the king now commands his postmaster for foreign parts to settle a running *post or two* to run night and day between Edinburgh and London, to *go thither and come back again in six days*." Enlarged postal arrangements were made by act of Parliament in 1657, "with a view to benefit commerce, convey the public despatches, and as the best means to discover and prevent many dangerous, wicked designs against the commonwealth *by the inspection of the correspondence*."

It seems curious and incredible, that, while the transmission of intelligence by relays of mounted couriers was in use among the Persians, and is accurately described by Herodotus, the high and liberal civilization of Greece and Rome should never have applied so simple an expedient to the popular benefit; and that, while kings occasionally gratified their impatience for news by such arrangements, the regular conveyance of letters for the general convenience was never thought of till the early part of the sixteenth century. Horse posts were at that date (under the reign of Maximilian I.) introduced into the Low Countries by a gentleman bearing the name of Francis de la Tour et Taxis, and were gradually but slowly introduced into other countries of Europe. So late was the plantation of that germ, which in about three centuries has expanded into a system which now binds together, by the regular and rapid interchange of intelligence, all the civilized nations of the world, and which, having subjected the powerful forces of steam and electro-magnetism to its service, promises at no distant period to put the whole human race in intimate and almost instantaneous connection. The introduction of posts for the carriage of letters has never been admitted to a place in the constellation of great inventions which distinguishes these latter centuries. Yet it would be difficult to mention one which has led on, step by step, to more brilliant discoveries, or has exerted a more powerful influence on the diffusion of knowledge, freedom, peace, and every constituent of human improvement and happiness. The rudely graven blocks of Costar did not more certainly initiate a train of inventions which has resulted in the gigantic operations of the steam-power presses of our day, than the horse posts of Francis de la Tour met the want and suggested the idea which have at length wrought out steam navigation and the electric telegraph, and are daily looking and striding forward towards new and yet more wonderful means for perfecting rapidity and accuracy of communication.

The extent of the correspondence before us appears the more astonishing, that it was kept up in the absence of all such conveniences. The conveyance of a letter, in the fourth century, continued to be the same simple affair as when, in an antiquity far beyond Homer, Bellerophon is said to have borne that which contained his own sentence of death,[3] from the court of Prœtus to Lycia. There were indeed, in the early days of the Roman empire, carriages with relays of horses along the military roads, so that any one furnished with the imperial *diploma* could travel night and day to the remotest region of the empire.[4] The *cursus publicus*, as this line of posts was termed, of the earlier Cæsars, reappears in the *res vehicularia* of Ammianus. One of the letters attributed to Julian, in this collection, invites Basil to "come with all speed to court, and to use the *public conveyance* in making the journey." But though public despatches were carried by these posts, they were never used for *mails*, in our sense of the word, or for the general conveyance of private letters. When Basil had occasion to transmit a letter, to however distant a place, he had no other resort (unless in the rare event of a trustworthy bearer presenting himself in the person of a casual traveller) than to send a special messenger to carry it, generally some "co-presbyter" or "co-deacon," and the tardy and precarious conveyance of his letters,[5] even when thus despatched, and their frequent loss and interception, are oftrecurring subjects of complaint. To Theodora, a devout and noble lady of uncertain residence, he thus writes:—

> "Excuse my tardiness in writing to you, my dear friend, as it is really caused by my uncertainty whether my letters have reached you. The faithlessness of messengers, added to the agitations and disorders which now pervade the whole world, cause a multitude of my letters to fall into other hands. So that I await your own complaints and censures and urgent requests for more letters, before I am quite sure that you have received those already sent."— **"Ep. 173."**

A correspondence carried on in the midst of such difficulties, and yet extending almost to the remotest limits of the still undivided Empire,—to Edessa and Carrhæ beyond the Euphrates in the East, and to Gaul in the West, to Mœsia, possibly Sarmatia, in the North, and Egypt in the South, and thus making the influence of its writer felt throughout the civilized world,—is indeed a surprising monument of a vigorous mind, and of a large and philanthropic spirit; the more so, since it was achieved, as we shall presently see, in a condition of health which would have excused a man of ordinary energy from exertion of any kind. So indefatigable a letter-writer can hardly be matched in literary history. With all the advantages of modern times for writing and sending letters, there is no living man, probably there has been none since the Reformation, who has filled so wide a sphere, and filled it so influentially, by his correspondence, as this energetic church-leader of the fourth century.

Basil, it is true, had incomparable incentives to so wide a range of correspondence, and incomparable advantages for it, in the political and ecclesiastical condition of the world at that time. Christendom and the civilized world then constituted one Church and one State. There were no denominations in the former, no independent nations in the latter. One imperial will on the shores of the Bosphorus gave laws to the world, from the confines of Persia to the Atlantic, and from the Danube to the deserts of Africa. The Church, with the exception of her remote missionary outposts, had the same limits with the Empire, and was undergoing a rapid assimilation to it in political spirit and form. There were, it is true, the geographical divisions of the East and the West, and the doctrinal distinctions of Arianism with its subdivisions, over against the general faith of the Church as established by the Council of Nice. But there were no sectarian lines. The Church visibly, formally, and nominally was one.[6] This unity, at once political and ecclesiastical, brought the whole world-wide Church under the eye of such a man as Basil, active in intellect, fervent in spirit, intimately associated in his educational years with many of the leading men of the Church and Empire, conspicuous from the first for his abilities and zeal, self-released by the surrender of his property from all worldly cares and ties, and so thinking, caring, and living only for the Church and the Faith,—holding, too, so important a position as that of metropolitan of Cappadocia and leader of the Nicene interests after the death of Athanasius. Christendom is, in modern times, so divided by national lines, and mustered into sectarian encampments, that no one man, however eminent, can hold such a relation to the whole Church as that which was occupied by Basil in the fourth century.

The great variety of persons to whom these letters were addressed increases their interest and value. To say nothing of his correspondence with the Emperor Julian, which is of doubtful authenticity, and the single letter to Theodosius, which is clearly spurious, here are letters to persons of every political and social rank, from generals, counts, and governors of provinces to persons of the humblest grade; letters to the bishops of Antioch, Alexandria, Thessalonica, Milan, and other metropolitan churches, and to Christian ministers whose names are unnoticed in history, and their residences unknown to geography; letters to cities, senates, and bodies of magistrates; to national communities of Christians, to the bishops of the East and to the bishops of the West, to the bishops of the country and to the bishops of the sea-shore, to Christian congregations and to associations of recluses; letters to students, sophists, soldiers, courtiers, and exiles,—to widows, lapsed virgins, and "strong-minded women"; letters of introduction, of friendship, of counsel;—some, not more than three or four lines in length, containing some passing incident or expression of kindness, and not unfrequently of playful raillery,—a mere link to keep unbroken the chain of correspondence,—and others elaborating at great length some theological distinction pertaining to the controversies of the time, or clearing up some obscure passage of Scripture or case of conscience for the relief of an inquiring correspondent. Here we have an intercession with the government for poor miners, who found their taxes oppressive; there, a deprecation of imperial severity in behalf of a censitor whose accounts had become embarrassed; again, a solicitation of court patronage (never asked for himself) in behalf of a decayed gentleman; and yet again, an energetic remonstrance with despotic poewr against a *gerrymandering* scheme for cutting up Cappadocia. There are letters of advice to the young, of rebuke, tempered with true Christian lenity, to the fallen, and of eloquent consolation to the afflicted. So wide a range of subjects and of correspondents shows how the writer, though "pinned to his bed,"[7] as he expresses it, by almost continual illness, and scarcely able in the later years of his short life to attend a meeting of the synod in the next province without mortal peril, yet contrived to live all over the Church and Empire by his letters,— how keenly he watched every cloud that appeared above the horizon of the Universal Church,—and how widely and warmly he sympathized with every interest of humanity.

> "The letters of St. Basil," says Dupin, "are the most learned and the most curious of all his books, and perhaps of all ecclesiastical antiquity. They are written with inimitable purity, majesty, and eloquence, and contain an infinite number of things. One may see there all the history of his time described to the life, the different characters of men, the opposite interests of parties, the motives which actuated both sides, and the intrigues which they made use of for carrying on their designs. The state of the Eastern and Western Churches is there described in lively and natural colors. He handles an infinite number of questions of doctrine, of discipline, and of morality, which he decides with much learning and prudence. There one may find many letters of consolation or exhortation, which are very edifying and pathetic; and even those which are complimentary are full of wit, and abound in solid and useful thoughts."

The absence of chronological order, and the frequent omission of other material circumstances, in the ancient editions of these letters, has been matter of general complaint. The modern practice of affixing invariably place, date, address, and signature[8] to a letter, if used by the ancients, would have saved a vast amount of critical sifting and weighing in the chronological adjustment of such documents, without which they are of course almost valueless to history. But these are among those simple but inestimable expedients which have been suggested by the long experience of mankind, minute accessories of a highly finished civilization, the perfection of which, like that of a great and complicated machinery, has been attained through a long series of successive inventions. To have *dated* a letter in ancient times, would indeed have been a difficult matter; as there was no generally recognized era from which to reckon, the birth of Christ having been first used as an era about the beginning of the sixth century, and thenceforward gradually becoming the chronological centre whence all time was calculated and every document dated.

For ascertaining the place as well as time of an ancient letter, we are thrown entirely on internal evidence. It seems curious and unaccountable that the writer should not have told where he was when his letter was written. All we can say is that he did not, except in special cases and for special purposes. The letters of Plato, Cicero, Pliny, and Basil are utterly without designation of place, unless it be mentioned incidentally. Those of Basil, whether from primitive omission or later carelessness, are sometimes unaccompanied by the name of the writer or the person addressed. Dupin tried his hand at amending the "Vetus Ordo," which was mere confusion. The "Novus Ordo" of the indefatigable Benedictines is the last result of critical labor and skill in their adjustment. It is certainly an advance on anything of an earlier date. But it is the judgment of Romanists and monks, who, however learned and candid, could not be supposed without bias in a matter having important historical bearings on their Church and order.

In this "New Arrangement," the letters of Basil are distributed into three "Classes";—the first, consisting of forty-six, supposed to have been written before his episcopate, between A.D. 357 and 371; the second, containing two hundred and forty-six, written during his episcopate, from A.D. 370 to his death; the third, including the letters of uncertain date and doubtful authorship, and those bearing unquestionable evidence of other hands or later times.

Of Lives of Basil there has been no lack. Damascenus cites one by Helladius, his successor in the bishopric of Cæsarea. It is lost. Another has been attributed to Amphilochius. No man knew more profoundly the secrets of his soul, or was better able to appreciate his character at every point, than the excellent Bishop of Iconium. But the work which bears his name is allowed on all hands to be a late and poorly executed imposture. Gregory of Nyssa, his brother, and Gregory of Nazianzus, his intimate friend, both pronounced at his death funeral orations, which include biographical notices. But funeral orations are not very trustworthy sources of true biography. The naked facts they state are not to be questioned; but in an estimate of the character of Basil, and of the influence of persons and events in forming it, more reliance is to be placed on the modest photograph of his own letters, than on the highly colored portraits of his brother and friend, both of which are disfigured by the exaggeration and superstition then so prevalent, from which no eminent man of the time appears to have been so free as Basil.

He was born in Cæsarea of Cappadocia about A.D. 329, of a noble and opulent family. His ancestors had been distinguished for the offices they had borne in the army and state, but were more illustrious in the memory of the Church for their firmness in confessing Christ even to exile and death. His maternal grandfather is said to have suffered martyrdom. His ancestors on the father's side were driven from their country by persecution, and wandered about in the "deserts and mountains," the "dens and caves," of northern Pontus. Better times and Christian emperors had restored them to their worldly possessions before the birth of Basil. His early education was conducted by his father, who bore the same name with himself, and is represented by both the Gregories as a person of extraordinary endowments as well as piety. It is remarkable enough that Basil has nowhere mentioned him, nor his sister Macrina, who is also represented by the Gregories as having exerted a most important influence in the formation of his character, while he is profuse and fervid in his acknowledgments to his grandmother and mother. From the private tuition of his father he passed into the public school or university of Cæsarea, then a renowned seat of learning, resided for some time at Constantinople, and finished his education at Athens. He appears to have gone to Athens about the year 351, at the age of twenty-two, and to have left it in 355. Here he became acquainted with Julian, afterwards Emperor, and formed that close intimacy with Gregory Nazianzen which continued for life. He appears thus to have devoted a considerably longer period to study than is included in a full *cursus* of school and college education in these days. He had, however, given evidence of extraordinary talents (if we may believe the Gregories) before he entered on it; and the reputation which went before him from Constantinople to Athens, as Nazianzen assures us, joined with a certain shyness and austerity of manner, and probably his always infirm health, induced the students of the latter university to dispense, in his case, with *hazing*, or whatever initiatory torment was then in vogue. When he had completed his studies at Athens, he travelled extensively.[9] Egypt, Palestine, Cælesyria, and Mesopotamia were among the countries he visited, induced principally by the desire of seeing the religious life of the far-famed anchorites who abounded in those regions, for he was then agitated by deep spiritual anxieties and longings which had not yet found repose in Christ.

About this time he lost his younger brother, Naucratius. This young man, according to Nyssen, after giving

brilliant evidence of rare talents as an orator, had suddenly been "inspired by divine grace with disgust for the world," and had withdrawn into seclusion among the mountains of Pontus. The residence of his mother and sister was near enough to enable him to continue in the observance of filial and fraternal offices. A favorite servant, Chrysaphius, was his perpetual attendant. His principal occupation was to catch fish for the maintenance of some old and infirm recluses who lived around him. After living five years in this retirement, he was one day brought home dead with his attendant. The fertile imagination of Nyssen does not fail to throw a suggestion of mystery and miracle over his sudden death.

This event may have served to give a more serious turn to the thoughts of Basil. Nyssen says that his sister Macrina, observing that he aspired with idolatrous enthusiasm to the culture of eloquence, and was elated with an intellectual pride which looked down with austere contempt even on earthly greatness and honor, sought earnestly to draw him to a Christian life, and succeeded the more easily on account of the satiety and disgust he already felt for the world.[10]

Basil himself speaks only of an interior efficacy[11] in the following account of his conversion, which occurs in a letter written long afterward to Eustathius of Sebaste:—

> "After I had spent a long time in vanity, and wasted nearly all my youth in laboriously doing nothing,— inasmuch as I had passed it in the acquisition of that wisdom which God hath made foolish,—at length, awaking as from a deep sleep, I beheld the marvellous light of the truth of the Gospel, and I saw how utterly worthless is the wisdom of the princes of this world, who shall come to naught. I then wept much over my miserable life, and prayed that a hand might be extended to me to guide me to the doctrines of godliness. And, first of all, my care was to correct my way of life, which had been perverted by long association with evil men. And then when I read the Gospel, and learned therein that it is a very great help towards perfection to sell one's goods and make distribution to the poor brethren, and to live absolutely without care of this life, and to have the soul distracted by no sympathy with the things that now are, I prayed that I might find some brother who had chosen this way of life, so that with him I might pass together over this short wave of existence. And indeed I found many such at Alexandria, many in the rest of Egypt, others still in Palestine and Cælesyria and Mesopotamia: whose temperate way of life I admired; I admired, too, their fortitude in labors; I was amazed at the intense fervor of their prayers, and how they overcame sleep, and were bowed by no physical necessity, but maintained always a lofty and indomitable temper of soul, in hunger and thirst, in cold and nakedness, paying no attention to the body, nor allowing themselves to waste any thought upon it, but, living as if in the body of another, they showed

indeed what it is to sojourn among the things here and to have one's conversation in heaven. I admired what I then saw, and esteemed the life of those men happy, because they show what it is in reality to bear about in the body the dying of the Lord Jesus, and I prayed that I too, as far as it was attainable by me, might resemble those men."—**"Ep. 222."**

He appears to have planned with his friend Gregory, while at Athens, a retirement from the world for the purposes of study and devotion. Gregory declined the immediate execution of the project on account of the age and infirmities of his parents, which he thought made it wrong for him to absent himself from them. Basil, therefore, determined to accomplish his purpose alone.

This "secessus" of Basil[12] is a matter of considerable historical interest. It forms the principal ground on which he is represented by later historians as the father and founder of monastic institutions in that highly organized and widely extended form which gave them so powerful and baneful an influence in the subsequent history of the Church. This theory is neither true to history nor just to the character of Basil. To say the least, no adequate proof can be brought to sustain it from his own letters, though the Benedictine editors have done their best, by means of title, translation, margin, notes, and index, to bring them to that complexion. The ultimate ground of proof must of course be the example of Basil in his own "secessus." He alludes to it so often in the course of his letters, that there is no difficulty in showing how little it had in common with the monastic life of later times.

Impatient, he says, of the delays of his friend, he went off to explore Pontus in quest of a hermitage. He found a place in every way suited to his purpose on the banks of the river Iris. He thus describes it in a letter to his friend:[13]—

"I believe I have at last found the end of my wanderings; my hopes of uniting myself with thee—my pleasing dreams, I should rather say, for the hopes of men have been justly called waking dreams—have remained unfulfilled. God has caused me to find a place, such as has often hovered before the fancy of us both; and that which imagination showed us afar off, I now see present before me. A high mountain, clothed with thick forest, is watered towards the north by fresh and ever-flowing streams; and at the foot of the mountain extends a wide plain, which these streams render fruitful. The surrounding forest, in which grow many kind of trees, shuts me in as in a strong fortress. This wilderness is bounded by two deep ravines; on one side, the river precipitating itself foaming from the mountain forms an obstacle difficult to overcome; and the other side is enclosed by a broad range of hills. My lodge is so placed on the summit of the mountain, that I overlook the extensive plain, and the whole course of the Iris, which is both more beautiful, and more abundant in its waters,

than the Strymon near Amphipolis. The river of my wilderness, which is more rapid than any which I have ever seen, breaks against the jutting precipice, and throws itself foaming into the deep pool below,—to the mountain traveller an object on which he gazes with delight and admiration, and valuable to the native for the many fish which it affords. Shall I describe to three the fertilizing vapors rising from the moist earth, and the cool breezes from the broken water? Shall I speak of the lovely song of the birds, and of the profusion of flowers? What charms me most of all is the undisturbed tranquillity of the district; it is only visited occasionally by hunters; for my wilderness feeds deer and herds of wild goats, not your bears and your wolves. How should I exchange any other place for this! Alcmæon, when he had found the Echenades, would not wander farther."—**"Ep. 14,"** *Gregorio Sodali.*

In this romantic retreat, which he assures his friend surpasses the island of Calpyso, as described by Homer, he by no means lived from

A scrip with herbs and fruit supplied,
And water from the spring.

How well he was attended there comes to light incidentally from a letter to Candidianus (a magistrate, perhaps the governor of the province, and evidently associated with him by literary and friendly ties), in which he claims redress for an outrage on his dwelling.

"A servant of mine lately died. One of the peasants living in my neighborhood here at Annesi, without even the pretence of a claim on him, without any previous notice or request to me, assailed my dwelling with a band of rude fellows like himself, broke open the doors, beat the women servants in attendance, and carried off everything, taking part for himself, and leaving the rest to be plundered by his companions."—**"Ep. 3."**

He demands the protection of Candidianus, and says that he must be perpetually exposed to such outrages, unless they are repelled by the energetic interposition of his official friend. He adds, however, that he would be satisfied if the man were "arrested by the pagarch, and shut up in jail a little while."

We do not expect to find men-servants and women-servants in attendance upon the abode of a veritable anchorite. Its contents would be hardly worth plundering. The last request, too, scarce breathes the spirit of a monk or a martyr. The beginning of this same letter "to Candidianus" is as little redolent of monastic austerity.

"My impressions on receiving your letter were worth telling. I shrank from it, expecting that politics, or public business, would be its burden; and while I was breaking the wax, I looked at it with a dread such as no Spartan under impeachment ever felt on handling the scytale. But when I had opened and read it, I had a good laugh,—partly from relief on finding that it contained no news, and partly from a comparison of your condition with that of Demosthenes. When he was obliged to take charge of a chorus, he said that he ought no longer to be called Demosthenes, but Choragus. But you, who have more than ten thousand soldiers in charge, write me in the same quiet strain as usual, and are as much as ever addicted to your books."

"Annesi," which he mentions above as the place of his retirement,—and the name occurs nowhere else but in two of his letters,—appears to have been a hamlet on the Iris, perhaps an estate belonging to his family; for just beyond the river was a residence of his mother, with whom he was "in communion night and day," not on subjects suggested by natural affection, but on those "spiritual things" which were uppermost in both their hearts. It was by this good, kind mother that his residence on the Iris was furnished and supported. Her society and her liberal arrangements for his comfort alike forbid the idea of a properly monastic isolation and austerity.

Such a retreat, surrounded by scenery of romantic beauty, in a most comfortably-appointed home, with beloved and accomplished relatives within call, and cheered by occasional visits from his friends, is quite another thing from the "hairy gown and mossy cell," and studied self-privations and self-tortures, which were essential to the later monachism. And when we add, (a circumstance to which Basil gives a tempting prominence in his description to Gregory,) that the region abounded in deer and fish, we cannot help thinking there would be no lack of cenobites, even in these self-indulgent days, who would relish just such a "secessus," and who go annually to Moosehead Lake and the Adirondacks in quest of a retirement not *materially* differing from this far-famed hermitage of Basil on the banks of the Iris.

That passionate delight in nature which the delicate criticism of Humboldt has traced in the writings of Basil, added to a natural love of retirement so strong that, he says, he "shrank from publicity," and "courted solitude," and "no life seemed to him more happy than one of complete seclusion from the world,"—probably had much to do with his retired sojourn in Pontus. The general impulse which, from Egypt and the East, was then spreading to other parts of Christendom, doubtless strengthened these constitutional tendencies. But often as he has alluded to that period of his life in his letters, he nowhere speaks of the maceration of the body by privations and austerities as forming any part of his design. He went into retirement, he says, "to form his plan of life," and "to escape the tumults of political life."

"A longing came upon me," he writes, "for divine truth, and undisturbed meditation upon it. How,

thought I, can I subdue the depravity which dwells within us? Who shall become Laban to me, and shelter me from the pursuit of Esau? Who shall take me by the hand and lead me to the highest wisdom?"—**"Ep. 8."**

How far the hopes of spiritual melioration which had drawn him into retirement were fulfilled, may be learned from a very fine passage in one of his letters to Gregory. To Basil's tempting description of his retreat, Gregory had replied, that it did not so much matter where he was, as what he was about, and how he was succeeding in the object which they both had at heart. Basil rejoins:—

"I knew your letter as people know the children of their friends by their likeness to their parents. That remark, that the charms and advantages of my retreat could not tempt you to join me unless you knew the way I was passing my time and the progress I was making, was just like yourself,—a true expression of that spirit which esteems the things of this life as nothing in comparison with the blessedness laid up for us in the promises. Well, then, what I am doing night and day in this remote solitude I really am ashamed to tell you. For I forsook the crowd and bustle of the city as the occasion of innumerable ills, but *I have not been able to leave myself behind.* I am, in truth, like people at sea, unaccustomed to navigation, and therefore ill at ease and sea-sick, who fret at the great size of the vessel, as if that were the cause of the rolling and pitching, and so get out into a cock-boat or pinnace, and still roll and pitch and retch, and are as sea-sick as ever; for their discomfort, with the disturbed bile which causes it, goes along with them. My case is very much the same. For carrying about with me as I do my indwelling lusts,[14] I am everywhere in the like disquietude. So that *I have derived no great advantage from this solitude."*—**"Ep. 2."**

A memorable confession, which ought to have gone far to correct any monastic tendencies in his writings or his example.

Basil's ideas of Christian culture and virtue, and of the Christian life, are such as cannot be reconciled with the maxims and the spirit of fully-developed monachism. Take, for example, the following fine letter "To a Soldier":—

"My late journey left me many occasions of gratitude to my gracious Lord, and I esteem as one of the greatest of them, the opportunity it afforded me, honored sir, of forming your acquaintance. In you I beheld a man giving actual proof that, even in a military life, it is possible to maintain, in its utmost fervor and constancy, the love of God, and that a Christian should be distinguished, not by the peculiarity of his dress, but by the disposition of his soul. My intercourse with you inspired me with great affection for you; and the pleasure it gave me is renewed at every remembrance of it. Quit thyself, therefore, like a man; be strong; give all diligence to cherish the love of God and to increase it many fold, that the ministration of his blessings to you may also abound more and more. Of your kind remembrance of me I need no other proof than the testimony of your actions."—**"Ep. 106."**

A gentleman who had resigned an important magistracy from the love of retirement he thus exhorts to resume his office, for the glory of God and the public welfare:—

> "You write me that public life is annoying and oppressive to you. I knew it before. It was long ago observed, that those who are laboring to form themselves to virtue are disinclined to public offices. The life of magistrates is in this respect like that of physicians. They behold sad sights, and go through painful experiences. They feel the calamities and sufferings of others as if they were their own. I speak, of course, of those magistrates who deserve the name. For those who look upon life as a mere mercantile speculation, who are ever on the watch for gain, and dote upon honor and notoriety,—such men esteem it the greatest blessing to be an office-holder, since it enables them to advance their friends, to crush their enemies, and to gratify their own wishes. But you are not a man of that stamp. You have withdrawn of your own accord from a high political station; and when it was in your power to rule a city as if it were a single family, you have preferred a tranquil and untroubled life, esteeming a quiet and humble lot a greater blessing than the haughty elevation which others prize so highly. But since it is the will of the Lord that Iboris should not be under the rule of knaves and hucksters, and that the appraisement and taxation should not be like the dealings of a slave-market, but that every man should be registered, rated, and taxed fairly and according to justice, accept the office, however disagreeable it be to you, as giving you an opportunity of pleasing and of serving God. Fulfil it without the fear of power or the contempt of poverty; but maintaining towards those you govern an equity more delicate than the poise of the most accurate scales. So shall your zeal for justice be manifest to those who have confided the office to you, and you will win the general esteem. Or if you even fail of that, our God will not forget you, who encourages us to good works by the promise of great rewards."— **"Ep. 299."**

These letters certainly do not breathe the spirit of an eremite. That Basil felt and yielded to the influence then moving over Christendom like a breeze which gradually stiffens into a furious and resistless gale, is not to be doubted. His own temporary seclusion, the association for religious culture formed under his auspices at Cæsarea, and many things in his letters, as well as other writings, prove this. But, without attempting nicely to estimate his historical relations to the monachism of the Middle Age, we only affirm that

what he taught and practised was a totally different thing. He assumed no religious vows, and we may naturally conclude that he imposed none upon others; his system did not include community of goods; he says nothing in disparagement of marriage, or of domestic and social affections and duties, and his societies (if he really formed any besides that which he mentions at Cæsarea) appear to have been associations more or less isolated from the world, and passing their time in prayer, praise, and the study of the Scriptures, laboring with their own hands to support themselves and to minister to the poor.[15] We do not discern in this system the severer features of the later monachism.

About seven years seem to have intervened between the completion of his course at Athens and his full entrance on the Christian ministry. He does not appear to have been ordained presbyter till the year 364, when he was thirty-five years old. This scrupulous tardiness in assuming the ministerial office was a characteristic of the period. Basil, however, was not idle the meanwhile. He wrote his **Moralia**, perhaps his books against Eunomius, within that interval. He kept up an extensive correspondence. He was probably employed as a teacher of youth, his admirable **Discourse to the Young** on the study of the ancient Greek writers having been evidently addressed to young men under his care. Several of his letters appear to have been written to his pupils and to their parents. How long a portion of this interval he passed in his retirement in Pontus it is impossible to determine. In one of his letters to the Neo-Cæsareans he alludes to his having spent several years at a retired and modest residence of his family near their city, which had been inherited by his brother Peter, to escape the tumults of the world, and give himself to undisturbed study and meditation. We cannot well find room for these "several continuous years" in any other part of his life than the interval between his departure from Athens and his entrance on the ministry at Cæsarea.

The letters contained in the second "Classis" are supposed to have been written during the episcopate of Basil. His predecessor in that office at Cæsarea was Eusebius. Basil several years before had received some affront from him which induced him to withdraw from the scene of his labors at Cæsarea and indulge his love of retirement by another "secessus." A reconciliation was, however, brought about by the good offices of Gregory, and Basil, says Gregory, had so commended himself after his return by his reverential deportment and pastoral assiduity, that the good, though somewhat infirm and mutable Eusebius, "peacefully breathed out his soul in the arms of Basil," about A.D. 370.

Great was the anxiety with which the election to so important a place was anticipated. The bishops were still chosen by the general suffrages of the congregation. The language of Ammianus in describing the competition of Damasus and Ursinus for the bishopric of Rome indicates that the popular sovereignty was still acknowledged even there.[16] A letter of Basil himself to the people of Neo-Cæsarea on the death of their bishop thus summons them to a conscientious and earnest discharge of their collective duty of providing a successor.

"Fierce wolves, hiding their treacherous nature under sheep's clothing, are everywhere rending the flock of Christ. Against such you must defend yourselves by the guardianship of some watchful pastor. To seek him is yours,—and in doing this, purify your souls from all strife and love of leadership; to point him out to you is the Lord's,—who since the great Gregory presided over your church, down to him who has just departed, has ever added and adapted one to another, so as to make the history of your church beautiful as a setting of very precious stones. You are not therefore to despair of the future. For the Lord knoweth them that are his, and can bring before us those whom we look not for. . . . I adjure you, therefore, by your fathers, by the pure faith of your church, by this excellent man whom you have lost, to stir up your souls, and, each one esteeming the matter in hand his own proper concern, and remembering that he must share in the consequences of the measures now taken, whether for good or evil, not to devolve on his neighbor the care of the common interest; and afterwards, in consequence of each one making light of his share of responsibility, all unconsciously draw upon themselves the calamitous consequences of neglect."—**"Ep. 28,"** *Ecclesiæ Neo-Cæsariensi Consolatoria.*

Basil ends a letter of consolation to the church of Ancyra, under the like circumstances, with these words,—after dwelling on the happy unanimity which the church had enjoyed under the care of its deceased pastor: "There is no small peril lest the strifes and dissensions which spring up at the election of a bishop should overturn all his work."

It was not uncommon for vacant churches to invite bishops of approved piety and wisdom to assist them in the choice of a pastor. A bishop deemed it in every way appropriate to his office to visit a church bereaved of their pastor, and offer them his sympathy and counsels. When the church was that of a metropolis, as in the case of Cæsarea, the presbyters sometimes sent such invitations. Both the clergy and people of Cæsarea had on this occasion requested the good and venerable Gregory, Bishop of Nazianzus, father of Basil's friend of the same name, (for a bishop might still honestly be a father,) to come without failure to Cæsarea, and use his influence to bring the pending election to a good result. This urgent request called forth the following letter from Gregory to Eusebius of Samosata.

"O that I had wings like a dove! O that this aged frame might renew its youth, so that I might hasten to you, my dear friend, and at once gratify the longing I have to see you, and disclose to you the sorrows of my soul, and through you find some consolation in my troubles! The good Eusebius has gone to sleep! And no small anxiety has come upon us lest those who have for some time been lying in ambush for the church of our metropolis, and trying to fill it with the tares of heresy, may seize on this opportunity and root out the seeds of piety which have been sown in the souls of men, and replace them with their own mischievous doctrines, and so break up the unity of this church, as they have of many others. And since I have received letters from the clergy entreating me not to be out of sight on so important an occasion, I have looked about in every direction, and have bethought myself of you, dear brother, and of your pure faith, and of the zeal which you always have for the churches of God. And for this cause I have sent the beloved Eustathius, our fellow-deacon, to entreat you, reverend sir, and to importune you, to add this also to all your labors for the churches; and to refresh my old age by your fellowship; and to establish in this church of pure faith that piety which is spoken of throughout the world, by giving to it along with me (if I shall be deemed worthy to share the labor with you) a pastor after the will of the Lord, who shall be able to guide his people. We have, in fact, before our eyes a man who is not unknown to you. If we shall succeed in obtaining him, I feel sure that we shall acquire great confidence towards God, and confer a very great blessing on the people who have summoned us. I entreat you, therefore, again and often, to put aside every hinderance, and to come before the severities of the winter have set in."

The candidate so mysteriously hinted at by the good Gregory in the above letter—it was perilous in those days to put confidential matters on paper[17]—was Basil. Eusebius obeyed the summons of his friend, and, with the two Gregories, exerted himself to procure the election of a candidate equally known and esteemed by them all. The extremely feeble health of Basil was objected; but the elder Gregory reminded the people that they were going to choose, "not a boxer, but a bishop," and that "the strength of the Lord was made perfect in the weakness of his servant." The choice fell upon Basil; and in the year 370, when he was about forty-one years old, he entered on the charge of the metropolitan church of Cæsarea.

How assiduously he fulfilled this office, with what unwearied exertions as a preacher, a pastor, and a curator of the young and the poor, he ministered to his own immediate flock; with what public spirit he watched over the interests of his country, and labored to shield it from oppression, and to advance its welfare by the exertion of his influence with the great; how earnestly he toiled for the unanimity and peace of all Christendom, seeking a "Broad Church" comprehension which should bind together the East and the West in the bonds of a common faith, communion, and affection; with what a large humanity he strove to do good to men everywhere, always on the principle that the Gospel includes a remedy for every disorder and misery of mankind,[18]—these letters and his other works, as well as the funeral eulogies of his friends and the testimonies of Church historians, give ample proof.

Many interesting details of his ministrations come to light in his letters and homilies. They quite surpassed anything in modern times, in the way of frequent services. He held morning and evening services in his church for prayer, praise, and exposition of the Scriptures. The terms used will by no means admit of being understood in our sense of *forenoon* and *afternoon* assemblies. They were held at the dawn and close of the day. He says in one of his homilies, that he brought the service to a close in order that those who were occupied with labor for their daily subsistence might go to their customary occupations, meditating the meanwhile on what they had heard, and seasoning their repasts with the recollection and discussion of it, and return, with minds released from worldly cares, to "an evening banquet on the word of God." Their assemblages could not, therefore, have been held exclusively on the Lord's day, which was appropriated to rest and worship. Some of his most elaborate and admired productions were delivered at these morning and evening meetings. His homilies on the Creation are among them. A free and colloquial tone pervades all his public discourses, and they appear to have been delivered extemporaneously.[19] He speaks of the eagerness with which the people crowded to hear the word of God, and yet there were some who stood around him to mock and ridicule. On one occasion he accounts for his late appearance at the service by saying that he had just come from ministering to a distant church,—a proof that he fulfilled the office of a bishop in the primitive way, by doing at the same time "the work of an evangelist." Even here, too, we are reminded of the ill-health under which he constantly labored, when he tells the congregation that "the failure of his voice by reason of the infirmity of his body" compelled him to bring his discourse to an end.

The Neo-Cæsareans accused him of introducing novelties into divine worship in his church at Cæsarea. His defence, completed from incidental notices in his homilies, presents us with a very full and distinct picture of the service. "With us," he says, "the people go at the dawn, before it is light, to the house of prayer, and in labor and affliction and continual tears confess their sins to God. At length they rise from prayer," (which would thus seem to have been offered in a kneeling posture,) "and engage in singing psalms." He speaks of prayers at the dawn and in the evening as a customary practice in the churches. He says that there arose from his congregation a mingled sound of the voices of men, women, and little children, as the sound of many waters, adoring God. It is quite plain, therefore, that the whole congregation took an audible part in the service. He insists much on the use of the voice by every member of the congregation in public worship, often citing that passage, "In his temple doth *every one speak* his praise." But there were no forms of prayer. He recommends that each one should compile from the Scriptures prayers adapted to his own wants. Every worshipper was supposed to offer up the congregational confession, with a mental application to his own particular sins.[21] The communion was administered four times a week. Litanies or confessions of sin, it appears, were also a part of public worship in the church of Neo-Cæsarea. Thus Basil replies to his accusers:—

"You accuse me of innovation because I have introduced certain changes in the worship of the Church. You say, such things were not in use in the time of the great Gregory. But neither were the litanies which are now part of your worship. I do not say this to accuse you. I could wish that you all passed your lives in tears order, for those who have the care of the church, the attendants on divine service,—the common use of which is open to you, our rulers, and your suites. And whom do we wrong when we build lodging-places for strangers,—both those who are mere passers-by, and those who are sick, and therefore need attendance and medical treatment,—and when we provide all that is necessary to their comfort and relief, such as nurses, physicians, bearers, escorts? Such arrangements must necessarily include various arts, both those which are needful to life and those which have been invented to adorn and elevate it, as well as houses and shops for mechanics and artisans. All these buildings are an ornament to the place, and a reputable thing for our governor, to whom the credit of them redounds. . . . And let not your excellency suppose that this is a mere scheme of ours; for we are already at work, and have accumulated the materials. So much for my defence before you as governor of Cappadocia. But as to the carpings of malicious fault-finders, the vindication which I owe you as a Christian and a friend who has my reputation at heart,—I shall not attempt that now, for my letter has already exceeded the due length; and besides, some things which I have to say it is not safe to intrust to a lifeless letter. I shall have an interview with you erelong. But, lest your kind estimation of me should suffer some interruption from the calumnies of certain persons in the mean time, do as Alexander did. When an information was presented to him, it is said, against one of his officers, he turned one ear to the accuser and closed the other firmly with his hand, signifying that he who would form a just judgment must not give himself up altogether to the party who gets the first hearing, but reserve half of the audience, without preoccupation or prejudice, for the absent defendant."—"**Ep. 94.**"

The governor seems to have interposed no further opposition to the bold and vigorous bishop, and that the execution was at least equal to the project appears from the following passage in the funeral discourse of Gregory Nazianzen, where he speaks of this extensive suite of buildings as one of the monuments of the large philanthropy of his friend.

> "Step forth beyond the walls of the city, and you will see a new city, that treasure of piety, that deposit of wealth, where not only the superfluities of the rich but the necessaries of the poor were, by his exhortations, accumulated; thus shaking off moths, disappointing thieves, escaping the decays of time;— where sickness is at once nursed and instructed, where sympathy is exercised, and misfortune itself becomes a blessing. What, now, in comparison with such a work, the sevengated Thebes, and all the glories of Egypt, and the Babylonian walls, and the Carian Mausoleum, and store of Corinthian bronzes, and temples once vast and magnificent, now deserted and ruinous, which conferred nothing but a short-lived celebrity on their builders."[22]—*Op. Greg. Naz. Tom. I. pp. 316 et seq.*

It appears, then, that he derived the means for the great outlay which such a scheme required from the free contributions of Christians. Gibbon's statement, that the "Emperor subscribed the donation of a valuable estate" towards the object, does not appear to be supported by any historical evidence. If imperial bounty had borne so large a share in the expense, Gregory, from his relations to Constantinople and the court, would doubtless have noticed the circumstance. It is inconsistent, too, with Basil's letter to Helias, in relation to this very matter, where he simply expresses the hope that "our great sovereign, observing the solicitudes that press upon us, will *leave us to administer the churches by ourselves*,"[23] but neither acknowledges nor asks any assistance from the royal treasury. The whole enterprise stands forth as a gratifying proof of the power of the "voluntary principle," even under the despotic system of the fourth century.

Such gigantic enterprises contrast strangely with his own personal poverty. He speaks of "this poverty wherein I abide with God." In a letter to some unknown friend he alludes to his foster brother, "who," he says, "is at much inconvenience for my support, inasmuch as I have, as you well know, no private property, but am supported by my friends and relatives." These letters are supposed to have been written before he entered on his episcopate. But some of those which were written afterward are in the same strain. To the collector of revenues he says: "No man knows my poverty so well as your excellency, who have sympathized with me and borne with my unavoidable delays, to the utmost possible extent, without allowing your kind heart to be turned from its purpose by the threats of those in power." His letters were retarded by the want of a scribe or copyist. He excuses himself for retaining a volume sent him by Diodorus on the same plea, adding, "I have not yet been able to obtain the services of a copyist,—to such a degree of poverty have the boasted riches of Cappadocia been reduced."

He here alludes to the disastrous effects of the division of Cappadocia. That extensive province, corresponding formerly to the ancient kingdom of Cappadocia, was divided by the Emperor Valens, about A.D. 372, into two parts, Cappadocia Prima and Secunda. Basil's opposition to the measure has been imputed to prelatical ambition, chagrined by the curtailment of his diocese and the diminution of his suffragans. His own correspondence in relation to it would lead us to form a more charitable opinion of his motives. His account of the effects of the division on the once opulent and splendid metropolis, Cæsarea,[24] his own native city and the scene of his labors, is as follows:—

> "Those assemblies, lectures, and coteries of learned men about the forum,—all, in fact, that erewhile made our city famous, are no longer here. The barbaric rudeness of multitudes of Scythians and Massagetæ has taken their place. The voice of exactors and the cry of the oppressed under the strokes of the scourge are the sounds we now hear. The porticos everywhere re-echo the dismal sound. The Gymnasia are shut up, *the streets no longer illuminated.* A part of the Senators have forsaken the city, preferring a perpetual exile at Podandum to a residence at home."—**"Ep. 74."**

The death of that loving and generous mother, whose society cheered and solaced him, while her thoughtful kindness mitigated the severities of his voluntary poverty, is thus alluded to in a letter to "the friend of his soul," Eusebius of Samosata:—

> "If I should tell you of all the causes which to this time have hindered me from coming to see you, as I wished to do, it would be an endless story. One attack of sickness after another, a severe winter, continual occupations,—all these are well known to you, my excellent friend, and so I forbear to repeat them. But now I have a new sorrow. She who was the only consolation of my life, my mother, has, for my sins, been taken away from me. Do not now smile that a man of my age should bewail his orphanage. But pardon me rather for bearing with so little fortitude the loss of one whom the whole world that survives cannot replace to me. Again, therefore, sickness is upon me: again I am laid on my bed, and the little strength left in me so utterly shaken, that every hour that passes I am ready to look upon as the last. The churches are in a condition very much like that of my body,—no good hope appearing,[25] and things tending ever from bad to worse. . . . Wherefore, faint not in prayer, nor cease to importune God in behalf of the churches."—**"Ep. 30."**

None of these letters, probably, are more illustrative of the man and of the times than those which were written in the ordinary fulfilment of the cure of souls,—a work which, physically disabled as he was, he must, to an unusual extent, have performed with the pen and in the shape of letters. Of this class is the following, "To

Harmatius,"—a Pagan highly esteemed for his social virtues,—whose son had been converted to Christianity. Basil thus deprecates the displeasure of the father, and pleads for the liberty of the son. The absolute power with which the Roman law invested the father will account for the earnestness of its tone.

> "Do not consider me intrusive, if I intercede with you in behalf of your son. In all things else I admit that you justly claim his obedience; for he is in subjection to you as it respects the body, both by the law of nature and by these civil relations which bind us together. The soul, however, which is derived from a diviner source, we must regard as subject to another, and that it owes an obedience to God which has priority of all other obligations. Since, then, your son has chosen our God, the God of the Christian, the true God, in preference to the numerous divinities whom you worship through material symbols, be not offended with him; rather admire his moral courage, that he has thought it of greater importance to become one of the household of God through the knowledge of the truth and a holy life, than even to comply with the promptings of filial fear and reverence. Nature itself will plead with you, and that mildness and humanity which characterizes you on all occasions, not, for a moment even, to make him the object of your resentment. Do not reject also my intercession in his behalf, rather, I might say, the intercession through me of all your fellow-citizens, who, because they love you, and pray for all blessings upon you, really thought, when they heard of your son's conversion, that you had yourself become a Christian. Such a general joy did the sudden news of the event diffuse through the city."—**"Ep. 276."**

Cæsarius, brother of Gregory Nazianzen, had an extraordinary escape from the great earthquake which overwhelmed Nice, A.D. 368. Though embedded in the masses of ruined buildings, he was uninjured. Basil addressed to him, on the occasion, the following letter:—

> "Thanks to God who has shown forth his marvellous works in you, and from so great a death has preserved you to your country,[26] and to us who love you! It remains for us not to be unthankful or unworthy of such signal kindness, but to publish, as far as we can, the wonderful works of God, and to sing the praises of that goodness we have experienced; and not in words only to make grateful returns for it, but in act and life. You have already served God. Serve him, I entreat you, yet more earnestly; ever increasing in his fear, and going on to perfection, that we may be wise stewards of that life which he has given us to dispense. For if it is enjoined on all to present themselves to God as those who are alive from the dead, how much more on those who have been lifted up from the gates of death! And this, I think, will be best accomplished, if we resolve always to retain that state of mind which we had in the very moment of peril. For then I think the mind is deeply penetrated

with the thought of the vanity of life, and that there is nothing stable or trustworthy in human things, which are liable to such quick vicissitudes. Then, too, repentance is awakened by the review of the past; and for the future, a purpose, if our life is preserved, of serving God and watching over ourselves with all diligence. Such, or something like them, were, I suppose, the thoughts which passed through your own mind, if the apprehension of impending death left you the power of reflection. We are, therefore, under a debt to God which a grateful life must pay. Full of gratitude that God has given you back to us, and deeply anxious too for the consequences of the event, I have ventured to make these suggestions to you. Receive them kindly and favorably, as you have always done what I have spoken to you in person."—**Ep. 26."**

A Christian lady desired an interview with him in some unexplained affliction or perplexity. He thus replies:—

> "I hope to find a convenient day for the interview you request, after certain meetings which I am about to appoint in the hill country. No other opportunity of meeting you, except it be in the way of public ministration, appears, unless the Lord should order it, beyond my expectation. . . . But since you have the teaching and consolation of the divine Scriptures, you will not need me nor any other to assist you to the perfect discovery of duty, having the all-sufficient counsel of the Holy Spirit, and his guidance to that which is best."—**"Ep. 283,"** *Ad Viduam.*

In this multifarious correspondence the Christian and the Christian minister seldom disappear. Even the shortest notes often contain a direct and fervid exhortation to piety. From secular or church business, and from the language of friendship or of compliment, he passes, without apologetic transition, to "this one thing," as if with a majestic assertion at once of his right and duty, to "warn every man and teach every man," "in season and out of season."

He had borrowed some mules from a noble lady. To the courteous acknowledgment with which he returns them, he adds some brief spiritual admonitions; among others, "continually to keep before her eyes her departure from this world, and to have her whole life in harmony with the defence which must then be made before a Judge who cannot be deceived, and who will reveal the secrets of all hearts in the day of his visitation. Present my salutations," he adds, "to your noble daughter. I entreat her continually to study the oracles of God, that her soul may be nourished in good doctrine, and that she may grow in mental even more rapidly than in bodily stature."

A note of some half a dozen lines, without epigraph, but apparently addressed to some friend who had risen to high political position, thus concludes:—

"I pray God to advance you more and more in honor and dignity, and to make your virtue a blessing to us and to your whole country. And I exhort you, in all your life, to remember God who created you and has raised you to honor; that, as you have had a brilliant career in this life, you may also obtain the heavenly glory; for which we must do all things and shape our whole life to that blessed hope."—**"Ep. 326."**

A letter bearing the inscription, "To Chilo, his Disciple,"[27] contains the following counsels:—

"By little and little withdraw from the world, abolishing gradually thy circle of habits and acquaintance, lest, making war upon all pleasures at once, thou bring upon thyself a host of temptations."—**"Ep. 42."**

This breathes, though in a moderate form, the ascetic spirit. Perhaps it may be found, to a fully equal extent, in Leighton's "Rules and Directions for a Holy Life," which are quite as much out of tone with his sermons and commentaries, as the *Regulæ* of Basil, and some passages in his letters, with the general strain of his writings. He adds:—

"With manifold temptations is the believer tried; with worldly losses, calumnies, controversies, persecutions. Under all these be thou quiet, not forward in speech, not contentious, not disputatious, not desirous of vainglory, . . . ever ready to learn rather than to teach."

His letters of consolation are among the finest in the collection; and certainly manifest a warmer sympathy with domestic losses and sorrows than could be expected from a thoroughgoing ascetic. Here are some of the consolations which he addresses "To Nectarius," on the death of an only son in infancy:—

"God only knows how he apportions to each one that which is best, and why he sets such unequal limits to our life. It is utterly inscrutable to men why it is that some are removed hence so soon, and others left to toil and suffer on for a long while, in this troublous life. We must therefore adore, in all things, the kindness and love of God towards man, and not think hardly of his allotments; calling to mind the noble sentiment uttered by that great combatant, Job, when he saw ten children crushed in a moment at the same table: 'The Lord gave, the Lord hath taken away; as it seemed good to the Lord, so hath it happened.' Let us make that admirable state of mind our own. . . . We have not been bereaved of the child; we have but given him back to Him who lent him. His life has not been extinguished, it is only transfigured into a better. The earth has not hid our beloved one, heaven has received him. Let us wait a little, and we shall be with him whom we mourn and long for. The time of separation will not be long, since we are all on the way—this present life—which leads to the same resting-place. One has already arrived there, another

is just entering, another presses on,—all will soon reach the same end. If he has finished the journey sooner, yet we are all accomplishing it, and the same abode awaits us all. May we, too, by purity and simplicity of heart, be prepared for the rest which is the portion of babes in Christ."—**"Ep. 5."**

He thus consoles the mother of the same child:—

"To the Wife of Nectarius.

. . . Not without a Divine Providence are the things that befall us, since we have learned in the Gospel, that not even a sparrow falleth to the ground without our Father. So that whatever has happened has been by the will of Him who created us. And who hath resisted God? Let us rather accept what he allots. . . . Great is your sorrow, I confess that. But . . . when you became a mother, and looked on your child, and gave thanks to God, you knew full well that, a mortal mother, you had given birth to a mortal son. What wonder is it, then, if a mortal has died? 'But,' you say, 'it was so untimely, that is what afflicts us.' We know not but it has happened in very good time. Since our knowledge is far too narrow to make us capable of choosing what is for the true interest of souls, and to mark out the limits of human life. Look around on the whole world in which you dwell, and consider that all things visible are mortal. Look up at the heavens, they shall pass away; at the sun, even that shall not remain. All the stars, all animated creatures on land and in water, all the beautiful things of earth, the earth itself, all are corruptible, all, after a little while, will be no more. Let the thought of these things mitigate your affliction. Do not look at your bereavement by itself. It will be insupportable. But when you compare it with the general human lot, you will find relief in the comparison. One consideration I add of great force,—spare your husband. Be a consolation to one another. Do not make his sorrow heavier by consuming yourself with grief. After all, I well know that words have little power to comfort. Prayer is our only refuge in such a calamity. And I do therefore pray the Lord himself, by his unutterable power, to touch your heart, and to kindle up the light of good thoughts in your soul, so that from within you may have suggestions of consolation."—**"Ep. 6."**

His comforting words "To Maximus," on the death of his wife, could hardly have come from a monk:—

"I have been intimate with your excellency from our first acquaintance, and also with that happy spirit which has departed. And verily I thought I saw that expression in the Book of Proverbs fulfilled in you, *the wife is fitted by God to the husband.*[28] So were your qualities mutually adapted, that each, as it were in a mirror, presented an individual image of the other. . . . But grieve not at your present loss; rather give thanks to Him who bestowed your former happiness. For to die is the lot of all who are partakers of this nature. But to live happily with a good wife is the lot of few, even of those who are deemed fortunate. In fact, the very tears with which you deplore your separation are no small proof of the goodness of God, if you look at the matter rightly. For I have known many people who have welcomed the dissolution of an ill-assorted marriage as the laying aside of a burden. We are parts of a perishing creation, and only receive what falls to us of the common lot. Marriage itself is a suggestion of death, since it was not given for continuance, but is the plan of the Creator to perpetuate life by the succession of the race. Nor let us mourn that she was so soon taken from us, nor envy her that she was not required to drink the whole cup of this life's sorrows, but, like a flower in full bloom, left us while we still loved and delighted in her. Above all, let the doctrine of the resurrection draw away your mind from brooding over its grief, for you are a Christian, and live in the hope of future blessings. Let reason shake off the burden of sorrow, and take thought how, for the time that is left to us, we may so live as to be well-pleasing to the Lord."—**"Ep. 301."**

These letters abound in historical and antiquarian suggestions, as might be expected in letters not written for the mere sake of letter-writing, but to meet the claims arising from wide and actual relations with the living world.

It appears from **"Ep. 298"** that Priessnitz must relinquish the honor of having originated the water-cure. There was an institution, it would seem, with all the pretension of Gräfenberg, in the fourth century. Basil was evidently no convert to hydropathy.

> "I am surprised that the delusion of this man has infected you, and that you have come to believe in the efficacy absurdly ascribed to water; and that, too, while there is no substantial testimony to confirm the report. There is not one of those who have been there who has received any of the bodily relief he hoped for, small or great; unless it be some little alleviation from accidental causes, such as men often find from sleep, and other processes, from the mere efficacy of the laws of life. But this man, renouncing charity, persuades silly people to ascribe effects which are quite accidental to the efficacy inherent in water. Experiment will show you, if you choose to make it, that my opinion is right."

The imperial patronage inaugurated by Constantine by no means, it would seem, secured Christian ministers from severe straits for the means of support. He speaks of an excellent and very able man, (whom he recommends as eminently suitable for a bishopric to which a friend had requested him to name a candidate,) who "had not wherewith to get his bread, but *wove out* a subsistence by the labor of his hands." This may have been a case of voluntary poverty. But he says elsewhere, that "the majority of the numerous body of the clergy" of Cæsarea, though they "did not embark in merchandise, labored in the sedentary arts, and thence obtained the means of daily subsistence."

The cheerful tone which everywhere pervades this correspondence is one of its most remarkable aspects. Earnest and strenuous as he was, suffering too from almost constant bodily pain and weakness, assailed by a tempest of calumny which never seemed to slacken till at his death it changed into an equally extravagant and indiscriminate adulation, feeling all the inconveniences of the poverty to which he had voluntarily subjected himself, and profoundly afflicted by the divisions and calamities of the Church, the hilarity of his spirit shines out through circumstances of the deepest gloom. A large element of his cheerfulness would seem to have been a humor which, as Gregory says, shed a fascinating charm over his conversation, and of which there are many traces in his correspondence. "I put," he says, "the agreeables and disagreeables into the opposite sides of the scale, and when the latter seem to preponderate, I throw my *will* into the better side." He tells the Neo-Cæsareans, (who showed a singularly bitter and implacable spirit towards him,) that, full as they were of dissensions on all other subjects, they were *unanimous in hating him.* Vexed and afflicted as he was by the division of Cappadocia, he cannot suppress a joke on the subject, saying, that "the imperial project of dividing Cappadocia was like cutting in two a horse or an ox with the expectation of making two out of one." Cassian reports that a Senator named Syncletius proposed to adopt the life of a recluse, and to surrender his property; but, upon further reflection, concluded to retain a sufficient provision "for a rainy day." "Syncletius," said Basil, "you have spoiled a gentleman and not made a monk." To his physician, Meletius, he expresses his regret that he cannot "migrate with the cranes, and escape the discomforts of winter."

A better and more abiding source of cheerfulness he seems to have found in the anticipations of that "long and ageless life," the hope of which animated him in all labor and cheered him in all calamity.

As years advance, the indications of increasing suffering and failing energies multiply. He speaks of "long diseases urging on to the inevitable end,"—of being "*used up*[30] by fever and complaint of the liver,"—"oppressed by old age," though in years he scarcely reached the prime of life. He closes a short note by saying, "I have just enough of life to breathe." To Amphilochius, his "beloved son," he addresses this touching request: "I entreat you, pray first of all that the Lord would grant me release from this burdensome body, and that he would give peace to his own churches."

His laborious and suffering life came to an end, before he had completed his fiftieth year, A. D. 379. His last words, as reported by Gregory, were, "Into Thy hands I commend my spirit."

Upon the whole, Basil seems justly entitled to the fame of a Christian hero,—by no means free from the ascetic trammels of his time, nor untainted by those incipient tendencies to wrong which were afterwards developed into such enormous evils, but still a great teacher and a bold confessor of Christian truth, and a shining example of Christian virtue.

Notes

[1] "Quas qui legat, non multum desideret historiam contextam eorum temporum."—Cornelius Nepos in Vit. Attici, 16.

[2] Rather a free translation, perhaps, of . . . ("Ep.329.").

[3] If the . . . . [text] (Iliad, VII. 155 *sqq.*) *was* a letter.

[4] This system appears to have been organized by Augustus. Suetonius, *Octavius*, 49.

[5] He speaks of the severe and protracted winter having interrupted his correspondence with Theodotus. (Ep. 121, Theodoto Episcopo, &c.)

[6] "All who hope in Christ," says Basil ("Ep. 161"), "are one people, . . . all who are Christ's are now one Church, . . . though it be named from different *places*." The only denomination, then, was that derived from *place*. . . .

[8] The ancient letter seems to have been identified by the *handwriting* of the author. Basil ("Ep. 223"), defending himself against a charge founded on a letter said to have been written while he was at Athens to Apollinarius, says that the very letter itself which formed the ground of the charge was doubtful. "They could not know it," he adds . . . (ex subscriptionis signis), *"inasmuch as they had not in their possession the original letter, but a copy."* This shows that the . . . [names] were not the *signature* as understood by us, i. e. the name subscribed, but the proof of authorship by the handwriting. When an amanuensis was employed, *an autograph postscript* was the sign of genuineness. So Paul (2 Thes. iii. 17) says, "The salutation by the hand of me, Paul, which is *the sign* in every epistle,"—"a token whereby all my letters may be known." (Conybeare and Howson.) This was like putting an autograph signature to a letter written by another hand.

[9] . . . ("Ep. 204.") The allusion must be to this period of his life, for in later years he tells us that his infirmities fixed him in one spot *"like a tree planted in the soil."* . . . That he sometimes, however, made tours of Christian labor and visitation through the different regions of Asia Minor, is evident from some even of his latest letters, e. g. "Ep. 216."

[10] Vit. Mac., p. 181. In his discourse on the Resurrection, which was occasioned by the death of Basil, he calls this accomplished and excellent lady at once "the sister and teacher" of his departed brother. . . . She survived him; and this discourse on the Resurrection is in the form of a conversation with her. Its abstruse and metaphysical ideas are a proof of the extent to which the culture of Christian females was carried in the fourth century. Basil too ("Ep. 223") says that his mature Christian knowledge and faith were nothing more than a development of the sentiments implanted in his mind . . . by his mother and grandmother. The discourse on the Resurrection is preserved in Wolfii Anecdota Græca, Tom. II.

[11] Which he calls elsewhere "the grace of him who hath called us with a holy calling to the knowledge of himself." The expression occurs in the course of a retrospect of his early religious life, "Ep. 204," Ad Neo-Cæsarienses.

[12] Called by himself [*apokhoresis eskhatia*].

[13] The passage here quoted is inserted by Humboldt in his Cosmos, as an instance of the high appreciation and enjoyment of nature which is discernible in the writings of the Christian Fathers. He thus introduces it: "I begin with a letter of the great Basil, which has long been an especial favorite with me."

[14] . . . This description of his inner life may be compared with a remark of his cited by the Benedictine biographer from Cassianus: "Fertur S. Basilii Cæsariensis episcopi districta sententia: *Et mulierem*, inquit, *ignoro, et virgo non sum.*"

[15] Such at least was the theory. . . . ("Ep. 207.") Gregory says ("Ep. 8") they would have starved if their wants had not been supplied by the timely bounty of Basil's mother. The later history of manual-labor institutions has been much the same.

[16] Amm. Marc. Valentin. et Valens, XXVII. 3. This election took place A.D. 367.

[17] So Basil says ("Ep. 9"), and warns his friend to come to him for a personal interview. . . .

[18] He says ("Ep. 261") that "our Lord went through all things pertaining to ministration to the race of men". . . .

[19] . . ."Ep. 223." . . .

[21] . . . No other confessional is hinted at by Basil than "the throne of grace."

[22] "This noble and charitable foundation," says Gibbon, alluding to the same work, "(almost a new city), surpassed in merit, if not in greatness, the pyramids, or the walls of Babylon."—Dec. and Fall, Vol. IV. p. 269, n.

[23] . . . ("Ep. 94.") We remember no instance in which Basil, either for himself or for the Church, asks any favors from the government. He was in spirit, and in practice as far as the age would permit, a "voluntary." His letter "to Demosthenes," "Ep. 225" (*cf.* 238), shows a vivid sense of the degradation and weakness incurred by the Church in accepting the patronage, and of course the dictation, of the state. It began already to be apparent, to use the striking words of Bunsen, that "evangelical and apostolical freedom received its death-blow from the same police crutch which had been given it for support."

[24] "Cæsarea, the capital of Cappadocia, was supposed to contain four hundred thousand inhabitants."—Gibbon, Vol. IV. p. 439.

[25] . . . often used of the first light of the dawn.

[26] Cæsarius held an important post in Bithynia.

[27] In the Codex Regius 2895, this letter is ascribed to St. Nilus, who lived a century later; and it certainly presents ascetic ideas in a more developed form than the unquestioned writings of Basil.

[28] Sept. translation of Prov. xix. 14. . . .

[30] . . . "Ep. 138." Liver-complaint he calls his "old affliction," which, he says, "excluded me from food, drove sleep from my eyes, and held me on the confines of life and death, allowing me to live just so much as to be sensible of the pains it caused me."—*Ibid.*

Edmund Venables (essay date 1877)

SOURCE: "Basilius of Caesareia" in *A Dictionary of Christian Biography*, Vol. I, A-D, Little Brown, and Company, 1877, pp. 282-97.

[*In the excerpt reprinted below, Venables provides a detailed narrative of Basil's life and career, highlighting the tactics Basil employed to gain the episcopate of Caesarea, consolidate his power and authority, and defend the orthodox faith against a variety of challenges. The abbreviations "Ep." and* De Sp. Sancto *used throughout stand for "epistle" and* De Spiritu Sancto, *respectively.*]

Basilius, bishop of Caesareia in Cappadocia, commonly called Basil the Great, the strenuous champion of orthodoxy in the East, the restorer of union to the divided Oriental Church, and the promoter of unity between the East and the West, was born at Caesareia (originally called Mazaca), the capital of Cappadocia, towards the end of the year 329. His parents were members of noble and wealthy families, and were Christians by descent. His grandparents on both sides

had suffered during the Maximinian persecution. His maternal grandfather was deprived of his property and life. Macrina, his grandmother on his father's side, and her husband, were compelled by the severity of the persecution to leave their home in Pontus, of which country they were natives, and to take refuge among the woods and mountains of that province, where they are reported to have passed seven years (Greg. Naz. *Or.* xx. p. 319) [Macrina]. His father, whose name was also Basil, was an advocate and teacher of rhetoric whose learning and eloquence had brought him a very large practice. He was also celebrated for his Christian virtues. Gregory Nazianzen speaks of this elder Basil in terms of the highest commendation as one who was regarded by the whole of Pontus as "the common instructor of virtue" (*Orat.* xx. p. 324). His mother's name was Emmelia [Emmelia]. Basil and Emmelia had ten children, five of each sex, of whom a daughter, Macrina, was the eldest, and a son named Peter, whose birth was almost contemporaneous with his father's death, the youngest. Basil was the eldest of the sons, two of whom besides himself, Gregory Nyssen and Peter, attained the episcopate. One son died in infancy. Naucratius, the second son, died a layman when about 27 years of age [Naucratius]. Four of the daughters were well and honourably married. Macrina the eldest embraced a life of devotion, and exercised a very powerful influence over Basil and the other members of her family [Macrina, No. 2]. Basil had a paternal uncle named Gregory, who took his father's place after his decease, and was present with other bishops of Cappadocia at his nephew's ordination. Basil was indebted for the care of his earliest years and the formation of his opening mind to his grand-mother Macrina, who brought him up at her country house, not far from Neocaesareia in the province of Pontus (Bas. **"Ep. 210,"** 1). The rule on which Macrina sought to form her grandson's religious character was the teaching of Gregory Thaumaturgus which she had received from those who had been his auditors. On leaving infancy the boy Basil passed to the hands of his father, probably at Neocaesareia, who was his instructor not only in rhetoric and secular learning, but also in religion and the virtues of a Christian life. The date of Basil's baptism is uncertain, but it hardly admits a doubt that, according to the prevalent custom, his admission into the church was deferred until he reached man's estate, and did not take place until he formally renounced the world after his return from Athens. For the completion of his education, Basil was sent by his father first to his native city of Caesareia, where he soon gained great reputation not only with his tutors and fellow pupils, but also among the people of the city, for the brilliancy of his talents and his virtuous life (Greg. Naz. *Or.* xx. p. 325). From Caesareia he passed to Constantinople where, if the correspondence between Libanius and Basil is genuine, which has been questioned by Garnier on insufficient grounds, he studied under that famous sophist. The letters of Libanius shew that there was a close intimacy between them, and express a high degree of admiration of Basil's eloquence and his life of gravity and self-restraint in the midst of the temptations of such a city as Constantinople (Bas. **"Ep. 335-339"**; Liban. *Vita,* p. 15). According to Socrates and Sozomen (Socr. iv. 26; Soz. vi. 17) the scene of the intercourse between Libanius and Basil was Antioch. But there is no reason to believe that Basil ever studied there, and these writers have evidently confounded him with his namesake, Basil of Antioch, Chrysostom's early associate. On leaving Constantinople Basil proceeded to Athens, where he prosecuted his studies from the year 351 to 356, chiefly under the sophists Himerius and Prohaeresius. He had as his fellow-student and inseparable companion Gregory Nazianzen, whom he had known previously at Caesareia, who had entered the university of Athens a short time before. Gregory's report of the eminent qualities and high attainments of his old friend, strengthened by the influence he had already gained over his fellow-students, secured Basil from the boisterous reception and rough practical jokes which were the lot of most freshmen. The acquaintance between the two young men speedily ripened into an ardent friendship which subsisted with hardly any interruption through the greater part of their lives. The painful estrangement that followed Gregory's forced consecration to the see of Sasima will be narrated in its proper place. The feeling was more enthusiastic on the side of Gregory, who looked on his friend with the most absorbing admiration, but it was returned with no degree of coldness by Basil. The most complete union subsisted between them. They occupied the same chamber and ate at the same table. They studied the same books and attended the same lectures, and stimulated each other in the pursuit of the highest Christian philosophy. In the midst of the distractions and excitements, the shows and the games of Athens, they lived a life of sobriety and self-restraint, seldom leaving their lodgings except for the schools or for church. Gregory's funeral oration on his friend (Greg. Naz. *Or.* xx. 328 sq.) and his poem *de Vita Sua* (tom. ii. p. 4, 15) supply many other interesting details of their joint college career, presenting a curious picture of university-life in the 4th century. Athens afforded Basil the opportunity of familiar intercourse with a fellow-student whose name was destined to become unhappily famous, the nephew of the emperor Constantius, Julian. The future emperor conceived a warm attachment for the young Cappadocian, with whom—as the latter reminds him when the relations between them had so sadly changed—he not only studied the best models of literature, but also carefully read the sacred Scriptures (**"Ep. 40, 41"**; Greg. Naz. *Orat.* iv. *adv. Julian.* p. 121 sq.). Basil remained at Athens till the middle or end of the year 355, when with extreme reluctance he quitted the scene of his studies, tearing himself from the fellow-students and friends who by their expostulations, entreaties, and tears endeavoured to retain him. His friend Gregory confesses his own

inferior strength of mind in yielding to the urgency of his companions and allowing Basil to depart alone (*Orat.* xx. p. 334). Basil's first object in quitting Athens was to profit by the instructions of a philosopher named Eustathius, a native of Cappadocia, who still adhered to the old pagan faith, probably the same spoken of with high commendation by Eunapius (*de Vit. Sophist.* c. iii. iv.) whom he had hoped to find at Caesareia. He passed through Constantinople without halting, and reached his native city, but was disappointed of meeting Eustathius (**"Ep. 1"**). By this time his father was dead. His mother Emmelia was residing at the village of Annesi, . . . near Neocaesareia. Basil's Athenian reputation had preceded him, and he was received with much honour by the people of Caesareia, who, when he consented to settle there as a teacher of rhetoric, are said, in the tumid language of his panegyrist, to have regarded him as "a kind of second founder and protector of their city" (Greg. Naz. *Or.* xx. p. 334). He practised the profession of a rhetorician with great celebrity for a considerable period (Rufin. ii. 9), and, according to a letter of Libanius, assigned to this period, was not unwilling to undertake the troublesome charge of the education of boys (Basil, **"Ep. 358"**). So great was Basil's reputation that the people of Neocaesareia sent a deputation of the leading persons of the city to entreat him to remove thither and undertake the education of their youth. Basil declined. But on a subsequent visit to his mother the citizens endeavoured to overcome his objections, and used all measures short of actual force to detain him (**"Ep. 210,"** 2). Gregory Nazianzen repudiates the idea of either Basil or himself—for by this time he had joined his friend—having been in any degree influenced by ambition or love of human praise, asserting that they had only yielded for a while to the importunities of their fellow-citizens and sacrificed themselves to the world . . . (Greg. Naz. *Or.* xx. p. 334). But Basil's excellent sister Macrina judged him less indulgently and more truly. His brother, Gregory Nyssen, reports that she found him on his return from Athens inordinately elated, puffed up with the pride of philosophy and science, and looking down with contempt on his superiors in dignity and rank (Greg. Nyss. *Vit. S. Macr.* p. 181). At this time also, we may gather from an amusing letter of the other Gregory, Basil had adopted something of the airs and habits of a fine gentleman, and without being stained with the vices of the city was not altogether insensible to its pleasures (Greg. Naz. *Ep.* 6). It was a period of some peril to the young and ardent rhetorician, the object of universal admiration. Macrina proved his good genius. Her warnings and counsels were effectual to guard him from the seductions of the world, and eventually to induce him to abandon it altogether and devote himself to a religious life (Greg. Nyss. *u. s.*). Basil in a letter to Eustathius of Sebaste describes himself at this period as one awaked out of a deep sleep, and in the marvellous light of gospel truth discerning the folly of that wisdom of this world in the study of which nearly all his youth had vanished. His first care was to reform his life corrupted by long intercourse with evil. He sought eagerly for some one to take him by the hand and lead him into the doctrines of godliness. Finding in the Gospels that nothing tended so much toward perfection as to sell all that he had and free himself from worldly cares, and feeling himself too weak to stand along in such an enterprise, he desired earnestly to find some brother who might give him his aid (**"Ep. 223"**). No sooner did his determination become known than he was beset by the remonstrances of his friends entreating him, some to continue the profession of rhetoric, some to become an advocate. But his choice was made, and his resolution was inflexible. His resolution in favour of a Christian life called forth the admiration of his old instructor Libanius (Bas. **"Ep. 336"**). Basil's baptism may be placed at this epoch. He was probably baptized by Dianius bishop of Caesareia, by whom not long afterwards he was admitted to the order of reader (**De Sp. Sancto**, c. xxix. 71). Basil's determination in favour of a life of devotion would be strengthened by the death of his next brother, Naucratius, who had embraced the life of a solitary, and about this period was drowned while engaged in works of mercy (Greg. Nyss. *de Vit. S. Macr.* p. 182). About the year 357, when he was still under thirty, Basil left Caesareia to pursue his search after the most celebrated ascetics, who might exhibit a model of the life he had resolved to embrace. For this purpose he visited Alexandria and Upper Egypt, Palestine, Coelesyria, and Mesopotamia. He records his admiration of the abstinence and endurance of the ascetics whom he met with in these countries, their mastery over hunger and sleep, their indifference to cold and nakedness, as well as his desire to imitate them (**"Ep. 223,"** 2). His feeble health and frequent sicknesses interrupted his journeys, and prevented his pursuing Eustathius, whom he was still anxious to meet, to his place of retirement (**"Ep. 1"**). The year 358 saw Basil again at Caesareia resolved on the immediate carrying out of his purpose of retiring from the world. He and his friend Gregory had already resolved to abandon the world together, and Basil having fixed on Pontus as his place of retirement wrote to his friend to remind him of his engagement. But Gregory had a father and mother both advanced in years, and filial duty forbade his leaving them (Greg. Naz. *Or.* xx. p. 334). His eager desire for the companionship of his early associate led Basil to propose to exchange Pontus for the district called Tiberina, in which Gregory's home, Arianzus, was situated. But he found the place on trial cold and damp, and intolerably muddy, "the very pit of the whole earth" (**"Ep. 14"**), and he quitted it in disgust, and returning to his original destination, selected for his retreat a spot near Neocaesareia, close to the village of Annesi where his father's estates lay, and where he had passed his childhood under the care of his grandmother Macrina. To Annesi his mother Emmelia and his sister Macrina had retired after the death

of the elder Basil, and were living a semi-monastic life. Basil's future home was only divided from Annesi by the river Iris, by which and the gorges of the mountain torrents a tract of level ground was completely insulated. A wooded mountain rose behind. There was only one approach to it, and of that he was master. The natural beauties of the spot, with its ravines, precipices, dashing torrents, and waterfalls, the purity of the air and coolness of the breezes, the abundance of flowers and multitude of singing-birds ravished him, and he declared it to be more beautiful than Calypso's island (**"Ep. 14"**). His glowing description of its charms at length tempted Gregory to visit him. But he did not find the place so much to his taste, and in a bantering epistle addressed to Basil after his return, he reproached him with the wretchedness both of the lodging and the fare, and the severity of the toil he had compelled him to share. "But for Basil's lady-mother he would have been starved to death" (Greg. Naz. *Ep.* 7, 8).

A more serious letter written to soothe Basil's somewhat wounded feelings shews that he sojourned some considerable time with his friend and studied the Scriptures with him (*Ep.* 9), together with the Commentaries of Origen and other early expositors. At this time they also compiled their collection of the 'Beauties of Origen,' or **'Philocalia'** (Socr. iv. 26; Soz. vi. 17; Greg. Naz. *Ep.* 87). In this secluded spot Basil passed five years, an epoch of no small importance in the history of the church, inasmuch as it saw the origin under Basil's influence of the monastic system in the coenobitic form. Eustathius of Sebaste had already introduced monachism into Asia Minor, but monastic communities were a novelty in the Christian world, and of these Basil is justly considered the founder. To his calm and practical mind the coenobitic life appeared much more conducive to the exercise of Christian graces than that of the solitary. "God," he said, "has made us, like the members of our body, to need one another's help. For what discipline of humility, of pity, or of patience can there be if there be no one to whom these duties are to be practised? Whose feet wilt thou wash— whom wilt thou serve—how canst thou be last of all— if thou art alone?" (Basil. ***Reg. Resp.*** vii.). His rule, like that of St. Benedict in later times, united active industry with regular devotional exercises, and by the labour of his monks over wide desert tracts, hopeless sterility gave place to golden harvests and abundant vintages. Not the day only but the night also was divided into definite portions, the intervals being filled with prayers, hymns, and alternate psalmody. The day began and closed with a psalm of confession. The food of his monks was limited to one meal a-day of bread, water, and herbs, and he allowed of sleep only till midnight, when all rose for prayer (**"Ep. 2, 207"**). On his retirement to Pontus Basil devoted all his worldly possessions to the service of the poor, retaining them, however, in his own hands, and by degrees divesting himself of them as occasion required. His life was one of the most rigid asceticism. He had but one outer and one inner garment; he slept in a hair shirt, his bed was the ground; he took little sleep, no bath; the sun was his fire, his food bread and water, his drink the running stream (Greg. Naz. *Or.* xx. p. 358; Greg. Nyss. *de Basil.* p. 490). The severe bodily austerities he practised emaciated his frame and ruined his already feeble health, sowing the seeds of the maladies to which in later years he was a martyr. His friend describes him as "without a wife, without property, without flesh, and almost without blood" (Greg. Naz. *Or.* xix. p. 311). Basil's reputation for sanctity collected large numbers about him. Monasteries sprang up on every side. He repeatedly made missionary journeys through Pontus, and the result of his preaching was the establishment of many coenobitic industrial communities, and the erection of monasteries for both sexes, by which the whole face of the province was changed, while the purity of the orthodox faith was restored by his preaching (Rufin. ix. 9; Soz. vi. 17; Greg. Nyss. *de Basil.* p. 488). Throughout Pontus and Cappadocia Basil was the means of the erection of numerous hospitals for the poor, houses of refuge for virgins, orphanages, and other homes of beneficence. His monasteries had as their inmates children he had taken charge of, married persons who had mutually agreed to live asunder, slaves with the consent of their masters, and solitaries convinced of the danger of living alone (Basil, **Regulae**, 10, 12, 15).

After two years spent in these labours Basil was summoned from his solitude in 359 to accompany Basil of Ancyra and Eustathius of Sebaste, who had been delegated by the council of Seleuceia to communicate the conclusions of that assembly to Constantius at Constantinople. Basil seems from his youth and natural timidity to have avoided taking any part in the discussions of the council that followed, 360, in which the Anomoeans were condemned, the more orthodox Semiarians deposed, and the Acacians triumphed. But when Constantius endeavoured to force those present to sign the creed of Ariminum, Basil left the city and returned to Cappadocia (Greg. Nyss. *in Eunom.* p. 310, 312; Philost. iv. 12). Not long after his return George of Laodiceia arrived at Caesareia as an emissary of Constantius, bringing with him that creed for signature. To his intense grief the bishop, Dianius, a gentle undecided man, whose creed always inclined to that of the strongest, and who valued peace above orthodoxy, but for whom Basil felt great respect and affection, was persuaded to sign the heretical document Basil felt it impossible any longer to hold com munion with his bishop, and fled to Nazianzus to find consolation in the society of his dear friend Gregory ("**Ep. 8, 51**"). He denied with indignation the report that he had anathematized his bishop, and when two years afterwards (362) Dianius was stricken for death and entreated Basil to return and comfort his last hours, he at once ac-

ceded to his request, and the aged bishop died in his arms, protesting with his last breath that he had never intentionally departed from the faith as declared at Nicaea, and had signed the creed of Ariminum in the simplicity of his heart ("**Ep. 51**"). [Dianius.] The choice of Dianius' successor gave rise to violent dissensions at Caesareia. The clergy were divided into parties, each urging the claims of a favourite candidate. At last the populace, wearied with the indecision, took the initiative, and chose Eusebius, a man of high position and eminent piety, but as yet unbaptized. In spite of his reluctance, they forcibly conveyed him to the church where the provincial bishops were assembled, and compelled the unwilling prelates first to baptize and then to consecrate him. The subsequent desire of the provincial bishops to annul the election on the ground of violence was overruled by the elder Gregory of Nazianzus, and Eusebius occupied the episcopal seat of Caesareia for eight years (Greg. Naz. *Or.* xix. 308. 309).

Shortly before the death of Dianius Julian had ascended the throne (Dec. 11th, 361). It was the desire of the new emperor to surround himself with the friends and associates of his early days (Greg. Naz. *Or.* iv. 120). Among the first whom he invited was his fellow-student at Athens, Basil. Basil at first held out hopes of accepting his old friend's invitation. Julian was delighted at his readiness, and placed the public conveyances at his disposal, begging him to come as soon as he could and stay as long as possible, but giving him full liberty to leave whenever he might be so inclined (*Julianus Basilio*, Basil. "**Ep. 39**"). Basil delayed his journey, and Julian's declared apostasy from the Christian faith soon gave him sufficient cause to relinquish it altogether. Julian concealed for a time his indignation at the non-fulfilment of his promise, which however stung him to the quick, as an implied censure from one whom he knew to be worthy of all respect. The following year afforded Julian an opportunity of displaying his irritation. On his progress through Asia Minor to Antioch he received the intelligence that the people of Caesareia, so far from apostatizing with him, and building new temples as he had desired, had pulled down the only one still standing, that of Fortune (Greg. Naz. *Or.* iii. 91; xix. 309; Socr. v. 4). His indignation at this contempt of his authority knew no bounds. He expunged Caesareia from the catalogue of cities, made it take its old name of Mazaca, imposed heavy payments, compelled the clergy to serve in the police force, and put to death two young men of high rank, named Eupsychius and Damas, who had taken part in the demolition of the temple. Before reaching Caesareia he despatched a minatory letter to Basil demanding a thousand pounds of gold, for the expenses of his Persian expedition, and threatening in default of payment, to rase the city to the ground. The letter ends with the familiar paranomasia, also (according to Sozomen, *H.*

E. v. 18) addressed by him to Apollinaris, who had remonstrated with him on the folly of idolatry . . . (Bas. **"Ep. 40"**). Basil's dauntless reply reminds the apostate emperor of the time when they two studied the Holy Scriptures together, and nothing escaped him. But now Demons had raised him to so proud a height that he exalted himself against God and the church, the nurse and mother of all. He upbraids him with the folly of demanding so vast a sum from him, the poorest of the poor, who had not enough to purchase himself a meal; and concludes by retorting his play upon words on himself— . . . (Bas. **"Ep. 41"**). The displeasure of Julian against Caesareia was still further exasperated by the election of Eusebius as bishop, a choice which had robbed the state of a valuable magistrate (Greg. Naz. *Or.* xix. 309). The principal responsibility for this election lay with Basil and Gregory. These therefore he reserved with the cruel kindness of the Cyclops (Hom. *Odyss.* i. 369, 370) to be the last to suffer on his triumphant return from his Persian campaign (Greg. Naz. *Or.* iv. 132). The death of the apostate (June 26th, 363) delivered Basil from this imminent peril and preserved him for future labours in defence of the orthodox faith and for the promotion of the unity of the church.

It has been remarked that Julian considered Basil to have been one of those chiefly responsible for the choice of Eusebius as bishop of Caesareia. Nor is it at all improbable that his belief was well grounded. Basil, keeping in the background, may have secretly directed the popular movement, hoping thereby to secure a triumph for the cause of orthodoxy, and promising himself to have in the new bishop, suddenly raised from the ranks of the laity to an office of such great difficulty, a pliant instrument for carrying out his own purposes. The result will shew how far his anticipations were realised.

One of the first acts of Eusebius was to compel the reluctant Basil to be ordained priest. His friend Gregory had been ordained a little before, and his language seems to indicate that, as was by no means uncommon, both had been the victims of artifice, if not of violence (Greg. Naz. *Ep.* 11, p. 775). Eusebius was very naturally desirous to avail himself of the theological knowledge and intellectual powers of Basil to compensate for his own deficiencies. At first he employed him very largely. But when he found himself completely eclipsed he became jealous of his popularity and treated Basil with a marked coldness, amounting almost to insolence, which awoke a feeling of hostility to himself in the majority of the Christians of Caesareia, of whom Basil was the idol. A rupture was the consequence. We are ignorant of its immediate cause, but probably both parties were more or less to blame. If Eusebius's personal dignity was wounded by Basil's too evident superiority, Basil himself fretted under the official priority of his intellectual inferior, and yielded unwilling submission to his claims to obedience (cf. Bas. *in Esaiam*, i. 57). A schism was imminent, which Basil might have easily precipitated. It happened that at this time some western bishops, Eusebius of Vercelli being probably among them, were at Caesareia. They warmly espoused Basil's cause. A word from him was only wanted, and they would have ordained him bishop, a step which would have been received with enthusiasm not only by the populace, but by the chief inhabitants of the city. But Basil had strength of mind to resist the temptation. He refused to strengthen the hands of the heretical party by creating divisions among the orthodox, and retired with his friend Gregory to Pontus, where he devoted himself to the care of the monasteries he had founded (Greg. Naz. *Or.* xx. p. 336, 337; Soz. vi. 15).

Basil had passed about three years in his Pontic seclusion when, in 365, the blind zeal of the emperor Valens for the spread of Arianism brought him back to Caesareia. As soon as it was known that Valens was approaching that city, the popular voice demanded the recall of Basil as the only bulwark against the attack on the true faith and its adherents meditated by the emperor. Eusebius sought to make a compromise by inviting Gregory to his side. But Gregory, true to his friendship, refused to come so long as Basil was rejected. He acted the part of a wise mediator. Soothing the irritation of Eusebius, softening Basil's offended feelings, leading each to regard the conduct of the other in a more friendly light, he finally brought about a complete reconciliation (Greg. Naz. *Ep.* 19, 20, 169; *Or.* xx. p. 339). Nothing could surpass the Christian temper and wisdom manifested by Basil on his return to Caesareia. He treated Eusebius with the honour due to his position and his age, and by his deferential conduct dissipated the unworthy suspicions he had entertained. He was always at his side as his counsellor and sympathizing friend. He proved himself, in the words of Gregory, the staff of his age, the support of his faith; at home the most faithful of his friends; abroad the most efficient of his ministers (*ib.* 340). The consequence was that while the one had the name, the other had the reality of power, and while all was being really done by him, with happy adroitness he persuaded his superior that he was doing all himself (Greg. Naz. *Or.* xx. 340).

The first designs of Valens against Caesareia were interrupted by the news of the revolt of Procopius (Amm. Marc. 26, 27). He left Asia to quell the insurrection which threatened his throne. Basil availed himself of the breathing-time thus granted in organizing the resistance of the orthodox against the Eunomians or Anomoeans who were actively propagating their pernicious doctrines through Asia Minor; supporting the weakness of some, awakening the consciences of others, healing divisions, and uniting the Cappadocians in loyal devotion to the truth. The year 368 afforded

Basil occasion of displaying his large and universal charity. The whole of Cappadocia was desolated by drought and famine, the visitation pressing specially on Caesareia on account of the largeness of its population and its distance from any seaport. The poor were the chief sufferers, and Basil devoted his whole energies to their maintenance. Some rich merchants having sought to turn the famine to their own profit by buying up all the remaining corn, Basil employed all his powers to bring them to a better mind, never ceasing from his expostulations until he had led them to open their stores to the famishing multitude. Setting an example himself, he sold the property he had inherited at the recent death of his mother, and devoted the sum thus realised to feeding the poor. Not content with this, he raised a large subscription in the city with which he purchased stores of provisions, the distribution of which he regulated himself. None were refused. He gave his own personal ministrations to the wretched, feeding them with his own hand and washing their feet, and while he fed their bodies he was careful to nourish their souls also with the bread of life (Greg. Naz. *Or.* xx. 340-342; Greg. Nyss. *in Eunom.* i. 306).

Eusebius died towards the middle of the year 370, breathing his last in the arms of Basil (Greg. Naz. *Or.* xix. 310; xx. 342). Basil persuaded himself, and not altogether unwarrantably, that the cause of orthodoxy in Asia Minor was involved in his becoming his successor. His election must be ensured at all risks. Unable to assert his claims personally, he at once sent for his friend Gregory, by whose influence and exertions he hoped his election would be put beyond doubt. But fearing lest Gregory, if apprised of the real nature of the business for which his services were required, would decline to undertake a task of so much delicacy, Basil employed artifice to cloke his design. He happened to be suffering from one of the attacks of illness to which he was subject, and he wrote to his friend begging him to come and see him before he died, and receive his last commands. The affectionate heart of Gregory allowed no delay. He started instantly, before the news of Eusebius's death had reached him. But halfway to Caesareia the sight of the bishops hastening to that city for the election of a new prelate disclosed the deceit that had been put upon him. With very natural indignation, instead of pursuing his journey, he wrote a letter of earnest remonstrance to Basil, not only refusing to come to Caesareia himself, but urging him, if he wished to avoid unfriendly suspicions, to leave the city until the election was over. Such affairs were not managed by men of piety, but by men of power and popularity: nor could it be fitting that Gregory should be prominent in a business in which Basil was unwilling to appear. When all was over he would visit his old friend, and upbraid him as he deserved (Greg. Naz. *Ep.* 21). Basil, disappointed of the assistance he had confidently anticipated from the younger Gregory, now betook himself to his father, the aged bishop of Nazianzus of

the same name. The momentous importance of the juncture was more evident to the elder man. Orthodoxy was at stake in Basil's election. "The Holy Spirit must triumph" (Greg. Naz. *Or.* xx. 342). No exertion therefore was spared by him; no means of influence left untried. Using his son as his scribe, he dictated a letter to the clergy, monks, magistrates, and people of Caesareia, calling on them earnestly to lay aside all party feeling and choose Basil as bishop, and followed this up by another to the electing prelates, exhorting them not to allow Basil's weakness of health to counterbalance his marked pre-eminence in spiritual gifts and in learning (Greg. Naz. *Ep.* 22, 23). He felt himself too old to venture on so long a journey, while he clearly saw that the delicate temperament of his son was unsuited for the guidance of a factious constituency and a successful resistance to cabals and intrigues. No orthodox prelate had at that time a deservedly greater influence than Eusebius of Samosata. Gregory wrote to him and persuaded him to visit Caesareia and undertake the direction of this difficult business (Bas. **"Ep. 47"**). On his arrival, Eusebius found the city divided into two opposite factions. All the best of the people, together with the clergy and the monks, warmly advocated Basil's election, which was as vigorously opposed by other classes. The bishops were jealous of his superior powers: the rich were uneasy at his uncompromising preaching of charity: the authorities looked with alarm on a prelate of his resolute will, and dreaded the displeasure of Valens. The influence and tact of Eusebius overcame all obstacles. The people warmly espoused Basil's cause; the bishops were compelled to give way, and the triumph of the orthodox cause was consummated by the arrival of the venerable Gregory, who on learning that one vote was wanting for the canonical election of Basil, while his son was still hesitating full of scruples, and refused to quit Nazianzus, left his bed for a litter, and had himself carried to Caesareia at the risk of expiring on the way, and with his own hands consecrated the newly elected prelate, and placed him on his episcopal throne (Greg. Naz. *Ep.* 29, p. 793, *Or.* xix. 311, xx. 343). Basil's election filled the orthodox everywhere with joy. Athanasius, the veteran champion of the faith, congratulated Cappadocia on possessing a bishop whom every province might envy (Athan. *ad Pallad.* p. 953, *ad Joann. et Ant.* p. 951). At Constantinople it was received with far different feelings. Valens regarded it as a serious check to his designs for the triumph of Arianism. Basil was not an opponent to be despised. He must be either forced to bend to the emperor's will, or be got rid of. As bishop of Caesareia Basil's power extended far beyond the limits of the city itself. He was metropolitan of Cappadocia, and exarch of Pontus. In the latter capacity his authority, more or less defined, extended over more than half Asia Minor, and embraced as many as eleven provinces. Ancyra, Neocaesareia, Tyana, among other metropolitan sees, acknowledged him as their ecclesiastical superior.

Basil's first disappointment in his episcopate arose from his inability to induce his dear friend Gregory to join him as his coadjutor in the government of his province and exarchate. He wrote to Basil expressing his exceeding delight at his election, but excusing himself from coming to him both on Basil's account, lest he should seem to be collecting his partisans about him with indecency and heat, and for his own peace and reputation. He feared that he should excite jealousy, and only increase his friend's difficulties (Greg. Naz. *Ep.* 24, *Or.* xx. 344). When at last he yielded to Basil's importunities, he sedulously kept himself in the background, and declined all the public attentions and marks of dignity which Basil was anxious to confer on him. He refused all that Basil offered, and made Basil approve his refusal (Greg. Naz. *Or.* xx. 344). His sensitive and retiring disposition unfitted him for life in a large city, and Eusebius's affection for Basil and the sense of the services he might render him in his difficult charge, were insufficient to retain him long at Caesareia, and he returned to Nazianzus. Difficulties soon thickened round the new exarch. The bishops who had opposed his election, and who had manifested their ill-feeling by refusing to take any part in his consecration, now exchanged their open hostility for secret opposition. While professing outward union, they withheld their support in everything. They treated Basil with marked slight and shewed a complete want of sympathy in all his plans (**"Ep. 98"**). He complains to Eusebius of Samosata that they refused to help him, and were of no real use to him in anything. It was impossible to please them. They were angry if he neglected to invite them to the commemoration of the martyrs, and if he did invite them they would not come. On one occasion the report of his death having got abroad, they hastened to Caesareia to choose a successor. But finding him alive, they had to receive from him a sharp admonition. They manifested extreme contrition and lavished promises of amendment; but no sooner had they got back to their dioceses than they resumed their former opposition (Bas. **"Ep. 48, 141, 282"**). This disloyal behaviour filled Basil with despondency, and was the cause of repeated attacks of illness. It is true he overcame all his opponents in a few years by firmness and kindness, but their secret opposition and half-hearted support greatly increased the difficulties of the commencement of his episcopate. The alienation of his uncle Gregory, whom he had reason to regard with affection and respect as a second parent, who had superintended the completion of his education after the death of his father, was extremely painful to him. The aged bishop for some unknown cause took offence and joined the party of opposition. Basil's brother, the simple-minded but unadroit Gregory Nyssen, tried to put an end to the estrangement, but only made matters worse. With an almost inconceivable want of judgment he wrote forged letters to Basil in his uncle's name. Basil acted on them, and when they were repudiated by the aged bishop

the estrangement was deepened. Each heartily desired reconciliation, but neither would take the first step. The uncle refused to humble himself to his nephew: the metropolitan to his suffragan. Basil, on discovering the deception that had been practised, wrote with just indignation to his brother upbraiding him with his unbrotherly conduct. He does not refuse to visit his uncle, but he declines to come until he has been properly invited (Bas. **"Ep. 58"**). At last the love of peace and a sense of the scandal of a quarrel between such near relations prevailed with Basil, and he wrote a letter breathing affection and duty to his uncle. The old Gregory had only waited for this. He at once sent back his other nephew with a pacific reply. Basil answered thanking him for his forgiveness, and leaving all arrangements as to the time and place of the interview to him (Bas. **"Ep. 59, 60"**). The misunderstanding was thus happily healed and peace restored. Basil had been bishop little more than twelve months, when he was brought into open collision with the emperor Valens, who was traversing Asia Minor with the fixed resolve of exterminating the orthodox faith and establishing Arianism. No part of Basil's history is better known, and in none do we more clearly discern the strength and weakness of his character. While every unprejudiced reader will repudiate Gibbon's offensive verdict, that Basil's assertion of "the truth of his opinions and the dignity of his rank" was due to "inflexible pride," rather than to an uncompromising zeal for the truth as declared by the Nicene Fathers, a calm review of the circumstances may lead him to accept the judgment of a later historian. "The memorable interview with St. Basil," writes Dean Milman, "as it is related by the Catholic party, displays, if the weakness, certainly the patience and toleration of the sovereign—if the uncompromising firmness of the prelate, some of that leaven of pride with which he is taunted by St. Jerome" (Milman, *Hist. of Christianity*, iii. 45).[1] Four years before, A.D. 367, the designs of Valens against the Catholics of Caesareia had been interrupted by the revolt of Procopius. Bat he had never relinquished them, and he was now approaching with the determination of reducing to submission one whom he knew to be the chief champion of orthodoxy in the East. The progress of Valens hitherto had been one of uniform victory. The Catholics had everywhere fallen before him. Bithynia had resisted and had become the scene of horrible tragedies. The fickle Galatia had yielded without a struggle. The fate of Cappadocia depended on Basil. His house, as the emperor drew near, was besieged by ladies of rank, high personages of state, even by bishops, who entreated him to bow before the storm and appease the emperor by a temporary submission. Their expostulations were rejected with indignant disdain. A band of Arian bishops headed by Euippius, an aged bishop of Galatia and an old friend of Basil's, preceded Valens' arrival with the hope of overawing their opponents by their numbers and unanimity. Basil took the initiative, and with prompt decision separated himself from their communion (Bas. **"Ep. 68, 128, 244, 251"**). These prelates were followed by the members of the emperor's household, who indulged in the most violent menaces against the archbishop. One of the most insolent of these was the eunuch Demosthenes, the superintendent of the kitchen. Basil met his threats with quiet irony, bidding him go back to his kitchen fire. The archbishop was next confronted by Modestus, the prefect of the Praetorium, commissioned by the emperor to offer Basil the choice between deposition or communion with the Arians. This violent and unscrupulous imperial favourite accosted Basil with the grossest insolence. He refused him the title of bishop: he threatened confiscation, exile, tortures, death. But such menaces, Basil replied, were powerless on one whose sole wealth was a ragged cloak and a few books, to whom the whole earth was a home, or rather a place of pilgrimage, whose feeble body could endure no tortures beyond the first stroke, and to whom death would be a mercy, as it would the sooner transport him to the God to Whom he lived. Modestus expressed his astonishment at hearing such unusual language (Greg. Naz. *Orat.* xx. 351; Soz. vi. 16). "That is," replied Basil, "because you have never before fallen in with a true bishop." Modestus finding his menaces useless changed his tone. He counselled prudence. Basil should avoid irritating the emperor, and submit to his requirements, as all the other prelates of Asia had done. If he would only yield he promised him the friendship of Valens, and whatever favours he might desire for his friends. Why should he sacrifice all his power for the sake of a few doctrines? (Theodoret, iv. 19.) But flattery had as little power as threats over Basil's iron will. The prefect was at his wit's end. Valens was expected on the morrow. Modestus was unwilling to meet the emperor with a report of failure. The former interview had been a private one. The aspect of a court of justice with its official state and band of ministers prepared to execute its sentence, might inspire awe. But judicial terrors were equally futile (Greg. Nyss. *in Eunom.* p. 315). Modestus, utterly foiled, had to announce to his master that all his attempts to obtain submission had been fruitless. "Violence would be the only course to adopt with one over whom threats and blandishments were equally powerless" (Greg. Naz. *Orat.* xx. p. 350). Such Christian intrepidity was not without effect on the feeble impressionable mind of Valens. He refused to sanction any harsh measures against the archbishop, and moderated his demands to the admission of Arians to Basil's communion. But here too Basil was equally inflexible. To bring matters to a decided issue, the emperor presented himself among the worshippers, in the chief church of Caesareia on the Feast of the Epiphany, A.D. 372. The service had commenced when he arrived, and he found the church flooded with "a sea" of worshippers whose chanted psalms pealed forth like thunder, uninterrupted by the entrance of the emperor and his train. Basil was at the altar celebrating the eucharistic sacrifice, standing,

according to the primitive custom, behind the altar with his face to the assembled people, supported on either hand by the semicircle of his attendant clergy. "The unearthly majesty of the scene," the rapt devotion of the archbishop, erect like a column before the holy table, the reverent order of the immense throng, "more like that of angels than of men," overpowered the weak and excitable Valens, and he almost fainted away. When the time came for making his offering, and the ministers were hesitating whether they should receive an oblation from the hand of a heretic, his limbs failed him, and but for the aid of one of the clergy he would have fallen. Basil, it would seem, pitying his enemy's weakness, came forward himself and accepted the gift from his trembling hand (Greg. Naz. *Orat.* xx. p. 351). The next day Valens again visited the church, and listened with reverence to Basil's preaching, and made his offerings, which were not now rejected. The sermon over, Basil graciously admitted the emperor within the sacred veil, and discoursed with him at considerable length on the orthodox faith. He was rudely interrupted by the cook Demosthenes, who was in attendance on the emperor. Demosthenes was guilty of a gross solecism. Basil smiled and said, "We have, it seems, a Demosthenes who cannot speak Greek; he had better attend to his sauces than meddle with theology." The retort amused the emperor, who retired so well pleased with his theological opponent, that he made him a grant of lands for the poorhouse Basil was erecting (Theod. iv. 19; Greg. Naz. *Orat.* xx. 351; Basil. **"Ep. 94"**). The vacillating mind of Valens was always influenced by the latest and most imperious advisers, and when Basil remained firm in his refusal to admit them to his communion, the Arians about the emperor had little difficulty in persuading him that he was compromising the faith by permitting Basil to remain, and that his banishment was necessary for the peace of the East and the maintenance of the faith. The emperor yielded to their importunity, and ordered Basil to leave the city. Basil at once made his simple preparations for departure, ordering one of his attendants to take his tablets and follow him. He was to start at night to avoid the risk of popular disturbance. The chariot was at his door, and his friends, Gregory among them, were bewailing so great a calamity, when his journey was arrested by the sudden and alarming illness of Galates, the only son of Valens and Dominica. The empress attributed her child's danger to the divine displeasure at the treatment of Basil. The emperor in abject alarm sent the chief military officials of the court, Terentius and Arinthaeus, who were known to be his friends, to entreat Basil to come and pray over the sick child. Galates was as yet unbaptized. On receiving a promise that the child should receive that sacrament at the hands of a Catholic bishop and be instructed in the orthodox faith, Basil consented. He prayed over the boy, and the malady was alleviated. On his retiring the Arians again got round the feeble prince, reminded him of a promise he had made to Eudoxius, by whom he himself had been baptized, and the child received baptism from the hands of an Arian prelate. He grew immediately worse, and died the same night (Greg. Naz. *Orat.* xx. 352, 364; Theod. iv. 19; Socr. iv. 26; Soz. iv. 16; Eph. Syr. *opud* Coteler. *Monum. Eccl. Graec.* iii. 63; Rufin. xi. 9). Once more the unwearied enemies of Basil returned to the attack, and with the usual result. Valens always yielded to pressure. Again Basil's exile was determined on, but the pens with which Valens was preparing to sign the decree refused to write, and split in his agitated hand, and the supposed miracle arrested the execution of the sentence. Valens left Caesareia, and Basil remained master of the situation (Theod. iv. 19; Ephr. Syr. *u. s.* p. 65). Before long his old enemy Modestus, attacked by a severe malady, presented himself as a suppliant to Basil, and attributing his cure to the intercessions of the saint, became his fast friend. So great was Basil's influence with the prefect that persons came from a distance to secure his intercession with him. We have as many as six letters addressed by Basil to Modestus in favour of different individuals (Basil. **"Ep. 104, 110, 111, 279, 280, 281"**; Greg. Naz. *Orat.* xx. pp. 352, 353). Another striking evidence of Basil's power is recorded by his friend Gregory. A rich widow, whose hand had been vainly demanded in marriage by the judge's assessor, took refuge from his violence in Basil's cathedral. The vicar of Pontus demanded the fugitive, and ordered a domiciliary visit of the archbishop's residence. Failing to discover the lady he commanded Basil to be brought before him, and menaced him with tortures and a horrible death. On his threatening to tear out his liver, Basil calmly replied that he should be very much obliged to him to do so, since where it was it gave him a great deal of trouble. The news of Basil's danger spread through the city. The populace rushed to the prefect's court to rescue their beloved bishop. So violent was the commotion that Basil had to calm the mob and rescue the vicar by his intercessions from the consequences of his own rash insolence (Greg. Naz. *Orat.* xx. pp. 353, 354; Greg. Nyss. *de Bas.* p. 435).

The issue of these unsuccessful assaults was to place Basil in a position of inviolability, and to leave him at leisure for the internal administration of his diocese and exarchate, where there was much that needed his firm and unflinching hand. In the course of his visitation many irregularities were discovered which he sternly repressed. The chorepiscopi were in the habit of admitting men to the lower orders of the ministry who had no intention of proceeding to the priesthood, or even to the diaconate, merely to purchase immunity from military service (**"Ep. 54"**). Too many of his suffragans were guilty of simony in receiving a fee for ordination (**"Ep. 55"**). Men were raised to the episcopate from motives of personal interest, and to gratify private friends (**"Ep. 290"**). The perilous custom for unmarried priests to have females . . . residing with them as "spiritual sisters" called for animadversion (**"Ep. 55"**).

A fanatic deacon, named Glycerius, who had collected a band of professed virgins, whom he forcibly carried off by night, and wandered the country dancing and singing to the scandal of the faithful, caused him much trouble (**"Ep. 169, 170, 171"**). To heal the fountainhead, he made himself as far as possible master of episcopal elections, and steadily refused to admit any but those whom he deemed worthy of the office. So high was the reputation of his clergy that other bishops sent to him for presbyters who might be their coadjutors and become their successors (**"Ep. 81"**). Marriage with a deceased wife's sister he denounced as prohibited both by the laws of scripture and of nature (**"Ep. 160"**). Feeble as his health was, Basil's activity was unceasing. He was to be found in every part of his exarchate, and maintained a constant intercourse by letter with confidential friends who kept him informed of all that passed, and were ready to carry out the instructions they received. He pushed his episcopal activity to the very frontiers of Armenia. In 372 he made an expedition by the express command of Valens, obtained by the urgency of his fast friend the count Terentius, to strengthen the episcopate in that country by the appointment of new bishops and the infusion of fresh life into those already in office (**"Ep. 99"**). He was very diligent in preaching, not only at Caesareia and other cities, but in the country villages. The details of public worship occupied his attention. Even while a presbyter he arranged forms of prayer . . . , probably a liturgy, for the church of Caesareia (Greg. Naz. *Or.* xx. p. 340). He established nocturnal services, in which the psalms were chanted by alternate choirs, which, as a novelty, gave great offence to the clergy of Neocaesareia (**"Ep. 207"**). These incessant labours were carried out by one who, naturally of a weak constitution, had so enfeebled himself by austerities that, "when called well, he was weaker than persons who are given over" (**"Ep. 136"**). His chief malady, a disease of the liver, caused him repeated and protracted sufferings, which often hindered him from travelling when most needful, the least motion bringing on a relapse (**"Ep. 202"**). The severity of the winter often kept him a prisoner not only to his house but even to his room (**"Ep. 27"**). A letter from Eusebius of Samosata arrived when he had been fifty days ill of a fever. "He was eager to fly straight to Syria, but he was unequal to turning in his bed. He hoped for relief from the hot springs" (**"Ep. 138"**). He speaks of himself as having received "sickness upon sickness, so that his shell must certainly fail unless God's mercy extricate him from evils beyond man's cure" (**"Ep. 136"**). At forty-five he calls himself an old man. The next year he had lost all his teeth. Three years before his death all remaining hope of life had left him (**"Ep. 198"**). He died prematurely aged at the age of fifty. Seldom did a spirit of so indomitable activity reside in so feeble a frame, and, triumphing over its weakness, make it the instrument of such vigorous work for Christ and His church.

The year 372 saw Basil plunged into a harassing dispute with Anthimus, bishop of Tyana, touching ecclesiastical jurisdiction, which led to the chief personal sorrow of his life, the estrangement of the friend of his youth, Gregory of Nazianzus. The circumstances were these. Towards the close of the year 371 Valens determined on the division of Cappadocia into two provinces. Podandus, a miserable little town at the foot of Mount Taurus, was named at first as the chief city of the new province, to which a portion of the executive was to be removed. The inhabitants of Caesareia, who would thus lose much of their gains, and be subjected to double civil burdens, were stunned with the blow. They entreated Basil to go to Constantinople himself, and petition the authorities to rescind the edict. The weakness of his health prevented Basil from acceding to their desire, and he wrote letters to Sophronius, a native of Caesareia, who held a high official position about the court, and a man of influence named Aburgius, begging them to employ all their power to alter the emperor's decision. They could not, however, prevent the division of the province. All they could obtain was the substitution of Tyana for Podandus (Bas. **"Ep. 74, 75, 76"**).

This was only the commencement of Basil's troubles. Anthimus, bishop of Tyana, insisted that the ecclesiastical division should follow the civil, and claimed the rights of a metropolitan over several of Basil's suffragans. Basil appealed to ancient usage in vain. The new metropolitan called a council of the bishops who having opposed Basil's election continued secretly his enemies, and were not indisposed to exalt his rival. Anthimus strengthened his faction partly by flattery, partly by intimidation, and partly by the removal of those who opposed his wishes. Basil's authority was at a blow reduced to a nullity in one-half of his province (Greg. Naz. *Or.* xx. p. 355, *Ep.* 31, 33; Bas. **"Ep. 259"**). In his difficulty Basil at once summoned his friend Gregory. He replied that he would come to his assistance, though Basil wanted him no more than the sea wanted water. He warned Basil at the same time that his difficulties were increased by the suspicions created by his intimacy with Eustathius of Sebaste and his friends, whose reputation for orthodoxy was not undeservedly low (Greg. Naz. *Ep.* 25). On Gregory's arrival the two friends started together for the monastery of St. Orestes on Mount Taurus, in the second Cappadocia, the property of the see of Caesareia, to collect the produce of the estate. This roused Anthimus's indignation, and notwithstanding his advanced age, he occupied the defile through which the train of mules had to pass with his armed retainers, and a serious affray took place, in which Gregory fought bravely in his friend's defence (Greg. Naz. *Or.* xx. 356, *Ep.* 31, *Carm.* i. 8). To strengthen himself against his rival, Basil determined to erect several new bishoprics as defensive outposts. One of the new sees chosen was Sasima, a miserable little posting station, and seat of a

frontier custom-house at the junction of three great roads not far from the source of the disputed revenues, St. Orestes; hot, dry, and dusty, vociferous with the brawls of muleteers, travellers, and excisemen. No place could have been more distasteful to one of Gregory's delicate temperament; but here Basil, with disregard to his friend's sensitive nature, determined to place him. Gregory's weaker character bowed to the iron will of Basil, and he was most reluctantly consecrated bishop of Sasima. Basil's object, however, was not gained. Anthimus appointed a rival bishop, and Gregory took the earliest opportunity of escaping from a position into which he had been thrust by the despotic will of a friend from whom he had expected far other treatment, and which he could only maintain at the risk of continual contest and even bloodshed [Gregory Nazianzen, Anthimus]. A peace was ultimately patched up between the contending bishops, apparently through the intercession of Gregory, assisted by the mediation of Eusebius of Samosata, and the senate of Tyana. Anthimus was recognized as metropolitan of the new province, each province preserving its own revenues (Bas. **"Ep. 97, 98, 122"**). Basil's conduct at this juncture Gregory could never forgive or forget. He attributed it to a high sense of duty, and admired and reverenced him even more than before. But the wound inflicted on their mutual attachment was never healed, and even after Basil's death he reproaches him with his unfaithfulness to the laws of friendship, and laments the perfidy of which he had been the victim. "This lamentable occurrence took place seven years before Basil's death. He had before and after it many trials, many sorrows; but this probably was the greatest of all."[2]

The *Ptochotropheion,* or hospital for the reception and relief of the poor, which Basil had erected in the suburbs of Caesareia, afforded his untiring enemies a pretext for denouncing him to Helias, the new president of the province. This establishment, which was so extensive as to go by the name of the "New Town" . . . (Greg. Naz. *Or.* xx. p. 359), and subsequently the "Basileiad" after its founder (Soz. vi. 34) included a church, a palace for the bishop, and residences for his clergy and their attendant ministers; *hospices* for the poor, sick, and wayfarers; and workshops for the artisans and labourers whose services were needed, in which the inmates also might learn and practise various trades. There was a special department for lepers, with arrangements for their proper medical treatment, and on these loathsome objects Basil lavished his chief personal ministrations. By such an enormous establishment Basil, it was hinted, was aiming at undue power and infringing on the rights of the civil authorities. But Basil adroitly parried the blow by reminding the governor that apartments were provided in the building for him and his attendants, and suggesting that the glory of so magnificent an architectural work would redound to him[3] (Bas. **"Ep. 84"**).

Far more harassing and more lasting troubles arose to Basil from the double dealing of Eustathius, the unprincipled and time-serving bishop of Sebaste. Referring the reader to his own article for further particulars [Eustathius of Sebaste], it will be enough here to state that the heretical antecedents and connexions of Eustathius, who had been a pupil of Arius at Alexandria, and had been ordained at Antioch by the Arians, failed to close the large heart of Basil against him. The austerity of his life, his seeming holiness, his strict adherence to truth, his zeal against more developed Arianism, gave him a high place in Basil's esteem, which after-intercourse warmed into real friendship. Eustathius visited Basil at his monastery on the Iris, where, as well as during the journeys they took together to visit various religious communities, he acquired an intimate knowledge of Basil's mind and character, which he afterwards employed against him. Eustathius was one of those who are always found on the side of those in authority. A semi-Arian under Constantius, he professed Arian doctrine under Valens. Basil was slow to believe evil of one to whom he was so much attached, and maintained his intimacy with him notwithstanding the suspicions it caused of his own heterodoxy, and the hindrances created in the effective management of his diocese. He attributed his heterodoxy to over-subtlety or want of clearness of mind, not to unsoundness of belief—sought to detach him from his old Arian connections, and to confirm him in the true faith.

Basil's intercourse with Eustathius was productive of many mortifications and disappointments in his episcopal work. Towards the middle of June 372, the venerable Theodotus, bishop of Nicopolis, a metropolitan of Lesser Armenia, a prelate of high character and unblemished orthodoxy, deservedly respected by Basil, had invited him to a festival at Phargamon near his episcopal see. Meletius of Antioch, then in exile in Armenia, was also to be there. Sebaste was almost on the road between Caesareia and Nicopolis, and Basil, aware of the suspicion entertained by Theodotus of the orthodoxy of Eustathius, determined to stop there on his way, and demand a definite statement of his faith. Many hours were spent in fruitless discussion until, at three in the afternoon of the second day, a substantial agreement appeared to have been attained. To remove all doubt of his orthodoxy, Basil requested Theodotus to draw up a formulary of faith for Eustathius to sign. To his mortification not only was his request refused, but Theodotus plainly intimated to Basil that he had no wish that he should visit him at Nicopolis. Basil had already felt hurt at the want of due formality in the invitation, and the absence of the usual escort. While hesitating whether he should still pursue his journey, he received letters from his friend Eusebius of Samosata stating his inability to come and join him.

This at once decided Basil. Without Eusebius' help he felt himself unequal to face the controversies his pres-

ence at Nicopolis would evoke, and he returned home full of despondency at the ill-fortune which for his sins rendered his labours for the peace of the church unavailing ("**Ep. 98, 99**"). A few months later the sensitive orthodoxy of Theodotus prepared another mortification for Basil. In carrying out the commands of Valens, mentioned above, to supply Armenia with bishops, the counsel and assistance of Theodotus as metropolitan was essential. As a first step towards cordial co-operation, Basil sought a conference with Theodotus at Getasa, the estate of Meletius of Antioch, in whose presence he made him acquainted with what had passed between him and Eustathius at Sebaste, and his acceptance of the orthodox faith. But Theodotus could tell him of the effrontery with which Eustathius had denied that he had come to any agreement with Basil. To bring the matter to an issue, Basil again proposed that a confession of faith should be prepared on his signing which his future communion with Eustathius would depend. This apparently satisfied Theodotus, who invited Basil to visit him and inspect his church, and promised to accompany him on his journey into Armenia. But on Basil's arrival at Nicopolis he spurned him with horror . . . as an excommunicated person, and refused to join him at either morning or evening prayer. Thus deserted by one on whose co-operation he relied, Basil had little heart to prosecute his mission, but he continued his journey to Satala, where he consecrated a bishop, established discipline, and promoted peace among the prelates of the province. Basil well knew how to distinguish between the busy detractors who rejoiced to find a pretext for their malevolence in his intercourse with Eustathius, and one like Theodotus animated with a true zeal for the orthodox faith. Generously overlooking his former rudenesses, he reopened communications with him the following year, and visiting Nicopolis employed his assistance in once more drawing up an elaborate confession of faith embodying the Nicene creed, for Eustathius to sign (Bas. "**Ep. 125**"). Eustathius did so in the most formal manner in the presence of witnesses whose names are appended to the document. But no sooner had this slippery theologian satisfied the requirements of Basil than he threw off the mask, broke his promise to appear at a synodical meeting called by Basil to seal the union between them and their respective adherents, and openly assailed him with the most unscrupulous invectives ("**Ep. 130, 244**"). He went so far as to hold assemblies in which Basil was charged with heterodox views, especially on the Divinity of the Holy Spirit, and with haughty and overbearing behaviour towards his chorepiscopi and other suffragans. At last Eustathius pushed matters so far as to publish a letter written by Basil 25 years before to the heresiarch Apollinaris. It was true that at that time both were laymen, and that it was merely a friendly letter not dealing with theological points, and that Apollinaris had not then developed his heretical views and stood high in the esteem of Athanasius. But its circulation served Eustathius's ends in strengthening the suspicion already existing against Basil as a favourer of false doctrine, by proving that he had not scrupled to hold communion with an acknowledged heretic. The letter as published by Eustathius had been disgracefully garbled, and was indignantly repudiated by Basil. By a most shameful artifice some heretical expressions of Apollinaris, without the author's name, had been appended to Eustathius's own letter accompanying that attributed to Basil, leading to the supposition that they were Basil's own. Basil was overwhelmed with distress at being represented in such false colours to the church, while the ingratitude and treachery of his former friend stung him deeply. He restrained himself, however, from any public expression of his feelings, maintaining a dignified silence for three years (Bas. **"Ep. 128, 130, 224, 225, 226, 244"**). During this period of intense trial Basil was much comforted in 374 by the appointment of his youthful friend Amphilochius to the see of Iconium [Amphilochius]. But the same year brought a severe blow in the banishment of his intimate and confidential counsellor Eusebius of Samosata. At the end of this period (375) Basil, impelled by the calumnies heaped upon him on every side, broke a silence which he considered no longer safe, as tending to compromise the interests of truth, and published a long letter nominally addressed to Eustathius, but really a document intended for all the faithful, in which he briefly reviews the history of his life, describes his former intimacy with Eustathius, and the causes which led to the rupture between them, and defends himself from the charges of impiety and blasphemy so industriously circulated (**"Ep. 223, 226, 244"**). It was time indeed that Basil should take some public steps to clear his reputation from the reckless accusations which were showered upon him. He was called a Sabellian, an Apollinarian, a Tritheist, a Macedonian, and his efforts in behalf of orthodoxy in the East were continually thwarted in every direction by the suspicion with which he was regarded. Athanasius, bishop of Ancyra, misled by the heretical writings that had been fathered upon him, spoke in the harshest terms of him (**"Ep. 25"**). The bishops of the district of Dazimon in Pontus, giving ear to Eustathius's calumnies, separated themselves from his communion, and suspended all intercourse; and were only brought back to their allegiance by a letter of Basil's, written at the instance of all the bishops of Cappadocia, characterized by the most touching humility and affectionateness (**"Ep. 203"**). The alienation of his relative Atarbius and the church of Neocaesareia of which he was bishop, was more difficult to redress. To be regarded with suspicion by the church of a place so dear to Basil, his residence in youth, and the home of many members of his family, especially his sainted grandmother, Macrina, was peculiarly painful. But the tendency of the leading Neocaesareians was Sabellian, and the emphasis with which he was wont to assert the distinctness of the Three Persons was offensive to them. They took umbrage also at the favour he showed to

monasticism, and the nocturnal services he had established. To heal these offences Basil wrote in terms of affectionate expostulation to the church of Neocaesareia, and took advantage of the existence of his brother Peter's monastic community at Annesi to pay the locality a visit. But as soon as he was known to be in the neighbourhood a strange panic seized the whole city; some fled, some hid themselves; Basil was everywhere denounced as a public enemy. Atarbius abruptly left the synod at Nicopolis which he was attending, on hearing of Basil's approach. [Atarbius.] Basil returned from his visit mortified and distressed (**"Ep. 126, 204, 207, 210"**). Among other charges Basil was widely accused of denying the proper divinity of the Holy Spirit. Gregory Nazianzen tells an amusing story of an old monk who at a feast at Nazianzus, while the rest of the company were lauding Basil to the skies, vehemently charged him with unsoundness on this point, inasmuch as at the recent festival of St. Eupsychius he had passed very superficially over the Godhead of the Spirit while declaring that of the Father and Son most explicitly. Gregory warmly defended his friend's orthodoxy. But the company at table declared themselves against him, and mockingly applauded Basil's discreet silence (Greg. Naz. *Ep.* 26, 27; Bas. **"Ep. 71"**). This charge which when made by some Cappadocian monks had been already sternly reproved by Athanasius (Athan. *ad Pall.* ii. 763, 764) was revived at a later time on the plea that he had used a form of the doxology open to suspicion, "Glory be to the Father, through the Son, in the Holy Spirit"[4] (*De Sp. Sanct.* c. 1, vol. iii. p. 3). Self-defence was again reluctantly forced on the victim of calumny. He prayed that he might be deserted by the Holy Ghost for ever if he did not adore Him as equal in substance and in honour . . . with the Father and the Son (Greg. Naz. *Or.* xx. 365). Similar charges made at the festival of St. Eupsychius in the year 374 were the occasion of Amphilochius requesting him to declare his views on this subject, which led to his writing his treatise *de Spiritu Sancto* (1; **"Ep. 231"**). Maligned, misrepresented, regarded with suspicion, thwarted, opposed on all hands, few champions of the faith have had a heavier burden to bear than Basil. The history of the Eastern church at this period is indeed little more than a history of his trials and sufferings.

Basil's was not a nature, however, to give way before difficulties the most tremendous and failures the most disheartening. The great object he had set before himself was the restoration of orthodoxy to the Eastern church, and the cementing of its disorganized fragments into one compact body capable of withstanding the attacks of hostile powers. And this object he had pursued with undaunted perseverance notwithstanding the constant interruptions caused by his feeble health, "which might rather be called the languor of a dying man."

Cut to the heart by the miserable spectacle which surrounded him, the persecution of the orthodox, the triumphs of false doctrine, the decay of piety, the world-liness of the clergy, the desecration of the episcopate by ambition and covetousness, rival bishops rending asunder the venerable church of Antioch, Christians wasting in mutual strife the strength that should have been spent in combating the common foe, feeling himself utterly insufficient in his isolation to work the reformation he desired, Basil had looked round eagerly for effectual aid and sympathy.

He naturally turned first to that "great and apostolic soul who from boyhood had been an athlete in the cause of religion," the great Athanasius (**"Ep. 69, 80, 83"**). In the year 371 he begged his assistance in healing the unhappy schism of Antioch by inducing the Western church to recognize Meletius, and persuading Paulinus to withdraw. He called on him to stir up the orthodox of the East by his letters, and cry aloud like Samuel for the churches (**"Ep. 66, 69"**).

In his request about Antioch, Basil "was inviting Anthanasius to what was in fact impossible even to the influence and talents of the primate of Egypt; for being committed to one side in the dispute he could not mediate between them. Nothing then came of the application" (J. H. Newman, *Church of the Fathers*, p. 105). Basil had other requests to urge on Athanasius. He was very desirous that a deputation of Western prelates should be sent to help him in combating the Eastern heretics and reuniting the orthodox, whose authority should overawe Valens and secure the recognition of their decrees. He asked also for the summoning of a council of all the West, which should confirm the decrees of Nicaea, and annul those of Ariminum (**"Ep. 66, 69"**).

Basil next addressed himself to the Western churches. His first letter in 372 was written to Damasus, bishop of Rome, lamenting the heavy storm under which almost the whole Eastern church was labouring, and entreating of his tender compassion, as the one remedy of its evils, that either he, or persons like-minded with him, would personally visit the East with the view of bringing the churches of God to unity, or at least determining with whom the church of Rome should hold communion (**"Ep. 70"**). Basil's letters were conveyed to Athanasius and Damasus by Dorotheus, a deacon of Antioch, in communion with Meletius. He returned by way of Alexandria in company with a deacon named Sabinus (afterwards bishop of Piacenza) as bearer of the replies of the Western prelates. These replies were eminently unsatisfactory. They abounded with expressions of sympathy, but held out no definite prospect of practical help. Something, however, was hoped from the effect of Sabinus's report on his return to the West, as an eye-witness of the lamentable condition of the Eastern church. Sabinus was charged with several letters on his return to Italy. One bearing the signatures of thirty-two Eastern bishops, including besides Basil, Meletius of Antioch, Eusebius of Samosata, Gregory

Nyssen, &c., was addressed to the bishops of Italy and Gaul; another was written in Basil's own name to the bishops of the West generally. There were also private letters to Valerian of Aquileia and others. These letters give a most distressing picture of the state of the East. "Men had learnt to be theorists instead of theologians. The true shepherds were driven away. Grievous wolves, spoiling the flock, were brought in instead. The houses of prayer were destitute of preachers, the deserts full of mourners. The faithful laity avoided the churches as schools of impiety. Priestly gravity had perished. There was no restraint on sin. Unbelievers laughed, the weak were unsettled. . . . Let them hasten to the succour of their brethren, nor allow the faith to be extinguished in the lands whence it first shone forth" (**"Ep. 92, 93"**). No help, however, came. A Western priest named Sanctissimus, who visited the East towards the end of 372—whether travelling as a private individual or deputed by Damasus is uncertain—again brought assurances of the warm attachment and sincere sympathy of the Italian church; but words, however kind, were ineffectual to heal their wounds, and Basil and his friends again sent a vehement remonstrance beseeching their Western brethren to make the emperor Valentinian acquainted with their wretched condition, and to depute some of their number to console them in their misery, and sustain the flagging faith of the orthodox (**"Ep. 242, 243"**). These letters transmitted by Dorotheus—probably a different person from the former—were not more effectual than those which had preceded them. The only point gained was that a council—confined, however, to the bishops of Illyria—was summoned in 375 through the instrumentality of Ambrose, by which the consubstantiality of the Three Persons of the Trinity was declared, and a priest named Elpidius despatched to publish the decrees in Asia and Phrygia. Elpidius was supported by the authority of the emperor Valentinian, who at the same time promulgated a rescript in his own name and that of his brother Valens, who dared not manifest his dissent, forbidding the persecution of the Catholics, and expressing his desire that their doctrines should be everywhere preached (Theodor. iv. 8, 9). But the death of Valentinian on November 17th of that same year frustrated his good intentions, and the persecution revived with greater vehemence.

The secret of the coldness with which the requests for assistance addressed by the Eastern church were received by the West, was partly the suspicion that was entertained of his orthodoxy in consequence of his friendship with Eustathius of Sebaste, and other doubtful characters, and the large-heartedness which led him to recognise a real oneness of belief under varying technical formulas, but principally the refusal of Basil to recognize the supremacy of the bishop of Rome. His letters were usually addressed to the bishops of the West, and not to the bishop of Rome individually. In all his dealings, Basil treats with Damasus as an equal, and asserts the independence of the East. In his eyes the Eastern and Western churches were two sisters with equal prerogatives; one more powerful than the other, and able to render the assistance she needed; but not in any way her superior. The want of deference in his language and behaviour offended not Damasus only, but Jerome and all who maintained the supremacy of Rome over all churches of Christendom. Jerome accused Basil of pride, and went so far as to assert that there were but three orthodox bishops in the East, Athanasius, Epiphanius, and Paulinus (*ad Pammach.* 38). The most impassioned appeals proving ineffectual, and no heed being paid to his warnings that heresy unchecked might spread and infect the West also, Basil's tone respecting Damasus and the Western prelates underwent a change. He began to suspect the real cause of the apathy with which his entreaties for aid had been received, and to feel that no relief could be hoped from their "Western superciliousness," . . . and that it was in vain to send emissaries to "one who was high and haughty and sat aloft and would not stoop to listen to the truth from men who stood below; since an elated mind, if courted, is sure to become only more contemptuous" (**"Ep. 215, 239"**). But while his hope of assistance from the West lessened, the need for it increased. The persecution of the orthodox by the Arians grew fiercer. "Polytheism had got possession. A greater and a lesser God were worshipped. All ecclesiastical power, all church ordinances were in Arian hands. Arians baptized; Arians visited the sick; Arians administered the sacred mysteries. Only one offence was severely punished, a strict observance of the traditions of the fathers. For that the pious were banished, and driven to deserts. No pity was shewn to the aged. Lamentations filled the city, the country, the roads, the deserts. The houses of prayer were closed; the altars forbidden. The orthodox met for worship in the deserts exposed to wind and rain and snow, or to the scorching sun" (**"Ep. 242, 243"**). In his dire extremity he determined once more to make trial of an appeal to the West. He now adopts the language of indignant expostulation. "Why," he asks, "has no writing of consolation come to us, no visitation of the brethren, no other of such attentions as are due to us from the law of love? This is the thirteenth year since the war with the heretics burst upon us. Will you not now at last stretch out a helping hand to the tottering Eastern church, and send some who will raise our minds to the rewards promised by Christ to those who suffer for Him?" (**"Ep. 242"**). These letters were despatched in 376. But still no help came. His reproaches were as ineffectual as his entreaties. A letter addressed to the Western bishops the next year (377) proves that matters had not really advanced a single step beyond the first day. We find him still entreating his Western brethren in the most moving terms to grant him the consolation of a visit. "The visitation of the sick is the greatest commandment. But if the Wise and Good Disposer of human affairs forbids that, let them at least write something that may comfort those who are so grievously

cast down." He demands of them "an authoritative condemnation of the Arians, of his enemy Eustathius, of Apollinaris, and of Paulinus of Antioch. If they would only condescend to write and inform the Eastern churches who were to be admitted to communion and who not, all might yet be well" (**"Ep. 263"**). The reply brought back by the faithful Dorotheus overwhelmed him with sorrow. Not a finger was raised by the cold and haughty West to help her afflicted sister. Dorotheus had even heard Basil's beloved friends Meletius, and Eusebius of Samosata, spoken of by Damasus and Peter of Alexandria as heretics, and ranked among the Arians. What wonder if Dorotheus had waxed warm and used some intemperate language to the prelates? If he had done so, wrote Basil, let it not be reckoned against him, but put down to Basil's account and the untowardness of the times. The deep despondency which had seized Basil is evidenced by his touching words to Peter of Alexandria: "I seem for my sins to prosper in nothing, since the worthiest brethren are found deficient in gentleness and fitness for their office from not acting in accordance with my wishes" (**"Ep. 266"**).

Foiled in all his repeated demands; a deaf ear turned to his most earnest entreaties; the council he had begged for not summoned; the deputation he had repeatedly solicited unsent; Basil's span of life drew to its end amid blasted hopes, and apparently fruitless labours for the unity of the faith. It was not permitted him to live to see the Eastern churches, for the purity of whose faith he had devoted all his powers, restored to peace and unanimity. "He had to fare on as he best might—admiring, courting, but coldly treated by the Latin world, desiring the friendship of Rome, yet wounded by her superciliousness—suspected of heresy by Damasus, and accused by Jerome of pride."[5]

Some gleams of brightness were granted to cheer the last days of this dauntless champion of the faith. The invasion of the Goths in 378 gave Valens weightier cares than the support of a tottering heresy, and brought his persecution of the orthodox to an end on the eve of his last campaign, in which he perished, after the fatal rout of Hadrianople (Aug. 9, 378). One of the first acts of the youthful Gratian was to recall the banished orthodox prelates, and Basil had the joy of witnessing the event so earnestly desired in perhaps his latest extant letter, the restoration of his beloved friend Eusebius of Samosata (**"Ep. 268"**). Basil died at Caesareia, an old man before his time, Jan. 1st, 379, in the fiftieth year of his age. Though so far from advanced in years, his constitution was worn out by labours and austerities, as well as by the frequent severe diseases from which he had suffered. He rallied before his death, and was enabled to ordain with his dying hand some of the most faithful of his disciples. "His deathbed was surrounded by crowds of the citizens, ready," writes his friend Gregory, "to give part of their own life to lengthen that of their bishop." He breathed his last with the words "into Thy hands I commend my spirit." His funeral was attended by enormous crowds, who threnged to touch the bier or the hem of his funeral garments, or even to catch a distant glimpse of his face. The press was so great that several persons were crushed to death; almost the object of envy because they died with Basil. Even Jews and Pagans joined in the general lamentations, and it was with some difficulty that the bearers preserved their sacred burden from being torn to pieces by those who were eager to secure a relic of the departed saint. He was buried in his father's sepulchre, "the chief priest being laid to the priests; the mighty voice to the preachers; the martyr to the martyrs" (Greg. Naz. *Or.* xx. 371, 372).

In person Basil is described as tall and thin, holding himself very erect. His complexion was dark; his face pale and emaciated with close study and austerities; his forehead projecting, with retiring temples. A quick eye, flashing from under finely arched eyebrows, gave light and animation to his countenance. His speech was slow and deliberate. His manner manifested a reserve and sedateness which some of his contemporaries attributed to pride, others to timidity. Gregory, defending him from the former charge, which seems to have been too commonly urged to be altogether groundless, says that he supposes "it was the self-possession of his character, and composure and polish which they called pride," and refers not very convincingly to his habit of embracing lepers as a proof of the absence of superciliousness (*Or.* xx. p. 360). Basil's pride, indeed, was not the empty arrogance of a weak mind; but a wellgrounded confidence in his own powers. His reserve arose partly from natural shyness—he jestingly charges himself with "the want of spirit and sluggishness of the Cappadocians" ("**Ep. 48**").—partly from an unwillingness to commit himself with those of whom he was not sure. It is curious to see the dauntless opponent of Modestus and Valens charged with timidity. The heretic Eunomius after his death accused him of being "a coward and a craven skulking from all severer labours," and spoke contemptuously of his "solitary cottage and close-shut doors, and his flustered look and manner when persons entered unexpectedly" (Greg. Nyssen. *adv. Eunom.* i. p. 318). Philostorgius also speaks of Basil as "from timidity of mind withdrawing from public discussions" (*H. E.* iv. 12). The fact seems to be that Basil was like many who, while showing intrepid courage when once forced into action, are naturally averse from publicity, and are only driven by a high sense of duty to leave the silence and retirement in which they delight. Basil was a great lover of natural beauty; his letters display abundant proofs of his delight in scenery. The playful turn of his mind is also shewn in many passages of his familiar letters, which sufficiently vindicate him from the charge of austerity of character. In manner he united Oriental gravity with the finished politeness of the Greeks, and was the charm of society from his happy union of sedateness and

sweetness: his slightest smile was commendation, and silence was his only rebuke (Greg. Naz. *Or.* xx. 260, 261).

The voice of antiquity is unanimous in its praise of Basil's literary works. To adopt the words of Cave (*Hist. Lit.* i. 239) "plenae sunt omnium paginae, totus veneratur antiquitatis chorus, plaudit tota eruditorum cavea." His former tutor, Libanius, acknowledged that he was surpassed by Basil, and generously rejoiced that it was so, as he was his friend (Bas. "**Ep. 338**"). Nor has the estimate of modern critics been less favourable. "The style of Basil," writes Dean Milman, "did no discredit to his Athenian education. In purity and perspicuity he surpasses most of the heathen as well as Christian writers of his age" (*Hist. of Christianity*, iii. 110). . . .

Notes

[1] The passage of St. Jerome referred to by Milman is quoted from the *Chronicle,* A.D. 380. It is not found in Scaliger's edition, but was exhumed by Isaac Vossius who, to quote Gibbon's words, "found it in some old MSS, which had not been reformed by the monks." The Benedictine editor allows the genuineness of the passage, but asserts that the words refer not to Basil but to Photinus. Jerome, however, was no friend to Basil, who had incurred his displeasure by espousing the cause of Meletius against that of Paulinus, the favourite with the Western church, and by want of deferential behaviour towards pope Damasus. The passage as given by Gibbon from Vossius runs thus: "Basilius Caesarlensis Episcopus Cappadociae clarus habetur. . . . qui multa continentiae et ingenii bona uno superbiae malo perdidit."

[2] J. H. Newman's *Church of the Fathers,* p. 144.

[3] Basil had established similar almshouses in the country dioceses of his province, . . . placed under the care of a *chorepiscopus* ("Ep. 142, 143").

[4] Compare Hooker's remarks on this subject (*Eccl. Polity*, V. xlii. 12), "Till Arianism had made it a matter of great sharpness and subtilty of wit to be a sound believing Christian, men were not curious what syllables or particles of speech they used. Upon which when St. Basil began to practise the like indifferency, and to conclude public prayers, glorifying sometime the Father *with* the Son and the Holy Ghost, sometime the Father *by* the Son *in* the Spirit, whereas long custom had inured them to the former kind alone, by means whereof the latter was new and strange in their ears; this needless experiment brought afterwards upon him a necessary labour of excusing himself to his friends, and maintaining his own act against them, who because the light of his candle too much drowned theirs, were glad to lay hold on so colourable a mat-

ter, and exceedingly forward to traduce him as an author of suspicious innovation."

[5] J. H. Newman, *Church of the Fathers*, p. 115.

W. M. Ramsay (essay date 1906)

SOURCE: "Life in the Days of St. Basil the Great" in *Pauline and Other Studies in Early Christian History,* Hodder and Stoughton, 1906, pp. 369-406.

[*In the essay reprinted below—a revised version of a book review first published in the mid-1890s—Ramsay focuses on Basil's letters, finding in their style the same contradiction that biographers have discerned in Basil's character: even-handedness and civility toward his friends, yet misleading hyperbole and bitterness toward his critics. Ramsay also points out that the writings of the Cappadocian fathers provide a wealth of detail about social, cultural, and economic life during the late Roman Empire.*]

The publication of three volumes of selections from the works of the great Cappadocian Fathers of the fourth century[1] may well attract notice even in this busy time; and the careful and excellent scholarship displayed by the translators and editors thoroughly deserves more generous recognition than it has yet received. The work has been well done; it was well worth doing; and it was by no means easy to do. Gregory of Nyssa is a really difficult author. The style of Basil is, like his own character, direct, vigorous, and much too intense to become so complicated as that of his brother. But even Basil presents numerous difficulties to the comprehension of his readers; and the scholar, who studies an author of this period, with few and poor editions, has a much more difficult task than the translator of some author that has attracted the attention of generations and centuries of learned leisure. Dr. Wace is responsible for the editing of the whole volume of Gregory Nyssen, and part of the volume of Basil; and the many difficulties and questions that confront the translator in every page must all have been weighed anew by him in the execution of a peculiarly thankless, but important task.

It is not our intention to enter into minute questions of translation and criticism, but to attempt to illustrate the usefulness of work like this, by giving some examples of what is to be learned from the selected portions of the three authors. We shall disregard entirely the theological side of their writings, and only quote some of the passages bearing on the condition of society and life at the time and in the land where the three Fathers lived. It is from Basil that we learn most, partly because he had a much more practical and statesmanlike mind than either his brother or his friend, partly because almost the whole collection of his letters, which

come into nearer relations to actual life than the theological treatises, is here translated,[2] whereas only a small selection of the letters of Gregory Nazianzen is given (and these seem chosen more for their theological or personal interest than for their bearing on the state of society), and only a very few letters of Gregory Nyssen have been preserved. We shall, as far as possible, narrate each incident in the original words, partly to preserve the true colouring, partly in order to bring out incidentally the success with which the work of translation has been performed.

The modernness of tone that is often perceptible in the literature of the Roman Empire strikes every reader; it corresponds to and expresses a certain precocious ripeness—or, possibly, rottenness—in a too rapidly developed social system. In the Eastern provinces an interesting problem is presented to us; this precocious Western civilisation and education was there impressed upon Oriental races, backward in development and unprogressive in temperament, by the organising genius of Rome and the educative spirit of Greece. It is an interesting process, whereby Western manners and ideas were for a time imposed on, and in a small degree even naturalised among, an Oriental people, and then died out again, either because the circumstances of the Byzantine Empire were uncongenial, or because all civilisation and ideas were destroyed by the Turks. That long process will some time find a historian; a single moment in it is revealed in the pages of the three great Cappadocians.

One of the most interesting passages for our purpose is Gregory Nyssen's satirical sketch of the early life of the two heretics, Ætius and Eunomius. Their history, as told by Gregory, is quite a romance; though it is doubtful how far the account which he gives of theological opponents is to be trusted. Ætius was originally a serf, bound to the soil on a vine-growing estate.

> Having escaped—how, I do not wish to say, lest I be thought to be entering on his history in a bad spirit—he became at first a tinker, and had this grimy trade quite at his fingers' end, sitting under a goat's-hair tent,[3] with a small hammer and a diminutive anvil, and so earned a precarious and laborious livelihood. What income, indeed, of any account could be made by one who mends the shaky places in coppers, and solders holes up, and hammers sheets of tin to pieces, and clamps with lead the legs of pots?

As the story goes, "a certain incident necessitated the next change in his life". A woman, attached to a regiment, gave him a gold ornament to mend; he returned to her a similar one of copper, slightly gilt, "for he was clever enough in the tinker's, as in other, arts to mislead his customers with the tricks of trade". But the gold got rubbed off, and he was detected; "and as some of the soldiers of her family and nation were roused to indignation, she prosecuted," and secured his condemnation. After undergoing his punishment, he "left the trade, swearing that . . . business tempted him to commit this theft". He then became assistant to a quack doctor, and

> made his attack upon the obscurer households and on the most abject of mankind. Wealth came gradually from his plots against a certain Armenius who, being a foreigner, was easily cheated, and . . . advanced him frequent sums of money. He next wanted to be styled a physician himself. Henceforth, therefore, be attended medical congresses, and, consorting with the wrangling controversialists there, became one of the ranters, and, just as the scales were turning, always adding his own weight to the argument, he got to be in no small request.

From medicine Ætius turned to theology. Arius had already started his heresy,

> and the schools of medicine resounded then with the disputes about that question. Accordingly Ætius studied the controversy; and, having laid a train of syllogisms from what he remembered of Aristotle, he became notorious for even going beyond Arius in the novel character of his speculations.

At this point the inconsistency of this "veracious" narrative strikes the reader; if the life of Ætius as serf, tinker, quack's assistant, and quack principal is rightly recorded, when had he found time and opportunity to study Aristotle?

Eunomius, the pupil of Ætius, had (according to his theological opponent) an almost equally varied, though much less disreputable, career. He was born at a small village—Oltiseris—of the Korniaspene district, in the north-western part of Cappadocia, near the Galatian frontier. His father was a peasant farmer,—

> an excellent man, except that he had such a son . . . . He was one of those farmers who are always bent over the plough, and spend a world of trouble over their little farm; and in the winter, when he was secured from agricultural work, he used to carve out neatly the letters of the alphabet for boys to form syllables with, winning his bread with the money these sold for.

This is an interesting picture of the farmer's life in a remote and obscure corner of Cappadocia; and it suggests that the knowledge of letters and writing had penetrated to a very humble stratum of society, if a peasant farmer could make money in this way during the long winter season, when the ground was covered with snow for months. Facts like these make it all the more remarkable that a bishop who was present at the Council of Constantinople, in 448, had to get a friend to sign on his behalf, *eo quod nesciam literas*. The Phrygian Church, which had been so flourishing in the second and third centuries, was destroyed with fire and sword by Diocletian, and the country never properly recovered from that crushing persecution; education and prosperity were for a time almost annihilated. But Cappadocia had not been so thoroughly Christianised before the time of Diocletian, and hence it escaped more easily. In reading over the *Acta Sanctorum*, every student must observe that a much larger number of Cappadocian than of Phrygian martyrs are recorded under that great persecution; but the fact is that the destruction in Phrygia was so thorough that the memory of individuals was not preserved. Where a whole city with its population was burned, who would record the martyrdom of any single hero? In Cappadocia many martyrs were tried and condemned, and their memory embalmed in history: in Phrygia the Church in considerable districts was obliterated for the time, and its tone permanently depreciated.

Eunomius, perceiving that his father led

> a life of laborious penury, said good-bye to the plough and the mattock and all the paternal instruments, intending never to drudge himself like that; then he sets himself to learn Prunicus' skill of short-hand writing; and having perfected himself in that he entered at first, as I believe, the house of one of his own family, receiving his board for his services in writing; then, while tutoring the boys of his host, he rises to the ambition of becoming an orator.

Here, again, we are struck with the development of education in this obscure district, when a shorthand clerk could be found worth board and lodging in a family, which must have been either rustic or of a small provincial town.

Gregory draws a veil over the subsequent stages in the life of Eunomius, until the epoch when he saw that his toil "was all of little avail, and that nothing which he could amass by such work was adequate to the demands of his ambition". He accordingly turned to heresy-mongering, and found that this was a much more lucrative profession. "In fact, he toiled not thenceforward, neither did he spin; for he is certainly clever in what he takes in hand, and knows how to gain the more emotional portion of mankind." He made religion pleasant to his hearers and dupes; "he got rid of 'the toilsome steep of virtue' altogether"; and Gregory declares that he initiated them in practices and vices which it would not be decent even in an accuser to mention.

Considering the style in which religious controversy was carried on by almost all parties at this time, we cannot attach any special credibility to Gregory's accusation that Eunomius's teaching was so profoundly immoral. But it is of some interest to observe that the charge of appealing to the excitability and to the vices of the public was mutual. Eunomius declared that his great opponent Basil, the brother of Gregory, was "one who wins renown among poor old women, and practises to deceive the sex which naturally falls into every snare, and thinks it a great thing to be admired by the criminal and abandoned".

In these descriptions of Ætius and Eunomius, and in many other occasional touches in the writings of Basil and Gregory, we observe traces of a certain contempt for the low-born persons who had to make their living by their own work. The family of Basil and Gregory possessed considerable property in land, and their tone is that of the aristocrat, brought up in a position of superiority, and voluntarily accepting a life of asceticism and hardship to which they were not trained. Basil is distinctly a champion of the popular cause against the dominant power of the Emperor and of the wealthier classes; but his position is not that of Cleon and Hyperbolus, claiming rights for the class from which they sprang, and not free from a touch of vulgarity in their speeches and a taint of selfishness in their aspirations. His spirit and his aims are like those of Tiberius Gracchus, actuated by sincere and Divine sympathy for the wrongs and miseries in which he had no part, and showing perhaps want of judgment, but not selfishness.

From the Apostle Paul onwards it was, as a general rule, the local aristocracy that produced the leading figures in Anatolian history during the Roman period. Education was indispensable to advancement and influence under the Empire; and the poorer classes were cut off from the opportunity of getting education by a chasm which very few could cross. The Imperial system never attempted to spread education more widely; rather, it almost discouraged any movement of this kind. Only private individuals,[4] or the cities of the provinces, made some attempt to increase the educational opportunities for their own people. Basil and Gregory of Nazianzos belonged to the class of landed proprietors whose fortune opened to them the path of education and enabled them to study in Athens or some other of the leading Universities.

Such families belonged originally to a conquering class of land-owners, who dwelt as a country aristocracy amid an older conquered population. They dwelt in a kind of building which was called Tetraypyrgion or Tetrapyrgia: quadrangular farm steadings enclosing an open courtyard, with towers at the corners and over the gate. Such buildings were made to be defensible; and Eumenes found that regular military operations were necessary to reduce them.[5] Their plan has been preserved to the present day in the great Khans, built along the principal roads by the Seljuk Sultans to defend the trade from the wandering and unruly Nomads.

According to Gregory of Nyssa, Christianity was the nearly universal religion of Cappadocia in the second half of the fourth century. He says in his *Epistle on Pilgrimages* that,

> if it is really possible to infer God's presence from visible symbols, one might more justly consider that He dwelt in the Cappadocian nation than in any of the spots outside it. For how many Altars[6] there are there, on which the name of our Lord is glorified. One could hardly count so many in all the rest of the world.

There is, doubtless, some truth in this picture; but it has been considerably heightened in colour, even setting aside the Oriental hyperbole of the last words, which were not meant to be taken literally. Basil, who is always more trustworthy than Gregory, because he was more honest and more earnest, and stood closer to real life, gives a somewhat different account. He sees how far the Christian spirit was from having extirpated the pagan spirit, even where it had triumphed in outward appearance. He gives, for example, an interesting account of the Magusæi, a people who were settled in Cappadocia "in considerable numbers, scattered all over the country, settlers having long ago been introduced into these parts from Babylon". Probably they had been transplanted to Asia Minor by the Persian kings, to strengthen their hold on the country; and they had remained for nearly eight centuries unmixed with the other inhabitants, preserving their own religious customs and separateness of blood. In a recent book on Turkey,[7] it has been pointed out as one of the worst evils in the country that the different races remain apart, divided by difference of custom, and by consequent mutual hatred; and the existence of the same evil in ancient time might have been stated even more strongly than it is in that work. In the fourth century Roman rule and the influence of the Church had alike failed, as yet, entirely to obliterate racial differences; but it is only in incidental references like this to the Magusæans, that the existence of such despised races is admitted by the Cappadocian Fathers. As Basil says, "Their manners are peculiar, as they do not mix with other men. . . . They have been made the prey of the devil to do his will. They have no books; no instructors in doctrine." Basil means, of course, Christian books: it is not improbable that in secret they preserved and used Magian books. "They are brought up," as he goes on to say, "In senseless institutions." Besides more obvious characteristics, "they object to the slaying of animals as defilement; and they cause the animals they want for their own use to be slaughtered by other people. They are wild after illicit marriages: they consider fire divine," and so on. These illicit marriages are described by Eusebius[8] as being between such near relatives as father and daughter, brother and sister, son and mother; and the same writer says that the Magusæi were very numerous in Phrygia and Galatia, and everywhere retained the social customs and mysterious religious ritual which they had brought with them from Persia.

Illicit marriages were not confined to the Magusæi, but were still admitted among the general population of Cappadocia, as is evident from the Canonical Letters, and from some incidental references.

Apparently, the Magusæi made a superficial pretence of Christianity, but retained their pagan customs almost unaltered; as at the present day some races in the same country put on an outward appearance of Mohammedanism, though wanting its real character. Such, for example, are the Takhtaji (woodmen), about whom every traveller, who has seen much of Asia Minor, speaks: Dr. Von Luschan, *Reisen in Lykien*, ii., p. 199, vouches on personal knowledge for the survival among them of the custom of marriage between brother and sister, and they are as much despised by the Turks now as the Magusæi were by the Christians of Basil's time. But even among the Cappadocians proper, who had embraced Christianity in a more thorough way, there continued to exist many customs belonging to their pre-Christian state, which the Church had either tacitly acquiesced in, or at least failed to eradicate. Basil belonged to the Puritan party, and waged stern war with many of these customs. His invectives against them have preserved their memory; and the student of ancient society will turn to these passages with a very different spirit and interest from that which Basil felt.

Marriage by capture was still a common practice, justified and supported by common opinion. In **"Letter 270"** Basil speaks of this "act of unlawfulness and tyranny against human nature and society," and prescribes the treatment which is to be meted out to the offenders. The nature of the punishments shows that he is writing to some church official, probably one of his subordinate bishops, or village bishops, or presbyters.

> Wherever you find the girl, insist on taking her away, and restore her to her parents, shut out the man from the prayers, and make him excommunicate.[9] His accomplices, according to the canon which I have already put forth, cut off, with all their household, from the prayers. The village which received the girl after the abduction and kept her, or even fought against her restitution, shut out with all its inhabitants from the prayers; to the end that all may know that we regard the ravisher as a common foe like a snake or any other wild beast.

It is clear, then, that the whole neighbourhood approved the capture as preliminary to enforced marriage; and even the clergy to some extent acquiesced in the popular opinion, for Basil says that "if you had all been of one mind in this matter, there would have been nothing to prevent this bad custom from being long ago driven out of your country".

Basil was not so severe on some superstitions which had clothed themselves in a thoroughly Christian form. He regards it as quite praiseworthy that sick persons should have recourse for cures to the prayers of hermits; and he promises to try to find some relics of martyrs for a new church built by Bishop Arcadius (**"Ep. 49"**). Gregory Nazianzen declares that the mere visit of Basil almost cured the sick son of the Emperor Valens, and would have done so completely, had not his saving influence been counteracted by the presence of Arian heretics (*Or.* xiiii., 54). Yet Basil writes a noble eulogy of the medical profession: "To put that science at the head and front of life's pursuits is to decide reasonably and rightly" (**"Ep. 189"**). But the lively interest taken by the physicians of the time in theological controversy, as proved by that very letter, and by the life of Ætius described above, is not suggestive of good; and, on the whole, we may gather that the medical profession had degenerated seriously from the scientific spirit of the old Greek medical schools.

On the other hand, he was very severe on the *Panegyreis*, or local festivals, which, along with religious observances and sermons, united a good deal of social enjoyment of a kind that was in his opinion objectionable (**"Ep. 42"**). We should be glad to learn more about these festivals. There can be no doubt that they were a Christianised form of the earlier pagan festivals, celebrated at the places which have continued to be the great centres of religion in all ages of history. The festivals were, in the first place, "spiritual gatherings," where might be heard "expositions of the teaching of the Apostles, lessons in theology," and so on; but, besides, there were presented before the assemblies plays, music, mountebanks, jests and follies, drunken men and—worst of all in Basil's estimation—beautiful women. The most interesting of these festivals took place at Venasa, the old seat of one of the three great temples of Cappadocia; and it corresponds to the modern festival of St. Macrina at Hassa-Keui, a few miles south of Venasa (which is now purely Turkish), to which Mohammedans as well as Christians resort, bringing sick animals to be cured on the holy occasion. The quaint and interesting story of the Deacon Glycerius is associated with that festival (**"Ep. 169"** ff.); but it is too long for our space, and, moreover, has been very fully discussed elsewhere.[10]

Again, Basil condemns unsparingly the evils and abuses that existed in the Church of his time. He forbade an old unmarried presbyter of seventy to have a woman living in his house, and when the presbyter wrote to explain that there was no evil relation between them, he rebuked him with growing sternness, ordering him to expel her from his house and "establish her in a monastery". Basil also strenuously denounced the practice of taking money from candidates for ordination: "They think that there is no sin because they take the money not before but after the ordination; but to take is to take at whatever time" (**"Ep. 53"**). He strove to reintroduce "the ancient custom observed in the Churches," that ministers should be tested by examination as to their moral character and their whole past life before being admitted, and to put down the ordinary practice among the village-bishops of allowing "presbyters and deacons to introduce unworthy persons, without any previous examination of life and character, by mere favouritism, on the score of relationship or some other tie" ("**Ep. 54**").

The clergy had not yet become a distinct order, wholly separate from the laity: they practised trades in order to make their living. Basil had difficulty in finding any clergyman to whom he might entrust a letter to Eusebius, Bishop of Samosata, "for though our clergy do seem very numerous, they are men inexperienced in travelling, because they never traffic and prefer not to live far away from home, the majority of them plying sedentary crafts, whereby they get their daily bread" ("**Ep. 198**").

From the letter just quoted, and many others, it is clear that Basil usually tried to find clerical letter-carriers; and we may understand that in many other cases, where no exact information is given, this was the case, *e.g.*, in "**Epist. 19**" to Gregory Nazianzen, where he explains that he could not reply on the spot to Gregory's letter, "because I was away from home, and the letter-carrier, after he had delivered the packet to one of my friends, went away". But other convenient opportunities were sometimes used: *e.g.*, magistrates travelling were often asked to carry letters for their friends ("**Ep. 215, 237**").

The number of travellers was evidently far greater on the roads leading to Constantinople or Athens than towards Armenia. Basil has "no expectation of finding any one to convey a letter to Colonia in Armenia, which is far out of the way of ordinary routes" ("**Ep. 195**"). On the other hand, he speaks of a continuous stream of travellers coming from Athens to Cappadocia ("**Ep. 20**"); and though the letter, addressed to Leontius the Sophist, bears the stamp of the rhetorical style, sacrificing fact to effect, yet it implies that a considerable number of Cappadocian students, like Basil and Gregory Nazianzen, attended the University of Athens.

The important road to Samosata in Syria would be probably well frequented; and, when Basil speaks of difficulty in finding messengers thither, either he is speaking of the winter season, when the passes were blocked by snow, or he requires to find a trustworthy special messenger for an important letter.

On the whole, the impression given by the letters is that the custom of travelling, which had increased under the early Roman Empire to an extent almost unknown until the present century, was fully maintained in the fourth century.

Travelling on pilgrimage to the holy places of Palestine was not very much approved by the Cappadocian Fathers. Basil says here little on the subject. Gregory, having been entrusted with the duty of "visiting the places where the Church in Arabia is on the confines of the Jerusalem district," desires also to "confer with the Heads of the Holy Jerusalem Churches". He describes his journey thus:—

> Our most religious Emperor had granted us facilities for the journey, by postal conveyance, so that we had to endure none of those inconveniences which in the case of others we have noticed; our waggon was, in fact, as good as a church or monastery to us, for all of us were singing psalms or fasting in the Lord during the whole journey.

But, though he took advantage of this opportunity of visiting Jerusalem, he did not approve of going on pilgrimage. He thought that there was nothing to be gained, even for men, by pilgrimage, except the more vivid appreciation of the fact "that our own places are far holier than those abroad"; and he considered that people should stay at home till they died, and that it was better for "the brethren to be absent from the body, to go to our Lord, rather than to be absent from Cappadocia, to go to Palestine". As to women going on pilgrimage, the difficulties of travelling made it still more unbecoming and improper.

> For instance, it is impossible for a woman to accomplish so long a journey without a conductor; on account of her natural weakness, she has to be put upon her horse and to be lifted down again; she has to be supported[11] in difficult situations. Whichever we suppose, that she has an acquaintance to do this service or a hired attendant to perform it, either way the proceeding cannot escape being reprehensible; whether she leans on the help of a stranger or on that of her own servant, she fails to keep the law of correct conduct; and as the inns and hostelries and cities of the East present many examples of licence and of indifference to vice, how will it be possible for one passing through such smoke to escape without smarting eyes?

The evil reputation of the inns and taverns on the great roads of the Empire, to which Gregory here alludes, is confirmed by many other testimonies. Under the pagan Empire, the hosteries were for the most part little better than houses of ill-fame;[12] and under the Christian Empire there seems to have been no serious improvement. The story of the birth of St. Theodore of Sykea in Galatia, about A.D. 560, bears witness to a singularly depraved condition of public feeling; and in the Middle Ages matters seem to have been equally bad for the Pilgrims to the Holy Land. Felix Fabri of Ulm, about 1480, says that "the inns on the isles of the sea are houses of ill-fame," and warns every "good and godly pilgrim" at night to "return to his galley and sleep therein safe in his berth".[13] The character of the public hostelries was, doubtless, one of the reasons that weighed with Basil in making his great foundation near Cæsareia, including not merely an almshouse and hospital, but also

> a place of entertainment for strangers, both those who are on a journey and those who require medical treatment on account of sickness, and so establishing a means of giving these men the comfort they want, doctors, means of conveyance, and escort.

A foundation like this shows Basil's practical character; he diagnosed the real character of the evil, and struck out the cure; and, as we believe, his foundation became so important that it gradually attracted the city to itself, and the ancient site is now deserted, while Basil's site is the present Kaisari.[14]

The frequent allusions to the severity of winter weather will surprise those who do not know the country. Although Cappadocia does not lie so high, and the winters are not so severe, as in Armenia, yet Cæsareia is 3,500 feet above sea-level, and the border-land between the valleys of the Halys and Sarus and Euphrates is a good deal higher; and at that elevation winter is long and hard. Basil speaks of "such a very heavy fall of snow that we have been buried, houses and all, beneath it, and now for two months have been living in dens and caves" (*i.e.*, under the surface of the snow, like the underground dwellings—dens and caves—used in some parts of Cappadocia) ("**Ep. 48**"). Even an unusually mild winter "was quite enough to keep me not merely from travelling while it lasted, but even from so much as venturing to put my head out of doors" ("**Ep. 27**").[15]

In another letter he mentions that "we have had a winter of such severity that all the roads were blocked till Easter" ("**Ep. 198**"). Again, "the road to Rome is wholly impracticable in winter" ("**Ep. 215**"). Even a meeting with the Bishop of Iconium must be arranged "at a season suitable for travelling" ("**Ep. 191**"), though the road from Cæsareia to Iconium traverses only level country and crosses no hills or passes except that of the Boz-Dagh, about 600 feet above the plain.

As to the state of peace and order in the country, there are many indications that the administration of government was both arbitrary, weak and ineffective. Basil writes to Candidianus, the governor or a high official of the province Pontus,[16] shortly after his return from Athens, probably about A.D. 360, asking redress for a serious wrong: the house on his farm had been broken into, part of the contents stolen, and his servants beaten, by a band of rude persons from the neighbouring village of Annesi. Basil himself seems to have been living at the time in his retreat in the gorge of the river Iris, near the farm. The farm was managed by a steward, who had died; and a creditor in Annesi had taken

this disorderly way of recovering a debt which he claimed. We have, of course, only a statement of one side of the case; but the main facts cannot be doubted. We are struck, however, by the fact that Basil makes no attempt to get redress by ordinary process of law. He writes direct to a high officer, and asks that, as a punishment, the man be "apprehended by the district magistrate and locked up for a short period in the jail". Basil had too much of the aristocratic tone to take proceedings before the district magistrate against a vulgar rustic. His claim is that the governor should act at once on his representation, and should give a slight lesson to the neighbours that Basil was not a person whose property and house could be lightly insulted, even in his absence. It was probably after this event that Basil gave the use of the estate and the slaves on it for life to his foster-brother, Dorotheos, the presbyter of the village, reserving to himself an annual rent from it for his support. Mr. Blomfield Jackson has rightly brought out that this act had not the character, which has often been attributed to it, of a total renunciation of the property. Basil was not a man to retire wholly from the world and live in pure asceticism. He recognised rightly the duty incumbent on him of action in the world; and he knew that he could act far more usefully, if he were not in a position of penury. He was used to the position of a country gentleman with means and influence; and the thought of abandoning this position and entering on a life of real poverty evidently never occurred to him as a serious possibility. When the assessment on the property was raised, he protested vigorously and asked that the ancient system of rating should be retained, as Dorotheos might throw up the property, making Basil himself responsible for the whole of the rate ("**Ep. 36**").

Gregory Nazianzen in his *Panegyric on St. Basil*, 56, tells how "the assessor of a judge was attempting to force into a distasteful marriage a lady of high birth, whose husband was but recently dead," and used all the powers of his position against her and Basil, who was trying to protect her, until the populace rose in defence of their bishop,

> especially the men from the small-arms factory and from the imperial weaving-sheds; for men at work in these trades are specially hot-tempered and daring, because of the liberty allowed them. Each man was armed with the tool he was using, or with whatever else came to hand at the moment. Torch in hand, amid showers of stones, with cudgels ready, all ran and shouted together. . . . Nor were the women weaponless; . . . they were by the strength of their eagerness endowed with masculine courage.

In the end Basil's help alone preserved the official from their violence.

The events which called forth "**Letters 72-73**" illustrate this subject. They seem to have been the following, though the allusive way in which Basil refers to what was familiar to his correspondents makes several of the details doubtful. A certain Callisthenes, a man of great influence, probably an official (see p. 403), resided in some city of South-west Cappadocia. At Sasima (the town of which Gregory Nazianzen was made bishop, much against his will, by Basil), where three great roads met, and where there was, doubtless, a post-station and a vast amount of traffic and travellers, there had occurred a quarrel between Callisthenes and a set of slaves belonging to Eustochius, who was apparently a merchant residing at or near Cæsareia. Some dispute about precedence, or other incident of travelling, caused such angry feeling that the slaves had even used personal violence to Callisthenes; and they had made themselves liable to some serious punishment. Callisthenes seems to have been sole arbiter of their fate; and the owners of the slaves, perhaps a trading company to which Eustochius belonged, had no way of preventing him from exacting the extreme penalty. Eustochius appealed to Basil, who exerted himself to the utmost to secure milder treatment for the slaves. He wrote to Callisthenes a letter (not preserved), and received a very polite reply, couched in that Oriental style of elaborate courtesy which means nothing, professing to leave the decision with Basil, but insisting that the slaves should come to Sasima to submit to punishment, and giving no pledge as to the penalty which would satisfy him. Basil replied, acknowledging the courtesy of the letter, but pointing out clearly that, unless Callisthenes gave some distinct promise before the slaves went to Sasima, the politeness of the letter was merely a matter of words. He allowed that, if Callisthenes insisted, the slaves must go to Sasima; but he hoped and begged that Callisthenes would be satisfied with their appearance there and submission to his will, and would remit further punishment. Especially, he desired a promise that Callisthenes would himself be present at Sasima, and not let himself be detained by business on the road, leaving to others the exaction of the legal penalty. This desire implies that, if Callisthenes were not present to remit the penalty, no other person would have the power to do so; and that the slaves had been condemned to appear and suffer a certain punishment, unless Callisthenes chose to be satisfied with less. What the penalty was is not stated by Basil, but his language implies that it was very serious, possibly death. The decree had apparently been pronounced at Cæsareia, whither Callisthenes had sent a soldier to demand satisfaction, and his vigorous complaint at headquarters secured an order in his favour from the governor of the province.

Basil also wrote to Hesychius, who lived in the same city as Callisthenes, and was apparently an official of the Church. He sent a deacon to carry these letters, and instructed him to take other steps in the business. The amount of trouble which Basil took furnishes a proof of the interest which he felt in the condition of slaves, and of the way in which he was ready to use the whole strength of the Church, as well as his own, to secure milder treatment for them (see p. 403).

Complaints about the burden of taxation were evidently often made. Thus: "everything nowadays is full of taxes demanded and called in . . . for even the Pythagoreans were not so fond of their Tetractys, as these modern tax-collectors of their four-times-as-much" (a rule imposing quadruple payment for arrears); an estate "is now left and abandoned on account of the weight of the rates imposed on it". In **"Ep. 110"**: "give orders that the tax paid by the inhabitants of iron-producing Taurus may be such as it is possible to pay". A new system, whereby the burdens on the clergy were much increased, is referred to elsewhere. The harsh treatment of the clergy by Maximus, the governor of Cappadocia, is complained of. The governors seem to have been far from just or good. We hear of the same Maximus, persecuted by the next governor of Cappadocia, and of a governor in Africa so bad as to be excommunicated by the Church. The arbitrary conduct of governors, in violation of formal law or of equity, is a frequent subject of complaint.

In **"Ep. 54"** we learn that "a large number of persons are presenting themselves for the ministry through fear of the conscription". The strong dislike for military service, by making the mass of the people entirely incapable of self-defence, undoubtedly rendered them an easier prey to the ravages of Parthians and afterwards of Saracens.

As to the conditions of labour, we learn little from the works here translated, though there are materials in the other works for a much more elaborate picture. In **"Ep. 18"** Basil mentions the hired labourers engaged on a farm during the heat of summer; in the winter, when all agricultural work was suspended, they would not be needed. He distinguishes these hired farm-servants from the agriculturists proper, some of whom turned to other industry during the winter, like the father of Eunomius. The slaves who cultivated such estates as Basil's at Annesi must be distinguished from both hired labourers and free agriculturists.

Famine-relief operations were organised by the Church officials; for scarcity seems to have been common. Basil says that "the dearth is still with us, and I am therefore compelled to remain where I am, partly by the duty of distribution, and partly out of sympathy for the distressed" [**"Ep. 31"**]. The letter is ordinarily assigned to A.D. 369, and was certainly earlier than the death of Eusebius, Bishop of Cæsareia, in A.D. 370.[17] It was followed by a long and severe scarcity which was raging at Nazianzus in A.D. 373, when Gregory Nazianzen delivered his Oration xvi. to his suffering and terrified congregation.

It is a highly elaborated and artificial civilisation that is set before us in these works; but there are many signs of the bad administration, which went from bad to worse during the following century and a half, until Justinian made a great and noble effort to reform the whole executive. His *Novellae* present a terrible picture of provincial oppression and misgovernment;[18] but a rigorous diagnosis of the evil, such as is there given, is the first step towards improvement. Whether the changes in the executive which he made were ill-advised, or the evil was too deeply seated to be reached by changes on the surface, little permanent improvement was attained; but the attempt which was made to cure the evil, as well as the unsparing statement of its character and causes, deserve different treatment from the brief paragraph of unlimited condemnation, in which Gibbon sums up the character of the *Novellae* in his chapter xliv., quoting and apparently endorsing the opinion of Montesquieu, that "these incessant and for the most part trifling alterations can be only explained by the venal spirit of a prince, who sold without shame his judgments and his laws". Change was urgently necessary, both on the surface and at the heart. In St. Basil of Cæsareia we have a great administrator, whose plans of cure for the deeper evils affecting his country were wise and statesmanlike, though, as was natural, too purely ecclesiastical to be complete. But he could make no provision to ensure a succession of Basils. The Roman Empire had too much neglected its duty of creating a sufficient educational system for the people; and the society of the Roman Provinces was not fertile and vigorous enough to produce a series of men like Basil.

Twelve years ago, the greatest of living historians, Professor Theodor Mommsen, said to the present writer that, if he were now beginning a new life of scholarship, he would take up the period between Diocletian and Justinian. The scholar who devotes himself to that period will be filled with a growing admiration for Basil; and he will recognise the merits and the scholarly insight of the books which we have taken as the text of this paper. Any ambitious young scholar, who wishes to do real service by increasing our knowledge of past history, will find here an open field; and he could not better begin than by a systematic study of the society presented to us in the pages of the three great Fathers. The voluminous writings of the three contemporary Cappadocians, Basil and the two Gregories, apart from the purely theological and ecclesiastical interest, possess a high value as storing up many facts about the state of society and of education, about the administration and law of the late Roman Empire as practically affecting the people, about the taxpayers' views on taxation, the travellers' views as to the roads and the seasons, the householder's views on the safety of his property, the merchants' and the investors' views on the public credit and the standard of commercial honesty; in short, about the ordinary life of a highly organised community, in which the Oriental style of society and manners was being replaced by the Euro-

pean; and, above all, they show us the views entertained by three men of power and education as to the duties of the Church in its relation to all these various interests. A study of the three great Cappadocians from this point of view would make a most instructive and interesting work.

After this glance at the times and surroundings of Basil, it is fair to look at the man himself.

He was probably the most vigorous, striking and manly figure in the Church of Asia Minor under the Empire of Constantinople, though some blemishes of temper and of pride have combined with a certain hardness and want of sympathy in his nature to render him an object of less interest in history than he deserves. Mr. Jackson's translation is at once pleasant to read as English, and true to the letter and to the spirit of the original; and we may hope that it will succeed (as it deserves) in drawing more attention on the part of classical scholars to the varied interest of the Christian writers of the period in question.

In Mr. Jackson's prolegomena we have a careful account of the life of Basil, and a very full account of the works which are not translated here. In the biography, the results of earlier writers, Tillemont and Maran (the Benedictine editor), are worked up; and there is added to them a much more precise localisation of the scenes, in which recent geographical discoveries are utilised. Naturally, however, the biography is secondary to the translation; and there is still need for a careful study of the life of Basil and for a more exact determination of the dates of his letters as well as of the larger works. Several interesting incidents in his history seem to me not to have been properly understood; and the dates assigned to some letters by the Benedictine editor (and accepted by Mr. Jackson) are in several cases not convincing and even quite unsatisfactory.[19] While we cannot enter on any such wider questions within our narrow limits, we may profitably devote some few pages here to studying, under the guidance of Mr. Jackson, a few passages which bring out some personal characteristics of "St. Basil the Great"; and, at the same time, the quotations will exemplify the spirit and excellence of the translation in this volume.

The letter which faced me, as I first opened the volume, "**No. 135,**" may be taken as a specimen, selected at random, of the translation and of Basil's expression. Basil acknowledges two books which Diodorus, Presbyter of Antioch (afterwards Bishop of Tarsus), had sent him for perusal. "With the second," he says, "I was delighted, not only with its brevity . . . but because it is at once full of thought and so arranged that the objections of opponents and the answers to them stand out distinctly. . . . The former work, which has practically the same force, but is much more elaborately adorned with rich diction, many figures, and niceties of dialogue, seems to me to require considerable time to read and much mental labour, both to gather its meaning and retain it in the memory. The abuse of our opponents and the support of our own side, which are thrown in, although they may seem to add some charms of dialectic to the treatise, do yet break the continuity of the thought and weaken the strength of the argument by causing interruption and delay. . . . If the subject of the dialogue be wide and general, digressions against persons interrupt its continuity and tend to no good end. . . . So much I have written to prove that you did not send your work to a flatterer. . . . I have, however, now sent back the larger and earlier of the two volumes, after perusing it as far as I have been able.[20] The second I have retained with the wish to transcribe it, but hitherto without finding any quick writer."[21]

This letter conveys a very favourable impression (and a correct impression) of Basil's tone to his friends, and to those who thought like himself: it is judicious in its criticism, pointed and simple in expression, polite and kindly in tone; it advises without assumption, and encourages without flattering.

Everywhere the warmth of Basil's affection for friends and relatives, and the pleasant recollection of old associations, combined with his good sense and lofty tone, convey a most favourable impression. Take a few examples: "One would rather see his friend, though angry with him, than anybody else, flattering him. Do not, then, cease preferring charges like the last! The very charge will mean a letter; and nothing can be more precious or delightful to me" (**"Ep. 21"**). Or this: "Now for my sins, I have lost my mother, the only comfort I had in life. Do not smile if, old as I am, I lament my orphanhood. Forgive me if I cannot endure separation from a soul, to compare with whom I see nothing in the future that lies before me. So once more my complaints have come back to me; once more I am confined to my bed, tossing about in my weakness, and every hour all but looking for the end of life" (**"Ep. 30"**). Or again, these recollections of childhood from (**"Ep. 271"**): "To travel once again in memory to our young days, and to be reminded of old times, when for both of us there was one home, one hearth, the same schoolmaster, the same leisure, the same work, the same treats, the same hardships, and everything shared in common! What do you think I would not have given to recall all this by actually meeting you, to rid me of the heavy weight of my old age, and to seem to be turned from an old man into a lad again!"

But it was not pleasant to be on the opposite side from Basil. Speaking of the Arians, he is hardly to be trusted even as to facts. He felt too bitterly; and he exaggerated so rhetorically, that his words cannot be taken literally. Thus in **"Ep. 242"** he declares that in the thirteen years of Arian persecution "the Churches have

suffered more tribulations than all those that are on record since Christ's gospel was first preached"—an utterly unjustifiable statement (against which Mr. Jackson rightly, perhaps too mildly, protests, as "not to be taken literally"). The harsh and rude invective which Basil uses about his opponents is the fault of his age, and, while we regret it, we cannot wonder at it.

Difficult, however, as it is to appreciate the real character of the Arian controversy as a question of social life, on the whole we gather, I think, that the progressive tendencies were on the side of Basil, and acquiescence in the existing standard of morality characterised the Arian point of view. The "Orthodox" Church was still the champion of higher aspirations, and Basil, however harsh he was to all who differed from him, was an ennobling and upward-struggling force in the life of his time. At a later period the facts changed; and, in the Iconoclast period, the sympathy of the modern student must, I think, be almost wholly against the successors of Basil, and in favour of the maligned and despised heretics.

The contest in which Basil was involved against the Imperial power in regard to the division of Cappadocia into two provinces produced the most striking scenes of his life, and displayed both his strongest qualities and his worst faults of character. The questions at issue in this contest seem not to have been correctly apprehended by writers on the life of Basil. The policy of the Byzantine rule had been uniformly directed to subdividing the great provinces, and thus diminishing the power of provincial governors. Subdivision was the natural result of the centralisation of authority, the exaggeration of the power of the court, and the diminishing of the power of officials at a distance from the court. Cappadocia was by far the largest of the provinces; its turn had now come to be subdivided, and in 371 the Arian Emperor Valens resolved on this step. He may probably have been roused to it by the fact that the influence of Cæsareia, under its vigorous and uncompromising "orthodox" bishop, was dead against his ecclesiastical policy. It was natural that he should wish to diminish that influence; but in itself the subdivision would naturally have been soon made even by an orthodox emperor; and at a later time Justinian divided Cappadocia into three parts. The bias of Valens was shown, however, by his leaving the smaller part of Cappadocia to the metropolis Cæsareia, and making the new province of Secunda Cappadocia decidedly larger. The officials who lived at Cæsareia, and the business which came to it, were much diminished, as the province of which it was the metropolis shrank to less than half its former size. The city, naturally, regarded the change with dismay, and protested strongly. Basil exerted himself to the utmost; but the three letters which he wrote intreating the intercession of certain influential persons with Valens in favour of Cæsareia, are among the poorest in the collection.[22] They are inflated and exaggerated in their description of the loss that would result to Cæsareia; they show no appreciation either on the one hand of the real causes that recommended the subdivision, or on the other of the weighty reasons that might have been urged against the centralising policy. In fact the whole system of the Orthodox Church was in favour of centralisation; and Basil himself would have been the most vigorous supporter of that policy in any case where it did not affect his own city and his own archbishopric. He could not argue on strong grounds against the change, for his whole system of thought debarred him from those grounds, and his protests are weak and hysterical.

The true greatness of Basil, however, shone forth immediately afterwards, when Valens came to Cæsareia. The archbishop triumphantly resisted the efforts made by the creatures of Valens to overawe him and bend him to the will of the Arian Emperor. Valens himself was not blind to the nobility and dignity of Basil's character; he left the archbishop in secure possession of his rank and the freedom of his opinions; he attended Divine service performed by him in the cathedral; he held private conference with him; and he gave land[23] to endow Basil's new foundation, the hospital, etc., near Cæsareia. Considering how bitter was the quarrel at this time between the Arian and the orthodox party, Valens deserves more credit in this case than he has generally received. But, as to Basil, every one must say, with Mr. Jackson, that "his attitude seems to have been dignified without personal haughtiness, and to have shown sparks of that quiet humour which is rarely exhibited in great emergencies except by men who are conscious of right and careless of consequences to self".

But, in the following months, the quarrel with Anthimus, Bishop of Tyana, the metropolis of the new province of Cappadocia Secunda, shows Basil at his worst. He struggled to maintain his former rights over the churches and monasteries of the new province with undignified pertinacity. He created new bishoprics, not on account of the needs of the Church, but to increase the number of his supporters and their weight; and his old friend Gregory of Nazianzus could hardly forget or forgive the way in which Basil used him for his own purposes by almost forcing him to become Bishop of Sasima, one of these new sees. He went in person to collect the revenues of St. Orestes (what Gregory calls sarcastically his "supply of sucking-pigs and poultry from St. Orestes"), and his servants came almost to a battle with those of his rival. Basil certainly would have justified his action in the same terms that Innocent, Bishop of Rome, used shortly afterwards, about 408, that it was not right that the Church of God should be altered to suit the changes of this world.[24] But every attempt made to maintain that principle, fine as it seems in words, was a failure under the Empire, and must be a failure. The classification of dioceses was not of the

essence of the Church; it naturally and properly varied with the changes of society, and prosperity, and political arrangement. The reason why Cæsareia had been an ecclesiastical centre lay originally in its being the political capital, and therefore the natural centre from which the province could best be affected and its churches directed. But, when Tyana had become the metropolis of considerable part of Cappadocia, it was merely introducing confusion to maintain that the cities of that province should look to Cæsareia ecclesiastically, when they must look to Tyana in political, legal and social respects. Neither Anthimus nor Basil showed in this case true dignity, or self-respect, or the respect due to a colleague; but, while no one cares about Anthimus, it is painful to those who respect and admire a great man to read about Basil's action, and above all to read his condemnation in the estrangement of his old friend Gregory, who had at first supported him in the case.

Many touches of the raillery which became rude and unpleasant towards his opponents,[25] appear in a much more pleasant style when he writes to his friends.

He has found out that "there does seem something thinner than I was—I am thinner than ever".

In **"Ep. 4"** he acknowledges a gift under the guise of a complaint that the giver is "evicting from our retreat my dear friend and nurse of philosophy, Poverty".

Twitting Gregory with the shortness of his letters, he says, "The letter is shown to be yours, not so much by the writing as by the style of the communication: in few words much is expressed".

The tone of these quotations doubtless gives the key to explain the rather enigmatic **"Ep. 1,"** where he speaks as if his travels through Syria and Egypt had been undertaken for the single purpose of meeting Eustathius, the philosopher to whom the letter is addressed.

In **"Ep. 56,"** apologising for leaving a letter unanswered until his correspondent wrote again, he says, "I naturally forget very easily, and I have had lately many things to do, and so my natural infirmity is increased. I have no doubt, therefore, that you wrote to me, although I have no recollection of having received any letter from your excellency. . . . Really this letter of mine, as it is more than twice as bulky (as yours), will fulfil a double purpose. You see to what sophisms my idleness [surely laziness] drives me. . . . But, my dear sir, do not in a few words bring serious charges, indeed the most serious of all. Forgetfulness of one's friends, and neglect of them arising from high place, are faults which involve every kind of wrong. . . . I shall begin to forget you when I cease to know myself. Never, then, think that, because a man is a very busy man he is a man of faulty character."

The dignity, mingled with humility and desire for peace, shown in the two letters to his uncle Gregory, **"59, 60,"** may be referred to as illustrating the graver and loftier side of his character.

As examples of the sound and high judgment, which placed him on the right side in most great social questions, we may quote the opinion which, when he writes to a physician, he states about his profession as being at the head and front of life's pursuits (see p. 380).

He refers in **"Ep. 191"** with longing admiration to the hospitable intercourse which "was once the boast of the Church. Brothers from each Church, travelling from one end of the world to the other, were provided with little tokens, and found all men fathers and brothers. But now," he says, "we are confined each in his own city, and every one looks at his neighbour with distrust".

Basil was ready to defend the weak against the strong. In **"Ep. 73"** he uses the whole influence of his position and of the Church to save some slaves from harsh punishment at the hands of Callisthenes, a government official[26] to whom they had behaved rudely. "Though you have sworn to deliver them to execution as the law enjoins, my rebuke is still of no less value, nor is the Divine law of less account than the laws current in the world." See p. 388.

Basil's tone in addressing women lacks the charming ease that generally characterises his letters to his male correspondents. An illustration is supplied in the two letters which he addressed to Nectarius, a noble of Cilicia, and his wife, on the death of their only son. The letter to Nectarius (**"No. 5"**), in spite of the rhetorical touch (which may be pardoned, as it stands alone), "if all the streams run tears, they will not adequately weep our woe," is very fine, and the conclusion is charming, "Let us wait a little while, and we shall be once more with him. The time of our separation is not long, for in this life we are all like travellers on a journey, hastening on to the same shelter"; and so on in terms that have now become, through familiarity and repetition, less impressive than they were to Basil's contemporaries. But the letter to the bereaved mother is far inferior. "Alas, for the mighty mischief that the contact with an evil demon was able to wreak. Earth! what a calamity thou hast been compelled to sustain! If the sun had any feeling, one would think he might have shuddered," etc. After these bombastic commonplaces of rhetoric, he addresses the bereaved mother in almost equally frigid consolations. "When first you were made a mother, . . . you knew that, a mortal yourself, you had given birth to a mortal. What is there astonishing in the death of a mortal? . . . Look round at all the world in which you live; remember that everything you see is mortal, and all subject to corruption. Look up to heaven, even it shall be dissolved; look at the sun, not even the sun will last for ever. All the stars together," etc., etc., "are subject to decay." In the early part of the letter Basil says, "I know what a mother's heart is"; but Mr. Jackson, in his note on the words, well remarks that the mother might have replied in the words of Constance to Pandulph: "He talks to me that never had a son". A certain externality and hardness of tone characterises the letter, and makes it more of a rhetorical exercise than a spontaneous outburst of sympathy.

A few passages occur to me in which it may be doubted whether Mr. Jackson has fully caught the meaning. For example, **"Ep. 8,"** 1, when, evidently, Basil is replying to a letter of the people of Cæsareia, asking him to return from his sojourn with Gregory, he says: "Give me, therefore, I beg you, a little time. I am not embracing a city life." Mr. Jackson adds the note: "*i.e.,* the life of the city, presumably Nazianzus, from which he is writing". But surely a person who writes to the great city of Cæsareia from the small town of Nazianzus, and speaks of "city life" . . . , must be referring to life in Cæsareia, not life in Nazianzus. Moreover, I cannot doubt, both from the context and the localities, that Basil was at the moment dwelling, not in Nazianzus, but in Carbala or Caprales (still called Gelvere), where Gregory's home was situated, where he was (as he intimates) enjoying the life of retirement and contemplation, and where to this day the memorials of Gregory are preserved, and the rock-cells mark the abode of many hermits in the succeeding ages.[27] I should venture to suggest that a thought has been left unexpressed by Basil from brevity and rapidity, and that the sense is, "a little time, pray, a little time grant me, I beg; [and then I shall come to you,] not welcoming the life of cities (for I am quite well aware of the danger caused to the soul in that life), but judging that the society of the saints [as contrasted with the solitary life of the hermit] is the most practically useful. [But grant me the delay,] for in the constant free interchange of ideas [with 'Gregory, Christ's mouth'] I am acquiring a deep-seated habit of contemplation." Elsewhere, also, Basil declares plainly his opinion that the life of action and public work is the more honourable, as it is the more wearisome and difficult and unpleasant side of the truly religious life.

As another example, take **"Ep. 190,"** 1: "The most careless observer must at once perceive that it is in all respects more advantageous for care and anxiety to be divided among several bishops". This reads like a general maxim intended for wide application; but the Greek seems to me to need a different sense, applying solely to the case of Isaura, now under consideration, "it is more advantageous that the care of the district be divided among several bishops". The case, which had been referred to Basil by Amphilochius, Archbishop of Iconium, for advice, was a remarkable one. The large district round the great city Isaura had fallen into utter disorganisation (probably owing to the unruly character of the Isaurians, who were frequently in rebellion). Several bishops were needed for the care of so large a district. Basil would prefer that a bishop for the city should first be appointed, who might afterwards associate others with himself, as his experience showed him that they might be most usefully placed. But, owing to the danger that the bishop might be tempted by ambition to rule over a larger diocese, and might not consent to the ordination of others, he felt it safer to appoint in the first place bishops . . . to the small towns or villages which were formerly the seats of bishops, and thereafter to select the bishop of the city.[29] We have here a good example of the decay of bishoprics in political troubles, of the revival of disused bishoprics, and of the trouble that might be caused by an ambitious prelate.

Some other examples have struck me where opinions as to the meaning are likely to differ. But when we consider how little care has been devoted to the elucidation of Basil, and contrast it with the voluminous studies that have contributed to the long and difficult growth of the interpretation of Horace, or Virgil, or Sophocles, we can better appreciate the difficulties that Mr. Jackson had to face, and better estimate the gratitude we owe him.

Notes

[1] *Select Library of Nicene and Post-Nicene Fathers of the Christian Church.* Edited by Dr. Henry Wace, Principal of King's College, London, and Dr. Philip Schaff, Professor of Church History in Union Seminary, New York.

Vol. V., *Select Writings and Letters of Gregory of Nyssa.* Translated with prolegomena, etc., by W. Moore, M.A., Rector of Appleton, late Fellow of Magdalen College, Oxford, and H. A. Wilson, M.A., Fellow and Librarian of Magdalen College, Oxford.

Vol. VII.: Part II., *Select Orations and Letters of S. Gregory Nazianzen.* Translated with prolegomena, etc., by C. G. Browne, M.A., Rector of Lympstone, Devon, and J. E. Swallow, M.A., Chaplain of the House of Mercy, Horbury.

Vol. VIII., *Letters and Select Works of St. Basil.* Translated with prolegomena, etc., by Blomfield Jackson, M.A., Vicar of St. Bartholomew's, Moor Lane, and Fellow of King's College, London.

The variety in the titulature of the three Saints suggests a certain difference of view among the translators.

[2] The first 299, with a few specimens of the rest (including the doubtful or spurious correspondence), are included in Mr. Jackson's volume. Our references to ["Ep."] are to be understood of Basil's letters, unless another name is mentioned.

[3] The translation is certainly right, though "camel's hair" is a commoner sense of the Greek word. Such tents are, and doubtless always have been, common in the country.

[4] Pliny the younger may be taken as typical of a class.

[5] Plutarch, *Enm.,* 8; *Studies in the Eastern Roman Provinces,* p. 372 f. (Hodder & Stoughton, 1906); *Cities and Bishoprics of Phrygia,* ii., p. 419.

[6] " . . . the sanctuaries (with the Altar), into which at this time no layman except the Emperor might enter."

[7] *Impressions of Turkey,* p. 95.

[8] *Præp. Ev.,* vi., pp. 275, 279, Viger.

[9] In the canonical letter to Amphilochius, p. 238, the total duration of the punishment in its various degrees is specified as four years.

[10] *Church in the Roman Empire before* 180, ch. xviii.

[11] Gregory seems to have had the lowest possible idea of women's capacity: they could not even sit on a horse, without being held to prevent them falling off.

[12] See Friedländer, *Sittengeschichte Roms,* ii., p. 44.

[13] Translation in *Palest. Pilgrims' Text Society,* i., p. 163; compare p. 21.

[14] [*pandokseion*] at Constantina in Osrhoene, *B. C. H.,* 1903, p. 200, was founded in 514, *hotellerie ecclesiastique pour pelerins.*

[15] Contrast with this the account given of a modern missionary in my *Impressions of Turkéy,* p. 222. The winter weather does not prevent travellers of Western origin from going about; but the Eastern people are not great travellers, and regard winter as a closed season.

[16] Not Cappadocia, as editors think, for Annesi was in Pontus.

[17] This famine and the relief operations are also described by Gregory Nazianzen, *Panegyric,* 34-36.

[18] Entirely confirmed by other evidence, *e.g.,* an inscription recently found in Pisidia of the year 527 (*Bulletin de Corresp. Hellénique,* 1893, p. 501 ff.).

[19] The biography of Basil in *Dictionary of Christian Biography,* meritorious and useful as it is, is too much guided by the earlier modern authorities.

[20] The effect of this rather suggestive statement is toned down in the original by a sentence here omitted about Basil's weak health.

[21] This shows a rather low standard of the book-trade in Cæsarea, one of the greatest commercial cities of the East. Without such scribes, the publication of an edition of a book was impossible. A similar statement is made by Gregory Nyss., "Ep. 15" (Migne).

[22] "Epp. 74, 75, 76." The first is addressed to Martinianus, who had some personal friendship with Basil; otherwise he is unknown, but he evidently was not a Cappadocian official. The profusion of literary allusions in the letter, and the compliments to the knowledge of history and of mankind that Martinianus possessed, suggest that he was a philosopher or man of letters. He evidently lived at some distance both from Constantinople and from Cappadocia. Mr. Jackson's statement that he was an official of Cappadocia rests on no ancient authority, and seems to me not to suit the letter.

[23] Mr. Jackson's suggestion that they were part of the Imperial estate of Macellum, beside Cæsareia, is very probable.

[24] See *Historical Geography of Asia Minor,* p. 93.

[25] As when ("Ep. 231") he calls one (perhaps Demosthenes, the agent of Valens) "the fat sea-monster" and "the old muleteer".

[26] He is shown to be an official by his having the power to send a soldier to Cæsareia with a message on the subject.

[27] The exact localisation of the home of Gregory, on the estate Arianzos, beside the village Carbala (or Caprales, Basil, "Ep. 308"), about eight miles southwest of Nazianzus (now called Nenizi), is made in *Historical Geography of Asia Minor,* p. 286; see also Sir C. Wilson's *Handbook to Asia Minor,* etc. (Murray), p. 169. The modern village of Gelvere is built in the Tiberina, described by Gregory Naz., "Ep. 6, 7," a narrow, rocky, picturesque glen, like a hole in the plain (4,500 feet above sea-level), "the very pit of the whole earth," as Basil calls it (*Ep.* 14). . .

[29] On the desire of bishops to extend their authority over smaller cities and to diminish the number of bishops, see *Studies in the History and Art of the Eastern Provinces* (Hodder & Stoughton, 1906), p. 28 f.

Roy J. Deferrari (lecture date 1917)

SOURCE: "The Classics and the Greek Writers of the Early Church: Saint Basil," *The Classical Journal,* Vol. XIII, No. 8, May, 1918, pp. 579-91.

[*In the following excerpt, originally delivered as a lecture in 1917, Deferrari calls attention to Hellenistic influences in Basil's writings, particularly his "Address to Young Men," the* Hexaemeron, *the* Homilies on the Psalms, *and his letters. In the critic's judgment, these works demonstrate the value that Basil placed on classical learning as well as his indebtedness to Aristotle, Plutarch, and—most particularly—Plato.*]

The purpose of this paper[1] is to serve as a reminder of the close bond which exists between the masters of classical literature and many of the early Christian writers and to emphasize the great value in studying at least certain of the church authors for the acquirement of the fullest understanding of the great minds of antiquity. At the same time we would warn against an over-accentuation of classical elements in the products of later periods and the consequent lack of appreciation of the true value and place of the post-classical in the history of civilization.

St. Basil the Great, of Caesarea, is an excellent example of the Christian Father, a study of whom is very compensating to the classicist. He lived in a period (the fourth century) when the elements of Christianity and pagan life were most closely united. Theodosius the First had made Christianity the state religion, and paganism was from that time on to suffer constant persecution and gradual extermination. Christianity, which had hitherto been fighting desperately for its very existence, and had thus been averse to any principle of life in any way reminiscent of paganism, now, in a feeling of security, readily took over many of the pagan elements of the older civilization. This reaction, as one would expect, is reflected strongly in the literature of the period. It seems, indeed, like one of the ironies of history that scarcely had the church begun to triumph when paganism began to make greater and greater inroads, not only into the literature, but also into the customs, thoughts, and life of the people.

The earliest literary productions of Christianity show very little contact with Hellenism, and in form are almost entirely independent, with some Jewish and oriental influences.[2] The Apocalypse is the only early Christian literary composition which has a foreign source, and this is Jewish.

From this earliest period down to Clement of Alexandria (latter part of the second century) is the time of transition from a literature hostile to all culture and everything worldly to a literature influenced by a very careful Hellenistic training. The literary products of the third and fourth centuries show the closest contact with Hellenism without lacking at the same time every quality of originality. Not only do we see very marked Hellenistic influences, but we find open declarations of the high value of the classics,[3] and accompanying this we notice a correspondingly high level of culture. Basil is one of the foremost authors of this patristic *floruit*.

It is very noteworthy that the older Greek Fathers, in explaining the nature of the Holy Ghost, had recourse to Platonic formulae, particularly to the doctrine of the soul of the universe. . . . It has been observed that Origen made use of the theory in describing the Holy Spirit,[4] and Gregory Nazianzus[5] frankly compares this idea with the Christian doctrine of the Holy Ghost. Basil also makes free use of these formulae in his work on the Holy Spirit . . . , so much so that an effort has been made to establish a direct relation between this treatise and the writings of Plotinus.[6] Although the resemblances in thought are striking and numerous, it is difficult to establish any direct dependency. The arguments contained therein were generally known in Basil's time through the teachings of the popular philosophy and, as we have indicated, through the work of the earlier Christian Fathers. Basil therefore may be depending on the earlier Christian writers (e.g., Origen), or, what is more probable, on the current teachings of the neo-Platonists in general. Furthermore, since Basil's intimate acquaintance with Plato is very marked in some of his other works, it is not too rash to presume that here also he is drawing somewhat on the great master himself.

The influence of the popular diatribe is seen in the form of what are known as the longer and shorter rules for monks. . . . Both of these works are written in the regular diatribe form of question and answer, and are known as the ***Monks' Catechism of Morals and Obligations***.

The work which best displays Basil's attitude toward the ancient classics is his address to Christian youths on the benefit to be derived from pagan literature.[7] . . . Life eternal, he says, is the supreme goal of every Christian, and Holy Writ is the guide to this life. Since young men cannot appreciate the deep thoughts contained therein, they should study the profane writings, in which truth appears as in a mirror. As leaves are a protection and an ornament to the fruit of a tree, so is pagan wisdom to Christian truth. In reading pagan literature one must distinguish between the morally helpful and the morally injurious. Since the life eternal is to be obtained through virtue, one must pay particular attention to those passages in which virtue is praised—such examples as may be found in Hesiod, Homer, Solon, Theognis, and Prodicus. Almost all eminent philosophers have extolled virtue, and we must try to realize their words in this life. Every man is divided against himself who does not make his life conform to his words, but who says with Euripides, "The mouth indeed hath sworn, but the heart knows no oath."[8] To seem to be good when one is not so is, if we are to respect the opinion of Plato[9] at all, the very height of injustice. In pagan literature virtue is praised in deeds as well as in words, wherefore one should study the acts of noble men which coincide with the teachings of the Scriptures—for example, the deeds of Pericles, Euclid, Socrates, Alexander, and Cleinias. The young man, then, in thought and action must never lose sight of his aim in life. Thus, like the athlete Polydamas and the musician Timotheus, he must bend every energy to one task, the winning of the heavenly crown. This end is to be obtained by freeing the soul from its association with the senses, by scorning riches and reputation, and by subordinating all else to virtue. This ideal will be matured later by the study of the Scriptures, but at present it is to be fostered by the study of the pagan writers. From these should be stored up knowledge for the future.

This résumé in itself tells much about Basil's knowledge of ancient classics. In addition, throughout the whole a strong Platonic influence is felt in the method of expression and in the development of the theme. As often, it is difficult to distinguish between the influence of popular philosophy and a direct relationship with Plato. In certain portions, however, the resemblance to Plato is too marked to admit of doubt—for example, in the early part of the address, where Basil, in considering the merits and demerits of the poets, is clearly basing his remarks on Plato's *Republic* 376 E ff. Plutarch's [*Pos dei ton. . .*] bears many similarities to Basil's work, not so much in content as in methods of argument. Any connection with Basil, however, is probably very slight, as in these cases of likeness we have to do with *topoi* which may have a common source in the popular philosophy of the time.

Basil's homilies show the most evident dependence on the classics. The ***Hexaemeron***, a series of nine sermons on Genesis, is strikingly influenced by the *Timaeus* of Plato and the *Historia animalium* of Aristotle, colored here and there by reminiscences of Origen and Philo.[10] The very statement of the subject recalls the *Timaeus*. It is a treatise [*Peri phoseos*] [11] just as the *Timaeus* is said to be.[12] To mention only a few of the most important parallels: both Basil and Plato say that God bound the elements together by a bond of friendship;[13] the universe is visible and tangible, and the visibility is due to fire, the tangibility to the hardness of the earth.[14] The last parallelism has a remarkable similarity in phraseology. Other parallels in phraseology as well as in thought are the statements that God kindled the sun and made it of sufficient brightness to shine on the whole universe;[15] the commonplaces on the division of time;[16] the expressions about the origin of flesh;[17] and the respiration of fish.[18] An attempt has been made[19] to show that for the most part Basil made use of Posidonius' commentary on Plato's *Timaeus*. This is only partially true, as the outstanding resemblances cannot be explained simply by the study of a mere commentary.

This dependence on Plato is found to the greatest extent in the first four sermons, which treat especially of the creation of the universe in contrast to the formation of creatures. After a consideration in the next two homilies of the nature of the universe and the question of the divisions of time, Basil proceeds to the formation of creatures, discussing respectively the creeping things, the creatures of the air, the creatures of the waters, and the creatures of the land. In those questions, which are treated in the last three homilies, Basil's chief source is Aristotle's [*Peri zoou*].[20] Basil did not make use of the discussions of Genesis which were written before his time, as the preserved fragments of these works show no connection with Basil whatsoever. Some assert an influence from the *Physiologus*. Kraus,[21] however, convincingly dates the *Physiologus* at the end of the fourth century or after Basil's time, and Plass (*loc. cit.*) sees no resemblance striking enough to warrant the slightest idea of dependency. An examination of the two works reveals many passages which have been taken almost verbatim from Aristotle, many which Basil saw fit to expand or curtail, and others which Basil enlarged by adding information from other sources, Aelian and Oppian.[22]

The influence which Philo and Origen exerted on Basil's **Hexaemeron** has been summarized thus:

> Basil probably derived from Philo directly or indirectly the reason why the luminaries were not created until the fourth day, and the notion that both birds and fish swim. Both likewise speak of underground veins of water, and Basil evidently refers to Philo and his school when he says that certain Jews assert that the plural verb in the command "let us make man" signifies that the angels are addressed.[23]

> It is difficult to tell how much Basil drew from Origen, because so much of the work of the latter has been lost. It is generally supposed, however, that in asserting so firmly his belief that the upper waters are real water, and rejecting an allegorical interpretation of the passage, Basil directs his arguments against Origen, with whom allegory was a favorite method of exegesis.[24] Basil owes many of his arguments against astrology to Origen, and the idea that it is impious to assert that God is ever inactive is common to Origen and Basil.[25]

The homilies on the psalms are naturally of a more popular nature. If it is true that Basil composed these sermons extempore,[26] we cannot doubt that he poured forth his mind with perfect freedom on every topic. Thus it is only natural that we should find that in these sermons Basil did not excerpt from any particular author, but spoke sentiments which were the composite product of his training in the schools of rhetoric and his studies in the ancient pagan and later Christian authors.

Homily VI . . . is such a composition. Although many passages therein agree with certain sentiments of the Cynics and Stoics, it does not follow that Basil leaned to their teachings. Such passages have their source in the popular philosophy of the day.

Homily VII . . . bears very manifest traces of Plutarch and Clement of Alexandria. The parallelism between this sermon and Plutarch's [*Peri philoploutias*] and Clement's *Paedagogus* are so close that we suspect that Basil read these works very shortly before he delivered his talk. Starting out with the words of the Scripture (Matt., chap. 19) he mingles his own sentiments with the words of a Christian and a pagan.

Basil's homily on Psalm 14 . . . bears a very close resemblance to Plutarch's [*Peri ton me dei*].[27] As in Homily VII, the resemblances are so close that Basil must have read Plutarch's work but a short time previously.

Homily XXI . . . has very marked indications of being an extempore speech. All the sentiments of this sermon are met with in others of Basil's works. Expressions from the Cynic and Stoic, Plato, Plutarch, Clement of Alexandria, and Origen, are all woven together into a composite mass.

In the field of epistolography Basil stands out as one of the leading writers of Greek literature. He has left us a group of vigorous letters of high literary value, a mine of information for the life of the times. In these private communications it is impossible to trace any direct connection with another author, except where occasionally a letter on some theological question develops into a small treatise. In such cases Basil presents views necessarily influenced in part by the earlier Christian Fathers. Yet Basil's training in the classics and in schools of rhetoric is everywhere apparent if only in his manner of expression. Furthermore, he makes many allusions to classical authors and subjects. In **"Letter 1"** he speaks of passing the city on the Hellespont more unmoved than any Ulysses passing Sirens' songs.[28] In **"Letter 74"** he says: "Not then would I pray that I might listen to you, like Alcinous to Ulysses, only for a year, but throughout all my life." In **"Letter 239,"** Basil quotes Homer directly: "I am moved to say as Diomed said—

> 'Would God, Atrides, thy request were yet to undertake,
> . . . . he's proud enough.'"[29]

In **"Letter 3"** Basil mentions Plato (*Rep.* vi. 10): "You do not give up the study of literature, but, as Plato has it, in the midst of the storm and tempest of affairs, you stand aloof, as it were, under some strong wall, and keep your mind clear of all disturbances."[30] Anecdotes apparently taken from Plutarch occur about Demosthenes in **"Letter 3 ,"**[31] and about Solon in **"Letter 74,"**[32] Other echoes from classical antiquity may be seen in **"Letters 4," 8, 14, 21, 39, 133, 112, 291,"** and **"339."** These references are by no means all that exist in Basil's letters, but only a small portion collected at random.

In touching upon Basil's language there is need of great caution. We classicists are very apt to forget that elementary principle of philology which declares that language, totally distinct from literature, experiences no rise and decline, but ever changes and develops. Consequently we often erroneously speak of the quality and purity of a writer's Greek, of a decline in the use of moods, etc. However, if we may compare Basil's Greek with that which we know as Attic, we can say that the resemblance is very close. Certain words, to be sure, bear a slightly different meaning. There is a tendency to make a minimum use of the moods. Yet the differences on the whole are very slight.[33] Since he was born in Cappadocian Caesarea, the son of a worthy rhetor and lawyer, trained by his father from the beginning in rhetorical studies, and then for several years taught in the University at Athens, it is difficult to understand how Basil could write anything but Greek, very closely resembling the classical.

In a literary way, then, Basil belongs to those Church Fathers in whom classical culture and Christianity are most closely united. He is well read in profane literature and knows how to employ his wide reading fittingly. He has an intimate first-hand knowledge of Aristotle and Plutarch, but is especially well acquainted with Plato, particularly the *Republic*. The popular philosophical tracts of the Cynics, a long rhetorical training, and a careful study of the earliest Christian Fathers have all shown their influence on Basil. His theology is colored by Platonic and Stoic ideas. As for his language, he unconsciously rather than consciously follows the method of the second Sophistic in imitating Attic as his norm. Although Basil may not have appreciated the importance of classical culture in all its phases, he did recognize in it a lasting and imperishable worth for the cultivation of men's minds, and he did much to preserve the intellectual product of Hellenic culture for later generations.

Aside from the literary and purely theological and ecclesiastic interest which Basil's writings-possess, we cannot pass over a value which has never been fully recognized. Indeed we may make the same statement about the voluminous writings of his brother Gregory of Nyssa and his friend Gregory of Nazianzen. They possess great worth as storing up many facts about the condition of society and education in the late Roman Empire, about the administration and law as practically affecting the people, about the taxpayer's views on taxation, the traveler's views as to the roads and the seasons, the householder's views on the safety of his property, the merchant's and the investor's views on the public credit, and the standard of commercial honesty—in short, about the ordinary life of a highly organized community, in which the original style of society and manners was being replaced by the European. Above all, however, these writings show us the views entertained by a man of power and education as to the duties of the church in its relation to all these various interests.[34] . . .

Notes

[1] Delivered at the meeting of the American Philological Association at the University of Pennsylvania, December 28, 1917.

[2] E.g., the Epistles to the Hebrews and the so-called first letter of St. Clement show a strong rhetorical and slightly stoical influence. Cf. P. Wendland, *Christentum und Hellenismus in ihren litterarischen Besiehungen* (Leipzig, 1902); E. Norden, *Die Antike Kunstprosa* (Leipzig and Berlin, 1909), II, 460; E. Hatch, *Griechtum und Christentum* (Freiburg, 1892).

[3] Cf. Jerome, *Ad magnum oratorem;* Basil, *Homily on Education* 3. 584 C7; *Epistles* 4. 1092 C10; 4. 572 C8.

[4] Baumgarten-Crusius, *Histor. Dogm. T.H.,* p. 1025.

[5] *Or.* 37.

[6] Jahnius, *Basilius Magnus Plotinizans* (Bernae, 1838); Carolus Gronau, *De Basilio, Gregorio Nazianzeno Nyssenoque Platonis Imitatoribus* (Goettingae, 1908).

[7] Cf. Georg Buettner, *Basileios des Grossen Mahnworte an die Jugend über nützlichen Gebrauch der heidnischen Literatur* (München, 1908); Shear, *The Influence of Plato on St. Basil* (Baltimore, 1906); Eichoff, *Zwei Schriften des Basilius und des Augustinus als geschichtliche Dokumente der Vereinigung von klassischer Bildung und Christentum*; de Vos, *De legendis gentilium libris in scholastica adolescentium institutione quid sit sentiendum, quid S. Baslius M. senserit* (Warendorf, 1855); Padelford, *Essays on the Study and Use of Poetry by Plutarch and Basil the Great* (New York, 1902).

[8] Hippolytus 612.

[9] *Rep.* ii. 361.

[10] Cf. Shear, *loc. cit.;* Robbins, *The Hexaemeral Literature* (Chicago, 1912); Plass, *De Basilii et Ambrosii excerptis ad historiam animalium partinentibus*; Müllenhoff, "Aristotles bei Basilius," Hermes, II, 252; Jahn, *Neue Jahrb.*, XLIX, 397; Hiller, *Neue Jahrb.*, CIX., 174.

[11] Bas. 1. 8A1.

[12] *Tim.* 27A.

[13] *Tim.* 32C; Bas. 33A.

[14] *Tim.* 31B; Bas. i. 25 A14.

[15] *Tim.* 39B; Bas. 137B.

[16] *Tim.* 39B; Bas. 137B.

[17] *Tim.* 82C; Bas. 168A.

[18] *Tim.* 92A; Bas. 149B.

[19] Gronau, *loc. cit.*

[20] Cf. Müllenhoff and Plass, *loc. cit.*

[21] *Geschichte der christlichen Kunst* (Freiburg, 1896).

[22] Cf. (*a*) Basil 149A; Aristotle (Aristotelis opera ed. Acad. Reg. Borussica Berolini) 754*a*, 21: B. 152C; A. 675*a*, 3 and 675*a*, 5: B. 152C, 5; A. 591*a*, 7 and 22 and 25: B. 157B; A. 601*b*, 16 and 598*b*, 3: B. 169B; A. 486*a*, 23: B. 172B; A. 487*b*, 33: B. 180A; A. 563*b*, 7, etc.; (*b*) Basil 149A; Aristotle 489*a*, 35: B. 149B; A. 479*b*, 8: B. 177A; A. 542*b*, 4: D 184D; A. 541*b*, 9, etc.; (*c*) Basil 149D; Aristotle 566*b*, 16; Oppian *De piscat.* 1. 734: B. 153C; A. 622*a*, 8; O. ii. 233: B. 180A; A. 756*a*, 15 and 539*a*, 30; Aelian (ed. R. Hercher), p. 35, 22, etc.

[23] *Hex.* 205B; *De op. mund.* 25. 17.

[24] *Hex.* 76A; Origen, *Hom. in Gen.* 148A.

[25] Cf. Origen, *De prin.* iii. 5. 3; Basil 32B; Philo 2. 12. The quotation is from Robbins, *op. cit.*, p. 44.

[26] Cf. Fialon, *Étude littéraire et historique sur St. Basile* (Paris, 1869), p. 183.

[27] Cf. A. Jahn, *Animadversiones in St. Basilii opera, fasc. 1. Accadunt emblemata Plutarchea ex Basilii homilia in Ps. XIV* (Bern. 1842).

[28] Hom. *Od.* xii. 158.

[29] *Il.* ix. 694-95 (Chapman). Hom. *III.* 346 is quoted in "Letter 348," but the authenticity of this letter is questioned.

[30] Plato is mentioned in "Letter 348," but the genuine character of this letter is questioned.

[31] Cf. Plut. [*Pol paragg*]. xxii.

[32] Cf. Plut. *Solon* 30. Note reference to Alexander from Plutarch's *Alexander* in doubtful "Letter 272."

[33] Cf. J. Trunk, *De Basilio Magno sermonis Attici imitatore* (Stuttgart, 1911).

[34] Cf. W. M. Ramsay, "Basil of Caesarea," *Expositor,* January, 1896, pp. 49-61 (a criticism of Jackson's translation of St. Basil's letters).

Margaret Mary Fox (essay date 1939)

SOURCE: "Christian Society" in *The Life and Times of St. Basil the Great as Revealed in His Works,* The Catholic University of America Press, 1939, pp. 137-65.

[*In the essay reprinted here, Fox surveys the customs and practices of the Caesarean church during Basil's episcopate. Using information derived from his letters, she discusses Basil's innovative establishment of charitable institutions, his veneration of martyrs and their relics, and his relations with congregants as well as clergy.*]

A Bishop and His Congregation

Numerous references reveal the informality that existed between St. Basil and the vast congregation that filled the great church of Caesarea, and also the intimate union that was established between the pastor and his flock. St. Basil tells us that his congregation at Caesarea included, besides the rich, artisans and workmen, some of whom were scarcely able to eke out an existence by their daily labor.[1] It was for these working men and women standing around him in crowds that he often shortened his discourses in order not to keep them too long from their work.[2] Sometimes, however, fearing lest "many of the congregation, when dismissed, would at once resort to the gambling table," St. Basil prolonged his sermons purposely to detain his people longer in church.[3] He tells us that he preached at Mass on Sundays and on anniversaries of the martyrs, both morning and evening during Lent, and during the fast days which preceded the great feasts.[4] In order to secure attention and to make his words effective, St. Basil advised his people to make his sermon the subject of conversation at their evening meal.[5] Twice in the same homily he refers to their attentiveness and interest, although we know from other references that his audience never hesitated by "looks and signs" to manifest their displeasure.[6]

Again we see by the familiar reflections with which he intermingles his homilies the informality which exists between the Saint and his congregation. Once we find him praising his flock and thanking them for waiting for him until noon at a martyr's shrine.[7] He acknowledged the fact that even if he spent himself for them as a mother for her children, his sermons bore their own fruit, which gave him consolation.[8] On the other hand, the Saint complains elsewhere of the "great noise that the enemy is making outside the church," so that he cannot be heard.[9] On another occasion, he says bitterly that "they ask for sermons not to profit by them, but only to slander him and to accuse him of disseminating new ideas."[10] He is alluding to someone who is apparently envious of his eloquence and who is criticizing him unfavorably.

It is certain that the Saint knew his people well, that he spoke to them from his heart, and that they reciprocated his friendliness. They often interrupted his sermons to remind him of something he had omitted.[11] The Saint sometimes improvised his sermons in order to make them more applicable to the occasion, even though they suffered in rhetorical style. Toward the close of one sermon, someone in the audience urged St. Basil not to omit to mention the miracle which the Lord had wrought for them on the previous day, when their church had been saved from fire by a sudden change of wind.[12] Again, while preaching one of the homilies on Creation, his people reminded him by looks and signs that in his enthusiasm he had forgotten to mention the birds. "Some may wonder why I have just made a considerable pause in my sermon, but my more attentive hearers know the reason of it; those, namely, who by their looks at one another and their signs, have called my attention to them and brought back my thoughts to what I had omitted."[13] And on another occasion he says, "I noticed long ago that you were displeased with my sermon; I can almost hear you saying that I am spending my time upon points which are admitted, that I am avoiding more pertinent questions."[14]

From another reference we may learn of the curiosity displayed by St. Basil's audience, who were anxious to hear as much as possible about nature, and we may see the concern that a fourth-century ecclesiastic showed for the interests of his flock. "What trouble you have given me in former discourses," exclaims St. Basil, "by asking me why the earth was invisible, when all bodies are imbued with color, and all color comes under the sense of sight? Perhaps the reason I gave did not seem sufficient to you. . . . Perhaps you will ask me new questions."[15] St. Basil gratifies their curiosity concerning the world of nature with many details from his store of Greek learning. He tells his hearers that as "anyone not knowing a town is taken by the hand and led through it," so he will guide them "through the mysterious marvels of this great city of the universe."[16] Thus he raised their hearts to God through contemplation of nature by explaining to them the marvels of creation.

Yet we know that with the religion of the common people there were evidently mingled superstitions, and beliefs in astrology and in charms, for St. Basil reproaches those Christians who have recourse in the sickness of their children to magicians, and hang a talisman around the patient's neck,[17] or those who have

the Chaldean astrologers ready at the birth of their children to forecast their destinies.[18] The Saint says that "those who give themselves to this imaginary science and those who listen to them openmouthed, as if they could learn the future, are supremely ridiculous."[19]

In regard to congregational singing, we may conclude from St. Basil's comments that he approved and encouraged it, and his people responded and enjoyed it. St. Basil writes of the singing: "If the ocean is good and is worthy of praise before God, how much more beautiful is the assembly of a Church like this, where the voices of men, women, and children arise in prayer to God, mingling and resounding like the waves which beat upon the shore."[20] Delayed until noon in reaching a martyrion on a feast day, St. basil found that the assembly had spent the time singing hymns.[21] In a letter to the bishops of the West, describing the sad conditions of the Eastern Church in the midst of the Arian persecution, St. Basil laments among other things that there is "no evening singing of hymns."[22] St. Basil evidently encouraged his monks to sing also, for in his Rules he writes: "And it is perfectly possible to pray and to sing at the same time that we work."[23]

We know also that St. Basil employed the antiphonal chanting of hymns, dividing the faithful into two choirs, replying to each other. The Saint refers to it thus: "And now indeed divided into two groups they sing antiphonally. . . . Then again after entrusting to one person to lead the chant, the rest sing the response."[24] That this was an innovation we learn from the fact that St. Basil's method became a subject of suspicion and accusation in other churches where a different system of singing the psalms was used.[25] The new method, however, soon spread through the churches of the East. Both Flavian, bishop of Antioch, and Diodorus, bishop of Tarsus, are reported to have made use of it.[26]

Synods and Religious Festivals in their Social Aspects

A close study of St. Basil's writings discloses three types of gatherings, each described by the term "synod": namely, the assembly of the faithful to commemorate the feast of a martyr;[27] a meeting of the bishops usually held on the day before the festival;[28] and a meeting of the country presbyters held whenever St. Basil visited their district.[29] In connection with the festivals, a country fair was also held for the purpose of displaying and exchanging goods.[30]

St. Basil's disapproval of the mingling of the religious and commercial elements at these festivals is seen in a strict prohibition to his monks. Although they are permitted to dispose of their goods at fairs under certain conditions, the frequenting of the fairs held at the martyrs' shrines is never permitted and the penalty is that "inflicted by Christ on the buyers and sellers in the Temple."[31]

The necessity for St. Basil's disapproval may be seen in several references to the evils likely to result when such a large concourse of people were brought together. It was at "the local festival" at Venasa, when "a great crowd from all sides, as was natural, was gathering," that the outburst of fanaticism on the part of the deacon Glycerius occurred.[32] Of another synod, St. Basil writes, "At this synod some have been arrested who were engaged in wicked deeds, and in stealing, contrary to the Lord's commandment."[33]

St. Basil gives a vivid description of the vices and evils prevalent at such festivals:[34] "Indeed, when once I attended the spiritual festivals, I found with difficulty one single brother who in appearance at least had fear of the Lord; but in fact he was under the mastery of the devil, and I heard him tell witty stories and tales fabricated for the deception of those whom he met. After meeting him I fell in with many thieves. . . . I saw the shameful sight of drunkards. . . . I also saw the beauty of women. . . . I heard many a discourse edifying to the soul, but in none of my teachers did I find a virtue worthy of their discourses. Next I listened to countless songs, clothed however in wanton music. Again I listened to a sweetly-sounding lyre, a clatter of clogdancers, the voice of buffoons, much folly and ribald wit, and the clamor of an enormous crowd."[35]

Of the spiritual advantages and benefits to be derived from religious festivals, St. Basil gives us the following details: "The enigmas of the Proverbs are revealed, the teachings of the Apostles are explained, the ideas of the gospels are set forth. There are lectures on theology, and conversations with spiritual brethren, who by the mere sight of their faces confer great benefits upon those they meet."[36]

Even though St. Basil was extremely averse to having his monks attend the fairs held in connection with the synods, nevertheless the Saint urged attendance of all the other clergy at the martyrs' festivals, which usually attracted large concourses of people to hear the eulogies of their local saints.[37] On one occasion at the feast of a martyr, the people assembled at the martyrion and waited overnight until midday for the arrival of St. Basil, spending the time singing hymns.[38] Allusions to festivals in June and September would seem to indicate that these were the usual months for holding the synods.[39]

St. Basil himself made every effort to attend celebrations which generally combined official meetings of the bishops and the clergy with the annual memorial services in honor of different martyrs. He tells us that in spite of serious illness, which should have kept him at home, he risked traveling to the martyr's chapel, only to suffer another attack of illness that hindered a meeting he had planned with Amphilochius.[40] **"Epistle 157"** informs us also that these gatherings were utilized by friends as opportunities to have pleasant visits with one another. In this letter St. Basil expresses disappointment in not having met a certain Antiochus, the nephew of Bishop Eusebius, during the summer. In **"Epistle 278"** he writes to another friend: "I longed to see your Nobility when I was in Orphanene (in Armenia Minor). For I expected that you, living at Corsagena, would not hesitate to cross over to us if we should be at Attagena holding the synod. But when I failed of that synod, I longed to see you at the mountain."

The necessity for synods in the midst of the dangers of heresy is seen in the purpose stated by St. Basil on the occasion of a second synod during the trouble with Eustathius: "So that our brethren throughout the diocese might come together and unite with one another and so that our communion in the future might be genuine and without guile."[41] Other difficulties that arose may be seen in the following letter. One year St. Basil was going to make use of the assembly of chorepiscopi at the synod for the martyr Eupsychius, to introduce them to the *numerarius* of the prefect,[42] but since the latter failed to appear, St. Basil had to write a letter of introduction for each bishop, when necessity required a favor from the official.[43]

We find mention, too, of the fact that although these synods and festivals were held annually on the same date, formal invitations to attend were sent to the bishops, who were strongly urged to attend in order to add to the dignity and solemnity of the festival.[44] St. Basil tells one bishop that the people will be looking for him,[45] and on another occasion the people of Samosata regretted St. Basil's absence.[46] In the course of another letter St. Basil assures the bishops "that a reward is laid up for the honoring of the martyrs," and that "all who hope in the Lord seek eagerly to honor the martyrs."[47] Bishops may display their loyalty to their common Master by their disposition towards the martyrs, "their fellow-servants who have won renown."[48] In **"Epistle 282"** we learn that a bishop complained that he was not invited, although St. Basil said that he paid no attention when he was invited. Nevertheless, St. Basil sent another invitation for "it is not right to neglect the martyrs in whose commemoration he is invited to join." Even though the bishops do not care to give pleasure to St. Basil personally, they should come to the martyrs' festivals and "grant the favor to those held in the highest honor."[49]

"Epistle 252" is a general invitation to all the bishops of the diocese of Pontus to attend the festival in honor of Eupsychius and Damas, "most celebrated martyrs, whose memory is observed yearly by our city and by all the surrounding country."[50] "The Church," St. Basil writes, "calls upon you to take up your ancient custom of making the visit."[51]

We have another invitation sent to Amphilochius, bishop of Iconium, to attend the festival "which it is the custom of our church to celebrate annually in honor of the martyrs," Damas and Eupsychius.[52] St. Basil urges the bishop, his spiritual son, to come early, at least three days before the synod, "to anticipate the days of the synod, so that we may converse at leisure with each other."[53] Again, in 375 A.D., St. Basil reminds Amphilochius to remember the martyr Eupsychius, and not to wait for a second invitation to the festival but to "anticipate it and make us happy."[54]

On the other hand, St. Basil himself did not attend the festivals at Nicopolis in June of 372, because he says "the perfunctory manner of those who had invited me came to my mind—that, after extending a passing invitation through Hellenius, regulator of taxes at Nazianzus, they did not think it worth while to send a messenger to remind us of this same matter again or to act as our escort."[55]

Cult of Martyrs

It was only in the fourth century, with the freedom granted to the Church in the age of Constantine, that churches could openly establish festivals to commemorate publicly the death and the anniversaries of the martyrs.[56] St. Basil testifies that his people communicated at Caesarea every Sunday, Wednesday, Friday, Saturday, and on all the feasts of the martyrs.[57] Thus during the fourth century the festivals assumed wider proportions until they obtained definitely recognized places in the liturgical year.

Several references confirm the fact that St. Basil summoned all bishops—even those of the diocese of Pontus, annually to honor the memory of their famous fellow-citizens, Eupsychius, Damas, and their companions.[58] These martyrs had been condemned under Julian for the part they took in the demolition of a temple of Fortune in 362 A.D. Sozomen says that Eupsychius was a nobleman of Caesarea, who had recently been married. The anger of Julian was aroused against all the inhabitants of Caesarea, so that any who had taken part in the action were either condemned or banished. Eupsychius had been cruelly tortured and beheaded.[59] At the martyrion in Caesarea, erected in the place of the pagan temple which they had been accused of demolishing, the festival took place on September seventh. St. Basil did not inaugurate this festival, for he mentions that the memory of these martyrs is observed yearly by Caesarea and all the surrounding country, and that it is an "ancient custom."[60]

St. Basil's interest in, and enthusiastic devotion to the martyrs is explained somewhat by the description he gives of the tortures inflicted on martyrs by their executioners. It gives an idea also of the barbarous cruelties that the fourth-century Christians might experience. St. Basil speaks of the persecution of the Christians under Athanaric, King of the Ostrogoths, when St. Sabas and his companions were martyred; "But your story—contestants confronting each other, bodies torn to pieces for religion's sake, barbarian rage treated with contempt by men undaunted of heart, the various tortures applied by the persecutors, the firm resistance of the contestants throughout, the beam, the water—these are the instruments for the perfecting of martyrs!"[61] St. Sabas suffered martyrdom in the second year of St. Basil's episcopate, 372 A.D., in a local persecution. He had endured long, cruel torments before he was drowned. The Christian Duke of Scythia, Julius Soranus, a native of Cappadocia, had taken charge of the martyr's bones; and **"Epistle 155,"** which is considered one of the earliest references to the preservation of the relics of martyrs, was written to this duke of Scythia, a relative of St. Basil.[62] St. Basil requested Soranus to send him some relics of the Gothic martyrs. "You will do well if you send the relics of martyrs to your native land, since, as you have written us, the persecution which is taking place there is even now making martyrs to the Lord."[63]

The next year St. Basil thanks Soranus for his prompt compliance in sending the relics of St. Sabas. St. Basil writes thus: "With a martyr, who but lately finished his struggle in the barbarian land neighboring your own, you have honored the land which bore you, sending, like a grateful husbandman, the first fruits back to those who supplied the seed. Truly worthy of Christ's athlete are the gifts: a martyr of the truth who had just been wreathed with the crown of righteousness. We not only received him with joy, but also glorified the God who among all the Gentiles has already fulfilled the gospel of his Christ."[64] Thus St. Basil rejoiced to have secured the relics of this Saint, who had so recently shed his blood for Christ at a time when the Church in Cappadocia was torn by the Arian heresy and as yet had no martyrs, as the Saint explains: "Though grievous are our afflictions yet nowhere is martyrdom, because those who harm us have the same appellation as ourselves."[65]

The martyrdom of the Gothic Saint recalled the Cappadocian martyr, Eutyches, who received special honor annually at Caesarea. Ascholius reminded St. Basil of Eutyches who, after laboring zealously among the Goths, was taken prisoner by them in 260 A.D., in the reign of Gallienus, in a raid into Cappadocia.[66] Through the teaching of Eutyches and other captives before their martyrdom, many had been converted. Thus it was through the kindness of Ascholius, the bishop of Thessalonica, that the body of the third-century martyr was sent to St. Basil. In his letter of thanks to Ascholius, thinking again of the Arian heresy, St. Basil writes: "You have exalted our fatherland for having by itself furnished the seed of our religion; you cheered us by calling up the past, but distressed us by exposing the conditions which we see today. For no one of us is comparable to Eutyches in virtue."[67]

In a discourse on St. Mamas, St. Basil omits praise of the martyr in order to point out the lessons to be learned from his life, but, not to disappoint the expectations of the audience who came to hear an encomium, he says: "Remember the martyr, all who have enjoyed a sight of him in dreams, all who have listened in this place and have had him for a helper in prayers, all whom he has helped at work, when invoked by name, all whom he has brought home from wayfaring, all whom he has raised up from sickness, all to whom he has restored children already dead, all whose life he has prolonged. Bring all the facts together; work him up an encomium by common contribution, then distribute it to each other, and let each one impart his knowledge to the ignorant."[68] This solemnity celebrated at the tomb of Mamas aroused the whole city and the surrounding country.

From the honor paid at the tombs of the dead and of martyrs it follows that their relics were held in veneration. St. Basil shows his own respectful and devout regard for them when he asks to have sent to him some relics of those who died in the persecutions in Scythia and whom he considered martyrs.[69] St. Julitta had suffered martyrdom at Caesarea about 306 A.D., and it was generally believed that her body had sanctified the region where she was buried. St. Basil states that the earth, blessed by receiving the martyr into its bosom, "sent forth a delightful spring," whose waters prove both a preservative for the healthy, a comfort for the sick, and a source of pleasure to all the city, "while all the neighboring waters are brackish and salt."[70]

St. Basil's veneration for relics and his enthusiasm to honor the martyrs are expressed again, when, after thanking Bishop Arcadius for the special confidence he has placed in him, he promises the bishop relics for his new church, "if we can discover any relics of martyrs."[71] For then, "The just shall be had in everlasting remembrance," and "we shall certainly share in the blessed memory which will accrue to you from the saint."[72]

Nowhere do we find greater reverence expressed for relics than in the scrupulous care taken by St. Basil to send back to Bishop Ambrose of Milan the relics of St. Dionysius of Milan who died in Cappadocia, to whom the same honor was given as to a martyr. Dionysius had become bishop of Milan in 346 A.D., but had later been banished by the Arian Emperor Constantius to Cappadocia, where he died in 357.[73] In the first year of his episcopacy, St. Ambrose asked St. Basil to have the relics of the bishop, who had acquired a high reputation for sanctity, returned to his native city. In reply, St. Basil praised St. Ambrose eloquently for his interest in, and zeal for the relics of his predecessor. St. Basil says that this one act bears witness to much virtue, for "he who honors those who have contended for the Faith shows that he has an equal zeal for the Faith."[74]

Then St. Basil assures St. Ambrose of the authenticity of the relics in the strongest terms: "This is indeed that unconquerable athlete. These bones the Lord recognizes, for they shared in the contest along with his soul. . . . One coffin received that honored body. No one lay beside him. His burial was glorious, and the honor given to him was worthy of a martyr. Christians who had received him as a guest, with their own hands laid him away then, and have taken him up now. They wept as though they were being bereft of a father and protector, but they sent him on, considering your joy of greater worth than their own consolation. . . . Nowhere has there been deceit, nowhere fraud, we ourselves bear witness to this. Let the truth be free from all calumny on your part."[75]

St. Basil's almost exaggerated insistence on the authenticity of the relics is especially impressive, and can be explained perhaps by the abuse of relics which later became prevalent. St. Ambrose's care in securing the relics is also noteworthy. He was careful in his selection of clerics to receive them and to know the piety and scrupulous care of those who surrendered them.

St. Basil's sermons on the Forty Martyrs and on St. Barlaam exemplify further his enthusiasm in honoring the martyrs and his veneration of relics, before which, he says, the people in every necessity seek intercession and are heard.[76] Perhaps no martyr's festival was observed with greater pious enthusiasm than that of the Forty Martyrs in Caesarea where a portion of their precious relics was kept. They had been procured by the holy parents of St. Basil, and some of them had been given by his mother to the church of Annesi.[77] They were honored by miracles according to St. Gregory of Nyssa, who also tells us that he buried his sister, Macrina, with his parents near the relics of these holy martyrs at Annesi.[78] From an inscription of 301 A.D., we learn that although many desired, few obtained the privilege of burial near martyrs.[79]

In speaking of these relics St. Basil says: "You often labor to find one to pray for you; here are forty. Where two or three are met in the Lord's Name, God is there, but where there are forty, who can doubt His presence? These are they who guard our country like a line of forts. They do not shut themselves up in one place, but they are sojourners already in many spots, and adorn many homes, and the strange thing is that they are not divided asunder on their visits to their entertainers, but are mingled with one another, and make choral practice unitedly. Divide them into a hundred, and they do not exceed their proper number; bring them together in one and they are forty still, like fire."[80]

Through the homilies in honor of St. Julitta and St. Gordius,[81] we know that there were also martyria to these saints,[82] where the annual festival or synod was held, of which St. Basil made use to inspire his

Cappadocians with enthusiasm, and with devotion to imitate the virtuous lives of the saints.[83]

St. Basil's interest in a hospice for travelers was no doubt increased because of the evil reputation of the inns and taverns on the great roads of the Empire.[84] The Saint expresses keen admiration for the hospitable intercourse which " . . . was once the boast of the church, . . . Journeying with little tokens from one end of the world to the other, the brethren from each church found all men as fathers and brothers."[85] But now the Saint writes: "This boast along with everything else, the enemy of Christ's churches has taken from us, and we are circumscribed city by city, and we each hold our neighbor in suspicion."[86] Consequently St. Basil established by alms near Caesarea his celebrated hospice,[87] which eventually derived its name from himself; for the Saint considered Christian hospitality to strangers as an essential duty of Religious.[88] The monk, the Saint writes, is to care not only for the perfection of his soul, but for all suffering mankind. Monks gave up all their possessions when they entered religion, and this helped to support the numerous almshouses and asylums which were under the direction of the bishop and chorepiscopi.[89] And in all this St. Basil set the example to his monks. He used all his wealth to build the vast charitable institution, which St. Gregory Nazianzen called a "second city."[90] It included hospitals, one for the sick and one for contagious diseases, a home for the poor, and a hospice for travelers and strangers—in fact, everything that the state might have furnished for alleviating misery. In addition to establishing hospices, the Saint took care that his monks should maintain them.[91] These great charitable enterprises are thought to have inspired the Emperor Julian to plan hospices for strangers and poor houses for his pagans. Julian wrote: "Establish hostelries in every city, so that strangers from neighboring and foreign countries may reap the benefit of our philanthropy, according to their respective needs."[92]

There are several brief allusions to the Saint's other houses for the poor in letters asking for immunities from taxation,[93] and testifying to the fact that St. Basil was not satisfied with one vast hospice but that similar institutions were established throughout the province under the supervision of chorepiscopi, who delegated authority over them to the clergy and to monks.[94] It has been suggested that St. Basil was the first in establishing poor houses in all cities and towns and in organizing social work on a large scale. We wish that he had told us more about his hospices.[95]

With St. Basil hospices were a subject of importance to which he must have given very much thought, time, attention, and money. Yet we find slight reference in St. Basil's letters or other writings to the hospice, that beautiful monument of his charity. We are greatly indebted to his friend St. Gregory Nazianzen, therefore,

for what he tells us, also to a certain Heraclidas who lived at the hospice, and to Amphilochius, a relative of St. Gregory Nazianzen,[96] to whom a letter is addressed, written supposedly by Heraclidas,[97] but which was in reality dictated by St. Basil himself. Amphilochius had met with reverses in fortune and was living a secluded life with his aged father. St. Basil thought he had a religious vocation and sent him a letter urging him to visit the hospice, where he would find his friend Heraclidas, who was a lawyer, living in retreat at the hospice, where he met St. Basil whenever "according to his custom he visited the hospice," and where he often had the opportunity to discuss religious topics with the Saint.[98] In St. Basil's letter, we learn the situation of the hospice: "But when I came near enough to Caesarea to observe the situation, refraining, however, from visiting the city itself, I took refuge in the neighboring poorhouse, that I might gain there the information I wished."[99] Thus we learn that the hospice was near the city, but not in Caesarea itself. In another letter St. Basil implies that the hospice is adjacent to the martyrion of St. Eupsychius. He is urging Amphilochius to come three days before the festival to St. Eupsychius, "in order that you may also make great by your presence the memorial chapel of the hospice for the poor," or the ptochotrophion.[100]

We know that St. Basil's charitable institutions developed on such a vast scale that their size and importance became a subject of much concern to the civil authorities. In one letter the Saint is pleading in behalf of his great work and is defending himself from slanders reported to the governor of Cappadocia concerning his charitable works. The Saint pleads thus:

> I wish, however, that those who keep annoying your honest ears be asked what harm the state receives at our hands; or what, either small or great, of the public interests has suffered injury through our government of the churches; unless, indeed, someone may say that it inflicts injury upon the state to raise in honor of our God a house of prayer built in magnificent fashion. . . . Nor was it, indeed, on this account that you have been forced to give attention to our affairs—that, namely, by reason of the magnitude of your wisdom, you are competent single-handed to restore the works which have fallen into ruin, to people the uninhabited areas, and, in general, to transform the solitudes into cities! Was it, therefore, the more consistent course to harass and insult the man who cooperates with you in these works, or rather to honor him and show him every consideration? And do not think, most excellent Sir, that our protest consists of words alone; for we are already in action, being engaged meanwhile in getting our materials together. So much, then, for our defence to you as the governor.[101]

The Saint acknowledges in this letter "the magnificence" of the great church which stands in the center of the group of buildings. Around it are the bishop's residence, "a generous home," the Saint says; also a number of single houses for the clergy, "arranged in order," or in streets. Then there are "the hospices for strangers, or for those who visit us while on a journey, and also for those who require care because of sickness. . . . Whom do we wrong when we build these hospices?" St. Basil pleads, ". . . access to all of which is alike free to you magistrates yourselves and to your retinue."[102]

In addition, St. Basil tells us that the stranger will find at his command all that can contribute to his welfare and comfort. Physicians and nurses resided within the walls, and workshops were provided for artisans. But "all of these buildings," St. Basil states, "are an ornament to the locality, and a source of pride to our governor," since their fame redounds to his credit.[103] Then for the traveler who would continue his way, horses and guides are placed at his disposal.

This letter testifies to the principles that St. Basil endeavored to inculcate in his Cappadocian clergy: Christian hospitality, the dignity of labor, and active participation in dispensing charity. St. Basil was a true philanthropist himself, for we find him writing: "The famine has not yet released us, so that it is incumbent upon me to linger on in the city, partly to attend to distribution of aid, and partly out of sympathy for the afflicted."[104] The necessity for St. Basil's active interest may be learned from another epistle sent to the Western bishops in which among the evils of Eastern churches is stated the fact that unscrupulous officials "squander on their pleasures and for the distribution of gifts" the funds intended for the poor.[105] Thus, although the clergy are immune from taxation, they are contributing "a great benefit to the public revenues" by the generous relief they give to the poor and "to those who are at any time in distress."[106]

We realize how important this establishment at the gates of Caesarea was when we learn that it so attracted people to settle near and around it that gradually the ancient site of the city was abandoned, and the site of St. Basil's hospice, which is designated as a "new city,"[107] still retained this name a century later, and is the site of the modern Kaisari.[108]

Bishops

A study of St. Basil's works yields valuable information on the moral and religious conditions of Christian society in the fourth century. The *Letters* reveal many details of the religious situation, which was sadly affected by the "death-dealing fruits" of the Arian heresy. One situation that must have caused grief, anxiety, and indignation to St. Basil was the fact that abuses had arisen in the matter of appointing bishops. Ambition and lack of true religious vocation were among the causes of the abuses that called forth vehement criticism from St. Basil. The epistles dealing with this subject reveal the unworthy characters who "intruded the fold" during the struggle with Arianism.

On account of the extent of the province of Cappadocia a large number of suffragan bishops was necessary to assist the archbishop.[109] These assistants were called chorepiscopi,[110] and exercised their episcopal authority in the more remote country districts, assisting St. Basil in watching over the priests and deacons of their district, and ordaining candidates for minor orders. In "**Epistle 53**" we learn that reports had reached St. Basil of abuses in connection with these ordinations. A great many young men had evidently offered themselves who did not have a true vocation for the priesthood, but who desired only to escape the burden of civil offices, military service, or taxation. The chorepiscopi who received the candidates evidently forgot their duty and consented to ordain the unworthy aspirants, from whom they accepted money.[111] To be sure, St. Basil continues, the bishops had not accepted the money until after the ordinations, but St. Basil is firm with such men: "To take is to take, whenever it happens," even "covered up under the name of piety," as a proof of the giver's good will. His letter is a very severe protestation against such a practice.[112] It seemed "incredible" to him, and he asserts that "these things must not be done in this way."[113] These bishops had sold "the gift of God," and made ordinations a matter of commerce, bringing "the huckster's traffic into spiritual affairs and into the Church where we are entrusted with the Body and Blood of Christ."[114]

Another serious abuse spoken of at the same time and "already approaching the incurable" had been introduced by bishops who not only had permitted priests and deacons to select aspirants for Sacred Honors without having examined into their character, but had failed to report their choice to St. Basil, arrogating to themselves the entire authority.[115] As a result, every village had many clerics in minor orders but "not one worthy to conduct the service at the alter," that is, suitable for the priesthood.[116] Consequently St. Basil sent out this epistle, evidently in one of the early years of his episcopate, to remind his bishops that the canons of the Fathers must be enforced. He insists that all candidates accepted by priests "after the first year of the indiction" are to return to the ranks of the laity.[117] This meant that all accepted since 358 A.D., had to be re-examined and voted for again, and all names of the ordinandi had to be submitted to St. Basil. St. Basil would thus purge the Church of all unworthy candidates by carefully investigating their conduct in every detail, first, to learn if they were "railers, or drunkards, or quick to quarrel, and whether they so controlled their youthful spirits as to be able to achieve holiness. . . . Otherwise," he concludes simply and sternly, "rest assured that he who has been received into the subdeaconate without my approval will be still a layman."[118]

We see St. Basil "aflame with righteous indignation" against a certain Timotheus, a chorepiscopus, whom he has known from childhood, and who has been wasting his time—"mingling too much in the turmoils of civil life."[119] In a courteous but firm manner the pastoral admonition is expounded that "no man can serve two masters."[120] Again, the Saint is greatly grieved and annoyed over the fact that "bishops are going about without laity and clergy, bearing an empty name, and accomplishing nothing for the promotion of the Gospel of peace and salvation."[121]

It happened at one time in a small community of a remote country district, which had been long without a bishop, that the people had unanimously elected a pious slave, in spite of his protestations. St. Basil and St. Gregory Nazianzen, moved no doubt by the zeal manifested by the people, ordained the man without the consent of his owner Simplicia, a wealthy lady, who asserted her right of ownership and threatened St. Basil with the vengeance of her slaves and eunuchs.[122] For this she was severely rebuked by him in an indignant reply to her threats.[123] In connection with this point we might add that St. Jerome gives evidence of many slaves among the clergy in his time. However, the canons forbade raising a slave to the priesthood or episcopate without the consent of the master, who would naturally grant freedom at the same time.[124]

In describing the abuses of the Arian leaders St. Basil refers to the "wretched men, even slaves," who have assumed the name and office of bishop.[125] "The lust for office on the part of men who do not fear the Lord," St. Basil says, "leaps upon the positions of high authority," with the result that none of the Christians are willing to set themselves up in opposition. In fact, no event in history can compare with the actions of the "monstrous and wicked" Arian leaders, except those attending the capture of Jerusalem by Titus.[126] St. Basil's brother Gregory, bishop of Nyssa, was replaced by a "slave, worth only a few obols," whom the Arians appointed.[127] They sent another slave to Doara, "an orphan's domestic, who ran away from his masters . . ., insulting the poor name of the episcopal office."[128] Again, at Nicopolis, Fronto was installed in the episcopal office but had already become "a common abomination of all Armenia," and soon fell into heresy.[129]

It is in his appeal for help to the Western bishops that St. Basil reveals the fatal effects of the Arian heresy upon the priesthood of the Eastern church. "Gone is the dignity of the priesthood," St. Basil writes. "None are left to tend the flock of the Lord with knowledge, and ambitious men squander sums collected for the poor on their own pleasure and for the distribution of gifts. The strict observance of the canons has been weakened."[130]

The Saint deplores the license to commit sin. The Arians "who have come into office through the favor of men take this very means of returning thanks for the favor," namely, of granting concessions to sinners to do "what ever will conduce to their pleasure."[131] The leaders who secured power for themselves through the favor of men are now "the slaves of those who have conferred the favor."[132] Thus we see that at least certain evils found in the episcopacy in the fourth century are due to the "death-dealing fruits" of the Arian heresy, which reached its height in St. Basil's time in Cappadocia.[133]

St. Basil admits to Amphilochius,[134] at the time he was considering the appointment of bishops to the Isaurian church, that "it is not easy to find worthy men;" and, although he would like the Church to have the advantage of more bishops in order that it might be governed more strictly, still he would not risk encouraging "indifference" among the laity through the "unworthiness" of their shepherds. "Whatever the rulers are, such for the most part the characters of those governed are accustomed to become."[135] The Isaurian church has been under the ecclesiastical jurisdiction of Amphilochius, bishop of Iconium, and in his reply to a letter asking for advice, St. Basil congratulated him on his zealous care of the church in the past. The disorganization is due in part to the unruly character of the Isaurians, who were frequently in rebellion and always threatening their neighbors with invasion, and, in part, to the political disturbances of the Arian persecution. Therefore, St. Basil suggests to Amphilochius, with whom he had always been in very close friendship, that it would be even more advantageous to divide the burden with its care and anxiety among several bishops.

It would be preferable, St. Basil says, to appoint bishops to all the vacant sees immediately, but "since it is not easy to find worthy men," his next plan would be to send one bishop to preside over the whole province of Lycaonia, a man "of proved worth," of courage and resolution, a man who, if he felt unable to cope with all the work, would associate others with himself.[136] According to this plan, however, a bishop might be tempted to such ambition that in his desire to rule a larger diocese he might not consent to the creation of minor sees and to the curtailment of his own power. St. Basil considered it wiser, therefore, to appoint only overseers or chorepiscopi to the small towns and villages which formerly had an episcopal seat, and later to select a bishop for the whole province. In this way he would forestall any trouble that might be caused by an ambitious prelate.

The following incident will show the great necessity for vigilance and care on St. Basil's part, and also his personal power to withstand unprincipled appeals from a man whose friendship he held in high esteem. Nectarius wrote to St. Basil to present the claims of a friend as a candidate at the approaching election of suffragan bishops.[137] Although St. Basil valued his friendship with Nectarius very highly, for it dated from childhood, and although he tactfully welcomed the testimony which was sincerely given, nevertheless the final selection, he said, must be the result of prayer alone, for "a steward" must not "barter the gift of God for human friendships," and no unworthy subject might enter the clergy in Cappadocia.[138]

It is evident that the laity had participated in the election of bishops, and that St. Basil, without taking away their right to vote, did all he could to restrain and minimize their influence in the choice of candidates.[139] St. Gregory Nazianzen testifies to the abuses in appointments to the episcopacy at this time, and names as candidates, collectors of the tribute, seamen, ploughmen and soldiers.[140] Even before St. Basil became archbishop, he wrote a consolatory letter to the Church of Neocaesarea on the death of Musonius, their late bishop, urging the people to purge their souls of all rivalry and ambition for preferment as they petition for a new bishop, since it is God's part to designate his representative on earth. "He knows who are His," and the laity must accept the choice, even when it is someone whom they do not expect.[141] From then on it would seem that St. Basil controlled the elections, seldom submitting to the will of the people. However, in an emergency that same year, St. Basil writes to Amphilochius that since the one on whom he had planned has now become incapacitated for service through illness, although the laity has left the choice to him, he prefers in this pressing need to let the laity propose one of their own number, preferably a newly baptized.[142]

Later, in 374, we find St. Basil telling Amphilochius, bishop of Iconium, to appoint "overseers for the small towns and villages which formerly had an episcopal seat,[143] for already the Isaurian bishop has ordained some of his neighbors. "Hereafter, however, the right should be reserved for ourselves on the proper occasion to appoint as bishops men whom we ourselves judge most suitable, approving of them after careful examination.[144] It is interesting to note that among those bishops who were candidates of St. Basil's own choice are his brother, St. Gregory of Nyssa,[145] his best friend, St. Gregory Nazianzen,[146] a relative, who was the "apple of his eye," Poemenius of Satala,[147] Euphronius, the bishop of Armenia, on whom he relied very much and whom Poemenius transferred from Colonia to Nicopolis, and Amphilochius, a spiritual son who remained a steadfast friend. All are prelates well known in history as eminent and loyal churchmen.

The next year we find St. Basil exhorting the civil magistrates of Nicopolis to accept Euphronius as their bishop,[148] and to gain for him the good will of the people of the district. "The management of the churches is in the hands of those who have been entrusted with their guidance, but they are strengthened by the laity . . . thus what was in the power of the most God-beloved bishops has been completed; what remains now looks to you, . . . to cleave to the bishops who have been given to you."[149] In this way he insists that the choice of a candidate belongs to the bishop, and he tries to prove his teaching by his example. The clergy, civil magistrates, and people have only to ratify this choice.

Clergy

In several letters St. Basil reveals some of his disciplinary difficulties with the clergy. We see from these letters that although St. Basil was untiringly vigilant in trying to preserve the spirit of celibacy, nevertheless there were abuses. For monks only he prescribed an explicit vow of celibacy, while he allowed bishops, priests, and deacons to retain their wives.[150] He insisted, however, that all other women be dismissed from presbyteries according to the decrees of the Nicaean Council.[151] We find an instance cited of a country priest, seventy years of age, Paregorius by name, who desired very much to have a woman as servant and housekeeper in his presbytery.[152] But St. Basil compelled Paregorius to dismiss her and suggested that she be placed in a convent, not because he doubted the virtue of the aged presbyter, but because he felt convinced that he must maintain discipline and enforce the Nicaean Canon for the preservation of celibacy.[153]

St. Basil insisted that his clergy employ the same vigilance as himself, in order to correct any other abuses still prevalent in the country. Consequently, on one occasion, when a priest failed to show indignation similar to St. Basil's own at the evil of ravishment, the Saint's grief and indignation knew no bounds. The Saint asserts that this evil was common in Cappadocia and that if all felt as indignant as he, "this wicked custom, an unlawful outrage and a tyranny against life itself, would have been abandoned long before."[154] In a small village, where the evil of ravishment was rife, it happened that the priest did not seem to exert himself against it. On this particular occasion, St. Basil learned that the man guilty of ravishment had accomplices and that the neighboring village where the girl was taken, "not only kept her, but even fought to keep her."[155] The Saint condemned the entire affair unhesitatingly, commanded the priest "to take the girl by force, wherever he found her, and return her to her parents, and to declare the ravisher "a common foe, like a snake or any other wild beast,"[156] whom he wishes the people "to pursue accordingly and to champion those who are wronged by him."[157] The accomplices in this affair and their whole households were excommunicated for three years, and also all the inhabitants of the village where the girl was detained. By taking such drastic measures St. Basil hoped to inspire his clergy to be as zealous and active as he was himself in condemning evil.

On another occasion the conduct of an eccentric deacon, Glycerius by name, attached to one of the churches in St. Basil's diocese, caused St. Basil much grief, since "the whole order of monks" was put to shame by his folly and insubordination.[158] Although St. Basil was aware that Glycerius was a self-willed character when he ordained him deacon of the church of Venasa, he had shown considerable aptitude for routine work. After his appointment, however, he neglected his work and without any authority began to train a company of youths and maidens for singing and dancing, not from any motive of piety, St. Basil states, but because he preferred this way of making a livelihood. Assuming the title and robes of a patriarch, Glycerius caused great disturbance in the local church, where he disregarded the commands of his venerable presbyter, scorned his chorepiscopus, and even St. Basil himself. Then, threatened with punishment, he fled with his band of maidens and young men to a local festival where he amused or shocked by the dance of his chorus, according to their dispositions, a great assembly of persons. When the parents wished their young people to return home, Glycerius refused, as well as the maidens, and insulted the parents. He and his followers took refuge with a bishop, Gregory by name, who evidently took the band under his protection. St. Basil remonstrates with him about this in a second letter in which he condemns the delay in sending the group back to their homes.[159]

It is interesting to find that the aged presbyter, Gregory, "a man who is venerated both for his conduct and his age, and whose gray hairs and kindness of heart" St. Basil himself respected, pleaded, together with many others, on behalf of Glycerius.[160] As a consequence, St. Basil wrote to the deacon and promised pardon if he would repent.[161] We do not learn the conclusion of this strange episode except that St. Basil was filled with indignation and shame.

Non-Christian Environment

A letter to Epiphanius, bishop of Salamis in Cyprus, yields interesting details on a strange isolated race the Magusae, that had settled in Cappadocia. St. Basil tells us that these strange people are "widely scattered amongst us throughout almost the whole country."[162] The Bishop of Salamis has evidently asked St. Basil for information concerning them, and in reply St. Basil gives him a detailed account about "these nations of the Maguseans . . . colonists who long ago were introduced into our country from Babylon." They claimed they were descended from Abraham and that a certain Zarnuas was the founder of their race. However, St. Basil writes, "No one of the Magi has up to the present told any myths about this."[163]

They still practiced their own peculiar customs, and did not mingle with the Cappadocians. It is quite impossible, St. Basil states, to reason with them, "inasmuch as they have been preyed upon by the devil according to his wish." They had their own peculiar religious beliefs and customs, which must be handed down by oral tradition only, for they had "neither books, nor teachers of doctrine among them, but were brought up in an unreasoning manner."[164] St. Basil says that the foregoing facts are well known to all Cappadocians.

They also retained other peculiar customs. "They reject the slaying of animals as defilement, and have others slaughter the animals necessary for their use. They indulge in unlawful marriages, they believe in fire as God, and other things of like nature."[165]

We find, on the other hand, that there were genuine conversions from paganism which St. Basil encouraged and which pagan relatives resented. Harmatius, a pagan, was displeased about his son's conversion, but St. Basil urged him to feel no resentment, and rather to let his paternal authority yield before the dictates of the conscience of his son, who had sacrificed filial respect for union with the true God. In speaking thus St. Basil stated that he was writing in the name of all those citizens who were fond of Harmatius and were overjoyed by the recent report which had spread through the city that he too had become Christian.[166]

Notes

[1] *Hex.* III, 22 C.

[2] *ibid.*

[3] *Hex.* VIII, 79 C-D.

[4] *Hex.* III, 32 D.

[5] *Hex.* VII, 69 D; IX, 88 D; III, 22 B. St. Gregory Nazianzen assures us that they spoke with admiration of their brilliant orator in the evening at table.

[6] *Hex.* VIII, 71 E.

[7] *In Ps.* CXIV, 199 B. Cf. p. 140, *infra.*

[8] *In Ps.* LIX, 188 E.

[9] *De Judicio Dei,* 587 A.

[10] *Adv. Calumn. Trin.,* 160 A.

[11] Cf. note 13 *infra.*

[12] *Quod mundanis,* 170 A.

[13] *Hex.* VIII, 71 E.

[14] *Contr. Sabell.,* 193 B. St. Basil is referring to an exposition of the doctrine of the Holy Ghost.

[15] *Hex.* IV, 34 A.

[16] *Hex.* VI, 50 B.

[17] *In Ps. 45,* 171 C.

[18] *Hex.* VI, 54 E.

[19] *ibid.,* 55 B.

[20] *Hex.* IV, 39 D-E.

[21] *In Ps.* CXIV, 199 B.

[22] Epist. 243. Cf. Fliche and Martin, III, 400.

[23] *Reg. fus. tract., Interr.* 37, 382 E-383 A.

[24] Epist. 207, 311 B-C, written in 375 A.D. For antiphonal singing in the East, cf. Theodoret, II, 24; Socrates, VI, 8; cf. also article "Antiphone dans la Liturgie Grecque" in DACL, I, 2461-2488.

[25] *ibid.,* 311 A.

[26] Cf. Fliche and Martin, III, 401. St. Ambrose employed antiphonal singing in Milan in 386 A.D., after St. Basil's death.

[27] Epist. 141; 176. Cf. article "Agape" in DACL, I, especially 816-820.

[28] Epist. 142.

[29] Epist. 283.

[30] Cf. p. 18, *supra.*

[31] *Reg. fus. tract., Interr.* 38.

[32] Epist. 169. For the Glycerius affair, cf. p. 163, *infra.*

[33] Epist. 286. Cf. also p. 126, *supra.*

[34] Cf. Deferrari, (1) I, 258, n. 1.

[35] Epist. 42.

[36] *ibid.*

[37] Epist. 176; 200; 202; 252; 282.

[38] *In Ps.* CXIV, 199 B.

[39] Epist. 95; 176.

[40] Epist. 202.

[41] Epist. 244.

[42] Cf. p. 130, n. 191, *supra.*

[43] Epist. 142.

[44] Epist. 176; 252.

[45] Epist. 176.

[46] Epist. 141.

[47] Epist. 252.

[48] *ibid.*

[49] Epist. 282.

[50] Epist. 252.

[51] *ibid.*

[52] Epist. 176.

[53] *ibid.*

[54] Epist. 200.

[55] Epist. 98. . . .

[56] Cf. Fliche and Martin, III, 373.

[57] Epist. 280. Cf. article "Martyr" in DACL, X, especially 2430-2438; also article "Reliques" in d'Alès, IV, 909-930; cf. also Delehaye.

[58] Epist. 100; 176; 252.

[59] Cf. Soz. V, 11.

[60] Epist. 252; 100.

[61] Epist. 164.

[62] Cf. Deferrari, II, 380, n. I. For Soranus, cf. p. 70, n. 237, *supra.*

[63] Epist. 155. For St. Sabas, cf. DCB, IV, 566.

[64] Epist. 165.

[65] Epist. 164.

[66] For Eutyches, cf. DCB II, 404 (2); Philostratus, II, 5. For Ascholius, the bishop of Thessalonica, who later baptized Theodosius in 380 A.D., cf. Baudrillart (1), IV, 901 (2).

[67] Epist. 164.

[68] *In Mamantem* 185 C-D. Although the *Acta* of the Saint are obscure, it seems likely that this Saint died at

the age of twelve in the persecution under Aurelian in the third century at Caesarea. St. Basil's panegyric perpetuates the memory of his existence, occupation, and place of martyrdom. Cf. DCB, III, 789.

[69] Epist. 155. Cf. article "Martyr" in DACL, X, especially 2438-2441.

[70] *Hom. in Julittam*, 35 A. Julitta was a wealthy woman of Caesarea, who had been unjustly deprived of her fortune, which consisted of many farms, cattle, goods, and slaves, and had been denounced as a Christian in court without the right of appeal in 303 A.D. Condemned to death by fire, her body remained miraculously incorrupt. Practically nothing is known of this Saint beyond what is contained in St. Basil's panegyric. Cf. DCB, III, 526 (2).

[71] *Epist.* 49.

[72] *ibid.*

[73] Dionysius had defended St. Athanasius against the Emperor Constantius at the synod of Milan in 355 A.D. His relics were buried in his own church in Milan until 1533, when they were transferred to the cathedral.

[74] Epist. 197.

[75] *ibid.*

[76] *Hom. in XL Mart.* 155B; *Hom. in Barlaam* 139 B-C. St. Barlaam was a pious peasant, who endured torture and martyrdom during the persecution of Diocletian in 304 A.D. at Antioch. He was cruelly scourged, hoisted on the rack, and near the end of his torture he permitted live coals with incense to burn through his hand rather than to shake them off and thus be accused of offering sacrifice. Cf. DCB, I, 260; also Baudrillart (1), VI, 812 (1). Baudrillart questions the authenticity of this homily of St. Basil. St. John Chrysostom has a homily on this martyr also, entitled *Hom. in St. Barlaam*.

[77] Cf. St. Gregory of Nyssa, *Or. II in XL Mart.*, 994 C.

[78] *ibid.*

[79] De Rossi, I, 142, cf. DCA, II, 1131.

[80] *Hom. in XL Mart.*, 155 B.

[81] *Hom. in Julittam*, 34 E; *Hom. in Gordium*, 141 D. St. Basil compares the crowd gathered around the tomb of St. Gordius to a hive of bees. Cf. *In Gordium*, 141 C-D. Gordius was a Caesarean soldier (143 C-D) who had retired into solitude in 304 A.D., but later reappeared in the stadium during a festival (145 B) and addressed the crowd in his zeal for converts (145 E).

He was seized and beheaded, (148 E). St. Basil's panegyric has perpetuated his memory, and is the main source for his life.

[82] For a detailed description of a fourth-century martyrion built in the form of a cross, cf. St. Gregory of Nyssa, Ep. XXV, 1096 A-1100 B.

[83] Cf. St. Gregory of Nyssa's *Encomium* of his brother delivered on the first or second anniversary of St. Basil's death in order to establish a feast day for St. Basil, and to place him in the martyrology. Cf. Stein, p. XXXII.

[84] Cf. Friedländer, II, 44; cf. also article "Caupona" in DS, I, 2, 973-974.

[85] Epist. 191.

[86] *ibid.*

[87] The Emperor Valens donated to the large hospice St. Basil founded "considerable landed property," from the income of which the Saint was able to support the poor of his diocese. Cf. Seeck, V, 81; also cf. Fliche and Martin, III, 261.

[88] *In Divites*, 52 C.

[89] Epist. 140. Cf. note 110, *infra.*

[90] . . ."New Town." Cf. *Or. 43,* 63; Sozmen, VI, 34.

[91] Epist. 94.

[92] Epist. 49, p. 338. Cf. also Fliche and Martin, III, 372.

[93] Epist. 142; 143; 144. Cf. p. 130, *supra.*

[94] Epist. 176.

[95] Cf. Gorce, 146. According to PW, VI, 1449-1450, and to Fliche and Martin, III, 253, Eustathius, bishop of Sebaste, 300-377 A.D., had already founded poorhouses and hospices, and placed monks in charge of them.

[96] For Amphilochius, cf. note 134, *infra.*

[97] For Heraclidas, cf. DCB, II, 901 (3).

[98] Epist. 150.

[99] *ibid.*

[100] Epist. 176.

[101] Epist. 94.

[102] *ibid.*

[103] *ibid.*

[104] Epist. 31.

[105] Epist. 92.

[106] Epist. 94.

[107] Cf. note 90, *supra.*

[108] Cf. Ramsay, (3), 384.

[109] Epist. 53. According to St. Gregory Nazianzen, St. Basil had fifty chorepiscopi under his jurisdiction. Cf. *Carmen de vita sua*, v. 2.

[110] Cf. article "Chorévêques" in DACL, III, 1423-1440. Cf. also Fliche and Martin, II, 396-397. Cf. p. 51, *supra.*

[111] Epist. 54.

[112] Epist. 53.

[113] *ibid.*

[114] *ibid.*

[115] Epist. 54.

[116] *ibid.*

[117] On the method of reckoning time by indiction, cf. article "Indiction" in DACL, VII, 530-535.

[118] Epist. 54.

[119] Epist. 291.

[120] *ibid.*

[121] Epist. 265.

[122] For Simplicia, cf. DCB, IV, 688. Although very generous in her gifts to the Church, Simplicia had been suspected of unsoundness in her faith. St. Gregory Nazianzen appealed to her to sanction the ordination made against her will, as the renewal of her claim would only strengthen the suspicion felt of her heterodoxy. Cf. St. Gregory Nazianzen, Epist. 38.

[123] Epist. 115.

[124] Epist. 82.

[125] Epist. 239.

[126] *ibid.*

[127] Epist. 239. Cf. p. 115, *supra.*

[128] *ibid.*

[129] *ibid.*

[130] Epist. 92.

[131] *ibid.*

[132] *ibid.*

[133] *ibid.*

[134] Amphilochius was a former orator and lawyer of Constantinople, who retired from active life in the world and came under the influence of St. Basil. They remained steadfast friends and many of the Saint's letters are addressed to this spiritual son. Appointed to the new metropolis of Lycaonia, Amphilochius proved a worthy heir of his master, as bishop. Cf. article "Amphiloque" in DTC, I, 1121-1123. Cf. also article "Amphiloque" in *Dictionnaire d'Histoire et de Géographie ecclésiastique*, II, 1346-1348. Cf. also Fliche and Martin, III, 444; PW, I, 1937.

[135] Epist. 190.

[136] *ibid.*

[137] For Nectarius, cf. p. 114, *supra.*

[138] Epist. 290.

[139] Epist. 230, *passim.*

[140] *Carmen de Episcopis,* V, 156.

[141] Epist. 28.

[142] Epist. 217.

[143] Epist. 190. . . .

[144] *ibid.*

[145] St. Gregory was the last survivor of St. Basil's family. A theologian, orator, and writer, he was consecrated bishop of Nyssa in 372 A.D. by St. Basil. He was banished by the Arian faction, but was restored to his see in 387 A.D. where he died in 395 A.D., or shortly after. Cf. article "Grégoire de Nysse" in DTC, VI, 1847-1852.

[146] St. Gregory Nazianzen was consecrated bishop of Sasima by St. Basil. Later he was transferred to Constantinople, but he resigned that bishopric and retired to Nazianzus where he died in 389. Cf. article "Grégoire de Nazianze," DACL, VI², 1667-1710.

[147] Epist. 101, 122. Epist. 229, written three years later,

shows that Poemenius proved worthy of the confidence St. Basil placed in him when sent to Satala in the northeast of Armenia Minor.

[148] Epist. 229.

[149] *ibid.*

[150] Epist. 199.

[151] According to the Council of Nicaea, c. 27. Cf. Mansi, II, 906.

[152] Epist. 55.

[153] According to Council of Nicaea, c. 3; cf. Mansi, II, 669. Cf. also *Theod. Cod.* IV, 22.

[154] Epist. 270.

[155] *ibid.*

[156] *ibid.* Severe imperial laws had been passed against those guilty of rape. Cf. *Theod. Cod.*, IX, XXIV, 1, Apr. 1, 326 A.D. Cf. Fliche and Martin, III, 61.

[157] *ibid.*

[158] Epist. 169.

[159] Epist. 171.

[160] Epist. 170.

[161] *ibid.*

[162] Epist. 258, p. 44. The Magusae were also found in Media, Egypt, Phrygia, and Galatia. Epiphanius states that the Magusae disliked the Persian idols but still venerated them. They worshiped fire, the sun, and the moon. Cf article "[*Magoi*]" in PW, XIV, 509-518, especially 510.

[163] *ibid.*, p. 45.

[164] *ibid.*

[165] *ibid.*

[166] Epist. 276, *passim.*

Select Bibliography

Translations

Deferrari, R. J. *St. Basil's Letters with an English Translation*, 4 vols. . . .

Special Works on Asia Minor

Ramsay, W. M. (3) *Cities and Bishoprics of Phrygia,*

London, 1895-1897. . . .

Other Works

1. General

Baudrillart, A. (1) *Dictionnaire d'histoire et de géographie ecclésiastiques.* Paris, 1912-1935. . . .

D'Alès, A. *Dictionnaire apologétique de la foi catholique.* 4 vols. Paris, 1911-1922. . . .

Delehaye, H. *Les légendes hagiographiques.* 3rd ed. Brussels, 1927. . . .

Fliche, A. and Martin, V. *Histoire de l'Église depuis les origines jusqu' à nos jours.* Vol. III. J. B. Palanque, G. Bardy, and P. De Labriolle, De la paix constantinienne à la mort de Théodose, Paris, 1936.

Friedländer, L. *Darstellungen aus der Sittengeschichte Roms in der Zeit von August bis zum Ausgang der Antoninen.* Revised by G. Wissowa. 4 vols., 9th and 10th ed. Leipzig, 1921-1923. The English translation of this work is under the title: *Roman Life and Manners under the Early Empire*, 4 vols. London and New York, 1908-1913. . . .

Mansi, G. D. *Sacrorum Conciliorum Nova et Amplissima Collectio.* Vols. VI and VII. Venice, 1771. Reprinted Paris, 1901 ff. . . .

Seeck, O. *Geschichte des Untergangs der antiken Welt.* Vol. V. 3rd ed. Berlin, 1910-1921. . . .

2. Special

Deferrari, R. J. "St. Augustine's Method of Composing and Delivering Sermons," *American Journal of Philology*, 43 (1922): 106-110.

Delehaye, H. *Les origines du culte des martyrs.* 2nd ed. Brussels, 1933. . . .

Gorce, D. *Les voyages, l'hospitalité et le port des lettres dans le monde chrétien des IVe et Ve siècles.* Paris, 1925. . . .

Stein, Sister James Aloysius. *Encomium of Saint Gregory, Bishop of Nyssa, on his Brother Saint Basil, Archbishop of Cappadocian Caesarea. A Commentary, with a Revised Text. Introduction and Translation.* Catholic University of America Patristic Studies, Vol. XVII. Washington, D. C., 1928. . . .

Abbreviations

Works of Reference

DACL Dictionnaire d'archéologie chrétienne et de

liturgie Cabrol-Leclercq

DCB Dictionary of Christian Biography Smith and Wace

DTC Dictionnaire de théologie catholique Vacant et Mangenot

PW Realencyclopädie der klassischen Altertumswissenschaft Pauly-Wissowa-Kroll

Works of St. Basil

. . . Hex.—Hexaemeron . . .

In Ps. XIV—In partem Psalmi XIV, et contra feneratores

In Ps. LXI—In Psalmum LXI

Quod Mundanis—Quod rebus mundanis alhaerendum non sit, et de incendio extra ecclesiam facto

Reg. fus. tract.—Regulae fusius tractatae . . .

I. P. Sheldon-Williams (essay date 1967)

SOURCE: "The Cappadocians" in *The Cambridge History of Later Greek and Early Medieval Philosophy,* edited by A. H. Armstrong, Cambridge University Press, 1967, pp. 432-39.

[*In the excerpt below, Sheldon-Williams explicates the* Hexaemeron, *noting that Basil views the universe as a hierarchy whose parts are bound together in harmonious sympathy. The critic maintains that Basil's conception of creation, time and motion, and material elements is derived from the writings of Greek natural philosophers such as Aristotle and the Stoics, as well as from scripture.*]

The Cappadocians inherited the Alexandrian Gnosis through Origen, though each departed from the position of their master, St Basil most of all. He was more interested in the moral and pastoral than in the philosophical implications of the Faith, distrusted allegory,[1] and clung to the literal interpretation of Scripture, to which the pagan learning was to supply rational corroboration as required rather than combine with it to form a synthesis. Therefore, as was to be the case with the Aristotelian Christians,[2] he made greater use of the physics of the pagans than of their metaphysics, and in his *Homilies on the Hexaëmeron*,[3] intended as a scientific defence of the Mosaic account of creation, he drew chiefly on the current cosmology, meteorology, botany, astronomy and natural history.[4]

As a consequence, the Christian theory of creation assumed certain pagan features, of which the most important were the implied identification of the Platonic Demiurge with Yahweh,[5] the Aristotelian division of the universe into the supralunar and sublunar spheres, and the notion of a universal harmony . . . :[6] 'Although the totality of the universe is composed of dissimilar parts, he binds it together by an indissoluble law of friendship into one communion and harmony, so that even the parts that from the positions they occupy seem most distant from one another are yet shown to be united by the universal *sumpatheia.*'[7]

Nature is the work of God, who created her in time, or rather created time in the process of creating her.[8] Matter is a part of creation, for if it were uncreated God would have been dependent upon it for bringing his plan to fruition;[9] and if matter were independent of God there would not be that reciprocity between agent and patient which is everywhere apparent.[10]

Although Scripture does not speak of the four elements, it mentions earth and implies fire (for since Moses limits his theme to the created universe[11] he must mean by heaven the highest part of the physical world, of which the substance is fire[12]), and by speaking of the highest and the lowest it infers the two intermediaries.[13] Fire (or light) is the substance of heaven because, although the elements were originally intermingled, each tends towards its proper level: fire at the top, extending downward as far as the Firmament;[14] then air; then water; then earth at the base.

Each element also has its proper quality: fire is warm, air moist, water cold, earth dry.[15] But none is found wholly in its place or with its quality unmixed: fire is found below the Firmament, and there are waters above it;[16] earth, as it is experienced, is cold as well as dry, and so can combine with water; water moist as well as cold, and so can combine with air; air warm as well as moist, and so can combine with fire; and finally fire is dry as well as warm, and therefore can mingle with earth. This cyclic movement of the elements[17] produces the variety of combinations out of which all sensible beings are created.[18]

This is Aristotelian and Stoic doctrine, except for 'the waters above the Firmament', which is part of revealed truth. The Alexandrians interpreted these allegorically as the intelligible world, separated from the sensible by the Firmament, or First Heaven:[19] Basil characteristically insists on the literal sense on the ground that Moses is only concerning himself with the physical universe. There is water above the Firmament to abate the fiery substance and prevent the Stoic conflagration. . . . [20]

The *Homilies on the Hexaëmeron* demonstrate that the truth discovered by man's reason is not different, so far as it goes, from the truth revealed by Scripture. But Scripture also reveals truths inaccessible to man's reason: the Nature of God, which is wholly incomprehensible, as well as the basic principles of the intelligible and sensible worlds. The incomprehensibility of the Divine Nature[21] was one of the points on which the Cappadocians were at issue with Eunomius, the champion of Arianism; for Eunomius,[22] following his master Aëtius,[23] contended that reason is equal in value and power to revelation, and that therefore if the Divine Nature is known through revelation it is also accessible to reason. He further argued that if what we know of God is his Essence, and if we know of him that he is Father, Son, and Holy Spirit, then each of the three is his Essence; but that, on the other hand, we deduce that God is not more than Trinity, and that therefore all names given to him by Scripture beyond these Three must be mere metaphor. For instance, the Begotten Word cannot literally be God since God is unbegotten. This line of reasoning imposed upon Basil and the other Cappadocians the task of examining the problem of the Divine Names.[24] Basil's answer was that any epithet could be applied to God, but that all fall into one of two classes: those that indicate what he is not . . . , of which 'unbegotten' is an example; and those which affirm that he is not other than this . . . , such as 'righteous', 'judge', 'creator'.[25] The former can lead the reason to a partial knowledge of God by what the Neoplatonists called *aphairesis*, the progressive stripping away of every concept that the mind can form about God in the certainty that every one will be inadequate.[26] *Aphairesis* by itself, however, will lead to sheer negation;[27] and this would be all that could be known of God, did not Scripture reveal that he is, and that he possesses the Attributes with which it endows him. The Scriptural Names or Attributes are therefore outgoings . . . of God's Nature to the human understanding,[28] and are thus the authentic Names of his *Energeiai*.

The intelligible world is only accessible to reason in its function of substantiating the sensible. By revelation it is known as the angelic world,[29] outside time . . . ,[30] not with the absolute eternity of God, but with that eternity which is consistent with its being a creature; for *aion* is a limit which precludes even the intellectual activity of man from being infinite.[31] The angels are substantial and occupy a substantial world, but one which does not share a common matter with the sensible world. It has an intelligible matter,[32] which Basil identifies with the light[33] which illuminates the material world, and is therefore the common ground of the whole universe, intelligible and sensible. This leads him to give to Ps. ciii. 4[34] a literal interpretation which St Gregory Nazianzen treats with reserve,[35] and St Gregory of Nyssa rejects.[36]

It follows that light is a more general nature than time,[37] for time is found only in the sensible world. Because light is not limited to time it was universally diffused at the moment of its creation,[38] as it fills the whole room in which a lamp is kindled. Between the intelligible and the sensible worlds the Firmament acts as a barrier, of which the solidity implied by its name is such that light may pass through it (though in a diluted form), but time cannot break out to the world above.[39]

Bounded within the Firmament, time is the principle of the sensible world, which is more explicable to reason than the intelligible, but still not wholly so; otherwise there would be no purpose in the translucency of the Firmament. It is by revelation that we know that it is not eternal, for reason would suggest the contrary.[40] It was created with time, or as a logical consequence of time . . . , which is itself a necessary consequence of the creation of the Firmament rotating in space; for time, motion, and spatial extension[41] are mutually interrelated. Not only can there be no motion without time, but time is only time when measured by motion. Therefore, since there can be no motion that is not from one place or state to another, there can be no first moment of time, and Moses is careful to call the 'First Day' of creation not the first but 'one day':

> The God who created the nature of time appointed the periods of the days as its measures and marks, and ordains that the week, by returning upon itself, shall count the motion of time. The week is the fulfilment of the one day seven times returning upon itself: for this is the way of the circle, that it starts from itself and ends in itself. In this it resembles the aeon, which returns upon itself endlessly. Therefore he called the origin of time not a first day but one day, to show that time retains its kinship with eternity.[42]

But this does not mean that time and eternity are identical or that the physical universe is eternal. In the passage just quoted the last sentence (which is also reproduced in almost the same words by Johannes Lydus)[43] comes from a Pythagorean source, but whereas the Pythagoreans held that time was intrinsically eternal, Basil only claims for it an affinity . . . with eternity. He agreed with Plato[44] that it is the copy of eternity, but only in so far as what is created can be a copy of what is not. Eternity has no beginning: time has no beginning *in itself.* The beginning . . . is 'not even the smallest part of time',[45] but quite outside the temporal process, and therefore no part of the creative act takes place within time. God creates 'in the beginning' . . . and therefore not in time. . . . [46] The Firmament is created 'before' the earth not in a chronological sense, but as the container precedes the content, and the light the shadow cast by an interposed body.[47] The creation of the extratemporal circumference was necessarily the cause of the temporal content, and therefore of motion and extension. The effect of extension is that the divine *energeiai,* which in the intelligible world are one in the Nous or Logos,[48] now become many, and the effect of motion is to bring them into association to form sensible bodies,[49] and to separate them again to bring about the dissolution of those bodies. Basil agrees with Aristotle that whatever comes into being in time must perish in time,[50] for time, as we have seen,[51] cannot pass through the Firmament.

But Aristotle was wrong to apply this principle to the soul, for although the soul is involved in the spatio-temporal world, she is not of it, and therefore is destined to pass beyond it.[52] By nature she belongs to the intelligible world, and is like the angels a creature of light, to which the Firmament is not a barrier.[53] For the same reason the incarnate soul's mode of cognition, which is discursive, is not precluded from the knowledge which is the object of Nous. Since time is the offspring of eternity and resembles it, the content of the temporal world is a copy in this extended medium of the non-extended prototype, as that in its turn is the expression of the Thoughts of the Divine Mind. Thus the entire universe is linked together by a chain of likeness and exhibits a harmonious sympathy.[54]

As time is co-existent with, and a kind of secondary substance of, the sensible world, so this sympathy is the primary substance of the whole creation, intelligible and sensible, being the mode in which the *energeiai* express the divine unity. Where it does not reach creation does not reach, and this is the realm of evil, which is no substance, but the absence of good.[55] It is probably to be identified with the darkness which covered the face of the earth 'before' its creation.[56]

For St Basil, as for every Christian philosopher, the central theme is God, his dealings with the world, and especially with man. God creates the world, and sets in it his own image, man.[57] But this is man's eternal, not his contemporary condition. Created in the intelligible order, he falls into the sensible; designed for eternity, he is enmeshed in time, and in danger of a further fall into the total dissolution which is a concomitant of temporality, that is to say, into absolute evil. The philosopher's task is to reverse this trend, converting the descent into an ascent, first by a purification of the carnal passions, which leads to the First Heaven, the Firmament; then by the acquisition of wisdom to which the soul, no longer clouded by these obscurities, now has access, and by which she rises, illumined, to the summit of the intelligible world, which is the Second Heaven; from which she is finally drawn up to the Third Heaven of deification. . . .

Notes

[1] Cf. *Hex.* IX I (*PG* 29. 188B-C).

[2] Below, p. 478.

[3] *PG* 29. 4A-208C, ed. S. Giet, Paris, 1950 (*Sources chrét.* 26). References are to this edition by numbers of columns in *PG*.

[4] Giet, *op. cit.* 56-69. Cf. St Greg. Naz. *Orat.* XLIII (*PG* 36. 528A).

[5] Below, p. 439.

[6] Cf. Philo *ap.* É. Bréhier, *Les Idées philosophiques et religieuses de Philon d'Alexandrie* (Paris, 1925), pp. 158-61.

[7] *Hex.* II 2, 33A. Cf. Proclus, who taught that the Hierarchies are connected by love . . . or friendship . . . which is [*enopoios*]. (*In Tim.* 155-6, II 53. 24 - 54. 25 Diels (Leipzig, 1904)). See also below, p. 437.

[8] Cf. below, pp. 437; 447; 487; 501.

[9] *Hex.* II 3, 32A-B. Cf. Origen, *De princ.* II I. 4 (*PG* 11. 185C-D, 110. 1 - 111. 1 Koetschau).

[10] *Hex.* II 3, 33B-C. See below, p. 500.

[11] See below, p. 440.

[12] See below, p. 448.

[13] *Hex.* I 7, 20B-C. For air and water as intermediaries cf. Plato, *Tim.* 32B.

[14] See below, p. 448.

[15] Cf. Aristotle, *De gen. et corr.* II 3, 331a4.

[16] Gen. i. 6.

[17] Cf. Aristotle, *op. cit.* II 4, 331b2.

[18] *Hex.* IV 5, 89B-92A. See below, pp. 437; 448; 520. The doctrine that the elements pass into one another is a Stoic variation of the Heraclitean theory of flux.

[19] See below, p. 448.

[20] See below, pp. 479-80.

[21] See below, p. 460.

[22] Cf. Eunomius *ap.* Socrates, *Hist. eccl.* IV 7. 13-14, 482. 10-14 Hussey (Oxford, 1853); Theodoret, *Haeres. fat. comp.* IV 3; idem, *In Dan.* VIII.

[23] Cf. Aëtius *ap.* Theodoret, *Hist. eccl.* II 24 (*PG* 82. 1072C2-5).

[24] . . . St Greg. Naz. *Orat.* xxx 16 *ad fin.* (134. 17-18 Mason). See below, p. 441.

[25] St Basil, *Adv. Eun.* I 10.

[26] St Basil, *Ep.* ccxxxv 2 (*PG* 32. 869C1-2); *Adv. Eun.* 114 (*PG* 29. 544A10-B15); cf. Plotinus, v 5 [32] 13, 11-13. See below, p. 440; ps.-Dionys. pp.468-70.

[27] Plotinus, v 5 [32] 6, 11-13. See below, p. 468.

[28] This is the subject of the ps.-Dionysius' treatise *On the Divine Names*, for which see below, p. 461. Cf. above, p. 431.

[29] . . . *Hex.* I 5, 13A. Cf. St Greg. Nyss. below, p. 454 ps.-Dionys. below, p. 464.

[30] *Hex. loc. cit.* See below, p.

[31] Cf. St Greg. Nyss. *C. Eun.* 1 (*PG* 44. 365C (I 135 Jaeger)); Lossky, *op. cit.* p. 97.

[32] St Basil, *Hom. in ps. xlviii,* 8 (*PG* 29. 449B (I 148E ed. Maur.)).

[33] Idem, *Hex.* II 5, 40C-41A. See below, pp. 437; 507-8.

[34] Quoted by St Paul, Hebr. i. 7.

[35] St Greg. Naz. *Orat.* XXVIII 31 (70. 3-7 Mason) (*PG* 36. 72A). See below, p. 443.

[36] According to Greg. Nyss. fire is intermediary between the intelligible and sensible nature (*C. Eun.* II (XII B/XIII) (*PG* 45. 1004A, I 306 Jaeger); *In Hex. PG* 44. 80D-81A; 81C-D; 116B; 121A), and therefore the angelic intelligences are of a higher order than fire. See below, p. 448.

[37] Proclus identified light with space, which he held to be an immovable, indivisible immaterial body: idem *ap.* Simpl. *Phys.* ed. Diels (Berlin, 1882), pp. 611-12.

[38] *Hex.* II 7, 45A.

[39] See below, p. 437.

[40] See above, p. 426.

[41] St Bas. *Adv. Eun.* I 21 (*PG* 29. 560 B, 1 233 A-B ed. Maur.). The identification of time and extension is Stoic: see Simplicius, *In Categ.* 350 Kalbfleisch; Plutarch, *Quaest. plat.* 1007; Philo, *Leg. alleg.* 11 2.

[42] *Hex.* II 8, 49 B-C.

[43] Ioan. Lyd. *De mens.* III 3, 39. 4-14 Wuensch. Cf. J. Daniélou, 'La typologie de la semaine au ivᵉ siècle', *Recherches de science religieuse*, XXXV (1948), p. 399. For Lydus, see also below, p. 522.

[44] *Tim.* 37D. Cf. Plotinus, III 7 [45] 13, 23-5.

[45] *Hex.* I 6, 16C.

[46] *Hex.* IX 2, 189 B.

[47] *Hex.* II 5, 41 A-B.

[48] See above, p. 429.

[49] See above, p. 433.

[50] *Hex.* I 3, 9C. Cf. Aristotle, *De caelo* I 12, 288 b 4; St Greg. Nyss. *De hom. opif.* XXIII (*PG* 44. 209 B); Baudry, *Le Problème de l'origine et de l'éternité du monde dans la philosophie grecque de Platon à l'ère chrétienne* (Paris, 1931), p. III; below, p. 496.

[51] Above, p. 435.

[52] *Hex.* I 5, 12C.

[53] See above, p. 435. Cf. H. Urs von Balthasar, *Présence et pensée* (Paris, 1943), pp. 8-9.

[54] *Hex.* II 2, 33A. See above, p. 432. The idea comes from Plato (cf. *Tim.* 32A), and plays an important part in the philosophy of Posidonius: cf. Cleomedes, *De motu circ.* I I, 4, 8 Ziegler; Sextus Empiricus, *Adv. math.* IX = *C. phys.* I 78-80; Karl Reinhardt, *Kosmos und Sympathie* (Munich, 1928), pp. 52 f. However, L. Edelstein, 'The physical system of Posidonius', *American Journal of Philology*, LVII (1936), p. 324, considers that its importance for Posidonius has been overrated.

[55] *Hex.* II 4, 37 C-D. This definition of evil, which derives from Plotinus (cf. I 8 [51] II, 8-9; III 2 [47] 5, 25-6), was held in common by all the Cappadocians, and was developed at length in the Neoplatonic tradition that was drawn upon by Proclus and the ps.-Dionysius.

[56] *Hex.* II 5, 41 B.

[57] St Basil left his exposition of the theme uncompleted, for the *Homilies on the Hexaëmeron* break off at the point where God creates man in his own image. A treatise on this was promised, but the promise was long deferred. See below, p. 449.

Abbreviations

. . . *PG* Migne, *Patrologia Graeca* . . .

SC Sources Chrétiennes . . .

ARISTOTLE

. . . *De gen. et corr. De generatione et corruptione* . . .

PLUTARCH

. . . *Plat qu.* . . . *Platonicae quaestiones* . . .

PHILO

. . . *Leg. Alleg. Legum Allegoriae* . . .

ORIGEN

. . . *Princ. De principiis* . . .

PROCLUS

. . . *In Tim. In Platonis Timaeum commentarii* . . .

PSEUDO-DIONYSIUS

. . . *CH De caelesti hierarchia* . . .

ST BASIL

. . . *Hex. Hom. in Hexaëmeron*

Adv. Eun. Adversus Eunomium

ST GREGORY NAZIANZEN

Orat. Orationes

Orat. theol. Orationes theologicae

ST GREGORY OF NYSSA

C. Eun. Contra Eunomium . . .

De hom. opif. De hominis opificio . . .

PLATO

. . . *Hippias major* . . .

Timaeus . . .

Select Bibliography

ST BASIL

Works, PG 29-32.

Homiliae in Hexaëmeron, ed. and tr. S. Giet (*Sources Chrétiennes*). Paris, 1950.

On the Holy Spirit, ed. and tr. B. Pruche (*Sources Chrétiennes*). Paris, 1947.

ST GREGORY NAZIANZEN

Works, PG 35-8.

Orationes 27-31 (*Orationes theologicae*), ed. A. J. Mason. Cambridge, 1899.

ST GREGORY OF NYSSA

Works, PG 44-6.

Works, ed. W. Jaeger, H. Langerbeck, etc. Leiden, 1952- , in progress. . . .

PSEUDO-DIONYSIUS

Works, PG 3.

De caelesti hierarchia, ed. and tr. R. Roques, G. Heil, M. de Gandillac (*Sources Chrétiennes*). Paris, 1958. . . .

Eric Osborn (essay date 1976)

SOURCE: "Basil the Great" in *Ethical Patterns in Early Christian Thought*," Cambridge University Press, 1976, pp. 84-113.

[*In the essay reprinted below, Osborn examines Basil's views on the moral and ethical obligations of a Christian. Drawing especially on the* Moralia *and the* Longer *and* Shorter Rules, *the critic contends that Basil's guidelines for devoting one's life to the glory of God were intended for the laity as well as for members of the monastic community, even though Basil believed that only an ascetic could achieve perfect righteousness.*]

Basil was born in Caesarea of Cappadocia about 330 of rich but honest parents.[1] His father was a teacher of rhetoric, a lawyer and a wealthy land-owner. One of his grandfathers had died a martyr. The piety and devotion of Basil's mother was reflected in her children, three of whom became bishops, one a nun and another a monk. Three of these children were canonised. After careful training at home, he studied rhetoric and philosophy in Caesarea and Constantinople. In 351 he went to Athens where for five years he took advantage of its rich intellectual life. He returned to Caesarea as a professor of rhetoric for two years, and then turned from the bright prospects of his academic future, was baptised and entered a life of religious discipline. After visiting Egypt and Syria to observe the monks, he selected a quiet country retreat, and gathered a few others who wished to live a hermit's life. He wrote in moving terms of the rich beauty of his surroundings and of its silence. Seeing the dangers of solitary life, he organized monks into a community. He gave to his community a set of rules and a detailed pattern of life. Far more than Pachomius had done in Egypt, he put emphasis on the common life which members shared. Together with his learning, sancity and perception, he had great powers of organisation. Monasticism in the East has retained the shape which he gave it. His programme of social relief produced hospitals and homes for the poor.[2] The Emperor Julian tried to bring him from his place of retreat to the splendour of the court, for they had been students together. This and other efforts to move him failed, but in 364 he was ordained and took an active part in the fight against Arianism. In 370 he became Bishop of Caesarea, and held this office until his early death in 379. From these years he is remembered as the defender of the Nicene faith in the face of imperial Arianism. The Emperor Valens came to Cappadocia, determined to stamp out opposition. The rest of the province yielded; but Basil stood firm against all threats. Confiscation of property meant nothing to him, since he only had an old cloak and a few books. Exile was nothing to a stranger and pilgrim in all the earth. Pain and death held no terrors. When a threatening prefect expressed surprise at Basil's stand he was told that he had not met a proper bishop before. The emperor talked with Basil on problems of faith with his household cook, one Demosthenes, in attendance. When the latter entered the discussion, Basil suggested that a Demosthenes who could not speak Greek would be better making sauces in the kitchen than improvising at theology. He once replied to a threat of torture which included tearing out his liver with the comment that he would be obliged for the treatment since his liver gave him a lot of trouble where it was. He showed no consideration for himself or for his few friends, once making Gregory of Nazianzus the bishop of a desolate but strategic outpost.[3] His theological work was crucial but he saw small reward for the struggles of his strenuous life. Jerome and others accused him of pride. He was reserved, conscious of his abilities and deeply concerned by the doctrinal dangers of his time. The body, which he ill-treated, gave him great pain and he declared himself an old man at forty-five. He died five years later, two years before the second ecumenical council at Constantinople, to be remembered as Basil the Great.[4]

His chief theological work concerned the Holy Spirit. The Spirit must be 'counted with' and not 'counted below' the Father and Son. 'We glorify the Spirit with the Father and the Son because we believe that he is not foreign to the divine nature.'[5] Basil did not write in the abstract. His founding of monastic communities grew from a direct awareness of the varied gifts of the Spirit. The 'enthusiasm' of the earliest church had been exemplified in the behaviour of the Corinthians to whom Paul wrote. They wanted 'spirit without letter' and believed that the fullness of the last days was already on them. The second century rejected the Montanist movement which claimed even greater heights of spiritual ecstasy. The third century faced the brief problem of Cyprian's contemporaries who demanded martyrdom. Monasticism saw the revival of enthusiasm on a wide scale. The spiritual gifts of the anchorites were not immediately disruptive because they were exercised, in isolation, for the perfection of the individual. They

displayed all the intensity of those who would take the kingdom by storm. In time the ideal of Antony led to excesses and the reforms of Pachomius had moderating effects. It was left to Basil, however, to establish the common life (cenobitism), through an appreciation of spiritual gifts and their interdependence. Basil saw in the successors to Antony a new hope for the church. God was pouring out his Spirit and the day of Pentecost had come again. The community of monks, indwelt and endowed by the Spirit, reproduced the earliest Christian community. Their charismatic endowments were not for their own elevation but for the enrichment of a common life. With sound theological judgment Basil turned to scripture for the direction and rule of his community. He cites more than 1500 verses of New Testament.[6] His exhaustive knowledge and continuous use of scripture point to profound insight. Spirit without letter would be just as disastrous as letter without spirit. The challenge and opportunity of his time caused him to discover afresh the ethical patterns of the New Testament. His rigour, enthusiasm and devotion cannot fail to move the twentieth-century reader one way or another. Yet these are only half of Basil. The other half is integration of these qualities in a fellowship of the Spirit and an obedience to the Word. God has made us, like members of one body, to need one another's help.[7] The need for community is evident because Basil 'once saw a swarm of bees flying in military formation according to the law of their nature and following their king[!] in good order'.[8] Renunciation of the world is joined to an affirmation of its order and beauty. The length of the elephant's trunk is due to stiffness of legs which is due to weight of body.[9] Every season brings its special fruits. Spring is the time for flowers, summer for wheat harvest, autumn for apples and winter is the time for talking.[10]

Basil is a strenuous Christian. The pictures of the soldier, the athlete and the child come readily to his mind.[11] His monk is the Christian soldier who takes the kingdom by force, the athlete who throws everything into the contest and the child who is saved with simplicity and trust. Not that Basil ever loses his pride or activism; but they are tempered by submission to the king, for whom he fights and in whose love he finds his only rest.

RIGHTEOUSNESS

(i) Rigorism

The righteousness of the Christian is marked by excess. It abounds in every way, goes beyond that of the scribes and Pharisees, and is governed by the single standard of the Lord's teaching.[12] Frequent reference to the teaching of the Lord determines the quality of this righteousness. The Lord sent his followers to teach *all* that he had commanded and not, 'to observe some things and neglect others'. If all commands had not been essential, all would not have been written down. This righteousness is always superior to that of the law, and goes beyond literal requirements. The Christian must neither speak evil, do violence, fight or avenge himself. He never returns evil for evil, but rejects anger, is patient and suffers, not in order to justify himself, but rather to reform his brother. He must not slander his brother secretly, nor may he joke, laugh or be idle. While he lives a temperate life, he never thinks of himself as his own master. He does not complain in time of need or weariness. Every action and word is governed by one obedience. He is never glad when others go wrong and always looks for reconciliation.[13]

With this extreme account of righteousness there is an insistence on the gravity of all kinds of sin. There is no distinction between one fault and another. Basil was troubled by the effects of sin and disobedience in a divided church. From scripture he knew that all sin is a revolt against God and must be punished. The New Testament makes no distinction between large and small sins. He who commits sin is the slave of sin, and the word will judge him: whoever does not obey the Son will not see life, but the wrath of God dwells upon him. The only possible distinction between sins is between those which dominate us and those which do not. The large sin is one which is our master, the small sin is one which we have mastered. So every thought should be obedient to God and every disobedient thought must be punished. God does not condemn the number of our sins, nor their relative seriousness; he condemns the plain contradiction of his will; so it is wrong to be tolerant towards some sins and to condemn others. At this point Basil is close to the Stoics who insisted that it was as easy to drown in one foot of water as in ten feet; but the New Testament also told him what happened to those who broke the least commandment, while the Old Testament warned those who swerved to the right or the left. As all sin is condemned, so all men are called to virtue. The will and commandments of God are found in scripture, which is interpreted according to concrete situations. Distinctions may be introduced, but severity and rigour remain. The letter of scripture is followed, for example, when he who calls his neighbour a fool is condemned to hell, although Basil explains, 'What is Raca? A vernacular word of mild insult, used among friends and relations.'[14]

With God it must be all or nothing, obedience or disobedience. Sin is the only source of evil. Like Clement and Origen, Basil strictly separates evil from God and attributes it to man's free choice. Reason in relation to conduct is called conscience. All men have an elementary sense of good and evil. Man's pursuit of good should take the practical route of conquering sin. Sin must be torn out. The words of the Lord show the need for vigilance. He who defends a sinner is worse than he who has made one to stumble and earned a millstone around his neck. The unrepentant sinner is like the eye which should be plucked out and cast away.[15] True repentance brings joy to the Lord. The sinner who will not repent becomes as a Gentile and a tax-gatherer.[16] With fear and tears the lost soul must turn from sin.[17] Repentance must be obvious.[18] Great care must be taken before a sinner is trusted with any office in the brotherhood.[18] Penitence is central in the life of every monk. While love is the supreme virtue, the monk lives in continual penitence through his desire to obtain remission of past sins. He prays for the freedom of his soul. He practises mortification and good works which help him to stamp out sin. He does not laugh because his Lord has condemned laughter and because there are so many sinners to be mourned. Sleep brings slackness in thoughts of God and, when overdone, leads men to despise God's judgements.[20] Every idle word earns judgement. It may be a good word; but, if it does not fulfil a purpose in the Lord, if it does not edify faith, then it grieves the Holy Spirit.[21] On the other hand if a sister does not sing psalms with fervour, 'Let her either correct herself or else be expelled.'[22]

In the church of God a minister must be upright. His life is examined before his admission to office.[23] Unworthy ministers should be dismissed and not replaced until worthy candidates are available. Yet the church has fallen upon sad days. Its laws are in confusion. There is no just judgement and no limit on vice.[24] The righteousness of God is the justice which all shall know when they receive the reward of their works. At present men enjoy the long-suffering of God, but in that terrible day, his justice will be made clear to all.[25] He is the one God of mercy and judgement,[26] who will duly reward those who have done well. Generosity, for example, earns his blessing. Whoever gives to the afflicted gives to the Lord and shall receive his reward from the Lord.[27] The soul looks to the great day when all creation shall stand before the judge to give an account of its deeds. That day and that hour must ever be remembered so that life may be lived in the fear of God.[28] The body is trained to work hard and the soul is accustomed to trials; but the end of everlasting blessedness with the saints is never forgotten.[29]

(ii) Rule

Basil's discourse on morals sets out in separate prescriptions what the New Testament tells Christians to do.

> Let us now try to fulfil in the name of our Lord Jesus Christ our promise concerning the ***Morals***. As many things as we find in the New Testament in scattered passages forbidden or approved, these to the best of our ability we have tried to gather into summarised rules for the easy comprehension of whoever wants them.

The Rules fulfil the ministry of the word for the perfecting of souls. The life of the monk is governed in every aspect. His clothing, food, sleep, in fact, every part of his life is regulated. Many laws or canons cover particular sins and prescribe punishment in a wide variety of special cases.[30] Basil, an enemy of compromise, is always practical in his outlook. 'The saints that have gone before teach us that the use of the girdle is necessary . . . It is especially necessary that he who means to do work in person should be neatly dressed and able to move without hindrance.'[31]

Punishment is remedial and beneficial rather than retributive. A just judge requires that an evil doer should pay his debt with interest, 'if he is to be made better by punishment and render other men wiser by his example'. Such punishment is to be received willingly, 'as befits a son who is sick and at death's door'.[32] Correction and cure must be prescribed according to individual need. 'There is no fault that cannot be cured by care or overcome by the fear of God.' The privileged patrician needs a very distasteful job to help him to achieve the Lord's humility.[33] Special responsibility hangs heavily upon the superior, who shares the condemnation of a brother if he has not warned the brother concerning his sin and taught him a way of reformation. One of the greatest faults is to give wrong guidance and cause a brother to go astray.[34] A superior heals the weak brother, just as a doctor heals those who are sick in body. Surgery may be painful or drugs may be bitter, but they can achieve a cure. Godly sorrow is necessary.[35] The same principle is applied to heal diseases of body and of soul.

> We must take care so to use the art of medicine, if need arise as not to assign to it the whole cause of health or sickness, but to accept the use of its remedies as designed for the glory of God and a type of the care of souls . . . For as with the flesh both the putting away of foreign elements and the addition of what is lacking are necessary; so also with our souls, it is fitting that what is foreign be removed and what is according to our nature be received. Because 'God made man upright' and created us for good works that we should walk in them.[36]

The corporate aspects of sin are clear within the brotherhood. If one allows another to sin, one is guilty of that sin. As our Lord said to Pilate, 'He that delivered me to you has the greater sin.' We must not be silent when others sin. The Old Testament tells us to rebuke our neighbours and the gospel tells us to show our brother his faults.[37] Within the community any offence requires direct and drastic action. A man may provide such offence by transgressing the law, leading another to transgress it, preventing someone from doing God's will, or encouraging a weak man to do something which is wrong. There is intricate variety in the apportioning of blame.[38] Various community problems are considered. Laziness is linked with sin because one should be zealous and endure to the end.[39] Spiritual sickness may show itself in eating delicacies or in eating too much.[40] When a good man falls into sin, his condition is different from that of an indifferent man who has committed the same sin. The latter is corrupt in his whole nature and requires more drastic action.[41] Obedience is the answer to sin. When monks dispute among themselves and reject the commands of their Lord, the king is no longer among them.[42] Disobedience must be punished and if punishment does not cure the ill, then the diseased member must be cut off from the community. 'Insubordination and defiance are the proofs of a multitude of sins, of tainted faith, of doubtful hope, of proud and overweening conduct.'[43]

Moderation, quiet and self-control should rule the lives of those who receive what God gives from the wealth of his universe. The providence of God rules justly over all things and must never be questioned.[44] The true good of man is his soul, uniquely his soul and man should know himself, or as scripture says, take heed to himself. Health, beauty, youth, long life, riches, glory and power, must be regarded with moderation. Reason helps moderation. Basil answers reasonably the unreasonable question, 'if a brother having nothing of his own be asked by another for the actual thing he is wearing, what ought he to do, especially if he who asks is naked?' The matter of giving and receiving is a question of stewardship and there is happily a Pauline principle, 'Let each man abide in that wherein he was called.' Another problem shows moderation of appetite, 'How can a man avoid taking pleasure in eating?' The answer is that one must hold to the criterion of what is fitting and useful and regard pleasure as irrelevant.[45]

(iii) Order and Natural Law

The beauty of nature inspires quietness in the soul.[46] Basil marvels at the ordered beauty of the creation, and uses philosophy to explain the links between the ordered universe, the providence of God, and human responsibility. He rejects any argument which would threaten man's responsibility and freedom. The design of the creator is seen on every side. Appropriate herbs are provided to heal the various sicknesses of the body. Man must use God's world in a right way. The rich man must care for those in need. Divine judgement falls on the selfish. Money should not be lent or borrowed at interest, and if it is, both lender and borrower are selfishly at fault.[47] Basil's sermons on the six days of creation show how the order of nature is important to moral life. Nature teaches us by her example to show vigour in producing good works.[48] The serpent symbolises the fickleness and shiftiness of sin. Justice and honesty must go together.[49] Fishes which move by regular laws of migration indicate obedience to the law of God. They have no reason in them but the inward law of nature tells them what to do.[50] The ox and the ass know their master and can even follow a known track when a man has lost his way. Man is not always able to show his superiority over dumb creatures.[51] Storks show qualities of kindness and care which shame many men. When the old lose their feathers others surround them to keep them warm. Man can learn also from the industry of the swallow who builds a nest by perseverance and before whose example no man can plead his poverty.[52] Nature is a good teacher. Man by standing upright on his two feet looks to his heavenly country, while cattle with their four feet bend towards the earth. 'Raise your soul above the earth. Draw from its natural shape the rule of your conduct; fix your way of life in heaven.'[53] The care which irrational creatures take of their lives warns us to watch over the salvation of our souls. The bear, the fox and the tortoise all know how to heal their wounds.[54] Basil does not hesitate to read off from nature recommendations concerning human conduct. Porphyry writes in similar vein of the lessons to be drawn from nature. Ants, bees and other gregarious animals preserve a communal and reciprocal justice. Doves are very strong on chastity and storks on kindness to parents.[55] Both these writers have a strong dualistic tendency which does not diminish their allegiance to natural order. Basil draws one violent conclusion from nature. The body is like a charging beast that must be whipped by reason to calm it down.[56]

DISCIPLESHIP

(i) Seized by a Vehement Desire to Follow Christ

Throughout Basil's account of Christian discipleship, there sounds a ruthless call to self denial. Asceticism is required of all. He who is attached to this life or tolerates 'anything which even to a small degree draws him away from the commandment of God'[57] cannot be a disciple of the Lord. The glory of God is declared by doing his will.[58] Confession of the Lord and possession of spiritual gifts cannot save the disobedient from condemnation.[59] It is no help to live with others who please God and to preserve an outward appearance of virtue when one has no real virtue within. God must be obeyed in God's way.[60] Every offensive thing must be cut away however necessary and dear it may seem.[61] The Law condemns bad deeds but the gospel goes further and condemns the inner passions of the soul. There is an initial act of renunciation which cannot be avoided. The soldier must enlist. 'For if a man has not first succeeded in denying himself and taking up his cross, he finds, as he goes, many hindrances to following, arising from himself.'[62] One must renounce the devil, fleshly lusts, physical relationships, human friendships, all behaviour contrary to the gospel, worldly affections, parents, relations and possessions.[63] 'Accordingly perfect renunciation consists in a man's attaining complete passionlessness as regards actual living and hav-

ing "the sentence of death" so as to put no confidence in himself.' The first disciples show the way. John and James left their father 'and even the boat, their sole source of livelihood'. Matthew left all and followed, not only leaving the profits behind, 'but also despising the dangers that were likely to come upon himself and his family at the hands of the authorities for leaving the accounts of the custom-house in disorder'. All of this shows that anyone 'who is seized by the vehement desire of following Christ can no longer care for anything to do with this life'.[64] Yet all is gain, for the things which are given up are no better than dung, and what is gained is the pearl of great price. Renunciation looses the chains which bind us to all present, material and transitory things, and releases us from human obligation 'making us more ready to start on the way to God'.[65] So Basil's message is good news, because man is able to fulfil all the commandments of God. God forgives all sins when we produce fruits of repentance, and are washed in the blood of Christ. An inner spark of divine love enables us to keep the commandments of God. For if we love him we will keep his commandments, and the two commandments to love God and our neighbour are all the law and the prophets. Yet the promise does not remove the need for constant vigilance. None of the saints of old won their crowns by living in luxury. They all passed through the fire of affliction. The Christian follows the commandment of his Lord and the example of the holy men of old who showed in adversity their greatness of soul.[66] The athlete of Christ fights for victory over sin, by straining every muscle. Christians struggle and suffer together. They fight in the arena for the common heritage 'for the treasure of the sound faith, derived from our fathers'.[67] Those who are being attacked by Arians are congratulated on their good fortune. They have won the blessings of persecution in a period of peace.[68] A soldier does not worry about rations or lodging, but faces dangers and death for the reward of nearness to his king, the friendship and favour of his king. 'Come, then, soldier of Christ, take to heart these small lessons from human affairs and consider eternal blessings.'[69] Ascetic life is a peaceful substitute for martyrdom, the peak of perfection. As with Clement, each Christian should order his life as a preparation for martyrdom. So Basil kept a direct link between the life of the monk and the perseverance which gave to martyrs their perfection.[70]

(ii) His Glory as Object and Desire

The ascetic life is not an end in itself. It is a means to the end of the glory of God. 'Ever to be pressing the soul on beyond its strength to do the will of God, having his glory as its object and desire.'[71] Prayer should be unceasing but special times of the day have been chosen as appropriate for the remembering of the blessings of God. These times are the dawn, the third, sixth and ninth hour with a final service at midnight.[72] All must be done to the glory of God.[73] Prayer is governed by a sense of God's presence. When one talks with a ruler or a superior, one fixes one's eyes upon him. Much more, when one prays, one fixes one's mind upon God.[74]

Man and woman are equal before God[75] and possess two chief faculties, reason and free choice. The beginning of the moral life comes with the Delphic injunction, 'Know thyself', or the theme of Deuteronomy, 'Take heed to yourself.'[76] Self-knowledge is a condition of the good life. One must consciously choose between animal life and higher spiritual life. Quietness of mind and freedom from distraction enable a soul to fix its gaze on God. The wax tablet must be smoothed out before it can be written on.[77] Prayer should leave imprinted a clear idea of God. In this way God dwells in the soul which becomes his temple.[78] The inner man consists of contemplation and since the kingdom of heaven is within, this kingdom must be contemplation.[79] Basil praises the quietness and beauty of his new home in the country. 'However, the best thing to be said about the place is that being suitable for growing fruits of every kind, it nurtures what to me is the sweetest fruit of all, quietness.'[80] The life of a religious community enjoys tranquillity of soul through solitude. It is here, and here alone, that one may live the spiritual life, away from the noise and distractions of the world.

The **Longer Rules** begin with the exhortation to apply ourselves to the care of our souls for the love of Jesus Christ,[81] who calls us back from death to life and who has shared our weakness and disease that we might be healed. Only through him may we regain the image and likeness of God which man possessed in paradise before his fall.[82] The fear of God is important for all who begin to practise piety.[83] To follow God we must loosen all chains of attachment to this life. We must remove from our previous environment and forget all former habits. No distraction must threaten the achievement of our aim. If our minds wander we cannot hope to succeed in loving God and our neighbour. This art is to be learnt by concentration.[84] Solitude is a great help to a soul which wishes to avoid distraction.[85] To follow the Lord Jesus Christ means taking up the cross after him.[86] We must suffer and endure for Christ's sake,[87] continue in prayer and in vigils to the end that we may be disciples of Christ and conform to his pattern. As sheep we follow him who is our shepherd, as branches we bear fruit in him, as members of his body we are equipped with the gifts of the Spirit. We are the bride of Christ, temples of God, a sacrifice to him and 'children of God, formed after the likeness of God according to the measure granted to men'. It is a mark of the Christian that he sees his Lord always before him.[88]

We are called to be made like God.[89] We cannot become like God unless we know what he is like. Theo-logical inquiry is necessary to find the truth which rules the goal of human life.[90] Perfection of life can only be found in the outward and inward imitation of Christ, the following of his example in life and death. Paul spoke of being made like the death of Christ.[91] As every man is made in the image of God, the blasphemy of the Arians, who deny that the Son is like God, is all the more outrageous.[92]

Perfection calls man to continence, to the renunciation of every worldly relationship, to fasting, to the study of scripture and to watching. There has been disagreement on the shape of Basil's thought. Some have maintained that he describes a progress in gradual stages towards the direct love of God, moving through an *ordo amoris* like that of Augustine. A stronger case can be made for seeing his initial drive of life and thought towards God alone. Duty to the world, neighbour and church,[93] develop from this point. The perfect Christian is considered on the Stoic pattern of the wise man. Moses too is described as a sage.[94] Man must advance by degrees until he is completely like God. He always has to fight against temptations and his life is a continual struggle. Perfection is not secure or stationary. Life must be lived either for or against God. There is no neutrality. The Christian life is always a battle against demons and evil passions. Spiritual perfection can build on the basis of the fear of God, whose terrible judgements are always before us, and whose demnation will consign sinners to hell. The discipline of the monk is simply a continuation of the discipline which is imposed on every baptised Christian. There is one morality of the gospel, and it is this gospel which the discipline of Basil is concerned to realise, a gospel of perfection. Passionlessness, a goal of Christian living, is constancy, perseverance under suffering, and freedom from passion through self-rule.[95] All of these are universal features of Christian moral exhortation; but as Basil develops them they show his Hellenic background and personal extremism.

(iii) *Ever Pressing the Soul on Beyond its Strength*

Basil understands soul and body in much the same way as did Plato and the later Platonists. The true self is the soul which has been made in the image of God. The body is simply a dependent possession of the soul. Basil shows admiration for the beauty of physical things, and he shares with Plato an admiration for the excellence of man's physical form. But the soul, for Plato and Basil, is the essential part of man. It is what belongs to man as man. The soul must be liberated from its prison within the body. It must be purified from the passions. Here Basil talks like Plato, the Pythagoreans and the Stoics; Marcus Aurelius spoke of man as a soul carrying a corpse. Yet Basil's account of temperance is based on Paul, and he quotes Galatians 5:16-18 and Romans 7:14ff. The Christian soldier fights against the flesh and against the devil. Body and soul are irreconcilable. The soul can only be strong through the body becoming weak. The victory of the soul is the defeat of the body. An emaciated body is a sign of piety.[96] We must be grateful when woken for prayer because the soul perceives nothing in sleep but meets God in prayer.[97] If anyone is annoyed when woken, he deserves 'temporary separation and deprivation of food'.[98] There is a tricky problem concerning the possession of a night shirt, if that shirt is a hair shirt. More than one garment is forbidden; but hair cloth is special. 'For its use is not on account of bodily necessity but for afflicting and humiliating the soul.'[99]

Continence or self-rule, listed by Paul among the gifts of the Spirit, is that self-mastery which comes through restraint, the suffering of hardship and the buffeting of the body. Incontinence was the cause of man's first disobedience while all the saints have practised continence.[100] Laughter can be incontinent if it lacks moderation and control and should not be confused with spiritual joy or hilarity.[101] Continence mortifies the body, introduces eternal blessings and takes the sting out of pleasure.[102] The demons know and fear the power of continence as the Lord said that 'this kind does not go out except by prayer and fasting'.[103] The monk must therefore chastise and mortify his body, for the athlete of Christ trains his body in self-control.[104] The fear of God purifies soul and body. It penetrates the soul so that the soul no longer tolerates sin, and refuses to do anything contrary to the divine commands.

The monastic virtues are poverty whereby the monk treats nothing as his own and cares for the property of his community, and obedience by which the monk is subject to the authority of his superior. His obedience must be perfect, enthusiastic and exact. Like the little hungry child when it hears its nurse calling it to eat, he obeys commands with enthusiasm, for his life springs from their fulfilment.[105] The monk lives in isolation from worldly pursuits, in detachment from the world, and from himself. His renunciation is shown in purity of conscience, poverty, humility and obedience. He mortifies himself both physically and spiritually. His love and his renunciation must bear fruit in prayer throughout the day, in work which all monks must do, and in charitable service to those in need. He must dress in a way appropriate to the temperate life, showing humility and avoiding softness. The purpose of clothing is to hide nakedness and to protect from the heat and the cold. The monk from his poverty will have only one tunic. He is temperate in eating and eats whatever is put before him. He eats what is necessary in order to live and observes a mean between indulgence and self-torture. Fasting can get out of hand if it depends upon the will of the individual, and it should be done under the direction of a superior. All forms of luxury are to be avoided.[106]

The members of the brotherhood are not to be distracted. Their parents and relations are no longer their private concern.[107] Under no circumstances may the monk leave his community for the sake of his family. He must no longer think in terms of what is his, but in terms of what belongs to the community. Visits from his parents may awaken memories of his past life, and it is generally forbidden for monks to speak with their parents or with strangers. There may be some exception to this rule if spiritual advancement can be seen as a result. When a monk talks with a nun he must do so under the direction of their superiors who will choose persons, time and place for the conversation. There should be two or three monks and two or three nuns of a serious disposition. A' monk must never meet a nun by herself. Basil writes also of the danger of homosexual behaviour to the common life of the monastery. The monk abhors such tendencies.[108]

It has been common to look for philosophical interest in Basil's asceticism and tendency to dualism. While Basil's account of the Spirit[109] shows some awareness of Plotinus, his pessimistic view of the world is closer to Porphyry. Not that God made a bad world; he is not the source of evil.[110] Evil is separation from God and has no being.[111] But man remains a wanderer or fugitive in the world. Only through the incarnation of the Son and the gift of the Spirit can his release be secured.[112]

A world-denying strain of Platonism may be distinguished from a world-affirming strain in the tradition from Plato to Philo and the Hermetic literature.[113] The two strains continue in later Platonism. Plato commended the study of astronomy provided it left the stars alone.[114] Plotinus, for all his optimism, still pleaded for the flight of the alone to the alone.[115] The stronger pessimism of Porphyry is evident in his *On Abstinence from Animal Food*. The philosopher turns from the body and its passions to pure intellect and the supreme God.

Senses and passions work always on the irrational part of the soul, food and drink can poison the soul with passions. To stand against these things is a great struggle but there is no other way of purity.[116] As far as we can we should avoid contact with all that incites passions. That is why the Pythagoreans live away from the noises of the world. Plato chose an unhealthy part of Athens as the place for his Academy.[117] The philosopher meditating on death despises luxury and lives free from want on a slender diet. 'For he who in this way mortifies the body will obtain all possible good through self sufficiency and be made like the divine.'[118] The worship of the supreme God can employ neither material sacrifice nor verbal utterance—only silent contemplation is appropriate.[119]

This is the kind of Platonism which Basil knows and understands. In his *"Discourse to the young,"* he argues for the similarity of classical and Christian moralities. Socrates, when attacked, turned the other cheek. Alexander would not look at the daughters of Darius because after capturing men he did not want to be conquered by women; he was in effect fulfilling the precept against committing adultery in the heart.[120] But, to sum up, the body in every part should be despised by everyone who does not want to be buried in its pleasures as if in slime.' Both Plato and Paul warn us against the body. We should not pander to it but whip it with the lash of reason until it settles down. Pythagoras is quoted on the body as the prison of the soul.

> It was for this reason, in fact that Plato also, as we are told, providing against the harmful influence of the body, deliberately settled in the disease-infested part of Attica, the Academy, in order that he might prune away, as one prunes the vine of its excessive growth, the excessive well-being of his body. And I myself have heard physicians say that extreme good health is even dangerous.[121]

However wrong this estimate of Plato may be,[122] it is the one which Basil knows, a Platonism which is more dependent on Porphyry than on Plotinus. Like Clement he wishes to show that Christian sage can excel pagan philosopher. He admires the scorn of Diogenes for worldly things and his claim to superior wealth because he had fewer needs than the king.[123] Julian, of course, was critical of the moral influence of Christianity and the free forgiveness which it offered.[124] Basil could not afford to offer a morality less stringent than that of his imperial friend.

On the other hand Basil was no Manichee. He maintained a unity between the ascetic and the created world. The 'world' which he rejected was an attitude to life, a 'system of purely human values which takes no account of the judgement of God'.[125] The ascetic 'renounces also all the affections of this world which can hinder the aim of godliness'.[126] Yet the flesh can hamper us in the vision of God.[127] It is the heavy prison house of the soul.[128]

There is also a positive side to Basil's Platonism. With the sense of man's temporality and hostility between soul and body, there is that yearning for absolute beauty which only God can satisfy. God is beauty itself to whom all things look and from whom all things flow. He is the ever-springing fount of pure grace, and a treasure which can never be spent.[129] It is God's will that all should participate in his life.[130]

FAITH

(i) Sound Faith and Godly Doctrines

Faith for Basil is the apostolic rule of faith. It must be guarded and kept. Sound faith is the only basis for good living. 'For by these two things the man of God is perfected.'[131] The exposition of the faith requires care and discernment, for the devil is always trying to destroy faith. Faith which works through love is a mark of the Christian. 'I think it both fitting and necessary that I should now expound our sound faith and godly doctrines concerning the Father, Son and Holy Spirit, and then add the discourse on morals.'[132] Such faith is simple, strong, quiet and full of light. Belief in the word of God is a living faith which works by love and shows itself in good works. Faith is an unhesitating assent to that which we learn from God. It is the full conviction of the truth which is declared and taught to us by the grace of God. Faith is firm and unshakeable, pure and exact, founded upon scripture. Scripture is divinely inspired and is the source of all doctrine.[133]

If we are asked why we are Christians, we must answer that it is through our faith.[134] Faith is linked with baptism as inseparable in salvation. 'Faith is perfected through baptism, baptism is established through faith.'[135] Faith is directed to the Father, Son and Holy Spirit, and they who deny the trinity are acting against faith.[136]

Basil's faith is more static than Clement's. It does not go beyond essentials. Christians should not puzzle over anything superfluous but stand firm in the ancient faith. Let them confess one Name and one God and avoid all kinds of novelty.[137] Yet there is continuity, for Basil simply takes over all of Origen's negative theology.[138] God cannot be known in the way other things are known. Eunomius has shown insufferable pride and presumption in his attempt to enter the being of God;[139] 'to know God is to keep his commands'.[140] For Clement the mystery of God is an invitation to pilgrimage from faith to knowledge, for Basil it is a warning against intellectual impertinence.

The faith of the fathers stands as a fixed point of reference in times of uncertainty. 'Now I charge you by the fathers, by the true faith, by our blessed friend, lift up your souls.'[141] The struggle against heresy is a constant fight in defence of the faith.[142] One should not waver concerning what the Lord has said but be convinced that every word of God is true and possible. A man who doesn't trust the Lord in small things will believe him far less in great things.[143] Human conditions can never cancel out the commandments of God.[144] Faith must be steadfast and immovable from the good things which are in the Lord.[145] The mark of a believer is to hold fast to the faith which is 'unhesitating conviction of the truth of the inspired Word.' What is not of faith, as the apostle says, is sin.[146] The power of faith is recognised by animals, for with it one may walk upon serpents and scorpions. The snake did not hurt Paul because it found him full of faith. On the other hand, 'if you have not faith, do not fear wild animals so much as your lack of faith, through which you make yourself susceptible to all corruption.'[147]

When the waves of trouble seem to overwhelm Basil, he asks for prayer that he might please God. He does not wish to be a wicked servant who thanks his master only for what is good and refuses to accept the chastisement of adversity. Rather, 'Let me gain benefit from my very hardships, trusting most in God when I need him most.'[148] Against the heretics the struggle must go on. Christians are called upon to fight their way through temptations for the prize of the truth. They must never cease to fight the good fight, nor throw away the achievement of past toil.[149] Anxiety is a good thing if it does not lead to dejection and despair. We must trust in the goodness of God, knowing that, if we turn to him, he will not cast us off for ever, since he is with us always.[150] The trial may be heavy, but no one who avoids the dust and the blows of battle can win a victor's crown. The mockery of the devil and the onslaughts of his minions are troublesome but despicable. They combine wickedness with weakness. We should not cry too loud when we are hurt. There is only one thing which is worth deep sorrow, and that is 'the loss of one's own self', which comes from denying God and losing the eternal reward.[151] The endurance of the Christian philosopher is the endurance of the man of faith and is marked by the new virtue of humility.[152]

(ii) Whose Feet Will You Wash?

Faith must always be linked to humility. We should not be proud of our good deeds,[153] nor should we choose any but the lowest seat at a meal.[154] Simple clothing shows humility.[155] Within the brotherhood the ideal of humility is shown by a superior as he performs acts of service to lower brethren. The brethren must readily receive such service and not resist. The dangers of pride and the need for humility are recognised in the ordering of communities.[156] Our Lord spoke of the dangers of exalting oneself and the apostle pointed the way of lowliness and humility.[157] The humility and endurance of the monk has many forms, and leads to patience and sweetness. Basil expounds humility with great persuasion, and shows how it should be practised. Humility is the virtue which places us in our right place in the order of being. It places us truly in the presence of God and springs from a sense of his glory. In a sermon on humility, Basil speaks of the moving example of the humility of the Word of God, who became flesh, descending from heavenly glory and abasing himself for our sake. He shows the child in the manger, the young boy in the carpenter's shop, always obedient and subject to his parents. He shows Jesus receiving baptism at the hands of his servant John and giving himself up as an innocent victim to his enemies, receiving injury, outrage, humiliation, and finally a shameful death. We are to imitate this humility of Christ, a humility which his apostles have also followed, and such humility will gain eternal glory. One may gain humility, not by the extravagance of ascetic extremes, but by quietness and moderation in daily life. Humility is bound to a recognition of the grace of God and to humble dependence upon him. It always sees the wonder of God's providence and trusts in that providence.[158] Humility cannot be practised except within a community. How can one follow our Lord's pattern of humility unless one has brethren who have feet to be washed? 'Whose feet will you wash? For whom will you care? If you live by yourself to whom will you come last?'[159] With humility goes silence.[160] 'For there are a tone of voice, a symmetry of language, an appropriateness of occasion and a special vocabulary which belong to godly men . . . These can only be learned by one who has unlearned his former habits. Now silence both induces forgetfulness of the past through lack of practice and affords leisure to learn good habits.'[161] Silence brings peace and unity, removing causes of tension. There can be a time for speaking, when the time for silence is past.[162] Yet even theological opinions do not normally provide a ground for breaking silence.[163]

(iii) Free Will

Sin does not come from God, but from man's misuse of his free will. Sin is man's work. Basil's system, following Origen, is built upon the fact of free will which enables man to strive towards perfection. Sin may be seen negatively as the absence of good in the universe, positively as a revolt against God, a self-willed disobedience.[164] Greek thought, especially as mediated through Origen, moulds Basil's insistence on free will.[165] In the homily **"That God is not the author of evil,"** Basil declares, 'The origin and root of sin is what is in our own control and our free will.' In the sixth homily of the *Hexaemeron* he refutes astrology, using the anti-fatalist arguments of Carneades.[166] If man's affairs are governed by fate then there is no such thing as human responsibility; there can be no ground for the processes of law and no one can be blamed for moral faults. Fatalism is absurd. 'Under the reign of necessity and of fatality there is no place for merit, the first condition of all righteous judgement.'[167] Man is free to choose good or evil.

LOVE

(i) Wounded With Love

Basil begins the *Morals* with a reference to the first and great commandment to love God with all the heart, and the second to love one's neighbour as oneself. Only by keeping God's commandments can love for him be proved. The keeping of the commandments of Christ is linked with the endurance of his suffering even to death.[168] 'Love to God cannot be taught.' We were not taught to rejoice in life or to hold on to life nor did anyone show us how to love our parents. There is sown in the hearts of men the word which inclines to the love of God and shows that there is nothing comparable with the beauty and magnificence of God. The yearning of the soul for God as it cries, 'I am wounded with love' points to the beauty which cannot be seen, but is desired with an insatiable desire. The beauty of the morning star and the brightness of the sun and moon cannot compare with the glory of God.[169] To be separated from God is worse than all the punishment of hell. We cling to him who is our maker and whose goodness is evident on every hand. Apart from the beauties of creation, we learn the divine goodness in the humility and suffering of Christ. It is not possible to say everything about the love of God but it is important to remind the soul of it and to stir up a longing for God.[170] The love of God is the first duty of the Christian life, the perfection of virtue, and the supreme object of every baptised child of God. As the centre of all religious and moral activity, it gives to the discipline of the monastery and to the whole life of perfection the one aim of union with God in love. The soul is moved by love of God to prayer in which it is renewed and strengthened. Prayer gives to the soul a clear notion of God. God dwells in the soul so that it may become his temple and be conscious of him at all times, undistracted by worldly cares and passions. Prayer, constant prayer, is union with God.[171] The love of wisdom begins with the love of God whose wisdom made all things; it is this love which grows to perfection.[172]

(ii) The Sure Sign of Christ's Disciples

A Christian must be pure from hatred and must love his enemies. He must love his friends and be prepared to lay down his life for them. 'A sure sign of Christ's disciples is their mutual love in him.' One does not have the love of Christ towards a neighbour if one harms him in any way even though the harmful act may be permitted by scripture. The Christian is a man of peace and tries to pacify any man who may be vexed with him; but in love the Christian may grieve another for the other's good.[173] Hospitality should be practised among Christians in a quiet and frugal way.[174] One will not go to law even for the clothes on one's back, but one will strive to bring others to the peace which is in Christ.[175] Basil puts persistent stress on the need for neighbourly love. All begins with love of God. This is the first and greatest commandment, but a pure love of the glory of God is not yet fully Christian. The lover of God must also be a lover of his brother. This theme runs through all Basil's letters and is the reason why they were written.[176] He is delighted to know that Maximus the philosopher had discovered the highest good which is love to God and to one's neighbour.[177] The monk who treads the way to the mansions of the Lord has a love to the Lord God, which takes up all his heart, strength and mind;[178] and he must love when he is hated.[179] Friends know that to lose is to win, for love bears all things and never fails. 'He who subjects himself to his neighbour in love can never be humiliated.'[180]

The love of one's neighbour shows too in the requirements of social ethics. Marriage brings duties for husband and wife, for children and parents. Society brings obligations to all its members, especially to those who rule. The animals display a pattern of ordered community. The church is charged to follow the same way of peace. The clergy and the bishops have their obligation to one another. The care of poor and sick springs from personal interest; for there is a natural as well as a Christian law which requires this duty. It is wrong to give money only in old age or after death. Generosity should have personal discernment, and charity should have particular objects.[181] Man's response to God's infinite love and mercy is in both commandments, for love of God and neighbour go together. What is done for the least of his brothers is done for the Lord.[182] Love for God and neighbour are both implanted in every human heart. At the moment of its creation the soul receives from God seeds of reason which prompt this love. Weakened by sin, love needs to be restored by grace which can lead it on to perfect communion with God.[183]

(iii) One Body Having Christ as Head

The monks are members of Christ, and their community is his body. Souls are united and find concord and peace in him. The Holy Spirit distributes gifts in abundance and thereby maintains the life of the community. Every spiritual gift goes with a charge or an office which the gift should fulfil. The charge of the superior implies a special gift for commanding and ordering. Love of the brethren brings fulfilment of all the duties of the community. It is shown by good example, by prayer, by the work of our hands, by teaching or by hospitality. It cares for the sick, for travellers, for orphans. All this is a way of fulfilling the command to love the brethern. Common life is the core of Basil's message. Men must live together in no superficial way, but by sharing in a common love. Only in the community can one avoid the dangers of the solitary life and practise brotherly love and true humility. Only here can one grow towards fullness of love and life in the Holy Spirit. The health of the monastery depends upon the proper use and co-ordination of the many gifts which the Spirit has given. The second commandment, like all God's law, simply cultivates and grows the innate abilities which are planted in us like seeds. 'Who does not know that man is a tame and sociable animal, and not a solitary and fierce one? For nothing is so characteristic of our nature as to associate with one another, to need one another, and to love our kind.'[184] The implanted seed of love must grow as must the love of God which is implanted by the Holy Spirit. The intention of man is there, but the achievement of such love is only possible through rigorous discipline and painful obedience. The unity of Christians in the body of Christ is a unity of love. Christ loves and gives, Christ receives and is loved. The spiritual union of Christ with believers is the basis of the love of the brethren.[185]

The community must still have its rules. To avoid disorder there must be a way to bring disputes before the brotherhood or the superior.[186] The idle man must either be brought to diligence or treated as a persistent sinner.[187] Through the common life the individual is able to recognise and overcome his sins.[188] Basil reformed but did not abandon the system of Pachomius. Basil's scheme is more humane and more intimate than the earlier form of community life. He also sees an important place for the community of monks in the life of the whole church, which should be ordered like a community.[189]

Basil declares his work to be that of restoring the laws of ancient love and the peace of the fathers.[190] The 'brotherhood' is another name for the church.[191] He speaks of 'the good old times when God's churches flourished, rooted in faith, united in love, all the members being in harmony, as though in one body'. Then Christians were truly at peace and the loss of this peace is the saddest feature of his day.[192] The first Christians shared a common life, common thoughts and sentiments and ate from one table. They showed brotherhood without division and love without pretence. They were one body in outward solidarity, and in inward unity. For Basil the monastic community is a renewing of the primitive church of Jerusalem. The need is sadly urgent. Love is cold, 'brotherly agreement is destroyed, the very name of unity is ignored, brotherly advice is heard no more, nowhere is there Christian pity, nowhere falls the tear of sympathy.' Christians have no concern for one another and are worse than animals who at least herd together. 'But our most savage warfare is with our own people.'[193]

The whole of Basil's moral teaching is drawn together by his account of love. 'For Basil charity is the first of the virtues, and the monastic life has only one end— charity and union with God.'[194] The first and great commandment is to love God, the second is to love one's neighbour,[195] and a proof of our love for God and for his Son is that we keep his commandments. These we keep even to death, bearing all suffering and tribulation for love of him.[196] The love of God moves us to fulfil his commandments. Basil explains how this works, the love of God is implanted in our souls and it responds to the need of our hearts. The first motive which inspires us to love God is God's unspeakable beauty. The second reason is that we are rational creatures and are therefore obliged to love a creator who is infinitely good. The third reason is the consideration of the many blessings we have received from God.

God has ordered the whole creation for the benefit of men. He made man in his image and when man fell he did not desert the human race. Through the old and new dispensations he has loved man and wrought man's redemption, through Jesus. We are moved also by the fear that we might neglect the love of God and of Christ, and so give to the devil the opportunity to triumph on our account at the terrible day of judgment.[197]

Basil's ethics are of permanent value. As an account of Christian living they possess clarity and imagination. He is sensitive to later Platonism; but the most ardent index-maker could hardly deny his main impulse to the New Testament. As the first expositor of the ascetic way he illuminates the subsequent course of Christianity. His account of justice shows tendencies to legalism. He is fond of rules and prolific in producing them. His rigorism runs to literalism. His greater righteousness involves keeping rules more carefully; yet there is a strong strain of individualism and an extended plea for freedom as essential to morals. He is an advocate of natural law and sees beauty in natural order; yet he pleads for violence and excess in storming the kingdom. His chief danger would seem to lie in the ascetic extremes. Clement's right use of the world and care of the body for the good of the soul have both disappeared. The body is whipped or starved, not tended. The path of renunciation is so demanding that it can easily become an end in itself. Basil is aware of this danger and declares no other end than the glory of God. The opposite tendency to mystic contemplation is not far away. Origen had shown the way and Basil is ever ready to follow. Yet the sheer mass of practical prescription and the prevalence of the theme of following maintain the sovereignty of the Lord over his disciple. Faith is tied to creed, firm and exact. Yet Basil has even more to say on the faith that trusts through adversity 'trusting most in God when we need him most'. Freedom never becomes licence. Love is certainly threatened by fraternal duties but these also form a check against vague sentiment. The notion of reward supplants sovereign grace. He who gives to the afflicted gives to the Lord and will be rewarded by the Lord. The common life springs from enthusiasm.

In each section there is tension and sensitivity. The great retreat lies in the attitude to the physical world. Basil could enjoy natural beauty when its quietness soothed him; but he could not see how the way of righteousness might be trodden by body and soul together or how the path of discipleship could lead into the world of people and daily work. Work was a curse on man consequent to the Fall.

Basil poses two insoluble problems. First, there is the question of a double standard for monk and layman. In fact there was a single standard but only the monk could achieve it. Basil meant to unify Christian morality so this point has to be handled very carefully. The asceticism of the monk was simply the continuation of the life of every believer. 'The monk is the authentic and courageous Christian who strains to live out his Christianity to the full, and to practise with greater fidelity all the virtues of the Gospel.' Basil did not want to put a barrier between the simple believer and the monk nor to divide Christian ethics into two parts. 'There is only one morality, that of the Gospel. But only the monastic life in community reaches the perfection, . . . of the ideal of the Gospel.'[198] At the same time Basil expected an élite, a Christian nobility,[199] and he could not tolerate mediocrity. As an enthusiast, he wanted the fresh movement of the Spirit to stir a sluggish church. When, by placing asceticism in the centre of the church, he made a double standard inevitable, it was the opposite of his desire. History does not give men unlimited choice. Clement had to choose between a closed fatalist amoral élitism and an open, ethical élitist optimism of grace. Basil had to choose between an élite estranged from the church and an élite within one community and one gospel.

The evidence remains ambiguous. Christianity cannot approve a plurality of moral standards. Yet from early days there was a distinction between a path of perfection and a lower way. This distinction between 'precepts' and 'counsels' existed in the second century and the *Didache* described two ways.[200] Yet the opposition to Gnosticism maintained the perfection of baptismal faith and denied the predetermined categories of spiritual and carnal Christians; the passing of the Gnostic threat made it easier for later writers like Ambrose to distinguish clearly precepts and counsels. 'Every duty is either ordinary or perfect.'[201] Porphyry had used the customary distinction between the philosopher and the common herd. Things are permitted to the many which are not permitted to the best of men. The philosopher follows divine laws.[202] Whenever Christianity drew on the philosophic ideal, as it did in Clement and Basil, some trace of this distinction lingered on.[203]

Basil remains unclear at this point because as an enthusiast he put no limits on the spread of perfection. He wanted the whole church to follow the way the monks had shown.[204] The transformed life of those few who follow the one way of Christ is the best way to preach and to change the world.[205] He never saw the monks as an enclosed order; they were the beginning of a reformation for the whole church.[206] So Basil deliberately tried to discard the two ways or double standard of Christian living. Too many Christians chose the easy way, selecting the convenient commandments. Basil demanded total renunciation and total obedience for all who would enter the kingdom. Did this mean that all should be monks? No, but it would be very difficult for those who live in the wrong environment. Speaking carefully he says it will be most difficult, not to say wholly impossible.[207] When less careful he claims that pleasing God[208] is impossible for one surrounded by the distractions of the world. There is some distinction between the three great demands.[209] Obedience and poverty are required of all. Poverty means the dedication of one's wealth, not necessarily ceasing to be its legal owner. Chastity in the sense of celibacy or married abstinence is put forward as good but not obligatory; but Basil continues to regard his disciples as a celibate élite.[210] The general conclusion remains that, in opposition to sectarian asceticism, Basil directed his teaching to the church as a whole; but on this point it is better to understand his inconsistency than to fight for his consistency.

However much we may admire the spirit and heroism of Basil and the early ascetics, we should remember that their contribution was neither distinctively Christian nor ultimately harmless. Asceticism was everywhere. The community at Qumran was strangely similar to that of Basil in spite of their separation in time and space. The harmful aspects of asceticism are important because 'much in the traditional ascetic disciplines is morally objectionable at just the points where it is not true to Christian theism'.[211]

This points to a second insoluble problem: the right assessment of asceticism in general and monasticism in particular. It is wise to see Basil in his historical setting where he stands as a moderator, and reformer. There is an ascetic tendency in most virtue. 'What has the man of virtue learnt?' asks a modern philosopher; 'He has learnt to conquer the obscuring effects of passion upon his judgements of good and evil.'[212] It is unlikely that we might achieve an assessment of final praise or blame in the matter. There can be general agreement that Basil, by largeness of mind and sensitivity of spirit, gave to the ascetic movement a tendency which lifted and held it higher.[213] On the negative side, critics of the monastic movement will find many unhappy elements in its varied development. One unbalanced verdict ran: 'A hideous, sordid, and emaciated maniac, without knowledge, without patriotism, without natural affection, passing his life in a long routine of useless and atrocious self-torture, and quailing before the ghastly phantoms of his delirious brain, had become the ideal of the nations which had known the writings of Plato and Cicero and the lives of Socrates and Cato.'[214] Historians are never kind to enthusiasts and the monks have been blamed for disrupting the unity of the church and for ensuring the later triumph of Islam.[215] Christian asceticism has long been an object of 'widespread and constant moral repugnance'.[216]

But an equally forceful statement may be found on the opposing side. Basil shaped Christian asceticism which in turn shaped later Christian morals. The originality of the life of faith was 'its reverence for the lowly, for sorrow, suffering, and death, together with its triumphant victory over these contradictions of human life'.[217]

In his moral theology of the cross,[218] we may find 'the root of the most profound factor contributed by Christianity to the development of the moral sense, and contributed with perfect strength and delicacy'.[219] Later centuries were to go wrong as this insight changed into 'an aesthetic of spiritual agony and raptures over suffering'. There had always been some tendency of this kind. 'Yet, however strongly we feel about the unsightly phlegm of this corruption, and however indignantly we condemn it, we should never forget that it represented the shadow thrown by the most profound and at the same time the most heroic mood of the human soul in its spiritual exaltation; it is, in fact, religion itself, fully ripe.'[220] This is too much. Ripeness and consistency were not to be found in Basil. But he saw clearly where it should all lead: through the desert, to God. For Basil as for the New Testament, ethics point beyond themselves to religion and finally to God, 'das Wunder in den Wüsten, das Ausgewanderten geschieht'.[221]

Notes

[1] The following abbreviations will be used in this chapter: *M.=Moralia; L.R.=Longer Rules; S.R.=Shorter Rules; Ep.=Letter; H.=Hexaemeron; S.=On the Spirit.* The first three works are quoted with some modifications from the translations of W. K. L. Clarke, *The Ascetic Works of Saint Basil* (London, 1925). See also the translation of B. Jackson (Oxford, 1845).

[2] 'For the first time, the hospital, the almshouse, and school become regular adjuncts of a monastic settlement.' K. E. Kirk, *The Vision of God* (London, 1932), p. 266. See for extended treatment, S. Giet, *Les idées sociales de S. Basile* (Paris, 1941).

[3] Sasima. See S. Giet, *Sasimes* (Paris, 1941).

[4] See Gregory Nazianzus, *Oration* 20; Gregory of Nyssa, *Funeral Oration, Life of St Macrina;* Ephraem Syrus, *Encomium on Basil the Great;* Socrates, *H.E.* 4.26; Sozomen, *H.E.* 6.15-17; Jerome, *De vir. illust.,* 116; *Dictionary of Christian Biography, in loc.*

[5] *Ep.* 159.2.

[6] See J. Gribomont, 'Les règles morales de S. Basile et le NT', *Studia Patristica* 11 (Berlin, 1957), 417ff.

[7] *L.R.* 7.

[8] *On the Judgement of God,* 214E. For 'king' bees compare Ambrose, *Hex.* 5.21.68, and Seneca, *De Clem.* 1.19.2. Dr A. Lenox-Conyngham has drawn my attention to these parallel references.

[9] *H.* 9.5.

[10] *Ep.* 13.

[11] K. Holl comments, 'Eine merkwürdige Mischung kindlicher Einfalt und heiligen Ernstes ist die Signatur des griechischen Christentums in seinen liebenswürdigsten Vertretern, ein naiver Sinn und eine abgeschlossene Stimmung, die uns immer zugleich an die Jugendzeit des Christentums und an das Sterbegefühl der alten Völker erinnern', p. 282, *Ueber das griechische Mönchtum, Ges. Aufsätze* 11 (Tübingen, 1928).

[12] *M.* 80.22.318C.

[13] *Ep.* 22.

[14] *S.R.* 51. For the general point, see S. Giet, 'Le rigorisme de S. Basile'. *Revue des Sciences Religieuses* 23, (1949), 333-42, and also D. Amand, *L'ascèse monastique de S. Basile* (Maredsous, 1948), pp. 164-75.

[15] *S.R.* 7.

[16] *S.R.* 9.

[17] *S.R.* 10.

[18] *S.R.* 14.

[19] *S.R.* 18.

[20] *S.R.* 32.

[21] *S.R.* 23.

[22] *S.R.* 281.

[23] *Ep.* 54.

[24] *Ep.* 92.2.

[25] *L.R.* Preface 328 and 329.

[26] *L.R.* Preface 329 and 330.

[27] *Ep.* 150.3.

[28] *Ep.* 174.

[29] *Ep.* 42.4.

[30] *Ep.* 188, *Ep.* 199, *Ep.* 217.

[31] *L.R.* 23.

[32] *S.R.* 158.

[33] *L.R.* 10.

[34] *L.R.* 25.

[35] *L.R.* 52.

[36] *L.R.* 55.

[37] *S.R.* 46-7.

[38] *S.R.* 64.

[39] *S.R.* 69.

[40] *S.R.* 71.

[41] *S.R.* 81.

[42] *On the Judgement of God,* 214.

[43] *L.R.* 28.

[44] *Ep.* 2.6 and *Ep.* 6.2.

[45] *S.R.* 91 and 126.

[46] *Ep.* 14.

[47] On usury, see *Hom. on Psalm 14* and *Hom. on avarice.*

[48] *H.* 5.7.

[49] *H.* 7.3.

[50] *H.* 7.4.

[51] *H.* 8.1.

[52] *H.* 8.5.

[53] *H.* 9.2.

[54] *H.* 9.3.

[55] *On Abstinence,* 3.11.

[56] *To the young,* 9(7).

[57] *M.* 2.

[58] *M.* 4.

[59] *M.* 7.

[60] *M. 16* and *M.* 18.

[61] *M.* 41.

[62] *S.R.* 237.

[63] *L.R.* 8.348f.

[64] *L.R.* 8.349.

[65] *L.R.* 8.350.

[66] *Ep.* 206.

[67] *Ep.* 243.4.

[68] *Ep.* 257.1.

[69] *Preliminary sketch of the ascetic life,* 200A.

[70] *Ep.* 252: 'the bond, as it were, of blood which binds the life of strict discipline to those perfected through endurance'.

[71] *S.R.* 211.

[72] *L.R.* 37.383f.

[73] *L.R.* 55.401.

[74] *S.R.* 201.

[75] *Hom. on Psalm 1.3* Sec S. Giet, *Les idées sociales de S. Basile* (Paris, 1941), pp. 71-5.

[76] When all has been said of hospitals and school, the monk's chief work was to 'take heed to himself'. 'Von der Erkenntnis aus, dass die sittliche Aufgabe in der Vollendung der eigenen Persönlichkeit besteht, ist das Mönchtum zu einer intensiven Selbstbeobachtung geführt worden': K. Holl, *Ueber das griechische Mönchtum, Ges. Aufsätze,* II (Tübingen, 1928), p. 277.

[77] *Ep.* 2.2.

[78] *Ep.* 2.4.

[79] *Ep.* 8.12.

[80] *Ep.* 14. H. von Campenhausen comments, 'Anyone who is able to enjoy solitude to that extent cannot expect it to last forever', *The Fathers of the Greek Church* (London, 1963), p. 89.

[81] *L.R.* Preface 327.

[82] *L.R.* 2.339.

[83] *L.R.* 4.341.

[84] *L.R.* 5.341.

[85] *L.R.* 6.344.

[86] *L.R.* 8.348f.

[87] *M.* 55.

[88] *M.* 80.

[89] For the closely-woven Platonism of Basil's thought, there is no better summary than the account of his ethical outlook in the *Homilies on the Psalms,* given by A. Benito y Duran, 'Filosofía de san Basilio Magno', *Studia Patristica,* v, *Texte and Untersuchungen* 80 (Berlin, 1962).

[90] *S.* 1.2.

[91] *S.* 15.35.

[92] *H.* 9.6.

[93] Basil remains sensitive to social relationships. A strong case has been made out for his social concerns, by S. Giet, *Les idées sociales de S. Basile*; but a concluding reference to Basil's 'inlassable et géniale activité' (p. 425) overstates the case.

[94] T. Spidlik, *La sophiologie de S. Basile* (Rome, 1961), pp. 24f.

[95] A. Dirking, 'Die Bedeutung des Wortes Apathie beim heiligen Basilius dem Grossen', *Theolisches Quartalschrift,* 134 (1954), 211f.

[96] M. Viller and K. Rahner, *Aszese und Mystik in der Väterzeit* (Freiburg, 1939), p. 127.

[97] *S.R.* 43.

[98] *S.R.* 44.

[99] *S.R.* 90.

[100] *L.R.* 16.358.

[101] *L.R.* 17.

[102] *L.R.* 17.360.

[103] *L.R.* 18.362.

[104] *L.R.* 17.361. Amand, *L'ascèse monastique de S. Basile*, p. 201f.

[105] Amand, *op. cit.,* pp.318-35.

[106] *Ibid.* pp. 212-42.

[107] *L.R.* 32.375.

[108] Amand, *L'ascèse monastique de S. Basile,* p. 242ff.

[109] H. Dehnard, *Das Problem der Abhängigkeit des Basilius von Plotin* (Berlin, 1964), examines common expressions in Basil and Plotinus. The similarities between Plotinus, Origen and Gregory are due to a common philosophical tradition (p. 31). In *De Spiritu*, Basil has drawn on Plotinus' metaphysical formulae to complete Gregory's account of the Spirit and uses Plotinus' account of the world soul to describe the activity of the Spirit; there is no evidence of any real influence of Plotinus. Basil uses the common terms because they are the best he can find (p. 87). Dehnard can find no trace of any dependence of Basil on Porphyry (p. 88)! D. Amand, *op. cit.,* pp. 351-64, shows that Basil has taken over the metaphysical dualism of later Platonism. The extent of Basil's debt to later classical thought has been the subject of discussion. Courtonne shows that his debt to classical literature is not great; Y. Courtonne, *S. Basile et l'hellénisme* (Paris, 1934).

[110] Hom. *That God is not the author of evils, passim.*

[111] *Ibid.* 5.

[112] See L. Vischer, *Basilius der Grosse, Untersuchungen zu einem Kirchenvater des 4. Jahrhunderts* (Basel, 1953), pp. 29-38.

[113] See A. J. Festugière, *La révélation d'Hermès trismégiste,* II (Paris, 1949), x ff.

[114] *Republic* 530.

[115] Plotinus, *Enneads,* VI.9.9-11.

[116] *On Abstinence,* 1.33-5.

[117] *Ibid.* 1.36.

[118] *Ibid.* 1.54.

[119] *Ibid.* 2.33.

[120] *To the young,* 7(5).

[121] *Ibid.* 9(7).

[122] Nevertheless, it remains true that 'Neither Christians nor Platonists, if they are to be faithful to their deepest convictions, can simply be negative in their attitude to the body and the world, regarding them as wholly evil and alien. Their fundamental belief that the material world, with all that is in it, is good, and made by a good power simply because of his goodness, prevents them from becoming Gnostics or Manichees': A. H. Armstrong, *St. Augustine and Christian Platonism* (Villanova University Press, 1967), p. 10.

[123] *To the young,* 9(7).

[124] A. von Harnack, *Mission and Expansion* (ET, London, 2 ed. 1908) 2, 215.

[125] J. Gribomont, 'Le renoncement au monde dans l'idéal ascétique de S. Basile', *Irénikon* (1958), pp. 282-307 and 460-75, esp. p. 298.

[126] *L.R.* 8.

[127] 'Because of the weakness of the flesh which enfolds us', *Hom. on Psalm 33*.11.

[128] *Hom. on Psalm 29*.6.

[129] *Hom. on Psalm 1*.3.

[130] *Hom. on Psalm 29*.4.

[131] *De Fide* and Preface to *S.R.*

[132] *On the Judgement of God*, 223C.

[133] *Ep.* 2.3.

[134] *S.* 10.26.

[135] *S.* 12.28.

[136] *S.* 18. For additional comment on true faith, see Vischer, *Basilius der Grosse*, pp. 66-72.

[137] *Ep.* 175.

[138] See also J. Gribomont, *L'Origénisme de S. Basile, L'homme devant Dieu, Mélanges offerts à H. de Lubac* (Paris, 1963), 1,294, 'Des héritiers d'Origène le plus discret est Basile.' Thanks to Basil's discretion, the influence of Origen lived on, 'ramenée à l'essentiel et décantée'.

[139] *Against Eunomius*, 1.12.

[140] *Homily on the Martyr Mamas* 4. See Vischer, *Basilius der Grosse*, pp. 89f., for the contrast with Origen's unrelenting enquiry.

[141] *Ep.* 28.3.

[142] *Ep.* 125.

[143] *M.* 8.

[144] *M.* 12.

[145] *M.* 39.

[146] *M.* 80.

[147] *H.* 9.6.

[148] *Ep.* 123.

[149] *Ep.* 140.1.

[150] *Ep.* 174.

[151] *Ep.* 240.2.

[152] Morison points out that Basil does not describe his monk as a philosopher: *St. Basil and his Rule, A Study in Early Monasticism* (Oxford, 1912), p. 35; but the influence of the idea is clear.

[153] *M.* 57.

[154] *L.R.* 21.

[155] *L.R.* 22.

[156] *L.R.* 35.

[157] *S.R.* 56.

[158] Amand *L'ascèse monastique de S. Basile*, pp. 312-18.

[159] *L.R.* 7.345-8.

[160] See Vischer, *Basilius der Grosse*, pp. 112-15, for a developed account of the following points.

[161] *L.R.* 13.

[162] *Ep.* 223.1.

[163] *Ep.* 9.3.

[164] Amand, *L'ascèse monastique de S. Basile*, pp. 146-51.

[165] Epictetus speaks similarly of self-determination: *Diss.* 2, 2, 3; 4, 1, 56; 4, 1, 62; 4, 1, 68; 4, 1, 100; see M. Spanneut, 'Epiktet', *RAC* 5, 642-5.

[166] Cf. Sextus Empiricus, *adv. math.* v; Origen, *Philocalia*, 23, 17.

[167] *H.* 6, 7. D. Amand, *Fatalisme et liberté dans l'antiquité grecque* (Louvain, 1945), chapter 8, pp. 383ff.

[168] *M.* 3. See, for example, Vischer, *Basilius der Grosse*, pp. 38f., on 'Die Motive des asketischen Lebens'.

[169] *L.R.* 2.336-7. See Amand, *L'ascèse monastique*, pp. 295ff.

[170] *L.R.* 2.338-40.

[171] Amand, *L'ascèse monastique*, p. 91.

[172] T. Spidlik, *La sophilogie de S. Basile* (Rome, 1961) pp. 24f.

[173] *M.* 5.

[174] *M.* 38.

[175] *M.* 49-50.

[176] 'God gave to those, who could not see one another in person, the great comfort of communication by letters', *Ep.* 220. See Vischer, *Basilius der Grosse*, p. 61, 'Ein grosser Teil der Korrespondenz des B. dient einzig dieser Absicht: Gemeinschaft herzustellen'.

[177] *Ep.* 9.1.

[178] *Ep.* 23.

[179] *Ep.* 43.

[180] *Ep.* 65.

[181] See J. Rivière, *S. Basile* (Paris, 1925), pp. 208-87. Also the comprehensive treatment of S. Giet, *Les idées sociales de S. Basile* (Paris, 1941), covers many aspects of the subject.

[182] *L.R.* 3.

[183] See G. M. Cossu, "Il motivo formale della carita in S. Basilio Magno', *Bollettino della Badia Greca di Grottaferrata* (1960), pp. 3-30, and 'L'amore naturale verso Dio e verso il prossimo', *ibid.* pp. 87-107.

[184] *L.R.* 3. Basil's reasons (*L.R.* 7) for the superiority of the cenobite over the anchorite are summarised by W. K. L. Clarke, *St. Basil the Great* (Cambridge, 1913), pp. 85f.: we are not self-sufficient in provision of bodily needs, solitude goes against the law of love, we need someone to correct our faults, we have duties to others, we are members one of another, we have different gifts, we are in danger of thinking that we have arrived at perfection.

[185] See D. M. Nothomb, 'Charité et unité', *Le Proche-Orient Chrétien*, 4 (1954), 321.

[186] *L.R.* 49.

[187] *S.R.* 61.

[188] *L.R.* 26, 28, 29: see Vischer, *Basilius der Grosse*, p. 44.

[189] Church and community react on one another: Vischer, *op. cit.*, p. 49, 'Er gestaltet die Kirche nach dem Bild des Klosters.'

[190] *Ep.* 70.

[191] *Ep.* 133; *Ep.* 255; *Ep.* 266.1. See Vischer, *op. cit.*, p. 54.

[192] In her persecutions, the church found true peace and real unity, *Ep.* 164.1. See Vischer, *op. cit.*, p. 53.

[193] *S.* 30.78.

[194] Amand, *L'ascèse monastique*, p. 295.

[195] *S.R.* 163.

[196] *M.* 3. 1-2.

[197] Amand, *L'ascèse monastique*, pp. 296-303.

[198] *Ibid.* pp. 12f.

[199] Cf. Jerome's commendation of a 'holy arrogance'. *Ep.* 22.16.

[200] *Didache* 6.

[201] *De officiis* 1.36.

[202] *On Abstinence* 4.18.

[203] That it was there is indicated by evidence brought against it in discussions of the early church. Basil could not, as a bishop, restrict perfection to monks, in the opinion of K. Holl (*Ueber das griechische Mönchtum*, p. 278). But Vischer comments, 'Dabei übersieht Holl jedoch, dass Basilius der Mcinung ist, die Kirche müsse nach dem Vorbild des Mönchtums gebildet werden' (*Basilius der Grosse,* p. 50). Reluctance to admit non-Christian elements in monasticism is typified by the comment of R. N. Flew, *The Idea of Perfection in Christian Theology* (Oxford, 1934), p. 159, 'The soil for the plant of monachism may have been prepared by many movements of the mind . . . but the seed itself is easily recognizable, and it is sown by those at work within the garden of the Church.' The same writer however, does not hesitate to say of Basil, 'It is clear that we have to do with the Stoic ideal of *apatheia*': p. 176.

[204] Vischer, *Basilius der Grosse,* p. 167.

[205] J. Gribomont, 'Le renoncement au monde', *Irénikon* (1958), p. 475.

[206] J. Gribomont, 'Les règles morales', p. 417. Gribomont goes on to describe the historical setting of Basil's rules in the conflict between Eustathian enthusiasm and the rest of the church, p. 423.

[207] *L.R.* 6.

[208] *S.R.* 263.

[209] See J. Gribomont, 'Le monachisme au IVe siècle en Asie-Mineure: de Gangres au Messalianisme', *Studia Patristica* II (Berlin, 1957), 400-15.

[210] *Ibid.* p. 413.

[211] D. Cupitt, *Crises of Moral Authority* (London, 1972), p. 47.

[212] G. H. von Wright, *The Varieties of Goodness* (London, 1963), p. 147.

[213] Amand, *Fatalisme et liberté,* p. 349, 'le grand réformateur du cénobitisme oriental'. W. K. L. Clarke summarises Basil's work as the organisation of asceticism, the moderation of austerities, the introduction of the common life and the bringing of monasticism into the service of the church. See *St. Basil the Great* (Cambridge, 1913), p. 115.

[214] W. E. H. Lecky, *History of European Morals* (1884), 2, 107.

[215] N. Zernov, *Eastern Christendom* (London, 1961), p. 80.

[216] D. Cupitt, *Crisis of Modern Authority,* p. 30.

[217] A. von Harnack, *Mission and Expansion,* I, 217.

[218] The centrality of the cross comes out most clearly in the final sections of *Morals.* The mark of a Christian is to be cleansed in the blood of Christ, to eat in memory of him who died, to live for him who died for them and to love as Christ loved: *Morals,* 72.22.

[219] Harnack, *Mission and Expansion,* p. 218.

[220] *Ibid.*

[221] R. M. Rilke, *Stundenbuch.*

Abbreviations

ABR Australian Biblical Review

ATR Anglican Theological Review

BHT Beiträge zur historischen Theologie

CQ Classical Quarterly

CR The Classical Review

CSEL Corpus Scriptorum Ecclesiasticorum Latinorum

DCB Dictionary of Christian Biography

DR Downside Review

GCS Die griechischen christlichen Schriftsteller

JBL Journal of Biblical Literature

JR The Journal of Religion

JTS Journal of Theological Studies

MSR Mélanges de Science Religieuse

NTS New Testament Studies

POC Le Proche-Orient Chrétien

RA Recherches augustiniennes

RAC Reallexikon für Antike und Christentum

RAM Revue d'Ascétique et Mystique

RB Revue Biblique

REA Revue des Études Augustiniennes

REG Revue des Études Grecques

RHPR Revue d'Histoire et Philosophie Religieuses

RP Historia Philosophiae Graecae, H. Ritter et L. Preller (8th edition, 1898)

RSR Recherches de Science Religieuse.

RevSR Revue des Sciences Religieuses

SA Studia Anselmiana

SC Sources Chrétiennes

SVF Stoicorum Veterum Fragmenta, von Arnim

TU Texte und Untersuchungen

TWNT Theologisches Wörterbuch zum Neuen Testament, Kittel

VC Vigiliae Christianae

ZAM Zeitschrift für Aszese und Mystik

ZNW Zeitschrift für die Neutestamentliche Wissenschaft

Paul Jonathan Fedwick (essay date 1979)

SOURCE: "The Church in the Life and Works of Basil of Caesarea" in *The Church and the Charisma of Leadership in Basil of Caesarea,* Pontifical Institute of Medieval Studies, 1979, pp. 1-201.

[*In the following excerpt, Fedwick explains Basil's concept of the church as a community of believers drawn together by love of God and each other, and spiritually secluded from those who reject the teachings of Christ. The critic traces the expressions of this idea in Basil's ascetic writings, in the treatises* Against Eunomius *and* On the Holy Spirit, *and in several of the homilies.*]

The term by which Basil of Caesarea most commonly addresses the communities of Christians is "church," "churches of God."[1] Obviously referred to are not simply liturgical gatherings but established bodies of Christians living in a locality.[2] It would be inappropriate to ask whether Basil employs the term [*Ekhanoia*] with reference to the universal or local church. Throughout his writings the bishop of Caesarea shows no awareness of such a distinction as every local body is for him but the manifestation of a universal reality—the reality of being reached and grasped at a certain point of time by the saving action of God the Father acting for man's sake through the Son in the Holy Spirit.[3] The church is the body of Christ and the fellowship of the Spirit.[4] As the work of God, the Almighty, the church cannot be confined to one people, culture, or social order. Neither can it be circumscribed spatially.[5] By its very essence, the church provides the place and opportunity for humans to rediscover their common nature,[6] so that those who were before their calling opposed to each other because of social, cultural or national differences might become "through the instrumentality of the church habituated to each other in love."[7] Consequently, the end of the Christian church and the general end of human existence converge: both consist in being totally possessed and ruled by God.[8]

Basil first experienced the church in the bosom of his religious family. Although in his panegyric Gregory of Nazianzus speaks foremost of the cultural and intellectual upbringing of the future leader of the church of Caesarea, Basil himself, in recalling his childhood, maintains an eloquent silence on the matter. He acquaints us instead with his early contacts with religion in its various applied forms. The fullness of assurance that Scripture and tradition are of equal weight and authority in the establishment of orthodoxy, which echoes throughout Basil's writings, seems to have originated from his domestic experience.[9] Whereas from his parents Basil and Emmelia, Basil learned "from infancy the Holy Scriptures," Macrina, his grandmother, was the link for his acquaintance with an evolved (spiritual rather than speculative) form of Origenism, embodied since the time of Gregory Thaumaturgus in the liturgical tradition of the church of Neocaesarea.[10] There can be little doubt that Basil became first acquainted with the "words and sayings" of Gregory before he knew anything about the symbol of Nicaea.[11] One of the fundamental principles of Neocaesarean theology, the radical distinction between creator and creature, lord and servant, will later find wide application in Basil's controversy with the Arians (Son as the intermediate hypostasis), Anomoeans (unlikeness of Father and Son), and the Pneumatomachi (creaturehood of the Son and of the Holy Spirit).[12]

Another distinctive characteristic acquired by Basil early in his life was a strong awareness of the Christian faith as a holocaust not only of human freedom but also, whenever necessary, of human life.[13] Macrina and her husband, it is known, barely managed to escape the persecution of the second Maximinus.[14] The narrative of the severe hardships, the long wanderings of his ancestors through the wilderness of Pontus, put Basil from the beginning in contact with a church of martyrs, a church founded on the blood of Christ and that of many of his followers.[15]

If one may assume that the church of Neocaesarea was at the time under the influence of Eustathian asceticism, Basil must also have perceived a continuity between the family type of religion as practiced in his household and the religion of the ascetics living in communities nearby the urban churches.[16] This experience further establishes in his consciousness the close link and even total inseparability of Christian life and ascetic practice which we find prominently represented in his early writings.

Outside the family environment there was another aspect of the church which Basil was soon destined to discover and which was to fill his heart not only with sorrow and grief but also with the desire to correct it later in life. The fellowship that claimed apostolic origin and martyrdom within its ranks was to reveal itself also as a community of sinners whose members hindered its expansion rather than contributed to its growth.[17] His own words in the first preface to the *Moralia* seem to indicate the uneasiness he experienced from having become acquainted during his travels abroad with the state of many churches strongly divided against each other:

> Seeing a great and exceeding discord on the part of many men both in their relations with one another and their views about the divine Scripture, . . . and what was most horrible of all, its very leaders differing so much from one another in sentiment and opinion and wondering, moreover, what and whence was the cause of so great an evil, first of all I lived as it were in profound darkness and was inclining, as it were on scales, first in this direction and then in that. Now one man would attract me, now another.[18]

That Basil did not let this negative dimension prevail over his consciousness we find evidenced in his early decision to give up a promising career as a sophist-rhetorician, and in his rejection of the eremitic type of asceticism on grounds that it does not serve the common interests of Christians but tends to separate one individual from the other, thus aggravating even more the dissension in the churches.

As we shall see Basil's full support and further elaboration of the communal type of asceticism was aimed at healing the church's wounds caused by internal divisions.

After these preliminary remarks based mostly on Basil's own recollections and those of others regarding his first experiences of the church, we will now briefly review some of his writings. We shall consider only those in which some reference is made to the church and its ministerial structure. Because of the uncertainty surrounding the exact chronology of Basil's writings, we can review them here in only an approximate order.

A. *Contra Eunomium* 1 - 3

One of the earliest writings to be considered in which the term "church" occurs is the *Against Eunomius*, Books 1 - 3, written *ca.* 364.[19] The overall plan of the work is to refute Eunomius' attempt to couch Christian truths in Aristotelian categories and to expose the danger which might follow for Christians from the encroachment of philosophical ideas upon the "simplicity" of expression of their ecclesiastical faith.[20] Prior to writing his apologies, Basil had taken part in a public debate with the Semi-Arians at the Council of Constantinople in January of 360, but apparently without attracting much attention. Thus the treatises against Eunomius constitute his first major contribution to the defence of orthodox Christianity. The rationale for writing the refutation was to protect the faith of those members of the orthodox community who were unskilled ("weak") in Arian sophistries.

What emerges from the opening paragraphs of the first apology against Eunomius is Basil's awareness of a church founded on the "simplicity" . . . of the evangelical witness and the apostolic traditions.[21] By emphasizing simplicity Basil shows opposition to any "private" reelaboration or restatement of the ecclesiastical formulae handed down by past generations. He is not so much opposed to knowledge as to the arrogance and self-sufficiency that a man like Eunomius exhibits by calling into question the viability of past formulae and by trying to replace them with some of his own.[22] Also salient throughout Basil's treatises is a strong consciousness of the centrality of the person of Christ in the economy of salvation. Only through Christ is there access to true knowledge.[23] People who do not believe in the divinity of Christ are, as it were, dead and nonexistent. . . . [24]

Very characteristic of Basil's understanding of the church's role in establishing the truth is the inclusion of past authorities in the apologies.[25] The use of authorities is most conspicuous in the third book, in which the main thesis that the Spirit is not a creature is entirely drawn from liturgical evidence.[26]

B. *The Theme of the Church and its Charismatic Structure in the Homilies*

The hearers of Basil's homilies belonged to varied classes and occupations, with the poor class predominating. Among the people attending his sermons were architects, builders, merchants, husbandmen, soldiers, probably members of the clergy, and also ascetics of the family and communal type.[27] The catechumens seem to have constituted the majority of church members at the time belonging to all of the aforementioned walks of life with the exception of the clergy and the ascetics. Thus, most of Basil's homilies can be interpreted as exhortations to baptism and thereby the acceptance of the ascetic life.

Indeed, "Homily 11," chronologically the first of those to be reviewed here, deals with the subject of envy. It was probably in replying to an outbreak of jealousy that Basil made an excursus on the charismatic structure of the church. Some of his colleagues—the custom then being that several preachers addressed the public on a single occasion—or perhaps some members of the congregation, coveted his charisma of brilliant eloquence. At any rate, the point was made by Basil that neither natural endowments, nor riches, nor strength, nor power are ends in themselves but instruments . . . of virtue.[28] They only provide blessedness if used for the purpose of serving the neighbours. Particularly practical wisdom . . . and the competence to interpret the words of God are devices and charismata of the Holy Spirit given for the good of others.

> It is your good, and it is for your sake that your brother was endowed with the gift of teaching, if only you are willing to accept it. . . . Why then do you refuse to lend your ears gladly to the spiritual word so profuse in the church, and gushing forth like a river from the pious heart filled with the charismata of the Spirit? Why do you not with gratitude take advantage of the benefits?[29]

Per se charismata are instruments intended more for the good of others than the one possessing them.[30] The lesson for the church conveyed in this incidental remark is that, like material possessions, spiritual gifts are also to be regarded not as a privategood but as the common property of all.

"Homily 13" hinges upon the instrumentality of the *logos* as a means of communication and discipleship among people.[31] Basil speaks with approval of the exercise of the various crafts . . . in the church. These crafts, whose introduction is elsewhere attributed to the period after the Fall, are highly regarded as outstanding achievements of the human *logos*.[32] Despite their characteristic of being not "us" or "ours" but things "around us," they are used by Basil as incentives to cheer up the poor and destitute.[33] They should, however, be put in the perspective of the gospel requirements. Basil feels that each disciple of the *logos* is a minister in charge of one of the activities . . . demanded by the gospel.

> In the great house, which is the church, there are not only vessels of every kind—golden and silver, of wood and earthenware—but also manifold crafts. Indeed the house of God, that is, the church of the living God, houses hunters, travellers, architects, builders, husbandmen, shepherds, athletes, soldiers.[14]

Basil then proceeds to attribute a higher meaning to each of these occupations, interpreting them symbolically, as significant of higher mysteries.[35]

The theme of the church as a house is developed also in the **"Homily on Psalm 29."** The church is the new house of David, built by Christ. "The renovation of the church must be understood as the renewal of the mind, which takes place through the Holy Spirit in each, individually, of those who complete . . . the body of the church of Christ."[36] Again, the **"Homily on Psalm 48"** represents the church as housing people of all walks and pursuits of life "in order that no one may be left without its aid."[37] Through the kerygma of the Holy Spirit people of all races and cultures are called to fill its ranks. The church's function in history is described as that of leveling all differences of racial and cultural background or origin. There is one common goal assigned to all: strive to be ruled by God.

In the **"Homily on Psalm 44"** the church is treated within a christological perspective. The homily relates the words of the psalm to the various aspects of Christ's divinity and humanity: Christ the Word of the Father (393A), Christ the Man anointed by the Spirit (405A), Christ Man and the church, his body (397C), the preaching and the preachers of the gospel (396C; 401A). According to this homily, every believer is a member of the body of Christ.[38] The church is the only perfect dove of Christ "which admits to the right hand . . . of Christ those who are conspicuous by their good works, discerning them from the evil ones, as a shepherd discerns the sheep from the goats."[39] Then the preacher proceeds to talk about the soul not subject to sin whom he calls queen and bride standing at the right hand of the "bridal Word."[40] "As the doctrines are not of one kind but variegated and manifold, comprising moral, natural and mystical sayings . . . , Scripture . . . declares that the garment of the bride is variegated."[41]

Returning again to the church, Basil refers to it by the names bride of Christ and daughter of the King, adopted through love.[42] Through the words of the psalmist, God summons the church to abjure its former parent who begot it for destruction, to reject the teachings of the demons and instead to apply itself to the study and observance of the commandments. Through love for God the church becomes his daughter.[43] Only after the

church's mind . . . has been purified of evil teachings and its natural pride overcome through obedience to the humble account of the gospel does it acquire a mind capable of ascending . . . from contemplation . . . of the visible order to recognition of its Creator.[44] Although he ascribes to the church many of the attributes of Christ the Man, Basil maintains that not the church, but Christ its head is the object of Christian worship. . . . [45]

The church is not only endowed with words but also with many deeds, and therefore it is capable of bringing virgins to the King, but only virgins that keep close to the bride of the King and "do not deflect from the ecclesiastical discipline. . . ."[46] In the context of the church generated through the proclamation of the gospel, Basil regards the Old Testament patriarchs as the fathers of the church "because for them through Christ were born children doing the works of Abraham."[47] At the end of this long exposition Basil invites his hearers to ponder the greatness of the authority . . . of the church in constituting . . . and ordaining . . . princes all over the earth, that is, saints.[48] For them all the church, the bride of Christ, is a mother, whom all people remember through their confession of benefits and thanksgiving. . . .[49]

In the **"Homilies on Psalm 45 and 59,"** Basil applies to the church the Stoic notion of the city, "an established community . . . , administered . . . according to law."[50] However, the church is a city only of a special kind, that is, "fortified by the faith encompassing it," and a dwelling "made joyful by the inflowing of the Holy Spirit."[51] The notion of the Greek *polis* is applied both to the historical and eschatological community.[52] The latter is in a certain sense identified with the "church of those who [here on earth] have their conversation in heaven."[53]

The **"Homily on Psalm 59"** brings out also the idea that to the tradition of the Christian church belong the books of the Old Testament which were actually written more with the purpose of serving the Christians ("those who accepted the change") than the Jews.[54]

According to the **"Homily on Psalm 28,"** although between the two Testaments there is a continuity of teaching, after the advent of Christ the church is the sole "holy court" where God should be adored and worshipped.[55] In the same homily the Jewish synagogue is called "parasynagogue"—illicit assembly.[56]

The **"Homily on Psalm 33"** presents the idea of Christians as children generated through apostolic preaching and ecclesiastical instructions; it speaks also of the bond of charity, peace and harmony binding together the stronger members to the weaker.[57]

The homilies on the **Hexaemeron,** delivered in a time of relative calm, probably 378, afford only incidental remarks. Their main concern is the "edification" of the hearers (the church) for whose spiritual benefit Basil presents an account of the origins of the universe based largely on the reading of the Genesis in the light of contemporary scientific ideas. More than popularizing philosophical theories, Basil's objective is to show that Moses' account of the origins of life in the universe is more trustworthy than that of all Greek philosophers. Already in the expositions of the Psalms we saw Basil crediting the church with the authority . . . to discern . . . between what is good and viable and what is evil and objectionable. The same is claimed here with regard to scientific knowledge. Only the church, and consequently only a Christian as a result of being delivered from sin and ignorance, has a mind . . . capable of knowing and deciding what cosmogonic account is genuine.

Many objections have been and perhaps could yet be raised regarding Basil's assumptions and treatment of science and its methods.[58] It should perhaps be remembered that science . . . for him more than for anyone else was not a neutral field, nor an independent body, but part of a larger, more general and fundamental world view which implied the acceptance or rejection of an ultimate cause.[59] Because, as he understood them, the philosophical speculations of the Greek intellectuals led a great many of them to the negation of God, Basil, in his **Hexaemeron,** tried to discredit them on that score in the eyes of his audience.[60] Naturally the image of the church conveyed by such polemic is not one of openness and dialogue with the world of scientists, but one that is by and large determined by claims of "ideological" superiority.[61]

C. The Church as the Community of Complete Christians in the Ascetic Writings

To appreciate fully Basil's contribution to the understanding of the church and the functions of its leaders, it is important to preface the analysis of his ascetic writings with an historical note.[62]

Beginning with the accession to power of Julian in 361, the milieu of the church changed. Until that moment, Christian religion, despite internal difficulties and struggles, enjoyed some recognition and assistance from the state. Under the auspices of the emperors who regarded themselves not only as heads of the state but also as "external bishops" of the church, that is, the supreme lawgivers and defenders of Christian public and private interests, it was natural for Basil to feel comfortable in his retreat in Pontus.[63] The peaceful coexistence between church and state, which had occasionally been somewhat strained in the past, was forcefully interrupted by Julian and was not to be restored completely until after the death of

Basil in 379. In his solitude Basil must soon have become aware of the change. **"Epistle 18"** encourages two young Christians living in the imperial court to persevere in their convictions. By the time Basil made his appearance in Caesarea in 362, the proposals of the emperor-philosopher for revitalizing the ancestral religion had already been made public.[64] Julian's reform posed a menacing challenge to the church. His religion, more than a revival of old beliefs, was a curious but also updated blend of Neoplatonic and Christian elements. Julian indeed "wanted to smite the Galileans with their own weapons, wanted to build up an organization of pagan clergy on the Christian pattern, wanted to train his priests on principles and for tasks which he had learned among the Christians."[65]

Basil must have been impressed with the careful selection and high moral standards demanded of the new hierarchy by the philosophizing emperor. In one of his letters addressed to the High Priest Theodore, Julian was also stressing the importance of the social aspect—something hitherto unheard of among pagans:

> The Jews do not allow any of their own people to become beggars, and the Christians support not only their own but also our poor; but we leave ours unhelped. . . . It is matters like this which have contributed most to the spread of Christianity: mercy to strangers, care for burying the dead, and the obvious honourableness of their conduct. . . . And the people must learn to give part of their possessions to others; to the better placed—generously, to the indigent and the poor—sufficient to ward off distress; and, strange though it sounds, to give food and clothing to one's enemies is a pious duty, for we give to men as men, not to particular persons.[66]

Whether or not Basil was in Caesarea at the time of Julian's reprisal-visit to that city in September of 362, the confiscation of church property, the subordination of the clergy to the military authority, and the burden of heavy taxes imposed on all Christians of Caesarea by the emperor must have made clear to Basil, as to any one else, that in order to survive the church needed a different kind of structure and arrangement that would make its well-being less dependent on the state.[67] The strengthening of internal unity and the autonomy of the bishops in the administering of its affairs had to be given priority.[68] If at the time Basil had come up with concrete plans and tried a solution, he did not succeed in putting his projects into practice. A conflict arose between him and the bishop Eusebius, and to avoid the threat of an internal schism Basil retreated to Pontus.[69] The reign of Julian, in any event, was short-lived.[70]

Whatever thoughts on the church and the functions of its leaders Basil might have had during his exile in Pontus, we see him busily engaged in the organization of ascetic communities. The corporate type of Christian life had definitively prevailed in his mind over the individual one. From the moment when in 365, with a visit of Valens imminent, Eusebius recalls him to Caesarea, Basil will be seen as uncompromisingly committed to the project of church reform on the pattern of the pre-Constantinian model or, better yet, of the apostolic community of Jerusalem.

The desire to strengthen the internal organization, the distinctiveness and self-sufficiency of the church as a society of its own is characteristic of Basil's activities displayed during the period 365-378. It would be easy perhaps simply to read his ascetic works from that period and draw conclusions from the material evidence.[71] The issue, however, becomes complicated from the moment when we firmly realize that Basil was above all an ascetic. In the fourth century there were various existing models of perfect Christian life. However impartial we may try to be in the analysis of Basil's writings concerned with his awareness of the church, conclusions will largely depend upon whether we make of him a tributary of the desert type of asceticism represented in its organized form by Pachomius, or of the urban version practiced under the instigation of Eustathius of Sebaste in the northern provinces of Asia Minor. Since the question of Basil's indebtedness to either of these two representatives of Christian asceticism in the fourth century has been long debated, and although the opinion of modern scholars tends somewhat to favour Eustathius' influence on Basil, because of its undeniable import we have tried to reopen this question in two Appendices placed at the end of this work.[72] The following discussion of the church as a community of complete Christians presupposes some of the results reached in our two Appendices, and the reader, if in doubt, would be well advised to become acquainted with them first.

As we mentioned earlier, during the period commencing in 362 Basil became an uncompromising advocate of the ecclesial type of asceticism. This asceticism in his original intention was to be developed not on the margins of the local churches but as a sequel to the sacrament of baptism. All Christians, independently of sex, race, social condition and even age, were, within their limits, to practise the ascetic life.[73] Whereas the form could vary, the quality of the desire to become similar to God, so far as this is humanly possible, was to be the same.[74]

Basil's thought on the corporate character of Christian perfection is developed mainly in his *Asceticons*.[75] His recommendation of the corporate type of sanctity is based upon the premise "that all men by nature desire beautiful things, despite the fact that they differ as to what is supremely beautiful."[76] While some of the Gentiles have declared that the end is theoretical knowledge . . . , others, practical activity . . . , others, some profitable use of life and body, and others, simply

pleasure . . . , Christianity transcends them all by placing man's end in "the blessed life in the world to come," which will consist in being "ruled by God."[77] "Up to this time," Basil observes, "nothing better than the latter idea [life under the rule of God] has been found in rational nature."[78]

Christian righteousness and holiness are identified by Basil with the observance of all divine commandments: "There is one rule and canon prescribed for our works, to fulfil God's commandments in a manner pleasing to Him."[79] The disposition . . . of complete subordination to the divine rule is identified with the knowledge . . . of God.[80] *Gnosis* in Basil's terminology is thus not the same as the abstract *epist m* of the Platonist philosophers. It is rather a religious intimacy and communion between man and God grounded on love. When Basil insists that all divine commandments ought to be implemented without distinction, his ideal of evangelical sanctity may be suspected of formalistic legalism. However, Basil expressly distinguishes between the character of the gospel and the Jewish law precisely on the score "that as the law forbids bad deeds, so the gospel forbids the very hidden sins of the soul," and so on.[81] It is here that we arrive at the core of Basil's ascetic teaching. Before stating that moral perfection consists in the implementation of all divine commandments, Basil makes clear that God's decrees act only as reminders and stimuli to man's inborn tendency to love. They do not force themselves upon man's faculty of self-determination from the outside but only activate and cultivate the *logos spermatikos* implanted in man from his first constitution.[82]

Love, Basil teaches, is such a moral action . . . that, although it is only one, as regards power it accomplishes and comprehends every commandment; hence all commandments issue in love.[83] This is an important conclusion that Basil reaches at the very beginning of his "systematic" part of the *Asceticon*. For the man seeking happiness and fulfillment there is one simple thing to be done: to let himself be moved by the love of God and of his neighbours. "For 'he that loveth me', saith the Lord, 'will keep my commandments'. And again: 'On these two commandments hang all the law and the prophets'."[84] Moreover, the Lord

> demanded as a proof [. . . syllogistic demonstration] that we are His disciples, not signs and marvellous works—and yet He bestowed the working of these too in the Holy Spirit—but what does He say? 'By this shall all men know that ye are my disciples, if ye have love one towards another.'[85]

The two commandments of love are so bound up together that the Lord

> transfers to Himself benefits conferred on one's neighbours. For He says: 'I was hungry and ye gave

me to eat,' and so on. To which He adds: 'Inasmuch as ye did it to one of the least of these my brethren, ye did it unto me.'[86]

At this point, an inescapable conclusion imposes itself: If all commandments and virtues are indeed represented in love as their most genuine form and expression, *Christian perfection cannot be individual, but can flourish and achieve perfection only in a life of communion . . . with God and one's neighbours.* We have thus reached the topic Basil deals with in the first chapter of his *Asceticons*: the corporate or ecclesial dimension of Christian perfection.[87]

"*Interrogations* 1-3" of the *Small Asceticon* and the "*Longer Questions* 1-7" of the *Great Ascetion*, basically deal with the environmental problem, that is, with the ideal conditions for leading a life in conformity with the divine commandments. Two aspects are involved: (1) Should Christians converted to the gospel continue to live among those who hold in contempt the divine commandments . . . ? (2) If not, should they live by themselves, in solitude, or should they come together with like-minded brethren . . . and form communities of their own?[88] Both questions are very important from the ecclesial point of view despite the fact that some passages of Basil's ascetic works can be interpreted as favouring the constitution of particular ("monastic") communities within the universal community of the church.[89] In spite of such ambiguities, his *Asceticons* offer a valuable contribution for the understanding of the church as a community of baptized people trying to live a perfect life not only in the monastic seclusion but also in the middle of the world.

In referring to the subject treated in the first chapters of both *Asceticons* we called it an environmental problem. The fourth century was a time of numerous critical changes in the church's internal and external organization. When Basil insists in his treatises on the quality rather than the form of Christian life, and when he maintains that to be perfect it is not enough to follow some more convenient norms and ignore the rest, he is trying to protect the church's elements of distinctiveness, sacredness, and secrecy which so significantly, in his opinion, characterized early Christianity.[90] The fourth century saw crowds of people flocking into the church not for the sake of improving the spiritual character of their lives, but often for the mere convenience of becoming eligible for public offices and careers.[91] With the indiscriminately swelled ranks, the church's awareness of being a sacred community distinct from earthly society was in danger of disappearing. There was hardly any *disciplina arcani* left to keep church doctrines, rites and customs out of reach of the unworthy.[92] More as a solicitous pastor than a "monastic legislator," Basil, following a service in the church, evidences readiness to answer questions from those who are willing to inquire further "concerning

that which belongs to sound faith and the true method of right conduct according to the gospel of our Lord Jesus Christ" by means of which "the man of God is perfected."[93] If they are sincerely determined to redress their morals, to take up their cross as true disciples of the Lord and to deny themselves completely, he asks this elite not "to mix with those who are fearlessly and scornfully disposed towards the exact observance of the commandments."[94]

Life in the "world," that is, among people who despise the teaching of Christ, is described by Basil as full of overt and hidden dangers.[95] Basil does not advocate a physical separation or total withdrawal from this environment, at least not as a permanent measure. The concept of the *fuga mundi*, it has been noticed, does not occur in this context at all, and the description of Christians as having their "citizenship in heaven" appears to be more ethical than institutional in nature.[96] In a letter written from his Pontic retreat, where Basil retired to amend his way of life "long perverted by the intimacy with wicked people," he states:

> One way of escaping . . . all this [that is the cares . . . of life] is separation . . . from the whole world. However, separation from the world . . . not through bodily withdrawal from it . . . but through severance of the soul's sympathy with the body, so as to live without city, home, goods, society, possessions, means of life, business engagements, intercourse, human learning, that the heart may readily receive every impression of divine doctrine.[97]

It is obvious that what counts most is spiritual withdrawal from the environment of sinners and outsiders. However, as a temporary measure, seclusion from people and also withdrawal from the political community are recommended at the beginning of one's conversion to "philosophy"—the life according to the gospel.[98] Basil himself spent some time in the solitude of his estate. But, as his own letters show us, during his retreat Basil continued to be in touch with the world of friends, magistrates, public servants.[99] Whereas at one point he perhaps thought that he should cut off these relations too, later on he understood that quiet . . . lies not so much in physical separation as in freeing oneself from ties caused by a passionate attachment to life, in the avoidance of distractions, and giving up of all unnecessary worldly cares. . . . [100] The criterion, however, for discerning and judging what things *in concreto* should be avoided is a very subjective one: it is anything that, in one's opinion, seems to interfere with the way of piety . . . and the strictness of the gospel.[101]

Undoubtedly Basil advocates the necessity of abandoning the world in order to serve God adequately, not the world as such—for our anxieties will pursue us everywhere—but the world conceived as the society of outsiders-sinners . . . , people hostile to the teaching and the spirit of Christ.[102]

Next Basil speaks in his **Asceticons** against withdrawing from the company of the like-minded, that is, from those who share sound views on the commandments and on the gospel.[103] Many in the fourth century, affected adversely by the evils of the world and of the church, fled to the desert. Basil categorically rejects such a solution as unchristian (unscriptural) and inhuman. Instead, Basil wishes his converts to come together, to live together . . . as closely as possible in one body, with Christ as the head and the Holy Spirit as the soul.[104]

W. K. L. Clarke had already noticed that the doctrine contained in the **Longer Rule** 7 on the disadvantages of eremitic life and benefits of community life can be applied "equally well to a Christian life in the world."[105] There can be no doubt that Basil meant something more than a convent when he spoke of the benefits of sharing . . . spiritual gifts (charismata) and material possessions with others. He assuredly intended his new church to be patterned on the model of the first Christian community of Jerusalem, whose members "were together and had all things in common."[106] We shall, then, summarize Basil's teaching from his **Longer Rule** 7.[107] Concomitantly, we shall adduce parallel passages from Basil's other writings in order to see whether his doctrine on the corporate type of Christian life is applicable to all members in the church.

Basil's arguments in favour of communal Christianity are contained in the following general principles:

(1) No man is individually self-sufficient. . . . By nature he needs the assistance of other fellow members in providing for his bodily needs.[108]

(2) The *logos* of Christian love does not allow each man to look to his own good exclusively. "For 'love', we read, 'seeketh not its own'."[109]

(3) It is harmful to the soul when men have no one to rebuke them for their faults.[110]

(4) The solitary life is idle and fruitless for it allows only a partial implementation of the commandments.[111]

(5) "All of us who have been received in one hope of our calling are one body having Christ as head, and we are severally members of one another. But if we are not joined together harmoniously in the close links of one body in the Holy Spirit, but each of us chooses solitude, not serving the common welfare in a way well-pleasing to God but fulfilling private desires, how, when we are thus separated and divided off, can we preserve the mutual relation and service of the limbs one to another, or their subjection to our head, which is Christ?"[112]

(6) A charisma is a gift of the Holy Spirit given and accepted for the benefit of others.[113] No person can possess all the charismata. But "when a number live together," a man enjoys not only his own charisma, but he multiplies it "by imparting it to others, and reaps the fruits of other men's charismata as if they were his own."[114]

(7) Life in the company of many provides a good protection against the plots of the enemy, and the presence of others is a good means for the correction of one's own faults.[115]

(8) In a structure that allows no personal relations it is impossible to practice many of the Christian virtues such as humility, mercy or long-suffering. Scripture provides only the theory of perfection; theory without practice is void.[116]

It was perhaps only natural that in the course of later institutional developments such an exposition of the advantages of the communal life, strongly motivated by scriptural and philosophical arguments, should be almost exclusively applied by many Christians to monastic institutes. Basil, in such a view, would be speaking here not to all Christians but only to those who have decided to practice not only the commandments but also the so-called evangelical precepts. Such an attempt to limit the scope of Basil's projected reform of the contemporary church to one small portion of it should, however, be dismissed as ill-founded and anachronistic.[117]

As we observed earlier, throughout his works Basil never employs a special name to designate his close followers. His disciples, even those addressed in the shorter interrogations of the **Great Asceticon**, are active members of the local church. Through them Basil expects to revive the ideal of the first apostolic community, whose members were "of one heart and one soul," and had all things in common with no one seeking what is his own but only what is for the good of others.[118] The communal life in Basil's terminology is the "apostolic life"; it is Christian life grounded on and nurtured by love; it is in other words "faith working through love."[119] As the **Moralia**, the manual for ascetics living in the world, puts it,

> the *logos* wishes Christians to be: as disciples of Christ, conformed only to the pattern of what they see in Him, or hear from Him; . . . as members of Christ, who are perfect in the working of all the commandments of the Lord, or equipped with the charismata of the Holy Spirit according to the worthiness of the head, which is Christ; . . . as light in the world, so that both they themselves are not receptive of evil and enlighten those who approach them to a knowledge of the truth, and these either become what they should be or reveal what they are; as salt in the world, so that they

who communicate with them . . . are renewed in the spirit unto incorruptibility.[120]

Between his churches as communities of perfect Christians and the world . . . Basil does not think any friendship . . . possible, for no one can be a friend of the wicked and undiscerning. . . .[121] He does, however, admit a beneficial relationship with a view to winning the wicked to the church.[122]

As we mentioned earlier, in his long exposition of the benefits resulting for the individual from the adoption of a communal standard of life. Basil had also tried to deprive the eremitic experience of reasonable foundation by declaring it to be inhuman and unscriptural. Previously he had identified the requirement to abandon the world with the demand to flee and resist the company of outsiders not physically, but so far as friendship was concerned. His further appeal to constitute new fellowships of perfect Christians alongside the officially supported societies of the [hoi exothei] was aimed at the formation of a new nucleus of authentic practitioners of the gospel, whose conversation would be in heaven, from where the light of the gospel would diffuse to all.

Basil's plea to Christians to adopt a corporate concept of sanctity acquires further moment if considered in its historical context. Fourth-century churches were mostly found in the cities or near populated areas. Many Christians perhaps, in view of the scarcely edifying urban life, would have preferred to spend their time after baptism in some quiet spot, far from those centres of corruption and loose morality. Basil himself, after suffering a similar crisis of Christian identity, realized that . . . spiritual peace, and . . . freedom from sins, was to be found not through "bodily separation" from the world "but in the severance of the soul's sympathy with the body."[123] Through his action, he thus prevented the questionable Egyptian experiment of Christians deserting the churches from repeating itself in Asia Minor.

D. The Holy Spirit and Life in the Brotherhood: The Basilian Brotherhood as the Body of Christ

The term [adelphotes] is indiscriminately applied by Basil to both the ascetic community and the local church.[124] Basil's cenobia were clearly structured on the pattern of the first community of Jerusalem—the ideal church, according to Basil, in which all things were common, whose members were united by the same faith and brotherly love, "all in common seeking in the one Holy Spirit the will of the one Lord Jesus Christ."[125] These communities of perfect Christians patterned on the model church of Jerusalem were designed to serve as models for the contemporary local churches.[126] Since we shall continually speak of the Holy Spirit as being for Basil the main architect of

the church, we here propose to outline first the notion of charisma in Basil's writings, notably in the *Moralia* and the *De Spiritu Sancto*, and second the idea of the Christian life as a life in the body of Christ characterized by the presence and riches of the Holy Spirit. Our intent is to indicate briefly that the Basilian brotherhoods—the ascetic communities and ideally all the local churches—are organic unities, whose life and functioning depends directly upon the charismatic operation of the Holy Spirit.

i. *What is Charisma?*

From time to time throughout this chapter we have heard Basil speak of the charismata and the charismatic structure of the church. We must now consider more closely the significance of this term in his theological vocabulary, especially in view of its frequent occurrence in the *Moralia* and the *De Spiritu Sancto*. As Basil seems to derive his notion of charisma from Paul, we shall first outline Paul's concept inasmuch as he is the first to introduce this term into the Christian theological vocabulary.[127]

Although the reality signified by the word 'charisma' is familiar to other New Testament writers, Paul is the first to give it a precise theological significance.[128] The basic notion of charisma can be found in Romans 6.23: "The charisma of God is eternal life in Christ Jesus our Lord." "Other charismata only exist because of the existence of this one charisma to which they are all related, and they only exist where the gift of eternal life is manifested in the eschatologically inaugurated dominion of Christ."[129] In our opinion, the key passage to study in considering Paul's notion of charisma is 2 Corinthians 13.13. . . . As it stands, this text admits of two equally possible renderings, "The participation [fellowship] *of* the Holy Spirit," or, "The participation [fellowship] *in* the Holy Spirit."[130] This is precisely what charisma is: It is a participation or communion both in the objective and subjective sense; that is, it is a fellowship *of* and *in* the Holy Spirit.

Charisma points first towards the event of man's participation in the eschatological riches imparted by the death and resurrection of Jesus Christ. In this latter sense it is referred to by Paul also by the terms [klesis] and [phanerosis tou Pneumatos] (cf. 1 Cor 12.7). In the second place or rather concomitantly with the first sense, charisma is a participation in the fate and sufferings of others. Paul identifies it with the *diakonia*, the service which Christians render to their fellowmen (1 Cor 12.4 ff.). The term that comprehends all these aspects of charisma is . . . , the calling from God addressed to each person individually to participate in his life through his Son in the Holy Spirit and to render the necessary services to our neighbours (Rom 11.29; 1 Cor 7.7, 17 ff.).

Charisma essentially is a *koinonia* in and of the Holy Spirit through which Christians are called by the Risen Lord to serve his cause by serving their neighbours. The Pauline concept of charisma encompasses the whole range of human actions which under the influence and guidance of the Holy Spirit are performed for the specific purpose of proclaiming the lordship of Christ and edifying his church. Reacting against the Enthusiasts of Corinth, the apostle reminds them that they should not restrict this notion exclusively to the supernatural and miraculous phenomena such as ecstasies and glossolalia (1 Cor 12.22 ff.). As the Antichrist can also produce signs, wonders and powers (see Mt 24.24; Mk 13.22 and 2 Thess 2.9), the possession of the former is not yet a guarantee of participation in eternal life. Conversely, Paul points out that such inconspicuous and ordinary tasks as tending the sick or providing physical welfare for the poor *can be* charismata of the Spirit *if* accompanied by faith in the lordship of Christ and the intention to edify his community, the church. In other words, the true measure of charisma is the way in which, in and for the Lord, an existing set of natural circumstances is transformed by the new obedience to the Risen Lord. My previous condition of life becomes charisma as soon as in baptism the Spirit transforms and takes possession of me. From that moment on nothing is secular or unclean for me as a Christian anymore, but everything becomes holy and purified as long as I use it to proclaim the lordship of Christ and to build up his church.[131] It is in virtue of this comprehensive conception that Paul could speak of marriage, of virginity, of widowhood, of the condition of being slave or free, male or female, etc., as charismata, that is, possible callings and services.[132] As Käsemann observes:

> Charisma is no longer the distinguishing mark of elect individuals but that which is the common endowment of all who call upon the name of the Lord, or, to use the phraseology of the primitive Christian tradition as we have it in Acts 2.17 ff., a demonstration of the fact that the Spirit of God has been poured out on all flesh.[133]

In summing up Paul's teaching on charismata, the same author writes:

> Paul's teaching on the subject of charismata constitutes the proof, first, that he made no basic distinction between justification and sanctification and did not understand justification in a merely declaratory sense; further, that he binds justification by faith tightly to baptism, so that it is not permissible to drive a wedge into his gospel, separating the juridical from the sacramental approach; and finally, that he considers faith to be actually constituted by the new obedience.[134]

In view of Basil's use of the term charisma in other contexts, we should add also Paul's application of this term in the description of the "social" relations among the Christians as members of the church, the body of Christ. First, in his teaching on charismata, Paul rules out any ecclesiastical egalitarianism.

> God does not repeat himself when he acts, and there can be no mass production of grace. There is differentiation in the divine generosity, whether in the order of creation or of redemption. Equality is not for Paul a principle of Church order.[135]

It is within such contexts that we often hear Paul saying. "To each his own" (Rom 12.3; 1 Cor 3.5; 11.18; 12.7).

> Within the ranks of the community there are to be found both strong and weak, aristocrat and proletarian, wise and foolish, cultured and uncultured. No one, according to 1 Cor 12.21, may say to his brother 'I have no need of you.' Over them all stands the sign [*kathos bouletai ethelesei*] (1 Cor 12.11, 18); this expresses the sovereignty of the divine grace and omnipotence, which is both liberal and liberating, which puts an end to worry and envy by giving individually to every man.[136]

The second watchword coined by Paul in the context of his doctrine on the charismata is, "For one another" (1 Cor 12.23).

"The third watchword designed to stifle self-will is to be found in Rom 12.10, Phil 2.3, 1 Peter 5.5 and with special force in Eph 5.21. It runs, 'Submit yourselves to each other in the fear of Christ'."[137] The humble subordination in love to one's neighbour by rendering him a service, without thereby exercising an act of authority is the truly Christian way of witnessing to the power of the one who "did not count equality with God a thing to be grasped, but emptied himself, taking the form of a servant. . . . And being found in human form he humbled himself and became obedient unto death, even death on the cross" (Phil 2.6-8).

Did Basil, who was familiar with all these passages, understand Paul in the very way we perceive him today? If Paul had indeed contended that there is no opposition between body and spirit, and that the bodily and material are the sphere of operation of the *Pneuma* (the Power and Grace of the Risen Lord),[138] at least on this point Basil along with other early writers seems to be in closer agreement with the Platonist than the Pauline tradition. His homily entitled, "Take Heed of Yourself," it is true, incorporates all life occupations and stations under the rubric of charismata.[139] Also, his understanding is that each charisma or calling expresses itself in a specific praxis. At the conclusion of the homily Basil pays a high tribute to the body . . . as the place where divine wisdom, love, generosity, goodness and beauty reveal themselves.[140] But elsewhere, in a quite thoroughgoing manner, he almost completely surrenders to the philosophical dictum that the body is a tomb. . . . [141] On the other hand, Basil expands the

Pauline notion of charisma to include earthly goods as well.[142] Not only the sharing of spiritual endowments produces the unity in the Body of Christ, but also the *koinonia* in the material possessions contributes to edifying the Christian fellowship. It is precisely in such a perspective that the opposition between spirit and matter is resolved through the realization that nothing material is intrinsically evil.[143] On the contrary, Basil admits, through an act of "dedication" anything can be converted into an instrument . . . of love and virtue.[144]

After these preliminary comparisons between the thinking of Paul and Basil let us now take a closer look at Basil's notion of charisma. Although nowhere in his writings do we find what we might call a technical definition of the term, it is clear that the two Pauline criteria for validating charismata—the confession of the lordship of Christ and the edification of the church—have found ample expression in his writings. The confession of Christ, however, does not necessarily assume a dogmatic form. It is understood rather as a *gnosis* of God, that is, as the unconditional observance of all divine commandments.[145] This is the most telling proof authenticating all kinds of claims to charismata.[146] The other variable of this motif is the renunciation of one's own self-will through complete surrender to the authority of the Holy Scriptures.[147]

The "edification of the church" as a criterion for testing and discerning the spirits is also often found in Basil.[148] Sometimes it assumes the form, known also to Paul, of the search for the "common good" of others.[149] This in its turn entails the renunciation of self-love and even private property.[150]

We have already indicated that under the rubric of charisma Basil places all natural goods and services. Nowhere is this better attested perhaps than in the *Moralia*. Any condition or status in life is suitable to proclaim the "death of Christ" in our bodies and to take part in the victorious advance of the gospel through various parts of the world.[151]

His more detailed treatment of the individual charismata Basil precedes with a summary description of the nature of charisma:

> Since the charismata of the Spirit are different, and neither is one able to receive all nor all the same, each should abide with sobriety and gratitude in the charisma given to him, and all should be harmonious with one another in the love of Christ, as members in a body. So that he who is inferior in charismata should not despair of himself in comparison with him that excels, nor should the greater despise the less. For those who are divided and at variance with one another deserve to perish.[152]

Strongly emphasized here is the non-egalitarian principle, on the one hand,[153] and the unitary character of

the action of the Spirit, on the other. Charismata are the grounds of Christian unity, eschatological peace and deep love because they stem from the one and same Holy Spirit who is their only cause and source. At the same time charismata manifest the manifold and variegated character of the Bride of Christ.[154] This unity in diversity and diversity in unity is explained by the idea of the Holy Spirit acting as a whole in parts:

> In relation to the distribution of charismata, the Spirit is to be conceived as a whole in parts. For we all are 'members one of another, having different charismata according to the grace of God that is given us' (Rom 12.5-6). Wherefore 'the eye cannot say to the hand, I have no need of thee; nor again the head to the feet, I have no need of you' (1 Cor 12.21), but all together complete the body of Christ in the unity of the Spirit, and render to one another the needful aid that comes of the charismata. 'But God hath set the members in the body, every one of them, as it hath pleased Him' (cf. 1 Cor 12.18, 11). But 'the members have the same care for one another' (1 Cor 12.25) according to the spiritual communion of their inborn sympathy. . . . And as parts in the whole so are we individually in the Spirit, because we all 'were bap-tized in one body into one spirit' (cf. 1 Cor 12.13).[155]

Because of the dialectical nature of charismata moderation and restraint . . . should accompany their use and exercise.[156]

The extent to which Basil admitted the principle of charismatic ordering in his communities is difficult to determine simply by reading his works. A more thorough study will almost certainly show that the ministerial structure of his brotherhoods was rather loose, flexible, and open, allowing considerably more freedom for the charismatic manifestations than one would be ready or willing to admit. The ***Shorter Interrogation*** 114 is a case in point: the commands of anyone who has passed the test of the Scriptures—a criterion similar to the one for the validation of all charismata—should be obeyed as if they had the same authority as the will of God (1160A ff.). Anyone who has unselfishly dedicated himself to his brothers "in the love of Christ" (***Reg. br.*** 146: 1177D) is capable of contributing through his individual charismata to the edification of the body of Christ as long as he does not arbitrarily volunteer his services but offers them in response to the needs of others.

ii. *Life in the Spirit*

While the Egyptian Christians, desirous of working out their salvation and sanctification, were advised to abandon through physical withdrawal the world of human relations and to seek in the wilderness the ideal environment for their vocation, Basil, dealing with the same subject, proposes what he terms a "paradoxical" statement: the "ambiance" . . . of Christian sanctification and worship is not to be found in any physical or geographical location but essentially consists in living and in being in the Holy Spirit who is the [*hora*] of those being sanctified.[157] The withdrawal of passions and the subsequent quiet . . . are precisely intended to facilitate this contact and even the entry of the soul into the "ambiance" called the Holy Spirit.[158]

Baptism is the means by which every single member is introduced into the life in the Holy Spirit.[159] Through this sacrament of Christian regeneration humans not only bury themselves with Christ and die to sin, but they are also positively enabled to become "that very thing" of which they were born anew, that is to say, they receive from the Spirit the power to become assimilated to God:

> Shining upon those that are cleansed from every spot, the Spirit makes them spiritual . . . by fellowship . . . with Himself. Just as when a sunbeam falls on bright and transparent bodies, they themselves become brilliant too, and shed forth a fresh brightness from themselves, so souls wherein the Spirit dwells, illuminated by the Spirit, themselves become spiritual, and send forth their grace to others. Hence come foreknowledge of the future, understanding of mysteries, apprehension of what is hidden, distribution of charismata, heavenly citizenship, a place in the chorus of angels, joy without end, abiding in God, being made like to God, and, what is most desirable, being made God. . . . [160]

In virtue of this deifying principle apportioned to every single member of the body of Christ, the church is referred to by Basil as the place of the fellowship . . . in and of the Holy Spirit.[161] In it humans communicate with each other by sharing their material and spiritual goods and through the mutual (social) exchange of services.[162]

As Basil is explicit, on the one hand, that the members of his brotherhoods are people filled with the Spirit and his endowments, so he is very firm, on the other, in asserting the organic unity of his communities as the body of Christ. To the question "Ought one in the brotherhood to obey what is said by every one?" Basil replies:

> The answer to this question is fraught with considerable difficulty. In the first place the question indicates disorder when it mentions things said by every one, for the apostle says: 'Let the prophets speak by twos and threes and let the others discern' (1 Cor 14.29). And the same writer in dividing charismata has assigned the proper rank (order) of each of the speakers. . . . And by his example of the members of the body he shows clearly that the lot of the speaker is to speak in turns. . . . [163]

Basil then proceeds to explain the structure of the brotherhood basically as consisting of those entrusted with the charisma of leadership and those entrusted with the charisma of obedience.[164]

The Holy Spirit, as it is not difficult to illustrate from Basil's works, is present not only in each member of the community. His lifegiving and sanctifying presence and operation, besides being universal and comprising all intelligent beings, as apparent particularly in the mysteries of the church—the sacraments of baptism and confirmation, the inspired writings of the Old and New Testament, the proclamations . . . of the church; that is, homilies, ordinances, decisions made by spiritual men, instructions, the exchange of letters and visits, consultations and spiritual advice, as well as in meetings for the purpose of edifying the faith and in the prayers of the church.[165]

E. The Brotherhood of Churches

If Basil often appealed to the need for order and decency within his ascetic brotherhoods, in doing so he was far from basing his claims on conciliar decisions or "rules" drawn up by himself or others to that effect.[166] The only commandment of vital importance and urgency for Basil was the commandment of love, often referred to as the first fruit and charisma of the Holy Spirit.[167] As we shall see in more detail in Chapter Four the *logos* of love should not only bind the Christian communities together internally, but it should also compel each individual community to seek intercourse and communion with the others. Thus, in place of a hierarchical system, we find in Basil an order of brotherhood intended to regulate not only individual but also intercommunal relations.

Basil's design provided that the ascetic communities be the prime model in this. In the **Longer Rule**[35] Basil first advocates the welding together . . . of several brotherhoods existing in the same parish. . . . [168] The rule invoked is the apostolic command, "Not looking each to his own things, but each also to the things of the others" (Phil 2.4). Basil explains:

> For I reckon this cannot be carried out in separation, when each section takes care for its fellow denizens, but thought for the others is outside its ken, which, as I said, is clearly opposed to the apostolic command. And the saints in the Acts bear witness to this frequently, of whom it is written in one place: 'The multitude of them that believed were of one heart and soul' (Acts 4.32), and in another place, 'All that believed were together, and had all things common' (Acts 2.44). So it is obvious that there was no division among them all, nor did each live under his own authority, but all had one and the same care—and that too although the total number was five thousand, and with such a number one would think perhaps there were no few obstacles to union. But where men living in a single parish are found so inferior in numbers to those, what in reason allows them to remain separated from one another?[169]

But Basil is not satisfied with this first step of union among local brotherhoods. The same reasons of convenience and of better provision for the private needs of the individuals compel him to formulate a more far-reaching wish:

> Would that it were possible, that not only those in the same parish were thus united, but that a number of brotherhoods existing in different places might be built up into a community under the single care of those who are able without partiality and wisely to manage the affairs of all in the unity of the spirit and the bond of peace![170]

That Basil sought the implementation of the same apostolic pattern of union and brotherhood for all the churches spread throughout the *oikoumene* is easy to gather from his correspondence and the ***De Spiritu Sancto***. As I shall deal more extensively with this subject in the fourth chapter, it should suffice here to provide additional evidence indicating Basil's interest in seeing all churches amalgamated into one universal brotherhood. It can hardly be said that Basil considered the church as a monad.[171] Time and again throughout his writings he shows a consciousness of the church as a brotherhood of all believers in Christ: "All believers in Christ are one people; all Christ's people, although He is hailed from many regions, are one church."[172] As we shall see in Chapter Four, the concrete circumstances in which Basil lived were far from ideal for the realization of a union of all Christians. The scene, particularly east of Illyricum, dominated by endless theological squabbles, personal rivalries and partisanship, rather resembled a storm at sea, "as when at sea many ships sailing together are all dashed one against the other by the violence of the waves, and shipwreck arises in some cases from the sea being furiously agitated from without, in others from the disorder of the sailors hindering and crowding one another."[173] Some bishops, if they were not in open warfare with their neighbours, tried to ignore them and live in confinement in their own cities. Basil, although fully conscious of his personal sins which he considered to be the major obstacle to friendship and to achieving ecclesiastical unity, often made an appeal to more transcendental ties—the bond of love, of one Lord, one faith, one hope—as the only valid motives to be taken into account in the formation of a universal brotherhood of churches.[174] To the bishops of Pontus unsettled by the Eustathian propaganda about his orthodoxy, Basil wrote in an expostulatory letter:

> Nothing, brethren, separates us from each other, but deliberate estrangement. We have one Lord, one faith, the same hope.... For we are assured, that though you are not present in body, yet by the aid of prayer, you will do us much benefit in those most critical times. It is neither decorous before men, nor pleasing to God, that you should employ such words which not even the Gentiles who know

no God have employed. Even they, as we hear, though the country they live in be self-sufficient for all things, yet, on account of the uncertainty of the future, make much of alliances with each other, and seek mutual intercourse as being advantageous to them.[175]

It was not only the uncertainty of the situation under a hostile government that compelled Basil to seek the establishment and reinforcement of the brotherhood among Christian communities spread throughout the world, but the principle that no Christian or individual community can adequately take care of oneself or itself while ignoring the interests of others. "General disaster involves individual ruin."[176] Wherefore "'whether one member suffereth, all the members suffer with it' (1 Cor 12.26), for 'there should be no schisms in the body, but the members should have the same care for one another' (1 Cor 12.25), according to the spiritual fellowship of their inborn sympathy, and being moved, no doubt, by the one indwelling Spirit."[177] But as we said earlier the situation was far from ideal for an enduring conciliation of the spirits on whom weighed heavily the consequences of the long war in which many churches became involved following the Council of Nicaea:

> We are confined now each in his own city, and everyone looks at his neighbour with distrust. What more is to be said but that our love has grown cold? Yet it is through [love] alone that, according to our Lord, His disciples are distinguished.[178]

The love of many has grown cold throughout, brotherly concord is destroyed, the very name of unity is ignored, brotherly admonitions are heard no more; ... but mutual hatred has blazed so high among fellow clansmen that they are more delighted at a neighbour's fall than their own success. . . . And to such depth is this evil rooted among us that we have become more brutish than the brutes; they do at least herd with their fellows, but our most savage warfare is with our own people.[179] . . .

Notes

[1] Other expressions include: "house of God," "church of Christ," "body of Christ," "dove of Christ," "bride of Christ," "city of God," "daughter of God," and also very frequently, "brotherhood." The names applied to Christians include: "brethren," "people of God," "members of the body of Christ," "believers in Christ," "God's flock," "disciples of the Lord," and "disciples of the gospel." Some of these expressions are studied below pp. 6 ff. In his work, *Early Christian Doctrines* (London, 1968), p. 401, J. N. D. Kelly quotes with approval the "customary" (*sic!*) view according to which "as contrasted with that of the West, Eastern teaching about the Church remained immature, not to say archaic, in the post-Nicene period." One could reply that

all such time-honoured designations, although obviously derived from the Bible, by being repeated in new historical contexts, reflect new realities, in the case of Basil the situation of the "imperial" church under Julian and Valens.

[2] See e.g. *In ps.* 45 and 59 quoted below p. 10. On the fourth-century church as an organization (society) competing with the state see A. Momigliano, *The Conflict between Paganism and Christianity in the Fourth Century* (Oxford, 1963), pp. 9 ff.

[3] See *In ps.* 48.1 discussed in n. 7, below; *Ep.* 161.1: Courtonne, 2:93; *De jud.*, 1:653A-B; *Ep.* 243.1: Courtonne, 3:68, and chapters 8 and 9 of the book *On the Holy Spirit*. For the theological impossibility of a distinction between universal and local church in general see H. M. Legrand, "The Revaluation of Local Churches: Some Theological Implications," *Concilium* 71 (1972) 57, and K. L. Schmidt, "[*Ekhansia*]" in *TDNT* (1965) 3: 501-536; see also J. D. G. Dunn, *Jesus and the Spirit* (London, 1975), pp. 262 ff.

[4] See below, pp. 41 ff., and 23 ff.

[5] See *Ep.* 161.1: Courtonne, 2:93; *In ps.* 59.2: 464B-C.

[6] See *Reg. fus.* 2.1: 908B ff.; *In ps.* 44.2: 392A f.

[7] *In ps.* 48.1: 433C-D. This important homily provides the essential elements of Basil's view on the universality (intrinsic and intentional catholicity) of the church. Before speaking of the Holy Spirit as the architect of the church . . . and of the church as the community of universal love (433A-D), Basil surveys the theories of the various philosophical schools concerning the end of human existence (432A-B). After the statement of the Christian position according to which the end of human life is "to be totally ruled by God," there follows a comprehensive list of all those called by the kerygma of the Holy Spirit to form the universal fellowship (433A). In order that no one may be left without the church's aid in the path to salvation, "there are three pairs of those called, in which every race of men is included". . . . Among those called by the Spirit are: non-Romans and Roman citizens . . . people of primitive culture and civilized men . . . the rich and the poor . . . whereby all social classes are comprised. See also *Hex.* 11.5: Smets-Esbroeck, 238:. . . . For the historical background of Basil's statements see Momigliano, *The Conflict*, pp. 12-16. On Gregory of Nazianzus' concept of universality and unity see Ph. Muraille, "L'église, peuple de l'oikouménè d'après s. Grégoire de Nazianze. Notes sur l'unité et l'universalité," *EThL* 44 (1968) 154-178, and E. Bellini, *La chiesa nel mistero della salvezza in san Gregorio Nazianzeno* (Venegono Inferiore, 1970), pp. 71-74. On Origen see briefly G. Bardy, *La théologie de l'église de saint Irénée au concile de Nicée* (Paris, 1947), pp. 160-161.

[8] Besides *In ps.* 48.1, see *De jud.*, 2:656A f.

[9] See *De jud.*, 1:653A. For the interpretation of *De sp. s.* 66: Pruche, 478 ff., see G. Florovsky, "The Function of Tradition in the Ancient Church," *GOTR* 9 (1963) 181 ff.; also T. Spidlik, *La sophiologie de saint Basile* (Rome, 1961), pp. 172-186. For the quite different domestic experience of the church of Gregory of Nazianzus see Bellini, *La chiesa*, pp. 13-14.

[10] See *De jud.*, 1:653A; *Epp.* 204.6: Courtonne, 2:178; 210.1: ibid., 190; 223.3: ibid., 3:1 ff. Whenever his orthodoxy was attacked or questioned Basil would appeal to the ties of his family with Gregory Thaumaturgus, apostle and founder of the church of Neocaesarea. K. Holl in *Amphilochius von Ikonium in seinem Verhältnis zu den grossen Kappadoziern* (Tübingen, 1904), pp. 117-119, has tried to show Basil's indebtedness to the theology, mainly as contained in the *Expositio fidei*, of Gregory Thaumaturgus. See also J. Gribomont, "L'origénisme de saint Basile," *L'homme devant Dieu. Mélanges H. de Lubac* (Paris, 1963), p. 281, and H. Dehnhard, *Das Problem der Abhängigkeit des Basilius von Plotin* (Berlin, 1964), pp. 19-32. But the authenticity of Gregory's *Expositio fidei* attributed to him by Gregory of Nyssa (PG 46, 912D-913A) has lately been challenged by L. Abramowski, "Das Bekenntnis des Gregor Thaumaturgus bei Gregor von Nyssa und das Problem seiner Echtheit," *ZKG* 87 (1976) 145-166. However, it is not at all impossible that Gregory of Nyssa is quoting in the symbol most or some of the *ipsissima verba* of the founder of the church of Neocaesarea as they were transmitted orally through his disciples, notably Macrina. There could be posterior additions by some of his successors in the see of Neocaesarea. The term [*hornios*] does not have to be necessarily derived from Plotinus; it is found already in Clement of Alexandria and Origen (see *PGL*, s.v.). For a comparison of Gregory's *Expositio fidei* with Arius' *Thalia* see A. Grillmeier, *Christ in Christian Tradition,* 2nd ed. (Atlanta, 1975), 1: 232-238.

[11] See the *Epistles* cited above, n. 10.

[12] For the evidences see Holl, *Am philochias*, pp. 127 ff., and n. 10, above.

[13] See *De sp. s.* 75: Pruche, 516; *Reg. mor.* 8.1: 712C-D; 70.19: 832B.

[14] See Gregory of Nazianzus, *Oration* 43.5-6: PG 36, 500B-D; Gregory of Nyssa, *Vita Macrinae*, 2 and 20: Maraval, 142 ff. (with the notes), and 206.

[15] On the inclusion of the cult of martyrs in the homilies of the Cappadocians see J. Bernardi, *La prédication des Pères cappadociens. Le prédicateur et son auditoire* (Paris, 1968), pp. 398-400.

[16] Probably Musonius, the bishop of Neocaesarea, was an ascetic (see *Ep.* 28.1: Courtonne, 1: 66-67). That many of the urban churches and schools were under the supervision of the Eustathians see below, pp. 162 ff., and 160 ff. Probably the whole family of Basil practiced the family type of asceticism which until 350 was in full vigour in Syria and Asia Minor; see E. Amand de Mendieta, "La virginité chez Eusèbe d'Emèse et l'ascéticisme familial dans la première moitié du IVe siècle," *RHE* 50 (1955) 777-820, esp. pp. 800 f.; Id. and M. C. Moons, "Une curieuse homélie grecque inédite sur la virginité adressée aux pères de famille," *RB* 53 (1953) 18-69; 211-238; also R. Metz, *La consécration des vierges dans l'Eglise romaine* (Paris, 1954).

[17] On the defection of Dianius, the bishop of Caesarea who baptized Basil, see *Ep.* 51.2; Courtonne, 1: 132-133. There was also the downfall of Hosius and Liberius.

[18] *De jud.*, 2 and 1 (conflated): 653c and B; Clarke, pp. 77 f. See also below, pp. 69, n. 149, and 75, n. 175.

[19] This, if we are to place the *Moralia* after 370; see below, pp. 149 ff., our Chronological Table. On Eunomius see M. Spanneut, "Eunome," in *DHGE* 15 (1963) 1399-1405 (with Bibliography). Among the most recent studies should be noted, L. R. Wickham, "The Date of Eunomius' *Apology*: A Reconsideration," *JThS* 20 (1969) 231-240 (Eunomius has *indeed* delivered his *Apology* at the Council of Constantinople), and E. Cavalcanti cited below, n. 22.

[20] *C. Eun.* 1.1: 497A ff.; 5: 516B ff.; 9: 532A. Cf. Kelly, *Early Christian Doctrines*, p. 249.

[21] See *C. Eun.* 1.1: 497A f.

[22] See *C. Eun.* 1.3: 505-508; 2.30: 641A; 7: 584B. Cf. *Ep.* 52.1: Courtonne, 1: 134; Spidlik, *Sophiologie*, pp. 211 ff. See also E. Cavalcanti, *Studi eunomiani* (Rome, 1976), pp. 34-46, and M. Girardi, "Le 'nozioni communi sullo Spirito Santo' in Basilio Magno," *VChr* 13 (1976) 278-283.

[23] See *C. Eun.* 1.26: 569C. Cf. *De sp. s.*, 17-19: Pruche, 302 ff.; *In ps.* 28.3: 288A-B.

[24] See *C. Eun.* 2.19: 612B-C.

[25] See *C. Eun.* 2.5: 585B-C; 19: 612C; 1.3: 508A ("multitude of Christians . . . endowed with all sorts of spiritual charismata").

[26] See in particular *C. Eun.* 3.2-3: 657C ff.

[27] The presence of clergy seems to be implied in *Hom.* 3.5: Rudberg, 30. See also the remark on *Hom.* 11.5

below, p. 7. On the two types of ascetics see Appendix B and C below, pp. 156-165. In his otherwise valuable work on the preaching of the Cappadocians Bernardi has failed to take notice of the preface to the *Small Asceticon* (PG 31: 1080A-B) which, in my opinion, implies the regular attendance of Basilian ascetics at the services and instructions held in the local churches. Moreover, many of the so-called *Shorter Rules* seem to have been occasioned by questions put to Basil following his homilies in the church. In some cases they appear as further explanations of some points raised during the sermons. As instances cf. *Reg. br.* 301: 1296A f. with *Hom.* 3.4: Rudberg, 28 f.; *Reg. br.* 164: 1189B ff. with *Hom.* 3.5: Rudberg, 30, etc.

[28] *Hom.* 11.5: 381C-D.

[29] Ibid., 384B.

[30] A similar thought is expressed in *Interrog.* 3: 495A.

[31] *Hom.* 3.1: Rudberg, 21 ff.

[32] Cf. *Hom.* 9.9: 394A-B; 3.6: Rudberg, 32-33.

[33] *Hom.* 3.3: Rudberg, 26. Cf. *Reg. fus.* 55: 1044B ff.

[34] *Hom.* 3.4: Rudberg, 28 f.; see *Hom.* 8.8: 328B.

[35] *Hom.* 3.4: Rudberg, 29-30. For a similar procedure see *In ps.* 28.1: 281A-B; 29.1: 308A; 48.1: 433B.

[36] *In ps.* 29.1: 308A.

[37] *In ps.* 48.1: 433B. See also above, p. 2, n. 7.

[38] *In ps.* 44.5: 397D.

[39] Ibid., 9: 408C. The authority . . . of discerning good from evil is attributed in *Reg. mor.* 80.15: 865A to one of the church members, the leader of the word, who in the body executes the function of the eye.

[40] *In ps.* 44.9: 408C.

[41] Ibid.

[42] *In ps.* 44.10: 409A; 11: 412C. On the theme of the church as bride of Christ in Origen see H. J. Vogt, *Das Kirchenverständnis des Origenes* (Cologne-Vienna, 1974), pp. 210-225.

[43] *In ps.* 44.10: 409A-B.

[44] Ibid., 10: 409A.

[45] Ibid., 10: 409C.

[46] Ibid., 11: 412C-D.

[47] Ibid., 12: 413B.

[48] Ibid., 12: 413C.

[49] Ibid., 12: 413D.

[50] *In ps.* 45.4: 421C-D; 59.4: 468B. On the sources of this definition see A. Harnack, *History of Dogma* (New York, 1961), 2: 81-82 (Platonic idea from the *Republic* found in Origen); also E. Hatch, *The Influence of Greek Ideas on Christianity* (New York, 1956), p. 211, n. 5 . . . . Cf. P. Scazzoso, *Reminiscenze della Polis platonica nel cenobio di s. Basilio* (Milan, 1970).

[51] *In ps.* 59.4: 468B; 45.4: 421C.

[52] *In ps.* 45.4: 421B-C.

[53] Ibid., 4: 421C; 8: 428C-429A. As a parallel to these passages see *Reg. fus.* 5: 920B ff., and 8: 933D ff. See also in this connection our remark below, p. 19 about the moral rather than institutional character of this "church in heaven."

[54] *In ps.* 59.2: 461B; see *In ps.* 1.2: 213A. On the idea of "change" in the sense of progress from the imperfect to the perfect see *In ps.* 44.1-2: 388A ff.; *De fide,* 2: 681B; *Ep.* 223.3: Courtonne, 3: 12. On the concept of excommunication from the church referred to *In ps.* 59.4: 468A, see *Ep.* 61: Courtonne, 1: 151-152.

[55] *In ps.* 28.3: 288A-C; cf. also *C. Eun.* 1.26: 569C.

[56] On the meaning of parasynagogue see *Ep.* 188, *c.* 1 discussed below, pp. 65-67.

[57] *In ps.* 33.8: 369A-B. This same homily emphasizes the non-egalitarian character of Christian calling: "Just as the bones by their own firmness protect the tenderness of the flesh, so also in the church there are some who through their own constancy are able to carry the infirmities of the weak," etc. (ibid., 13: 384B-C; Way, p. 272). See also below, p. 29, n. 153. For a possible identification of the stronger members see *Hex.* 5.6: Giet, 304, and *Epistles 28* and *29.* Cf. *C. Eun.* 1.1: 500A.

[58] See in particular the study of Y. Courtonne, *Saint Basile et l'hellénisme* (Paris, 1934), and S. Giet's introduction to his edition of Basil's *Hexaemeron* (Paris, 1968), pp. 32 ff., esp. 43 ff.

[59] See Spidlik, *Sophiologie,* pp. 143 ff.

[60] See *Hex.* 1.3: Giet, 96 ff.; 11.8: Smets-Esbroeck, 246 f.

[61] This is, however, an historical judgment. Basil's objective as we mentioned was of a religious rather than sociological nature. On Basil's attitude towards Greek science see Courtonne, *S. Basile et l'hellénisme,* and E. Amand de Mendieta, "The Official Attitude of Basil of Caesarea as a Christian Bishop towards Greek Philosophy and Science," in D. Baker, ed., *The Orthodox Churches and the West* (Oxford, 1976), pp. 25-49.

[62] Basil's *Corpus Asceticum* comprises the works listed foremost in his preface to the *Hypotyposis* (the text printed as spurious in PG 31, 1509-1513 has been vindicated as authentic by J. Gribomont, *Histoire du texte des Ascétiques de s. Basile* (Louvain, 1953), pp. 284-287; see there also, pp. 279-282, a critical edition of the Greek text). These works are: *De judicio, De fide, Moralia* and the *Great Asceticon.* However, it must be recognized that, in one way or another, all of Basil's writings bear the stamp of his ascetic training and background. Therefore in a study of his life and ideals connected with Christian asceticism one must also constantly refer to his sermons, letters and "dogmatic" writings. The existence of a previous edition of the *Great Asceticon* (known traditionally as the *Longer* and *Shorter Rules*) has been established only recently, thanks to the studies of F. Laun and J. Gribomont. It came to be known as the *Small Asceticon.* This early edition of Basil's *Asceticon* has been preserved only in two versions, the Latin of Rufinus from 397 (PL 103, 483-554), and in a less accessible Syriac translation from the sixth century. Both translations have been investigated and collated by Gribomont, *Histoire,* pp. 95-148. For reasons explained in the Chronological Table, I adopt the following chronology in the analysis of Basil's ascetic writings: *Small Asceticon*—between 365-369; *Great Asceticon*—370-376; *Moralia*—beginning with 360; final composition with the two prefaces, the *De judicio* and the *De fide,* from 376. The *Hypotyposis*—from 376.

[63] It is my contention that Basil became involved in the recruitment and organization of ascetic communities as a result, partially, of Julian's policies against the Christians and, partially, of emperor Valens' measures. Little consideration has been given until now in Basilian scholarship to the possible influence of these external factors on Basil's decision to switch from an isolated half-desert type of asceticism (Sarabaitism?) to one with closer ties with the church ostracized by the state. This change probably occurred during Basil's visit to Caesarea in 362, and his projects begun then were resumed on full scale on his return in 365. For the (Eastern) idea of the emperor as "always close to hand to his subjects," see P. Brown, *The World of Late Antiquity* (London, 1971), pp. 42-43.

[64] *Epistles 84* and *89* of Julian, in which the emperor-philosopher sketches his plans to revive the old religion, were written before June of 362. "On June 17, 362, a law was promulgated which made the giving of instruction in school everywhere dependent on the

permission of city authorities; and these were directed to test more the character of the applicants" (H. Lietzmann, *History of the Early Church* [Cleveland, 1961], 3: 274). If Eusebius was elected to succeed Dianius in June or July of 362 (see Maran, *Vita,* 8.4), Basil must have arrived at the summons of the dying Dianius either in May or June of the same year; see *Ep.* 51.2: Courtonne, 1: 133.

⁶⁵ Lietzmann, *History,* 3: 279.

⁶⁶ *Ep.* 89 quoted in Lietzmann, *History,* 3: 278-279.

⁶⁷ I place Julian's visit to Caesarea in September of 362 because on September 7 was the annual commemoration of the martyrdom of Eupsychius and Damas, who were executed by order of the emperor during his stay in Cappadocia; see *Epp.* 100, 176 and 252, and Maran, *Vita,* 8.5-6; L. Duchesne, *The Early History of the Christian Church* (London, 1912), 2: 265; Lietzmann, *History,* 3: 279-280 (I do not know on what evidence this author calls Eupsychius a bishop, 3: 280).

⁶⁸ Julian's policies had certainly affected Gregory of Nazianzus. Besides his *Invectives against Julian* from 363 (which were probably never pronounced in public), see *Orations 20, 42* and *43.* On the latter two see the important observation of Bernardi, *Prédication,* pp. 257-258.

⁶⁹ See Greg. Naz., *Or.* 43.29.

⁷⁰ The emperor died on June 26, 363, and was succeeded by the pious Jovian.

⁷¹ The same applies to his other works, see n. 62, above.

⁷² See below, pp. 156 ff.

⁷³ That Basil's ascetic ideal is addressed to all, independently of sex, social condition, and also very largely of age, can be proved from, *Interrog.* 6: 497D-498B; *Reg. fus.* 10.1: 944C ff.; 11: 948A-C; *Reg. mor.* 75.1: 856A; *Reg. fus.* 12: 948C ff.; 15.1-4: 952A-957A; *Reg. mor.* 73.1-6: 849D-853B; 76.1-2: 857A-B. The only remote condition seems to be baptism; see *Reg. fus.* 8.1: 936A and *Interrog.* 4: 498C, in the sense that catechumens, who in the local churches constituted the majority, would be excluded from Basil's "versions" of the church. That baptism was not an immediate condition can be inferred from Basil's account of his own ascetic renunciation in *Ep.* 223.2: Courtonne, 3: 10. Although regulations concerning the admission of slaves, married persons, and children appear only in the *Great Asceticon* it must be noted that the *Asceticons* are not systematic works but that their composition progressively developed as questions were raised; see *Scholion* 2, 3 and 4 in Gribomont, *Histoire,* pp. 152-154.

⁷⁴ See *De sp. s.* 2: Pruche, 252; *Reg. mor.* 80.8: 861D.

⁷⁵ We have in mind particularly the "systematic" part, the so-called "Longer Rules," in the *Small Asceticon, Interrogations* 1-11, and the *Reg. fus.* 1-54 of the *Great Ascetion.* While in all probability the titles of the shorter questions are original, that is, posited by the disciples of Basil, the headings of the longer ones were improperly added by the editors; see J. Gribomont, "Saint Basile," *Théologie de la vie monastique* (Paris, 1961), p. 104.

⁷⁶ See *Reg. fus.* 2.1: 909B; ibid.: 912A.

⁷⁷ Cf. *In ps.* 48.1: 432A-B. . . .

⁷⁸ *In ps.* 48.1: 432B.

⁷⁹ *Reg. fus.* 5.3: 921C; Clarke, p. 160.

⁸⁰ Cf. *Hom.* 23.4: 597A. . . .

⁸¹ *Reg. mor.* 43.1: 761C. See also ibid., 2: 761D; Clarke, p. 112: "That as the law makes a partial, so the gospel makes a complete demand as regards every good action," which confirms what was said above, pp. 15-16; see also *Reg. br.* 4: 1984C; 293, 1288C ff.

⁸² See *Reg. fus.* 2.1: 908B-C; 909A-B.

⁸³ See *Reg. fus.* 2.1: 908D; Clarke, p. 153.

⁸⁴ Ibid.

⁸⁵ *Reg. fus.* 3.1: 917A-B; Clarke, p. 157.

⁸⁶ Ibid.

⁸⁷ For the sake of brevity I shall quote mainly from the expanded text of the *Great Asceticon* unless there is an important difference in content, in which case I shall also cite the text of the *Small Asceticon.*

⁸⁸ The first question is taken from *Reg. fus.* 6.1-2: 925A-928B; the second, from *Reg. fus.* 7.1-4: 928B-933C, and the corresponding *Interrog.* 2: 493B-494A and *Interrog.* 3: 494B-496B.

⁸⁹ See below, pp. 163 ff.; Gribomont, "Renoncement," pp. 300-302.

⁹⁰ On the church's elements of sacredness, distinctiveness, and secrecy see *Ep.* 28.1: Courtonne, 1: 66-67; *De sp. s.* 66: Pruche, 478 ff.; E. Amand de Mendieta, *The 'Unwritten' and 'Secret' Apostolic Traditions in the Theological Thought of St. Basil of Caesarea* (Edinburgh, 1965); Idem . . . *JThS* 16 (1965) 129-142. However, I would be inclined to agree with the interpretation of the *De sp. s.* 66 given by G. Florovsky,

"The Function of Tradition in the Ancient Church," *GOTR* 9 (1963) 181-200, despite Amand's reservations in "The Pair," p. 136.

[91] In Cappadocia many tried to join the ascetic communities only to avoid taxes and military service. If Basil managed to deter many from joining the church for trivial reasons, he probably did so by making almost compulsory acceptance of ascetic renunciation part of the baptismal renunciation. This is not, however, so clear from the *Asceticons* alone, nor from Basil's homilies. See on the latter Bernardi, *Prédication*, p. 396.

[92] Besides n. 90 see Lietzmann, *History*, 4: 98-99.

[93] *Proem. in reg. br.:* 1080A; Clarke, p. 229.

[94] *Reg. fus.* 6.1: 925A; Clarke, p. 161; cf. ibid., 925C.

[95] For a definition of the "world" in the moral sense see *De sp. s.* 53: Pruche, 440 f.; see also n. 94.

[96] Cf. Gribomont, "Renoncement," pp. 295 and 300.

[97] *Ep.* 2.2: Rudberg, 158; cf. Jackson, p. 110; see also *Ep.* 223.2: Courtonne, 3: 10.

[98] Besides n. 97 see Gribomont, "Renoncement," pp. 305-306, and *Ep.* 210.1: Courtonne, 2: 190 . . . in *Ep.* 2.2: Rudberg, 158).

[99] See *Epistles* 3-6, 9, 11-13, 15, 17-18, 20-21.

[100] See *Reg. fus.* 5.1-3: 920A-924D, esp. 921A.

[101] Cf. Gribomont, "Renoncement," pp. 300-301.

[102] Cf. *Ep.* 2.1-2: Rudberg, 156 ff.

[103] Cf. *Reg. fus.* 7: 928B ff.; *Interrog.* 3: 494B ff.

[104] Besides *Reg. fus.* 7.2: 929C see *De jud.,* 3: 660A.

[105] *Saint Basil the Great. A Study in Monasticism* (Cambridge, 1913), p. 86, n. 2. Unfortunately this author often fails to draw the pertinent conclusions from many of his remarkable insights. For instance, on pp. 112-113 of the same work Clarke skillfully demonstrates that the term [*migas*] in Gregory of Nazianzus is used to describe the ascetic life lived in the world. However, he never follows up this accurate observation.

[106] Text from Acts 2.44 quoted in *Reg. fus.* 7.4: 933C. There do not seem to be substantial changes between the exposition in the *Reg. fus.* 7 and the *Interrog.* 3 regarding our subject. The only discrepancy I noticed is that Rufinus' text speaks also of prayer as drawing benefit from the communal life; see 495C. However, in the *Great Asceticon* there seems to be a certain

insinuation, but no more than that, as to the benefits of living in the same place.

[107] A rather "monastic" analysis of this interrogation can be found in E. Amand de Mendieta, *L'ascèse monastique de saint Basile* (Maredsous, 1949), pp. 118-128; see also Clarke, *Monasticism*, pp. 85-86.

[108] Cf. *Reg. fus.* 7.1: 928C-D. The concept of "insufficiency" is also expressed in *Ep.* 97: Courtonne, 1: 210. See also *Ep.* 203.3: Courtonne, 2: 170.

[109] *Reg. fus.* 7.1: 929A.

[110] Ibid.

[111] Ibid.: 929B.

[112] Ibid., 2: 929C; Clarke, p. 164.

[113] *Interrog.* 3: 495A: "quae [charismata] singula non tam pro se unusquisque quam pro aliis suscipit a Spiritu sancto."

[114] *Reg. fus.* 7.2: 932B; Clarke, p. 165.

[115] Ibid., 3: 932B-C.

[116] Cf. ibid., 4: 933A.

[117] For more on this see below, pp. 161-165.

[118] On the frequent use of Acts 2.44 and 4.32, see Amand de Mendieta, *Ascèse*, p. 129, n. 88.

[119] Cf. *Ep.* 295: Courtonne, 3: 169-170. Cf. also *Reg. mor.* 80.22: 868C: "What is the ethos of a Christian? Faith working through love."

[120] *Reg. mor.* 80.1, 4, 9-10: 860C-864A; Clarke, pp. 127-128.

[121] See *In ps.* 44.2: 392C. Compare Cicero, *De officiis* 1.17, 53-58: Miller, 56-60.

[122] See *Reg. mor.* 80.9-10: 864A; 18.6: 732C-D, and also below, pp. 74-75.

[123] See *Ep.* 2.2 analyzed above, pp. 19 f.

[124] See on the ascetic community, *Epp.* 223.5: Courtonne, 3: 14; 257.2: ibid., 100; and the *Great Asceticon, passim*. As applied to the church, see *Epp.* 133: Courtonne, 2: 47; 135.2: ibid., 50; 226.2: ibid., 3: 25; 255: ibid., 96. See also *Didascalia Apostolorum* and Firmilian's, among Cyprian's, *Epistle 175.25:* CSEL 3.2. Cf. also 1 Pet 5.9. However, beginning with the fourth century it is commonly restricted to the ascetic communities; see Greg. Nys., *Vit. Macr.* 16: Maraval, 194

and n. 1, ibid., references to Gregory of Nazianzus, Macarius, and Jerome.

[125] *De jud.*, 4: 660C-D; Clarke, p. 81.

[126] L. Vischer, *Basilius der Grosse* (Basel, 1953), p. 49, whose position Gribomont, "Renoncement," p. 474, endorses, has tried to reverse the statement of P. Humbertclaude by saying that Basil endeavoured to reform the local churches on the pattern of his cenobia, and not vice versa. It seems, however, that the most accurate statement to make is that Basil first built (or rebuilt) his ascetic communities on the pattern of the model church of Jerusalem, and that he then proceeded to apply that model to the contemporary churches: thus (a) church of Jerusalem; (b) ascetic community embodying that model; (c) the local church extending and perpetuating it. The interest in the model community of Jerusalem has been constantly present in the mind of many church reformers, from the early centuries through Basil and Augustine to the Middle Ages. In the absence of an overall study the reader may consult the works of A. Vööbus, *History of Asceticism in the Syrian Orient . . .* (Louvain, 1958, 1960), and P. C. Bori, *La chiesa primitiva* (Brescia, 1974).

[127] The following exposition of Paul's teaching on charismata is based largely on the works of E. Käsemann, "Ministry and Community in the New Testament," in *Essays on New Testament Themes* (London, 1964), pp. 63-94; Idem, "Worship in Everyday Life: a note on Romans 13," in *New Testament Questions of Today* (London, 1969), pp. 188-195; E. Schweizer, *Church Order in the New Testament* (London, 1961); Idem, *Jesus* (Richmond, Va., 1971); J. D. G. Dunn, *Jesus and the Spirit* (London, 1975). See also the articles "Charisma" (by H. Conzelmann) and "Pneuma" (by E. Schweizer) in *TDNT* and the homonymous entries in *PGL*.

[128] See Käsemann, "Ministry," p. 64.

[129] Käsemann, "Ministry," p. 64.

[130] For a discussion of these possibilities see L. S. Thornton, *The Common Life in the Body of Christ* (London, 1963), pp. 66 ff., and J. D. G. Dunn, p. 261.

[131] See Käsemann, "Ministry," p. 72. The term "new obedience" for the post-Easter faith is also taken from him; see also Idem, "Worship," p. 194, where it is demonstrated that for Paul there was no difference between the private and public realm.

[132] See for the biblical references Käsemann, "Ministry," p. 69; *contra*, Dunn, *Jesus*, pp. 206 f.

[133] "Ministry," pp. 73-74.

[134] Ibid., p. 75.

[135] Ibid., p. 76.

[136] Ibid.

[137] Ibid., pp. 77-78.

[138] Cf. Käsemann, "Worship," p. 191; "Ministry," pp. 67 f.

[139] *Hom.* 3.4: Rudberg, 29 f.; *Hom.* 9.5: 340B; *In ps.* 29.1: 308A.

[140] *Hom.* 3.8: Rudberg, 36-37; *Hex.* 10.1, 2, 6: Smets-Esbroeck, 166 ff., 178 ff.

[141] This is already indicated, guardedly though, in *Hom.* 3.3: Rudberg, 26 ff.; see Amand de Mendieta, *Ascèse*, pp. 191 ff.

[142] Before Basil this meaning is found only in the *Didache* 1.5; see *Hom.* 11.5: 384A ff.

[143] See *Reg. br.* 92: 1145c f.; *Hom.* 11.5: 381c ff.

[144] Ibid., and *Reg. fus.* 9.1: 941B ff.; *Reg. mor.* 48.2: 768D ff.

[145] See *Reg. mor.* 7.1: 712B; *Hom.* 23.4: 597A.

[146] *Reg. br.* 225: 1232B ff. and n. 145, above. The interpretation of this rule in Amand de Mendieta, *Ascèse*, p. 143 seems to us less correct. It is evident that throughout his writings, notably the *Moralia*, Basil is faced with the uncontrollable demands for freedom of the Messalians, the Enthusiasts of the fourth century; see the sources on their teaching in M. Aubineau, *Grégoire de Nysse, Traité de la Virginité* (Paris, 1967), pp. 534-536; cf. esp. p. 534, "they regard the zeal for the works of the commandments detrimental to their souls." See also J. Gribomont, "Les Règles Morales de s. Basile et le Nouveau Testament," *SP* 2 (Berlin, 1957) 416-426.

[147] The expression, "Submit to each other," is also strongly attested in Basil's writings; see briefly *Reg. br.* 1: 1081C, and Spidlik, *Sophiologie*, pp. 74 ff.

[148] See the references given below, pp. 90 ff.

[149] See *Reg. fus.* 7.2: 932A; *Ep.* 135.1: Courtonne, 2: 50; *Hom.* 11.5: 381D-384A.

[150] See *Ep.* 236.7: Courtonne, 3: 54-55; *Hom.* 6.7: 267B ff.; also Spidlik, *Sophiologie*, pp. 149 ff.

[151] See in general *Hom.* 5.2: 241A; *In ps.* 1.3: 217A; *Hom.* 3.4: Rudberg, 29-30, and also the inclusion of

the various life-situations in the *Moralia*; see *Reg. mor.* 70-79 preceded by the *Reg. mor.* 60 quoted next.

[152] *Reg. mor.* 60.1: 793A-B; Clarke, p. 117 (rev.).

[153] See also *Reg. br.* 235: 1240C, and *In ps.* 33.13 cited above, n. 57.

[154] See *In ps.* 44.9: 408C.

[155] *De sp. s.* 61: Pruche, 468 f. See also *De jud., 3:* 660A; *Reg. fus.* 7.2: 929C.

[156] See *Reg. mor.* 60 quoted above.

[157] *De sp. s.* 62: Pruche, 470. [*Hora*] could also be translated "the position" or "proper place" of a person in life.

[158] "Now the Spirit is not brought into intimate association . . . with the soul by local approximation. . . . This approximation results from the withdrawal of passions which, coming afterwards on the soul from its friendship to the flesh, have alienated it from its close friendship to God" (*De sp. s.* 23: Pruche, 326; Jackson, p. 15).

[159] See *De sp. s.* 61: Pruche, 470; *Reg. mor.* 80.22: 868D-869B.

[160] *De sp. s.* 23: Pruche, 328; Jackson, pp. 15-16 (rev.). Cf. also *Reg. mor.* 20.1-2: 736D ff.

[161] *Ep.* 90.1: Courtonne, 1: 195.

[162] On the social function of charismata see *Reg. br.* 253: 1252B-C; also the fine interpretation of the *Moral Rule* 58 by Amand de Mendieta, *Ascèse,* p. 139, n. 125; see also below, p. 119 and n. 74. B. Bobrinskoy, "Liturgie et ecclésiologie trinitaire de s. Basile," *VC* 89 (1969) 16 ff., has interpreted the words [*he koinonia tou Pneumatos*] which Basil obviously derives from 2 Cor 13.13, in the sense of a communion and participation in the Holy Spirit modelled on the eucharistic communion. Although some such meaning is possible according to Thornton, *The Common Life,* pp. 71 ff., if it is adopted "it must not be understood in a sense which excludes the other alternative," that is, "the human fellowship which the Holy Spirit brought into existence, the social entity which has the Holy Spirit for its creative author or fountain-source" (ibid., pp. 74 and 69; for such a sense in Basil see *In ps.* 48.1: 433A-D. Cf. S. Giet, *Les idées et l'action sociales de s. Basile* [Paris, 1941], p. 173). Cf. also Dunn, *Jesus,* pp. 260 f.: "shared experience."

[163] *Reg. br.* 303: 1296D-1297A.

[164] Ibid.: 1297B-C; see *Reg. br.* 235: 1240C-D. Besides the two mentioned charismata, Basil acknowledges the existence of others; see Amand de Mendieta, *Ascèse,* pp. 139 and 142-144. It should be noted that Basil is far from advocating an indiscriminate or blind obedience on the part of the subjects. In *Reg. br.* 303: 1297B-C the subjects are given the same rights to "test the spirits" as the hearers of the word in *Reg. mor.* 72.1-2: 845D ff.

[165] On the sanctification of angels by the Holy Spirit see the study of A. Heising, "Der Hl. Geist und die Heiligung der Engel in der Pneumatologie des Basilius von Caesarea," *ZKTh* 87 (1965) 257-308. On the "inspiration" of the Bible see the dissertation of B. B. Wawryk, *Doctrina Sancti Basilii Magni de inspiratione Sacrae Scripturae* (Rome, 1943). On the presence of the Spirit in other ecclesiastical actions see *Reg. mor.* 80.22: 868D; 20.2: 736D; *Ep.* 188, *c.* 1: Courtonne, 2: 123; *In ps.* 44.3: 396A; *Epp.* 229.1: Courtonne, 3: 33-34; 92.3: ibid., 1: 202-203; 207.4: ibid., 2: 187; and in general see the studies of J. Verhees, "Pneuma, Erfahrung und Erleuchtung in der Theologie des Basilius des Grossen," *Ostkirchliche Studien* 25 (1976) 43-59, and "Die Bedeutung der Tranzendenz des Pneuma bei Basilius," ibid., 285-302.

[166] The title "Longer" and "Shorter Rules" given in some MSS to the question-answers of Basil's *Asceticons* is illegitimate not only because of its being interpolated but also because in replying to the questions Basil acts less as a legislator than as a spiritual adviser.

[167] See *In ps.* 32.1: 324C; *Epp.* 65: Courtonne, 1: 155; 133: ibid., 2: 47; 172: ibid., 107; 204.1: ibid., 173. Cf. *In ps.* 33.13: 384C.

[168] . . . see PG 31, 1003A and Clarke, *Ascetic Works,* p. 201.

[169] *Reg. fus.* 35.3: 1008A-B; Clarke, pp. 203-204.

[170] Ibid.: 1008B; Clarke, p. 204.

[171] See ch. 4, B, i: "Intrinsic Limitations of the Local Church."

[172] *Ep.* 161.1: Courtonne, 2: 93; Jackson, p. 214.

[173] *Ep.* 82: Courtonne, 1: 184; Jackson, p. 172. The last words clearly refer to the internal difficulties.

[174] In his study, *Basilius der Grosse,* L. Vischer draws attention to the frequency with which Basil makes reference to personal sins as possible obstacles to the achievement of church's union; see e.g. *Epp.* 59.1: Courtonne, 1: 147; 124; ibid., 2: 29-30; 266.2: ibid., 3: 135; 204.4: ibid., 2: 175; 203.1: ibid., 168.

[175] *Ep.* 203.3: Courtonne, 2: 170; Jackson, p. 242.

[176] *Ep.* 136.2: Courtonne, 2: 52.

[177] Conflation of *De sp. s.* 61: Pruche, 470; Jackson, p. 39 and *De jud.*, 3: 657D-660A; Clarke, p. 80.

[178] *Ep.* 191: Courtonne, 2: 145.

[179] *De sp. s.* 78: Pruche, 526-528. See *De jud.* 3: 657c.

List of Abbreviations

1. *Abbreviations of the Works of Basil of Caesarea*

We refer to the works of Basil of Caesarea by the abbreviated Latin title and subdivision of the work. Books, chapters and paragraphs are indicated by arabic numerals. All references are to the Greek text either of Migne's Patrologia Graeca (=PG) volumes 29-32 quoted by volume, column and letter, or, if available, to the modern partial editions quoted by the name of the editor, volume and page number. Unless otherwise noted, English translations are my own. When used, the translations of others have always been checked against the Greek text and, if necessary, slightly revised. All such revisions are signalled by the abbreviation "rev." in parenthesis. The translations of W. K. L. Clarke and B. Jackson have been preferred to those of R. Deferrari, A. Way and M. Wagner as being more accurate.

C. Eun. 1-3 Contra Eunomium libri tres, PG 29, 497-669.

De fide De fide, PG 31, 676-692; Eng. trans. Clarke, *Ascetic Works*, pp. 90-99.

De jud. De judicio Dei, PG 31, 653-676; Eng. trans. Clarke, *Ascetic Works*, pp. 77-89. . . .

De sp. s. De Spiritu Sancto, PG 32, 68-217; ed. Johnston, *The Book of Saint Basil the Great on the Holy Spirit*; ed. and Fr. trans. Pruche, *Basile de Césarée, Traité du Saint-Esprit*; Eng. trans. Jackson, SLNPF, 8: 2-50.

Ep. 1-366 Epistolae 1-366, PG 32, 220-1112; ed. and Fr. trans. Courtonne, *Saint Basile, Lettres* 1-3; Eng. trans. Jackson, SLNPF, 8: 109-327; ed. and Eng. trans. Deferrari, *Saint Basil, The Letters. Epp.* 2, 150 and 173 are edited in Rudberg, *Etudes sur la tradition*, pp. 151-211.

Hex. 1-9 (11) Hexaemeron homiliae 9, PG 29, 4-208; ed. and Fr. trans. Giet, *Basile de Césarée, Homélies sur l'Hexaéméron*; Eng. trans. Jackson, SLNPF, 8: 52-107; *Homilies 10* and *11* are edited and translated into Fr. in Smets and van Esbroeck, *Basile de Césarée, Sur l'origine de l'homme*; see also the excellent edition of Hörner, *Auctorum incertorum . . . sermones.*

Hom. 1-29 Homiliae variae, PG 31, 163-481; 489-617; 1437-1476; 1488-1496. *Homily 3* is edited in Rudberg, *L'homélie de Basile.*

In ps. Homiliae in psalmos 1, 7, 14.1-2, 28, 29, 32, 33, 44, 45, 48, 59, 61, 114, 115 (PG 29, 307-494; 30, 104-116; Eng. trans. A. C. Way, *St. Basil, Exegetic Homilies*, pp. 151-359).

Interrog. 1-203 Interrogationes fratrum, PL 103, 483-554. Known also as *Small Asceticon;* see Gribomont, *Histoire*, pp. 237 ff. . . .

Reg. br. 1-313 Regulae brevius tractatae, PG 31, 1080-1305; Eng. trans. Clarke, *Ascetic Works*, pp. 230-351; for the additional 7 *Interrogations*, see Gribomont, *Histoire*, pp. 179-186.

Reg. fus. 1-55 Regulae fusius tractatae, PG 31, 905-1052; Eng. trans. Clarke, *Ascetic Works*, pp. 152-228.

Reg. mor. 1-80 Regulae morales, PG 31, 700-869; Eng. trans. Clarke, *Ascetic Works*, pp. 101-131.

2. *Other Abbreviations*

CSEL Corpus Scriptorum Ecclesiasticorum Latinorum (Vienna) . . .

DHGE Dictionnaire d'histoire et de géographie ecclésiastiques, edd. A. Baudrillart et al. (Paris: Letouzey, 1912—) . . . .

EThL Ephemerides theologicae lovanienses (Louvain) . . .

GOTR Greek Orthodox Theological Review (Brookline, Mass.) . . .

JThS Journal of Theological Studies (Oxford) . . .

PG Patrologia graeca, 161 vols., ed. J. P. Migne (Paris, 1857-1866). . . .

PGL A Patristic Greek Lexicon, ed. G. W. H. Lampe (Oxford: Clarendon, 1961-1965). . . .

RB Revue bénédictine (Maredsous) . . .

RHE Revue d'histoire ecclésiastique (Louvain) . . .

SCh Sources chrétiennes (Paris)

SCM Student Christian Movement (London) . . .

SLNPF A Select Library of Nicene and Post-Nicene Fathers of the Christian Church (New York: Grand Rapids) . . .

SP Studia patristica (Berlin)

SPCK Society for Promoting Christian Knowledge (London) . . .

TDNT Theological Dictionary of the New Testament, 10 vols., edd. G. Kittel et al. (Grand Rapids: Eerdmans, 1964-1976). . . .

VC Verbum caro (Taizé)

VCh Vigiliae christianae (Amsterdam)

VChr Vetera christianorum (Bari) . . .

ZK Zeitschrift für Kirchengeschichte (Stuttgart)

ZKTh Zeitschrift für katholische Theologie (Innsbruck) . . .

A. Select Bibliography

A. Editions and English Translations of Basil's Works

For an alphabetical listing with short references, see the List of Abbreviations, pp. ix-xii.

. . . Clarke, William Kemp Lowther, trans. *The Ascetic Works of St. Basil.* London: SPCK, 1925.

Courtonne, Yves, ed. & trans. *Saint Basile, Homélies sur la richesse.* Paris: Firmin-Didot, 1935.

————. *Saint Basile, Lettres.* 3 vols. Paris: Les Belles Lettres, 1957, 1961, 1966. . . .

Giet, Stanislas, ed. & trans. *Basile de Césarée, Homélies sur l'Hexaéméron.* 2nd ed. SCh 26bis. Paris: Editions du Cerf, 1968. . . .

Jackson, Blomfield, trans. *The Treatise De Spiritu Sancto, The Nine Homilies of the Hexaemeron and the Letters of Saint Basil the Great.* SLNPF, series 2, volume 8. New York, 1895; rpt. Grand Rapids: Wm. B. Eerdmans, 1968. . . .

Pruche, Benoît, ed. & trans. *Basile de Césarée, Traité du Saint-Esprit.* 2nd ed. SCh 17bis. Paris: Editions du Cerf, 1968. . . .

Rudberg, Stig Y., ed. *L'homélie de Basile de Césarée sur le mot: "Observe-toi toi même."* Stockholm: Almquist, 1962.

Smets, Alexis, and Michel van Esbroeck, edd. & trans. *Basile de Césarée, Sur l'origine de l'homme (Homélies x et x1 de l'Hexaéméron).* SCh 160. Paris: Editions du Cerf, 1970. . . .

Way, Agnes Clare, trans. *St. Basil, Exegetic Homilies.* Washington, D.C.: Catholic University Press, 1963. . . .

B. Other texts

Aubineau, Michel, ed. & trans. *Grégoire de Nysse, Traité de la virginité.* SCh 119. Paris: Editions du Cerf, 1966. . . .

Clémencet, Charles and Armand Benjamin Caillau, edd. & trans. *Sancti Gregorii Nazianzeni Opera omnia.* PG 35-38. . . .

Jaeger, Werner, et al., edd. *Gregorii Nysseni Opera.* Leiden: Brill, 1960—. (For works not comprised by any of the modern editions see PG 44-46).

Maraval, Pierre, ed. & trans. *Grégoire de Nysse, Vie de sainte Macrine.* SCh 178. Paris: Editions du Cerf, 1971. . . .

Miller, Walter, ed. & trans. *Cicero, De officiis.* London: Heinemann, 1928. . . .

C. Studies and General Works

Abramowski, Luise. "Das Bekenntnis des Gregor Thaumaturgus bei Gregor von Nyssa und das Problem seiner Echtheit." *ZKG* 87 (1976) 145-166. . . .

Amand de Mendieta, Emmanuel. *L'ascèse monastique de saint Basile. Essai historique.* Maredsous: Editions de Maredsous, 1949. . . .

————. "La virginité chez Eusèbe d'Emèse et l'ascétisme familial dans la première moitié du IVᵉ siècle." *RHE* 50 (1955) 777-820. . . .

————. *The "Unwritten" and "Secret" Apostolic Traditions in the Theological Thought of Saint Basil of Caesarea.* (Scottish Journal of Theology Occasional Papers, 13.) Edinburgh: Oliver & Boyd, 1965.

————. "The Pair 'Kerygma' and 'Dogma' in the Theological Thought of Saint Basil of Caesarea." *JThS* 16 (1965) 129-142. . . .

————. "The Official Attitude of Basil of Caesarea as a Christian Bishop towards Greek Philosophy and Science." In Derek Baker, ed., *The Orthodox Churches and the West*, pp. 25-49. Oxford: Blackwell, 1976. . . .

Bardy, Gustave. *La théologie de l'Eglise de s. Irénée au concile de Nicée.* Paris: Editions du Cerf, 1947. . . .

Bellini, Enzo. *La chiesa nel mistero della salvezza in san Gregorio Nazianzeno.* Venegono Inferiore: La Scuola Cattolica, 1970. . . .

Bernardi, Jean. *La prédication des Pères cappadociens. Le prédicateur et son auditoire.* Paris: Presses universitaires de France, 1968. . . .

Bobrinskoy, Boris. "Liturgie et ecclésiologie trinitaire de s. Basile." *VC* 89 (1969) 1-32. . . .

Bori, Piere Cesare. *Chiesa primitiva. L'immagine della communità delle origini—Atti 2.42-47; 4.32-37—nella storia della chiesa antica.* Brescia: Paideia, 1974. . . .

Brown, Peter. *The World of Late Antiquity.* London: Thames & Hudson, 1971. . . .

Cavalcanti, Elena. *Studi eunomiani.* Rome: Pontificio Istituto orientale, 1975.

Clarke, William Kemp Lowther. *Saint Basil the Great. A Study in Monasticism.* Cambridge: University Press, 1913. . . .

Conzelmann, Hans. [*Hariosma*]. *TDNT* (Grand Rapids, 1974), 9: 402-406. . . .

Courtonne, Yves. *Saint Basile et l'hellénisme. Etude sur la rencontre de la pensée chrétienne avec la sagesse antique dans l'Hexaéméron de Basile le Grand.* Paris: Firmin-Didot, 1934. . . .

Dehnhard, Hans. *Das Problem der Abhängigkeit des Basilius von Plotin.* Diss. Berlin: de Gruyter, 1964. . . .

Duchesne, Louis. *The Early History of the Christian Church.* 3 vols. London: Murray, 1909, 1912, 1924.

Dunn, James D. G. *Jesus and the Spirit. A Study of the Religious and Charismatic Experience of Jesus and the First Christians as Reflected in the New Testament.* London: SCM, 1975. . . .

Florovsky, Georges. "The Function of Tradition in the Ancient Church." *GOTR* 9 (1963) 181-200. . . .

Giet, Stanislas. *Les idées et l'action sociales de s. Basile.* Paris: Gabalda, 1941. . . .

Girardi, Mario. "Le 'nozioni comuni sullo Spirito Santo' in Basilio Magno." *VChr* 13 (1976) 269-288. . . .

Gribomont, Jean. *Histoire du texte des Ascétiques de s. Basile.* Diss. Louvain: Publications universitaires, 1953. . . .

———. "Les *Règles morales* de s. Basile et le Nouveau Testament." *SP* 2 (Berlin, 1957) 416-426.

———. "Le renoncement au monde dans l'idéal ascétique de s. Basile." *Irénikon* 31 (1958) 282-307; 460-475. . . .

———. "Saint Basile." In *Théologie de la vie monastique,* pp. 99-113. Paris: Aubier, 1961.

———. "L'origénisme de s. Basile." In *L'homme devant Dieu. Mélanges H. de Lubac,* 1: 281-294. Paris: Aubier, 1963. . . .

Grillmeier, Aloys. *Christ in Christian Tradition.* 1: *From the Apostolic Age to Chalcedon (451).* 2nd ed. Atlanta: Knox Press, 1975. . . .

Harnack, Adolf von. *History of Dogma.* 7 vols. New York: Dover, 1961.

———. *The Mission and Expansion of Christianity in the First Three Centuries.* 2 vols. London: Williams, 1904/1905.

Hatch, Edwin. *The Influence of Greek Ideas on Christianity.* New York: Torchbooks, 1957. . . .

Heising, Alkuin. "Der Hl. Geist und die Heiligung der Engel in der Pneumatologie des Basilius von Caesarea." *ZKTh* 87 (1965) 257-308. . . .

Holl, Karl. ["Basil's Trinitarian Teaching"]. In *Amphilochius von Ikonium in seinem Verhältnis zu den grossen Kappadoziern,* pp. 116-158. Tübingen: Mohr, 1904; rpt. 1969. . . .

Käsemann, Ernst. *Essays on New Testament Themes.* London: SCM, 1964.

———. *New Testament Questions of Today.* London: SCM, 1969.

Kelly, John Norman Davidson. *Early Christian Doctrines.* 4th ed. London: Black, 1968. . . .

Legrand, Hervé Marie. "The Revaluation of Local Churches: Some Theological Implications." *Concilium* 71 (1972) 53-64. . . .

Lietzmann, Hans. *History of the Early Church.* 4 vols. Cleveland: World, 1961. . . .

Malingrey, Anne Marie. *"Philosophia." Etude d'un groupe de mots dans la littérature grecque, des Présocratiques au IVᵉ siècle après J.C.* Paris: Klincksieck, 1961. . . .

Maran, Prudentius. *Vita s. Basilii Magni.* PG 29, v-clxxvii. See Julien Garnier and Prudentius Maran, edd. & trans. *Sancti Basilii Magni Opera omnia.* . . .

Metz, René. *La consécration des vierges dans l'Eglise romaine.* Paris: Presses universitaires de France, 1957. . . .

Momigliano, Arnaldo, ed. *The Conflict between Pa-*

ganism and Christianity in the Fourth Century. Oxford: University Press, 1963. . . .

Muraille, Philippe. "L'Eglise, peuple de l'oikouméné d'après s. Grégoire de Nazianze. Notes sur l'unité et l'universalité." *EThL* 44 (1968) 154-178. . . .

Scazzoso, Piero. *Reminiscenze della Polis platonica nel cenobio di s. Basilio.* Milan: Istituto Italiano, 1970. . . .

Schmidt, Karl Ludwig. [*Ekklesoa*]. *TDNT* (Grand Rapids, 1965), 3: 501-536. . . .

Schweizer, Eduard. *Church Order in the New Testament.* London: SCM, 1961.

————. . . . *TDNT* (Grand Rapids, 1965), 6: 389-455.

————. *Jesus.* Richmond, Va.: Knox, 1971. . . .

Spanneut, Michel. "Eunome." *DHGE* (Paris, 1963), 15: 1399-1405.

Špidlik, Thomas. *La sophiologie de saint Basile.* Rome: Pontificium Institutum Orientalium Studiorum, 1961. . . .

Thornton, Lionel Spencer. *The Common Life in the Body of Christ.* 4th ed. London: Dacre, 1963. . . .

Verhees, Jacques. "Pneuma, Erfahrung und Erleuchtung in der Theologie des Basilius des Grossen." *Ostkirchliche Studien* 25 (1976) 43-59.

————. "Die Bedeutung der Tranzendenz des Pneuma bei Basilius." *Ibid.*, 285-302.

Viller, Marcel & Karl Rahner. *Aszese und Mystik in der Väterzeit.* Freiburg-im-Breisgau: Herder, 1939.

Vischer, Lukas. *Basilius der Grosse. Untersuchungen zu einem Kirchenvater des vierten Jahrhunderts.* Diss. Basel: Rheinhardt, 1953. . . .

Vogt, Hermann Josef. *Das Kirchenverständnis des Origenes.* Diss. Cologne-Vienna: Böhlau Verlag, 1974.

Vööbus, Arthur. *History of Asceticism in the Syrian Orient. A Contribution to the History of Culture in the Near East.* 1: *The Origin of Asceticism. Early Monasticism in Persia.* (CSCO 184). 2: *Early Monasticism in Mesopotamia and Syria.* (CSCO 197). Louvain: Secrétariat du Corpus SCO, 1958, 1960. . . .

Wawryk, Basilius Boris. *Doctrina Sancti Basilii Magni de inspiratione Sacrae Scripturae.* Diss. Rome: Gregorian University, 1943. . . .

Wickham, L. R. "The Date of Eunomius' *Apology:* A Reconsideration." *JThS* 20 (1969) 231-240.

Philip Rousseau (essay date 1994)

SOURCE: "Basil on the World Stage" in *Basil of Caesarea,* University of California Press, 1994, pp. 270-317, 365-87.

[*In the essay reprinted below, Rousseau describes Basil's efforts to mediate ecclesiastical schisms and doctrinal disputes beyond the boundaries of the see of Caesarea. The critic contends that Basil's attempts to construct a cadre of like-minded bishops who would support the cause of orthodoxy were frequently motivated as much by collegiality and personal vindication as by theological ideology.*]

'Lifting his head high and casting the eye of his soul in every direction, he obtained a mental vision of the whole world through which the word of salvation had been spread'.[1] So Gregory of Nazianzus described his friend. 'A trumpet penetrating the immensity of space, or a voice of God encompassing the world, or a universal earthquake resulting from some new wonder or miracle, his voice and mind were all of these'.[2] Praise, indeed; and so it may have seemed in later years, with Basil's old enemies in retreat. But just what broader significance did he acquire during his struggles on behalf of orthodoxy? For he knew well enough that success would depend on carrying to the furthest possible limits the battle against error: 'Who will allow me to step upon the stage of the wide world? Who will give me a voice clear and penetrating like a trumpet?'.[3]

Correspondence examined in previous chapters—about the division of Cappadocia, about Eustathius, and about Antioch—points to a growing awareness of place. Basil's failure with Gregory and success with Amphilochius included an element of purely territorial interest. Once he had become a bishop, he began to develop a clear sense of the geography of his world; a geography that allowed him not only to pinpoint interests rivalling his own but also to associate with different localities—different sees, different groups of supporters and antagonists—the varying components of his own theology, the theology not only of the Trinity but also of human nature and the community within which that nature had to operate.

Antioch occupied a central place in that network;[4] Neocaesarea, and Armenia beyond it, also loomed large. A connection with Neocaesarea was only to be expected, given its prominence in Pontus, and the proximity of Basil's family property, some fifty kilometres to the west. We have already mentioned most of the important letters connected with the region. First came

Basil's response to the death of the bishop Musonius, near the end of 371. He naturally recalled the heritage of Gregory, Neocaesarea's first bishop; but he betrayed anxiety also that a change of leaders might rob him of a potential ally and generally weaken the city's resistance to error in those trying days. He hoped for 'a token either of neighbourly sympathy, or of the fellowship of men of like faith, or, more truly, of the fellowship of men who obey the law of love and shun the peril of silence'.[5] So he recalled the city's more recent resistance to error—'amid this great storm and tempest of affairs . . . unshaken by the waves'—and urged its people quickly to unite in their own defence around a new leader.[6]

The need to build up a community of churchmen who could present a common face against the forces that threatened them—the hope invested in Amphilochius not long afterwards—was felt most acutely at those moments when leaders died, and when the quality of their successors was uncertain. Basil struck the same note in a letter to Ancyra, following the death of its bishop Athanasius at around the same time: 'To whom shall we now transfer the cares of the churches? Whom now shall I take as partner in my sorrows? Whom as a sharer in my joy?'[7] 'There is no little danger', he continued with some pointedness, 'that many will fall together with this support which has now been taken from under them [i.e., Athanasius], and that the rottenness of certain persons will be laid bare'. 'The struggle', he concluded, 'is not slight, that we may prevent the springing up again, over the election of a superintendent, of strifes and dissensions, and the utter overturning, as the result of a petty quarrel, of all our labours'.[8]

At Neocaesarea, Musonius was succeeded by Atarbius, a distant relative of Basil. The man was not inspired thereby with automatic affection; and he seems to have made no move to acknowledge either Basil's anxieties or his sense of loyalty to Neocaesarea itself. Eventually, Basil decided to open communications himself, in 373. He was anxious still that Atarbius should bestir himself more effectively in the dangerous struggle against the enemies of orthodoxy:

> Unless we assume a labour on behalf of the churches equal to that which the enemies of sound doctrine have taken upon themselves for their ruin and total obliteration, nothing will prevent truth from being swept away to destruction by our enemies, and ourselves also from sharing in the condemnation, unless with all good zeal and good will, in harmony with one another and in unison with God, we show the greatest possible solicitude for the unity of the churches.

That was where Amphilochius had scored points, and where Atarbius had been particularly remiss:

Cast from your mind the thought that you have no need of communion with another. . . . Consider this—that if the evil of war which now goes on all about us should sometime come upon ourselves likewise . . . we shall find none to sympathize with us, because in the season of our tranquillity we failed to pay betimes our contribution of sympathy . . . to the victims of injustice.[9]

It was a theme very much to the fore at that moment, when not only was the policy of Valens, from a religious point of view, most oppressive, but also the division of the province had created new occasions for disunity. To the curia of Tyana, the see of his new rival, Anthimus, Basil wrote: 'We would never attribute so much to ourselves as to consider that single-handed we could surmount our difficulties, for we know very clearly that we need the help of each and every brother more than one hand needs the other'.[10]

Because of the way in which the controversy with Eustathius developed, Basil eventually accused Atarbius of Sabellianism. That represented, of course, a careful attempt to defend himself, and to preserve what allies he could, within the orbit of Neocaesarea itself. It is likely, however, that the opinions of Atarbius seemed bad enough in themselves, and deserving of censure, 'lest perchance, in addition to the countless wounds which the Church has suffered at the hands of those who have erred against the truth of the Gospel, still another evil may spring up'.[11] So he went about building up a wider circle of potential supporters. An obvious example was Olympius, a friend of long standing,[12] to whom he wrote about many aspects of the controversy, 'in order that you yourself may know the truth, and may make it clear to those eager not to let it suffer in the grip of injustice'.[13] The cultivation of locally influential lay persons, even in letters not explicitly theological in content, was an important means of maintaining one's position among ecclesiastical peers and rivals.[14] Nor was Olympius his only friend in the city.[15]

Basil actually travelled to Pontus in 376: so in a sense the letters discussed so far had been preparing the soil. The process continued in a long letter to the bishops of the coastal region. To some extent like Atarbius, they had been disturbingly quiet, slow to send either letters or envoys to comfort the embattled bishop of Caesarea. By this stage, several more reflective themes were beginning to come together in Basil's mind, following the breakdown with Eustathius and the continuing controversy over Apollinarius; and he now saw himself as the leader of the orthodox cause in Asia Minor generally: 'We, being publicly exposed to all, like headlands jutting out into the sea, receive the fury of the heretical waves'.[16] Such a sense of destiny had already been hinted at in his earliest correspondence with the newly consecrated Amphilochius—'awaiting the calm which the Lord will cause as soon as a voice is found worthy of rousing Him to rebuke the winds and the sea'[17]—and it seems confirmed in his letter to the curia at Tyana: 'If anyone follows us who are leading the way in this matter . . . , that is excellent, and my prayer is fulfilled'.[18] The same sense of changed circumstance was expressed quite clearly in his long, self-justificatory letter to Patrophilus, written also in 376 (the moment when he rose to new heights of self-confidence in the *De spiritu sancto*):

> Last year, having become ill with a most violent fever, and having approached the very gates of death, then being recalled by God's mercy, I was dissatisfied at my return, considering the evils upon which I was again entering; and by myself I inquired what in the world it was that lay in the depths of God's wisdom, whereby days of life in the flesh had again been granted to me. But when I understood these things, I considered that the Lord wished us to see the churches resting from the storm which they had experienced before this.[19]

Such was the spirit in which he wrote to his colleagues in Pontus. Yet Eustathius, Apollinarius, and Atarbius were never far from his mind: Basil wanted a local synod, in which he could be formally accused, instead of slandered behind his back, and where others could examine evidence, instead of merely listening to abuse.[20] He then went on to repeat, virtually, the imagery of his letter to Tyana, emphasizing the need for unity, just as limbs and organs in a body are in need of one another; and he repeated his warning to Atarbius not to think 'we who inhabit the sea-coast are outside of the suffering of the many, and have no necessity at all of aid from others'. He lamented the fact, as he had to Amphilochius, that no one felt shame in their being cut off from one another. The contrast was with that older model, represented by 'those fathers who decreed that by small signs the tokens of communion should be carried about from one end of the earth to the other, and that all should be fellow-citizens and neighbours to all'.[21]

From his temporary retreat in Pontus, Basil wrote three more long letters to Neocaesarea itself; and they probably represent the most carefully thought-out description of his state of mind on a number of issues beyond the immediate dissension.[22] Writing to the clergy of the city, Basil addressed the question of Sabellianism, making little attempt to hide the fact (for it would have been obvious) that he was attacking Atarbius. Yet the letter hints at other disputes, which may have been going on for a long time, and which probably do more to explain the atmosphere of sourness and suspicion in which recent misunderstandings had been able to flourish. There seems to have been division, in the first place, over the liturgy; the complaint being that, in singing the psalms, Basil and his congregation were departing from the practice inherited from Gregory Thaumaturgus. There had also been misgiving over

Basil's asceticism; in particular over the way in which he had introduced it into the very heart of his church. Such misgiving dated back, perhaps, to the early 360s, when Basil had made his choice between remote self-denial and involvement in church affairs. It reminds us not to expect total or automatic agreement among Basil's critics (in this case, between Atarbius and Eustathius).[23] In the second of the two later letters, Basil addressed the educated élite of Neocaesarea: that wider circle of potential allies from whom, for example, Olympius may have been drawn. To them he mentioned, as possible bases for sympathy, his family connections in the area, and the many years he had spent pursuing the ascetic life nearby.[24] He also recalled, as even more likely to awaken their sympathy, the way in which the city had tried to entice him there permanently, as a resident rhetor. The suspicions and disappointments of those years could now be forgotten: 'We do not consider the past, if only the present be sound'.[25] What mattered was to warn the informed and influential laity of the danger they faced: 'A subversion of faith is being contemplated among you, hostile to both apostolic and evangelical doctrines, and hostile to the tradition of the truly great Gregory and of those who followed after him up to the blessed Musonius, whose teachings are of course still fresh in your minds even now'.[26] He was referring to 'the evil of Sabellius'; but once again he became usefully specific: for the problem seems not to have been simply a general acceptance of the Sabellian tradition, but a debate within the city partly about the significance of not being able to 'name' the second person of the Trinity (for 'Only-begotten', was not, strictly speaking, a name), partly about supposedly ambiguous or obscure writings left behind by Gregory Thaumaturgus himself (writings that we no longer possess in full). So some of the philosophical and historical anxieties abroad in the region were quite specific, and older than any disagreement with Atarbius.[27]

Basil's first letter to the city (by a slight margin the longest of the three) was broader in its reference and implication. As we would expect from his contemporary letters to others in the region, he wanted above all a just hearing, which meant open confrontation with his accusers; and he wanted (since the current dispute was over matters of faith and doctrine) an examination of his suspect writings (if they could find any!) by competent critics.[28] He did not disguise, however, his genuine affection for the community: it was among 'the greatest of the churches', 'the church most dear to us'; and he implied sadly that its antagonism towards him had lasted 'for almost a whole generation'.[29] Against that coldness he asserted the rights of his own historical association with the city.

The thrust of his argument has been already discussed— the early allusion to 'blood relationships'; the fact that 'both you and we have not only the same teachers of

God's mysteries, but also the same spiritual fathers who from the beginning have laid the foundation of your church'; the evocation of 'the famous Gregory and all who . . . succeeded in turn to his chair'—preparing the way for the crucial passages, later in the letter, where he discussed both his family history and its relationship to, indeed its total involvement in, the ecclesial history of the region.[30] Now we can see the wider significance of his careful description of development—the development, as explained to Eustathius in the previous year, of the teachings of his grandmother Macrina.[31] His more explicit understanding of the doctrine of the Spirit, and his associated move away from any middle-of-the-road theological party towards a careful and limited gloss upon the simple teaching in Nicaea, were precisely the issues at stake; and they contributed to a new sense of where he stood, doctrinally, as well as to a new acceptance of the paths he had followed in his career to date. 'We are conscious', he wrote, 'of having received into our hearts no doctrine inimical to sound teaching, nor of having at any time defiled our souls by the abominable blasphemy of the Arians'. So he felt able to excuse any association he may have at one time countenanced between himself and churchmen who were later exposed as suspect in their theology (thinking, no doubt, of Apollinarius, but also of his old 'semi-Arian' friends): 'If we ever received into communion anyone who came from that teacher, they concealed the malady deep in their hearts and uttered pious words or at least did not oppose what was expressed by us, and thus we received them'.[32]

The last point embodied a principle he defended elsewhere: that one should not press too hard upon those in theological error, if they showed signs of repentance. Churchmen should ostracize and stigmatize as few as possible, enter into the warmest collegiality with the rest, and only then, when harmony had begun to do its work, press for additional 'clarification' . . . [33] He also brought to his defence a letter from Athanasius (not extant), 'in which he has clearly ordered that, if anyone wish to come over from the heresy of the Arians by confessing the faith of Nicaea, we should receive him without making any discrimination in his case'.[34] To that extent Basil had now carried the dispute onto a broader plane.

He continued in that vein, demanding nothing less (even *vis-à-vis* Neocaesarea) than a universal council, brought together simply (so it would seem) to discuss the matters at issue between them. It was more likely that he wished, even if only in passing, to draw Neocaesarea into his wider plans for church unity: it seems scarcely credible that Atarbius alone could have been the excuse for so momentous a congregation. Basil's true purpose was to bring home the isolation Neocaesarea threatened to bring upon itself:

> From the letters which are being conveyed from those regions [he listed more or less the provinces

of the whole empire!], and from those which are being sent back to them from here, it is possible for you to learn that we are all of one mind, having the same ideas. . . . So let him who flees communion with us, who cuts himself off from the whole Church, not escape the notice of your keen mind. Look around you, brethren, and see with whom you are in communion; once you are not received by us, who henceforth will acknowledge you?[35]

So he ended the letter bemoaning 'the wickedness of the age', which he contrasted, as on other occasions, with the practice of earlier days (thus clearly associating his programme for unity with an ancient model of the Church):

> Question your fathers and they will tell you that even if the parishes seemed to be divided by geographic position, they were yet one in mind and were governed by one counsel. Continuous was association among the people, continuous was mutual visiting among the clergy; and among the pastors themselves there was such love for one another that each used the other as a teacher and guide in matters pertaining to the Lord.[36]

The confrontation with Neocaesarea tells us a great deal about Basil's view of his own task and standing. It does so partly because it helps us to tie up loose ends in relation to Eustathius and Apollinarius, but mainly because it places firmly in its context the great exercise in self-definition *vis-à-vis* his own family, studied in the opening chapter. It also shows the extent to which, by 376, almost all the issues Basil faced were being drawn into the orbit of a universal ambition in the face of the Arian dispute. The ripples now covered the whole surface of the pond. We can see to what broader level of self-confidence he had now been able to raise himself—finding new friends, describing to his own satisfaction the path he had followed in life, articulating more clearly the principles he felt governed the inner lives of Christians, and identifying a single challenge and a single model within the Church, to which he might dedicate the energy of spirit miraculously reserved to him after so much sickness and disappointment. The sense of purpose is beyond doubt. Its fulfilment, as we shall see, was another matter.

. . . . .

Basil's activities in Armenia are no less difficult to disengage from his personal alarm, as he was faced with the errors of Eustathius and the suspicions of Theodotus of Nicopolis (a man with whom he had closely to work in his Armenian mission). Yet the circumstances were obviously of an importance far greater than could be encompassed by Basil's biography.[37]

The unity, independence, and eventually Christian character of the kingdom of Armenia, following the Roman defeat of Persia in 298, had made the area a sensitive buffer zone, and a scene of contentious struggle for influence, between the two rival empires. 'Unity' calls for some clarification. Armenia fell into at least three regions, which seem naturally divided one from another in the light of history and as a result of geography: the west, Armenia Minor, exposed to Hellenistic, Roman, and ultimately Christian influence; the north, more remote from both its powerful neighbours; and the south, adjacent to Syria, where local governors and aristocrats had long been susceptible to Roman influence, and where cities and peoples were naturally absorbed into Roman strategy, based upon Antioch, and reaching north as well as east.[38] Nor is 'independence' entirely appropriate. When Persian pressure induced fresh division, Constantine had been happy to appoint his nephew, Hannibalianus, king of what area he could control.[39] From then until 358, Rome demanded tax. During the middle years of the century, the interests of Armenia were easily sacrificed when it suited the emperors in Constantinople.

Events came to a new head in 363. Cut down unexpectedly in his grandiose war against Shapur II, and leaving no obvious successor, Julian bequeathed to the empire the need for a swift and bitter choice. War had to be abandoned, and a new emperor secured. Persia naturally took advantage of Roman embarrassment. Among the provisions of the treaty forced upon the empire, as Jovian strove to establish his authority, was an agreement (binding on both parties) not to interfere in the affairs of Armenia.[40] The result in practice was that the kingdom fell apart, to everyone's advantage but its own.

Arshak, the king, experienced particular humiliation. He had been, in latter years at least, a loyal friend to Rome. He had come to power around 350, when both Romans and Persians were preoccupied on other fronts—Constantius with the usurper Magnentius, and the Persians with frontier raids.[41] As time went by, he found it either useful or attractive to adopt a religious position more favourable to the Arianism espoused by Constantius. Inclination to the Roman cause brought tax relief in 358, and an arranged marriage with Olympias, daughter of Ablabius, Constantine's great Praetorian Prefect.[42] It also led soon after to the exile from Armenia of Nerses, the orthodox *catholicos*.[43] Nerses had been educated in Caesarea. His relationship with Gregory the Illuminator had made his succession as Christian leader in Armenia (after a period in the service of the king) impossible to challenge. He had been consecrated, also in Caesarea, in 353. It is not unlikely, therefore, that Basil, after his return from Athens to Cappadocia three years or so later, would have learned of this distinguished figure and might have begun to follow his career with some interest. Seeking the tax relief of 358, the successful Armenian embassy, led by the

catholicos, may have met the emperor in Caesarea itself.[44] Finally, Nerses had known, and had been influenced by, Eustathius of Sebaste, making it a mark of his administration to encourage both the ascetic life and the care of the poor and sick. All those associations would have encouraged the interest and admiration of Caesarea's future bishop.[45]

Nerses was not able to regain his see until 368 or 369. Arshak, meanwhile, fell victim to changed circumstance. As soon as Jovian had made his enforced peace, Shapur invaded Armenia, captured and imprisoned Arshak, and may have been directly responsible for his death soon after. The king's son, Pap, took refuge in Neocaesarea.[46] Gradually, Roman interest encouraged and supported Pap in a reclamation of his heritage. By the time Valens had completed his campaigns against the Goths in 369, Pap was on the path to full kingship. The *comes* Terentius was appointed *dux Armeniae* in that year and took a direct hand in regaining for Pap his royal authority.[47]

Nerses had not been idle since 359, cultivating his friends among the Armenian aristocracy. He returned to the kingdom in triumph on the back of Pap's own success, representing once again a temporarily welcome alliance with Rome. The visibly ad hoc friendship of emperor, king, and *catholicos*, however, could not last. Nerses had never been able to reserve his criticism—'Those whom he blessed were blessed, and those whom he cursed were cursed'[48]—and Pap resented his resistance to immorality and persecution.

Valens, meanwhile, found Pap difficult to keep in place. The Persians had not viewed recent events with equanimity; and in 371 it proved necessary to forestall, with a considerable show of strength, a Persian attack. Roman forces penetrated far to the east, to Bagravand, the high country between the upper valleys of the Aras and the Murat. It was what Themistius called 'saving Armenia'.[49]

Basil, in a sense, travelled in their wake, for it was in the context of that 'settlement' that he received the command from Valens to put in order the affairs of the churches in Armenia.[50] Judging by his subsequent correspondence, his responsibility (or at least his successful influence) was restricted to Armenia Minor in the west: he does not seem to have played any part in affairs further east than Satala, barely a hundred kilometres up the Lykos (Kelkit) valley from Nicopolis. It may seem unnecessary, therefore, to speculate about further relations with Nerses at that late stage; but one incident is bound to awaken our curiosity. At some point in 373, relations between Nerses and Pap reached breaking point, and Nerses was murdered at the command of the king himself.[51] Surely such an event would have coloured Basil's view of affairs, even in Armenia Minor, had he known of it. He did not make his journey until the middle months of the year and seems to have been back in Caesarea during August. Nerses may not have died until the end of July.[52] It leaves little time for an overlap. However, there is no way of telling whether Basil heard of the death of the *catholicos* while he was away from home, or whether he received the news of the funeral (conducted amidst Pap's carefully expressed grief) just across the border south of Satala, where Nerses had once resided and Pap had a fortified lodge.[53]

Pap continued to claim his attention. Before we examine what Basil actually did in Armenia, we should therefore pursue the more general story just a little further. Still within the context of the most recent Roman intervention, Pap himself was murdered, either in 374 or 375. Valens's long-term plan was to transfer support to his cousin Varazdat, who reigned until 378. Much more was involved, however, than simple dynastic strategy. The murder itself, ostensibly committed on the spur of the moment at a banquet, was the work of Traianus, *comes rei militaris* in the East since 371 and Roman commander in Armenia. Basil may have been his correspondent.[54] The deed seems likely to have won the approval, if not to have sprung from the intrigue, of Valens himself.[55] Terentius, no lover of Pap, and similarly in touch with Basil, may also have been involved. He had his connections with Samosata, where his daughters were deaconesses, and maintained friendships with orthodox aristocrats in the south of the kingdom (naturally aggrieved by, among other things, the treatment of Nerses). He had actually accused Pap to Valens's face and thereby engineered the king's virtual arrest for a time in Tarsus, from which he escaped only with some difficulty. His murder would have seemed no more than an astute alternative.[56] In the aftermath, Rome mounted a great drive in 377, to confirm its support of Varazdat. However, the Gothic revolt in the Balkans demanded a sudden and massive redeployment of troops. That could have opened the way for a significant reassertion of Persian might; but by one of those remarkable accidents of history, just in the year when Valens was meeting his death at Hadrianople, Shapur II died also. Armenia, divided now between two kings, was able to enjoy a brief period of fragmented independence.

With this survey of events, we seem to have thrust Basil onto the 'world stage' with a vengeance. It was, indeed, a moment of some importance for our understanding of his career and personal development. On the one hand, far from disappearing into the mountains on some obscure mission, he was thrust into the heart of a political and military situation crucial to the survival of the empire. On the other hand, many different incidents in his life were now given new significance by conjunction: the division of Cappadocia, the con-frontation with Valens, the estrangement from the two Gregorys and other bishops, the enmity of Demosthenes, the confrontation with Eustathius, the involvement with Neocaesarea, the correspondence with high officials, and the interest in Antioch. It has often seemed difficult to explain why Valens, so much a villain in sources closely associated with Basil himself, should have appointed him for a mission of such delicacy.[57] Yet Valens knew that he could not afford to sacrifice strategic security to theological passion, and that any potential division in Armenia was dangerous to the wider interest. The natural association of Caesarea with the Armenian church and Basil's personal connections around Neocaesarea would have made him an attractive envoy. Their meeting in 372 could not have disguised from Valens Basil's reputation and personal authority and may even have awakened his reluctant admiration. He knew, on the other hand, that the division of Cappadocia had clipped the bishop's wings a little, even if that had not been its direct intention. He knew that Basil's orthodoxy was still a relatively isolated and threatened advantage. He knew that lesser officials like Demosthenes could be relied on to keep the man in his place. He may even have known that Basil badly needed to maintain the friendship of bishops further east, not least Theodotus of Nicopolis himself, in order to gain the upper hand against Eustathius and to defend his own theological position. He was useful, in other words, but unlikely to prove offensive. It is sobering to observe how Basil might be thought of when viewed from such a height!

Setting out in June 373, Basil appears to have returned to Caesarea by August. It was from there that he sent a report of his conduct to Terentius, a personal friend, but, as we have seen, closely interested in Armenian affairs.[58] The *comes* had had a hand in transmitting to Basil the emperor's original wishes.[59] What Basil had to report was that 'I was not permitted to turn my desire into action', thanks to the unfriendly attitude of Theodotus, 'the bishop assigned to co-operate with us'. As we know, the cause of that problem was Eustathius. The letter proceeds to offer a long description of their dispute; but one new point commands attention: Basil seems to have travelled first, or certainly at a very early stage of his trip, to Getasa, where Meletius of Antioch was residing. His first significant port of call, in other words, in fulfilment of a government commission, was the temporary home of his Antiochene hero. That tells us something about the context in which Basil viewed his opportunity in Armenia, even if relations with Eustathius had also been at issue. However, Theodotus was there as well (it was at Getasa that he and Meletius taxed Basil further on the reliability of Eustathius's declarations to date). The plan was that they should travel on together to Satala. Theodotus did not do so. It is likely that Basil did, and that he received his rebuff at Nicopolis after that. He certainly went to Satala; and he described to Terentius what he achieved there: he 'established peace among the bishops of Armenia', urged them 'to put aside their habitual discord',[60] and supplied certain disciplinary 'rules . . . .' The Christians in Satala then asked him to appoint a bishop; and he reconciled their community with 'Cyril, the bishop of Armenia', against whom slander had been 'falsely fomented by the calumny of his enemies'. Basil was well aware that, beside his own difficulties, those achievements were 'trivial and of no importance' (for once, tactful humility was near the mark), and therefore not up to the emperor's expectations.[61]

Filling the bishopric at Satala seems not to have been an easy matter, nor swiftly accomplished: Basil had to make his eventual plans known by a later letter. The man chosen was a certain Poimenius, a long-standing friend and distant relative. His own city and family were very reluctant to see him go, and the probability is that Basil had drawn upon personal connections further west in making his choice.[62] When problems recurred in the region, Basil continued to address Poimenius with complete trust.[63]

He maintained his interest in Armenian affairs[64]—hence his anxiety in the face of a new problem that surfaced the following year (Poimenius may have been the first to hear of his complaints). 'Armenians', he warned, would be travelling through Satala, escorting one Faustus, consecrated (as *catholicos* of Armenia) by Anthimus of Tyana in direct opposition to Basil, who traditionally had that right, and who was reluctant for the moment to have anything to do with the man. A letter from Poimenius, however, would satisfy Basil that Faustus was orthodox; and he was prepared to overlook Anthimus's slight if Poimenius would speak on behalf of the new *catholicos*, 'bearing witness for him, if you see that the life of the man is good'. He could, moreover, if such were the case, 'urge the rest to do likewise'. Poimenius was thus authorized to exercise at least moral authority on Basil's behalf over the church in Armenia.[65] Basil sent a letter on the same topic to Theodotus of Nicopolis, expressing dismay that Faustus should have demanded consecration, when he had been unable to produce a reassuring letter 'from your Reverence and from the rest of the bishops'.[66] He also wrote finally to Meletius. He regarded the consecration of Faustus not only as an example of arrogance on the part of Anthimus but also as further evidence of opposition in Armenia to the Cyril mentioned in the letter to Terentius; 'In consequence Armenia has become filled with schisms'.[67]

Behind these developments lay the increasing estrangement of Pap from policies favourable to the empire, in church affairs as elsewhere. Rejection of Cyril was hardly likely to endear the king to such advocates of the orthodox cause as Terentius and Traianus. The

events do show, moreover, that Basil's association with Armenia proper was not just a consequence of his status as bishop of Caesarea but was directly connected with his responsibilities (albeit ad hoc) in Armenia Minor, and with his ability to place in a strategic frontier see a childhood friend who was also a member of his own family.

Events took another turn in the following year: Theodotus of Nicopolis died. Basil, with other bishops, was faced with the task of filling another vacancy. His solution was to recommend the transfer of Euphronius from his 'distant spot' at Colonia. The first task was to assuage natural dissatisfaction in Colonia itself (whose Christian citizens even threatened legal proceedings). Basil did so by recommending to the clergy of the city the broadest principles of church government. The decision had been no 'human arrangement . . . prompted by the reasoning of men' but had been made, rather, by 'those who are committed with the care of the churches of God' through their 'union with the Spirit'. The clergy of Colonia were exhorted, moreover, to 'impress this source of their action upon [their own] minds, and strive to perfect it . . . .'[68] Distrust of 'the reasoning of men . . . , dated back several years; but the reference to the Spirit was characteristic of Basil's more recent interests, with its accompanying exhortation to an inner change, and to moral improvement. He also wished to make it clear that Colonia was part of a wider world and would benefit from a secure succession at Nicopolis, whereas weakness in the mother church would undermine all efforts elsewhere. An accompanying letter to the leading citizens of Colonia was less intense in its address, asking more for 'pardon' than for ecstatic insight; but it did impress upon them, 'situated on the outskirts of Armenia', that they needed to take account of dangers and advantages just a little more distant than their own preoccupations.[69]

Then Basil had to assuage, for different reasons, the people of Nicopolis itself, where he had never found an easy reception. To the clergy he repeated his conviction that a task undertaken by 'pious persons' was pursued 'with the counsel of the Spirit': 'no human consideration is present', and 'it is the Lord who is directing their hearts'.[70] He was specific about the identity of those 'pious persons': chief initiator was no less a person than Poimenius of Satala. The plans set in motion in 373 were still having their effect. Nor was he the mere instrument of Basil's distant wishes: 'He did not resort to postponements of the matter and thus give an opportunity for defence to those who are opposing, . . . but he immediately brought his excellent plan to fulfilment'.[71] To the laity of the city, Basil was briefer in his comments, exhorting them to support in their own way the task of the new bishop.[72]

The outcome, perhaps predictably, was not a success. Eustathius in particular had seen the death of his old critic too good an opportunity to be missed. Not without the support of Demosthenes, he and others had intruded another candidate against Euphronius, named Fronto; and they proceeded to consecrate him as a rival bishop.[73] Fronto had at first succeeded in creating the impression of unsullied theological respectability, employing 'both words of faith and affectation of piety all for the deception of those who met him'.[74] Once he had emerged in his true colours, he became 'a common abomination to all Armenia'; but he could still muster enough accomplices to force those more amenable to Basil's viewpoint out of the city, at least to the extent that they were denied the use of the church and forced to worship in the open air.[75] That may call into question Basil's own assertion that Fronto's party represented only a minority, although it may also demonstrate how little a community could do, when faced with Arians confident of government support.[76] Other letters written later in that year continued to describe the depredations of Demosthenes.[77] All Basil was able to do was impress upon the clergy at Nicopolis that their misfortune was not unique in history. They should see themselves in a tradition of martyrs and confessors, whose enemies had not been able to triumph in the long run.[78]

. . . . .

By that time, Pap was dead. Although, for another year or so, Rome continued to play a forceful role in Armenian affairs, the diplomatic subtleties that may have seemed relevant in 373 might now have proved less useful. Failure at Nicopolis, and in the kingdom of Armenia itself (given the difficulties of Cyril), was a disappointing conclusion to Basil's efforts. Other preoccupations, however, had already begun to override the significance of the area in his mind. In the midst of his Armenian involvements, Eusebius of Samosata had been exiled, imparting a new emotional intensity to events in Syria. The need to maintain pressure on the Arian party had also drawn Basil further afield, at least in his correspondence. This is the moment, therefore, to marshal together the references, first to Antioch and its schism, and then to the Arian conflict, as fought out on a wider field. The question still remains, however: was Basil driven more by the fortunes of his own friends, and by a need to vindicate himself in the face of personal enemies, than by any elevated concern with ideological debate in the empire more generally? Was it possible for *any* bishop of the time to rise above divisions of language, cultural history, and political convenience, and to think in anything approaching 'universal' terms?

In the first place, the Arian conflict was consistently associated in Basil's mind with conflict in the church of Antioch itself. That conflict had been a feature of the city's life for decades already.[79] Eustathius had been chosen its bishop in 325; and for more than fifty years loyalty or opposition to his name and policy lay at the heart of the city's divisions. At Nicaea, he had been a clear opponent of Arius; but he subsequently tangled both with Eusebius of Caesarea (who accused him of too forceful a condemnation of Sabellius) and with Eusebius of Nicomedia (whom he accused in his turn of undermining all that Nicaea had attempted to achieve). Mostly as a result of that perceived impudence, Eustathius was deposed at a synod in Antioch in 330 and exiled to Thrace.

Not surprisingly, given the passions that Arius had aroused, and the accusations that had been bandied about between Eustathius and his immediate enemies, there followed a turmoil of succession to the see. Some of the effects we have noted already. The council held at Sardica in 343 calmed matters somewhat, largely because it made very clear the division of opinion (on Arianism as on other matters) between the eastern and western sectors of the empire (a division exacerbated by the shared rule and divergent opinions of Constans and Constantius, lasting until 350). Leontius, bishop from approximately 344 until 357, gained for Antioch a long and relatively stable period of church government, a period marked also by Constantius's engagements with Persia (always important for the city), and by the violent administration of the Caesar Gallus from 351. It was also the period during which Aetius began to come to prominence.[80] In 357, Leontius was succeeded by Eudoxius. The latter's appointment was not regular, and he maintained his position only with government support. In return, he agreed to the formula of Sirmium in 357, then supported more openly the Anomoean party, and maintained friendly relations with Aetius. It was after his deposition at Seleucia in 359 that the see passed to Meletius, whose position was confirmed at Constantinople in 360.[81]

Meletius, who maintained his rights in the see of Antioch for the rest of Basil's life and for a short while thereafter, and who will claim most of our attention, came originally from Melitene. He had been appointed formerly to the see of Sebaste in 358, in place of the other Eustathius; but he failed to gain acceptance there and lived at Beroea. In 359, at Caesarea in Palestine, he had signed the formula of Acacius, confirmed at Seleucia, which specified only that the Son was [*omoios*]. Evidently he came to regret the move. He later made a declaration of his revised opinions to Constantius, which represented certainly greater caution and probably orthodoxy.[82] Not surprisingly, he was exiled from Antioch (to Armenia Minor). His place was taken by Euzoius (who would later baptize the emperor Constantius as he headed north and west to meet the challenge of Julian).

At that point, matters became complicated in ways that would not be unravelled for at least two generations. With the pagan Julian in power (and it would not be unjust to describe his approach to Christian episcopal politics as meddlesome), Meletius was allowed back to Antioch. The city now had two bishops. Very shortly afterwards, a third appeared: Paulinus, consecrated in 362, with no respect for canonical regularity, by the unsavoury Lucifer of Cagliari. As a priest, Paulinus had long provided a focus in the city for those faithful to the memory of Eustathius himself. Consequently, he and his supporters were thought by others to incline towards Sabellianism. They had, nevertheless, the possibly dubious advantage of having been encouraged in their loyalties by Athanasius himself, who visited Antioch in 346. Yet they remained a minority. Most of the orthodox in Antioch had gathered around two other clerics, Diodorus and Flavianus, who had been unswerving in their opposition to Leontius and his immediate successor. They now transferred their allegiance to Meletius and were explicitly careful to avoid Sabellianist positions.

The confusing turn of events naturally caused concern elsewhere, not least in Alexandria (where Athanasius had also benefitted from Julian's 'tolerance'). A meeting of bishops was held there in 362; and part of the resulting synodal letter, which was widely addressed, attempted to wean some of Meletius's supporters away and awaken greater loyalty towards Paulinus. The document emphasized the formula of Nicaea and the belief that the Holy Spirit was not a creature. Its chief appeal was to the ideas of the Antiochene Eustathius, as expressed at the time of Nicaea itself; and it paid much less attention to the tangled legalities (or more often illegalities) of subsequent episcopal succession in the city.[83]

An embassy travelled to Antioch to announce the decisions reached at Alexandria. Perhaps fortunately, the churchmen involved were chary about the rights of Paulinus, for they soon discovered that matters were even more complicated than Athanasius and his immediate associates might have supposed. The two Apollinarii, father and son, at Laodicea had been firm supporters of Athanasius for many years; and the younger Apollinarius had sent a representative to Alexandria. He also had a finger in the Antiochene pie, bringing his influence to bear in the cause of the priest Vitalis, who was a firm adherent to the traditions of Nicaea and headed what was virtually a fourth party in the city. (More than ten years later, he managed to gain episcopal consecration also, although Damasus of Rome had eventually come to suspect his orthodoxy.)[84] The reputation of Apollinarius in the early 360s, and the seeming orthodoxy of his protégé, may have made Paulinus less obviously acceptable in the eyes of the delegates from Egypt. Later, when Apollinarius himself had become more compromised and

western support for Paulinus more entrenched, Vitalis was less able to maintain his claims.

The accession of Valens in 364 brought to an end the chaotic fruits of Julian's cynical indifference. Antioch's strategic position made its social stability important to the emperor; and he was bound to defuse tensions as far as he could. Meletius once again attracted censure and was exiled.[85] Collaboration with the West seemed to moderate parties the best way of strengthening their position against an emperor of uncertain orthodoxy. It was at that point that supporters of Basil of Ancyra, with Eustathius of Sebaste, went to the West, gained communion with Liberius of Rome, and returned in triumph to their synod at Tyana early in 367.[86] Yet endeavours of that sort were soon under serious threat. Meletius may have been able to return to Antioch briefly, while Valens was preoccupied with the revolt of Procopius and with his campaigns against the Goths in the late 360s; but he was certainly absent from the city again by 370.[87] The tone of eastern church affairs at that stage was best symbolized by the ambiguities and ill-defined promises of Demophilus, recently appointed to the see of Constantinople, and by the growing ambition and influence of Euzoius, even closer to Valens (who had soon moved to Antioch).[88]

We have come now to the beginning of Basil's own episcopate. It should be clear that the whole Antiochene saga had close connections with the Arian controversy. Eustathius of Antioch's original stand had been taken in that context; and successors and rivals had benefitted or suffered from the patronage or misfortune of conflicting parties in the dispute. There were elements, nevertheless, peculiar to Antioch itself. The clerical body in particular was obviously fractured by intense and local loyalties, which may have had little to do with the major theological issues of the day. As Basil put it, the city was not only 'completely divided by heretics' but also 'torn asunder by those who affirm that they hold identical opinions with one another'.[89] The support of great sees, such as Alexandria and Rome, or the shifting favour of the government of the day, may have been no more than opportunistic interference (when viewed from outside) or convenient but temporary reinforcement (when viewed from within).

We can avoid an extensive history of Antioch itself;[90] but it has to be added that its status in other respects had a direct effect on the course and variety of its religious difficulties. For the pagan Julian, it symbolized the vitality, cultic as well as political, of the traditional Hellenic *polis*. The degree to which he underestimated the strength of its ancient Christian traditions was revealed both in his own petulant comments and in the social unrest his intransigence appeared to unleash.[91] Like any great city in the empire, Antioch, with its large population, was always potentially volatile, making any tendency to faction a dangerous indulgence in the government's eyes.[92] Caution was increased by the fact that, from 371, Valens made the city his place of residence. Also established there, as a permanent feature, was the residence of the Praetorian Prefect of the East. Basil, as we have seen, was related to Antioch at that level also, in his dealings with Modestus.[93] The added presence of the emperor probably explains the vicious 'treason trials' that took place in Antioch, vividly described by Ammianus Marcellinus, and proof of the intrigue and paranoia that had infected the community at many social levels.[94]

Antioch was also the city of Chrysostom. It was there he developed his views of theology, discipline, and ecclesial order, long before he achieved prominence as the patriarch of Constantinople at the end of the century.[95] The city produced great literary figures also. There was Ammianus Marcellinus, already mentioned, whose view of the empire as a whole, of Valens, and of political ideology has done so much to colour our own interpretations of the age and springs so directly from much that is recognizably Antiochene.[96] There was Libanius, a correspondent of Basil himself, perhaps the greatest orator of the age, a loyal chronicler of the city he loved, and among the most vivid symbols of pagan literary and religious survival in a Christian empire.[97]

Finally, Antioch was, for Rome, the gateway to Persia. It was always the imperial headquarters in any military confrontation; and the significance of such confrontation would always dwarf (fatally, no doubt), in the imaginations of those in power, any threat or chance of glory on the Danube or the Rhine.[98] So the emperor was a frequent and sometimes lengthy visitor, and the army a constant presence.

In all those respects, Antioch was a microcosm of Roman society at the time; culturally, politically, religiously, and strategically. It set its face boldly against the Syrian interior and against Mesopotamia beyond, declaring itself the best symbol of all that was precious in the Hellenic past and of all that challenged the alternative polities of the Orient. How much less central, therefore, but how much more dangerous might its little schism now appear! How much easier it is to understand why Basil, placed midway at Caesarea on the major route between Antioch and the capital, would have found its affairs of importance in his provincial life.

Let us examine, therefore, in more detail the phases of his involvement. They related chiefly to embassies, sent or encouraged by Basil, to Alexandria and Rome; and to that extent they followed the major shifts of the Arian dispute itself. The first phase began in 371—almost at the beginning of Basil's episcopate.[99]

Dorotheus, a deacon of Meletius (now in exile again), was sent with a letter to Athanasius.[100] Basil had in mind at that stage a broad campaign: 'I recognize but one avenue of assistance to the churches in our part of the world—agreement with the bishops of the West'. Athanasius would be crucial in making such an appeal: 'What is more venerated in the entire West than the white hair of your majestic head?' So Basil exhorted the patriarch to send a deputation from Alexandria itself, 'a number of men who are mighty in the true doctrine'.

He also had much to say about Antioch. Athanasius should have a special sense of responsibility towards that church (Basil would have known, of course, of his earlier interventions), not least because unity achieved there would 'calm the confusion of the people, put an end to factional usurpations of authority, subject all men to one another in charity, and restore to the Church her pristine strength'.

Dorotheus carried also a letter to Meletius, to be delivered en route. In that note, Basil presented the embassy to the West as his own idea, designed to bring pressure to bear on the eastern government to rescind the various decrees of exile then current. He asked Meletius to prepare letters of his own, for Dorotheus to take to Italy, hoping that their western colleagues would then mount an embassy in the reverse direction.[101]

All those plans were apparently set awry by the arrival of a messenger from Alexandria. The news he brought prompted Basil to write instead a longer letter to Athanasius.[102] He still wanted the patriarch to provide companions for Dorotheus from his own church; but he now decided that they should carry a letter from himself to Damasus. Again, he wanted the West to send an embassy in return. He described his motives in cryptic terms: 'When all this has been done without the knowledge of any one [his chief hope being that they would formally reverse the compromises of Ariminum], our thought is that the bishop of Rome shall quietly, through a mission sent by sea, assume charge of affairs here so as to escape the notice of the enemies of peace'. Quite what species of unobtrusive infiltration he had in mind is hard to judge: presumably an attempt to persuade churchmen one by one, rather than to direct their address to the secular authorities, since the hoped-for ambassadors were to be 'capable, by the gentleness and vigour of their character, of admonishing those among us who are perverted'.[103]

There were other issues to be addressed. Basil hoped that such an embassy would declare itself strongly against Marcellus of Ancyra. His error (being, in Basil's eyes, at the other extreme from that of Arius) had escaped the desirable degree of censure in the West.

'Above all they must be solicitous for the Church at Antioch'.[104] There was a particular twist to those expectations, which we shall come across again. 'The result will be that henceforth we shall be able to recognize those who are of one mind with us, instead of being like those who fight a battle at night—unable to distinguish between friends and foes'.[105] That was a further hint of Basil's feeling that doctrinal division was often a front for more serious disloyalties, which raises at once the question of what he thought *were* the issues that divided him from other churchmen.

What Basil intended to say to Damasus himself we shall come to shortly. Unfortunately, yet another interruption postponed his plans. A certain Silvanus arrived from the West, with a letter; and this prompted Basil to write yet a third message to Athanasius, presumably to be substituted for the two already penned. It seems, in any case, that Dorotheus was not entirely happy with what Basil had said so far, demanding perhaps that he should make absolutely clear, both to Athanasius and to the West, that he was in favour of Meletius and confident that he could bring together the various factions in his city: 'He stands at the head of the whole body of the Church, so to speak, while the residue are, as it were, segments of its limbs'. Basil claimed (what is not altogether easy to believe) that Silvanus had brought a similar opinion from 'your co-religionists in the West'.[106]

Basil's drafted letter to Damasus gave central place to the Arian debate: 'The heresy, sown long ago by Arius, the enemy of truth, and now already grown up into shamelessness, and, like a bitter root, producing a deadly fruit, at last prevails'. What was required, therefore, was a delegation from the West: 'Send us men of like mind with us'. One should note the scale of anticipated achievements: the westerners 'will either reconcile the dissenters, or restore the churches of God to friendship, or will at least make more manifest to you those who are responsible for the confusion'. The last ambition may have been the most realistic, and the closest to Basil's heart: 'It will thus be clear to you also for the future, with what men it is proper to have communion'. Meletius was not mentioned by name; but what we know of the accompanying messages would have made that point entirely in his favour.[107]

Thanks to the many interruptions and delays, it is quite possible that none of that correspondence was carried further than Antioch—certainly no further than Alexandria.[108] A third visitor now arrived, calling into question the viability of the whole exercise: Sabinus of Milan, bringing with him a letter from Damasus, *Confidimus quidem*, which recounted decisions made at a synod in Rome in 368.[109] Amidst many other disappointments, the written material made no mention of Antioch. Basil decided to rethink his plans and wrote to Meletius, bringing him up to date (by this time it

was early 372). Once again, Meletius was to write his own letters to the West, to accompany what were now several from Basil, so that they could take advantage of Sabinus's return (although Dorotheus was to go as well). Nor had Basil lost all hope that Athanasius would help, even though communion between Alexandria and Meletius had not yet been achieved.[110] Yet it was the interests of Meletius that Basil had at heart, far more than any international front that might be mounted on the basis of Athanasius's reputation. It was loyalty to Meletius that now drove him to greater initiative and leadership, not any sense that he was about to take up the mantle of the great champion of orthodoxy (who was, after all, still very much alive).[111]

So, from that first phase, we have a series of letters that started and finished with a concern for Antioch and for the fortunes of its exiled bishop. Alexandria was drawn into play but then faded again. Relations with the West were yet to take on a clear form. The truth is that the issues at stake had engaged Basil's attention for some time before he hatched his plan to invite wider authorities to his aid. In a letter to Eusebius of Samosata, written early in 371, before the correspondence with Athanasius, he referred to 'the affairs of Antioch'.[112] A letter to Meletius himself may have been earlier again and hinted at some scheme that extended further in scope than his own troubles in Caesarea.[113] So the letters to Athanasius have to be read with some care, if we are to make correct sense of what Basil valued most in the eastern church, and of what he hoped might be achieved by an approach to Damasus and the bishops of the West.

Basil recognized in Athanasius a 'great solicitude for all the churches', as great as 'for the one especially entrusted to you'; and this at a time when 'most men deem it sufficient to look each to his own particular charge'.[114] The compliment summed up both his hopes and his convictions. Athanasius also possessed 'beyond the rest of us the guidance of the Spirit . . .', which made his 'counsels . . . more nearly unerring . . .'. 'Your years and your experience in affairs' also carried weight.[115] Soon Basil was able to feel that 'the Lord has appointed you the physician to heal the maladies of the churches'. 'You assuredly can see', he added, 'from the lofty watch-tower, so to speak, of your mental vision, what is happening on every hand'.[116] That was partly because Athanasius had been at the centre of the Arian dispute for so long—indeed, since Nicaea itself. He was a man 'who from childhood has struggled in the contests in defence of the faith',[117] a man 'who has experienced the pristine tranquillity and concord of the churches of the Lord touching the faith'.[118] 'Just as greater sorrow devolves upon your Excellency', Basil wrote, 'so we hold that it is proper for your prudence also to bear a greater solicitude for the churches'. The intensity of those appeals, and the broad theological terms in which they were expressed, make it all the more striking that Basil should have abandoned his appeal, as soon as he saw that antagonism between Alexandria and Antioch might render his efforts useless, if not disadvantageous.

Yet the correspondence of the first phase had afforded him an opportunity to express his views on the nature of the Church, seen now as extending beyond the confines of his recently acquired diocese. We find emphases already touched upon: in particular, that the laity were the chief victims of disunity, either docile in the face of confused leadership or enslaved by the enemies of orthodoxy.[119] We have also mentioned Basil's fear that apparent doctrinal division could overlay and even obscure the more fundamental problem of disloyalty to friends. Conveniently labelled factions set at odds with one another churchmen who should have been more effectively united against their true theological enemies. Petty, private scores were also being settled in the name of religion.[120] The central concept, which occurs significantly enough in his letter to Damasus, was that of an 'ancient love', . . . which had characterized in better days the life of the Church and relationships among its leaders.[121] As in the letters to Athanasius, appeal was made to a sense of shared destiny and mutual responsibility. That counted for more than (though it did not exclude) the seniority or reputation of this churchman or that. Basil was now applying on a world scale the principle of collegiality that had inspired him in his relations with bishops in Cappadocia and Armenia, joined with the same sense of history.

. . . . .

The second phase opened in 372 with the return journey of Sabinus to the West, accompanied by Dorotheus. They carried with them letters to churchmen in the West generally, to Valerian of Aquileia, and to bishops in Italy and Gaul. There were no doubt other letters in their baggage—from Meletius, for example, as Basil had requested.[122] No reply was received until the following year. Basil should have known, from the very character of Sabinus's original embassy, that his overtures were likely to fail. Damasus and his colleagues were working to different agenda. For them, Arianism had entered its final phase. Valentinian was proving a tolerant emperor favourable to the Nicene cause—which in itself raises the question of whether principles of church unity could be applied in a divided empire.[123] It was now possible to appoint orthodox bishops quite easily to vacant sees, and doctrinal positions and opponents were more clear-cut. As for Antioch, the position of Paulinus would be hard to undermine, in the face of what had been from the beginning a western commitment to his episcopacy.

For us, therefore, the chief interest attaching to the doomed missives carried by Dorotheus and his companion will continue to be the image of the Church that they so forcefully projected. Central still was the notion of the 'ancient love', hallmark of earlier days.[124] The vocabulary of admired antiquity was repeated elsewhere—'the old order of things', . . . the 'ancient glory of orthodoxy'.[125] . . . To accompany that clear historical appeal, Basil and his colleagues seem now to have acquired a broader sense of geography also. The crisis afflicted the whole of the East, 'from the borders of Illyricum to the Thebaid'; 'half the world [was] swallowed up by error'.[126] The West was seen as a contrasting territorial unit, where harmony and fearless proclamation of the truth were safely established. On the basis of that security, the West should now be able to come to the easterners' aid. History was still of relevance in that territorial contrast. A debt was about to be repaid, in return for the ancient expansion of the faith: 'There must come from you a renewal of the faith for the East, and in due time you must render her a recompense for the blessings which you have received from her';[127] 'Do not allow the faith to be extinguished in those lands where it first flashed forth'.[128]

In order to arouse further the sympathy of his readers, Basil and Meletius presented two pictures: one institutional, outlining the effect of error on the fabric of religious society; the other theological, describing the false formulae and the methods of argument now widely favoured among their enemies. In his general letter to the West, Basil complained that 'the shepherds are driven away, and in their places are introduced troublesome wolves who tear asunder the flock of Christ. The houses of prayer are bereft of those wont to assemble therein; the solitudes are filled with those who weep'. Again, an historical note was struck: 'The elders weep, comparing the past with the present; the young are more to be pitied, since they know not of what they have been deprived'.[129] In the more detailed letter to the bishops of Italy and Gaul, those points were expanded and more vividly expressed. 'Lust for office' . . . had taken possession of the Church. 'Those who have obtained power for themselves through the favour of men are the slaves of those who have conferred the favour'. As a result, church leaders no longer dared to say publicly what the laity had grown unaccustomed to hearing. They were eager, rather, to score points against one another, using 'the vindication of orthodoxy' . . . to further their 'private enmities'.[130] . . . Meanwhile, 'the laity who are sound in faith flee the houses of prayer as schools of impiety' and, 'having poured forth in front of the walls, offer up their prayers under the open sky, enduring all the discomforts of the weather with great patience, while they await assistance from the Lord'.[131]

When it came to theological method, the emphasis made was what we would expect of Basil himself: 'None are left to tend the flock of the Lord with knowledge'.[132] . . . In his general letter to the West, he lamented the casting aside of 'the teachings of the Fathers' and 'the apostolic traditions'. In their place 'the fabrications of innovators are in force in the churches', produced by men who 'train themselves in rhetorical quibbling and not in theology; the wisdom of the world takes first place to itself, having thrust aside the glory of the Cross'.[133] It was the language entirely of the **Contra Eunomium** and of its time,[134] and it included a characteristic reference to baptism: 'May the good teaching of our fathers who met at Nicaea shine forth again, so that the doxology in harmony with saving baptism . . . may be duly rendered to the Blessed Trinity'.[135]

What strikes one most in these letters is their intensity and logical rigour. Great stress was laid on consolation and hope, entirely in the spirit and with the same vocabulary we find in letters more technically designed to express sympathy. Basil was making those statements to western churchmen at exactly the time he was bringing such sentiments to bear upon his more personal sense of sinfulness, misfortune, isolation, and ineptitude.[136] 'The tempest-tossing and confusion in which we now find ourselves' would be calmed, he felt, by the prayers and intervention of the West. Their 'strict harmony and unity with one another' was at once a cause of hope and an assurance of healing and peace.[137] There was a melding, in other words, of various elements—the ancient love, the effect of unity, the contrasting 'famine of love' that afflicted the East. The very intensity of feeling with which anguish was betrayed and optimism asserted became, as it were, a model of the order and orthodoxy hoped for. Indeed, it made the Church most obviously and intimately present within the individual (in this case, Basil himself): 'Embracing us with your spiritual and holy yearning . . . you have engendered in our souls an ineffable affection'.[138] . . .

And what would that lead to? What was the outcome Basil hoped for? Here logic came into force. A series of steps was suggested, a recipe that would provide the ferment of a new church order. One of the fruits of western unity, so Basil wrote to Valerian, was 'that without hindrance the proclamation of the true faith is being made among you'.[139] . . . 'proclamation', was the crucial word. Basil expanded the argument in his general letter to the West:

> Let us also pronounce with boldness . . . that good dogma of the Fathers . . . which overwhelms the accursed heresy of Arius, and builds the churches on the sound doctrine . . . , wherein the Son is confessed to be consubstantial with the Father, and the Holy Spirit is numbered with them in like honour and so adored; in order that the Lord through your prayers and your co-operation may also bestow upon us that fearlessness in the cause of truth . . . , and that glory in the confession . . . of the divine and saving Trinity, which He has given to you.[140]

[*Kepugma*], therefore, and the accompanying [*pappesia*], represented a free-flowing clarity of expression among Christians, which was the only guarantee of sound structure, of that combination of healthy discussion, domestic balance, and simple adoration, which summed up for Basil the essence of the Church. Behind that conviction there lay, moreover, a traditional association between openness and order in ancient society.[141]

In these three letters, therefore, Basil achieved, with the support of his allies, a full and satisfying synthesis of ideas on the nature of the Church. Particularly impressive, in only the third year of his episcopate, was his ability to combine historical, geographical, theological, and personal elements in one ecclesial vision. Nor were his immediate ambitions petty in scale. It may even have been another council of the Church he had in mind:

> Remember that there is need of haste, if those who are still left are to be saved, and of the presence of several brethren, that they in visiting us may complete the number of the synod . . . , so that by reason not only of the high standing of those who have sent them, but also of the number of the delegates they themselves constitute, they may have the prestige . . . to effect a reform; and may restore the creed which was written by our fathers at Nicaea, may banish the heresy, and may speak to the churches a message of peace by bringing those of like convictions into unity.[142]

In his lifetime and on his terms, that was not to be; but the patterns of thought reflected in his letters to the West were equally prominent in correspondence of a more limited scale. His attachment to Athanasius continued to wane. In a letter to Ascholius of Thessalonica, he acknowledged that 'zeal . . . for the most blessed Athanasius gives the clearest possible evidence of your soundness in the matters of greatest importance'.[143] He was still recalling the patriarch's authority in 376, in his long letter to the people of Neocaesarea.[144] The new association with Ascholius led, however, to more protracted reflections, incorporating the broad view of church affairs that Basil had now developed. Reading Ascholius's letter,

> we thought that we were back in the olden times . . . , when the churches of God flourished, taking root in the faith, united by charity, there being, as in a single body, a single harmony of the various members; when the persecutors indeed were in the open, but in the open were also the persecuted; when the laity, though harassed, became more numerous, and the blood of the martyrs watering the churches nurtured many times as many champions of religion, later generations stripping themselves for combat in emulation of their predecessors. Then we Christians had peace among ourselves, that peace which the Lord left to us, of which now not even a trace any longer remains to us, so ruthlessly have we driven it away from one another.[145]

The theme was now familiar. In that period of 'old-time happiness . . . , one knew who was enemy and who was friend. Basil feared cautious deceit and a false sense of party almost as much as he feared error itself. How much more reassuring had been the conflicts of the martyrs, now no more than a memory. Their herosim had allowed issues to remain clear, whereas now the obscure and shifting intensities of schism made resolution all the harder.

Athanasius died at the beginning of May 373, having dominated the Arian debate for half a century. Basil felt obliged to build a new relationship with his successor, Peter. His first attempt was cautious. Gone was 'the intimacy engendered through long association' (which was an exaggeration, anyway): one had to fall back on 'true love . . . formed by the gift of the Spirit'. He hoped that Peter, 'having been the spiritual nursling of so great a man', would 'walk in the same spirit' as Athanasius, 'guided by the same dictates of piety'; but he took nothing for granted, asking simply for regular news and continued regard.[146] The sequel would prove that his caution had been justified.

He also kept in touch with Meletius, chiefly in connection with events in Armenia.[147] He maintained contact with Antioch, too. A letter on Christian style to Diodorus, written in late 372, we have examined elsewhere.[148] Now, towards the end of 373, he wrote a long and important letter on more specifically ecclesial matters to the whole community at Antioch, over which Diodorus, together with Flavianus, presided in Meletius's name. The themes of sin, trial, hope, and consolation were repeated once more. There was a hint that the end of suffering might be in sight: 'Presently He will come who will take our part; He will come and not delay. For you must look forward to affliction upon affliction, hope upon hope, for yet a little while, yet a little while'.[149]

. . . . .

The third phase began when at last news was brought back from the West. Evagrius (the later friend of Jerome, and translator of the *Life of Antony*) delivered (in 373) a specific request that Basil and other bishops should endorse *Confidimus quidem* and send a new delegation to Rome.[150] Basil relayed the news, together with his own misgivings, to Eusebius of Samosata.[151] With his close friend he was able to share a rather different view of how embassies should be conducted, both locally and further afield:

> And yet it does not seem best to me to estrange ourselves entirely from those who do not accept the faith, but we should show some concern for these men according to the old laws of charity . . . and should with one accord write letters to them, offering every exhortation of kindliness, and proffering to

them the faith of the Fathers we should invite them to join us [demanding, in other words, as little as possible, fearing to drive them otherwise into intransigent opposition]; and if we convince them, we should be united with them in communion; but if we fail, we should ourselves be content with one another, and should remove this present uncertainty from our way of life, taking up again that evangelical and guiltless polity in which they lived who from the beginning adhered to the Word.[152]

That was still how he felt the Arian dispute should be resolved, as also the schism at Antioch. Even more fundamental was the principle of consulting 'the good of our neighbours', since otherwise 'the ruin of each of us is involved in the common disaster'.[153] It was becoming clear, perhaps, that Damasus and his colleagues had rather more peremptory procedures in mind, which were likely to cause as much dissension as they relieved.

Even more shattering, however, was the news that Damasus had decided to give his unqualified support to Paulinus. Writing to Evagrius himself, Basil made no attempt to hide his dismay, or to play down his contrasting principles of mediation. The hope was still the same: that 'all those who are not divided from one another in mind [and that was the important point, so often obscured by the follies of party] shall fill the same assembly'.[154] Such an achievement would depend on delicacies of policy that Damasus, by implication, had failed to preserve: 'Evils which have been strengthened by time need time first of all for their correction'. Then 'the complete elimination of suspicions and of the clashes arising from controversies is impossible, unless there be some trustworthy man to act as a mediator in the interest of peace'.[155] Moreover, mediation had to be conducted face to face: letters were not enough. Basil took it also as a personal slight, not unnaturally, that in the midst of other tensions and disappointments Evagrius had seen fit not to share communion with Dorotheus—anticipating, of course, the sharper lines that were about to be drawn in Antioch.

As for setting up yet another embassy to the West, Basil was strikingly hesitant. He left it very much to Evagrius, saying that he could not think of anyone among his own circle who could either lead or take part in such a venture. Whether that arose from pique, which is far from impossible, or whether it reflected a sense of isolation on Basil's part, is hard to say. It may have been simply the result of his embroilments elsewhere: that was the year, after all, of his trip to Armenia. Subsequent journeys were undertaken, as we shall see, and may suggest that Basil had not lost hope in the West completely, as he had been forced to do in relation to Alexandria; but there is no doubt that the setback represented by Evagrius's mission seriously modified his view of what could be achieved in collaboration with Rome.

During the next two years Basil continued to afflict himself with indignation over the recognition of Paulinus. He also directed a number of letters to church communities in Syria, bemoaning above all the success of Valens in controlling their affairs. No doubt he saw a connection between the two problems.

In regard to the first preoccupation, a letter to the *comes* Terentius (appointed once again to a position of responsibility in Antioch) expressed his chief misgivings.[156] Paulinus and his followers had apparently received further written encouragement from Rome (this letter to Terentius was written towards the end of 376). Basil did not mince his words. The fresh correspondence from the West, he said, 'entrusts to them the episcopate of the church at Antioch' but also 'misrepresents the most admirable bishop of the true church of God, Meletius'. He asserted without hesitation that western churchmen were 'absolutely ignorant of affairs here . . .'. He wasted little time in pretending to respect opinions held in Rome: 'This is my position: not only shall I never consent to dissemble just because somebody has received a letter from human beings and is elated over it; nay, not even if it came from the very heavens but does not agree with the sound doctrine of faith, can I regard him as sharing in communion with the saints'.[157] He was careful to follow up this letter with shorter messages to Meletius and to Dorotheus.[158] In a slightly earlier letter to a community of ascetics, Basil showed how readily he connected affairs at Antioch with his own difficulties in relation to Eustathius of Sebaste. His more local opponents had begun to feel by this time that their interests might be additionally served if they sought an alliance with Euzoius in Antioch. In the process, therefore, they had begun to express more explicitly Arian doctrines, thus undermining, of course, the achievements they had boasted of, and the western support to which they had laid claim, at the synod of Tyana.[159]

As for his Syrian connections, Basil had been careful from the beginning of his episcopate to keep in touch with Christian communities in various parts of the region.[160] We have already discussed his long and cautious letter to the community at Chalcis, written in 375.[161] He also continued to encourage the church at Beroea: having received news of their' daily struggle and vigorous opposition on behalf of religion', he was able to assure them that 'your example has set many churches aright'.[162] Contacts of that sort continued during the next phase of events. The priest Sanctissimus (of whom we shall say more below) brought Basil news of the dispersal of some at least of the orthodox community at Beroea, and of similar disruptions in the church of Batnae.[163] All his letters of that period testify not only to continuing anxiety and involvement but

also to the success that Valens and the Arian party generally were enjoying in the churches of the region. Heroism and the postponement of hope were all that Basil now could bank on: 'In this we rejoice with you, and pray that the God of all, Whose is the struggle, Whose is the arena, and through Whom are the crowns, may create eagerness, may supply strength of spirit, and may bring your work to complete approval in His sight'.[164]

. . . . .

The fourth phase is represented by the preparations for, and the results of, a third journey undertaken to the West.[165] Events may have been precipitated by the exile of Eusebius of Samosata in 374. It was Eusebius who recognized, at the latest by 375, that some response would have to be made to the demands brought back by Evagrius in 373. That prompted Basil, early in 375, to write to Meletius, saddling him in effect with the responsibility of acting upon Eusebius's advice.[166] He suggested using the services of Sanctissimus, a priest from Antioch loyal to Meletius. The idea was that Sanctissimus would travel around various communities, seeking ideas and support for a new embassy. Basil's recent letters to Beroea and to Abramius of Batnae may be seen, therefore, as having taken the first steps; and Sanctissimus also carried back to Syria this very letter to Meletius.[167] A letter to Eusebius of Samosata, written towards the end of the process, shows us what Basil continued to regard as the important issues.[168] There is, it has to be said, more than a hint of confusion in his mind, which may explain why he passed on Eusebius's idea so quickly to Meletius in the first place: 'What message, then, I ought to send through them [Dorotheus and Sanctissimus], or how I am to come to an agreement with those who write, I myself am at a loss'. His enduring pessimism in regard to the bishop of Rome may be reflected in his observation that 'proud characters, when courted, naturally become more disdainful than usual'. After all, he said, 'if the Lord has been reconciled to us, what further assistance do we need? But if God's anger abides, what assistance can we have from the supercilious attitude of the West?' He did make a passing reference to Marcellus of Ancyra, which no doubt points to associations that endured in his mind; but otherwise all he could think of doing was sending a covering letter with Sanctissimus's eventual document, making the point that 'they should not attack those who have been brought low by trials nor judge self-respect to be arrogance'. His loss of confidence could not have been more clearly expressed.

Sanctissimus, meanwhile, had gathered together the threads of a new declaration to the West and had developed his own ideas about what should be emphasized. Basil betrayed once again that he was slightly out of touch with what was afoot: 'If the letter to the people of the West appears to contain anything that is important for us, be pleased to draft it and send it to us'.[169] There was only one point that he himself felt obliged to emphasize, and it had much more to do with his vision of church order than with the intricacies of the Arian controversy itself. He wanted to urge western churchmen

> not to receive indiscriminately . . . the communion of those coming from the East, but after once choosing a single portion of them . . . , to accept the rest on the testimony of these already in communion; and . . . not to take into communion everyone who writes down the Creed as a supposed proof of orthodoxy.[170]

In this way, presumably, he hoped that authorities in the West would not be able to ignore (as they seemed to have done in the case of Paulinus) a carefully prepared consensus, such as Sanctissimus and Dorotheus were about to present. Basil's motives were once again ecclesial rather than strictly doctrinal. He was dealing still with the old and different problem of people who opposed one another, even though they appeared to subscribe to the same doctrines. If the westerners did not follow his advice, they would 'find themselves to be in communion with men prone to fight, who often put forward statements of doctrine which are identical, but then proceed to fight with one another as violently as the men who are of opposite opinions'.[171]

As soon as the spring or early summer of 376 advanced, Sanctissimus and Dorotheus set out. Exactly what they carried with them, in the way of documentation, is not entirely clear from the surviving writings of Basil himself. Of the two letters that occur in the relevant section of his correspondence, one is clearly a draft of a letter already taken to the West by Dorotheus in 372. It is unlikely that it was taken again. The other is almost certainly a personal letter from Basil, designed to accompany and to endorse whatever documents Sanctissimus had been able to collect during his journey seeking support in the previous year.[172]

This second letter was filled with characteristic anxieties. It included a fairly mild version of his habitual grouse: some westerners with authority should come on a visit, 'in order that they may see with their own eyes the sufferings of the East, which it is impossible to learn by report, since no words can be found that can set forth our situation clearly to you'.[173] He then expressed a more fundamental misgiving: 'The most oppressive part of this is, that neither do those who are being wronged accept their sufferings in the certainty of martyrdom, nor do the laity reverence their athletes as being in the class of martyrs, because the persecutors are cloaked with the name of Christians'.[174] The lines of division, in other words, were obscured by the apparent theological unity of those in conflict.

A clear policy among the persecutors was laid bare by Basil's plea: 'Shepherds are being persecuted that their flocks may be scattered'. As a result, whole communities were torn apart. Basil described the destruction not in terms of theological argument but of decay in the conduct of cult. To begin with, 'the pious are driven from their native places, and are exiled to desert regions'. The results were quite specific:

> Our feasts have been turned into mourning; houses of prayer have been closed; idle are the altars of spiritual service. No longer are there gatherings of Christians, no longer precedence of teachers, no teachings of salvation, no assemblies, no evening singing of hymns, nor that blessed joy of souls which arises in the souls of those who believe in the Lord at the gatherings for Holy Communion and when the spiritual blessings are partaken of. It is fitting for us to say: 'neither is there at this time prince, or prophet, or leader, or oblation, or incense, or place of first-fruits before the Lord and no place to find mercy'.[175]

There was a frank admission, therefore, that theological oppression, so to speak, was in no way so powerful a weapon as manipulation of cultic practice:

> The ears of the more simple-minded . . . have become accustomed to the heretical impiety. The nurslings of the Church are being brought up in the doctrines of ungodliness. For what are they indeed to do? Baptisms are in the heretics' hands, attendance upon those who are departing this life, visits to the sick, the consolation of those who grieve, the assisting of those who are in distress, succour of all kinds, communion of the mysteries; all of these things, being performed by them, become a bond of agreement between them and the laity. Consequently after a little time has passed, not even if all fear should be removed, would there then be hope of recalling those held by a long-standing deception back to the recognition of the truth.[176]

Those emphases count for much more, in the letter as a whole, than do the half dozen or so sentences that make more explicit reference to theological argument.

There was also a specific point being made *ad hominem*, tailored, as Basil must have thought, to the prevailing indifference of the western church. 'Consider', he wrote, 'that our sufferings are yours'. Here he was recalling a point made in earlier correspondence with the West:

> Since the gospel of the kingdom, having begun in our region, has gone forth to the whole world, on this account the common enemy of our souls strives that the seeds of apostasy, having taken their beginning in the same region, may be distributed to the whole world. For upon whom the light of the knowledge of Christ has shone, upon these the darkness of impiety also contrives to come.[177]

The struggle was above all in defence of history, of tradition, of what Basil called 'our common possession—our treasure, inherited from our fathers, of the sound faith'.[178] Everything expressed here had already coloured entirely his conduct and attitude within the local church.

While the ambassadors were absent in the West, Basil had occasion to write to Epiphanius of Salamis. He refused to be drawn into a detailed discussion of the Arian issue, falling back in his characteristic way on the belief that 'we can add nothing to the Creed of Nicaea, not even the slightest thing, except the glorification of the Holy Spirit'.[179] He did have more to say about the situation at Antioch. He lamented once again the way in which 'orthodoxy has itself also been divided against itself'. He reasserted his support for Meletius, on the significant grounds of his 'great affection for him because of that steadfast and unyielding stand he made' (during 'that noble contest in the reign of Constantius'). He insisted that Athanasius had desired communion with Meletius at heart and had simply been misled 'through malice of counsellors'. As for himself, 'we have never accepted communion with any one of those who entered the see thereafter [including Paulinus, of course, as well as Euzoius], not because we considered them unworthy, but because we were unable to condemn Meletius in anything'. He recommended that Epiphanius should avoid taking sides and should concentrate more on effecting a reconciliation.[180] Basil was digging in his toes, in other words, and allowing himself to say less and less.

. . . . .

That brings us in effect to the fifth and final phase of Basil's 'international' career. Sometime in 377, Dorotheus and Sanctissimus came back from the West. They brought with them a letter from Damasus condemning Arianism in general terms, and also Apollinarius.[181] It was scarcely satisfactory; and the two long-suffering ambassadors were soon on their way to the West again, carrying a precise set of demands from Basil. Arianism, he said, was no longe the issue. That 'reckless and impudent heresy . . . being plainly cut off from the body of the Church, remains in its own error, and harms us but little . . . because their impiety is evident to all'.[182] Once again, it was internal enemies, appearing to share with him a common belief, who caused him most concern. He wanted them exposed, named formally, condemned explicitly by a general declaration from the West, so that they would no longer be able 'through an unguarded communion to share their own disease with their neighbours'.[183]

Who were those villains? They are by now familiar enough to us: Eustathius, Apollinarius, and Paulinus. Basil's portrayal of Eustathius was particularly skilful, given the diplomatic context. He had been able, as

Basil put it, to gain acceptance at the hands of the unsuspecting Hermogenes of Caesarea. He had then proceeded to undermine the purity of Nicaea at the various gatherings at Ancyra, Seleucia, and Constantinople. Then came his journey to the West, his favourable consultation with Liberius in Rome, and his triumphant return to Tyana. Basil implied, without much attempt at subtlety, that Liberius had been fooled. Certainly, 'this man now tries to destroy that creed on the basis of which he was received'. The bishops of the West had helped to create that situation: they should now take steps to correct it:

> Since, then, his power to harm the churches came from your quarter, and since he has used the privilege granted him by you for the downfall of the many, from ' you must come also his correction, and you should write to the churches what the conditions are on which he was received, and how now, having undergone a change, he nullifies the favour that was granted to him by the fathers of that time.[184]

Apollinarius, meanwhile, was having a pernicious effect, largely through the widespread distribution of his many writings, remarkable above all for their misleading obscurity. Finally, their protégé in Antioch, Paulinus, was 'inclined towards the teachings of Marcellus [of Ancyra]'. . . . [185]

Basil concluded that ideally a council of East and West together should expose those individuals once and for all, so that they would either seek communion on orthodox terms or find themselves publicly excluded from the unity of the Church.[186] Yet now, he said, was not the moment. That feeling may have been connected with his earlier admission that he currently lacked the authority to take part in such a gathering: 'Statements made by us are suspected by the many, on the ground that we perhaps, through certain personal quarrels, hold ill-will towards them'.[187] Quite frankly, Basil gave little sign here that he had made any attempt to extend himself beyond the orbit of his personal relationships and their attendant antagonisms.

The final embassy to the West had not been, in any case, a great success. All it managed to bring back was a deep sense of grievance and another ineffectual letter from the bishop of Rome.[188] It seems that the frustration of Dorotheus's hopes had been due to the intervention of Peter of Alexandria, who was in Rome at the time, and who commanded much more respect in western eyes, both because of the status of his see and because of his natural association with the reputation of Athanasius.[189] Peter had gone so far as to accuse Meletius and Eusebius of Samosata of Arian sympathies. The suggestion was, quite frankly, ridiculous and irresponsible; and Basil showed remarkable self-control in his subsequent letter to Peter himself. While continuing to defend his colleague in Antioch, he also warned the patriarch to tread more cautiously, if he wished to help in the achievement of any harmony among the eastern churches:

> We all need each other in the communion of our members, and especially now, when the churches of the East look to us, and will take your harmony as a start towards firmness and strength; but if they perceive that you are somewhat suspicious of each other, they will relax and will slacken their hands, so that they should not raise them against enemies of the faith.[190]

Basil seems to have reconciled himself, in any case, to the fact that authoritative aid from the West was no longer to be hoped for. He began, in his correspondence, to clarify for his own sake how matters now stood generally. Eustathius and Apollinarius still occupied the centre of the stage; but two other points made greater sense in relation to Antioch. First, Basil continued to associate Paulinus and his party with the teachings of Marcellus of Ancyra.[191] Second, he wished at least to create the impression that communication with the West had reinforced the weight of opinion against his own adversaries and had made more obvious their geographical isolation: 'Look about on the world, and observe that this portion which is unsound is small, but that all the rest of the Church, which from one end to the other has received the Gospel, abides by this sound and unchanged doctrine'.[192] He was still attempting to encourage his scattered allies to see themselves as belonging to a larger party, whose interests and beliefs they should take more carefully into account, before they accepted or rejected the leaders of this group or that.[193]

Conflict within Antioch itself did not end at that point. After the death of Valens at the battle of Hadrianople in 378, Meletius and Eusebius were able to return from exile. In the following year, Meletius held a synod at Antioch and seems to have gained recognition in the West. Certainly in 381, he presided over the Council of Constantinople, a vindication of his perseverance and perhaps the peak of his career. He lived long enough to see Gregory of Nazianzus briefly installed as bishop of the eastern capital; but he died shortly afterwards. It is a great sorrow that Gregory's funeral oration has not survived. Paulinus was still alive, and this might have been taken as the opportunity to settle matters once and for all; but a Meletian rival, Flaviánus, was also installed as bishop, and the schism continued for many years yet.[194]

By that time, Basil was dead. His final letters hint in several ways that he may have felt his enemies' days were numbered, and that the end of the Arian controversy was now in sight.[195] To Peter of Alexandria, he was willing to admit (and it may not have been merely self-deluding consolation) that the Church possessed

strengths scarcely affected by mere theological discord: 'We have given thanks to the Lord, that a remnant of the ancient good discipline . . . is being preserved in you and that the Church has not lost her strength in our persecution. For the canons . . . have not also been persecuted along with us'.[196] Yet he admitted also to a certain numbness of spirit, after so much struggle:

> But be informed, our most honoured and beloved brother, that continuous afflictions, and this great tumult which is now shaking the Churches, cause us to be astonished at nothing that takes place. For just as workers in smithies, whose ears are struck with a din, become inured to the noise, so we by the frequency of strange reports have at length become accustomed to keep our heart unmoved and undismayed at unexpected events. Therefore the charges that have from of old been fabricated by the Arians against the Church, although many and great and noised throughout the whole world, can nevertheless be endured by us.[197]

As usual, it was the hidden enemies, 'men of like mind and opinion with ourselves', that caused him more anxiety. Those remained much more closely associated in his eyes with the narrow arena of his own experience and preoccupation. The letter to Peter is the last from his pen that we can clearly date—in the moving words of one historian, 'le dernier écho qui nous soit parvenu de sa noble voix'.[198] It was the voice, we have to admit, of a man by now weary, isolated, and robbed of many hopes.

Notes

[1] GNaz *Orat.* 43. 41, tr. p. 62.

[2] GNaz *Orat.* 43. 65, tr. p. 83. The same sentiment occurs in GNaz *Ep.* 46. 2: . . . , ed. Gallay, 1: 59.

[3] *Hom.* 342. 1. Could Gregory have known of this sermon?

[4] The connection was emphasized strongly by Fedwick, *Charisma*, p. 102.

[5] *Ep.* 28. 3, C 1: 69f., D 1: 169. See chapter 3, at n. 102, and chapter 4, at n. 33.

[6] *Ep.* 28. 1, C 1: 67, D 1: 163.

[7] *Ep.* 29, C 1: 71, D 1: 173. Not that Athanasius had been the warmest of colleagues: see *Ep.* 25. Indeed, Musonius could have been placed in the same category: see *Ep.* 28. 3.

[8] *Ep.* 29; C 1: 71; D 1: 171/173, 173/175.

[9] *Ep.* 65, C 1: 156, D 2: 25/27.

[10] *Ep.* 97, C 1: 210, D 2: 163.

[11] *Ep.* 126, C 2: 36, D 2: 273.

[12] See *Ep.* 4, 12, 13.

[13] *Ep.* 131. 2, C 2: 46, D 2: 301; but Deferrari's slightly different text ends with obscurity. . . . See also *Ep.* 211.

[14] See *Ep.* 63. . . . It refers to news carried by one Elpidius (not the bishop mentioned below in n. 15), who fulfilled a similar function in *Ep.* 64 (more closely concerned with affairs in Cappadocia itself: see *Ep.* 72), and was associated with the disgraced official Therasius of *Ep.* 77 and 78. . . .

[15] See *Ep.* 208 and (perhaps) 209. In pursuit of the same general cause, he wrote assiduously to a bishop Elpidius, no friend of Eustathius (see *Ep.* 251. 3). He wanted above all, with Elpidius's help, to bring the bishops of the region together, 'to uproot the troubles which arise from our present suspicions of one another, and strengthen the love without which the Lord Himself has declared to us that the performance of every commandment is incomplete', *Ep.* 205, C 2: 182, D 3: 177.

[16] *Ep.* 203. 1, C 2: 168, D 3: 145.

[17] *Ep.* 161. 2, C 2: 93f., D 2: 415.

[18] *Ep.* 97, C 1: 211, D 2: 165.

[19] *Ep.* 244. 8, C 3: 81, D 3: 469. The extent to which he now felt that the hopes of earlier years were closer to fulfilment may be revealed by another comparison with that letter to Tyana: 'We ourselves, nevertheless, neither see nor hear anything but the peace of God and whatsoever leads to it. For even if others are powerful, and great, and confident in themselves, we, on the contrary, are nothing, and worth nothing', *Ep.* 97, C 1: 210, D 2: 161/163. His own confidence, if not self-piteous, would seem to have been bought at the cost of esteem and status.

[20] *Ep.* 203. 2.

[21] *Ep.* 203. 3, C 2: 170f., D 3: 149/151. . . .

[22] The two later letters appear to have responded to a silence that had greeted the first; and they did so by attending to quite particular points.

[23] *Ep.* 207 passim.

[24] This was the letter he wrote while staying with his brother Peter: see *Ep.* 216 and chapter 3, n. 18.

[25] *Ep.* 210. 4, C 2: 194, D 3: 207.

[26] *Ep.* 210. 3, C 2: 191f., D 3: 201. 'Even now . . . ' was a nice touch: it was still possible for them to segregate Atarbius from that respectable genealogy.

[27] The 'naming' anxiety was closely associated with central points of debate in the Arian dispute: for the ability to name, in a purely logical sense, the three persons of the Trinity was closely connected with the ability to distinguish characteristics of each one of them . . . , while safeguarding a unity of [*ousia*].

[28] On the importance of limiting disputes to written statements, see chapter 4, at nn. 94f.

[29] *Ep.* 204. 1, 7; C 2: 172f., 180; D 3: 155, 173.

[30] *Ep.* 204. 2, C 2: 173f., D 3: 157.

[31] *Ep.* 223. 3. For all these points, see chapter 1, at nn. 69f.

[32] *Ep.* 204. 6, C 2: 179, D 3: 169/171.

[33] *Ep.* 113 to Tarsus, C 2: 17, D 2: 225. See Fedwick, *Charisma*, p. 74 and n. 170. See also *Ep.* 114. For a fuller analysis of these letters, see Michael A. G. Haykin, 'And Who Is the Spirit? Basil of Caesarea's Letters to the Church at Tarsus'.

[34] *Ep.* 204. 6, C 2: 179, D 3: 171.

[35] *Ep.* 204. 7, C 2: 180, D 3: 173.

[36] *Ep.* 204. 7, C 2: 180, D 3: 173/175.

[37] Two general surveys have proved particularly useful: R. H. Hewsen, 'The Successors of Tiridates the Great: A Contribution to the History of Armenia in the Fourth Century'; and Roger C. Blockley, 'The Division of Armenia between the Romans and the Persians at the End of the Fourth Century A.D.'. Much can still be gained from Norman H. Baynes, 'Rome and Armenia in the Fourth Century': clarity and grace compensate for the imperfections of an older scholarship.

[38] See Matthews, *Ammianus*, p. 53.

[39] Matthews, *Ammianus*, pp. 136, 499 n. 14, with cautious comment on the nevertheless invaluable article by T.D. Barnes, 'Constantine and the Christians of Persia'.

[40] Ammianus Marcellinus 25, 7. 12f.

[41] Ammianus Marcellinus 14, 3. 1; 14, 5.

[42] Ammianus Marcellinus 20, 11. 1f.; *Cod. Theod.* 11, 1. 1. For the date (358 rather than 360), see Nina G. Garsoïan, 'Politique ou orthodoxie? L'Arménie

au quatrième siècle', p. 305. On Ablabius, see Eunapius *Lives* B 463f. in W 384f.

[43] Nerses did not have a metropolitan see, as was normal for church leaders within the empire, but exercised a wandering authority over bishops he had appointed.

[44] Ammianus Marcellinus 20, 9. 1, 11. 1-4. For Nerses' involvement, see Nina G. Garsoïan, 'Quidam Narseus? A Note on the Mission of St. Nerses the Great'.

[45] Nina Garsoïan, 'Nerses le Grand, Basile de Césarée et Eustathe de Sébaste', pp. 148f., was of the opinion that the connections dawned on Basil only later—perhaps an unnecessary caution: albeit 'remote' in Pontus, Basil could easily have heard reports. (I am much less open to Garsoïan's suggestion, p. 149, that the 'Narses' of *Ep.* 92 was the Armenian prelate.) For Nerses' own relations with Eustathius, see the same article, esp. pp. 164f., and her 'Sur le titre de *protecteur des pauvres*', esp. p. 29. The plentiful references to Basil in Armenian sources are frequently unreliable; but see Faustus of Byzantium 4, 3f.; 5, 24. For Faustus, I have relied on the French translation of Jean Baptiste Emine.

[46] Ammianus Marcellinus 27, 12. 9. For Pap specifically, see Roger C. Blockley, *Ammianus Marcellinus: A Study of His Historiography and Political Thought*.

[47] See *PLRE* 1: 881f., s.v. Terentius 2.

[48] Faustus of Byzantium 5, 21; tr. p. 289.

[49] Themistius *Orat.* 11, 149B . . . ed. Schenkl and Downey, 1: 224. See also Ammianus Marcellinus 29, 1. 2.

[50] *Ep.* 99. 1, C 1: 214 . . . See the points already made in chapter 5, at nn. 178f.

[51] The Armenian sources give wonderfully full accounts. See n. 45 above and n. 53 below.

[52] *PLRE* 1: 666, s.v. Papa, suggests with apparent confidence 25 July 373; but I have been unable to discover on what authority. Faustus and Moses (on whom see the following note) appear to be silent. The tenth-century *Généalogie de la famille de saint Grégoire et Vie de saint Narse*, 14, has the phrase (in the French translation, which I have been given no reason to doubt) 'dans le mois de hroditz [more properly, Hrotic'], le jour de jeudi', in *Collection des historiens anciens et modernes de l'Arménie*, ed. Victor Langlois, 2: 41. Hrotic' ran from early July to early August: V. Grumel, *La Chronologie = Traité d'études byzantines*, 1: 301. J. R. Russell was kind but equally at a loss.

[53] At Khakh and Til respectively. See Moses of Chorene (Moses Khorenats'i), *History of the Armenians,* 3. 38, tr. Robert S. Thompson, pp. 298f.

[54] See *Ep.* 148 and 149. *PLRE* 1: 921f., s.v. Traianus 2, seems assured, as is Garsoïan, 'Politique', 316f. See also Treucker, *Studien,* pp. 47, 51. Yet we cannot be completely certain that we are dealing with the same man.

[55] Ammianus Marcellinus was appalled, 30, 1. 18f., and one detects irony (obvious also to Traianus) in his phrase *'modo serenae mentis Valentis indices litteras tradens'*, 19, in Rolfe, 3: 304. Traianus remained in favour, acting as *magister peditum* in Thrace in 377; but he was killed at Hadrianople.

[56] Ammianus Marcellinus 30, 1. 2f. Compared with Traianus, Terentius may have experienced more censure (as much in relation to his own orthodoxy): *PLRE* 1: 881f., s.v. Terentius 2.

[57] Fedwick, *Charisma*, makes little reference; and the reasons adduced on p. 104 n. 9 are not corroborated. Gain's allusions are scattered in pursuit of other interests: 'ce qui ne manque pas de piquant, vu leur affrontement', *Église,* p. 81; and 's'explique par des raisons politiques', p. 322 n. 148. Courtonne, *Témoin,* esp. pp. 120f., places matters firmly in the context of the Arian controversy. Brennecke, *Geschichte der Homöer*, p. 195, may overestimate Basil's success ('im Auftrage des Kaisers, doch eigentlich gegen seinen Willen'), and he is surprisingly vague in assessing Valens's motives, picking out, as I would, Basil's impressive personality, and adding his friendships with those in high places and his reluctance to indulge in the fiery excommunication of Homoeans.

[58] *Ep.* 99. See also his earlier report concerning Apollinarius, *Ep.* 214.

[59] 'Both the Imperial ordinance and the friendly letter of your Honour': *Ep.* 99. 1, C 1: 214, D 2: 171/173.

[60] . . . not quite Deferrari's 'customary indifference'.

[61] *Ep.* 99. 4, C 1: 217f., D 2: 181/183.

[62] *Ep.* 102, with confirmation in 103.

[63] See *Ep.* 122, to be discussed shortly.

[64] Hence his improving relationship with Theodotus (*Ep.* 130), and other letters (now lost) addressed to the region (see *Ep.* 195).

[65] *Ep.* 122, C 2: 28, D 2: 251/253.

[66] *Ep.* 121, C 2: 27, D 2: 251.

[67] *Ep.* 120, C 2: 26, D 2: 249. See Gain, *Église*, pp. 77 (with n. 71), 81.

[68] *Ep.* 227, C 3: 30, D 3: 345. This letter was discussed in chapter 5, at n. 182.

[69] *Ep.* 228, C 3: 33, D 3: 351.

[70] *Ep.* 229. 1, C 3: 33f., D 3: 353.

[71] *Ep.* 229.1, C 3: 34, D 3: 353/355.

[72] *Ep.* 230. See chapter 5, at nn. 145f. It would seem that *Ep.* 127 and 128 to Eusebius of Samosata were written in 373 rather than in 375, which would bring all the Colonia and Nicopolis involvements closer together. *Ep.* 128 in particular is filled with reference to the Spirit and 'the old laws of charity'—matters touched upon already and to be touched upon again.

[73] *Ep.* 237. 2.

[74] *Ep.* 238, C 3: 58, D 3: 413. The same point is made in *Ep.* 239. 1.

[75] *Ep.* 239. 1, C 3: 60, D 3: 417. For other references to enforced worship in the open, see *Ep.* 238, 240. 2. Theodoret corroborates these other instances, *Hist. relig.* 2 (Julian). 15.

[76] See *Ep.* 238 at C 3: 58, lines 16f.; and 240. 3: 'Now that they have seen that the laity are provoked they are again pretending orthodoxy', C 3: 64, D 3: 425; . . .

[77] *Ep.* 246, 247.

[78] *Ep.* 240. 1; but the whole letter makes the point.

[79] In what follows I have depended heavily on the clear and detailed account given by Courtonne, *Témoin,* and with slightly more caution, the older study by Robert Devreesse, *Le Patriarcat d'Antioche, depuis le paix de l'Église jusqu'à la conquête arabe.* Behind both works stands F. Cavallera, *Le Schisme d'Antioche (IVᵉ-Vᵉ siècles).* Of comparable importance are the references to Antioch in Brennecke, *Geschichte der Homöer.* Note also his convincing scepticism about a persecution in Syria under Valens, pp. 233f. Basil's heroes and friends did most to isolate themselves from the mainstream of church opinion. Fedwick's chronology, *Charisma,* pp. 108f., is different from older works, but his narrative no less useful. Lukas Vischer, *Basilius der Große: Untersuchungen zu einem Kirchenvater des 4. Jahrhunderts,* is also particularly clear. A focus on Antioch is central to the argument of E. Amand de Mendieta, in an excellent and indispensable study, 'Basile de Césarée et Damase de Rome: Les causes de l'échec de leurs négociations', marred only by confessional anxieties over the status of the bishop of Rome (see, for example, nn. 126, 158 below). More balanced is the useful account by Justin Taylor, 'St. Basil the Great and Pope St. Damasus I'. He is content to leave Basil

at once orthodox and indignant, while showing a shrewd sympathy for Damasus's difficulties. His dating, however, is open to revision. Important criticisms are levelled on Basil's behalf by Wilhelm de Vries, 'Die Ostkirche und die Cathedra Petri'. Reference back to the early sections of chapter 4 may sometimes prove helpful.

[80] See chapter 4, at nn. 5f.

[81] The circumstances of those events, and the startling transfer of Eudoxius to the see of Constantinople, have all been discussed in chapter 4, as just noted above. It is important to stress the association of Meletius with the synod of Constantinople. Whatever move towards a clearer espousal of Nicaea he may have made, it happened gradually and later. See Brennecke, *Geschichte der Homöer,* pp. 69f.

[82] See Epiphanius *Panarion* 70. 3. 29f. Courtonne, *Témoin,* p. 248, observes: 'Le discours de Mélèce était d'un homme attaché à l'orthodoxie'.

[83] Athanasius *Tom. ad Ant.* 3f., *PG* 26. 798f.

[84] Vitalis actually went to Rome in 375 and gained some favour; but that ebbed with time. See Damasus's letter to Paulinus, *Per filium* (his *Ep.* 3), *PL* 13. 356f., together with his *Ep.* 7 against Apollinarius, *PL* 13. 369f. Also Epiphanius *Panarion* 77. 20f.; and Basil's *Ep.* 258, to which we shall return. Behind more recent accounts of the relations between Damasus and Basil lies the important textual study of E. Schwartz, 'Über die Sammlung des *Cod. Veronensis* LX'. See also his 'Zur Kirchengeschichte des vierten Jahrhunderts'.

[85] See Rochelle Snee, 'Valens' Recall of the Nicene Exiles and Anti-Arian Propaganda', p. 414. Jovian's brief reign had encouraged Meletius and his supporters to move closer to a Nicene position, chiefly because of their alarm at the conduct of Eunomius. Valens, restoring churchmen to the positions they had enjoyed under Constantius, simply (and successfully) ignored the intervening confusions caused by Julian and Jovian. See Brennecke, *Geschichte der Homöer,* pp. 173f., 209.

[86] See chapter 4, at n. 17, and chapter 7, at n. 24.

[87] Snee, 'Recall of the Exiles', p. 413 n. 103, following Gwatkin, is happy to think so. Brennecke, *Geschichte der Homöer,* p. 233 n. 64, implies as much.

[88] For Demophilus, see *Ep.* 48; for Euzoius, see Snee, 'Recall of the Exiles', pp. 414f. According to Brennecke, *Geschichte der Homöer,* p. 232, Valens's final settlement in Antioch ensured that Meletius would find no place in the city.

[89] *Ep.* 66. 2, C 1: 158, D 2: 33.

[90] See Glanville Downey, *A History of Antioch in Syria from Seleucus to the Arab Conquest*; A. M. J. Festugière, *Antioche païenne et chrétienne: Libanius, Chrysostome et les moines de Syrie*; Jones, *Cities*; J. H. W. G. Liebeschuetz, *Antioch: City and Imperial Administration in the Later Roman Empire*; Petit, *Libanius et la vie municipale à Antioche* (see chapter 2, n. 31); and D. S. Wallace-Hadrill, *Christian Antioch: A Study of Early Christian Thought in the East*. Recall the point made in chapter 3, n. 54, about Basil's early interest in Syria generally, and the usefulness of Theodoret's *Historia religiosa* (extensively quoted by several of the authors referred to above).

[91] His *Misopogon* gives the fullest impression. See especially the accounts of Bowersock and Browning, and Maude W. Gleason, 'Festive Satire: Julian's *Misopogon* and the New Year at Antioch'.

[92] In addition to the general material listed in n. 90, the following add useful reflections (even if dated) and references to sources: Glanville Downey, 'The Economic Crisis at Antioch under Julian the Apostate'; Robert Browning, 'The Riot of A.D. 387 in Antioch: The Role of the Theatrical Claques in the Later Empire'; and Timothy E. Gregory, 'Urban Violence in Late Antiquity'. The necessary caution had governed the imperial handling of church affairs in Antioch since the early days of Constantius's reign. See Brennecke, *Geschichte der Homöer*, pp. 66f.

[93] For Modestus, see appendix 2, at nn. 1f.

[94] See Ammianus Marcellinus 29, 1f.

[95] In addition to the study by Festugière mentioned in n. 90, see J. C. Baur, *John Chrysostom and His Time*; and Matthews, *Western Aristocracies*, pp. 121-45.

[96] See Matthews, *Ammianus*, esp. chaps. 2 and 18. Some excellent points are succinctly presented in his 'Ammianus' Historical Evolution'.

[97] For Libanius, see n. 90 and chapter 2, nn. 6, 16, 31.

[98] Julian's dismissive comment that the Goths were a less worthy enemy, for an emperor, than the Persians, may not have been idiosyncratic: Ammianus Marcellinus 22, 7. 8.

[99] Considerable difficulties attach to the dating of the various embassies between East and West. On the whole I have followed Fedwick, *Charisma*. Detailed variations very rarely affect my own argument; but a few alternatives will be noted as we proceed. I have numbered my phases simply in the interests of clarity. Different divisions are used by Courtonne, *Témoin*, Fedwick, *Charisma*, and Amand de Mendieta, 'Basile de Césarée et Damase de Rome'. A detailed account is contained in Charles Pietri, *Roma Christiana: Recherches sur l'Église de Rome, son organisation, sa politique, son idéologie de Mithrade à Sixte III (311-440)*, esp. 1:791-872. In spite of the fact that Basil's involvement was evident from 371, I question Taylor's view, 'Basil and Damasus', p. 187, that 'he came to his episcopal office with a grand strategy already worked out'.

[100] For what follows, *Ep.* 66, C 1: 156f., D 2: 27f.

[101] *Ep.* 68. The reference to Euippius brings the letter within the context of Arian conflict more generally but also relates to the growing dispute with Eustathius. See also *Ep.* 128.

[102] *Ep.* 69. I take it that this letter was to be carried by Dorotheus on the same first-planned journey: it appears from the text that he was still considered to need a full introduction; and Deferrari's 'we have *again* sent to your Piety' (2: 41) is an unjustified gloss on the Greek.

[103] *Ep.* 69. 1, C 1: 162, D 2: 43. One does need to keep constantly in mind the question of what Basil wanted from Damasus specifically: his early intentions must have coloured his later disappointment. Concerning Basil's relations with the bishop of Rome, in addition to the material cited above in n. 79, see Perikles-Petros Joannou, *Die Ostkirche und die Cathedra Petri im 4. Jahrhundert*—a book useful for bringing together documents and references, but lacking in overall judgement of any significance.

[104] *Ep.* 69. 2, C 1: 164, D 2: 47. On the prolonged and central attention to Marcellus, see Amand de Mendieta, 'Basile de Césarée et Damase de Rome, p. 144.

[105] *Ep.* 69. 2, C 1: 163, D 2: 47. See below, at nn. 122, 131.

[106] *Ep.* 67, C 1: 159f., D 2: 35. See chapter 4, n. 17.

[107] *Ep.* 70, C 1: 164f., D 2: 49f. This was the only letter Basil ever tried to write to Damasus personally.

[108] Fedwick, *Basil*, 1: 12 n. 72.

[109] Following Fedwick, *Charisma*, p. 109 n. 29. This is Damasus's *Ep.* 1, *PL* 13. 347-349, also edited by Schwartz, 'Sammlung'. Amand de Mendieta, 'Basile de Césarée et Damase de Rome, p. 127, follows Schwartz in dating the synod concerned to 372. Basil acknowledged receipt of the material in *Ep.* 90.

[110] We can almost certainly catch the final cadence of his optimism in another, vaguely expressed and vaguely dated, letter to the patriarch, *Ep.* 82.

[111] *Ep.* 89. 2.

[112] *Ep.* 48, C 1: 128f., D 1: 315.

[113] *Ep.* 57.

[114] *Ep.* 69. 1, C 1: 161, D 2: 39.

[115] *Ep.* 69. 1, C 1: 162, D 2: 41.

[116] *Ep.* 82, C 1: 184, D 2: 97.

[117] *Ep.* 82, C 1: 185, D 2: 99.

[118] *Ep.* 66. 1, C 1: 157, D 2: 27.

[119] The slavery image occurs at the beginning and end of *Ep.* 70, . . . and . . . C 1: 165f. Thus heretics were given satanic status: see *Hom.* 354. 3. In *Ep.* 66, it is not certain whether . . . [this] refers to bishops, C 1: 157; but episcopal leadership seems to be implied somewhere in the sentence, as the translations of Deferrari and Courtonne both suggest. For the associated misfortune of the laity see chapter 4, at n. 121, and, for the corresponding bond between clergy and laity, chapter 5, at nn. 126f.

[120] *Ep.* 69. 2. See above, n. 105. The theme was developed very fully in *Ep.* 92. 2, discussed below.

[121] *Ep.* 70, C 1: 164, D 2: 49. Deferrari's phrase '*an old affection*' appears to limit it to a description of the relationship between Basil and Damasus. The letter as a whole, however, makes clear reference to an ecclesiology, which 'we know through a continuous tradition', . . . C 1: 165, D 2: 51. Amand de Mendieta, 'Basile de Césarée et Damase de Rome', stresses with justice the importance of this . . . but is less successful in presenting it as a species of *history* (although note his discussion of 'la conception primitive', pp. 148f.). It is a major point in Pietri, *Roma Christiana*, that two different views of the Church were being stressed one against the other.

[122] It is difficult to decide who wrote what. Amand de Mendieta, 'Basile de Césarée et Damase de Rome', p. 127, follows Lietzmann in suggesting that *Ep.* 92 was written by Meletius, while 90 represented Basil's additional thoughts; but both letters bear Basil's mark.

[123] Snee, 'Recall of the Exiles', p. 415. I am not sure that Amand de Mendieta, however, makes suitable contrasts. Damasus was just as concerned as Basil with maintaining ecclesial alliances—as Amand de Mendieta, 'Basile de Césarée et Damase de Rome', p. 136, admits. 'Attention aux problèmes moraux et humains ainsi qu'à leurs solutions pratiques', p. 135, was not an attitude exclusive to the West! Nor should it be considered grounds for criticism, if Basil and

his colleagues were 'imbus d'hellénisme et épris de liberté intellectuelle', p. 158.

[124] In the opening phrase of *Ep.* 91.

[125] *Ep.* 92. 3; C 1: 201, 203; D 2: 141/143.

[126] *Ep.* 92. 2f., C 1: 201f., D 2: 137/141.

[127] *Ep.* 91, C 1: 198, D 2: 131.

[128] *Ep.* 92. 3, C 1: 202, D 2: 141. Concrete evidence that Damasus appreciated the point, while pleading more local preoccupations of his own, may be supplied in the inscription discussed by Henry Chadwick, 'Pope Damasus and the Peculiar Claim of Rome to St. Peter and St. Paul': 'Discipulos Oriens misit, quod sponte fatemur; . . . Roma suos potius meruit defendere cives'.

[129] *Ep.* 90. 2, C 1: 196, D 2: 125/127. See n. 119 above.

[130] *Ep.* 92. 2, C 1: 200, D 2: 137/139. See above, at nn. 105, 121.

[131] *Ep.* 92. 2, C 1: 201, D 2: 139/141. The same emphasis was made in the earlier draft of this letter (*Ep.* 242. 2)—see Fedwick, *Basil*, 1: 13. Similar events had been witnessed in Armenia: see above, at n. 75.

[132] *Ep.* 92. 2, C 1: 200, D 2: 137.

[133] *Ep.* 90. 2, C 1: 195f., D 2: 125.

[134] See chapter 4, esp. at nn. 97f., 125f.

[135] *Ep.* 91, C 1: 198, D 2: 131.

[136] As discussed in chapter 5, at nn. 73f.

[137] So *Ep.* 91, C 1: 197, D 2: 131; but the point was made extensively in the opening sections of *Ep.* 90, 92 (and 242), all with reference to storm and calm.

[138] *Ep.* 91, C 1: 197, D 2: 129.

[139] *Ep.* 91, C 1: 197, D 2: 131. See chapter 7, at nn. 160f.

[140] *Ep.* 90. 2, C 1: 196, D 2: 127. The contrast is with . . . *Ep.* 92. 2. . . . The civic echoes of such vocabulary should never be overlooked.

[141] See chapter 5, after n. 43 and at nn. 187f.

[142] *Ep.* 92. 3, C 1: 202, D 2: 141; but there is no hint of this in the draft, *Ep.* 242; which may support the view that a general council was Meletius's idea only (since *Ep*, 92 may have been his reworking of the

original text). See Taylor, 'Basil and Damasus', 196f. Basil did, however, entertain the notion eventually: see n. 186 below.

[143] *Ep.* 154, C 2: 79, D 2: 379.

[144] *Ep.* 204. 6. See above, at nn. 29f.

[145] *Ep.* 164. 1, C 2: 97f., D 2: 423.

[146] *Ep.* 133, C 2: 47, D 2: 303. *Ep.* 139 was also addressed to Alexandria and made the same points as the letter to Ascholius quoted above, *Ep.* 154. This seems an odd letter to have sent to Egypt, in that it suggests that, in better health, Basil would have travelled there; but we have no reason to doubt its editorial title. . . .

[147] It is useful to recall here *Ep.* 99 to Terentius, and events discussed above, at nn. 58f.

[148] *Ep.* 135. See chapter 2, at nn. 67, 76f.

[149] *Ep.* 140. 1, C 2: 61, D 2: 335. The importance of Flavianus and Diodorus (see above, after n. 82) was stressed by Theodoret *Hist. relig.* 8. 7. The vocabulary recurs in *Ep.* 238 of the year 376. We shall have occasion to discuss the theme further at n. 195 below. For other points connected with *Ep.* 140, see chapter 4, at n. 110, and chapter 5, at n. 98. *Ep.* 113 and 114 to Tarsus show how Basil thought open unity was best achieved: do not press those in error further than necessary. That point is well handled by Fedwick, *Charisma*, pp. 73f., and has occurred already in chapter 4, at n. 112 (and see chapter 6, n. 157).

[150] For Evagrius, see the several useful references made throughout his work by Kelly, *Jerome*. That one should have some sympathy for Damasus is a point made by Joannou, *Ostkirche*, pp. 14f.: he was caught between Liberius's earlier recognition of Meletius and Athanasius's persistent resistance. He also felt the need for a signed declaration of orthodoxy, as had been forthcoming from eastern delegates to Julius and Liberius before him. Basil, on the other hand, remembered such incidents precisely for their hidden tolerance of Marcellus of Ancyra and their encouragement of Eustathius's deceit. See Pietri, *Roma Christiana*, 1:801f.

[151] *Ep.* 138. 2: 'Our own letter he has brought back to us again on the ground that it was not pleasing to the more strict of the people there', C 2: 55f., D 2: 323. There was some irony in this attempt by Damasus to gain a clearer picture of Basil's theology: he may have remembered how Eustathius had fooled Liberius some ten years before—a point made, of course, by Basil himself! See n. 86 above, and Taylor, 'Basil and Damasus', p. 199.

[152] *Ep.* 128. 3, C 2: 39, D 2: 281/283. One should notice, again, how much interwoven with other concerns the point was: in this instance, affairs at Colonia, and Eustathius, discussed in the previous chapter. Compare the letters to Tarsus mentioned above in n. 149.

[153] *Ep.* 136. 2, C 2: 52, D 2: 315, also discussed in chapter 7, at n. 104.

[154] *Ep.* 156. 1, C 2: 82, D 2: 385.

[155] *Ep.* 156. 1f., C 2: 82, D 2: 387.

[156] *Ep.* 214. We have already examined this letter as an example both of theological advice to a layman and of Basil's wish that matters of discipline associated with heresy should be left to churchmen: see chapter 5, at nn. 151, 183 (and see chapter 3, at n. 47).

[157] *Ep.* 214. 2, C 2: 203f., D 3: 229/231. Here is perhaps the clearest indication that Basil rejected Damasus's point of view. It is probably true, however, that he did not fully understand the chief anxieties of the bishop of Rome; in which case, it is anachronistic to suppose he was preoccupied with the confessional issues that might later focus on papal expectations—see Amand de Mendieta, 'Basile de Césarée et Damase de Rome', p. 149. We are dealing here simply with his reaction to Vitalis's attempt to curry favour in the West, and to Damasus's *Ep.* 3: see n. 84 above.

[158] *Ep.* 214 and 215 (probably in that order, although any lapse of time between them would have been insignificant). It was in the latter that Basil criticized Gregory of Nyssa as a potential diplomat: see chapter 1, at n. 20.

[159] *Ep.* 226. It is not clear whereabouts this community was situated. Later editors have entitled the letter . . . ; but the content does not immediately suggest Basil was addressing people well known to him.

[160] For example, *Ep.* 184 to Eustathius of Himmeria, and *Ep.* 185 to Theodotus of Beroea.

[161] *Ep.* 222. See chapter 5, n. 89, and at n. 144, and chapter 7, at n. 37.

[162] *Ep.* 220, C 3: 4, D 3: 277/279. The Acacius mentioned here was later bishop of Beroea, which links this correspondence with that addressed to Dorotheus and Meletius, mentioned at n. 158 above. See Theodoret *Hist. relig.* 2 (Julian). 9. *Ep.* 221, also written in 375, makes the same points.

[163] See *Ep.* 256 (which also mentions Acacius). *Ep.* 132 was addressed to Abramius, bishop of Batnae, but then resident in Antioch.

[164] *Ep.* 221, C 3: 5, D 3: 281.

[165] Dating problems are numerous. I have accepted 376, taking into account the narratives of Devreesse and Courtonne and points made more recently by Fedwick, *Basil*, 1: 16, and Gain, *Église*, pp. 374f. This does not mean that I have unravelled the obscurities to my own satisfaction; and I have had to rest content with the ambition of describing ideas rehearsed by Basil over the course of a year or so. Note that this 'fourth' phase corresponds to Lietzmann's third—a solo journey by Dorotheus, made in 374—as described by Amand de Mendieta, 'Basile de Césarée et Damase de Rome', pp. 128f.

[166] *Ep.* 120. The move may have been associated with the burst of frustrated correspondence between Basil and Eusebius himself, discussed in *Ep.* 198 (of the same year).

[167] There is further confusion over dating. Fedwick, *Basil*, 1: 16, suggests, contrary to the accounts of Devreesse and Courtonne, that *Ep.* 253, 254, and 255, to Antioch, Laodicea, and Carrhae respectively, were also written at this juncture. The alternative suggestion is that they were written *after* the next journey to the West, announcing its success. Given the several references to recent western experience, I am inclined to agree with that view.

[168] For what follows, *Ep.* 239. 2, C 3: 60f., D 3: 419/421.

[169] *Ep.* 129. 3 (to Meletius, the year before), C 2: 41, D 2: 287.

[170] *Ep.* 129. 3, C 2: 41, D 2: 289.

[171] *Ep.* 129. 3, C 2: 41, D 2: 289.

[172] *Ep.* 242 and 243. The first is a draft of *Ep.* 92 (see nn. 125f. above). The detailed list of bishops at the beginning of *Ep.* 92 describes, no doubt, Sanctissimus's careful itinerary through Syria. The second reflects Basil's correspondence with Eusebius of Samosata, *Ep.* 239 (see n. 167 above).

[173] *Ep.* 243. 1, C 3: 69, D 3: 437.

[174] *Ep.* 243. 2, C 3: 69, D 3: 437.

[175] *Ep.* 243. 2, C 3: 70, D 3: 437/439, 441.

[176] *Ep.* 243. 4, C 3: 72f., D 3: 447. This preoccupation with cultic control was much more important to Basil than any sense of moral failing on the part of Arians: compare Amand de Mendieta, *Ascèse*, p. 175; and see chapter 4, at n. 121.

[177] *Ep.* 243. 3, C 3: 71, D 3: 443/445. See above, at nn. 127f.

[178] *Ep.* 243. 4, C 3: 71, D 3: 445.

[179] *Ep.* 258. 2, C 3: 101f., D 4: 41.

[180] *Ep.* 258. 3, C 3: 102f., D 4: 43/45. Basil was gaining much greater confidence in the face of the ambiguities involved. *Ep.* 257 was the herald, perhaps, of a new sense of release.

[181] According to Fedwick, *Charisma*, p. 110 and n. 33, this was *Ea gratia*. According to an older account, reflected in Amand de Mendieta, 'Basile de Césarée et Damase de Rome', p. 130, it was *Illud sane miramur*. Schwartz, 'Sammlung', considered these, along with *Non nobis*, to be fragments of separable letters, although they are presented as Damasus *Ep.* 2 in *PL* 13: 350-354. By this time, Damasus had had second thoughts about Vitalis and had committed himself much more to Paulinus (witness his *Per filium*): see n. 84 above. Taylor, 'Basil and Damasus', pp. 262f., may have a point in suggesting the influence of Jerome at this point; but other forces were sufficient to explain the hardening of western attitudes.

[182] *Ep.* 263. 2, C 3: 122, D 4: 91. If Basil died later in 377 (a possibility to be discussed in the next chapter and in appendix 3), this and associated letters can still easily be dated to the early months of that year.

[183] *Ep.* 263. 2, C 3: 122, D 4: 93.

[184] *Ep.* 263. 3, C 3: 124, D 4: 97.

[185] *Ep.* 263. 5, C 3: 125, D 4: 99.

[186] A universal council seems implied by Basil's phraseology . . . , *Ep.* 263. 5, C 3: 125. On a smaller scale, he had used the same technique against Neocaesarea in *Ep.* 204. 7: see above, at n. 35.

[187] *Ep.* 263. 2, C 3: 122, D 4: 93. Fedwick, *Charisma*, p. 65 n. 134, is anxious to stress that Basil did not wish to see Paulinus explicitly condemned, and that this was the first time the possibility of his heresy was raised. See also Gain, *Église*, pp. 371f.; Taylor, 'Basil and Damasus', pp. 192, 268. Amand de Mendieta, 'Basile de Césarée et Damase de Rome', p. 124, highlights the importance of Basil's perceived lack of authority.

[188] Probably *Non nobis quidquam* and *Illud sane miramur*: Fedwick, *Charisma*, p. 112 n. 43. See nn. 84 and 181 above.

[189] He had become, in Amand de Mendieta's words, 'Basile de Césarée et Damase de Rome', p. 127, 'le conseiller attitré pour les affaires d'Orient'. According to his account, all this would have predated the first journey made by Dorotheus and Sanctissimus.

[190] *Ep.* 266. 2, C 3: 135f., D 4: 127. On dating, see n. 182 above.

[191] *Ep.* 265. 3. See n. 104 above.

[192] *Ep.* 251. 4, C 3: 93, D 4: 17. See also *Ep.* 265. 3.

[193] Very much the point of *Ep.* 265, esp. 3. We have already touched upon this and *Ep.* 251 in chapter 7, at n. 37, and in chapter 4, at n. 98.

[194] The dating of these events will be discussed at the beginning of the next chapter and in appendix 3, in the light of Snee, 'Recall of the Exiles'.

[195] See *Ep.* 264 to Barses of Edessa. *Ep.* 267 suggests that this letter may not have reached its destination.

[196] *Ep.* 266. 1, C 3: 134, D 4: 123.

[197] *Ep.* 266. 1, C 3: 133, D 4: 121. The sentiment was in some ways analogous to the calculated humility of his letter to Tyana: see n. 19 above. Yet scarcely months before he had considered himself 'a byword all over the earth, and, I shall add, even over the sea', *Ep.* 212. 2, C 2: 199, D 3: 221. The resignation of tone in the letter quoted here seems the jaundiced successor of what might earlier have been taken as spirited confidence: 'The topsy-turvy condition of the times has taught us to be vexed at nothing', *Ep.* 71. 1, C 1: 167, D 2: 55.

[198] Devreesse, *Patriarcat*, p. 34; but Pierre Maraval, 'La Date de la mort de Basile de Césarée', p. 34, may reserve that distinction for *Ep.* 267. Fedwick, *Basil*, 1: 18, places *Ep.* 268, 269, and 196 in the year 378; but that must now be questioned in the light of the recent controversy over the date of Basil's death, to be discussed in the next chapter and in appendix 3.

Abbreviations

Adul. Basil *Ad adulescentes.*

B *Regulae brevius tractatae* = *Short Rules.*

C Yves Courtonne, editor of Basil's *Letters.*

CE Basil *Contra Eunomium.*

D Roy J. Deferrari, translator of Basil's *Letters.*

DSS Basil *De spiritu sancto.*

Ep. Epistula(e).

F *Regulae fusius tractatae* = *Long Rules.*

GCS Die griechischen christlichen Schriftsteller der ersten Jahrhunderte.

GNaz Gregory of Nazianzus.

GNyss Gregory of Nyssa.

HE Historia ecclesiastica.

Hex. Basil *Hexaemeron.*

Hom. Basil *Homilia(e).* (The numbering of Basil's homilies is explained in the supplement to the Bibliography.)

Jones, *LRE* A. H. M. Jones, *The Later Roman Empire, 284-602.* First published 1964. Reprinted in two paperback volumes. Oxford: Blackwell, 1986.

Laud. Gregory of Nyssa *In laudem fratris Basilii.*

N *Basilio di Cesarea, Discorso ai Giovani (Oratio ad adolescentes)*, ed. Mario Naldini.

Orat. Oratio(nes).

PG Patrologia Graeca, ed. J. P. Migne.

PL Patrologia Latina, ed. J. P. Migne.

PLRE The Prosopography of the Later Roman Empire, edited by A. H. M. Jones, J. R. Martindale, and J. Morris. Vol. 1, *A.D. 260-395.* Cambridge: Cambridge University Press, 1971.

R Rufinus's Latin translation of Basil's 'Rules'.

VMac. Gregory of Nyssa *Vita s. Macrinae.*

Bibliography

Sources

. . . Ammianus Marcellinus. The most convenient edition is the revised three-volume edition in the Loeb Classical Library, with an English translation by John C. Rolfe (London and Cambridge, Mass.: Heinemann and Harvard University Press, 1950, 1952).

Basil of Caesarea. *Ad adulescentes. PG* 31. 563-590. *Basilio di Cesarea, Discorso ai Giovani (Oratio ad adolescentes), con la versione latina di Leonardo Bruni*, ed. Mario Naldini (Florence: Nardini editore, 1984). See also *Saint Basil on the Value of Greek Literature*, ed. N. G. Wilson (London: Duckworth, 1975); and *Saint Basile, Aux jeunes gens sur la manière de tirer profit des lettres helléniques*, ed. and tr. Fernand Boulenger, Collection Guillaume Budé (Paris: Les Belles Lettres, 1952). English translation in *Saint Basil, The Letters*, 4: 379-435. . . .

———. *Epistulae. PG* 32. 219-1112. *Saint Basile, Lettres*, 3 vols., ed. and tr. Yves Courtonne, Collection

Guillaume Budé (Paris: Les Belles Lettres, 1957, 1961, 1966). English translation: *Saint Basil, The Letters*, 4 vols., tr. Roy J. Deferrari, Loeb Classical Library (reprint, London and Cambridge, Mass.: Heinemann and Harvard University Press, 1950-53). See also *Saint Basil, Letters*, 2 vols., tr. Sister Agnes Clare Way, Fathers of the Church 13, 28 (Washington, D.C.: Catholic University of America Press, 1951, 1955; reprint, 1965, 1969). . . .

―――. *Homilia(e)*. PG 29. 209-494; 31. 163-618, 1429-1514. English translations of homilies on the Psalms by Agnes Clare Way in *Saint Basil, Exegetic Homilies*, Fathers of the Church 46 (Washington, D.C.: Catholic University of America Press, 1963). . . .

Epiphanius. *Panarion* ['The Refutation of All Heresies']. *Epiphanius (Ancoratus und Panarion)*, ed. Karl Holl, vol. 3, GCS 37 (Leipzig: J. C. Hinrichs'sche Buchhandlung, 1933).

Eunapius. *Lives of the Philosophers and Sophists. Philostratus and Eunapius, The Lives of the Sophists*, tr. Wilmer Cave Wright, Loeb Classical Library, rev. ed. (London: Heinemann; Cambridge, Mass.: Harvard University Press, 1952).

Faustus of Byzantium. French translation by Jean Baptiste Emine in *Collection des historiens anciens et modernes de l'Arménie*, ed. Victor Langlois, 1: 209f. (Paris: Firmin-Didot, 1880). . . .

Gregory of Nazianzus. *Contra Julianum*. *Grégoire de Nazianze, Discours 4-5, Contre Julien*, ed. and tr., with intro. and notes, Jean Bernardi, Sources chrétiennes 309 (Paris: Éditions du Cerf, 1983). . . .

―――. *Epistulae. Saint Grégoire de Nazianze, Lettres*, 2 vols., ed. and tr. Paul Gallay, Collection Guillaume Budé (Paris: Les Belles Lettres, 1964, 1967). See also *Gregor von Nazianz, Briefe*, ed. Paul Gallay, GCS 53 (Berlin: Akademie-Verlag, 1969). . . .

―――. *Oratio* 43 (on Basil). *PG* 36. 493-605. English translation by Leo P. McCauley in *Funeral Orations*, pp. 27-99. . . .

Moses of Chorene (Moses Khorenats'i). *History of the Armenians*, tr., with notes, Robert S. Thompson (Cambridge, Mass.: Harvard University Press, 1978). . . .

Themistius. *Themistii orationes quae supersunt*, 3 vols., ed. Heinrich Schenkl, completed by Glanville Downey (Leipzig: Teubner, 1965-74).

Theodoret of Cyrrhus. . . .

Theodoret of Cyrrhus. *Historia religiosa. Théodoret de Cyr, Histoire des moines de Syrie: 'Histoire Philothé' I-*

XIII, 2 vols., ed. and tr., with intro. and notes, Pierre Canivet and Alice Leroy-Molinghen, Sources chrétiennes 234, 257 (Paris: Éditions du Cerf, 1977, 1979). English translation: *A History of the Monks of Syria by Theodoret of Cyrrhus*, tr., with intro. and notes, R. M. Price, Cistercian Studies 88 (Kalamazoo, Mich.: Cistercian Publications, 1985). . . .

Secondary Works

Amand de Mendieta, Emmanuel (David Amand). *L'Ascèse monastique de saint Basile: Essai historique*. N.p.: Éditions de Maredsous, 1949. . . .

―――. 'Basile de Césarée et Damase de Rome: Les causes de l'échec de leurs négociations'. In *Biblical and Patristic Studies*, edited by Birdsall and Thomson, pp. 122-66.

Barnes, T. D. 'Constantine and the Christians of Persia'. *Journal of Roman Studies* 75 (1985): 126-36. . . .

Baur, J. C. *John Chrysostom and His Time*. Translated by M. Gonzaga. 2d ed. Vaduz: Buchervertriebanstalt, 1988. . . .

Baynes, Norman H. *Byzantine Studies and Other Essays*. London: University of London Athlone Press, 1955.

―――. 'Rome and Armenia in the Fourth Century'. *English Historical Review* 25 (1910): 625-43. Reprinted in his *Byzantine Studies and Other Essays*, pp. 186-208. . . .

Birdsall, J. Neville, and Robert W. Thomson, eds. *Biblical and Patristic Studies in Memory of Robert Pierce Casey*. Freiburg: Herder, 1963.

Blockley, Roger C. *Ammianus Marcellinus: A Study of His Historiography and Political Thought*. Collection Latomus 141. Brussels, 1975.

―――. The Division of Armenia between the Romans and the Persians at the End of the Fourth Century A.D.'. *Historia* 36 (1987): 222-34. . . .

Bowersock, Glen W. *Julian the Apostate*. Cambridge, Mass.: Harvard University Press, 1978.

Bowie, Ewen Lyall. 'Apollonius of Tyana: Tradition and Reality'. In *Aufstieg und Niedergang der römischen Welt* II. 16. 2, edited by Wolfgang Haase, pp. 1652-99. Berlin and New York: Walter de Gruyter, 1978.

Brennecke, Hanns Christof. *Studien zur Geschichte der Homöer: Der Osten bis zum Ende der homöischen Reichskirche*. Beiträge zur historischen Theologie 73. Tübingen: Mohr (Siebeck), 1988. . . .

Browning, Robert. *The Emperor Julian*. London: Weidenfeld and Nicolson, 1975.

————. 'The Riot of A.D. 387 in Antioch: The Role of the Theatrical Claques in the Later Empire'. *Journal of Roman Studies* 42 (1952): 13-20.

Cavallera, F. *Le Schisme d'Antioche (IVᵉ - Vᵉ siècles)*. Paris: Picard, 1905. . . .

Chadwick, Henry. *History and Thought of the Early Church*. Collected Studies 164. London: Variorum, 1982.

————. 'Pope Damasus and the Peculiar Claim of Rome to St. Peter and St. Paul'. In *Neotestamentica et patristica*, edited by Van Unnik, pp. 313-18. Reprinted in his *History and Thought*. . . .

Coleman-Norton, P. R., ed. *Studies in Roman Economic and Social History in Honor of Allan Chester Johnson*. Princeton: Princeton University Press, 1951. . . .

Courtonne, Yves. *Un Témoin du IVᵉ siècle oriental: Saint Basile et son temps d'après sa correspondance*. Paris: Les Belles Lettres, 1973. . . .

Croke, Brian, and Alanna Emmett, eds. *History and Historians in Late Antiquity*. Sydney: Pergamon Press, 1983. . . .

Devreesse, Robert. *Le Patriarcat d'Antioche, depuis le paix de l'Église jusqu'à la conquête arabe*. Paris: Gabalda, 1945.

De Vries, Wilhelm. 'Die Ostkirche und die Cathedra Petri'. *Orientalia Christiana periodica* 40 (1974): 114-44. . . .

Downey, Glanville. 'The Economic Crisis at Antioch under Julian the Apostate'. In *Studies in Roman Economic and Social History*, edited by Coleman-Norton, pp. 312-21. . . .

————. *A History of Antioch in Syria from Seleucus to the Arab Conquest*. Princeton: Princeton University Press, 1961. . . .

Fedwick, Paul Jonathan, ed. *Basil of Caesarea: Christian, Humanist, Ascetic, A Sixteenhundredth Anniversary Symposium*. 2 vols. Toronto: Pontifical Institute of Mediaeval Studies, 1981.

————. *The Church and the Charisma of Leadership in Basil of Caesarea*. Studies and Texts 45. Toronto: Pontifical Institute of Mediaeval Studies, 1979.

Festugière, A. M. J. *Antioche païenne et chrétienne: Libanius, Chrysostome et les moines de Syrie*. Bibliothèque des Écoles françaises d'Athènes et de Rome 194. Paris: Boccard, 1959.

Gain, Benoît. *L'Église de Cappadoce au IVᵉ siècle d'après la correspondance de Basile de Césarée*. Orientalia Christiana analecta 225. Rome: Pontificium institutum Orientale, 1985. . . .

Garsoïan, Nina G. *Armenia between Byzantium and the Sasanians*. Collected Studies 218. London: Variorum, 1985. . . .

————. 'Nerses le Grand, Basile de Césarée et Eustathe de Sébasté. *Revue des études arméniennes*, n.s. 17 (1983): 145-69. Reprinted in her *Armenia between Byzantium and the Sasanians*.

————. 'Politique ou orthodoxie? L'Arménie au quatrième siècle'. *Revue des études arméniennes*, n.s. 4 (1967): 297-320. Reprinted in her *Armenia between Byzantium and the Sasanians*.

————. 'Quidam Narseus? A Note on the Mission of St. Nerses the Great'. In *Armeniaca: Mélanges d'études arméniennes*, pp. 148-64. Ile de Saint Lazare - Venise, 1969. Reprinted in her *Armenia between Byzantium and the Sasanians*.

————. 'Sur le titre de *protecteur des pauvres*'. *Revue des études arméniennes*, n.s. 15 (1981): 21-32. Reprinted in her *Armenia between Byzantium and the Sasanians*. . . .

Gleason, Maude W. 'Festive Satire: Julian's *Misopogon* and the New Year at Antioch'. *Journal of Roman Studies* 76 (1986): 106-19. . . .

Gregory, Timothy E. 'Urban Violence in Late Antiquity'. In *Aspects of Graeco-Roman Urbanism*, edited by Marchese, pp. 138-61. . . .

Grumel, V., ed. *La Chronologie*. Traité d'études byzantines, vol. 1, edited by Paul Lemerle. Paris: Presses universitaires de France, 1958. . . .

Haykin, Michael A. G. 'And Who Is the Spirit? Basil of Caesarea's Letters to the Church at Tarsus'. *Vigiliae Christianae* 41 (1987): 377-85. . . .

Hewsen, R. H. 'The Successors of Tiridates the Great: A Contribution to the History of Armenia in the Fourth Century'. *Revue des études arméniennes*, n.s. 13 (1978-79): 99-126. . . .

Joannou, Perikles-Petros. *Die Ostkirche und die Cathedra Petri im 4. Jahrhundert*. Päpste und Papsttum 3. Stuttgart: Anton Hiersemann, 1972.

Jones, A. H. M. *The Cities of the East Roman Provinces*. 2d ed. Oxford: Clarendon Press, 1971. . . .

Kelly, J. N. D. *Jerome, His Life, Writings, and Controversies.* London: Duckworth, 1975.

Langlois, Victor, ed. *Collection des historiens anciens et modernes de l'Arménie.* 2 vols. Paris: Firmin-Didot, 1880. . . .

Liebeschuetz, J. H. W. G. *Antioch: City and Imperial Administration in the Later Roman Empire.* Oxford: Clarendon Press, 1972. . . .

Maraval, Pierre. 'La Date de la mort de Basile de Césarée'. *Revue des études augustiniennes* 34 (1988): 25-38. . . .

Marchese, Ronald T., ed. *Aspects of Graeco-Roman Urbanism: Essays on the Classical City.* British Archaeological Reports, international ser., 188. Oxford, 1983. . . .

Matthews, John. 'Ammianus' Historical Evolution'. In *History and Historians in Late Antiquity*, edited by Croke and Emmett, pp. 30-41. Reprinted in his *Political Life and Culture.* . . .

———. *Political Life and Culture in Late Roman Society.* Collected Studies 217. London: Variorum, 1985.

———. *The Roman Empire of Ammianus.* London: Duckworth, 1989.

———. *Western Aristocracies and Imperial Court, A.D. 364-425.* Oxford: Clarendon Press, 1975. . . .

Petit, Paul. *Libanius et la vie municipale à Antioche au IVe siècle après J.-C.* Paris: Geuthner, 1955.

Pietri, Charles. *Roma Christiana: Recherches sur l'Église de Rome, son organisation, sa politique, son idéologie de Mithrade à Sixte III (311-440).* Bibliothèque des Écoles françaises d'Athènes et de Rome 224. Rome: Palais Farnèse, 1976. . . .

Schwartz, E. 'Über die Sammlung des *Cod. Veronensis* LX'. *Zeitschrift für die neutestamentliche Wissenschaft* 35 (1936): 1-23.

———. 'Zur Kirchengeschichte des vierten Jahrhunderts'. *Zeitschrift für die neutestamentliche Wissenschaft* 34 (1935): 129-213. . . .

Snee, Rochelle. 'Valens' Recall of the Nicene Exiles and Anti-Arian Propaganda'. *Greek, Roman and Byzantine Studies* 26 (1985): 395-419. . . .

Taylor, Justin. 'St. Basil the Great and Pope St. Damasus I'. *Downside Review* 91 (1973): 186-203, 262-74. . . .

Treucker, Barnim. *Politische und sozialgeschichtliche Studien zu den Basilius-Briefen.* Bonn: Habelt, 1961. . . .

Van Unnik, W. C., ed. *Neotestamentica et patristica: Eine Freundesgabe Herrn Prof. Dr. Oscar Cullmann zu seinem 60. Geburtstag überreicht.* Leiden: Brill, 1962. . . .

Vischer, Lukas. *Basilius der Große: Untersuchungen zu einem Kirchenvater des 4. Jahrhunderts.* Basel: Reinhardt, 1953. . . .

Wallace-Hadrill, D. S. *Christian Antioch: A Study of Early Christian Thought in the East.* Cambridge: Cambridge University Press, 1982. . . .

FURTHER READING

Amand de Mendieta, Emanuel. "The Pair 'Kerygma' and 'Dogma' in the Theological Thought of St. Basil of Caesarea." *Journal of Theological Studies* n.s. XVI, No. 1 (April 1965): 129-42.

> Analyzes Basil's idiosyncratic use of the term "dogma" in *On the Holy Spirit*. Amand de Mendieta maintains that here the word connotes a liturgical tradition known only to baptized communicants; thus Basil claims that although the church did not publicly affirm the full divinity of the Holy Spirit, this concept was an integral part of its instruction or "dogma."

Bamberger, John Eudes. " . . . The Psychic Dynamisms in the Ascetical Theology of St. Basil." *Orientalia Christiana Periodica* XXXIV, No. 2 (1968): 233-51.

> Evaluates the evidence of Basil's understanding of human psychology as revealed in his mystical writings and, particularly, in his monastic *Rules*. Bamberger argues that Basil had keen insight into the role of the unconscious in an individual's emotional and spiritual development.

Bonis, Constantine G. "The Problem Concerning Faith and Knowledge, or Reason and Revelation, as Expounded in the Letters of St. Basil the Great to Amphilochius of Iconium." *Greek Orthodox Theological Review* V, No. 1 (Summer 1959): 27-44.

> Focuses on Basil's discussion of the relation between epistemology and orthodox theology in "Letters 233, 234, and 235." Bonis sees this series of epistles as principally concerned with distinguishing between the knowable attributes of God and His unknowable essence, and acknowledging that both faith and knowledge are necessary for salvation.

Callahan, John F. "Basil of Caesarea: A New Source for St. Augustine's Theory of Time." *Harvard Studies in Classical Philology* LXIII (1958): 437-54.

Claims that Basil's concept of time as outlined in his *Against Eunomius* significantly influenced Augustine's definition of time in the *Confessions.* Callahan maintains that Augustine's use of scriptural references, the distinction he draws between quantitative and qualitative time, and his view of the relationship between time and motion are all drawn from Basil's treatise.

Campbell, James Marshall. "Ecphrasis." In his *The Influence of the Second Sophistic on the Style of the Sermons of St. Basil the Great.* Catholic University of America Patristic Studies II, pp. 128-45. Washington, D. C.: Catholic University of America, 1922.

Assesses Basil's rhetoric, particularly his restrained use of elaborate comparisons. These kinds of similes or word-pictures are most often found in his sermons, Campbell observes, where Basil adapts sophistic themes and conventions to further his principal goal of inspiring religious reverence.

Campenhausen, Hans von. "Basil the Great." In his *The Fathers of the Greek Church*, pp. 80-94. New York: Pantheon, 1955.

Examines Basil's ecclesiastical career, with special emphasis on tensions and conflicts in the fourth-century church. Basil was resolved to stabilize the church and its formal doctrines of faith, Campenhausen asserts, and as he carried out his duties as administrator, pastor, and theologian, he adopted strategies he believed would help accomplish this goal.

Deferrari, Roy J. Introduction to *Saint Basil: The Letters*, edited by Roy J. Deferrari, Vol. I, pp. xv-lv. New York: G. P. Putnam's Sons, 1926.

A biographical essay describing Basil's youth and education, important features of his monastic theory and practice, and his service as archbishop of Cappadocia. Deferrari also devotes a section of his introduction to the Arian controversy.

Gelsinger, Michael G. H. "The Epiklesis in the Liturgy of Saint Basil." *Eastern Churches Quarterly* X, No. 5 (Spring 1954): 243-48.

Considers the integrity of the clause invoking the Holy Spirit in the Basilean liturgical setting for the Eucharist. Although he acknowledges that the phrase is ambiguous, and that many revisers have either emended or deleted it, Gelsinger contends that this clause was part of the original formulation of the prayer.

Hanson, R. P. C. "Basil's Doctrine of Tradition in Relation to the Holy Spirit." *Vigilae Christianae* 22 (1968): 241-55.

Focuses on Basil's assertion, in *On the Holy Spirit*, of an extra-scriptural yet apostolic tradition of "general ideas" that supports the doctrine of the Spirit as a fully divine, independent essence within the Trinity.

Basil characterizes this tradition as secret or known to only a few—an innovative strategy that, in Hanson's judgment, was "unfortunate and unnecessary."

Mendieta, E. Amand de. "The Official Attitude of Basil of Caesarea as a Christian Bishop towards Greek Philosophy ad Science" in *The Orthodox Churches and the West,* edited by Derek Baker, pp. 25-49. London: Basil Blackwell, 1976.

Argues that Basil formally espoused a contemptuous attitude toward Greek philosophers. Citing the *Homilies on the Hexameron,* the critic maintains that in this work Basil frequently distorts or exaggerates the arguments of Greek philosophers, thereby revealing his deficient understanding of science as well as his zeal to affirm the authority of scriptural truth.

Newman, John Henry. "Labors of Basil" in *Essays and Sketches, Volume III,* edited by Charles Frederick Harrold, pp. 29-50. London: Longmans, Green, and Co., 1948, pp. 29-50.

Newman's essay, originally published in 1833, emphasizes the turmoil in the Eastern church in the years 375-76. He cites at length the letters from this period in which Basil describes the charges of heresy leveled against him, his estrangement fro his former colleagues and supporters, and his hopes that Western prelates will come to his aid.

Padelford, Frederick Morgan. "Introduction: The Life of St. Basil and the 'Address to Young Men.' " In *Essays on the Study and Use of Poetry by Plutarch and Basil the Great,* Yale Studies in English XV, edited by Albert S. Cook, pp. 33-43. New York: Henry Holt, 1902.

Briefly summarizes Basil's career and places the "Address to Young Men" in historical context. Padelford points out that Basil shared the viewpoint of some second- and third-century church fathers—Justin the Martyr, Athenagoras, Clement of Alexandria, and Origen—that familiarity with Hellenic literature provided valuable preparation for scriptural studies.

Prestige, G. L. "Basil and Apollinaris." In his *St Basil the Great and Apollinaris of Laodicea,* pp. 1-37. London: Society for Promoting Christian Knowledge, 1956.

Provides an extensive review of ecclesiastical politics and theological conflicts during the period 357-62, when "Letters 361-64," generally regarded as spurious, may have been written. Prestige believes they are authentic exchanges between Basil and Apollinaris, and he relates them to Eustace of Sebaste's accusation that Basil held Sabellian views.

Shear, Theodore Leslie. *The Influence of Plato on Saint Basil.* Baltimore, Md.: J. H. Furst, 1906, 60 p.

Asserts that Plato's influence on Basil was, in general, much less pronounced than on other early church fathers, though Basil did draw liberally from Plato when composing the *Homilies on the Hexaemeron* and the "Address to Young Men."

Way, Agnes Clare. *The Language and Style of the Letters of St. Basil*, Catholic University of America Patristic Studies XIII. Washington, D. C.: Catholic University of America, 1927, 229 p.

A detailed study of grammar and style in Basil's epistles. Way examines many technical aspects of the letters, including syntax, vocabulary, and rhetorical figures.

Bevis of Hampton

c. Fourteenth century

(Also known as *Sir Beves of Hampton* and *Beuve of Hamtoun*.) Medieval English romance.

INTRODUCTION

Among the many Middle English romances still in existence, *Bevis of Hampton* is one of the best known. Originally a French *chanson de geste,* or epic poem, it was enlarged and transformed into a celebrated romance by an unknown English poet in the late thirteenth or early fourteenth century. Orally composed and transmitted, *Bevis* comprises 4,620 lines, of which the first 474 are in tail-rhymed, six-line stanzas and the remainder in short rhyming couplets. It combines exotic settings and familiar ones as the action moves from England to Albania, from Arabia to Germany, and its final section is set in London. The tone is generally serious, though there are a number of scenes featuring grim and sometimes indelicate humor. The narrative is complex, building on repetitions and amplifications of traditional epic elements, including battles, betrayals, and imprisonments.

Commentators frequently assert that *Bevis of Hampton* was undoubtedly one of the most popular of all Medieval romances. Evidence of its popularity lies in the unusually large number of manuscript versions and copies of early printing that have survived. The most famous of these is the Auchinleck manuscript (Edinburgh), usually dated around 1330-1340; though it is the oldest English manuscript, and its lineation is the one most critics use in their citations, scholars do not believe the Auchinleck version is as close to the original as some others. Two fourteenth-century manuscripts are also extant, at Caius College, Cambridge, and the British Museum, but significant portions of the poem are missing from both of these. The complete text of *Bevis* survives in two fifteenth-century manuscripts, one in University College, Cambridge, and the other in the Royal Library of Naples. One leaf is lost from the *Bevis* manuscript in the Chetham Library, Manchester, but some scholars believe this version—also from the fifteenth century—is the most authentic. The only modern edition of *Bevis* is Eugen Kölbing's, prepared for the Early English Text Society and published over the period from 1885 to 1894.

The earliest form of the Bevis saga, *Beuve de Hantone* (also cited as *Beuves de Hanstone*), appeared in France during the twelfth century, and from there the story spread throughout Europe and the British Isles. At least six versions of the tale are extant in Italy, where the hero is called Bovo. It was also refashioned for audiences in Germany, Scandinavia, Ireland, and Wales. Scholars generally agree that the English *Bevis* is based on the Anglo-Norman *Boeve de Haumtone,* probably composed around 1200. To his original source, the English poet added three important episodes: the hero's clash with a group of Saracen warriors on Christmas Day, his struggle against the dragon of Cologne, and the pitched battle between Bevis and the citizens of London.

Many of the narrative elements in *Bevis of Hampton* are based on motifs found in folk tales, legends, and other romances, particularly the commonplace fable of the young hero who, driven into exile, wins fame in foreign lands and returns home to reclaim his patrimony and carry on the noble name of his family. Bevis is the son of the earl of Southampton, who late in life marries a woman who despises him. She has him murdered, marries the man who killed him, and sells their son into slavery. Bevis becomes part of the pagan household of the King of Armenia, whose daughter Josian falls deeply in love with him—though Bevis will have nothing to do with her until she converts to Christianity. Over the following years, Bevis engages in a series of perilous adventures, including conflicts with Saracens, giants, lions, and a dragon; he is also imprisoned for an extended period, returns to England to kill his father's murderer and witness his mother's death, and repeatedly endures the treachery of trusted aides and allies. Eventually, after Josian has been forced into two hateful marriages, she and Bevis are wed, and she gives birth to twin boys. In the concluding portion of the poem, Bevis and his sons become involved in a bitter civil dispute in England, narrowly winning a stunning victory over a mob of misguided London citizens.

Twentieth-century commentators have compared *Bevis* with other Middle English romances, analyzed its structure and principal characters, and evaluated its treatment of political issues. Scholars judge that *Bevis* is more fully developed in terms of literary form than some other romances of the period—for example, *King Horn* and *Havelok the Dane*. Many critics have pointed out that *Bevis* has some noteworthy parallels with *Guy of Warwick*, another extremely popular medieval saga, though several of them have also remarked that *Guy* is much closer than *Bevis* to the genre known as courtly or chivalric romance. Recently commentators have begun to challenge the traditional opinion that *Bevis* is a loosely constructed series of disparate episodes. Both Dieter Mehl and Sheila Spector have asserted that it has a unified design and was composed by a self-conscious artist who understood how to link together diverse narrative strands. But whereas Mehl has argued that the poem's dramatic unity stems from the actions of Bevis, Spector has maintained that it is Josian's development as a character that determines the formal order of the poem. Modern critics have generally viewed Bevis as both an epic hero and a defender of Christianity, though they have disagreed about whether he is more of a courtly knight or a popular hero. The only other character who has drawn close attention is Josian. In 1993 Geraldine Barnes evaluated the poem's portrayal of this sorely tried heroine, emphasizing her ingenuity as well as her moral strength, and noting that she continually devises clever strategies—both to gain the love of Bevis and to subvert the plans of villains who threaten her. Barnes has also assessed the significance of political issues in the final section of the romance, as has Susan Crane in her 1986 essay on *Bevis*. In Crane's estimation, *Bevis of Hampton* is deeply concerned with the political tensions that marked the late middle ages, when feudalism was in decline and a nationalist ideology was emerging to challenge the old order. This conflict, she has noted, reaches full expression when Bevis and his sons are assailed by the citizens of London acting in defense of the principle of monarchy.

PRINCIPAL ENGLISH EDITIONS

The Romance of Sir Beues of Hamtoun (edited by Eugen Kölbing) 1885-94

CRITICISM

Eugen Kölbing (essay date 1885-94)

SOURCE: "The Contents of the Romance" in *The Romance of Sir Beues of Hamptoun,* Kegan Paul, Trench, Trubner & Co., 1885, pp. xlv-lxvi, vii-xliii.

[*In the following excerpt, Kölbing provides a detailed summary of the narrative of* Bevis of Hampton, *generally following the plot line in the Auchinleck manuscript but drawing upon other texts as well.*]

. . . The story [of *Sir Beues of Hamtoun*] begins with our hero's father, Guy, Earl of South-Hampton, a most strong and valiant man, who unfortunately does not marry till he is old, exhausted and worn out by his battles and warlike expeditions. Then he makes up his mind to marry the daughter of the King of Scotland, a beautiful young lady, with whom the Emperor of Almaine, named Devoun, had been in love before. Her father refuses Devoun her hand, and gives her to Sir Guy. The result of this marriage is a pretty and bold boy, who receives the name Beves (l. 1-54).

After his birth, the lady feels unhappy at not having got a young and vigorous husband, instead of her old one, and she resolves to procure his death. She sends a messenger to the Emperor of Almaine, requiring him to come over to England on the first of May, go into a forest at the sea-side, and kill her husband, whom she will send there. When he has done this, he shall enjoy her love. The messenger promises to fulfil her wish (l. 55-108).

He gets to Almaine, and finds the Emperor at Rifoun, and gives him the message of his lady. The Emperor is very well pleased, makes the messenger a rich present, and bids him tell his mistress that he is entirely at her disposal. This the man does. On the first of May the Earl's wife pretends to be ill, and says she hopes to be cured by the flesh of a wild boar, which is in the forest at the sea-side (l. 109-192).

Thither her husband rides, armed only with a shield and sword, and accompanied by three attendants. He meets the Emperor, who has a large retinue. After a short conversation the Emperor throws Guy from his horse; but the Earl gets up again, draws his sword, and massacres many of his enemy's troops. But his own three men being killed, Guy kneels to the Emperor, and offers him all his possessions except his wife and son. The other refuses this demand, and strikes off Guy's head, which he sends to the lady, who promises him to become his wife the following day (l. 193-294).

Beves grieves enormously at his father's death, reproaches his mother with the murder, and calls her a whore. She boxes his ear so that he falls down; and in consequence, his fosterer Saber takes Beves away to his own house. Being desired by the lady to murder the boy, Saber does not refuse; but, in order to deceive her, he kills a pig, sprinkles the garments of Beves with its blood, and sends him, in the dress of a poor herd, to the field to tend his sheep. Saber also promises the youth that, in a fortnight, he will remove him to the court of an earl, and, when his education is finished, will help him to get back his patrimony (l. 295-378).

In the field, Beves hears from his father's palace the sounds of instruments and revelry. He cannot refrain himself, but goes there, staff in hand. As the porter refuses to let him in, and insults him, Beves kills him with one blow on the head, enters the hall, and peremptorily requires the Emperor to give him back his possessions. The Emperor calls him a fool, so Beves hits him three strokes with his club on the head, and he faints away. In spite of the lady's order to seize the boy, the knights let him pass. He repairs to Saber, confesses frankly that he has killed (as he believes) his stepfather, and is earnestly reproached for his imprudence (l. 379-474).

When the lady asks Saber for Beves, he shows her the bloody clothes, but without effect. As she threatens Saber, Beves leaves the secret room where Saber had shut him up, and shows himself fearlessly. His mother has him brought to the shore of the sea, and sold for a large sum to heathen merchants. These sail with Beves to Armenia, and present him to King Ermin, who has a beautiful only daughter, named Josian. Being asked by him for his name and native country, Beves gives Ermin a full reply; but, when the king wants him to turn heathen and to believe in Apolyn, Beves declines that demand positively. Still, the king makes him his chamberlain, and says that, after being knighted, he shall be his ensign-bearer in every battle. The king is very fond of Beves, but nobody at the court dares enter into a contest with him, since he is only fifteen years old (l. 475-584).

On Christmas-day he happens to ride out, accompanied by a number of Saracen knights, one of whom reproaches him for not knowing that it was the festival of the nativity of Christ. Beves has still one trick of Christendom in his mind, that on this day knights are wont to tourney; and he adds, that if he were as strong as his father, he would for God's love gladly undertake to fight against all his companions. The Saracen knights, offended by these words, attack and wound him severely with their swords; but he succeeds in wresting a sword from a heathen, and with that he kills the whole lot of them (l. 585-644).

While Beves retires to his own room to get relief from his wounds, the king, being told what has happened, swears that Beves shall be killed for this deed. But Josian, affirming that he acted only in self-defence, wants her father to allow him to speak for himself, a demand with which he willingly complies. Beves drives away roughly two knights, whom Josian had sent to fetch him; and so she, not at all intimidated by his refusal, makes up her mind to go herself to his room, accompanied by the knights. She does so, and persuades him by her affectionate words to follow her to the king. He, having heard the course of the whole adventure, gives up his wrath, and commands his daughter to do her best to heal Beves. The baths she prepares for him are so effective, that within a very short time he is entirely restored, and as fresh as he was before (l. 645-738).

There was in a neighbouring forest a boar of enormous size, which nobody had been able to kill. One night Beves bethinks himself of this animal, and the next morning he rides out, resolved to kill the boar. Josian sees him and falls in love with him. After a long fight, in the course of which Beves breaks his lance, he at last kills the animal, and cuts off its head (l. 739-836).

On his way to the king, Beves meets with twelve foresters, who intend to kill him. Having left his sword where he slew the boar, he has nothing to defend himself with but a piece of his broken lance.[1] With this he kills, not only the steward, but all his men too. This admirable feat is witnessed by Josian, who, in consequence, is utterly tormented by love for Beves. He presents the king with the boar's head (l. 837-908).

Some time afterwards, Brademond, King of Damascus, invades Armenia and demands Josian in marriage; else he will win her in battle and destroy the whole country. Still he is refused. The princess reminds her father of Beves's adventure in the wood, and wants him to knight the youth and make him leader of the Armenian army. The king agrees, and both he and Josian provide Beves with weapons, especially with the sword Morgelai; and finally she gives him the horse Arondel (l. 837-988).

Beves leads his host against the enemy, and himself kills Redefoun, the ensign-bearer of King Brademond. The result of the battle is that the whole host of the latter is destroyed, and the king takes to flight. Two knights of Beves's army, whom Brademond happens to meet on his way, he takes prisoners, but Beves rides after him, and throws him from his horse (l. 989-1040).

Brademond offers to become Beves's liege man; but he declines, refers Brademond to his master, King Ermin; makes him swear to keep the peace with Ermin, and submit to him. When Brademond has done so, Beves lets him go (l. 1041-1068).

Ermin receives the news of his general's victory with the greatest pleasure, and asks Josian to disarm Beves. This she does, and avails herself of this opportunity to tell him that she is deeply in love with him, and that she will die if he does not agree to love her again. When Beves refuses to become her lover, pretending that he is of too low degree to marry a princess, she is angry, and calls him a churl, who is not worthy to be in the company of pretty ladies. Beves is utterly offended, and, after having declared himself to be an earl's son and no churl, he adds, that she shall no more see him, and he retires to the town (l. 1069-1136).

Josian sends her chamberlain Bonefas to Beves, in order to make her peace; but though Beves gives her messenger a precious mantle, he refuses to comply with her wish. So she repairs herself to the apartments of the hero, and wins him by promising to adopt the Christian faith. In confirmation of this atonement he kisses her. Unfortunately the king is wrongly informed by the two knights freed by Beves from Brademond's hands, that he had deflowered his daughter (l. 1137-1218).

The king is very ill-pleased with this intelligence, and, on the advice of these villains, he writes a letter to

Brademond about Beves, and orders him to deliver it to the heathen king, without taking with him his sword Morgelay or his horse Arondel, or showing the letter to any one else (l. 1219-1262).

Saber sends out his son Terri, to seek Beves through all accessible foreign countries. In the neighbourhood of Damascus, Beves meets Terri eating his dinner in a meadow, and is invited by him to share his repast, an offer which Beves gladly accepts. After dinner, Terri asks his guest about a child named Beves, and gets the reply that Beves was hanged by the Saracens a few days ago. On hearing this bad news, Terri faints away. When he recovers he wants to read the letter, which he supposes dangerous for the bearer himself, but is refused. Then they separate. Terri tells his father of Beves's death; but Saber, from the Isle of Wight, continues to fight against the Emperor of Almaine (l. 1263-1344).

Beves pursues his journey towards Damascus, and there meets with a crowd of Saracens, who have just offered a sacrifice to their god Mahoun. Beves kills the priest, and throws the idols into the dirt. Then he addresses King Brademond in a very disrespectful way, and delivers him the letter. Having read it, Brademond orders his men to seize Beves and confine him in a deep dungeon. Here he lies for a long time, miserably fed, and obliged to defend himself against dragons and snakes with a stick, which he found at the prison door (l. 1345-1432).

When Josian asks her father about Beves, he pretends that the hero has returned to England and married the king's daughter there. Suspecting at once that some treason has been committed, when a new lover, King Yvor of Mombraunt, is obtruded on her, Josian does not oppose the marriage, but succeeds in preserving her virginity by a charm. When the appointed time of the marriage approaches, Yvor sends for the Soldan of Babylon and fifteen other vassal kings, to be present at the festivity (l. 1433-1482).

The wedding being solemnized, King Ermin presents his son-in-law with the horse Arondel and the sword Morgelay. But the former gift proves fatal; for, when Yvor mounts the horse, to ride triumphantly to his residence, it throws him so violently that he is near losing his life. From that time Arondel stands in its stable, fettered with iron chains (l. 1483-1534).

Now the story returns to Beves, who has lain for seven years in Brademond's horrible prison. When asleep one night, he is wounded by a flying adder, which he kills with his stick. This wound leaves a scar on his right eyebrow (l. 1535-1574).

One day he prays to Jesus and to Mary for his deliverance out of the dungeon. His two gaolers are so much offended by his prayer, that one of them comes down to murder him; but, instead, Beves kills his assailant with his fist. The other gaoler, who, intending to help his companion, has likewise descended by a rope, is pierced by Beves with the sword of his fellow-gaoler (l. 1575-1634).

After his gaolers are dead, Beves is entirely deprived of the hope of getting food. Three days having elapsed in this way, his prayer is answered, his fetters break, and the great stone on his body gives way. He gains the surface of the pit about midnight, provides himself with weapons and a horse, and, telling the porter that Beves has escaped from prison, he prevails upon the man to open the town gates. Thus he leaves Damascus in order to reach Armenia; but he unfortunately loses his way and rides back to Damascus, where, meanwhile, the news of Beves's flight has been reported to King Brademond. He, much ill-pleased, tells the fifteen kings, his vassals, and wants them to help him fetch Beves back. The first who gets a sight of Beves is King Grander, who possesses a very precious horse, called Trinchefis (l. 1635-1744).

After a long fight, Beves smites off the head of his adversary, mounts Trinchefis, and continues his flight, constantly followed by King Brademond and his vassals, until he comes to a rocky sea-shore, so that he is obliged either to swim over the sea or to fight with the Saracens. Having recommended himself to God in a prayer, he spurs his horse into the water, and Trinchefis is strong enough to bear him to the opposite shore. Though enfeebled by want of food, Beves continues his journey and comes to a castled town. On its tower he sees a lady, whom he beseeches to give him food sufficient for one meal. Though the lady answers that her lord is a giant, and a hater of all Christians, Beves insists upon his demand. The lady announces this to the giant, who seizes a club, rushes out of the door, and asks the stranger where he stole the horse Trinchefis, which had belonged to his brother Grander. Beves confesses, in scornful words, that he has killed him (l. 1745-1880).

Then they fight. After the giant has killed Trinchefis instead of the rider, Beves gets angry; and the end of the combat is, that he breaks the giant's neckbone. He now gets the dinner which he had formerly asked for in vain; then he orders a horse and leaves the castle. Being strengthened by meat and drink, he ardently wishes to meet Brademond and his army, to fight against them (l. 1881-1958).

He continues his journey to Jerusalem, where he confesses his sins to the Patriarch, who enjoins upon him, that he shall never marry a woman unless she is a pure virgin. Having left Jerusalem, Beves makes up his mind to take the road to Armenia; but, being told by a knight, an old friend of his whom he meets on the way, that king Yvor of Mombraunt has married Josian, he resolves upon going there. Having almost reached this rich and brilliant city, Beves exchanges dresses with a poor palmer, who informs him that the king is out hunting, and the queen in her apartment. At the gate he finds many pilgrims who wait for their share of food, which Josian is in the habit of distributing to poor palmers in the middle of the day, for the love of a knight called Sir Beves. Meanwhile, examining the exterior of the castle, Beves hears Josian in a turret complain of the falseness of her lover. Having returned to the gate, he enters with the rest of the poor, gets plenty of food, and in reply to Josian's question, professes to be an intimate friend of Sir Beves, who has told him of a horse, called Arondel, which he wants to see (l. 1959-2146).

The horse, hearing the name of its master, breaks its chains and rushes into the court of the palace. Beves approaches the horse, mounts it, and by that is recognized by Josian. She entreats him to take her home with him, and assures him that she is a pure virgin. Only on this condition does he comply with her wish (l. 2147-2208).

Bonefas, Josian's chamberlain, advises Beves to meet the king when he returns from hunting; and when he is asked for news, to tell King Yvor that his brother, the king of Dabilent, is in great danger of his life (l. 2209-2250).

Beves follows this advice, and pretends to Yvor that he has visited many countries and met everywhere with peace, except in the realm of Dabilent, the king of which is oppressed by his enemies (l. 2251-2280).

King Yvor, when he hears this, resolves at once to depart for Dabilent, to help his brother; and he leaves behind only an old king, named Garcy, to guard the queen. Bonefas contrives to give Garcy a soporific, which makes him sleep for four-and-twenty hours. During this time Beves, accompanied by Bonefas, carries off Josian; but Garcy, on awaking from his sleep, learns by a magic ring what has happened, and pursues the fugitives, though without success, as Bonefas has shown them a cave, in which they take refuge. Next day, whilst Beves is absent to get some venison to eat, two lions enter the cave and kill Bonefas, who most valiantly defends himself and his horse. Fortunately they cannot hurt Josian, for she is, at the same time, a king's daughter, a queen, and a pure virgin. On coming back from hunting, Beves will not let her hold fast one lion, whilst he fights the other, but he attacks both at the same time. First he kills the male lion (l. 2281-2464).

No sooner has he slain the lioness, than they meet with a most horrible giant, called Ascopart, who says he is sent by Garcy to fetch back the queen and to kill Beves. Beves answers that the giant will do neither (l. 2465-2532).

A fight ensues. Ascopart does not succeed in wounding Beves, and, at length, falls down while aiming a mighty blow at him. Beves is about to kill him, but spares his life at the intercession of Josian. The giant, in consequence, agrees to become Beves's page. All three proceed till they reach the sea, where they find a trading vessel, occupied by Saracens. Ascopart drives them out, and carries Beves, Josian, and Arondel into the ship, which bears them to Cologne. The bishop of this town, called Saber Florentin, who happens to be the uncle of Sir Beves, christens Josian, whilst Ascopart cannot be prevailed upon to enter a great font specially constructed for this purpose (l. 2533-2596).

After Josian's baptism, Beves achieves a most dangerous adventure, by killing a dreadful dragon. Two kings, one of Apulia, the other of Calabria, who had warred against one another during their whole life, were after their deaths transformed as a punishment into dragons; and, in this shape, they continue their fighting, until a holy hermit expels them by his prayers. One of them flies to St. Peter's bridge in Rome, where it will lie to the day of judgment; the other goes through Tuscany, Lombardy, and Provence, to the territory of Cologne. Sir Beves, moved by the groans of a knight, who suffers from the poison of this dragon, determines to attack it, attended by Ascopart, who, however, having heard the dragon's voice at some distance, is cowardly enough to go back. Still Beves proceeds alone to fight with the monster. His lance being broken, he attacks it with his sword, and the fight lasts till night. Then, in order to refresh himself, Beves dives into a well, which he has discovered in the neighbourhood (l. 2597-2802).

The fact that a virgin who lived in that country had bathed in the well, had rendered the water so holy that the dragon dares not come near it. After having drunk a gallon of this water, Beves leaves the well and renews his combat with the dragon, which spits so much poison on him, that his body looks like a leper's, and his coat of mail breaks in pieces. At last he tumbles into the well, where he recovers his strength and his health. After saying a prayer, he resumes the fight once more, and finally succeeds in cutting off the dragon's head. He sticks its tongue on his broken lance, and returns to Cologne, where the bishop and the people, who believed the dragon had killed him, receive him most triumphantly (l. 2803-2910).

Beves makes up his mind to go to England, attended by a hundred valiant knights, whom the bishop equips for him, in order to help Saber against his step-father Devoun. As to Josian, he takes his leave of her, and intrusts her to the care of Ascopart (l. 2911-2950).

Having landed in the neighbourhood of Southampton, Beves sends a knight to the Emperor of Almaine, with orders to say that a French knight, named Gerard, has arrived with a hundred men, and is ready to take his part in the war against Saber. In consequence, the Emperor invites Beves to supper, and gives him a very partial account of Beves's youth and of Saber's enmity against himself; Beves replies that if the Emperor will lend him arms and horses, he is willing to assault Saber (l. 2951-3022).

Beves carries both armour and horses to the Isle of Wight, and after having raised a flag with his arms on it, he lands, and is received by Saber with the utmost joy. Then, he instantly orders a messenger to return to Southampton, and to tell the Emperor that the knight who supped with him bore, not the name Gerard, but was Beves, and claims the lordship over Hamtoun. When the Emperor, who is at table, hears this unexpected news, he throws a knife at Sir Beves's ambassador, but misses him and pierces the body of his own son, a misfortune which gives the messenger a welcome opportunity of sneering at him. Sir Beves, when he learns what has happened, laughs, and is very much pleased (l. 3023-3116).

We return to Josian. In the neighbourhood of Cologne lives an earl named Miles, who is enamoured of her, and wants her to become his sweetheart. When she refuses him, saying that she relies on Ascopart, he forges a letter to that worthy, which he pretends is from Sir Beves, ordering his immediate presence in a castle on an island. Ascopart, having arrived there, is locked up in the castle, while Earl Miles returns, imagining that there is no further obstacle to his wishes. He tells Josian what he has done, and she sends a letter to Sir Beves, to inform him. Meanwhile she declares to Miles that she will surrender her person only to the man who has married her; and the Earl says that he has made up his mind to marry her against her will (l. 3117-3174).

Next day the wedding takes place. At night Josian is led to the wedding-chamber and the Earl follows her, attended by a lot of knights; but in compliance with her wish he agrees to turn out the guests and to shut the door. Then Josian makes a slip-knot in her girdle,[2] passes it round his neck, and strangles him (l. 3175-3224).

The following morning, when the Earl does not rise, Josian is obliged to confess that she has killed him. She is condemned to be burnt in a tun, outside the town. Ascopart, descrying from his castle the preparations for the burning, suspects that something is wrong, breaks the gate of the castle, seizes a fishing-boat, and rows to the opposite shore. There he is overtaken by Sir Beves, whose reproaches of having betrayed him Ascopart eas-

ily invalidates. They rescue Josian, and sail with her to the Isle of Wight (l. 3225-3304).

Meanwhile, Beves and Saber collect a great army, and the Emperor, on his part, summons his large host from Almaine, and is assisted by his wife's father, the King of Scotland. In the month of May, the Emperor lands with his army in Wight, and encamps before the castle in which Beves and Saber have collected their forces. Being aware of the approach of the enemy, Saber resolves at once to give them battle. He divides his host into three parts, one of which he leads himself, whilst the other two are led by Beves and Ascopart (l. 3305-3392).

In the middle of the fight, Beves throws his step-father from his horse, and would have beheaded him if his men had not rescued him in time. He calls on Ascopart, and wants him to seize the Emperor. Ascopart first kills the King of Scotland, and then takes hold of the Emperor, and carries both him and his horse to the castle. This decides the battle in favour of Beves and Saber. Beves's step-father dies, being cast into a kettle of molten lead. The countess, beholding the end of her husband, falls down from the top of the castle and breaks her neck. Beves rejoices as much at the decease of his mother as of his step-father. The lords of Hamtonshire render homage to Beves, who is very glad at having been able to take revenge on his father's murderer. Beves then sends for the Bishop of Cologne, who marries Beves and Josian (l. 3393-3482).

Sir Beves begets two children on Josian in the first year of their marriage. By Saber's advice, he proceeds to King Edgar in London, in order to be invested with his hereditary earldom. The king complies at once with his wish, and confers on him, at the same time, the dignity of his marshal (l. 3483-3510).

At Whitsuntide a horse-race is arranged, in which Sir Beves desires to take part, because he trusts in the speed of Arondel. On the appointed day he wins the race, in spite of two knights who started too soon. Beves takes the prize, and with the help of this and of other money he afterwards builds the castle of Arundel (l. 3511-3542).

The king's son, desiring to possess the horse Arondel, wants Beves to make him a present of it, which Beves decidedly refuses to do. During the dinner, which Beves had to attend in his duty as Marshal, the prince enters the stable, but, when he approaches the horse and is about to untie it, Arondel kicks him with its hind foot and kills him with one blow. King Edgar, eager to revenge the death of his only son, wants to have Beves hanged and drawn; but the barons do not agree with this sentence; they decide that the horse only must suffer death. Sir Beves, however, declares that he will rather leave England and make over his estates to Saber, than lose Arondel. This expedient being accepted, Beves departs from Hamton, and tells Josian and Ascopart what has happened. He makes Terri, Saber's son, his page, and all start for Ermony. But Ascopart, knowing which road they were to take, hastens to Mombraunt, with the intention of betraying his master (l. 3543-3594).

Ascopart promises King Yvor to fetch back the queen, and obtains from him a company of forty knights to go with him. In a forest, on the way to Ermony, Josian is seized with the pains of child-birth. Beves and Terri construct a hut, bring Josian into it, and retire for a short time. Scarcely is Josian delivered of two boys, when Ascopart comes with his companions and carries her off (l. 3595-3646).[3]

Beves, returning with Terri, and finding the two children quite alone, feels very uneasy. They wrap the children in their ermine mantles, and, continuing their journey, deliver one babe to a forester whom they meet on the way, charging him to christen it "Gii"; the other boy they consign to a fisher, who, according to their wish, christens it "Miles." That being done, Beves and his squire proceed on their voyage, until they arrive at a great town where a tournament has been proclaimed: the victor is to get the hand of the daughter and heiress of the King of Aumbeforce. Beves and Terri resolve to take part in the tournay; and their arms, when they ride through the town, excite general admiration (l. 3709-3792).

Beves tilts so brilliantly, that the princess falls in love with him and wants to marry him. When he objects that he has a wife, who has been stolen from him, she proposes that he shall be her lord in a pure manner, and that, if within seven years his real wife should appear, she will accept Terri as her husband. Beves declares his full agreement with these terms (l. 3793-3840).

One night, Saber dreams that Sir Beves was wounded, and that he had undertaken a pilgrimage to St. James's and St. Giles's. This dream he tells his wife; and she expounds it, that Beves has lost either his wife or a child. Saber thereupon equips twelve knights with pilgrims' robes, under which they wear complete armour, and embarks with them. When they overtake Ascopart, who carried off Josian, Saber kills the giant with the first stroke, and his companions knock down the Saracens who attend him.[4] Josian being rescued in this way, Saber disguises her as a palmer, and wanders about with her for seven years, in the hope of finding Beves and Terri (l. 3841-3898).

One day they come to a town in which Beves resides. Saber meets with his son Terri, and delivers Josian to her husband, who sends after his children, whilst Terri is married to the heiress of the land. (l. 3899-3962).

King Yvor makes war against King Ermin, and besieges him in his capital. Beves leads an army to Ermony, is reconciled with Ermin, and promises to fight against King Yvor. He vanquishes Yvor and sends him prisoner to King Ermin, who gives him his liberty on his paying a large ransom (l. 3963-4004).

When the old Ermin feels his end approaching, he sends for Guy, one of Beves' twin sons, and places the crown of Ermony on his head. Soon after he dies. Saber, desirous of seeing his wife, returns to England. In the service of King Yvor is a very sly thief, who manages to steal the horse Arondel, which he presents to King Yvor (l. 4005-4038).

This having happened, Saber dreams one night that Beves is in a very bad state and fearfully wounded. His wife, being told this dream, conjectures that Beves may have lost Arondel. When he hears that, Saber sets off without hesitation to see Beves, from whom he learns that his dream has been properly expounded. He at once starts for Mombraunt, and having taken away the horse (which is about to be watered) from a Saracen, he sets off speedily for Ermony, followed by a great number of heathen knights. From these he is rescued by Beves's two sons, who kill all the pursuers of his uncle (l. 4039-4108).

In order to take revenge, Yvor collects an enormous army, which he leads into Ermony. Having arrived there, he proposes to decide the war by a single combat between himself and Beves. This proposition is gladly accepted, and the two combatants betake themselves to a small island, where the fight is to be held. The combat is very long and fierce (l. 4109-4172).

At last, Beves hits his adversary such a blow that his right arm and his shoulder-bone fall on the ground. Beves in vain asks Yvor to be baptized,—the heathen thinking his to be the better faith;—he beheads the king, and all his attendants are killed likewise (l. 4173-4252).

After this victory, Beves is crowned king of the land over which King Yvor had held dominion. But his tranquility is interrupted by the arrival of a messenger, who informs Saber that King Edgar has deprived his son Robant of his estates. When Beves hears this ill news, he determines to accompany Saber to England, and to take with him a great army, his wife, his two sons, and Saber's son, Terri. They arrive in England, and Beves swears to take revenge on King Edgar (l. 4253-4286).

Beves leaves his army at Hamtoun, and, accompanied only by a few knights, repairs to the king at Westminster, and requests the restoration of his estates. Edgar and his barons are inclined to comply with Beves's wish; the steward alone contradicts, observing that Beves was an outlaw and a traitor. Hearing this, Beves gets very angry, leaves the court at once, and rides to London (l. 4287-4322).

The steward repairs to Cheapside, and proclaims to the people that the king commands them to take Beves prisoner as soon as possible. In deference to this proclamation, the citizens shut their gates, barricade the streets, and flock together in order to seize Beves. Beves arms quickly, mounts Arondel, and the first man he meets in the street is the steward, who calls him traitor, and summons him to surrender (l. 4323-4376).

Beves stabs the steward with his lance; but his knights are surrounded and slain by the citizens. He himself succeeds in cutting through the chains which confine him in a narrow lane, and advances to Cheapside, pursued by an immense crowd of people (l. 4377-4436).

Here he defends himself with the utmost bravery, assisted by his valiant steed. In the meanwhile, news is brought to Josian, whom he had left at Putney, that Beves has been slain in London. She relates this fact to her two sons, who resolve at once to revenge his death. They hasten to London-gate, and kill all who oppose them (l. 4437-4496).

Guy comes just in the nick of time to rescue his father from a traitorous Lombard. Miles follows at his heels, and then these three men stand up against all their assailants and gain a brilliant victory over them. At the opening of the night they fetch Josian to London, and hold a splendid festival there (l. 4497-4538).

When King Edgar hears of this dreadful slaughter, he determines to offer his only daughter to Miles with the prospect of becoming King of England after his death. His barons agree to this proposal, and the marriage takes place. Beves, having delivered his earldom of Hamtoun to Saber, repairs with Josian and his son Guy to Ermony, where the latter resumes the reins of government, leaves Terri at Aumbeforce, and then continues his journey to Mombraunt, of which he himself is king. When Josian, being seized with a mortal disease, finds that she will soon die, she sends for her son Guy, and for Terri. At the same time Beves enters his stable and finds Arondel dead. Returning to his dying wife, he folds her in his arms, and they both die together. Guy orders a chapel to be erected and dedicated to St. Lawrence, where the bodies of his father and mother are interred under the high altar. He also founds a monastery, in which the monks are to sing masses for the souls of Beves and of Josian (l. 4539-4620). . . .

Notes

[1] According to [the Auchinleck MS.], a steward at the court of King Ermin, out of envy of Beves, sallies out with four-and-twenty knights and ten foresters, in or-

der to kill him. Beves defends himself with the boar's head, until he succeeds in winning the sword Morgelai from the steward.

[2] According to [the Auchinleck MS.] she takes a towel instead.

[3] Iosian, being allowed to retire for a short time (l. 3646-3670), plucks and eats a herb, which has the power of making one look like a leper. The consequence is, that when Yvor sees her, he is very ill-pleased with the appearance of his wife, and wants Ascopart to take her to a castle in the neighbourhood of Mombraunt, and to guard her there (l. 3671-3708). This passage is only in [Auchinleck].

[4] According to [the Auchinleck MS.], Saber and his companions find out the castle where Josian is kept; she calls to them for relief. Ascopart, hearing that, goes to meet the strangers, but is killed by them. Josian, being relieved, renders her complexion clean by an ointment.

Prentiss C. Hoyt (essay date 1902)

SOURCE: "The Home of the *Beves Saga,*" *Publications of the Modern Language Association of America (PMLA),* Vol. XVII, No. 2, 1902, pp. 237-46.

[*In the essay reprinted below, Hoyt contends that the* Bevis *saga is of Anglo-Saxon derivation, not French or German. To support his argument, he calls attention to important parallels between the* Bevis *story and the tale of* King Horn—*an early-thirteenth-century English romance of indigenous origin.*]

The question of the original home of the *Beves* saga has often been discussed, but no satisfactory conclusion has been reached. The conjectures regarding it have been various, but as yet unconvincing.

Amaury Duval[1] places the scene of the story in France at Antonne, but without giving definite grounds for this supposition. Turnbull[2] and Kölbing[3] both adopt this view without argument. Pio Rajna[4] was the first to suggest a Germanic home for the saga, locating Hanstone (Hamtoun) on the continent near the French border of Germany. The arguments given are unimportant, but this view of the origin has been accepted by Gaston Paris,[5] although he takes exception to Rajna's wildest suppositions as to the name Hanstone. Albert Stimming[6] has exposed the weakness of Rajna's reasoning, but even he leaves the question still unsettled. Later in his introduction, he gives impartially the arguments in favor of French as well as those in favor of Germanic origin, but does not regard them as sufficient ground for forming an opinion. These comprise the conjectures thus far advanced, and all are weakly supported and inconclusive.

A resemblance between the **Beves** and the *Horn* seems to me to furnish at last the key to the complete solution of the problem. If the **Beves** can be shown to be but a romantically developed form of the *Horn* saga, its ultimate origin must at once be acknowledged to be the same as that of its more primitive base. Since such a relation can be proved, I present the proposition that the **Beves**, like its prototype, the *Horn*, is Anglo-Saxon and insular—not French, nor German.

The **Beves** romance is obviously a hotch-potch of adventures formed about a simple story. This simple base may be given briefly as follows:—A young man, driven from home, wins power in the service of a foreign king, gains the love of the king's daughter, returns home, and takes revenge on his enemies. This summary will be seen to serve admirably as an outline of the story of *King Horn*. Upon this relation, which has not been noticed heretofore, I base the proposition just given.[7]

A closer examination of the two poems shows that this resemblance is not merely that of two "expulsion and return" romances, but that the central story of the **Beves** parallels the *Horn*, incident for incident. Naturally, this parallelism is not exact, nor would we have it so. The differences, however, can be explained in accordance with the method of the **Beves**-writer, who was developing a long romantic story, zealously religious, from the *Horn*, which is itself simple and almost savage in its roughness.

Even a brief examination of the two romances will make clear the close resemblance in their essential elements, although they have always been regarded as entirely unlike.

The first incident—the *expulsion*—is the one most changed and developed in the **Beves**. In the *Horn,* the hero and his companions are set adrift by the "Saracens," who have conquered his father's land. The **Beves**, however, uses an entirely different motive—the cruel mother. Beves, after his father's murder, wildly accuses his mother of instigating the crime, and opposes her marriage with the murderer. Her first attempt on Beves's life is frustrated by the faithful old man, Saber, to whom she has given the boy to be put to death. He spares him, and shows the mother his coat dipped in the blood of a goat. Beves is too much enraged, however, to tend sheep quietly for his friend, and, rushing back to court, denounces his mother before them all. This time Saber is powerless to save him, and he is taken to the seashore and sold to some foreign merchants.

In this incident the *Horn* is absolutely simple, using only the conquest by the Saracens and the subsequent setting adrift of Horn and his noble friends. Such a situation would be obviously unfitted to the highly religious tone of the **Beves**; Saracens could not be permitted to destroy the hero's land, even in his youth. The author, therefore, in seeking an induction more suited to his purpose, made use of a well-known type of expulsion incidents, which had the additional advantage of giving him an opportunity for a wide romantic development later. This is exactly the treatment we should expect in the case of a late romance, developed from a simple early form. Any feature, not in accord with the author's time, would be changed to fit the later conditions. We seek, then, a similarity of fundamental elements only, and this we find in the retention of the "expulsion" itself, although the method employed is entirely different.

In the second incident—the *reception at the foreign court*—the two stories are closely parallel. Horn is at once received into favor by Aylmar, king of Westernesse, who is struck by the lad's beauty (l. 161 ff.). The king has him instructed in all arts and makes him his cupbearer (l. 229 ff.). In the **Beves**, also, the hero, by his beauty, wins immediate favor with King Ermin of Ermonie, to whom the merchants have presented him. Ermin at once appoints him chamberlain (l. 534 f. and 571 ff.[8]). The slight difference here is due to the difference in age of the two heroes. The numerous incidents of the expulsion in the **Beves** necessitate a youth of riper years than in the simpler *Horn*.

In the court, Horn is beloved by all who know him (ll. 245 ff.) and especially by Rymenhild, the daughter of the king. As soon as he learns of her love, Horn loves her in return, but seeks knighthood and honor that he may be worthy of her. In the **Beves**, religion plays a much more important part. Beves is loved by all who know him, as in the *Horn*, and especially by Josiane, the daughter of King Ermin (ll. 578 ff.). Beves, however, unlike Horn, will have nothing to do with Josiane for a long time, and only after her promise to embrace Christianity does he become her lover. The change is characteristic of the religious tone of the whole **Beves,** the author of which could not allow his Christian hero to love a Saracen, until she had offered to renounce her false faith. The marriage, in the **Beves** as in the *Horn*, is not consummated until long after, when vengeance has been taken upon the youth's enemies in his native land. It is noteworthy in this episode that the hero in each case is knighted by the king at his daughter's request, in order to defend the country against foreign foes.

The *banishment*, which forms the third incident, is also closely paralleled in the motiving. The meetings of the lovers are falsely reported to the king in each case.

Beves is betrayed by two knights, whom he had rescued in battle; Horn, by Fikenild, one of his twelve chosen comrades (*Horn*, 680 ff.; *Beves*, 1206 ff.). In the *Horn*, the king straightway banishes the hero, but, in the **Beves**, the incident is skilfully worked over to give an opportunity for the long episodes of Beves's imprisonment and his return adventures. This is accomplished by means of a sealed letter, which is given him to carry to Damascus. This letter contains instructions for Beves's instant death, but Brandimond, to whom it is delivered, throws him into prison instead. The difference in development is again perfectly characteristic; the author of the **Beves**, feeling the necessity of changing from the simple banishment of the *Horn* in order to lengthen his story, drew upon this well-known device of mediaeval fiction,—the Uriah or Bellerophon letter.

The fourth incident in the *Horn*, which occurs during this banishment, although not found in a corresponding place in the **Beves**, is nevertheless closely paralleled. Horn journeys to the land of King Thurston, and, by his valor in battle, wins the offer of the kingdom after the king's death, and of the hand of the princess. The corresponding episode in the **Beves** occurs during the wanderings of Beves and Terri (ll. 3759 ff.). They come upon the land of Aumberforce, and in a tournament—a natural change for the romantic author—Beves wins the hand of the Lady of Aumberforce and the promise of the succession after her father's death. Horn refuses King Thurston's offer, but promises to remain and serve him for seven years. Beves likewise refuses to accept Aumberforce and its princess, but is retained by her as her "lord in clene manere" for seven years.

It is to be noticed, also, that the ultimate outcome of the adventure is the same in both cases. Terri, Beves's foster-brother, gains the Lady of Aumberforce when Beves finds Josiane; Athulf, Horn's most intimate and faithful friend, marries Reynild, the daughter of King Thurston, when Horn returns to Rymenhild.

The fifth incident—the *first marriage*—shows the same close resemblance. During Horn's absence when banished by King Aylmar, Rymenhild is wooed by King Modi of Reynes and at last forced to wed him. Horn, however, returns just in time to prevent the consummation of the marriage. This differs little from Josiane's experience during Beves's imprisonment by Brandimond. She is forced to marry King Yvor, but preserves her virginity by means of a charm. Horn, on his opportune return just alluded to, disguises himself in a palmer's weeds to gain admittance to his love's presence. He is served by her own hands and reveals himself by means of a magic ring she had given him. Beves also returns after the same term of absence— seven years—although his adventures have been very different, as we are prepared to expect by the change in the method of banishment. He, too, gains admit-tance to his love's presence by adopting a palmer's weeds. Within the castle he is served by his mistress's own hands and reveals himself by his horse Arondel, which is endowed with supernatural powers. The parallel here is carried even into the replies which the assumed palmer makes to his lady's inquiries, granting always the partial rationalizing of the magic ring element by the substitution of the wonderful horse Arondel (cf. *Horn*, 1007 ff. with **Beves**, 2041 ff.). The plan of action after the recognition in the two stories is eminently characteristic. Horn straightway kills off most of his enemies; Beves, however, contrives to escape with Josiane in a highly romantic manner, well-calculated to bring in other adventures.

The *second marriage* forms the last important incident, and is, like the others, closely parallel in the two romances. Beves, before marrying Josiane, must set out from Cologne—where a long series of adventures has landed them—to relieve his foster-father Saber and to avenge himself upon his father's murderer. Horn in Westernesse will, also, neither marry nor rest until he has regained his hereditary kingdom. During Horn's absence, Rymenhild is again persecuted by Fikenild, whom Horn had unwisely spared. Horn a second time returns at the right moment; he assumes a harper's disguise to gain admittance to his enemy's castle, and this time makes his revenge more complete. After thus gaining his love again, Horn lives peacefully upon his own lands, crowning Arnoldin king of Westernesse and wedding Athulf to King Thurston's daughter. In the other story, Josiane, during Beves's absence, is importuned by Miles of Cologne and compelled by force to marry him. In desperation she succeeds in hanging him on the marriage-bed on the wedding evening. For this act she is condemned to be burned, and thus there is an opportunity for a romantic rescue. The **Beves** is then carried on, page after page, by means of incidents varying in the different versions. The end, however, resembles the ending of the *Horn*. The conquered territories are distributed among the hero's intimate friends, or relatives, and Beves and Josiane grow old in peace upon their own possessions. The final touch in the **Beves** is of course the more elaborate. Beves and Josiane die at the same time and are buried together; the *Horn* simply says "Nu are hi both ded," and commits their souls to God.

In the second marriage episode, it is noteworthy that, in the *Horn*, the repetition is an exact one—the opportune return, the disguise, and all. This shows a much more primitive stage of development than the **Beves**, where the story is artistically varied by the incidents of the murder in the bed chamber, the trial, and the rescue.

These parallels account for everything in the central story of the **Beves**—the story with which the author worked as his original. The omitted parts are non-essential elements. An examination of these plus-incidents shows that, without exception, they are repetitions or romantic commonplaces, and hence cannot be relied upon as giving any definite evidence for the original home of the saga.

Of these plus-incidents, three can be at once dismissed. These are important in the English *Beves*, but are not found in the Anglo-Norman version, which Stimming has proved to be the source of our English form. These late additions are Beves's fight with fifty Saracens over a question of religious belief (ll. 585-738), the dragon fight (ll. 2597-2910), and the encounter with the burghers of London (ll. 4287-4538).

Another class among the plus-incidents may be set aside also as unimportant in our discussion. There is no method of developing or enlarging a romance better recognized than that of repeating in a modified form one of the original incidents. This appears in the *Beves* in Josiane's second marriage. This very repetition is seen in the *Horn* as well. There, however, as I have already noted, it is an exact repetition—the simplest form of development. In the *Beves*, the repeated incident is carefully developed and this accounts fully for the changes. In the first marriage, Josiane preserves her virginity by means of a charm; in the second, the author gains variety by employing the well-known romantic feature of the murder in the bed chamber.

Other important repetitions may be seen in the numerous military expeditions (ll. 3303-3458, 3967-4004, 4109-4252). These repeat, with more or less variation, Beves's great battle against Brandimond immediately after being knighted (ll. 989-1068). This incident parallels, in its motiving, Horn's fight with the pagan freebooters, in which he proves his right to the knighthood just conferred upon him (Horn, 623-682).

A third class among the plus-incidents may comprise those features which are the direct outgrowth of feudal and chivalric conditions. Such features, unless they are parts absolutely essential to the story, are of course not portions of the simple original, which must have been formed in more primitive times. The sealed letter, the long imprisonment, the escape, and the many adventures of the return may safely be classed in this group. Here, too, we may place Beves's expedition in aid of Saber, and his subsequent journey to London to sue his estates.

Finally, there is a class of episodes which will at once be recognized as commonplaces of romance. The boar-fight, the encounter with the lions and the giant, Josiane's delivery in the forest, her capture by the treacherous page, and her search in minstrel's garments may be grouped here. No one of these is an essential part of the story, and each can be easily explained as a characteristic addition, or a change to fit the style of a more romantic writer.

These four classes include all the plus-incidents of the *Beves*,[9] which therefore have no weight against the proposition that the central story of the *Beves* is equivalent to the *Horn*. There is no essential incident in the *Beves* which is not found in the *Horn*, and, conversely, the *Horn* incidents reappear in the *Beves*, though with many romantic changes and developments. A more exhaustive study than is possible in this article shows that the close resemblance between the *Beves* outline and the *Horn* extends often to matters of minute detail.

The contention that the *Horn* is equivalent to the main story of the *Beves*, is strengthened by observing that the *Horn* shows a repetition which reappears in the *Beves*. This is the second marriage episode, which, in the *Horn*, is simply repeated, as I have shown. In the *Beves*, though more highly developed; it follows the outline of the *Horn* so closely as to be practically a proof of the correctness of the proposition. It is not held, of course, that the *Beves* is necessarily from the extant text of the *Horn*, but that it goes back to some form of the *Horn* saga, and is therefore Anglo-Saxon or Anglo-Danish—insular, and not continental. That the original was a developed form of the saga, the repetition of the marriage episode shows, and it may well have borne the name of Horn, although the mere name is of little importance.

The Anglo-Saxon origin thus contended for fits well with what has already been proved regarding the *Beves*. Stimming has shown that the Anglo-Norman is the oldest extant version, and that this Anglo-Norman form is an insular product. His thesis is strengthened when we prove that the original story was also of insular origin.

The theory of an insular home for the saga explains well the nautical character of the *Beves*, which is quite unlike the air of the French *chansons*, and associates the romance rather with English and Germanic material.

It suits, too, the name Hamtoun, which, in the earlier versions, is unquestionably English, despite the efforts of Duval and Rajna to prove it French or German.

Finally, it fits the historical Beves[10] mentioned by Elyot,[11] Fuller[12] and others. This Beves lived in the time of William the Conqueror, and, with a few followers, resisted ineffectually the power of the invaders. Whether this is real history or fiction, our proposition agrees well with it, especially as this Beves lived at first near Southampton, and nothing would be more natural than to group a series of adventures about a local hero.

Because we have seen that the central story of the **Beves** is equivalent to the *Horn*, and that its plus-incidents are easily accounted for as the work of a later romantic writer, and because all external evidence strengthens this proposition, we may confidently place the **Beves** in the rank of the *Guy*, the *Horn*, and the *Havelock* as insular and not continental material.

Notes

[1] *Histoire Litteraire de la France*, xviii, pp. 750 ff.

[2] *Sir Beves of Hamtoun*, pp. xv ff. (1837).

[3] *Sir Beves of Hamtoun* (E. E. T. S.), p. xxxiv (1885).

[4] *I Reali di Francia*, pp. 123 ff. (1872).

[5] *Romania*, II, 359.

[6] *Der Anglonormannische Boeve de Haumtone*, pp. clxxxi ff. (1899).

[7] Stimming, in his list of parallels, notices a resemblance in episodes only, not in the whole outline, and draws no conclusions. He says: "Das Liebesverhältnis zwischen Boeve und Josiane berührt sich in mehreren Punkten mit dem zwischen Horn und Rimel. Auch Horn wird von Winkle, gegen dem er sich freundlich bewiesen, verleumderischerweise angeklagt, Rimel beschlafen zu haben, und letztere soll gegen ihrem. Willen gewaltsam verheiratet werden." (p. cxc.)

[8] References in the *Beves* are to the A text of Kölbing's edition.

[9] Two episodes—Beves's swimming the sea on Trinchefis (1811-1818), and the island duel (4137-4239)—may, at first thought, be excluded from these classes. When considered in connection with their setting of commonplace romantic material, they show at once that they are elements quite unessential to the main story, and chosen by the author for variety only.

[10] This is probably what is alluded to as "a kernel of genuine English tradition" by Prof. George H. McKnight, p. vii of the introduction to his edition of *King Horn*, just published in the E. E. T. S. series (1901).

[11] Sir Thomas Elyot, *The Boke named the Governour*, H. H. S. Croft's edition, I. 184.

[12] Thomas Fuller, *Worthies of England*, under Souldiers of Hantshire.

Herbert L. Creek (essay date 1911)

SOURCE: "Character in the 'Matter of England' Romances," *The Journal of English and Germanic Philology*, Vol. X, 1911, pp. 429-609.

[*Here, Creek evaluates the relationship between characterization, plot, and setting in four Middle English romances:* Havelok the Dane, King Horn, Bevis of Hampton, *and* Guy of Warwick. *In terms of characterization, the critic claims,* Bevis *is closer to the simpler, more primitive forms of the genre—*Havelok *and* Horn—*but with respect to structural development, it is more akin to* Guy.]

For the student of medieval life and literature the *dramatis personæ* of the romances—conventional as they are, and conventional as the romancers' treatment of them often is—are of no little interest. Professor Comfort's studies in the *chansons de geste*[1] have shown the importance of a knowledge of the character types of the French epic for an appreciation of the ideals and culture of medieval France. In this paper an attempt will be made to investigate, on a somewhat broader plan,[2] the four most important of the "matter of England" romances—*King Horn*, *Havelok the Dane*, **Bevis of Hamtoun**, and *Guy of Warwick*.[3]

Character stands in a peculiar relation to the other narrative elements of the metrical romance. It is, of course, never emphasized. Yet when romance after romance has been read, and a host of incidents have been forgotten, characteristic personalities stand out, which, modern English literature proves, have been of abiding interest. The more distinguished names—Gawain, Kay, Lancelot, Tristram, Iseult—were the fruit of a romance-activity which stands in strong contrast with the more popular art of *Horn* and *Havelok*. Yet the heroes of this seemingly more primitive group typify, I think, ideals of permanent interest. Appearing, as they do, in situations and relations thoroughly stereotyped, they are perhaps more interesting for that reason, have more of the medieval flavor, gain in representative quality. If they are deficient in subtlety, they are not deficient in a crude strength of character and will, perennially attractive.

For these reasons it will be seen that characterization, to an unusual degree, perhaps, is bound up with plot on the one hand, and with the broad background of medieval life on the other, and it will be necessary, in discussing it, to trespass somewhat upon these other fields.

The Group

The well-known tendency of the *dramatis personæ* of medieval romance to fall into certain conventional relations is well illustrated by a group of characters which appears, with certain variations, in *Horn*, in *Bevis*, and in *Guy*. This group seems to belong naturally to stories of the exile-and-return type, but it is not restricted to them, as it appears very clearly in the *Guy*. Nor is it essential to the exile-and-return type, since it does not appear, unless faintly, in *Havelok*. The following table shows the correspondence:

The father
The hero
The old friend
The young friend
The foreign king
The foreign king's daughter
The defamer
The second lady

Horn
Murri
Horn
Aþelbrus
Aþulf
Aylmar
Rymenhild
Fikenhild
Reynild

Bevis
Guy
Bevis
Saber
Terri
Ermin
Josian
Two knights
King of Aumbeforce's daughter

Guy
[Syward]
Guy
Herhaud
Tirri
Ernis
Claris
Morgadour
Oisel

These lists might be paralleled, in part, with another from *Havelok*, as well as from romances far removed from this group, but as the relations of the *dramatis personæ* are not so clearly the same in these other cases, I have not thought it worth while to insist on the parallel. However, the possibility of making the table which here appears is not without significance, and a very fundamental resemblance will, I think, appear on closer investigation.[4]

In respect to the hero's father the resemblance is incomplete. *Guy of Warwick* is not a story of the exile-

and-return type, and Guy's father plays a comparatively unimportant part in the story. In *Horn* and in *Bevis* the resemblance is clear. In both cases the father is of very high rank, Murri being King of Suddenne and Guy the Earl of South Hampton, of noble character and approved prowess. Both are slain at the opening of the story, being overpowered by numbers, and their possessions, in both cases, are seized by those who have slain them—in the one case by the Saracens, and in the other by Devoun, Emperor of Almaine. Both leave young heirs who are helpless to protect their dominions. Birkabein, father of Havelok and King of Denmark, occupies an analogous position. He dies leaving his young heir in the power of a traitor, who seizes the kingdom. This situation is repeated in the same poem in the death of Aþelwold, leaving his daughter and the Kingdom of England in the care of a traitor. Thus in each of the three romances of the exile-and-return type there is a king who dies, leaving a young son in the hands of enemies.

The children of these three fathers[5] too early dead experience a similar fortune. Horn, sent out in a boat to find a grave in the sea, luckily reaches the coast of Westernesse. Bevis, narrowly escaping death at the hands of his own mother, is sold into slavery and borne across the seas to Armenia. Havelok, after heart-breaking sufferings, likewise crosses the sea in a boat to find a home at Grimsby. Guy had no such experiences in his earlier days, but gained manhood at his own home. It is his later career which brings him into the company of Horn and Bevis, as will appear in the discussion of the other typical characters.

Curiously enough, Horn, Bevis, and Guy each have for teacher a kind, brave man, who remains a steadfast friend. Aþelbrus taught Horn the craft of wood and river, as well as harping, carving, and serving the cup (vv. 229 ff.). Later he assists in the love affair of Horn and Rymenhild; and finally he is rewarded with a kingdom (vv. 1507 f.). However, the resemblance between *Guy* and *Bevis*, here as elsewhere, is much stronger. Saber is the "meister" of Bevis. After keeping Bevis concealed as long as he can, he is obliged to see him banished, but later sends his son to seek the lad; and he himself accompanies Bevis on some of his adventures. Almost the same thing happens in the case of Herhaud.

> Gij a forster fader hadde,
> þatte him lerd & him radde
> Of wodes & riuer & oþer game;
> Herhaud of Ardern was his name.

(vv. 169 ff.)

Herhaud, too, is a fellow-soldier of his friend, and himself seeks Guy when lost. Herhaud is also tutor to Guy's son Reinbrun, seeks him through many lands when he is stolen away, and in general stands in the same relation to the son that he did to the father. Like Saber, Herhaud has a warlike son who plays a part in the romance. Like him, too, he is warned in dreams when the hero is in need of assistance. Grim has certain points of contact with these characters, particularly with Saber. Both Grim and Saber are instructed to slay their charges, and both represent that they have done so. Thus in each of these romances there is an old friend who guards the early years of the hero; in three cases he is the tutor; and in the fourth case he stands in the general relation of guide and instructor, teaching, however, not knightly accomplishments, but the meaner duties of labor.

In three of the romances there is a young friend who is the faithful helper of his superior. In the fourth romance, *Havelok*, there is only the semblance of an equivalent in the three sons of Grim. But Aþulf in *Horn*, Terri in **Bevis**, and Tirri in *Guy*, occupy corresponding positions. In two of the cases the friend is presented with a bride and territory by the hero. Thus Reynild is given to Aþulf, and the daughter of the King of Aumbeforce agrees to become the wife of Terri when she learns that Bevis is beyond her reach. Guy also plays an important, though not similar, part in securing Oisel for Tirri. In the case of Terri and Bevis and of Tirri and Guy the friendship lasts through many battles in which the comrades fight side by side.

The term *foreign king* refers in *Horn* and in **Bevis** to the father of the heroine. The Emperor of Constantinople, in *Guy*, occupies a somewhat analogous position. Bevis and Horn are welcomed at the courts of the foreign kings. Each is granted honors, but later is the victim of a false friend (two in **Bevis**), who misrepresents the relations existing between the hero and the king's daughter. This, so far, is true of Guy at Constantinople also. But the Emperor of Constantinople is not misled, while both the King of Westernesse and the King of Armenia trust the informers, and as a consequence the hero in one case is banished (**Bevis**, vv. 1229 ff.) and in the other is sent on a mission which is intended to result in his death (*Guy*, vv. 3727 ff.). Thus in the portions of the stories connected respectively with the foreign kings the three romances show strikingly similar characteristics.

The term *defamer* indicates sufficiently well the characteristic quality of one of the conventional enemies of the hero in these romances. Thus Fikenhild tells Ailmar that Horn

> "liþ in bure
> Vnder couerture
> By Rymenhild þi doyter."

> (vv. 695ff.)

Similarly, the false knights whom Bevis had preserved in battle said of Bevis to the Emperor that

> "þe douyter he haþ now for-lain."

> (v. 1209)

In *Guy* it is the steward Morgadour who accuses the hero of having dishonored the Emperor's daughter.

> "Into his bour wiþ strengþe he yede
> & bi þi douhter his wille he dede."

> (vv. 3227 f.)

In these cases the resemblance between the villains lies chiefly in the identity of the charges which they make.

It is to be noted that the hero in each case has a love affair with the king's daughter. Clarice, it is true, does not become the wife of Guy; but the account of her relations with him has the characteristics of a romantic story, leading up almost to the marriage altar, when the hero recollects Felice in time. In the other cases the love results in marriage, and both Rymenhild and Josian take the initiative in the wooing. In both cases separation occurs as the result of the treachery of defamers, but the later fortunes of the heroines show wide divergence. However, so far as the general relations go, we again find strong similarity.

The last character of the group, the one I have called *the second lady*, is of slighter importance, and its presence here may be questioned. I mean by this Reynild in *Horn* and the King of Aumbeforce's daughter in **Bevis**, each of whom loves[6] the hero, but later becomes the wife of the hero's friend. Oisel, whose name I have placed in brackets in the table, can scarcely be included, except that it is through Guy's victories over Tirri's enemies that she becomes the wife of the hero's friend.

Of course I do not mean to say that the reappearance of this group of characters is sufficient ground for thinking that any one of this group of romances is derived directly or indirectly from any other.[7] But it does seem to me that there was a common narrative fund which every one felt at liberty to draw upon, which indeed was common property, since no one knew precisely whence it came. If we wish to know where it existed, it is not too vague to say that it existed in the stories already familiar, in the conventional incidents and characters which were found there, and which were being more and more conventionalized as they appeared again and again. Perhaps some elements were conventionalized out of existence; but one must think, from the state of the romantic literature which has been preserved, that the number of such was small.

It has been noted, no doubt, that in discussing this group of *dramatis personæ* nothing has actually been said about character. Rather has it not been plot, and are not the *dramatis personæ* (so viewed) merely the pegs to which the plot is tied? This question must be answered with a modified affirmative. What has been indicated thus far is that when a situation is used for a second or hundredth time in a romance, there is a strong tendency to place the new pegs about where the old ones were. Character, in the stricter sense, is then indicated only by the general relations of *dramatis personæ* to the plot. This, of course, does not sum up character; and a study of the characters as such will, I believe, add some confirming evidence of the existence of this recurring group.

Stock Dramatis Personæ

Before going on to discuss characters as distinguished from *dramatis personæ*, it is worth pointing out that there are in the romances, as indeed in fiction of a later date, stock figures who are of little or no value as characters, but who do mean something to the plot. Thus in *Horn* and in **Bevis** there is the conventional porter. The only function which he serves is to delay the action by supplying occasion for an altercation at the entrance to the castle. Thus in *Horn*:

> He com to þe gateward,
> þat him answerede hard.
> Horn bad undo softe,
> Mani tyme and ofte.
> Ne miyte he awynne
> þat he come þerinne.
> Horn gan to þe þate turne
> And þat wiket vnspurne.
> þe boye hit scholde abugge;
> Horn þreu him ouer þe brigge,
> þat his ribbes him to brake;[8]
> And suþþe com in atte gate."

(vv. 1067 ff.)

In **Bevis** the account is still more detailed. The hero, seven years of age, after getting the better of the porter in a word encounter, cleaves his head (vv. 394 ff.). The porter, it seems, nearly always stands at the gate to refuse admittance and to suffer for his refusal.[9]

The suggestion sometimes made that the minstrel is taking revenge for rebuffs suffered by his class is perhaps not altogether without foundation. The aim seems to be to make the porter a ridiculous figure. The humorous intention is sometimes marked.[10] Perhaps the porter in *Macbeth* is distantly akin to the porter of romance.

More intimately connected with the plot, and more important for the revelation of character in others, is the maid of the heroine. The fact that she does not appear in *Horn*, *Havelok*, or **Bevis** is a slight indication of the fact that they are not true romances of chivalry. Rymenhild may have sent a maid for Aþelbrus to summon him for the first interview, but, if so, there is no indication of the fact. When Josian desires to communicate with Bevis, she sends a man. The absence of the romantic element in *Havelok*, of course, almost precludes the possibility of such a character appearing. In *Guy* there is a hint of this personage. Guy has just made a declaration to Felice, and swoons from the violence of his emotions. Felice bids a maid to lift him, which she does, weeping.

> "Bi god of heuen," sche seyd,
> "& ich wer as feir a mayd,
> & as riche king's douhter were
> As ani in þis warld here,
> & he of mi loue vnder-nome were
> As he is of þine in strong manere,
> & he wald me so o lou yerne,
> Me þenke y no myyt it him nouyt werne."

(vv. 609 ff.)[11]

But Felice rebukes her for commiserating Guy. One need only glance at the French *Horn et Rimel*[12] to note a marked contrast with the maid of *Guy*. Here Herselote is the natural messenger of Rimel; she tells in the bower of what is going on in the hall; she receives her mistress's confidences, comforts her when distressed, praises the lover, and is on hand to assist in emergencies. This is the conventional part of the maid. It is to be found repeatedly. Lunete plays the part in Chrétien's *Ivain*. In *William of Palerne*, Alexandrine is not only a confidante; she plays almost the part of a fairy in bringing William and Melior together, having power to cause dreams. Iseult's maid is perhaps the most distinguished of all, performing more than one important service for her mistress.[13] Playing a part of far greater importance than the porter, the maid of romance has a more developed personality. She is faithful as a matter of course, loyal to lover as well as to mistress, resourceful, self-sacrificing, brave. But she belongs essentially to the chivalrous romance; she has no place in the very different type of romance to which the exile-and-return group belongs.

If the maid is a kind of good fairy in the romances, the steward is almost always a malevolent agency. Unlike the maid, he is well represented in our group. It is he frequently who envies the hero because of the favor bestowed upon him by the king, or because of his superior knightly qualities.

> A steward was wiþ King Ermin
> þat hadde tiyt to sle þat swin;

To Beues a bar gret envie
For þat he hadde þe meistrie.

(Bevis, vv. 837 ff)

The steward of the King of England also hates the hero. Bevis visits the king:

And alle þe barouns, þat þer were,
On Beues made glade chere,
Boute þe steward of þe halle
He was þe worste frend of alle.

(vv. 4303 ff.)

He later tries to slay Bevis and, like the steward of Armenia, pays for his treachery with his life. In *Guy* there are several stewards. The most typical, Morgadour, did his best to discredit Guy with the Emperor.

Traytour he was, and full of envy.

(v. 2962)

He, too, lost his life at the hands of the object of his envy. The steward of Duke Otous (vv. 4753 ff.) is slain by Guy while trying to lead away the wounded Tirri. After the death of Otous, his kinsman Berard becomes the Emperor's steward (v. 6497); persecutes Guy's friend Tirri; shows his lack of honor by wearing two coats of mail in his combat with Guy (st. 187) and by trying to rid himself of his dangerous antagonist by casting him in the sea with the bed on which he is sleeping; but finally he, too, succumbs to the hero's valor (sts. 208 ff.). Again, the steward of Earl Florentin attacks Guy while a guest in his master's castle, and his head is cleaved with an axe (vv. 6899 ff.). Thus in the romances of *Bevis* and *Guy* alone the appearance again and again of a treacherous, envious steward is striking. He appears very frequently elsewhere. The chief villain of *Generydes*, Amalok, is the steward of Auferius, King of India. He adds adultery with the Queen to treason against his lord. In *Sir Cleges* the steward commits the same offense and suffers the same punishment as did the porter.[14] The envious character of "Kay the seneschal," while not quite so offensive as that of most stewards, is perhaps due to the association of his position.[15] The typical steward, however, is treacherous as well as envious;[16] not a coward (for cowards are rare in medieval romance), yet with the manners, the sneakingness, so often associated with cowardice.[17]

Other lay figures are palmer, merchant, beggar. The palmer or beggar is frequently the hero disguised. But he may be merely the bearer of news. A palmer tells Guy of the war between the Emperor of Almaine and Duke Segyn (vv. 1803 ff.). It is from a palmer that Horn hears of the wedding preparations when he lands

in Westernesse with his Irish force (vv. 1027 ff.). No doubt the palmer was a natural bearer of news. Thus the false news which Bevis, disguised as a palmer, tells Yvor, is instantly accepted and acted upon. Bevis asks a palmer where to find King Yvor and his Queen, Josian, when he approaches Mombraunt (vv. 2049 ff.).[18] Beggars are necessary to show the hospitality of lord or lady and to furnish an opportunity for the disguised hero to slip in with the crowd. The number thirteen, so frequently mentioned, springs from the custom of inviting thirteen beggars to appear at wedding and other feasts in honor of Christ and the Apostles. Thus Guy is one of thirteen beggars fed by Felice when he finally returns home after his long pilgrimage (sts. 278 ff.). In *Ponthus and Sidone* the mother of Ponthus is discovered by him among the thirteen beggars at the feast celebrating the regaining of his kingdom (pp. 119 f.). In *Horn et Rimel* it is a beggar instead of a palmer whom Horn meets on his return to his beloved. Merchants, too, may be messengers. Guy learns from Greek merchants of the war between the Emperor of Constantinople and the Sultan (vv. 2801 ff.). Merchants are also used for taking away children. Bevis is sold to merchants (vv. 505 ff.), and Reinbrun is stolen by merchants who pass through the country (*Guy*, C. vv. 8680 ff.).[19] A large number of subordinate *dramatis personæ* of various sorts is naturally characteristic of the *roman d'aventure*, in which the social life is more complicated than in the *chanson de geste*.[20]

Typical Characters and Medieval Life

Looking again at this list of *dramatis personæ*, not this time as elements of the story, but as figures typical of medieval life, one sees at least four stand out as significant: (1) the king; (2) the knight; (3) the lady; (4) the vassal. These are not entirely exclusive of each other, as the knight may be king, and the vassal is, of course, usually a knight. However, the characteristic king is usually the father of the hero, or some lord under whom the hero takes service; the hero is nearly always an ideal knight; the hero's beloved is invariably represented as an ideal lady; and it is usually in a friend of the hero that faithful service to one's lord is best exemplified. So, for practical purposes, there is little or no confusion, and some light may be thrown, too, on the phase or phases of society for which the romances were produced, and also perhaps on the society in which they have enacted their subsequent history.

From the tremendous host of kings in medieval literature two great figures stand out—Charlemagne and Arthur—the one, at his best, the king of the *chanson de geste*, and the other, at his best, the king of chivalric romance; the one leading his hosts against the enemies of his country and fighting at their head; the other, for the most part at least, loosely controlling a band of knights errant, who are incessantly engaged in adventures for the sake of honor or for the sake of the "fair lady." In the so-called romance of Germanic origin, there is, of course, nothing to approach the splendor of either of these figures. But in these romances the kings are certainly more nearly related to Charlemagne than to Arthur. They are kings of national war. Murri, father of Horn, was such a man, although the primitive conditions which seem to underlie the story would make him little more than a tribal chief. With two knights he awaits the onset of the Saracens, and loses his life defending his territories. Nothing is said in the way of characterization, save that he was "gode king" (v. 33), as were also Ailmar of Westernesse (v. 219) and þurston of Ireland (v. 782).[21] Aþelwold, the father of Goldborough, was also a bold warrior.

> He was þe beste kniht at nede
> þat euere mihte riden on stede,
> Or wepne wagge, or folc vt lede;
> Of kniht ne hauede he neuere drede,
> þat he ne sprong forth so sparke of glede,
> And lete him knawe of hise hand-dede.

> (vv. 87 ff.)

In *Horn Childe* King Haþeolf is a bold warrior, fighting against the enemies of his country—the Danes and the Irish. In *Guy* Aþelstan is represented as leading the English forces in their struggle with the Danes. In other words, the kings in this group of romances are fighters, usually defending their country against invaders. The king who, like Arthur and Alexander, conquers the world, belongs to a different type of romance.

Of exceptional interest is the account of King Aþelwold in *Havelok*, because there is nothing precisely comparable to it elsewhere in the romances. Here is a king who is not merely a leader of warriors, but a lawgiver and a strong executive. We certainly have a picture of an ideal king as seen by the eyes of the middle and lower classes, by those who desired, not glory, but comfort and peace.[22] He loved God and holy church; he hated robbers and hanged outlaws. Chapmen might go through England with their wares fearlessly.

> þanne was Engelond at ayse.

> (v. 59)

Moreover, he was friendly to the fatherless (vv. 75 ff.) and

> Hauede he neure so god brede,
> Ne on his bord non so god shrede,
> þat he ne wolde þorwith fede
> Poure þat on fote yede"

> (vv. 98 ff.).

Here, surely, if anywhere, we get the ideal king of merchant and laborer.[23]

The heroes are more likely to be individualized than other characters. Nevertheless, the greater part of their traits are thoroughly typical. The ideal knight of this group is one of great personal beauty and strength, who hates infidels, enjoys battle, is a faithful lover of one woman. He is often rude, sometimes cruel, always pure. He stands opposed to the chivalrous, gentle, often immoral knight typified in Lancelot.

In these romances little is said, for the most part, regarding the personal appearance of the *dramatis personœ*. This is not so likely to be the case with the hero. Thus of Horn the author says at the beginning:

> Fairer ne miste none beo born
> Ne no rein vpon birine,
> Ne sunne vpon bischine:
> Fairer nis non þan he was.
> He was briyt so þe glas,
> He was whit so þe flur,
> Rose red was his colur.
> In none kinge riche
> Nas non his iliche.

> (vv. 10 ff.)[24]

His physical beauty continues to receive attention. He is the "faireste" (v. 173); Ailmar admires his "fairnesse" (v. 213); Aþulf says "he is fairere by one rib þan eny man þat libbe" (vv. 315 ff.); when he visits Rymenhild the bower is lighted "of his feire siyte" (v. 385);[25] Berild has never seen so fair a knight come to Ireland (v. 778); King þurston speaks of his "fairhede" (v. 798); and at the close the author says:

> Her endeþ þe tale of horn,
> þat fair was & noyt vnorn.

> (vv. 1525 f.)

Havelok likewise is very beautiful (v. 2133) and well-shaped (v. 1647). Bevis was a "feire child," and King Ermin said of him:

> "Be Mahoun, þat sit an hiy,
> A fairer child neuer i ne siy,
> Neiþer a lengþe ne on brade,
> Ne non, so faire limes hadde!"

> (vv. 535 ff.)

In *Guy*, too, not much is said of the personal appearance of the hero, not nearly so much as in *Horn*. There is nothing especially distinctive about the traces of description one finds, as they are the commonplaces.

The hero's strength and valor are of great prominence in all romances, but there are certain variations of greater interest than are found in descriptions of personal appearance. In *Horn* the hero's strength is frequently the object of direct praise from the *dramatis personæ*. The Admirad says to him, "þu art gret & strong" (v. 93), and adds that if he lived, in time he "scholde slen us alle" (v. 100); Ailmar says the strength of his hand shall become famous (vv. 215 ff.). The author of *Havelok* also takes great delight in his hero's physical prowess, and speaks directly to the audience:

> For þanne he weren alle samen
> At Lincolne, at þe gamen,
> And þe erles men woren alle þore,
> Was Hauelok bi þe shuldren more
> þan þe meste þat þer kan:
> In armes him noman ne nam
> þat he doune sone ne caste;
> Hauelok stod ouer hem als a mast.
> Als he was heie, so he was strong,
> He was boþe stark and long;
> In Engelond was non hise per
> Of strengþe þat euere kam him nere.

> (vv. 979 ff.)

Again and again this brute strength is brought out. Havelok eats more than Grim and his five children (vv. 793 f.); at Lincoln he upsets "sixtene laddes gode" and carries "wel a cart lode" of fish; his strength is admired by Ubbe, who thinks he should be a knight (v. 1650); he slays three men with one blow of a "dore-tre" (v. 1806); he puts the stone at the first throw so far that all competitors depart (vv. 1052 ff.). There is on the part of the author a certain simplicity of delight in the overwhelming strength of his hero that is almost unique. In the rapid succession of incidents in **Bevis** there is little time for commenting on the hero. However, there is a word at the beginning of his fighting career.

> Be þat he was fiftene þer olde,
> Kniyt ne swain þar nas so bolde,
> þat him dorste ayenes ride
> Ne wiþ wreþþe him abide.

> (vv. 581 ff.)

In *Guy* we have gone so far toward the romance of chivalry that the emphasis, so far as direct description goes, is on something else than strength, which is left to be inferred from many a deed of valor.[26]

On the other hand, the mental character and accomplishments of the hero are emphasized in *Guy*, especially on the knightly side, and in *Havelok* on the homely side, while in **Bevis** and in *Horn* they are neglected. Indeed, scarcely anything is said of Horn's mental or moral characteristics. He was "of wit þe beste" (v. 174), "wel kene" (v. 91). His teachableness and good nature are indicated.

> Horn in his herte layte
> Al þat he him tayte.
> In þe curt & ute
> & elles al abute
> Luuede men horn child.

> (vv. 243 ff.)

In *Havelok* again there is the unique quality which was noted in the account of the physical characteristics, but even more marked. The author probably had in mind that Havelok would make a good king like Aþelwold, but he has made him seem more like a strong, rather slow-witted, but happy peasant. His life at Winchester, which is described most fully, makes him seem to be a powerful, mild-tempered boy.

> Of alle men was he mest meke,
> Lauhwinde ay, and bliþe of speke;
> Euere he was glad, and bliþe,
> His sorwe he couþe ful wel miþe.
> It net was non so litel knaue, . . .
> For to leyken, ne forto plawe,
> þat he ne wolde with him pleye:
> þe children that yeden in þe weie
> Of him he deden al her wille,
> And with him leykeden here fille.

> (vv. 945 ff.)

Not only is his kindness shown by his playing with the children; it is shown in the care he later takes of his foster brothers and sisters and in the mercy offered to Godrich. He is as observant of law as Aþelwold. Only after due trial may Godard and Godrich be executed.

Thus does the author intend for us to see him—strong, cheerful, merciful, fearless, law-abiding. It may be questioned whether he intended that Havelok should so appear, but he surely was lacking in initiative. It is Goldborough who arouses in him the ambition, or at least stirs it to the acting point, to regain his kingdom. It is Ubbe who collects the friends of Havelok in Denmark. Havelok would have been a happy peasant. He is a true member of the lowly classes—strong in body and in mind, whole-hearted, loving peace better than war, but fearless when called upon to fight, rather than a fiery king, full of aggressive ambition, or a luxurious, generous monarch such as the nobility admired.

But Guy is a hero a chivalry—not of the Lancelot type, nor of the Galahad type, although approaching the latter in the religious devotion of his later years. He stands somewhere between Horn and Bevis, on the one hand,

and Lancelot and Galahad on the other. He has the knightly education which Horn had. He knows the craft

> Of wode, of Ryuer, of all game.

> (C. v. 171)

He is generous. He gives rich gifts to parsons and poor knights,

> And to other oft þeue he wolde
> Palfrey or stede, siluer and golde,
> Euery man after his good dede
> Of Guy vnderfangeth his mede.

> (C. vv. 181 ff.)

Moreover he became ill from loving too well, and fought long years merely for the sake of a woman. Guy stands in fairly strong contrast with the heroes of *King Horn*, of *Bevis*, and of *Havelok*, and approaches the heroes of another type of romance.[27]

Somewhat less need be said about the heroine in these romances. The part played by Goldborough is so small that she may be dismissed almost with a word. She is seen as a great lady, resenting her forced marriage to one apparently far beneath her in rank, and later urging her husband to regain his crown—a figure of strength, described as "swiþe fayr" (v. 111), the "faireste woman on liue" (v. 281), as bright (v. 2131), as chaste (v. 288), and

> Of alle þewes was she wis.
> þat gode weren, and of pris.

> (vv. 282 f.)

The absence of a love element prevents the development of her character. She is queen rather than woman.

The character of Rymenhild, on the other hand, is that of a woman, individual in some respects, yet typical of a class, of which Josian, in *Bevis of Hamtoun,* is a member. Her individuality may be said to lie largely in the very prominence of certain typical characteristics. Her appearance is passed almost without comment. She is "Rymenhild þe briyte" (vv. 382, 390) or "Rymenhild þe yonge" (v. 566). It is decidedly by her actions that she is interesting. It is a primitive, undisciplined nature. In love and in hate she is uncontrolled. She loved Horn "þat ney heo gan wexe wild" (v. 252). There is no reserve in her wooing. When Aþulf enters her bower she at once takes him in her arms. When she finds she has been deceived by Aþelbrus she is as unrestrained in her rage.

> "Schame mote þu fonge
> & on hiye rode anhonge . . .

> Wiþ muchel schame mote þu deie."

> (vv. 327 ff.)

When Horn refuses to plight his troth to Rymenhild, she swoons. She is all in tears over her dream of the net (v. 654). When she thinks Horn lost forever, she is ready to slay herself.

> Heo feol on hir bedde,
> þer heo knif huddle
> To sle wiþ king loþe
> & hure selue boþe,
> In þat vlke niyte,
> If horn come ne miyte
> To herte knif heo sette,
> Ac horn anone hire kepte,

> (vv. 1195 ff.)

She is as faithful as passionate. When she knows that she is about to be forced into a hateful marriage, she sends a messenger to seek Horn (vv. 933 ff.). She watches the sea for her absent lover (vv. 975 ff.). Even to the last she has Aþulf on the tower with his eyes searching the great expanse of water. Altogether she is a wilful, passionate creature of uncontrolled impulses, yet constant in love. The author does not think her worthy of direct description. Yet he has created a striking figure.[28]

As stated, Josian belongs to the same type. The account of her beauty is made somewhat more striking by the use of a figure of speech.

> So fair yhe was & briyt of mod,
> Ase snow opon þe rede blod.

> (vv. 521 f.)

She was also "hende" and "wel itau\??\t," although she knew nothing of Christian law (vv. 525 f.). Like Rymenhild she loves passionately, and it is her persistence and her willingness to change her faith which win her lover. Perhaps it is the same persistent courage which gives her the strength to slay her undesired husband. A strong woman, equal to emergencies, faithful to lover and husband—less attractive than Rymenhild, but by no means unworthy—is the heroine of *Bevis of Hamtoun*.[29]

But in Felice we have a lady of the romance of chivalry. Fifteen lines at the outset and more elsewhere are devoted to her beauty, although the author remarks that it is so great that he cannot describe it (v. 60).[30] Her accomplishments are equally remarkable.

> All the vii artis she kouthe well,
> Noon better that euere man herde tell.

His maisters were thider come
Out of Tholouse all and some;
White and hoore all they were,
Bisy they were that mayden to lere.

(c. vv. 81 ff.)[31]

In love she is as reserved and cruel as Rymenhild is
unrestrained and generous, promising her lover favor
repeatedly, only to withdraw it, until he has become
the most famous knight in the world. After that her
conduct shows a marked change. She seems a very
mild and dutiful wife. When Guy becomes a pilgrim,
she feeds the poor and prays for her absent lord, so
that there is no better woman in the world (st. 279). As
with Guy, there is in her traces of the ascetic ideal.
The best woman, as well as the best man, is one withdrawn from the common life.

Here again we find the *Guy* far removed from the other
romances. Josian and Rymenhild are passionate, primitive creatures, willing to do all and suffer all for their
lovers. Felice is a woman more cultivated, more self-
contained, more selfish, more of a "lady," and her later
piety and devotion but emphasize the fact that she is a
member of a class. Yet she in turn is far removed from
the Guinevere type, and farther still from the heroine
of so many of the later French romances—a married
woman who devotes her life to intrigues with a lover.[32]

While the type which I have called the *vassal* shows
less variety, it is extremely interesting. In Aþulf, in
Grim, in Saber, in Herhaud, as well as in other characters, one sees the relation of lord and follower at its
best. Aþulf, appearing only for an instant now and
then in the story of *Horn,* leaves a vivid impression.
There is never a hint of self-seeking. Not for an instant
will he take advantage of Aþelbrus's deception, when
Rymenhild, thinking him Horn, declares her love.
During Horn's long absence, he remains in Westernesse
to guard the mistress for her lover. Herhaud, Grim, and
Saber, likewise, are always willing to sacrifice all for
their respective lords. Here is a glimpse of the more
beautiful side of chivalry. However, it needs no emphasis here, as it is one of the most evident of the
attractive features common to the whole range of medieval romance.[33]

. . . . .

Minor Characters

There are in the romances, as in all narratives, figures
which flash for an instant before us, then pass away;
perhaps to return, and appear and disappear as before;
perhaps to be seen no more. Some of these we have
already noted as stock figures. Others do not seem to
be of that character. Whatever they are, it is interesting
to know who they are, what value they have for the

stories in which they are introduced, and what interest
the author has succeeded in attaching to them. Most
are beyond the pale of characterization. Some of them
are merely speaking persons, who appear unexpectedly, tell their stories, and disappear. In *Horn* there are
two of these—Aþulf's father, who greets Horn and his
companions when they land in Denmark, and tells them
what has been going on in their absence (vv. 1301 ff.),
and Arnoldin, who appears to tell Horn where
Rymenhild has been taken by Fikenhild (vv. 1443 ff.).
Again, there may be characters who are never named.
Of this class are nine of the twelve companions of
Horn—ornamental figures, who are dropped without
remark. Other characters may be talked about and never
actually get on the stage. Reynild is the sole member
of this class in *Horn*. Others still may merely add a
touch of pathos, as does Horn's mother. Lastly may be
mentioned Harild and Berild who, after performing one
or two insignificant acts, perish almost without rip-
pling the surface of the narrative.

Thus *Horn*, considering the brevity of the story, has a
fairly full background of *dramatis personœ*. If the
English version represents the earlier form of the story,
it is worth while to notice, in passing, how the minor
characters appear in such a developed, sophisticated
romance as *Horn et Rimel*. A number of the parts so
insignificant have become really important. Lemburc,
who plays the part of Reynild, and her brothers, Egfer
and Guffer, appear repeatedly in a series of highly
elaborated incidents. The account of Horn's father, told
in epic fashion by the son in the body of the romance,
is fairly full. A considerable addition to the stock of
characters is made to fill up the enlarged stage. Herselote
has already been mentioned. A nurse is introduced by
means of whom Rimel discovers that she is making love
to another than Horn. Rimel has attendants, unnamed,
ready to amuse the one who might disturb a tête-à-tête.
In the Irish part of the story, Gudburc and Sudburc,
mother and sister of Lemburc, and Eglaf, the chess-
player and athlete, are additions. Even the Irish kings
are named.[34] The divergence is extremely interesting,
for this elaborate treatment of so many minor *dramatis
personae* marks as well as anything else the long distance which must have been traveled by one or both of
these romances from the source common to both.

In *Horn* the lesser characters seem to spring, for the
most part, from a natural development of the plot. This,
I think, is less true of *Havelok*, *Guy*, and **Bevis**. There
may be, however, other sources of interest. In *Havelok*
the two sisters of the hero are essentially pathetic characters. Grim's wife, after playing an important part in
the realistic scene in Grim's "cleue," is never referred
to again. Her brutality to the unknown boy, like that of
Grim, leaves a blot on the family, if not on the story.

Vp she stirte, and nouht ne sat,
And caste þe knaue so harde adoune,

þat he crakede þer his croune
Ageyn a gret ston, þer it lay.

(vv. 566 ff.)

Grim's children and Ubbe play conventional parts. Bernard Brun is an innkeeper with a name. His chief part is a repetition of the story of the fight between Havelok and the sixty lads, which might very well have been dispensed with. The cook, Bertram, is merely a friendly helper. The Earl of Chester and the Earl of Lincoln furnish historical background, and the former, in addition, becomes husband of Gunnild, Grim's daughter. It is interesting to note that every one of these persons has a name, from Leue, the wife of Grim, to Bernard Brun, the innkeeper, and Bertram, the cook. Most of the minor characters, too, it will be noted, are of humble rank, and are an item in the popular character of the story. The prominence given to the family of Grim is probably due to the fact that the romance celebrates a particular place. If the minor *dramatis personae* of *Havelok* are less intimately connected with plot than those of *Horn*, they show greater realism and broader range.

In *Bevis* and *Guy* the greater part of the minor characters are principals in the incidents in which they appear. In these romances the story is a succession of adventures, each with its little plot. In *Bevis* these are usually brief and very slightly elaborated, three or four *dramatis personae* being sufficient for each incident. Many persons appear, only to be slain by the hero. Most of these are too colorless to be characterized. In general, it may be said that there is an absence of pathetic and ornamental figures. There is a fairly large number—including two messengers, two porters, two stewards, a palmer, and a giant—bearing no names. There is a concentration upon incidents. One figure, Ascopard, stands out somewhat, being intended, it seems, to produce a comic effect.[35]

Much of what was said about *Bevis* at the beginning of the preceding paragraph applies to *Guy* as well. The latter romance is much longer than the former; the incidents are told with greater detail; but there is the same succession of lifeless figures, among whom the hero displays his prowess. There is, moreover, no comic person to be placed beside Ascopard. The reference to the various ladies surrounding Felice is another element associating it with the courtly type of romance. There is, too, the account of the gathering of people at Warwick at Pentecost—

There were Erles, barons, and knyghtes,
And many a man of grete myghtes;
Ladies and maydens of grete renown,
The grettest desired ther to bee bown

(C. vv. 189 ff.)—

swhich furnishes a courtly setting. With the twelve companions of Horn may be compared the twenty sons of good barons who were dubbed knights with Guy. The list of *dramatis personae* is very great. Limiting the number to those introduced as individuals, there are almost a hundred, of whom about seventy are named.[36] In *Bevis* there are forty, of whom about twenty-five are named. In *Havelok* there are twenty-two, all named; in *Horn* twenty, of whom fifteen are named.

Dialogue and Soliloquy

Dialogue plays an interesting and important part in displaying character, and the manner of the dialogue goes far toward being the manner of the romance.

In *Horn* the vigorous dialogue serves to advance the narrative rather than to portray character. It is significant, too, that real soliloquy, to reveal intention or mood, is absent. In *Havelok*, on the contrary, in which dramatic situation is not emphasized, dialogue is of comparatively slight importance, while numerous soliloquies reveal mood and purpose.[37] In *Bevis* there is gain in dialogue with the author's superior sense of situation. However, it is a matter of plot primarily, although, with its brevity and passion, it is valuable for character too.[38] The seven soliloquies are brief and of slight importance. Both dialogue and soliloquy are of great importance in *Guy*. Dialogue is sustained, and emotions are presented fully.[39] The soliloquies are long and important. The one which shows Guy struck with remorse for his sins is both moving and true (sts. 21 f.). In dialogue and soliloquy *Guy* shows the characteristics of the chivalric romance.

Interest in Mental States

In reading this section much that has already been said should be kept in mind. The discussion of the individual characters, of dialogue, and of soliloquy includes much which might be treated here. But to avoid needless repetition, the attempt will be made to view the material already familiar from another angle, something being added to make the outlook sufficiently broad. The term "interest in mental states" is employed here loosely. The manner in which emotion is manifested by the *dramatis personae*, the degree to which the author delights in analyzing mental states, even the extent of the emotional appeal to the auditor, and the way in which it is produced, will come under review.

King Horn, which is the most ballad-like of all genuine English romances,[40] has, like the ballad, emotional value apart from any overt interest on the part of the author in character or mental states. The dialogue has frequently this emotional appeal. But of real interest in states of mind as such there is none. In the most dramatic scenes the auditor may be left without a hint of the emotions of the *dramatis personae* (e. g., the banishment of Horn, vv. 705 ff.).[41] In *Havelok* the situation is almost reversed. There is a certain amount of interest in mental states as such, but none of the ballad-like appeal to feelings by poignant situations such as we found in *Horn*. The author takes pleasure in reminding the hearers that Godrich is deceived and plotting his own ruin when he plans to marry Goldborough and Havelok.

> For he wende, þat Hauelok wore
> Sum cherles sone, and no more;
> Ne shulde he hauen of Engellond
> Onlepi forw in his hond
> With hire, þat was þer-of þe eyr,
> þat bope was god and swipe fair.
> He wende, þat Hauelok wer a þral,
> þer-þoru he wende hauen al
> In Engelond, þat hire riht was.

(vv. 1091 ff.)

We are told in some detail how the characters thought over situations. Thus Apelwold considers at length what best to do to protect his daughter's interests after his death. Havelok considers carefully before returning to Grimsby with his bride. In fact there is a good deal of downright thinking going on. To *Bevis* what was said about Horn in large measure applies. The situations in themselves are often moving, but the author does not dwell on the emotions of his characters, nor does he seem to insist on the emotional appeal to the reader. He is in too much of a hurry to get on. However, the dialogue is often characteristic enough to reveal the feelings of the characters. But the reader is left in doubt as to Bevis's feelings for Josian up to the time when she became a Christian. In the love affair it is only the heroine's feelings which are revealed. Scarcely anything is made of the loss of wife and children, when Ascopard carries Josian away and the two boys are left in the care of strangers. Whatever emotional appeal there is springs entirely from the imaginative sympathy of the audience with the situation. It need scarcely be said that there is far greater interest in emotional states of mind in *Guy*. So far as the hero's love and repentance are concerned, this was made clear in discussing the soliloquies. One may note, also, the accounts of the reunion of comrades after long separation (vv. 1749 ff.; sts. 142 ff.); the story of Guy's parting from father and mother (vv. 1217 ff.); the story of Oisel and Tirri; the story of Jonas. There is not so much analysis as in many French romances, but there is a decided interest in emotional states, a too-marked insistence on them often, which sets *Guy* far apart from *Horn*, *Havelok*, and *Bevis*.[42]

When one looks at the actual manner of manifesting emotion in the romances, he is at once in the midst of stock material. However, I believe that differences in the treatment of this stock material will appear. The expression of grief is most important. Wringing of the hands is, of course, a commonplace, and is not limited by age or sex.

> þe children hi broyte to stronde
> Wringende here honde.

(*Horn*, vv. 111 ff.)

When Rymenhild found her messenger drowned,

> Hire fingres he gan wringe.

(*ibid.*, v. 980)

Likewise of the child *Bevis*:

> yeme a wep, is hondes wrong.

(*Bevis*, v. 298)

Swooning is even more common. Rymenhild falls (presumably in a faint) three times: on Horn's refusal of her love "adun he feol iswoye" (v. 428); at Horn's departure for Ireland she "feol to grunde" (v. 740); and again she "feol iswoye" when Horn approached Fikenhild's castle singing (v. 1479). Swooning does not occur in *Havelok*, and in *Bevis* occurs but twice—curiously enough a man being the victim in each case. Thus Terri, when he was told that Guy was dead,

> fel þer doun and swouy,
> His her, his cloþes he al to-drouy.

(vv. 1309 f.)

And Bevis, when he finds his two newborn children. but no mother,

> fel þar doun and swouy.

(v. 3717)

Lovers were of course expected to faint, and Guy is a perfect lover. At the end of a confession of love,

> Adoune he felle swoune with that.

(v. 598)

Later in the story, what with bleeding wounds and sorrow for his slain friends, "adoun he fel aswon." Herhaud swoons from the shock of surprise and joy in meeting Guy (v. 1762), and again he "fel in swowe vpon his bedde"[43] because of anxiety for Guy, who was absent on a dangerous mission (v. 3999). Oisel faints over her wounded lover (v. 4896), and again when she sees him in bonds (v. 5903). Both Guy and

Felice swoon when he announces his intention to become a pilgrim (st. 32, v. 11). Tirri swoons when he learns that the unknown pilgrim who had slain his enemy Berard is in truth his old comrade Guy (st. 226, v. 3). Lastly, Felice swoons when she comes to the hermitage where her husband lies dead.

Weeping is too common an occurrence for anything like a full list here. While more often it is the manifestation of a woman's grief, it is not at all regarded as unworthy of heroes. In *Horn* there are the following examples:

> Heo sat on þe sunne
> Wiþ tires al birunne.

> (vv. 653 ff.)

> Alf weop wiþ iþe
> & al þat him isiye.

> (vv. 755 ff.)

> Horn iherd with his ires
> A spak with bidere teres.

> (vv. 887 ff.)

> Ne miste heo adriþe
> þat heo (Rymenhild) ne weop wiþ iye.

> (vv. 1035 f.)

> þe bride wepey sore.

> (v. 1049)

She was "sore wepinge & þerne" when Horn entered the hall where the wedding feast was being prepared; she wept "teres of blode" when imprisoned by Fikenhild (v. 1406). Aþulf, watching for Horn, says "for soreþe nu y wepe" (v. 1104). In Havelok there are only two or three examples. The lords whom Aþelwold summoned when he was at the point of death

> Greten, and gouleden, and gouen hem ille.

> (v. 164)

Havelok and his sisters, shut up in a castle, wept for hunger and cold (v. 416). Likewise, there is little weeping in **Bevis.** When the boy hero learned of his father's death, "þerne a wep" (v. 298). Josian weeps right sorely (vv. 1111, 1190) and Bevis hears her weeping and crying in the castle of Yvor (v. 2101). Guy, true lover that he is, weeps as well as faints from the violence of his passion (vv. 247, 261, 568). He weeps too over his fallen comrades (v. 1554). The kissing of men is associated with weeping sometimes, either for joy or for

sorrow. Once when Herhaud and his fellows rescue Guy pursued by Saracens,

> þe most hepe wepen for blis;
> þai kisten Gij alle for blis.

> (vv. 4072 f.)

When Guy and Tirri part,

> To gider þai kisten þo,
> At her departing þai wepen bo.

> (vv. 7111 f.)

And at another parting they

> kist hem wiþ eiye wepeing.

> (st. 232)

Weeping with both eyes seems intended to imply violent weeping (v. 4455, sts. 138, 226, 294).

The more violent tearing of hair and clothes is also a convention of romances. There are no cases in *Horn* or in *Havelok.* In **Bevis** there is the instance quoted above when Terri swooned and, apparently at the same time,

> His her, his cloþes he al todrouy.

> (v. 1310)

> In *Guy* the expression is common. Of Guy in
> love it is said
> His clothes he rende, his heer he drough.

> (v. 420)

The Sultan, enraged at his defeat, rends his clothes (Caius v. 3692). Earl Jonas, when Guy meets him, is rending his clothes and tearing his hair (st. 46).

Other ways of expressing grief may be mentioned. "Hise heorte began to childe" (*Horn*, v. 1148) has numerous parallels.[44] In **Bevis** there is

> þe childes herte was wel colde.

> (v. 511)

and

> þe kinges herte wex wel cold.

> (v. 553)

Less conventional is the account of Josian's woe when she thinks Bevis is leaving her:

Hire pouyte, þe tour wolde on hir falle.

(v. 1140.)[45]

Guy complains that, because of love, he cannot sit nor stand, rest nor sleep, eat nor drink (vv. 315 ff.). There is also in *Guy* an abundance of making "mone" and sighing "sore."

The expression of joy is also unrestrained. Kissing is often a token of joy.

Hi custe hem mid ywisse
& makeden muchel blisse.

(*Horn*, vv. 1209 f.)

When Terri discovered his father Saber in the palmer, he took him in his armes

& gonne cleppen and to kisse
And made meche ioie & blisse.

(vv. 3944 f.)

Almost the identical lines occur at another place (vv. 3057 f.). In *Guy* the meeting of old friends is accompanied by kissing.

To kissen Herhaud þai hem do,
Wel gret ioie þai maden þo.

(vv. 6655 f.)[46]

Swooning or falling down for joy is restricted to *Guy*. Herhaud's swooning (v. 1762) has been mentioned. When Oisel, forcibly held by Otous, saw Guy unexpectedly,

For blisse sche fel aswon adoun.

(v. 6297)

She swoons again when she meets Tirri:

For ioie sche swoned omong hem.

(v. 6533)

Unrestrained expression of emotion on the part of *dramatis personœ* is a characteristic pretty general in metrical romance.[47] In the group here studied, *Havelok*, which is the least romantic, is least emotional, and *Guy*, which is most romantic, is most emotional. The means of expressing feeling are thoroughly conventional, as the brief review here made clearly shows.[48] *Horn*, *Bevis*, and *Guy* represent types of literature which originally stood far apart. Yet we find them side by side on English soil, drawing from the same stock of

literary material. The sentimentalism of *Guy* brings with it a freer use of the extreme forms of expressing emotion.[49] In *Bevis*, where sentiment plays a small part, we find these stock expressions here and there; almost unexpectedly. In *Horn*, which is more truly romance, the expression of joy, less unrestrained than in *Guy*, is more appropriate than in *Bevis*. But the strong resemblance of these metrical stories is due, largely at least, to the recasting at the hands of Englishmen who did not distinguish types; who were familiar with stock romantic material, the well-known poses, rhyme phrases, etc., and in translating threw them in where convenient.[50]

In the English romances the expressions representing emotion are for the most part stock material, English material indeed, although no doubt French romance assisted in its creation. Perhaps there was a tendency in this respect to confuse types of narrative—that is, in the use of these stock emotional expressions—which brings the English romances nearer together than their sources.

The Human Relations

It is perfectly clear, even to him who reads running, that the medieval romances by no means deal in anything like a complete way with the various relations which make up human life. The name romance perhaps cuts out a certain portion of these; but modern romance has looked upon and cultivated great areas of life which medieval romance never dreamed about. To determine a little more clearly what are the human limits of the metrical romances, particularly the four now under examination, is the purpose of this section.

Love, as in all romance, is, next to war, the greatest interest. This means, of course, the love of the sexes. Other forms of love—of parent and child, of brother and sister, of brother and brother—are almost crowded out. War, of course, means comradeship, and the love of comrades for each other—sometimes of follower for lord—plays its expected part. But affections other than the love of man and woman, of warrior and warrior, are of insignificant interest.

In these four romances there are two types of love represented, the passionate and the chivalrous. The latter is, of course, the type at once associated with medieval romance—with Lancelot and with Tristram. In greater refinement it is represented by the love stories of Dante and Pertrach. It is the love of Arthur's court and of the court of love, of Chrétien at the beginning and Malory at the end of a literary period. This type of love is represented in *Guy*, imperfectly perhaps, yet not unattractively. The passionate type is represented in *Horn* and *Bevis*.

Curiously enough, in the passionate type it is the woman who woos. This is a situation appearing in *William of*

Palerne, in *Amis and Amiloun*,[51] as well as in *Horn* and in **Bevis**. There seems to be a greater popularity in the kind of love here represented. It is attractive by its simplicity, its frankness, its faithfulness, its healthy, unspoiled, primitive human nature. Sometimes there seems to be a certain disregard of the legal bond of marriage. Apparently Rymenhild cared little for it (vv. 531 ff.); we are not sure that Josian did (vv. 1093 ff.). William of Palerne's love for Melior had, at first, no legal sanction. Yet there is always the faithfulness which we associate with the marriage tie. It is the unmoral attitude of the ballads.

This passionate type of love is characteristic of the *chanson de geste* (cf. Gautier, I, p. 207). It is the lady who makes the advances, sometimes in a disgustingly bold manner.[52] Frequently it is a Saracen girl who shows this frank, sometimes brutal passion, which may not scruple at parricide to attain its end.[53] However, the general traits of female character seem much the same in Christian as in Saracen.[54] Prejudice against Saracen women who become Christians is not a trait of the *chansons de geste*.[55] Orable, the wife of *Guillaume de Orange*, is perhaps the most attractive of the heroines of the *chansons de geste*. This typical woman was never a person common in real life; but she probably does represent an earlier stage when women were of less importance socially, and when distinctively feminine traits were not held in the esteem which was felt by the society implied by the *roman d'aventure*.

In *Guy* it is the man who woos. The lady is unsusceptible, disdainful even. The hero must remain afar off, must wait for many years; and when he wins his love he is scarcely permitted to enjoy it. There is a strong undercurrent of asceticism. The love of woman leads to strife; many men have been and will be "to gronde y-brouyt" by women (vv. 1503 ff.); it is after renunciation that the noblest character is developed both in Guy and in Felice (st. 279). Even pure and chivalrous love is unworthy in the presence of religious asceticism.

It is well to bear in mind that there was an ideal of love in medieval literature, and life, too, perhaps, which insisted that the perfect relation was between a married woman and an unmarried man. At its best this ideal is beautiful, if unpractical and ultimately immoral. It sprang from a desire to preserve the first bright glow of young love before desire had darkened it. To do this meant to love the unattainable and unapproachable—a married woman. This of course is the love of Dante for Beatrice. It is the love which dictated the rules of the court of love. But in many of the French romances, as well as in their English analogues, we see the ideal breaking down, and another taking its place. The beloved is still a married woman, but not quite unapproachable, not quite unattainable. Here of course stand Lancelot and Guinevere, Tristram and Iseult, human and attractive, but sinners who must suffer. Later still

come the romances in which illicit love is represented not as sin, perhaps not involving evil consequences, or, if so, only accidentally as any pure love might. Under a slight varnish there is often all the grossness of *fabliau*. Yet the author will say that these were perfect lovers.[56] It is interesting to note that these grosser romances had no vogue in English. No doubt they were repugnant to medieval English moral standards, at least of the public which read the English romances, low as they often are. Contemporary with these immoral romances, with their ideal of courtly, illicit love, were romances in which love seems so primitive as in *Horn* and **Bevis**, and so pure as in *Guy*. The English were using the less fashionable of contemporary literary material.

More important is war—involving the emotions of hatred and envy, as well as hope of glory and joy of victory. Here we are concerned primarily with the human side—with the emotions concerned. These are implied rather than expressed. In *Horn* and in **Bevis** there is the opposition of Christian and Saracen; in *Havelok*, of the loyal and the traitorous; in *Guy of Warwick*, of national and foreign. In addition, we find in our romances hostility because of the appearance of an undesired suitor for the heroine's hand, or because some one has been dispossessed of his property, or because some one has been worsted in a tournament. On the whole it may be said that these hostile relations are dwelt upon only sufficiently to bring about the fascinating scenes when lances break and swords clash. To see more clearly how the human elements enter into war it will be sufficient to discuss vengeance, cruelty, and the emotions of the fight.

The emotions of the fight are anger and fear. In *Horn* and *Havelok* these scarcely appear. In the fight with his father's slayer

> Horn him gan agrise,
> & his blod arise

(vv. 868 ff.)

And Godard when captured "rorede als a bole" (*Hav.* v. 2438). In **Bevis**, however, there are numerous expressions to indicate the state of mind of combatants, especially of the hero. These are chiefly about physical sufferings. He is injured

> þat he miyte sofre namore.

(**Bevis,** v. 630)

When he got to his chamber, he

> leide him deueling on þe grounde
> To kolen is hertte in þat stounde.

(vv. 649 f.)

He became weary in his fight with the boar (v. 799). In the fight with the dragon "lim þouyte his herte to-brast" (v. 1792), and in his fight with the London crowd he was "wo be-gon" because of his wounds. In *Guy* combatants suffer for water (sts. 113, 120). When wounded, Amoraunt's "hert was full of ire and care" (v. 8541). Colbrond, when wounded, "was sore aschame" (st. 262). Guy in the same fight was sore dismayed and sore aghast when his sword broke. These are but a few of the cases in **Bevis** and *Guy* in which something is said about the emotions and physical sufferings of combatants. The simpler romances of *Horn* and *Havelok* have less fighting and therefore less material of this kind. Perhaps the most striking feature to be observed is the absence of fear.

Vengeance has an important part to play in many romances—and in three of this group, *Horn*, *Havelok*, **Bevis**. But the feeling of bitterness from which deeds of vengeance spring is almost absent. It is true that vengeance is secured. The Saracen enemies of Horn are slain; Godard and Godrich pay for their treachery with their lives; and the mother and stepfather of Bevis likewise perish. But of real hatred there is none except in the case of Bevis. Even in his case there is nothing to compare with the vengeance of Elizabethan drama. It is in the background of the story.

Of cruelty there is probably no more than medieval life would justify, In *Horn* there is mutual slaughter of Saracens and Christians, non-combatants as well as combatants (vv. 63 ff., 1377 ff.). But mortal enmity between Christians and infidels is merely part of the setting of much of medieval literature.[57] Even the Saracens did not have the cruelty to slay Horn and his companions outright. Fikenhild, after his death at Horn's hands, was drawn,[58] but that was the customary fate of traitors. The same remark applies to the tortures undergone by Godrich and Godard. They are condemned by their peers, and no one might do Godrich shame before trial (*Havelok*, vv. 1762 ff.). But there is no shrinking from legal cruelty. When Godard had been sentenced and shriven,

> Sket came a ladde with a knif,
> And bigan riht at þe to
> For to ritte, and for to flo
> So it were grim or gore.

(vv. 2493 ff.)

With like severity Godrich was bound to a stake and burned (vv. 2831 ff.). The cruelty of **Bevis** is of a much fiercer quality.[59] When Bevis was told that his half-brother[59] had been unintentionally slain by his father he

louy and hadde gode game.

(v. 3116)

When his stepfather was captured, he had him put to death by being thrown into a kettle of lead, and when his mother, beholding her husband thus perish, falls from the castle and breaks her neck,

> Alse glad he was of hire,
> Of his damme, ase of is stepsire.

(vv. 3463 f.)

Such brutality as this is entirely absent from *Guy*. Here is another instance of the distance by which this romance is removed from the others, particularly from **Bevis**, which in structure it so much resembles.

As has been said, not much is made of the family relations. The relation of husband and wife seems to be an exception, as it is a source of interest in *Havelok*, **Bevis**, and *Guy*. Yet not very much is made of it. In **Bevis** it is only the wife who seems much affected by the long separation. In *Guy* there is the tacit approval of the departure of the husband at a time when he is aware that he is to be a father. Scarcely anything is made of the relationship of mother and son. The meeting of Horn and Godhild, furnishing such a splendid chance for pathos, is barely mentioned (v. 1383).[60] In **Bevis** the mother's attitude is entirely unnatural. The mother of Havelok is not mentioned; and the mother of Guy is neglected after the beginning of the romance. The relation of father and son is of greater importance. It is necessary that the hero's father should be a man of rank and might as an assurance of the hero's qualifications. The death of the father may introduce the motive of quest for vengeance (*Horn*, **Bevis**); the hero may take pride in his father (**Bevis**, vv. 613 ff.). But scarcely anything is made of filial affection.[61] Much less is made of fraternal affection. As a rule the hero of romance is an only child, at least of both father and mother; so Guy, Horn, Bevis. The sisters of Havelok perish too early to play a significant part. It is true of romance literature in general that the fraternal relation is unimportant.[62] The relation of subject and lord is, as has already been indicated, one of importance. But when the most is made of all this, one need only think of Chaucer to realize that the appeal of these early metrical romances is to a limited range of emotion.

Summary

In order to see clearly what each of these romances has contributed to medieval character-writing, it is necessary to consider them separately, summarizing, for the most part, the conclusions already stated.

King Horn.—In this romance the characterization seems to harmonize perfectly with the rough, uncouth background of life and nature. Horn is a fighter first and a lover second. Indeed, as a lover, while faithful, he is not ardent. His long sojourn in Ireland does not seem sufficiently motivated if he is greatly in love. He does not absolutely refuse the Irish princess. He hesitates to accept Rymenhild's love when offered. His caution and self-command are almost too great. He is more anxious to receive knighthood and to become a warrior than to be the accepted lover of the royal princess. Yet he is a simple, manly, engaging figure. Rymenhild is equally simple, but her simplicity is that of primitive passion. Passionate love and passionate anger seem to bound her emotional range. The minor characters are barely sketched. Perhaps there is a touch of character contrast in the presentation of Fikenhild and Aþulf, both Horn's companions and subjects, both bound to him by ties of friendship, both receiving knighthood at his hands, but Fikenhild is throughout the type of the unfaithful as Aþulf is the type of the faithful vassal. Other characters are merely conventional figures—the porter, the palmer, Arnoldin, King Modi.

In presenting character, emotion, states of mind, use has been made of dialogue and action. A little is said of personal appearance, there is a hint here and there as to the feelings of the *dramatis personœ*, but these are comparatively unimportant. The dialogue reveals the progress of the love affair. The abundant action, of course, often reveals mood and attitude. Elsewhere all is left to the imagination of reader or hearer—the intention, the state of mind, even the character. The simplicity of character and emotion is emphasized by the sketchy presentation.

Of the human relations involved, only one is treated elaborately—namely, love. This is a human, popular, primitive passion, careless of fashion, free from coquetry, faithful, but without adoration. The woman woos, the man somewhat passively accepts the offered love. The love of comrades, manifested in Horn and Aþulf, while not developed, furnishes an additional interest, opposing the "envy" of Fikenhild, that scarcely understood hatred of the hero which apparently arouses very little resentment on the part of the one who suffers from it. The Saracens, however, arouse fiercer passions, although these are barely suggested. The darker passions remain unelaborated.

Havelok.—In *Havelok* the atmosphere has changed. Not knights, but the folk fill the stage. Havelok is a good servant, can put the stone beyond the farthest, and can break heads with a door-tree. He is good-natured, cautious, simple. There is no hint of passionate love or keen thirst for glory. Grim is a sturdy, loyal fisherman. The more vivid minor characters are fishermen (Grim's children), a cook, an innkeeper. Goldborough is scarcely the sketch of a queenly figure. Aþelwold, a character of some importance, is an ideal king from the point of view of the peaceful, law-abiding middle class. Godrich

and Godard, almost indistinguishable, are typical traitors. There is greater interest in states of mind than in *Horn*. There is greater individuality of character. This seems to be due to a changed point of view, as if the writer were not a minstrel seeing life through the spectacles of a courtly nobility, or even a crude, rough nobility, but some one—a priest, perhaps—who sees life with the eyes of the laborers or tradespeople of provincial England.

Here the author has more to say about his characters—Aþelwold, Havelok, Godard, and others. The soliloquies reveal both character and intention. With less dramatic situation, the dialogue is comparatively unimportant. Action, of course, is important for revealing character, especially as purpose and mood, out of which action arises, are made clear. On the other hand, there is far less passion than in *Horn*, since the situations are so much less vivid and emotionally significant. Character apparently is more consciously in the mind of the author, and is emphasized by the more obvious means—soliloquy, general narrative, and direct statement—but the emotions springing from dramatic situation are neglected.

The field of human relations is again comparatively narrow. Love is almost absent. The relation of subject and king is perhaps most important, exemplified by Grim, Ubbe, and Grim's children, and, negatively, by Godard and Godrich. There is a national outlook absent from *Horn*, not present to an equal degree in *Bevis* and *Guy*. The relation of parent and child is intimately connected with the deaths of Aþelwold and Birkabein. There is a glimpse, too, of the relation of servant and master. However, there is not the dramatic tension of strong passions which makes human relations of great significance for the story. The interest centers largely in the interaction of the hero and his environment—his conduct when famine reduces Grim to poverty, his conduct as the cook's servant, his success in the game of putting the stone, or of breaking heads. The chief emotion of the poem is the sense of triumph felt by the audience as it sympathetically followed the progress of the hero.

Bevis.—In *Bevis*, as in *Horn*, character has little interest for the author. He does not stop to describe character, and seldom to indicate mental states. Yet the main *dramatis personœ* are not unimpressive. We seen somehow to be again in the presence of fierce, primitive people and emotions. Bevis is a fighter, who joys in battle more than in love. He is fierce and even cruel—a stern, irresistible, brutal warrior, whose claim to admiration is unmeasured valor. Josian loves as Rymenhild loved—violently. She does not shrink from inflicting death on a persecutor. Other characters have an equal fierceness, without the redeeming faithfulness. Bevis's mother, the Emperor of Almaine, Ascopard, and most of the Saracens are people to inspire terror. There is not much said of states of mind, but so far as they are not purely conventional romantic material, due to the translator, they have the same fierceness and primitive, quality that mark the entire romance.

Character is presented by means of situation and dialogue. Not much is made of soliloquy. Scarcely anything is said in the way of direct characterization, and not much in regard to emotions. However, the dialogue is sharp and characteristic, and the situations swiftly succeeding one another have a cumulative effect, especially in connection with the impression made by the hero. It may be noted that there is a slightly humorous character in Ascopard.

What was said about human relations in *Horn* may almost be repeated here. There is the unrestrained love of the heroine, faithful and heroic; and there is, too, the lukewarmness of the hero. There is the development of the friendship of fellows-in-arms. There is the same background of Saracens versus Christians, as a basis for hatred and war. There is, however, greater fierceness and cruelty than in *Horn*. We are moving in the atmosphere of unrefined knighthood, of untempered fanaticism, and unbridled brutality, relieved somewhat by faithful love in wife and comrade.

Guy of Warwick.—*Guy* is a long step from **Bevis**. Here chivalry has softened warrior and war. Guy is an irresistible warrior like Bevis, but he is an adoring lover, and becomes a devoted palmer, doing penance for his sins. His character is less simple; he feels the conflict of love and religion; he suffers as well as triumphs. Felice is no Rymenhild, who invites her favorite to her bower that she may throw herself into his arms; she is to be won only after years of ardent seeking and repeated rebuffs. The stage is full of *dramatis personæ*. There is the maiden who plays the foil to Felice. Father and mother of Guy appear, playing natural, human parts. In addition, there is almost a host of *dramatis personæ* who are the conventional knights and kings and giants of romance. A greater elaboration distinguishes the character-material of *Guy* from that of **Bevis**, *Horn,* and *Havelok.*

Likewise more care and more time are devoted to the exposition of character and mental states. There are long soliloquies. Dialogue is sustained. There are definite statements from the author in regard to states of mind. At least one character—the maiden of Felice—is introduced to make feeling and attitude vivid by contrast. The action is very often significant of character. In the attention to character this romance is allied to *Havelok.*

But *Guy* differs very widely from *Havelok* in the field of human life from which character and emotion spring. Love is again of great interest—the love of knight for lady—an adoring, chivalrous love. This love conflicts

with the relation of man and the church, or of man and God, and succumbs to the exalted desire for penitential sacrifice. Thus there is an elevation above the normal emotions of *Horn*, **Bevis** and *Havelok*. There is here, again, the same or greater emphasis on love of comrades. There is a new touch of filial affection. There is a current of patriotism found in *Havelok*, but not in *Horn* and **Bevis**. Thus there is in *Guy* a broadening and heightening of character and feeling.

What remains to be said is merely this. In these four romances there are striking differences and striking resemblances in the treatment of character and emotion. The differences seem to indicate great variation of type. *Horn* is the representative of an undeveloped, unsophisticated, warlike society, and might well be at base a material version of a popular tale which had absorbed romantic motives. *Havelok* is written for and about provincial, lowly or middle class Englishmen. **Bevis** is essentially a *chanson de geste*. Guy is a *chanson de geste* made over into a romance of chivalry. Yet in the very structure of three of these metrical stories is the exile-and-return motive, with the *dramatis personæ* which it implies. Corresponding *dramatis personæ* appear in *Guy*, but belong less closely to the main structure of the romance. Nevertheless, this resemblance of the four romances in respect to *dramatis personæ* and the structure which they imply should not be made too much of in searching for the conditions from which the tales originally sprang. If they once were very similar, they became dissimilar. At least **Bevis** and *Guy* were worked over if not created by Frenchmen and developed into metrical tales of widely different type. But in the English dress in which we are examining them there is no evidence that the English redactors felt very keenly the distinction of types. Stock romantic material is found throughout, especially in *Horn*, in **Bevis**, and in *Guy*. There are the same stock *dramatis personæ*; there are the same stereotyped ways of expressing emotion; there are the same stereotyped phrases in the mouths of *dramatis personæ,* and in the mouths of the authors talking about the *dramatis personæ.* At least the stereotyped phrases are in a large measure the property of English romance, and the freedom with which they are employed everywhere seems to indicate that they were regarded as appropriate for any kind of story, that there was no distinction made between romantic and epic tale. What in France was intended for diverse audiences came in England into the hands of one set of minstrels reciting to one popular and undiscriminating audience, which welcomed a hodgepodge of narrative material that must have been very foreign to their natural interests. I must modify this statement by saying that in *Havelok* we seem to have a truly popular hero, not entirely created in the image of crude or chivalrous knighthood. But he is the exception that proves the rule. It is certainly not in the *dramatis personæ* of English metrical romances that we are to look for a clear image of medieval English life.

Notes

[1] "The Character Types in the Old French Chansons de Geste," *Pub. Mod. Lang. Asso.*, vol. xxi, pp. 279 ff.; "The Heroic Ideal in the French Epic," *Quarterly Review,* April, 1908.

[2] Many suggestions as to method have been obtained from the studies in narrative of Professor W. M. Hart, especially *Ballad and Epic*, Harvard Studies and Notes, vol. xi, Boston, 1907.

[3] References are made to the following editions: *King Horn*, ed. by Joseph Hall, Oxford, 1901; *Havelok the Dane*, ed. by W. W. Skeat, Oxford, 1902; *Bevis of Hamtoun,* ed. by E. Kölbing, E. E. Text Soc., Ex. Ser. xlvi, xlviii, lxv, London, 1885-1894; *Guy of Warwick,* Auchinleck and Caius Mss., ed. by J. Zupitza, E.E.T.S. Ex. Ser. xlii, xlix, lix, London, 1883-1891.

[4] Leo Jordan, *Über Boeve de Hanstone*, Beihefte zur *Zeitschrift für rom. Phil.* (xiv, Halle, 1908), pp. 41 f.; gives a list of *dramatis personæ* in French exile stories which is not quite the same as the one above. However, it is interesting as showing that practically this same group of characters appears in a number of *chansons de geste.* Among the English romances, *Generydes* furnishes the list of *dramatis personæ* most nearly parallel.

[5] Not counting Aþelwold, the father of a heroine.

[6] In *King Horn* it is not actually stated that Reynild loves Horn, though marriage is suggested to Horn by her father. However, in *Horn et Rimel* and *Horn Childe,* the love of Lembure and Acula (corresponding to Reynild) is a prominent feature.

[7] Nevertheless, cf. P. C. Hoyt, "The Home of the Beves Saga," *P.M.L.A.*, 1902, pp. 237 ff., who thinks the resemblance between *Bevis* and *Horn* sufficient to indicate that the former is derived from the latter.

[8] In *Horn Childe* the porter's shoulder bone was broken (HCh vv. 958 ff.).

[9] In *John de Reeue* (Percy Folio, vol. II), vv. 719 ff., is a similar dispute between hero and porter, with the result that John

> "hitt the porter vpon the crowne,
> With that stroke hee ffel downe,
> fforsooth as I you tell."

In *Sir Cleges* the hero gains admission to the king by agreeing to give the porter one-third of the gift he shall receive, and asks that the gift be twelve strokes, of which the porter gets his share in due time (vv. 247 ff.). Cf. Kölbing's note to *Bevis*, A 1. 419. Also see Hall's note to *Horn*, vv. 1067, 8; *Tristram*, vv. 619 ff.; Gautier, *Chivalry*, Eng. transl. by Henry Frith, London, 1891, pp. 369 ff.; C. Boje, *Über den Altfranzösischen Roman von Beuve de Hamtone*, Beihefte zur *Zeitschrift für rom. Phil.*, xix, Halle, 1909, pp. 71 f. The porter sometimes plays a different part; cf. *Gawayn and the Grene Knyght*, vv. 91 ff., and *Floris and Blancheflor*, vv. 749 ff.

[10] As in *Sir Cleges*; cf. note preceding.

[11] Cf. *Generydes*, vv. 4630 ff., where the maid takes the part of the knight against the reproaches of her mistress.

[12] Edited by Brede and Stengel, *Das Anglo-Normannische Lied vom Wackern Ritter Horn,* Ausgaben und Abhandlungen, vol. viii.

[13] From these instances it is evident that the maid plays in medieval romantic literature the same part which maid or attendant so often plays in the later dramatic literature.

[14] Referred to above, p. 436.

[15] For Kay at his worst, cf. the French romance *Ider,* in which he is guilty of the use of poison. See, too, G. Paris, in *Hist. Litt., XXXI*, p. 160, apropos of Kay in the *Escanor* of Girard d'Amiens: "Il parait avoir pris surtout le type du senechal dans les romans de Chrétien où, comme ici, sa mauvaise langue est le plus grave de ses defauts."

[16] Cf. *Arthur and Merlin*, vv. 80 ff.; *Squire of Low Degree*, vv. 283 ff., etc.; *Sir Triamore*, vv. 61 ff., etc.; *Merline*, vv. 47 ff.; *Amis and Amiloun*, vv. 205 ff.; *Sir Degrevant*, vv. 1633 ff.; also *"ffalse- steward"* in "Sir Aldingar" (Child, No. 59).

[17] Of course there are good stewards now and then, as is the case with Guy's father. However, the association of steward with self-seeking and an ugly disposition seems widespread. In this connection it is interesting to compare No. LXII of the *Fables* of Marie de France (ed. by Warnke, Bibliotheca Normannica, vol. VI), "De Aquila et Accipitre et Columbis".

[18] For cases in French medieval narrative where there is an exchange of clothing with a palmer, cf. Boje, p. 70.

[19] Cf. Prologue to "Man of Law's Tale" (*Cant. Tales*, B, vv. 127 ff.), where merchants are apostrophized:

Ye seken lond and see for yowre wynnynges;
As wise folk ye knowen al thestaat
Of regnes; ye been fadres of tidynges
And tales, bothe of pees and of debaat,
I were right now of tales desolaat,
Nere that a marchant—goon is many a yeere—
Me taughte a tale, which that ye shal heere.

[20] Two giants, brothers, whom the hero meets at different times and slays, seem a convention; cf. in *Bevis* Grander and his brother (vv. 1721 ff.; 1859 ff.); *Eglamore*, vv. 300 ff., 513 ff.; *Daurel* (*Hist. Litt.*, XXX, p. 137).

[21] This suggests the "s waes g d cyning" of *Beowulf*, although the term "good" is perhaps even more conventional in the romances.

[22] The very enumeration of the classes who loved him is suggestive.

It was a king bi are dawes,
þat in his time were gode lawes
He dede maken, an ful wel holden;
Hym louede yung, him louede holde,
Erl and barun, dreng and kayn,
Knict, bondeman, and swain,
Wydues, maydnes, prestes and clerkes,
And al for hise gode werkes.

(vv. 27 ff.)

[23] W. W. Comfort, "The Character Types in the old French *Chansons de Geste*", P.M.L.A., XXI, pp. 279 ff., distinguishes three treatments of the king in the *chanson de geste*. He is represented (1) as grandiose and epic, less only than God; (2) as weak, old, sometimes cowardly; (3) as a mere political necessity—this last under the influence of the Breton cycle where the king is only "a fixed point of support, on which the leading characters in the story are made to lean". The noble king of *Havelok* seems English. However, the weakness of the kings in *Horn*, *Bevis*, and *Guy* seems to relate them to class (2). The Emperor of Almaine (in *Guy*) is clearly of this class; his capture while on the chase is an incident connecting him with stories of Charlemagne.

It may be worth while to note here that both Bevis and Guy had fathers who were good stewards. They furnish the nearest parallels to the account of Aþelwold. Bevis's father Guy "kept well Englond in his days".

He set peas and stabelud the laws,
þat no man was so hardye,
To do another velanye.

(M. MS. vv. 43 ff.; passage missing from one set of **Bevis** MSS.)

In *Guy*, Syward was a steward of similar virtues.

þei a man bar an hundred pounde,
Opon him, of gold y-grounde
þer nas man in al þis londe
þat durst him do schame no schonde
þat bireft him worþ of a slo,
So gode pais þer was þo.

(vv. 137 ff.)

In Aþelwold's time one could carry red gold upon his back and find none to trouble him (*Havelok*, vv. 45 ff.).

If one thinks of Chrétien's romances, one recognizes how incongruous similar lines would appear if found in them. The same is equally true of nearly all of the super-refined chivalric romances. Compare, too, the Alexander romances. Generosity, not justice, is the chief virtue of the chivalric king.

[24] For numerous parallels, see Hall's notes. Medieval romancers were inclined to insist, as here, that their heroes were the most beautiful in the world; cf. *William of Palerne*, vv. 4437 f.

[25] The shining face is common, but more frequently belongs to women. In Chrétien's *Cliges* the hero and Fenice are so beautiful that they make the palace shine (vv. 2755 ff.).

[26] It is worth noticing here that something is said in regard to Guy's dress apart from armour; when he first calls on Felice he was arrayed in a "silken kirtell" that was so "well setting" that there was no need to amend it (vv. 211 ff.).

[27] Cf. W. W. Comfort, P.M.L.A., XXI, pp. 307 ff. on the Hero in the *chansons de geste*. See p. 325 for distinction between hero of earlier and later *chansons de geste*: "If any differentiation were attempted between the heroes of the earlier and those of the later poems, it would consist in this: the heroes of the later poems are less passionate, less flery, less implacable; they feel the softening influence of woman and of many of the principles of Christian charity which the later Middle Age included in the terms *chevalerie* and *courtoisie*." A comparison in these respects of *Bevis* and with *Guy* is suggestive. But even in the latest *chansons de geste*, according to Comfort, there remains in the hero "an unmistakable trace of his genealogical connection with the paladins of Charlemagne. In spite of his love adventures, and the lorn maidens, and the kind fairies, his mind harks back to his old-time foe, the Saracens, and to his duty to God. If we are not mistaken, this undercurrent of sturdy faith, this seriousness of purpose, was just the quality which was sought by a portion of the public as contrasted to the

more imaginative, fantastic, and *vain* heroes of the Breton cycle."

[28] As an instructive contrast, an examination of this same character elsewhere is valuable. In *Horn Childe* (the later English version) and *Horn et Rimel* she has lost her primitive traits. She is not wholly passionate; she devises plans. In HCh

> þe miri maiden hir bithouyt
> In what maner þat sche mouyt
> Trewe love for to ginne.

(vv. 364 ff.)

She wins Horn's favor first by costly gifts. Even more striking is the equanimity with which she learns of the deceit which the steward has practised in substituting Haþerof for Horn (vv. 349 ff.). The heroine of HR is also a highly developed character, eager, it is true, but not merely impulsive.

[29] Apparently of the same type, but interesting as tending away from it, is Melior, the heroine of *William of Palerne*. After falling in love with William, who apparently is somewhat mildly attached to her, she analyzes her feelings in a fashion which Josian and Rymenhild would never dream of. Yet she is the really active one of the pair; is the pursuer rather than the pursued indeed, acting, however, through her maid Alexandrine. William's love, it seems, becomes really passionate as the result of a dream which Alexandrine, by some magic power, introduces into his mind while he sleeps. Even then he merely stops eating, makes no effort to win the beloved; who comes to him while he is asleep in a garden. This figure is so much sophisticated as to seem considerably removed from Rymenhild and Josian. Yet she is not much farther removed from the type than is Rimel of *Horn et Rimel*.

[30] In the Celtic romances elaborate descriptions of dress as well as personal beauty are found. Cf. *Libeaus Desconus*, vv. 868 ff.; *Launfal*, vv. 926 ff. The brightness of the woman's face is characteristic. In *Richard Coer de Lion* a lady is "bryght as the sunne thorugh the glas" (v. 76); Cf. *Legend of Good Women*, Prologue B, vv. 232 f., *Le Bone Florence of Rome*, vv. 184 ff.; also the ballad "Lamkin" (Child No. 93), in which the head of a murdered woman, hung in the kitchen, makes the hall shine. On the personal appearance of women of chansons de geste, cf. Gautier, *Chivalry*, pp. 306 f.

[31] Josian was educated in "fysik and sirgerie" and "knew erbes mani and fale", by the use of one of which she was able to make herself undesirable. This accomplishment is hardly comparable to the learning of Felice. The manner of its introduction is also significant, as it is told merely to account for Josian's ability to pick

out the right herb. Knowledge of herbs, however, was not an unusual accomplishment and seems connected with skill in leechcraft. Acula, in HCh (vv. 790 ff.) and Gouernail in *Tristrem* (vv. 1200 ff.) are instances. This accomplishment is in no sense characteristic of the romance of chivalry, but is rather a popular element which survives in the romances.

[32] On frankness of speech and other characteristics of women of the *chansons de geste*, cf. Gautier, *Chivalry*, pp. 308 ff., and Comfort, *op. cit.*, pp. 359 ff. See discussion of love, pp.

[33] Cf. Comfort, *op. cit.*, pp. 307 ff., on the relations of vassal and lord in the *chansons de geste*.

[34] However, the companions of Horn are not named. In HCh, where less is made of minor characters than in HR, the companions are named and carefully disposed of. The twelve companions may be faintly reminiscent of the twelve peers of Charlemagne, who, in turn, go back to the twelve apostles; cf. Gautier, *Les Epopées* (1st ed.), I, pp. 173 ff.

[35] As comedy is rather rare in the romances, it seems worth while to enter into this feature in somewhat greater detail. Perhaps the chief comic scene in the romance is the one of the baptism of Ascopard.

> For Ascopard was mad a koue;
> When þe beschop him scholde in schoue,
> A lep anon vpon þe benche
> And seide: "Prest, wiltow me drenche?
> þe deuil þeue me helle pine,
> Icham to meche te be christine!"

(vv. 2591 ff.)

The incident of the dragon fight has also its comic opportunity. Bevis and Ascopard arrive in the neighborhood of the dragon, when

> Ascopard swore, be sein Ion
> A fote ne dorste he forther gon.
> Beues answerde and seide po:
> "Ascopard, whi seistow so?
> Whi schelt pow afered be
> Of ping pat pow miyt nouyt sen?"
> A swor, alse he moste pen,
> He nolde him neiper hire ne sen;
> "Icham weri, ich mot haue reste;
> Go now forp and do pe beste!"

(vv. 2747 ff.)

The "Icham weri, ich mot haue reste", coming from the mouth of the giant who carried the horse Arondel in his arm (v. 2564), in itself no doubt amusing to the medieval audience, must surely have raised a laugh.

Thus, slightly as the character of Ascopard is developed on the humorous side, and dangerous as he proved to be, here is a clear case of the introduction of a character with whom amusing incidents may naturally be connected.

Comic characters like Ascopard are found in a highly developed state in certain *chansons de geste*. Cf. W. W. Comfort, *op. cit.*, section entitled "Bourgeois and Vilain", pp. 279 ff. For other comic baptismal scenes see *Ferumbras*, vv. 5715 ff., and the *chanson de geste Aliscans*.

[36] That the scribes did not keep the *dramatis personœ* clearly in mind is evidenced by curious blunders. Thus Clarice, the daughter of the Emperor of Constantinople, is called "Blauncheflour" in both the Auchinleck and Caius MSS. at one point (v. 4497). Again, in a battle with the Saracens, the King of Nubia, after being struck down by Guy, immediately afterward is summoned by the Sultan to attack the Christians (v. 3506 ff.). This is only in the Auchinleck MS.; in the Caius MS. it is the King of Armenia whom the Sultan sends against the Christians, which, no doubt, is the correct reading.

[37] There are 137 lines in the poem, including the prayer of Havelok at Grimsby (vv. 1359 ff.), which possess the nature of soliloquy. An excellent example is the soliloquy in which Havelok determines that he must "swinken" for his "mete" (vv. 790 ff.).

[38] Cf. vv. 73 ff., 283 ff., 394 ff., 421 ff., etc.

[39] The second interview of Guy and Felice fills one hundred lines, and there is real progression, giving a clear view of the characters of the principal actors.

[40] Cf. Hart, *Ballad and Epic*, p. 56.

[41] With *King Horn* should be compared *Horn et Rimel*, the author of which shows decided interest in mental states. As has been stated, Herselote's importance lies in her part as Rimel's confidante. Rodmund can hardly decide on the fate of Horn and his companions. Rimel's impatience and anxiety to obtain an interview with Horn appear when she sends for the seneschal.

> Ele demaunde souvent dan Herlant quant
>   vendra.
>
>   (v. 529)

She gazes in her mirror and inquires anxiously as to her appearance (vv. 526 ff.). Herlant's mental distress at Rimel's request to see Horn, his sleeplessness, his arguments with himself, are related in detail (vv. 662 ff.). The scene in Rimel's chamber when Haperof is trying to convince Rimel that he is not Horn but is unable to do so, presents an interesting psychological situation. This interest in emotional states is prominent throughout the romance, and the length of this redaction is largely due to this characteristic.

[42] It may be noted that little is said about the heroine's feelings, as contrasted with *Horn et Rimel*, for instance, where there is a pretty thorough study made of the feelings of Rimel, much more subtle indeed than the study of the lover's feelings in *Guy*.

[43] Caius MS. only, v. 4013.

[44] See Hall's note to this line, Breul's note to *Gowther*, v. 546, and Schmirgel's list of stereotyped phrases in Bevis (in the Introduction to Kölbing's edition), p. XLVI.

[45] Kölbing says no parallels found.

[46] See Schmirgel for additional parallels, p. XLV.

[47] Sir Cleges (v. 90 of the romance so named) swoons from thinking of his misfortunes. In *William of Palerne* the Emperor swoons six times "for sorwe & for schame" when William elopes with Melior (v. 2098); in Chaucer's *Legend of Good Women* (v. 1342) Dido swoons twenty times (but this is hardly meant to be exact). Charlemagne and his hundred thousand followers faint for grief at the death of Roland (*Chanson de Roland*, v. 2916); in *Renaud de Montauban* the four sons of Aymon faint on seeing their paternal castle after an absence (Gautier, 1st ed., II, p. 192).

[48] Additional proof of conventionality of these and many other expressions may be obtained by consulting Schmirgel's list of typical phrases in the introduction to Kölbing's *Bevis*, the introduction to Zielke's edition of *Sir Orfeo*, as well as the notes to Kölbing's *Bevis*, Zupitza's *Guy of Warwick*, Hall's *Horn*, etc.

[49] Fainting, weeping, and tearing of the hair apparently run through medieval narrative literature. In the *roman d'aventure* the most violent grief is for unsuccessful love, in the *chanson de geste* for loss of comrades, although exceptions to this rule may be found. Sickness resulting from love is of course a strictly romantic feature. With Guy's illness may be compared the "fever" of Troilus in *Troilus and Criseyde*, v. 491. Fainting seems to have been almost a necessary part of romantic courtship. In the French *Amados & Ydoine* (cf. *Hist. Litt.*, XXII, p. 761) the scornful lady is won by the hero's fainting in her presence. In the *chanson* the fainting is more likely to be on the lady's side. In *Enfances Guillaume* when Orable, the Saracen maiden, is hearing from her brother an account of the beauty of Guillaume, whom she has never seen, she says she will faint if he says another word (Gautier, 2nd ed., IV, p. 297).

[50] A comparison of *Bevis* with the Old French *Boeve de Haumtone* (ed. by Stimming, Bib. Normannica, Halle, 1899), which represents pretty closely the version which the English translator had before him shows very few cases of parallclism of emotional expression.

[51] The love in *William of Palerne* is not quite of the *chanson de geste* type. But in *Amis and Amiloun* it very clearly is. Belisaunt threatens Amis with death if he does not accept her love (*Am. and Amiloun*, vv. 625 ff.). *Octavian* (S. Eng. version), vv. 1201 ff., tells of a Saracen maid loving a Christian knight, who makes advances to him and finally becomes a Christian.

[52] More than twenty girls go to the beds of knights in *chansons de geste*, according to Gautier 1st ed., I, p. 478.

[53] Cf. the English *Sir Ferumbras*, vv. 5763 ff. In this case Floripas, who has been converted, seems fired with religious zeal.

[54] Cf. the conduct of Charlemagne's queen Galienne in *Garin de Monglane* (Gautier, 2nd ed., IV, pp. 138 ff.). Three maidens seek Garin's love in *Enfances de Garin* (Gautier, IV, pp. 115 ff.). Even the *chanson de geste* hero wearies of the boldness of the women; cf. complaint of Girars de Viane, mentioned by Gautier, 1st ed., II, p. 90.

[55] Usually sexual relations with an unconverted Saracen woman were strongly condemned. Cf. *Merline* (Percy Folio, I, vv. 410 ff.):

> King Anguis had verament
> a daughter that was faire & gent,
> that was heathen Saracen;
> & Vortiger for loue fine
> vndertooke her for his wiffe,
> & liued in cursing all his life.

[56] Good summaries of several romances of this type may be found in Langlois, *Société Française au XIIIe Siècle D'après dix Romans d'Aventure* (Paris, 1904); cf. *Le Chatelaine de Couci*, for example.

[57] Even in war there was less consideration for Saracens than for Christian enemies; a twelfth century church council forbade the use of the crossbow against *Christian* enemies.

[58] Fikenhild hi dude todraþe (*Horn*, v. 1492).

[59] Possibly stepbrother?

[60] It is interesting to note that in *Ponthus and Sidone* the reunion of mother and son is elaborated and made the basis of pathetic appeal.

[61] The relation of father and son is more important in some romances; cf. *Generydes, Perceval, Libeaus Desconus*.

[62] Numerous references to the relationship are of course found; cf. Oliver and Aude, Percevale and his sister. But it is not made the basis of emotional appeal to any great extent.

Laura A. Hibbard (essay date 1911)

SOURCE: An introduction in *Three Middle English Romances*, David Nutt, 1911, pp. 1-2.

[*In the following excerpt, Hibbard alludes briefly to Bevis's genre classification, possible origins, metrical schemes, and wide popularity.*]

. . . *Beves of Hampton* differs materially from both *Horn* and *Havelok*. Although originally, perhaps, a viking tale of the tenth century,[16] in its extant forms it is a typical romance of adventure. There is no notably English feature in it save a few place-names and the obviously late addition telling of Beves's fight with the London citizens.[17] It would seem, rather, that Beves was an international character. Five versions of his story in French, six in Italian, others in Scandinavian, Dutch, and Welsh, attest his popularity; in Russia 'he was the most acclimated hero of the chivalric epic.'[18] The wide wandering of his story was like his own fabled adventurings, from England to Africa, and up and down the length and breadth of Europe.

Like a rolling ball it seems to have gathered up widely divergent motives and incidents, and in itself aptly illustrates the catholicity of mediaeval taste. There is scarcely an incident in it that may not be paralleled in some one of such famous romances as *Guy of Warwick* or *Lancelot de Lake*, which it mentions by name, or in *Tristram, William of Palerne*, or *Ferumbras*. Much of the phraseology is the stock-in-trade sort, long tried and dear to the children-like lovers of mediaeval story.[19] Traces of Germanic folk lore are found in the animal fights, and other motives suggest Greek,[20] Persian, Middle High German, and old French stories.[21] The influence of the Crusades is evident in the importance of Saracen conquest, and the belligerency of a militant age reveals itself in the detailed account of four single combats and five pitched battles. The romantic element is enlivened, as in most cases where Crusading influence entered in, by spirited wooing on the part of the young Saracen heroine; and the supernatural, through magic rings and herbs of healing, lends the ever delightful touch of mystery. Finally, the bourgeois element, indicative of the passing of romance from courtly lips and courtly audience, adds its touch of real and simple life. Like any little lad of a village house-wife, Beves is taken by the ear; he is a rude and awkward lover; Josian, in a scene like that of Brunhild in the *Nibelungenlied*, over which 'one can hear the old-time audience chuckling,' hangs her unwelcome husband on the wall; and Ascopard's attempted baptism is a scene of pure burlesque comedy.

From all this, then, it may be concluded that the author of **Beves** was of different character and purpose from those who wrote *Horn* and *Havelok*. These stories have in them more clearly the sound of the minstrel's voice; they were better, probably, in the telling than in the writing, but in **Beves** one feels a clerkly, fourteenth-century scribe at work. Though possibly inspired by local pride, for his Southern dialect would indicate a home in the neighbourhood of Southampton,[22] he wrote down no native English 'song,' but followed a French original, deviating from it only in the way of expanded detail and such additions as a typical dragon fight or a battle, which seemed to him necessary ingredients in the ample proportions of romance. He knew his 'olde bokes' and made industrious, generous use of them. The result is a tale of 4620 verses, interesting enough as a kind of summary of popular mediaeval motives, but well open to the elvish ridicule of a Chaucer, who jeers at such long-winded 'merriness' and solemnly parodies from it most of the metre of his *Sir Thopas*. The two entirely different metres of **Beves**, the tail-rhymed six-line stanzas of the first 474 lines, the short rhyming couplet of the remainder, may, perhaps, be explained by that lack of decisive literary consciousness which distinguishes the imitators from the originators of a popular literary fashion. In **Beves**, despite the old-fashioned, undying charm of a story for the story's sake, one may see clearly the forces that brought about the degeneracy of metrical romance.

Notes

. . . [16] Suchier, H., 'Bibliothethaca Normannica' VII. cxcv, 1899. But see also Leo Jordan, 'Uber Boeve de Hamtone,' p. 59, Halle, 1908, or R. Zenker, 'Das altfranzosische Epos von Boeve de Hamtone und der Ursprung de Hamlet Sage.' *Literarhistorischen Forschungen*, Band XXXII: Berlin, 1909.

[17] 'Beves of Hamtoun,' ed. E. Kolbing, p. xxxiv: E.E.T.S., 1894.

[18] Wasselofsky, A., Materiaux et Recherches pour servir a l'Histoire du Roman et de la Novelle, Tome III, 229-305. Reviewed in *Romania* XVIII, 313.

[19] Schmirgel, C. 'Typical Expression and Repetitions in "Sir Beves of Hamtoun," ' Kolbing's edition, p. xlv.

[20] Zenker, pp. 318, 398.

[21] Deutschbein, [M., 'Studien zur Sagengeschichte

Englands, Horn, Havelok, Tristram, Boeve, Guy'], pp. 194, 211 [Cöthen, 1906].

[22] 'Beves,' ed. Kölbing, p. xxv.

Laura A. Hibbard (essay date 1924)

SOURCE: "*Beves of Hampton*" in *Medieval Romance in England*, Oxford University Press, 1924, pp. 115-26, 321-26.

[*In the essay below, Hibbard offers an overview of nineteenth- and early-twentieth-century scholarship regarding the oldest versions, the sources, and the composition date of* Bevis of Hampton.]

Versions. The hero who bears the name of Beves of Hampton (Boeve de Hamptone, Hanstone) might well be described as an international character. The wide wandering of his story was like his own fabled adventuring from Hampton to Damascus. Versions in English, Welsh, Irish, French, Dutch, Scandinavian, Italian, attest the popularity of him who became even in Russia the most acclimated hero of the chivalric epic (Wesselofsky; cf. *Rom.* XVIII, 313). The story of the loss and recovery of his inheritance, his fights with Saracens and dragons, his marriage with a converted princess, his gaining of innumerable possessions, is distinctive chiefly for its amazing absorption of familiar *motifs* and for its blending of elements drawn from romance, fairy tale, saint legend, and heroic epic. Few stories better illustrate the catholicity of mediæval taste; and in this, perhaps, lay the secret of an influence which may be traced, not only through the wealth of manuscript material but through many literary allusions to the poem and through the representation of its incidents in different artistic forms.[1]

The length, the number, and the variety of the vernacular versions of **Beves** make the problem of their classification extremely difficult. Since the publication in 1899 of Stimming's edition of the Anglo-Norman version of **Beves**, the story has been the subject of many elaborate investigations, but for the purpose of enumeration it is convenient to disregard the maze of controversy and to note as the three principal versions the Anglo-French (*AF*), the Continental French (*CF*), and the Italian (Matzke, *Mod. Phil.* x, 20).

The first group, as Stimming made clear, has four branches, a thirteenth-century Anglo-Norman poem extant in two long supplementary fragments (ed. Stimming, 1899), a fourteenth-century prose version in Norse (ed. Cederschiöld, 1884), another of the thirteenth-century in Welsh (R. Williams, 1892), and one in Middle English verse (ed. Kölbing). The last, in the Auchinleck manuscript, has the first 474 verses in a six-line stanza and the remaining 4146 lines in short couplets. The popularity of the version, belonging originally, it would seem, to the south of England (Kölbing, XIII ff.), is attested by the six existing texts and by the six which Kölbing assumed as antecedent in order to explain the extant readings. These six manuscripts fall into two classes (A and SN; Mo-ME-C), in which the earliest, the (A)Auchinleck manuscript, is less near to the lost thirteenth-century Middle English original than is the fifteenth-century (M) Manchester manuscript, or even Pynson's old print. This original, from which the later manuscripts take over numerous references to a French original, was, in Stimming's opinion, derived from a lost Anglo-Norman version (x), the source also, through various lost intermediaries, of the extant Anglo-Norman and Welsh texts, and of the Norse account. The Middle English poet seems to have shortened his original at will, to have elaborated certain episodes, and to have made three important additions: (1) the account of Beves's first battle fought on Christmas day for the honor of God; (2) his great fight with the dragon of Cologne, an episode which suggests to the poet comparison of his hero with Lancelot, Wade, and Guy of Warwick; and (3) the heroic defense made by Beves and his sons against the London citizens when they are roused against him by the accusation that Beves has killed the king's son, a scene graphic enough to suggest some contemporary riot. Despite its prolixity and its constant borrowings from the commonplaces of Middle English romantic diction, which Schmirgel pointed out in Kölbing's edition, (pp. xlv-lxvi), the poem has a certain vigor of its own. Its popularity with a mediæval audience is not to be wondered at, nor is it strange that the traditional delight in this hero persisted even in the Elizabethan period.[2] An instance of the foreign interest in the Middle English *Beves* is a fifteenth-century Irish translation (ed. Robinson).

The Anglo-Norman (AF) text is generally thought to represent an independent version of the same story as that told by the continental French texts. Of these, nine manuscripts in verse and two in prose are now known. They fall apparently into three groups. The first is represented by the thirteenth-century Paris manuscript (P¹) published by Stimming in 1911. This version, Behrens (p. 77) believed, originated between 1230 and 1250, on the southern borders of Picardy. The second version, represented by an inedited and incomplete manuscript in Rome (R), another (W) of the fifteenth century in Vienna, and by another thirteenth-century Paris manuscript (ed. Stimming, 1913), was thought by Oeckel (p. 78) and Meiners (p. 239) to have been by the scribe, Pierot du Ries. The possibility that Pierot might have been the author was dismissed by Stimming (2, p. 4, 200). This version tends constantly to amplify the original by new episodes and so much delights in ecclesiastical detail that its author was presumably of the clergy. "Lokal patriotismus," however, gives now and then a secular touch to his story. The third group comprises the *Beves* texts of the thirteenth and the

fourteenth centuries found in manuscripts at Carpentras (C), Turin (T), and Venice (V); and finally a fragment now at Modena (Wolff and Paetz). Of these continental texts Boje (pp. 136-37) believed the oldest and truest form to be represented by the Rome and Paris manuscripts of the second group, and the original text to be the work of one man only. As a whole this continental French version is somewhat longer than *AF*, and, unlike it, places the hero's home on Gallic soil and names his stepfather Doon de Mayence. In the *AF* version Doon is Emperor of Almayn, and Beves's home is at Littlehampton (Hampton-sur-Mer, v. 2811), not more than two and one half miles from Arundel, the city named, according to the English romance, in honor of the race won by Arundel, Beves's famous horse. Finally it may be noted that the two fifteenth-century French prose versions of *Beves* and the five known sixteenth-century editions belong to the same redaction as the manuscripts P, R, W (Boje, p. 13).

The Italian version is preserved in at least six texts, of which the earliest is the fragmentary thirteenth-century Venetian manuscript (ed. Reinhold). The only complete form is the *Buova d'Antona* in the *Reali di Francia*, a late fifteenth-century composite which draws on the French as well as the Italian versions. The Italian version is shorter than the French; it differs in names and in sequence of events; and is, in the opinion of Rajna (*Ricerche intorno ai Reali di Francia*, pp. 135-40, Milan, 1872), of Jordan, and Matzke (3, p. 32), the prior form "independently transmitted from the original version of which the common source of *AF* and *CF* is another offspring."

Of the later popular versions of *Beves*, the first Dutch edition, printed at Antwerp, 1504, was derived from the *CF* version; and the sixteenth-century Russian and Jewish folk-books were from the Italian (Wesselofsky, *Rom.* XVIII, 302-14, 1889). In 1881 the Italian was translated into Roumanian (Groeber, 1901, 11, 3, 386). The fullest account of these and all the other versions is given by Boje (pp. 1-13).

The influence of *Beves* has been traced in the Middle High German poem, *Graf Rudolph* (cf. Bethmann, *Palæstra*, XXX; Deutschbein, p. 191), but the similar scenes are of the fairly conventional type concerning a Christian hero and a heathen princess. The Provençal poem, *Daurel et Beton* (ed. P. Meyer, Paris, 1880), is in part clearly a sequel to *Beves* (Jordan, 1, 102). Brockstedt's account (pp. 96-103) of this relationship is more convincing than his idea that the *Siegfriedlied* and the *Nibelungenlied* are variations of the Anglo-Norman *Beves*. The forest death of Beves's father, Beves's fight with the dragon of Cologne, and the bridal of Josian with Earl Miles, are in truth analogous to scenes in the German poems, but the inference made from the resemblance is over-large. Boje (p. 137) believed that the influence of the French forms of *Beves* was to be clearly traced in certain incidents in five poems; in *Florent et Octavian* (*Hist. Litt.*, XXVI, 316), in *Parise et Vienne* (*Rom. Forsh.*, XV, 1904), in *Ciperis* (*Hist. Litt.,* XXVI, 31), in *Valentin u. Namelos* (ed. Seelmann, 1884, p. 68) and, most interesting of all, in *Aucassin* (ed. Suchier), in the episode in which the heroine, disguised as a maiden minstrel, goes in search of her lost lover. On the whole, however, the influence of **Beves** is best attested by the long line of its own self-perpetuating versions.

Origin. **Beves of Hampton** is a typical *roman d'aventure* which moves within a certain "Ideenkreis" of a well-defined character. In his comparison of it with one hundred and eighty-seven Old French romances Boje distinguished the following characteristic details and incidents: the forest hunt, p. 62; the murder of Beves's father, the marriage of his mother with her husband's murderer, the stepfather's hostility to Beves, pp. 62-64; the disguise of Beves, coloring his face, p. 67, etc., to save his life; the exhibition of his blood-stained clothes as a proof of death, p. 66; the rude porter, p. 71; the feast broken up by a tumult, p. 66; the selling of the boy and his stay at the court of a foreign king, the love for him of the Saracen princess, the defeat through Beves of her cruel suitor, the false accusation brought against the lovers, the letter of death carried by Beves to a heathen king, pp. 74-80; the overthrow of the idols by Beves, p. 82; his imprisonment in Damascus, his escape and the vain pursuit, pp. 91-100; the beating of the idols by the heathen king, p. 100; Josian's forced marriage and the magic protection of her virginity, p. 106; Beves's disguise as a palmer and his horse's recognition of his master, pp. 108-09; the drugging of Josian's guard, p. 112; the elopement of the lovers, pp. 109-12; the grotesque giant Escopart and his comic baptism, pp. 113-14; Josian's second forced marriage, the killing of her husband, and Beves's rescue of Josian from the stake, pp. 115-17; Beves's homecoming, the rage of the usurper who throws a knife at the messenger, p. 90; the overthrow of the usurper by Beves in battle or by a judicial combat, pp. 82-88; the great race won by Beves's horse, p. 118; the horse theft attempted by the king's son, p. 131; the killing of the king's son, pp. 120-23; the second exile of Beves, the forest birth of Josian's twin sons, the separation of the family, pp. 123-24; Beves's nominal marriage with another lady, Josian's disguise as a minstrel, her search for her lost love, the recognition and reunion of husband and wife, pp. 128-31; the old age of Beves, the angelic warning and his death, pp. 132-33.

As no text of **Beves** antedates the thirteenth century, as linguistic studies, no less than a literary study of *motifs* such as Boje's, suggest nothing antecedent to 1200, it is probable that the original poem was not composed before that date. But numerous attempts have been made to find in the extant versions the signs of much more ancient origin. Suchier's belief (1, p. cxcv) based on the evidence of such names as Ivor, Bradmund, Rudefoun, etc., that the poem was basically a Viking saga, may be offset by reference to Langlois's *Tables des noms propres dans les chansons de geste*, Paris, 1904, from which it appears that these names appear in Old French poems for which no Viking origin can possibly be alleged. Deutschbein (p. 198) sought to connect the story with certain historical German antecedents and suggested identification of Doon, represented in **Beves** as the Emperor of Almayne who murders Beves's father in the forest in order to marry his mother, with Otto (Odon) the Great (929-947) who exiled his step-son, Duke Ernst of Swabia, or with the father of Ernst II of Swabia who was killed on a hunt and whose son revolted against his step-father, the Emperor Conrad II. Boje (pp. 62 ff.), however, proved the essentially literary character of this introductory part of the romance.

The question of origin has been constantly associated with the localization of the story. The apparently ample evidence of English place-names,[3] which led Stimming (pp. 183-85) to believe the poem of Anglo-Norman origin, has been brought into dispute by the contention that the Italian version, in which the English are supplanted by Continental names, is representative of the oldest and most authoritative version. Rajna in 1872 was one of the first to point out in his studies on the *Reali di Francia* that Hamtone or Hanstone might better be identified with Hunstein or Hammerstein on the Rhine than with Southampton, and others have stressed the importance of the clearly non-English elements in the romance. Nevertheless, Matzke, who did most to establish the independent value of the Italian version, thought (*Mod. Phil.*, X, 54) the question of insular or continental origin still an open one. Less cautious scholars, by considering limited portions of the story in the AF or CF group, which they take to represent the original nucleus of the story, have arrived at interestingly varied opinions. Settegast (pp. 282, 383) derived the history of Beves's first exile from an Armenian tale in which a king was killed on a hunting expedition, the throne was seized by an usurper and a young prince, the true heir, escaped in disguise as a shepherd boy. By the most dubious sort of etymology (p. 354) the names in this tale were made in some instances to coincide with those in **Beves**, and so made to argue an eastern origin for the romance. Deutschbein (p. 182), emphasizing different elements in this same part of **Beves**, the ill treatment of the boy by his relatives, the feast which he breaks up by shaming his enemy, was reminded of Karl Mainet and of an episode in *Jourdain de Blaivies*. The account of Beves's relations with his royal step-father still further suggested (p. 198) the twelfth-century German poem, *Herzog Ernst*, (ed. Bartsch, 1869), which relates the adventures of Ernst of Swabia, traditionally the rebellious stepson of Otto the Great. In *Graf Rudolph*, c. 1170 (Palœstra XXX) the eastern adventures of the hero, his escape from prison, his rescue of his beloved from a forced marriage, parallel to some degree similar incidents in **Beves**. These stories of Mainet and Ernst and Rudolph, which were known in their earliest versions in the district between Flanders and Picardy, were supposed by Deutschbein (p. 204) to have been carried to England by Flemish colonists who settled in Pembrokeshire in the neighborhood of Haverford (Aberford, in *AN. Beves*). There the stories were localized, and to some extent, perhaps, influenced by tales of the *Horn* type. The commonplace likeness between **Beves** and *Horn* in the hero's expulsion from home, his adventures at the foreign court, his banishment, his rescue of his betrothed, led Hoyt, on wholly insufficient grounds, to conclude that the home of the two stories must have been in England and that **Beves** was "but a romantically developed form of the Horn Saga."

The historical kernel for the story of Beves's second exile is to be found, according to Jordan (*Archiv*, CXIII, 98), in the story recorded under the year 870 by Regino of Prüm (*Mon. Germ.* I) of Carolus, the Frankish prince. In this anecdote a courtier, whose horse has been stolen in jest by the prince, unluckily wounds the royal youth and has to flee for his life. Deutschbein (p. 209) accepted Jordan's view and noted that Prüm was not far from the district from which he fancied some episodes in the first part of **Beves** to have been originally drawn. The theft of a famous horse as an episode in itself was, as Boje (p. 131) indicated, a popular incident.

Legendary sources for **Beves** have been found far and near. Zenker (p. 44) maintained that **Beves** and the Hamlet (Amlethus) legend told by Saxo Grammaticus were versions of the same story (p. 32), and that the common source probably originated in England. In the two stories the hero becomes the stepson of his father's murderer, vows vengeance, has a violent altercation with his mother, is sent (but for different causes) to a foreign court bearing a letter of death (Uriasbrief), escapes, and finally returns to accomplish his revenge on the step-father, the usurper of his heritage. Zenker believed that of these incidents the most distinctive was the use of the Uriasbrief, and paralleled it (p. 45) with numerous oriental tales, with the Greek Bellerophon story (pp. 283, 313), and the French *Dit de l'Empereur Coustant* (*Rom.*, VI, 162 ff.). But later students have shown that in most of these instances, with the exception of the Greek story, the letter, so rewritten as to command great rewards for the bearer, opened to him a new career of successful adventure. Such is the tale twice found in the Amlethus legend, but in **Beves** the original letter was delivered by the hero, and almost caused his death. This simpler use of the *motif* seems to be derived either from the ancient Biblical story (2 *Sam.* XI, 15) of David and Uriah or from "a folk-lore tale current in the East and introduced into **Beves** in the time of the Crusades."

A second important argument of Zenker's that *Amlethus* is the source of **Beves**, rested on the supposedly similar incidents of the double marriage of the two heroes. In **Beves** the hero, separated from his wife and children, comes to a city (*AF*, Aumberforce, *CF*, Civile); its ruler, one of many "Forth-Putting" ladies, offers herself to him, having been attracted by his military prowess; he enters reluctantly into a pretended marriage with her (*AF* version); and his true wife appears in time to prevent its consummation. In *Amlethus* the hero enters willingly into the second marriage, and the interest of the episode lies entirely in the Valkyrie-like character of the lady who, because of her vow of chastity, has long caused the death of all her suitors. The essential unlikeness of the episodes makes it improbable that one was derived from the other. To Jordan (2) the distinctive element in **Beves** was the hero's separation from his family—the separation and reunion *motif* that dominates such stories as *Guillaume d'Angleterre*, *Sir Isumbras*, *Die Gute Frau*, etc., narratives which are always in this episode in some way related to the Eustachius legend.

Although Zenker believed that the larger portion of **Beves** was to be derived from the northern Hamlet legend or its variants in the stories of *Havelok*, *Hrolf Hraka*, or the Icelandic *Anlopi*, which he thought basically related, he accounted for many of its eastern elements by traces which he detected in the Hamlet legend itself of the ancient Persian Chosro story found in the "King's Book" of the poet Firdausi (*cir.* 1011). This Chosro account in turn seems to show a fusion of the Brutus and Bellerophron legends. Beves's childhood resembles that of Chosro; for each has a faithful protector in the person of his father's friend, each acquires a wonderful horse whose recognition of his master is sometimes of vital consequence, each hero marries a king's daughter.

The Eastern names, the localization of so many incidents in eastern places, the perceptible flavor of the Crusading spirit in **Beves**, have led to other attempts to identify special incidents. Beves's imprisonment in Damascus was traced by Settegast (pp. 282, 338) to the similar experience of Bischen as recorded in Firdausi's book, and more significantly by Brockstedt (p. 35) to the French *Floovent*. In the Italian *Bovo* (Jordan, I, p. 17) the princess Malgaria loves and protects the imprisoned Beves; in *Floovent* the princess Maugalie, similarly tender-hearted, aids the hero to escape. The possible influence on the *Ur-Bueve* of *Floovent* or other stories of this exceedingly popular type must be admitted. Warren's study (*PMLA.* XXIX, 340-59) of the Enamoured Moslem Princess, showed that the type story greatly antedated the Crusading era, as he traced its earliest western form to the sixth *Controversia* of Seneca, the Rhetorician, and the earliest Crusade version to the account of Bohemond in the *Historia Ecclesiastica*, c. 1135, of Orderic Vitalis.

Brockstedt's argument, however, that the Italian version of **Beves**, because it borrowed the episode from *Floovent,* is a late form, was disputed by Matzke (*Mod. Phil.,* X, 25) who urged that the role of Malgaria must have belonged to the French source of the Italian poem, since she is to be recognized as the necessary second heroine of the story (which he believed the fundamental one in **Beves**), the so-called Legend of the Man with Two Wives ("Lay of Eliduc," *Mod. Phil.,* V, 211-39). In this type a youth exiled from his own home wins through his valor the love of a princess. He is slandered and is again forced to go into exile. In another court he wins the love of another lady but remains loyal to the first. He returns in time to rescue her from an unwelcome marriage, or she appears in time to prevent his marriage to the second lady. To Matzke (3, p. 41 ff.) the starting point of the legend is simply the doubling of the exile-and-return formula, and the consequent doubling of the love adventure of the hero. The doubled form appeared in such tales as *Horn, Ille et Galeron,* and, with certain variations in *Tristan, Eliduc, Lai del Fraisne,* and its derivative, *Roman de Galeran.* A comparison of the different versions of **Beves** seems to show that its original form was structurally of the same type as these.

Some of the earliest processes of accretion in **Beves** are set forth in Matzke's study of the St. George legend. In its ancient Eastern forms this legend had known only the monster-killing and martyrdom episodes, but in the course of its development in the west it absorbed the **Beves** story and became a typical *roman d'aventure,* as it appears, for instance, in Richard Johnson's *Seven Champions of Christendom,* London, 1592. In **Beves,** on the other hand, the influence of the saint legend is especially obvious in the scene in which Beves overthrows the heathen idol, in the account of his sufferings in the prison of Damascus, and his fight with the dragon of Cologne.

In regard to the authorship of **Beves**, the most important suggestion of recent years was that made by Boje. He urged that the original French version was the work of a single author sufficiently acquainted with contemporary romance to borrow from it freely. His belief that **Beves** was not a racial saga, that it was not of German, Anglo-Saxon, Celtic, or Viking origin, nor a gradual combination of elements drawn from Persian-Armenian, nor Græco-Roman story, but a literary romance, the work of one man, is in line with the whole tendency of modern criticism.[4]

Notes

[1] Scenes from *Beves* appear in the Smithfield Decretals and in the Taymouth Horæ. . . . *Notes and Queries,* 8th ser. XI (1897) referred to the hangings of Juliana de Leybourne, 1362, which were worked with the legend. W. G. Thompson, *Tapestry Weaving,* p. 26, mentioned two pieces of arras of *Beves* of the time of Henry V. The *Bull. de la Soc. des Antiquaires de France,* 1909, p. 237, shows a small stone mould (*c.* 1359) of the Musée de Cluny on which Beves and two lions appear. An inscription refers to "Bueve."

[2] Beves and Guy had an almost equal popularity, and the heroes were often mentioned together. . . .

[3] Cf. J. Westphal, *Englische Ortsnamen im Altfranzösischen.* Diss. Strassburg, 1891.

[4] Cf. Bédier, *Les Légendes Épiques,* Paris, 1908-13; L. Foulet, *Roman de Renard,* Paris, 1914; F. Lot, *Étude sur le Lancelot en prose,* Paris, 1918.

Bibliography

TEXTS, MIDDLE ENGLISH: (1), A, Auchinleck MS., ed. Turnbull, Maitland Club, Edin., 1838, rev. *Eng. Stud.* II, 317; E. Kölbing, *EETSES.* XLVI, XLVIII, LXV, 1885-86, 1894, rev. *Anglia,* XI, 325; *Eng. Stud.* XIX, 261; *Rom.* XXIII, 486; (2) C, Caius Coll. Cbg. 175, desc. *Eng. Stud.* XIV, 321; (3) S, Egerton 2862, desc. Brit. Mus. *Catalogue of Add. MSS,* 1905-10, p. 238, formerly the MS. of the Duke of Sutherland, desc. *Eng. Stud.,* VII, 191 ff.; (4) N, Royal Library, Naples, MS. XIII, B, 29; (5) C, Cbg. Univ. Libr. MS. Ff. II, 38; (6) M, Chetham Library, Manchester, MS. 8009, ed. Kölbing, *op. cit.;* cf. *Eng. Stud.* VII, 198. Early printed editions: L, "Douce fragments," no. 19, Bodleian; O, undated edition by Pynson, Bodleian. Editions from 1689-1711 listed by Esdaile, *English Tales,* pp. 163-64. Trans. L. Hibbard, *Three Middle Eng. Romances.*

FRENCH: Stimming, A. (1) "Der Anglo-Normannische Boeve de Haumton," *Bibliotheca Normannica,* VII, Halle, 1899; (2) "Der festländische Bueve de Hantone," Fassung I, *Gesellschaft f. rom. Lit.* XXV (1911); (3) Fassung II, *ibid.* XXX (1912); XLI (1918); Fassung III, *ibid.* XLII (1920).

IRISH: Robinson, F. N. "The Irish Lives of Guy of Warwick and Bevis of Hampton." *Zts. f. celt. Phil.* VI, 180-320 (1907). Text and trans. See also, *Eng. Stud.* XXIV, 463.

ITALIAN: Reinhold, J. "Die franko-italienische Version des Bovo d'Antone." *Zts. f. rom. Phil.* XXXV, 555-607; 683-714; XXXVI, 1-32 (1912).

STUDIES: Billings, *Guide,* pp. 40-1; Boje (see below) for MSS., pp. 1-13; Studies, pp. 43-49; Wells, *Manual,* pp. 765-66.

Behrens, L. *Ort u. Zeit der Entstehung der Fassung I des festländischen Beuve de Hantone.* Diss. 135 pp. Göttingen, 1913.

Bodtker, A. "Ivens Saga u. Bevis Saga in Cod. Holm. Chart. 46," *PB. Beiträge* XXXI, 261-71 (1906).

Boje, C. "Ueber den altfrz. roman v. Bueve de Hamtone." *Beihefte z. Zts. f. rom. Phil.* XIX, 145 pp. Halle, 1909. Rev. *Rom.* XLII, 314; *Zts. f. frz. Spr. u. Lit.* XXXV, 49.

Brockstedt, 1. *Floovent Studien.* Kiel, 1907. 2. *Von mittelhochdeut. Volksepen französischen Ursprungs.* Kiel, 1912. *Beves,* pp. 60-159. Rev. *Archiv.* CXXI, 170-72.

Deutschbein, M. *Studien z. Sagengeschichte Englands.* Die Wikingersagen: Horn, Havelok, Tristan, Boeve, pp. 181-215, Guy of Warwick. Cöthen, 1906.

Favaron, G. *L'elemento italiano nel period popolare toscano del epopea romanzesca; Saggio sul Buovo d'Antona.* 61 pp. Bologna (1900).

Gerould, G. See *Isumbras* here.

Groeber, G. *Gründriss,* II, 386 (1901).

Hibbard, L. A. "Beves of Hampton and the Nibelungenlied," *MLN.* XXVI, 159-60 (1911). "Jaques de Vitry and Boeve de Haumtone," *MLN.* XXXIV, 408-11 (1919).

Hoyt, P. C. "The Home of the Beves Saga," *PMLA.* XVII, 237-46 (1902).

Jordan, L. I. "Ueber Boeve de Hanstone," *Beihefte z. Zts. f. rom. Phil.* XIV. 197 pp. Halle, 1908. Rev. *Archiv.* CXXII, 412, *Zts. f. frz. Spr. u. Lit.* XXXIV, 25. 2. "Die Eustachiuslegende, Christians Wilhelmsleben, Boeve de Hanstone u. ihre orientalischen Verwandten," *Archiv.* CXXI, 340-62 (1908).

Kühl, H. *Das gegenseitige Verhältnis der Handschriften der Fassung II des festländischen Bueve de Hantone.* Diss. 63 pp. Göttingen, 1915.

Matzke, J. E. I. "Contributions to the Legend of St. George," *PMLA.* XVII, 464-535 XVIII, 99-171 (1902-03). 2. "The Legend of St. George; Its Development into a Roman d'Aventure," *PMLA.* XIX, 449-78 (1904). 3. "The Oldest Form of the Beves Legend." *Mod. Phil.* X, 19-54 (1912-13).

Meiners, J. E. *Die Handschriften P (RW), Fassung II d. festländischen Bueve de Hantone.* Diss. 268 pp. Göttingen, 1914.

Oeckel, F. *Ort. u. Zeit. d. Entstehung der Fassung II d. festländischen Boeve v. Hantone.* Diss. 88 pp. Göttingen, 1911.

Paetz, H. "Ueber das gegenseitige Verhältnis d. venetianischen, d. frankoitalienischen u. d. französischen gereimten Fassungen d. Bueve de Hantone." *Beihefte z. Zts. f. rom. Phil.* L. 133 pp. Halle, 1913.

Reinhold, See Texts, Italian.

Robinson, See Texts, Irish.

Sander, G. *Die Fassung T des festländischen Fassung d. Bueve de Hantone.* Diss. Göttingen, 1913.

Settegast, F. *Quellenstudien z. gallo-rom. Epik.* Leipzig, 1904. Ch. XVI, 338-69, *Beves, Generides.*

Schültsmeier, F. *Die Sprache d. Handschrift C d. festländ. Bueve de Hantone.* Diss. 200 pp. Göttingen, 1913.

Stimming, See Texts, French.

Wolf, S. *Das gegenzeitige Verhältnis d. gereimten Fassungen d. festländ. Bueve de Hantone.* Diss. Göttingen, 1912.

Zenker, R. "Boeve-Amlethus, Das altfrz. Epos Boeve de Hantone u. der Ursprung der Hamletsage." *Literarhist. Forschungen,* XXXII, 480 pp. Berlin, 1905. Rev. *Archiv.,* CXVIII, 226; *Eng. Stud.,* XXXVI, 284.

Abbreviations and References

. . . *Archiv* für das Studium der neueren Sprachen und Literaturen, ed. Herrig. Braunschweig, 1849- . . .

Mod. Phil. Modern Philology. Chicago, 1903- . . .

PMLA. Publications of the Modern Language Association of America, Baltimore, 1884-1901, Cambridge, 1902-

Rom. Romania. Paris, 1872- . . .

Rom. Forsch. Romanische Forschungen. Erlangen, 1883- . . .

Dieter Mehl (essay date 1967)

SOURCE: "*Sir Beues of Hamtoun*" in *Middle English Romances of the Thirteenth and Fourteenth Centuries,* Routledge & Kegan Paul, 1967, pp. 211-20.

[*In the following excerpt from a work originally published in German in 1967, Mehl analyzes the episodic structure of* Bevis, *describing it as consciously contrived to increase suspense and keep the audience's attention focused on the title character. The critic also maintains that the poem is a popular chronicle—chiefly concerned with the origins of a noteworthy family—not a courtly romance.*]

. . . *Sir Beues of Hamtoun* was probably one of the best known of the Middle English romances; in popularity it was probably second only to *Guy of Warwick* with which it has several features in common. Its wide appeal is attested by the transmission alone: the poem is preserved in six manuscripts and a number of early prints; there are also some versions that were current on the continent.[7] The English versions are mainly to be found in larger collections, like the Auchinleck Ms. (A) and Cambridge Ff. II. 38 (C), where they are put among other secular works, or Gonville & Caius 175 (E), Chetham 8009 (M) and Egerton 2862 (S), where they are copied together with some more historical and legendary works. (The sixth manuscript, Royal Library of Naples, XIII, B 29 (N), is of particularly mixed content.) It may be coincidence that *Sir Beues of Hamtoun* stands next to poems like *Arthour and Merlin* (in A), *Athelston* (in E) and *Richard Coeur de Lion* (in S) in some of the manuscripts, but it could also indicate that the novel was felt to be a kind of family chronicle or at least a tale from England's past which had some important bearing on the present.

In the poem's source, the Anglo-Norman *Boeve de Haumtone*, this is even more obvious; it belongs to the type, suitably described as 'ancestral romance' by M. D. Legge.[8] Its most characteristic motifs are the founding of a family, exile, and the achievement of extraordinary exploits abroad. The English version has taken over and dramatized just these 'native' qualities of the ancestral romances so that the term could also be applied to *Sir Beues of Hamtoun*, though perhaps in a wider and less specific sense.

The form of the work presents some problems. Unlike its source, it begins in tail-rhyme stanzas, which, however, break off after some four hundred lines; after that, the poem continues in rhyming couplets. As the Auchinleck version of *Guy of Warwick* has a similar change in metre, it is possible that the scribes of the manuscript or of its immediate source were responsible for the introduction of the tail-rhyme stanzas and, in the case of *Sir Beues*, simply continued in the metre of the preceding item (*Reinbrun*). *Horn Childe* and *Amis and Amiloun* show that this manuscript is particularly important for the history of the tail-rhyme romances.[9]

On the other hand, some other manuscripts, not immediately dependent on A, also have the strophic beginning. In two of them (S and N) there is an attempt to carry on the metre by adding a *cauda* (tail-line) after every couplet, though only for about a hundred lines, while in another version (M) the beginning is completely altered and consists of rhyming couplets only.

Thus it is hardly possible to say anything definite about the reasons which may have led the scribe to abandon the tail-rhyme stanzas in favour of couplets. All the same, the close relationship between the two metrical forms becomes apparent here. Kölbing maintained that the beginning of the romance could not originally have been written in couplets because he felt that many of the tail-lines were quite indispensable for the meaning;[10] this may be so, yet it is noticeable that the form of the tail-rhyme stanzas used here is quite different from that found in most of the tail-rhyme romances. Thus, only very few of the couplets are linked to each other by rhyme (see, for instance, ll. 301-5) and the tail-lines usually only rhyme in pairs; in other words, we have here six-line stanzas, not the usual twelve-line stanzas. The *caudae* are for the most part quite unimportant for the development of the plot; often they are only very loosely integrated in the syntax, just as in the passage of lines 409-509[21] of the manuscripts S and N, where it is obvious that the *caudae* are an afterthought. Essential parts of a sentence or of the plot are hardly ever contained in the tail-lines, as, for instance in *Reinbrun*.[11] Thus, it seems to me quite possible that the first part of the poem was also originally written in rhyming couplets which by slight alterations, in many cases merely by the insertion of *caudae*, were turned into tail-rhyme stanzas. The lines 409-509[21] in S and N prove that such a procedure was occasionally followed. The M-version, on the other hand, which is in rhyming couplets throughout, obviously belongs to a slightly different line of transmission. It is sometimes rather more formal than the other versions and occasionally tries to be more precise (cf. the indirect speech in M, ll. 708 ff., as compared with direct speech in A, ll. 917 ff., or the more exact details in M, ll. 241 ff. and the vaguer ones in A, ll. 301 ff.). Kölbing's 'stemma' describes very accurately the textual relationship between the individual manuscripts, but it is more than doubtful whether it gives an adequate explanation of the actual origins of the different versions.[12]

The plot of the poem has several points in common with *King Horn*. Both romances apparently go back to a *chanson de geste* and have some uncourtly, or rather pre-courtly characteristics, such as the resolute wooing by the lady, by which the knight is almost forced into loving her.[13] As in *King Horn*, the story combines the motifs of love, revenge and the progress of a knight from an inexperienced youth to a victorious fighter and king. In both poems the boy is deprived of his inheritance, and a long series of fights is necessary before he can win it back. The similarities between the two poems are hardly sufficient to prove that they have a common source, but they do show that this is a type of plot which was obviously a particular favourite in England.

An important difference between the two poems lies of course in their length. *King Horn* is a short tale, summarizing an extensive plot within a brief space, so that it could easily be read in one sitting, whereas *Sir Beues of Hamtoun* is a verse-novel of three times the length, with clear divisions and pauses, obviously aiming at a series of effective episodes rather than a unified whole. The work is not expressly divided into 'fitts' or *'partes'* (nor are any of the other verse-novels dealt with in this chapter), and so in reciting the poem, breaks could be introduced at various undetermined points, according to circumstances. However, the story itself suggests several clearly marked caesuras, dividing the novel into five almost equal sections of about nine hundred lines each.

The first part briefly describes the hero's youth, his escape and his first heroic deeds at the court of King Ermin. His boyish displays of strength already give a foretaste of his later glorious exploits, and his rescue by Josiane hints at the love relationship between the two. The injustice done to Beves and his vow of re-venge (ll. 301 ff.), foreshadowing later events, create enough suspense to hold the attention of the listeners and make them eager to hear the continuation of the story (see also the anticipation in ll. 328-30 and the repetition of his vow, l. 552). Thus, although complete in itself, this first part of the poem contains several motifs that prepare for the further development of the story. The opposition between Christians and heathens, too, which runs through the whole novel, is introduced at an early point. In the first description of Josiane we are expressly told that she is a pagan ('Boute of cristene lawe yhe kouþe nauyt', l. 526), and Beves soon has an opportunity of proving his loyalty to the Christian faith when Ermin offers to make him his heir and give him Josiane for a wife if he renounces his faith (ll. 555-68). Beves' determined refusal, which only increases Ermin's regard for him (ll. 569-70), is the more re-markable as he obviously only has a very vague idea of the Christian creed and has to have the meaning of Christmas explained to him by a heathen (ll. 585-606). That he can only remember the jolly tournaments and feasting in honour of Christmas from his early child-hood, but nothing about the deeper meaning of the festival, is quite characteristic of the unconcerned and at the same time realistic tone of the poem.

At line 909 a new section of the novel begins, out-wardly marked by the passing over of three years and by the appearance of Brademond as Josiane's suitor. What makes the break between the two parts particu-larly clear, is the detailed recapitulation of an episode told only a few lines earlier (ll. 934-59). This recapitu-lation is included in most of the English versions, but is lacking in M, which, as we noted before, is a more bookish redaction, less adapted to oral recitation. The repeated reference to Beves' heroic deeds at this point seems completely unnecessary and probably has no other function than that of giving the second part a certain amount of unity by providing a few helpful

clues for all those who would not recall every detail of the first part (or had not listened to it). The second section of the poem describes Josiane's wooing of Beves, his seven-years' imprisonment by Brademond and his miraculous rescue. On his way to Brademond, as well as after his escape from prison, he gives further examples of his prowess and gains victories against overwhelming odds, particularly, of course, against heathens. Beves is called 'þe cristene kniyt' (l. 1011), and there is a real crusading spirit in this part of the story, as in the English Charlemagne-romances and, by the way, in nearly all the verse-novels discussed in this chapter. The meeting with Terri recalls the first part of the poem with the story of Terri and Saber; both char-acters are to play an important part in the later course of the plot. Josiane's own fate, her despair at Beves' supposed infidelity and her marriage, are also described in this section. Thus, the second part, too, is in a way self-contained; it includes several complete episodes and all the most important characters of the story make their appearance.

Again at line 1959 a new section begins, which is also introduced by some glances at the previous parts of the story, reminding us of the most important elements in the plot that has already become somewhat compli-cated. Beves gives an account of his life-story up to this point and vows that he will only marry a virgin, a motif that may have something to do with the family-chronicle character of the poem and points forward to later events in the poem. The French version does not mention Beves' promise to marry a virgin at this point. The A-version of the poem has in addition some more recapitulations and backward glances (ll. 1991-2004, 2013-36). More recapitulations follow, usually extended by the English adapter, some in the form of dialogue. They recall Beves' own adventures (even the wicked part played by his step-father is briefly mentioned) and those of Josiane. The narrator also seems very inter-ested in the fate of Beves' horse Arundel (ll. 2139-46), presumably because of its association with the found-ing of Arundel castle.

Beves arrives at the conclusion that he is not yet in a position to reconquer his inheritance, and so first of all he sets out to find his lady again. The section which now follows gives an account of their flight together and their arrival in Cologne where Josiane is baptized. Another clear caesura in the plot can be discovered after line 2596, but the subsequent episode, which is only to be found in the English versions of the story (ll. 2597-2910), probably has to be counted as part of the previous section. Beves' glorious feat of killing a most dangerous dragon gives added importance to his sojourn in Cologne. The regaining of Beves' inherit-ance is again delayed by this interlude, as well as by Josiane's short marriage to Miles which is told in the following section (ll. 3117-3304). Thus, the third sec-tion of the poem (ll. 1959-2910) is just as long as the first two, whereas the fourth part, ending with Beves' reestablishment in his inheritance, and his marriage to Josiane, is somewhat shorter, though particularly rich in exciting incidents.

Between this and the following (fifth) section of the poem the division is less clearly marked;[14] indeed all the divisions suggested here are not meant as a strict scheme, but rather as reflecting the basic structure of the poem and the principle of its composition, with a view to oral recitation. These divisions are, however, by no means clearly marked in all the manuscripts. Just at this point (between the fourth and the fifth section) there is a very clear break in the plot, though not in the text of the poem. Beves has achieved his end, and the poem could quite conceivably stop here, but with the introduction of the English King new complications begin to arise, involving Beves' own sons and a number of his former enemies. They start with a quarrel about Arundel, the faithful horse, and a new separation from Josiane, lasting for seven years. At the end of the novel, Beves has won a kingdom for each of his sons, for Terri and for himself. After twenty years of happiness he and Josiane die, almost at the same moment, and Arundel, too, falls down dead.

This last part of the poem is of course linked to the preceeding sections by most of the characters taking part, but it still gives the impression of a later addition which is not absolutely necessary for the continuity of the story. On the other hand, we are at the end of the fourth part still in ignorance about the fate of Josiane's father and her first husband. Thus the poem is indeed a unified whole in so far that all the threads of the story are not tied up until the end; nevertheless there are several places where we can see that the plot is spun out in a purely episodic manner, suggesting that there was no very definite masterplan for the whole novel, such as we can discover in Chrétien's poems. The three extensive additions made by the English adapter can be quoted in support of this observation. They each consist of an episode, complete in itself (see ll. 585-738, 2597-2910, 4287-4538) and by no means clumsily inserted, but heightening the suspense; however, they seem to prove that the adapter was more interested in the individual episode than in the structure of the whole poem. Thus, the fight with the dragon is obviously added with the intention of putting Beves on an equal footing with Guy of Warwick and Lancelot, as the express reference to these two famous heroes shows. Beves has to be given a similar adventure as Guy. The fight is told almost in terms of a Saint's legend. It is prepared for by a dream, such as we would expect in a legend (ll. 2681 ff.), and Beves' victory is celebrated by bell-ringing and by a solemn procession (ll. 2893-2910).

The London street fight, too, has the effect of an independent insertion which was bound to appeal particu-

larly to an English audience of less refined tastes and must have been especially successful when read somewhere in the London area. The scene does not only prove that the poet had a pretty exact knowledge of the topography of London,[15] but also that he was capable of describing this battle against citizens of flesh and blood with more precision and artistic energy than the conventional encounters with bloodless monsters. It is less likely, however, that he wanted to allude to definite historical events. In this case, the wholesale slaughtering of London citizens would not have been an exploit apt to endear Beves and his sons to a London audience of the lower classes.

There are also some other aspects of the poem which give the impression that the author was mainly concerned with satisfying the audience's desire for simple amusement. Thus, we find quite a number of rather burlesque scenes, suggesting that the poet had no very subtle sense of humour, such as Ascopard's attempted baptism and his very unchivalrous way of fighting (ll. 3420 ff.), the messenger scene, obviously only included to raise a laugh (ll. 3061 ff.), and the description of Josiane's and Miles' wedding night (ll. 3117-3304). This whole episode is clearly not taken very seriously by the author; otherwise it would give rather an unfavourable picture of Beves' future spouse. There are also some other instances of the poet's grim and not very delicate humour.[16]

In spite of the episodic structure of the poem, there is no lack of coherence and tension, although we cannot detect a systematic plan or any sophisticated principles of composition. The dramatic unity of the poem is above all achieved by the character of the hero, who gets his revenge on his step-father, regains his inheritance, and founds a family which rules over several kingdoms. At the same time, the novel describes the career of a knight who by his natural valour alone overcomes all obstacles and all resistance. There is a certain climax in the series of his exploits. His first trials of strength (except his fight against Brademond) have something of the swaggering youth about them; his battles against his pursuers after his escape from prison are mainly fought in self-defence, but his great fight with the dragon shows him as a Christian champion who with God's help frees the country from a satanic plague and is honoured by the Bishop with a ceremonial procession. All the time Beves has to rely entirely on himself; indeed, he insists on being left to himself in all his fights and he twice rejects Josiane's offer of help (ll. 2413-20 and 2474-8), the second time with a brutal threat. Truly heroic courage and obstinate ambition seem to be closely related here, which fits in with the portrait of a popular hero rather than one of a courtly knight. The dramatic principle of increasing tension is applied time and again, but the repetition of similar episodes and the prominence of the external mechanism of the plot make it impossible for us to feel that this is a novel about the maturing and the chivalric education of a king, as is the case with *King Horn, Havelok,* and, to some extent, *Guy of Warwick.*

Beves is not only a valiant knight, but also a warrior of God who succeeds in decimating the heathens, freeing the Christians from wicked enemies and converting Josiane to the Christian faith. All this, however, does not amount to a consistent spiritual design, but is presented as part of the swiftly moving plot. The theory that the author of the original poem was a cleric could account for the pious tone of several episodes, but the style of the English versions is not so obviously religious that we are forced to assume the English adapter, too, must have been a cleric. The poem only shows once more to what extent love of God and hatred of the Saracens are part of the make-up of the perfect knight in many of the English popular romances and these qualities are just as important as physical superiority and courage. It is hardly surprising that these characteristics are particularly emphasized in a work describing the origins of a powerful English family and praising its famous ancestor. The term 'romance of prys' would be especially fitting in the case of this poem.

Apart from prowess and exemplary piety,[17] it is above all liberality by which the true knight is distinguished, and this is also a virtue which, in a somewhat watered-down form greatly appealed to the adapters of the English romances. Thus, Josiane's chamberlain who comes to Beves in order to reconcile him with his mistress, receives a princely reward from the knight, although his request is refused (ll. 1153 ff.), and it is just this reward that convinces Josiane that Beves cannot possibly be of low degree because

> . . . hit nas neuer a cherles dede,
> To þeue a maseger swiche a wede!
>
> (ll. 1173-4)

Indeed, it is this proof of his noble character that finally causes her to abandon her faith in order to win his love.

The on the whole very pointed and well-balanced structure of the poem shows that, within his modest limits, the English adapter had a conscious artistic design which, in spite of all episodic rambling and embellishment, he never quite lost sight of and tried to impress on his audience. Thus, even the Anglo-Norman version contains various prophetic hints, designed to create a feeling of suspense and to give some unity to the whole story. The English adapter took over some of these anticipations more or less literally (as, for instance, ll. 1063-8), extended them (as in ll. 205-10), or added new ones (ll. 832-6, 3637-8). They usually, however, refer to events that follow fairly soon, at least

in the same section of the poem, whereas the recapitulations, as we have seen, mainly serve to connect the various sections and help the audience to keep up with the somewhat intricate plot.

The frequent premonitions also have another function which is characteristic of the style of the poem. They give some prominence to the figure of the narrator by revealing his deep involvement in the events he has to relate. Thus, some of the premonitions are in the form of powerless complaints about the unavoidable disaster that is to befall one of the characters, as the distressed warning when Beves' father rides into the forest where he will meet his death (ll. 205-10).[18] The prayers for individual characters, particularly frequent in this poem, and the cursing of villains have a similar effect.[19] Such formulas are not infrequent in the source of the poem, but they can also be found in those passages that were added by the English adapter. The frequently inserted proverbs and general aphorisms are also characteristic of the style of the poem; they mostly seem to be added by the English adapter and are reminiscent of *Havelok,* particularly such homely truths as the following:

> For, whan a man is in pouerte falle,
> He haþ fewe frendes wiþ alle.
>
> (ll. 3593-4)[20]

These proverbial sayings also allow the narrator to come to the fore and to establish closer contact with his audience. In addition, there are the numerous conventional formulas, pointing out transitions and changes of scene or announcing some particularly exciting events, like 'Herkney now a wonder-cas!' (l. 1792) and similar clichés.[21] As in *Havelok,* the narrator in one place asks for a drink before he can continue his story:

> Ac er þan we be-ginne fiyte,
> Ful vs þe koppe anon riyte!
>
> (ll. 4107-8)

Here, too, we are not to think of an ale-house, but of some larger social gathering or a domestic circle. The passage, like several other formulas, creates a feeling of a community between the narrator and his audience, whether the invitation was really meant to be followed or, as is more likely, it is to be understood as a literary convention.

The narrative style of the poem has much in common with that of the Anglo-Norman poem which, as M. D. Legge says, 'has no nonsense about it'.[22] In spite of its length, the poem never seems monotonous or long-winded. The action develops rapidly throughout, and the narrator hardly ever troubles to give us a more detailed description of things and persons. Even the descriptions of feasts, so common in many other romances, are sometimes passed over by an *occupatio*, like the following:

> þouy ich discriue nouyt þe bredale,
> ye mai wel wite, hit was riale,
> þat þer was in alle wise
> Mete and drinke & riche seruise.

(ll. 3479-82)[23]

Only certain climaxes, like the fight with the dragon and the London street-fight, are related in more detail, but the long and elaborate speeches, so frequent in *Havelok*, are almost entirely absent here, although many events are portrayed in the form of brief scenes of dialogue in direct speech. Thus, in A (ll. 70-174), the sending of the messenger as well as the delivery of his message and his report on his return are presented in direct speech. In many ways, the style of the poem is much more like that of the shorter romances than that of *Havelok* or *Ywain and Gawain*.

Beues of Hamtoun, then, is an extremely lively and entertaining, though on the whole rather artless verse-novel, which is mainly concerned with presenting an exciting plot and with engaging the listeners' interest by a swift narrative and a wealth of colourful episodes. If the number of manuscripts is anything to go by, it was certainly very successful in this limited aim. . . .

Notes

[7] . . . See the very thorough edition by E. Kölbing, EETS, ES, 46, 48, 65 (1885, 1886, 1894), pp. vii ff.

[8] See her *Anglo-Norman Literature and its Background*, pp. 156-61, and A. Stimming's edition of *Boeve de Haumtone*, Bibliotheca Normannica, VII (Halle, 1899), especially pp. CXXX ff.

[9] The first twenty-four lines of *Richard Coeur de Lion* are also composed in tail-rhyme stanzas in the Auchinleck-manuscript. See K. Brunner's edition, pp. 25-6.

[10] See Kölbing's introduction, pp. x ff.

[11] See, however, ll. 19 ff.

[12] See Kölbing's stemma, p. xxxviii. We need to know a lot more about the copying of manuscripts and the methods of transmission before we can be very confident about such neat stemmata.

[13] See H. L. Creek, 'Character in the "Matter of England" Romances' [*Journal of English and Germanic Philology*, X (1911), 429-52 and 585-609], *passim*.

Creek repeatedly refers to the useful study by W. W. Comfort, 'The Character Types in the Old French *Chansons de Geste*', *PMLA*, XXI (1906), 279-434, which contains much interesting material.

[14] In most versions there is a clear break after line 3962 and again after line 4252. See also the prophetic hint, 4027-8, which connects several episodes.

[15] See Kölbing's edition, p. xxxvii.

[16] See ll. 1006-7 and the scene in which the Emperor tells Beves (whom he does not recognize) his (Beves') own story (ll. 2985 ff.), or the messenger's rough answer (ll. 3105 ff.).

[17] Beves' escape from the prison is a direct answer to his prayer (see ll. 1579 ff., 1645 ff., 1795 ff.).

[18] See also the prophetic hints in ll. 1200, 1204, 1328, 1388, etc.

[19] See ll. 510, 846, 1261-2, 1431-2, 2784, 3286 ff., 3619, 4016, 4352 (prayers for the hero or other characters) and 80-1, 1211 ff., 3458, 4030 (curses).

[20] See also ll. 46-7, 1192, 1215 ff., 3352.

[21] E.g. ll. 737-8, 848, 1068, 1263-4, 1345, 1433, 1527.

[22] *Anglo-Norman Literature*, p. 160.

[23] See also 1483-4 and 4563-8. . . .

Abbreviations

Archiv Archiv für das Studium der neueren Sprachen und Literaturen

EETS, ES Early English Text Society, Extra Series

ELH A Journal of English Literary History

GRM Germanisch-Romanische Monatsschrift (NF = Neue Folge)

JEGP Journal of English and Germanic Philology

MLN Modern Language Notes

MLR Modern Language Review

MP Modern Philology

PMLA Publications of the Modern Language Association of America

RES Review of English Studies

SP Studies in Philology

Select Bibliography

Editions of Romances

All quotations in the text are taken from the editions listed here. Other editions of individual poems and works that are only mentioned in passing will be found in the footnotes. The titles are sometimes abbreviated in accordance with usual practice.

Sir Beues of Hamtoun, ed. E. Kölbing, EETS, ES, 46, 48, 65 (1885, 1886, 1894). . . .

Richard Coeur de Lion, ed. K. Brunner (*Der mittelenglische Versroman über Richard Löwenherz*), Wiener Beiträge zur Englischen Philologie, XLII, Wien-Leipzig, 1913. . . .

Works of Reference and Criticism

LEGGE, M. D. *Anglo-Norman Literature and its Background*, Oxford, 1963. . . .

Sheila A. Spector (essay date 1976)

SOURCE: "Interlacing in *Bevis of Hampton*" in *Studies in "The Bovo Buch" and "Bevis of Hampton,"* 1976, pp. 22-49, 229-30.

[*In the excerpt below, Spector identifies a structural principle in* Bevis *known as interlacing, in which seemingly unrelated narrative threads are woven together—as in a silken tapestry or an illuminated letter in a medieval book of psalms—to achieve a unified whole. The poem begins with chaos and ends with the restoration of order, the critic argues, paralleling Josian's development from an unworthy pagan to an ideal Christian woman.*]

The fourteenth century romance, **Bevis of Hampton**, though certainly not a first-rate poem, has more merit than most of its critics are willing to grant it. At first glance, it may appear an "almost formless story,"[1] with "episodic rambling and embellishment,"[2] because of its unusual length;[3] but it does contain a structural principle which not only provides its unity, but also contributes to its total effect.

Eugène Vinaver, through his work with thirteen century French romances, provides the key for understanding **Bevis**. In his essay, "The Poetry of Interlace," he points out that nineteenth century critics tried to "rehabilitate" the medieval romance but invariably, this meant applying their own "artistic ideal" to the text, rather than studying the romances in the context of their own tradition.[4] Because medieval romances were so far re-

moved from the recognized norm of the nineteenth century, these critics lacked the "aesthetic notions" and "critical vocabulary" to deal with them.[5] Vinaver himself corrects their error by returning to medieval critics—Martianus Capella, Cassiodorus, Geoffrey of Vinsauf and John Garland—to whom *amplificatio* meant not "unity" but "multiplicity":

> The medieval variety of amplification was a horizontal rather than a vertical extension—an expansion or an unrolling of a number of interlocked themes. . . .

> Carried to its logical conclusion, this doctrine would not only justify but call for the very things that our conventional poetics condemn outright. It would call not for monocentric unity but for expansion and diversity, for growth, both real and hypothetical: real when a theme or a sequence of themes is lengthened within an existing work; hypothetical when the author projects a possible continuation into the future, to be carried out by a successor who in turn will bequeath a similar projection to those who will follow him.[6]

Vinaver calls this kind of poetry "the poetry of interlace." Through this technique the narrator is able to "give meaning and coherence to amorphous matter."[7] In other words, the romancer had at his disposal a number of strands of action revolving around a central character. Rather than selecting a single episode for his song, he would combine them all in an intricate design, analogous to a tapestry, where one theme would interrupt another which would interrupt a third, and so on; yet all would be kept in the reader's mind simultaneously, with earlier episodes contributing to the significance of later ones which, in turn, foreshadowed still later ones in a fabric from which one could not isolate the single thread but could perceive the unity of the total design.[8]

The term "interlace" is borrowed from medieval art which is notable for its very intricate ornaments. Though they appear to reflect no formal principle of construction,

> Historians of Romanesque art have shown us, among other things, that the so-called 'ribbon' ornament, which has no beginning, no end, and above all no centre—no 'means of guidance', as one critic puts it—is nevertheless a remarkably *coherent* composition. . . . Straightforward progression is abandoned in favour of intertwined patterns, 'the themes run parallel, or entwined, or are brought together as in a chequer of knotting and plaiting'.[9]

Although interlacing was a popular technique of the early Middle Ages, the advent of the *novella,* a relatively short tale with a unity of action, produced a resistance to interlacing in the later centuries of the period. The new reader was "unwilling . . . to be involved in structural complexities."[10] Consequently, the "minds and eyes" of twentieth century critics

> . . . have lost the art of perceiving the infinity of the great in the infinity of the small. The fascination of tracing a theme through all its phases, of waiting for its return while following other themes, of experiencing the constant sense of their simultaneous presence, depends upon our grasp of the entire structure—the most elusive that has ever been devised.[11]

What Kane and Mehl both overlooked in their evaluations of *Bevis* is that the narrator employs interlacing in the work, and it is through an analysis of his technique that a kind of unity emerges. Though certainly not on the level of a first rate romance writer like Chrétien, the *Bevis* narrator did have a reason for including what the twentieth century mind regards as padding and digressions.

The method differs slightly from that delineated by Vinaver, being more like a procedure of modification through repetition. That is, all constituent elements of *Bevis* are those found frequently in the romances of the time. Most of the plot and characters are stock, as can be attested to by the motif study by Christian Boje (*Über den altfranzösischen Roman von Beuve de Hamtone*).[12] In addition, there is a great deal of repetition in the story. One almost loses count of the number of men who try to take Josian from Bevis, or the number of times Bevis is betrayed by the Saracens. yet despite this apparent repetition, each particular incident is distinct. Earlier incidents of a particular type differ from later ones, as earlier characterizations of individuals within a type differ from later ones; and, most significantly, later incidents and appearances of characters are tempered by the earlier ones so that the growth of Bevis himself is marked by the change in scene as he progresses from Ermonie to England.

As the various threads come together at different points to produce these modified repetitions, the fact that they are not haphazardly joined becomes clear. Rather, the question of why certain strands interlace at a given moment takes on greater significance, especially from the perspective of the narrative as a whole. In this analysis, I will separate the three major interlaced elements: plot, theme and characterization. These three threads interlace to produce a unit which, if not equal to *Sir Gawain and the Green Knight*, does indeed reflect a degree of craftsmanship which may account for the considerable popularity of the romance.

Plot

The Beautus Initial of the Westminster Psalter is a good visual analogy for the plot of *Bevis*.[13] A quick glance at the illustration identifies it as an interlaced "B," but, in fact, as one continues to look closely at the intricacies of the design, the basic outline is obscured as the eye becomes lost in the maze of threads. Within the illumination, there is symmetry, though no identical repetition. The vertical line of the letter is punctuated by three round drawings, evenly spaced, at the top, middle, and bottom. Because of the shape of the letter, the center figure is only a semicircle, but the two ends are complete, each having spirals in the corner. The drawings within the circles are all different, and the two spirals are also different. In literary terminology, archetypically the circles are the same, though each is made distinct within its own context. Similarly, the two loops of the "B" are comparable, each having two interlocked circular figures running vertically along the left two-thirds of the loop, and a vertical figure (bordered by animals) along the right. Within the basic outline of the "B" are interlaced a myriad of threads, each merging with others, difficult to trace individually, yet necessary to the total composition.

Similarly, *Bevis* is an interlaced design woven around a linear outline, and like the "B," the intricacies of the threads obscure the outlines of the plot. Perhaps the major reason it has been difficult to recognize the unity of *Bevis* is that critics have assumed that, as with most narratives, the hero himself defined the outline of the story. But in analyzing the "B," once we defined the outline, we moved on to the more interesting figures and swirls within the outline. The initial only provided a frame—a necessary frame, certainly, yet only the skeleton of a drawing whose flesh and muscle make it artistic. In *Bevis*, the conflicts between the hero and his adversaries are the elements which interest us, but the composition as a whole is not given form by the succession of incidents. The form is built around the almost linear development of the character of Josian who progresses from heathen (archetypically a "siren") to Christian wife and mother. Around her outline are woven the innumerable repetitions of similar incidents which distract us from Josian as a character so that she becomes an almost passive object, constantly being kidnapped and rescued. But we must keep in mind the fact that it is her adventures which provide the organization of the plot.

The introductory section of the poem establishes not only Bevis's quest but also the major threads which are woven into the poem. This section also postulates the kind of character Josian is to be in the wish-fulfillment world of romance. The first 500 lines of the poem are a negative microcosm of the rest of the romance. In order to complete his quest, Bevis must undo every action performed by Devon against Guy, and Josian must prove herself to be the inverse of Brandonia. Virtually every major type of action repeated throughout the story is introduced in this section, but in an inverted form.

If the Bevis-Josian plot represents the typical happy-ending love story of romance, Brandonia and Guy are the embodiment of love gone wrong. This fact must be established immediately and decisively in the poem to avoid the audience's becoming too sympathetic with a character who is to die in the first episode. In order to do this, the narrator utilizes two techniques. First, he interrupts the narrative with editorial asides:

> Whan he was fallen in to elde,
> þat he ne miyte him self welde,
>   He wolde a wife take;
> Sone þar after, ich vnderstonde,
> Him hadde be leuer þan al þis londe,
>   Hadde he hire for-sake.
>
> (ll. 19-24)

> Man, whan he falleþ in to elde,
> Feble a wexeþ and vnbelde
>   þoury riyt resoun.
>
> (ll. 46-48)

Then he employs an almost heavy-handed foreshadowing:

> A knaue child be-twene hem þai hedde,
>   Beues a het.
> Faire child he was & bolde,
> He nas boute seue winter olde,
>   Whan his fader was ded.
>
> (ll. 50-54)

But even more important, he borrows the plot of the comic fabliau for the introduction of the tragedy of the story. Though the Guy episode provides the impetus for the action, it is actually a modified version of the cuckold plot of the January-May marriage. The result is that while we are horrified at Brandonia's treachery, we do not become too involved emotionally at the death of Guy to prevent our identifying with Bevis as a hero in his own right.

Basically, the cuckold theme revolves around the marriage of a foolish, old man and a buxom young woman who has no qualms about seeking her pleasure elsewhere, often in the arms of a young clerk who is only too willing to oblige her. The comic tone of the fabliau is easily sustained because the old man is egocentric enough to believe that a young girl would love him, yet insecure enough to fear that she will cuckold him. Thus, he watches her so closely that we, as well as the wife, enjoy the joke which she elaborately contrives to cuckold him. In **Bevis**, we have the basic outline with the January-May marriage and alternate suitor, but the elements are all modified for the milieu of a moralistic

romance. Thus, they provide impetus for the serious adventures of Bevis.

To begin with, while Guy's flaw is that he lacks judgment, he is not a foolish old man. In fact, the narrator attributes almost heroic proportions to the father of our hero:

> Of Hamtoun he was sire
> And of al þat ilche schire,
>   To wardi.
> Lordinges, þis, of whan y telle,
> Neuer man of flesch ne felle
>   Nas so strong
> And so he was in ech striue,
>
> (ll. 10-16)

But Guy's life was incomplete. He had never married. Hence, when an old man he decides to wed:

> And euer he leuede wiþ outen wiue,
>   Al to late and long.
> Whan he was fallen in to elde,
> þat he ne miyte him self welde,
>   He wolde a wif take;
>
> (ll. 17-21)

But even before the description of Brandonia, the narrator interjects his editorial, lest the reader might be led to believe that the marriage would be a happy one. He eliminates the possibility that the reader might sympathize with this young and beautiful daughter of the King of Scotland who was pitifully forced to marry a man she did not love. Actually, though, her lack of chastity was more significant than her lack of love. Long before Guy sued for her hand, she had had a paramour, one Devon, the Emperor of Almaine.

Guy is capable of performing sexually—we have Bevis as evidence—but not often enough to satisfy his wife whose sexual appetite is enormous:

> 'Me lord is olde & may nouyt werche,
> Al dai him is leuer at cherche,
>   þan in me bour,
> Hadde ich itaken a yong kniyt,
> þat ner nouyt brused in werre & fiyt,
>   Also he is,
> A wolde me louen dai and niyt,
> Cleppen and kissen wiþ al is miyt
>   And make me blis.'
>
> (ll. 58-66)

Again, the ambiguity of a cuckold theme in which one sympathizes with January rather than May is emphasized. In addition to Brandonia's excessive preoccupation with sex—desiring a young knight to love her day and night—she criticizes Guy's preference for the church to her bower.

In the fabliau, the action culminates in the cuckoldry, but Brandonia wants more than to sleep with Devon. Unable to adjust to life with Guy, she demands life without him:

> 'I nel hit lete for no þinge,
> þat ich nel him to deþe bringe
>   Wiþ sum braide!'

> (ll. 67-69)

And only after Devon kills Guy will she have sex with her paramour. In demanding Guy's death, she subverts all the principles upon which Guy had established his leadership in Southampton. She selects the appropriate instrument to execute her wiles, a man who will do anything, including commit murder:

> 'Sai, 'a seide, 'icham at hire heste:
> þif me lif hit wile leste,
>   Hit schel be do!'

> (ll. 145-147)

The battle between the two men is the antithesis of what is to be expected in the noble confrontation between knights, though it is perfectly in keeping with this episode of the romance. Guy is unarmed; Devon is armed, complete with a host of followers. Devon does not challenge Guy to combat, but insults him:

> 'Aþilt þe, treitour! þow olde dote!
> þow schelt ben hanged be þe þrote,
>   þin heued þow schelt lese;
> þe sone schel an-hanged by
> And þe wif, þat is so fre,
>   To me lemman i chese!'

> (ll. 217-222)

Guy swears to defend his wife and child and after losing the battle, offers Devon anything, save Brandonia and the life of Bevis, neither of which will Devon grant since those are the objects of his battle. Therefore, he kills Guy and sends the dead man's head to Brandonia, who invites the murderer to her bower that very night. The next day the marriage of Devon and Brandonia is celebrated with the attitude of "The king is dead; long live the king," the only mourners being Bevis and his loyal uncle Saber.

This episode represents the total subversion of order. Guy marries at the wrong time, old instead of young; Brandonia had a lover before marraige; both Brandonia and Devon place personal desire above social and moral responsibility; the battle is unfairly rigged—an old man who is unarmed against a young knight who is fully equipped; Brandonia sleeps with her new husband before marrying him; she tries to have her own son killed; and the people, in concert with their new lord, ignore the realities of the situation in favor of the appearance of order.

If the introduction represents chaos, the bulk of the poem is the re-establishment of order. If Brandonia is the symbol of the destruction of order, Josian's progress from paganism to her twenty-year reign as Christian queen, wife, and mother, is the antithesis of her mother-in-law's life and determines the order of the realm. It is therefore fitting that she also provide the linear unity of the poem. If Brandonia is Acrasia in the Bower of Bliss, Josian is Amoret in the Garden of Adonis. Venus brought Amoret to the Garden "To be vpbrought in goodly womanhed," (*FQ* III.vi.28, l. 7), and it is Josian's growth into Christian womanhood which provides the structure of the plot of *Bevis*.

An analysis of those incidents dealing directly with Josian indicates that as heroine of the story she is the direct inverse of Brandonia. She begins as a pagan who lusts after a young man, in contrast with Brandonia who is a nominal Christian, though her actions exceed the evil of the pagans Bevis meets on his adventures. Josian does convert to Christianity after proving herself worthy of the salvation of Christ. Brandonia, on the other hand, is most unworthy. Once Josian converts and proves her chastity (note the emphasis on Brandonia's lack of chastity), she and Bevis marry and produce two children. Brandonia, too, married and had a child, but she then had her husband killed and tried to kill her son. Guy and Miles love and respect their mother who teaches them to love, respect, and come to the rescue of their father when he is in trouble. Not only does Brandonia try to kill her son but, when she fails, she sells him to the Saracens. And finally, Josian lives out her life in peace, surrounded by a loving family and loyal subjects. Brandonia dies for her sins.

It is around this linear thread tracing the growth of perfect womanhood that the multiple incidents of the plot are interlaced. In addition to direct repetitions, where an incident is begun early in the romance but not completed until a later return, there are metaphoric or archetypal repetitions wherein types of incidents are repeated. The function of both kinds of repetition is the same. Josian progresses steadily throughout the poem, and the modifications worked on the repetitions reflect directly on her growth as they demonstrate her maturing responses to life in the world of romance.

The first part of the plot culminates in Josian's decision to convert. In a reverse of the situation between Guy, the King of Scotland and his daughter, the King of Ermonie and his daughter are Saracens. The daughter falls in love with Bevis at first sight. Ermin, too, recognizes Bevis's innate nobility and offers his daughter to him if only he will become a heathen. Bevis refuses, and though "þe kinges hertte wex wel cold," (l. 553), he makes Bevis his chamberlain and promises to knight him.

But Josian continues to love the Christian knight. When Bevis comes home from his first battles, she bathes his wounds, and when he presents her with the boar's head (the ironic repetition of Devon's sending Guy's head to Brandonia, especially since Guy had thought he was going to fight a boar), and defeats the envious steward (another ironic reference, this time to Devon's envying Guy), she is overtaken by a fit of love-longing, and prays to Mahomet:

> 'O Mahoun,' yhe seide, 'oure driyte,
> What Beues is man of meche miyte!
> Al þis world þif ich it hedde,
> Ich him þeue me to wedde;
> Boute he me loue, icham ded:
> Swete Mahoun, what is þe red?
> Loue-longing me haþ be-couyt,
> þar of wot Beues riyt nouyt.'
>
> (ll. 891-898)

This speech is a reversal of Brandonia's scornful comment about Guy's preferring church to her bower.

In the context of a Christian poem Mahomet, of course, is powerless, and the next thing we know, Brademond appears on the scene demanding Josian's hand. Here we have the first of the many triangles which develop, with Josian being in love with Bevis, though sued by someone else. In addition, we are reminded of Brandonia's being in love with Devon, though sued for by Guy or, possibly, her being married to Guy, though sued for by Devon. The ambiguity of the interlacing reflects the ambiguity of the situation. Though Josian loves Bevis, she is a Saracen, and hence, unfit for Bevis at this time. And it is her conversion which reconciles the situation.

Before she decides to convert, however, she undergoes the first of many metaphoric deaths and rebirths in the story. Unable to control her love any longer, especially in the light of Bevis's glorious defeat of Brademond and his forces, she confesses her feelings to the hero, and in doing so, offers her immortal soul in exchange for his physical love:

> 'Beues, lemman, þin ore!
> Ichaue loued þe ful þore,
> Sikerli can i no rede,
> Boute þow me loue, icham dede,
> And boute þow wiþ me do þe wille.'
>
> (ll. 1093-1097)

and

> 'Merci,' yhe seide, 'yet wiþ þan
> Ichauede þe leuer to me lemman,
> þe bodi in þe scherte naked,
> þan al þe gold, þat Christ haþ maked,
> And þow wost wiþ me do þe wille!'
>
> (ll. 1105-1109)

Her behavior, antithetical to Christian morality, is to be expected perhaps from a Saracen. Hearing her proposition Bevis in this way, we cannot help but remember Brandonia's proposition to Devon, though Brandonia demanded murder. Josian wants only physical gratification. But the offer itself demonstrates that she is not yet an appropriate mate for Bevis.

She curses him in the name of Mahomet, and denigrates his nobility. Of course, curses in the name of a false god are meaningless and, as Bevis reminds her, he is of noble origin:

> 'Damesele,' a seide, 'þow seist vnriyt;
> Me fader was boþe erl & kniyt:
> How miyte ich þanne ben a cherl,
> Whan me fader was kniyt & erl?'
>
> (ll. 1125-1128)

His identity is valid and her words cannot change it. Her identity, on the other hand, is based on false values. She must ascend to his level, and she does. When Bevis gives her messenger, Bonifas, an embroidered mantle, he demonstrates that he is truly noble and, through Bonifas's prodding, she does admit that the gift was not the action of a churl. She then goes to his chamber, prostrates herself, and vows to convert:

> 'Men saiþ,' yhe seide, 'in olde riote,
> þat wimmannes bolt is sone schote:
> For-yem me, þat ichaue misede,
> And ich wile riyt now to mede
> Min false godes al for-sake
> And cristendom for þe loue take!'
>
> (ll. 1191-1196)

It is only then that Bevis kisses her.

Her actual conversion is the focus of the second part of the narrative. It consists of three tests which she must undergo in order to prove herself worthy of Christ: Yvor, the lions, and Ascopart.

Acting on the lies of two envious knights, Ermin sends Bevis to Damascus where he is imprisoned by Brademond. Meanwhile, in order to quiet Josian's enquiries into her lover's whereabouts, Ermin says that Bevis returned home to marry the daughter of the King of England (ironic fore-shadowing of Bevis's son). Later, Ermin has her marry Yvor, King of Mombraunt, in a manner similar to the way the King of Scotland had married Brandonia to Guy when she was in love with Devon. In this case, the purpose of the interlacing is to show the difference between the two women. Whereas Brandonia accepts a mock sacrament, only eventually to have her husband killed, Josian, though having more justification than Brandonia, nevertheless refuses to accede to a loveless marriage. Instead, she professes faith in Bevis's fidelity:

> 'Beuoun,
> Hende kniyt of Souþ-Hamtoun,
> Naddestow me neuer for-sake,
> yif sum tresoun hit nadde make:'

(ll. 1463-1466)

And with the help of her magic ring, she protects her chastity:

> 'Ichaue,' yhe seide, 'a ring on,
> þat of swiche vertu is þe ston:
> While ichaue on þat ilche ring,
> To me schel noman haue willing,
> And, Beues!' yhe seide, 'be god aboue,
> I schel it weren for þe loue!'

(ll. 1469-1474)

While Bevis languishes in prison, Josian spends the seven years questioning palmers for news of him. When he finally escapes, and after several intermediary adventures, Bevis comes to Josian disguised as a palmer to test her faith. In the tradition of the disguise motif, Bevis answers all of Josian's questions ambiguously so that they are literally true to those who know the truth. When she asks him if he knows Bevis, he replies:

> 'þat kniyt ich knowe wel inouy!
> Atom,' a seide, 'in is contre
> Icham an erl and also is he;'

(ll. 2136-2138)

And when they go to the stable, she tells the faithful Bonifas:

> 'Be þe moder, þat me haþ bore,
> Ner þis mannes browe to-tore,
> Me wolde þenke be his fasoun,
> þat hit were Beues of Hamtoun!'

(ll. 2153-2156)

And when the horse permits his master to mount him, Josian knows that it is Bevis:

> 'O Beues, gode lemman,
> Let me wiþ þe reke
> In þat maner, we han ispeke,
> And þenk, þow me to wiue tok,
> When ich me false godes for-sok:
> Now þow hast þin hors Arondel,
> þe swerd ich þe fette schel,
> And let me wende wiþ þe siþþe
> Hom in to þin owene kiþþe!'

(ll. 2182-2190)

The identification works both ways. By naming him, she is not only giving him the identity which had lain dormant for seven years, but since she is the only one who recognizes him, she is proving her own worth by responding to the innate qualities of the hero. This is an interlacing of the earlier episode when she had misidentified him as a churl, only to find herself mistaken. That incident resulted in her promise to convert. Josian has passed her first test of a seven-year false marriage (compare this with Brandonia's seven years with Guy).

The next adventure, the encounter with the lions, symbolically reinforces the previous incident. While they attack and kill Bonifas, and ferociously fight against Bevis, they will not touch Josian:

> But þey ne myyt do hur no shame,
> For þe kind of Lyouns, y-wys,
> A kynges douyter, þat maide is,
> Kinges douyter, quene and maide both,
> þe lyouns myyt do hur noo wroth.

(ll. 2390-2394)

Because she is a king's daughter and a maid and will twice be a queen, she is immune to their attack. Unfortunately, her steward is killed, but they soon encounter Ascopart who, in Josian's mind, will be a suitable replacement.

Ascopart is not just a test of faith but one of judgment. After Bevis defeats the giant in battle, Josian mercifully begs that Ascopart's life be spared. This excess of Christian charity reminds us of Bevis's sparing Brademond's life at their first encounter and Devon's denial of mercy to Guy. Mercy is a Christian virtue, but one must have the judgment to determine when it is justified. Though by now Bevis has that kind of knowledge ("'Dame, a wile vs be-trai!'" [l. 2371]), Josian, new to Christianity, has not. Although she is ready for her conversion, she is not yet the woman she is to become.

After Ascopart joins the party, the three of them go to Cologne where Josian is converted. But she must be tested yet another time before Bevis can marry her.

Having already proven her chastity, in this episode she must prove her willingness to defend it to whatever lengths are necessary. The previous assaults against her chastity were outright—Brademond simply attacked Ermin, and Yvor's suit was openly granted by her father. And her defenses were appropriate. Ermin, with Bevis's help, defeated Brademond, and her magic ring protected her from the marriage bed. This third assault, however, is accomplished through duplicity; consequently, Josian must go to extraordinary lengths to protect herself.

At this point, Bevis returns to England to regain his heritage, leaving Josian in Cologne under the protection of the bishop and Ascopart. Josian, for her part, feels secure in Bevis's absence because "While ichaue Ascopard,/ Of þe nam ich noþing afard," (ll. 3133-3134). But this is a typical romantic twist of irony: it is fairly certain that if she feels that she will be safe with Ascopart, he will be unable to protect her. And this is precisely what happens. Miles sends Ascopart a letter ostensibly from Bevis (reminiscent of Bevis's Uriah letter, and Brandonia's original message to Devon betraying Guy), requesting the giant's presence in England. He goes, leaving Josian unprotected, but she, on her own, sends Bevis a letter which ultimately counteracts Miles's treacherous one.

Once her protection is gone, Miles appears but Josian gives him the correct response for a Christian woman in her position:

> 'Nouyt, þey i scholde lese me lif,
> Boute ich were þe weddede wif;
> þif eni man me scholde wedde,
> þanne mot ich go wiþ him to bedde:
> I trowe, he is nouyt now here,
> þat schel be me wedde-fere!'

> (ll. 3163-3168)

This situation has occurred repeatedly in this poem but the significance of this scene is that the interlacing of the thread is completed. She enunciates the necessity for married love and, thus, compensates for her original lustful proposition to Bevis. Earlier, she had said she would die if she did not have him; now, she would rather die than fornicate. This reverses the travesty of love represented by Brandonia.

Words, of course, are not enough. Miles is not particularly concerned about the marriage vows:

> 'Y schel þe wedde ayenes þe wille,
> To morwe y schel hit ful-fille!'
> And kiste hire anon riyt.
> And sente after baroun & kniyt

> And bed hem come leste & meste,
> To anoure þat meri feste.

> (ll, 3169-3174)

His kiss is reminiscent of Bevis's when Josian decided to convert. That kiss became the source of Bevis's betrayal by Ermin who wrongly believed it to be lustful. This time it does represent lust, only Josian has no one to protect her from it, and must handle the problem herself.

She requests one favor from Miles:

> 'Ich bidde, þow graunte me a bone,
> And boute þow graunte me þis one,
> I ne schel þe neuer bedde none;
> Ich bidde þe at þe ferste frome,
> þat man ne wimman her in come;
> Be-lok hem þar oute for loue o me,
> þat noman se our priuite!'

> (ll. 3194-3200)

She speaks the literal truth since one boon is all she will ever need from him. The irony parallels that used by Bevis when he came to Yvor's castle dressed as a palmer. Then, irony was used to identify Bevis; now Josian uses irony to protect her identity, for after this episode she will have proven her right to be Bevis's wife.

Once she has killed Miles, she does not run away but stays in her bed and waits. Though she knows that certain retribution will follow the murder, she feels that her action is justified—she has defended herself against an assault on her chastity—and as a Christian, she must face the consequences. To run away would indicate guilt, but she has committed murder under special circumstances and must defend it as such:

> 'þestendai he me wedded wiþ wrong
> & to niyt ichaue him honge:
> Doþ be me al youre wille,
> Schel he neuer eft wimman spille!'

> (ll. 3253-3256)

Still, the townsmen decide to burn Josian at the stake. She is stripped and the fire is started when, in timely fashion, Bevis and Ascopart come to the rescue. Symbolically, Josian undergoes the death of her old self, and is reborn as wife to Bevis. In addition, the episode reflects back to the introduction of the poem. On the literal level, Josian parallels Brandonia in that both were forced into loveless marriages, and arranged the deaths of their respective husbands in order to marry the preferred suitors. However, one must keep in mind the character of Brandonia in contrast to that of Josian.

Brandonia was unchaste and did not have her husband killed for the sake of chastity but for that of lust. Even more significant is the contrast between the reactions of the townsmen. While Miles's kin demand revenge against a justifiable murder, the people of Southampton not only ignore the murder of Guy but celebrate the wedding of their treacherous queen and her lover. The contrast cannot have been overlooked by the fourteenth century audience. Bevis not only embodies the heroic aspects of romance but also represents a national hero who rectifies the political injustice of Edgar's reign. Though he has not yet literally avenged his father's murder, he has done so metaphorically, by choosing a wife who is the inverse of Brandonia.

Once Josian is safe, Bevis returns to England, kills Devon, sees his mother die ("yhe fel and brak hire nekke þer fore." [1. 3462]), and he and Josian marry. At this point, the past has been rectified. Guy's murder has been avenged, his mother is dead and he can retrieve his birthright. But as a nationalistic romance postulating the ideals of society, the poem cannot end here. Before the author can rest, he must establish stability for the future.

Bevis is an interlaced narrative and the future is not a simple linear progression. In a comedy, for example, marriage frequently signifies the defeat of the old society and birth of a new one.[14] Even in *Love's Labour's Lost*, where the action is cut off before that moment, the projection of a happy ending suffices since we are confident that after their year's penance, the academicians will marry and live happily ever after. In *Bevis*, however, such a relaxed attitude towards the future does not work. Because Christians have been assaulted by treacherous Saracens, and even by other Christians, every loose thread must be interlaced completely into the fabric, lest future happiness might unravel. Consequently, the romance must continue until its natural resolution, the establishment of a realm of peace.

The fourth section of the narrative culminates in the reunion of Bevis and his family. Once Josian is married and bears children, chastity is replaced by motherhood as the central issue. It is in this section that Bevis's prophecy about Ascopart is fulfilled, when the giant becomes the Iago of the story. He remains loyal to Bevis and Josian until he is denied promotion in favor of another—Bevis makes Terry his swain. Then, in revenge, Ascopart betrays Josian to Yvor. He had earlier betrayed Yvor when Bevis defeated him in combat, but now, he returns to his original master.

When Josian is about to deliver twins, she sends Bevis and Terry away:

'For godes loue,' yhe seide, 'nai,
Leue sire, þow go þe wai,
God for-bede for is pite,

þat noman þoury me be kouþe:
Goþ and wende hennes nouþe,
þow and þe swain Terry,
And let me worþe & oure leuedy!'

(ll. 3627-3634)

On the one hand, this speech directs our attention to her one boon from Miles, only that time she pretended modesty to make her new husband's retainers leave the chamber; but this time she is literally modest. Both incidents result in the elimination of a suitor. On the other hand, the speech also reminds us of the earlier time she had sent Bevis away. Then, the lions symbolically attested to her chastity; now, she will have to use trickery to preserve it. In addition, the result of the earlier incident was the introduction of Ascopart to the retinue; the ultimate result of this one will be the elimination of the traitor.

As soon as the twins are born, Ascopart arrives with forty Saracens and captures her on behalf of Yvor. This is the third time that Josian is forced to be with a man other than Bevis, and each time her defense is appropriate to the point in the story. Miles had threatened rape in the guise of marriage; consequently, a violent response was indicated. In the first episode with Yvor, she had been legally married though as yet unbaptized. Thus, the ordeal of a seven-year temptation was an apt way of demonstrating her worthiness of becoming a Christian. This time, however, it is only a matter of simple protection; therefore, she protects herself in the simplest way possible. She ingests an herb which gives her the appearance of a leper and makes her look so repulsive that Yvor locks her away for a year and a half. She is in absolutely no physical danger. The fact that Saber and not Bevis rescues her underscores the lack of danger.

Josian and Saber then search for Bevis who remains for seven years at Amberforce. Unlike the earlier reunion between the two, which was protracted to permit them to test each other, this one is resolved in less than ten lines. They retrieve their children from the fisherman and forester, and then move on. Though the incident is short in itself, its association with the introduction of the romance gives it great significance. Guy and Brandonia had been married for seven years when she had him killed. She then tried to have her son killed and failing that, sold him to the Saracens. This episode reverses that procedure. Bevis and Josian are separated for the seven years following the birth of their children who are given to strangers to raise. Each is tempted to commit adultery; both withstand the temptation. They are then reunited and retrieve their sons. In the previous episode the treachery against Guy was avenged. Now, with the reunion of Bevis and his children, this thread which began when Brandonia exiled her son, is completed. If Guy symbolized the past, Bevis represents the present, and now we can move on to a future marked by a generation of peace.

The emphasis of the final episode is social. Bevis and Josian have already proved themselves worthy of their identities, and now they fulfill those identities by converting the Saracens and reforming evil Christians, spacially moving back to England in the reverse of Bevis's original exile. Bevis converts the land of Ermonie which its king then leaves to Bevis's son, Guy. Bevis kills Yvor, who refuses to convert, and becomes King of Mombraunt. Both of these episodes are reminiscent of the beginning when, first of all, Ermin offered his kingdom and daughter to Bevis provided he become a Saracen, and when after that, Ermin had his daughter married to the King of Mombraunt.

In the final section, Josian withdraws from the action, performing only one last act. When the London mob attacks Bevis for being a traitor, she sends her sons to defend their father. She thus completes the final thread begun by Brandonia. Probably even more important to young Bevis than the fact that his mother had had his father murdered was his inability to help Guy. Now this situation is resolved as Bevis's own sons assist him. And in order to establish peace, Edgar, now old (like Ermin and Guy—Bevis's father), gives his daughter in marriage to Bevis's son Miles.

Finally, all of the loose threads have been woven into the fabric. The Saracens have been disposed of, and everyone has a realm to rule: Bevis has Mombraunt; Guy, Ermonie; Miles, England; Terry, Amberforce; and Bevis gives his earldom in Hampshire to Saber.

The emphasis on monarchy is necessarily strong. In the beginning, the townspeople feasted at an occasion which should have provoked rioting. At the end, a bloodthirsty mob unjustly attacks Bevis. Coming as it does at the end of the romance, the social commentary is significant. The people of London require a strong ruler to lead them, lest they be betrayed by unscrupulous usurpers. As a whole, from beginning to end, the people lack the wisdom to rule themselves and only a Bevis of Hampton, married to a Josian, producing a line of Guys and Miles', can assure order and stability. This they all do. . . .

Notes

[1] George Kane, *Middle English Literature* (New York: Barnes and Noble, 1951), p. 50.

[2] Mehl, p. 218.

[3] Baugh, "The Middle English Romance," 23-24.

[4] Eugène Vinaver, "The Poetry of Interlace," in *The Rise of Romance* (New York: Oxford University Press,

1971), pp. 68-98.

[5] Ibid.

[6] Ibid., pp. 75-76.

[7] Ibid., p. 68.

[8] Ibid., p. 76.

[9] Ibid., p. 77.

[10] Ibid., p. 95.

[11] Ibid., p. 81.

[12] (Halle: Max Niemeyer, 1909).

[13] The illustration is reproduced from Vinaver, p. 81.

[14] Frye, p. 163. . . .

Works Cited

. . . Baugh, Albert C. "The Middle English Romance: Some Questions of the Creation, Presentation, and Preservation." *Speculum*, 42 (1967), 1-31. . . .

Kane, George. *Middle English Literature*. New York: Barnes and Noble, 1951. . . .

Mehl, Dieter. *The Middle English Romances of the Thirteenth and Fourteenth Centuries*. London: Routeledge and Kegan Paul, 1968. . . .

Vinaver, Eugène. *The Rise of Romance*. New York: Oxford University Press, 1971. . . .

Susan Crane (essay date 1986)

SOURCE: "Land, Lineage, and Nation" in *Insular Romance,* University of California Press, 1986, pp. 53-91, 225-51.

[*In the following excerpt, Crane examines the competing principles of feudalism and nationalism in* Bevis of Hampton *as well as in the Anglo-Norman version of the poem and other Middle English romances. She contends that Bevis merely pays lip service to the notion that national ideology is more important than the interests of noble families; in reality, she asserts, it celebrates ancestral heriage, opposition to royal authority, and aristocratic autonomy.*]

The conventional notion of what constitutes medieval English romance—much bloodshed, great length, marvels and wonders, action rather than reflection—comes close to perfect embodiment in the stories of Guy of

Warwick and Bevis of Hampton. Lord Ernle's assessment typifies modern reaction to these romances: "The austere simplicity of the older forms is overlaid with a riot of romantic fancy; their compactness of structure is lost. The romances are swollen to a prodigious length, in which incident is threaded to incident, adventure strung to adventure, and encounter piled on encounter."[1] They are as long as novels, and their detractors often fault them for failing by modern fictional standards,[2] while their admirers class them with popular detective novels or thrillers.[3] But "novel" content, design, technique, and invention by no means characterize the aesthetic of these works, nor are they particularly strong on mystery or thrills. Rather, they develop earlier romances' interest in baronial issues of land and lineage; their design, the kinds of events and problems they treat, and their stylistic procedures convey images of noble life that give their "riot of romantic fancy" a meaning worthy of the success they enjoyed.

This chapter treats the thirteenth-century Anglo-Norman romances of English heroes, their English descendants, and some later fourteenth-century romances as well. *Sir Beues of Hamtoun*[4] and *Guy of Warwick* (both ca. 1300) are so closely related to Anglo-Norman versions that some critics have treated them as translations. But textual studies demonstrate that no English manuscript translates an extant Anglo-Norman manuscript, so that their differences cannot be considered evidence of direct poetic reworking. Instead, the various versions of each story, like the versions of Horn and Havelok, are related works whose differences may be more accurately understood in terms of insular generic and historical developments than in terms of textual revision.

The longer romances of English heroes usually connect exile and return to feudal dispossession and reinstatement, and double the hero's winning of land with his winning a bride to continue the lineage. As for Horn and Havelok, the law and the courts are important sources of justification for Bevis, Guy, and Fulk—though this confidence in law breaks down in the later *Athelston* and *Gamelyn*. In addition, the diffuse longer works incorporate new sources of validation for noble heroes. Motifs from epic, saints' legends, and courtly poetry demonstrate heroic worth by other standards than winning a heritage. Where these standards conflict, uneasy accommodations reestablish the heritage as the dominant value for adventuring heroes.

Des Aventures e Pruesses Nos Auncestres

Central to all these works is the English hero's status as fictional forebear and defender of his nation. The opening lines of *Fouke le Fitz Waryn* (ca. 1280) illustrate this emphasis by revising the topos that spring's renewal stimulates human activity. Rather than inspiring love as in much lyric poetry, or warfare as epitomized in Bertran de Born's "Be'm platz lo gais temps," here springtime prompts reflection on the deeds of English ancestors:

> En le temps de averyl e may, quant les prees e les herbes reverdissent e chescune chose vivaunte recovre vertue, beauté e force, les mountz e les valeyes retentissent des douce chauntz des oseylouns, e les cuers de chescune gent pur la beauté du temps e la sesone mountent en haut e s'enjolyvent, donque deit home remenbrer des aventures e pruesses nos auncestres, qe se penerent pur honour en leauté quere.[5]

> In the season of April and May, when meadows and plants become green again and every living creature regains its nature, beauty, and force, the hills and valleys echo with the sweet songs of birds, and people's hearts soar and gladden at the beauty of the weather and the season, then we should remember the adventures and deeds of prowess of our ancestors, who labored to seek honor in loyalty.

Fulk is loyal to his lineage and to feudal law: the "aventures e pruesses nos auncestres" typically continue to arise from disputed land tenure and a family's cyclical self-renewal. This is evident in the first of the later romances of English heroes, the Anglo-Norman *Boeve de Haumtone*, composed somewhat later than the *Lai d'Haveloc* but probably not long after 1200. More than in the Old French *Bueve de Hantone*, in *Boeve* a clearly discernible line of interest in land and family runs through a varied range of motifs and adventures.[6]

Boeve, which closely resembles the story of Horn in plot,[7] unites the hero's first exile loosely around his first disinheritance. Like Horn, Boeve becomes a model vassal who defends the feudal hierarchy at home and in exile, refuses to marry until his patrimony is secured, and makes plans to avenge his father's death and rewin his own rights.[8] His subsequent confrontations with King Edgar inspire the most politically cogent section of the work. Unique to the insular versions of the story are Boeve's refusal to pay the inheritance fee because of Edgar's failure to protect his rights, his request for permission to build Arundel Castle, and his warning to Edgar not to interfere with his land while he is again in exile.[9]

Boeve's second exile develops insular concerns in the more emotive sphere of family feeling. The hero's line of descent and that of his old tutor Sabaoth become intermixed in one extended family that shares Boeve's exile, conquests, and return to power in England.[10] Boeve and his companion Tierri, Sabaoth's son, value their wives primarily as mothers and take great delight in their children.[11] Boeve's two sons obediently play up to their father's pride in their emerging likeness to himself:

> Dist l'un a l'autre: 'le champ traversez,
> si pensom de joster! Contre moi venez;

ke ne savom, kant serrom esprovez.
Kant nus vera mun pere li alosez
nos armes porter, si serra mult lez.'
Ore purrez vere cops de chevalers.
'Par mon chef!' dist Boves, 'cil erent
    bachelers;
s'il vivent longes, il atenderunt lur per. . . .
Sainte Marie, dame!' dist Boves li alosez,
'dame, merci! les enfans me gardez.'

(3346-53, 3357-58)

One said to the other: 'Cross the field, and let's
think on jousting! Come at me, for we don't know
when we will be tried. When our renowned father
sees us bearing our arms, he will be very happy.'
Then you could see the blows of knights! 'By my
head!' said Bevis, 'these are fine aspirants to
knighthood; if they live long, they'll catch up to
their father. . . . Holy Mary, Lady!' said worthy
Bevis, 'Lady, your grace! Guard these children for
me.'

The family continuity that Boeve sees represented in
his children culminates when his two sons share in
achieving his heritage and when he realizes at his death
two weeks later that his children can successfully hold
his property:

'Sire, ke tendra vos riches cassemens?'
'Dame, jeo n'en ai cure, a deu lur command;
la merci deu, uncore ay trois enfans,
ke purrunt tenir nos riches cassemens.'

(3814-17)

'My lord, who will hold your great fiefs?' 'Lady, I
have no concern for them, I commend them to God;
thanks to God I still have three children who can
hold our great fiefs.'

Here the familial devotion running through the work
finally comes to support the political concept of land
tenure.[12] Through much of the romance, however, the
influence of baronial concerns operates on the level of
emotionally felt impulse rather than of consciously
articulated political principle.

In *Fouke le Fitz Waryn* the "aventures e pruesses nos
auncestres" all center more closely around the disputed
patrimony. This romance, exceptionally, tells not of
legendary pre-Conquest figures but of a historical
family's fortunes from the time of the Conquest through
the reign of King John. Nearly half the romance recounts (with many historical distortions) the exploits
of Fulk's ancestors as they establish the lineal claims
he must defend from King John's depredations. Fulk's
defense is double, with two escapes abroad from John's
unjust anger, two promises of restoration, and numer-

ous minor adventures that support the legal rights of
family members and other barons to land.

The central crisis occurs when, upon the death of Fulk's
father, King John denies Fulk's inherited right to
Whittington in favor of another's claim. Fulk turns
outlaw with a resounding denunciation of John's failure to provide just administration:

'Sire roy, vous estes mon lige seignour, e a vous su
je lié par fealté tant come je su en vostre service, e
tan come je tienke terres de vous; e vous me dussez
meyntenir en resoun, e vous me faylez de resoun e
commune ley, e unqe ne fust bon rey qe deneya a
ces franke tenauntz ley en sa court; pur quoi je vous
renk vos homages.' (24.26-32)

'Sir king, you are my liege lord, and I am bound to
you in fealty as long as I am in your service and as
long as I hold lands from you; and you ought to
sustain me in justice, and you fail me in justice and
common law; and there was never a good king who
refused his free tenants law in his court; wherefore
I renounce my allegiance to you.'

Fulk's language of fealty and his appeal to law recall
the *Romance of Horn*, yet here the situation is directly
historical. The era of Magna Carta is the only post-
Conquest period for which it is easy to imagine baronial victories comparable to those in the romances of
English heroes. The historical John, like the fictional
Edgar in the story of Bevis or Edelsi/Godard in the
story of Havelok, appeared a wrongheaded and in the
end intimidated king who had to concede the rights he
unjustly sought to deny. Similarly, the Welsh border is
perhaps the only post-Conquest setting that provided
something like the military autonomy with which the
English heroes demonstrate the worthiness of their
claims. The Marcher lords enjoyed rights to private
armies, to waging war and winning land, and to considerable judicial freedoms, in contrast to the rest of
England's barony.[13] In *Fouke* a remarkable historical
moment, an exceptional setting, and a heavily romanticized account of the Fitz Warin family's affairs allow
the ideal fictional pattern of baronial victory to play
itself out in a situation from the insular barony's own
history.

To regain his holdings, in these later romances as in
earlier ones, the hero must establish or sustain his family dynasty. Women's roles (except in the story of Guy)
support the hero's efforts and contrast to roles from
the literature of *fine amor*. Fulk secretly marries
Matilda, whom he has never even seen before the
wedding, partly to discomfit her suitor, King John, and
partly because he "savoit bien qe ele fust bele, bone e
de bon los, e qe ele avoit en Yrlaunde fortz chastels,
cités, terres e rentes e grantz homages" [knew well that
she was fair, good, and of good reputation, and that
she had in Ireland strong castles, towns, lands and
income, and great fiefs] (30.20-22). The insular Bevis

versions lack even the superficially decorous customs of deference that ornamented political alliances in the *Romance of Horn*. Rather, Josian courts Bevis with pleas and insults, while he shows energetic pique at her advances, walks out on her show of indignation, and, when she follows him to his room, snores in a futile attempt to get rid of her (AN 670-772, ME A 1093-199). After their betrothal, this freedom from the conventions of *fine amor* allows Josian to become an active helper to the hero, very like his wonderful horse Arundel, with whom she is in fact sometimes equated. Bevis's wife and horse both assist him in his dynastic victory and, despite their servile status, achieve a measure of dignity and repute as the appanage of Bevis's great merit.[14]

Sir Beues of Hamtoun undertakes an important development, whose beginnings are barely discernible in *Boeve*, from the perception of the baronial family as a political unit owing personal allegiance to rulers on the basis of reciprocal support, to a wider perception of national identity and the importance of national interests. The adventures of Horn and Havelok as they lose and gradually regain power correspond directly with the loss and the need of their people. This is a simple and effective means of heroic justification: what is good for Horn and Havelok turns out to be good for everyone. *Fouke le Fitz Waryn* shares this confident assessment. In the romances of Bevis and Guy, the needs and desires of the whole nation do not constantly coincide with those of the noble hero. But in compensation, patriotic sentiment reinforces the value of the hero's actions. Whatever his private baronial goals, he nonetheless represents his nation by occupying England's fictional history as an ancestral figure of diverse and superlative accomplishments.

The process is just beginning in *Boeve de Haumtone*, where a marginal sense of the hero's Englishness may be suggested by echoes of the legend of St. George, whose feast day became a national holiday in 1222.[15] Boeve's crusading fervor against pagans and his imprisonment in Damascus, as they recall St. George's exploits, reflect the gradual development of England's national identity through the impact of the Crusades, the loss of Normandy in 1204 and of the Angevin territories by 1243, and the increasing centralization of rule: "By the thirteenth century the fully developed medieval state [of England] had reached a momentary equilibrium, and if it was still 'feudal,' it was also, in its way, a national state."[16] To sustain the national state, a sense of pride in and commitment to it developed, expressed during the thirteenth century in antiforeign sentiment and more positively in the country's mobilization against the crises of the 1290s. Maurice Powicke concludes from Edward I's handling of these crises that "it was in Edward's reign that nationalism was born."[17]

A powerful sense of national commitment renders obsolete and even subversive the older feudal belief that lord and vassal have mutual duties and that vassals can maintain some spheres of autonomous action. Fulk's resistance to John goes unquestioned, but the Middle English *Beues* recognizes and adjusts to the challenge of nationalism by adding references to England and Bevis's Englishness on the one hand while supporting and even strengthening Bevis's feudal claims on the other.[18] Introducing an interpolated combat with a dragon, the poet ranks Bevis's achievement with similar victories by the English Wade and Guy of Warwick (2599-608). Told in the manner of a saint's legend, the dragon-killing extends the correspondences suggested in Anglo-Norman between the hero and St. George, patron saint of the English army from the earliest Crusades.[19] By these associations the Middle English version implies that Bevis's merit is national, even while extending references to his personal claims.

The conclusion of *Beues* also recognizes that the more dominant national ideology becomes, the more questionable a baron's commitment to his family and resistance to royal authority will become. *Boeve de Haumtone* reaches its resolution when Boeve, in response to Edgar's disseisin of Sabaoth's son, returns to England to bring the king into line. Edgar sweats with fear at the news of Boeve's arrival and, deferentially greeting the hero as "'sire roi'" (3767), settles Boeve's claim by arranging with his parliament to offer his daughter in marriage to Boeve's son (3738-49). The tensions in the feudal hierarchy that provide the terms of *Boeve*'s conclusion are obfuscated in the conclusion of *Beues*. The vassal no longer intimidates the king; even though Edgar had wrongly denied Bevis's rights he simply returns the heritage "bleþeliche" (A 4301). But the inescapable tension between them erupts in a street battle instigated by the king's steward, who recalls Bevis's role in the death of Edgar's son during the son's attempted theft of Arundel:

'Hureþ þe kinges comaundement:

                                       Hear

Sertes, hit is be-falle so,

                                    Truly

In your cite he haþ a fo,
Beues, þat slouy þe kinges sone;

                                    slew

þat tresoun ye ouyte to mone:

                                    lament

I comaunde, for þe kinges sake,
Swiþe anon þat he be take!'

                               Right away

Whan þe peple herde þat cri,
þai gonne hem arme hasteli.

                          (A 4332-40)

It may seem surprising that a hero would be memorialized in British literature for slaughtering so many citizens of London "þat al Temse was blod red" (A

4530).[20] The carnage does resolve the charge that Bevis had betrayed the king: "'þus men schel teche file glotouns [vile rascals] / þat wile misaie [speak evil of] gode barouns,'" the hero concludes self-righteously as he delivers the coup de grace to King Edgar's steward (A 4387-88). In terms of the poem's professed national feeling, the best we can do is to read this episode non-mimetically as a "good baron" triumphing over slander.[21]

But it is important that, however Bevis's Englishness or his relations with Edgar may be *described*, his *actions* still defend his heritage, defy the king, and maintain his autonomy. Deprived of direct confrontation with Edgar, he exercises indirect opposition with relish; during this battle his sons' devoted support is crucial (A 4415-18, 4457-74, 4523-26). The romance denies its own assertions with respect to nationhood whenever those assertions interfere with Bevis's access to rights and rank. The underlying impetus of **Beues of Hamtoun** remains baronial, and any conflicting elements of national ideology are resisted. . . .

Notes

[1] Ernle, *Light Reading*, p. 78.

[2] Charles W. Dunn writes that *Guy of Warwick*'s "incidents are unduly repetitive and prolix; the Middle English adapters show no inventiveness or critical sense. . . . The extent of its appeal is presumably dependent more upon the fame of Warwick Castle than upon its literary merit" (Severs, ed., *Manual*, I, 31).

[3] E.g., Richmond, "*Guy of Warwick*: A Medieval Thriller"; McKeehan, "*Guillaume de Palerne*: A Medieval 'Best Seller'"; Ramsey, *Chivalric Romances*, pp. 1-7.

[4] *Beues of Hamtoun*, ed. Kölbing. On its dependence on the AN *Boeve*, see Kölbing, edition, p. xxxv; and Baugh, "Improvisation," pp. 431-32. The eight MSS and early printed versions used in Kölbing's edition differ considerably, although three main versions may be classified from them. See Kölbing, pp. vii-viii; Baugh, "Convention and Individuality," pp. 126-29. I cite the Auchinleck (A) MS, except where variants are significant to the discussion.

[5] *Fouke le Fitz Waryn*, ed. Hathaway et al., p. 3, lines 1-8. The editors summarize research on the relationship between the extant prose version (ca. 1330) and its lost verse source (ca. 1280), pp. xxxiii-xlvii.

[6] *Boeve de Haumtone*, ed. Stimming. Legge, *Anglo-Norman Literature*, p. 157, suggests a late twelfth-century date, but cf. Stimming, edition, pp. lvii-lviii. Stimming, pp. clxxx-cxciii, and Matzke, "Beves Legend," summarize debate over the origin of the story and the relationship of the AN version to the three continental versions (*Bueve de Hantone*, ed. Stimming). Recent opinion supports continental dependence on the AN version (Rickard, *Britain in Medieval French Literature*, pp. 140-41).

[7] During Bevis's first period of exile from his patrimony in England he is wooed by Josian, the daughter of the foreign king he serves, and in consequence suffers a long imprisonment in Damascus. A second exile from England (after his horse Arundel kicks King Edgar's son to death) follows Bevis's marriage to Josian and a temporary reacquisition of his lands and titles. This exile repeats the pattern of foreign success and wooing by a foreign princess found in Bevis's first exile, with many added adventures of separation and reunion. Finally, Bevis's twin sons participate in the acquisition of three kingdoms, those of Josian's father, Josian's pagan husband Yvor, and England.

[8] *Boeve*, 635-46, 683-87, 977-79, 1412-16, 1945-46, 2375-77, 2380-82. Martin [Weiss], "Middle English Romances," pp. 95-107, believes that different poets composed the first 165 laisses and the remainder of the poem. Errors and illogicalities do trouble the later stages of narration, e.g., the designation "François" for Boeve's supporters (3156-59, 3604-28). Cf. Stimming, edition, pp.xxii-lvii.

[9] *Boeve*, 2428-50, 2508-22, 2545-50, 2615-21.

[10] Boeve gives Sabaoth his land (2598-600); Boeve's second (chaste) wife subsequently marries Tierri (3001-6); Boeve is godfather to their son Boeve (3200), who is to be married to Boeve's daughter Beatrice (3520).

[11] The account of Boeve's marriage stresses the conception of his sons (2389-96); see also 3064, 3195-200, 3205-6, 3265-71, 3512-13.

[12] In addition, a few events in the second half of the work reinforce or echo Boeve's political claim in England: he defends the claim of the Dame de Civile (2824-47) and of Sabaoth's son (3702-5); he returns to England, as he warned Edgar he would, when Edgar dispossesses Robant, who holds Boeve's lands for him (2611-21).

[13] Davies, *Lordship and Society*, pp. 67-85, 149-75, 217-28; Meisel, *Barons*, pp. 34-54, 87-100, 132-38.

[14] Arundel is her gift to Bevis; both she and the horse are one-man creatures who resist appropriation by others (e.g., Yvor's attempts, AN 981-1031, ME A 1457-534, 2031-35). In two AN warning dreams losing Arundel represents losing Josian (2731-42) and harm to Boeve indicates the loss of one or the other helper (3436-43).

[5] Matzke, "Contributions," p. 125; Weiss, "*Sir Beues of Hamtoun*," p. 72.

[16] Galbraith, "Nationality and Language," pp. 113-14; Powicke, *Thirteenth Century*, pp. 29-31, 100-103, 218-19; Wood, *Age of Chivalry*, pp. 125-38; Rickard, *Britain in Medieval French Literature*, pp. 38-40.

[17] *Thirteenth Century*, p. 528; see also Keeney, "Military Service."

[18] The English adapters add these references to Bevis's claims: *Beues*, A 1126-28, 1263-88, 1339-44, 2916-20, 2938-40, 3039-46, 3070, and M 901. But they omit passages on the children's charms and their growing prowess; Terri has no son and Bevis no daughter.

[19] A 2597-910; Weiss argues that "patriotic sentiment" inspires these and other developments in *Beues* ("*Sir Beues of Hamtoun*," p. 72); see also Matzke, "Contributions," pp. 125, 150-56.

[20] That the steward's chief ally is a Lombard, or in later versions crowds of Lombards (A 4497-516; MO 4102, 4233), gives the episode a more conventionally nationalist coloring, yet in all versions surely most of the thirty thousand or more citizens whom Bevis slays must be Englishmen. On antiforeign sentiment in the thirteenth century, see H. W. C. Davis, *England under the Normans*, pp. 415-16, 421-22, 433-34; Rickard, *Britain in Medieval French Literature*, p. 40.

[21] Mehl recognizes the problem but assumes it would not be recognized by an audience of "less refined tastes" (*Middle English Romances*, p. 216); Weiss seeks national feeling in the street fight's analogies to certain oppositions between barons and London merchants during the reform period ("*Sir Beues of Hamtoun*," pp. 73-76).

Abbreviations

ANTS Anglo-Norman Text Society . . .

EETS Early English Text Society . . .

MÆ Medium Ævum

M&H Medievalia et Humanistica . . .

MHRA Modern Humanities Research Association . . .

MP Modern Philology . . .

PAPS Proceedings of the American Philosophical Society . . .

TRHS Transactions of the Royal Historical Society . . .

Bibliography

Primary Sources

Primary sources are listed alphabetically by author, if known, or by the key word in the title. Phrases preceding the key word are bracketed. . . .

[*The Romance of Sir*] *Beues of Hamtoun.* Ed. Eugen Kölbing. EETS, e.s. 46, 48, 65. London, 1885, 1886, 1894.

[*Der anglonormannische*] *Boeve de Haumtone.* Ed. Albert Stimming. Bibliotheca normannica, No. 7. Halle, 1899.

[*Der festländische*] *Bueve de Hantone.* Ed. Albert Stimming. 5 vols. Gesellschaft für romanische Literatur, Nos. 25, 30, 34, 41, 42. Göttingen, 1911-20. . . .

Fouke le Fitz Waryn. Ed. E. J. Hathaway et al. ANTS, 26-28. Oxford, 1975. . . .

Secondary Sources

. . . Baugh, Albert Croll. "Convention and Individuality in the Middle English Romance." In *Medieval Literature and Folklore Studies: Essays in Honor of Francis Lee Utley.* Ed. Jerome Mandel and Bruce Rosenberg. New Brunswick, N.J., 1970, pp. 123-46.

———. "Improvisation in the Middle English Romance." *PAPS,* 103 (1959), 418-54. . . .

Davies, R. R. *Lordship and Society in the March of Wales, 1282-1400.* Oxford, 1978.

Davis, H.W.C. *England under the Normans and Angevins, 1066-1272.* London, 1905. . . .

Ernle, R.E.P. *The Light Reading of Our Ancestors: Chapters in the Growth of the English Novel.* London, 1927. . . .

Galbraith, V.H. "Nationality and Language in Medieval England." *TRHS,* 4th ser., 23 (1941), 113-28. . . .

Keeney, Barnaby C. "Military Service and the Development of Nationalism in England, 1272-1327." *Speculum,* 22 (1947), 534-49. . . .

Legge, Maria Dominica. "Anglo-Norman Hagiography and the Romances." *M&H,* n.s. 6 (1975), 41-49.

———. *Anglo-Norman Literature and Its Background.* Oxford, 1963; corr. repr. 1971. . . .

McKeehan, Irene P. "*Guillaume de Palerne:* A Medieval 'Best Seller.'" *PMLA*, 41 (1926), 785-809. . . .

Martin [Weiss], Judith Elizabeth. "Studies in Some Early Middle English Romances." Diss. Cambridge, 1967. . . .

Matzke, John E. "The Oldest Form of the Beves Legend." *MP*, 10 (1912), 19-36.

Mehl, Dieter. *The Middle English Romances of the Thirteenth and Fourteenth Centuries.* London, 1968.

Meisel, Janet. *Barons of the Welsh Frontier: The Corbet, Pantulf, and Fitz Warin Families, 1066-1272.* Lincoln, Nebraska, 1980. . . .

Powicke, Maurice. *The Thirteenth Century, 1216-1307.* 2nd ed. Oxford, 1962. . . .

Ramsey, Lee C. *Chivalric Romances: Popular Literature in Medieval England.* Bloomington, 1983. . . .

Richmond, Velma Bourgeois. "*Guy of Warwick:* A Medieval Thriller." *South Atlantic Quarterly*, 73 (1974), 554-63. . . .

Rickard, Peter. *Britain in Medieval French Literature, 1100-1500.* Cambridge, 1956. . . .

Severs, J. Burke. *A Manual of the Writings in Middle English, 1050-1500.* Vol. I, *Romances.* New Haven, 1967. . . .

Weiss, Judith. "The Major Interpolations in *Sir Beues of Hamtoun.*" *MÆ*, 48 (1979), 71-76. . . .

Wood, Charles T. *The Age of Chivalry. Manners and Morals, 1000-1450.* London, 1970. . . .

Geraldine Barnes (essay date 1993)

SOURCE: "*Beves of Hamtoun*" in *Counsel and Strategy in Middle English Romance*, D. S. Brewer, 1993, pp. 60-90, 139-58.

[*In the excerpt below from an essay that emphasizes the significance of good counsel in several medieval romances, Barnes traces Bevis's growing maturity, linking it to his willingness to accept the judgment or advice of others. She also discusses the issues of kingship and tyranny raised in the final section of the poem.*]

. . . An adaptation, with some emendations and interpolations,[44] of the Anglo-Norman *Boeve d'Hamtoune*,[45] **Beves of Hamtoun** shares certain superficial similarities of theme and structure with *Guy of Warwick*. In this instance, however, the role of counsel in the hero's life is not directed towards an understanding of the ethos of chivalry but to the overcoming of tyranny and injustice.

Although they are not marked by a change in verse form, **Beves**, like *Guy*, falls into two distinct and self-contained parts on the diptych pattern, which chart the loss and restoration of the hero's patrimony.[46] The first, and longer, section (to l. 3510)[47] deals with Beves's fight against a private wrong motivated by lust; the second, his efforts to overcome a public act of royal tyranny, precipitated by material greed, which has far-reaching consequences for the kingdom. Whereas *Guy* is the account of the life of a national hero, whose defence of England against the threat of Danish invasion is only one, albeit the greatest, of his chivalric exploits, the political concerns of **Beves** are actually closer to those of *Havelok*. Like Guy, Beves progresses from a disregard for good counsel to the recognition of its importance for knightly success, but his ultimate mission is to save England, not from the external threat of dragons, giants, or invasion, but from the internal threat of royal tyranny.

As a child, Beves is the helpless victim of evil counsel. When he is seven years old, his mother conspires with her lover, Devoun, emperor of Almaine, to murder her elderly husband Guy, Earl of Southampton. The first explicit act of 'counsel' in the narrative is one of conspiracy, in which Beves's mother reveals her plot against his father to a 'messenger': 'Anon riyt þat leuedi fer/ To consaile cleped hir masager' (ll. 70-71). As acknowledged by Beves's uncle, tutor, and designated killer, Saber, who saves Beves and fakes evidence of his death by soaking his clothes in pig's blood (ll. 347-52), it is her *red* to have her son murdered as well: 'Dame,' a seide, 'ich dede him of dawe/ Be þe red and be þe sawe' (ll. 481-82).

Attired in poor clothes and unrecognized, Beves receives, and rejects, his first piece of *red*, which takes the form of an abusive warning ('Scherewe houre son, y þe rede,' l. 398) by a porter against entering the family castle, now occupied by Devoun. Nevertheless, Beves enters the hall and 'counsels' the usurper in a similar vein: 'Aris! Fle hennes, I þe rede' (l. 436). He rants, raves ('Beues was niy wod for grame,' l. 439), and strikes the emperor with a club in a display of impotent anger which serves merely to illustrate his youthful vulnerability. Only another, more reasoned form of action restrains the tyrannical exercise of authority and saves him from death, when the knights in the hall, distressed on the child's account, ignore his mother's demand that they seize him (ll. 452-56).

Alarmed at the possible consequences of Beves's actions, Saber warns that unless he heeds his counsel ('Boute þow be me consaile do,' l. 472), both of them will be imperilled. Beves, like Guy, ignores the sage advice of his elder—in this case, to remain in hiding[48]—and soon, on his mother's orders, finds himself captured and sold into heathendom, where he soon becomes the prized property of King Ermin of Armenia and object of the love of the king's daughter, Josian. Beves repeats his mistake later in the narrative when Terry, Saber's son, offers him life-saving advice in different circumstances: rightly guessing that a letter in Beves's possession actually contains his death warrant on a false charge of seducing Josian, Terry asks to read it.[49] Just as Beves has previously ignored Saber's advice, he rejects Terry's request, walks straight into the trap (ll. 1387-88), and spends the next seven years in a snake-infested dungeon.

The fortunes of Beves begin to improve only when he learns to act on good advice, beginning with that of Josian's servant, Boniface. Although she loves Beves, Josian is wooed by another, unwanted suitor. Boniface counters Beves's rash proposal to flee with the princess, now the reluctant but virgin bride of King Yvor of Mombraunt, with a plan of his own: 'Sire, þe is beter do be me rede!' (l. 2210). 'It schel be so!,' says Beves (l. 2236). The first part of the strategy, to remove Yvor from the scene, is successful, and Boniface prefaces the details of the next step—to drug old King Garcy, who has been left to guard Josian, and then to flee—with the words: 'þif þe wil by my consaile do' (l. 2296). When Beves declares that he is, in fact, ready to do battle with Garcy and all his host (ll. 2332-38), Boniface once more sagely counsels discretion: 'Sir, þow is better do by my reed' (l. 2340). Beves heeds this counsel, the plan is successful, and he and Josian take ship for Cologne. Three times Boniface has tendered his counsel, and three times Beves has curbed his rashness and successfully followed good advice.[50]

Having conclusively proved his prowess in battle with a dragon who has taken up residence in Cologne, Beves is now fully qualified, physically and mentally, to reclaim his inheritance. In a significant step towards maturity, he actively solicits wise counsel before taking action and, instead of following his own rash inclinations, seeks advice, this time from another uncle, Saber Florentin, bishop of Cologne: 'Leue em, what is to rede/ Of me stifader Deuoun,/ þat holdeþ me londes at Hamtoun?' (ll. 2912-14). The bishop duly provides *red* (l. 2922), in the form of one hundred men to support Beves and Saber in mounting an attack on the emperor. Following hard upon this indication of maturity is the first endorsement of Beves's own credentials as counsellor; converted and baptised by Saber Florentin but stranded in Cologne, Josian appeals to him as he prepares to leave for England: 'Who schel me þanne wisse & rede?' (ll. 2942).

It is not, however, until Beves and his company are one mile out of Southampton that he is represented as a military leader, capable of providing battle strategy.

He addresses his men thus: 'Lordinges,' to his men a sede,/ 'ye scholle do be mine rede!' (ll. 2957-58), the plan being to trick Devoun into thinking that the force, led by a certain 'Gerard', has come to lend assistance against attacks by Saber. Beves's good counsel here is, however, directly challenged by evil, when his mother re-enters the narrative with her own strategy for the emperor ('Sire,' yhe seide, 'doute þow nouyt!/ Of gode consaile icham be-þouyt,' ll. 3313-14): to muster forces from Almaine and Scotland. Beves is nevertheless victorious, has Devoun put to death—his mother, beside herself with grief at the sight of her husband 'in þe pich' (l. 3460) conveniently falls and breaks her neck—and, within the space of thirty lines, marries Josian and follows Saber's advice to go to King Edgar in London to claim his patrimony (ll. 3487-88), a request which is immediately granted. Like his father before him, Beves becomes the king's marshall.

Marriage and restoration of birthright are usually signals to narrative closure, and the rapidly moving events of these thirty-five lines (ll. 3475-510), which also make reference to the children of Beves and Josian, constitute a stereotyped conclusion to a Middle English romance.[51] But *Beves* has some thousand lines to go, and the concerns of this last quarter of the narrative enter the arena of public affairs. At issue are the duties of kingship and the problem of tyranny. Tyranny is shown to be an insidious thing: some despots may be instantly recognizable, like Devoun, but they may also be less immediately obvious, like the apparently worthy King Edgar. In the first part of *Beves*, a criminal act robs the hero of his father and his birthright; in this last part, the abuse of legitimate authority drives him from his lands and leads to the loss of his wife and children.

Beves's second exile is precipitated by the attempted theft, by Edgar's foolish son, of Josian's gift, the magnificent warhorse Arundel, who retaliates by kicking out the prince's brains (ll. 3561-63). Arundel has been left unattended only because Beves has left the stable to fulfil the obligations of the office of king's marshall, a point emphasized by the narrative:

> Hit is lawe of kinges alle,
> At mete were croune in halle,
> & þanne eueriche marchal
> His yerde an honde bere schal.
> While Beues was in that office,
> þe kinges sone, þat was so nice,
> What helpeþ for to make fable?
> A yede to Beues stable.

> (ll. 3551-58)

Disregarding Beves's adherence to his duty on the one hand and his son's felonious action on the other, Edgar orders the hero's execution. But, taking into account his previous record of loyal service, the barons exercise their right of counsel and suggest that Arundel be hanged instead (ll. 3571-74), a proposal to which Beves responds by making his estate over to Saber and emigrating to Armenia. This incident, where royal tyranny is restrained only by baronial counsel, offers something of a parallel with events in the early part of the narrative, when refusal by the knights of Southampton to comply with an unjust order saves Beves from the homicidal wrath of his mother.

Creating an impression of competing narrative modes, *chanson de geste* and 'political romance', this last part of *Beves* presents a striking contrast between the lurid and fantastic nature of those episodes which take place abroad, mainly in 'Armenia', and the more 'realistic' tenor of those set in England.[52] Take, for example, the two attempts to steal Arundel, the unsuccessful one by Edgar's son and a second, successful one in Armenia: whereas we are given the plausible details and consequences of the English prince's actions, Arundel is simply whisked away in Armenia by unspecified 'charmes' (l. 4033). Beves achieves his goals in Armenia by the sword, but in England he regains his patrimony 'Ase hit was lawe and riyt vsage' (l. 3470).[53] Deviating from the topographical vagueness of *Boeve d'Hamtoune*,[54] the final episodes of *Beves* convey an impression of geographical versimilitude. We are a long way from exotic and unhistorical 'Armenia' when the narrative moves into the concrete and recognizable world of London and its environs: Putney, the Thames, Westminster, Cheapside, Ludgate.

The events of Beves's second exile parallel those of the first. Having originally lost his birthright and his father to the evil machinations of his mother, he is now deprived of the family assets through royal tyranny and of his wife through the treachery of the giant, Ascopard, who abducts Josian after she delivers twins in a forest enroute to Armenia. In Armenia, Beves inspires the love of another lady, who persuades him to marry her in a bigamous but chaste union (ll. 3829-40). The work of conversion continues, too: with the aid of his son, Guy, Beves forcibly brings Christianity to the entire kingdom of Armenia (ll. 4019-20), to which the dying Ermin makes Guy heir (ll. 4008-13). After defeating Yvor in single combat, Beves himself is crowned king of Mombraunt (ll. 4253-54). He has achieved all that the exotic world of *chanson de geste* can offer but is a dispossessed person in the 'real' world of England.

Beves makes a final journey to his homeland, this time with a force of 60,000 (l. 4276), to lend support to Saber's son, Robant, in the face of the ursurpation of the ancestral lands by King Edgar. Beves argues his case before the king's court in Westminster, but there is a lone dissenter to the decision of king and barons to restore his property in the person of Edgar's steward. The steward's denunciation of Beves as outlaw

and traitor to the king (ll. 4309-14) and to the people of London (ll. 4324-38) leads to a conflict of epic proportions—32,000 die and the Thames turns red with blood (ll. 4530-32)—in claustrophobically familiar surroundings.[55]

This episode is one of two major interpolations by the English adapter of *Boeve de Haumtone*,[56] and, despite its likely association with the incident involving Simon de Montfort and a crowd of Londoners in December, 1263,[57] its immediate narratorial significance is not overtly clear. Dieter Mehl suggests that it is intended for local appeal to English, specifically London audiences, 'of less refined tastes',[58] and Susan Crane, that: 'In terms of the poem's professed national feeling, the best we can do is to read this episode non-mimetically as a "good baron" triumphing over slander.'[59] The episode can, however, be interpreted as another illustration of the power of malign counsel to corrupt justice and promote anarchy, a notion supported by the more forthcoming version of *Beves* in Gonville and Caius manuscript 175, where the baleful effects of the steward's *red* are presented in a similar light to the potentially dire consequences of Wymound's slanderous *counseil* in *Athelston*, which, as it happens, follows *Beves* in that manuscript. The Gonville and Caius narrator ascribes the bloodshed to 'þe fals stywardys red' (l. 198, p. 213), commenting, like his counterpart in *Athelston*, that: 'Falsnesse cam neuere to good endyng' (l. 200, p. 213);[60] likewise, the Gonville and Caius Edgar summons his earls, barons, and knights in order to make the same attribution: 'And tolde hem, hou hys men were ded/ þorwy þe false stywardys red' (l. 214, p. 214).

Edgar's crime is not, like Athelston's, to act upon the advice of one evil counsellor, but not to act at all. This *redeless* king offers no response to the steward's slanderous attack upon Beves and simply disappears from the narrative until the battle is all but over. The steward's actions in the king's name (he incites the Londoners by claiming that Beves has been outlawed by royal *comaundement* [l. 4332]) remain unchecked, and the next we hear of Edgar is that he is eager to make peace by marrying his daughter to Beves's son, Miles (ll. 4539-60).

As in *Guy*, love is a problematic issue in *Beves*, but instead of being a seductive obstacle on the hero's path to a true understanding of chivalry, it is actively eschewed by him from the outset. Whereas *Guy* initially subscribes to the 'courtly' values of love service, *Beves* displays a consistent streak of misogyny: Guy eventually denounces the negative effects of 'courtly' love upon chivalry and acknowledges God, rather than Felice, as the inspiration for his noble deeds, but Beves, although spurred throughout by Christian zeal, is also driven by the desire for vengeance upon his mother. In the *curriculum vitae* with which he identifies himself to Ermin, he accuses his mother of treacherously engineering his father's death, condemns the wickedness of many other women, and swears vengeance for Earl Guy, without making any reference to Devoun, the willing instrument of the deed itself:

> 'For gode,' a seide, 'ich hatte Bef,
> Iboren ich was in Ingelonde,
> At Hamtoun, be þe se stronde;
> Me fader was erl þar a while,
> Me moder him let sle wiþ gile,
> Wikked beþ fele wimmen to fonde!
> Ac sire, yif it euer so be-tide,
> þat ich mowe an horse ride
> And armes bere & scheft to-breke,
> Me fader deþ ich schel wel wreke!'

(ll. 542-52)

It is tempting, although it credits the narrative with an unwarranted depth of psychological insight, to see the influence of his childhood trauma in all of Beves's dealings with women, which end in disaster, or near disaster, until his mother is dead. The single kiss which he gives Josian at the announcement of her pending conversion (ll. 1194-99), for example, leads directly to the false accusation of seduction (ll. 1200-10) and his seven-year incarceration in Brademond's dungeon. Then, having escaped and been advised by the bishop of Jerusalem to marry only a virgin (ll. 1967-69), he returns to Armenia to learn that King Yvor has Josian 'to bord and to bedde' (l. 2012).

Other incidents, too, recall the horrific events of Beves's early years. Like Guy, he kills a wild boar; but while Guy's boar fight and subsequent killing of Florentine's son illustrate the wrongful use of chivalric prowess, Beves's despatch of the beast, whose head he presents to Ermin, has a different, symbolic significance. His mother's plot to murder his father begins with a feigned illness, which, she tells her husband, can be cured only by the meat of a wild boar (ll. 184-86). When Guy duly sets out on the hunt, Devoun waylays him with a company of 10,000 knights, kills, and beheads him. Beves's boar slaying is a reverse metaphorical representation of that murder:[61] Devoun sends Guy's head to his mistress as a trophy (ll. 277-85), whereas Beves intends giving the boar's to Josian (l. 832). In the course of the hunt, Beves is also assailed, by Ermin's wicked steward; but after defeating his attackers, he presents the head to Ermin (ll. 903-04) without further reference to Josian.[62]

Although Josian eventually becomes his wife, and on one occasion is called Beves's *lemman* (l. 1984) by the narrator and, on another, by Beves himself (l. 713), he remains the passive and reluctant partner in their relationship. The first, and decidedly ill-timed, offer of her hand comes from King Ermin, who makes his proposal immediately after the statement of disgust for his mother

and all womankind with which Beves introduces himself. The hero's declaration, in response to Ermin's offer, that 'I nolde for-sake in none manere/ Iesu, þat bouyte me so dere' (ll. 565-66) is explicitly a rejection of heathendom, but also, implicitly, of sexuality. Beves ceases his comically brutal rejection of Josian's advances (ll. 1093-132; 1179-99)[63] when she announces her readiness to embrace Christianity, but not until Devoun and his mother are dead, and Beves is said, for only the second time in his life,[64] to be 'glad & bliþe' (l. 3471), do they marry.

The talented, loving, and faithful Josian is the antithesis of Beves's lascivious mother and the (initially) aloof Felice, but she is also the object of his transferred resentment and, as Lee Ramsey argues, 'clearly punished'[65] for her first two marriages, unwanted and unconsummated though they are. Condemned to death for the murder of her second husband, Earl Miles, she is stripped to her shift and tied to the stake before Beves rides to the rescue (ll. 3289-93). Even after marriage to Beves, and moments after giving birth to twin sons on the flight from England to Armenia, she is beaten, bound, and kidnapped.

During and despite these hardships, Josian, well-versed in the Eastern arts of magic and trickery and possessed of healing and musical skills, is no passive Griselda and emerges as one of the most enterprising women in Middle English romance. Her ingenuity gives her more in common with *Ywain and Gawain*'s Lunet than with *Guy of Warwick*'s Felice. Like Felice, she dispenses charity to Christian pilgrims for her beloved's sake during his seven years of imprisonment (ll. 2080-88), but her outstanding quality is her talent for *gyn*. While Beves shows himself to be progressively more receptive to wholesome counsel, Josian, successfully contriving to remain a virgin throughout her first two marriages, becomes an exponent of stratagem to virtuous ends. The means by which she manages this in the first instance are not revealed, but she avoids consummation of the second forced union by strangling the bridegroom (ll. 3175-224). No practical use is made of Felice's education in *Guy*, whereas Josian uses the knowledge of medicine she has acquired from the 'meisters grete' (l. 3672) of Bologna and Toledo to give herself the temporary appearance of a leper in order to discourage the renewed advances of Yvor (ll. 3671-700). She exercises her healing skills upon Beves when he is wounded in a skirmish with Ermin's knights on Christmas Day (ll. 715-34) and is also well-tutored in music, a talent which she employs to practical advantage to support herself and the temporarily ailing Saber (ll. 3906-16), after he rescues her from her postpartum abductor (ll. 3852-88), and they commence a seven-year search for Beves.

Nevertheless, even on her deathbed, Josian fails to capture her husband's full attention. Mortally ill, she summons her son, Guy, and Beves's cousin, Terry, to her side. The first mention of Beves in this final scene concerns his thoughts not for Josian, but for Arundel. Upon the arrival of Guy and Terry, Beves goes abruptly to the stables, where he finds his horse dead (ll. 4595-97). Stricken with grief, he returns to see, apparently for the first time, that Josian is on the brink of death. He embraces her, and they die together.

Like the first, the second conclusion of **Beves of Hamtoun** returns to the conventional framework of romance, with the marriage of Edgar's daughter and Beves's son, and the reconciliation of king and hero. Instead of returning to Southampton, however, Beves bestows his earldom upon Saber and returns to Armenia to take up residence in Mombraunt, where he and Josian spend the last twenty years of their lives. Beves thus fulfils a threefold mission in life: personal, patriotic, and religious. Through his efforts to regain his patrimony and the family honour, he delivers England from tyranny and Armenia from heathendom. The continued success of these achievements is assured by the succession of his sons, Guy and Miles, to these respective kingdoms, and achieved in no small part through the faithful lifetime service of his uncle, Saber.

Beves follows a pattern, common to *Havelok, Gamelyn,* and *Guy,* in which the hero's maturity is signalled by his capacity to receive, to act upon, and to impart wise counsel. With the exception of Havelok, who never rejects good advice, the heroes of these romances progress from initially ignoring sage *red* and *counseil* to heeding their mentors and showing themselves to be capable givers of counsel. Knights who spurn wholesome counsel invite failure and dishonour; *unrede* kings, like Athelston (*Athelston*), the king of Maydenland (*Ywain and Gawain*), Costentine (*Of Arthour and of Merlin*), and Edgar (*Beves*), who are deficient in judgment and receptive, actively or passively, to evil counsel, or averse to good, are either cyphers or tyrants.

Notes

. . .[44] See Judith Weiss, 'The Major Interpolations in *Sir Beues of Hamtoun*,' 48 (1979), 71, 76.

[45] Which probably dates from: 'in its existing shape . . . the last decade of the twelfth century' (Judith Weiss, 'The Date of the Anglo-Norman *Boeve de Haumtone*,' *Medium vum* 55 [1986], 240).

[46] There is, however, a switch in verse form from stanzas to couplets early in the narrative, at line 475. Fewster sees this metrical shift as having thematic significance in that it constitutes 'a new opening that points to the establishment of Beues as the hero of this romance. Like the *Guy* metrical change, the break signals a new set of adventures for the hero' (*Traditionality and Genre*, p. 48).

[47] References, unless otherwise indicated, are to the Auchinleck version of *Beves*, in Kölbing, *The Romance of Sir Beues of Hamtoun*. On the relationships between the manuscripts and printed versions, see Mehl, *The Middle English Romances*, pp. 211-13; Jennifer Fellows, 'Editing Middle English Romances,' in *Romance in Medieval England*, ed. Mills, Fellows, Meale, pp. 7-10.

[48] Although Ellis is of the opinion that, by concealing Beves in a closet, 'Saber was unable to devise any counsel worth following' (*Specimens of Early English Metrical Romances*, p. 243), this seems to be a logical strategy in the circumstances.

[49] Unlike Josian, the heroine of the romance, Beves never receives a scholarly education.

[50] The pagan Boniface now appears to have served his purpose and is slain by lions (ll. 2378-86).

[51] 'The reader will now be disposed to flatter himself that this prodigious and eventful history is terminated; that Sir Bevis will in future sleep quietly in his bed, Arundel in his stable, and Morglay in its scabbard' (Ellis, *Specimens of Early English Romances*, p. 272).

[52] On the geographical boundaries of *Beves,* see Metlitzki, *The Matter of Araby*, pp. 126-33.

[53] As Crane comments: 'Bevis wins back his heritage from King Edgar not by invasion but by pressing his legal claim and winning the support of the king's counselors' (*Insular Romance,* p. 87).

[54] See Albert C. Baugh, 'Convention and Individuality in the Middle English Romance,' in *Medieval Literature and Folklore Studies. Essays in Honor of Francis Lee Utley*, ed. Jerome Mandel and Bruce A. Rosenberg (New Brunswick, N.J., 1970), pp. 138-39.

[55] As Judith Weiss remarks: 'His Pass of Roncesvalles is Gose Lane' ('The Major Interpolations in *Sir Beues of Hamtoun*,' p. 73).

[56] The other being the dragon fight in Cologne (see Weiss, 'The Major Interpolations,' pp. 71-72).

[57] See Weiss, 'The Major Interpolations,' p. 74, and above, ch. 1, p. 37.

[58] *The Middle English Romances*, p. 216.

[59] *Insular Romance*, p. 61.

[60] 'Lystnes, lordyngys þat ben hende,/ Off falsnesse, hou it wil ende' (*Athelston*, ll. 7-8).

[61] And, to engage in speculation about unconscious symbolism, possibly of his desired revenge upon

Devoun: the boar is castrated (l. 815), although Devoun meets his end in a cauldron of boiling pitch and brimstone (ll. 3451-57).

[62] To venture into Beves's subconscious once again, possibly he associates his plan to give the boar's head to Josian with the attack which follows almost immediately (ll. 837-88).

[63] On Josiane's wooing of Boeve in *Boeve de Haumtone* and its comic potential, see Judith Weiss, 'The wooing woman in Anglo-Norman romance,' in *Romance in Medieval England*, ed. Mills, Fellows, Meale, pp. 152-53. On the figure of the 'bele Sarrasine', see also William Calin, 'Rapports entre chanson de geste et romans courtois au XIIe siècle,' in *Essor et Fortune de la Chanson de geste dans l'Europe et l'Orient latin. Actes du XIe Congrès International de la Société Rencesvals pour l'Etude des Epopées Romanes (Padoue-Venise, 29 août - 4 septembre 1982),* 2 vols. (Modena, 1984), II, 415-16.

[64] The first (l. 2497) follows his victory over two lions in the forest where he and Josian take refuge after their flight from Garcy and Yvor.

[65] *Chivalric Romances,* p. 59.

Bibliography

Primary sources

. . . *The Romance of Sir Beues of Hamtoun. Edited from Six Manuscripts and the Old Printed Copy, with Introduction, Notes, and Glossary,* ed. Eugen Kölbing, EETS, e.s. 46, 47, 48 (London, 1885, 1886, 1894). . . .

Secondary sources: critical and historical works

. . . Baugh, Albert C. 'Convention and Individuality in the Middle English Romance,' in *Medieval Literature and Folklore Studies. Essays in Honor of Francis Lee Utley,* ed. Jerome Mandel and Bruce A. Rosenberg (New Brunswick, N.J., 1970), 123-46. . . .

Calin, William. 'Rapports entre chanson de geste et romans courtois au XIIe siècle,' in *Essor et Fortune de la Chanson de geste,* pp. 407-24. . . .

Crane, Susan. *Insular Romance. Politics, Faith, and Culture in Anglo-Norman and Middle English Literature* (Berkeley, Los Angeles, London, 1986). . . .

Ellis, George. *Specimens of Early English Metrical Romances, to which is prefixed an Historical Introduction on the Rise and Progress of Romantic Composition in France and England,* new edn., revised by J.C. Halliwell (London, 1848). . . .

Fellows, Jennifer. 'Editing Middle English romances,' in Mills, Fellows, Meale, ed., *Romance in Medieval England,* pp. 5-16. . . .

Fewster, Carol. *Traditionality and Genre in Middle English Romance* (Cambridge, 1987). . . .

Mehl, Dieter. *The Middle English Romances of the Thirteenth and Fourteenth Centuries* (London, 1968).

Metlitzki, Dorothee. *The Matter of Araby in Medieval England* (New Haven and London, 1977). . . .

Mills, Maldwyn, Jennifer Fellows and Carol M. Meale, ed. *Romance in Medieval England* (Cambridge, 1991). . . .

Ramsey, Lee C. *Chivalric Romance. Popular Literature in Medieval England* (Bloomington, 1983). . . .

Weiss, Judith. 'The Major Interpolations in *Sir Beues of Hamtoun,' Medium Ævum* 48 (1979), 71-76.

————'The Date of the Anglo-Norman *Boeve de Haumtone,' Medium Ævum* 55 (1986), 237-40.

————'The wooing woman in Anglo-Norman romance,' in Mills, Fellows, Meale, ed., *Medieval Romance in England,* pp. 149-61. . . .

FURTHER READING

Brownrigg, Linda. "The *Taymouth Hours* and the Romance of *Beves of Hampton.*" In *English Manuscript Studies 1100-1700,* edited by Peter Beal and Jeremy Griffiths, Vol. I, pp. 222-41. Oxford: Basil Blackwell, 1989.

Focuses on the illustrations that accompany an excerpt from *Bevis of Hampton* which appears in the fourteenth-century manuscript known as the *Taymouth Hours.*

De Vries, F. C. "A Note on *The Owl and the Nightingale* 951, 1297." *Notes and Queries* n.s. 16, No. 12 (December 1969): 442-44.

Points out that although the reflexive form of the verb "to understand" is rarely found in fourteenth-century English texts, this usage appears in line 319 of the Auchinleck version of *Bevis of Hampton.*

Hibbard, Laura A. "Jacques de Vitry and *Boeve de Haumtone.*" *Modern Language Notes* XXXIV, No. 7 (November 1919): 408-11.

Proposes that a tale related in a sermon by a French cleric is the source of the episode in the Anglo-Norman version of *Boeve de Haumtone* in which Bevis escapes from his Saracen foes by a masterful display of horsemanship.

Matzke, John E. "The Legend of Saint George: ItsDevelopment into a *roman d'aventure*." *PMLA* XIX, n.s. XII, No. 3 (1904): 449-76.

Compares early English versions of *Bevis of Hampton* with the story of Saint George as recounted in Richard Johnson's *Seven Champions of Christendom* (1592). Matzke concludes that Johnson's depiction of George as both a valorous hero and a religious martyr was adapted from a version of *Bevis*—now lost—in which elements of the stories of Beves and George had already been fused.

————. "The Oldest Form of the *Beves* Legend." *Modern Philology* X, No. 1(July 1912): 19-54 1-36.

Argues that the essential outline of Italian variants of the *Bevis* story stems from an independent tradition. Matzke determines that both the Italian forms on the one hand and the Anglo-Norman and continental French versions on the other originally derived from a French tale that is no longer extant.

Turnbull, William B. D. D. "Preliminary Remarks." In *Sir Beves of Hamtoun: A Metrical Romance*. Publication 44 of the Maitland Club, edited by William B. D. D. Turnbull, pp. xi-xix. Edinburgh: 1838.

Comments briefly on Bevis's historical prototype and the poem's French predecessors, and summarizes the plot.

Hypatia

c. 370-415

Greek mathematician and philosopher.

INTRODUCTION

Widely regarded as the first female mathematician, Hypatia was famous during her lifetime as a scholar and educator. She taught astronomy and philosophy as well as algebra and geometry, and composed treatises on the writings of other mathematicians. Endowed with uncommon intellect and strength of character, she achieved a degree of academic eminence that was rare for women of her day. Hypatia's written works are no longer extant, but over the centuries she has inspired her own literary tradition, as poets, dramatists, historians, and novelists have adapted and reformulated the story of her life—and particularly her violent death.

Biographical Information

Contemporary sources provide only a bare sketch of Hypatia's biography, and scholars have pointed out that even these are a mixture of fact, bias, and conjecture. A birth date of c. 370 has been accepted by many commentators, though some have suggested it was several years earlier. Hypatia was born and spent most of her life in Alexandria, a center—with Athens—of late fourth-century Greek intellectual activity. Her father, Theon, was a noteworthy mathematician, astronomer, and teacher in the city's institution of higher education, known as the Museum. He supervised her early education and training, and exerted a major influence on her life. Some scholars believe that Hypatia also studied philosophy in Athens. She began her teaching career while still a young woman, instructing a privileged circle of students in private classes at her home and later adding public lectures as her fame increased. She was reputed to be a woman of modesty and dignity, who wore her mantle of celebrity with grace. Despite the widespread respect she enjoyed in Alexandria—or perhaps because of it—Hypatia apparently became the object of factional hatred in a city troubled by conflicts between Christians, Jews, and pagans. In 415 she was attacked by a mob in the streets of Alexandria and brutally murdered.

Twentieth-century scholars have noted how the legend of Hypatia grew out of early accounts of her life and career. Substantial evidence of her significance as an educator appears in the letters of Synesius of Cyrene (c. 370-413), a philosopher and churchman who stud-

ied with Hypatia for many years and was devoted to her. Synesius's correspondence shows that many of her students, who were the sons of wealthy and noble families, later became important ecclesiastical and imperial figures. Synesius also refers to Hypatia's mechanical abilities and credits her with several inventions, including astronomical instruments and an apparatus that measured the density of liquids. Socrates Scholasticus, a near contemporary (c. 379-450), documented Hypatia's life in his *Ecclesiastical History;* his narrative is based at least in part on eyewitness accounts. He reported that she attracted students from throughout Egypt and beyond, and that she had considerable influence in Alexandria's political and social life. Socrates also provided a detailed account of her death: he implicated the Alexandrian church, named a monk called Peter as the chief assassin, and claimed that Hypatia was killed because of her close association with Orestes, the city Prefect. A third important source of information about Hypatia comes from the *Suda*, an anonymous tenth-century historical and literary collection.

According to the *Suda*, she was much admired for both her beauty and her intellect, and was awarded an official appointment as public lecturer in philosophy, drawing audiences from the highest ranks of society as well as from the academy. The *Suda* also relays the accusation contained in Damascius's *Life of Isidore* (c. 526) that Cyril, the Bishop of Alexandria, envied Hypatia's eminence and induced some of his monks to kill her. The testimony of Socrates and the *Suda* against the Alexandrian Christians eventually became an integral part of her story—generally accepted as truth by writers who embellished her personal narrative and focused on her savage murder. Few of these authors paid much attention to her principal writings.

Major Works

Commentators usually attribute three major works to Hypatia: a commentary on the *Arithmetica*, Diophantus's great treatise on algebra; an edition, with commentary, of the geometrician Apollonius of Perga's *Conic Sections*; and the *Astronomical Canon*. This last work deals with the movement of the planets, and some critics regard it as more of a commentary on Ptolemy's theories than an original essay on astronomy. These writings have all been lost, though a few scholars have identified fragmentary revisions of Hypatia's work embedded in the mathematical treatises of later writers. There are also reports that she composed philosophical essays, but no titles have survived. In addition, she assisted her father in his magnum opus, a multi-volume edition of Ptolemy's *Almagest*; while it is generally believed that Hypatia helped Theon prepare book three of this edition, scholars disagree about the extent of her contribution.

Critical Reception

The modern reception of Hypatia begins in the early eighteenth century. In 1720 John Toland, a British deist and self-described free-thinker, published an essay on Hypatia in which he charged Cyril and other Alexandrian clergy with direct responsibility for her death. More than a decade later, in an essay on religious fanaticism, the French poet and philosopher Voltaire characterized her as a martyr to Christian intolerance. In 1788 Edward Gibbon included a vivid account of Hypatia's death in a section of *The History of the Decline and Fall of the Roman Empire* in which he deprecates Cyril of Alexandria; Gibbon's representation of her murder is often quoted by critics and commentators. The English novelist Charles Kingsley published, in 1853, a novel entitled *Hypatia, or, New Foes with an Old Face,* loosely based on her life. This was frequently reprinted and translated into several languages, though Kingsley was also censured for his lurid treatment of sexual motifs and his anti-Catholic bias. In the second half of the nineteenth century, French Romantic poets and dramatists portrayed Hypatia as

the last of the classical Greeks—a symbol of the lost world of harmonious relations between art and philosophy, science and religion. More recently, Hypatia has become an icon for feminists such as Ursule Molinaro (1989) who see her murder as an act of vindictiveness against independent-minded women. While dramatists and novelists in Europe and North America continue to refashion her story, a few scholars have attempted to present an objective view of Hypatia's life and work. In 1965, for example, J. M. Rist assessed her philosophical teachings, determining that despite the tradition of associating her with Neoplatonism, she was actually a relatively conservative Platonist. Without concrete evidence of Hypatia's writings, it is difficult to assess her contribution to philosophical or mathematical scholarship. Yet Maria Dzielska, the author of a book-length study (1995) of Hypatia and the literary legend that has accrued to her, notes that all reliable sources attest that she was an inspired teacher as well as "a model of ethical courage, righteousness, veracity, civic devotion, and intellectual prowess."

---

*PRINCIPAL WORKS

Arithmetica (commentary)

Conic Sections (edition and commentary)

Astronomical Canon (essay)

Almagest (editor, with her father, Theon)

*All of Hypatia's works have been lost and their dates of composition are not known.

CRITICISM
Edward Gibbon (essay date 1788)

SOURCE: "Nestorius, Patriarch of Constantinople" in *The History of the Decline and Fall of the Roman Empire,* John Murray, 1872, pp. 14-5.

[*In the following excerpt from a work originally published in 1788, Gibbon fixes the responsibility for Hypatia's death on Cyril of Alexandria, charging that the bishop used her as a scapegoat to resolve a breach between church and state.*]

. . . Hypatia, the daughter of Theon the mathematician,[25] was initiated in her father's studies; her learned comments have elucidated the geometry of Apollonius and Diophantus; and she publicly taught, both at Athens and Alexandria, the philosophy of Plato and

Aristotle. In the bloom of beauty, and in the maturity of wisdom, the modest maid refused her lovers and instructed her disciples; the persons most illustrious for their rank or merit were impatient to visit the female philosopher; and Cyril beheld with a jealous eye the gorgeous train of horses and slaves who crowded the door of her academy. A rumour was spread among the Christians that the daughter of Theon was the only obstacle to the reconciliation of the prefect and the archbishop; and that obstacle was speedily removed. On a fatal day, in the holy season of Lent, Hypatia was torn from her chariot, stripped naked, dragged to the church, and inhumanly butchered by the hands of Peter the reader and a troop of savage and merciless fanatics: her flesh was scraped from her bones with sharp oyster-shells,[26] and her quivering limbs were delivered to the flames. The just progress of inquiry and punishment was stopped by seasonable gifts; but the murder of Hypatia has imprinted an indelible stain on the character and religion of Cyril of Alexandria.[27]

Notes

. . . [25] For Theon and his daughter Hypatia, see Fabricius, Bibliothec. tom. viii. p. 210, 211. Her article in the Lexicon of Suidas is curious and original. Hesychius (Meursii Opera, tom. vii. p. 295, 296) observes that she was persecuted . . . ; and an epigram in the Greek Anthology (l. i. c. 76, p. 159, edit. Brodæi) celebrates her knowledge and eloquence. She is honourably mentioned (Epist. 10, 15, 16, 33-80, 124, 135, 153) by her friend and disciple the philosophic bishop Synesius.

[26] . . . Oyster-shells were plentifully strewed on the sea-beach before the Cæsareum. I may therefore prefer the literal sense without rejecting the metaphorical version of *tegulæ,* tiles, which is used by M. de Valois. I am ignorant, and the assassins were probably regardless, whether their victim was yet alive.

[27] These exploits of St. Cyril are recorded by Socrates (l. vii. c. 13, 14, 15); and the most reluctant bigotry is compelled to copy an historian who coolly styles the murderers of Hypatia . . . At the mention of that injured name, I am pleased to observe a blush even on the cheek of Baronius.

Elbert Hubbard (essay date 1908)

SOURCE: "Hypatia" in *The Complete Writings of Elbert Hubbard,* The Roycroft Shop, 1908, pp. 51-79.

[*In the essay below, Hubbard offers an elaborate account of Hypatia's life and thought, stressing her independent mind and spirit as well as her indebtedness to Plato and Plotinus. Throughout, Hubbard uses details of her biography to express his personal antipathy to formal systems of religion.*]

The father of Hypatia was Theon, a noted mathematician and astronomer of Alexandria.

He would have been regarded as a very great man had he not been cast into the shadow by his daughter. Let male parents beware! At that time, astronomy and astrology were one. Mathematics was useful, not for purposes of civil engineering, but principally in figuring out where a certain soul, born under a given planet, would be at a certain time in the future. No information comes to us about the mother of Hypatia—she was so busy with housework that her existence is a matter of assumption or *a-priori* reasoning; thus, given a daughter, we assume the existence of a mother.

Hypatia was certainly the daughter of her father. He was her tutor, teacher, playmate. All he knew he taught her, and before she was twenty she had been informed by him of a fact which she had previously guessed—that considerable of his so-called knowledge was conjecture. Theon taught his daughter that all systems of religion that pretend to teach the whole truth were to a great degree false and fraudulent. He explained to her that his own profession of astronomy and astrology was only for other people.

By instructing her in all religions she grew to know them comparatively, and so none took possession of her to the exclusion of new truth. To have a religion thrust upon you, and be compelled to believe in it or suffer social ostracism, is to be cheated of the right to make your own. In degree it is letting another live your life. A child does not need a religion until he is old enough to evolve it, and then he must not be robbed of the right of independent thinking, by having a fully prepared plan of salvation handed out to him. The brain needs exercise as much as the body, and vicarious thinking is as erroneous as vicarious exercise.

Strength comes from personal effort. To think is natural, and if not intimidated or coerced the man will evolve a philosophy of life that is useful and beneficent. Religious mania is a result of dwelling on a borrowed religion. If let alone no man would become insane on religious topics, for the religion he would evolve would be one of joy, laughter and love, not one of misery or horror. The religion that contemplates misery and woe is one devised by priestcraft for a purpose, and that purpose is to rule and rob. From the blunt ways of the road we get a polite system of intimidation which makes the man pay. It is robbery reduced to a system, and finally piously believed in by the robbers, who are hypnotized into the belief that they are doing God's service. "All formal dogmatic religions are fallacious and must never be accepted by self-respecting persons as final," said Theon to Hypatia. "Reserve your right to think, for even to think wrongly is better than not to think at all." Theon gave lectures, and had private classes in esoterics, wherein the innermost secrets of divinity were imparted.

Also, he had a plan for the transmutation of metals and a recipe for perpetual youth. When he had nothing else to do, he played games with his daughter. At twenty-one Hypatia had mastered the so-called art of Rhetoric, or the art of expression by vocal speech. It will be remembered that the Romans considered rhetoric, or the art of the rhetor, or orator, as first in importance. To impress people by your personal presence they regarded as the gift of gifts. This idea seems to have been held by the polite world up to the Italian Renaissance, when the art of printing was invented and the written word came to be regarded as more important than the spoken. One lives, and the other dies on the air, existing only in memory, growing attenuated and diluted as it is transferred.

The revival of sculpture and painting also helped oratory to take its proper place as one of the polite arts, and not a thing to be centered upon to the exclusion of all else. Theon set out to produce a perfect human being; and whether his charts, theorems and formulas made up a complete law of eugenics, or whether it was dumb luck, this we know: he nearly succeeded. Hypatia was five feet nine, and weighed one hundred thirty-five pounds. This when she was twenty. She could walk ten miles without fatigue; swim, row, ride horseback and climb mountains. Through a series of gentle calisthenics invented by her father, combined with breathing exercises, she had developed a body of rarest grace. Her head had corners, as once Professor O. S. Fowler told us that a woman's head must have, if she is to think and act with purpose and precision.

So having evolved this rare beauty of face, feature and bodily grace, combined with superior strength and vitality, Hypatia took up her father's work and gave lectures on astronomy, mathematics, astrology and rhetoric, while he completed his scheme for the transmutation of metals. Hypatia's voice was flute-like, and used always well within its compass, so as never to rasp or tire the organs. Theon knew the proper care of nose and throat, a knowledge which with us moderns is all too rare. Hypatia told of and practised the vocal ellipse, the pause, the glide, the slide and the gentle, deliberate tones that please and impress. That the law of suggestion was known to her was very evident, and certain it is that she practised hypnotism in her classes, and seemed to know as much about the origin of the mysterious agent as we do now, even though she never tagged or labeled it.

One very vital thought she worked out was, that the young mind is plastic, impressionable and accepts without question all that it is told. The young receive their ideas from their elders, and ideas once impressed upon this plastic plate of the mind can not be removed.

Said Hypatia: "Fables should be taught as fables, myths as myths, and miracles as poetic fancies. To teach superstitions as truths is a most terrible thing. The child-mind accepts and believes them, and only through great pain and perhaps tragedy can he be in after-years relieved of them. In fact, men will fight for a superstition quite as quickly as for a living truth—often more so, since a superstition is so intangible you can not get at it to refute it, but truth is a point of view, and so is changeable."

Gradually, over the mind of the beautiful and gifted Hypatia, there came stealing a doubt concerning the value of her own acquirements, since these were "acquirements," and not evolutions or convictions gathered from experience, but things implanted upon her plastic mind by her father. In this train of thought Hypatia had taken a step in advance of her father, for he seems to have had a dogmatic belief in a few things incapable of demonstration; but these things he taught to the plastic mind, just the same as the things he knew. Theon was a dogmatic liberal. Possibly the difference between an illiberal Unitarian and a liberal Catholic is microscopic. Hypatia clearly saw that knowledge is the distilled essence of our intuitions, corroborated by experience. But belief is the impress made upon our minds when we are under the spell of or in subjection to another. These things caused the poor girl many unhappy hours, which fact, in itself, is proof of her greatness. Only superior people have a capacity for doubting. Probably not one person in a million ever gets away far enough from his mind to take a look at it, and see the wheels go round.

Opinions become ossified and the man goes through life, hypnotizing others, never realizing for an instant that in youth he was hypnotized and that he has never been able to cast off the hypnosis. This is what our pious friends mean when they say, "Give me the child until he is ten years old and you may have him afterward."

That is, they can take the child in his plastic age and make impressions on his mind that are indelible. Reared in an orthodox Jewish family a child will grow up a dogmatic Jew, and argue you on the Talmud six nights and days together. Catholic, Presbyterian, Baptist, the same. I once knew an Arapahoe Indian, who was taken to Massachusetts when four years old. He grew up not only with New England prejudices, but a New England accent, and saved his pennies to give to missionaries that they might "convert" the Red Men.

When the suspicion seized upon the soul of Hypatia that her mind was but a wax impression taken from her father's, she began to make plans to get away from him. Her efforts at explanations were futile, but when placed upon the general ground that she wished to travel, see the world and meet people of learning and worth, her father acquiesced and she started away on her journeyings. He wanted to go, too, but this was the one thing she did not desire, and he never knew nor could know why.

She spent several months in Athens, where her youth, beauty and learning won her entry into the houses of the most eminent. It was the same in Rome and in various other cities of Italy. Money may give you access to good society, but talent is always an open sesame. She traveled like a princess and was received like one, yet she had no title nor claim to nobility nor station. Beauty of itself is not a credential—rather it is an object of suspicion, unless it goes with intellect. Hypatia gave lectures on mathematics; and there was a fallacy abroad then as there is now that the feminine mind is not mathematical. That the great men whom Hypatia met in each city were first amazed and then abashed by her proficiency in mathematics is quite probable.

Some few male professors being in that peculiar baldheaded hypnotic state when feminine charms dazzle and lure, listened in rapture as Hypatia dissolved logarithms and melted calculi, and not understanding a word she said, declared that she was the goddess Minerva, reincarnated. Her coldness on near approach only confirmed their suspicions.

. . . . .

Just how long a time Hypatia spent upon her pilgrimage, visiting all of the great living philosophers, we do not know. Some accounts have it one year, others ten. Probably the pilgrimages were extended over a good many years, and were not continuous. Several philosophers proved their humanity by offering to marry her, and a prince or two did likewise, we are creditably informed. To these persistent suitors, however, Hypatia gently broke the news that she was wedded to truth, which is certainly a pretty speech, even if it is poor logic. The fact was, however, that Hypatia never met a man whose mind matched her own, otherwise logic would have bolstered love, instead of discarding it. Travel, public speaking and meeting people of note form a strong trinity of good things. The active mind is the young mind, and it is more than the dream of a poet which declares that Hypatia was always young and always beautiful, and that even Father Time was so in love with her that he refused to take toll from her, as he passed with his hourglass and scythe.

In degree she had followed the example of her great prototype, Plotinus, and had made herself master of all religions. She knew too much of all philosophies to believe implicitly in any.

Alexandria was then the intellectual center of the world. People who resided there called it the hub of the universe. It was the meeting-place of the East and the West. And Hypatia, with her Thursday lectures, was the chief intellectual factor of Alexandria.

Her philosophy she called Neo-Platonism. It was Plato distilled through the psychic alembic of Hypatia. Just why the human mind harks back and likes to confirm itself by building on another, it would be interesting to inquire. To explain Moses; to supply a key to the Scriptures; to found a new School of Philosophy on the assumption that Plato was but right, but was not understood until the Then and There, is alluring. And now the pilgrims came from Athens, and Rome, and from the Islands of the Sea to sit at the feet of Hypatia.

. . . . .

Hypatia was born in Three Hundred Seventy, and died in Four Hundred Thirty.

She exerted an influence in Alexandria not unlike that which Mrs. Eddy exerted in Boston. She was a person who divided society into two parts: those who regarded her as an oracle of light, and those who looked upon her as an emissary of darkness. Strong men paid her the compliment of using immoderate language concerning her teaching. But whether they spoke ill or well of her matters little now. The point is this: they screeched, sneezed, or smiled on those who refused to acknowledge the power of Hypatia.

Some professors of learning tried to waive her; priests gently pooh-poohed her; and some elevated an eyebrow and asked how the name was spelled. Others, still, inquired, "Is she sincere?" She was the Ralph Waldo Emerson of her day. Her philosophy was Transcendentalism. In fact, she might be spoken of as the original charter-member of the Concord School of Philosophy. Her theme was the New Thought, for New Thought is the oldest form of thought of which we know. Its distinguishing feature is its antiquity. Socrates was really the first to express the New Thought, and he got his cue from Pythagoras.

The ambition of Hypatia was to revive the flowering time of Greece, when Socrates and Plato walked arm in arm through the streets of Athens, followed by the greatest group of intellectuals the world has ever seen. It was charged against Hypatia that Aspasia was her ideal, and that her ambition was to follow in the footsteps of the woman who was beloved by Pericles. If so, it was an ambition worthy of a very great soul. Hypatia, however, did not have her Pericles and never married.

That she should have had love experiences was quite natural, and that various imaginary romances should have been credited to her was also to be expected. Hypatia was nearly a thousand years removed from the time of Pericles and Aspasia, but to bridge the gulf of time with imagination was easy. Yet Hypatia thought that the New Platonism should surpass the old, for the world had had the Age of Augustus to build upon.

Hypatia's immediate prototype was Plotinus, who was born two hundred four years after Christ, and lived to be seventy. Plotinus was the first person to use the phrase "Neo-Platonism," and so the philosophy of Hypatia might be called "The New Neo-Platonism." To know but one religion is not to know that one.

In fact, superstition consists in this one thing—faith in one religion, to the exclusion of all others. To know one philosophy is to know none. They are all comparative, and each serves as a small arc of the circle. A man living in a certain environment, with a certain outlook, describes the things he sees; and out of these, plus what he imagines, is shaped his philosophy of life. If he is repressed, suppressed, frightened, he will not see very much, and what he does see will be out of focus. Spiritual strabismus and mental myopia are the results of vicarious peeps at the universe. All formal religions have taught that to look for yourself was bad. The peephole through the roof of his garret cost Copernicus his liberty, but it was worth the price.

Plotinus made a study of all philosophies—all religions. He traveled through Egypt, Greece, Assyria, India. He became an "adept," and discovered how easily the priest drifts into priestcraft, and fraud steps in with legerdemain and miracle to amend the truth. As if to love humanity were not enough to recommend the man, they have him turn water into wine and walk on the water. Out of the labyrinth of history and speculation Plotinus returned to Plato as a basis or starting-point for all of the truth which man can comprehend. Plotinus believed in all religions, but had absolute faith in none. It will be remembered that Aristotle and Plato parted as to the relative value of poetry and science—science being the systematized facts of Nature.

Plotinus comes in and says that both are right, and each was like every other good man who exaggerates the importance of his own calling. In his ability to see the good in all things, Hypatia placed Plotinus ahead of Plato, but even then she says:

"Had there been no Plato there would have been no Plotinus; although Plotinus surpassed Plato, yet it is plain that Plato, the inspirer of Plotinus and so many more, is the one man whom philosophy can not spare. Hail Plato!"

. . . . .

The writings of Hypatia have all disappeared, save as her words come to us, quoted by her contemporaries.

If the Essays of Emerson should all be swept away, the man would still live in the quotations from his pen, given to us by every writer of worth who has put pencil to paper during the last fifty years. So lives Sappho, and thus did Charles Kingsley secure the composite of the great woman who lives and throbs through his book. Legend pictures her as rarely beautiful, with grace, poise and power, plus. She was sixty when she died. History kindly records it forty-five—and all picture her as a beautiful and attractive woman to the last. The psychic effects of a gracefully gowned first reader, with sonorous voice, using gesture with economy, and packing the pauses with feeling, have never been fully formulated, analyzed and explained.

Throngs came to hear Hypatia lecture—came from long distances, and listened hungrily, and probably all they took away was what they brought, except a great feeling of exhilaration and enthusiasm. To send the hearer away stepping light, and his heart beating fast—this is oratory—all of which isn't so much to bestow facts, as it is to impart a feeling. This Hypatia surely did. Her theme was Neo-Platonism. "Neo" means new, and all New Thought harks back to Plato, who was the mouthpiece of Socrates. "Say what you will, you 'll find it all in Plato." Neo-Platonism is our New Thought, and New Thought is Neo-Platonism.

There are two kinds of thought: New Thought and Secondhand Thought. New Thought is made up of thoughts you, yourself, think. The other kind is supplied to you by jobbers. The distinguishing feature of New Thought is its antiquity. Of necessity it is older than Secondhand Thought. All genuine New Thought is true for the person who thinks it. It only turns sour and becomes error when not used, and when the owner forces another to accept it. It then becomes a secondhand revelation.

All New Thought is revelation, and secondhand revelations are errors half-soled with stupidity and heeled with greed. Very often we are inspired to think by others, but in our hearts we have the New Thought; and the person, the book, the incident, merely remind us that it is already ours. New Thought is always simple; Secondhand Thought is abstruse, complex, patched, peculiar, costly, and is passed out to be accepted, not understood. That no one comprehends it is often regarded as a recommendation. For instance, "Thou shalt not make unto thyself any graven image," is Secondhand Thought.

The first man who said it may have known what it meant, but surely it is nothin to us. However, that does not keep us from piously repeating it, and having our children memorize it. We model in clay or wax, and carve if we can, and give honors to those who do, and this is well. This commandment is founded on the fallacy that graven images are gods, whatever that is.

The command adds nothing to our happiness, nor does it shape our conduct, nor influence our habits.

Everybody knows and admits its futility, yet we are unable to eliminate it from our theological system. It is strictly Secondhand—worse, it is junk. Conversely, the admonition, "Be gentle and keep your voice low," is New Thought, since all but savages know its truth, comprehend its import, and appreciate its excellence. Dealers in Secondhand Thought always declare that theirs is the only genuine, and that all other is spurious and dangerous. Dealers in New Thought say, "Take this only as it appeals to you as your own— accept it all, or in part, or reject it all—and in any event, do not believe it merely because I say so." New Thought is founded on the laws of your own nature, and its shibboleth is, "Know Thyself."

Secondhand Thought is founded on authority, and its war-cry is, "Pay and Obey." New Thought offers you no promise of paradise or eternal bliss if you accept it; nor does it threaten you with everlasting hell, if you don't. All it offers is unending work, constant effort, new difficulties; beyond each success is a new trial. Its only satisfactions are that you are allowing your life to unfold itself according to the laws of its nature. And these laws are divine, therefore you yourself are divine, just as you allow the divine to possess your being. New Thought allows the currents of divinity to flow through you unobstructed.

Secondhand Thought affords no plan of elimination; it tends to congestion, inflammation, disease and disintegration. New Thought holds all things lightly, gently, easily—even thought. It works for a healthy circulation, and tends to health, happiness and well-being now and hereafter. It does not believe in violence, force, coercion or resentment, because all these things react on the doer. It has faith that all men, if not interfered with by other men, will eventually evolve New Thought, and do for themselves what is best and right, beautiful and true. Secondhand Thought has always had first in its mind the welfare of the dealer. The rights of the consumer, beyond keeping him in subjection, were not considered. Indeed, its chief recommendation has been that "it is a good police system."

New Thought considers only the user. To "Know Thyself" is all there is of it. When a creator of New Thought goes into the business of retailing his product, he often forgets to live it, and soon is transformed into a dealer in Secondhand Thought.

That is the way all purveyors in Secondhand revelation begin. In their anxiety to succeed, they call in the police. The blessing that is compulsory is not wholly good, and any system of morals which has to be forced on us is immoral. New Thought is free thought. Its penalty is responsibility. You either have to live it, or else lose it. And its reward is Freedom.

. . . . .

It was only a little more than a hundred years before the time of Hypatia that the Roman Empire became Christian. When the Emperor Constantine embraced Christianity, all of his loyal subjects were from that moment Christians—Christians by edict, but Pagans by character, for the natures of men can not be changed by the passing of a resolution.

From that time every Pagan temple became a Christian Church, and every Pagan priest a Christian preacher. Alexandria was under the rule of a Roman Prefect, or Governor. It had been the policy of Rome to exercise great tolerance in religious matters.

There was a State Religion, to be sure, but it was for the nobility or those who helped make the State possible. To look after the thinking of the plain people was quite superfluous—they were allowed their vagaries. The Empire had been bold, brazen, cruel, coercive in its lust for power, but people who paid were reasonably safe.

And now the Church was coming into competition with the State and endeavoring to reduce spoliation to a system. To keep the people down and under by mental suppression, by the engine of superstition, were cheaper and more effective than to employ force or resort to the old-time methods of shows, spectacles, pensions and costly diversions. When the Church took on the functions of the State, and sought to substitute the gentle Christ for Cæsar, she had to recast the teachings of Christ. Then for the first time coercion and love dwelt side by side. "Depart from me, ye cursed, into everlasting fire prepared for the devil and his angels," and like passages were slipped into the Scriptures as matters of wise expediency.

This was continued for many hundred years, and was deemed quite proper and legitimate. It was knavery under a more subtle form. The Bishop of Alexandria clashed with Orestes the Prefect. To hold the people under by psychologic methods was better than the old plans of alternate bribery and force—so argued the Bishop. Orestes had come under the spell of Hypatia, and the *Republic* of Plato was saturating his mind. "To rule by fettering the mind through fear of punishment in another world is just as base as to use force," said Hypatia in one of her lectures. Orestes sat in the audience, and as she spoke the words he clapped his hands. The news was carried to the Bishop, who gently declared that he would excommunicate him. Orestes sent word back that the Emperor should be informed of how this Bishop was misusing his office by making threats of where he could land people he did not like, in another world. Neither the Bishop nor the Prefect could unseat each other—both derived their power from the Emperor. For Orestes to grow interested in the teachings of Hypatia, instead of siding with the Bishop, was looked upon by the loyalists as little short of treason.

Orestes tried to defend himself by declaring that the policy of the Cæsars had always been one of great leniency toward all schools of philosophy. Then he quoted Hypatia to the effect that a fixed, formal and dogmatic religion would paralyze the minds of men and make the race, in time, incapable of thought.

Therefore, the Bishop should keep his place, and not try to usurp the functions of the police. In fact, it was better to think wrongly than not to think at all. We learn to think by thinking, and if the threats of the Bishop were believed at all, it would mean the death of science and philosophy. The Bishop made answer by declaring that Hypatia was endeavoring to found a Church of her own, with Pagan Greece as a basis. He intimated, too, that the relationship of Orestes with Hypatia was very much the same as that which once existed between Cleopatra and Mark Antony. He called her "that daughter of Ptolemy," and by hints and suggestions made it appear that she would, if she could, set up an Egyptian Empire in this same city of Alexandria where Cleopatra once so proudly reigned.

The excitement increased. The followers of Hypatia were necessarily few in numbers. They were thinkers—and to think is a task. To believe is easy. The Bishop promised his followers a paradise of ease and rest.

He also threatened disbelievers with the pains of hell. A promise on this side—a threat on that! Is it not a wonder that a man ever lived who put his honest thought against such teaching when launched by men clothed in almost absolute authority! Hypatia might have lived yesterday, and her death at the hands of a mob was an accident that might have occurred in Boston, where a respectable company once threw a rope around the neck of a good man and ran him through streets supposed to be sacred to liberty and free speech.

A mob is made up of cotton waste, saturated with oil, and a focused idea causes spontaneous combustion. Let a fire occur in almost any New York State village, and the town turns wrecker, and loot looms large in the limited brain of the villager. Civilization is a veneer.

When one sees emotionalism run riot at an evangelistic revival, and five thousand people are trooping through an undesirable district at midnight, how long think you would a strong voice of opposition be tolerated?

Hypatia was set upon by a religious mob as she was going in her carriage from her lecture-hall to her home.

She was dragged to a near-by church with the intent of making her publicly recant, but the embers became a blaze, and the blaze became a conflagration, and the leaders lost control. The woman's clothes were torn from her back, her hair torn from her head, her body beaten to a pulp, dismembered, and then to hide all traces of the crime and distribute the guilt, so no one person could be blamed, a funeral-pyre quickly consumed the remains of what but an hour before had been a human being.

Daylight came, and the sun's rays could not locate the guilty ones. Orestes made a report of the affair, resigned his office, asked the Government at Rome to investigate, and fled from the city.

Had Orestes endeavored to use his soldiery against the Bishop, the men in the ranks would have revolted. The investigation was postponed from time to time for lack of witnesses, and finally it was given out by the Bishop that Hypatia had gone to Athens, and there had been no mob and no tragedy. The Bishop nominated a successor to Orestes, and the new official was confirmed. Dogmatism as a police system was supreme. It continued until the time of Dante, or the Italian Renaissance. The reign of Religious Dogmatism was supreme for well nigh a thousand years—we call it the Dark Ages.

John A. Zahm [pseudonym of H. J. Mozens] (essay date 1913)

SOURCE: "Women in Mathematics" in *Woman in Science*, University of Notre Dame, 1913, pp. 136-41.

[*In the following excerpt from an essay describing the earliest female mathematicians, Zahm outlines what is known of Hypatia's life and works.*]

"All abstract speculations, all knowledge which is dry, however useful it may be, must be abandoned to the laborious and solid mind of man. . . . For this reason women will never learn geometry."

In these words Immanuel Kant, more than a century ago, gave expression to an opinion that had obtained since the earliest times respecting the incapacity of the female mind for abstract science, and notably for mathematics. Women, it was averred, could readily assimilate what is concrete, but, like children, they have a natural repugnance for everything which is abstract. They are competent to discuss details and to deal with particulars, but become hopelessly lost when they attempt to generalize or deal with universals.

De Lamennais shares Kant's opinion concerning woman's intellectual inferiority and does not hesitate to express himself on the subject in the most unequivocal manner. "I have never," he writes, "met a woman who was competent to follow a course of reasoning the half of a quarter of an hour—*un demi quart d'heure.* She has qualities which are wanting in us, qualities of a particular, inexpressible charm; but, in the matter of reason, logic, the power to connect ideas, to enchain principles of knowledge and perceive their relationships, woman, even the most highly gifted, rarely attains to the height of a man of mediocre capacity."

But it is not only in the past that such views found acceptance. They prevail even to-day to almost the same extent as during the ages of long ago. How far they have any foundation in fact can best be determined by a brief survey of what woman has achieved in the domain of mathematics.

Athenæus, a Greek writer who flourished about A.D. 200, tells us in his *Deipnosophistœ* of several Greek women who excelled in mathematics, as well as philosophy, but details are wanting as to their attainments in this branch of knowledge. If, however, we may judge from the number of women—particularly among the hetæræ—who became eminent in the various schools of philosophy, especially during the pre-Christian era, we must conclude that many of them were well versed in geometry and astronomy as well as in the general science of numbers. Menagius declares that he found no fewer than sixty-five women philosophers mentioned in the writings of the ancients[1]; and, judging from what we know of the character of the studies pursued in certain of the philosophical schools, especially those of Plato[2] and Pythagoras, and the enthusiasm which women manifested in every department of knowledge, there can be no doubt that they achieved the same measure of success in mathematics as in philosophy and literature.[3]

The first woman mathematician, regarding whose attainments we have any positive knowledge, is the celebrated Hypatia, a Neo-platonic philosopher, whose unhappy fate at the hands of an Alexandrian mob in the early part of the fifth century has given rise to many legends and romances which have contributed not a little toward obscuring the real facts of her extraordinary career. She was the daughter of Theon, who was distinguished as a mathematician and astronomer and as a professor in the school of Alexandria, which was then probably the greatest seat of learning in the world. Born about the year 375 A. D., she at an early age evinced the possession of those talents that were subsequently to render her so illustrious. So great indeed was her genius and so rapid was her progress in this branch of knowledge under the tuition of her father that she soon completely eclipsed her master in his chosen specialty.

There is reason to believe—although the fact is not definitely established—that she studied for a while in Athens in the school of philosophy conducted by Plutarch the Younger and his daughter Asclepigenia. After her return from Athens, Hypatia was invited by the magistrates of Alexandria to teach mathematics and philosophy. Here in brief time her lecture room was filled by eager and enthusiastic students from all parts of the civilized world. She was also gifted with a high order of eloquence and with a voice so marvelous that it was declared to be "divine."

Regarding her much vaunted beauty, nothing certain is known, as antiquity has bequeathed to us no medal or statue by which we could form an estimate of her physical grace. But, be this as it may, it is certain that she commanded the admiration and respect of all for her great learning, and that she bore the mantle of science and philosophy with so great modesty and self-confidence that she won all hearts. A letter addressed to "The Muse," or to "The Philosopher". . . was sure to be delivered to her at once. Small wonder, then, to find a Greek poet inditing to her an epigram containing the following sentiment:

> "When I see thee and hear thy word I thee adore; it is the ethereal constellation of the Virgin, which I contemplate, for to the heavens thy whole life is devoted, O august Hypatia, ideal of eloquence and wisdom's immaculate star."[4]

But it was as a mathematician that Hypatia most excelled. She taught not only geometry and astronomy, but also the new science of algebra, which had but a short time before been introduced by Diophantus. And, singular to relate, no further progress was made in the mathematical sciences, as taught by Hypatia, until the time of Newton, Leibnitz and Descartes,—more than twelve centuries later.

Hypatia was the author of three works on mathematics, all of which have been lost, or destroyed by the ravages of time. One of these was a commentary on the *Arithmetica* of Diophantus. The original treatise—or rather the part which has come down to us—was found about the middle of the fifteenth century in the Vatican Library, whither it had probably been brought after Constantinople had fallen into the possession of the Turks. This valuable work, as annotated by the great French mathematicians Bachet and Fermat, gives us a good idea of the extent of Hypatia's attainments as a mathematician.

Another of Hypatia's works was a treatise on the *Conic Sections* by Apollonius of Perga—surnamed "The Great Geometer." Next to Archimedes, he was the most distinguished of the Greek geometricians; and the last four books of his conics constitute the chief portions of the higher geometry of the ancients. Moreover, they offer some elegant geometrical solutions of problems which, with all the resources of our modern analytical method, are not without difficulty. The greater part of this precious work has been preserved and has engaged the attention of several of the most illustrious of modern mathematicians—among them Borelli, Viviani, Fermat, Barrow and others. The famous English astronomer, Halley, regarded this production of Apollonius of such importance that he learned Arabic for the express purpose of translating it from the version that had been made into this language.

A woman who could achieve distinction by her commentaries on such works as the *Arithmetica* of Diophantus, of the *Conic Sections* of Apollonius, and occupy an honored place among such mathematicians as Fermat, Borelli, and Halley, must have had a genius for mathematics, and we can well believe that the glowing tributes paid by her contemporaries to her extraordinary powers of intellect were fully deserved. If, with Pascal, we see in mathematics "the highest exercise of the intelligence," and agree with him in placing geometers in the first rank of intellectual princes—*princes de l'esprit*—we must admit that Hypatia was indeed exceptionally dowered by Him whom Plato calls "The Great Geometer."

There is still a third work of this ill-fated woman that deserves notice—namely, her **Astronomical Canon**, which dealt with the movements of the heavenly bodies. It is the general opinion that this was but a commentary on the tables of Ptolemy, in which event it is still possible that it may be found incorporated in the work of her father, Theon, on the same subject.

In addition to her works on astronomy and mathematics, Hypatia is credited with several inventions of importance, some of which are still in daily use. Among these are an apparatus for distilling water, another for measuring the level of water, and a third an instrument for determining the specific gravity of liquids—what we should now call an areometer. Besides these apparatus, she was likewise the inventor of an astrolabe and a planisphere.

One of her most distinguished pupils was the eminent Neo-platonist philosopher, Synesius, who became the Bishop of Ptolemais in the Pentapolis of Libya. His letters constitute our chief source of information respecting this remarkable woman. Seven of them are addressed to her, and in four others he makes mention of her. In one of them he writes: "We have seen and we have heard her who presides at the sacred mysteries of philosophy." In another he apostrophizes her as "My benefactress, my teacher,—*magistra*—my sister, my mother."

In science Hypatia was among the women of antiquity what Sappho was in poetry and what Aspasia was in philosophy and eloquence—the chiefest glory of her sex. In profundity of knowledge and variety of attainments she had few peers among her contemporaries, and she is entitled to a conspicuous place among such

luminaries of science as Ptolemy, Euclid, Apollonius, Diophantus and Hipparchus.[5] . . .

Notes

[1] "Ipse mulieres Philosophas in libris Veterum sexaginta quinque reperi," *Historia Mulierum Philosopharum*, p. 3, Amstelodami, 1692.

[2] Plato had inscribed above the entrance of his school, . . . Let no one enter here who is not a geometer.

[3] Menagius in referring to this matter, op. cit., p. 37, writes as follows: "Meritrices Græcas plerasque humanioribus literis et mathematicis disciplinis operam dedisse notat Athenæus."

[4] The sentiment of the Greek epigram is well expressed in the following Latin verses:

> "Quando intueor te, adoro, et sermones,
> Virginis domum sideream intuens.
> E coelis enim tua sunt opera,
> Hypatia casta, sermonum venustas,
> Impollutum astrum sapientis doctrinæ."

[5] Among modern works on Hypatia may be mentioned *Hypatia, die Philosophin von Alexandria*, by St. Wolt, Vienna, 1879; *Hypatia von Alexandria*, by W. A. Meyer, Heidelberg, 1886; *Ipazia Alessandrina*, by D. Guido Bigoni, Venize, 1887, and *De Hypatia*, by B. Ligier, Dijon, 1879.

J. M. Rist (essay date 1965)

SOURCE: "Hypatia," *Phoenix*, Vol. XIX, No. 3, Autumn, 1965, pp. 214-25.

[*In the excerpt below, Rist focuses on Hypatia's philosophical position, but he also attempts to separate the legends surrounding her from the accounts given in Socrates's* Ecclesiastical History *and the* Suda. *She was more closely aligned with traditional Platonism than with advanced Neoplatonism, he asserts, and her achievements in the field of philosophy have been inflated because of the circumstances of her death.*]

Presumably for English-speaking readers the trouble began with Gibbon,[1] who knew the tragic end of Hypatia, daughter of Theon, and used his knowledge, as had some of his predecessors in antiquity, to vilify Cyril, Patriarch of Alexandria. Gibbon's account should be quoted at length, so that its full force may be grasped and the problems of understanding the circumstances of the career and teachings of Hypatia may be clarified. After describing Cyril's various aberrancies as patriarch, Gibbon continues as follows:

He soon prompted, or accepted, the sacrifice of a virgin, who professed the religion of the Greeks and cultivated the friendship of Orestes [the prefect of Egypt; see below]. Hypatia, the daughter of Theon the mathematician, was initiated in her father's studies; her learned comments have elucidated the geometry of Apollonius and Diophantus; and she publicly taught, both at Athens and Alexandria, the philosophy of Plato and Aristotle. In the bloom of beauty, and in the maturity of wisdom, the modest maid refused her lovers and instructed her disciples; the persons most illustrious for their rank or merit were impatient to visit the female philosopher; and Cyril beheld, with a jealous eye, the gorgeous train of horses and slaves who crowded the door of her academy. A rumour was spread among the Christians that the daughter of Theon was the only obstacle to the reconciliation of the praefect and the archbishop; and that obstacle was speedily removed. On a fatal day in the holy season of Lent, Hypatia was torn from her chariot, stripped naked, dragged to the church, and inhumanly butchered by the hands of Peter the Reader and a troop of savage and merciless fanatics: her flesh was scraped from her bones with sharp oyster-shells, and her quivering limbs were delivered to the flames. The just progress of inquiry and punishment was stopped by seasonable gifts; but the murder of Hypatia has imprinted an indelible stain on the character and religion of Cyril of Alexandria.

This is fine polemic, though the details of the assassination have been rendered even more lurid than they actually were, and it admirably fulfils its author's intention of arousing emotional hostility to Christianity. When Bertrand Russell quoted a part of Gibbon's narrative, he added that "after this Alexandria was no longer troubled by philosophers,"[2] a dramatic and false conclusion. Yet the memory of Hypatia and of Alexandrian philosophy is no better served by this partisan treatment than are those of the victims of the concentration camps by a recent author who in his novel of Nazi Germany introduced explicitly erotic tones into an account of the meeting of his beautiful Jewish heroine with Hitler at a gala occasion in the Berlin of the thirties. For the Alexandrian philosopher has not escaped the attentions of the perverted clergyman Charles Kingsley, whose novel *Hypatia* is full of sadistic eroticism and whose account of the heroine's death reminds Professor Marrou of the writings of Pierre Louÿs.[3]

From imagination and the emotional backwash of history we must turn to facts. Gibbon claims that his account of Hypatia derives primarily from Socrates the ecclesiastical historian (H.E. 7.15). This is not, of course, the only source for the events he describes, and indeed much of his information is drawn from the notice of Hypatia in the *Suda*. The information in the *Suda* probably comes from Damascius' *Life of Isidore*,[4] and additional evidence from that source is preserved by

Photius. Further material is to hand in various letters of Synesius,[5] and vague scraps of information have reached the pages of Malalas[6] and Philostorgius.[7] From all this we can see a little more clearly than has sometimes been supposed the true character of the work and importance of Hypatia, especially if we also take into account the views of her immediate successors in Alexandria as they are represented by Hierocles.[8]

Hypatia was born about 370 A.D.[9] and was murdered in 415. Her father Theon was the author of a number of mathematical works and was associated with the Museum at Alexandria;[10] there is no evidence that he was a philosopher, and indeed it was for mathematical as much as for philosophical activity that Hypatia herself became famous, as the letters of Synesius and the lists of her writings show. According to the *Suda* she commented on the mathematical writings of Diophantus, a third-century Alexandrian, and wrote on the "astronomical canon"—probably, as Tannery and Lacombrade propose,[11] a commentary on Ptolemy—and on Apollonius' *Conic Sections*. Yet although she followed her father's footsteps in mathematics, and although Damascius, comparing her unfavourably with his idol Isidore, can say that he surpassed her not only as a man surpasses a woman but as a real philosopher surpasses a geometrician (*Vit. Isid.* 164), it is as a philosopher that her fame has principally reached posterity.

Mathematics might in turbulent times be a dangerous science, and the *Suda* suggests that it was not only to her philosophical wisdom that Hypatia owed her death, but in particular to her ability in the field of astronomy, a science which might look like astrology to the credulous and sometimes to the practitioners themselves. Astronomy, however, even if it had degenerated into astrology, was still a "Platonic" science, though only a propaedeutic one. But what about the keystone of the Platonic education, dialectic itself? What do we know of Hypatia's activities here? At first sight the prospect does not look encouraging.

According to the *Suda* Hypatia gave public lectures on Aristotle, Plato, and other philosophers;[12] according to Socrates she took over the Platonic way of thinking from Plotinus; and Lacombrade is quite prepared to admit that in some respects Hypatia was reasonably represented by Synesius as a successor of Plotinus.[13] But there is little evidence for this latter idea, while the exposition of Plato and Aristotle was the general preoccupation of the philosophers of the day. It is interesting in this connection to consider the nature of the thought of Synesius. Certainly he knows Plotinus, but his debts to Plotinian philosophy are not extensive. Taking his letters as a rough and ready guide, Fitzgerald[14] claimed 126 quotations from Plato, 36 from Plutarch, 20 from Aristotle, but only 9 from Plotinus and 3 from Porphyry. This gives an idea of Synesius' interests: Plotinus, though known, is far from holding a position of honour. It should be added that his doctrines are no more in evidence than are quotations from his text. It is curious, if Hypatia was a Plotinian, that Synesius, her close friend and contemporary as well as her pupil, is so little interested in Plotinian Neoplatonism. It hardly looks as though Hypatia spent much time studying it with him.

Nor is Hypatia interested in the Platonism of Athens, where perhaps the influence of Plotinus was somewhat stronger than at Alexandria.[15] Letter 136 of Synesius is important here. It was written by Synesius at Athens to his brother. The writer is full of complaints that the good old days have passed. Athens, he says, is a city of great names, but nothing more. While in Egypt there flourishes the fruitful wisdom of Hypatia, in Athens there is nothing more than bee-keepers to interest the visitor. There are a couple of wise Plutarchians—he seems to mean Plutarch and Syrianus—whose eloquence is so inadequate that they have to bribe students with pots of honey from Hymettus if they want an audience! It seems certain from this that, whatever the teachings of the Athenian school, Synesius was not disposed to learn from them. Might one say that he had already come to feel some distaste for philosophy which differed from that traditionally taught at Alexandria?

But what was traditionally taught at Alexandria? What did people think of Plotinus there in the fifty years before A.D. 400? Henry has reminded us that Plotinus' whole vast work was virtually ignored in the East in the fourth century:[16] "Si l'on excepte quelques citations tacites des ['*Aphoria*'] de Porphyre, ouvrage dont on ignore la date de composition, mais qui est vraisemblablement antérieur a la publication des Ennéades [probably in A.D. 301], si l'on excepte les extraits d'Eusèbe qui proviennent de l'édition d'Eustochius [this may or may not have existed], si l'on excepte enfin quelques très vagues allusions de Jamblique et les adaptations très libres de saint Basile, on ne rencontre en Orient, dans tout le cours du quatrième siècle, aucune trace des oeuvres de Plotin." Synesius' own writings indicate that he was at least slightly informed of the work of Plotinus, and during the fifth century the great Alexandrian came into his own all over the Greek East. Yet Alexandria itself had been in no hurry to recognize his importance.

We know comparatively little of philosophy in Alexandria during the fourth century. We do not know who carried the Platonic torch between the pupils of Ammonius Saccas, such as Origen, and the contemporaries of Theon, father of Hypatia. What we do know indicates that Plotinus was not the dominating influence. But if Hypatia did not learn of Plotinus from her teachers, perhaps it was she who revived interest in him at Alexandria. The attitude of Synesius does not indicate that Plotinus was a favourite of his teacher,

but Synesius was a Christian and perhaps the Plotinian stream could more easily be transmitted to non-Christian Neoplatonists.

Our next task, therefore, is to determine what happened to philosophy at Alexandria after Hypatia's death in 415. Synesius himself died before his teacher, and the fellow-pupils whom he mentions in his letters are mostly little known figures. Yet we do know the name of the next major Platonist in Alexandria; it was Hierocles. And an enquiry into the nature of Hierocles' thinking may shed light on the kind of philosophical tradition left behind in Alexandria after Hypatia's death.

About Hierocles we are fairly well informed, not only through the accounts of his work on Providence preserved by Photius (*Biblioth.* 214, 251), but also through his commentary on the *Carmen Aureum*.[17] He is, as scholars of Alexandrian thought agree, a very old-fashioned Platonist, whose work once again bears little mark of the influence of Plotinus, or of the Athenian school, but which harks back at least to Origen and beyond him to the Middle Platonists of the second century of our era. Like Hypatia Hierocles had both Christian and pagan pupils; and Praechter has suggested[18] that his thought likewise bears marks of Christian influence, though this is much more doubtful. It is true that there are many parallels between Christian thought and the Platonism of Hierocles, but these could easily exist without the necessity of postulating the influence of Christianity on the pagan master. After all Hierocles himself admits (*Biblioth.* 214) that Origen the pagan is one of his mentors, and Origen composed a treatise, possibly in opposition to Plotinus, which might well have pleased Christian ears: it was called *The King, The Sole Creator*.[19] The King, of course, is the first God of the Middle Platonic systems.

We learn from Photius something of Hierocles' philosophical training. Hierocles apparently regarded himself as in the main stream of Platonic thinking which stemmed from Ammonius Saccas (*Biblioth.* 241, 285H). He claims as links between himself and Ammonius, Plotinus, Origen, Porphyry, Iamblichus, and his successors down to Plutarch of Athens. We should not attach much weight to this as far as doctrines are concerned. There may well be some similarity between the positions of Hierocles and those of Origen, but Plotinus is not a major influence on Hierocles, as we have seen, and the traces of Iamblichus seem negligible. The matter of Plutarch of Athens is important, however, for he is commonly regarded as the founder of the Athenian school which attained its greatest development under Syrianus and Proclus. On the basis of this section of Photius, . . . , Zeller[20] named Hierocles as one of Plutarch's pupils, thus in effect linking him with the introduction of Plotinian or Iamblichan Neoplatonism into Alexandria.

If Zeller was right to believe that Hierocles was a pupil of Plutarch, we should have to conclude that he learned practically nothing from his master; for although it may be true[21] that Plutarch was hostile to the excesses of religiosity that were acceptable to Iamblichus, and later to Syrianus and the Athenian school, there can still be little doubt that he is far from that freedom from credulity and superstition which characterizes Plotinus. Fortunately Zeller need not be right. We do not have to assume that because Hierocles refers to Plutarch as his [kathegetes] he necessarily studied under him at Athens.[22] It need only mean that Hierocles accepted Plutarch as one of his eminent predecessors. Hierocles then is a very traditional Platonist. Origen the pupil of Ammonius is perhaps his major authority, as Weber believes,[23] though something of Porphyry may also be detected. As Damascius tells us, his teachings included an exposition of Plato's *Gorgias*,[24] and it seems likely that he regarded himself as primarily a commentator on Plato or "Pythagoras" and a corrector of those whose novelties offended against the master's text.

Our enquiry into the teachings of Hierocles was undertaken in order to determine the nature of Alexandrian philosophy after Hypatia's death. We can now see that our view that Hypatia was not an exponent of the philosophy of either Plotinus or Iamblichus is given further confirmation: these philosophies do not appear to have been established in Alexandria until long after her death. In fact Alexandria seems only to have abandoned its "old-fashioned" Platonism when the effects of the pupils of Proclus made themselves felt in the latter part of the fifth century. Hypatia, then, as far as we can determine, taught a Platonism like that of Hierocles, though with more emphasis on mathematics—an emphasis which was appropriate in her scientific city and serves to link her still more closely to the Middle Platonic, un-Plotinian tradition to which Origen, the pupil of Ammonius, and Hierocles also largely belonged.

Do such conslusions provide the only knowledge we have of Hypatia's philosophical ideas? Her writings have not survived and the only example of her conversation to have been preserved by Synesius is the description of himself as an [allotrion agathon] (*Ep.* 81). Yet, as Lacombrade indicates, the account in the *Suda* gives the patient enquirer a little more help.[25] Hypatia not only lectured to initiates and close disciples like Synesius; she had some kind of public position. She was, as the *Suda* and Socrates agree, a well-known public figure. In fact there is little doubt that she gave public lectures in virtue of some kind of official appointment. . . . This seems to indicate, as Lacombrade supposes, that she held an official teaching post in the city.

But the fact that she was a woman must never be forgotten. Female philosophers were a comparative rarity in antiquity and were regarded as a marvellous phenomenon. The robe of Athena did not prevent many of the auditors of such blue-stockings from thinking in terms of the Birth of Venus. Generally speaking, famous intellectual women of antiquity are free and easy in matters of sexual morality, for the mere act of being a philosopher would involve abandoning the traditional pursuits of women and entering into debate with men. Men for their part protected themselves by treating such intrusions as acts of immodesty; the female philosophers tended to retaliate by shocking their frivolous male detractors or distractors into respectful silence. As told by Diogenes Laertius, the story of the aristocratic Hipparchia, wife of the Cynic Crates, is instructive. An unusual feature of her life, according to Diogenes, was that she went to banquets with her husband. On one such occasion, when she had silenced a fellow-guest named Theodorus with an ingenious piece of sophistry, she found that his reaction was so far from philosophical that he tried to remove her [hymation] (D.L. 6.97). Such happenings help us to understand the case of Hypatia. Socrates (*H.E.* 7.15) speaks of her as follows: "She was not ashamed to be present in the company of men: for all respected and stood in awe of her the more because of her surpassing [sophrosyne]" The treatment of this matter in the *Suda* is more elaborate and more revealing: "She also took up the other branches of philosophy [other than mathematics], and though a woman she cast a [tribon] around herself and appeared in the centre of the city." Such manners in the Greek world must remind us of the Cynics, as Lacombrade has pointed out,[26] though he has not observed that Hypatia even wears the [tribon], the rough cloak which was virtually the uniform of the Cynic preachers and their monastic successors. And Hypatia, as female philosopher, is in some ways more striking than Hipparchia, for even though Hipparchia apparently "lived with" her husband in public . . . , she at least had a husband. Hypatia's public appearances were not under the protection of a man, though fortunately for Kingsley and the other writers of romance she is attested by the *Suda* to have remained not only [sophron] and virgin,[27] but also very beautiful and possessed of fine features.

Hipparchia had to seek out her partner Crates; Hypatia had no desire of partners but had to employ Cynic means to keep them off. A certain youth became enamoured of her and revealed his passion to her. The *Suda* gives two versions of what happened, one clearly designed to remove the Cynic element in what seems certainly to have been the true and original story. According to [apadentoi logoi] Hypatia recalled the youth to higher things by reminding him of the nature of culture. But the truth is, says the *Suda*, that cultural interests had long faded from his mind, and that she only brought him to his senses by throwing the ancient version of a used "feminine napkin" at him with the remark [tonton eras, o neaniske, kalou de oudenos].

This display of [*to symbolov tes akathartou geneseos*] so shamed and amazed the youth, as the story goes, that his soul was turned to righteousness and he lived [*sophronesteron*] ever after.

Here then is further information about Hypatia; her Platonism is at least in part the Platonism of the Cynic preacher. This is another feature which links her with the popular semi-Platonic teachers of the second century A.D.; and Socrates speaks of her [*semne parresia*]. The unkind might almost hear the Cynic dog barking.

We must now turn from her doctrines and public attitudes to her public position and therefore inevitably to the causes of her death. Here there are a number of matters which deserve consideration. First of all it seems most unlikely that she was murdered *because* she was a philosopher. Despite occasional disturbances there was never the great hostility in Alexandria between the pagan teachers and the Christians that later arose in Athens. Hypatia certainly had Christian pupils, as did her successor Hierocles, and such pupils, including persons of some eminence like Synesius, would not have attended her school against the expressed wishes of the leaders of the Christian community. It is true that violence could and did occur in the philosophical schools in theological disputes. Zacharias records that in about 486 certain pagan students murdered a fellow-student named Paralios who, having delivered himself of public abuse of the goddess Isis, announced his intention of becoming a Christian.[28] But this is an exceptional circumstance, an occasion of what was virtually provocation to violence. A public denunciation of Isis among her worshippers could be construed as the expression of an over-pious desire for martyrdom. But this kind of situation clearly did not arise in the case of Hypatia. It is highly unlikely that she had anything public to say about Christianity. It may be added further that if Hypatia's philosophical teachings had a Cynic, popularly Platonic, rather than a Plotinian or Iamblichan ring, they would certainly not have immediately aroused public hostility. The Cynics, if any philosophers, were tolerated by the Christians of later antiquity.

What Philostorgius has to say about Hypatia's death can be discounted. His bald statement that she was lynched by the orthodox party . . . can be regarded as the malevolence of an Arian who hated Alexandria, home of the great enemy Athanasius. And in this matter the *Suda* seems as unreliable as Philostorgius. According to that source on one occasion the patriarch Cyril passed Hypatia's house, and, noticing the great crowd of men and horses coming and going, grew so envious that he plotted her assassination, which was, as the author writes, doubtless choosing his words carefully, the most unholy assassination of them all. The implication would be that Cyril was the most unholy bishop of them all.

That Cyril was a violent and hot-headed man, his dealings with Nestorius and the general tenor of his administration of his see make clear. But there is nothing in his career which would suggest that he would plot a murder through mere envy of someone else's popularity, as the *Suda* suggests. No evidence is offered by the *Suda* that Cyril had any hand in the crime. All that the *Suda* knows is that the actual criminals were [*theriodeis anthropoi*] by which he certainly means monks. Monks were men who renounced city life; and such a renunciation made them for the average Greek "either beasts or gods," as Aristotle puts it in the *Politics* (1253A 29). For the authors of the murder of Hypatia "beasts" is clearly the more likely alternative.

The failure or unsatisfactory nature of our other sources compels us to rely mainly on Socrates for an account of what actually happened in 415. Socrates' narrative has the immediate advantage that the murder of Hypatia is placed in context. Chapters thirteen and fourteen of the *Ecclesiastical History* show how there had been considerable rioting in Alexandria, a not infrequent phenomenon, how much of this had taken the form of conflict between Jews and Christians, and how the prefect Orestes and the bishop Cyril had found themselves on opposite sides. Various monks had come down to Alexandria from their monasteries in Nitria and on one occasion had attacked and insulted the prefect as he was driving through the city. Their charges against him were that he sacrificed to the ancient gods and that he was a "Hellene," meaning a supporter of the Greek way of life.

We should remember that religious tension at Alexandria was still high at this time. The Christians were by now the dominant party, but they were still nervous of the demonic aid granted to their adversaries. A few historical facts should be recalled: it was in 391 that the Emperor Theodosius had forbidden all pagan cults and indeed passed a specific law against such cults in Egypt. The destruction of the great temple of Serapis at Alexandria followed amid considerable civic disorder.[29] The years 392-394 saw the last struggle of the pagan cause in the West under the leadership of Eugenius and Flavianus and the inevitable defeat of the pagan party. Yet these events of twenty years back doubtless still worried the men of 415. They could recall that, thirty years before Eugenius, Julian the Apostate sat on the Imperial throne.

With this in our minds we can see that the charge against Orestes of sacrificing to the ancient gods was a serious one. He was lucky to escape with his life, but escape he did, and his rescuers arrested a monk named Ammonius who had struck the prefect with a stone. Ammonius was put to death with torture, to the intense indignation of Cyril who not only reported the whole affair to the Emperor but hailed Ammonius as a martyr for his faith. According to Socrates even the moderate

Christians thought this action of Cyril's intolerable and he found it expedient to let the matter drop. But hostility between the bishop and the prefect remained intense.

Such is the context of the murder of Hypatia as Socrates describes it. Feelings were running high; fanatical monks were roaming Alexandria prepared to murder if necessary. Hypatia was, according to Socrates, a close associate of Orestes and the rumour spread that it was her influence which prevented the bishop and the prefect from being reconciled. This opinion grew up "among the church people" . . . there is no suggestion that Cyril himself held it. It is far more likely, as the passage itself suggests, that the fanatical rabble, maddened by fastings—it was during Lent that the murder occurred—conceived the notion that Hypatia was trying to play the role of Maximus of Ephesus to Orestes' Julian. It is, of course, highly unlikely that this was the case, for, although we know from other sources, for example, Synesius, that Hypatia had considerable influence, there is no evidence whatever to show that she exploited her power to forward the political position of Neoplatonism. Let us listen to Synesius speaking of Hypatia's position: "You always have power and long may you have it and make good use of that power. I recommend to your care Nicaeus and Philolaus, two excellent young men united by the bond of relationship. In order that they may come again into possession of their own property, try to get support for them from all your friends, whether private individuals or magistrates."

It is likely enough both from this story and from what we know of the adherents of Platonism generally at this time that many of the followers of Hypatia would be men of influence. Philosophy was very frequently an aristocratic pursuit; many even of the eminent Cynics were of aristocratic origin. It was from these friends that Hypatia's danger came; they formed a group unsympathetic to Christianity and potentially hostile to it. Among such dangerous friends we should not perhaps include a large percentage of Hypatia's most serious-minded philosophical students, although some men of rank, like Synesius himself, were serious enough. But philosophy in ancient times always attracted the able aristocrat, the Alcibiades or the Critias, men who were impressed by the personalities of the teachers, though not sufficiently to warrant their adopting a philosophical life themselves. The circle of Socrates is illuminating: we see three types of individual: Alcibiades, Chaerophon, Plato. Alcibiades is the aristocratic dilettante, Chaerophon the serious bourgeois professional, Plato the aristocratic professional. If Synesius corresponds to Plato, then the Christians might fear that Orestes and his circle corresponded to Alcibiades.

According to the *Suda* Hypatia was [*emphrona te kai politiken*]. It seems that it was to this public activity and to her public position rather than to her purely philosophical or even astronomical interests that she owed her death. There appears no reason to implicate Cyril in the murder itself; Cyril's crime was more probably to try and hush the matter up—bribery is mentioned in the *Suda*—in the vain hope of turning the spotlight of publicity away from such a disreputable event in the history of the Alexandrian church. His efforts to secure this only led to the belief, so welcome to such writers as Philostorgius and so gleefully accepted by latter-day haters of ecclesiastical power, that he himself was the organizer of the assassination.

Hypatia's fame then is in many ways unrelated to her historical position in the sequence of Alexandrian thinkers. Within the context of Platonism she appears as merely another to pass on the torch. Untouched or virtually untouched by the influence of Plotinus she accepted, taught, and handed on a conservative Platonism to a mixed pagan and Christian audience. The fact that she was a woman increased her fame in an age where the educated woman was comparatively rare; her dreadful end secured her a posthumous glory which her philosophical achievements would never have warranted. Her reputation in her lifetime was great; her death ensured that although we hear little of her in the philosophical writings of her successors she could win the admiration of that less professional audience which to this day has reacted so favourably towards her. . . .

Notes

[1] Edward Gibbon, *The Decline and Fall of the Roman Empire*, ch. 47 (The Modern Library: New York n.d.) 2.816.

[2] *History of Western Philosophy* (London 1946) 387.

[3] H. I. Marrou, "Synesius of Cyrene and Alexandrian Neoplatonism," in *The Conflict between Paganism and Christianity in the Fourth Century* (Oxford 1963) 127. For Kingsley's general manner of proceeding in matters of virginity and cruelty see Meriol Trevor, *Newman: Light in Winter* (New York 1963) 326-327. For detailed treatment of the "after-life" of Hypatia in European traditions see R. Asmus, "Hypatia in Tradition und Dichtung," *Studien zur vergleichenden Literaturgeschichte* 7 (1907) 11-44.

[4] Cf. Damascius' *Vita Isidori* (to be found with Diogenes Laertius, ed. Cobet) and P. Tannery, "L'article de Suidas sur Hypatie," *Ann. de la Fac. des Lettres de Bordeaux* 2 (1880) 199 ff.

[5] Letters 10, 15, 16, 33, 81, 124, and 154 are to Hypatia herself. She is referred to in 133, 136, 137, and 159.

[6] *Chronogr.* 14 (*PG* 97, 536A).

[7]Philostorgius H.E. 8.9. (GCS 21, p. 111 Bidez).

[8] The chief previous attempts to determine the importance of Hypatia are those of R. Hoche, "Hypatia die Tochter Theons," Philologus 15 (1860) 435-474, K. Praechter, art. "Hypatia," RE 9[1] cols. 242-249, E. Zeller, Die Philosophie der Griechen 3[2] (5th edition Leipzig 1923) 801-803, and C. Lacombrade, Synésios de Cyrène (Paris 1951) 38-46.

[9] Cf. Suda (ed. Adler) 4.644; Socrates H.E. 8.9; Lacombrade (see note 8) 39. Lacombrade notices that the remark of Malalas (see note 6) that at the time of her death Hypatia was a [palaia rune] need not conflict with these dates, as was supposed, for example, by Hoche (see note 8) 439.

[10] Suda, s.v. "Theon."

[11] P. Tannery (see note 4) 199; Lacombrade (see note 8) 41-42.

[12] The idea of certain moderns that these lectures were given both at Alexandria and at Athens is due to a misinterpretation of a passage of the Suda (4.645.2). What the Suda says is that, while Hypatia was teaching, politicians were among the followers of philosophy, as they had once been in Athens. Hypatia herself did not teach in Athens.

[13] Lacombrade (see note 8) 46.

[14] The Letters of Synesius trans. A. Fitzgerald (Oxford 1926) 16.

[15] For Plutarch's position in the Athenian school see below.

[16] P. Henry, Plotin et l'Occident (Louvain 1934) 15. Henry is a little too sweeping. He has not, for example, mentioned Gregory of Nyssa.

[17] Printed by Mullach in Fragm. philos. Graec. 1. 416-486.

[18] K. Praechter, "Christlich-neuplatonische Beziehungen," BZ 21 (1912) 1-27.

[19] Porph. Vita Plotini 3.

[20] Zeller (see note 8) 812. This view is also held by A. H. Armstrong, "Platonic Eros and Christian Agape," Downside Review 79 (1961) 120.

[21] For this view of Plutarch see E. Evrard, "Le Maître de Plutarque d'Athènes," L'Antiquité Classique 29 (1960) 396.

[22] For this view, with reference to the treatise on Provi-

dence, see K. Praechter, art. "Hierocles (18)," RE 8, cols. 1481-1482 and R. Beutler, art. "Plutarch (3)," RE 21,[1] col. 963.

[23] K-O. Weber, Origenes der Neuplatoniker: Versuch einer Interpretation (Zetemata 27, Munich 1962).

[24] Cf. Vita Isidori 54.

[25] Lacombrade (see note 8) 44-45.

[26] Lacombrade (see note 8) 44-45.

[27] The Suda contradicts itself on this point. In one place the heroine . . . (4.644.20); in another she is the wife of the philosopher Isidore (4.644.2). Fortunately we can be sure, as has been generally noticed, that the reference to Isidore is an absurd interpolation. Isidore's floruit is at least sixty years after Hypatia's death.

[28] Zacharias Vita Severi (Patrologia Orientalis 2) p. 38 Kugener.

[29] For the suppression of paganism see now H. Bloch, "The Pagan Revival in the West at the end of the Fourth Century," The Conflict between Paganism and Christianity in the Fourth Century (Oxford 1963) 198. . . .

Lynn M. Osen (essay date 1974)

SOURCE: "Hypatia 370-415" in Women in Mathematics, The MIT Press, 1974, pp. 21-32.

[In the following excerpt, Osen presents an overview of Hypatia's life, emphasizing her skill in mathematics.]

During the pre-Christian era, the philosophical schools of Plato and Pythagoras served to create a favorable social climate in which at least some women could pursue an academic career. Because the emphasis on and love of mathematics was so strong in these schools, this tradition persisted long after the Christian era began.

Athenaeus, a Greek writer (ca. A.D. 200), in his Deipnosophistoe, mentions a number of women who were superior mathematicians, but precise knowledge of their work in this field is lacking. It is probable that there were many women who were well educated in the general science of numbers at this time, judging from the pervasive interest in the subject and the rigor with which women sought an education.

A few Greek women enjoyed comparative freedom in these pursuits, although the class of women known as hetaerae attracted the most public notice. These slave women were usually paramours of the ruling class, although some were freed women or women of free birth;

many of them, particularly those from Ionia and Aetolia, strongly impressed themselves on the Greek conscience with their intelligence, wit, and culture. They had keen intellects, and their work in abstract studies made some of them apt students and competent teachers. No doubt the legacy left by these women over the ensuing centuries contributed also to an auspicious social climate within which the formidable genius of Hypatia could flourish in the later part of the fourth century A.D.

Hypatia was the first woman in mathematics of whom we have considerable knowledge, but the story of her life that has come down to us is not a particularly happy one. Despite the good fortune of her legendary talents, her beauty, her long life of hard work, and her celebrated accomplishments in mathematics and astronomy, the story of her eventual martyrdom excites almost the same sympathies as a classic Greek tragedy. Although nearly a thousand years separated her from the time of Aspasia, in many ways Hypatia was also a true daughter of Greece.

Hypatia was born around A.D. 370, and her father, Theon, was a distinguished professor of mathematics at the University of Alexandria. He later became the director of the University, and Hypatia's early life was spent in close contact there with the institute called the *Museum*.

We know little about Hypatia's mother, but the family situation must have been a fortunate one, for Theon was determined to produce a perfect human being. As Elbert Hubbard (1908, p. 83) remarked, " . . . whether his charts, theorems and formulas made up a complete law of eugenics, or whether it was dumb luck, this we know: he nearly succeeded."

From her earliest years Hypatia was immersed in an atmosphere of learning, questioning, and exploration. Alexandria was the greatest seat of learning in the world, a cosmopolitan center where scholars from all the civilized countries gathered to exchange ideas. As Theon's daughter, Hypatia was a part of this stimulating and challenging environment. In addition, she received a very thorough formal training in arts, literature, science, and philosophy.

Theon was his daughter's tutor, teacher, and playmate; his own strong love of the beauty and logic of mathematics was contagious. We know that he was influential in this part of Hypatia's intellectual development, which was eventually to eclipse his own.

At the time, mathematics was used mainly for calculating such obscure problems as the locus of a given soul born under a certain planet. It was thought that mathematical calculations could determine precisely where such a soul would be on a future date. Astronomy and astrology were considered one science, and mathematics was a bond between this science and religion.

These disciplines were a part of Hypatia's early training, and, in addition, Theon introduced her to all the systems of religion known to that part of the civilized world. He had a rare talent as a teacher, and he was determined to transmit to Hypatia not only the accumulated fund of knowledge but the discrimination needed to assimilate and build upon this fund. Toward this end, he was particularly concerned that she be discriminate about religion and that no rigid belief take possession of her life to the exclusion of new truths. "All formal dogmatic religions are fallacious and must never be accepted by self-respecting persons as final," he told her. "Reserve your right to think, for even to think wrongly is better than not to think at all" (Hubbard 1908, p. 82).

Theon also established a regimen of physical training to ensure that Hypatia's healthy body would match her formidable, swift, well-trained mind. He devised a series of gentle calisthenics that she practiced regularly; she was taught to row, swim, ride horseback, and climb mountains, and a part of each day was set aside for such exercise.

To the Romans the art of the rhetor, or orator, was one of the most consequential of the social graces; the ability to impress others by one's personal presence was indeed a most extraordinary gift. As part of the preparation for becoming the "perfect human being" that Theon had determined she should be, Hypatia was given formal training in speech, and there were lessons in rhetoric, the power of words, the power of hypnotic suggestion, the proper use of her voice, and the gentle tones considered pleasing. Theon structured her life minutely and precisely, leaving little to chance or circumstance, but he was not content to produce such a powerful personality without giving her an understanding of her responsibility to others. He cautioned her about the vulnerability of the permeable, impressionable mind of the young, and he warned her against using the cosmetic effect of rhetoric and pretense to influence or manipulate others. His training urged her toward becoming a sensitive, gifted, and eloquent teacher, and these qualities are reflected in her writing:

> Fables should be taught as fables, myths as myths, and miracles as poetic fancies. To teach superstitions as truths is a most terrible thing. The child mind accepts and believes them, and only through great pain and perhaps tragedy can he be in after years relieved of them. In fact men will fight for a superstition quite as quickly as for a living truth— often more so, since a superstition is so intangible you cannot get at it to refute it, but truth is a point of view, and so is changeable (Hubbard 1908, p. 84).

As a further part of her education, Hypatia traveled abroad and was treated as royalty wherever she went. Some accounts say that Hypatia's travels extended over a period of 10 years; others say she spent only a year or so in travel. It is probable that her trips extended over a long period of time and were not continuous, but it is known that for a while she was a student in Athens at the school conducted by Plutarch the Younger and his daughter Asclepigenia. It was here that her fame as a mathematician became established, and upon her return to Alexandria, the magistrates invited her to teach mathematics and philosophy at the university. She accepted this invitation and spent the last part of her life teaching out of the chair where Ammonius, Hierocles, and other celebrated scholars had taught.

She was a popular teacher; Socrates, the historian, wrote that her home, as well as her lecture room, was frequented by the most unrelenting scholars of the day and was, along with the library and the museum, one of the most compelling intellectual centers in that city of great learning. She was considered an oracle, and enthusiastic young students from Europe, Asia, and Africa came to hear her lecture on the *Arithmetica* of Diophantus, the techniques Diophantus had developed, his solutions of indeterminate problems of various types, and the symbolism he had devised. Her lectures sparkled with her own mathematical ingenuity, for she loved mathematics for its own sake, for the pure and exquisite delight it yielded her inquisitive mind.

Hypatia was the author of several treatises on mathematics. Suidas, the late-tenth-century lexicographer of Greek writings, lists several titles attributed to her, but unfortunately these have not come down to us intact. Most were destroyed along with the Ptolemaic libraries in Alexandria or when the temple of Serapis was sacked by a mob, and only fragments of her work remain. A portion of her original treatise **On the Astronomical Canon of Diophantus** was found during the fifteenth century in the Vatican library; it was most likely taken there after Constantinople had fallen to the Turks.

Diophantine algebra dealt with first-degree and quadratic equations; the commentaries by Hypatia include some alternative solutions and a number of new problems that she originated. Some scholars consider these to have been in Diophantus' original text, but Heath (1964, p. 14) attributes them to Hypatia.

In addition to this work, she also wrote **On the Conics of Apollonius**, popularizing his text. It is interesting to note that, with the close of the Greek period, interest in conic sections waned, and after Hypatia, these curves were largely neglected by mathematicians until the first half of the seventeenth century.

Hypatia also wrote commentaries on the *Almagest*, the astronomical canon of Ptolemy's that contained his numerous observations of the stars. In addition, she coauthored (with her father) at least one treatise on Euclid. Most of these works were prepared as textbooks for her students. As was the case with her commentaries on *Conics*, no further progress was made in mathematical science as taught by Hypatia until the work of Descartes, Newton, and Leibniz many centuries later.

Among Hypatia's most distinguished pupils was the eminent philosopher Synesius of Cyrene, who was later to become the wealthy and influential Bishop of Ptolemais. His letters asking for scientific advice have furnished us with one of the richest sources of information concerning Hypatia and her works, and they indicate how keenly he valued his intellectual association with her (see, for example, Hale 1860, p. 111).

References are found in Synesius' letters crediting Hypatia with the invention of an *astrolabe* and a *planesphere*, both devices designed for studying astronomy. His letters also credit her with the invention of an apparatus for distilling water, one for measuring the level of water, and a third for determining the specific gravity of liquids. This latter device was called an *aerometer* or *hydroscope*.

Hypatia's contemporaries wrote almost lyrically about her great genius. Socrates, Nicephorus, and Philostorgius, all ecclesiastical historians of a persuasion different from that of Hypatia, nevertheless were generous in their praise of her characteristics and learning. Her popularity was wide and genuine, and it is said that she had several offers of marriage from princes and philosophers, but to these proposals she answered that she was "wedded to the truth." This pretty speech was no doubt more an evasion than a verity; it is more likely that she simply never met a suitor whose mind and philosophy matched her own. Although she never married, she did have love affairs, and various imaginary romances have been credited to her.[1]

Her renown as a philosopher was as great as her fame as a mathematician, and legend has it that letters addressed to "The Muse" or "The Philosopher" were delivered to her without question. She belonged to a school of Greek thought that was called neo-Platonic: the scientific rationalism of this school ran counter to the doctrinaire beliefs of the dominant Christian religion, seriously threatening the Christian leaders. These pietists considered Hypatia's philosophy heretical, and when Cyril became patriarch of Alexandria in A.D. 412, he began a systematic program of oppression against such heretics. Because of her beliefs and her friendship with Orestes, the prefect of Egypt, whose influence represented the only countervailing force against Cyril, Hypatia was caught as a pawn in the political reprisals between the two factions.

Cyril was an effective inquisitor. He began by inflaming the passions of the populace, setting mobs on his detractors, leveling the synagogues, and almost completely usurping the state and authority of a civil magistrate. The turbulent mood of his own faithful and the political events that followed his actions convinced him in A.D. 415 that his own interests would be best served by the sacrifice of a virgin. At his direction, a mob of religious fanatics set upon Hypatia, dragging her from her chariot while she was on her way to classes at the university, pulling out all of her hair, and subsequently torturing her to death. Edward Gibbon wrote (1960, p. 601)

> In the bloom of beauty, and in the maturity of wisdom, the modest maid had refused her lovers and instructed her disciples; the persons most illustrious for their rank or merit were impatient to visit the female philosopher; and Cyril beheld with a jealous eye the gorgeous train of horses and slaves who crowded the door of her academy. A rumour was spread among the Christians that the daughter of Theon was the only obstacle to the reconciliation of the prefect and the archbishop; and that obstacle was speedily removed. On a fatal day, in the holy season of Lent, Hypatia was torn from her chariot, stripped naked, dragged to the church, and inhumanly butchered by the hands of Peter the reader and a troop of savage and merciless fanatics; her flesh was scraped from her bones with sharp oyster-shells, and her quivering limbs were delivered to the flames. The just progress of inquiry and punishment was stopped by seasonable gifts; but the murder of Hypatia has imprinted an indelible stain on the character and religion of Cyril of Alexandria.

Orestes felt a responsibility for Hypatia's cruel death and did what he could to bring the culprits to justice. He reported her death to Rome and asked for an investigation. Then fearing for his own life, he quit the city. The investigation was repeatedly postponed for "lack of witnesses," and finally it was given out by the Bishop that Hypatia was in Athens and there had been no tragedy. Orestes' successor was forced to cooperate with the Bishop, and as one historian phrased it, "Dogmatism as a police system was supreme" (Hubbard 1908, p. 102).

Hypatia's place in history seems relatively secure. Indeed, very often she is the only woman mentioned in mathematical histories. Her life and times have been romanticized by Charles Kingsley in his book *Hypatia: or New Foes in Old Faces* (1853), but his novel almost totally ignores Hypatia's significant work in mathematics. Neither is it to be recommended as a reliably authentic source of information, either about Hypatia or life in Alexandria during the fifth century A.D. . . .

Notes

1 Although Suidas (ca. tenth century) implies that Hypatia was married to Isidorus of Gaza, the

Neoplatonist, most historians discount this as fiction rather than fact. The romantic aspect of her life has inspired a great deal of speculation; see J. Toland, *Hypatia, or the History of a Most Beautiful, Most Vertuous, Most Learned . . . Lady* (London, 1720).

References

. . . Gibbon, Edward, 1960. *The Decline and Fall of the Roman Empire.* (An abridgement by D. M. Low). New York: Harcourt, Brace, and World. . . .

Hale, Sarah Josepha, 1860. *Women's Record: or Sketches of All Distinguished Women from the Creation to A. D. 1854.* New York: Harper & Brothers Publishers.

Heath, Thomas L., 1964. *Diophantus of Alexandria: A Study in the History of Greek Algebra.* New York: Dover Publications. . . .

Hubbard, Elbert, 1908. *Little Journeys to the Homes of Great Teachers.* Vol. 23. New York: The Roycrofters. . . .

Kingsley, Charles, 1853. *Hypatia or New Foes with Old Faces.* Chicago: W. B. Conkley Company.

Margaret Alic (essay date 1986)

SOURCE: "Hypatia of Alexandria" in *Hypatia's Heritage,* The Women's Press, 1986, pp. 35-49.

[*In the following excerpt, Alic summarizes Hypatia's career within the context of the political and intellectual climate of early-fifth-century Alexandria.*]

> She was a person who divided society into two parts: those who regarded her as an oracle of light, and those who looked upon her as an emissary of darkness. (Elbert Hubbard, p. 280)

A slight scientific renaissance occurred in fourth-century Alexandria, illuminated by the most famous of all women scientists until Marie Curie. For fifteen centuries Hypatia was often considered to be the *only* female scientist in history. Even today, for reasons that have more to do with the romanticising of her life and death than with her accomplishments, she is frequently the only woman mentioned in histories of mathematics and astronomy.[6]

Hypatia is the earliest woman scientist whose life is well documented. Although most of her writings have been lost, numerous references to them exist. Furthermore, she died at a convenient time for historians. The last pagan scientist in the western world, her violent death coincided with the last years of the Roman

Empire. Since there were to be no significant advances in mathematics, astronomy or physics anywhere in the West for another 1000 years, Hypatia has come to symbolise the end of ancient science. Though the decline had already been in progress for several centuries, after Hypatia came only the chaos and barbarism of the Dark Ages.

When Hypatia was born in AD 370, the intellectual life of Alexandria was in a state of dangerous confusion. The Roman Empire was converting to Christianity and more often than not the Christian zealot saw only heresy and evil in mathematics and science: ' "mathematicians" were to be torn by beasts or else burned alive.'[7] Some of the Christian fathers revived the theories that the earth was flat and the universe shaped like a tabernacle. Violent conflicts among pagans, Jews and Christians were spurred on by Theophilos, Patriarch of Alexandria. It was not a propitious era in which to become a scientist, or a philosopher.

Hypatia's father, Theon, was a mathematician and astronomer at the Museum. He closely supervised every aspect of his daughter's education. According to legend, he was determined that she develop into a 'perfect human being'—this in an age when females were often considered to be less than human! Hypatia was indeed an exceptional young woman. She travelled to Athens and Italy, impressing all she met with her intellect and beauty. Upon her return to Alexandria, Hypatia became a teacher of mathematics and philosophy. The Museum had lost its pre-eminence and Alexandria now had separate schools for pagans, Jews and Christians; however, Hypatia taught people of all religions and she may have held a municipal Chair of Philosophy. According to the Byzantine encyclopaedist Suidas, 'she was officially appointed to expound the doctrines of Plato, Aristotle, &c.'[8] Students converged on Alexandria to attend her lectures on mathematics, astronomy, philosophy and mechanics. Her home became an intellectual centre, where scholars gathered to discuss scientific and philosophical questions.

Most of Hypatia's writing originated as texts for her students. None has survived intact, although it is likely that parts of her work are incorporated in the extant treatises of Theon. Some information on her accomplishments comes from the surviving letters of her pupil and disciple Synesius of Cyrene, who became the wealthy and powerful Bishop of Ptolemais.

Hypatia's most significant work was in algebra. She wrote a commentary on the *Arithmetica* of Diophantus in 13 books. Diophantus lived and worked in Alexandria in the third century and has been called the 'father of algebra'. He developed indeterminate (Diophantine) equations, that is, equations with multiple solutions. (A common example of this type of problem is the variety of ways of changing a pound using different denominations of pence—50p, 20p, etc.). He also worked with quadratic equations. Hypatia's commentaries included some alternative solutions and many new problems subsequently incorporated into the Diophantus manuscripts.

Hypatia also authored a treatise **On the Conics of Apollonius** in eight books. Apollonius of Perga was a third-century-B.C. Alexandrian geometer, the originator of epicycles and deferents to explain the irregular orbits of the planets. Hypatia's text was a popularisation of his work. Like her Greek ancestors, Hypatia was fascinated by conic sections (the geometric figures formed when a plane is passed through a cone). After her death, conic sections were neglected until the beginning of the seventeenth century when scientists realised that many natural phenomena, such as orbitals, were best described by the curves formed by conic sections.

Theon revised and improved upon Euclid's *Elements* of geometry and it is his edition that is still in use today. Hypatia probably worked with him on this revision. Later she co-authored with him at least one treatise on Euclid. Hypatia also wrote at least one book of Theon's work on Ptolemy. Ptolemy had systematised all contemporary mathematical and astronomical knowledge in a 13-book text which he modestly called a *Mathematical Treatise*. Mediaeval Arab scholars renamed it the *Almagest* ('Great Book'). Ptolemy's system remained the leading astronomical work until Copernicus in the sixteenth century. Hypatia's tables for the movements of the heavenly bodies, the *Astronomical Canon,* may have been part of Theon's commentary on Ptolemy, or a separate work.

In addition to philosophy and mathematics, Hypatia was interested in mechanics and practical technology. The letters of Synesius contain her designs for several scientific instruments including a plane astrolabe. . . . The plane astrolabe was used for measuring the positions of the stars, planets and the sun, and to calculate time and the ascendant sign of the zodiac.

Hypatia also developed an apparatus for distilling water, an instrument for measuring the level of water, and a graduated brass hydrometer for determining the specific gravity (density) of a liquid.

Fourth-century Alexandria was a centre for neoplatonic scholars. Although Hypatia may have studied at the neoplatonic school of Plutarch the Younger and his daughter Asclepigenia in Athens, she subscribed to a more tolerant, mathematically-based neoplatonism.[9] There was rivalry between the neoplatonic schools of Alexandria and Athens, with the Athens school emphasising magic and the occult. But to the Christians, all Platonists were dangerous heretics.

That Hypatia became enmeshed in Alexandrian politics is indisputable. Her student Hesychius the Jew wrote:

> Donning the philosopher's cloak, and making her way through the midst of the city, she explained publicly the writings of Plato, or Aristotle, or any other philosopher, to all who wished to hear . . . The magistrates were wont to consult her first in their administration of the affairs of the city.[10]

As a pagan, an espouser of Greek scientific rationalism and an influential political figure, Hypatia thus found herself in a very dangerous position in an increasingly Christian city. In 412 Cyril, a fanatical Christian, became Patriarch of Alexandria, and intense hostility developed between Cyril and Orestes, the Roman Prefect of Egypt, a former student and long-time friend of Hypatia. Soon after taking power, Cyril began persecuting Jews, driving thousands of them from the city. Then, despite the vehement opposition of Orestes, he turned his attention to ridding the city of neoplatonists. Ignoring Orestes' pleadings, Hypatia refused to abandon her ideals and convert to Christianity.

Hypatia's murder is described in the writings of the fifth-century Christian historian, Socrates Scholasticus:

> All men did both reverence and had her in admiration for the singular modesty of her mind. Wherefore she had great spite and envy owed unto her, and because she conferred oft, and had great familiarity with Orestes, the people charged her that she was the cause why the bishop and Orestes were not become friends. To be short, certain heady and rash cockbrains whose guide and captain was Peter, a reader of that Church, watched this woman coming home from some place or other, they pull her out of her chariot: they hail her into the Church called Caesarium: they stripped her stark naked: they raze the skin and rend the flesh of her body with sharp shells, until the breath departed out of her body: they quarter her body: they bring her quarters unto a place called Cinaron and burn them to ashes. (p. 380)

This took place in March 415, just over a century after the pagans had murdered Catherine, a Christian Alexandrian scholar. Hypatia's murderers were Parabolans, fanatical monks of the Church of St Cyril of Jerusalem, possibly aided by Nitrian monks. Whether Cyril directly ordered the murder remains an open question. At the very least he created the political climate that made such an atrocity possible.[11] Cyril was later canonised.

Orestes reported the murder and asked Rome to launch an investigation. He then resigned his office and fled Alexandria. The investigation was repeatedly postponed for 'lack of witnesses' and eventually Cyril proclaimed that Hypatia was alive and living in Athens. Hypatia's brutal murder marked the end of platonic teachings in Alexandria and throughout the Roman Empire. . . .

Notes

. . . [6] Elbert Hubbard's portrait of Hypatia was fanciful and sarcastic. Following the *Chronicle* of John of Nikiu, a Coptic bishop who rewrote history to fit his Christian prejudices, Hubbard asserted that Hypatia hypnotised her students with satanic wiles (see Parsons, p. 379). Other writers identified her as an alchemist. Charles Kingsley, the popular nineteenth-century novelist, also fictitiously portrayed the life of Hypatia. Kingsley had her killed at the age of 25 instead of 45, and imagined her as a fanatical neoplatonist caught up in political intrigue. Hypatia never married and for centuries historians haggled over the question of her chastity.

Richardson's *The Star Lovers* exemplifies the treatment accorded women scientists in histories, on those occasions when they are discussed at all. Although he includes a chapter on women astronomers, he ignores some of the most important ones and generally ridicules those he does mention. Much of the chapter is devoted to the moon craters named after women astronomers! Heading the list is Hypatia: 'A learned woman who died defending the Christians [sic].' She is followed by Catherina: 'an extremely learned young woman of noble family who died in AD 307 defending the Christians' (p. 173).

[7] McCabe, p. 271.

[8] Quoted in Marrou, p. 134.

[9] The Athenian school was later taken over by Asclepigenia's daughter, Asclepigenia the Younger. This eastern branch of neoplatonism also included other women such as Sosipatra, wife of the prefect Cappadocia. It has commonly been assumed that Hypatia was a neoplatonist in the tradition of Plotinus; but Rist presents evidence that the philosophy of Plotinus did not become well established in Alexandria until late in the fifth century, and that neither Hypatia nor Synesius were particularly interested in his doctrines.

[10] Quoted in McCabe, p. 269.

[11] Edward Gibbon (II, 816) implied that Cyril was so jealous of Hypatia's influence and popularity that he 'prompted, or accepted, the sacrifice of a virgin, who professed the religion of the Greeks'. Rist (p. 223) suggests that the mob was maddened by Lenten fastings.

. . .

Bibliography

Gibbon, Edward, *The Decline and Fall of the Roman Empire,* 3 vols. New York: Modern Library [n.d.]. . . .

Hubbard, Elbert, *Great Teachers,* Vol. 10 of *Little Journeys to the Homes of the Great.* Cleveland: World Publishing, 1928. . . .

Kingsley, Charles, *Hypatia: Or New Foes with an Old Face.* 1853; rpt. New York: Hurst, 1910. . . .

Marrou, H.I., 'Synesius of Cyrene and Alexandrian Neoplatonism', in *The Conflict between Paganism and Christianity in the Fourth Century*, ed. Arnaldo Momigliano. London: Oxford University Press, 1963, pp. 126-50. . . .

McCabe, Joseph, 'Hypatia', *Critic*, 43 [1903], 267-72. . . .

Parsons, Edward Alexander, *The Alexandrian Library: Glory of the Hellenic World: Its Rise, Antiquities, and Destructions.* Amsterdam: Elsevier, 1952. . . .

Richardson, Robert S., *The Star Lovers.* New York: Macmillan, 1967. . . .

Rist, J.M., 'Hypatia', *Phoenix*, 19 (1965), 214-25. . . .

Socrates Scholasticus, 'The Murder of Hypatia', in *A Treasury of Early Christianity*, ed. Anne Fremantle. New York: Viking, 1953, pp. 379-80. . . .

Ursule Molinaro (essay date 1989)

SOURCE: "A Christian Martyr in Reverse," *Hypatia*, Vol. 4, No. 1, Spring, 1989, pp. 6-8.

[*In the prose poem reprinted below, Molinaro recreates the life and death of Hypatia from the perspective of a feminist poet and novelist.*]

The torture killing of the noted philosopher Hypatia by a mob of Christians in Alexandria in 415 A.D. marks the end of a time when women were still appreciated for the brain under their hair.

The screams of a 45-year-old Greek philosopher being dismembered[1] by early-5th-century Christians, in their early-5th-century church of Caesareum, in Alexandria, center of early-5th-century civilization, reverberated between the moon gate & the sun gate of that civilized Egyptian city.

Before the philosopher's broken body was thrown into the civilized Alexandrian gutter, for public burning.

& smoke signals rose from the disorderly chunks of her charring flesh, warning future centuries of reformers & healers that they must hush their knowledge if they wished to avoid burning as heretics, or witches. If they wished to stay alive.

In a world run by a new brand of Christians, politicians of faith, who out-lawed independent thought. Especially when thought by women. Whom they offered a new role model of depleasurized submission as they converted the great & lusty earthmother goddess into a chaste mother of a martyred god.

Whose teachings they converted into an orthodox church.

Which converted heresy—a word that used to mean: choice; of a view of life other than the norm—into the crime of otherness. Punishable by torture.

—The sudden heresy of astrology.

Which St. Augustine repudiated　　together with the suddenly heretic Christianity of the Manichees, & the pagan philosophy of the Greeks　　after the repudiated stars warned him of the sudden heresy of all his former beliefs. & sources of knowledge.

As they warned Theron, Alexandria's foremost Greek astrologer & mathematician, of the impending martyrdom of his only daughter. The 45-year-old Greek philosopher Hypatia.

Whose chart Theron had cast at the moment of her birth. Taking pride in her strong Mercury that promised eloquent intelligence in fortunate aspect to her Jupiter. That gave her early recognition; a renown greater than his own. Rejoicing at her Moon exalted in the sign of the Bull, that made her clear strong voice turn logic into music. Shaking his head at her Venus in the sign of the Ram, which made her willful in matters of emotion & aesthetics.

Although he had to smile when he recognized that willful Venus in his 4-year-old daughter's request to wear golden sandals on her feet.

& when the 12-year-old started to bind her thick red hair in golden nets.

He was still smiling　　though with thinner lips　　when the already renowned young philosopher started to have lovers.

Whose charts he also cast.

& when she married the philosopher Isidore. Whose charted philosophical acquiescence to his willful wife's many amorous friendships made Theron shake his head. & wonder if his brilliant daughter was perhaps abusing the power over men seemingly granted to her by the stars.

Which seemed to turn against her, suddenly, as she approached her 45th year. When the lined-up planets foreshadowed an event of such horror that Theron's civilized early-5th-century mind refused to believe what he saw in her progressions.

Which he recast & recast, until belief in his science outweighed his belief in civilized early-5th-century humanity. & he warned his daughter. Urging her to slip out of the city. To travel to Sicily, perhaps, where earlier Greek philosophers had lived out disgraced lives in quiet meditation, & discreet teaching.

But Hypatia refused to listen to her father.

Or perhaps she did listen, but refused to leave a city that used to sit at her feet, listening to her learning. That seemed to be the only city in her civilized world. Where her current lover lived also.

Or perhaps Hypatia was sensing the end of an era, beyond which she had no desire to live.

Her era, that had allowed her to be learned. More learned than her learned astrologer/mathematician father Theron. Than her philosopher husband Isidore.

& to share her learning. With students as illustrious as Synesius of Cyrene. The only Christian she knew to laugh a hearty laugh. Who had just recently become Bishop of Ptolomais. Who was writing her many affectionate, admiring letters.

An era that had allowed a woman to think. & to become known because of her thoughts.

That allowed the known thinking woman to have lovers, besides having a philosophical philosopher husband.

Powerful lovers, like Orestes, the pagan prefect of Egypt. Her current lover, whom she refused to leave behind in Alexandria.

Whom the Christian gossip of that city had taking orders from his known philosopher-mistress. Whom gossip suspected of being behind the pagan prefect's opposition to Alexandria's Christian patriarch St. Cyril.

Who denied having expressed the unchristian wish to see the accursed woman dead. To his reader Peter.

Who denied having repeated the Christian patriarch's unexpressed unchristian wish   casually, after a mass to a group of lingering clergy.

Who denied having mentioned the known 45-year-old philosopher by name, in various exhortations

—about the adulterous conduct of pagan wives   the insidious influence of adulterous sex on the minds of

pagan politicians; which had led to the martyrdom of earlier Christians in the past—

addressed to various gatherings of their faithful.

Who stopped the unmentioned known 45-year-old philosopher's carriage on its way to her lecture hall. & forced it to go instead to their Christian church of Caesareum.

Where the gathered faithful pulled the philosopher from her carriage.

By the long red hair. In its habitual net of fine gold, that instantly disappeared beneath a faithful cloak.

& by the feet   with their polished toe nails   in their habitual golden leather sandals. That instantly disappeared.

& by her tunic. Which tore. & left her nude.

Standing for another instant   staring wide-eyed across a sea of bodies that were pausing briefly, getting ready to charge   into the new Christian era in which she had no desire to live.

Until she realized how long it took a healthy 45-year-old woman's body to be torn fingers from hands from wrists from elbows from shoulders toes from feet from ankles from knees from thighs. For the 45-year-old heart to stop beating. For her brain to lose its exceptional consciousness.

Note

[1] According to *The Women's Encyclopedia of Myths and Secrets (1983):* the martyring Christians scraped the flesh off Hypatia's bones with oyster shells.

References

Walker, Barbara. 1983. *The woman's encyclopedia of myths and secrets.* New York: Harper & Row.

Maria Dzielska (essay date 1995)

SOURCE: "The Literary Legend of Hypatia" in *Hypatia of Alexandria,* Harvard University Press, 1995, pp. 1-26.

[*Below, Dzielska surveys the confusion of fact and fiction that constitutes Hypatia's posthumous fame, evaluating the literary works of European and North American writers from the mid-eighteenth century to 1989, as well as the ancient sources that gave rise to that literary tradition. Dzielska points out that over the centuries, Hypatia's legendary story has been used to support a diverse range of view-points and ideologies.*]

The Modern Tradition

Long before the first scholarly attempts to reconstruct an accurate image of Hypatia, her life—marked by the dramatic circumstances of her death—had been imbued with legend. Artistically embellished, distorted by emotions and ideological biases, the legend has enjoyed wide popularity for centuries, obstructing scholarly endeavors to present Hypatia's life impartially, and it persists to this day. Ask who Hypatia was, and you will probably be told: "She was that beautiful young pagan philosopher who was torn to pieces by monks (or, more generally, by Christians) in Alexandria in 415." This pat answer would be based not on ancient sources, but on a mass of belletristic and historical literature, a representative sample of which is surveyed in this chapter. Most of these works present Hypatia as an innocent victim of the fanaticism of nascent Christianity, and her murder as marking the banishment of freedom of inquiry along with the Greek gods.

Hypatia first appeared in European literature in the eighteenth century. In the era of skepticism known historically as the Enlightenment, several writers used her as an instrument in religious and philosophical polemic.

In 1720 John Toland, in youth a zealous Protestant, published a long historical essay titled *Hypatia or, the History of a Most Beautiful, Most Virtuous, Most Learned and in Every Way Accomplished Lady; Who Was Torn to Pieces by the Clergy of Alexandria, to Gratify the Pride, Emulation, and Cruelty of the Archbishop, Commonly but Undeservedly Titled St. Cyril.* Though basing his account of Hypatia on sources such as the tenth-century encyclopedia *Suda*, Toland begins by asserting that the male part of humanity has been forever disgraced by the murder of "the incarnation of beauty and wisdom"; men must always "be ashamed, that any could be found among them of so brutal and savage a disposition, as, far from being struck with admiration at so much beauty, innocence, and knowledge, to stain their barbarous hands with her blood, and their impious souls with the indelible character of sacrilegious murderers." In unfolding the story of Hypatia's life and death, Toland focuses on the Alexandrian clergy, headed by the patriarch Cyril: "A Bishop, a Patriarch, nay a Saint, was the contriver of so horrid a deed, and his clergy the executioners of his implacable fury."[1]

The essay produced a stir in ecclesiastical circles and was speedily answered by Thomas Lewis in a pamphlet, *The History of Hypatia, a Most Impudent School-Mistress of Alexandria. In Defense of Saint Cyril and the Alexandrian Clergy from the Aspersions of Mr.*

Toland.[2] But for the most part Toland's work enjoyed a favorable reception among the Enlightenment elite. Voltaire exploited the figure of Hypatia to express his repugnance for the church and revealed religion. In a style not unlike Toland's, he writes about Saint Cyril and the Alexandrian clergy in *Examen important de Milord Bolingbroke ou le tombeau du fanatisme* (1736). Hypatia's death was "a bestial murder perpetrated by Cyril's tonsured hounds, with a fanatical gang at their heels."[3] She was murdered, Voltaire asserts, because she believed in the Hellenic gods, the laws of rational Nature, and the capacities of the human mind free of imposed dogmas. Thus did religious fanaticism lead to the martyrdom of geniuses and to the enslavement of the spirit.

Voltaire returns to Hypatia in his *Dictionnaire philosophique.* There he asserts that she "taught Homer and Plato in Alexandria during the reign of Theodosius II" and that the events leading to her death were instigated by Saint Cyril, who "loosed the Christian rabble on her." Though not neglecting to divulge his sources—Damascius, *Suda,* and "the most learned men of the age"—Voltaire makes quite cavalier use of them; and in the midst of serious accusations against Cyril and the Christians, he offers a coarse, asinine salon witticism about his favorite heroine: "When one strips beautiful women naked, it is not to massacre them." In truth, we are left in the dark as to whether the "sage of Ferney" is deriding his readers, the ideas that he is promulgating with such enthusiasm, or Hypatia. Voltaire expresses hope that the patriarch Cyril asked God for forgiveness and that God indeed had mercy on him; Voltaire himself prays for the patriarch: "I beseech the merciful father to have pity on his soul."[4]

Toland's and Voltaire's reductive accounts of Hypatia mark the genesis of a legend that mixes truth and falsehood. Had they consulted their ancient sources with greater perception, they would have detected in them a far more complex personality. This "victim of superstition and ignorance" not only believed in the redemptive powers of reason but also sought god through religious revelation. Above all, she was stubborn and intensely moral, no less a proponent of asceticism than the dogmatic Christians whom Voltaire and others depicted as ruthless enemies of "truth and progress."

Influenced by Enlightenment ideas, neo-Hellenism, and Voltaire's literary and philosophical style, Edward Gibbon elaborated the legend of Hypatia. In *The Decline and Fall of the Roman Empire* he identifies Cyril as the perpetrator of all conflicts in Alexandria at the beginning of the fifth century, including the murder of Hypatia.[5] According to Gibbon, Hypatia "professed the religion of the Greeks" and taught publicly in both Athens and Alexandria. I do not know the source of Gibbon's first claim; the latter reflects an erroneous interpretation of Damascius' account in *Suda.* Like

Toland and Voltaire, Gibbon retails Damascius' story about Cyril's burning envy of Hypatia, who was "in the bloom of beauty, and in the maturity of wisdom," surrounded by disciples and persons "most illustrious for their rank or merit" and always "impatient to visit the female philosopher." Hypatia was murdered by "a troop of savage and merciless fanatics" instigated by Cyril, and the crime was never punished, apparently because "superstition [Christianity] perhaps would more gently expiate the blood of a virgin, than the banishment of a saint." This representation of "the Alexandrian crime" perfectly fitted Gibbon's theory that the rise of Christianity was the crucial cause of the fall of the ancient civilization. He used the circumstances of Hypatia's life to document this thesis and to show the difference between the old world and the new: reason and spiritual culture (Hypatia) versus dogmatism and barbaric absence of restraint (Cyril and Christianity).[6]

The figure of Hypatia appears briefly and allusively in many other eighteenth-century works, including Henry Fielding's droll satiric novel *A Journey from This World to the Next* (1743). Describing Hypatia as "a young lady of greatest beauty and merit," Fielding states that "those dogs, the Christians, murdered her."[7]

But it was in the mid-nineteenth century that the literary legend of Hypatia reached its apex. Charles Leconte de Lisle published two versions of a poem titled *Hypatie*, one in 1847 and another in 1874.[8] In the first version Hypatia is a victim of the laws of history and not of a Christian "plot," as Voltaire contended.[9] Leconte de Lisle views the circumstances of Hypatia's death with historical detachment, from the perspective that history cannot be identified with a single culture or system of belief. The era of Hypatia simply faded away, replaced by a new one with its own rules and forms. As a believer in the old deities and a lover of reason and sensual beauty, she became a symbolic victim of the changing circumstances of history. "Mankind, in its headlong course, struck you and cursed you."[10]

In the second version of the poem Leconte de Lisle reverts to an anti-Christian interpretation of Hypatia's death. It is Christians who are guilty of the crime, not "historical necessity":

> The vile Galilean struck you and cursed you;
> But in falling, you became even greater! And now, alas!
> The spirit of Plato and the body of Aphrodite
> Have withdrawn forever to the fair skies of Hellas!

This version echoes Toland's anticlerical, and specifically anti-Catholic, motif.[11] As the legend develops, that motif is reinforced.

Both of Leconte de Lisle's Hypatia poems manifest confidence in the permanence of the essential values of antiquity. As one of the founders of the Parnassian school of poetry, which drew inspiration from classical antiquity, Leconte de Lisle loved classical literature. He not only translated Greek poets and dramatists; he regarded Hellenism as the fulfillment of the ideals of humanity, beauty combined with wisdom. Thus for Leconte de Lisle, despite her death Hypatia lives on in the Western imagination as the embodiment of physical beauty and the immortality of the spirit, just as the pagan ideals of Greece have molded Europe's spirituality.

> She alone survives, immutable, eternal;
> Death can scatter the trembling universes
> But Beauty still dazzles with her fire,
>   and all is reborn in her,
> And the worlds are still prostrate beneath her
>   white feet!

Leconte de Lisle's admiration for the Greeks' excellence and Hellenic ideas about the supernatural world is also expressed in a short dramatic work, "Hypatie et Cyrille" (1857).[12] In it we find the same Romantic longing for ancient Greece, where people lived in harmony with the beauty of divine nature and in conformity with the teachings of their philosophers—the same longing that resonates in Hölderlin's poems, the classics of "Weimar humanism," and the works of the English neo-Hellenists. Here Leconte de Lisle attempts to reconcile pagan philosophy with Christianity.

Plato's beautiful and wise disciple tries to convince the stern patriarch Cyril that there is only a small difference between Neoplatonism and Christianity: "The words are slightly different, the sense is very much the same." Hypatia admits that the person of Christ is holy to her, but she also feels affinity with the gods enrobed in the eternal fabrics of the cosmos. The deities reveal themselves in the beauty of nature, in the intelligence of the astral bodies, in the wonder of art, in the spirituality of sages searching for truth. Cyril's pronouncement, "Your gods are reduced to dust, at the feet of the victorious Christ," elicits Hypatia's passionate credo:

> You're mistaken, Cyril. They live in my heart.
> Not as you see them—clad in transient forms,
> Subject to human passions even in heaven,
> Worshiped by the rabble and worthy of
>   scorn—
> But as sublime minds have seen them
> In the starry expanse that has no dwellings:
> Forces of the universe, interior virtues,
> Harmonious union of earth and heaven
> That delights the mind and the ear and the
>   eye,
> That offers an attainable ideal to all wise men

And a visible splendor to the beauty of the
    soul.
Such are my Gods!

"Hypatie et Cyrille," full of exaltation and Romantic
rapture over the Greeks' "heaven," ends with a description of the bishop's anger. He has no understanding of Hypatia's belief in the world of divine intelligences and the natural beauty of the universe. Cyril
threatens her and her world with the curse of oblivion,
extinction of the ancient culture.

Leconte de Lisle's poems were known and widely read
in the nineteenth century; and the image of Hypatia in
love with the ideal forms of the visible world—in
contrast to the closed spheres of Cyril's rigidly dogmatic Christianity—has survived to our time. Even
today we tend to associate the figure of Hypatia with
de Lisle's line, "Le souffle de Platon et le corps
d'Aphrodite," the spirit of Plato and the body of
Aphrodite.

Leconte de Lisle's younger contemporary Gérard de
Nerval referred to Hypatia in an 1854 work,[13] and in
1888 Maurice Barrès published a short story about
Hypatia, "La vierge assassinée," in a collection titled
Sous l'oeil des barbares. Barrès states in his preface
that he wrote the story at the request of Leconte de
Lisle, his "Parnassian master."[14] "La vierge assassinée"
combines bucolic elements with a cool and austere
presentation of philosophy and moral virtues.

The story opens as young Lucius meets the charming
and beautiful Alexandrian courtesan Amaryllis on the
banks of the Nile canal overgrown with water lilies.
The marble of a temple and Greek sculptures glimmers
beyond the trees, and we also see town buildings and
ships anchored in the port. However, rich and beautiful Alexandria is in decline: "The town extends its
arms over the ocean and seems to call the entire universe to its perfumed and feverish bed, to lend assistance during the death throes of a world and the formation of the ages to come."[15]

Walking to the Serapeum, where Hypatia (who is called
Athénée in this story) is usually to be found, Lucius
and Amaryllis encounter a crowd of Christians who
are chasing Jews out of the city. The audience awaiting Athénée/Hypatia in the library of the Serapeum
talk with alarm about "the Christian sect, which says it
owes its convictions to the fact that the lenient temples
have fallen into disrepute and age-old traditions have
been abandoned." They recall that the Emperor Julian
perished at the hands of a Christian while fighting to
defend holy monuments of the past. One member of
the audience attempts to induce the "Hellenes" to defend themselves against the "barbarians" using their
methods, that is, cruelty and violence; otherwise "those
barbarians will destroy you."

In the meantime a crowd of Christians begins to assail
the Serapeum, calling for the death of Athénée, the
symbol of paganism in the city. The mob forces its
way into the interior of the shrine, where Athénée
delivers a speech in praise of the Hellenic past and
takes an oath of fidelity to the monuments of the past
now being destroyed. Impressed by her speech, the
mob desists, but its most zealous members continue to
incite action. Athénée calmly awaits death. Lucius,
Amaryllis, and their friends attempt to lead her out of
the temple, but she refuses to abandon "the library and
the statues of our forebears." Covering her face with a
long veil, she gives herself up to the mob, which tears
her to pieces. The Roman legions, which have just
entered the city, are unable to rescue her. In the evening
Amaryllis and Lucius find the divine remains "of the
virgin of Serapis." Barrès assures us that the martyrdom of "the last of the Hellenes" will become the source
of her apotheosis and enduring legend.

While Leconte de Lisle, Barrès, and others were writing about Hypatia in France, the English clergyman,
novelist, and historian Charles Kingsley elaborated her
legend in a long book titled *Hypatia or the New Foes
with an Old Face* (1853).[16] Though originally intended
as a historical study based on the author's research on
Greek culture of the late empire and the history of
Alexandria, it in fact took the form of a mid-Victorian
romance with a strong anti-Catholic flavor. Kingsley
detested priests and monks, with their vows of celibacy and their seclusion from the affairs of this world.
In the book Cyril and the clergy around him exemplify
the Catholic hierarchy and the segment of the Anglican clergy that opposed Kingsley; good Christians could
find their virtues represented in the young monk, the
converted Jew, the courtesan Pelagia, and Hypatia
herself.

The action of the novel occurs chiefly in Alexandria.
This large port city of the East, wealthy and poor,
enlightened and primitive, with a heterogeneous population of Greeks, Egyptians, Jews, and—as Kingsley
would have it—Goths, provides an appropriate medley
of nationalities, trades, beliefs, and social classes, out
of which emerge the central characters of the novel:
the pagan philosopher Hypatia, the dogmatic and despotic patriarch Cyril, the ambitious and power-hungry
prefect of Egypt Orestes, and the monk Philammon.

Hypatia incarnates "the spirit of Plato and the body of
Aphrodite." Though barely twenty-five years old, she
gives lectures in the Museion on Platonic and
Neoplatonic philosophy. Throngs of young people surround her; she knows all the important people in the
city and is herself a very influential person. Hypatia
writes commentaries on Plotinus' works and, with her
father Theon, studies the writings of ancient masters in
mathematics and geometry. Her pagan erudition is an
irritant to Christian circles in Alexandria. The patri-

arch Cyril sees to it that young Christians do not attend her lectures; he does not want them exposed, under her tantalizing influence, to Greek science and philosophy. When the young monk Philammon expresses a desire to attend, Cyril describes Hypatia to him as "subtler than the serpent, skilled in all the tricks of logic" and warns, "you will become a laughing-stock, and run away in shame."

Beautiful, wise, and virtuous, Hypatia displays some surprising features: a fierce hatred of Christianity and a Voltairean obdurateness rather than Neoplatonic benignity. She is full of contempt for the monks and the clergy, supercilious toward the creed that is alien to her civilization. She characterizes monks as "bigots, wild beasts of the desert, and fanatic intriguers, who in the words of Him they call their master, compass heaven and earth to make him twofold more the child of hell than themselves."

The monk Philammon is one of those whom Hypatia despises. He has been brought up in the desert and is completely under the spiritual influence of the patriarch. Prompted by curiosity and interest in Hypatia's fame, he attends one of her lectures with a view to condemning her teachings and converting her. Instead, he becomes one of her most devoted and loyal disciples. He discovers in Hypatia a deep religiosity that transcends simple belief in the Homeric deities, and their friendship, mixed with erotic overtones, lasts until Hypatia's death.

Kingsley presents the prefect Orestes as a cunning schemer, drunken and dissolute, with far-reaching political ambitions. Hoping to become emperor of Egypt and Africa and, perhaps later, the East, he supports the revolt of Heraclian, governor of West Africa. He draws Hypatia into these plans by proposing marriage to her. He arranges sumptuous gladiatorial games, dance performances, and other public revelries, promising Hypatia that they portend a renaissance of paganism. He assures her that these manifestations of a simple religiosity are only a transitory phase meant to win people's hearts; they will be soon replaced by a religiosity of a higher order.

Heraclian, in whom Orestes vests all his hopes, suffers defeat at the gates of Rome. Only then does Hypatia realize that she has been a victim of Orestes' deceptions and machinations. Her honesty, nobility, and faith in the sublime ideals of a resurrected Hellenic religiosity have been betrayed.

Kingsley's story of the conflict between Orestes and Cyril follows the account by the fifth-century church historian Socrates Scholasticus. A series of incidents bring escalating tensions between the prefect's people and the church. During street actions provoked by the monks the prefect himself sustains an injury. A rumor

is spread that Hypatia is the cause of the unrest in the city, the sower of discord. And although at the last she is converted and baptized into Christianity, she is murdered by monks, the parabolans or church servants, and a Christian mob under the leadership of Peter the Reader. The murder provides an outlet for fanaticism, ignorance, and hidden lusts—Kingsley strongly emphasizes the erotic aspect of the act committed on the beautiful young woman.

Before her death Hypatia, deceived and disappointed by Orestes' lies, undergoes a spiritual crisis. Her conversion is effected through the beneficent influence of a former disciple, the Jew Raphael Aben-Ezra. After Hypatia's death he demands that Cyril identify the perpetrators. When the bishop refuses, Raphael warns Cyril that the kingdom of God he is erecting may turn out to be the kingdom of Satan, to which the patriarch may be condemned.

The memory of the crime against Hypatia lives on in Alexandria. Science and philosophy wither away, and with them the intellectual life of Alexandria. "Twenty years after Hypatia's death, philosophy was flickering down to the very socket. Hypatia's murder was its death-blow." The nascent Christian church in Egypt suffers disgrace and loses itself in trivial sectarian disputes and quarrels among clerics.

Kingsley's book was translated into several European languages, and several German historians even wrote dissertations on it.[17] His broad novelistic vision of "the last of the Hellenes" entertained readers around the world. His figure of Hypatia functions as a symbol of passing civilization, as the last victim of the struggle for the rescue of the perfect Grecian world of harmony, art and metaphysics, divinity and materialism, soul and body. Far more than the accounts of Toland, Voltaire, Barrès, or Leconte de Lisle, Kingsley's book promoted and sustained the notion that with the death of the last idealist of Hellenism, Greek values disappeared.

In the second half of the nineteenth century American and British positivists presented Hypatia as primarily a scientist, the last scholar in the Greek East. Thus the American scientist J. W. Draper, described as a "valiant defender of science against religion," considered Hypatia a heroic figure in the contest between two powers in European history: the free mind searching for truth in the material world versus superstitious religion (represented by the church) enslaving reason. This perspective renders the history of European thought very simple: from the death of Hypatia until the age of the Enlightenment Europe was draped in darkness; the Enlightenment (with its revolt against the authority of the church, revelation, and dogmas) conquered the darkness and reopened the clear sky of knowledge. The death of Hypatia was "one of those moments in which great general principles embody themselves in individuals. It is Greek philosophy under the appropriate form of Hypatia; ecclesiastical ambition under that of Cyril." After a graphic description of Hypatia's horrible death, Draper adds: "Though in his privacy St. Cyril and his friends might laugh at the end of his antagonist, his memory must bear the weight of the righteous indignation of posterity." He concludes: "Thus in the year 414 of our era, the position of philosophy in the intellectual metropolis of the world was determined; henceforth science must sink into obscurity and subordination. Its public existence will no longer be tolerated."[18]

Bertrand Russell, expressing similar sentiments, opens his history of Western European thought with a characterization of Saint Cyril: "His chief claim to fame is the lynching of Hypatia, a distinguished lady who, in an age of bigotry, adhered to the Neoplatonic philosophy and devoted her talents to mathematics . . . After this Alexandria was no longer troubled by philosophers."[19]

Hypatia became a figure in modern Italian literature as early as 1827, when Contessa Diodata Roero di Saluzzo published a two-volume poem, *Ipazia ovvero delle Filosofie*.[20] This work ventures beyond the legend into a fanciful biography of Hypatia that connects Hypatia with Christianity. This is a venerable tradition: elements of Hypatia's life were inscribed in the legend of Saint Catherine of Alexandria, for example.[21] Saluzzo portrays Hypatia as a disciple of Plotinus living with him in the "Alexandrian Lyceum" and unhappily in love with the Egyptian prince Isidore who fights for independence from Rome. Hypatia parts company with Isidore and, having been converted by Bishop Cyril, links her fate with that of the Christians. She dies in a church, at the foot of the Cross, killed with three blows of a sword by a treacherous priest.

Other Italian works present Hypatia in the context of the struggle between expiring paganism and an ascendant Christianity that destroys old values and imposes its own truths. In the chapter "Ipazia e le ultime lotte pagane" in his book on great men in history, Carlo Pascal reiterates the theme that connects Hypatia's death with the decline of philosophy and Mediterranean civilization in general.[22] Pascal, however, also introduces a new element into the literary tradition of Hypatia, one that resonates in our time: Hypatia's death is seen as an antifeminist act. "Obviously the persecution against Hypatia stemmed to a great extent from this insolent and superstitious antifemale tendency." It brought about a profound change in the treatment of women. Formerly free, intellectually independent, and creative, they were suppressed into silence.

In 1978 two thematically related dramas by Mario Luzi were published in one volume: *Libro di Ipazia* and *Il messagero*, the latter about Synesius of Cyrene. *Libro di Ipazia* is not only a historical work, as G. Pampaloni remarks in his introduction;[23] it is also a drama of historicism. The story of Hypatia is meant to serve as testimony to the irreversibility of historical phases: the decline of Greek culture and the victory of the new order were inevitable. The drama begins in Alexandria, then moves to Cyrene, where Bishop Synesius fights the barbarians who are both threat and heralds of the destination of history.

A lament for the political and social decay of Alexandria opens the play. Its greatness is gone, and there are almost no traces of those "perennial flowerings" that made her famous. Orestes, the prefect of Egypt, complains to George, a well-known and respected Alexandrian, about the weakness and impotence of Alexandria's civil government. Insoluble problems confront them as a result of the forceful presence of pagans and fanaticism of the Christian masses. Orestes says that the city's Hellenes, the disciples of Proclus and Plotinus, "pour oil on water." But the daughter of Theon is kindling hostility and passions; as the gentle and wise woman philosopher turns into a formidable adversary, "her sweetness becomes horrible." Orestes is afraid of Cyril and incapable of restricting Hypatia's freedom of speech and that of her friends. So he asks George to join the ranks of the pagan intellectuals and to do everything in his power to stop them from publicly teaching Greek philosophy and religion.

The second act takes place in Synesius' house. Jone, a woman who lives with Synesius, and George beg Synesius to act in the cause of peace and order in the city and quell the storm that has been brewed by "the enchantress Hypatia." Synesius interprets the disturbances as a manifestation of the law of history: the Greek mind must be reconciled with the Christian logos; the highest reason calls for harmony between these two worlds.

In the third act Hypatia conducts a dialogue with herself. Her inner voice tells her that her time has come: "prepare yourself. Your hour is approaching." Weeping, Hypatia prepares for death: "Let me cry a little while longer and then I will come to wherever you may call me." At this moment Synesius enters; he begs her to stop propagating pagan philosophy and religion, for the entire city is in an uproar and in danger of a disaster. He tells her that the prefect has lost control over the situation; in addition, the prefect has quarreled with the bishop. Hypatia, however, stands by her truths and conduct. Synesius leaves Hypatia's house with the premonition that he will never see her again, but he is afraid of saying good-bye. He only blurts out, "Until tomorrow."

In the fourth and final act Synesius tells George about his failed mission. As he reiterates his opinion of

Hypatia, Jone bursts in with the news of the murder and, at Synesius' behest, relates the circumstances in detail:

> "Well, she was speaking in the square to
>   many people,
> speaking about the present God and they were
>   listening to
>   her in silence,
> in a stupor, both followers and adversaries.
> But a fanatic horde interrupted,
> hands and hands came down upon her,
> they tore her clothes and her flesh,
> they pushed her into the church of Christ,
> and there they finished her. There she died on
>   the floor
>   of the temple."

Dying (her death is a historical moment), Hypatia articulates her attitude toward the god of the Christians. She looks far ahead into the future; her eyes are open to the course of the world. In two lines George sums up the knowledge of the inevitable direction of history—knowledge that they all have already comprehended:

> "In this way the dream of Hellenic Reason
>   ended
> In this way, on the floor of Christ."

Luzi interprets Hypatia's death in Christian terms. Hypatia stands very close to Christ, and her sacrifice becomes a martyrdom. The fanatics who murder her are not the evil Christians portrayed by Kingsley, but the ever-present powers of evil and crime inherent in any crowd. The defining structures and concepts of Christian Europe have burgeoned from the soil of the Alexandrian convulsions and dramas, from Hypatia's sacrifice, from fanaticism and despair. Christian Europe is the consummation of the ancient world. Luzi's drama enriches the thin tradition of Hypatia's presence in Christian literature.

Hypatia appears as a character in other contemporary literature, either in works devoted to her or in novels set in the late Roman empire.[24] In Germany Arnulf Zitelmann's recent historical novel *Hypatia* has been a great popular success.[25] Zitelmann's Hypatia remains a pagan to the end. Intending to found a Platonic state behind the Pillars of Hercules, she journeys to Athens and visits Plutarch, the head of the Platonic Academy; subsequently she travels to Delphi, Dodona, Nicopolis, and Phaistos on Crete. After returning to Alexandria, she delivers a speech in the forum directed against Cyril and his supporters. She is murdered by monks in the company of a Christian mob. Zitelmann describes the event in what are by now familiar terms: the book abounds in descriptions of the perfidiousness, greed, and obscurantism of the church. In the epilogue he repeats the claim made by others: "The attack on Hypatia marks the end of antiquity." He adds: "Hypatia, the daughter of Theon, was the first martyr to that misogyny which later rose to a frenzy in witch hunts."

Canada, too, has produced two novels about Hypatia, André Ferretti's *Renaissance en Paganie* (Montreal, 1987) and Jean Marcel's *Hypatie ou la fin des dieux* (Montreal, 1989).[26] Both express viewpoints close to those of Kingsley and Zitelmann.

The latest development in the legend of Hypatia concerns her appeal to feminists. Two scholarly feminist journals have taken her name: *Hypatia: Feminist Studies*, published in Athens since 1984; and *Hypatia: A Journal of Feminist Philosophy*, published at Indiana University since 1986. In 1989 the latter featured a vivid poetic prose portrait of the life and death of Hypatia as seen through the eyes of feminist poet and novelist Ursula Molinaro.[27] The introduction to the text reiterates a theme voiced earlier in Claudio Pascal: "The torture killing of the noted philosopher Hypatia by a mob of Christians in Alexandria in 415 A.D. marks the end of a time when women were still appreciated for the brain under their hair."

In Molinaro's account Hypatia's father, Theon, has been warned by the stars about the approaching martyrdom of his daughter. We learn that while still an adolescent, but already famous as a philosopher, she commenced taking lovers and then married the philosopher Isidore, who tolerated his wife's "many amorous friendships." The same stars that had granted Hypatia power over men also divined her tragic death. Aware of his daughter's doom, Theon wants her to move to Sicily, the ancient seat of Greek philosophers, but she rejects the suggestion. She wants to continue to teach her students, among them Synesius. Besides, Hypatia senses the passing of the epoch in which women are permitted to think and to achieve a level of erudition that makes them superior to men; she herself is superior to her father and her husband, Isidore. Moreover, she does not want to leave behind her current lover, the prefect Orestes.

The rumor circulates in Alexandria that Hypatia has formed an alliance with the pagan Orestes against the patriarch Cyril. Cyril incites the faithful and his supporters, headed by Peter the Reader, to rebel against Hypatia. The patriarch begrudges Hypatia her success, and he cannot condone the "adulterous conduct of pagan wives." He therefore makes preparations for her death. After describing Hypatia's death at length and in detail, Molinaro suggests that such will be the lot of women in Christian times, in which Hypatia "had no desire to live." Subsequently Hypatia's murderers (Christians) constrained all free thought and offered women "a new role model of depleasurized submission."

Through its arbitrariness, fabrications, and alterations Molinaro's text goes considerably beyond previous literary mythologizing seeking to justify through Hypatia various perspectives on history, religion, and Greek antiquity.

Hypatia has also been commemorated in feminist art. In the controversial sculptural work of the feminist artist Judy Chicago exhibited in the San Francisco Museum of Modern Art in 1979, Hypatia is presented as a participant—together with other famous and talented women of Western civilization—at a dinner party that dazzles by its sheer size (but not elegance).[28]

The Origins of the Legend

Few ancient sources underlie the literary tradition about the beautiful young Hypatia, famous philosopher and mathematician, admired by her fellow pagans and despised by Christians, especially by the patriarch Cyril, who with his people delivered her to an undeserved and cruel death, and so on, and so forth—rehearsed in diverse variations.

A few rudimentary elements of the legend originate in Socrates Scholasticus' fifth-century ecclesiastical history. Socrates not only waxes eloquent about Hypatia's virtues, her erudition, and her popularity in the city; he also provides the most detailed description of her murder, including the name of the leader of the band that killed her: Peter, who is mentioned in almost all subsequent narratives about Hypatia. Here is part of Socrates' account:

> It was at that time that envy arose against this woman. She happened to spend a great deal of the time with Orestes, and that stirred up slander against her among people of the Church, as if she were one who prevented Orestes from entering into friendship with the Bishop. Indeed, a number of men who heatedly reached the same conclusion, whom a certain Peter (who was employed as a reader) led, kept watch for the woman as she was returning from somewhere. They threw her out of her carriage and dragged her to the church called Caesarion. They stripped off her clothes and then killed her with broken bits of pottery [*ostraka*]. When they had torn her body apart limb from limb, they took it to a place called Cinaron and burned it.[29]

Socrates, however, leaves open the question of Cyril's complicity in the crime.

The only clear and unequivocal accusation of the patriarch and the Alexandrian Christians occurs in Damascius' *Life of Isidore.*[30] Before the reconstruction and separate publication of this work, the following fragment was preserved as the entry on Hypatia in *Suda.* According to this account, Cyril sought the fulfillment of his ambition by having Hypatia murdered, and his bestial supporters performed the deed and went unpunished. The crime is described as a street scene in which the patriarch himself is a participant:

> Cyril, the bishop of the opposing party, went by Hypatia's house and noticed a great throng at her door, "a jumble of steeds and men." Some came, some went; others remained standing. He asked what this gathering meant and why such a tumult was being made. He then heard from his retainers that the philosopher Hypatia was being greeted and that this was her house. This information so pierced his heart that he launched a murderous attack in the most detestable manner. For when Hypatia was going out as usual, several bestial men, fearing neither divine vengeance nor human punishment, suddenly rushed upon her and killed her: thus laying their country both under the highest infamy and under the guilt of innocent blood. And indeed the Emperor was grievously offended at this matter, and the murderers had been certainly punished, but that Aedesius did corrupt the Emperor's friend: so that his Majesty it is true remitted the punishment but drew vengeance on himself and posterity, his nephew paying dearly for this action.

Writers of the eighteenth and nineteenth centuries found this version of the murder of the pagan philosopher in popular histories of the church as well as in widely known and highly esteemed histories of antiquity such as those of Sébastien Le Nain de Tillemont or Edward Gibbon. Gibbon's description of the events of 415 well served those who wanted to portray the disappearance of Greek civilization as well as those who wished to tarnish the relatively new and rising church. About Cyril, the Alexandrian church, and Hypatia, Gibbon wrote:

> He [Cyril] soon prompted, or accepted, the sacrifice of a virgin who professed the religion of the Greeks . . . Hypatia, the daughter of Theon the mathematician, was initiated in her father's studies; her learned comments have elucidated the geometry of Apollonius and Diophantus, and she publicly taught, both at Athens and Alexandria, the philosophy of Plato and Aristotle. In the bloom of beauty, and in the maturity of wisdom, the modest maid refused her lovers and instructed her disciples; the persons most illustrious for their rank or merit were impatient to visit the female philosopher; and Cyril beheld with a jealous eye the gorgeous train of horses and slaves who crowded the door of her academy. A rumour was spread among the Christians that the daughter of Theon was the only obstacle to the reconciliation of the prefect and the archbishop; and that obstacle was speedily removed. On a fatal day, in the holy season of Lent, Hypatia was torn from her chariot, stripped naked, dragged to the church, and inhumanly butchered by the hands of Peter the reader and a troop of savage and merciless fanatics: her flesh was scraped from her bones with sharp oyster-shells, and her quivering limbs were

delivered to the flames. The just progress of inquiry and punishment was stopped by seasonable gifts; but the murder of Hypatia has imprinted an indelible stain on the character and religion of Cyril of Alexandria.[31]

In describing Hypatia's fate Gibbon avails himself of both Socrates and *Suda*, but in his anti-Christian fervor he fails to perceive the small yet puzzling fact that Damascius sets the murder of Hypatia on a religious basis. Passing by Hypatia's house, the jealous patriarch Cyril is called "the bishop of the opposing party" (*hairesin*). We later learn that Damascius has in mind a particular group headed by the bishop. Thus Damascius, who elsewhere in the *Life of Isidore* describes Hypatia's paganism and her teaching of Plato and Aristotle, here places on one level her followers and the Christian environment of the bishop of Alexandria. Does he not therefore treat Hypatia as a person aligned with some Christian movement?

It is possible that Hypatia became affiliated with a Christian creed early in her life, as suggested by a contemporary chronicler of the church, the Arian Philostorgius, who blamed adherents to the Nicene Creed, orthodox Christians, for her death.[32] But Philostorgius' description may be historical intrigue resulting from his steadfast allegiance to Arianism: it is gratifying to blame one's opponents for a crime. So we must seek other clues. They disclose that Damascius may have read texts connecting Hypatia with the theology promulgated by Nestorius.

Diverse authors writing about Hypatia quote a letter of Hypatia's (which is an anonymous fraud) addressed to Cyril, titled "Copy of a letter from Hypatia, who taught philosophy at Alexandria, to the blessed Archbishop Cyril," which contains Hypatia's urgent appeal to Cyril asking him to exercise consideration and understanding for Nestorius and his views on the nature of Christ.[33] Hypatia is thus a presumed Nestorian, that is, a follower of the heresy of Christ's double nature, and "she" writes to Cyril:

> For, as the Evangelist [John 1:18] said, "No one has ever seen God." So how, they say, can you say that God was crucified? They say, too, "How can someone who has not been seen have been fixed to a cross? How could he have died and been buried?" Nestorius, then, who has recently been placed in exile, explained the Apostles' teaching. Now I, who learned long ago that Nestorius himself professed that Christ exists in two natures, say to him who said that, "The gentiles' questions are resolved." Therefore I say that your holiness did wrong in summoning a synod when you hold views contrary to his and that you contrived in advance that his deposition should take place as a result of the dispute. As for me, after starting this man's exposition a few days ago and comparing the

Apostles' teaching, and thinking to myself that it would be good for me to become a Christian, I hope that I may become worthy of the rebirth of baptism.

It is easy to guess the source of the connection between Hypatia and Nestorius. Cyril was a staunch personal opponent of this "heresiarch," as well as of Arianism and Arius' successors. This circumstance probably influenced Philostorgius' account of Hypatia's death, which he attributed to the "homousiasts"—that is, to Cyril and his adherents.

Cyril's differences with Nestorius, his theological and political rival in Constantinople, were fierce and deep. The two patriarchs argued about Christ's divine and human nature, and about Mary. Nestorius referred to her only as the "Mother of Christ" and not as the "Mother of God." Cyril used the contention with Nestorius to promote the cult of Mary in Christian circles, and Nestorius was defeated, condemned at the Council of Ephesus in 431 and declared a heretic. Deprived of his Constantinople patriarchate, he returned to his monastery in Antioch; later "interned" in Egypt, he came under Cyril's rule.

Since the letter mentions Nestorius' banishment, we presume that the fraud—so strangely connected with Hypatia—must have been perpetrated after the Council of Ephesus in 431. It therefore appears that at the close of antiquity there arose a legend linking Hypatia with unorthodox Christianity since two sources—Philostorgius and the anonymous author of the letter to Cyril—seem to have observed her among its sects. At the beginning of the sixth century Damascius showed familiarity with these tendencies in his *Life of Isidore*, an account that was disseminated through *Suda*. Hypatia's association with Christianity persisted, extended by the instigators of the legend of Saint Catherine the Alexandrian, which was constructed on elements drawn from Hypatia's biography. Nor have modern writers hesitated to connect Hypatia with Christianity. Kingsley would have liked to make her a Protestant; Luzi endowed her with a momentous historical mission and linked it to the emergence of Christian Europe from antiquity. The later tradition, however, does not assign her a role in the theological controversies on the nature of divine being.

Eventually, Hypatia returns in the modern literary tradition through a sort of mysterious rebirth of the idea of the past in the poet's soul—an image of Hypatia as Cyril's instructor—in the beautiful poem by Leconte de Lisle. The image persists to our day as we descry it, for example, in Luciano Canfora's book: "celebrated Hypatia who studied geometry and musicology and whom the Christians, convinced in their ignorance that she was a heretic, barbarously murdered in 415."[34] All works devoted to Hypatia, whether literary, scholarly, or popular, quote an epigram that celebrates the exceptional personal qualities of a woman called Hypatia. Its authorship is connected with the name of an Alexandrian poet of the fourth century, Palladas.[35] He was probably born around 319; thus he was a contemporary of Theon rather than of Hypatia. He lived and wrote when Hypatia was still young, and although we are ignorant of the year of his death, it is difficult to assume that he lived long enough to see Hypatia's death and to know of her achievements. Yet the poem celebrates a person of mature excellence and wisdom elevating her above earthly forms to the stars, to the "heavenly" existence she deserves because of her accomplishments:

> Whenever I look upon you and your words, I
>   pay reverence,
> As I look upon the heavenly home of the
>   virgin.
> For your concerns are directed at the
>   heavens,
> Revered Hypatia, you who are yourself the
>   beauty
>   of reasoning,
> The immaculate star of wise learning.[36]

As G. Luck demonstrates, there is no convincing evidence that the epigram was composed in honor of "our" Hypatia, philosopher and mathematician.[37] Luck believes that it is a poem by an anonymous author addressed to a pious woman named Hypatia, probably the founder of a church ("home of the virgin" in Byzantine poetry refers to a church devoted to Mary). In this reading the walls of the church are decorated with stars and a picture of a woman who is the addressee of the poem. And the poem portrays Hypatia in the context of the constellation Virgo, the astronomical sign of the virgin. Luck's other arguments also appear credible—such as the erroneous identification of Palladas as the poem's author; he was probably confused with another poet, Panolbios.[38] Indeed, in *Suda* we read that Panolbios wrote an epitaph in tribute to Hypatia, the daughter of a high Byzantine official, Erythrius, who in the second half of the fifth century was thrice appointed to the prestigious post of praetorian prefect of the East.[39]

After studying the epigram some scholars, such as Wolfgang Meyer, have inferred that there were two Hypatias: Theon's daughter, at the turn of the fourth and fifth centuries, and Erythrius' daughter, in the second half of the fifth century.[40] This conclusion, however, is only partly correct, for we know that there were more women named Hypatia, including a benefactress of the church in the mid-fifth century (see Sources). The name was by no means uncommon, and it was not confined to pagan women.

Modern historians of the church have taken note of Hypatia. At the beginning of the seventeenth century Caesar Baronius, in his *Annales Ecclesiastici*, wrote ecstatically about her, drawing on a mixture of information from *Suda* and Socrates Scholasticus: "she made such progress in learning that she far surpassed all philosophers of her time"; and he continues: "We can learn from the philosopher Synesius, of whom I have spoken at greater length above, that she shone forth as the most celebrated of all philosophers of that period."[41] Baronius does not explicitly blame Cyril for her death, but he writes with scorn about the Alexandrian church and the bloody event that remains associated with his name.

Toland's perspective on Cyril, however, is foreshadowed by another church historian, G. Arnolds, in his *Kirchen und Ketzer-Historie* (1699).[42] Praising Hypatia's wisdom and ethical perfection, he attributes to Cyril, and the Alexandrian clergy associated with him, criminal intentions toward Hypatia, justified by their struggle to protect the young Christian creed. Arnolds describes Cyril's relentlessness toward theologians promulgating views in conflict with those officially endorsed, and his methods in the struggle to preserve the Nicene orthodoxy.

Le Nain de Tillemont—the historian of antiquity and the church who was most esteemed by Gibbon—also writes about Hypatia.[43] He too dissolves in praise of Hypatia's soul, character, and ascetic and virginal life. Describing her achievements, he asserts that in her own time she was a widely known and respected philosopher. By proclaiming that she was teaching philosophy in Athens and Alexandria, enjoying great respect in both cities, he makes the same error repeated by Gibbon later. Like other contemporary historians, he confuses fact and fiction when writing about Hypatia; he condemns Cyril but at the same time conjectures about the real perpetrators of the murder; he gullibly relies on *Suda*, but he also questions its data.

Johann Albert Fabricius likewise relies on *Suda*, repeating the tale invented by Hesychius, and preserved in *Suda*, that Hypatia was married to the philosopher Isidore.[44] He also disseminates the view that Hypatia was a worshiper of pagan gods, a philosopher devoted to pagan culture. He is equivocal in his assessment of the events connected with her death, although he describes Cyril as "a headstrong and arrogant man."

The first treatise on Hypatia with scholarly aspirations appeared as early as 1689,[45] followed sixty years later by J. C. Wernsdorff's dissertation.[46] But not until the second half of the nineteenth century, with improved critical methods of studying antiquity, did more substantial works on Hypatia appear. In 1860 R. Hoche collected all the primary material on Hypatia then known, in an article titled "Hypatia die Tochter Theons." This was followed by three small monographs: a biography by Stephan Wolf, *Hypatia die Philosophin von Alexandrien* (1879); Hermann Ligier's *De Hypatia philosopha et eclectismi Alexandrini fine* (1879); and Wolfgang A. Meyer's *Hypatia von Alexandrien. Ein Beitrag zur Geschichte des Neuplatonismus* (1886). All three monographs, however, reflect Romantic and neo-Hellenic influences and are uncritically admiring, characterizing Hypatia as a heroically wise and great Hellenic woman. Like contemporary fictional accounts, they contain long descriptions of Hypatia's death, with the patriarch Cyril as the chief instrument.

The same account and accusations persist today in historical studies of Hypatia, in various kinds of dictionaries and encyclopedias, in histories of mathematics, and in works dealing with women's contributions to the history of science and philosophy. Thus, the *Dictionary of Scientific Biography* (1972) characterizes her as "the first woman in history to have lectured and written critical works on the most advanced mathematics of her day." A. W. Richeson, writing about "the celebrated mathematician-philosopher Hypatia," asserts that after her death "we have no other mathematician of importance until late in the Middle Ages."[47] Similarly, R. Jacobacci states that "with her passing there was no other woman mathematician of importance until the eighteenth century."[48] M. Alic describes Hypatia as the most eminent woman scientist before Marie Curie.[49] B. L. Van der Waerden reiterates the theme that Alexandrian science ceased with her death: "Hypatia, a very learned woman, heroine of romantic atrocity tales. She was handsome, she was eloquent, she was charming, she wrote learned commentaries on Diophantus and on Apollonius . . . After Hypatia, Alexandrian mathematics came to an end."[50]

And now Hypatia has been incorporated into the political, social, and cultural history of Africa. B. Lumpkin assumes that Hypatia, "one of the universal geniuses of antiquity," "the last great woman scientist of antiquity," and "woman algebraist, martyr to science," must have been African, not Greek, because of the way she conducted herself: her appearing in public places, her unrestrained behavior and speech.[51] And M. Bernal, writing about Afro-Asian sources of classical civilization, asserts: "Twenty-five years later [after the destruction of the Serapis temple] the brilliant and beautiful philosopher and mathematician Hypatia was gruesomely murdered in the same city by a gang of monks instigated by St. Cyril. These two acts of violence mark the end of Egypto-Paganism and the beginning of the Christian Dark Ages."[52]

Notes

[1] J. Toland, *Tetradymus*, chap. 3 (London, 1720), p.

103.

[2] T. Lewis, *The History of Hypatia* (London, 1721); I have not seen it. C. P. Goujet represents a similar position in "Dissertation sur Hypatie où l'on justifie Saint Cyrille d'Alexandrie sur la mort de cette savante," in P. Desmolets, *Continuation des Mémoires de littérature et d'histoire*, V (Paris, 1749), pp. 138-191.

[3] Voltaire, *Mélanges*, Bibliothèque de la Pléiade, 152 (Paris, 1961), pp. 1104 and 1108. On eighteenth-century philosophy see, among others, P. Gau, *The Enlightenment: An Interpretation,* I: *The Rise of Modern Paganism* (New York, 1967).

[4] In *Oeuvres complètes de Voltaire*, VII: *Dictionnaire philosophique* (Paris, 1835), pp. 700, 701. Voltaire also writes about Hypatia in the treatise *De la paix perpétuelle* (1769), describing her as "de l'ancienne religion égyptienne" and spinning an improbable tale about her death. See R. Asmus, "Hypatia in Tradition und Dichtung," *Studien zur vergleichenden Literaturgeschichte* 7 (1907):26-27.

[5] E. Gibbon, *The Decline and Fall of the Roman Empire* (London, 1898), pp. 109-110.

[6] M. R. Lefkowitz expresses a similar view in *Women in Greek Myth* (Baltimore, 1986), p. 108.

[7] In the edition of Gotha (1807), p. 76.

[8] Edgard Pich, *Leconte de Lisle et sa création poétique: Poèmes antiques et Poèmes barbares* (1852-1874) (Lille, 1974), pp. 160ff.; *Oeuvres de Leconte de Lisle, Poèmes antiques* (Paris, 1897), p. 97.

[9] Leconte de Lisle shared this view with other writers and literary theorists of the period, including F. R. Chateaubriand, P. Proudhon, E. Renan, Numa-Denis Fustel de Coulanges (Pich, *Leconte de Lisle,* p. 186 and nn. 83 and 86).

[10] Pich, *Leconte de Lisle*, p. 160 n. 8.

[11] Ibid., p. 165: "Le martyre d'Hypatie a été considéré comme l'une des manifestations les plus claire du fanatisme catolique."

[12] *Oeuvres de Leconte de Lisle*, pp. 275-289.

[13] G. de Nerval, *Nouvelles*, I: *Les Filles du feu. Angélique* (1854; reprint, Paris, 1931), p. 32: "La bibliothèque d'Alexandrie et le Serapéon, ou maison de secours, qu'en faisait parti, avaient été brulés et détruits au quatrième siècle par les chrétiens—qui en outre massacrèrent dans les rues la célèbre Hypatie, philosophe pythagoricienne." C.-P. de Lasteyrie in-

cluded a life story of Hypatia in *Sentences de Sextius* (Paris, 1843), pp. 273-304, under the characteristic title *Vie d'Hypatie, femme célèbre, professeur de philosophie, dans le deuxième siècle à l'école d'Alexandrie*, in which he laid heavy charges against Cyril.

[14] M. Barrès, *Sous l'oeil des barbares*, 2d ed. (Paris, 1904), preface, p. 6.

[15] Ibid., p. 13 and passim to p. 58.

[16] I use here the third edition (London, 1906).

[17] H. von Schubert, "Hypatia von Alexandrien in Wahrheit und Dichtung," *Preussische Jahrbücher* 124 (1906):42-60; B. Merker, "Die historischen Quellen zu Kingsleys Roman 'Hypatia'" (Diss. Würzburg, 1909-10); Asmus in *Studien der vergleichenden Literaturgeschichte* 7 (1907), pp. 30-35. Asmus also writes about German authors imitating Kingsley (pp. 35-44). Kingsley's book is also discussed by S. Chitty, *The Beast and the Monk: A Life of Charles Kingsley* (New York, 1975), pp. 151-156.

[18] J. W. Draper, *History of the Intellectual Development of Europe* (New York, 1869), pp. 238-244. On Draper see *Dictionary of Scientific Biography,* IV (New York, 1971), pp. 181-183.

[19] B. Russell, *History of Western Philosophy and Its Connection with Political and Social Circumstances from the Earliest Times to the Present Day* (London, 1946), p. 387.

[20] The contents of the work and data on it are collected by G. Arrigoni, "Tra le donne dell' antichità: Considerazioni e ricognizioni," in *Atti del Convegno nazionale di studi su la donna nel mondo antico, Torino, 21-23 aprile 1986* (Turin, 1987), pp. 68-69.

[21] Today, too, we find Hypatia presented as a defender of the faith and confused with Saint Catherine. See, for example, R. Richardson, *The Star Lovers* (New York, 1967), writing of Hypatia on p. 173 that she "died defending the Christians. She is followed by Catharina, an extremely learned young woman of noble family who died in A.D. 307, defending the Christians." See the discussion later in this chapter.

[22] C. Pascal, "Ipazia," in *Figure e caratteri (Lucrezio, L'Ecclesiaste, Seneca, Ipazia, Giosue Carducci, Giuseppe Garibaldi)* (Milan, 1908), pp. 143-196.

[23] G. Pampaloni, "La poesia religiosa del Mutamento," introduction to M. Luzi, *Libro di Ibazia e Il messagero* (Milan, 1978), p. 14.

[24] I need mention only Lawrence Durrell's reference to Hypatia in *The Alexandria Quartet*. He sings his beloved Alexandria thus: "Walking those streets again in my imagination I knew once more that they spanned, not merely human history, but the whole biological scale of the heart's affections—from the painted ecstasies of Cleopatra (strange that the vine should be discovered here, near Taposiris) to the bigotry of Hypatia (withered vine-leaves, martyr's kisses)"; *Clea* (London and Boston, 1968), p. 660.

[25] A. Zitelmann, *Hypatia* (Weinheim and Basel, 1989).

[26] Discussed in E. Lamirande, "Hypatie, Synesios et la fin des dieux: L'histoire et la fiction," *Studies in Religion (Sciences religieuses)* 18 (1989):467-489.

[27] U. Molinaro, "A Christian Martyr in Reverse: Hypatia, 370-415 A.D.," *Hypatia: A Journal of Feminist Philosophy* 4 (1989):6-8.

[28] See *Art in America*, April 1980, pp. 115-126; *Art International* 25.7-8 (Sept.-Oct. 1982):52-53. In our day a well-known star of pornographic films adopted Hypatia as her first name.

[29] Socrates, *Historia Ecclesiastica* VII.15.

[30] *Suda,* s.v. Hypatia (4.645.4-16 Adler) = Dam. frag. 102 (pp. 79.18 and 81.10 Zintzen).

[31] Gibbon, *Decline and Fall*, pp. 109-110.

[32] Philostorgius, *Historia Ecclesiastica* VIII.9.

[33] The letter is in Mansi, *Conciliorum omnium amplissima collectio*, V (Florence, 1751), col. 1007 (*Synodicon,* chap. 216). On the apocryphal nature of the letter see Hoche, pp. 452-453. The letter seems to have originated at the end of antiquity.

[34] L. Canfora, *The Vanished Library* (New York, 1990), p. 87.

[35] See *Prosopography of the Later Roman Empire*, I, 657-658. On Palladas also see A. Cameron, "Palladas und Christian Polemic," *Journal of Roman Studies* 55 (1965):17-30.

[36] In *Anthologia Palatina*, IX, 400 (Stadtmüller).

[37] G. Luck, "Palladas Christian or Pagan?" *Harvard Studies in Classical Philology* 63 (1958):455-471.

[38] *Suda,* s.v. Panolbios (4.21 Adler); *Prosopography of the Later Roman Empire*, II, 829; A. Cameron, "Wandering Poets: A Literary Movement in Byzantine Egypt," *Historia* 14 (1965):470-509.

[39] *Prosopography of the Later Roman Empire*, II, 401-

402 and 576 (Hypatia 3).

[40] Meyer, p. 52.

[41] C. Baronius, *Annales Ecclesiatici* (12 vols., 1597-1609), VII (Paris, 1816), p. 56 (46-47).

[42] G. Arnolds, *Kirchen und Ketzer-Historie*, I (Frankfurt, 1699), pp. 229-230.

[43] S. Le Nain de Tillemont, *Mémoires pour servir à l'histoire écclesiastique des six premiers siècles* (Paris, 1701-1730), XIV, 274-276.

[44] J. A. Fabricius, *Bibliotheca Graeca*, VIII (Hamburg, 1717), pp. 219-221; IX (Hamburg, 1719), pp. 718-719; also Aegidius Menagius, *Historia mulierum philopharum* (Amsterdam, 1692), p. 28. At the end of the seventeenth century the priest and historian C. Fleury included Hypatia in his *Histoire écclesiastique*, V, 23, 25 (Paris, 1697), 434-435.

[45] D.J.A. Schmid, *De Hipparcho, duobus Theonibus doctaque Hypatia* (Jena, 1689).

[46] J. C. Wernsdorff, "De Hypatia philosopha Alexandrina," in *Dissertationes*, IV: *De Cyrillo episcopo in causa tumultus alexandrini caedisque Hypatiae contra Gothofredum Arnoldum et Joannem Tolandum defenso* (Wittemberg, 1747-48).

[47] A. W. Richeson, "Humanismus and History of Mathematics," ed. G. W. Dunnington, *National Mathematics Magazine* 15 (1940):74-82.

[48] R. Jacobacci, "Women of Mathematics," *Arithmetic Teacher* 17.4 (April 1970):316-324.

[49] M. Alic, *Hypatia's Heritage* (Boston, 1986), p. 41. Also introduced into the history of mathematics as a distinguished mathematician by T. Perl, *Math Equals: Biography of Women Mathematicians and Related Activities* (Menlo Park, Calif., 1978), pp. 13-28; M. E. Waithe, ed., *A History of Women Philosophers* (The Hague, 1987), pp. 169-195, uncritically collects old and new views on the erudition and fortunes of Hypatia.

[50] B. L. Van der Waerden, *Science Awakening* (New York, 1963), p. 290.

[51] M. Bernal, *Black Athena: The Afroasiatic Roots of Classical Civilization* (New Brunswick, N.J., 1987), pp. 121-122.

[52] B. Lumpkin, "Hypatia and Women's Rights in Ancient Egypt," in *Black Women in Antiquity, Journal of African Civilization* 6.1 (1984, rev. ed., 1988), pp. 155-156.

Mary Ellen Waithe (essay date 1996)

SOURCE: "Finding Bits and Pieces of Hypatia" in *Hypatia's Daughters,* Indiana University Press, 1996, pp. 1-26.

[*Here, Waithe focuses on Hypatia's accomplishments as a scholar and educator, emphasizing in particular her application of philosophic analysis and methodology to the exposition of mathematics and astronomy. Waithe also examines the texts of possible early editions or prototypes of Hypatia's writings that appear in the work of later authors.*]

When *Hypatia: A Journal of Feminist Philosophy* was founded in 1983 and the decision was made to name it after a famous ancient woman philosopher, the received wisdom was that *none of Hypatia's writings survived.* As it turned out, the conventional wisdom was false. In the present chapter I will describe what we can surmise about Hypatia's life, her students, her teaching and her writing.[1]

Hypatia was probably born *circa* 370-375, although some scholars claim (on questionable grounds) a much earlier date.[2] Hypatia was already teaching in Alexandria and was sufficiently well known throughout northern Africa by the year 390, when Synesius came from Cyrene to become her student. Accounts of outrageous tactics that Hypatia used to counter a male student's sexual harassment by throwing the fifth-century equivalent of a used sanitary napkin at him may be apocryphal (Toland 1720; Lewis 1921). Nevertheless they provide insight into the personality of a woman philosopher who was determined to be an outstanding teacher and scholar in a brutally misogynist environment. A traditional middle platonist, Hypatia was sympathetic to Plotinian and Porphyryian metaphysics and to stoicism. In 415, she was savagely murdered, allegedly by a gang of monks. According to the Suda[3] *Lexicon*, her corpse was then hacked into pieces and burned.

The converse of what happened to her corpse happened to the *corpus* of her works. Scholars have been finding and analyzing bits and pieces of scattered mathematical and astronomical writings deriving from the time and place she lived. Like forensic experts who have found scattered body parts, they have independently and in some cases, tentatively, identified these remains as hers.

To date, the best analysis of Hypatia the teacher has come from a study of one of Hypatia's students, Synesius of Cyrene. After studying with Hypatia, Synesius converted to Christianity and soon became Bishop of Ptolemais. His letters to Hypatia have survived, and were translated and analyzed during the nineteenth and twentieth centuries (Lapatz 1870;

Fitzgerald 1926). Letters from Hypatia to Synesius probably have not survived. Synesius' letters are full of clues: names of persons who may have been her students and to whom some copy of Hypatia's works might have been loaned, names of cities to which her works might have been sent.

Hypatia of Alexandria by the Polish scholar Maria Dzielska (1995) pieces together a magnificent analysis of Hypatia's teachings and personality based almost exclusively on Synesius' letters. Apparently unknown to Dzielska her analysis of Hypatia's personality and teachings corresponds nicely with that given by the historian of science and mathematics, Wilbur Knorr (1989). And while Dzielska may be accused of somewhat overstating the case by attributing almost every view of Synesius' to Hypatia, Knorr is scrupulous to a fault (if such a thing is possible) when it comes to reserving judgment about identifying particular works as originating with Hypatia.

The connection between philosophic analysis with religious practice may seem a strange one to contemporary secular philosophers. *Our* philosophical views about metaphysics and epistemology have little to do with how we act. But it is impossible to understand and appreciate Hypatia's without understanding two basic things. One is that the philosophical *is* the personal. Holding certain philosophical views about metaphysics implies seeing the world in a particular way. Two, mathematics and astronomy are sciences that apply particular metaphysical views and are the key to achieving personal ethical and religious knowledge. For Hypatia and for her students, the Plotinian interpretation of Plato's metaphysics implied a way of life. Philosophy was not just a job, the teaching of its content was not mere academic exercise, having nothing to do with daily life. Philosophy *was* life. Dzielska brings that point home in a clear and convincing way. For Hypatia, mathematics and astronomy were ways of applying or verifying metaphysical and epistemological features of neo-Platonic Plotinian philosophy. Most mathematicians and astronomers of fourth-century Alexandria, including Hypatia's father, Theon, were not philosophers. Their interests were more technical than philosophical. But Hypatia sought for greater meaning, so the truths of mathematics and astronomy needed to fit into a greater cosmological and ethical framework. This was consistent with the ancient traditions in philosophy from Pythagorean times when philosophy implied a way of life. It is the Pythagoreans with whom *harmonia* was first identified as a mathematical, musical *and* ethical principle. Dzielska reminds us that Synesius called mathematics:

> "divine geometry," and its "holy" principles, we remember were applied to the achievement of reciprocal friendly relationships. (*Ep.* 93).

> Of all mathematical sciences auxiliary to metaphysical knowledge, Hypatia regarded astronomy as the highest. . . . Synesius preserves her view that "astronomy is itself a divine form of knowledge." (Dzielska 1995, 54)

Dzielska identifies as disciples of Hypatia not only Synesius, but also Herculianus, Olympius, and Euoptius who was Synesius' younger brother. There are others: Ision, Hesychius, an Alexander who was Synesius' uncle, Athanasius, Theodosius, and Gaius. In addition, Dzielska names some as possible students: Herculianus' brother Cyrus, Syrus, Petrus, Paeonius, and Auxentius. These are names mentioned by Synesius as "companions," those regarding whom exists a connection to "Alexandria," "our Mother, Hypatia," "sacred/holy philosophy/mysteries," or to "time spent profitably in our youth," "in study," "in contemplation," etc. Dzielska may cast Hypatia's net too far on the basis of Synesius' "evidence." Synesius seems to have been a blowhard, a braggart, and a self-aggrandizing name-dropper. But Dzielska's conjecture is plausible and warrants further scrutiny. In addition to the regular students, Dzielska says that notable public figures may have been occasional attendees at quasi-public lectures given by Hypatia. On this list Dzielska includes Orestes, the augustal prefect of Alexandria, and possibly Pendadius and Heliodorus, the archontes, Ammonius the curialis, Isidore of Pelusium (later, St. Isidore), Simplicius the military commander, and other unnamed officials. On Dzielska's view, (and, assuming that she's got Hypatia's roster correct, I'm tempted to agree, here) Hypatia taught only wealthy young male aristocrats from politically powerful families. On that account Hypatia is described by Dzielska as an elitist who did nothing to advance the education of women. But while Synesius appeared to study geometry and metaphysics with Hypatia, it is clear that other students studied much more. You have only to look at the works attributed to Hypatia to get a sense of her scholarship and her teaching activities.

Hypatia of Alexandria was a deeply committed educator and scholar. At Alexandria during Hypatia's time, the practical applications of mathematics and astronomy were often to be found in the works of the geographers, the architects, the observational astronomers, and the astrologers. The technical and theoretical aspects of mathematics and astronomy were still taught in the schools, often as applied philosophy; i.e., as applied metaphysics. Hypatia was a philosopher of this stripe. A work by the historian of mathematics, Montluca (1960) mentioned that Hypatia's father, Theon had "ascribed" one of the books (Book III) of his *Commentary on Ptolemy's Syntaxis Mathematica* to the authorship of Hypatia. The Belgian astronomer, Rome, located the only two copies of that *Commentary* that contained Book III in the

Vatican collection early this century. During and following the time Rome was establishing the text he published a number of articles describing various parts of the commentary, but always describing it either as by Theon or as by Theon and Hypatia. Rome's final, established text (Rome 1943) summarized the idiosyncrasies of style (didactic, very terse, formal language) and content (greater mathematical precision) found within Book III (and some later books, too). Paul Tannery, a French engineer by training, but a historian of science and mathematics by profession, identified a set of problems in the surviving editions of Diophantus' *Arithmetica*[4] as deriving from Hypatia (Tannery 1893-1895). Those problems were also noted by the mathematician Thomas Heath (1960) and translated from Tannery in my *History of Women Philosophers* (Waithe 1987).

The writings Hypatia prepared were for the teaching of students and ancient copies succumbed to the vagaries of time and happenstance (including the burning of the Library at Alexandria). Hypatia's work has a character not unlike that which philosophy has today vis-à-vis medicine. Today, philosophy of medicine and bioethics use philosophy as a tool with which to impose rigor on the science of medicine and with which to analyze ethical issues arising in medical practice. In order to do this well, bioethicists must learn in some depth (but limited breadth) the relevant content areas within the medical sciences. I think that Hypatia used philosophy in exactly the same way when teaching mathematics and astronomy.

In addition to philosophy, Hypatia taught algebra, geometry, and astronomy, preparing for her students critical editions of the texts of her predecessors (Diophantus, Apollonius Pergaeus, Ptolemy, Euclid, Archimedes, Pappus, Zenodorus, etc.). But she is always a philosopher, and so she corrects these texts. Unlike texts by her father and by some of her predecessors, she doesn't play the role of the brilliant scholar who is too knowledgeable to have to complete her proofs. Unlike her father Theon, she is not satisfied with approximations and rounding-off. Sometimes she improves the rigor of theorems by finding and then filling in gaps to achieve greater completeness. Sometimes she plays with the theories, extending computations to many additional place values, thereby achieving greater accuracy which improves the predictability of astronomical calculations. Sometimes she pushes the classical proofs to improve their soundness by devising direct proofs where only indirect proofs existed before. Sometimes she connects geometrical theorems to their astronomical applications and to Platonic metaphysics and cosmology. One of the hallmarks of Hypatia's *corpus* (to the extent that we can guarantee that the works are hers) is the symmetry with which she lays out the elements of her proofs, following each with related alternative cases.

When possible, she comes up with two seemingly competing hypotheses and works the proof twice, as if to show that no matter how you reasonably might conceptualize the problem, you can get the correct result. The impression here is of a teacher taking into account different students' different learning styles, and their different intuitions. She is not the officious professor full of a sense of her own importance. She doesn't force her students into her mode of thinking about things. She nurtures them, she cultivates diversity. She sees the larger picture, beyond the narrow proof. Hypatia makes no attempt at rhetorical innovation so characteristic of philosophical writing that would appear during the 11th and 12th centuries; her language is terse, precise, repetitive, methodical. It's the beauty of the logic of the proofs, not the aesthetics of the prose that Hypatia cares about. Knorr (1989, esp. ch. 11 and 12) has given an argument that is more compelling than he himself seems willing to believe concerning a group of works ascribable to Hypatia.[5] When we piece together the old evidence I assembled from Halley, Heath, Rome, and Tannery with new evidence from Knorr, the following may tentatively be attributed to Hypatia:

(1) A*, an edition of Diophantus' *Arithmetica* including new lemmas and other original problems. (Tannery 1893-1895; Heath 1960)

(2) CS*, the lost prototype based on Archimedes' *Sphere and Cylinder* surviving only as CS: John of Tynemouth's *De curvis superficibus*. (Knorr 1989)

(3) AI*, the anonymous (lost) prototype that relied heavily on Zenodorus' text on isoperimetric figures, but is now incorporated into *Introduction to the Almagest* by an anonymous author. (Knorr 1989)

(4) DC*, the lost prototype commentary edition of Archimedes' *Dimension of the Circle*. (Knorr 1989)

(5) C*, a commentary edition of Apollonius Pergaeus' *Conics* that formed the basis for later commentary editions. (Waithe 1987)[6]

(6) SM, an edition (partly concordance, partly revision) of work begun by Theon in Book III (and perhaps other books) of Theon's *Commentary of Ptolemy's Syntaxis Mathematica.* (Rome 1943)

In each case, except SM, it is important to remember that we do not have Hypatia's original writings extant; nor do we have a faithful copy seasoned only with obvious corrections and *marginalia*. We are identifying within the context of a surviving later work, an earlier edition or a prototype (indicated by *). This earlier edition or prototype differs from the larger work within which it is found in some one or more ways. It may use a different style of writing, betray a higher level of sophistication, etc. That is how it is possible to mark out Hypatia's material subsequently incorporated (without citation!) by later writers.

On my reading of Knorr's findings, we can supplement the Suda's description of three works by Hypatia[7] with three additional works. I elsewhere suggest (Waithe n.d.) evaluating the entire *corpus* for the respective levels of complexity of technical knowledge required to prepare each work. When we do so, the above ordering I think, suggests the possible order of their composition by Hypatia.

It is my hypothesis that work requiring the least technical knowledge such as algebra and plane geometry may be assumed to have been composed earlier than works requiring the additional mastery of astronomy. On this theory, A* on Diophantus' algebra, would be an early work.[8]

CS*, AI* and DC*, however are works on Archimedean geometry. According to Knorr (1990), the Latin CS appears to translate and incorporate an earlier Greek document, CS*, by Hypatia. Hypatia's CS* differs from what is known about the original *Sphere and Cylinder* by Archimedes in several ways:

> (a) it gives a condensed account of Archimedes' chief results on the surface area and volume of the sphere;

> (b) it is lacking entirely Archimedes' results on spherical sectors and segments;

> (c) it contains other results not attributable to Archimedes' own writings;

> (d) it adopts forms of proof not recognizably Archimedean, including citations to Euclidean theorems (from *Elements*) in each proposition.

These differences between the Hypatian prototype and Archimedes' *Sphere and Cylinder* reflect Hypatia's purely pedagogical interests in condensing Archimedes' material from the form in which it then existed, and focussing it on special topics. It also reflects her scholarly interests in incorporating her own cases, reporting her own results, demonstrating her improved methodology, and providing broader theoretical foundations for the proofs from Euclid, from the commentary literature on Hero's *Metrica* and *Stereometrica*, from her father's *Commentary on Ptolemy's Syntaxis Mathematica Book I*.

An identifying feature of Hypatia's work in CS* and also in AI* perhaps is that she prefers Euclidean methodology over the Archimedean in formulating the results of certain problems. Where the identical problems are treated in other tracts by Pappus, by *his* student Theon, and by others, only Hypatia interjects the philosophically preferable direct proof in favor of what for Pappus and Theon was the traditional standard: Archimedean indirect proof.

AI* is a brief but condensed passage applying the insights of Zenodorus in his *On Isoperimetric Figures* to Archimedean spherical geometry. It is very much like similar tracts by Pappus and Theon, but the differences betray a philosopher's touch (Knorr 1989, 689-751 and 774-80). Some language alludes to Plato's argument in *Timeaus* regarding the shape of the universe. Hypatia's tract explores mathematical explanations for the perfect creation of the universe as a circle moving within a circle. Her reasoning here is that such a construction would be more spacious than any other isoperimetric configuration of the universe and therefore would be able to contain more intelligible beings than would a universe of any other shape. This tract is really no more than a paraphrase of CS* (see above). Although it is a separate document in summary form, it would be stretching the point to denote this as a genuinely separate work.

The lost prototype DC* is a Commentary on Archimedes' *Dimension of the Circle*. Hypatia is believed to be responsible for preparing an adaptation of Theon's Commentary edition of Archimedes' *Dimension of the Circle*. It is a loosely adapted account of Archimedes' original work, but not based directly on the original. Hypatia introduces and partly deconstructs the substance and results of *Dimension of the Circle*, and adds relevant secondary source materials on plane geometry, including clarifications and amplifications from Pappus and Theon, and Hypatia's own improvements to these. The original Archimedean work is not itself highly technical, but requires understanding of Euclid's *Elements XII*, and Hypatia's apparent penchant for doing long computations, something we see later, in SM.

If we trace the paths that this single work DC*, has taken since Hypatia's death, we get a glimpse of the kind of influence her works had, and the seriousness with which later scholars took her contributions, albeit, in time, without her name attached to the documents. A copy of this particular work DC*, went to Baghdad, and during the 9th century was translated into Arabic at the Baghdad court of caliph al-Ma'mun by Qusta ibn Luqa. Adaptations were produced by the Banu Musa (sons of Musa: Muhammad, Ahmad and Hassan—9th century) who included the substance of DC* in their *On the measurement of plane and curved figures* (which also contained their adaptation of CS* *supra*.) Other versions derived from that of Qusta ibn Luqa were produced by Abu 'l-Rashid 'Abd al-Hadi (*circa* 12th century), and by Nasir al-Tusi (13th century). It surfaced in two 12th-century Latin versions (by Plato of Tivoli and by Gerard of Cremona), and also in a Hebrew version likely by Kalonymos ben Kalonymos,[9] (sometimes Qalonymous, etc.) a 14th century Jewish philosopher who was born in Provence but lived mostly in Rome.

Let me return to the issue of the development of Hypatia's work. CS*, AI*, and DC* bear textual affinities to each other, according to Knorr (1989, 805ff). It is my conjecture that due to their similarities, they may have been written closely together in what we might call Hypatia's middle period. C*, on Apollonian geometry, is more sophisticated than CS*, AI* and DC* in part because it adopts Pappus' results and improves upon them (Knorr 1982, 1-24). C* and SM may, therefore, represent Hypatia's late period.

A decade ago it was noted that:

> The Suda *Lexicon*, Fabricus in *Bibliotheca Graecorum* and Socrates Scholasticus in *Historiae Ecclesiasticae* all mention that Hypatia authored a commentary on Apollonius of Perga's *Conic Sections*. This Commentary appears to be the only one of the three Hypatian writings reported lost which has actually failed to survive. Edmund Halley, the 17th century British astronomer, collected the ancient Latin and Arabic versions of *Conic Sections* in an attempt to reconstruct the original and to separate scholia and commentary from the original text. This was apparently an insurmountable task, at least with respect to identifying the Hypatian commentary, for although Halley's text lists Hypatia's commentary among its contents, there exists only a title page without additional text. I have not been successful in locating the materials that Halley was working from, but there appears to be little reason to hope that Hypatia's commentary on Apollonius' *Conic Sections* has in fact survived. (Waithe 1987, 191)

Subsequently Professor Knorr[10] mentioned a tantalizing alternative reading of Halley, namely, that Halley intended readers to understand that the collected commentary editions in his volume were based on Hypatia's commentary. The ***Commentary on Apollonius Pergaeus' Conics*** (C*), to my knowledge does not exist as a separate document, but if I understand Knorr's comment correctly, it may be imbedded in the surviving Halley edition. C*, if indeed it can be teased out from the successor commentary editions, would be the least securely attributed work by Hypatia. C*, whatever it is, presumably formed the basis for other accounts of Apollonius' work, including the Commentary by Eutocius of Askalon on Books I-IV for which he acknowledges his indebtedness to "the copies." Knorr (1982 and 1989) suggests that Eutocius' reference is to commentaries including that (which, for Eutocius would have been the most recent) by Hypatia. In the (unlikely?) event that all dif-

ferences between the Eutocius and Apollonian texts were to be attributed solely to Hypatia (and not to any other intermediary commentators and scholiasts), we could hazard the following wild guess regarding her possible contribution. By demonstrating connections between remarks by Pappus and her own adaptation of Euclid's theorems on the circle, Hypatia sketches a proof of two original theorems that had been hypothesized, but not demonstrated by Pappus. C* shows that Hypatia was no mere authority on Pappus. She contributes a small but significant improvement to mathematical theory on the projection of the cone: an essential geometric feature of every earth-bound astronomical observation. This is the work of no merely competent professor. Hypatia is an innovative scholar contributing to the theory of her disciplines. I suggest therefore, that C* is likely to be a later work than the Archimedean tracts, CS*, AI* and DC*.

Theon attributes to Hypatia the preparation of at least Book III, "On the Motions of the Sun," in his *Commentary on Syntaxis Mathematica* (SM). Rome (1943) and Knorr (1989) suggest that Hypatia possibly had a hand in Books IV and IX as well. Theon's identification at the beginning of Book III of Hypatia as "the Philosopher" indicates that she had already risen to the top of her career and was a well-established senior scholar with an independent reputation as a philosopher. That Hypatia is acknowledged by her father to have revised what was then and would remain (until Copernicus) the most influential work on mathematical astronomy, is clear evidence of her reputation as a mathematician and theoretical (perhaps not an observational) astronomer. The preparation of C* would have made that reputation indisputable. This view accords with my hypothesis that Hypatia's algebraic and geometrical writings preceded SM. SM is a lengthy work of significant complexity and the only astronomical work of Hypatia's *corpus*. In part because it is on Ptolemaic astronomy as derived through Pappus, I am inclined to view it as a more mature work which relied, nevertheless, on the prior development of C*. The expertise required to produce SM would need to build upon precisely the kinds of expertise demonstrated in all of the prior works. Theon was probably very old by the time of the preparation of the written *Commentary on Syntaxis Mathematica,* and ready to prepare a final edition of the lectures he (and Hypatia?) had given to students. In this work, Hypatia modelled a particular didactic innovation on that of Pappus. To enable students to make quicker and more accurate calculations, Hypatia introduced a system of long division in the sexagesimal system utilizing a table of divisors and dividends. The tables facilitate quicker and more accurate calculations, carrying the results to more integer places than generally recommended by Theon and Pappus. Why is this significant? It is significant because one of the difficulties with the works of the ancient astronomers was that predictability of astronomical events became less precise the further in time they were projected from that of the original observation. One method Hypatia employed to correct for this was to refine and redefine original calculations and to provide resources with which to carry out the results to greater accuracy. In addition, numerous examples are proved twice, employing competing hypotheses. Hypatia noticed some errors in Ptolemy's geocentric model that caused her to be concerned whether it always accurately predicted the position of the sun. I am not sure whether anything should be made of her cryptic comment, but it would be interesting to see whether later astronomers noticed it, and whether it influenced reconsideration of the heliocentric model.

Scholars have often wondered at the identification of Hypatia as a philosopher, and at the curiosity that the titles of her works mentioned by her late contemporary Suidas were scientific and mathematical. Where were her philosophical writings? Clearly, her writings themselves provide significant evidence that what in the modern era are identified as mathematical and astronomical theories needed the touch of a philosopher's conceptual analysis and methodology. And just as bioethics is now considered part of philosophy, so in early 5th-century Alexandria, were the problems of mathematics and astronomy considered to fit squarely within the sphere of philosophy.

When we consider the characteristics of her writings and the description of her philosophical views decipherable through the writings of Synesius of Cyrene, the Hypatian fingerprint begins to emerge. It is the mark of a philosopher who introduces beginning students to Platonic metaphysics, addressing moral and cosmological concerns fleshed out in Plotinian mysteries, tinged with the deep personal religious awe and quasi-mystical contemplation of the One. But the truths of mathematics, especially "divine geometry" prepare one for consideration of higher philosophy. Developing technical expertise in astronomy is part and parcel of testing cosmological theories. For Hypatia, doing so involves filling in significant gaps in the logic of geometrical and astronomical theory. As a scholar, she becomes adept at doing so. But she is also an educator who delights in honing students' abilities to become philosophers. She is a dedicated teacher who prepares for her student a careful, symmetrical exposition of elements of mathematical and astronomical proofs with the introduction of a series of related alternative cases, all expressed in extremely precise application of technical terminology. But all along, her efforts are philosophically motivated: she

is on and takes her students along on a quest for completeness, instilling in them a desire to consider all possibilities. She was a model for us all.

Notes

[1] See also Waithe (1987).

[2] Notably Dzielska (1995). See below.

[3] The conventional wisdom on this changes with the wind. Traditionally, the author has been referred to as "Suidas." Then it was considered an erroneous appellation and the Suda were revealed to be a committee or group of authors who composed the *Lexicon*. More recently, I am again seeing references to "Suidas." I use the names interchangeably.

[4] Not *Arithmeticorum* as I originally cited it.

[5] I Make this paradoxical comment because the original articles by Knorr on the separate documents considered in his book are generally silent about his conjecture that Hypatia is the common source of the prototypes CS*, AI*, and DC*, e.g., "Archimedes and the Measurement of the Circle: A New Interpretation," (1976), "Ancient Versions of Two Trigonometric Lemmas," (1985), "Archimedes' *Dimension of the Circle*: A View of the Genesis of the Extant Text," (1986). And although these works have understandably been somewhat revised by the later interpretations made in Knorr's book, the absence of mention of his hypothesis that Hypatia is the author of the prototype CS* from which is derived Johannes de Tinnemue's Latin translation in Knorr's 1990 paper "John of Tynemouth *alias* John of London: emerging portrait of a singular medieval mathematician," *BHJS*, (1990), 23: 293-330 leaves me worried that Knorr has abandoned his hypothesis (for which I admit a bias).

[6] I made reference to this in my original chapter (Waithe, 1987) on Hypatia. Knorr wrote to me suggesting that what I may not have understood was that the entire edition Halley prepared may be based on the Hypatian edition of Apollonius. Halley, 1710.

[7] Knorr (1989) assumes (p. 755-6) that Suidas' mention of an "Astronomical Table" as one of the three works by Hypatia refers to something other than the tables that are part of the *Syntaxis*. I am inclined to agree with Tannery's conjecture here " . . . that Hypatia commented on the *Astronomical Tables* that are part of the *Almagest*, just as her father Theon commented on the manual tables [*Canones Procheiroi*] of Ptolemy that formed a separate {part of that} work. (Tannery, "L'Article de Suidas Sur Hypatia," *Annales de la Facuite des Letters de Bordeaux*, (1880), p. 199, translation and material in {brackets} mine.

[8] Hypatia's introduction of new problems and of alternative solutions to original problems helps illustrate the abstractness and generalizability of algebraic theory. Diophantus' original problems often appeared to be mere puzzles rather than illustrations of general theorems, corollaries, etc. Hypatia demonstrated the generality and indeterminateness of a problem by substituting for assumed unknowns numeric values which themselves are unrelated (e.g., not surds, multiples, powers, fractions, or square roots) to the original value. Therefore, although algebraic, the purpose of A* fits squarely within the tradition of philosophy of mathematics.

[9] Kalonymos ben Kalonymos also translated treatises on Euclid, Apollonius, Ptolemy and Averroes.

[10] Professor Knorr to Professor Waithe, personal communication, November, 1987.

References

Dzielska, Maria. 1995. *Hypatia of Alexandria.* Cambridge: Harvard University Press.

Fitzgerald, A. 1926. *The letters of Synesius.* London: Oxford University Press.

Halley, Edmund. 1710. *Apollonius Pergaeus conic sections.* Oxford.

Heath, Thomas. 1960. *Diophantus of Alexandria.* New York: Dolphin.

Knorr, Wilbur. 1982. Observations on the early history of the conics. *Centaurus* 26:1-24.

————. 1989. *Textual studies in Ancient and Medieval geometry.* Boston: Birkhauser.

————. 1990. John of Tynemmouth *alias* John of London: Emerging portrait of a singular Medieval mathematician. *BHJS.*

Lapatz, F. 1870. *Lettres des Synesius. Traduit pur la premier fois et suivies d'etudes sur les derniers moments de l'Hellenisme.* Paris.

Lewis, Thomas. 1921. *The history of Hypatia, a most impudent schoolmistress of Alexandria.* London: Bickerton.

Montluca, J. 1960. *Histoire des mathematiques.* Paris: Librarie Scientifique et Technique.

Rome, A. 1943. *Commentaires de Pappus et de Theon d'Alexandrie sur l'Almageste, Tome III., Theon d'Alexandrie Commentaire sur les Livres 3 et 4 d l'Almageste, Studi e Testi.* Citta del Vaticano; Biblioteca Apostolica Vaticana.

Tannery, Paul. 1880. L'article de Suidas sur Hypatia. *Annales de la Faculte des Lettres de Bordeaux.*

————. [1893-95]. 1974. *Diophanti Alexandrini opera omnia.* Two volumes. Stugardiae: Teubner.

Toland, John. [1720]. 1921. Hypatia; or, The history of a most beautiful, most virtuous, most learned, and every way accomplish'd lady; who was torn to pieces by the clergy of Alexandria, to gratify the pride, emulation, and cruelty of their Archbishop Cyril. In *Tetradymus.* London: J. Brotherton.

Waithe, Mary Ellen. 1987. *A history of women philosophers, Volume 1: Ancient women philosophers.* Dordrecht: Kluwer Academic Publishers.

FURTHER READING

Cameron, Alan. "Isidore of Miletus and Hypatia: On the Editing of Mathematical Texts." *Greek, Roman, and Byzantine Studies* 31, No. 1 (Spring 1990): 103-27.

Examines in detail conflicting theories about the extent of Hypatia's contribution to Theon's edition of Ptolemy's *Almagest*. Cameron hypothesizes that she was responsible for editing the text of Books III through XIII but that her father wrote all the commentary.

Dzielska, Maria. "Hypatia and Her Circle." In her *Hypatia of Alexandria.* Revealing Antiquity 8, G. W. Bowersock, general editor, pp. 27-65. Cambridge, Mass.: Harvard University Press, 1995.

Focuses on Hypatia's coterie of students and her mode of instruction, citing many letters of Synecius of Cyrene, together with pertinent details from Socrates Scholasticus's *Ecclesiastical History* and Damasc-ius's *Life of Isidore.* Dzielska emphasizes the secret-iveness of Hypatia's community of philosophical protégés as well as the intellectual and moral elitism of her students.

Kingsley, Charles. *Hypatia, or, New Foes with an Old Face.* London: Oxford University Press, 1915, 459 p.

A historical novel noted for its lively and authentic descriptions of fifth-century Alexandria, its lurid account of Hypatia's death, and its rancorous portrayal of the early church. First published in serial form in 1851, the novel was issued in book form in 1853.

Waithe, Mary Ellen. "Hypatia of Alexandria." In *A History of Women Philosophers*, edited by Mary Ellen Waithe, Vol. 1, pp. 169-95. Dordrecht, The Netherlands: Martinus Nijhoff.

A general discussion of what is known—or conjectured—about Hypatia's life, her role as a teacher, and her major commentaries. Waithe also describes the principal recensions of Hypatia's works.

Martial

c. 38-41 - c. 104

(Full name Marcus Valerius Martialis.) Roman poet.

INTRODUCTION

Martial is universally acclaimed as the greatest writer of epigrams in literary history. Though earlier Greek and Latin poets had used this verse form, Martial perfected it, giving it the wit and pointedness that remain its chief characteristics to this day. He depicted the world around him with such realistic detail that his poems are frequently praised as much for their historical value as their literary merit. Martial's forte was the satiric epigram, and the objects of his satire run the gamut of human faults and vices. His best poems are marked by concrete imagery, memorable phrases, masterful use of rhetorical devices, and originality of expression. Over the centuries, Martial's reputation has ebbed and flowed according to the tastes of particular ages. For some commentators, his prodigious aesthetic skills are insufficient compensation for two recurring features of his epigrams: excessive flattery of his patrons and undisguised obscenity.

Biographical Information

Virtually everything that is known about Martial's life has been deduced from information that he gives about himself in his epigrams. He was born around 38-41 in Bilbilis, a small city in the region of northeastern Spain now known as Aragón, and he celebrated his birthday on the first of March, but scholars are unsure whether that was his actual birth date. Though he was a Roman citizen, his ancestry was a mix of Celtic and Iberian strains, and he frequently expressed great pride in this heritage. Martial's parents, whom he refers to in one poem (5.34) as Fronto and Flaccilla, furnished him with a good education, principally in literary subjects. In 64 he left Spain to seek fame and fortune in Rome. He hoped that his celebrated Spanish compatriots, Lucian and the younger Seneca, would help advance his career, but within a year of his arrival they were implicated in a conspiracy against the emperor Nero and were executed. Henceforth Martial became a client of a variety of patrons, eking out a meager living from allowances and gifts. In exchange for financial support, clients such as Martial were obliged personally to attend their patrons almost on a daily basis. This left little time for writing poetry, as Martial frequently complained, but during this period he regularly prepared verses for his patrons' recitations and dinner parties, and undertook commissions to write commemorative lines for special occasions. As a young man he

lived in a third-floor apartment on the Quirinal, but in later years he was able to exchange this for a small townhouse in the same area. He also acquired—perhaps as a gift—a small farm near Nomentum, about thirteen miles from Rome, to which he regularly repaired to escape the clamor of the city and the demands of his patrons. In his middle years, he was awarded several important honors, including the *ius trium liberorum* ("right of three children"), which, though ostensibly reserved to fathers of three, was often conferred on childless or unmarried men and made them eligible for significant financial benefits. Martial was also named an honorary military tribune, giving him the status of equestrian, or knight. The publication in 86 of the first two books of his epigrams established him as an important literary figure, and over the next ten years his fame increased steadily. During this decade, however, he also became closely identified with the emperor Domitian, and after 96—when Domitian was assassinated—the poet was unable to secure the favor of Nerva, the next emperor, or Trajan, Nerva's designated heir. Around 99 or 100, Martial left Rome and returned to Bilbilis, where a generous patroness named Marcella had given him a villa and a small estate outside the town. Throughout his years in Rome, he had often expressed nostalgia for the Spanish countryside, but he was soon bored by solitude and small-town life. He particularly missed the liveliness of the imperial city, the critical judgment of his audience there, and the companionship of his lifelong friends. Martial died in Spain, sometime around 104. His death was lamented that year by Pliny the Younger, a friend and patron, who attested to Martial's ready wit and good nature but expressed reservations about whether the poet's fame would live on after him.

Major Works

Selections of Martial's early work were probably in circulation before 80, but that year saw the publication of his first collection, the *Book of Spectacles*. Scholars believe that the thirty-three surviving pieces represent about half of the original anthology, which was written to commemorate the emperor Titus's opening of the Flavian Amphitheater, now known as the Colosseum. These verses shed light on the lavish shows and bloody contests, lasting for one hundred days, that inaugurated the arena. About five years later, Martial published two collections of mottoes that could be used to accompany gifts: *Xenia* and *Apophoreta;* in modern editions, these are generally represented as Books 13 and 14 of Martial's epigrams. *Xenia* comprises 127 pieces—all except three in the form of couplets—appropriate for gifts of food and wine. The *Apophoreta* includes 223 verses, also in distichs; these would serve for a wide array of both cheap and expensive "gifts to take home" after Saturnalia celebrations—including housewares, toiletries, objects d'art, and pets.

Martial's literary reputation generally rests on his mature work, the epigrams in Books 1-12. These were published almost yearly beginning in 86; he completed the final volume while he was in retirement in Spain. The vast majority of these verses are written in elegiac meter, but 238 are in hendecasyllabic meter and 77 in choliambic, also known as scazon. The epigrams are of varying length, from one line to as many as fifty-one, though approximately half are couplets and more than thirty contain between twenty and thirty lines. An important characteristic of his epigrams is what is known as "the sting in the tail": a word or phrase at the close that takes the reader by surprise—although in the best examples of Martial's verses, the poet subtly prepares the way for the final ingenious turn of thought. As might be expected with such a large collection, the quality of the epigrams is uneven. Nevertheless, Martial's writing is consistently polished, showing the effect of a literary craftsman who took his efforts seriously, even though he often alluded to his verses as jokes or nuggets and, with mock-modesty, made light of their merit. The chief features of his epigrammatic style are compression, candor, wit, and irony. His explicit treatment of sexual topics has earned him the censure of many commentators over the ages; however, some late twentieth-century critics have suggested that only a comparatively small proportion of Martial's epigrams are truly obscene. In the preface to Book 1, anticipating the charge of lewdness, he notes that he writes in the tradition of Latin epigrammatists who preceded him—including Catullus, Marsus, Pedo, and Gaetulicus—who also wrote candidly about sexual matters. Elsewhere, like other writers of obscenity before and since, he avers that, though his verses may be salacious, his personal life is above reproach.

Martial wrote in a variety of tones and for a variety of purposes. The majority of the epigrams in Books 1 through 12 are satiric, and the objects of his derision are manifold. Martial's principal targets are hypocrisy and pretentiousness, though he also makes sport of the patronage system, physical afflictions, sexual deviation, drunkenness, and bad manners. Furthermore, he parodies foreigners, freedmen, and vain or assertive women, though—as with all his satires—he either portrays them as character types or assigns them fictitious names. Many of Martial's non-satiric poems are addressed to or mention various patrons or benefactors—complimenting them, pleading for their support, or thanking them for favors granted. His extravagant praise of the emperor Domitian in scores of epigrams strikes most modern readers as arrant flattery, and critics have noted that Martial's panegyrics to his imperial patron—concentrated in Books 4 through 9—are among the least successful of his verses, because of their artificial expression as well as their fawning tone.

Martial also wrote many poems about the nature of poetry and its practice; formal addresses of congratulation or farewell; affectionate tributes to his friends; testimonials to virtuous men and women; homages to the dead; and reflections on what is meaningful in life. He repeatedly mocked the pretentiousness of mythological epics, dramas, and elegies, and vigorously defended his short, realistic verses. His obituary epigrams include three on the death of Erotion, a slave child who died just days before her sixth birthday; of these, 5.34 is particularly celebrated for its beauty and poignancy. He addressed more than a dozen poems to his closest friend, Julius Martialis, including two of the most frequently translated ones: 5.20, which expresses profound regret that they are both living their lives for others—men of power and influence—rather than for themselves; and 10.47, the most famous of Martial's epigrams, which describes, with simplicity and sincerity, the elements of a happy life.

Critical Reception

Martial has had a significant impact on European literature, and he has been widely read: between 1471 and 1993 there were at least twenty complete editions of his work—and numerous collections of his selected verse—in many languages. The earliest writer on whom he had a major influence was Juvenal (c. 55-60 - c. 130), whose indebtedness to Martial with respect to both subject and style is extensive. Moreover, Spanish historians and critics regard Martial as one of the founders, together with Seneca and Lucian, of their literary tradition. The first of Martial's many English imitators was the neo-Latin poet Godfrey of Winchester (c. 1050 - 1107). Beginning in the thirteenth century, Italian humanists rediscovered the beauty of form in Martial's verses, and subsequently neo-Latin writers throughout Europe found in his epigrams a model for their own poetry. In the fourteenth, fifteenth, and sixteenth centuries, Martial was read, translated, and imitated by such authors as Petrarch and Poggio in Italy, the Pleiades in France, and Desiderius Erasmus and Sir Thomas More in England. From the beginnings of the English Renaissance and throughout the Elizabethan, Jacobean, and Restoration periods, Martial's influence was at its peak in that country. His translators and emulators included Henry Howard, Earl of Surrey, Sir John Harington, Ben Jonson, Robert Herrick, and Abraham Cowley. Among his less famous imitators was the seventeenth-century satirist Thomas Brown, who, as an Oxford undergraduate, reworked Martial 1.32—a distich about a physician named Sabidius—into the well-known rhyme "I do not like you, Dr. Fell. . . . "[4] Though Martial profoundly affected the practice and style of Augustan poetry, his reputation began to decline in the eighteenth century. It plummeted during the Victorian period, when he received little praise for form or style and much opprobrium for flattery of patrons and obscene jokes. In the twentieth century, Martial's literary stature has improved. Poets and scholars in England, Italy, Spain, and central Europe are once more translating his work, and philologists in Germany have carried out important textual studies. However, controversy continues as to whether Martial is one of the preeminent classical writers and whether a brief epigram can ever be considered a great poem.

PRINCIPAL WORKS

Liber de Spectaculis (also *Liber Spectaculorum*) [Book of Spectacles] (epigrams) 80

Apophoreta (Book 14 in modern editions) [Gifts for Saturnalia] (mottoes) 84-5

Xenia (Book 13 in modern editions) [Guest-gifts] (mottoes) 84-5

Epigrammaton libri (Books 1-12) (epigrams) 86 to 101

PRINCIPAL ENGLISH TRANSLATIONS

Selected Epigrams of Martial Englished (translated by Thomas May) 1629

Select Epigrams of Martial (translated by William Hay, Abraham Cowley, and others) 1755

The Epigrams of Martial, Translated into English Prose, Each Accompanied by One or More Verse Translations from the Works of English Poets, and Various Other Sources (edited by Henry George Bohn) 1860

Select Epigrams from Martial (translated by F. A. Paley and W. H. Stone) 1868

One Hundred and Twenty Epigrams of Martial (translated by J. H. Westcott) 1894

The Ancient Editions of Martial, with Collations of the Berlin and Edinburgh MSS (translated by W. M. Lindsay) 1903

Martial: Epigrams (translated by W. C. A. Ker) 2 vols. 1919, 1920; 1925; revised edition 1968

Martial's Epigrams: Translations and Imitations (translated by A. L. Francis and H. F. Tatum) 1924

Martial, the Twelve Books of Epigrams (translated by J. A. Pott and F. A. Wright) 1924

The Pensive and the Antic Muse: Translations from Martial (translated by Ralph Marcellino) 1963

Martial: Selected Epigrams (translated by Ralph Marcellino) 1968

Epigrams from Martial: A Verse Translation (translated by Barriss Mills) 1969

Epigrams of Martial (translated by Palmer Bovie) 1970

Martial: The Epigrams Selected and Translated (translated by James Michie) 1973

Epigrams from Martial (translated by Richard O'Connell) 1976

A Commentary on Book One of the Epigrams of Martial (translated by Peter Howell) 1980

More Epigrams from Martial (translated by Richard O'Connell) 1981

Letter to Juvenal: 101 Epigrams of Martial (translated by Peter Whigham) 1985

Martial Book XI: A Commentary (translated by N. M. Kay) 1985

Epigrams of Martial Englished by Divers Hands (edited by J. P. Sullivan and Peter Whigham) 1987

Martial: Epigrams (translated by D. R. Shackleton Bailey) 3 vols. 1993

Martial Book XIV: The Apophoreta (translated by T. J. Leary) 1996

Martial in English (edited by J. P. Sullivan and A. J. Boyle) 1996

CRITICISM

Pliny the Younger (essay date c. 104)

SOURCE: "To Cornelius Priscus" in *Pliny Letters,* William Heinemann, 1915, pp, 267, 269.

[*In this letter to his friend Cornelius Priscus, written around 104, Pliny eulogizes Martial, commending the poet's wit, incisiveness, and good nature. He also describes their patron-client relationship and raises doubts about the endurance of Martial's epigrams.*]

I have just heard of the death of poor Martial, which much concerns me. He was a man of an acute and lively genius, and his writings abound in both wit and satire, combined with equal candour. When he left Rome I complimented him by a present to defray the charges of his journey, not only as a testimony of my friendship, but in return for the little poem which he had written about me. It was the custom of the ancients to distinguish those poets with honours or pecuniary rewards, who had celebrated particular persons or cities in their verses; but this practice, with every other that is fair and noble, is now grown out of fashion; and in consequence of having ceased to act laudably, we consider applause as an impertinent and worthless tribute. You will be desirous, perhaps, to see the verses which merited this acknowledgement from me; and I believe I can, from my memory, partly satisfy your curiosity, without referring you to his works: but if you are pleased with this specimen of them, you must turn to his poems for the rest. He addresses himself to his Muse, whom he directs to seek my house upon the Esquiline, and to approach me with respect:

> "Go, wanton Muse, but go with care,
> Nor meet, ill-tim'd, my Pliny's ear.
> He, by sage Minerva taught,
> Gives the day to studious thought,
> And plans that eloquence divine,
> Which shall to future ages shine,
> And rival, wond'rous Tully! thine.
> Then, cautious, watch the vacant hour,
> When Bacchus reigns in all his power!
> When crown'd with rosy chaplets gay,
> E'en rigid Catos read my lay."

Do you not think that the poet who wrote in such terms of me, deserved some friendly marks of my bounty *then,* and that he merits my sorrow *now*? For he gave me the most he could, and it was want of power only, if his present was not more valuable. But to say truth, what higher can be conferred on man than fame, and applause, and immortality? And though it should be granted, that his poems will not be immortal, still, no doubt, he composed them upon the contrary supposition. Farewell.

Gotthold Ephraim Lessing (essay date 1771)

SOURCE: "The Seventeenth and Eighteenth Century Reception" in *The Classical Heritage,* edited by J. P. Sullivan, Garland Publishing, Inc., 1993, pp. 124-27.

[In the following excerpt from an essay originally published in 1771, Lessing salutes Martial as the first and best of the epigrammatists. In his discussion of the lewdness of some of Martial's verses, Lessing cautions against the assumption that the views expressed by the first-person narrator necessarily represent Martial's own opinions.]

There were countless poets before Martial, Greek as well as Roman, who wrote epigrams, but there had never been an epigrammatist before him. By this I mean that he was the first to treat the epigram as a genre in its own right and to devote himself entirely to this genre.

Before him the epigram lay indistinguishable amid the whole throng of short poems, a mass of such infinite variety that no one would have been able or even willing to attempt further classification. Titles were given to all short poems indiscriminately: *epigrammata, idyllia, eclogae* were entirely synonymous designations, indeed Pliny the Younger still left it to the reader to choose from these a name for his poetic dabblings, which he himself had simply named after the metre common to all of them [*elegidia*].

Martial was, as I have said, the first to form for himself a clear, well-grounded conception throughout. As diversified as his epigrams may be with regard to their ideas, they are all exactly alike with regard to their inner structure. The poorest and the best, the longest and the shortest bear without exception the mark by which even a reader who is nothing less than he is a judge of literature can recognize that they are akin and that they belong to the same category.

Moreover, just as Martial must rightly be honoured as the first epigrammatist chronologically speaking, he is also, even to this day, the first in terms of excellence. Only few have composed as many epigrams as he did; and no one amongst as many just as many good ones, or as many quite superb ones. Of all ages and nations the one poet who can still compare the most closely with Martial is our [Christian] Wernike [1661-1725]. The fullness and wealth of both is almost equally vast, the only difference being that, in the case of the German, the toil and sweat which his wealth cost him are a little too noticeable. Martial came by his amongst people and from people; Wernike mined for his, often risking his life, in Nature's womb. Wernike had more of the metals used to make coins, while more of the minted coins passed through Martial's hands.

No more talk of Martial's false wit! Which epigrammatist has none of this? But how many have that which alone makes false wit tolerable and which in Martial is so abundant? Martial knows that it is false wit and does not pretend that it is anything else. His idle fingers toy a little and no sooner is the bauble ready than he blows it from his hand. Others, however, hardly know what they are cutting and polishing, whether it is a real gem or false; they put as much effort into the one as they really only should into the other; with an unchanging grave, solemn, upright expression they ask the same price for the real and the false.

Furthermore, I could scarcely think of any example where Martial mixes false and genuine wit in one and the same epigram. He very often shows true wit, be the subject ever so trifling, ridiculous and ignoble. But he never displays false wit where the subject is serious, dignified and grand, and this alone is the true touchstone for the man of wit, the man whose wit cannot be judged his own disgrace. The best defence for him on this point would be a comparison with modern epigrammatists who itch to vie with him at being thus seriously charged. I wish to name only one such example and choose to this purpose the epigram on the death of Porcia.

I could also feast on Muretus, for whom Martial was nothing but a *scurra de trivio*. Howbeit he did still imitate Martial rather frequently in his poems and this always quite unfortunately. The only thing in which he could outdo the old buffoon was in making puns. However, Muretus' poems are called *Juvenilia*, and he passed his critical judgement as—pray to God—a mature adult.

I shall therefore leave the man in peace and simply add only this one last point with regard to Martial's quality as a poet. If Aelius Verus, who called Martial his Vergil, meant nothing more than that Martial was in his little genre what Vergil was held to be in his grand one— a view shared by various learned men—, then no one need be ashamed of having a similarly refined taste. It is, however, undeniable that this Caesar meant more than that, and indeed there has never been any lack of men in his position who quite seriously prefer an amusing, salacious ditty to the greatest work of genius, the appreciation of which merely requires a little effort. They overrate things that please them, without troubling their heads as to what ought to please them.

Only the writer himself could possibly be forgiven for such overrating. Martial too was always inclined to believe that his epigrams were just as valuable as the heroic poems and tragedies of other authors, for in order to excel at something it is indeed necessary not to think lightly of it. One must rather look upon it as one of the most important things in the world, otherwise there can be no enthusiasm, without which nothing outstanding can be achieved in any field. For the author a very expedient self-deception, but woe betide the reader who allows himself to be carried away by this! In the end he will not be able to tell what is grand or small, what important or unimportant, and will ultimately belittle everything.

Nothing has been more detrimental to Martial's reputation in modern times than the lewd contents of quite a number of his epigrams. Not that one would wish to maintain that a thing cannot be aesthetically beautiful which is not also morally good. But it is not so very unreasonable to view with disfavour those things of beauty in which this goodness is not immediately recognizable.

Thus those who preferred to cut out all Martial's itchy, diseased, infectious parts, rather than see him barred altogether from the innocent hands and delicate brows of readers, meant well by him after all. Ramires de Prado must have been dull-witted to use honest Rader so cruelly for having such good intentions. It would have been a different matter, had the parts removed then been destroyed, or if it were still easy to arrange for things which are suppressed in *one* edition to disappear completely as a result.

Martial's own excuse as regards obscenity:

> Lasciva est nobis pagina? vita proba est—

does not go very far. And yet those who are of the opinion that no objections can be raised against the lewdness, have not even stretched his excuse to a point where it would be more or less acceptable. They have not even explained to us how an untainted life style can be compatible with such tainted poems, or what the criterion is if it be no longer permissible to draw any conclusions from the one as to the other. For the sake not so much of voicing actual agreement with their opinion, but rather of contributing something towards a better understanding of the poet, I would like to set down a few observations on this point.

1. As is the case with men who treat bodily defects, those who undertake to remedy moral turpitude have accordingly always been allowed to use frank language as well, to name all things by their proper names— something which common decency would either forbid entirely or at least require to be disguised, except when done to these two purposes. This being so, what is there to stop us from looking upon Martial as one of those who follow the latter? It is at least evident that he had no intention of glorifying even one of the coarse, unnatural forms of lust, the mere naming of which in his poems causes such disgust; on the contrary, where he does mention any of these, it is never otherwise than in derision and scorn. . . .

2. I was hoping that by now no further pleas would be needed in defence of Martial. However, one important argument ought still to be brought forward, so that Martial will not be burdened with additional charges arising from these epigrams in which he is clearly not criticizing or deriding anything, but talking about himself, expressing wishes and demands for himself. Thus the following might perhaps be said in favour of these poems, were the object to prove that Martial was as little infected as possible with the corruptness of his age.

It is wrong to assume that the epigrammatist intends everything he says in the first person to be interpreted as having to do with his own person. Brevity and rondure, two such essential qualities of this type of poetry, often force him to present something in the first person which neither his heart nor his reason could share. That Martial too came across such a situation and that Martial too had no qualms about it, is entirely plausible.

Lord Byron (essay date 1821?)

SOURCE: "Martial" in *The Works of Lord Byron,* edited by Ernest Hartley Coleridge, John Murray, 1821, p. 74.

[*The poem below, believed to have been written in 1821, is Byron's famous imitation of Martial 1.1, on the poet's fame.*]

> He, unto whom thou art so partial,
> Oh, reader! is the well-known Martial,
> The Epigrammatist: while living,
> Give him the fame thou would'st be giving;
> So shall he hear, and feel, and know it—
>   Post-obits rarely reach a poet.

Thomas Babington Macaulay (essay date 1857)

SOURCE: "Chapter XIV" in *The Life and Letters of Lord Macaulay,* Harper & Brothers, 1877, p. 378.

[*In the following excerpt, dated 1857, from Macaulay's journal, the distinguished British statesman and historian records his generally disparaging appraisal of Martial. Though Macaulay remarks on the poet's lively imagery, he is deeply offended by Martial's obscenity and mendicancy.*]

. . . I have now gone through the first seven books of Martial, and have learned about three hundred and sixty of the best lines. His merit seems to me to lie, not in wit, but in the rapid succession of vivid images. I wish he were less nauseous. He is as great a beast as Aristophanes. He certainly is a very clever, pleasant writer. Sometimes he runs Catullus himself hard. But, besides his indecency, his servility and his mendicancy disgust me. In his position, for he was a Roman knight, something more like self-respect would have been becoming. I make large allowance for the difference of manners; but it never can have been *comme il faut* in any age or nation for a man of note—an accomplished man—a man living with the great—to be constantly asking for money, clothes, and dainties, and to pursue with volleys of abuse those who would give him nothing. . . .

Gaston Boissier (essay date 1900)

SOURCE: "The Poet Martial" in *Tacitus and Other Roman Studies,* translated by W. G. Hutchison, G. P. Putnam's Sons, 1906, pp. 248-54.

[*In the following excerpt from an essay first published in 1900, Boissier focuses on Martial's incisive portraits of character types in the fashionable society of his day and on the poet's attitude toward women.*]

. . . We possess nothing of Martial's save epigrams, and probably he did not write anything else: he seems to have made a speciality of this form of verse. We know that the word *epigram* had among the ancients a much wider significance than it has to-day. It was, properly speaking, a short inscription of a few lines, and it denoted the epitaph on a tomb, or the dedication of an altar, as well as some malicious skit scribbled on a wall. With Martial satire predominates in the epigram. It is scarce more in his case than a few lines of verse, sprightly, vivacious and witty, which humorously tells some anecdote, banters an eccentricity, or cracks a joke. As the interest is mainly in the quip with which it concludes, he prepares his reader for it in advance, and, from the start, all leads up to the final sting. This method of proceeding, which is nearly the same in all, risks making them seem in time monotonous, and when a large number are accumulated, one upon another, the monotony grows still more sensible. Martial, as a man of taste, was aware of it, and so he is careful to apologise for his epigrams. From the outset he frankly confesses that all is not irreproachable in his works: 'There are good things in them, there are middling, there are yet more that are bad.' But we must not be too hard on epigrams. If but one half be good, that suffices; the rest must stand excused. Besides what need of reading them all at once? Do you think there are too many? then only read a few; you will turn to the others later. This counsel is sound: Martial is one of those authors who should be taken in moderate doses and at intervals.

But the true method for finding pleasure in his study is to put yourself back in his time, to pass with him for a moment into his life and that of the people with whom he associated. It was a wealthy society, restricted and select; he is very careful to tell us that he does not address himself to everybody: 'Others write for the multitude; for my part I only aim at pleasing the few'; he wishes to divert men of taste, men of wit accustomed to light conversation, who are not startled at a risky story, who pardon a piece of foolery, if it be but neatly put. His book seems to deserve another fate than that of being solemnly stored in a library cheek by jowl with works of philosophy and science, and from time to time being consulted by persons of a serious turn of mind. As it is compact in form, of agreeable aspect and quite portable, it can be carried under the toga and taken out and read under the porticoes or carried to those dinner-parties where a good company is assembled. Towards the end of the repast, when the guests are tired of talking charioteers and horses, or retailing the scandal of the day, they will pass to Martial's latest epigrams and regale themselves therewith. It is hardly a change of subject, for Martial too likes to speak of all that attracts the frivolous curiosity of the idlers of the fashionable world; he is always chatting of the minor incidents of the public games—of the snow which fell one day in the middle of the performance without either Emperor or public leaving their places; of the actor who played the part of Mucius Scævola, and so bravely held his hand in the flaming brazier; of the lion which devoured its keeper, and played with a little hare which had taken refuge between its paws; to these add the good stories current in town, naughty anecdotes and other improprieties, to which the ladies are besought not to listen, so as to make sure that they will strain their ears the better to hear them.

It cannot be said that Martial tells us much that is very new about contemporary society; he was not free enough to speak of it as he would have wished; in his position of dependence on the people about him, it was inadvisable to find fault with any one. He is constantly protesting against those who would find malicious allusions in his verses; *ludimus innocue.* So timid a man could not be a very profound observer. For fear of compromising himself he lingers in the commonplaces of everyday ethics; he attacks the misers and the prodigals, those who do nothing and those who do too much; the rich man who permits the belief that he is poor, for fear he may be forced to be generous; the poor man who wants to pass for being rich and at night, to defray the day's expenses, pawns his ring; the insolent upstart, for ever bragging of his fortune; the legacy-hunter; the parasite in quest of a dinner; the poet who assassinates every one in his verses, and so on. These are real and vital figures, but of slight originality and not drawn in strong relief.

His painting of women is not carried to the point of blackness as in Juvenal. At bottom, however, he forms pretty nearly the same estimate of them. It is clear from what he says that they are quite emancipated from the servitude and seclusion of old; they go into society, they accompany their husbands to banquets; seated on their high chairs, they await their visitors who come to pay their respects and tell them the news. What caused their independence was that they held their fortune apart from their husbands', and guarded it jealously,[1] so as to be able to carry it off on the day of divorce—and divorces were so frequent! To administer their property they selected a steward, and, if we are to believe that evil tongue of Martial's, this steward was sometimes a very pretty boy: 'Tell me, my dear Marianus, who is that little curled darling, who never quits your wife's side, who leans on the back of her chair, and is for ever bending down to whisper some sweet nothing in her ear? His legs are free of every hair, and dainty rings crowd his every finger. You answer me that he is her steward. Poor fool!—how fit are you to play the part of simpleton at the theatre by the side of Latinus! 'Tis not your wife's business that he does, but rather

yours.'[2] It is evident that the women were not content to use the independence they had won; many abused it. To prove conclusively to themselves and convince the whole world that there was no inequality between themselves and men, they assumed their weaknesses, made a display of their absurdities, and invaded their professions; they affected no longer to speak anything but Greek, they posed as bluestockings and pedants, they studied philosophy, they wrote poems, even love poems. One of them, Sulpicia, the wife of Calenus, was famous for her terribly passionate poems; it is true they were addressed to her husband, which disarms the severest critic. Martial admires her like every one else, he compares her to Sappho and the nymph Egeria.[3] But, in speaking thus, he does not quite express what he thinks: in reality these talents which women are seeking to acquire cause him disquietude. He longs, for his own part, that she whom he marries—if he ever does marry—will not be too learned; the equality they would fain establish betwixt men and women is to him of no good omen, and he avails himself of old Cato's saying: 'On the day they are our equals they shall be our masters':—

> *'Inferior matrona suo sit, Prisce, marito.*
> *Non aliter fient femina virque pares.*

To complete this picture of fashionable life of which Martial affords us a glimpse, we must place beside the woman who tricks herself out, who bedizens herself, who paints her face, 'who dreads the rain because she has powdered herself, and the sun because she has laid on rouge'—her companion, the man of fashion, whom the poet calls the coxcomb or the curled exquisite, *bellus homo, crispulus.* He is somewhat of a newcomer in Roman society; he was almost unknown at the Republican epoch, and so he never figures in the comedies of that age. Perhaps we might find him in the mimes of the Augustan epoch, when private life was readily put on the stage, where you could see the lover, surprised by the unexpected return of the husband, taking refuge in a chest. There are already some traces of his presence in Ovid's *Art of Love,* but it is Martial who has depicted him to the life. 'A coxcomb is a man whose hair has a well-made parting always smelling of perfumes, who hums between his teeth the ditties of Egypt and Spain, and can beat time with his hairless arms; who never, the whole day, stirs from the ladies' chairs and has always something to tell them, who reads through the letters they have received from various quarters and undertakes to reply to them; whose one great object in life is to preserve his clothes from being rumpled by his neighbour's elbow, who knows the tattle of the town and will tell you the name of the woman of whom such an one is enamoured, who is a constant diner-out and can rehearse the whole pedigree of the horse Hirpinus.'[4] Here, in a few lines, we have a finished portrait, which puts the fellow before our eyes.

People have been right in trying to discover who the persons are to whom Martial addresses his epigrams[5]: they consist of nearly the whole of the distinguished society of the time. We first come across the servants, the freedmen of the prince, those, that is to say, who, under his name, govern the Empire; then, what remains of the old aristocracy, much diminished and sorely impoverished by the tyranny of the Cæsars, and the new nobility in course of replacing it; provincial governors, generals of armies, senators who have for long held high place; others, less known but already making their mark, like that Palfurius Sura, Trajan's friend, for whom the future reserved so brilliant a fortune. Add to these the wealthy patrons of the arts, the amateurs, the collectors, the lettered men of the world of society—Silius Italicus, who had written an epic poem, and that Arruntius Stella, a king of fashion and a writer of precious little poems, 'into which he put as many pearls and brilliants as he wore upon his fingers.' Tacitus is not included in the list; he was too serious a person for that, and must have been mildly horrified by Martial's playful muse; but we find in it his friend, the younger Pliny, whom the poet only approaches with respect, and who reminds him of Cato. One of the most curious in the list is that Antonius Primus who had his hour of celebrity. He belonged to Toulouse, and his compatriots had, in the patois of their country, surnamed him Becco (the man with the big nose). Condemned under Nero for the crime of forgery, he had found means to remount the saddle, and, on the death of Otho, he commanded a legion in the army of Pannonia. He resolutely declared for Vespasian, threw himself upon Italy, though he had been ordered to do nothing of the kind, defeated Vitellius in defiance of everybody, pillaged and burnt Cremona, and took Rome by storm. His soldiers worshipped him, and would follow no other leader; he fascinated them by his audacity, by his ready tongue. In the councils of war he talked more loudly than the others, so as to be heard by the centurions outside the tent. In the thickest of the fight he passed through the ranks, finding a word for each, encouraging the brave, treating the cowards as *pékins* (*pagani*), always ready, if he saw them wavering, to snatch up the eagle and throw himself upon the foe. He was one of those heroic soldiers of fortune whom factions use during a struggle, and who are given the cold shoulder after success has been won. He, the war at an end, disappears from history, and we should not know what became of him, did we not find him again in Martial. He had gone back to Toulouse and was peacefully waxing old there. As he was well pleased that accounts of the life of Rome should still reach him in his retirement, he read Martial's epigrams; the poet had been careful to forward them to him himself, remarking that a book has more value when it comes directly from the author than when it is purchased at the bookseller's. This individual truly deserves to be never forgotten; he is the first Gascon whose memory has been kept green.

Notes

[1] From the praise accorded by Martial to one of them who merged her fortune in her husband's, we find that was a very rare exception.

[2] v. 61

[3] x. 35; vii. 69.

[4] iii. 63.

[5] See Giese, *De personis a Martiale commemoratis.* See also the *index nominum,* which Mommsen has inserted in the second edition of Keil's letters of Pliny. The persons of whom Martial speaks are often to be found in Pliny.

H. E. Butler (essay date 1909)

SOURCE: "Martial" in *Post-Augustan Poetry, from Seneca to Juvenal,* Clarendon Press, 1909, pp. 251-86.

[*In the essay below, Butler offers a variety of judgments regarding Martial's life and work. He complains that Martial lacks seriousness and is guilty of lewdness, yet he credits the poet with an elegant style and a realistic view of his own abilities.*]

Marcus Valerius Martialis, like Quintilian, Seneca, and Lucan, was a Spaniard by birth, and, unlike those writers, never became thoroughly reconciled to life at Rome. He was born at Bilbilis,[1] a small town of Hispania Tarraconensis. The exact year of his birth is uncertain; but as the tenth book of his epigrams, written between 95 and 98 A.D., contains a reference (x. 24) to his fifty-seventh birthday, he must have been born between 38 and 41 A.D. His birthday was the 1st of March, a fact to which he owes his name Martialis.[2] Of the position of his parents, Valerius Fronto and Flaccilla,[3] we have no evidence. That they were not wealthy is clear from the circumstances of their son. But they were able to give him a regular literary education,[4] although, unlike his fellow-countrymen whom we have mentioned above, he was educated in his native province. But the life of a provincial did not satisfy him. Conscious, perhaps, of his literary gifts, he went, in 64 A.D.,[5] like so many a young provincial, to make his fortune at Rome. There he attached himself as client to the powerful Spanish family of the Senecas, and found a friendly reception also in the house of Calpurnius Piso.[6] But fortune was against him; as he was congratulating himself on his good luck in starting life at Rome under such favourable auspices, the Pisonian conspiracy (65 A.D.) failed, and his patrons fell before the wrath of Nero.[7] His career must be commenced anew. Of his life from this point to the reign of Domitian we know little. But this much is certain, that he endured all the indignities and hardships of a client's life,[8] and that he chose this degrading career in preference to the active career of the Roman bar. He had no taste for oratory, and rejected the advice of his friend Gaius[9] and his distinguished compatriot Quintilian to seek a livelihood as an advocate or as a politician. 'That is not life!' he replies to Quintilian:

> vivere quod propero pauper nec inutilis annis,
>   da veniam: properat vivere nemo satis.
> differat hoc patrios optat qui vincere census
>   atriaque immodicis artat imaginibus.

(ii. 90. 3)

His ideals and ambitions were low, and his choice had, as we shall see, a degrading effect upon his poetry. He chose rather to live on such modest fortune as he may have possessed, on the client's dole, and such gifts as his complimentary epigrams may have won from his patrons. These gifts must have been in many cases of a trifling description,[10] but they may occasionally have been on a more generous scale. At any rate, by the year 94 A.D., we find him the possessor of a little farm at Nomentum,[11] and a house on the Quirinal.[12] Although he must presumably have written a considerable quantity of verse in his earlier years, it is not till 80 A.D. that he makes an appearance on the stage of literature. In that year the Flavian amphitheatre was consecrated by the Emperor Titus, and Martial celebrated the fact by the publication of his first book, the *Spectaculorum Liber.* It is of small literary value, but it was his first step on the ladder of fame. Titus conferred on him the *ius trium liberorum,* although he seems not to have entered on the enjoyment of this privilege till the reign of Domitian.[13] He thus first came in touch with the imperial circle. From this time forward we get a continual stream of verse in fulsome praise of Domitian and his freedman. But his flattery met with small reward. There are many poems belauding the princeps, but few that thank him. The most that he acquired by his flattery was the honorary military tribunate and his elevation to the equestrian order.[14] Of material profit he got little,[15] save such as his improved social position may have conferred on him indirectly.

Four years after the publication of the *Spectaculorum Liber* (i.e. later in 84 and 85)[16] he published two books, the thirteenth and fourteenth, composed of neat but trifling poems on the presents (Xenia and Apophoreta) which it was customary to give at the feast of the Saturnalia. From this point his output was continuous and steady, as the following table will show:[17]

I, II. 85 or early in 86.

III. 87 or early in 88.

IV. December (Saturnalia) 88.

V. Autumn, 89.

VI. Summer or Autumn, 90.

VII. December, 92.

VIII. 93.

IX. Summer, 94.

X. 1. December, 95.

X. 2. 98.

XI. 97.

XII. Late in 101.

His life during this period was uneventful. He lived expensively and continually complains of lack of funds and of the miseries of a client's life. Once only (about 88) the discomfort of his existence seems to have induced him to abandon Rome. He took up his residence at Forum Cornelii, the modern Imola, but soon returned to Rome.[18] It was not till 98 that he decided to leave the capital for good and to return to his Spanish home. A new princeps was on the throne. Martial had associated his work too closely with Domitian and his court to feel at his ease with Nerva. He sent the new emperor a selection from his tenth and eleventh books, which we may, perhaps, conjecture to have been expurgated. He denounced the dead Domitian in a brilliant epigram which may have formed part of that selection, but which has only been preserved to us by the scholiast on Juvenal **(iv. 38):**

> Flavia gens, quantum tibi tertius abstulit heres!
>   paene fuit tanti non habuisse duos.

> How much thy third has wronged thee,
>   Flavian race!
> 'Twere better ne'er to have bred the other
>   brace.

Anon.

But he felt that times were changed and that there was no place now for his peculiar talent for flattery **(x. 72.** 8):

> non est hic dominus sed imperator,
> sed iustissimus omnium senator,
> per quem de Stygia domo reducta est
> siccis rustica Veritas capillis.
> hoc sub principe, si sapis, caveto
> verbis, Roma, prioribus loquaris.

>   an emperor
> Is ours, no master as of yore,
> Himself the Senate's very crown

Of justice, who has called from down
In her deep Stygian duress
The hoyden Truth, with tangled tress.
Be wise, Rome, see you shape anew
Your tongue; your prince would have it true.

A. E. Street

Let flattery fly to Parthia. Rome is no place for her **(x. 4)**. Martial had made his name: he was read far and wide throughout the Empire.[19] He could afford to retire from the city that had given him much fame and much pleasure, but had balanced its gifts by a thousand vexations and indignities. Pliny assisted him with journey-money, and after a thirty-four years' sojourn in Italy he returned to Bilbilis to live a life of *dolce far niente*. The kindness of a wealthy friend, a Spanish lady named Marcella,[20] gave him an estate on which he lived in comfort, if not in affluence. He published but one book in Spain, the twelfth, written, he says in the preface, in a very few days. He lived in peace and happiness, though at times he sighed for the welcome of the public for whom he had catered so long,[21] and chafed under the lack of sympathy and culture among his Spanish neighbours.[22] He died in 104. 'Martial is dead,' says Pliny, 'and I am grieved to hear it. He was a man of genius, with a shrewd and vigorous wit. His verses are full of point and sting, and as frank as they are witty. I provided him with money for his journey when he left Rome; I owed it to my friendship for him, and to the verses which he wrote in my honour'—then follows Mart. **x. 20**—'Was I not right to speed him on his way, and am I not justified in mourning his death, seeing that he wrote thus concerning me? He gave me what he could, he would have given more had he been able. And yet what greater gift can one man give another than by handing down his name and fame to all eternity. I hear you say that Martial's verses will not live to all eternity? You may be right; at any rate, he hoped for their immortality when he wrote them' (Plin. *Ep.* iii. 21).

Of Martial's character we shall have occasion to speak later. There is nothing in the slight, but generous, tribute of Pliny that has to be unsaid.

Of the circles in which he moved his epigrams give us a brilliant picture; of his exact relations with the persons whom he addresses it is hard to speak with certainty. Many distinguished figures of the day appear as the objects of his flattery. There are Spaniards, Quintilian, Lucinianus Maternus and Canius Rufus, all distinguished men of letters, the poets Silius Italicus, Stertinius Avitus, Arruntius Stella, the younger Pliny, the orator Aquilius Regulus, Lentulus Sura, the friend of Trajan, the rich knights, Atedius Melior, and Claudius Etruscus, the soldier Norbanus, and many others. With Juvenal also he seems to have enjoyed a certain intimacy. Statius he never mentions, although he must

have moved in the same circles.[23] His intimates—as might be expected—are for the most part, as far as we can guess, of lower rank. There are the centurions Varus and Pudens, Terentius Priscus his compatriot, Decianus the Stoic from the Spanish town of Emerita, the self-sacrificing Quintus Ovidius, Martial's neighbour at Nomentum and a fellow-client of Seneca, and, above all, Julius Martialis. His enemies and envious rivals are attacked and bespattered with filth in many an epigram, but Martial, true to his promise in the preface to his first book, conceals their true names from us.

Of his *vie intime* he tells us little. As far as we may judge, he was unmarried. It is true that several of his epigrams purport to be addressed to his wife. But two facts show clearly that this lady is wholly imaginary. Even Martial could not have spoken of his wife in such disgusting language as, for instance, he uses in **xi. 104**, while in another poem **(ii. 92)** he clearly expresses his intention not to marry:

> natorum mihi ius trium roganti
> Musarum pretium dedit mearum
> solus qui poterat. valebis, uxor,
> non debet domini perire munus.

The honorary *ius trium liberorum* had given him, he says, all that marriage could have brought him. He has no intention of making the emperor's generosity superfluous by taking a wife. He preferred the untrammelled life of a bachelor. So only could he enjoy the pleasures which for him meant 'life'. He is neither an impressive nor a very interesting figure. He has many qualities that repel, even if we do not take him too seriously; and though he may have been a pleasant and in many respects most amiable companion, he has few characteristics that arrest our attention or compel our respect. More will be said of his virtues and his vices in the pages that follow. It is the artist rather than the man that wakens our interest.

In Martial we have a poet who devoted himself to the one class of poetry which, apart from satire, the conditions of the Silver Age were qualified to produce in any real excellence—the epigram. In a period when rhetorical smartness and point were the predominant features of literature, the epigram was almost certain to flourish. But Roman poets in general, and Martial in particular, gave a character to the epigram which has clung to it ever since, and has actually changed the significance of the word itself.

In the best days of the Greek epigram the prime consideration was not that a poem should be pointed, but that it should be what is summed up in the untranslatable French epithet *lapidaire;* that is to say, it should possess the conciseness, finish, and relevance required for an inscription on a monument. Its range was wide; it might express the lover's passion, the mourner's grief,

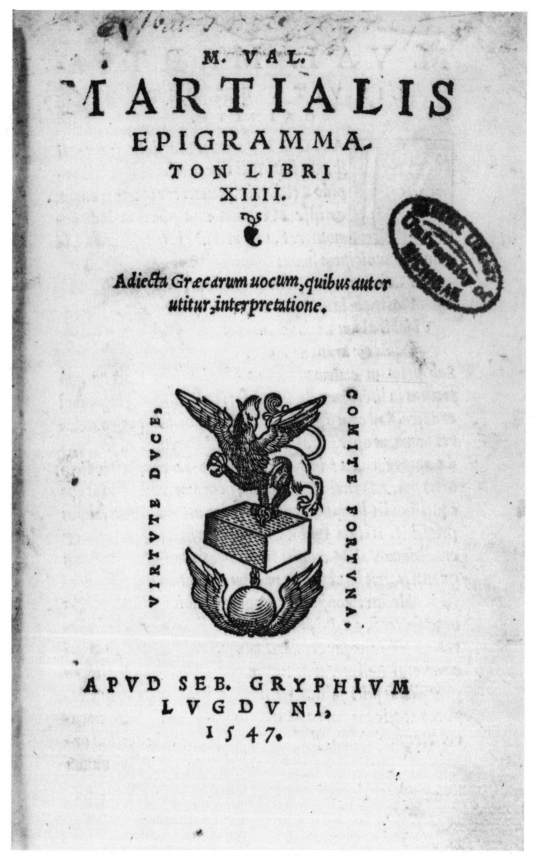

Title page of a 1547 edition of Martial's Epigrams.

the artist's skill, the cynic's laughter, the satirist's scorn. It was all poetry in miniature. Point is not wanting, but its chief characteristics are delicacy and charm. 'No good epigram sacrifices its finer poetical substance to the desire of making a point, and none of the best depend on having a point at all.'[24] Transplanted to the soil of Italy the epigram changes. The less poetic Roman, with his coarse tastes, his brutality, his tendency to satire, his appreciation of the incisive, wrought it to his own use. In his hands it loses most of its sensuous and lyrical elements and makes up for the loss by the cultivation of point. Above all, it becomes the instrument of satire, stinging like a wasp where the satirist pure and simple uses the deadlier weapons of the bludgeon and the rapier.

The epigram must have been exceedingly plentiful from the very dawn of the movement which was to make Rome a city of *belles-lettres*. It is the plaything of the dilettante *littérateur,* so plentiful under the empire.[25] Apart from the work of Martial, curiously few epigrams have come down to us; nevertheless, in the vast majority of the very limited number we possess the same Roman characteristics may be traced. In the non-lyrical epigrams of Catullus, in the shorter poems of the *Appendix Vergiliana,* there is the same vigour, the same coarse humour, the same pungency that find their best expression in Martial. Even in the epigrams attributed to Seneca in the *Anthologia Latina,*[26] something of this may be observed, though for the most part they lack the personal note and leave the impression of mere juggling with words. It is in this last respect, the attention to point, that they show most affinity with Martial. Only the epigrams in the same collection attributed to Petronius[27] seem to preserve something of the Greek spirit of beauty untainted by the hard, unlovely, incisive spirit of Rome.

Martial was destined to fix the type of the epigram for the future. For pure poetry he had small gifts. He was endowed with a warm heart, a real love for simplicity of life and for the beauties of nature. But he had no lyrical enthusiasm, and was incapable of genuine passion. He entered heartwhole on all his amatory adventures, and left them with indifference. Even the cynical profligacy of Ovid shows more capacity for true love. At their best Martial's erotic epigrams attain to a certain shallow prettiness,[28] for the most part they do not rise above the pornographic. And even though he shows a real capacity for friendship, he also reveals an infinite capacity for cringing or impudent vulgarity in his relations with those who were merely patrons or acquaintances. His needy circumstances led him, as we shall see, to continual expressions of a peevish mendicancy, while the artificiality and pettiness of the life in which he moved induced an excessive triviality and narrowness of outlook.

He makes no great struggle after originality. The slightness of his themes and of his *genre* relieved him of

that necessity. Some of his prettiest poems are mere variations on some of the most famous lyrics of Catullus.[29] He pilfers whole lines from Ovid.[30] Phrase after phrase suggests something that has gone before. But his plagiarism is effected with such perfect frankness and such perfect art, that it might well be pardoned, even if Martial had greater claims to be taken seriously. As it is, his freedom in borrowing need scarcely be taken into account in the consideration of our verdict. At the worst his crime is no more than petty larceny. With all his faults, he has gifts such as few poets have possessed, a perfect facility and a perfect finish. Alone of poets of the period he rarely gives the impression of labouring a point. Compared with Martial, Seneca and Lucan, Statius and Juvenal are, at their worst, stylistic acrobats. But Martial, however silly or offensive, however complicated or prosaic his theme, handles his material with supreme ease. His points may often not be worth making; they could not be better made. Moreover, he has a perfect ear; his music may be trivial, but within its narrow limits it is faultless.[31] He knows what is required of him and he knows his own powers. He knows that his range is limited, that his sphere is comparatively humble, but he is proud to excel in it. He has the artist's self-respect without his vanity.

His themes are manifold. He might have said, with even greater truth than Juvenal, 'quidquid agunt homines, nostri est farrago libelli.' He does not go beneath the surface, but almost every aspect of the kaleidoscopic world of Rome receives his attention at one time or another. His attitude is, on the whole, satirical, though his satire is not inspired by deep or sincere indignation. He is too easy in his morals and too good-humoured by temperament. He is often insulting, but there is scarcely a line that breathes fierce resentment, while his almost unparalleled obscenity precludes the intrusion of any genuine earnestness of moral scorn in a very large number of his satiric epigrams. On these points he shall speak for himself; he makes no exacting claims.

'I hope,' he says in the preface to his first book, 'that I have exercised such restraint in my writings that no one who is possessed of the least self-respect may have cause to complain of them. My jests are never outrageous, even when directed against persons of the meanest consideration. My practice in this respect is very different from that of early writers, who abused persons without veiling their invective under a pseudonym. Nay more, their victims were men of the highest renown. My *jeux d'esprit* have no *arrières-pensées,* and I hope that no one will put an evil interpretation on them, nor rewrite my epigrams by infusing his own malignance into his reading of them. It is a scandalous injustice to exercise such ingenuity on what another has written. I would offer some excuse for the freedom and frankness of my language—which is, after all, the language of epigram—if I were setting any new precedent. But all epigrammatists, Catullus, Marsus, Pedo, Gaetulicus, have availed themselves of this licence of speech. But if any one wishes to acquire notoriety by prudish severity, and refuses to permit me to write after the good Roman fashion in so much as a single page of my work, he may stop short at the preface, or even at the title. Epigrams are written for such persons as derive pleasure from the games at the Feast of Flowers. Cato should not enter my theatre, but if he does enter it, let him be content to look on at the sport which I provide. I think I shall be justified in closing my preface with an epigram

> To Cato
>
> Once more the merry feast of Flora's come,
> With wanton jest to split the sides of Rome;
> Yet come you, prince of prudes, to view the
>   show.
> Why come you? merely to be shocked and
>   go?'

He reasserts the kindliness of his heart and the excellence of his intentions elsewhere:

> hunc servare modum nostri novere libelli;
>   parcere personis, dicere de vitiis.

> **(x. 33)**

> For in my verses 'tis my constant care
> To lash the vices, but the persons spare.

> Hay

Malignant critics *had* exercised their ingenuity in the manner which he deprecated.[32] Worse still, libellous verse had been falsely circulated as his:

> quid prodest, cupiant cum quidam nostra
>   videri
>   si qua Lycambeo sanguine tela madent,
> vipereumque vomant nostro sub nomine virus
>   qui Phoebi radios ferre diemque negant?

> **(vii. 12. 5)**

> But what does't avail,
> If in bloodfetching lines others do rail,
> And vomit viperous poison in my name,
> Such as the sun themselves to own do shame?

> Anon., 1695

In this respect his defence of himself is just. When he writes in a vein of invective his victim is never mentioned by name. And we cannot assert in any given case that his pseudonyms mask a real person.

He may do no more than satirize a vice embodied and typified in an imaginary personality.

He is equally concerned to defend himself against the obvious charges of prurience and immorality:

> innocuos censura potest permittere lusus:
>   lasciva est nobis pagina, vita proba.[33]

> **(i. 4. 7)**

> Let not these harmless sports your censure
>   taste!
> My lines are wanton, but my life is chaste.

> Anon., seventeenth century

This is no real defence, and even though we need not take Martial at his word, when he accuses himself of the foulest vices, there is not the slightest reason to suppose that chastity was one of his virtues. In Juvenal's case we have reason to believe that, whatever his weaknesses, he was a man of genuinely high ideals. Martial at his best shows himself a man capable of fine feeling, but he gives no evidence of moral earnestness or strength of character. On the other hand, to give him his due, we must remember the standard of his age. Although he is lavish with the vilest obscenities, and has no scruples about accusing acquaintances of every variety of unnatural vice, it must be pointed out that such accusations were regarded at Rome as mere matter for laughter. The traditions of the old *Fescennina locutio* survived, and with the decay of private morality its obscenity increased. Caesar's veterans could sing ribald verses unrebuked at their general's triumph, verses unquotably obscene and casting the foulest aspersions on the character of one whom they worshipped almost as a god. Caesar could invite Catullus to dine in spite of the fact that such accusations formed the matter of his lampoons. Catullus could insert similar charges against the bridegroom for whom he was writing an *epithalamium*. The writing of Priapeia was regarded as a reputable diversion. Martial's defence of his obscenities is therefore in all probability sincere, and may have approved itself to many reputable persons of his day. It was a defence that had already been made in very similar language by Ovid and Catullus,[34] and Martial was not the last to make it. But the fact that Martial felt it necessary to defend himself shows that a body of public opinion—even if not large or representative—did exist which refused to condone this fashionable lubricity. Extenuating circumstances may be urged in Martial's defence, but even to have conformed to the standard of his day is sufficient condemnation; and it is hard to resist the suspicion that he fell below it. His obscenities, though couched in the most easy and pointed language, have rarely even the grace—if grace it be—of wit; they are puerile in conception and infinitely disgusting.

It is pleasant to turn to the better side of Martial's character. No writer has ever given more charming expression to his affection for his friends. It is for Decianus and Julius Martialis that he keeps the warmest place in his heart. In poems like the following there is no doubting the sincerity of his feeling or questioning the perfection of its expression:

si quis erit raros inter numerandus amicos,
    quales prisca fides famaque novit anus,
si quis Cecropiae madidus Latiaeque Minervae
    artibus et vera simplicitate bonus,
si quis erit recti custos, mirator honesti,
    et nihil arcano qui roget ore deos,
si quis erit magnae subnixus robore mentis:
    dispeream si non hic Decianus erit.

(i. 39)

Is there a man whose friendship rare
With antique friendship may compare;
In learning steeped, both old and new,
Yet unpedantic, simple, true;
Whose soul, ingenuous and upright,
Ne'er formed a wish that shunned the light,
Whose sense is sound? If such there be,
My Decianus, thou art he.

Professor Goldwin Smith

Even more charming, if less intense, is the exhortation to Julius Martialis to live while he may, ere the long night come that knows no waking:

o mihi post nullos, Iuli, memorande sodales,
    si quid longa fides canaque iura valent,
bis iam paene tibi consul tricensimus instat,
    et numerat paucos vix tua vita dies.
non bene distuleris videas quae posse negari,
    et solum hoc ducas, quod fuit, esse tuum.
exspectant curaeque catenatique labores:
    gaudia non remanent, sed fugitiva volant.
haec utraque manu complexuque adsere toto:
    saepe fluunt imo sic quoque lapsa sinu.
non est, crede mihi, sapientis dicere 'vivam'.
    sera nimis vita est crastina: vive hodie.

(i. 15)

Friend of my heart—and none of all the band
    Has to that name older or better right:
Julius, thy sixtieth winter is at hand,
    Far-spent is now life's day and near the night.
Delay not what thou would'st recall too late;
    That which is past, that only call thine own:
Cares without end and tribulations wait,

Joy tarrieth not, but scarcely come, is flown.
Then grasp it quickly firmly to thy heart,—
    Though firmly grasped, too oft it slips away;—
To talk of living is not wisdom's part:
    To-morrow is too late: live thou to-day!

Professor Goldwin Smith

Best of all is the retrospect of the long friendship which has united him to Julius. It is as frank as it is touching:

triginta mihi quattuorque messes
tecum, si memini, fuere, Iuli.
quarum dulcia mixta sunt amaris
sed iucunda tamen fuere plura;
et si calculus omnis huc et illuc
diversus bicolorque digeratur,
vincet candida turba nigriorem.
si vitare voles acerba quaedam
et tristes animi cavere morsus,
nulli te facias nimis sodalem:
gaudebis minus et minus dolebis.

(xii. 34)[35]

My friend, since thou and I first met,
    This is the thirty-fourth December;
Some things there are we'd fain forget,
    More that 'tis pleasant to remember.
Let for each pain a black ball stand,
    For every pleasure past a white one,
And thou wilt find, when all are scanned,
    The major part will be the bright one.

He who would heartache never know,
    He who serene composure treasures,
Must friendship's chequered bliss forego;
    Who has no pain hath fewer pleasures.

Professor Goldwin Smith

He does not pour the treasure of his heart at his friend's feet, as Persius does in his burning tribute to Cornutus. He has no treasure of great price to pour. But it is only natural that in the poems addressed to his friends we should find the statement of his ideals of life:

vitam quae faciunt beatiorem,
iucundissime Martialis, haec sunt:
res non parta labore sed relicta;
non ingratus ager, focus perennis;
lis numquam, toga rara, mens quieta;
vires ingenuae, salubre corpus;
prudens simplicitas, pares amici,
convictus facilis, sine arte mensa;
nox non ebria sed soluta curis.
non tristis torus et tamen pudicus;
somnus qui faciat breves tenebras:

quod sis esse velis nihilque malis;
summum nec metuas diem nec optes.

(x. 47)

What makes a happy life, dear friend,
If thou would'st briefly learn, attend—
An income left, not earned by toil;
Some acres of a kindly soil;
The pot unfailing on the fire;
No lawsuits; seldom town attire;
Health; strength with grace; a peaceful
   mind;
Shrewdness with honesty combined;
Plain living; equal friends and free;
Evenings of temperate gaiety;
A wife discreet, yet blythe and bright;
Sound slumber, that lends wings to night.
With all thy heart embrace thy lot,
Wish not for death and fear it not.

Professor Goldwin Smith

This exquisite echo of the Horatian 'beatus ille qui procul
negotiis' sets forth no very lofty ideal. It is frankly, though
restrainedly, hedonistic. But it depicts a life that is full of
charm and free from evil. Martial, in his heart of hearts,
hates the Rome that he depicts so vividly. Rome with its
noise, its expense, its bustling snobbery, its triviality, and
its vice, where he and his friend Julius waste their days:

   nunc vivit necuter sibi, bonosque
   soles effugere atque abire sentit,
   qui nobis pereunt et imputantur.

(v. 20. 11)

Dead to our better selves we see
   The golden hours take flight,
Still scored against us as they flee.
   Then haste to live aright.

Professor Goldwin Smith

He longs to escape from the world of the professional lounger and the parasite to an ampler air,
where he can breathe freely and find rest. He is no
philosopher, but it is at times a relief to get away
from the rarified atmosphere and the sense of strain
that permeates so much of the aspirations towards
virtue in this strange age of contradictions.

Martial at last found the ease and quiet that his soul
desired in his Spanish home:

   hic pigri colimus labore dulci
   Boterdum Plateamque (Celtiberis
   haec sunt nomina crassiora terris):
   ingenti fruor inproboque somno

quem nec tertia saepe rumpit hora,
et totum mihi nunc repono quidquid
ter denos vigilaveram per annos.
ignota est toga, sed datur petenti
rupta proxima vestis a cathedra.
surgentem focus excipit superba
vicini strue cultus iliceti, . . .

sic me vivere, sic iuvat perire.

(xii. 18. 10)

Busy but pleas'd and idly taking pains,
Here Lewes Downs I till and Ringmer plains,
Names that to each South Saxon well are
   known,
Though they sound harsh to powdered beaux
   in town.
None can enjoy a sounder sleep than mine;
I often do not wake till after nine;
And midnight hours with interest repay
For years in town diversions thrown away.
Stranger to finery, myself I dress
In the first coat from an old broken press.
My fire, as soon as I am up, I see
Bright with the ruins of some neighbouring
   tree. . . .

Such is my life, a life of liberty;
So would I wish to live and so to die.

Hay

Martial has a genuine love for the country. Born at a
time when detailed descriptions of the charms of scenery had become fashionable, and the cultivated landscape at least found many painters, he succeeds far better
than any of his contemporaries in conveying to the reader
his sense of the beauties which his eyes beheld. That
sense is limited, but exquisite. It does not go deep; there
is nothing of the almost mystical background that Vergil
at times suggests; there is nothing of the feeling of the
open air and the wild life that is sometimes wafted to us
in the sensuous verse of Theocritus. But Martial sees
what he sees clearly, and he describes it perfectly. Compare his work with the affected prettiness of Pliny's
description of the source of the Clitumnus or with the
more sensuous, but over-elaborate, craftsmanship of
Statius in the *Silvae*. Martial is incomparably their superior. He speaks a more human language, and has a far
clearer vision. Both Statius and Martial described villas
by the sea. We have already mentioned Statius' description of the villa of Pollius at Sorrento; Martial shall
speak in his turn:

   o temperatae dulce Formiae litus,
   vos, cum severi fugit oppidum Martis
   et inquietas fessus exuit curas,
   Apollinaris omnibus locis praefert. . . .

hic summa leni stringitur Thetis vento:
nec languet aequor, viva sed quies ponti
pictam phaselon adiuvante fert aura,
sicut puellae non amantis aestatem
mota salubre purpura venit frigus.
nec saeta longo quaerit in mari praedam,
sed a cubili lectuloque iactatam
spectatus alte lineam trahit piscis. . . .

frui sed istis quando, Roma, permittis?
quot Formianos imputat dies annus
negotiosis rebus urbis haerenti?
o ianitores vilicique felices!
dominis parantur ista, serviunt vobis.[36]

(x. 30)

O strand of Formiae, sweet with genial air,
Who art Apollinaris' chosen home
When, taking flight from his task-mistress
    Rome,
The tired man doffs his load of troubling
    care. . . .

Here the sea's bosom quivers in the wind;
'Tis no dead calm, but sweet serenity,
Which bears the painted boat before the
    breeze,
As though some maid at pains the heat to ban,
Should waft a genial zephyr with her fan.
No fisher needs to buffet the high seas,
But whiles from bed or couch his line he
    casts,
May see his captive in the toils below. . . .

But, niggard Rome, thou giv'st how
    grudgingly!
What the year's tale of days at Formiae
For him who tied by work in town must stay?
Stewards and lacqueys, happy your employ,
Your lords prepare enjoyment, you enjoy.

A. E. Street

These are surely the most beautiful *scazons*[37] in the Latin tongue; the metre limps no more; a master-hand has wrought it to exquisite melody; the quiet undulation of the sea, the yacht's easy gliding over its surface, live before us in its music. Even more delicate is the homelier description of the gardens of Julius Martialis on the slopes of the Janiculum. It is animated by the sincerity that never fails Martial when he writes to his friend:

Iuli iugera pauca Martialis
hortis Hesperidum beatiora
longo Ianiculi iugo recumbunt:
lati collibus imminent recessus
et planus modico tumore vertex

caelo perfruitur sereniore
et curvas nebula tegente valles
solus luce nitet peculiari:
puris leniter admoventur astris
celsae culmina delicata villae.
hinc septem dominos videre montes
et totam licet aestimare Romam,
Albanos quoque Tusculosque colles
et quodcumque iacet sub urbe frigus.

(iv.64)

Martial's few acres, e'en more blest
Than those famed gardens of the West,
Lie on Janiculum's long crest;
Above the slopes wide reaches hang recessed.
The level, gently swelling crown
Breathes air from purer heavens blown;
When mists the hollow valleys drown
'Tis radiant with a light that's all its own.
The clear stars almost seem to lie
On the wrought roof that's built so high;
The seven hills stand in majesty,
And Rome is summed in one wide sweep of
    eye.
Tusculan, Alban hills unfold,
Each nook which holds its store of cold.

A. E. Street

Such a picture is unsurpassed in any language.[38] Statius, with all his brilliance, never came near such perfect success; he lacks sincerity; he can juggle with words against any one, but he never learned their truest and noblest use.

There are many other themes beside landscape painting in which the *Silvae* of Statius challenge comparison with the epigrams of Martial. Both use the same servile flattery to the emperor, both celebrate the same patrons,[39] both console their noble friends for the loss of relatives, or favourite slaves; both write *propemptica*. Even in the most trivial of these poems, those addressed to the emperor, Statius is easily surpassed by his humbler rival. His inferiority lies largely in the fact that he is more ambitious. He wrote on a larger scale. When the infinitely trivial is a theme for verse, the epigrammatist has the advantage of the author of the more lengthy *Silvae*. Perfect neatness vanquishes dexterous elaboration. Moreover, if taste can be said to enter into such poems at all, Martial errs less grossly. Even Domitian—one might conjecture—may have felt that Statius' flattery was 'laid on with a trowel'. Martial may have used the same instrument, but had the art to conceal it.[40] There are even occasions where his flattery ceases to revolt the reader, and where we forget the object of the flattery. In a poem describing the suicide of a certain Festus he succeeds in combining the dignity of a funeral *laudatio* with the subtlest and most graceful flattery of the princeps:

indignas premeret pestis cum tabida fauces,
   inque suos voltus serperet atra lues,
siccis ipse genis flentes hortatus amicos
   decrevit Stygios Festus adire lacus.
nec tamen obscuro pia polluit ora veneno
   aut torsit lenta tristia fata fame,
sanctam Romana vitam sed morte peregit
   dimisitque animam nobiliore via.
hanc mortem fatis magni praeferre Catonis
   fama potest; huius Caesar amicus erat.

(i. 78)

When the dire quinsy choked his guiltless
   breath,
   And o'er his face the blackening venom
      stole,
Festus disdained to wait a lingering death,
   Cheered his sad friends and freed his
      dauntless soul.
No meagre famine's slowly-wasting force,
   Nor hemlock's gradual chillness he endured,
But like a Roman chose the nobler course,
   And by one blow his liberty secured.
His death was nobler far than Cato's end,
For Caesar to the last was Festus' friend.

Hodgson (slightly altered)

The unctuous dexterity of Statius never achieved such
a master-stroke.

So, too, in laments for the dead, the superior brevity
and simplicity of Martial bear the palm away. Both
poets bewailed the death of Glaucias, the child favourite
of Atedius Melior. Statius has already been quoted in
this connexion; Martial's poems on the subject,[41] though
not quite among his best, yet ring truer than the verse
of Statius. And Martial's epitaphs and epicedia at their
best have in their slight way an almost unique charm.
We must go to the best work of the Greek Anthology
to surpass the epitaph on Erotion (v. 34):

hanc tibi, Fronto pater, genetrix Flaccilla,
   puellam
   oscula commendo deliciasque meas,
parvola ne nigras horrescat Erotion umbras
   oraque Tartarei prodigiosa canis.
inpletura fuit sextae modo frigora brumae,
   vixisset totidem ni minus illa dies.
inter tam veteres ludat lasciva patronos
   et nomen blaeso garriat ore meum.
mollia non rigidus caespes tegat ossa nec illi,
   terra, gravis fueris: non fuit illa tibi.

Fronto, and you, Flaccilla, to you, my father
   and mother,
   Here I commend this child, once my delight
   and my pet,

So may the darkling shades and deep-mouthed
   baying of hellhound
   Touch not with horror of dread little Erotion
   dear.
Now was her sixth year ending, and melting
   the snows of the winter,
   Only a brief six days lacked to the tale of
   the years.
Young, amid dull old age, let her wanton and
   frolic and gambol,
   Babble of me that was, tenderly lisping my
   name.
Soft were her tiny bones, then soft be the sod
   that enshrouds her,
   Gentle thy touch, mother Earth, gently she
   rested on thee!

A. E. Street.

Another poem on a like theme shows a different and
more fantastic, but scarcely less pleasing vein (v. 37):

puella senibus dulcior mihi cycnis,
agna Galaesi mollior Phalantini,
concha Lucrini delicatior stagni,
cui nec lapillos praeferas Erythraeos
nec modo politum pecudis Indicae dentem
nivesque primas liliumque non tactum;
quae crine vicit Baetici gregis vellus
Rhenique nodos aureamque nitellam;
fragravit ore quod rosarium Paesti,
quod Atticarum prima mella cerarum,
quod sucinorum rapta de manu gleba;
cui conparatus indecens erat pavo,
inamabilis sciurus et frequens phoenix,
adhuc recenti tepet Erotion busto,
quam pessimorum lex amara fatorum
sexta peregit hieme, nec tamen tota,
nostros amores gaudiumque lususque.

Little maiden sweeter far to me
   Than the swans are with their vaunted
   snows,
Maid more tender than the lambkins be
   Where Galaesus by Phalantus flows;
Daintier than the daintiest shells that lie
   By the ripples of the Lucrine wave;
Choicer than new-polished ivory
   That the herds in Indian jungles gave;
Choicer than Erythrae's marbles white,
   Snows new-fallen, lilies yet unsoiled:
Softer were your tresses and more bright
   Than the locks by German maidens coiled:
Than the finest fleeces Baetis shows,
   Than the dormouse with her golden hue:
Lips more fragrant than the Paestan rose,
   Than the Attic bees' first honey-dew,
Or an amber ball, new-pressed and warm;
   Paled the peacock's sheen in your compare;

E'en the winsome squirrel lost his charm,
   And the Phoenix seemed no longer rare.
Scarce Erotion's ashes yet are cold;
   Greedily grim fate ordained to smite
E'er her sixth brief winter had grown old—
   Little love, my bliss, my heart's delight.

A. D. Innes

Through all the playful affectations of the lines we get the portrait of a fairy-like child, light-footed as the squirrel, golden-haired and fair as ivory or lilies.[42] Martial was a child-lover before he was a man of letters.

Beautiful as these little poems are, there is in Martial little trace of feeling for the sorrows of humanity in general. He can feel for his intimate friends, and his tears are ready to flow for his patron's sorrows. But the general impression given by his poetry is that of a certain hardness and lack of feeling, of a limited sympathy, and an unemotional temperament. It is a relief to come upon a poem such as that in which he describes a father's poignant anguish for the loss of his son (**ix. 74**):

effigiem tantum pueri pictura Camoni
   servat, et infantis parva figura manet.
florentes nulla signavit imagine voltus,
   dum timet ora pius muta videre pater.

Here as in happy infancy he smiled
Behold Camonus—painted as a child;
For on his face as seen in manhood's days
His sorrowing father would not dare to gaze.

W. S. B.

or to find a sudden outbreak of sympathy with the sorrows of the slave (**iii. 21**):

proscriptum famulus servavit fronte notata,
   non fuit haec domini vita sed invidia.[43]

When scarred with cruel brand, the slave
   Snatched from the murderer's hand
His proscript lord, not life he gave
   His tyrant, but the brand.

Professor Goldwin Smith

Of the *gravitas* or dignity of character specially associated with Rome he shows equally few traces. His outlook on life is not sufficiently serious, he shows little interest in Rome of the past, and has nothing of the retrospective note so prominent in Lucan, Juvenal, or Tacitus; he lives in and for the present. He writes, it is true, of the famous suicide of Arria and Caecina Paetus,[44] of the death of Portia the wife of Brutus,[46] of the bravery of Mucius Scaevola.[45] But in none of these poems does he give us of his best. They lack, if not

sincerity, at least enthusiasm; emotion is sacrificed to point. He is out of sympathy with Stoicism, and the suicide doctrinaire does not interest him. 'Live while you may' is his motto, 'and make the best of circumstances.' It is possible to live a reasonably virtuous life without going to the lengths of Thrasea:

quod magni Thraseae consummatique Catonis
   dogmata sic sequeris salvus ut esse velis,
pectore nec nudo strictos incurris in enses,
   quod fecisse velim te, Deciane, facis.
nolo virum facili redimit qui sanguine famam;
   hunc volo, laudari qui sine morte potest.

(i. 8)

That you, like Thrasea or Cato, great,
Pursue their maxims, but decline their fate;
Nor rashly point the dagger to your heart;
More to my wish you act a Roman's part.
I like not him who fame by death retrieves,
Give me the man who merits praise and lives.

Hay

The sentiment is full of common sense, but it is undeniably unheroic. Martial is not quixotic, and refuses to treat life more seriously than is necessary. Our complaint against him is that he scarcely takes it seriously enough. It would be unjust to demand a deep fund of earnestness from a professed epigrammatist dowered with a gift of humour and a turn for satire. But it is doing Martial no injustice to style him the laureate of triviality. For his satire is neither genial nor earnest. His kindly temper led him to avoid direct personalities, but his invective is directed against vice, not primarily because it is wicked, but rather because it is grotesque or not *comme il faut*. His humour, too, though often sparkling enough, is more often strained and most often filthy. Many of his epigrams were not worth writing, by whatever standard they be judged.[47] The point is hard to illustrate, since a large proportion of his inferior work is fatuously obscene. But the following may be taken at random from two books:

Eutrapelus tonsor dum circuit ora Luperci
   expingitque genas, altera barba subit.

(vii. 83)

Eutrapelus the barber works so slow,
   That while he shaves, the beard anew does
   grow.

Anon., 1695

invitas ad aprum, ponis mihi, Gallice, porcum.
   hybrida sum, si das, Gallice, verba mihi.

(viii. 22)

You invite me to partake of a wild boar, you set before me a home-grown pig. I'm half-boar, half-pig, if you can cheat me thus.

pars maxillarum tonsa est tibi, pars tibi rasa
  est,
  pars volsa est. unum quis putet esse caput?

(viii. 47)

Part of your jaws is shaven, part clipped, part has the hair pulled out. Who'd think you'd only one head?

tres habuit dentes, pariter quos expuit omnes,
  ad tumulum Picens dum sedet ipse suum;
collegitque sinu fragmenta novissima laxi
  oris et adgesta contumulavit humo.
ossa licet quondam defuncti non legat heres;
  hoc sibi iam Picens praestitit officium.

(viii. 57)

Picens had three teeth, which he spat out altogether while he was sitting at the spot he had chosen for his tomb. He gathered in his robe the last fragments of his loose jaw and interred them in a heap of earth. His heir need not gather his bones when he is dead, Picens has performed that office for himself.

summa Palatini poteras aequare Colossi,
  si fieres brevior, Claudia, sesquipede.

(viii. 60)

Had you been eighteen inches shorter, Claudia, you would have been as tall as the Colossus on the Palatine.

Without wishing to break a butterfly on the wheel, we may well quote against Martial the remark made in a different context to a worthless poet:

tanti non erat esse te disertum.

(xii. 43)

'Twas scarce worth while to be thus eloquent.

There is much also which, without being precisely pointless or silly, is too petty and mean to be tolerable to modern taste. Most noticeable in this respect are the epigrams in which Martial solicits the liberality of his patrons. The amazing relations existing at this period between patron and client had worked a painful revolution in the manners and tone of society, a revolution which meant scarcely less than the pauperization of the middle class. The old sacred and almost feudal tie uniting client and patron had long since disappeared,

and had been replaced by relations of a professional and commercial character. Wealth was concentrated in comparatively few hands, and with the decrease of the number of the patrons the throng of clients proportionately increased. The crowd of clients bustling to the early morning *salutatio* of the patronus, and struggling with one another for the *sportula* is familiar to us in the pages of Juvenal and receives fresh and equally vivid illustration from Martial. The worst results of these unnatural relations were a general loss of independence of character and a lamentable growth of bad manners and cynical snobbery. The patron, owing to the increasingly heavy demands upon his purse, naturally tended to become close-fisted and stingy, the needy client too often was grasping and discontented. The patron, if he asked his client to dine, would regale him with food and drink of a coarser and inferior quality to that with which he himself was served.[48] The client, on the other hand, could not be trusted to behave himself; he would steal the table fittings, make outrageous demands on his patron, and employ every act of servile and cringing flattery to improve his position.[49] The poor poet was in a sense doubly dependent. He would stand in the ordinary relation of *cliens* to a *patronus,* and would be dependent also for his livelihood on the generosity of his literary patrons. For, in spite of the comparative facilities for the publication and circulation of books, he could make little by the public sale of his works, and living at Rome was abnormally expensive. The worst feature of all was that such a life of servile dependence was not clearly felt to be degrading. It was disliked for its hardship, annoyance, and monotony, but the client too often seems to have regarded it as beneath his dignity to attempt to escape from it by industry and manly independence.

As a result of these conditions, we find the pages of Martial full of allusions to the miserable life of the client. His skill does not fail him, but the theme is ugly and the historical interest necessarily predominates over the literary, though the reader's patience is at times rewarded with shrewd observations on human nature, as, for instance, the bitter expression of the truth that 'To him that hath shall be given'—

semper pauper eris, si pauper es, Aemiliane;
  dantur opes nullis nunc nisi divitibus;

(v. 81)

Poor once and poor for ever, Nat, I fear,
None but the rich get place and pension here.

N. B. Halhead

or the even more incisive

pauper videri Cinna, vult: et est pauper

(viii. 19)

I have no money, Regulus, at home. Only one thing
is left to do—sell the gifts you gave me. Will you
buy?

But we soon weary of the continual reference to dinners and parasites, to the snobbery and indifference
of the rich, to the tricks of toadyism on the part of
needy client or legacy hunter. It is a mean world, and
the wit and raillery of Martial cannot make it palat-
able. Without a moral background, such as is provided by the indignation of Juvenal, the picture soon
palls, and the reader sickens. Most unpleasing of all
are the epigrams where Martial himself speaks as client
in a language of mingled impertinence and servility.
His flattery of the emperor we may pass by. It was no
doubt interested, but it was universal, and Martial's
flattery is more dexterous without being either more
or less offensive than that of his contemporaries. His
relations towards less exalted patrons cannot be thus
easily condoned. He feels no shame in begging, nor
in abusing those who will not give or whose gifts are
not sufficient for his needs. His purse is empty; he
must sell the gifts that Regulus has given him. Will
Regulus buy?

> aera domi non sunt, superest hoc, Regule,
>   solum
>   ut tua vendamus munera: numquid emis?

(vii. 16)

Stella has given him some tiles to roof his house; he
would like a cloak as well:

> cum pluvias madidumque Iovem perferre
>   negaret
>   et rudis hibernis villa nataret aquis,
> plurima, quae posset subitos effundere nimbos,
>   muneribus venit tegula missa tuis.
> horridus ecce sonat Boreae stridore December:
>   Stella, tegis villam, non tegis agricolam.

(vii. 36)[50]

When my crased house heaven's showers
   could not sustain,
But flooded with vast deluges of rain,
Thou shingles, Stella, seasonably didst send,
Which from the impetuous storms did me
   defend:
Now fierce loud-sounding Boreas rocks doth
   cleave,
Dost clothe the farm, and farmer naked leave?

Anon., 1695

This is not the way a gentleman thanks a friend, nor
can modern taste appreciate at its antique value abuse
such as—

> primum est ut praestes, si quid te, Cinna,
>   rogabo;
>   illud deinde sequens ut cito, Cinna, neges.
> diligo praestantem; non odi, Cinna, negantem:
>   sed tu nec praestas nec cito, Cinna, negas.

(vii. 43)

The kindest thing of all is to comply:
The next kind thing is quickly to deny.
I love performance nor denial hate:
Your 'Shall I, shall I?' is the cursed state.

The poet's poverty is no real excuse for this petulant
mendicancy.[51] He had refused to adopt a profession,[52]
though professional employment would assuredly have
left him time for writing, and no one would have complained if his output had been somewhat smaller. Instead, he chose a life which involved moving in society,
and was necessarily expensive. We can hardly attribute
his choice merely to the love of his art. If he must beg,
he might have done so with better taste and some show
of finer feeling. Macaulay's criticism is just: 'I can make
large allowance for the difference of manners; but it can
never have been *comme il faut* in any age or nation for
a man of note—an accomplished man—a man living
with the great—to be constantly asking for money,
clothes, and dainties, and to pursue with volleys of abuse
those who would give him nothing.'

In spite, however, of the obscenity, meanness, and exaggerated triviality of much of his work, there have been
few poets who could turn a prettier compliment, make
a neater jest, or enshrine the trivial in a more exquisite
setting. Take the beautifully finished poem to Flaccus in
the eighth book **(viii. 56)**, wherein Martial complains
that times have altered since Vergil's day. 'Now there
are no patrons and consequently no poets'—

> ergo ego Vergilius, si munera Maecenatis
>   des mihi? Vergilius non ero, Marsus ero.

Shall I then be a Vergil, if you give me such gifts
as Maecenas gave? No, I shall not be a Vergil, but
a Marsus.

Here, at least, Martial shows that he could complain of his
poverty with decency, and speak of himself and his work
with becoming modesty. Or take a poem of a different
type, an indirect plea for the recall of an exile **(viii. 32):**

> aera per tacitum delapsa sedentis in ipsos
>   fluxit Aratullae blanda columba sinus.
> luserat hoc casus, nisi inobservata maneret
>   permissaque sibi nollet abire fuga.
> si meliora piae fas est sperare sorori
>   et dominum mundi flectere vota valent,
> haec a Sardois tibi forsitan exulis oris,
>   fratre reversuro, nuntia venit avis.

A gentle dove glided down through the silent air and settled even in Aratulla's bosom as she was sitting. This might have seemed but the sport of chance had it not rested there, though undetained, and refused to part even when flight was free. If it is granted to the loving sister to hope for better things, and if prayers can move the lord of the world, this bird perchance has come to thee from Sardinia's shore of exile to announce the speedy return of thy brother.

Nothing could be more conventional, nothing more perfect in form, more full of music, more delicate in expression. The same felicity is shown in his epigrams on curiosities of art or nature, a fashionable and, it must be confessed, an easy theme.[53] Fish carved by Phidias' hand, a lizard cast by Mentor, a fly enclosed in amber, are all given immortality:

artis Phidiacae toreuma clarum
pisces aspicis: adde aquam, natabunt.

(iii. 35)

These fishes Phidias wrought: with life by
   him
They are endowed: add water and they swim.

Professor Goldwin Smith

inserta phialae Mentoris manu ducta
lacerta vivit et timetur argentum.

(iii. 41)

That lizard on the goblet makes thee start.
Fear not: it lives only by Mentor's art.

Professor Goldwin Smith

et latet et lucet Phaethontide condita gutta,
   ut videatur apis nectare clusa suo.
dignum tantorum pretium tulit illa laborum:
   credibile est ipsam sic voluisse mori.

(iv. 32)

Here shines a bee closed in an amber tomb,
As if interred in her own honey-comb.
A fit reward fate to her labours gave;
No other death would she have wished to
   have.

May

Always at home in describing the trifling amenities of life, he is at his best equally successful in dealing with its trifling follies. An acquaintance has given his cook the absurd name of Mistyllos in allusion to [a] Homeric phrase. . . . Martial's comment is inimitable:

si tibi Mistyllos cocus, Aemiliane, vocatur,
   dicatur quare non Taratalla mihi?

(i. 50)

He complains of the wine given him at a dinner-party with a finished whimsicality:

potavi modo consulare vinum.
quaeris quam vetus atque liberale?
Prisco consule conditum: sed ipse
qui ponebat erat, Severe, consul.

(vii. 79)

I have just drunk some consular wine. How old, you ask, and how generous? It was bottled in Priscus' consulship: and he who set it before me was the consul himself.

Polycharmus has returned Caietanus his IOU's. 'Little good will that do you, and Caietanus will not even be grateful':

quod Caietano reddis, Polycharme, tabellas,
   milia te centum num tribuisse putas?
'debuit haec' inquis. tibi habe, Polycharme,
   tabellas
   et Caietano milia crede duo.

(viii. 37)

In giving back Caietanus his IOU's, Polycharmus, do you think you are giving him 100,000 sesterces? 'He owed me that sum,' you say. Keep the IOU's and lend him two thousand more!

Chloe, the murderess of her seven husbands, erects monuments to their memory, and inscribes *fecit Chloe* on the tombstones:

inscripsit tumulis septem scelerata virorum
   'se fecisse' Chloe. quid pote simplicius?

(ix. 15)

On her seven husbands' tombs she doth impress
'This Chloe did.' What more can she confess?

Wright

Vacerra admires the old poets only. What shall Martial do?

miraris veteres, Vacerra, solos
nec laudas nisi mortuos poetas.
ignoscas petimus, Vacerra: tanti
non est, ut placeam tibi, perire.

(viii. 69)

Vacerra lauds no living poet's lays,
But for departed genius keeps his praise.
I, alas, live, nor deem it worth my while
To die that I may win Vacerra's smile.

　　　　　　　　Professor Goldwin Smith

All this is very slight, *merae nugae;* but even if the humour be not of the first water, it will compare well with the humour of epigrams of any age. Martial knows he is not a great poet.[54] He knows, too, that his work is uneven:

iactat inaequalem Matho me fecisse libellum:
　si verum est, laudat carmina nostra Matho.
aequales scribit libros Calvinus et Vmber:
　aequalis liber est, Cretice, qui malus est.

　　　　　　　　　　　(vii. 90)

Matho makes game of my unequal verse;
If it's unequal it might well be worse.
Calvinus, Umber, write on one dead level,
The book that's got no up and down's the
　　devil!

If there are thirty good epigrams in a book, he is satisfied (vii. 81). His defence hardly answers the question, 'Why publish so many?' but should at least mollify our judgement. Few poets read better in selections than Martial, and of few poets does selection give so inadequate an idea. For few poets of his undoubted genius have left such a large bulk of work which, in spite of its formal perfection, is morally repulsive or, from the purely literary standpoint, uninteresting. But he is an important figure in the history of literature, for he is the father of the modern epigram. Alone of Silver Latin poets is he a perfect stylist. He has the gift of *felicitas* to the full, but it is not *curiosa*. Inferior to Horace in all other points, he has greater spontaneity. And he is free from the faults of his age. He is no *virtuoso,* eaten up with self-conscious vanity; he attempts no impossible feats of language; he is clear, and uses his mythological and geographical knowledge neatly and picturesquely; but he makes no display of obscure learning. 'I would please schoolmasters,' he says, 'but not *qua* schoolmasters' **(x. 21.** 5). So, too, he complains of his own education:

at me litterulas stulti docuere parentes:
　quid cum grammaticis rhetoribusque mihi?

　　　　　　　　　　　(ix. 73. 7)

My learning only proves my father fool!
Why would he send me to a grammar school?

　　　　　　　　　　　　　　Hay

As a result, perhaps, of this lack of sympathy with the education of his day, we find that, while he knows and admires the great poets of the past, and can flatter the rich poetasters of the present, his bent is curiously unliterary. He gives us practically no literary criticism. It is with the surface qualities of life that he is concerned, with its pleasures and its follies, guilty or innocent. He has a marvellously quick and clear power of observation, and of vivid presentation. He is in this sense above all others the poet of his age. He either does not see or chooses to ignore many of the best and most interesting features of his time, but the picture which he presents, for all its incompleteness, is wider and more varied than any other. We both hate him and read him for the sake of the world he depicts. 'Ugliness is always bad art, and Martial often failed as a poet from his choice of subject.'[55] There are comparatively few of his poems which we read for their own sake. Remarkable as these few poems are, the main attraction of Martial is to be found not in his wit or finish, so much as in the vividness with which he has portrayed the life of the brilliant yet corrupt society in which his lot was cast. It lives before us in all its splendour and in all its squalor. The court, with its atmosphere of grovelling flattery, its gross vices veiled and tricked out in the garb of respectability; the wealthy official class, with their villas, their favourites, their circle of dependants, men of culture, wit, and urbanity, through all which runs, strangely intermingled, a vein of extreme coarseness, vulgarity, and meanness; the lounger and the reciter, the diner-out and the legacy-hunter; the clients struggling to win their patrons' favour and to rise in the social scale, enduring the hardships and discomfort of a sordid life unillumined by lofty ideals or strength of will, a life that under cold northern skies would have been intolerable; the freedman and the slave, with all the riff-raff that support a parasitic existence on the vices of the upper classes; the noise and bustle of Rome, its sleepless nights, its cheerless tenements, its noisy streets, loud with the sound of traffic or of revelry; the shows in the theatre, the races in the circus, the interchange of presents at the Saturnalia; the pleasant life in the country villa, the simplicity of rural Italy, the sights and sounds of the park and the farm-yard; and dimly seen beyond all, the provinces, a great ocean which absorbs from time to time the rulers of Rome and the leaders of society, and from which come faint and confused echoes of frontier wars; all are there. It is a great pageant lacking order and coherence, a scene that shifts continually, but never lacks brilliance of detail and sharply defined presentment. Martial was the child of the age; it gave him his strength and his weakness. If we hate him or despise him, it is because he is the faithful representative of the life of his times; his gifts we cannot question. He practised a form of poetry that at its best is not exalted, and must, even more than other branches of art, be conditioned by social circumstance. Within its limited sphere Martial stands, not faultless, but yet supreme.

Notes

[1] On the modern Cerro de Bambola near the Moorish town of El Calatayud.

[2] Cp. ix. 52, x. 24, xii. 60.

[3] Cp. v. 34.

[4] ix. 73. 7.

[5] In x. 103. 7, written in 98 A.D., he tells us that it is thirty-four years since he left Spain.

[6] iv. 40, xii. 36.

[7] He is found rendering poetic homage to Polla, the wife of Lucan, as late as 96 A.D., x. 64, vii. 21-3. For his reverence for the memory of Lucan, cp. i. 61. 7; vii. 21, 22; xiv. 194.

[8] Cp. his regrets for the ease of his earlier clienthood and the generosity of the Senecas, xii. 36.

[9] ii. 30; cp. l. 5:

> is mihi 'dives eris, si causas egeris' inquit.
> quod peto da, Gai: non peto consilium.

[10] Vide his epigrams *passim*.

[11] xiii. 42, xiii. 119. Perhaps the gift of Seneca, cp. Friedländer on Mart. i. 105.

[12] ix. 18, ix. 97. 7, x. 58. 9.

[13] Such is the most plausible interpretation of iii. 95. 5, ix. 97. 5:

> tribuit quod Caesar uterque
> ius mihi natorum (uterque, i.e. Titus and
> Domitian).

[14] iii. 95, v. 13, ix. 49, xii. 26.

[15] iii. 95. 11, vi. 10. 1.

[16] xiii. 4 gives Domitian his title of Germanicus, assumed after war with Chatti in 84; xiv. 34 alludes to peace; no allusion to subsequent wars.

[17] I, II. Perhaps published together. This would account for length of preface. II. Largely composed of poems referring to reigns of Vespasian and Titus. Reference to Domitian's censorship shows that I was not published before 85. There is no hint of outbreak of Dacian War, which raged in 86.

III. Since bk. IV contains allusion to outbreak of revolt of Antonius Saturninus towards end of 88 (11) and is published at Rome, whereas III was published at *Cornelii forum* (1), III probably appeared in 87 or 88.

IV. Contains reference to birthday of Domitian, Oct. 24 (1. 7), and seems then to allude to *ludi saeculares* (Sept. 88). Reference to snowfall at Rome (2 and 13) suggests winter. Perhaps therefore published in *Saturnalia* of 88.

V. Domitian has returned to Italy (1) from Dacian War, but there is no reference to his triumph (Oct. 1, 89 A.D.). Book therefore probably published in early autumn of 89.

VI. Domitian has held his triumph (4. 2 and 10. 7). Julia (13) is dead (end of 89). Book probably published in 90, perhaps in summer. Friedländer sees allusion to Agon Capitolinus (Summer, 90) in vi. 77.

VII. 5-8 refer to Domitian's return from Sarmatic War. He has not yet arrived. These epigrams are among last in book. He returned in January 93. His return was announced as imminent in Dec. 92.

VIII. 21 describes Domitian's arrival; 26, 30, and others deal with festivities in this connexion. 65 speaks of temple of Fortuna Redux and triumphal arch built in Domitian's honour. They are mentioned as if completed. 66 speaks of consulate of Silius Italicus' son beginning Sept. 1, 93.

IX. 84 is addressed to Appius Norbanus Maximus, who has been six years absent from Rome. He went to Upper Germany to crush Antonius Saturninus in 88. 35 refers to Agon Capitolinus in summer of 94.

X. Two editions published. We possess later and larger. Cp. x. 2. 70. 1 suggests a year's interval between IX and X. X, ed. 1 was therefore perhaps published in Dec. 95. X, ed. 2 has references to accession of Trajan, Jan. 25, 98 A.D. (6, 7 and 34). Martial's departure for Spain is imminent.

XI. 1 is addressed to Parthenius, executed in middle of 97 A.D. xii. 5 refers to a selection made from X and XI, perhaps from presentation to Nerva; cp. xii. 11.

XII. In preface Martial apologizes for three years' silence (l. 9) from publication of X, ed. 2. xii. 3. 10 refers to Stella's consulship, Oct. 101 or 102. Three years' interval points to 101. It was published late in the year; cp. 1 and 62. Some epigrams in this book were written at Rome. But M. says that it was written *paucissimis diebus*. This must refer only to Spanish epigrams, or the book must have been enlarged after M.'s death.

For the whole question see Friedländer Introd., pp. 50 sqq.

[18] iii. 1 and 4.

[19] Cp. xi. 3.

[20] xii. 21, xii. 31. There is no reason to suppose with some critics that she was his wife.

[21] xii. praef. 'civitatis aures quibus adsueveram quaero.'

[22] Ib. 'accedit his municipalium robigo dentium.'

[23] See p. 271. It is hard to avoid the conclusion that this silence was due to dislike or jealousy.

[24] Mackail, *Greek Anthol.*, Introd., p. 5.

[25] Domitius Marsus was famous for his epigrams, as also Calvus, Gactulicus, Pedo, and others.

[26] See p. 36.

[27] See p. 134.

[28] The best of his erotic poems is the pretty vi. 34, but it is far from original; cp. the last couplet:

> nolo quot (sc. basia) arguto dedit exorata
> Catullo
> Lesbia: pauca cupit qui numerare potest.

[29] Cp. Cat. 5 and 7; Mart. vi. 34; Cat. 2 and 3; Mart. i. 7 and 109 (it is noteworthy that this last poem has itself been exquisitely imitated by du Bellay in his poem on his little dog Peloton).

[30] Cp. Ov. *Tr.* ii. 166; Mart. vi. 3. 4; Ov. *F.* iii. 192; Mart. vi. 16. 2; Ov. *A.* i. 1. 20; Mart. vi. 16. 4; Ov. *Tr.* i. 5. 1, iv. 13. 1; Mart. i. 15. 1. His imitations of other poets are not nearly so marked. There are a good many trifling echoes of Vergil, but little wholesale borrowing. A very large proportion of the parallel passages cited by Friedländer are unjust to Martial. No poet could be original judged by such a test.

[31] There is little of any importance to be said about Martial's metre. The metres most often employed are elegiac, hendecasyllabic, and the seazon. In the elegiac he is, on the whole, Ovidian, though he is naturally freer, especially in the matter of endings both of hexameter and pentameter. He makes his points as well, but is less sustainedly pointed. His verse, moreover, has greater variety and less formal symmetry than that of Ovid. On the other hand his effects are less sparkling, owing to his more sparing use of rhetoric. In the hendecasyllable he is smoother and more polished. It invariably opens with a spondee.

[32] Cp. vii. 72. 12, x. 3.

[33] Cp. vii. 12. 9, iii. 99. 3.

[34] Catull. xvi. 5; Ov. *Tr.* ii. 354; Apul. *Apol.* 11; Auson. 28, *cento nup.;* Plin. *Ep.* vii. 8.

[35] We might also quote the beautiful

> extra fortunam est quidquid donatur amicis:
> quas dederis solas semper habebis opes.

> (v. 42)

> What thou hast given to friends, and that alone,
> Defies misfortune, and is still thine own.

> Professor Goldwin Smith

But the needy poet may have had some *arrière-pensée*. We do not know to whom the poem is addressed.

[36] Cp. the description of the villa of Faustinus, iii. 58.

[37] Their only rival is the famous Sirmio poem of Catullus.

[38] Even Tennyson's remarkable poem addressed to F. D. Maurice fails to reach greater perfection.

[39] e. g. Arruntius Stella and Atedius Melior. Cp. p. 205.

[40] Cp. the poems on the subject of Earinus, Mart, ix, 11, 12, 13, and esp. 16; Stat. *Silv.* iii. 4.

[41] Mart. vi. 28 and 29.

[42] The remaining lines of the poem are tasteless and unworthy of the portion quoted, and raise a doubt as to the poet's sincerity in the particular case. But this does not affect his *general* sympathy for childhood.

[43] i. 101 provides an instance of Martial's sympathy for his own slaves, Cp. l. 5:—

> ne tamen ad Stygias famulus descenderet
> umbras,
> ureret implicitum cum scelerate lues,
> cavimus et domini ius omne remisimus aegro;
> munere dignus erat convaluisse meo.
> sensit deficiens mea praemia meque patronum
> dixit ad infernas liber iturus aquas.

[44] i. 13.

[45] i. 42.

[46] i. 21. He is perhaps at his best on the death of Otho (vi. 32):

cum dubitaret adhuc belli civilis Enyo
    forsitan et posset vincere mollis Otho,
damnavit multo staturum sanguine Martem
    et fodit certa pectora tota manu.
sit Cato, dum vivit, sane vel Caesare maior:
    dum moritur, numquid maior Othone fuit?

When doubtful was the chance of civil war,
And victory for Otho might declare;
That no more Roman blood for him might
    flow,
He gave his breast the great decisive blow.
Caesar's superior you may Cato call:
Was he so great as Otho in his fall?

                             Hay

[47] It is to be noted that even in the most worthless of his epigrams he never loses his sense of style. If childish epigrams are to be given to the world, they cannot be better written.

[48] Cp. Juv. 5; Mart. iii. 60, vi. 11, x. 49; Plin. *Ep.* ii. 6.

[49] v. 18. 6.

[50] This is doubly offensive if addressed to the poor Cinna of viii. 19. Cp. the similar vii. 53, or the yet more offensive viii. 33 and v. 36.

[51] More excusable are poems such as x. 57, where he attacks one Gaius, an old friend (cp. ii. 30), for failing to fulfil his promise, or the exceedingly pointed poem (iv. 40) where he reproaches Postumus, an old friend, for forgetting him. Cp. also v. 52.

[52] See p. 252.

[53] Cp. the elaborate and long-winded poem of Statius on a statuette of Hercules (*Silv.* iv. 6) with Martial on the same subject, ix. 43 and 44..

[54] Cp. viii. 3 and 56.

[55] Bridge and Lake, Introd., *Select Epigrams of Martial.*

Kirby Flower Smith (essay date 1918)

SOURCE: "Martial, the Epigrammatist" in *Martial, the Epigrammatist and Other Essays,* The John Hopkins Press, 1918, pp. 13-36.

[*In the following excerpt, Smith offers a vigorous response to Martial's detractors, particularly those who have charged him with obsequiousness toward patrons. Smith stresses the tradition of the patron-client rela-* *tionship—before as well as after Martial—and praises the poet's keen powers of observation, his candor, and his sense of proportion.*]

. . . I know of no ancient writer whose personal character has been more bitterly assailed by modern critics of a certain class. I know of few who have deserved it so little. We may say, at once, that all Martial's faults are on the surface. Otherwise, many of his critics never would have discerned them at all. The just and sympathetic appreciation of an ancient author demands a much larger background of knowledge and experience than seems to be generally supposed. It is, of course, obvious that, first of all, before attempting to criticize an author one ought to read his entire works with care and understanding. In the case of a man like Martial, one must also be thoroughly acquainted with all of the conditions of his life and times; one must know all about the history of the antique epigram as a department, one must be able to realize the peculiarities of the Latin temperament as such, and make due allowance for them.

For example, most prominent and most widely circulated—indeed, with many persons, the only association with the name of Martial—is the charge that both in subject and in language his epigrams are offensive to modern taste. To a certain extent this is true. We should add, however, that Martial himself cannot be held responsible for it. The conventional tradition of the epigram demanded that a certain portion of one's work should be of this character. That in Martial's case the peculiarity is more the result of this convention than of individual taste, is shown by the fact that it does not run through his entire text. On the contrary, it is confined to certain epigrams, and those epigrams do not represent his best and most characteristic work. Lastly, the proportion of these objectionable epigrams is by no means as large as the majority of people appear to suppose. The text of Martial contains 1555 epigrams. The Delphin edition of 1660 excluded 150 of this number. The standards of another age and a different nationality would probably exclude about 50 more. All told, hardly a seventh of the total. This leaves more than 1200 little poems into which anyone may dip without hesitation, and on this residuum Martial can easily support his claim to be called one of the wittiest, one of the most amusing, and at the same time one of the most instructive, writers in any period of the world's history.

Martial's flattery of Domitian is a charge easily disposed of. Flattery of the reigning emperor has been the rule since Augustus. By this time it was almost as conventional as our titles of nobility. What do these mean when we interpret them literally? Moreover, Martial is outdone not only by his predecessors but, which is more to the point, by his graver contemporaries, Statius and Quintilian. Still more to his credit is the fact that he did not revile the memory of Domitian after his death. Finally, we must remember that Martial was a Spaniard and a provincial. Why should he care about Domitian's vices or virtues, or about his moral fitness or unfitness to be a Roman emperor?

The third and, on the face of it, the most serious charge against Martial is his relation to his patrons. To state the matter baldly as well as briefly, it is Martial's idea that his patrons owe him a living, and if he has reason to think that they are forgetting it, he does not hesitate to refresh their memories. For instance, he frequently reminds his readers in general, and his patrons in particular, that a poet is a person who needs money. Again, he makes pointed reference to the depleted condition of his wardrobe. Once, he reminds Stella that unless he is moved to send him some new tiles, the farmhouse at Nomentum will have to go on leaking as before.

Now all this is unpleasant to us, but we must not forget that, as a matter of fact, Martial's patrons actually did owe him a living. Such were the habits and standards of his time, the accepted and unavoidable conditions of his life. That life was the life of a brilliant provincial who came to the city without an independent fortune and chose literature as his profession. Nowadays, the most of us are familiar with the idea that an author is entitled to a share in the success of his book, that he draws his income for literary work from that source. But this idea was not generally entertained until the nineteenth century; and our recent experience with the law of international copyright shows that the idea is still rudimentary in many minds. In antiquity, therefore, unless an author possessed independent means, his only alternative was patronage; and until 1800 patronage was the general rule of literature.

The relation of client to patron was an ancient and honorable institution in Roman society. There was nothing to criticize in the relation of Vergil and Horace to Mœcenas and Augustus. And at the time of his death Vergil possessed not less than half a million in our money. But whatever Vergil was worth, the bald fact remains that practically all of it was acquired by gift. It was only through the generosity of a patron that a poor author could secure the leisure for literary composition. In return, he undertook to immortalize his patron in his works. He also attended him in public from time to time, he went to his regular morning receptions, and if his patron invited him to dinner, he made himself agreeable. In short, he made every return in his power for the favors he had received or hoped to receive.

It will easily be seen that this relation—like the fee to the waiter—was peculiarly liable to abuse. The pages of Martial, Pliny, and Juvenal show how much it had deteriorated by the time of Domitian. Both sides were to blame. Prices were outrageous, and wealth the standard of life. The rich were largely the descendants of dishonest nobodies, and with habits, tastes, and views to match; the poor had lost their pride, their independence, their spur of ambition. Each class despised the other, and each class was justified in it. Both Juvenal and Martial tell us that men of birth and education, men of high official position, even men with fortunes of their own, were not ashamed to take the *sportula* (originally the basket of food for the day, now the dole of money) given to those who had made the regular morning call. One is reminded of the retainers of a noble house in the Middle Ages, or of the poor courtiers under the old régime in France and England.

Not pleasant, this custom; but it existed, and Martial in paying court to a patron was only following the universal rule of his time. He had the further justification of necessity, and it is also clear that he made all the return for it in his power. Indeed, it was characteristic of the man, and, all things considered, rather to his credit, that he insisted upon the business aspect of it, and refused to pretend that it was anything else. So far, therefore, from severely criticizing Martial's relation to his patrons, it seems to me that in a situation which he could not avoid, and for which he was not responsible, he showed himself a better man than most of his contemporaries would have done under the same conditions.

It was a hard, uncertain, Bohemian sort of life in many respects. But to a certain degree Martial was himself a genuine Bohemian. The type is excessively rare in the annals of Roman literature. The one other striking example whom I now recall is that brilliant old reprobate Furius Bibaculus. Martial's combination of improvidence and gaiety is distinctly Bohemian. He also seems to have had the peculiarly attractive personality by which that temperament is sometimes accompanied. At any rate, his epigrams show not only that he knew everybody in Rome who was worth knowing, but that few men as great as he have at the same time been so universally liked by their contemporaries. Some of Martial's best epigrams are to his friends. In one of his last poems (**xii, 34**)—it is addressed to Julius Martialis, whom he had known and loved for four-and-thirty years—the poet closes by saying: "If you would avoid many griefs, and escape many a heartache, then make of no one too dear a friend You will have less joy, but you will also have less sorrow." This can only be the observation of a man who has had real friends, and has really loved them.

Another attractive side of his nature was his evident devotion to little children. I content myself with a single illustration. This is his epitaph for Erotion, a little girl belonging to his household who died at the age of six. Martial, who was then a man of nearly fifty, was deeply affected by the loss of his little favorite. The poem, which is one of three devoted to her memory, recommends the child to the care of his own parents, who had long been dead—a touchingly naïve conception quite in harmony with antique methods of thought, but inspired with a simple and homely tenderness for which there are few parallels in the annals of literature **(v, 34)**;

> Dear father and dear mother: Let me crave
> Your loving kindness there beyond the grave
> For my Erotion, the pretty maid
> Who bears these lines. Don't let her be afraid!
> She's such a little lassie—only six—
> To toddle down that pathway to the Styx
> All by herself! Black shadows haunt those
>   steeps,
> And Cerberus the Dread who never sleeps.
> May she be comforted, and may she play
> About you merry as the livelong day,
> And in her childish prattle often tell
> Of that old master whom she loved so well.
> Oh earth, bear lightly on her! 'Tis her due;
> The little girl so lightly bore on you.

Lines like these help us to understand why under continual provocation he could still be patient with a fussy, dictatorial, old slave who was utterly unable to realize that the boy he had spanked forty or fifty years before had now arrived at years of discretion.

The only contemporary reference to Martial which has happened to survive is found in the passage of Pliny to which I have already alluded. He describes the poet whom he knew as "acutus, ingeniosus, acer"—clear-sighted, clever, shrewd. And, truly, as a keen observer of men and things, Martial has rarely been equalled. The world of Rome was an open book before him. He read the text, fathomed its import, and wrote his commentary upon it in brilliant and telling phrases, and in a literary form of which he was undoubtedly the master.

But, after all, the mainspring of Martial's character and career, the real secret of his abiding greatness as an epigrammatist, is found as soon as we learn that he possessed the quality which Pliny calls *candor. Candor* means frankness, genuineness, sincerity. It was one of the highest tributes to character that a Roman could pay.

Here we have, according to Pliny's showing, a man who was witty, yet kindly, who was clear-sighted, yet tolerant, who was shrewd, yet sincere. This is the character of one who is never blind to the true proportion of things. And, as a matter of fact, a sense of proportion, a conception of the realities as applied to life, conduct, thought, art, literature, style, everything, is the leading trait of Martial's character, the universal solvent of his career and genius. All is expressed in . . . "avoid extremes," that phrase so characteristic of

antiquity, the summary of its wisdom and experience, its most valuable contribution to the conduct of life.

So it was that in spite of his surroundings and associations Martial remained simple, genuine, and unaffected to the end. In an age of unutterable impurity he had no vices. In an age of cant, pedantry, affectation, and shams of every sort and description, he was still true to himself. In an age as notable for exaggeration as is our own, Martial knows that strength does not lie in superlatives. He tells us again and again in his own characteristic fashion that the secret of happiness has not been discovered by the voluptuary, nor the secret of virtue by the ascetic. The present is quite good enough for him; to live it heartily and naturally as it comes, to find out what he is best fitted to do, and then to do it— this is the sum of his philosophy. It is true enough that most friendship is mere feigning. But there are real friends. Let us, therefore, bind them to us with bonds of steel. It is true that life is hard and bitter. But we have to live it. Let us, therefore, find the sunshine while we can. In **v, 58,** he says (Cowley's translation):

> To-morrow you will live, you always cry.
> In what far country does this 'morrow' lie,
> That 'tis so mighty long ere it arrive?
> Beyond the Indies does this 'morrow' live?
>
> 'Tis so far-fetched, this 'morrow,' that I fear,
> 'Twill be both very old and very dear.
> "To-morrow I will live," the fool does say;
> To-day itself's too late—the wise lived
>   yesterday.

The sentiment is as characteristic of antiquity as it is of Martial. Not very elevated, perhaps, but Martial is not a reformer. Like most men of the world he is generally indifferent on the subject of other people's vices. He is not an enthusiast, for he has no illusions. Nor is he a man of lofty ideals. But he is natural and sensible as he is witty and brilliant. Therefore he was in harmony with his own days, and would have been equally in harmony with ours. For if Martial seems so intensely modern, it is not because he has advanced beyond his own time. It is because he is universal. Martial is a cosmopolitan poet and, with the single exception of Menander, the most pronounced example of the type in all classical antiquity.

The prose preface to Martial's first book indicates very clearly some of his views with regard to the sphere and character of the epigram. It also illustrates the man. "I trust," he says, "that the attitude I have maintained in these books of mine is such that no reasonable man can complain of them. They never make their fun at the expense of real people, even of the humblest station—a thing quite absent from the old epigrammatists. Those men not only attacked and vilified people by their real names, but also attacked people of consequence. I do not care to buy fame at such a price. My witticisms contain no innuendoes. I want no malicious commentators who will undertake to rewrite my epigrams for me. It is unfair to be subtle in another man's book. For my free plainness of speech, that is, for the language of the epigram, I should apologize if the example were mine. But so Catullus writes, so Marsus, so Pedo, so Gœtulicus—so everyone who is read through. Still, if there is anyone so painfully Puritanical that in his eyes it is unholy to speak plain Latin in a book, he would better content himself with the preface or, better still, with the title. Epigrams are written for those who attend Flora's entertainments. Cato should not come into my theatre. But if he does come in, let him take his seat and look on with the rest."

Perhaps I ought to add, by way of explanation, that the theatrical performances regularly given at the spring festival of the Floralia were proverbial for their gaiety and license. Once upon a time, the younger Cato, a proverb of Stoic virtue and gravity, went into the theatre during this festival, but finding that his presence put a damper on the occasion, he walked out again. The Stoics of the Empire were never weary of repeating this anecdote of their patron saint. We might expect a man of Martial's temperament to detect the essential ostentation of such a performance. Witness the closing words of his preface:

> Pray tell me, when you knew 'twas Flora's holiday,
>   With all the license, all the sport expected then,
> Why, Cato, came you stalking in to see the play?
>   Or was it that you might go stalking out again?

So, too, referring to the theatrical way in which the contemporary Stoics preached and practised their favorite doctrine of suicide, Martial says (**i, 8, 5-6**): "I care nothing for a man who buys fame with his blood—'tis no task to let blood. Give me the man who can deserve praise without dying for it." That the ostentatiousness of the proceeding was the cause of his criticism, is shown by the fact that he yields to none in his admiration of real heroism where real heroism is needed. Ostentation in vice is quite as repellent to him. "Tucca," he says, "is not satisfied to be a glutton, he must have the reputation of it."

All this goes back to his doctrine of *Nil nimis*—temperance in the real meaning of the word. Neither virtue nor happiness is compatible with excess of any sort. Writing to his friend Julius Martialis, he says (**x, 47**, translated by Fanshawe):

> The things that make a life to please,
> Sweetest Martial, they are these:

> Estate inherited, not got;
> A thankful field, hearth always hot;
> City seldom, lawsuits never;
> Equal friends, agreeing ever;
> Health of body, peace of mind;
> Sleeps that till the morning bind;
> Wise simplicity, plain fare;
> Not drunken nights, yet loos'd from care;
> A sober, not a sullen spouse;
> Clean strength, not such as his that plows;
> Wish only what thou art, to be;
> Death neither wish, nor fear to see.

It is extremely difficult to reproduce the exquisite poise and simplicity of Martial's style and thought. No one knew better than he how hard it was to write good epigrams. "Some of your tetrastichs," he says to one Sabellus (**vii, 85**), "are not so bad, a few of your distichs are well done. I congratulate you—but I am not overpowered. To write one good epigram is easy, to write a bookful is another matter." To those who insisted that no epigram should exceed the length of a distich, his characteristic reply was (**viii, 29**). "If a man confines himself to distichs, his object, I suppose, is to please by brevity. But, pray tell me, what does their brevity amount to, when there is a whole bookful of them?"

Everyone knows his famous judgment of his own work (**i, 16**):

> Sunt bona, sunt quœdam mediocria, sunt mala plura
>   Quœ legis hic: aliter non fit, Avite, liber.

> Good, fair, and bad
> May here be had.
>   That's no surprise!
> 'Twere vain to look
> For any book
>   That's otherwise.

So good a criticism of books in general, and of books of epigrams in particular, that one might almost be excused for overlooking the fact that Martial himself is really an exception to his own rule. At any rate, no one has written so many epigrams, and at the same time has contrived to produce so many good epigrams. It is clear that he was one of those rarest of men who have resolution enough to throw their bad work into the waste-basket.

So far as they illustrate the life of contemporary Rome, many of Martial's themes are also to be found in the letters of that literary Bostonian of antiquity, the Younger Pliny. They are, likewise, the same which Juvenal worked into his satires twenty years after—when Domitian was safely dead. Each of these three has pictured the situation from his own point of view. It was Martial who really saw it. So far as that situation applies to our own life, much has always been familiar, some has grown familiar during the last decade, and the remainder will probably come home to us with the advancing years of the twentieth century.

A marked feature of this age was the feverish production of literature. One may say without exaggeration that it was really the fashion to write books. In fact, the situation politically and socially was such that for an ambitious Roman of birth and education, literature was one of the few avenues to fame which was still open. No wonder Juvenal and Martial believed that neither literature nor learning was a paying investment. "There are quite too many persons of quality in the business," says Martial in one place, "and who ever knew an author who was interested in other people's books?" "Of course **(x, 9)**, one may become famous through one's books. I myself, for example, am well known all over the Empire—almost as well known, I may say, as Andrœmon, the race-horse!"

But although literature may bring fame, it never brings a large income. "I understand, Lupus," he says in another epigram **(v, 56)**, "that you are debating on the best training for your son. My advice is, avoid all professors of literature and oratory. The boy should have nothing to do with the works of Vergil or Cicero. Let him leave old Professor Tutilius to his own glory. If he makes verses, disown the poet. If he wants to follow an occupation that will pay, let him learn the guitar or the flute. If he proves to be dull, make an auctioneer of him or an architect."

The business of an auctioneer was despised, but it was proverbially lucrative. Hence the point of the following epigram **(vi, 8)**:

> Two prætors, seven advocates,
> Four tribunes and ten laureates—
> Such was the formidable band
> Of suitors for a maiden's hand.
> All twenty-three approached her sire,
> All twenty-three breathed their desire.
> Father dismissed that deputation
> Without a moment's hesitation,
> And straight bestowed his daughter dear
> On Eulogus, the auctioneer.

Of course, we hear a great deal about the deadly *recitatio* and all its attendant horrors, such as the amateur poet, the Admirable Crichton in literature, etc., etc. The ostensible and legitimate object of the *recitatio* was to allow an author to read his work to his friends and get their criticisms of it. But this unfortunate invention of Vergil's friend Asinius Pollio had become literally pestiferous by the time of Domitian, and more especially for its inordinate length and intolerable frequency. Martial speaks in all seriousness of the entire

days which politeness or policy often obliged him to waste on these things. Pliny attended them religiously. But Pliny performed all the functions of his life religiously. Moreover, Pliny was himself an author. He was, therefore, as Horace said, an 'auditor et ultor'— in a position to get even now and then by giving a reading himself.

Martial is only too well acquainted with all the types. Here is Maximus **(iii, 18)** who begins his reading by saying that he has a bad cold. "Why then do you recite?" inquires Martial solicitously.

"Gallicus," he says in another epigram **(viii, 76)**, "you always say, 'tell me the exact truth about my poetry and my oratory. There is nothing which I would rather hear.' Well, Gallicus, listen then to the great truth of all. It is this: Gallicus, you do not like to hear the truth."

"Mamercus," he says **(ii, 88)**, "you wish to be considered a poet, and yet you never recite. Be anything you like, Mamercus, provided you don't recite!"

Of course, the reader often gave a dinner to his hearers. But in Martial's opinion such dinners are quite too dear at the price. In **iii, 45,** he observes: "They say the Sun god turned backward that he might flee from the dinner of Thyestes. I don't know whether that is true or not. But I do know, Ligurinus, that I flee from yours. I don't deny that your dinners are sumptuous, and that the food you furnish is superb. But absolutely nothing pleases me so long as you recite. You need not set turbot and mullet before me; I don't care for mushrooms, I have no desire for oysters. Just be still."

The most important and characteristic feature of Roman social life was the dinner party. Martial accepted the invitations of his patrons as a matter of course; and it is inconceivable that a man of such unrivalled wit and social qualities could have failed to be in constant demand elsewhere. Between the two, he probably saw as much, if not more, of this side of life than any other man of his time. No wonder he did not live to be seventy-five, in spite of his temperate habits!

Nothing has been added to Roman experience in the methods of giving a dinner. Singing, for example, music, vaudeville, and the like, which some of our wealthy contemporaries are just beginning to discover, were already old when Martial began his career. His own opinion is **(ix, 77)** that "the best kind of a dinner is the dinner at which no flute-player is present." Doubtless there are some in these days who will agree with him.

But of all the persons one met at these large entertainments the best known and the most frequently mentioned is the professional diner-out, the 'dinner-hunter.'

One of Juvenal's best satires is devoted to this character. But not even Juvenal can surpass Martial's observation of this specific type of 'dead-beat.' "Some of these people carry off as much food as they can conceal in their napkins. The next day they either eat it themselves or sell it to someone else. They try to make you believe that they don't care to dine out, but this is false. Others, on the contrary, swear that they never dine at home, and this is true—for two reasons."

But the Nemesis of the dinner-hunter is the stingy host. The stingy host has many ways of displaying his really remarkable ingenuity. He can blend good and bad wines, he can give a different wine to his guests from that which he drinks himself—though he sometimes tries to conceal it by giving them poor wine in good bottles. He can allow his guests the privilege of watching him eat mushrooms. Or if he does give them something good, he may give them so little of it as to be merely an appetizer. Such, for example, is Mancinus, who set out one poor, little, unprotected boar for no less than sixty hungry men. Or the stingy host never invites a man except when he knows that he has a previous engagement. Again, he furnishes handsome decorations at the expense of the dinner, or he gives a poor dinner and tries to excuse himself by abusing the cook. You will observe, however, that these persons are only niggardly with other people. In their own pleasures they are extravagant enough.

The strangest type, however, are those who are too stingy to do anything even for themselves. A curious anomaly, the miser. Here is Calenus, for example. Calenus never became stingy at all until he had inherited a fortune and could afford to be generous. The twin brother of the miser is the spendthrift, and they are both alike in their inability to realize the value of money.

One of the most tedious duties of a client was the necessity of presenting himself at the daily receptions of his patrons. These took place regularly at daylight. On the whole, it was the heaviest burden of Martial's life in Rome. He often complained that his literary work was sadly interfered with by this duty. And there is no real affection in it, he says. Some patrons, for instance, insist upon having all their titles. Nor is there much profit in it. The only ones who get anything are the rich, or those persons who know too much about their patron. And as for the sportula, it is so small and so poor that foreign competition for it is quite discouraged. For example, there was my countryman Tuccius **(iii, 14)**:

> Poor Tuccius, quite starved at home,
> To seek his fortune here in Rome
>   Came all the way from Spain.
> But when he reached the city gate,
> He heard about the dole—and straight
>   Went posting back again.

No one knows better than Martial all the possible varieties of the genus Millionaire. The type which we have recently named 'the migratory rich' is nothing new to him, and his comment is, that "a man who lives every-where lives nowhere." He knows the sort who cherish a high temper, "because it is cheaper to fly into a passion than it is to give." Another one gives, but he never ceases to remind you of the fact. He knows the wealthy invlid and recommends, free of charge, one dose of real poverty. Nor does he fail to observe the rich upstart who is forever trying to steal a Knight's seat in the theatre, or who attempts to get into society by changing a too significant name. Mus is a small matter—as Horace says, "ridiculus mus." But observe what a difference it makes between Cinnamus, the ex-slave, and Cinna, the patrician.

Martial devotes more than one caustic epigram to that large class in Rome who lived beyond their means— "ambitiosa paupertate," as his friend Juvenal puts it— eking out what they lack by all sorts of shifts and hypocrisies, the mere counterfeit presentment of wealth in an age of high prices and vulgar ostentation. Most hopeless of all is the semi-respectable person, too indolent to work, too self-indulgent to be independent.

"You say you desire to be free **(ii, 53)**. You lie, Maximus, you do not desire it. But if you should desire it, this is the way. Give up dining out. Be content with *vin ordinaire*. Learn to smile at dyspeptic Cinna's golden dinner service. Be satisfied with a toga like mine. Submit to lower your head when you enter your house. If you have such strength of mind as this, you may live more free than the Parthian king."

Nor are the fortune-hunters forgotten **(ii, 65)**: "Why are you so sad?" says Martial to his acquaintance Saleianus. "Why, indeed? I have just buried my wife." "Oh great crime of Destiny!" Martial cries with exaggerated sympathy, "Oh heavy chance! To think that Secundilla is dead—and so wealthy too—she left you a million sesterces, didn't she? My broken-hearted friend, I cannot tell you how much I regret that this has happened to you."

No new observations have been made on the various professions since Martial's day, and surely no classical scholar would venture to guess how long it has been since anything new has been contributed to the theme of lovely woman.

"Diaulus **(i, 30)** began as a doctor. Then he became an undertaker. Really, a distinction without a difference. In either case he laid us out."

"In the evening Andragoras supped gaily with me. In the morning he was found dead. He must have dreamed that he saw Dr. Hermocrates!" **(vi, 53)**.

"The artist (**i, 102**) who painted your Venus must have intended to flatter Minerva." The point of this criticism is seen as soon as we recollect that the only time Minerva ever contended in a beauty-show was on that memorable occasion when Paris was umpire and gave the prize to Venus. Perhaps Martial was justified in his suspicion that if the severe and unapproachable goddess of wisdom was sufficiently human to enter such a contest, she was also sufficiently human to enjoy seeing her victorious rival so dreadfully caricatured by the artist.

"All of Fabulla's friends (**viii, 79**) among the women are old and ugly to the last degree. Fabulla thoroughly understands the value of background."

To Catulla, fascinating but false, Martial says (**viii, 53**):

> So very fair! And yet so very common?
> Would you were plainer, or a better woman!

Which is really far superior to Congreve's famous song which ends:

> Would thou couldst make of me a saint,
>   Or I of thee a sinner!

Many of Martial's best epigrams may be grouped under the head of character sketches. So many of these men are quite as familiar to us as they were to him eighteen centuries ago.

Here is Cinna (**i, 89**) who takes you aside with a great air of mystery to tell you that "it is a warm day."

Here is Laurus (**ii, 64**) who all his life has been intending to do something great, but has never been able to decide what it shall be.

We all know Nœvolus (**iv, 83**). Nœvolus is never polite or affable except when he is in trouble. On the other hand, we also know Postumus (**ii, 67**). Postumus is the painfully civil person. If he saw you from a merry-go-round, he would say "how do you do?" every time he passed.

And which one of us has failed to meet Tucca (**xii, 94**), the Admirable Crichton, the Jack-of-all-trades, the man who knows it all? Tucca always reminds me of the Welsh Giant in my old copy of Jack the Giant-killer. Whenever you have done anything, he at once lets you know that "Hur can do that hursel."

Poor Tom Moore, among his titled friends, finds his prototype in Philomusus (**vii, 76**), of whom Martial says:

> Delectas, Philomuse, non amaris,—

"You divert them, Philomusus; you are not an object of their regard."

Another type is represented by Linus (**vii, 95**). Linus is the affectionate person with a long beard and a cold nose who never misses the chance of kissing you on a winter's day. "Pray put it off," Martial cries, "put it off, until April!" These kissers, these 'basiatores,' as he calls them, were the poet's *bête noire*. "You cannot escape them," he complains (**xi, 98**), "you meet them all the time and everywhere. I might return from Spain; but the thought of the 'basiatores' gives me pause."

One other familiar type in Rome was also the poet's especial dislike. This was the 'bellus homo'—the pretty man, the beau.

"Pray tell me," he inquires of Cotilus in **iii, 63**, "what is a 'bellus homo' anyhow?" "A bellus homo," Cotilus replies, "is one who curls his locks and lays them all in place; who always smells of balm, forever smells of cinnamon; who hums the gay ditties of the Nile and the dance music of Cadiz; who throws his smooth arms in various attitudes; who idles the whole day long among the chairs of the ladies, and is always whispering in someone's ear; who reads little billets-doux from this quarter and from that, and writes them in return; who avoids ruffling his dress by contact with his neighbor's sleeve; he knows with whom everybody is in love; he flutters from entertainment to entertainment; he can give you to the uttermost degree every ancestor of the latest race horse." "That, then, is a bellus homo? In that case, Cotilus, a bellus homo is a monstrously trifling affair."

Sextus the money-lender (**ii, 44**) hates to say no, but has no intention of saying yes:

> Whenever he observes me purchasing
> A slave, a cloak, or any such like thing,
> Sextus the usurer—a man, you know,
> Who's been my friend for twenty years or
>   so—
> In fear that I may ask him for a loan,
> Thus whispers, to himself, but in a tone
> Such as he knows I cannot choose but hear:
> "I owe Secundus twenty thousand clear,
> I owe Philetus thirty thousand more,
> And then there's Phœbus—that's another
>   four—
> Besides, there's interest due on each amount,
> And not one farthing on my bank account!"
> Oh stratagem profound of my old friend!
> 'Tis hard refusing when you're asked to lend;
> But to refuse before you're asked displays
> Inventive genius worthy of the bays!

Of a fascinating but moody friend Martial says (**xii, 47**, translated by Addison):

> In all thy humours whether grave or mellow
> Thou'rt such a touchy, testy, pleasant fellow,

Hast so much wit and mirth and spleen
　　about thee,
There is no living with thee or without thee.

It is high time, however, for me to bring this imperfect sketch of Martial and his work to a close. I have said nothing of the history, form, and style of the antique epigram. One should be well acquainted with them in order really to understand and appreciate Martial. I have also said nothing of his supreme position in the later history of his department. His influence on the English poets is a large chapter by itself. So, too, a few of his happy phrases still linger in cultivated speech. But, so far as I know, only one of his epigrams, as such, has penetrated our popular consciousness. This is **i, 32:**

　　Non amo te, Sabidi, nec possum dicere quare:
　　　Hoc tantum possum dicere, non amo te.

An epigram which through a lawless Oxford undergraduate of the seventeenth century is responsible for the proverbial jingle:

　　I do not love thee, Doctor Fell,
　　The reason why I cannot tell;
　　But this I know, and know full well,
　　I do not love thee, Doctor Fell.

I have also said nothing of Martial's occasional tenderness, of his frequent touches of real poetry, and of many other important matters. I trust, however, that I have succeeded in giving some idea of the scope and character of his genius.

Not altogether a pleasant period, those evil days of Domitian. It is always saddening to watch the long senescence of a great nation. But after dwelling in the gloom of Tacitus, after being dazzled by the lightning of Juvenal's rhetoric, it is well for us that we can see that age in the broad sunlight of Martial's genius, that we can use the keen and penetrating yet just and kindly eyes of one who saw it as it really was. And bad as it may have been, there was at least a large reading public which was highly cultivated, and the great traditions of literary form and style were still intact. Patronage was unpleasant enough, but I fancy that one could find authors in this age who would prefer the slavery of patronage to slavery to the modern descendant of Scott's "Gentle Reader."

However that may be, the genius of Martial was the genius of one who knew how to write for time, and time has justified his methods. As he himself said, "his page has the true relish of human life." And in its essentials human life is unchangeable. Thus it was that the first and last great poet whom the Provinces gave to the literature of Imperial Rome could also take his place among the few who have written for all men and for all time.

Keith Preston (essay date 1920)

SOURCE: "Martial and Formal Literary Criticism," *Classical Philology,* Vol. XV, No. 4, October, 1920, pp. 340-52.

[*In this essay, Preston assesses Martial's opinions—as expressed in the epigrams—of his artistic predecessors, and compares them to the more formal literary commentary offered by some of Martial's contemporaries.*]

What constitutes real literary criticism is always debatable, in the case of Martial as much perhaps as anywhere. Martial does not give us the masses of criticism that we find in Horace, nor are his critical ideas systematized as Horace's are. No doubt this is what is meant by Mr. H. E. Butler[1] when he says in his essay on Martial, "He gives us practically no literary criticism." But Martial, at first sight not a bookish poet, has a surprising amount of informal literary comment and reflection. Along certain lines he imitated largely, and imitation is at least the softer side of criticism. His imitations, collected in special studies and swallowed, if not bolted, in Friedlander's commentary, are a field in themselves. In specific references to Greek and Latin writers as well as to theories of composition Martial also richly repays sifting. On contemporaries he is as uncritical as Pliny; both, for slightly different reasons, must be subject to heavy discount. But on the elder writers, and on writing in general, Martial's views have interest and value, especially for comparison with Quintilian, Tacitus, and Pliny. Not only did these three have forensic interests to which their criticism was in some degree adapted, but they represented, much more directly than Martial could, one phase at least of the cultivated or school tradition of the age. Martial, as but slightly interested in oratory, and professedly popular in his appeal, might be expected to supply an independent, if not insurgent, critical position. How far he does so is what we wish to determine.

The archaist movement was making itself felt in Martial's time. Quintilian, as a moderate Ciceronian, posts himself midway between Horace and the professional "lovers of Lucilius" (*Inst.* x. 1. 93-94), but he prefers the work of Horace in satire. Martial exceeds Quintilian or even Horace in his opposition to the archaists and their chief fetish. Adopting Horace's comparison of the muddy torrent, to which Quintilian had filed a mild objection, Martial condemns the early satirist for his bumpy style, cascading over rocks. He takes pains to submit his lemma, **xi. 90. 1-4:**

　　Carmina nulla probas molli quae limite currunt,
　　　Sed quae per salebras altaque saxa cadunt,
　　et tibi Maeonio quoque carmine maius habetur,
　　　"Lucili columella hic situst Metrophanes."[2]

Lucilius is, however, the representative of satire (Martial xii. 94. 7). In the cited epigram, flinging out a tag of Ennius, *terrai frugiferai,* Martial fleers at the cult of Ennius, to which Quintilian (*Inst.* x. 1. 88) accords respect without adherence. Ennius is contracted unfavorably with Vergil (Mart. v. 10. 7). On Accius and Pacuvius, two more totems of the archaists, Martial (xi. 90. 6) is frankly spiteful,

> Accius et quidquid Pacuviusque vomunt.[3]

To these, Quintilian (*Inst.* x. 1. 97) allows perfunctory praise, excusing blemishes of form as the fault of their times. An interesting feature of Martial's criticism of the archaists is his associating with the antiquaries in literature those who affected a similar taste in architecture (Mart. v. 10. 3-6):

> Hi sunt invidiae nimirum, Regule, mores,
> praeferat antiquos semper ut illa novis.
> sic veterem ingrati Pompei quaerimus umbram,
> sic laudant Catuli vilia templa senes.[4]

In this case as elsewhere when Martial reflects on old fogies a compliment to Domitian is implied. How far old-fashioned tastes in art went with political intransigence is an interesting question. In general Martial seems opposed to the ancients as a smooth joiner of verses would naturally despise a clumsy craftsman. With this reasoned prejudice blends the usual anger of moderns against such critics as demand the seasoned classic, a feeling which comes out very well in the pert epigram to Vacerra who "liked his poets high," Mart. viii. 69.

Not far from the archaists, and in some cases identical, stood the obscurantists or over-learned poets, with whom Martial had nothing in common. Quintilian, who was no pedant, sneers civilly at this class (*Inst.* x. 1. 97). *Virium tamen Attio plus tribuitur; Pacuvium videri doctiorem, qui esse docti affectant, volunt.* Martial x. 21, attacks a gentleman who prefers Cinna to Vergil and whose works require a corps of grammarians, nay, Apollo himself, to interpret them. Mere learning, he says, can save no poem from oblivion (vi. 61 [60]):

> nescioquid plus est, quod donat saecula chartis:
> victurus genium debet habere liber.

Hoping he may change to please the grammarians, Martial notwithstanding aims to win his public without benefit of grammarians (x. 21. 5-6):

> mea carmina, Sexte,
> grammaticis placeant, ut sine grammaticis.

Sotadean juggling, echo verses, trick stuff of any kind, Martial sensibly pronounces trivial. Even the *Attis* of

Catullus with its galliambies, a brilliant *tour de force* (*luculentus*), so Martial concedes to general opinion, has no message for him:

> Turpe est difficiles habere nugas
> Et stultus labor est ineptiarum.[5]

Much erudition was at this time going into various mythological confections, such as the star myths, . . . done into flowing elegiacs by Pliny's young friend Calpurnius Piso, *eruditam sane luculentamque materiam,* as Pliny remarks, with many other encomiums (v. 17. 1). Such things as this, along with the parlor epic and the closet drama, Martial condemns alike for bombast (Mart. iv. 49. 7-8), and for the deadly staleness of the themes. They are the lucubrations of long-faced dullards and the bane of school children (viii. 3. 15-18). The man who would be completely dead to the world of reality is urged to bury himself n the *Aetia* of Callimachus (Mart. x. 4. 11-12). Listing repeatedly the stock epic and tragic themes, Martial pronounces them a waste of time and paper.[6] Whether any of this vehemence was aimed at Statius, whom Martial does not directly mention, has been much and uselessly discussed. Certainly Martial does not admire the *genre.* Mythology serves him mostly as a kind of shorthand, by the Ovidian system. Orestes and Pylades suggest friendship, Hecuba and Andromache, sorrow, Nestor, Priam, Pelias, or Hecuba, age, and so through a wide range of types. Few obscure myths find reference in the epigrams, though Martial seems particularly well primed on the myths of Hercules, in whose cult Domitian had a peculiar interest (cf. Mart. ix. 64; ix. 65; ix. 101; and v. 65). In tributes, dedications, bread-and-butter poetry generally, Martial falls into myth easily and with his eyes open. For his compliments to Domitian it made by far the best vehicle. In estimating the element of flattery in Martial, one should consider the coin in which he renders payment to Caesar. As the coin of compliment, mythological comparisons were as cheap as Russian rubles. Quintilian flatters quite as grossly and with a clumsier touch. Despite his contempt for stale erudition and for anything resembling pedantry, Martial respects learning. The epithet *doctus* on his lips seems sincerely though vaguely complimentary.[7] He covets this quality in his own work (x. 20 [19]. 1), courts learned criticism (iv. 86. 1-3), and affects dread of the grammarian Probus iii. 2. 12. His deferebtuak address to Quintilian has perhaps little value as evidence. More informing are his mentions of the Attic tradition; Attic charm and Attic salt are frequently on Martial's lips. He flares up at a pretender to Atticism, vi. 64. 16 ff.

> Sed tibi plus mentis, tibi cor limante Minerva
> acrius et tenues finxerunt pectus Athenae.
> Ne valeam etc.[8]

Mention of particular writers and types of writing is exceedingly common in Martial but often quite perfunctory. On the Greek side, his provincial education left him well enough read in Homer to play with Homeric tags, as in **i. 45** and **i. 50** and to allude intelligently. Homer he couples with Vergil, and Vergil with Silius Italicus.[9] Archilochus comes in with the conventional reference to the sensitive and high-strung Lycambes (Mart. **vii. 12.** 6). Sappho, whom Quintilian ignores, presumably on moral grounds,[10] Martial calls *amatrix,* comparing Lesbian morals unfavorably with those of the chaste Theophila (**vii. 69.** 9-10). If Sappho could have had lessons from the poetess Sulpicia she would have been more learned and less experienced (Mart. **x. 35.** 15-16). Of Greek tragedians, Martial mentions only Sophocles. Martial, like Quintilian, rates Menander high, making him, not incompatibly, share a distich with Ovid (Mart. **v. 10.** 9-10). A neat play on the comic rule of three actors occurs (Mart. **vi. 6).** Callimachus, otherwise the "limbo of learned poets," is first among the Greeks in epigram, but the comparison to Martial's friend Brutianus does not flatter the Greek (Mart. **iv. 23.** 4-5).[11] Excepting for his knowledge of Homer, a few imitations of the late Greek epigrammatist Lucillius, and a propensity for feeble punning on Greek proper names, Martial's information on Greek letters might have come at second hand.

On the Latin side, we have seen that Martial, rating form even before content, rejects the older poets as far down as Catullus, who was, along with Domitius Marsus, Martial's avowed model and master. His epithets for Catullus are *doctus, tenuis, argutus, lepidus,* and *tener.*[12] His imitations and references go mostly to the shorter poems of Catullus, especially to his hendecasyllabics, which are certainly straightforward and unassuming. In slighting the more ambitious work of Catullus, Martial is like Quintilian, who passes judgment on Catullus only as an iambic poet, commending his *acerbitas* (*Inst.* x. 1. 96), and Pliny, who quotes Catullus in defense of epigrammatic license (iv. 14. 5). Martial defends his own drastic vein by the same precedent. The deftness of Catullus shows in several details of Martial's technique. For example, the type of epigram which consists of a piling up of comparisons, sometimes agreeable, and sometimes, as in **ix. 57,** quite the reverse, seems a direct legacy from Catullus. Martial and his contemporaries admired the "pet" poems of Catullus extravagantly.[13] The Lesbia cycle also delighted Martial, but real passion was foreign to his experience. Lesbia, says Martial (**viii. 73.** 7), inspired Catullus; love made the elegists and Vergil; give me a Corinna or an Alexis, and neither Ovid nor Vergil will have cause to scorn me. Compare, however, Mart. **viii. 55. (56)** and **xi. 3.** 7-10, where the fatal lack is leisure and a patron like Maecenas.

To Martial, as to others of his age, Vergil was unique, above criticism. His appropriate epithets are *sacer, cothurnatus.* The Aeneid is often referred to, and quoted, Mart. **viii. 55 (56).** 19 and **xiv. 185.** 1; for a reference to the *Ecologues* cf. **viii. 55 (56).** 17-18. We are indebted to Martial for a testimony on the *Culex* with a suggestion of criticism **viii. 55 (56).** 20:

> Qui modo vix Culicem fleverat ore rudi

cf. also **xiv. 185,** where the *Culex* is recommended as light verse for after-dinner consumption. That technique of citation which coupled the elegiac poets regularly with their amorous inspirations, Martial extends to Vergil, persistently associating him with the boy Alexis.[14] Vergil could have shone first in any field of poetry (Mart. **viii. 18.** 5-8).

To Martial, as to Quintilian, Horace is the type of Latin lyric poetry (Mart. **xii. 94.** 5), *fila lyrae movi Calabris exculta Camenis.* Reminiscences, not confined to the odes, are fairly common, including some of Martial's few touches of parody[15] (cf. Martial **iv. 55.** 5-7 and **xii. 17),** where Fever mounts behind the horseman, bathes beside the bather, and trenches on the trencher man (because there is no verbal handle this reminiscence seems to have slipped the commentators). Martial's odd impression that Horace was a Calabrian (**v. 30.** 2, **viii. 18.** 5, and **xii. 94.** 5), is one of several blunders in literary history. This one may go back to a blurred recollection of Horace, *Odes* ii. 6. 9-16.

A much more lively personal interest on Martial's part seems indicated for Domitius Marsus and the elegiac group. Marsus was Martial's master no less than Catullus, and his debt to the former was undoubtedly large. Had Martial found a Maecenas, he would not have been a Vergil but a Marsus (**viii. 55 [56].** 21-22). He modestly deprecates comparison with Marsus and Catullus (**ii. 71.** 3). Marsus, along with Catullus, Pedo, and Gaetulicus, supplies sanction for calling a spade a spade (Mart. **i. pref.** 12). Martial, consistently enough, slights Marsus' epic, the *Amazonis* (Mart. **iv. 29.** 8). As for Marsus' elegies, Martial lets us know that they were addressed to a pronounced brunette, *fusca Melaenis* (Mart. **vii. 29.** 8). The epigrams, *Cicuta,* seem to have inspired Martial's regard for Marsus. Tibullus, as we have seen, Martial rates high, agreeing in this with Quintilian, x. 1. 93, who calls him first in elegy, *tersus atque elegans.*[16] References to Gallus, and to Propertius, *lascivus* (Mart. **viii. 73.** 5), and *facundus* (**xiv. 189.** 1) are not particularly significant. Much more to Martial's liking was Ovid, all of whose works he seems to have read and assimilated. Metrical dexterity, smooth and polished phrasing, and verbal prettiness[17] were his chief lines of imitation. Ovid's excesses in rhetoric he sensibly avoids, but the whimsical way with myths which is so pleasant in Ovid appealed to Martial (cf. Ovid *Met.* i. 173, *Ibis* 81, with Mart. **viii. 49 [50].** 3-4).[18]

The poets so far considered include those who did most to influence Martial's style. He approves also the vogue of Persius (**iv. 29.** 7), as does Quintilian (x. 1. 94). Both comments remark the fact that Persius was a "one book" wonder. On Lucan, Martial seems to recognize and differ from the academic verdict. Quintilian, praising Lucan's rhetoric, declares him a model for orators rather than poets (*Inst.* x. 1. 90). Martial (**i. 61.** 7), calls Lucan *unicus,* citing also (**xiv. 194),** the "best seller" argument for his poetical pre-eminence:

> Sunt quidam qui me dicunt non esse poetam:
> Sed qui me vendit bibliopola putat.

Of course Martial had personal grounds for a kindness toward Lucan. A clear allusion to formal criticism comes in Martial's distich for a copy of Sallust, **xiv. 191:**

> Hic erit, ut perhibent doctorum corda virorum,
> primus Romana Crispus in historia.

Cf. Quint. *Inst.* x. 1. 32. The series of little book mottoes in Martial's *Apophoreta* **xiv. 183-96** might be called the beginning of book advertising and tabloid reviewing.

Coming now to epigram, a field in which Martial's critical views deserve peculiar respect, we may first consider the status of the type as Martial found it. Epigram was one variety, not too clearly defined, of that brief occasional verse, *lusus, nugae, ineptiae,* the vogue of which Pliny amply attests. Pliny defines the *genre* (vii. 9. 9-10): *Fas est et carmine remitti, non dico continuo et longo (id enim perfici nisi in otio non potest) sed hoc arguto et brevi, quod apte quantas libet occupationes distinguit. Lusus vocantur.* Collections of such verse went under a variety of titles, as Pliny notes when considering a title for his own collection; Pliny iv. 14. 9-10: *Proinde sive epigrammata sive idyllia sive eclogas sive, ut multi, poematia seu quod aliud vocare malueris licebit voces, ego tantum hendecasyllabos praesto.* Pliny chose to call his poems "Hendecasyllabics" because "this title is bound by no law but that of meter." Sentius Augurinus, Pliny iv. 27, entitled a similar collection *poematia.* The content was as various as the titles. A lively play of shifting emotions was desirable (cf. Pliny iv. 14. 3; iv. 27. 1). The honorific element was large. For example, the estimable Capito, Pliny i. 17, besides collecting portraits of distinguished republicans, wrote verse in praise of great men, quite possibly to go with the portraits.[19]

Epigram, then, was one name for a short poem on almost any subject. Neither Pliny nor Martial pays much attention to Greek epigram, though both mention the epigrams of Callimachus and contemporary imitations. Pliny, in discussing his hendecasyllabics, and Martial, on his epigrams, stress Roman tradition and Roman examples. According to this tradition epigram was characterized by *sal Romanum,* which differed from Attic salt chiefly by a superior crudity. More specifically, Latin epigram had developed license of tone and theme,

lascivia, petulantia, sharpness and asperity, *amaritudo, acerbitas, bilis,* and a brutal directness of language, *simplicitas.*[20] Both Martial and Pliny eagerly defend these qualities, on much the same sanction. Pliny, as an orator, cites mainly those statesmen and orators who had composed epigrams in odd moments (cf. Pliny v. 3. 5-6). He admits that by giving a public reading of his verses he had perhaps gone farther than his precedents. Martial cites mainly poets in his own defense. Catullus, Gaetulicus, Lucan, and the Emperor Augustus are cited by both. The matter of definite personalities in epigram was treated similarly by Pliny and Martial. Though Pliny has nothing to say of his own practice we can hardly suspect him of hurting anyone's feelings, and his theory comes out in comment on the plays of Vergilius Romanus.[21] Martial abstained from definite personalities, following the procedure which had long been a convention for satire (Mart. **vii. 12; x. 33.** 9-10):

> Hunc servare modum nostri novere libelli,
> parcere personis, dicere de vitiis.

Yet Martial abhorred the saccharine type of epigram, **vii. 25:**

> Dulcia cum tantum scribas epigrammata
> semper
> et cerussata candidiora cute,
> nullaque mica salis nec amari fellis
> in illis
> gutta sit, O demens, vis tamen illa legi!
> Nec cibus ipse iuvat morsu
> fraudatus aceti,
> nec grata est facies cui gelasinus abest.
> Infanti melimela dato fatuasque
> mariscas:
> nam mihi, quae novit pungere, Chia sapit.

Martial was himself criticized for saccharine tendencies, probably in his flattering epigrams (Mart. **x. 45):**

> Si quid lene mei dicunt et dulce
> libelli,
> si quid honorificum pagina blanda sonat,
> hoc tu pingue putas

Martial makes no very satisfactory defense. It is worth recalling that Pliny also was criticized for puffing his friends.[22]

We have been at some pains to compare the light verse of Pliny and Martial, not that Pliny's hendecasyllabics were probably worth their salt, but for evidence on the convention of Roman epigram. It appears that epigram was a popular medium, saddled firmly with certain conventions of crudity, which required constant apology, and held lightly or rather not handled at all by the higher critical opinion. Pliny made some effort to assert the dignity of epigram; cf. his comment on Martial, Pliny iii. 21, and ix. 25. 2. *Incipio enim ex hoc genere studiorum non solum oblectationem verum etiam gloriam petere post iudicium tuum.* Martial seems rather hopeless of critical approval for his medium. In addition to the conventions already noted we might add a convention of meter. Martial himself regarded hendecasyllabics and elegiacs as his principal meters (Mart. **x. 9.** 1). But he makes exceptions and finds precedent for them (Mart. **vi. 65.** 1-2):

> "Hexametris epigramma facis" scio dicere
>   Tuccam.
> Tucca, solet fieri, denique, Tucca, licet.

The convention of brevity in epigram was clearly recognized and when Martial exceeds average length he meets criticism by citing precedents (Mart. **vi. 65.** 3).

"Sed tamen hoc longum est." Solet hoc quoque, Tucca, licetque: Marsus and Pedo, says he, often wrote one epigram to fill two pages (Mart. **ii. 77.** 5-6). Curiously enough, Martial does not seem conscious of originality in that insistence upon point which is the peculiar virtue of his epigrams. He is annoyed with the spoiled reader who demands nothing but point. All point and no padding is hard on the artist, Mart. **x. 59:**

> Non opus est nobis nimium lectore guloso;
>   hunc volo, non fiat qui sine pane satur.

This epigram asserts that body is necessary to explain and develop the subject, *lemma;* it also insists on the intrinsic merit of this exegesis. Martial speaks as a lecturer who suspects that his audience wants nothing but the slides. He sneers at the popular demand for distichs, nothing but distichs (Mart. **vi. 65.** 4; **viii. 29.** 1-2). On the other hand, belittled by a critic because of his brevity, Martial hotly defends his *genre,* comparing the miniature in plastic art (Mart. **ix. 50.** 5-6):

> Nos facimus Bruti puerum,[23] nos Langona
>   vivum:
>   tu magnus luteum, Gaure, Giganta facis.

With so much that was conventional in his literary creed, Martial was and felt himself to be original in some very important respects. The choice of live subjects was his first tenet (cf. **xi. 42.** 1-2):

> Vivida cum poscas epigrammata, mortua ponis
>   lemmata. Qui fieri, Caeciliane, potest?

The colors of life must be in his work, **viii. 3.** 19-22:

> At tu Romano lepidos sale tinge libellos:
>   adgnoscat mores vita legatque suos.
> Angusta cantare licet videaris avena,
>   dum tua multorum vincat avena tubas'.

Cf. also **x. 4.** 9-12,

> non hic Centauros, non Gorgonas Harpyiasque
>   invenies: hominem pagina nostra sapit.
> Sed non vis, Mamurra, tuos cognoscere mores
>   nec te scire: legas Aetia Callimachi.

Martial appreciates to the full the essentially personal nature of epigram **(ii. pref.** 4-8), "I can see why tragedy or comedy should carry a letter of introduction, for they may not speak for themselves: epigrams need no herald and are pleased to hail you with their own saucy tongue." Martial's book expresses him better than a picture **(vii. 84.** 6). In all of this we have a code of realism, modernism, and personal expression perhaps unique in Martial's time. By no means all his epigrams fit the creed, as he was the first to recognize, **vii. 81:**

> Triginta toto mala sunt epigrammata libro.
>   Si totidem bona sunt, Lause, bonus liber est.

Martial does not subscribe to Quintilian's doctrine of *aequalitas* (Mart. **vii. 90**):[24]

> Iactat inaequalem Matho me fecisse libellum:
>   si verum est, laudat carmina nostra Matho.
> Aequales scribit libros Calvinus et Umber:
>   aequalis liber est, Cretice, qui malus est.

As the seamy side of Martial's modernism may be urged his insistence on popularity, his use of booksellers' arguments, and his admission that *mime* had influenced his technique. The aims that Martial ascribes to the harlequin Latinus (Mart. **ix. 28**) are essentially his own (cf. **ix. prefatory poem** lines 5-8; **I. pref.** 15-21; **1. 4.** 5-6).[25] But on the whole Martial represents an entirely wholesome reaction against a stagnant literary age. Despite this reaction he shows himself docile as regards literary tradition and amenable to the best critical opinion.

Notes

[1] H. E. Butler, *Post-Augustan Poetry from Seneca to Juvenal* (Oxford, 1909), p. 284. [*Classical Philology* XV, October, 1920]

[2] *Salebrae* was already technical in criticism, as the citations show. Cf. the adjective *salebrosus,* Martial xi. 2. 7: *Lectores tetrici salebrosum ediscite Santram.* Friedlander infers from this passage that Santra must have done verse as well as prose, but the supposition is not essential.

[3] This extreme position toward the archaists appears also, Tac. *Or.* 21: *Pacuvium certe et Accium non solum tragoediis sed etiam in orationibus suis expressit; adeo durus et siccus est ibid. 23 isti qui Lucilium pro Horatio et Lucretium pro Vergilio legunt.* It is worth noting

that Quintilian is much more drastic in his comment on the old masters in his own field of oratory than he is where poetry is concerned. Cf. his warning against the Gracchi and Cato (*Inst.* ii. 5. 21).

[4] The two arts are conjoined also, Tac. *Or.* 20. *Quid enim, si infirmiora horum temporum templa credas, quia non rudi caemento et informibus tegulis extruuntur, sed marmore nitent et auro radiantur?* Tacitus also illustrates archaism from the stage, *ibid.* 20, *nec magis perfert in iudiciis tristem et impexam antiquitatem quam si quis in scena Roscii aut Turpionis Ambivii exprimere gestus velit.* The tendency to associate the arts in criticism seems especially strong in this age. Pliny compares sculpture and painting to literature. i. 20. 5; iii. 13. 4. Martial compares epigram and figurines, ix. 50. 5. Comparisons from the gastronomic art are very common in Quintilian, Martial, and Pliny.

[5] Cf. Mart. ii. 86. 1-12, with Friedlander's excellent note on ingenious poetry. On the same ground, pettiness, Martial (xii. 43. 1-11) condemns some didactic poetry of licentious content, which he compares to Elephantis. Martial would not have cared for the hokku.

[6] Cf. Mart. iii. 45. 1-2; iv. 49. 3-6; v. 53. 1-2; x. 4. 1-10; x. 35. 5-7; xiv. 1. 11.

[7] *Doctus* is applied by Martial to Homer, Catullus, Sappho, Nero, Pedo, and Seneca as well as to various contemporaries. In this connection we even suspect Martial of conferring the Doctorate in commerce.

[8] The epithet *tenues* recognizes the doctrine of Attic *tenuitas* or the plain style, cf. Quint (*Inst.* xii. 10. 21). *Quapropter mihi falli multum videntur, qui solos esse Atticos credunt tenues et lucidos* (*ibid.,* 25-26). *Quid est igitur, cur in iis demum qui tenui venula per calculos fluunt, Atticum saporem putent?. . . . Melius de hoc nomine sentiant credantque Attice dicere esse optime dicere.* Martial's idea of Atticism would be close enough to this last (cf. 1. 25. 3; iii. 20. 9; iv. 23. 6; iv. 86. 1).

[9] Pliny speaks his real mind about Silius, who does not seem to have been an intimate, but Pliny's friend Paulus does elegies that are true-Propertian, and lyrics you couldn't tell from Horace; cf. Pliny ix. 22. 2.

[10] A bias against the erotic suggests itself throughout Quintilian's catalogue, cf. his remarks on Afranius (*Inst.* x. 1. 100). Martial takes high ground on such themes as Scylla and Biblis, x. 35. 7-8, commending the *castos et probos amores* of Sulpicia, but he can hardly qualify as a consistent purity advocate.

[11] Pliny also compares a friend's epigrams to Callimachus iv. 3. 3-4 (Quintilian x. 1. 58 considers only his elegies). These comparisons have a certain interest as characteristic of an age of logrollers.

[12] On *doctus* cf. Friedlander's note on Mart. i. 61. 1. *Tenuis* is high praise, cf. *supra* p. 5 n. 1. Martial employs the word *tenuis* for Tibullus and for Nerva "the Tibullus of our time" cf. viii. 70. 5 *tenui corona* (compare viii. 3. 21) of himself, *angusta avena. Tenuis* connotes a proud simplicity. *Argutus,* a hard word to pin down (Martial uses it of a painter's deft brush work), is applied also to Tibullus and to Martial's own epigrams.

[13] Cf. Stella's Columba (Mart. i. 7), Martial's Issa. (i. 109), Statius Silv. ii. 4 and 5.

[14] Cf. Martial v. 16. 12 with Friedlander's note.

[15] The lack of parody in Martial is really surprising, seeing that he was fairly well read and could turn the trick when he wished to. A neat parody of the elegiac style occurs ix. 49:

> *Haec est illa meis multum cantata libellis,*
> *Quam meus edidicit lector amatque togam.*

[16] Mart. v. 30. 4, *cultis aut elegia comis,* indicates a similar regard for polish in elegy. Other epithets for elegy and elegists in Martial are *levis, tenuis, lascivus* (a). *Lascivus,* in Quintilian used to denote any exuberance of style, seems to stand for erotic content in Martial.

[17] Cf. Martial iv. 22 with Ovid *Met.* iv. 354 ff. Martial would seem to have written a little poem quite out of his usual style and devoid of valid point simply to incorporate some pretty images from Ovid.

[18] The whole matter of reminiscences in Martial needs extreme caution. Many of those listed by the commentators were certainly *clichés,* common to all poets since the early Augustans.

[19] Compare the numerous epigrams which Martial wrote to fit statuary, paintings, and other works of art.

[20] Critics of epigram were more opposed to the crude diction than to the licentious subject-matter. Pliny believed in both, practiced the latter, but lacked the moral courage to be boldly vulgar; cf. Pliny iv. 14.4: *summos illos et gravissimos viros qui talia scripserunt non modo lascivia rerum sed ne verbis quidem nudis abstinuisse; quae nos refugimus, non quia severiores (unde enim?), sed quia timidiores sumus.* Quintilian, though not recognizing epigram, seems to condemn both qualities. For *verba parum verecunda,* Quintilian *Inst.* x. 1. 9, grudgingly allows a certain license in iambic poetry and the old comedy, though he denies such language to the orator.

[21] Pliny vi. 21. 5-7: *non amaritudo, non dulcedo, non lepos defuit: ornavit virtutes, insectatus est vitia, fictis*

nominibus decenter, veris usus est apte. The words would serve to describe Martial's practice.

[22] On the matter of harsh personalities in epigram, one recalls the distinction between the wit and the buffoon, *scurra,* which Horace insists upon. Martial does not use the word *scurra,* though Pliny does. But he makes the same distinction, in comment on the lampoons which had been attributed to him (x. 3. 1). *Vernaculorum dicta, sordidum dentem,* etc., cf. also (i. 41. 1-2). *Urbanus tibi, Caecili, videris. Non es, crede mihi. Quid ergo? verna.* Later in the same epigram Caecilius is compared to noted *scurrae.* Cf. also Mart. 7. 12. Martial emphasizes a distinction between *urbicus* and *urbanus* (i. 41. 11).

[23] For the "Boy of Brutus" cf. Friedlander on Mart. ii. 77. 4. Also Mart. xiv. 171. For Martial's literary thesis cf. Pliny vi. 21. 4: *scripsit mimiambos tenuiter argute venuste, atque in hoc genere eloquentissime; nullum est enim genus quod absolutum non possit eloquentissimum dici.* This was no doubt a very liberal admission on Pliny's part. Critical opinion at this time was apt to measure genius in terms of lamp oil and elbow grease.

[24] Cf. Quintilian *Inst.* x. 1-54 (*Apollonius*) *non tamen contemnendum edidit opus aequali quadam mediocritate et quantum eminentibus vincimur, fortasse aequalitate pensamus* (*ibid.* x. 1. 86-87).

[25] The stage is recognized by Tacitus as a vicious influence for oratory; cf. *Or.* 26: *quo plerique temporum nostrorum actores ita utuntur ut lascivia verborum et levitate sententiarum et licentia compositionis histrionales modos exprimant.* On popularizing generally cf. Quintilian x. 1. 43: *alios recens haec lascivia deliciaeque et omnia ad voluptatem multitudinis imperitae composita delectant.*

T. K. Whipple (essay date 1925)

SOURCE: "Martial" in *Martial and the English Epigram from Sir Thomas Wyatt to Ben Jonson,* The University of California Press, 1925, pp. 285-99.

[*In the following excerpt, Whipple discusses Martial's principal themes and classifies the epigrams by their content. He also provides a detailed analysis of their structure, emphasizing the poet's masterful use of rhetorical figures to enhance the essence and effect of his verses.*]

No author was ever more completely the product of his environment than Martial. Both in the material which he treats and in his attitude toward it, he is representative of Rome in the latter half of the first century after Christ. The same statement holds true of the form in which he casts his epigrams; it is the natural result of the rhetorical training of the time.

In the first place, his subject-matter is limited only by Rome as Martial knew the city, under Nero and Domitian. He has left us a remarkably detailed picture of his surroundings. He occupied a most advantageous position from which to view the life of the imperial capital. He himself was evidently poor and lived in bohemian fashion on his doles as client and the gifts he could obtain with his verses. However lacking in dignity and manliness this manner of life may have been, it at least brought him into contact with all sorts and classes of people. As a client and as a distinguished poet, he had the acquiantance of the aristocracy and the literary cliques; whereas his hand-to-mouth way of living made him see much of the poorer class and especially of those who like himself were dependent upon the caprices of the rich.[4]

The vivid picture he gives us shows Roman life as brilliant on one side as it is squalid on the other. His laudatory epigrams, addressed for the most part to the Emperor Domitian and to members of the imperial court, show to what lengths flattery can can go without discomposing its object, and how the resources of the most highly developed literary art may lend themselves to heightening the effect of fulsomeness. The flattery which Martial addresses to the favorite slaves and freedmen of those in power sheds some light on the state of society in which could flourish the cliques and intrigues that centered about the emperor. On the other hand, when he addresses his friends and acquaintances, most of whom seem to have been more prosperous than himself, we see the best side of contemporary life; for his friends were men of culture with philosophic and literary interests, many of them authors in their own right, connoisseurs of art, and the like. When to one of these friends Martial sends an invitation to dinner, or congratulations on marriage, or a gift accompanied by an epigram, we see him at his most likable; for he is at his best in dealing with the theme of friendship, which seems to have been the deepest and most sincere emotion he experienced.

The second class of his epigrams—the gnomic or reflective—are usually addressed to these friends. His moralizings aspire to no elevation; he professes an epicurcanism even less exalted and less attractive than Horace's. *Carpe diem*—eat, drink, and be merry—is the burden of his advice: to have as good a time as possible, without worrying about anything more remote than the pleasure offered by the present moment. His real point of view is mildly cynical, strictly speaking, rather than epicurean, though neither harsh nor bitter. He sums the matter up in the well-known *Vitam quae faciunt beatiorem,*[5] in which he wishes for a modest income, health, peace and quiet, and a farm. He seldom presents himself so pleasingly.

The taste for country life indicated in the epigram just mentioned is one of Martial's outstanding characteristics. Many of his epigrams are concerned with rural Italy—with the life on the country estate of the rich city man, that is, rather than with the life of the real farmer or the peasant. Martial has all the enthusiasm for the country usually shown by dwellers in large cities, not the less sincere because called forth by the glamor of distance and contrast. These epigrams usually take the form of epistles to his friends, and are closely allied to those of the preceding type, the reflective. Martial is entirely free from the pastoral convention. In his writing we see the real Italian countryside, not an ideal land of shepherds and their loves.

Martial wrote a number of epitaphs. A few of these are satirical, but for the most part they display to perfection that vein of sentiment and pathos, often half-playful, in which he excelled. Many of the best are on children, chiefly young slaves, or on animal pets. Others are composed for the benefit of his friends. Closely akin to these, but more conventional and of less merit, are his mere *jeux d'esprit,* concerning his friends' pets, or dealing cleverly with objects of art or natural curiosities, such as the bee enclosed in amber.[6]

Friendship, pathos, sentiment, mark the height to which Martial rises in poetic feeling; when dealing with love he is at his worst. To be sure, most of the epigrams which relate to that theme have to do with other people's love affairs and treat them satirically. But those in which he talks of his own amatory concerns are devoid of passion, with the possible exception of a few addressed to favorite slaves. It would scarcely be going too far to say that love, as an inspiration to poetry, is absent from Martial's work.

Finally we arrive at his epigrams which depict more specificaly the city life of ancient Rome. Most of these, but by no means all, are satiric. Favorite themes with Martial are the spectacles in the arena, food and drink, and presents. He asks for gifts, he—less often—returns thanks for them, he writes verses to accompany those he gives his friends. He sends verses as an excuse for not calling in person on his patrons. Many of his epigrams are no more than detailed descriptions of dinners, which often include invitations to his friends to dine with him. In describing the spectacles, he finds occasion to flatter the emperor who provided them.

Generally, however, he sees in the life about him occasion for amusement, for contempt, once in a while for disgust. The vast majority of his epigrams are satiric. Especially he attacks all the forms of hypocrisy and pretence to which such a society as he knew gives birth. The poor who pretend to wealth, the lowborn who pretend to high station, the old men and women who pretend to youth, the dissolute who pretend to rugged virtue—all provide him with material for his jests. The literary life in which he took part also furnishes him with a fertile field, and he attacks poetasters, bad reciters, and plagiarists. But in truth the objects of his satire are as varied as the life of the metropolis. Sycophants, dinner-seekers, newsmongers, social upstarts, gourmands, sots, dandies, misers, bad lawyers and doctors, courtesans, legacy-hunters—he lampoons them all. In terms of unrivaled obscenity he describes the debauchery and vice of the time. We see the streets of the capital with their contrasts, their extreme luxury and extreme poverty, their dirt and noise; we go to the baths; we wait for hours in the great man's antechamber to be presented with the price of a dinner. All this is depicted without moral indignation; Martial fell in with the spirit of the age, and it is to this fact that we owe the extraordinary vividness of the picture he has drawn of Rome in the days of Domitian.

There has been a tendency to underestimate the variety in Martial's work. It has become common to refer to the satiric pointed epigram as the "Roman" or the "Martial" type. For this reason the wide range and the varied treatment both of material and of form in the *Epigrammata* need to be emphasized. And yet there is of course some excuse for the over-insistence on Martial's satire. Certainly as a class his satiric verses are more amusing and have therefore won more popularity than his others. The point I make is only that this portion of his work must not be allowed to obscure the rest, that we must not forget his epitaphs, his praises of country life, his reflective verse, his eulogies.

In form, likewise, Martial exhibits a considerable variety. His epigrams range in length from a single verse to fifty lines and more. Many of them an English reader would not call epigrams at all. They might with equal propriety be termed epistles, epodes, short satires. Some of them differ only in meter from certain odes of Horace. A few fail to terminate in a 'point.' Yet the author apparently regarded them all as epigrams, although even in his own time there seem to have been demurrers on this point.[7] I emphasize Martial's variety because much has been said of the restricting influence which he has exerted upon the modern epigram.

That this restriction has been associated with his influence will not be denied. The reason lies in the fact that with him the pointed epigram is the rule, the unpointed the exception. In giving an account of the form of his epigrams, we shall therefore confine ourselves to this, the representative and preponderating type.

In the form of Martial's epigrams, the first thing to note is the structure. On the basis of structure, most of his work may be divided into two groups: those epigrams which consist merely of exposition and conclusion; and those which contain also a transition from the one to the other.

In the first group, exposition and conclusion usually take one of the three following forms: statement and comment; statement and question; question and answer. The simplest type of epigram is that in which the exposition consists of a mere statement in the third person, the conclusion containing the poet's comment. An illustration is **III 21:**

> Proscriptum famulus servavit fronte notatus.
>   Non fuit haec domini vita, sed invidia.

This type, however, is rare in Martial; more frequently the statement is in the second person, or is an indirect quotation:

> Bellus homo et magnus vis idem, Cotta,
>   videri:
>   sed qui bellus homo est, Cotta, pusillus
>   homo est.

> **(I 9)**

> Dicis formonsam, dicis te, Bassa, puellam.
>   istud quac non est dicere, Bassa, solet.

> **(V 45)**

Instead of comment, the conclusion may take the form of a question:

> Iurat capillos esse, quos emit, suos
> Fabulla: numquid [ergo], Paule, peierat?

> **(VI 12)**

Or the exposition, instead of statement, may take the form of question, the conclusion containing the answer, or some comment, perhaps in the form of another question:

> Quid mihi reddat ager quacris, Line,
>   Nomentanus?
>   Hoc mihi reddit ager: te Line, non video.

> **(II 38)**

> Abscisa servom quid figis, Pontice, lingua?
>   nescis tu populum, quod tacet ille, loqui?

> **(II 82)**

The preceding illustrate the simplest type of epigram; much more numerous are those which contain also a third element, a transition from the exposition to the conclusion. In **III 15,** for instance:

> Plus credit nemo tota quam Cordus in urbe.
>   'Cum sit tam pauper, quomodo?' Caecus
>   amat—

we have one of Martial's favorite methods of constructing an epigram: by a statement in the exposition, a transitional question, and an answer in the conclusion. Sometimes he develops a little dialogue out of this form:

> Petit Gemellus nuptias Maronillae
> et cupit et instat et precatur et donat.
> Adeone pulchra est? Immo foedius nil est.
> Quid ergo in illa petitur et placet? Tussit.

> **(I 10)**

Another form to which he is partial is a combination of question, answer, and comment:

> Esse quid hoc dicam quod olent tua basia
>   murram
>   quodque tibi est numquam non alienus odor?
> hoc mihi suspectum est, quod oles bene,
>   Postume, semper:
>   Postume, non bene olet qui bene semper
>   olet.

> **(II 12)**   ·

Martial's favorite ways of opening an epigram, then, are with a statement in the second person, a question, an indirect quotation. He uses habitually some form of direct address. In addition to the varieties already mentioned, he employs apostrophe, exhortation, exclamation: "I, felix rosa" **(VII 89);** "Sili, Castalidum decus sororum" **(IV 14);** "Barbara pyramidum sileat miracula Memphis" **(Spec. 1);** "Quantus, io, Latias mundi concentus ad aras" **(VIII 4).**

Occasionally he will develop one of the three simple elements of exposition, transition, and conclusion to a considerable length. One of his methods of doing this has already been mentioned: his use of several questions and answers so as to produce a short dialogue. Another of his methods is enumeration, of details or of specific instances. An example is **III 63:**

> Cotile, bellus homo es: dicunt hoc, Cotile,
>   multi.
>   audio: sed quid sit, dic mihi, bellus homo?
> 'Bellus homo est, flexos qui digerit ordine
>   crines,
>   balsama qui semper, cinnama semper olet;
> cantica qui Nili, qui Gaditana susurrat,
>   qui movet in varios bracchia volso modos,
>   *etc.*[8]

Much like the preceding are those epigrams which he develops by a series of comparisons, such as **II 43** or **VIII 33.** But the simple epigrams are more numerous and more typical of Martial than the developed, which remain after all the exception, not the rule.

A thorough classification of Martial's ways of making a point is perhaps impossible. Only an indication of some of the more frequent will be attempted here. A great many of his epigrams depend for their point upon surprising or startling the reader. This surprise is effected by several means. Sometimes what the poet says is in itself startling, because of its apparent impossibility or its incongruity, as in the conclusion of **Spec. 11:**

> deprendat vacuo venator in aere praedam,
> > si captare feras aucupis arte placet.

The same device appears in **II 78,** although here it is used with an ironical implication:

> Aestivo serves ubi piscem tempore, quaeris?
> > In thermis serva, Caeciliane, tuis.[9]

More often, however, the surprise is less in what Martial says than in the way he says it. He likes to work up a suspense or deliberately to mislead the reader, so that the solution of the difficulty, when it comes, is contrary to the reader's expectation. This device, technically known as paraprosdokia, is used with signal effect in **VI 51:**

> Quod convivaris sine me tam saepe, Luperce,
> > inveni noceam qua ratione tibi.
> irascor: licet usque voces mittasque rogesque—
> > 'Quid facies?' inquit. Quid faciam? veniam.[10]

Other and not dissimilar means of securing this effect are antithesis, paradox, oxymoron, and hyperbole. Antithesis gives point to the conclusion of **II 68:**

> servom si potes, Ole, non habere,
> et regem potes, Ole, non habere.

Paradox is one of Martial's favorite figures; in **XII 46** we find it combined with oxymoron:

> Difficilis facilis, iucundus acerbus es idem:
> > nec tecum possum vivere nec sine te.[11]

The whole point of **III 35,**

> Artis Phidiacae toreuma clarum
> pisces aspicis: adde aquam, natabunt—

depends upon mere hyperbole; more often, however, we find the hyperbole combined with some other figure. In **III 25** it is combined with an ambiguity, a play upon the two kinds of frigidity:

> Si temperari balneum cupis fervens,
> Faustine, quod vix Iulianus intraret,
> roga lavetur rhetorem Sabineium.
> Neronianas is refrigerat thermas.

Furthermore, even plainer than in the preceding is the ironical implication of the hyperbole in **VI 53:**

> Lotus nobiscum est, hilaris cenavit, et idem
> > inventus mane est mortuus Andragoras.
> Tam subitae mortis causam, Faustine, requiris?
> > In somnis medicum viderat Hermocraten.

Irony, in fact, is one of Martial's most frequent satirical weapons. It rarely takes the form of downright sarcasm; he does not often say the opposite of what he means. Rather, he deals in innuendo, he damns by implication. Straightforward, bludgeoning abuse is not his line; even if his satire sounds far from over-delicate or subtle to modern ears, it yet involves a certain indirection. In **VII 59,** for instance,

> Non cenat sine apro noster, Tite, Caecilianus.
> > bellum convivam Caecilianus habet—

or in **VI 24,**

> Nil lascivius est Charisiano:
> Saturnalibus ambulat togatus—

although no doubt the point is obvious enough, still the method employed is not direct statement.[12] We have already seen how the same effect is sometimes secured by means of a surprising incongruity or an hyperbole. Another device which Martial often uses for ironical effect is ambiguity. See, for instance, the ironical *double entendre* in the close of **IV 33:**

> Plena laboratis habeas cum scrinia libris,
> > emittis quare, Sosibiane, nihil?
> 'Edent heredes' inquis 'mea carmina.'
> > Quando?
> tempus erat iam te, Sosibiane, legi.[13]

Sometimes by a question at the end he will import an ironical equivocation into what has preceded, as in **IX 15,** or in **VI 12** (quoted above) on Fabulla's hair. Or by his final statement he will give a new satiric sense to what before was dubious or obscure, as in **I 10** (quoted above) by the final word 'Tussit.'

Word play furnishes the point of many of Martial's epigrams. Sometimes he plays with the meaning, sometimes with the sound, of a word. In **III 15,** although the point is in the unexpected resolution of a difficulty, it depends upon the double meaning of *credit:*

> Plus credit nemo tota quam Cordus in urbe.
> > 'Cum sit tam pauper, quomodo?' Caecus amat.

The twofold sense of *nil* gives point to **III 61:**

> Esse nihil dicis quidquid petis, inprobe Cinna:
> > si nil, Cinna, petis, nil tibi, Cinna, nego.

The point of such epigrams as these, depending as they do altogether upon meaning, is not lost in translation. When, however, Martial plays with sound, the point is lost in translation. The pun in **IX 21** or in **III 34,** which depends upon the similarity of the name Chione to the Greek word for snow, is an illustration:

> Digna tuo cur sis indignaque nomine, dicam.
>   Frigida es et nigra es: non es et es Chione.

Perhaps the most extreme case in Martial of playing with sound is **I 100:**

> Mammas atque tatas habet Afra, sed ipsa
>   tatarum
>   dici et mammarum maxima mamma potest.

But mere sound play is not habitual with Martial; it is scarcely, indeed, common enough to be called characteristic of him.

Martial employs two other devices for securing point. One of them is his manner of ending an epigram with an implied comparison or analogy, as in the following:

> Muneribus cupiat si quis contendere tecum,
>   audeat hic etiam, Castrice, carminibus.
> nos tenues in utroque sumus vincique parati:
>   inde sopor nobis et placet alta quies.
> Tam mala cur igitur dederim tibi carmina,
>   quaeris?
>   Alcinoo nullum poma dedisse putas?

> **(VII 42)**

Finally, Martial makes very large use of aphoristic material. One of his most frequent ways of concluding an epigram is with a pithy generalization: "hunc volo, laudari qui sine morte potest"; "qui bellus homo est, Cotta, pusillus homo est"; "sera nimis vita est crastina: vive hodie"; "ille dolet vere qui sine teste dolet."[14]

Besides the structure of Martial's epigrams, and besides his methods of introducing, developing, and concluding an epigram, there are other features of his style which must be noted. Most important of these are the parallelism and the balance which so pervade all Martial's work as to constitute an outstanding feature of his style. Especially in those epigrams which he develops by an enumeration of details or instances or by a series of comparisons, he makes use of parallelism for the sake of clearness and emphasis. He is particularly fond of putting a balanced antithesis in chiastic order, as in the familiar line, "Lasciva est nobis pagina, vita proba."[15] Usually the parallelism is strengthened by the repetition of words or phrases. Martial uses every conceivable species of repetition. He repeats the same words at the beginning of consecutive clauses, or at the end of them:

> Hermes Martia saeculi voluptas,
> Hermes omnibus eruditus armis,
> Hermes et gladiator et magister, etc.

> **(V 24)**

> Appellat rigida tristis me voce Secundus:
>   audis et nescis, Baccara, quid sit opus.
> pensio te coram petitur clareque palamque:
>   audis et nescis, Baccara, quid sit opus.
> esse queror gelidasque mihi tritasque lacernas:
>   audis et nescis, Baccara, quid sit opus.

> **(VII 92, vv. 3-8)**

> Primum est ut praestes, si quid te, Cinna,
>   rogabo;
>   illud deinde sequens ut cito, Cinna, neges.
> diligo praestantem; non odi, Cinna, negantem:
>   sed tu nec praestas nec cito, Cinna, negas.

> **(VII 43)**

The repetition at the end of clauses is usually, as in the preceding, varied by the use of different forms and constructions. Sometimes Martial combines these two types of repetition, as in the first two lines of **XII 79:**

> Donavi tibi multa quae rogasti;
> donavi tibi plura quam rogasti.

Again, Martial uses the first words of one clause as the last of the next, or the last of one as the first of the next; he even does both:

> Pauper videri Cinna vult; et est pauper.

> **(VIII 19)**

> Cogit me Titus actitare causas
> et dicit mihi saepe 'Magna res est.'
> Res magna est, Tite, quam facit colonus.

(I 17)

> [*Koina philon*] haec sunt, haec sunt tua,
>   Candide, [*koina*].

> **(II 43, v. 1)**

Finally, as an illustration of the lengths to which repetition can be carried, **IX 97** may be cited:

> Rumpitur invidia quidam, carissime Iuli,
>   quod me Roma legit, rumpitur invidia.
> rumpitur invidia quod turba semper in omni
>   monstramur digito, rumpitur invidia.
> rumpitur invidia tribuit quod Caesar uterque
>   ius mihi natorum, rumpitur invidia, etc.

He uses the same words, but in opposite relations—that is, with a reversal of the thought:

> Insequeris, fugio; fugis, insequor; haec mens
>   est:
> velle tuum nolo, Dindyme, nolle volo.

(V 83)

Martial's method of fitting the structure of his epigrams and the devices of parallelism and repetition just enumerated into the structure of his verse is also noteworthy. He commonly ends exposition, transition, and conclusion at the end of a line, often in his shorter pieces allotting to each element a couplet or a single verse. Frequently he begins with a couplet of exposition, makes the transition in a line, and devotes the final verse to making the point; or he opens with two couplets of rhetorical questions and gives over the final couplet to the conclusion. Again, he likes to save his point until the final word of the last line, especially when it is intended to surprise the reader. In that case, all save the final word will usually be filled with a transitional question. The same strictness of form is exhibited in his treatment of parallelism and repetition; he arranges to have the repeated words at the beginning or the end of lines, or at least in the same metrical position in succeeding lines. He is especially given to introducing the name of the victim of his satire in line after line in this fashion, so as to produce a sneering effect.

In form as in substance Martial's work is typical of his age. He lived at a time when the art of rhetoric was as highly developed as it has ever been, and when, moreover, it constituted the chief—almost the only—subject of education. The natural result is seen in his masterly control of devices for heightening the effect and point of his epigrams, for upon them he lavishes all the resources of the most elaborate rhetoric. His brilliance, his polish and vivacity, are in large measure due to his use of parallelism and repetition. Both these devices and also his use of question and answer, of quotation direct and indirect, of the first and second persons, of dialogue, of exclamation and apostrophe, impart to his style an emphasis, a liveliness and animation, which are among its most conspicuous characteristics. With all that terseness and concision which is essential to the successful epigram and which is in none more evident than in Martial's, he has managed to secure a colloquial ease which makes his way of writing as unconstrained as a casual conversation. This quality too is the result of his way of constructing and developing his epigrams.

It is therefore in large measure due to the devices which we have been discussing that his epigrams have attained their effect of reality and individuality, that in reading them we seem to be overhearing the talk of two real men. In many if not most of his epigrams he speaks in the first person; he addresses some one by name, and refers to a common acquaintance. When he begins, "Do you see that fellow yonder, Decianus, that needs a haircut?"[16] we seem to be present at the gossip of the baths or the porticos. It is thus that Martial contrives to give the air of writing about, and to, definite and actual people.

Both his manner and his matter are calculated to render as clear to us as possible the world he lived in. He draws his material from the ordinary life and the everyday interests of himself and his acquaintances, and he treats it, though in the most finished style and with the most finished art, yet without imagination and without emotion. We see both the author and the age through the least distorting of mediums. And this quality is the quality of the time: in fresher, less sophisticated, and more imaginative periods there is no demand for this microscopic realism, for these *minutiae* of common life and this mirror-like verisimilitude.

Martial's spiritual quality, or rather his lack of it, is also significant. For all his sentimental pathos and his genuine expression of friendship, he is wanting in poetic feeling and imagination. Superficial both in feeling and in vision, he was above all observant and easy-going, but easy-going without benevolence, even without good nature. He makes no pretense to that earnestness which most satirists affect if they do not feel. Although sharp and clever, quick of eye and of wit, a finished workman and complete master of his medium, he gives at best an accurate rendering of the outside of a society which even in its brilliance was frivolous and squalid.

If we ask ourselves, then, when we may expect to find Martial influencing modern literature, we need be at no loss for an answer: in an age which appreciates his literary skill, which is interested in his subject-matter, and which sympathizes with his spirit. An age which exalts Martial, we may be sure, is a disillusioned and skeptical, a sophisticated and cynical age; it holds up realism as the end of art, for it understands and has faith in only the concrete and the immediate. Martial cannot appeal to an imaginative and idealistic age which trusts enthusiasm and generous aspiration, which cherishes high hopes and thinks more of the possibilities of human life than of the spotted actuality.

Notes

. . . [4] For Martial's life, see Friedlaender's ed., I, 3 ff. See H. E. Butler, *Post-Augustan Poetry,* for a general characterization of Martial and his work.

[5] X 47. References throughout are to W. M. Lindsay's edition in Oxford *Classical Texts.*

[6] IV 32.

[7] VI 65:

> 'Hexametris epigramma facis' scio dicere
>   Tuccam.
>   Tucca, solet fieri, denique, Tucca, licet.
> 'Sed tamen hoc longum est.' Solet hoc quoque,
>   Tucca, licetque:
>   si breviora probas, disticha sola legas.
> conveniat nobis ut fas epigrammata longa
>   sit transire tibi, scribere, Tucca, mihi.

See also II 77, III 83.

[8] For examples of various kinds of enumeration, see II 14, VII 10, VII 92.

[9] See also IV 2 and V 17.

[10] See also I 10, I 28, III 57, V 47.

[11] See also II 80, III 10, V 81, VI 41.

[12] For other illustrations see II 58, II 71, V 29, V 53, VII 11.

[13] See also II 65.

[14] I 8, 9, 15, 33.

[15] I 4. "Vis dare nec dare vis" (VII 75) might also be cited, but it contains the additional element of repetition.

[16] I 24: Aspicis incomptis illum, Deciane, capillis?

Bibliography

. . . BUTLER, H. E., *Post-Augustan Poetry,* Oxford, 1909. . . .

MARTIAL, M. VAL., *Epigrammata,* ed. W. M. Lindsay, Oxford, n.d. (*Script. Class. Bibl. Oxon.*)

Epigrammaton libri, ed. L. Friedlaender, 2 vols., Leipsig, 1886.

John W. Spaeth, Jr. (lecture date 1928)

SOURCE: "Martial Looks at His World," *The Classical Journal,* Vol. XXIV, No. 5, February, 1929, pp. 361-73.

[In the essay below, originally delivered as a lecture in 1928, Spaeth evaluates Martial's opinion of four categories of first-century Roman professionals: physicians, teachers, lawyers, and poets.]

It has been observed by an eminent writer on Roman life and manners that our extant Latin literature is descended wholly from a sphere of society "which had more contempt than interest for the lower orders, the men who, day by day, tucked in their tunics behind the counter, or stood in apron and cap by their bench in the workshop, where nothing noble could be made, only the daily bread earned."[1] No doubt this reflection is largely true of the poet Martial, as of others; but in his case it deserves some qualification. For he did not view the lower ranks of society from the fixed standpoint of a die-hard aristocrat, nor did he reserve his abundant flow of derision to be expended on them only. His reach was far greater. He evinces a decided interest in the lower orders—usually not a sympathetic interest, to be sure, but the curiosity of one whose *penchant* it is to study life and to see it whole. In fact, he was interested in life at all levels. He took it as he found it, and wherever he sensed matter fit for quip or jest or stinging satire, he made use of it, generally regardless of whom he offended, in order, as he remarks, that life might be cognizant of its ways.[2] If his hand was stayed at all, it was only because of the fair prospect of a meal or of a new toga; and even then, if the prospect proved to be vain, his vitriolic pen moved faster than ever. Rich and poor, the high and the lowly, male and female—all were sharers both of his contempt and of his interest. It is just this candid treatment that makes of Martial's books such rich storehouses of valuable information on life and manners at Rome under the early Empire.

Now in writing his epigrams, the poet tells us, it was his purpose to spare the individual while he discussed his faults.[3] As an earnest of this endeavor he makes use of assumed names to conceal—rather ineffectively, we imagine—real persons. With Martial, in most cases, the point of the epigram was everything; and the point could be achieved with a false name about as readily as with a true one, although, of course, the laugh was louder and longer when the reader recognized the actual persons. In such epigrams as these it would not be difficult for the author to express his opinions about an entire class by lampooning the weaknesses apparent in a fictitious member of that class. It will be my endeavor in this paper, from a serious study of his poems—insofar as we can take them seriously—to present Martial's attitude and reaction toward certain of the professions of his day.

But at the outset we must needs be wary. We must bear in mind that Martial's opinions may be derived, in part at least, from the traditional attitude which he inherited from his predecessors and shared in common with his contemporaries. For, in spite of his Spanish origin, Martial was very much a Roman and was sensitive of Roman prejudices. Even as with us today there are certain occupations which are proverbially held in disrepute, so at Rome in Martial's day there were even more numerous vocations which the free-born Roman looked at askance and, moreover, with a feeling much more radical than ours in that it directly reflected the social conscience. In interviewing Martial for his opinions of various trades and professions we must also beware of unwarranted generalizations. Our poet would rather particularize than generalize. He never meant to *typify* the lawyer or the teacher or the doctor after the manner of a Theophrastus. In each profession, to be sure, he saw certain common traits and emphasized them; but always the individual members were to him like his own poems, "some good, some middling, and more bad" **(I, 16).** Within the circles with which he was most familiar he found men of varying habits and capacities, and he attacked follies and vices where they existed and meted out praise where he saw cause for it. Martial passed judgment on the man. This is partly the implication in his assertion that his page "smacks of humanity."[4] He was a shrewd and searching discerner of human nature, the most variable of God's creations.

Rome in the first century of the Empire presents the appearance of a very busy city, in spite of the fact that it was not, in any strict sense, a manufacturing center and that its exports were negligible. But it was the administrative center of the Western World, and it had much to do to supply the needs of its own huge population. There existed a highly specialized division of labor, both skilled and unskilled, into many crafts and guilds. There were, moreover, merchants of different grades, a vast horde of professional entertainers of all sorts, and the higher professions with their different branches. But all of these were not equally or freely accessible to the true-born Roman. In a society where slaves and freedmen performed most of the drudgery it is natural to find that honest manual labor, in particular, was held in very low esteem. Under the Republic, especially, this attitude had been most exacting. There were then very few professional callings to which a Roman gentleman might direct his energies and at the same time preserve his social caste. A political career leading to the higher magistracies, gentleman farming, and the professions of the lawyer and the soldier just about made up the approved list. Many of what are today our highest callings were under the social ban. Ordinary banking was no noble occupation, a medical career was unheard of, teaching was not to be considered. Under the Empire the traditional Roman attitude tended to become modified and even to disappear as time went on, especially after the incoming of Christianity. But in Martial's day there was still much anti-labor prejudice in the upper levels of Roman society, and of this we must take account if we are to evaluate the poet's own attitude at all correctly. Many a poverty-stricken proletarian chose to trust himself to the bounty of the state or the chance benevolence of wealthy patrons rather than turn an honest penny at a vocation that he considered beneath his Roman dignity. And many a knight, like Martial himself, as his funds decreased and his toga wore thin, preferred to preserve his proud and lofty station to recuperating his fortunes

by dint of honest work. Even our poet could see the grim humor in this situation, though it is to be doubted whether he ever allowed himself much thought on the anomaly of it.

Martial makes mention, more or less casually, of upwards of sixty different occupations at Rome, ranging from magistrates and lawyers to actors, hucksters, and mule-drivers. He has merely touched upon the field, it is true; but the number and variety of the pursuits he has alluded to give an indication of the breadth of his interests. He rubbed elbows with men in all walks of life: none was too high or too low. Some draw from him no comment at all. Against others, such as auctioneers, barbers, cobblers, undertakers, and charioteers, his general reaction seems to be the bitter complaint that they have means and he has not. To one of Martial's inclinations, of course, this disparity was a grievous fault. But in others, like the doctor, the teacher, and the lawyer, he found more fruitful ground for laughter and contempt; and it is on these professions that we can best pass judgment along with him.

Doctors

Physicians of all kinds were among Martial's pet aversions. Here is one point at which he and the strait-laced Cato the Elder would have been in perfect accord. If we are to believe our poet, there was scarcely a member of the healing profession about whom it could not be said, in the words of Dryden, "for every inch that was not fool was rogue." The practitioner Herodes is caught with a stolen drinking-ladle (*trulla*) on his person and tries to get off with a quick evasion **(IX, 96).** A certain Baccara is running a heavy risk, thinks Martial, in entrusting the care of his person to a doctor who happens to be his rival in love **(XI, 74).** Diaulus the surgeon has become an undertaker's assistant. Well, remarks the poet, it isn't such a great change: he is still putting his patients to bed in his old effective way **(I, 30, and 47)!** Similarly, in another epigram, it is thought that a certain eye-specialist (*opthalmicus*) who has turned gladiator (*oplomachus*) is probably putting out no more eyes than he did before **(VIII, 74).** These epigrams are very significant as showing how little removed the medical profession was, at least in the opinion of Martial, from pursuits of the lowest rank. Then there is the professor-doctor Symmachus who stalks into the sick chamber attended by a host of a hundred eager learners. A hundred hands, chilled by the north wind, paw the patient. "I *had* no fever, Symmachus," wails Martial; "now I *have*" **(V, 9).** It is no wonder that Andragoras, though left in the best of health and spirits, is found dead in the morning, when a poetical autopsy discloses that he has seen Dr. Hermocrates in his dreams **(VI, 53).** Happy indeed is the man who can afford to point the finger of scorn at these rascals.[5]

In all the epigrams not a single individual emerges to redeem the profession from this general and utter condemnation. One other fact is puzzling. We are well informed elsewhere that, in spite of its low estate, the medical calling was often very profitable. Yet among the quite numerous physicians whom Martial mentions not one is singled out as the unworthy possessor of a superabundance of worldly riches. Here our poet must have nodded.

Teachers

From the doctor to the teacher is only a step. The pointed remark, found in the Greek writer Athenaeus (XV, 66), to the effect that "if there were no physicians there would be nothing more stupid than grammarians," might well have been made by Martial. In his youth his sunny disposition must have been clouded forever by some *plagosus Orbilius* or other; for certain it is that as an adult he has little time for the pedagogical tribe. A teacher's position at Rome in Martial's day was far from being an unadulterated joy. It was anything but honorable, and, except for a few outstanding instances, it was poorly paid. Martial is not alone, therefore, in painting a gloomy picture of it.

Some distinction should be made between the elementary teachers (the *ludi magister* and the *grammaticus*) and the teacher in the rhetorical school (*rhetor*). The former our poet seems to treat with utter contempt, not unmixed with bitterness; for the latter he appears to entertain a pitying disdain. In the first place, many an early morning's sleep is lost on account of the din which the elementary pedagogue and his curly-headed troop are wont to raise even before cockcrow (**IX, 68; XII, 57,** 4 f.). For if it isn't the tyrant's raucous voice that breaks the early silence,[6] it is the resounding thwacks of his ferule as they fall athwart the anatomies of his luckless charges, louder than the ringing blows of the smith on his anvil or the thundering shouts of the amphitheater (**IX, 68**). This ferule, so hateful to the pupil, was the delight of the master, says Martial (**XIV, 80**). Perhaps it was an essential instrument of instruction where discipline was necessarily severe. How the poet shudders at the thought of his verses being dictated in blatant tones by some pompous pedagogue (**VIII, 3, 15**).[7] When Martial scornfully tells Cinnamus, once a barber but now a knight, that he is fit to become nothing else, not a teacher of rhetoric (*rhetor*) nor a secondary teacher (*grammaticus*) nor a primary teacher (*ludi magister*), does he mean to imply that these positions are low enough in the social scale but still above the reach of Cinnamus (**VII, 64**)? Teachers of rhetoric, in the person of Apollodotus, remind one of the proverbial absent-minded professor of more recent fiction. Having had difficulty in attaching the proper name to the proper face in the circle of his acquaintances, Apollodotus finally adopted the plan of writing down the names and learning them by heart. What a marvel

it was when, without consulting his notes, he was able to greet Calpurnius extemporaneously (**V, 21, 54**)! Sabineius the rhetorician chilled the warm baths of Nero whenever he entered them (**III, 25**). Martial, be it understood, abhors all pedantry.[8] He is not a bookish man himself; and so he advises one Lupus, who is anxious for the material success of his son, to steer clear of all teachers of grammar and of rhetoric and to let him have nothing to do with the books of Cicero and Vergil (**V, 56**). Such learning does not make for a profitable career.

In the face of this scornful utilitarian view, and of all that the poet has had to say in derision of teachers and teaching, it is reassuring to read the brief but honest tribute which he pays his countryman Quintilian, the most famous of all Roman rhetoricians—"Quintilian, illustrious guide of errant youth, glory of the Roman toga" (**II, 90**). It is but further evidence of his ability to detach himself from his prejudices and to view men as individuals, not as types.

Lawyers

The case is much the same with the legal profession. Whether in the form of the pleader (*orator* or *patronus*) or of the consulting barrister (*iurisconsultus*), this was the most distinguished of all the civil callings at Rome, alike honorable for the knight and senator, and the obvious road to eminence for the ambitious plebeian. The profession tended to become overcrowded under the Empire, when the craze for litigation had nearly reached the point of being a fashionable vice. Many noted writers in this period of Rome's history were members of the bar; such were Seneca, Suetonius, Quintilian, Fronto, and the two Plinys. But it is quite clear that Martial personally had no ambitions in this direction, in spite of the gratuitous but unwelcomed advice of certain of his acquaintances. For him the work of the lawyer involved too much noise and bustle, too much anxious responsibility, too much loss of sleep. "Let me have my days without lawsuits," is his curt judgment (**II, 90,** 10). His was not a legalistic nature.[9]

It is but natural, therefore, that Martial should find, among certain members of the bar, traits that called forth his laughter and his disgust. Here is a pompous fellow in the Forum, unduly impressed with the weighty responsibility of his station, as he dictates to a crowd of stenographers nearby and examines with a severe countenance the numerous documents that are thrust at him from all sides. The condescension of a cordial "How-do-you-do?" would be utterly impossible for him (**V, 51**). Then there is Postumus who, in pleading a case involving three lowly she-goats, rings the changes on all the mighty tribulations and past glories of Rome, like a veritable Fourth of July orator. "Now, Postumus," ventures the poet, cuttingly, "say something about my three she-goats!" (**VI, 19**).

Long-winded harangues seem to have been not uncommon. One Caecilianus, having been granted seven water clocks' allowance of time by the judge, is speaking long and furiously, ever and anon stopping to moisten his throat from a drinking flask. Martial suggests that Caecilianus might satisfy both his oratory and his thirst by drinking from the water clock **(VI, 35)**. A certain Cinna takes ten hours to say nine whole words **(VIII, 7)**. From which statement we are to infer that during most of the time allotted him he has rambled on but said nothing. On the other hand Naevolus has a habit of speaking only when everybody else is shouting and drowning him out, but he *thinks* himself a pleader nevertheless **(I, 97)**.

Some lawyers, moreover, are not as independent professionally as they might be. Ponticus will undertake no case that offends the wealthy or influential **(II, 32)**. No doubt the reason is that he is well aware of the most abundant source of his income. Under the Roman Republic a barrister was forbidden by law (the *lex Cincia de donis et muneribus,* of 204 B.C.) to collect stated fees from clients, and even under the Empire fees were permitted only up to a certain limit,[10] but there were, usually, ample rewards forthcoming in the shape of gifts and legacies. In many individual cases the profession proved to be quite lucrative. Cicero, for example, was a man of considerable wealth. Martial makes frequent mention of the client's gifts to the lawyer, especially on the occasion of the Saturnalia.[11] Pannychius, as a suburban farmer, is buying products which, as a lawyer, he used to receive in such abundance that he sold them **(XII, 72)**. In one epigram, however, our poet suggests that, sometimes at least, the monetary return was not so good. He attempts to dissuade his friend Sextus from coming to Rome to practice law by reminding him that neither Atestinus nor Civis, former lawyers, had earned his full rent **(III, 38)**. But usually the testimony is quite otherwise. There is in another poem the old jest about the lawyer's charges that eat up the contested funds and leave the plaintiff in debt. "The judge is looking for his fee and the pleader for his. I advise you, Sextus, to pay your— creditor!" **(II, 13)**. Cyperus, a former baker who is now pleading cases, aims to make the equivalent of $10,000 a year, a tidy income in Martial's day **(VIII, 16)**. And elsewhere our poet laments that law is much more profitable than the pursuit of the Muses and none too gently hints that he would like to see the inequality removed.[12] Indeed, it was, no doubt, the general fact of the lawyer's good financial standing that established Martial on terms of amity with so many members of the profession and led him to maintain a respectful attitude toward them in spite of his natural antipathy to their work.

For it seems to be certain, from the testimony of his verses, that Martial numbered many friends among the lawyers of his day. We have already mentioned the high tribute that he pays to the Spanish Quintilian, barrister and rhetorician **(II, 90)**. He has a similar warm regard for the younger Pliny, learned and eloquent member of the bar **(X, 20)**. Pomponius Auctus, "steeped in law and versed in the many-sided practice of the gown," doubly merits the poet's esteem in that he is a fond admirer of his verse **(VII, 51)**. The poet Silius Italicus was a noteworthy practitioner at law, Martial tells us admiringly, before he essayed the sacred art of poesy **(VII, 63)**. Fronto, Maternus, Restitutus, and Rufinus are other representatives of the legal profession about whom or to whom he speaks in terms of affection and esteem. But the most notable recipient among the lawyers of Martial's complimentary remarks is the famous advocate Regulus. The poet felicitates him twice upon his narrow escape from death beneath a collapsed portico **(I, 12 and 82)**, makes his scholarly renown comparable to his piety **(I, 111)**, congratulates him upon his eloquence **(VI, 64, 11)** and his popularity **(II, 74)**, and sketches a pretty picture of his son's admiration for the father's skill **(VI, 38)**. But in view of Pliny's pronounced aversion for this same Regulus[13]—the sole mortal whom the gentle Pliny seems to have detested—we are a little sceptical of the genuineness of the feeling that called forth Martial's praise. In fact, with a man of Martial's character—or lack of character, as some would have it—there is always difficulty in deciding whether we are reading mere flattery or heartfelt esteem. But we should like to regard it as a safe assumption that in at least some of the cases which we have mentioned Martial entertained real friendship with lawyers, mostly on account of their outstanding personalities, but partly, we believe, because of the honorable Roman calling that our poet admired at the same time that he rejected it for himself.

Poets

With this we have approached the end of our excursion. We have glanced at a few of the Roman professions and have observed that the poet Martial gave but scant approval to any of them. What, then, our patient reader may justly ask, in the face of this sweeping negation, was Martial's own *métier*? To which question we might promptly reply—as Martial himself might have done—that a man with his innate nonchalance did not consider it essential to have any. But there *was* one pursuit that our poet cherished with all the earnestness of which he was capable. It was an avocation rather than a vocation, though with Martial it was both. I refer to the calling of authorship. On almost every other page of the *Epigrams* we can find evidence of the high regard in which he held good literature, especially poetry, and of the professional attitude that he maintained toward the literature of his day. He looked upon authorship as a trust which he must guard jealously and devotedly. The names of writers, from Homer down, whom he mentions with varying degrees of praise and affection would make a list tediously long.[14] His favorite among the classic poets of bygone days is Catullus. But Martial is not merely a *laudator temporis acti.* In fact, he strongly resents the narrow attitude that can see nothing of literary excellence among the writings of the present **(VIII, 69):**

> "You honour, Vacerra, the ancients alone,
> And never praise poets unless dead and gone.
> Your pardon, if unceremonious I seem,
> But it's not worth while dying to gain your
>   esteem."[15]

He has a high regard for the work of many of his literary contemporaries, notably Silius Italicus, Lucan, and Decianus, as well as a warm affection for them personally. Indeed, it is among literary men that Martial finds his truest friends.

But not all poets are worthy, any more than all school teachers are impossible; and Martial is as scathing in his denunciation of a poor poet as he is fulsome in his praise of a good one. To him a poor poet is a blot upon the escutcheon of the highest of all arts. He is especially severe in his judgment of plagiarizers—those numerous Mr. Faithfuls (*Fidentanus*), as he likes ironically to call them, who parade under false colors and win the applause that rightfully belongs to another **(I, 38; II, 20).**

Criticism of the right sort he welcomes and solicits, but the carping and quibbling fault-finding of those who have little or no adequate knowledge of poetry as an art moves him to stinging rejoinders:

> "You damn every poem I write,
> Yet publish not one of your own.
> Now kindly let yours see the light,
> Or else leave my damned ones alone."[16]

Anyway, as he says, he prefers that the dishes which he has served at his literary repast should please the guests rather than the cooks **(IX, 81).**

Martial, as a poet, is thoroughly conscious of his own art and many times theorizes about the qualities of his epigrams—their subjects, their metres, their length, their freedom. Poets are the darlings of Apollo and the Muses, but they are not on that account freed from all responsibility for their work. Nor can they be successful bards unless they are afforded the leisure and financial independence that a wealthy patron can give them. A Maecenas plays a vital part in the success of a Vergil; and Martial continually complains that lack of the wherewithal of leisure is the greatest obstacle in his path of ascent to the Parnassian heights.[17] He is also experienced in all the hardships of a Grub-Street existence and bitterly laments that almost any trade is productive of greater material rewards than is the work of a poet.

In his own day many a successful bard is neglected and unsung. Men spend their praise on more worldly achievements than poetry. Fame comes late **(I, 1, 6; V, 10).** But the immortality which a true poet achieves is well worth all the tribulations which his mortal existence has cost him. His name will still ring in the ears of men when the perishable splendor of the world's Croesuses has passed away **(X, 2).** And so, in spite of all its hardships and inequalities, Martial never despairs of poetry as the highest of all possible callings for him. It has its sublime recompense. We can close no more fittingly than by listening to our poet as he replies proudly to a certain Callistratus whom the world has made wealthy **(V, 13):**

> I am poor, I admit, and I always have been, Callistratus, and yet I am no unknown, unheralded knight; no, I am read by many in all parts of the world, and people say of me, "Look! There he is!" and what death has given to only a few, life has given to me. But your roof rests on a hundred columns, and your money chest keeps close guard on a freedman's wealth; broad acres of Syene on the Nile acknowledge you as master, and Gallic Parma clips for you numberless flocks. Such, we are, you and I; but what I am you cannot be; what you are any one at all can be.

Notes

[1] Ludwig Friedländer, *Roman Life and Manners under the Early Empire,* English translation: New York, E. P. Dutton and Co. (1908), I, 150.

[2] VIII, 3, 20: *adgnoscat mores vita legatque suos.* (The references in this paper are to W. M. Lindsay's edition, *M. Val. Martialis Epigrammata:* Oxford, The Clarendon Press (1902).)

[3] X, 33, 10: *parcere personis, dicere de vitiis.*

[4] X, 4, 10: *hominem pagina nostra sapit.*

[5] Like Cotta, in VI, 70. With Martial VIII, 74 compare *Anthologia Palatina* XI, 115; with VI, 53 compare *ibidem* XI, 257.

[6] V, 84, 2 (*clamoso—magistro*); VIII, 3, 15 (*rauca voce*); IX, 68, 11 (*garrule*).

[7] Horace, too, it will be recalled, had gloomy forbodings of a similar fate; *Epist.* I, 20, 17 f.

[8] Cf. X, 21.

[9] For passages illustrative of this paragraph cf. I, 17; II, 30, 5 f; I, 49, 35; I, 97; III, 46, 7; IV, 8, 2; V, 20, 6; VIII, 67, 3.

[10] The Emperor Claudius fixed it at 10,000 sesterces. Cf. Cicero, *De Sen.* 10; *Ad Att.* I, 20, 7; Tacitus, *Ann.* XI, 5, 7.

[11] *E.g.* IV, 46; V, 16; VII, 72, 5; X, 87; XII, 72; XIV, 219.

[12] V, 16, 5 f.; cf. I, 17; II, 30, 5.

[13] Cf. *Epist.* I, 5; II, 20; IV, 2, 7.

[14] See Ludwig Friedlaender, *M. Valerii Martialis Epigrammaton Libri:* Leipzig, S. Hirzel (1886), II, 367-369 (Register 3, Autoren).

[15] Marcus S. Dimsdale, *A History of Latin Literature:* New York, Appleton and Co. (1915), 473. Cf. Martial XI, 90.

[16] I, 91, rendered by Paul Nixon, *Martial and the Modern Epigram:* New York, Longmans, Green, and Co. (1927), 131. See his *A Roman Wit:* Boston, Houghton, Mifflin Co. (1911), 12. (Unfortunately the latter book is now out of print).

[17] I, 107; VIII, 55; XII, 3. Mr. T. R. Glover takes exception to this complaint of Martial (*Studies in Virgil:* London, Edward Arnold [1904], 26): "Martial was wrong; if any one man made Virgil, it was rather the *barbarus* than Maecenas, but all the king's horses and all the king's men, veterans and ministers, could never make a Virgil—least of all out of a Martial." See, too, Martial X, 58, 70; XI, 24.

John W. Spaeth, Jr. (essay date 1932)

SOURCE: "Martial and the Roman Crowd," *The Classical Journal,* Vol. XXVII, No. 4, January, 1932, pp. 244-54.

[*In the essay below, Spaeth surveys Martial's depiction of men whose occupations he either scorned as contemptible or envied because they were lucrative—cobblers and booksellers, moneylenders and pawnbrokers, merchants and undertakers, and charioteers and musicians, among others.*]

The epigrams of Martial have long served as a rich source of supply for those who would seek a more intimate knowledge of life as it was lived at Rome in the first century of the Empire. This is quite as it should be, for Martial was one who freely obeyed his own command to live in the present[1] and at the same time he had been endowed by nature with a keen sense of vision and an agile mind, which he used with unsurpassed success in describing what he saw and experienced. The simplicity and sparkling vividness of his little poems make them immediately appealing and expressive. His vignettes of Roman life are based upon a familiar background into which they naturally merge; but oftener than not this is true because of the very wealth of detail which he himself has supplied. Both

by virtue of necessity and by deliberate intent the epigrammatist knew life at close range and from that knowledge derived both entertainment and a livelihood. No one knew the contemporary scene better than he; no one observed it with so professional an interest.

Moreover, if it be objected that Martial's pictures are too frequently vitiated by exaggeration, the result of prejudice and a straining after effect, it must also be acknowledged that the character of the man is so clearly revealed in his verse that the exaggeration can easily be discounted by the discerning reader. For Martial's prejudices are seldom so deep-seated as to be very vicious; Juvenal erred much more in that direction. The epigrammatist scanned the surface, wearing his heart on his sleeve, so to speak, and submitting to no close philosophic attachment. His interests were generally broad rather than deep. It was thus that he touched life closely at all levels and was enabled, by his gift of pointed expression, to invite his many readers to a feast of such richness and variety.

Representatives of practically all walks of Roman life are mentioned and criticized by Martial in the course of his fifteen books. Sometimes the mention is a brief one; in other cases the poet is moved, more often by animosity than by sympathy, to give his pen freer play. Of the sixty or more Roman occupations, high and low, to which he alludes there are very few which find much favor in his sight. In an earlier essay[2] I presented his views on doctors, teachers, lawyers, and poets, about whom he permitted himself considerable eloquence. The purpose of the present paper will be to follow the poet's course as he ranges more widely through the heterogeneous Roman mob, in the fora, the Subura, the parks, and the porticoes, making note as he passes of each flagrant example of vice or folly which may serve him later as the subject for an epigram.

Let us turn first to the world of the petty tradesmen. These were in many cases slaves or freedmen who acted as agents for their betters. There were all sorts, but for Martial they might all be lumped together as necessary evils that must be tolerated. And yet the poet admits that some of them at least, like the butcher, barber, and taverner, are indispensable aids to a livable existence. The noisy baker (*pistor*), like others of his genus, robs one of an hour or two of sleep before daybreak (**XII, 57,** 4f), a heinous sin for which Martial can never forgive him.[3] Then there is, too, the crafty taverner (*copo*) who tries to sell his cheap wine unmixed with the more precious water (**I, 56; III, 57**). At this rate, thinks Martial, it is about time for him to be giving a gladiatorial show to his native town, as a cobbler and a fuller have already done for theirs (**III, 59**). Even book-sellers (*bybliopolae*) are thriving beyond their deserts. Tryphon is selling Martial's thirteenth book (the collection of *Xenia* or "Guest-Gifts") for twenty cents, whereas at half the price it would yield him a decent profit **(XIII, 3)**. But, in passing, the poet pays to the book-dealer Quintus Pollius Valerianus the compliment of remarking that it is through him that his poems are not permitted to disappear from public view **(I, 113)**; and, for advertising purposes, he informs us that another of his publishers is Secundus, freedman of learned Lucensis **(I, 2)**.

The depth of degradation is very nearly reached when one descends to the level of the petty huckster. Wishing to be especially abusive to one Caecilius who has dared to regard himself as a man of polish and wit, Martial likens him to the common street vender and much else besides—the hawker who trades sulphur chips for broken glassware **(X, 3, 3f)**, the peddler of pease-pudding, the vile slaves of the salt-fish merchant (*salarius*),[4] the raw-voiced purveyor of smoking sausages **(I, 41)**. The foul debauchee is merely in the same category. The dealer in slaves (*mango*) offends by his greed **(IX, 5, 4)** and still more by the din he makes **(IX, 29, 5)**. This was a combination that Martial could not stomach. The self-imposed pomposity of the merchant (*negotiator*) in Agrippa's Saepta **(X, 87, 9)** and the frenzied haste of the business man in the fora **(VIII, 44)** move him to scorn. He is prompted to warn Titullus, as he observes him rushing about from forum to forum in the busy hours of the morning, sweating and mud-bespattered, that his wealth is an evanescent thing after all: "Plunder, hoard, pilfer, possess; you must finally leave it all."[5] How the poet exults in the edict of Domitian that forbade these pushing fellows to overflow the whole street in the ambitious promotion of their trade! Thanks to the emperor, no longer must a praetor tramp through the mud in the middle of the street; no longer does the reckless barber brandish his razor dangerously close to the ears of pedestrians, nor the smoky cook-shop (*nigra popina*) monopolize most of the walk. "Barber, taverner, cook, and butcher (*lanius*) are keeping to their own thresholds. Now Rome actually does exist; recently it was but one huge shop" **(VII, 61)**. This world of business was not for Martial. It was too noisy, too nervously busy, and too undeservedly profitable; on these grounds alone it would justly have merited our author's unrighteous indignation. But, in addition, it was one side of Roman life that the prouder Roman should not tolerate, and Martial's disapproval is merely superimposed upon this traditional attitude and buttressed by it.

The tale is not much different among the handicraftsmen and those who contracted for their services. We are still in the realm of slave and freedman. What an outrage, exclaims the poet, this kissing craze has become at Rome! You are bussed on one side by the weaver (*textor*), on the other by the fuller (*fullo*), and again by the cobbler (*sutor*) who has just been kissing his hide **(XII, 59)**. What could be more disgusting? Yet these same fullers, greedy like the rest **(VI, 93, 1)**, gather in their inordinate gains and, at least in the case of one of their number, can entertain their native mu-

nicipalities with gladiatorial shows **(III, 59)**. The metalworker (*aerarius*) and the money-lender (*faenerator*) are among those who rob Rome of its matutinal slumbers and so, of course, could never rise at all in Martial's esteem **(XII, 57, 6f)**. These money-lenders were loathsome creatures anyway to a man like Martial, who was in a continual state of insolvency and would rather receive a *gift* of money than put up surety for a loan. Sextus, one of these fellows, at the approach of our poet, murmurs to himself very audibly that he hasn't a cent (*quadrans nullus*) in his chest. "Vile worm!" mutters Martial; "it is bad enough to refuse a loan when you are asked, but much worse to do so beforehand" **(II, 44)**. Cladus, another pawn-broker, advances less than forty cents on a customer's ring **(II, 57)**. One of Martial's particular banes among this class was Secundus, stern-voiced and without a trace of human benevolence **(VII, 92, 3)**. A contractor (*redemptor*) for construction work is very likely to be an arrant cheat, and a good five-foot rule, says Martial, is a handy weapon to have on hand to combat his fraud **(XIV, 92)**. Even the brazen mule-driver (*mulio*), knowing that his asinine subjects cannot complain intelligibly about him, will rob them of their barley and sell it to the innkeeper **(X, 2, 9f; XIII, 11)**.

Undertakers' menials (*vispillones*), too, are a tribe to be scorned, being on a par with hangmen (*carnifices*) and neither better nor worse than doctors **(I, 30; I, 47; and II, 61, 3f)**; and this, as we have seen,[6] is contempt indeed. Barbers (*tonsores*) are especially exasperating. It is hard to do without them **(II, 48, 2)**, and yet they goad one almost to the verge of despair. The sidewalk barber, in particular, is a menace to life on this planet **(VII, 61, 7)**. The slashing Antiochus, barber by trade, will disfigure a customer more effectively than any other known agent. Avoid him if you are not yet prepared to meet the god of the lower world. The he-goat of all beasts alone seems to have good sense: he chooses to go bearded in order to escape Antiochus' razor **(XI, 84)**. The barber Eutrapelus (Mr. Skillful), on the other hand, works so slowly and deliberately that another beard has grown by the time he has finished shaving the original one **(VII, 83)**.[7] Yet one of these worthless fellows, Cinnamus, "the most noted barber in the whole city," has been made a knight through the generosity of a female acquaintance, only to find, as Martial tauntingly observes, that he is, by nature, fitted to be nothing else than a barber **(VII, 64; cf. also VI, 64, 26)**. Martial is here voicing, in his own pungent manner and with his own unique comments, the opinions of his day and generation. For the pursuits which all these men represented met with scant respect from any trueborn Roman citizen. They were all out of caste.

Certain trades in particular Martial regarded as especially conducive to ill-deserved gain; and about these, for this reason if for no other, his pen is more fluent than ever. The job of public crier or auctioneer (*praeco*), like that of undertaker (*libitinarius*), was held in general contempt.[8] So when the auctioneer Gellianus, mentioned by Martial, kissed the slave girl in order to prove her qualities, he immediately lost all chances of making a sale (**VI, 66**). Yet such vileness did not prevent the trade of auctioneer from being one of the most profitable in the imperial city. Our poet advises a friend, Lupus, to avoid all higher learning for his boy: if he is dull, make him an auctioneer and his fortune is assured (**V, 56**).[9] Just so the *praeco* Eulogus (Mr. Plausible) wins the hand of an eligible maiden in the face of competition from two praetors, four tribunes, seven lawyers, and ten poets; and Martial is quite cynically convinced that the old father has done wisely and well by his daughter (**VI, 8**).[10] Cobblers (*sutores*) seem to have furnished another special butt for Martial's disesteem. He abominates their kisses as he would those of a viper (**XII, 59**). In three epigrams (**III, 16, 59, and 99**) he applies to a cobbler the term *cerdo*, which was used for slaves or tradesmen of the lowest class. Such creatures are outcast; but this fact does not hinder them in the accumulation of wordly treasure. Here is one who has become possessed of the estate of his deceased patron. "*My* parents taught me latters," bitterly exclaims the poet; "but what is the use to me of teachers of grammar and of rhetoric if a shoe can give a cobbler a gift like that?" (**IX, 73**). Another cobbler, like his mate the fuller, is affluent enough to spend his surplus on a gladiatorial show for his home town (**III, 16 and 59**), and Martial is rather fiendishly amused when he has got the fellow angry by twitting him about it (**III, 99**).

Charioteers (*aurigae*) are another low-lived lot which the public honors with both praise and wealth. Here we can well imagine that it is the real Martial himself who is speaking. One Catianus is rogue enough to "pull" his team in a race, probably in order to gratify some patron who has staked his money on a different color (**VI, 46**). Yet in polite conversation his fellows Scorpus and Incitatus will take precedence over topics of art and literature (**XI, 1, 15f**), just as Messrs. Ruth and Tunney, in our own sporting circles, have little competition from Barrie or Shaw. Scorpus, when victorious, carries off in a single hour fifteen bags of gold, whereas the client Martial spends a whole feverish day to receive a few spare pennies (**X, 74**; cf. also **X, 76**). In view of this bitterness we are tempted to wonder who paid our poet for writing the lament on Scorpus' death and the eulogistic epitaph that we find in the tenth book of the *Epigrams* (**X, 50 and 53**). Or may it be, rather, that here we read the sportsman Martial's genuine tribute to the individual, whereas elsewhere we have his stinging scorn for an overprized profession? Musicians, too, were a well-paid tribe—too well paid, of course, for Martial's satisfaction. The same parent whom we have already mentioned is advised to make his boy into a lyre-player (*citharoedus*) or a flute-player (*choraules*) if he shows an aptitude for money-making arts (**V, 56**). The poet belittles the

pride of a certain wealthy Rufinus by reminding him that Philomelus the musician has more than he (**III, 31**); and he replies to a hypothetical query as to when he will return to Rome from a sojourn in Cisalpine Gaul with the words, *veniet cum citharoedus erit* (**III, 4**). In spite of their wealth, as well as because of it, these musicians were a bother; and the best entertainment of all, Martial thinks, is one in which there is no lyre-player to din one's ears (**IX, 77**).

Architecture was another lucrative pursuit at Rome, but it was also generally held in higher esteem than the others already mentioned. Martial is hardly different in his own attitude. While he grieves to note that this calling is highly rewarded while the profession of letters is not (**V, 56**), he is ready to pay a very flattering tribute to Rabirius, the architect (*architectus*) of Domitian's palace on the Palatine (**VII, 56**).[11] The fact remains, however, that Martial could not view with perfect serenity the professional status of the auctioneer, the cobbler, the charioteer, the musician, and the architect so long as they were paid well and the pursuit of poetry was a career of beggary. This was a perversion of nature that he could never condone.

The charioteer and the musician were not the only professional entertainers that our poet disliked. He spurned them all; and we can imagine that here, too, he was sustained in his position by the best elements of Roman society. Gladiators (*gladiatores*) were, in most cases, slaves, though under the Empire they were, on occasion, even *equites* and senators; and they merited little esteem from any respectable person. Yet, to be sure, many of them were idolized, like our own athletic heroes. Martial himself pays a tribute to the fighter Hermes (*et gladiator et magister*) in a peculiar poem of fifteen lines, every one of which begins with the idol's name (**V, 24**).

The gladiatorial trainers (*lanistae*) were by general consent little more than brutes, so that Martial was probably echoing sentiment in using the name of this occupation, along with other obviously vile terms, as an epithet to apply to a certain Vacerra whom he despised. Even here the poet cannot refrain from inveighing against riches in his customary manner. "I wonder, Vacerra," he concludes, "why you are not wealthy!" (**XI, 66**). The boxing master (*magister*) with his cauliflower ear (*fracta aure*) was probably not much better (**VII, 32, 5**). The keeper and trainer of snakes (*custos dominusque viperarum*) and the foul dancing master from Gades were of the lowest rank of disrepute, classed with those petty hucksters whom we have already introduced as stigmatized by Martial as the very dregs of humanity (**I, 41**).

Of actors (*mimi*)[12] the poet has little of importance to say.[13] He mentions the *mima* Thymele and the *mimi* Latinus and Panniculus in terms that would suggest that the performances in which they participated were not the highest and purest forms of histrionic art. In fact, the acting profession was, like some others, confined almost entirely to freedmen, foreigners, and slaves; the citizen who performed professionally, at least under the Empire, suffered legal *infamia,* thus being barred from holding public office.[14] Accordingly, the social esteem in which actors as such were held could not have been very high,[15] though individual performers were complimented, flattered, and materially rewarded. Martial seems to be paying a high tribute to the famous Latinus in an epigram that is echoed by Ben Jonson's lines on Shakespeare.[16] There the actor, styling himself "the sweet idol of the stage, the glory of the games, the darling of your applause," defends his private life from attack on the grounds of his actions on the stage (**IX, 28**). So, too, the actor Paris is honored in an epitaph as "the darling of the city and the wit of the Nile, art and grace itself, playfulness and joy, the Roman theater's glory and bereavement, and all the Venuses and Cupids incarnate" (**XI, 13**).[17]

Official position *per se* held no charm for Martial, particularly if the incumbent himself was unworthy. He was pleased enough to commend in verse the tenure of the consulship by his friend Silius Italicus in the year 68 (**VII, 63**, 9f) and to felicitate him when the same high office fell to one of his sons some twenty-five years later (**VIII, 66**); and he prays earnestly to Apollo, god of bards, that a like honor may be granted to his poet friend Stella (**IX, 42**). Even under the Empire the consulship was an honorable distinction, though it was not much more. But some holders of public office were worthy of nothing but contempt. Such is the consul who attends "a thousand morning levees (*mane salutator limina mille teras*), crowding out poorer and humbler brethren who find it hard to compete against his official purple for their patron's alms (**X, 10**). In such cases the rewards are bound to be unequal: the poor client may be asked to dinner, but the consul, by his assiduous lobbying, gains a rich province to plunder (**XII, 29**). Moreover, courting a praetor or a consul was a burdensome bore, when at any moment of the day he might expect a crowd of clients to escort him home from some function or other (**X, 70**, 9; cf. also **II, 74**; and **XI, 24**). Yet holding high office involved heavy expense, too; and Martial gives a knowing wink to one Proculeia who has divorced her husband, the praetor, at the very beginning of the year, when, as we might say, the bills for his lavish entertainments are about due to arrive (**X, 41**). After all, these great and mighty magistrates did not rate so high in the scale of wealth, for, as we have already seen, one auctioneer has outbid two praetors, four tribunes, and seven lawyers for the privilege of marrying an old man's daughter (**VI, 8**). In Domitian's day Martial was safe in taking but a languid interest in politics. Nor was it his rôle, either, to play upon the heavier instruments of war (**VIII, 3**, 13f). He has little to say in general about

military offices, confining his observations to a few personal remarks about hardy centurions[18] with whom he was acquainted and several of whom had fallen on foreign fields while engaged in the service of Rome.[19]

Finally, in matters of religion Martial was a Roman.[20] He observed the proper forms, but it is highly doubtful that he ever experienced a surge of religious devotion. For the imported cult of Cybele and her emasculated priests (*Galli*) he can entertain only utter disgust (**I, 35**, 15; **V, 41**, 3; **VII, 95**, 15; and **IX, 2**, 13f). These are simply rascals that practice vice under the guise of religion, and when hungry they are not above selling the brazen cymbals which are used in their crazy rites.[21] The bald-pated, linen-clad priests of Isis, with their noisy crowd of followers (*linigeri fugiunt calvi sistrataque turba*), were scarcely much better (**XII, 28**, 19; cf. also **IX, 29**, 6). Yet, even in Martial's day, there did exist religious devotees who were not rogues and impostors. Such is the Roman Carpus whom the poet praises in one of his laudatory epigrams as a duteous high priest (*pius antistes*) who devotes his gifts to the pursuit of wisdom (**VII, 74**).[22] Thus there was still real worth to be found in the holy profession. The witch or fortune-teller (*saga*) and the astrologer (*astrologus*), we might say in passing, draw from Martial only a few casual remarks (**VII, 54**, 4; **IX, 29**, 9; **IX, 82**, 1; and **XI, 49**, 8). "Garrulous" he calls the former (**XI, 49**, 8). Probably his contempt for such charlatanism was too eloquent even for words.

Not all the canvases in Martial's gallery have been passed in review in this survey. But sufficient have been produced to prove the kaleidoscopic quality not only of his literary output but also of the Roman world in which he lived, a world which will stand comparison with our own in many striking particulars. Obviously Martial is one of the most modern of the ancients. But it is to be noted in addition that he is a zealous and exceedingly realistic reporter of many humbler walks of life that the more elevated Roman literature is wont to disregard. For our comprehensive knowledge of these lower levels of society we shall always remain his debtors.

Notes

[1] Cf. I, 15, 12: *Sera nimis vita est crastina: vive hodie;* also V, 20; V, 58; and VIII, 44. The references in this paper are to W. M. Lindsay, *M. Val. Martialis Epigrammata:* Oxford, Clarendon Press (1902).

[2] "Martial Looks at His World," *Classical Journal* XXIV (1929), 361-73.

[3] Cf. IX, 29; IX, 68; X, 74; XII, 18; and XII, 68, 5f.

[4] Or it may be "sellers of salt"; cf. IV, 86, 9f. The more usual term for sellers of salt-fish is *salsamentarii.*

[5] Cf. VIII, 44, 9: *Rape, congere, aufer, posside: relinquendum est.*

[6] Cf. the *Classical Journal* XXIV (1929), 364f.

[7] Cf. VIII, 52, where, however, another interpretation is possible.

[8] By the terms of the *Lex Iulia Municipalis* (45 B.C.), 94-97, *praecones* and *libitinarii* were excluded from standing for municipal offices; cf. C. G. Bruns, *Fontes Iuris Romani Antiqui*[7]: Tübingen, P. Siebeck (1909), 107; and E. G. Hardy, *Six Roman Laws:* Oxford, Clarendon Press (1911), 155f. Cf. also Cicero, *Ad Familiares* VI, 18, 1.

[9] Cf. Petronius, *Satiricon* XLVI, 7.

[10] Cf. Juvenal VII, 5f, where poets are forced to turn *praecones* in order to make a living.

[11] Of course we cannot be sure that this was not an indirect shaft of flattery aimed at the master through the servant. We must always, in reading Martial, be wary of such commendations.

[12] Martial nowhere in his epigrams employs the word *histrio*.

[13] Cf. I, 4, 5; II, 72, 3f; III, 86, 3f; V, 61, 11f; IX, 28; and XI, 13. There is a subtle hint in VII, 64, 9.

[14] Cf. Livy VII, 2, 12; Suetonius, *Aug.* XLV, 3f; *Digest* III, 2, 2, 5; also Tenney Frank, "The Status of Actors at Rome," *Class. Phil.* XXVI (1931), 11-20.

[15] Cf. Seneca, *Epist. Mor.* XLVII, 17; Tacitus, *Ann.* I, 77; Juvenal VII, 90; Suetonius, *Aug.* XLV, 3f; and *Digest* XXIII, 2, 44.

[16] "Th' applause, delight, the wonder of our stage."

[17]

Urbis deliciae salesque Nili,
ars et gratia, lusus et voluptas,
Romani decus et dolor theatri
atque omnes Veneres Cupidinesque.

[18] Cf. XI, 3, 4 (*rigido centurione*).

[19] Cf. I, 31; VI, 58; XIII, 69 (*Pudens*): I, 93 (Fabricius and Aquinus): and X, 26 (Varus, fallen in Egypt): also VI, 76 (Fuscus, in Dacia).

[20] Cf. E. E. Burriss, "Martial and the Religion of His Day," the *Classical Journal* XXI (1926), 679f.

[21] Cf. XIV, 204 (Cymbala). The *esuriens Gallus* of this epigram recalls Juvenal's famous *Graeculus esuriens* (III, 78); the sentiment in both cases is, no doubt, similar—a strong feeling of contempt for easterners.

[22] In line 7 some MSS read *Caro* or *caro* instead of *Carpo.*

Francis L. Jones (essay date 1935)

SOURCE: "Martial the Client," *The Classical Journal,* Vol. XXX, No. 6, 1935, pp. 355-61.

[*In the essay below, Jones describes the patron-client system, emphasizing both the humiliation Martial endured under various patrons and the poet's frequent evasion of the responsibilities he was supposed to fulfill as a client.*]

In the Rome of the first century of our era there were many who preferred to be client to one or more patrons rather than to earn a precarious living by hard work. One of these was Martial. Coming to Rome from Spain, probably in the year 64 A.D., he successively flattered the emperor and paid court to wealthy patrons in the hope of gaining a livelihood. His failure was as marked as his persistence, for he was nearly always begging and nearly always on the verge of poverty. Martial found the thirty-four years of his life at Rome disappointing but out of them he wove a vivid pattern of the seamy side of life in the Rome of his time. Especially is this true of his experiences as a client.

Martial felt deeply about the trials of a client, for he knew from experience the inconveniences, hardships, and insults that a client had to undergo. He detested the *salutatio*. He must break off his sleep and, clad in his toga, the official dress, plow through the muddy streets in order to present himself at daybreak at the house of his patron. He must salute his patron as the latter entered the *atrium* with the words "*Salve, domine.*" Some patrons were exacting in allowing no violation of this etiquette. When Martial unthinkingly saluted Caecilianus with "*Salve, Caeciliane,*" he was docked of his dole for the day.[1] But the trials of a client did not end here. Decianus was seldom at home when Martial went to salute him, and if he was, he had his doorkeeper trained to say that he was not at leisure. Martial tells Decianus that it is not irksome to walk two miles to see him but that it is irksome to trudge four miles and then not see him.[2] Another difficulty was that Maximus owned so many houses in town that Martial could not tell where to find him: "A man who lives everywhere," declares Martial, "lives nowhere."[3]

The other duties of a client were almost equally tedious to Martial. After the *salutatio* the patron, surrounded by his band of clients, set out for the forum. It was considered a mark of honor to have a large number of clients as an escort, but there were practical reasons as well. Clients as well as slaves carried the patron's sedan chair or trudged on ahead to clear a passage through the narrow streets, while others followed as escort. If the patron went on foot, one of his clients walked on his left to protect him from assault, while others cleared the way. If the patron was pleading a case, his clients must shout applause. If he gave a *recitatio,* they must rise from their seats and applaud. In short, as Martial puts it, they must praise whatever he said or did.[4] Martial, moreover, found fault with the long working hours, for he must attend his patron from daybreak until late afternoon.[5]

> *Lassus ut in thermas decuma vel serius hora*
> *te sequar Agrippae.*

Many times he even had to escort his patron back home. This constant attendance on his patron prevented him from writing epigrams:[6]

> *Dum te prosequor et domum reduco,*
> *aurem dum tibi praesto garrienti,*
> *et quidquid loqueris facisque laudo,*
> *quot versus poterant, Labulle, nasci.*

While these duties cannot be called burdensome, they were calculated to destroy a man's self-respect and independence of spirit. Martial with his poetic temperament and aversion to manual labor naturally hated the inconvenience of the *salutatio,* the indifference of individual patrons, and the tedium of performing such menial tasks.

Hating the system as he did, Martial spared no efforts to evade his obligations. He sent his book to salute Proculus, whom he had neglected, explaining that he could not have written the book if he had been a regular attendant at the *salutatio.*[7] He sent his freedman to attend Candidus, pointing out how much better an attendant he would make:

> I shall hardly be able to keep up with your sedan chair; he will even carry it. If you fall into a crowd, he will elbow his way through; my side is too weak for such hard work. Whenever you plead a case in court, I myself shall have to keep silence, but he will shout "bravo" for you.[8]

The patron was expected to reward his clients for services rendered. First, he was expected to give them legal advice and to plead their cases in court. This service was sometimes of doubtful value. Sometimes it was refused. Martial attacked one of his patrons for declining to plead his case against one of the emperor's freedmen or a wealthy widow.[9] Next, at irregular intervals or at the Saturnalia the patron was supposed to send his clients gifts. Martial warned Labullus not to think himself a generous patron merely because he sometimes sent some silver plate, a threadbare toga that would keep nobody warm, or a few pieces of money. For although Labullus might be more liberal than the general run of patrons, Martial considered him stingy when compared with the patrons of other days.[10]

Another of Martial's patrons had been accustomed each Saturnalia to send silver plate weighing one pound. When instead of this he sent a half-pound of pepper, Martial objected that pepper at that price was too expensive.[11]

But the most common reward of the client took another form. In the days of the Republic the patron was expected to invite his clients to a dinner (*cena recta*). As clients increased in number, this practice was abandoned and a basket of food (*sportula*) was given. Later a dole of money (*centum quadrantes*) was substituted, while under Domitian the *cena recta* was revived. Patrons, however, were too selfish to treat their clients fairly. Martial tells how Caecilianus invited a crowd, not to dine with him, but to watch him eat a choice variety of mushrooms alone.[12] Mancinus, after inviting a throng of clients, served nothing but a boar, and that only as large a one as a dwarf might slay. None of the "fixings" were served and, besides, the guests had an opportunity only to look at the boar. It was not a dinner but a spectacle.[13] Annius, another patron, had the dinner served by slaves instead of on a table. The slaves removed the dishes so rapidly that none of the guests had a chance to eat. Martial took offense at a "dinner on wheels."[14] At best, the clients were served inferior food. Martial complains that he and his patron Ponticus are not served the same quality of food. While Ponticus is eating Lucrine oysters, Martial himself tries to suck the juice of a mussel through a hole in the shell. While Ponticus enjoys a luscious, fat turtledove, Martial is served a magpie that had died in its cage.[15] In short, the restoration of the *cena recta* was so unsatisfactory that it was again replaced by the money dole.

The clients seem to have preferred the money dole. Martial tells of a starveling Spaniard who set out for Rome. Upon hearing when a few miles north of Rome that the money dole had been replaced by the *cena recta,* he immediately retraced his steps.[16] Martial himself bade a sad farewell to the "*centum quadrantes*" although he did call them "*miselli*":[17]

> *Centum miselli iam valete quadrantes*

In the light of what has been said about the *cena recta* of Domitian's time it is not difficult to understand the preference. Furthermore, the money dole, although very small (about thirty cents) did allow the client a measure of independence. By careful saving he might scrape together enough to buy a toga and pay the rent for his dingy lodings. But the client paid dearly for even this modicum of independence, for some patrons were irregular in the payment of the money dole.[18] There was also the expense of the toga, which the client must wear at the *salutatio* and during attendance on his patron. Martial laments that even twice the amount of the money dole will not buy a toga, and, therefore, his is old and threadbare.[19] Again, at least one patron paid in counterfeit money.[20] Clearly the preference of the client for the money dole was a preference for the less annoying of two evils. Neither the *cena recta* nor the money dole was an adequate means of support. Martial indicts the whole system as a means of livelihood when he says.[21]

> *Vix tres aut quattuor ista*
> *res* [being a client] *aluit, pallet cetera turba*
> *fame.*

The system of patron and client had many ramifications. When Martial one morning reached the home of his patron Maximus, he was told that Maximus had gone to salute his own patron.[22] Martial refused to be client to a client: "It is bad enough to be a slave; I have no desire to be the slave of a slave."[23] This criticism, however, loses some of its force when we discover that Martial had a client of his own.[24] Even consuls did not blush to be clients. The consul Paulus had no scruples about carrying the litter of his patron, plowing his way through the mud, or indulging in the grossest kind of flattery.[25] To Martial's scorn for a consul who would obsequiously perform the tasks of a client is added his anger against Paulus, whom he regards as a competitor. What can the poor client do in the face of such competition? Paulus' *toga praetexta* has put Martial's poor toga out of business.[26]

Martial was constantly changing patrons. He bade adieu to After and Decianus who were never at home to be saluted, to Caecilianus and Mancinus who served such poor dinners. In these instances it is probable that the patrons were at fault. Yet sometimes it was Martial who was to blame. We have seen that he sought every excuse to escape his duties. Many of his farewells, therefore, were written in answer to charges of neglect. Candidus objected because Martial had sent his freedman as a substitute. Martial replied that his freedman would make a better client than he could ever be.[27] Postumus objected because Martial had not presented himself for a whole year at the *salutatio*. Martial, admitting the charge, replied that he was none the poorer.[28] Thus while Martial was often treated unfairly by his patrons, he himself was not above reproach.

Martial's criticism of the system, his efforts to dodge his responsibilities, and his frequent adieus to his patrons show clearly that he and the system were incompatible. After allowance is made for the indifference of Decianus, the meanness of Mancinus, or the parsimony of Postumus, it is evident that Martial and his patrons had entirely differing objectives. Martial loathed the *salutatio*. His patrons insisted that he attend it regularly. Martial desired exemption from the servile tasks of the client. His patrons were interested in him primarily as a client who would swell their train and perform these same tasks.[29] When he failed to discharge his duties, they considered that he was not playing the game according to the rules, and they resented it. Martial above

all was in search of a patron of literature, a Maecenas, as he so often expressed it, who could and would give him freedom from the necessity of earning a living and so leisure in which to cultivate the Muses:[30]

> *Olia da nobis, sed qualia fecerat olim*
> *Maecenas Flacco Vergilioque suo.*

This was his goal alike in seeking wealthy friends and in flattering the emperor and his favorites as well as in becoming client to numerous patrons. Consequently, it is not surprising that he was continually in difficulties with his patrons.

Yet there was one class of patrons with whom Martial was on good terms: those who themselves were literary men. Even to them, however, he did not discharge his duties with any great regularity. We recall that he sent a book of his epigrams to Proculus in order to make amends for neglecting the *salutatio*.[31] In apologizing to Frontinus he declared that regular attendance on one's patron was not the only way in which to show affection.[32] It is likely, then, that Proculus and Frontinus were willing to excuse Martial's disregard of the *officium*. Since he was a literary man, Proculus could appreciate Martial's argument that he would not have had time to write the book he was sending if he had attended the *salutatio* regularly.[33] Since he was a literary man, Frontinus could appreciate Martial's plea that a poet ought not to waste his time attending his patron.[34] In other words, while the typical patron merely desired Martial as one more client to swell his train of attendants, Proculus and Frontinus could understand a poet's desire for leisure in which to write and so were willing to overlook his neglect. This is further evidence that Martial and the system were incompatible.

Thus Martial's life as a client was most humiliating. He had to push his way through the crowd up the steep, muddy street leading to the Esquiline Hill to greet Paulus, who was not at home. He had to waste his time attending Labullus all the day when he wished to be at home writing epigrams. He was reprimanded by Candidus for neglecting his duties. He was docked of his dole by Caecilianus. Mancinus served only a boar. Since any one of these experiences was sufficient to evoke his wrath, the result each time was an epigram which was to preserve for us the record of one more bitter experience in the life of a client of the first century of our era.

Notes

[1] Cf. Martial VI, lxxxviii.

[2] II, v, 5-8.

[3] VII, lxxiii, 6.

[4] XI, xxiv, 3.

[5] III, xxxvi, 5 f.

[6] XI, xxiv, 1-4.

[7] I, lxx.

[8] III, xlvi, 3-8.

[9] II, xxxii.

[10] XII, xxxvi.

[11] X, lvii.

[12] I, xx.

[13] I, xliii.

[14] VII, xlviii.

[15] III, lx.

[16] III, xiv.

[17] III, vii, 1.

[18] IV, xxvi.

[19] IX, c, 5 f.

[20] X, lxxiv, 4.

[21] III, xxxviii, 11 f.

[22] II, xviii, 3 f.

[23] II, xviii, 7 f.

[24] VIII, xlii.

[25] X, x, 7-10.

[26] X, x, 11 f.

[27] III, xlvi.

[28] IV, xxvi.

[29] XI, xxiv, 10 f.

[30] I, cvii, 3.

[31] I, lxx.

[32] X, lviii, 11 f.

[33] I, lxx, 18.

[34] X, lviii, 12.

J. Wight Duff (essay date 1938)

SOURCE: "Varied Strains in Martial" in *Classical and Medieval Studies in Honor of Edward Kennard Rand*, edited by Leslie Webber Jones, Books for Libraries Press, 1938, pp. 87-99.

[*In this essay, Duff stresses—and commends—Martial's realism, which he regards as the primary impulse behind the poet's variety of tone, perspective, and subject matter. Duff sees further evidence of Martial's realistic viewpoint in the poet's acknowledgment of his artistic limitations.*]

In an author like Martial who makes the true assertion that his writing smacks of mankind (*hominem pagina nostra sapit*), there must inevitably be a wide variety of persons and themes. This clever Spaniard of the first century A.D. had only to use his well-nigh unsurpassed faculty of keen observation in the cosmopolitan Rome where he spent thirty-four years of his life to find infinite material for the epigrams, largely but by no means entirely satiric, in which he proved his mastery. It is the range of human character portrayed in his poems that first and most obviously impresses a reader; for there is little in the Rome of his day that is not set in clear outline before the mind's eye.

Yet to concentrate on this aspect alone would give an imperfect view of his manysidedness. Some years ago in a paper[1] I isolated the tender sentiment which makes so lovable a strain in his nature: and more recently I have discussed his use of the epigram for satire.[2] Here I desire to range more widely over the multiplicity of elements which mixed in him, and throw out a few reminders about his realism, but also about the almost chameleon-like changes of a spirit which could combine cringing and coarseness, hatred and affection, admonition and aspiration; about fluctuations in his literary quality, his deftness in stylistic variation, the composite literary influences acting upon him, his different metres, and his various pronouncements on literature.

In 64 A.D., he came, a young well-educated man, from Spain to Rome with claims on the attention of his fellow-Spaniards, Seneca and Lucan, and although that connection was severed abruptly through their implication in the Pisonian plot against Nero, yet Martial succeeded in maintaining relations, not always as profitable as he would have liked, with many men of high social standing, while at the same time poverty made him acquainted with the lowest grades in the community. In Domitian's reign he could address, amuse, and overpraise the Emperor himself, while studying all ranks of his subjects for 'copy.' The result is a gallery of what in varying proportion to the length or the shortness of a poem may be called portraits, miniatures or mere thumbnail sketches, but all marked by a marvellous realism.

It is worth while noting how his figures re-create the society of the times. We meet the senator as well as the swaggerer in senatorial seats who has risen from servitude. So too with the knights—an ex-slave wears the equestrian ring (**III, 29**), and some people are only pretended knights (**V, 35**). Social usages lent themselves to comment: dinner-parties, dinner-hunters, mean hosts, legacy-hunters (*captatores*) were traditional subjects for satire. Thus we have the man who never dines at home unless he fails to hook an invitation (**V, 47**); the systematic diner-out ever hoping for better offers (**V, 44**) or inventing the latest news (**IX, 35**); the niggardly patron who has mushrooms served to him, while his guests receive none (**I, 20**), whereas host and guests in equity and etiquette ought to enjoy the same fare (**III, 60**); for it is hard at a meal to get perfumes and nothing else (**III, 12**). There is the terrible literary host whose *recitatio* from his works spoils a dinner (**III, 45 and 50**), or his fit fellow, the antiquarian bore, chattering about his silver goblets (**VIII, 6**). But guests also may misbehave by filching dainties (**II, 37; VII, 20**) or by noisy talkativeness.

The legacy-hunters, courting childless wealthy folk with presents, come in for scathing ridicule. The rich men, whom they secretly wish dead, may go on living, or, worse still, may die without making them heirs (**IV, 56 and 61; V, 39; VI, 63; VIII, 27**). The morning *levée* (*salutatio*), at which patrons received clients in the formal toga, is denounced as a physical burden, an expense, a waste of time (**III, 36; V, 22; VII, 39**); and the whole Roman day is summarised with inimitable neatness (**IV, 8**).

Widely various human types—more or less oddities inviting satire—are presented in profusion: the skin-flint, parsimonious, although he has inherited two millions (**I, 99**: cf. **I, 103**), the acquaintance who gives advice instead of a loan (**II, 30**), the man who quotes 'Friends go shares' in Greek . . . but fails to put the maxim into practice (**II, 43**), or one who possesses a well-stocked wardrobe but no clothes for a shivering friend (**II, 46**), or another whose gifts grow shabbier each December (**VIII, 71**). There are fussy triflers (*ardaliones*) who know other people's business best (**II, 7; IV, 78**). There is the nuisance of a fellow who haunts shops, examining countless *objets d'art* and late in the day departs with two small cups bought for a penny (**IX, 59**); and there is the pretentious dandy who is 'A 1 in cloaks' (*alpha paenulatorum*) but has to pawn his ring to get a dinner (**II, 57**).

The professions undergo castigation. We meet the advocate who gets and, no doubt, deserves trumpery presents at the Saturnalia (**IV, 46**), or the surly lawyer incapable of uttering a polite greeting ([*haire*], **V, 51**), or your counsel who takes an unconscionable time to say next to nothing (**VIII, 7**), or the other who sagaciously blushes in preference to stating his client's case

(**VIII, 17**). In an adaptation of a Greek epigram, an amusing picture is drawn of the pleader in a lawsuit about three she-goats who dragged in with vociferous rhetoric some great names in Roman history and who is at last implored by his client to come back to the three she-goats (**VI, 19**: cf. *Anth. Pal.* XI, 141). Medical men are no less a theme for jest than they were in Greek epigrams. So Martial laughs at Dr. Doublecourse (*Diaulus*) who exchanged the profession of healing for that of funeral undertaker—the same thing in the end! (**I, 47**), or the physician who brings a band of students to paw his patient, thereby infecting him with the fever he had not got before (**V, 9**), or the light-fingered doctor who, after stealing a winecup from his patient, pretends he has done it to keep him teetotal (**IX, 96**). A remonstrance by an invalid to another doctor declares that he has had one professional visit already and a continuance would make him seriously ill (**VIII, 25**). The climax comes with the man who died solely because he dreamt about his doctor—another Greek imitation (**VI, 53**; cf. *Anth. Pal.* XI, 257). Teachers are also subjected to mockery—the schoolmaster whose stridency and whacks before cockcrow prevent folk from sleeping (**IX, 68**), and the noisy rhetor who, if he does not crack columns, as in Juvenal's exaggeration, at least plagues the ears of others more than he does his own throat (**IV, 41**). Martial, in a flippant mood, questions the wisdom of his parents in getting him rhetorical instruction (**IX, 73, 7-8**). Elsewhere he caustically places such money-making arts (*artes pecuniosas*) as an auctioneer's business above a literary education (**V, 56**); but on those principles we should never have had the epigrams of Martial.

Women make frequent appearance—some attractive, some repulsive. The young bride, good and pretty (**IV, 13**) and the faithful Arria on the verge of accompanying her husband through the gates of death (**I, 13**) are offsets to the cruel mistress who beats her slave for one badly arranged curl (**II, 66**), the much-married woman about to wed her tenth husband (**VI, 7**), artificial beauties who are all make-up, toothless or nearly toothless crones, an ugly beldame careful to keep a retinue of still uglier creatures so as to shine by contrast, and many others, expert in loathsome vice. Some women were skilled enough in poisoning, as Juvenal reminds us, to be dangerous to a husband, or to lady friends, as was one whom Martial calls Lycoris (**IV, 24**). A different Lycoris becomes the theme of a frank avowal of altered affections:

> Lycoris, once 'mong women you were queen:
> Now queen of women Glycera is to me.
> *You* can't be she: *she'll* be what you have been.
> Time's work! I wanted *you;* but now—'tis *she*!

(**VI, 40**)

The common trades of Rome are touched on in their infinite variety, perhaps nowhere more realistically than in the terse catalogue of pedlars on a Roman street, including the hawker who barters pale sulphur matches for broken glass **(I, 41)**.

But it is not only persons to whom Martial directs attention. Concrete things as well as characteristic features of the times demanded record from him. He has an eye for the beautiful, in natural landscape, and in art—the imposing baths of Claudius Etruscus **(VI, 42)**, a winebowl that was a triumph of skill **(VIII, 51)**, an old statuette of Hercules in bronze by Lysippus **(IX, 43)**, or a pretty name like 'Earinos' **(IX, 11)**. Now, he contrasts the nerve-racking din of Rome with rural peace **(XII, 57)**; now, he praises the attractions of his native Spain. He introduces us to most of the prominent writers of the day, and, as we shall see, some of his satire is aimed at literary tendencies like archaizing. Even personal confessions and the author's preferences (a traditional feature in classical satire) tell us much about the characteristics of his age.

It is natural, and certainly most enjoyable and profitable, in surveying Martial's range, to draw instances chiefly from the twelve books which contain his most representative work, produced from 85 to 102 A.D. But one must not overlook his earlier extant writings; firstly, the book of *Spectacula,* as we entitle it, on the games celebrating the opening of the Flavian Amphitheatre by Titus in 80 A.D.; and, secondly, the two collections (*ca.* 83-86 A.D.) of mottoes, mostly in couplets, for gifts to guests, *Xenia* and *Apophoreta,* now numbered, out of due order of composition, as **Books XIII** and **XIV.** The *Liber Spectaculorum* has been subjected to a meticulous investigation by Weinreich,[3] and one result brought out is the background of mythological learning which at this period rather beset Martial, though it is striking how he shows independence of originals by a kind of Ovidian gift of variation in expression and motif. The theme of the 'Wonders of the World' in the introductory epigram on the Amphitheatre is an old one freshly handled by Martial. When he takes to writing three elegiac epigrams (*Spect.* **12, 13, 14**) about the pregnant sow killed in the imperial hunt, he varies his treatment by using mythology in two of these and dropping it in the third. They are exercises in variation, just as in **Book I,** by devoting seven poems (six elegiac, one hendecasyllabic) to the incident of the hare spared by a lion, he proves his skill in ringing changes on a single theme. The ingenious rather than thrilling poems on different animals in the arena, including a *pius elephas,* which exhibit instinctive reverence for the Emperor's *numen,* bear a significance for Caesar-worship; and Weinreich left over for a pupil a comparison between the Caesar-cult of Statius and that of Martial.[4] The *Xenia* might be called one long elaborate menu, for, with four exceptions, the mottoes deal with eatables and drinkables—vegetables,

cheeses, savouries, fish, poultry, wines and so forth. The *Apophoreta,* 'things to be taken away,' are concerned, on the whole, with a different sort of gifts, expensive or cheap, such as writing-tablets, dice-box, tooth-pick, sunshade, cloak, table, ivory tusk; but, at the close, we come back to cereal dainties for a very early morning meal:

> Rise! bakers now sell breakfast to the boys—
> Dawn's chaunticleers all round crow out their
>   noise.

>   **(XIV, 223)**

Mostly in elegiac distichs, with some hendecasyllabics, those two books have a value as showing at once Martial's range of subject and his advance from apprenticeship to skill in that condensed expression which made a factor in his epigrammatic power.

When we study his personality, we are struck with its prodigiously extensive range. Variety of spirit, variety of attitude, lend to his poems an aspect of medley so multifarious as almost to constitute a new kind of *satura.* We find copious indecency wilfully indulged in with the warning that much will shock propriety and with the conventional excuse that a poet can be clean though his verses be filthy. They are another aspect of his realism. Knowing well that lubricity would not please a staid emperor, he feels obliged to make a bowdlerized anthology for Norva. We suffer too a tedious surfeit in the adulation of Nerva's predecessor, Domitian, disfigured by far-fetched conceits, which, as a rule, are foreign to Martial's forthright and unrhetorical style. Here he pays for insincerity by an artificiality of ideas beyond the verge of absurdity. I give a single instance. In **IX, 3** he goes the length of arguing that even the gods could never repay all that Domitian has done for them in the way of temple-building. They are bankrupt debtors, and he assembles Roman business terms (*creditor, auctio, conturbare, decidere*) to elaborate his point. If the deities were to sell off to meet their obligations, Atlas would go smash and Jupiter fail to raise a penny in the shilling (*non erit uncia tota*). Martial is not often so silly, and of such flatteries he explicitly repented under Nerva and Trajan **(X, 72)**.

Other qualities attesting his composite nature are a brutal savagery of attack, mitigated, no doubt, by his censuring under disguised names, and, in contrast, that vein of tender sentiment to which we owe his beautiful poems of friendship and touching tributes of affection to the dead. The genuine accents of a warm heart ring through his verses to friends like Decianus and Julius Martialis no less than through his *In memoriam* poems, lamenting the death of the little slave-girl Erotion **(V, 34 and 37; X, 61)** or a young friend who will never come back from the East **(VI, 85)**. Death in childhood or youth affects him, as it affected the Greek epigram-matists. But Martial's note is his own. He has a breadth of human sympathy which includes bond and free, as seen in his obituary lines on a slave hairdresser:

> Here lies Pantagathus whose youthful years
> Cut short have brought his master grief and
>   tears.
> His steel that clipped scarce touched each
>   wandering hair
> And trimmed the bearded cheek with deftest
>   care.
> Earth, be thou kind and light as fitteth thee:
> Lighter than his skilled hand thou canst not
>   be.

>   **(VI, 52)**

Allied to this vein of sentiment is his love for beautiful scenery, his raptures over the fine view of the city across the Tiber from the Janiculum, his enjoyment of farm-life on his little property out at Nomentum, his homesick longings for Spain, his distress over the landscape wrecked by the eruption of Vesuvius

>   where but late mid vines
> Green shadows played, and noble clusters
>   filled
> The brimming vats.

In that ruined country-side he sees, with poetic imagination, a lost sporting-ground for the fabled creatures of mythology:

> On this same mount the satyrs yesteryear
> Did foot their frolic dance;

and his reflections lead to the melancholy conclusion:

> Now all lies whelmed in fire and ashes dread.

>   **(IV, 44)**[5]

Other poems reveal him in a mood of serious admonition, and here it should be noted that he objects to have his *nugae* and *lusus* dismissed as unconsidered trifles. Thus, he uses epigrams to proffer sound advice. In one he strikes the time-honoured philosophic note that to be 'free' you must have cheap tastes and despise luxury **(II, 53)**; in another, he declares that big purchases argue a small mind **(III, 62)**. He advocates a good use of time (e.g. **IV, 54**) and sighs with honest aspiration after the leisure essential for an author's work and guaranteed by patronage **(I, 107; XI, 3,** 6-10), a cardinal point, we shall see, in his literary creed.

Varying strains are further exemplified by the difference of literary quality in his epigrams. About this he is disarmingly frank—'some bits are good, some so-so,

and more are bad,' he recognizes **(I,16)**: 'that's how a book is made.' It is an implicit and defensive exposure of the hypocritical pretence that abusive criticism, by concentrating wholly on faults in a work, indicates honesty on the part of a critic. Indeed, Martial is still more emphatic in a later book. In **VII, 90,** fastening on the term *inaequalis,* which a critic had applied to his work, he contends that a book to be good must be uneven in quality: *inaequalis,* then, he takes as a compliment (*laudat carmina nostra*); for a dead level means dulness, and no one will charge Martial with that blemish, if his works be taken as a whole. A quite cursory examination confirms his avowal. He is not his best self either in his coarser or in his adulatory pieces; and he cannot always be equally successful in securing polish or point. Some of the dedicatory epigrams are frigid compared with Greek parallels, although there are others where his genius and response to Roman environment have brilliantly eclipsed his models.

The different strains in Martial may be in part set down to the variety of literary influences acting upon him—influences inherited consciously and unconsciously from Greece and Rome. The Roman predecessors to whom he specifies indebtedness are Catullus in Ciceronian times, Domitius Marsus and Albinovanus Pedo, two Augustans, and Lentulus Gaetulicus, put to death by Caligula. The latter is possibly the author of nine epigrams.... So insignificant are the fragments of Marsus and Pedo that their influence cannot be disentangled; Catullus, however, is not only quoted and parodied by Martial but is the chief pattern for his hendecasyllabic and choliambic poems. True, he shows metrical independence in restricting the first foot of his hendecasyllables to a spondee; but he owes much to the satiric spirit of Catullus[6] in both of these metres and in elegiac verse. One hendecasyllabic piece, in a tone of withering contempt, might have been written by Catullus to Lesbia after their breach. It shows his method of free adaptation; for he echoes *quot sunt quotque fuere* from Catullus' lines to Cicero (XLIX, 2) and applies the name 'Catulla' to the woman whom he addresses:

> Loveliest of women now or long ago,
> Vilest of all who are or e'er have been,
> Catulla, how I wish that you could grow
> A woman not so lovely but more clean!

>   **(VIII, 53)**

In elegiacs, although influenced by Ovid, he does not accept rigorously the Ovidian disyllabic close of the pentameter, but resembles Catullus in endings like *amicitiae* and *ingenio.* For technique and phraseology Martial was also indebted to Virgil and Horace.[7] One influence, however, he never specifies, presumably because it was obvious to his mind. This is the influence of Greek epigrams, long imitated by Latin poets. A generation before Cicero, poets in the circle of Q.

Lutatius Catulus freely drew upon them as models.[8] Many distinguished Greek epigrammatists, now represented in the *Anthologia Palatina,* had spent part of their lives in Rome; and it was the ordinary thing for literary men in the coterie of Martial's friend, the younger Pliny, to try their hand at such brief compositions in Latin.[9] It will be conceded that Greek epigrammatic themes and conventions influenced Martial profoundly, although they did not rob him of a free power of adaptation; and some Greek epigrams such as those by Lukillos of the Neronian age, contain resemblances too striking to be dismissed as mere coincidences.[10]

Nor must his variety of metrical form be neglected. It is a variety appropriate to his miscellaneous content. Of his 1561 epigrams, 1235 are elegiac, 238 hendeca-syllabic, 77 choliambic: a few are iambic or hexametric. Pieces in hexameters alone are thus comparatively rare; but their importance for him in theory appears to be seldom appreciated. He makes a strong plea for the right to use them in light poetry. An objector in **VI, 65** holds that epigrams should be not in continuous hexameters but in distichs. This criticism is intentionally placed immediately after a poem of thirty-two hexameter lines. Martial's defense is that this verse is both permissible and customary: his critic may read distichs only, if he prefers what is short: he may skip (*transire*) long epigrams, provided that Martial is allowed to write them! The significant point is that he virtually places himself, for the moment, alongside of his friend Juvenal, within the domain of *satura,* whose conventional form since the time of Lucilius had been the hexameter. But it was not the high-flown epic hexameter which either of them found to their taste: for Martial it was too much associated with a mythology that had wearied him, and Juvenal makes fun of its style in his description of the Privy Council which deliberated upon the monster-fish presented to Domitian (Satire IV: cf. *consedere duces,* VII, 115, borrowed from Ovid).

It remains to indicate his varied views on his own poetry and on literary questions. What he craved for himself was a niche beside Pedo, Marsus and Catullus (**V, 5,** 5-6). Of these the only rival to his fame in modern times is Catullus, and that for lyric rather than for epigrammatic power. Martial is conscious of his contemporary vogue: his *juvenilia* can still be had (**I, 113**), and he mentions different booksellers who stock his poems (**I, 2** and **117; IV, 72**). Rome repeats his verses (**VI, 60**); but he is known far more widely than in the capital (*toto notus in orbe Martialis* **I, 1, 2**; cf. **III, 95,** 7-8; **V, 13, 3**). He is read or quoted on the Rhone (**VII, 88**), in Rhaetia (**IX, 84**), even in distant Britain (**XI, 3**). His hendecasyllables have brought him notoriety, though, he admits, not equal to that of a circus horse (**X, 9**): but certainly he is pointed out in the streets (*monstramur digito* **IX, 97**). He is convinced that his poetry, because it will live, can confer immortality on

those mentioned in it (**V, 10, 12**)—why, then, condescend to mention a snarling detractor (**V, 60**)? And yet, as regards individuals, he insists that in his censures he avoids personalities (**VII, 12, 3; IX, 95** B) and substitutes fictitious names.[11] The principle observed has been

> To spare the sinner, but denounce the sin,

> (**X, 33, 10**)

safeguarding, as he tells us in his valuable prose preface to **Book I,** the respect due even to persons of lowliest degree (*salva infimarum quoque personarum reverentia*). Thus, he declines to say who 'Postumus' is: and indeed Postumus must be partly a lay figure and parly a Horatian reminiscence when admonished for postponement of 'living' (**V, 58**). Nor is it likely that the same person is meant by the Postumus, half of whose kisses are still half too much (**II, 10**); or the over-scented Postumus (**II, 12**); or the Postumus whose dole as a patron is stingy (**IV, 26**); or Postumus, the rhetorical advocate who bellows out Roman historical instances in the lawsuit already mentioned (**VI, 19**). Martial's *ioci* are *innocui,* not meant to hurt (**I, 4,** 7; **V, 15; VII, 12,** 9); and they amuse, although they may not pay (**I, 76**). Naturally, then, he objects to finding scurrilous verses circulated under his name (**VII, 72,** 12-16; **X, 3** and **33**); for he is not vitriolic toward actual persons, however bitter in exposing the offender as a type. A poet to whom we owe poems of true friendship and sympathy could not be heartless: indeed, he marks the man without a heart as an object for commiseration (**V, 28,** 9). Yet this is not to suggest that his poems are compact of sentiment; for he is well aware that epigrams without 'salt' and 'gall' must be insipid (**VII, 25**). To his own poetry his attitude is, as we should expect, a varying one: sometimes he stresses the light nature of his *nugae,* sometimes he is anxious to proclaim that he harbours a serious purpose (**IV, 49,** 1-2). His claim may be conceded, even if he has no constructive system to propound; for an observer so acute and incisive cannot fail to produce a positive effect: his coarsest poems unmask the hideousness of vice and stimulate a revulsion of feeling toward moral health.

A pleasant strain of common sense runs through his literary pronouncements. Writing nice epigrams, he says, looks easy work—yes, but to write a whole book is hard (**VII, 85**). Conscious that the epigram is his specialty, he naïvely instances an able friend who would no more compete with him in that field than Virgil would compete with Horace in odes or Virgil with Varius in tragedy (**VIII, 18**). With equal frankness he mentions an admirer who likes his epigrams next to the satires of the now lost Turnus (**VII, 97**). Patronage he favours because it guarantees leisure for the creation of literature: it might not make Martial a Virgil, but it would at any rate make a Marsus of him (**VIII, 56**, 24). The same poem summarises this doctrine in one of his familiar lines: *Sint Maecenates, non derunt, Flacce, Marones.*

Writing, however, may be overdone. There is unwisdom in an author's publishing books too frequently—his came out almost annually. The risk is that readers may be satiated:

> What hurts my books, dear Pudens, is the rout
> Of constant issues wearing readers out.
> Rare things delight: first apples charm the
> more:
> By winter-roses men set ampler store.
> So pride commends the wench that fleeces
> you:
> An ever-open door keeps no youth true.
> The single book by Persius wins more praise
> Than all light Marsus' epic length of lays.
> Think, when you read again a book by me,
> That it's the only one: more choice 'twill be.

(IV, 29)

Some editors have doubted whether the *levis Marsus* of this poem can be the same as the one mentioned among his models. The line *quam levis in tota Marsus Amazonide* is the single extant allusion to his *Amazonis,* an epic apparently in more than one book on a war with the Amazons. It is likely that, had Martial meant a different Marsus, he would have made this clear; and *levis* may be used here not in the derogatory sense of 'trivial' but to suggest that Marsus' province was light poetry like Martial's *nugae,* and that it would have been better if Marsus had shared his distaste for epic.

Prompted either by common sense or by a more penetrating discernment, and conscious of the vital force within him, he states a great literary truth when he declares

> To live, a book must have indwelling power.
> (*Victurus Genium debet habere liber:* **VI, 60,**
> 10).

Such is the conviction that entitles him to anticipate literary immortality. He knows that his *métier* is to hold the mirror up to the facts of life. Once—it is in **Book VIII**—he hesitates whether he should go on writing: five books were surely enough, six or seven rather too much, and now an eighth is in progress. But a rebuke, which is also an encouragement, comes from Thalia, the Muse of light poetry. He has a mission from which she will not discharge him. 'Ingrate!' she exclaims, 'can you abandon your pleasant trifles? What else could Martial compose but *nugae*? Not tragic drama, surely? nor epic?'

> Nay, dye your Roman booklets smart with wit,
> That Life may read and own the portraits fit.

(VIII, 3, 9-10)

And so there comes in a later book his triumphant proclamation of his literary position. 'Why,' he asks, 'read mythological twaddle about Oedipus or Thyestes, Colchian witches like Medea, or monsters like Scylla?'

> Read this which makes Life say 'It is my
> own.'
> No Centaurs, Gorgons, Harpies here you'll
> find:
> My pages have the smack of human-kind.

(X, 4, 8-10)

This return to the Terentian *humani nil a me alienum puto* reveals the basis of both the pleasant and the unpleasant in Martial. He concludes with the advice: 'if it is not your wish to recognize the manners of men or to know yourself, then take up the study of an Alexandrine mythological poet like Callimachus.'

Such is, definitely announced and in practice maintained, the programme of Realism that explains most of his literary antipathies. He dislikes, we have seen, mythological themes. This hardly needs further illustration; but one short piece may sum up. In **V, 53,** which is based upon a Greek epigram preserved in *Anth. Pal.* XI, 214, he reasons with Bassus against writing tragedies on Medea, Thyestes, Niobe and Andromache, already overdone in Latin literature (we know of half a dozen attempts at a Thyestes drama).[12] The most suitable *materia* for such work would be Deucalion or Phaëthon: it should, that is to say, be drowned in water or consumed in fire!

He dislikes bombast. This follows from his disclaimer of anything like the epic grand manner, though in the same breath he parodies it:

> Lo! I the man for trifles unsurpassed,
> I mayn't o'erawe you, yet I hold you fast.
> Great themes are for great bards: enough to see
> You oft re-reading my light poetry.

(IX, praef.)

Another of his dislikes is obscurity. Himself preferring the straight-forward style of an essential realist, free from the enigmatic and the precious, he was out of sympathy with such Alexandrine poets and such of their imitators as followed that cult of the obscure which is a recurrent ideal of decadents in ancient and modern poetry. A literary contemporary preferred to Virgil the recondite *Zmyrna* of Cinna for its difficulty, and Martial banters him on his hard style:

It's not a reader but Apollo's light
  Your books require:
As Cinna, matched with Virgil, was like night,
  You rank him higher!

(X, 21, 3-4)

Further he felt an objection to compositions written merely to display technical skill—lines . . . such as those that read backward as well as forward or those 'echoic' elegiacs where the words constituting the opening two and a half feet of the hexameter are repeated at the close of the pentameter. Such ingenious trifles he dismisses with the sentence 'silly is the labour spent on puerilities' (*stultus labor est ineptiarum:* **II, 86,** 10).

Likewise he shares Horace's contempt for slack composition, advocating care in writing, and stigmatizing the glib versifier who tosses off 200 lines per day, but doesn't recite them—for a fool, how wise! **(VIII, 20).** And he dislikes the archaistic tendencies of some contemporaries, reducing *ad absurdum* the idea that dead poets are necessarily the best **(VIII, 69: cf. XI, 90).**

His interest in standard poets and prose-writers is shown in couplets suited for copies of their works, in **Book XIV, 183-195.** It was an interest fostered by friendship with the chief literary men of his day. Most of them he mentions, but he never names Statius, though L. Arruntius Stella was the poet-patron of both **(I, 7; IV, 6, 5; V, 11, 2; VII, 14, 5).** Statius' mythological poems would not attract Martial: a *Thebaid* or an *Achilleid* were too remote from life around. His concern was not with mythical heroes but with men. One practice, however, he shares with Statius, that of prefixing to some books explanatory prefaces in prose. Indeed, Statius in certain of his *Silvae* handles the same subjects as Martial in his epigrams: and occasionally they use similar expressions more like borrowings than coincidences (e.g. Mart. **I. 41,** 4-5; Stat. *Silv.* **I, 6,** 73). In Martial's aspersions on mythological epics (he does not appear to feel the same objection to Silius' historical epic, the *Punica*), he must have had Statius in mind, just as Statius can hardly have failed to think of Martial, when in his introduction to *Silvae,* Book II, he apologises for some of his own light poems (e.g. on a parrot) as *leves libellos quasi epigrammatis loco scriptos.* What they felt was in all likelihood not deep animosity but incompatibility of taste and temperament.[13]

It is pleasant to take leave of Martial as one of a literary circle, in which his gift for friendship was an asset. He honoured Lucan's memory, keeping the anniversary of his birth and maintaining relations with his widow Polla **(VII, 22; X, 64).** He respected Silius for the reverence he showed to 'great Virgil's monument' on land he had bought **(XI, 48 and 49);** as an epic poet he is 'the pride of the Castalian sisterhood'

(IV, 14). His activities as advocate, consul and poet are celebrated **(VII, 63);** and Martial is so proud of his admiration that he asks how a detractor dare carp at poetry valued by Silius **(VI, 64,** 6-15). To Juvenal he was linked by a share of his satiric outlook and a warm affection **(VII, 24 and 90; XII, 18).** The younger Pliny, of whose seriousness he affected to be half afraid **(X, 19),** was another good friend, who supplied him with the expenses of his final journey home to Spain. A common interest in literature animates the friendly note to the prose author Frontinus **(X, 58)** and the commendation of Sulpicia's writings **(X, 35 and 38)** as poetry of honourable love and healthy jest. The general effect is that of a versatile man with sympathies broad enough to enable him to understand literature and human beings of the most various types.

Martial is at his best where he is most himself—where he adheres to the theme of humanity which he recognized as his own. When he has beasts of the arena or an imperial *dominus et deus* for his subject he is tempted into artificiality. Here the quest for variety of style makes a display of skill that over-reveals itself. But humanity he can depict, disdain, loathe, pity with a convincing truth which brings into play simple style and fitting metres used with consummate mastery. This realism and his literary genius for reserving to the end the point or sting in many of his most celebrated epigrams are, amidst all his manysidedness, the sure pillars of his fame.

Notes

[1] J. Wight Duff, *Martial: Realism and Sentiment in the Epigram* (Cambridge University Press, 1929, printed for Leeds Classical Association).

[2] J. Wight Duff, 'Martial: the Epigram as Satire,' in *Roman Satire: Its Outlook on Social Life* (Berkeley: University of California Press, 1936), 126-146.

[3] O. Weinreich, *Studien zu Martial* (Stuttgart, 1928).

[4] F. Sauter, *Der römische Kaiserkult bei Martial und Statius* (Stuttgart, 1934).

[5] The whole poem is translated by J. Wight Duff, *A Literary History of Rome in the Silver Age* (London, 1927), 527.

[6] J. Wight Duff, *Roman Satire* (Berkeley: University of California Press, 1936), 128-129.

[7] E. Wagner, *De M. Valerio Martiale poetarum Augusteae aetatis imitatore* (Regimonti = Königsberg, 1888).

[8] R. Buttner, *Porcius Licinus u. der litterarische Kreis des 2. Lutatius Catulus* (Leipzig, 1893), ch. 9.

[9] J. Wight Duff, *A Lit. Hist. of Rome in Silver Age,* 555-6; cf. p. 536 for Pliny's own light poetry.

[10] O. Autore, *Marziale e l'epigramma greco* (Palermo, 1937) gives a judicious estimate of Martial's debt to Greek epigrams. Cf. K. Prinz, *Martial u. die griechische Epigrammatik* I (Wien, 1910); E. Pertsch, *De Valerio Martiale graecorum poetarum imitatore* (Berlin, 1911); R. Schmook, *De M. Valeri Martialis epigrammatis sepulcralibus et dedicatoriis* (Weidae Thuringorum, 1911).

[11] See L. Friedlaender, *M. V. Martialis Epigrammaton libri* (Leipzig, 1886), II, Register 6, 'Wirkliche und fingirte Privatpersonen aus Martials Zeit.'

[12] O. Ribbeck, *Tragicorum Latinorum Reliquiae:* (Leipzig, 1852), index.

[13] H. Heuvel, 'De inimicitiarum, quae inter Martialem et Statium fuisse dicuntur, indiciis,' *Mnemosyne* (1937), 299-330.

Franklin B. Krauss (essay date 1944)

SOURCE: "The Motive of Martial's Satire," *Classical Weekly,* Vol. 38, No. 3, October 16, 1944, pp. 18-20.

[*In the essay below, Krauss maintains that Martial's early and continuing failure to find a generous, sympathetic patron led to deep personal resentment and a proclivity for satire. The critic also speculates about why Martial's acerbic verses were so popular with his contemporary audience.*]

Marcus Valerius Martialis, the son of Celtic parents, migrated to Rome from Bilbilis, his birthplace, in Hispania Tarraconensis in A.D. 64, when he was already in or approaching his middle twenties. The incentive, doubtless, was the quite natural desire of an aspiring provincial writer to realize his literary ambitions in the city which was the cultural, as well as the political, center of the empire. It appears that soon after his arrival he not only gained the patronage of his eminent and well-to-do fellow countrymen, Seneca the Philosopher, the latter's brothers, Gallio and Mela, and the poet Lucan, Mela's son, but also that through them he came to the favorable notice of Calpurnius Piso, a prominent representative of one of the oldest and most distinguished Roman gentes. Certainly he was justified in believing that under these auspicious beginnings he could embark in his career amply provided with the sort of social entrée and freedom from pecuniary cares that Vergil, Horace, and Propertius had enjoyed through the bounty of Maecenas. It is not likely that he was aware that in the emperor's greedy and jealous mind all these sponsors were already suspect. His prospects, however enviable they may have appeared to him, were destined to be short-lived, indeed, for in the following year (A.D. 65) these supporters were swept away because of their real or alleged participation in Piso's conspiracy against the life of Nero.

What a severe shock Martial suffered through this abrupt reversal of his expectations and to what social humiliation he thereby was exposed are reflected in the significant silence which he maintained regarding the events of his life during the succeeding fifteen years of his residence at Rome. Doubtless these were for him years of bitter disappointment and of gross disillusionment, years spent in observing and experiencing the seamy side of a morally bankrupt society. From his later writings we can readily deduce that he must have felt degraded by the necessity of having to associate competitively with that large and heterogeneous army of freeborn citizens whom economic circumstances or overweening ambition impelled to search perennially for patronal support in quarters high and low.

Accordingly, when his hopes for an early and brilliant career faded through his failure to find a liberal and sympathetic patron, and as his provincial 'simplicitas' was repeatedly and incurably bruised by the callous sophistication of the imperial city, he evolved into a confirmed satirist. His native Celtic wit and passion were stimulated into protest against the prevalent snobbishness and demoralizing superficiality of an age which recognized mercenary gain and political advancement as the sole criteria of achievement. The denial of the dignity of the individual and of the freedom of individual expression created a multitude of social injustices that only the pen of the satirist could adequately attack. To this dubiously popular form of literature Martial was impelled by his chargin and attracted by his peculiar genius.

The fact that Martial determined the function of the Latin epigram is a commonplace of literary history. It is of more immediate interest to us to know that, in spite of the inevitable carping of critics, his caustic verses had an inherent attraction for the rank and file of the reading public. We can understand why this was so, since the epigrams are comparable in their psychological appeal to our cartoons and comic strips. The sensational novelty of his themes and particularly of his treatment of these depended on a synthesis of factors that was Martial's own: his almost complete preoccupation with a merciless and frequently indiscreet expose of Roman foibles; his extensive use of trenchant wit to relieve otherwise unpleasant observations; and his ingenious practice of reserving the element of surprise to the last verse, or even the last word, of the epigram. Since his avowed purpose was to portray Roman life realistically, he delighted and dismayed by turns, through the range and accuracy of his thumbnail sketches, individuals and social groups as they beheld others or themselves pitilessly caricatured.

What, then, did Martial's readers find so amusing, so piquant and provocative, in his verses? He catered to the Italic propensity to laugh at physical defects by his burlesque representation of smooth-pated Labienus, Phoebus, and Marinus (**5.49; 6.57; 10.83**), of sparse-toothed Aelia, Maximina, and Picens (**1.19; 2.41; 8.57**), of one-eyed Thais, Lycoris, and Philaenis (**3.8, 11, 39; 2.33; 4.65; 12.22**), or full-breasted Spatale (**2.52**), of the physical degeneration of Afra, Vetustilla, and Lesbia who refused to act their obvious ages (**1.100; 3.93; 10:39**), and of Phoebus whose legs were so bowed that they resembled the horns of the moon (**2.35**).

Undoubtedly, Martial won the applause of many readers by his denunciation cap-a-pie of the 'bellus homo' (**1.19; 3.63**), that dandified pest of questionable sex whose activities the depravity of the age encouraged. Similarly, he ridiculed other only slightly less offensive male types: the man who is careful to make a great show of being exceedingly busy, although actually he accomplishes nothing (**1.79**); the person who dabbles neatly in everything, yet fails to do anything well (**2.7**); the old busybody who disgraces his grey hairs by roaming up and down the town to feed his insatiable curiosity (**4.78**); the chronic whisperer who makes such pretense of imparting important information (**1.89; cf. 3.28**); the foreign fop who assumes a distasteful air of familiarity (**10.65**); the bounder who turns expensive shops inside out, yet ultimately purchases only two inexpensive articles and even carries them off in his own hands (**9.59**); the well dressed bluffer who attempts to occupy a seat in the theater to which his social rank does not entitle him (**5.8, 14, 23; 5.25.1-2; 5.35.5**); the defaulter who is brazenly indifferent to his obligations (**1.75, 98; 2.3, 13, 58; 8.10; cf. 4.15**); and the boor who boasts of his urbanity (**1.41; cf. 6.44**).

Martial also lampooned physicians (**1.30, 47; 5.9; 6.53; 8.74; 9.96; cf. 6.70.1-6**), lawyers (**1.97; 6.35; 8.7, 17; cf. 5.33**), and auctioneers (**1.85; 5.56.10-1; 6.8**), because, no doubt, he envied them their superior incomes from vocations which he regarded as inferior to his own. He stigmatized husbands and wives who disposed of one spouse after another by manifestly criminal means (**8.43; 9.15, 78; 10.43; cf. 4.69; 10.16[15]**). In an age of "emancipated women," he denounced the penalty that one incurred by marrying a rich woman, namely, the forfeiture of a husband's rights (**8.12; 9.95**).

These inimitable characterizations of universally recognizable types are on the amusing or shocking side of human relations. Decidedly more subjective both in motivation and approach are Martial's attacks on individuals who made a false pretense to riches (**2.57; 5.35**), and particularly on those wealthy persons who made a shabby use of their means. Whereas the sentiments expressed in these outcries of exasperation are clearly

enough Martial's own, they must have been seconded heartily by many free-born Romans who were hopelessly enmeshed in the economic toils of the time.

Rome is an inhospitable place, indeed, Martial asserts (**3.38** cf. **12.51; 4.5** cf. **Iuv. 3.21-4**), to the poor man who has nothing more to recommend him than an honest ambition to succeed. If you are. poor, you will always be poor, since wealth is bestowed on none but the wealthy (**5.81**). In fact, the existence of a poor and upright man at Rome is a matter of sheer fortuity (**3.38**.14; cf. **3.30**.5-6). Though the indigent should not envy those who can make a display of fine attire, sedan chairs and carriers, large retinues of clients, and of grand homes served by a legion of slaves, only with the aid of the pawnbroker (**2.57**), yet they have much reason to decry the irresponsible and irresponsive wealthy.

Consider the millionaire who once was approachable and generous to his friends but who, now that his fortune has increased fivefold, has been transformed into the most despicable sort of miser (**1.99**; cf. **1.103; 4.51**). Even more infuriating is the man of means who pompously mouths fine phrases to the effect that he ever stands ready to assist a needy friend, but who never gives a much-needed gift to an obviously impecunious client (**2.43; 7.92**; cf. **10.15[14]**). How shameless, too, are some men of property who cite the costs of their endless building projects as an excuse for refusing to grant a loan (**9.22, 46**). Equally aggravating is the 'rex' who keeps a client on tenterhooks by neither rejecting outright a request for a loan nor acceding to it without further ado (**7.43**; cf. **2.25; 10.17[16]**). Condone, if you can, the inhumanity of creatures such as Mancinus who persists in keeping his helplessly poor friends informed of every increase in his already large fortune (**4.61**).

How contemptible, moreover, is the practice of many rich hosts who deliberately insult their dinner guests by serving them food and wine inferior to that which they themselves openly consume (**1.20; 3.49, 60; 4.68, 85; 6.11; 10.49; 12.27[28]**). What an exhibition of gluttony there is in high places (**3.32; 10.31; 11.86; 12.17**), the while a vaga turba of dinner hunters crowds the baths, taverns, colonnades and Forum in desperate search of an invitation to partake, at the least, of the leavings from the rich man's table (**2.11, 14, 27, 69; 5.47; 12.82**).

Why, in fact, should self-respecting free men, simply because they are poor, be forced as clients to dance attendance, year in and year out (**3.36, 46; 10.56, 74**), on patrons who grudgingly requite this attention with a mere pittance (**3.7, 14; 4.26; 6.88; 9.100**), or, worse still, with an unsatisfying dinner (**1.43; 2.19; 3.12; 7.48**)? Furthermore, what chance does a poor client have to improve his status by this form of service, when actually he must compete with senators and consuls for the notice and favors of wealthy nobodies (**10.10; 12.29[26]**), and must abase himself by being a client even to a client (**2.18**)? However lordly the patron may be, he is habitually slow to recognize his clients' need of new and seasonable clothing (**2.85; 5.26; 7.36; 10.76**), and thus carelessly subjects them to ridicule and embarrassment (**2.58; 6.82**). It is not surprising, therefore, that the indigent client and the money-lender are acquaintances of long standing (**2.44.**3-4).

Naturally, Martial did not stimulate the hearts of many patrons to generosity by such tactless and indiscriminate, albeit truthful, censure. His precarious income remained small, because he was too pert toward those who worshiped wealth and position, too clever in mocking those who were inflated with unwarranted pride, too outspoken against a degrading and degraded system of social dependence. Either he could not or would not see the glaring fact that the economic instability and the political tyranny of the time had made the fortunate few unconscionably hard and self-centered. Consequently, he contradicted his chances of improving his position by flouting the very sources from which alone amelioration could come. He departed too often from his canon of "sparing the person, denouncing the vice" (**10.33.**9-10) by denouncing the person and publishing the vice.

Under the adverse conditions which the inadequate system of 'clientela' imposed on the poor 'white-collar' constituents of Roman society, Martial fretted and fumed for thirty-four years; against its inflexible demands and distinctions he hurled the epigrammatic barbs of his satire. He stubbornly persisted in believing that by the merits of his literary efforts he eventually could arouse the unresponsive 'Zeitgeist' to acknowledge his right to handsome patronal support. Yet, leisure that was firmly secured against petty pecuniary worries he never acquired (**10.58.**6-10); and even his fame as a poet, he bitterly admitted in later years, was no more widespread than that of the race horse Andraemon (**10.9;** cf. **1.1.**4-6; **1.61; 5.13.**3-10; **7.88**). As the years dragged on without bringing an appreciable improvement in his economic status, he was forced to recognize that, whereas Rome had accepted and acclaimed him, she had no intention of rewarding him on his own terms. In fact, so completely had he become inured to the rôle in which circumstance and his own disposition had cast and confined him that, even though there was a sharp improvement in the social and economic outlook at Rome through the accession of Nerva and of Trajan, he lacked the will to renew the struggle for what had been denied him so long. He may have perceived in a moment of poignant consciousness that he could not under any emperor, whether good or bad, surmount the obstacle of his own satiric temperament or control the irresistible dictates of his peculiar genius.

Accordingly, as the unremitting and unremunerative duties of client estranged Martial from Rome (**12.68**), so an increasing nostalgia for the friends and places of his youth drew this proud provincial home (**4.55; 10.13[20]**). The deliberate manner in which he made his departure suggests a man who is embarking on a journey from which he does not expect to return. He made his adieus, commissioned his friend Flavus who was preceding him to Spain to procure for him a small and inexpensive retreat near Bilbilis (**10.104.**12-5), heralded his return after an absence of thirty-four years with a somewhat lofty greeting to his townsmen (**10.103**), and eagerly looked forward to recapturing a life of simple ease in a congenial environment far removed from the scene of his prolonged disappointment (**10.96;** cf. **1.49.**27-36; **10.47**).

Yet, when he was comfortably established in the house and on the land which a Spanish lady, Marcella, had provided for him (**12.18, 31**), he missed the libraries, the theaters, the public squares, the crowds, the incentive to literary activity, in short, the vibrant stimulation of the metropolis (**12. Introd. Ep.**). Moreover, as he rather had anticipated (**10.103.**11-2), he found most of his provincial neighbors, with the notable exception of Marcella (**12.21**), uninteresting, envious, and spiteful, and, therefore, felt all the more acutely the separation from his intimate friends at Rome (**12. Introd. Ep.; 12.34**).

Most probably, Martial believed that his ill-starred Fortune by having again introduced a mirage of unsubstantial prospects had tricked him quite as maliciously upon his return to Spain as she had during the first years of his residence at Rome. His unreflective mind failed to uncover the essential fact that through the unrestrained exercise of his wit he had purchased popularity at the expense of both propriety and affection, and that he had emphasized Rome's social evils without searching sincerely for their correction. His personal chagrin and resentment rather than a genuine hatred of the wrongs of the age accounts for the almost total absence of moral tone in his work. Whether this deficiency would have been avoided, if his early prospects had materialized, is purely a matter of conjecture. It is possible that under such conditions we might have had another Juvenal, but certainly not another Horace. For Martial's insistence (**1.107; 8.55[56]; 11.3**) that literature of the more elevated sort can be produced only with favorable patronal support reflects a certain meanness of character, inertia of the creative will, and misconception of literary motivation.

One cannot fail to detect a deep-seated feeling of frustration operating throughout the body of Martial's epigrams. Yet, it is to this negative goad to his genius that we are indebted for the most intimate and comprehensive survey of Roman society in the early empire.

Martial's merits as a poet are his keen eye, sharp stylus, and rare faculty for delineation. These literary virtues more than offset his deficiencies as a man.

Skuli Johnson (lecture date 1952)

SOURCE: "The Obituary Epigrams of Martial," *The Classical Journal,* Vol. 49, No. 6, March, 1954, pp. 265-72.

[*In this essay, originally delivered as a lecture in 1952, Johnson examines Martial's epigrams on death and dying. He calls attention to the poet's use of conventional tropes—especially from mythology—but he also remarks on the originality and genuine emotion in several of these obituary epigrams.*]

There are some twenty-five obituary epigrams[1] in Martial's corpus of 1561 poems.[2] If one includes all the pieces pertaining to death the total is considerably increased. To these Pliny's[3] familiar appraisal of Martial *par excellence* applies. Though wit is less appropriate in them than pathos[4] it is present here, but, as one would expect, well within bounds. A sufficiency of *fel* is assuredly to be found in his satirical epigrams on the blame-worthy dead. However, in the majority of his obituary pieces Martial qualifies for Pliny's *candor.* The term may mean *'sincerity', 'purity', 'kindness of heart',* or *'good nature',*[5] and any one of these meanings is easily evidenced in Martial. The vein of sentiment discernible in him is particularly noticeable in his attitude to the dead, his genius for friendship, and his love of nature.[6] Quite a few of Martial's obituary pieces combine the first two of these elements; there are some in which all three are present. Several sympathetic critics of Martial have noticed Martial's love of children,[7] and, in general, he is genuinely grieved at the passing of the young with all their beauty and promise.

Martial's thoughts on death are the commonplaces found in Latin lyrics, in the literature of consolations, in the inscriptions, and in the anthologies, both Greek and Latin. No doubt his wide acquaintance with these sources was due to the literary education which his foolish parents, as he calls them, gave him.[8] The piling up of literary parallels, as has been done by some editors,[9] will not however deprive Martial of all claims to originality.[10] With him originality consists largely of a novel combination of established ideas. Indeed with the *poetae docti* it was *de rigueur* to do this, and Martial, being one of these, was merely carrying on a traditional practice.[11] For him Graeco-Roman mythology was an open book from which to cull. This is not to say with Aelius Spartianus that Martial is our Vergil; only a person who cherished equally the *Amores* of Ovid and the culinary *Recipes* of Caelius Apicius could be guilty of such a judgment.[12] On the other hand the

devastating indictments of Martial[13] by his adverse critics overlook the fact that he is in a Graeco-Roman succession. This is particularly true of his significant sepulchral pieces. In these if anywhere Martial is entitled to the appellation of "noble Martiall" bestowed on him by the English laureate, John Skelton.[14]

It remains to illustrate some of these general statements by citations from Martial. Home-made versions reflecting the *ipsissima verba* of the poet seem to be most serviceable. May their readers not feel prompted to hurl at their author the ejaculation of Robert Burns on reading Elphinston's wretched translations of Martial: "O thou whom poetry abhors! / Whom prose has turned out of doors! / Heards't thou that groan? Proceed no further; / 'Twas laurel'd Martial roaring murther!"[15]

Quite a few of Martial's obituary pieces may be quickly passed by for the reason that they, for the most part, are conventional. The friendship of the centurions Fabricius and Aquinus, rival officers who now are reunited in Elysium, was for Martial more significant than their military records **(1.93).** Another centurion Varus, who died in Egypt, will be immortal in Martial's verse,[16] unless indeed the Nile has power to withhold this comfort too **(10.26).** To the epigram on Fuscus, a prefect of the praetorians, who fell in Dacia, there is added Roman imperiousness: "The Dacian bears our mighty yoke upon his neck subdued, / And Fuscus' shade victorious holds the subjugated wood." **(6.76).** The death of Antistius Rufus in Cappadocia derives a solace from the affection of Nigrina his widow: Martial makes the point that she seemed twice bereaved. **(9.30).** The passing of Saloninus, buried in Spain, is softened by the thought that he still lives in the part[17] which he preferred: in his friend Priscus **(6.18).** Camonius Rufus, who succumbed in Cappadocia, is asked to accept *in absentia* the tribute of his poet-friend: "Receive with his sad tears thy friend's brief lay, / And deem these incense from him far away." **(6.85).** The epigram on Etruscus, "that ancient hoar / Who both his lord's[18] moods with no meekness bore," proceeds on usual lines: there is a tribute to his character, he was buried by his duteous offspring by the side of his wife, he had reached high old age, with his wife he now dwells in Elysium. Martial ends with the observation that his son's grief for him might suggest that he had died prematurely **(7.40).** Similar to this is the epigram on the parents of Rabirius, Domitian's architect who, Martial asserts elsewhere **(7.56),** earned for himself immortality for his skill and for his services to his master: they lived together for sixty years, their deaths were gentle, they were burnt on the same pyre: their son must not lament them as if they had died untimely **(10.71).**

An obituary piece on an unnamed noble lady of Tarentum **(10.63)** teems with conventional ideas uttered, as usual, by the departed: "Albeit tiny is this sepulchre[19] / On which you read these lines, o traveller, / Yet will it not in fame be vanquished by / The Pyramids or Mausoleum." are her opening words. She had lived long enough to see the Secular Games twice; Juno had given her five sons and five daughters[20] who all sealed her eyes; her wedded glory was that her chastity had known only one consort.[21] The type is well described by Nicholas Grimald in his lines *Upon the Tomb of A.W.* which begin thus: "Myrrour of matrones, flowr of spouslike loue, / Of fayr brood fruitfulle norsse, poor peoples stay . . ." (*Tottel's Miscellany*, p. 113).

Occasionally Martial deviates into side issues. In the epigram to Silius Italicus on the death of his son Severus (**9.86**) he says nothing of the lad, but lauds the sire's literary attainments. In a rather involved manner he proceeds to have Apollo console Calliope for her loss, by pointing out that the Tarpeian Thunderer (i.e. Jupiter) and the Palatine Thunderer (i.e. Domitian) had also been bereaved.[22] The conclusion is neatly put: when you see that the divinities are exposed to the harsh rule of destiny, you may acquit them of envy.

Sometimes Martial introduces his mythological material somewhat awkwardly. An instance of this is the epigram to Sempronia (**12.52**) who had lost her husband. Before proceeding far the reader comes here upon the rape of Helen and other items. In this excursus is imbedded the comforting thought about Rufus that "His very ashes with affection blaze / For thee, Sempronia . . ."[23] Less felicitous is the final thought of the poem: Sempronia's seizure will endear her to Proserpine in Elysium.

On the other hand mythology is very happily introduced into Martial's epigram on the hunting-hound Lydia (**11.69**):

Within the amphitheatre
The trainers gave me nurture; there
Instruction also they gave me:
A huntress I was taught to be.
Amid the woodlands I was wild,
But I within the house was mild,
Lydia called, most loyal to
My lord and master Dexter who
Would not have had instead of me
The famed hound of Erigone,[24]
Nor yet the one from Dicte's land
Which Cephalus attended, and,
Translated with him, dwells upon
The constellation of the Dawn.[25]
Me carried off not life's brief day,
Nor bore me useless eld away:
To have such ending was the doom
Of house-hound of Dulichium.[26]
I was with lightning-thrust undone
By foaming boar: such monstrous one
Thy boar was, Calydon,[27] or thine,
O Erymanthus. . . . [28]

Lydia's comfort is that she could not have died more nobly. It is strange that this delightful "toy-consolation" is not included in a well-known doctoral dissertation[29] where those of Catullus, Ovid and Statius are adduced and Martial's obituary poems receive due notice.

Rarely do legalistic matters find their way into Martial's obituary pieces. Of the two poems on Antulla (**1.114; 116**) the latter, the more significant one, brings out the consolation that her parents will be buried in the same plot, for it belongs everlastingly to the dead—an obvious reference to the legal formula: *Hoc monumentum sive sepulchrum heredem non sequitur.*[30]

In his epigram on the actor Latinus the poet has him speak of himself much in the same way as Ben Jonson spoke of Shakespeare: *Th' applause, delight, the wonder of our stage.* He defends his morals, albeit an actor, and easily passes on to praise the Emperor Domitian as *censor morum* (**9.28**). No such extraneous matter mars the epigram on Paris, the accomplished actor of mimes from Alexandria, whom Domitian murdered:

Whoso the Way Flaminian fare,
Traveller, this famed sepulchre
Pass you not by. Here Rome's delight,
The witticisms of Egypt's wight,
Art, grace, and play and pleasure lief,
The glory of Rome's stage, and grief,
All Venuses and Cupids room
Have found, interred in Paris' tomb.

(**11.13**)

On the popular charioteer Scorpus Martial wrote two epigrams.[31] In the one he makes the point that Scorpus, in the race of life as in the races of the Circus, was swift to reach his goal with his swart-hued steeds (**10.50**). In the other, Martial is more brief but equally pointed. Lachesis, counting his victories—according to an inscription[32] they were 2048, though Scorpus was only twenty-seven—concluded that he was old and so cut his thread. Nike in the Anthology[33] similarly counted a man's victories, and the Parcae, according to Ben Jonson,[34] made the same mistake about S(alomon) P(any), 'one of the Companye of Reuells to Queene Elizabeth who died scarce thirteen': "And did act (what now we mone,) / Old men so duely / As sooth the Parcae thought him one / He plai'd so truely." Martial's epigram runs thus:

I'm Scorpus, Rome, whom Circus'
shouts acclaimed;
Thy short-lived pet, thy plaudits I
received.
In my ninth triad Lachesis me claimed;
My wreaths she counted and me old
believed.

(**10.53**)

Glaucias, the freedman of Melior, also receives two epigrams. The one pays tribute to his popularity, his purity and his youthfulness; he is buried by the Flaminian Way; may the passerby who weeps for him have no other cause for woe! (6.28) The other reasserts his endowments and declares that Melior manumitted him from pure affection;[35] it concludes with these lines: "The well-endowed of humankind obtain / A life-span short, and seldom old age gain. / Whate'er you cherish supplicate that such / You may not seek to cherish overmuch." (6.29). The old idea that the good die young is perhaps most familiar from Gloucester's aside, *"So wise so young they say do ne'er live long."*[36] The thought of the last two lines of Martial's epigram Ben Jonson borrowed for his lines on his son, who died at the age of seven: "For whose sake henceforth all his vowes be such / As what he loues may never like too much."[37]

The epigram on Alcimus, a young slave, is genuinely elegiac, and has imbedded in it a vignette of natural beauty:

> Alcimus, whom from thy lord snatched
> away
> In growing years, the Lavicana Way
> With light turf veils, receive no Parian
> stone
> Of nodding weight that will be over-
> thrown,
> Which labour vain bestows upon the
> dead,
> But yielding box-trees here receive in-
> stead;
> Receive thou too the dusky palm-tree's
> shade,
> And meadow green, by my tears dewy
> made.
>
> Dear lad, memorials of my grief I give;
> For thee this honour evermore will live.
> When Lachesis has spun my last years
> I
> Ordain my ashes in like mode should
> lie.

(1.88)

The epigram on Canace, a young slave girl, is also deeply affecting. She had died from a dreadful canker of the mouth; Martial makes the point that her lips had to be impaired lest her sweet utterance might win the Fates to mercy:

> Canace of Aeolis lies buried in this
> tomb,
> The lass's seventh winter was her last
> one: sore woe!
> Yet wait awhile, o stranger, before thou
> weep'st her doom:

> One may not here complain of how
> quickly life must go.
>
> Sadder than death was death's mode:
> upon her dear mouth sate
> Disease foul; her fair features de-
> spoiled its wastage dire;
> Her very lips so loving its cruel canker
> ate,
> So came she sorely blemished to her
> sad fun'ral pyre.
>
> Ah, if her end was fated to come with
> flight so fleet,
> Its means should have been better;
> The passage of her breath
> The Lord of Doom sealed swiftly for
> fear her voice so sweet
> Might move to ruth the Maidens who
> reign o'er life and death.

(11.91)

Martial composed three poems on his own little slave-girl Erotion ("Sweetie"). In one of these, each successive owner of her grave-plot is requested to pay annual dues to her departed spirit (10.61). Leigh Hunt's paraphrase of it is well known.[38] Perhaps a closer version is the following:

> Here rests Erotion's hastened phantom
> whom
> Her winter-season sixth with crime of
> doom
> Destroyed. Thou, whosoever thou wilt
> be
> The master of my farm-plot after me,
> On her slight spirit yearly dues bestow,
> So be thy Lar forever safe, and so
> Thy household too, and may this tear-
> ful stone
> Upon thy little farmstead stand alone.

In another epigram (5.37) Martial rather extravagantly dwells on the charms of Erotion and her endearing ways. This piece has been regarded as 'a clear case of the maxim *trop de zèle*.'[39] The overstatement may however be a true measure of his affection and of his sorrow. The poet however proceeds to mar the genuine pathos of the piece and the simple sincerity of his grief by adding a sarcasm at the expense of a certain Paetus, who has urged Martial not to mourn for a mere slave-girl. Paetus, though he has recently lost a wife who was *nota, superba, nobilis* and *locuples,* has the fortitude to live on! The remaining poem on Erotion is regarded by many as Martial's masterpiece (5.34). It has been said of it that it is 'inspired with a simple and homely tenderness for which there are few parallels in the annals of literature'.[40]

O mother mine Flaccilla and Fronto
    too my sire!
  To you I trust this maiden, my
    darling precious,
Lest little Sweetie shudder before the
    shades so dire,
  And dread the monstrous mouths of
    the Hound of Tartarus.

Just six times she'd have finished the
    winter-season's cold,
  But six days still were lacking when
    Death to claim her came.
O may she sport and play now anigh
    her guardians old,
  And mid her lovely babbling, o may
    she lisp my name!

Her bones so young and tender en-
    shroud in pliant sod,
  And, Earth, lie lightly on her: on thee
    she softly trod.

Robert Louis Stevenson in a translation of this poem compares her lightness with that of thistle-burr.[41] This is not necessarily a Scottish touch: it is also classical; for example, Theocritus[42] speaks of Galatea as being 'wanton as the dry thistle-down'.

Martial has several variations on the inscriptional *motif* of the last line, viz. *Sit Tibi Terra Levis* (STTL). One is the *jeu d'esprit* on the tiny farmer: "This farmer, heirs, do not inter: / So slight is he / That for him any earth whate'er / Would heavy be." (11.14). In his epigram on Pantagathus ("All-good"), the slave-barber, Martial makes the point that the lightness of the earth over him cannot match the lightness of his craftsman's hand (6.52). Usually barbers are made the butts of sarcasms.[43] Another lad Eutychus ("Lucky"), despite his name, drowned prematurely at Baiae: the earth and water are asked to be gentle to him (6.68). There is a similar request in the Greek Anthology: "O earth crowded with tombs and sea that washest the shore, do thou lie light on the boy, and do thou be hushed for his sake."[44]

English literature abounds in instances of this literary device. Lovers of Herrick will readily recall his concluding lines of a concise epitaph on a little lass: "Give her strewings: but not stir / The earth that lightly covers her."[45] Scotchmen remember with relish the epigram of Robert Burns on a Noted Coxcomb: "Light lay the earth on Billy's breast, His chicken heart so tender. / But build a castle on his head, / His skull will prop it under."[46] Dean Swift affords however the best parallel, in his epitaph on the architect Vanbrugh: "Lie heavy on him, earth, for he / Laid many a heavy load on thee."[47] A very recent instance of the *Sit Tibi Terra Levis* idea appeared in the Reader's Digest (Novem-

ber, 1951, p. 96); there under *In Memoriam* is cited the verse on the tombstone of Mark Twain's daughter, Olivia Susan Clemens, of which the third line is: *"Green sod above, lie light, lie light."*[48]

Some of Martial's epigrams pertaining to death appear to be written primarily to score rhetorical points. The one on the lad killed by an icicle concludes with the paradoxical question: "And does not death bide lurking everywhere / If, water, you become a murderer?" (4.18). In another piece a lad is poisoned by a viper in the mouth of a brazen bear: the wicked deed was due to the fact that the wild bear was not real! (3.19) An epigram on the words *Chloe fecit* (quoted from a tombstone) affords Martial excellent material for a *double entendre:*

On the tombs of criminal Choe's seven
    husbands she
Has inscribed that she had done it:
    what could clearer be?

                    (9.15)

Another notorious dame was Galla who has now met more than her match:

After the death of seven husbands you
    then, Galla, wed
Picentinus: you wish, Galla, to pursue
    your dead.

                    (9.78)

Phileros ("Philanderer") apparently had earned much wealth by burying his wives:

Wives seven you, Philanderer, have
    buried / Within this field. /
Philanderer, to none else does the farm-
    stead / More profit yield.

                    (10.43)

One way of getting rid of such marriage-monsters is to match them:

Fabius lays out wives for funeral;
Crestilla puts her husbands on their
    pall.
Both of them brandish o'er the mar-
    riage-bed
The baneful torch-flame of a fury dread.
Match thou the victors, Venus: there'll
    remain
One end: one fun'ral will bear out the
    twain.

                    (8.43)

Yet lustful hags like Plotia keep their propensity even in death.[49]

The most extensive satirical piece of Martial is addressed to Philaenis, a beldame mentioned several times elsewhere by him.[50] One is tempted to quote this epigram in full:

> When thou hadst passed the eld of Nestor
>   through,
> So swiftly wert thou snatched, Philaenis, to
> Dis's infernal waters? Thou didst not
> As yet in life's span emulate the lot
> Of the Euboean Sibyl: by months three
> The prophetess in age exceeded thee.
> Ah, what a tongue is mute! Not slaves for
>   sale
> On thousand platforms could o'er it prevail,
> Nor crowd that loves Serapis Egypt-born,
> Nor teaching-master's curly troop at morn;
> Nor does the Strymon's bank, when it around
> The flocks of birds have gathered, so resound.
> What beldame will with rhomb Thessalian
>   now
> To draw the moon from heaven down know
>   how?
> What go-between will now like her know well
> How bride-beds, these and those, for bribes to
>   sell?
> *May earth on thee lie lightly, and be thine*
> *A covering of sand both thin and fine,*
> *In order that the dogs enabled be*
> *To dig thy buried bones up easily.*

(9.29)

Unfortunately for Martial the thought of the last four lines is by no means original; it is easily paralleled from the Greek Anthology: "May the dust lie lightly on thee under the earth, wretched Nearchus, so that the dogs may easily drag thee out."[51] Philaenis appears also in this anthology, for instance where she protests that she was not lascivious with men or a public woman.[52]

Martial occasionally writes on famous cases of suicide. That of Porcia, the wife of Brutus, who met her death as a true daughter of Cato Uticensis, is quite melodramatic. Better known is the shorter epigram on two other Stoics, Arria and Paetus:

> When Arria chaste her Paetus gave the sword
> Which she herself from out her vitals drew,
> 'My wound pains not, if truth be,' was her
>   word,
> 'What pains me is the wound you'll deal to
>   you.'

(1.13)

Elsewhere Martial has other things to say about suicide. How foolish was Fannius who in flight dealt himself death in fear of dying! **(2.80)**. More seriously he says in another place: "In adversity it is easy to despise life; the truly brave man is one who can endure to be miserable." **(11.56)**. In Martial's epigram rendered familiar to Englishmen by the translation of it by the Earl of Surrey,[53] the poet lists the elements of a happy life; his last entry is: 'life's final day / To fear not, yet not for it pray.' **(10.47)**.)

In general Martial in his obituary poetry deals with the harrowing experience of death and bereavement in the spirit of a gentle humanist. Although Martial constantly uses the conventional phraseology about death and dying,[54] he leaves the reader puzzled about his real beliefs. Of his own narrow escape from death Martial speaks conventionally yet convincingly;[55] he hopes that when he comes to die, he may seek the grove of the Elysian Lass (= Persephone), while he is still not disabled by protracted old age, yet having accomplished the three stages of life.[56] Return of the dead to the world of the living is mentioned by Martial only hypothetically.[57] As to the possibility of communication between the departed and the living, Martial is equally inconclusive: for instance he merely expresses the wish that the spirit of the dead poet Lucan may be aware of the affection of his widow Polla.[58] This is precisely the vagueness one finds in the Greek anthology[59] as well as throughout the Latin lyric poets.[60] Whether the dead retain their old likes and dislikes is also indefinite: although, according to Martial, Romulus still eats *rapa* (turnips) in heaven, this may be a mere echo of Seneca.[61] Another echo of Seneca is seen in Martial's short epigram on the fate of the Pompeys.[62] In general, death by violence is an anathema to the gentle poet; in speaking of Lucan's enforced death at the hands of Nero, his heart cries out against the crime: "Cruel Nero, made / More hateful by no other phantom-shade, / Alas this cursèd crime at any rate / Thou should'st not have had pow'r to perpetrate."[63] Again, when Martial beheld the destruction that had been perpetrated by the gods in the eruption of Vesuvius he concludes that "The gods might wish that they had not / Had pow'r to do what here they've wrought."[64] Nowhere in Martial is the dominance of death put more potently than in the concise epigram on "Crumb", the little dining-room that looked out on the Mausoleum of the Caesars.[65] Despite the many clichés and commonplace ideas in this portion of Martial's poetry, his obituary pieces are assuredly exempt from the disdainful query of Lord Byron: "And then what proper person can be partial / To all those nauseous epigrams of Martial?"[66]

Notes

[1] A paper delivered at the Fifth University of Kentucky Foreign Language Conference, Lexington, Kentucky, April 24-26, 1952.

[2] In a total of 1561 Epigrams in the *Spectacula* and fourteen other books, 1235 are in elegiac metre, 238 in hendecasyllabic and 77 in choliambic or scazon. There are besides a few in hexameter and iambic verse (J. Wight Duff: *A Literary History of Rome in the Silver Age.* London: T Fisher Unwin, 1927, 512.)

[3] Pliny: *Ep.* 3.21. *Erat homo ingeniosus acutus acer, et qui plurimum in scribendo et salis haberet et fellis nec candoris minus.*

[4] Cf. M. S. Dimsdale: *Latin Literature.* New York: Appleton and Co., 1915, 475 (re obituary pieces of Martial) "point is less appropriate than pathos."

[5] So Merrill took it *(Selected Letters of the Younger Pliny,* edited by E. T. Merrill. London: Macmillan and Co., 1912, 294.)

[6] J. Wight Duff: *op. cit.* 524. Butler remarks that "Martial has a genuine love for the country" (H. E. Butler: *Post Augustan Poetry.* Oxford: Clarendon Press, 1909, 268); in Martial's obituary verse this comes to view in little nature touches in regard to the surroundings of the sepulchre.

[7] Cf. Butler (*op. cit.* 274) "Martial was a child-lover before he was a man of letters;" H. J. Rose: (*A Handbook of Latin Literature.* London: Methuen and Co., 1936, 403.) "it was one of his amiable qualities that he loved children;" Kirby Flower Smith (*Martial the Epigrammatist and Other Essays.* Baltimore: John Hopkins Press, 1920, 18.) "Another attractive side of his nature was his evident devotion to children."

[8] Martial 9.75. *At me litterulas stulti docuere parentes.*

[9] Conspicuously by L. Friedländer. *M. Valerii Martialis Epigrammaton Libri.* 2 vols. Leipzig: Verlag von S. Hirzel, 1886.

[10] Butler (*op. cit.* 260 *fn.* 2) points out that a very large proportion of the parallel passages cited by Friedländer is unjust to Martial, "No poet could be original judged by such a test."

[11] J. F. D'Alton: *Roman Literary Theory and Criticism.* London: Longmans, Green & Co., 1931, 431-432.

[12] *Aelius Spartianus:* Aelius ch. 5, sec. 9, *Atque idem Apicii Caelii* relata idem Ovidii libros amorum in lecto semper habuisse, idem Martialem epigrammaton poetam Vergilium suum dixisse.*

*Recipes of Caelius Apicius de re coquinaria libri X

[13] E.g. by J. W. MacKail: *Latin Literature.* London: John Murray, 1913, 194-195.

[14] Cf. *The Complete Poems of John Skelton* edited by Philip Henderson. London: J. M. Dent and Sons, 1931, 136: *Poems Against Garnesche:* "If thou wert acquainted with all / The famous poets satircall / As Persius and Juvenall / Horace and noble Martiall."

[15] *The Poetical Works of Robert Burns.* London: George Bell and Sons, 1878 (The Aldine Edition) Vol. ii, 194-195. *Epigram on Elphinstone's (sic) Translation of Martial's Epigrams.*

[16] Martial, like many another poet, believed his verse bestowed immortality. Of this his friend Pliny was doubtful (*Ep.* 3.21).

[17] Cf. *Greek Anthology* XII.52; Callim. *Ep.* 42 (echoed in the expression *aufugit mi animus* of Q. Catulus); Arist. . *Eth. Nic.* 9.4.5; Hor. *Od.* 1.3.8; 2.7.5.

[18] *Utrumque deum,* i.e. Domitian whether adverse or auspicious. For an analogous use cf. Cat. 31.3 *Uterque Neptunus.*

[19] Cf. *Greek Anthology* 7.2B; 18: 380.

[20] Cf. *Ibid.* 7. 331 (woman boasts that she was the wife of one husband and left him and ten children alive); *ibid.* 7.224 (woman boasts that she had 29 children and left them all living).

[21] Martial's epigram closes with an indecent expression (10.63.8). For the woman's boast cf. *Greek Anthology* 7.324 (woman declares that she loosed her zone for one man alone.)

[22] In 4.3, Martial fancies that the deified son of Domitian is throwing down from the skies snowballs at his father sitting at the games.

[23] This is as lovely as the line in Propertius (4.11.74) *haec cura et cineri spirat inusta meo* (which inspired Gray in the Elegy: *E'en in our ashes live their wonted fires*).

[24] Maera, the hound of Icarius, placed with his daughter Erigone in the heavens as the constellation Virgo; cf. Ovid *Fasti* 5.723.

[25] Laelaps ("Hurricane") a hound of Crete given to Procris by Diana and by Procris to Cephalus. When Cephalus was elevated to the heavens by Aurora the loyal dog went with him; cf. Ovid *Met.* 3.211; 7.771.

[26] *Dulichio cani* i.e. Argus the hound of Odysseus (Hom. *Od.* 17.291-293, 326-327).

[27] The Calydonian boar *(sus)* sent by the enraged Diana, and killed by Meleager; cf. Ovid. *Met.* 8.324.

[28] The Erymanthian boar was slain by Hercules; cf. Ovid *Her.* 9.87; *Met.* 5.608.

[29] S'ster Mary Edmond Ferns: *The Latin Consolatio as a Literary Type.* St. Louis, Missouri, 1941. The "toy-consolations" are dealt with in ch. XI.

[30] cf. Wilmanns *Ex. Inscr.* 2.693 sq.

[31] In 10.74 Martial satirizes his quick acquisition of wealth, and in the preface to 11.1 refers to the gossip about him and another charioteer Incitatus (who is mentioned also in 10.76).

[32] CIL 6.2, 10048.

[33] Cf. *Anthol. Palat.* 3.18.

[34] Cf. Ben Jonson: *Epigrammes CXX (Ben Jonson* edited by C. H. Herford, Percy and Evelyn Simpson, [Oxford Clarendon Press, 1947] VIII. 77).

[35] Martial himself manumitted his beloved secretary Demetrius, before he died. (1.101). His friend Pliny similarly set free his dying slaves (*Ep.* 8.16).

[36] Shakespeare: *King Richard III* 3.1.79.

[37] Ben Jonson: *Epigrammes XLV On My First Sonne (op. cit.* 41).

[38] *The Poetical Works of Leigh Hunt* edited by H. S. Mitford, Oxford: Oxford University Press, 1923, 427.

[39] E. E. Sikes: *Roman Poetry.* London: Methuen and Co., 1923, 10.

[40] Kirby Flower Smith: *op. cit.* 18; H. E. Butler: *op. cit.* 272: "And Martial's epitaphs and epicedia at their best have in their slight way an almost unique charm."

[41] *Robert Louis Stevenson: Collected Poems* edited by Janet Adam Smith. London: Rupert Hart-Davis, 1950, 292: "That swam light-footed as the thistle-burr / On thee: O mother earth, be light on her." In another version Stevenson however discards the simile: "That ran so lightly footed in her mirth / Upon thy breast—lie lightly, mother earth." *(Robert Louis Stevenson Poems.* II. 176 in the Tusitala edition. London: Heinemann, XXIII, 1923).

[42] Theocritus. *Id.* 6. 15-16; cf. Hom. *Od.* 5. 328 ff.

[43] E.g. in 11.84 Martial satirizes at length the barber Antiochus; more briefly in 7.83 he pokes fun at the slowness of barber Eutrapelus ("Nimble"): "While barber Nimble made the round amowing / Old Wolfeman's face, / And smoothed his cheeks, another beard came growing / To take its place."

[44] *Greek Anthology* 7.628; cf. *ibid.* 372, 461, 476, 583; Kaibel: *Epigrams.* 329, 538, 551, 569; *Anthol. Lat.* (Meyer) 1349.

[45] Robert Herrick: *Upon a Child That Dyed* (For Herrick's indebtedness to Martial see Paul Nixon's article, *CP* V (1910) 189-202. Cf. Ben Jonson (*op. cit.* 33-34). *Epigrammes XXII On My First Daughter.* (The girl was less than six years old).

[46] Robert Burns. *op. cit.* II 144, *Epigram on a Noted Coxcomb.*

[47] Cf. *Greek Anthology* 7.401. "Earth, who hast espoused an evil bridegroom, rest not light or thinly scattered on the ashes of the deformed being." Cf. *ibid.* 7.204 (on a partridge killed by a cat).

[48]

> "Warm summer sun, shine kindly here;
> Warm southern wind, blow softly here;
> Green sod above, lie light, lie light;
> Good night, dear heart, good night, good
>   night."

[49] 10.67. 6-7: *Hoc tandem sita prurit in sepulcro Calvo Plotia cum Melanthione.*

[50] 2.33; 4.65; 7.67; 70; 9.62; 10.22; 12.22.

[51] *Greek Anthology,* 11.226.

[52] *Ibid.* 7.345.

[53] The translation of Lord Henry Howard, Earl of Surrey, appeared in the first edition of *Tottel's Miscellany,* June 5, 1657. Martial was recognized a good deal earlier: Sir Thomas Elyot in his first edition of *The Boke named the Governour,* I. 128) in 1531 said of Martial: "Martialis whiche for his dissolute wrytynge is mooste seldom radde of men of moche gravite hath not withstandynge many commendable sentences and right wise counseils. . . ." (and he gives a version of Martial 12.34.8-11.) Indeed the poet as recognized by Puttenham, in 1589, "was cheife of this skil among the Latines." *(The Arte of English Poesie,* Arber Reprint, 1895, 68.)

[54] E.g. 1.36.5; 11.84.1; 4.60.4; 12.90.4; 1.78.3; 10.23.4; Metaphorically in 5.25.6 'not to want to approach the Stygian pools' = 'to desire immortality'; similarly Truth has been recovered from the Stygian abode by Trajan because he has resuscitated her (10.72.10); and Martial's readers save him from the sluggish waves of ungrateful Lethe, i.e. from oblivion (10.2.7-8). His book also, if critized by his friends Secundus and Severus, will not behold the restless rock of tired Sisyphus, i.e. will not be condemned to oblivion (5.80.10-11). Whether Martial really believed in the traditional punishments

in Hades is uncertain: when he is imprecating against a slanderous poet punishments after death, he finishes with the expression *delasset omnes fabulas poetarum* (10.5.17) i.e. may he exhaust all the *fabled torments* the poets mention.

[55] 6.58.3-4. "O how nearly had I been carried off from you to the waters of the Styx and seen the dusky clouds of the Elysian plain."

[56] 10.24.8-10.

[57] 4.16.5; 10.101.1; 11.5.5-6; 13-14.

[58] 7.23.3-4. *Tu, Polla, maritum / Saepe colas et se sentiat ille coli. /*

[59] *Greek Anthology* 7.23.6: "If indeed any delight touches the dead;"

[60] Cf. *Intimations of Immortality in the Major Lyric and Elegiac Poets of Rome,* a paper by the present writer, Proceedings of the Royal Society of Canada, XLIV (1950) 61-93.

[61] 13.16; cf. Seneca: *Apocoloc.*9.5. *cum sit e republica esse aliquem qui cum Romulo possit ferventia rapa vorare.*

[62] 5.74. In 11.61 Martial says that the plane-tree at Cordova was not planted by Pompeian hands: it was planted by Caesar. Martial's regret at the murder of Pompey is however genuine though it was less heinous that that of Cicero (3.66; 5.69): Pothinus slew Pompey to serve his master, Antony had Cicero murdered to serve his private viciousness, but all in vain for "All men will commence / To speak for Tully's muted eloquence."

[63] 7.21.

[64] 4.44.

[65] 2.59.

> Crumb I am called: a little diningroom
> Thou know'st: from me thou look'st on
>   Caesar's Tomb.
> Crush couches, drink. don roses, ointed be:
> 'Remember death' the god himself bids thee.·.

[66] Lord Byron: *Don Juan;* Canto 1. 43. 7-8. Byron employed the same rhyme in his single translation from Martial (1.1).

W. H. Semple (lecture date 1960)

SOURCE: "The Poet Martial," *Bulletin of the John Rylandds Library,* Vol. 42, No. 2, March, 1960, pp. 432-52.

[*In this essay, Semple touches on a wide range of topics associated with Martial's life and work. He gives an extended treatment of the patron-client system as the writer's only means of financial support; the accuracy and sincerity of the epigrams praising Domitian; and Martial's poetic style and tone.*]

As I thought about a scheme for this lecture, my main difficulty was this. Here were 1,200 short poems, on many different topics and themes, but with no single co-ordinating plan. There is no unity in their variety: they preach no doctrine: they advance no cause: they are not related to any one end. The individual poems are separate entities; and, though massed together in books, they stand there as isolated units, without cohesion of subject or purpose. I am reminded of what the Emperor Gaius said of Seneca's writings: "harena sine calce" ("sand without lime"): there is no lime, no mortar, in Martial to bind the individual pieces into a cohesive whole; and this caused my difficulty in preparing to write about them. But, as I considered, there emerged three possible groupings of the poems which would supply some interesting material for my talk—first, some glimpses of how a poor man, a poet, lived at Rome in the first century A.D.; then, the surprising portrait of the Emperor Domitian that Martial presents to us; and finally, some account of his own methods, aims, and opinions as a man-of-letters. I shall have to quote a good deal, often in translation and in prose (for the verse translations are unsatisfactory): and I warn you that in translation the pointed sharpness of a Latin epigram is often blurred: but I shall try to quote pieces that are intrinsically interesting as well as useful for my purpose. And I may as well add that, in the 1,900 years since Martial lived, nothing of what I now say has failed to be said before.

Let me state at once that, if I now appear as a literary critic dealing with an ancient poet, I do not conceive a literary critic to be primarily or mainly a fault-finder. It is not his duty to come before you as an accuser or indeed as an advocate: his first duty is to exercise judgment—to discern between good and evil, I mean literary good or literary evil, not necessarily moral. He must base his judgment on no predetermined doctrine: he must know thoroughly the time and milieu and intellectual atmosphere in which his author worked: he must judge the success of a book by its attainment or otherwise of its professed intention, with due allowance for the handicap of circumstances or personal conditions. I deprecate that type of modern criticism by which the author is put in the dock and subjected to a third-degree examination, and is often condemned for errors which are not typical or symptomatic. If errors are occasional and localized, they are no doubt regrettable but venial. If they are embedded in the structure of the work and endemic, then and then only are they significant. It is as much the duty of the critic to praise where he justly admires as to blame where he is justly indignant. In fact, good criticism is generally neither praise nor blame, but a mixture of both: for a book is a human document, not perfect, but in spite of human failings striving towards perfection. Martial himself puts it very well in a poem (I. 16) to his friend Avitus:

> sunt bona, sunt quaedam mediocria, sunt mala plura
> quae legis hic: aliter non fit, Avite, liber.

And when the censorious critic, Lausus, says (VII. 81) with heavy displeasure,

> triginta toto mala sunt epigrammata libro,

Martial makes the very apt rejoinder,

> si totidem bona sunt, Lause, bonus liber est.

The known facts of Martial's life are soon stated. He was a Spaniard, like several other distinguished men-of-letters at Rome in the first century A.D., Quintilian, the Senecas father and son, and Lucan: he was born about 40 A.D. at Bilbilis, a steel-making town in Hispania Tarraconensis in central north-east Spain. He was given a good education by his parents, that is, he had been to the grammarian's school to study language and literature both Latin and Greek, and to the more advanced school of the rhetorician to study oratory. He comments (IX. 73) on the folly of his parents in having him taught these literary subjects which were never of any material advantage to him in making a living:

> at me litterulas stulti docuere parentes:
> quid cum grammaticis rhetoribusque mihi?

"My foolish parents had me taught the rudiments of literature: but what good are grammar teachers and rhetoric teachers to me now?"

He came to Rome in the early sixties of the century, in the reign of Nero, and for thirty-five years he existed as a man-of-letters in the capital, under Nero, Vespasian, Titus, Domitian, Nerva and Trajan, gaining such a livelihood as he could, and finally retiring to his native Bilbilis about 98 A.D. He lived there for a few years more and published from there his twelfth book of epigrams in 101 A.D. During all his time in Rome, he took no part in politics: there is barely a single political reference all through his works, though he does of course mention such public events as the Emperor's campaigns and triumphs. He was a man about town, poor, dependent on his own resources, making his way by his talent as a poet and by his faithful attendance as a client on rich patrons against whose meanness and grudging appreciation of literary merit he inveighs frequently. We have no knowledge of his first fifteen years in Rome. In 80 A.D. he published a collection of epigrams known as the *Liber Spectaculorum* to celebrate the opening of the Colosseum by Titus. He then published twelve successive books of epigrams, of which the first nine were published under Domitian: each book contains about 100 poems, some as short as a couplet, some quatrains, many of them twelve or fourteen lines long, some few running to twenty or thirty lines, mostly in elegiacs, iambic scazons, or hendecasyllables, the tone and style of the poems being mostly satirical and based on the epigrams of Catullus, whose disciple and follower in the art of the epigram Martial professed himself to be. He acquired a very considerable reputation; in his own day he was much read, imitated, plagiarized, and criticized; he was the maker of the epigram as we know it: he could justly be called the greatest epigrammatist of the world.

What has a perpetual social interest is the fact that Martial, a man without (as far as we know) inherited private means, lived for some thirty-five years at Rome and appears to have supported himself on the tenuous income derived from the relationship of patron and client. Like many other freeborn Roman citizens, he depended on the small daily allowances which the wealthier men gave to those who attended them as clients—and from the hundred farthings, the "centum miselli quadrantes", which constituted the client's daily dole, there had to be paid his lodgings, his clothes, his amenities and comforts. The patron expected his presence at the "salutatio", the early morning levee in his house: the client had to rise early and make his way through the dark streets in order to be present punctually between six and eight o'clock. Then along with others he would accompany his patron down to the centre of the city, perhaps to the forum, perhaps to a literary reading, perhaps to the law-courts, the throng of clients in their formal togas giving importance to the movement of the great man through the streets. The morning's duties extended till nearly midday, and then the afternoon was given more or less to one's own pursuits. The picture that Martial gives us of patrons is not an attractive or pleasant one. All through the books of poems he attacks their churlish treatment of the clients from whom they have exacted such a continuous round of social duties. At the morning "salutatio" they are haughty and remote: at the dinner to which they sometimes invite a client they make a difference in food and drink—a fine menu for the lord and his close friends, an inferior meal for the client: sometimes they make him a gift of clothing, but not on any regular system, so that the formal toga in which he pays his official calls has become worn and shabby and needing repair, but he has no means of replacing it. The Emperor Domitian in his queer conservative way had tried to bring the patron-client relationship back to the old-time style in which it was formed by a genuine social protection which the patron extended to his poor dependants: at this earlier period there was no money payment, the client dined in the afternoon at the table of his protector: and Domitian had ordered a return to the original system, so that the "sportula", the "centum quadrantes", the money dole, had to be replaced by a regular meal—a "cena recta". The clients were appalled at such reactionary legislation: they had lost their only means of subsistence: there was so much complaint that the change lasted only for a short time. We have a pleasant little poem (**III.7**) from Martial about it, in which he asks his fellow-dependants how they regard the new arrangement:

> centum miselli iam valete quadrantes,
> anteambulonis congiarum lassi, . . .
> quid cogitatis, o fames amicorum?
> regis superbi sportulae recesserunt.

And they answer in one voice:

> nihil stropharum est: iam salarium dandum est.

> "Goodbye to you now, wretched hundred farthings, distributed as our dole for acting as weary escort. What do you think, my starving friends? The dole the haughty patron gave us is now abolished. What about it?"

And their answer comes:

"There can be no dodging it: he must pay us a salary as well as a dinner."

But what of the dinner itself to which the client, no longer a paid attendant, is invited by his patron? Let Martial tell us in a poem (**III. 60**) written to his patron:

> cum vocer ad cenam non iam venalis ut ante,
>   cur mihi non eadem, quae tibi, cena datur?
> ostrea tu sumis stagno saturata Lucrino,
>   sugitur inciso mitulus ore mihi:
> sunt tibi boleti, fungos ego sumo suillos:
>   res tibi cum rhombost, at mihi cum sparulo:
> aureus inmodicis turtur te clunibus implet,
>   ponitur in cavea mortua pica mihi.
> cur sine te ceno, cum tecum, Pontice, cenem?
>   sportula quod non est, prosit: edamus idem.

"Why, Ponticus, when I, no longer a dole-paid client, am invited by you to dinner,
    Why is it not the same dinner served to me as to you?
You take oysters fattened in the Lucrine Lake:
    I suck a mussel, cutting my lips on the shell.
You have mushrooms: I get funguses.
    You tackle a turbot, but I a brill.
You gorge yourself on the super-fatted haunches of a golden-brown turtle dove:
    Before me is set a magpie that has died in its cage.

Why do I dine at a different table from you though I am dining with you?
    Let me have some benefit from the abolition of the money-dole: let us eat the same food."

And since I am quoting, let me quote the amusing little poem (**VII. 39**) about a client who became so utterly weary of walking round with his patron and of having his morning broken up and of meeting with supercilious disdain when he saluted the great men, that he decided to simulate an attack of gout as a good excuse for absenting himself: but he made his malingering so realistic that he actually convinced himself he had a genuine bout:

> discursus varios vagumque mane
> et fastus et ave potentiorum
> cum perferre patique iam negaret,
> coepit fingere Caelius podagram.
> quam dum volt nimis adprobare veram
> et sanas linit obligatque plantas
> inceditque gradu laborioso,
> (quantum cura potest et ars doloris!)
> desit fingere Caelius podagram.

"Wishing to prove that it was absolutely genuine, he plasters and bandages his perfectly healthy feet, and walks with a hobbling gait. Well—such is the powerful effect of scientifically shamming pain—it's no longer a *pretended* gout that Caelius has got."

About all this treatment of clients, Martial, like his contemporary, Juvenal, feels bitterly. The condition of a slave, he tells us, is much preferable to that of a free poor citizen. The slave is not dunned for debts he cannot pay, nor bothered by social duties: he is fed, given shelter, and a place to sleep quietly: and thus he is three times as well off as his master. This need for money and the general lack of money among clients at Rome undoubtedly led to the degrading and shameful practice of cultivating the aged and childless wealthy and so ingratiating oneself by constant attendance and gifts that a fat legacy would be the outcome on the death of the testator. Martial sees all this with his peculiarly sharp vision and he leaves us almost a photographic record of what takes place: he writes (**VI. 63**) to a rich old man, Marianus:

"You know, Marianus, that you are being fished for, and you know the rapacity of the fisherman who is angling for you, and you know the fisherman's purpose. Yet, you foolish man, in your last will and testament you name him your heir and you mean him to take your place. You say, 'oh! but the gifts he sent me were splendid.' Yes, but he sent them as bait on a hook. Can the fish really love the fisherman? Will this man mourn your death with any genuine grief? If you want him to feel sorrow, Marianus, *leave him nothing*."

However, it is pleasant to record the experience of one "captator" (**X. 97**) which turned out unexpectedly: his intended victim, the aged and stricken invalid, was at his last gasp: his life was despaired of: all the preparations for the funeral are complete, pyre, ointments, grave, bier and funeral-director. It only remains for him to make his will and name the "captator" as his heir. Well, what happened?

> dum levis arsura struitur Libitina papyro,
>   dum murram et casias flebilis uxor emit,
> iam scrobe, iam lecto, iam pollinctore parato
>   heredem scripsit me Numa: convaluit.

> "While the lightly built pyre was being laid
>   with papyrus for kindling,
> While the weeping wife was buying myrrh
>   and casia,
> When the grave and the bier and the
>   undertaker were ready,
> Numa inscribed me in his will as heir,
>   and—recovered!"

Martial is bitter enough about the indignities put upon a freeborn client at Rome, but often he is even more indignant at the lack of reward for a man-of-letters in the capital of the world. It is indeed a hard life for a poet. In those days there were no royalties from publishers, no copyright, no literary agents to look after a writer's interests: there is no clear evidence that any author of the first century A.D. got any financial benefit from the publication of his work. The bookseller, of course, charged for the copies of it: but he took the risk and bore the expense of having it transcribed by his copyists. If the author was successful, he acquired reputation: and if he had a wealthy patron, and had flattered him by a dedication or a special mention, he might be given a sum of money or some other material reward; but as often as not, all he got was applause—for Helicon has all the ornamental trappings, but no solid benefit for the poet (**I. 76**):

> praeter aquas Helicon et serta lyrasque dearum
>   nil habet et magnum, sed perinane,
> sophos.

"Isn't it strange," Martial says (**X. 76**), "how Fortune distributes her gifts! Yonder is a Roman citizen, Maevius, not a slave, not an immigrant from Syria, Parthia, or Cappadocia, 'sed de plebe Remi Numaeque verna,' a pleasant and friendly man, honest too and blameless, educated in both Greek and Latin, altogether an admirable person, but having one fault and no small fault—'quod est poeta:' that's why he goes cold in a black cowl, while the mule-driver Incitatus walks in flaming scarlet." The fact is (and Martial expresses it bitterly in many of his poems) if a man is coming to live in this city of Rome and means to keep himself in any comfort, he need not count on any qualities of character to help him on, nor any qualities of mind. If he wants to have money, he ought to become a popular musician. Indeed Martial for a while left Rome and went to Forum Cornelium in Cisalpine Gaul because he could no longer put up with the useless social duties required of a client; and if Rome wonders where he is and why he went and when he will return, he sends her a message that will explain all (**III. 4**): the self-exiled poet is undergoing a change: he will return when he has got a profitable profession—

> poeta
> exierat: veniet cum citharoedus erit.

Therefore if you are educating your son for life in the city, you must watch carefully what you have him taught (**V. 56**): guard him from the unremunerative literary subjects: the aim of education should be profitableness:

> cui tradas, Lupe, filium magistro
> quaeris sollicitus diu rogasque.
> omnes grammaticosque rhetorasque
> devites moneo: nihil sit illi
> cum libris Ciceronis aut Maronis,
> famae Tutilium suae relinquat;
> si versus facit, abdices poetam.
> artes discere vult pecuniosas?
> fac discat cithareodus aut choraules.
> si duri puer ingeni videtur,
> praeconem facias vel architectum.

"You have long been anxiously enquiring and asking what kind of master to send your son to, Lupus. Well, I advise you to avoid all teachers of literature and of oratory; keep him clear of the works of Cicero and of Virgil: don't let him emulate Tutilius' fame as a lawyer: and if he writes poetry, disinherit the poet. But suppose he wants to learn the money-making arts? See that he learns to be a harp-player or a flute-player—or if he seems to be dull-witted, make him an auctioneer or an architect."

Martial therefore concludes that, if great works of literature are to be produced, writers must not be expected to depend on a mean pittance but should have a competency, adequate recognition, and complete freedom from anxiety; and it is only the patrons who can confer such a boon (**I. 107**),

> otia da nobis, sed qualia fecerat olim
>   Maecenas Flacco Vergilioque suo.

Martial again and again calls for a Maecenas (**VIII. 56**) who will endow literature and thus make possible a revival of poetry:

> sint Maecenates, non deerunt, Flacce,
> Marones.

But the age of wealthy nobles was past. The only patron of letters who could now provide pensions for poets was the Emperor. Caesar must become the universal patron: only the head of the State could adequately reward writers whose work was of service to the State. Teachers and professors had been well provided for. Vespasian had instituted a class of teachers graded and salaried on a systematic and permanent scheme: why could not some comparable benefit be conferred on poets? The only fault in the age of Domitian, says Martial **(V. 19)**, an age which he claims to have surpassed all earlier ages in most respects, is the fact that the poor man, the penniless writer, is not cared for and there is no one to befriend him in his poverty: the triumphs of Domitian's age, the favours bestowed on it by heaven, the enlargement and adornment of the city—these, says the poet, had never before been equalled:

> est tamen hoc vitium, sed non leve, sit licet
>   unum,
>   quod colit ingratas pauper amicitias.

Therefore to remedy this one fault in an almost perfect age, Caesar must be the patron of poets and writers:

> esto tu, Caesar, amicus:
> nulla ducis virtus dulcior esse potest.

In fact, Titus and Domitian had each conferred on Martial the "ius trium liberorum" (which brought him whatever privileges the actual father of three children could have) and a tribuneship which carried with it the honorary status of knight. At some time towards the latter part of his career he owned a small estate at Nomentum about twenty miles north-east of Rome, and later he also acquired a town-house in Rome: but his circumstances were never easy: and after the death of Domitian and succession of Nerva, either because he found the new régime less sympathetic or because his finances were still difficult, or because, as he grew older, the chances of ease in Rome seemed less, he decided to return to Spain, where through the kindness of friends and the liberality of a Spanish patroness, Marcella, he was given a small estate sufficient for his needs. He lived there not unhappily till his death in 104 A.D.

The Roman historians have not much good to say about the Emperor Domitian. The fifteen years of his reign (81-96 A.D.) are described by Tacitus in the *Agricola* as a grim tyranny in which the liberal arts and all freedom and indeed even speech itself were suppressed by this jealous and ruthless Emperor. The impression we get is of a haughty, morose, vain, suspicious man, who at the same time was ambitious, impulsive and dangerous. The portrait given by Suetonius is little better. And the Younger Pliny in his *Panegyricus*, addressed to Trajan, uses every trait of Domitian as a foil to heighten the virtues and glories of the new Emperor

whom he is extolling. I feel that the Roman writers were all too prone to emphasize these extremes of contrast: they adored antithesis not only of phrase, but of character: it was part of their rhetorical education. Scipio Africanus and Hannibal are contrasted in Livy, Caesar and Pompey in Lucan, Aeneas and Turnus in Virgil; and so the unpopular Domitian is set over against his brother Titus who was acclaimed as "deliciae populi Romani". Now, contrast is a powerful and useful device, but in Roman hands it tended to make the black blacker so as to intensify the radiance of the white; and I am not sure that a more subtle or controlled gradation of the difference between virtue and vice might not have given Domitian a rather less repellent reputation. Certainly, coming from the pages of Tacitus, Pliny, Suetonius, and Juvenal, one is surprised to find the transfiguration (I can use no other word) which has befallen Domitian. As Martial sees him, or chooses to portray him, he is a very different figure—angelic, noble, generous, the vice-regent on earth of Jupiter, approachable, willing to be entreated, interested in the arts especially poetry, and exercising a cleansing moral influence in the life of the State. He is a successful general, not the organizer of a sham triumph as he appears in Tacitus: he has won victories over the Germans, the Sarmatians, and the Dacians. Like Augustus, he has given his name to the calendar—to two months, for September in which he came to the throne he has decided to call "Germanicus", and October in which he was born is to be called "Domitianus". Hence Martial **(IX. 1)** speaks of the first day of September as "Germanicarum magna lux Kalendarum". The Emperor's Sarmatian campaign was so enthralling **(VII. 6 and 7)**, especially when dispatches of victory began to arrive, that the Romans' minds were far away from Rome—with Caesar in the field, and not a man of them could have told you which of the favourite horses was running in the Circus that day:

> adeoque mentes omnium tenes unus
> ut ipsa magni turba nesciat Circi
> utrumne currat Passerinus an Tigris.

The Emperor in his achievements is like Hercules: he has come through many labours to final acknowledgement of his greatness. This theme is one that appeals both to Emperor and poet. Domitian built a temple to Hercules on the Appian Way and erected beside it a huge golden statue of the god—but with his own head and features imposed on top of it. Martial develops the theme with zest: Jupiter now, he says **(IX. 65)**, will have no hesitation in accepting Hercules as his true son or in acknowledging the sonship and godhead of Alcides,

> postquam pulchra dei Caesaris ora geris;

and if the original Hercules had had these features, Juno's heart would have been won and the twelve labours avoided. The twelve labours were great: but what of the labours that Domitian has accomplished? how do they compare with those of the ancient and lesser Hercules? They are so surpassing that the likeness of Domitian on the statue of Hercules is not enough: let the Emperor give his features to Jupiter Capitolinus **(IX. 101)**:

> templa deis, mores populis dedit, otia ferro,
>   astra suis, caelo sidera, serta Iovi.
> Herculeum tantis numen non sufficit actis:
>   Tarpeio deus hic commodet ora patri.

"He has given temples to the gods, sound morals to his nation, peace to the sword, deification to his father and brother, stars to the firmament, and wreaths to Jupiter. The divine personality of Hercules is not enough for such achievements: let this god of ours lend his features to the statue of Jupiter."

This ascription of divinity to the Emperor was completely in accord with Domitian's wishes as we learn from Suetonius (*Dom.* xiii), and it is everywhere present in the poems. In **V. 8** he speaks of the "edictum domini deique nostri"; he calls Domitian "dux sanctus, praeses mundi, summe mundi rector et parens orbis". His safety and preservation are the surest proof that the gods exist and are beneficent **(II. 91),**

> rerum certa salus, terrarum gloria, Caesar,
>   sospite quo magnos credimus esse deos.

Jupiter, in fact, doesn't want to be bothered with human petitions when a power so generous and willing exists on earth **(VI. 10)**: "When I was recently praying to Jupiter for a few thousands, he answered: 'the one on earth who gave me the temples, he will provide for you,'

> "ille dabit" dixit "qui mihi templa dedit."

So in future when he supplicates Jupiter, it will be a prayer for the Emperor only: all personal prayers he will address to Domitian **(VII. 60),** and he begs Jupiter not to misunderstand:

> nil pro me mihi, Iuppiter, petenti
> ne succensueris velut superbo:
> te pro Caesare debeo rogare:
> pro me debeo Caesarem rogare.

When, therefore, he ventures to address a prayer to Domitian, he begs fervently that it may be granted **(VIII. 24):** but if not—giving a clever turn to the poem, he prays that at least the request may be allowed to be made, because it is not the image-maker who creates the gods, but the worshipper and petitioner:

> qui fingit sacros auro vel marmore vultus,
>   non facit ille deos: qui rogat, ille facit.

In fact, if he were invited to dinner by a summons simultaneously from Jupiter and from Domitian, it would be a nice problem of protocol to decide which to accept **(IX. 91)**; but he is sure what his answer would be:

> astra licet propius, Palatia longius essent,
>   responsa ad superos haec referenda darem:
> 'quaerite qui malit fieri conviva Tonantis:
>   me meus in terris Iuppiter, ecce, tenet.'

"Though the sky was nearer and the Palace farther away, I would give this answer to be returned to the Gods of Heaven: 'Find someone who would prefer to be the guest of Jupiter: don't you see, I'm engaged with my own Jupiter here on earth.' "

It is with equally avowed admiration, and sometimes also with a little brisk fun, that he greets some of Domitian's legislation in the State. You will recall how Domitian assumed the office of censor early in his reign and, contrary to all precedent, held on to it for the rest of his life. Politically, this gave him control of the Senate and he could advance to that order or degrade from it at his own will and choice. But he also exercised the censorial powers to institute a kind of moral purge of the city by re-instituting certain lapsed laws, notably the Lex Julia against adultery, with the result that there was a considerable rush on the part of offenders to get married. Martial refers to it seriously, but he cannot help joking about it too. For example he addresses Domitian **(VI. 4)** in tones of magniloquent eulogy:

> censor maxime principumque princeps,
> cum tot iam tibi debeat triumphos,
> tot nascentia templa, tot renata,
> tot spectacula, tot deos, tot urbes:
> plus debet tibi Roma, quod pudica est.

"Greatest of censors and prince of princes,
  Although Rome is indebted to you for so
    many victories,
  For so many new temples being built, and so
    many old ones reconstructed,
  For so many spectacles, so many gods, so
    many cities,
  Yet Rome is still more indebted to you for
    making her chaste."

But listen to this in a different vein **(V. 75)**:

> quae legis causa nupsit tibi Laelia, Quinte,
>   uxorem potes hanc dicere legitimam.

"Laelia who married you to comply with the
  law, Quintus,
  you can now surely call your *lawful* spouse."

And this **(VI. 7)** is a characteristically satirical comment on the law:

> Iulia lex populis ex quo, Faustine, renata est
>   atque intrare domos iussa Pudicitia est,
> aut minus aut certe non plus tricesima lux est,
>   et nubit decimo iam Telesilla viro.

"Faustinus, it is now the thirtieth day, perhaps less, certainly not more, since the Julian law was reinstituted and chastity officially ordered to enter our homes—it is just about the thirtieth day and already Telesilla is marrying her tenth husband."

Domitian also re-enacted the Lex Roscia by which the two highest orders in the state, the senators and the knights, were assigned special places in the theatre—the senators having the orchestra seats in a semicircle in front of the stage, and the knights having the next fourteen rows. Martial as a military tribune had the standing of a knight, and was very proud of his privilege at the theatre. **Book V** is full of references to comical scenes in the theatres when well-dressed and wealthy upstarts tried to occupy a knight's seat and argue it out with the vigilant attendants. There is for example **V. 35**, which describes a scene in the theatre when Leïtus the attendant attempts to expel from the knights' stalls an indignant scarlet-clad Greek who wishes to be taken for a rich freedman of equestrian rank, and who protests that he has the full legal income for a knight, since he draws 200,000 sesterces a year from his farm at Patrae and as much again from his property near Corinth; and as for family, he has an attested pedigree running back to Leda and the swan. As the altercation proceeded, there dropped out of the magnificent pretender's clothes a large key, a doorkeeper's key, which revealed him for what he was, a slave:

> dum suscitanti Leïto reluctatur:
> equiti superbo, nobili, locupleti
> cecidit repente magna de sinu clavis.
> nunquam, Fabulle, nequior fuit clavis.

"While he was struggling against Leïtus, who was removing him, out of the robe of this proud, aristocratic, wealthy knight there suddenly tumbled a large door-key. Never, Fabulus, was there a more perverse key."

How far can these complimentary poems about Domitian be trusted? How true is the evidence they afford? It may be said in their favour that **Book V,** being specially intended for Domitian's reading, has been made to conform to the new standard of at least legal morality which the Emperor has instituted, and the tone of the book has been very much improved, so that the Emperor may read it with face unashamed in the very presence of his patron goddess Pallas Athene **(V. 2)**; but readers who enjoy "nequitiae procaciores salesque nudi" are referred back to the first four books already published. Similarly in **Book VIII,** which is specifically dedicated to the Emperor, he states that his epigrams have not been allowed to speak with as much playful licence as before **(VIII. proem.)** though, of course, he does allow a certain admixture of jest. "As the greater part, and better part, of my book is attached to the Majesty of your sacred name, it should remember that only those cleansed by religious purification ought to approach the temple"; and therefore in the first poem he dismisses Venus and welcomes Pallas the patroness of Caesar:

> nuda recede Venus; non est tuus iste libellus:
>   tu mihi, tu Pallas Caesariana, veni.

And it must be said that the tone of these two books is such that they could indeed be read, as Martial claims, by "matronae, puerique, virginesque".

On the other hand, it is notable that **Book X,** which had passed into circulation just before Domitian's death, was in fact withdrawn, remodelled, and republished two years later; and the only conclusion one can draw is that the first draft contained poems in praise of Domitian which would have been unacceptable to the new régime, however liberal that régime was. This is supported by the fact that in the new edition there is a kind of apology or palinode **(X. 72),** in which the poet dismisses *Blanditiae* from his books so as to make room for sincere and truthful praise of the new Emperor Trajan,

> frustra, Blanditiae, venitis ad me,
> adtritis miserabiles labellis . . .

"In vain, Flatteries, do you come to me, wretched creatures with your hackneyed lips. I am not now intending to address anyone as Master and God: no longer in this city is there any place for you . . . there is no *Master* here now, but a commander, but a senator the most just of them all, by whose action plain unadorned Truth has been brought back from her exile in the underworld: if you are wise, Rome, under such an Emperor you will beware of speaking in your former tones."

This change of note, this renunciation of flattery, seems to me to cast considerable doubt on the genuineness of his praise of Domitian: he had very quickly adjusted himself to the character of the new ruler.

Martial has written twelve books of epigrams with nearly a hundred poems in each and a total of between 700 and 750 verses in each book. (I omit from consideration the introductory book called the *Liber Spectaculorum,* because it is not really of great poetic interest: and I equally omit **Books XIII** and **XIV** which consist of couplet-mottoes meant for inscription on gifts and presents.) So the whole collection of epigrams amounts to between 8,000 and 9,000 verses—about the same length as the *Aeneid,* except that most of Martial's lines are shorter than hexameters. The poems are short, crisp and pointed. There is nothing aimless or loose in them. The poet knows what he wants to say and the effect he wishes to produce, and he does it with the utmost economy of words and terseness of diction. I have heard his poems described as mechanical, as if he turned them out by automation. I don't agree. The simplicity and precision and rapidity of his execution are such that the technical excellence of his artistry can be missed. What strikes me most is the inevitability of his phrasing: it could not be bettered: it has no surplusage, no fat tissue: it is lean, athletic and swift: he puts it well himself **(II. 77)** in reply to one of his critics:

> non sunt longa quibus nihil est quod demere
> possis,

"a poem is just right in length if there is nothing that can be omitted without spoiling it": such a poem has become a natural entity: it is self-sufficient, existing in its own right.

Martial is not a poet of war. In his books no trumpets blare, and no legions march. Nor is he a learned poet. In him there is very little mythology, no recondite allusions, no abstruse echoes of older poets, no laboured effects, no enigma variations. The tone is conversational, direct, plain, neat and crisp, free from that curse of Roman poetry—rhetorical ornament and rhetorical emphasis. He makes no great claims for his verse: he calls it **(X. 19),**

> nec doctum satis et parum severum
> sed non rusticulum nimis libellum.

But this absence of academic learning, this unpuritan gaiety, and this air of unaffected urbanity—all these constitute its charm. And when you cast your mind over Latin poetry, this kind of writing is something unique.

His subject-matter was the Rome of his day and the multifarious people whom he saw or met in the houses, the forum, the baths, the Campus, the theatres and streets. He was a poet of life: his books are, in his own phrase, "Roman books dipped in sprightly wit" in which "Life can read and recognize her own manners" **(VIII. 3).** His little poems are like snaps, sharp and vivid, of real scenes. He had a great contempt for the poets who produced long epics and dramas on such traditional literary subjects as Oedipus and Thyestes, Colchian witches, Scyllas, and monsters **(X. 4):**

> hic non Centauros, non Gorgonas, Harpyiasque

invenies: hominem pagina nostra sapit.

"Here in my poems you won't find Centaurs, Gorgons, and Harpies: it is of living humanity that my page smacks." And he has equal scorn for those other escapists from life, the archaizing poets **(XI.90),** who adore the rough measures and expressions of Accius and Pacuvius, and who love such a hexameter ending as "terrai frugiferai", and who praise as better than Homer such a vile pentameter as "Lucili columella hic situ' Metrophanes".

The tone of his epigrams is generally satirical and mocking, but never sour like Juvenal's. As Pliny said of him, "plurimum in scribendo et salis (habebat) et fellis nec candoris minus": "a lot of wit, a lot of gall, but no less good nature." He had no wish to win notoriety by attacking persons openly by name and damaging their reputation: "ludimus innocui", he says **(VII. 12).** He enjoyed the human scene: and laughter, dry and astringent, is the dominant note in his verse. He has no use for an epigrammatist whose poems are merely sweet **(VII. 25):**

> nullaque mica salis, nec amari fellis in illis
> gutta est; o demens, vis tamen illa legi?

"Not a single grain of wit, not a single drop of gall—and yet do you expect your poems to be read?"

Martial, on the contrary, requires that his own poems shall have a sharp tang—and he is generally successful. These short disciplined epigrams are made to sting and bite. For example, he attacks a critic who thinks that, because Martial wrote small poems, he had therefore only a small talent. This critic Gaurus had composed a grand epic in twelve books on the wars of Priam. Does this vast work therefore prove him to be a great man? "Not at all", says Martial: "I make my small works live: you, Gaurus, make a giant of a poem, but an inert clay giant" **(IX. 50).**

> tu magnus luteum, Gaure, Giganta facis.

There are obscenities in Martial's poems. It would be a mistake not to mention this feature which he himself so often mentions and excuses and defends. The licentiousness is sometimes so gross that the Loeb translation renders it into the language of the Decameron. He was criticized in his own day for the *luxuria* of his pages **(III. 69):** one critic complained **(I. 35)** that he wrote (and this is putting it mildly)

> versus . . . parum severos
> nec quos praelegat in schola magister.

In his introduction to the **First Book** he speaks of the naughty realism of the language, "lascivam verborum veritatem", which he claims to be the proper kind of language for epigrams, because the fashion was set by Catullus who to him is the "magister". I imagine that in some ways Roman society in its talk must have been a great deal coarser than our own (there is evidence of this in many anecdotes in Suetonius), and Martial naturally mirrors this society. He argues that the type of epigram which he terms Catullan cannot give entire pleasure without an element of bawdiness: this is not introduced because the poet or his readers are depraved: it is not evidence that their character and morals are corrupt: it belongs to the accepted convention of the literary genre **(I. 35)**,

> lex haec carminibus data est iocosis,
> ne possint, nisi pruriant, iuvare.

> "This is the law appointed for amusing poems; they can't please unless bawdy."

And for this reason he refuses to have his poems emasculated or expurgated. He does not attack known or recognizable persons: he uses fictitious names: it is always his intention **(X. 33)**

> parcere personis, dicere de vitiis.

I would not say that Martial reveals any serious or idealistic philosophy of life. He had no religious belief, no faith, as far as I can discover. He makes no profession of philosophic belief: there is nothing in his poems that indicates his adhesion to any particular school of thought. On the whole, I would call him a realist, a man with no illusions about life, with no great ambitions; he desires only such common pleasures as bring comfort without pain or regret—a mildly optimistic hedonist who knows what he would enjoy but not always how to get it. He has left us his view of what constitutes for him the best in life in a number of poems scattered through the collection, and some of these are in my judgment among the very best that he wrote. His claims on life are not high: the same sentiments have been expressed by other Latin poets perhaps more eloquently: but I find in Martial a simple directness of statement which is in keeping with the plainness of his hopes. You will, perhaps, remember the well-known poem **(II. 90)** addressed to his countryman Quintilian, the great teacher and professor of rhetoric. It sounds as if Quintilian had been rebuking him for his unwillingness to settle down to a serious profession such as the law, or teaching, which would bring him a settled income. But this is not what Martial wants: he admits he is poor and not too old to begin a profession, but he doesn't want to be tied, he wants to live,

> vivere quod propero pauper nec inutilis annis,
> da veniam: properat vivere nemo satis.

> "Forgive me, Quintilian, for being in a hurry *to*

live, to enjoy life . . . ; no man ever makes enough speed in enjoying life."

His wants are few. He has no desire for power or wealth. His tastes are simple and not beyond attainment: he sets them out for Quintilian very simply: here they are:

> me focus et nigros non indignantia fumos
>   tecta iuvant et fons vivus et herba rudis.
> sit mihi verna satur, sit non doctissima
>   coniunx,
>   sit nox cum somno, sit sine lite dies.

> "What gives me pleasure is a fire on the hearth, and rafters with the black smoke eddying through them, and a well of spring water, and a plot of untrimmed grass. I would like to have a well-fed slave, and a wife educated but not a bluestocking, a sound night's sleep, and a day without a lawsuit."

That theme, which insists on the urgent immediacy of living *now,* recurs through all Latin poetry; but again and again in these poems it comes with a delightful freshness and charm. Pleasures are fugitive: we must clutch them with both hands **(I. 15)**,

> non est, crede mihi, sapientis dicere "vivam":
>   sera nimis vita est crastina: vive hodie.

> "Believe me, it's not the part of a wise man to say 'I intend to live': living tomorrow is too late: live today, my friend."

In fact, neither living tomorrow nor living today is good enough: the only wise man is he who has already lived yesterday **(V. 58)**:

> cras te victurum, cras dicis, Postume, semper.
>   dic mihi, cras istud, Postume, quando venit?
> quam longe cras istud, ubi est? aut unde
>   petendum?
>   numquid apud Parthos Armeniosque latet? . .

> cras vives? hodie iam vivere, Postume, serum
>   est:
>   ille sapit quisquis, Postume, vixit heri.

> "Tomorrow you say you will live, Postumus,
>   always tomorrow.
>   That tomorrow of yours, when does it
>   arrive? Tell me.
> How distant is it? Where is it? Where is it to
>   be found?
>   Is it hidden somewhere in Parthia or
>   Armenia? . . .
> Tomorrow will you live? To live to-day it's
>   too late even now.

He's the wise man who really lived
  yesterday."

And what is this living, this enjoyment of life, this realization of a swiftly passing existence, that Martial speaks about so feelingly? He tells us in two poems which I consider to be among the very best he wrote. They are both addressed to Julius Martialis, his closest friend at Rome for thirty-three years. The first is **V. 20:** in it he gives utterance to the deep hatred he has come to feel for the conventional life of the retainer whose time belongs not to himself but is given to his patron. He wishes to be free to enjoy the social company and talk and freedom of the Roman capital:

> "If you and I, my dear Martial, had the chance to enjoy together unworried days, and to have our time unoccupied by business and our own to dispose of, and both alike to have leisure for genuine life, we shouldn't have anything to do with the halls or mansions of the great or grim lawsuits or the gloomy forum or lordly families: but the promenade, the conversation, the notices, the Campus Martius, the colonnade, the coolness of the shade, the baths—these would always be our haunts and this our work. But as it is, neither of us sets the plan for his own life. We see the good sunny days slipping away and passing beyond recall, days that are lost to us and yet are included in our reckoning. Does any man, if he knows how to live, put off beginning?"

                    bonosque
soles effugere atque abire sentit,
qui nobis pereunt et inputantur.
quisquam, vivere cum sciat, moratur?

And the second poem (**X. 47**) simply states the things which in the poet's opinion make for a happier life—and they are not all to be found in a Welfare State:

vitam quae faciant beatiorem,
iucundissime Martialis, haec sunt:
res non parta labore, sed relicta;
non ingratus ager, focus perennis;
lis numquam, toga rara, mens quieta;
vires ingenuae, salubre corpus;
prudens simplicitas, pares amici;
convictus facilis, sine arte mensa;
nox non ebria, sed soluta curis;
non tristis torus, et tamen pudicus;
somnus, qui faciat breves tenebras:
quod sis, esse velis, nihilque malis;
summum nec metuas diem nec optes.

> "What makes life happier, my genial friend
>   Martial, are things like these:
> Means not gained by work but inherited by
>   bequest;
> A pleasantly rewarding demesne, a fire on the
>   hearth perpetually alight;

> No lawsuits, the formal toga seldom worn, a
>   mind at peace;
> A free man's natural vigour, a healthy body;
> Candor with discretion: congenial friends;
> Good-natured companionableness: a menu not
>   elaborated.
> An evening not intoxicated but relaxed and
>   carefree;
> A wife who is jolly and yet chaste;
> Sleep so sound that it's morning before you
>   know;
> To be content with what you are and not wish
>   to be something else:
> Neither to dread your final day nor to wish
>   for it."[1]

Walter Allen, Jr., et al. (essay date 1970)

SOURCE: "Martial: Knight, Publisher, and Poet," *The Classical Journal,* Vol. 65, No. 8, May, 1970, pp. 345-57.

[*In the following essay, Allen and a group of his students challenge the image of Martial as a desperately poor poet who regarded his verses as ephemeral or insignificant. Citing a variety of evidence to support their claim that Martial was financially secure and enjoyed a respectable social position, they argue that he was deeply involved in the publication of his books and believed strongly in the merit of his epigrams.*]

Martial, like Tibullus and Ovid before him,[1] was a Roman knight. That simple fact colors our acceptance of what the poet says about himself and his patrons. While a literal interpretation of Martial's conventional epigrammatic treatment of literary patronage could produce a picture of Martial as the shabby, starving poet of the third-floor garret, our author has deliberately included in his epigrams autobiographical material that he must have intended as a correction to such a false impression. Martial desired patronage and tangible rewards, of course, but it is the view of the modern reader, and not the view of Martial, that such gifts are demeaning for the poet who requests and accepts them. He is careful to inform his contemporary reader that such patronage was not required as a means of rescuing him from the ranks of the proletariat.

We refer in particular to three significant honors conferred upon Martial in the course of his life at Rome, honors the poet himself emphasizes a number of times when he is speaking about historical facts.[2] He was granted the *ius trium liberorum* by two emperors, presumably Titus and Domitian (**2.92, 3.95.**5 f., **9.97.**5 f.); he held a tribunate (**3.95.**9); and he was a knight (**5.13.**2, **9.49.**4, **12.29.**2). We must keep in mind, however, that the poet did not necessarily receive these honors in the order in which he mentions them nor in the order of the present discussion.

It is significant that Martial gained the *ius trium liberorum* at his own request when he was definitely childless (**2.91.5**)[3] and perhaps, at least when it was granted, not even married (**2.92.3**). Suetonius, by contrast, gained the same favor only through Pliny's urgent intercession with Trajan (*Ep.* 10.94, 95). Pliny himself acquired the *ius trium liberorum* through the influence of his friend Julius Servianus (*Ep.* 10.2.1). The granting of the *ius trium liberorum* conferred the privileges of exemption from the duties of guardian and *iudex,* and priority of claim to magistracies.[4] It is easy, then, to understand the poet's pride in this enhancement of his social position by his own successful request of the emperor.

Martial expressly states that he was a *tribunus,* but without further specification (**3.95.9**: *vidit me Roma tribunum*). It is possible that he was a *tribunus supra numerum,* a title instituted by the emperor Claudius.[5] Conceivably, the poet may have held a *tribunatus semestris* (*sexmestris*), which Juvenal seems to refer to when he writes of the pantomime Paris encircling the poets' fingers with the "six-month ring" (**7.89**); he also speaks of that pantomime producing tribunes and prefects (**7.92**).[6] According to Marquardt,[7] these *tribuni semestres* probably served nominally for one year, but in actual fact only for six months, although their pay of 25,000 sesterces was a full year's salary.[8]

Closely related to his tribunate is Martial's status as a knight. We learn explicitly of his title of *eques* initially in **5.13.2**,[9] and he often makes mention in this book of the knights' seats in the theater (e.g., **8, 14, 23, 27**). He was probably an *eques equo publico,* since this appears to have been the standard type of knight under the Empire. He exhibits, moreover, a certain preoccupation with the *equus* of a knight (e.g., **5.23.8, 38.4**).

The fact of Martial's knighthood, at any rate, implies that he must have possessed at least the requisite equestrian census of 400,000 sesterces. Although not a large sum by the standards of his day, it might, nonetheless, have allowed the poet to live in better circumstances than he often leads us to infer.

There remains the problem of whether Martial became an *eques* as a result of his tribunate, as Horace did,[10] or whether he was a knight before then. Mayor[11] feels that the legionary tribune "became as a matter of course an *eques.*" He says that the office of *tribunatus semestris* was conferred by the emperor on those who did not intend to pursue a military career but "retired as *equites* into private life." Against this theory we have the opinions of Mattingly, Hirschfeld, and Kromayer-Veith[12] that army officers (tribunes and prefects) were appointed from among the knights. Helm and Friedländer[13] both think that Martial became a knight by virtue of his tribunate which, Friedländer suggests, might have been granted by Titus. The problem is by no means settled, but it is perhaps enough for us that we can couple the rank of *eques* and the office of *tribunus.*

It is generally believed, as has been mentioned already, that Martial received the *ius trium liberorum* from Titus and that it was subsequently confirmed by Domitian.[14] Attempts to date the reception of his tribunate and knighthood, however, can be far less successful since the poet himself gives no clear indication of when they were granted. This very vagueness allows us to propose a new suggestion, based on the fact that the tribunate was appropriate for a young man, while the *ius trium liberorum* was not.

Martial could have been content, indeed well-advised, merely to mention his tribunate and knighthood, without indicating their source, if he had received these honors from Nero. He would, moreover, have been, in the early 60's A.D., just about the right age to receive a tribunate, especially if he did see some active duty, however token it may have been. This theory is reinforced by the fact that he stresses, and expresses gratitude for, the *ius trium liberorum,* apparently a Flavian gift, while simply stating his possession of the other two titles without comment.

If the foregoing theory be correct, then we might suggest that Martial perhaps came to Rome a few years before the commonly accepted date of A.D. 64, pursued an equestrian career, with the help of the Senecas and Piso, fell from favor as a consequence of the Pisonian conspiracy, and then turned to poetry. The bestowal of the *ius trium liberorum* in A.D. 79 or 80 (when Martial was about forty years old) would mark a return to imperial favor which continued under Domitian. Martial was gratified by the *ius trium liberorum,* and could scarcely have expected anything more in the way of a renewed official career.

Another indication of Martial's good social position can be seen in some of the people with whom he was intimate, especially those patrons whom he shared with Statius—viz., Claudius Etruscus, L. Arruntius Stella, Novius Vindex, Atedius Melior, and Lucan's widow, Polla Argentaria. Statius has been called the "Poet Laureate" of Domitian's court[15] and Howard[16] thought that he "lived on terms of intimate friendship . . . with many rich and cultured Romans." Yet Martial, who belonged to the same circles as Statius, is usually looked upon as the grovelling pauper who survived on *sportulae.* We might conclude with J. W. Duff[17] that Statius and Martial did indeed belong to the "same social grade" and that both enjoyed the imperial favor, if not largess.

There are substantial indications of Martial's influence at court. We find, for example, that, in addition to winning favors for himself, he was instrumental in gaining citizenship for others (**3.95**.11). The poet also claims that he was read by the emperor and other important men "of the city and law courts" (**6.64**.8-15). It is doubtful that he would have been so insolent as to make such a claim if it were not true.

The fact that Pliny the Younger supplied Martial with money for his journey back to Spain has been generally taken as conclusive proof that Martial was indigent and left Rome penniless. Pliny, however, indicates in a letter (**3.21**) that the sum of money was presented in gratitude for Martial's complimentary poetic address (**10.20**), and Pliny gives no suggestion that his monetary gift was a necessary act of charity.[18] The supposition that Martial could not have returned to Spain without this *viaticum* from Pliny is not substantiated by Pliny's own statement on the matter.

Martial is of course our only source for his biography except for this letter of Pliny (**3.21**). While his information must always be viewed in the light of his careful observance of the tradition of his genre, some of his poetical statements about himself are capable of yielding more signs of modest affluence than the three honors that we have found capable of further interpretation with regard to Martial's finances and his early life at Rome.[19]

No later than A.D. 63 or 64 Martial came to Rome, where he stayed for thirty-four years (**10.103**.7, **104**.10; **12.18**.16, of which the last seems to be an approximation). Although he was not in Rome continuously for the thirty-four years, he seems to have considered it his residence, and he specifically states that he did not return to Bilbilis during this time (**10.103**.7 f., **104**.9 f.).

Virtually nothing is known of Martial's life from his arrival in Rome until the publication of the ***Liber spectaculorum*** in A.D. 80. He does, however, seem to have made the acquaintance of the influential personages of the day, and he was apparently well received in the capital.

From his frequent references to speaking and pleading in the courts, Martial appears to have at least an intimate dislike of that profession. He tells Titus that he would sooner be a farmer than a lawyer (**1.17**). When Gaius advises him to be a lawyer and grow rich, Martial does not mind letting him know that the advice was not appreciated (**2.30**). He informs Quintilian as to what he thinks of the law when he describes the ideal life and emphatically states that one of the requirements for happiness is the lack of lawsuits (**2.90**). In addition, he complains (seriously?) to Sextus for not paying his bill for pleading a case (**8.17**). All these

references, many of which are in the early part of the corpus, suggest that he knew the profession and had probably practiced it. He does tell us, somewhat bitterly, that his parents had procured a rhetorical education for him (**9.37**.7-10).

More significant, perhaps, is the fact that Martial, to our knowledge, did not publish poetry regularly until the advent of the Flavians. If we recall that Horace turned to poetry to mend his shattered fortunes (*Ep.* 2.2.51 f.), we should have to conclude that Martial's was not a similar case despite his pleas for patronage. Martial was, by contrast, about forty years old when his first book appeared and, if our previous suggestions are acceptable, he was already a knight and of some means. A Maecenas is always desirable, of course, and it was a Maecenas that Martial wanted, not a niggardly patron (**1.107, 8.55 [56]**).

Martial's housing situation in Rome is also relevant, but hard to interpret. In the first book he says that his *cenacula* look out on the Vipsanian laurels (**1.108**.3), and adds that he has become a *senex in hac regione* (**1.108**.4). He says that he lives up *tribus scalis* (**1.117**.7)[20] and that it is an effort to get to his dwelling. From these comments it would seem necessary to place him near the *Porticus Vipsania* and the *Campus Agrippae*[21] in the vicinity of the Campus Martius. Martial complains about his neighbor who lives so close that Martial could touch him by reaching his hand out of the window, but who creates a rather unpleasant situation because he does not visit or dine with Martial (**1.86**).

The next fact that we have on Martial's life is that he was in Gual at the time of the publication of **book 3** in 87-88. There naturally follows the question of what became of the original home of which he wrote in **book 1**. It appears that he gave up his apartment and, on his return, bought a *domus*. He no longer uses the Vipsanian laurels or the *Porticus Vipsania* to locate his house, as he had done previously, but rather the Temple of Flora (**5.22**.4, **6.27**.1) and the Old Temple of Jove (**5.22**.4), both of which were on the Quirinal.[22] He also begins to invite guests for dinner (**5.44, 78; 9.35**.11), and he even states that he has a cook and a kitchen (**5.50**.7 f.), both of which would have been unusual in an *insula*.

A further evidence of Martial's holdings in urban real estate is in **9.18**, where he asks to hook on to the city water supply, namely the Aqua Marcia. The opening lines, *Est mihi—sitque precor longum te praeside, Caesar—/rus minimum, parvi sunt et in urbe lares,* are usually taken to refer to his country estate and to his *domus* in Rome. On the basis of the arguments, however, that the country estate has no real purpose in the poem, and that Martial elsewhere uses the phrase *rus in urbe* (**12.57**.21) to describe the *domus* of a wealthy man, it seems to us that he is here referring to the grounds or gardens that surround his house in the city, rather than to his country estate. The Marcia, moreover, would be the appropriate aqueduct to supply the Quirinal, and, according to Grimal,[23] its water was then used for gardens.

The fact that Martial again refers to the Aqua Marcia in a later book **(11.96)** suggests that he is then still in the same region. It seems plausible to suggest also that the *horti* and *rus* mentioned in **9.18** are the same as the gardens which he states that he bought in **5.62.** They seem to have been complete with dwelling and furniture, although not in good repair. The request for a connection with the Aqua Marcia shows an effort on Martial's part to improve his property.

Aside from the *domus* in the city, Martial often speaks of his Nomentan Farm, even in some of his very early poems **(13.119; 2.38; 6.43.3; 7.31.6-8, 49, 93; 9.60).** Although he does offer some wine from his farm as a gift **(13.119),** he indicates that the farm really produces nothing to speak of **(7.31.8, 49; 9.60).** The farm is therefore not a commercial enterprise, but rather a pleasurable retreat where he can withdraw from the people he does not like **(2.38)** and the excitement of fashionable resorts **(6.43).** Another advantage of the farm is that his dear friend Quintus Ovidius is his neighbor **(7.93.5 f.).** The farm was apparently not very far from the city, since in one poem he claims that he prefers it to resorts and adds **(6.43.9):** *nunc urbis vicina iuvant facilesque recessus.* In **7.49** he sends *suburbani munuscula horti,* and in **8.61.6** he calls it *sub urbe rus . . . aestivum.*

Although Martial is often complaining of worn out togas (as in **9.49),** he would appear to have been financially secure. When he tells Quintilian **(2.90.3)** that he is poor but happy, or boasts that he has fame and popularity even though he is poor, or complains that poetry does not bring in enough money, it is probably realistic not to take him too seriously. A man who owns a country estate, a town house with grounds, the proper amount of money to qualify him to be a knight, and the means to ask a friend to purchase a place for him in Spain **(10.104.**14), could hardly be considered poor, and indeed his total resources could have exceeded the minimum requirement for the census of a Roman knight.

Not only did Martial take these pains to clarify his own social position for his readers; he also indicated that he was the publisher of his own poetry. We are using the term "publish" in its modern meaning, with the understanding that the ancient *bibliopola* of Martial's day combined the modern functions of print shop and retail store. Earlier poets had set a precedent, notably Ovid with his two editions of the *Amores,* but Martial presents us with some novelties that reward

further study. We accept the dating of most of Martial's individual books from internal evidence, the work of the last half of the nineteenth century that achieved definitive formulation in the work of L. Friedländer. W. M. Lindsay has also put us in his debt by his superb discussion of the significance of the three archetypes of our tradition.[24]

Yet the poems, as printed in a modern edition, are likely to present a deceptive appearance to the reader, for the fragmentary *Liber spectaculorum* survives in only one manuscript tradition, the florilegia of A[a]. All three manuscript traditions are quite explicit about dividing the remaining fourteen books into the *Epigrammaton libri* XII and the *Xenia* and *Apophoreta.* The numbering of the last two as **books 13** and **14** is a modern innovation.[25]

The most interesting and important problems concern the twelve *Epigrammaton libri.* The dating of the *Liber spectaculorum* and the *Xenia* and *Apophoreta* was examined and settled as adequately as possible by Friedländer.[26] Internal evidence impels us to the conclusion that the fourteen complete books that we possess were issued originally and individually as papyrus *volumina.*[27] How, when, and by whom they were united into the present collection, we do not know.

With Martial, there is no need to consider the possible discrepancies between the datable poems and the dates of the publishing of the books. He ostentatiously and repeatedly numbers his books **(2.93; 5.2, 15; 6.85; 7.17; 8.***praef.***, 3; 10.2; 12.5).**[28] The erratic location of the numbering within the roll precludes any merely technical explanation of the poet's frequent mention of the books' numbers. He also takes care to let us know the date, when he wishes us to know it **(4.11; 5.3; 6.3, 13; 7.5-8; 8.2** [Domitian returned in January]**; 9.23, 24, 84; 10.6, 7).** When he does not tell us, we have to make do with the principle of a book a year **(10.70.**1). We shall try to suggest how these facts ought to affect our attitude towards the evidence.

In **3.1** Martial suggests a contrast between **book 3,** written at Forum Corneli in Gallia Togata, and an earlier work, *liber prior,* written at Rome *(verna liber).* This must be a reference to **book 2,** wherein the last poem **(93)** is a conversation between Martial and his patron Regulus:

> "Primus ubi est," inquis, "cum sit liber iste
>   secundus?"
>   Quid faciam si plus ille pudoris habet?
> tu tamen hunc fieri si mavis, Regule, primum,
>   unum de titulo tollere iota potes.

Now whatever the ambiguous second verse may mean, the last two seem to say, "If you erase one of the two iotas of the *titulus,* for all practical purposes this will be the first book, *liber primus.*" This translation helps to clear up any difficulty in verse 2. *Pudor* does not refer to the book as less *lascivus.* Instead, since it has not yet been published, it is described as being shy.

By the time that **book 5** is published, the problem of numbering has disappeared, for **5.2.5 f.** tell the wanton reader: *lascivos lege quattuor libellos,/quintus cum domino liber iocatur.* **Book 5** is datable, appearing after the embassy of Degis (**5.3**), possibly in the fall of 89. **Book 3** probably preceded the revolt of Saturninus (88) mentioned in **4.11**, and is plausibly dated to 87 or early 88. Within these two dates either a **book 1** is written, or **book 2** is expanded to the size of two books.[29]

If we now examine the circumstances surrounding the two editions of **book 10**, the first edition is dated by Friedländer to the Saturnalia of 95. Yet, after the publication of **book 11** (probably in late 96), Martial goes to the trouble not only of reworking and reissuing **book 10** in a revised and expanded form, but also of informing us of the fact in a prominent place in the volume (**10.2**).[30]

It is difficult to find a satisfactory explanation for the revision. Although one immediately thinks of a now (mid-98) unwise obsequiousness to Domitian, it is difficult to imagine greater flattery than had appeared in **book 8.** Furthermore, the letters of Pliny preserve evidence that the social atmosphere of the circles in which Martial moved was not greatly influenced by the death of the last Flavian.[31] Finally, and this is especially striking, it is not easy to understand why a new edition of **book 10** would cause the suppression of an embarrassing earlier edition.

We are thus faced with a significant problem. Why does Martial go out of his way to tell us that **book 1** was published later than **books 2** and **3,** and that the present **book 10** is a revision of an earlier edition? The most adequate solution to this question seems to have been suggested, in passing, by Th. Birt.[32] He cited an interesting sentence in the *praefatio* to **book 8:** *Hic, tamen, qui operis nostri octavus inscribitur, occasione pietatis frequentius fruitur;* and he suggested that Martial was attempting to write a coherent corpus of poetry, publishing each volume as it was finished. Columella's publication of *De re rustica* was cited as a parallel.

With these considerations in mind, it becomes remarkable that the number of books is twelve, a number reminiscent of epic completeness and not without influence on writers in other genres. Martial's veneration for Vergil is a case in point here, as well as the concern for serious poetry that his oft-remarked distaste for Statius implies.[33]

To find some order in the above facts, we must posit in Martial a poet who looked upon the epigram as significant poetry when it reports or reflects the life and spirit of the contemporary world.[34] He attempted to write a body of poetry that would be true to his standards. He places emphasis on the correct numbering of his books and makes clear (**2.93, 3.1**) that his numbering is not just an indication of chronological order.[35] He tells us dates only when they are of importance to his artistic purpose, e.g., the chronicling of Domitian's rise to supreme glory, reflected in **books 4-9.** When he for some reason modifies his design by a revision of **book 10**, Martial still insists that the book is to be numbered tenth.

We turn now to the curious fact that Martial, at about the halfway point in his production of twelve books, brought out an edition that should be a landmark in the history of publication and of text criticism. The studies of modern scholars can be used to substantiate the accuracy of what Martial says at the beginning of **book 1** (**1.2.3 f.**): *hos eme, quos artat brevibus membrana tabellis:/scrinia da magnis, me manus una capit.* The word *membrana* at first surprises the reader who recalls that the papyrus roll is thought to have been the usual form of the book until the parchment codex supplanted it nearly three centuries after Martial's time.[36] We cannot, however, ignore the facts that Martial expressly calls his book *membrana,* and firmly rejects the *scrinia,* or book boxes for papyrus rolls, in a poem that seems to serve as an introduction to a collection of books.[37]

Martial, further, gives his name, his fame, and the title of his book in **1.1.1-3:**

> Hic est quem legis ille, quem requiris,
> toto notus in orbe Martialis
> argutis epigrammaton libellis.

He thereby uses this poem in lieu of a title page, a matter of some importance in confirming that the form of his book was a codex. The papyrus rolls almost always bore their titles at the end of the roll, and on the outside or on a tag, but rarely at the beginning of the roll.[38]

The indisputable evidence given by Martial in **1.1** and **1.2,** and elsewhere,[39] that parchment codices did in fact exist in the first century A.D. is overlooked by Kenyon, who cites only the poems in **book 14 (183-195)** as relevant, and claims that most of these passages could easily refer to ordinary rolls of papyrus. The rest of these poems in **book 14,** he submits, describe gifts of an unusual nature by the very words *in membranis* and can therefore not be used as evidence that parchment codices were in common circulation.[40] R. P. Oliver, moreover, cited above in connection with the titulature of papyri, overlooks **1.1.** in his claim that "the exiguous fragments of earlier [earlier than the great vellum codices in rustic capitals after the second century A.D.]

texts do not include . . . a single example of a title or subscription."[41] In support of the claim that parchment codices were definitely in existence in the first century A.D. is the discovery at Oxyrhynchus of a fragment of parchment written on both sides, first published in 1898, and discussed in a later article by Jean Mallon.[42] This ten-line historical fragment, now entitled *De bellis Macedonicis,* was originally ascribed to the third century A.D. because of the forms of certain letters, and particularly because it was a codex and made out of parchment. Mallon, however, fixes the date of this fragment at about A.D. 100, but fails to mention that Martial's codex edition of collected epigrams, prefaced by **1.1** and **1.2**, probably antedated *De bellis Macedonicis.* Before Mallon's study of this fragment, no codex had been found to date before the fourth century A.D.

Mallon, who reconciles the forms of the letters in question to the classical system of writing in the first century A.D., bases his evidence for the early appearance of the codex almost entirely on Martial. Martial, he says, not only gives us clear evidence that parchment codices were in existence but also provides a *terminus a quo,* since Martial, in addition to listing in one of his "advertisement poems" the great advantages of the codices over the *volumina* (compactness and portability),[43] tells us that codices were just then being manufactured for the first time.[44] We can therefore set the earliest date for the appearance of the codex at about A.D. 88 from the date of Martial's collection of the first four (or first seven) books, although Mallon's fragment is from the first extant codex and dates from the end of the first century, circa A.D. 100.

Besides accounting for the fact of the apparent existence of the codex in as early a period as the first century A.D., we must also deal with another troublesome word, *charta.* The appearance of this word in **2.1.4**, and the mention of the use of Roman numerals for numbering in **2.93.3** f., which certainly indicates a papyrus roll, make it necessary for us to postulate that in this period of flux between parchment and papyrus Martial must have regularly published his individual books separately on papyrus, but then published some of his books in a collection on parchment,[45] for which **1.1** and **1.2** serve as prefatory poems.

A poet so concerned about his own rank and about the publication of his books can naturally be expected to display equal concern about his verses, even though his genre is not so noble as epic. In Martial's statements about his own art and his own place as a poet, we are faced with two sets of apparent contradictions. On the one hand, we can see numerous traditional elements in his poetry that had been used frequently as the epigram was developed by the Greeks and Romans.[46] Yet, throughout the epigrams, we find indications that Martial felt somewhat bound to justify himself in regard to certain new techniques or subjects. Another paradox can be seen in Martial's dismissal of his poems as mere trifles, alongside of his repeated claims to fame both present and future.

Reitzenstein, in his article on "Epigramm" in Pauly-Wissowa,[47] shows that, by the time of Martial, the epigram had developed to the point where it not only encompassed poems of an inscriptional nature, but also versified expressions on practically every conceivable subject in a variety of meters (elegiacs, hendecasyllabics, various lyric meters). It is, however, evident from statements in Martial's epigrams that tradition had established certain limits and conventions upon the genre.

In the first place, there must have been some normal length for the epigram. Otherwise Martial would not have anticipated the criticism of **6.65** where Tucca complains of the length of the preceding epigram.[48] In addition to this suggestion that epigrams were most often brief distichs, the second inference can be drawn from this poem that the hexameter was not a usual meter for the epigram.[49] The third general area in which Martial appears to be very conscious of traditions is in the limitation of his audience according to the type of poem. He calls his poems *lascivi* (**3.86**; **4.14**.12; **5.2**; **7.17.4, 51, 68**; **11.16**.3, 20) and *nequitias* (**6.82**.5; **11.15**.4, **16.7**). Apparently, a slightly caustic tone with an element of obscenity was a requisite for epigrams; he speaks of the necessary *sal* and *fel* (**7.25.3**),[50] and he reminds Cornelius (**1.35**.10 f.):[51] *lex haec carminibus data est iocosis,/ne possint, nisi pruriant, iuvare.* In **3.68** he explicitly tells us that henceforth the poems in this book are not for the *matrona;*[52] elsewhere he dedicates poems to a modest audience (**5.2**.1 f.): *Matronae puerique virginesque,/vobis pagina nostra dedicatur.* In the preface to **book 8** the poet informs us that his poems are less licentious than is usual for the genre: *ego tamen illis non permisi tam lascive loqui quam solent.*

In addition to warning his readers when to expect certain types of poems, Martial is careful to point out both his personal morality and his lack of personal vindictiveness. He makes the claim common to writers of erotic poetry (**1.4.8**; cf. **11.15.13**):[53] *lasciva est nobis pagina, vita proba,* and we can see traces of Roman satire in such disavowals of personal rancor as (**5.15.2**):[54] *et queritur laesus carmine nemo meo.* His poems, like satire, speak of vices, not of individuals (**10.33**.10): *parcere personis, dicere de vitiis.*

Throughout these poems that define his genre and what is expected of him, we find indications that Martial was not the first to make slight departures from the norm. He frequently refers to such predecessors and models as Catullus, Marsus, Pedo, Gaetulicus (**1.*praef.*;** **2.71, 77; 8.55 [56].24; 10.78.16**). Unfortunately, with the exception of Catullus, we cannot make comparisons with Martial, but it is likely that in the period between Catullus and Martial the epigram, strongly influenced by Roman satire and rhetoric,[55] began to develop along the lines indicated by Martial's arguments and justifications.

In the light of Martial's acute awareness of his art, it is natural that we are puzzled by his frequent dismissals of his poems as *nugae, ludi,* or *ioci,*[56] as well as *apinae* and *tricae.*[57] Horace of course had referred to his artistic and carefully composed *Odes* as *nugae.*[58] Catullus also, in his first poem, seemed to pass his poems off lightly by calling them *nugas.* A. L. Wheeler pointed out how common was the use of the word *nugae* in reference to short, light poems and suggested that in Catullus it was to be applied to one small book dedicated to Nepos, not to the entire collection as we have it.[59] Later, in 14b, Catullus' poems are called *ineptiae.*[60] Martial himself limits the importance we should attach to the terminology when he states that his poems are more than mere trifles (**4.49.**1 f.): *Nescit, crede mihi, quid sint epigrammata, Flacce,/qui tantum lusus illa iocosque vocat.* In **10.2.**3 he clearly indicates his habit of revision and the use of the *lima.*

On the other hand, we have evidence for the use of the same terms for seemingly more extemporaneous endeavors. Pliny (*Ep.* 4.14.1) refers to the poems that he is offering to Paternus as *lusus,* and the letter goes on to indicate the usual themes expressed in such poems as well as the customary places for their composition:

> . . . hendecasyllabos nostros, quibus nos in vehiculo
> in balineo inter cenam oblectamus otium temporis.
> His iocamur ludimus amamus dolemus querimur
> irascimur. . . .

We might also note that the composition of epigrams was not confined to a few persons of chiefly literary repute, for *Suetonius*[61] records that the Emperor Augustus composed epigrams *tempore balinei,* and Martial suggests in **9.26.**9 f. that Nero dabbled in the *lascivum opus.*

Perhaps the most convincing argument for not taking *nugae, ioci,* etc., too literally is the frequent claim that Martial makes to fame both in his own time and for the future. He often repeats the theme of (**1.1.**2):[62] *toto notus in orbe Martialis;* while we learn that such important persons as Domitian read and praised his poems.[63] In life Martial has been given what few men gain even by death (**5.13.**4): *quodque cinis paucis hoc mihi vita dedit.* The notion that Martial regarded his poems as transitory and inconsequential again collapses when one reads that Martial expected the occurrence of someone's name in his poetry to bring everlasting fame to that person.[64] Here again we can see just how

close to tradition he was, for both Horace and Catullus expected or hoped for everlasting fame[65] from their *nugae.*

In search of support for Martial's assertion that he is to be taken seriously as a poet, we shall examine a part of just one aspect of his work that shows him operating within the tradition of rhetoric. It is not surprising to find him making copious use of mythological references, but it is valuable to consider how conventionally and continually he does this. In the study of his entire corpus, we find that his use of mythology can best be described as the extension and development of a few basic rhetorical tropes.

Martial found in myth, exactly as he found in contemporary and historical reality,[66] a source of material to decorate, clarify, illustrate or emphasize his chosen subjects, material that he used in rhetorical ways. Quintilian's discussion of two tropes, metonymy and antonomasia, is enough to demonstrate how closely Martial follows the rules that Quintilian lays down for both orator and poet (*Inst. orat.* 8.6). We shall use his definitions and *exempla* as a guide, although we, with Quintilian, are well aware that boundary lines among tropes are indistinct.

Quintilian thus defines metonymy (8.6.23 f.):

> . . . metonymia, quae est nominis pro nomine positio.
> . . . Haec inventas ab inventore et subiectas res ab obtinentibus significat, ut 'Cererem corruptam undis'. . . . Refert autem, in quantum hic tropus oratorem sequatur. Nam ut 'Vulcanum' pro igne volgo audimus et 'vario Marte pugnatum' eruditus est sermo, et 'Venerem' quam coitum dixisse magis decet, ita 'Liberum et Cererem' pro vino et pane licentius, quam ut fori severitas ferat.

Martial's use of metonymy is in accord with Quintilian's injunctions.[67] He uses all the conventional substitutions: "Venus" for "passion,"[68] "Mars" for "war,"[69] "Lares" or "Penates" for "house" or "household,"[70] "Bacchus" for "wine,"[71] "Pallas" for "olive tree,"[72] but he also stretches the trope to even its poetical limits. "Libitina" thus stands for "pyre" (**10.97.**1), "Thetis" not only for "the sea" (**10.30.**11) but also for "a salt-water bath" (**10.14[13].**4), "Bacchus" for "wine" and also for the *comissatio* after a meal,[73] while anything Athenian is "Cecropian."[74]

Antonomasia is so closely allied to metonymy that it is sometimes hard to distinguish. Quintilian says (8.6.29): *Antonomasia, quae aliquid pro nomine ponit, poetis utroque modo frequentissima.* . . . He mentions two basic types: (1) the name may be replaced by an epithet ("Tydides" for "Diomedes" is his example), or (2) by the most striking characteristics or actions of the person:

Oratoribus etiam si rarus eius rei, nonnullus tamen usus est. Nam ut 'Tydiden' . . . non dixerint, ita dixerint 'impios et parricidas'; . . . 'Romanae eloquentiae principem' pro Cicerone potuisse non dubitem (8.6.29 f.).

Although Martial is at home with the substitution of an epithet for a personal name,[75] his most frequent use of antonomasia is for identification of places, topographical or geographical, in the following format: "Agenoris puella" or "ubi Sidonio taurus amore calet" means "the portico of Europa in the Campus Martius,"[76] "limina Inachidos" stands for "the temple of Isis" (**11.47.4**), Marcellus in the far North is said to be "prope Promethei rupes" (**9.45.**3 f.), etc.[77] The latitude Martial allows himself in this trope is neatly illustrated in the phrase "Hersiliae civis et Egeriae," which means simply "a Roman" (**10.68.**6).

These samples should be enough to show, moreover, that it is true that Martial made wide use of standard rhetorical tropes, but they should also demonstrate that his use of the tropes is enlivened and expanded both by the greater license allowed poets and by his own most original wit.

Notes

[1] Regrettably we can only note the title of a paper by Prof. L. R. Taylor, "Republican and Augustan writers enrolled in the equestrian centuries," on the APA program in Toronto for Dec. 28, 1968, and announced while we were writing our article.

[2] We are using throughout the text and the numbering of the poems in W. M. Lindsay's OCT edition.

[3] This poem, of course, refers to Martial's request of Domitian for a renewal of the *ius* granted by Titus. We have no knowledge of the procedure by which the *ius* was originally obtained from Titus.

[4] Apparently, the possession of the *ius trium liberorum* entitled the holder to receive legacies, which would be denied in whole or in part to a person who was technically *caelebs*: Steinwenter, s. v. *"Ius liberorum,"* RE 10 (1919) 1281; Plin. *Ep.* 10.94.

[5] Suet. *Claud.* 25: . . . stipendiaque instituit et imaginariae militiae genus, quod vocatur supra numerum, quo absentes et titulo tenus fungerentur.

[6] See also Plin. *Ep.* 4.4; Lengle, s.v. "Tribunus," RE 6A² (1937), p. 2448.

[7] J. Marquardt, *Römische Staatsverwaltung*³ (completed by H. Dessau and A. v. Domaszewski) vol. 2 (Darmstadt 1957; reprint of second ed. of 1881), p. 368, n. 2.

[8] For the view that the *tribunus semestris* received only half the year's pay of *tribunus legionis:* J. Kromayer-G. Veith, *Heerwesen und Kriegführung der Griechen und Römer* (Munich 1928), p. 511, n. 12.

[9] Martial hints at his knighthood as early as 3.95.10, where he says: et sedeo qua te suscitat Oceanus.

[10] L. R. Taylor, "Horace's equestrian career," *AJP* 46 (1925) 161-170.

[11] *Thirteen satires of Juvenal* (London 1889) 1.290 f. R. E. Colton holds essentially this same view: "Juvenal and Martial on the equestrian order," *CJ* 61 (1965-66) 158.

[12] H. Mattingly, "Equester ordo," *OCD* 336; O. Hirschfeld, *Die kaiserlichen Verwaltungsbeamten bis auf Diocletian*² (Berlin 1905), p. 226; Kromayer-Veith (above n. 8), p. 511. For the same view, see also Lengle (above, n. 6), p. 2445; F. F. Abbott, *Roman political institutions*³ (Boston 1911), p. 393 f.

[13] R. Helm, "M. Valerius Martialis," *RE* 8A¹ (1955), p. 56 f.; L. Friedländer, *M. Valerii Martialis epigrammaton libri* (Amsterdam 1961; reprint of Leipzig ed. of 1886) 1.6.

[14] See especially 2.91, 92; 3.95.5 f.

[15] D. A. Slater, *The Silvae of Statius* (Oxford 1908), p. 17.

[16] J. H. Howard, *Selected Silvae of P. Papinius Statius* (University of South Dakota 1911), p. 3; cf. *Teuffel's history of Roman literature,* revised by L. Schwabe, translated by G. C. Warr (London 1900), 2.116 f.

[17] *A literary history of Rome in the Silver Age,*³ ed. by A. M. Duff (New York 1964), p. 376. For a discussion of the parallels in the lives of the two poets: G. Boissier, *Tacitus and other Roman studies,* translated by W. G. Hutchison (London 1906), p. 254 f.

[18] Pliny writes:

> Prosecutus eram viatico secedentem; dederam hoc amicitiae, dederam etiam versiculis, quos de me composuit. Fuit moris antiqui eos, qui vel singulorum laudes vel urbium scripserant, aut honoribus aut pecunia ornare. . . . Quaeris qui sint versiculi quibus gratiam rettuli?

L. Friedländer also feels that Pliny's gratuity was given from a sense of obligation in return for the poet's praise: *Roman life and manners under the early empire*[7] (New York 1965, reprint) 3.50.

[19] In a highly interesting article that touches upon some

of our points in a different way, U. Scamuzzi also believes that it is wrong to consider Martial indigent: "Contributo ad una obiettiva conoscenza della vita e dell'opera di Marco Valerio Marziale," *Rivista di studi classici* 14 (1966) 149-207.

[20] In the only other verse in which Martial uses *scalae* (7.20.20: *per ducentas . . . scalas*) it is usually taken to mean "steps" instead of "staircases." If one were to read "steps" in our passage, it might suggest that Martial was living in a ground floor apartment, or possibly that he was living in his own *domus* instead of in an *insula*. A. Wotschitzky has discussed the problem of the *ducentae scalae,* and he seems to interpret the word to mean "steps" (200 *Stufen*): "Hochhäuser im antiken Rom," *Natalicium Carolo Jax . . . oblatum* (Innsbrucker Beiträge zur Kulturwissenschaft 3, 1955) 151-158.

[21] The laurels were probably in the gardens of the *Porticus Vipsania* (Portico of Europa?), which was in part of the *Campus Agrippae:* M. Reinhold, *Marcus Agrippa: a biography* (Geneva, N. Y., 1933), p. 136, n. 57; P. Grimal, *Les jardins romains à la fin de la république et aux deux premiers siècles de l'empire* (Bibliothèque des Écoles françaises d'Athènes et de Rome, fasc. 155, Paris 1943), p. 192.

[22] The evidence, largely literary, is adequately reviewed by S. B. Platner, *The topography and monuments of ancient Rome*[2] (Boston and New York 1911), p. 486 f., 489.

[23] Frontin, *Les aqueducs de la ville de Rome,* ed. P. Grimal (Paris 1944), p. 31, n. on chapter 67.

[24] Friedländer (above, n. 13), *Einleitung,* p. 50-67, and *passim* in commentary; Friedländer (above, n. 18) 4.298-304; W. M. Lindsay, *Ancient editions of Martial* (Oxford 1903); also Lindsay's *OCT* edition. For other references cf. Schanz-Hosius, *Geschichte der römischen Literatur* (Munich 1935) 2.548-552; Helm (above, n. 13) 79-83.

[25] Lindsay, *Ancient editions* (above, n. 24), p. 11, n. "r," and the appendices. There is also a good discussion in the *praefatio* to his *OCT* edition, where he remarks on an unnumbered page: Sic, i. e. Xenia et Apophoreta, appellantur in omnibus tribus archetypis duo ultimi libri Martialis, non 'lib. XIII' et 'lib. XIV.'

[26] Friedländer (above, n. 13) 1.51 f.

[27] The significant poems are cited by O. Immisch, "Zu Martial," *Hermes* 46 (1911) 482 f.

[28] Of the five books not numbered internally, 1 is mentioned in 2.93, and 3 and 4 are implied in 5.2 and mentioned in 8.3.

[29] Friedländer (above, n. 13) 1.54 f. (on book 3), 1.56 (on book 5); E. T. Sage, "The publication of Martial's poems," *TAPhA* 50 (1919) 174 f.

[30] Friedländer (above, n. 13) 1.62-65; Lindsay, *Ancient editions* (above, n. 24), p. 14.

[31] Especially Pliny's letters on Regulus: 1.5, 2.20, 4.2, 4.7, 6.2; Veiento dining with Nerva (4.22); and elsewhere.

[32] *Kritik und Hermeneutik, nebst Abriss des antiken Buchwesens* (Munich 1913), p. 350.

[33] There is a brief listing of literary works in twelve books in E. Wölfflin, "Die hexadische Composition des Tacitus," *Hermes* 21 (1888) 158. For Vergil: Martial 12.67, where Vergil's birthday is regarded as a sort of holy day; J. W. Spaeth, Jr., "Martial and Vergil," *TAPhA* 61 (1930) 19-28. For Statius: see our n. 34; and Friedländer (above, n. 13) 1.8 f., 21, and commentary under 4.49; R. B. Steele, "Interrelation of the Latin poets under Domitian," *CP* 25 (1930) 328-342.

[34] Especially 4.49; 8.3.19-22; 9.50; 10.4; 10.21.5 f.

[35] The numbering is not used to distinguish among editions issued by the varying *bibliopolae* mentioned by Martial, which is a matter discussed by Sage (above, n. 29) 168-176. Tryphon, mentioned in 13.3, appears in 4.72. Three other *bibliopolae* are named, all in book 1, whose wares are quite distinct: 1.2, codices; 1.113, *juvenilia;* 1.117, a five-denarius *volumen.*

[36] Cf. H. A. Sanders, "The beginnings of the modern book: the codex of the classical era," *University of Michigan quarterly review* 44 (1938) 95-111, esp. 106; C. H. Roberts, "The codex," *Proceedings of the British Academy* 40 (1954) 169-204. Both scholars provide thorough accounts of the history of the codex, but they fail to acknowledge the evidence for a very early codex in Martial 1.1, 2.

[37] Immisch (above, n. 27) 481-517; Friedländer (above, n. 18) 4.299 f. Both authorities recognized that Martial 1.1, 2 indicated a parchment codex. Immisch postulated that Martial 1.1, 2 served as introductory poems to a collected edition of books 1-7 (on the basis of 7.17.6). His observation that 1.1, 2 refer to a collection in the format of a parchment codex is well taken, although it seems more probable to the authors of this article that, on the basis of 4.89; 5.2, 15, the collection contained books 1-4 and not books 1-7. Book 1 was not published first, but appeared later, sometime between books 3 and 5 (cf. 5.2). Cf. also on the matter of publication in codex form, Helm (above, n. 13), p. 79, 83.

[38] R. P. Oliver, "The first Medicean manuscript of

Tacitus and the titulature of ancient books," *TAPhA* 82 (1951) 243. Cf. also Verg. *Georg.* 4.559-66, Hor. *Epist.* 1.20.19-28, both of which take the place of the names of the author and the work normally expected at the end of the roll.

[39] It is convenient to cite at this point the major occurrences of the two words, *charta* and *membrana*. *Membrana* appears much less frequently: 1.2.3; 14.7.1 (and title); 14.184, title; 14.186.1 (and title); 14.188.1 (and title); 14.190, title; 14.192, title. This word occurs also in 1.66.11, used in connection with a papyrus roll and meaning the purple outer wrapping. *Charta* occurs in: 1.66.7; 4.82.7; 4.86.11; 5.6.7; 10.93.6; 13.1.7; 14.84.2. In addition to these passages, in which *charta* seems definitely to refer to papyrus, the word appears in other epigrams in which it denotes writings in general, sheets of paper, letters, or official dispatches: 1.25.7; 1.44.2; 2.1.4; 2.8.1; 5.18.2; 6.61(60).9; 6.64.23; 7.6.5; 7.51.8; 8.24.2; 9.35.5; 9.99.2; 10.2.11; 11.3.7; 12.3(4).4; 14.10.2 (and title); 14.11.2 (and title); 14.196.2; and elsewhere. Finally, several passages describe a papyrus roll without actually mentioning the word *charta*: 1.66.6, 10 f.; 1.117.16; 3.2.7-11; 4.10.1 f.; 6.85.9; 8.61.4; 8.72.1 f.; 11.1.2, 4, 13.

[40] F. G. Kenyon, *Books and readers in ancient Greece and Rome*[2] (Oxford 1951), p. 94 f.

[41] Oliver (above, n. 38) 241.

[42] "Quel est le plus ancien example connu d'un manuscrit latin en forme de codex?" *Emerita* 17 (1949) 1-8; idem, *Paléographie romaine* (Madrid 1952), p. 77-89, 177 f. (plate X.2).

[43] 1.2; 14.184, 186, 188, 190.

[44] Mallon does not cite an exact reference for this fact, and there is no one epigram that clearly states that codices were just then being manufactured for the first time. There are, however, certain epigrams that imply the novelty of the codex form: 14.7, 184, 186, 190, 192.

[45] We have already noted that Martial makes a special effort to number each book, usually near the beginning, and that he indicates that the books were published separately at first and in individual *volumina*. We have no way of knowing whether this parchment codex of four (or seven) books appeared after just those books had been published or after all twelve books had been published. The former possibility appears the more likely, since it hardly seems possible that Martial, after his return to Spain, would have seen to the issue of a collection of fewer books than he had already published.

[46] Note the frequent similarities between Martial's epigrams and those of the *Palatine anthology:* e.g., 1.57 and *Anth.* 5.42; 5.53 and *Anth.* 11.214; 6.19 and *Anth.* 11.141; 6.53 and *Anth.* 11.257; 9.29.11 f. and *Anth.* 11.226; 12.17.10 and *Anth.* 11.403; 12.23 and *Anth.* 11.310; 12.74 and *Anth.* 11.39. These more apparent similarities, and others, are fully discussed by P. Laurens, "Martial et l'épigramme grecque du 1ᵉʳ siècle après J.-C.," *REL* 43 (1965) 315-341. Laurens also points out that many of these Greek epigrams are by Martial's contemporaries.

[47] R. Reitzenstein, "Epigramm," *RE* 6 (1909), p. 105-111.

[48] See also 2.77, 8.29, 9.50.2, 10.59, 11.108.

[49] For Martial's adherence to strict metrical traditions, see 9.11.11-17, 10.9.1.

[50] The *epigrammaton linguam* of the *praef.* of book 1. For *sal* and *fel,* see also 8.3.19.

[51] Plin. *Ep.* 3.21.1 also gives some of the characteristics of the genre and the poet: *homo ingeniosus, acutus, acer, et qui plurimum in scribendo et salis haberet et fellis nec candoris minus.*

[52] See also 11.2 and 11.15.

[53] G. R. Throop, "The lives and verse of Roman erotic writers," *Washington University studies* (St. Louis 1920) 1.160-183.

[54] See also 7.72.

[55] C. W. Mendell, "Martial and the satiric epigram," *CP* 17 (1922) 1-20. The similarities between the two genres can be further seen in their common claim of *hominem pagina nostra sapit* (10.4.10; cf. 8.3.19 f.).

[56] 1.35.13; 1.113.6; 4.10.4, 8; 5.15.1; 6.64.7 f.; 6.82.5; 6.85.9 f.; 7.11.4; 7.12.2; 7.26.7; 7.28.8; 7.51.1; 9.*praef.* 5; 10.64.2; 11.6.3; 11.16.7; 13.1.7; 13.2.4.

[57] 1.113.2, 14.1.7.

[58] *Ep.* 1.19.42.

[59] *Catullus and the traditions of ancient poetry* (Berkeley 1934), p. 20 f. P. 50-58 of this book discuss *nugae*, and other words such as *ludi, ineptiae,* etc., as they are used by other writers (including Martial).

[60] Cf. Martial 11.1.14.

[61] *Aug.* 85.2; cf. Martial 12.61 for an improper locale suitable for epigrams of inferior quality.

[62] 5.13.3; 5.16.3; 6.60(61); 6.82.6; 7.17.10; 8.3.4; 8.61.3; 9.81.1; 9.97; 10.9.3 f.; 10.103.3; 11.3.4; 11.24.5-

9; 12.3.17 f.; 12.11.8.

[63] 4.27.1; 6.64.9; 7.26; 8.*praef.*; 8.82.1; 12.3.15 f.; 12.11.6.

[64] 5.15.3 f.; 5.60.3 f.; 9.76.10; 10.26.7. See also Plin. *Ep.* 3.21.6, in reference to Martial's poems: At non erunt aeterna quae scripsit: non erunt fortasse, ille tamen scripsit tamquam essent futura.

[65] Hor. *Carm.* 3.30; Catull. 1.10.

[66] For an excellent survey of Martial's use of historical personages, A. Nordh, "Historical *exempla* in Martial," *Eranos* 52 (1954) 224-238, who remarks on p. 229: "The rhetorical *exemplum* means a kind of synecdoche of the general conception of a personality, an isolation of a quality, an action or a situation, conceived as characteristic of the man. The name is used as a formula or symbol, the individual becomes a type."

[67] Metonymy in Martial is only briefly touched on by M. Platnauer, "Spicilegia Valeriana," *Greece and Rome* 17/18 (1948/49) 12-17.

[68] 2.34.4; 2.53.7; 3.75.6; 6.45.2; 11.60.1; 12.43.5, etc.

[69] 6.25.7; 6.32.3; 7.6.6, etc. For battle in the arena, *Spect.* 24.5; 2.75.9; 5.24.1, 14. "Diana" for *venationes* in the arena: *Spect.* 12.1.

[70] 1.70.11; 3.5.6; 3.31.2; 4.64.29; 8.1.1; 9.18.7; 11.82.2; 12.57.2, etc.

[71] 13.22.1; 13.23.1; 13.114.1.

[72] 7.28.3, a rare but not original use: see Ovid, *Am.* 2.16.8.

[73] 4.82.6; 5.78.18.

[74] 1.25.3; 1.39.3; 1.53.10; 4.23.6; 6.34.4; 7.32.2; 7.69.2, etc. For other novel metonymy: 10.21.3; 10.26.3; 11.18.19.

[75] 2.14.6; 4.32.1; 7.15.3; 11.43.5-8; 14.178.2; *Spect.* 16B.2.

[76] 11.1.11; 7.32.12. Other such references to the same spot: 2.14.3, 5; 3.20.12.

[77] 2.43.7; 4.25.2-6; 5.1.1 f., 5; 5.22.4; 6.47.3 f.; 7.44.5; 7.73.1, 3 f.; 8.33.21; 10.48.1; 14.114.2, etc.

William S. Anderson (essay date 1970)

SOURCE: "Lascivia vs. Ira: Martial and Juvenal" in *Essays on Roman Satire*, Princeton University Press, 1982, pp. 362-95.

[*In the essay below, Anderson contrasts the function of wit in Martial and Juvenal by an extended comparison of their poetry, particularly Martial's epigram 3.52 and Juvenal's third satire. He calls attention to significant differences in tone and purpose—even when the basic material is the same—and distinguishes between Martial's primary interest in humor and Juvenal's subordination of wit to serious thematic issues.*]

Sandwiched between two lighthearted epigrams on the dubious physical attractions of a Galla and a Chloe, there appear in Martial's **Third Book** the following four elegiac lines:

> empta domus fuerat tibi, Tongiliane, ducentis:
> abstulit hanc nimium casus in urbe frequens.
> conlatum est deciens. rogo, non potes ipse videri
> incendisse tuam, Tongiliane, domum?

(3.52)

Martial has so contrived his development that each line begins with a crucial verb, each marking an important stage in the total situation, and the final one driving home the witty point. The first couplet establishes the situation in general terms: the cost of the house, then its total destruction (cause unspecified). To correct the impression of disaster, however, to make sure that we grasp Martial's attitude and correctly view the character of Tongilianus, the second couplet reports the huge profit made from the fire because of public contributions (again, cause undefined), then ever so politely raises the question of arson. What might have been mistaken for sympathy in the first couplet has changed to ridicule, while Tongilianus has been transformed from a pitiable victim to a criminal.[1] The careful placing of *domus* close to the start of line 1 and *domum* at the end of line 4; the alliterative use of personal pronoun *tibi* and possessive *tuam* with vocative *Tongiliane* respectively in 1 and 4; the variation between the structure of the first couplet (one clause in each line) and of the second (one clause in a half-line, the next expanding to a line and a half); the use of three verbs to express the various nuances of Martial's suspicions in 3 and 4—these are some of the principal artistic devices employed to enhance this witty epigram. The incident with which it plays was no doubt one of the common scandals of the day, somewhat analogous to cases of arson today when a man sets fire to his house or factory in order to collect fraudulently on insurance. And Martial has treated this arson with the naughty laughter which is so typical of him.

Twenty to twenty-five years after the appearance of Martial's epigram, Juvenal published Satire 3, in which there occurs a sequence remarkably like that of those four elegiac lines.

si magna A
sturici cecidit domus, horridamater,
pullati proceres, differt vadimonia praetor.
tum gemimus casus urbis, tunc odimus ignem.
ardet adhuc, et iam accurrit qui marmora
    donet,
conferat impensas; hic nuda et candida signa,
hic aliquid praeclarum Euphranoris et
    Polycliti,
haec Asianorum vetera ornamenta deorum,
hic libros dabit et forulos mediamque
    Minervam,
hic modium argenti. meliora ac plura reponit
Persicus orborum lautissimus et merito iam
suspectus tamquam ipse suas incenderit aedes.

(3. 212-222)

Juvenal has devoted eleven lines to his development, which he presents as a number of related scenes leading up to the same point as Martial's. Instead of talking to the arsonist, the speaker addresses the audience. Thus, he does not inquire or report the price of the mansion, but focuses on the disaster to the building and the immediate public outcry that it provokes. The first three lines, it might be said, represent an elaboration of the single line in which Martial recorded and affected to deplore the total destruction of Tongilianus' house. Martial's equally terse and generalized report of contributions is also amplified here by a list of six contributors and donations, five of which are organized by means of anaphora with the initial demonstrative. After devoting a full line in 217, 218, and 219 to three contributors, Juvenal rapidly closes the list after the first half of 220. Then he starts to develop his point on the arson. First of all, what may have been somewhat puzzling in Martial, namely, why people should contribute so heavily to a victim of fire, receives explanation from Juvenal: his arsonist Persicus is one of the richest men in Rome and has no immediate heirs; hence, people are contributing so as to earn a profitable place in his will. Then, with the conjunction *et* followed by *merito* and a monosyllable, Juvenal deliberately creates a harsh ending to the hexameter of 221 and a jerky beginning of the enjambement into 222. Instead of the mockingly polite construction of three verbs employed by Martial, Juvenal cleverly exploits the line division to hold us in suspense as to what Persicus has "deservedly" accomplished, before placing *suspectus* in its prominent position at the beginning of 222. Martial's naughty question becomes a statement, and the satirist voices a decisive bias about the popular scandal: it has a likely basis in fact.

Martial and Juvenal have worked with the same kind of scandalous incident and built towards the same witty point, though Juvenal has gone at the situation with greater amplitude than Martial. Taken in isolation, too, this Juvenalian scene might appear to be using its wit in the same amused and amusing way as that of the epigram. Suppose we knew Juvenal's poetry only through this excerpt, found in some anthology of the tenth century: could we accurately assess its tone? Might we not be tempted to believe, especially after seeing the parallel in Martial, that the speaker of these lines was not seriously engaged with the criminal behavior of Persicus, but, like Martial, intent on the manipulation of words and details so as to extract from the well-told anecdote the maximum amount of wit for the audience's pleasure? The problem which I have set myself forms part of the larger traditional problem involving Martial and Juvenal. For years, scholars have inquired into the connections between epigrammatist and satirist, in an attempt not only to define but also to explain them. I shall briefly review this scholarship, then proceed to the particular problem involving Martial and Juvenal which seems to have the most contemporary importance for us. I may put it this way: to what extent does Juvenal accept, along with the material, the basic method of Martial; to what extent is his wit a clever variation on Martial's? In terms of my title, to what extent can we regard Juvenal's announced mood of *indignatio* and *ira* as an instrument of a dominant wit that closely parallels the integrated witty mood of *lascivia* proclaimed by Martial?

In reviewing the main facts about the relationship of Juvenal and Martial and the theories erected on these facts, we may classify the facts as biographical and literary. Evidence can be drawn from the life and times of the two poets and (as has been done at the beginning of this paper) from common material in their poetry. To begin in conventional manner with the biographical facts of the older poet, Martial, born in Spain about A.D. 40, came to Rome in the early sixties, hoping perhaps to gain advancement through the other Spaniards who had acquired influence at the court of Nero, for example, Seneca and the family of Lucan.[2] Although the Pisonian Conspiracy ended that particular hope, Martial remained in Rome nearly thirty-five years, at first forced to struggle for survival, then gradually establishing himself as a clever poet who merited patronage, whose epigrams deserved not only to be recited in Rome but also to be published and read all over the empire. He produced a slight volume to mark the inauguration of the Colosseum in 80, when Titus ruled; his major works, however, twelve books of Epigrams, appeared more or less year by year after 85, all but the last during the reign of Domitian.[3] Success came to him, then, when he was about 45. Having been conditioned by early years in Spain, by the chaos of Nero's last years, and by the decade of Vespasian's sound rule, Martial flourished under the Flavian brothers, as Rome somewhat relaxed from the necessarily austere ways of their father.

Juvenal arrived in Rome during those years when Martial first began to enjoy fame. Born about 60 and raised, it appears, in the Italian town of Aquinum, he proceeded to Rome at approximately the same period as his contemporaries Tacitus and Pliny, though with entirely different hopes.[4] They immediately entered upon the political career to which their background and influence entitled them; both progressed steadily and had reached high positions during the reign of Domitian while Juvenal remained insignificant.[5] Since we hear nothing of Juvenal's political career, indeed virtually nothing at all of his experience, we assume that his background and influence (not his innate talent) were negligible.[6] He apparently settled for a literary career, first perhaps as a teacher of rhetoric, then later as a more or less independent poet under the patronage of various men of wealth. Martial counted Juvenal as a friend by 92, for in **Book 7** published that year, he mentioned him twice (**7.24** and **91**). Exactly when Juvenal began to develop his satiric talents and write the Satires we now possess, is uncertain. Most of the earliest poems, it is generally agreed, were written during the reign of Trajan; and Book I does not seem to have been published before 110.[7] Since Martial had by then been dead five years and since Juvenal avoids giving specific details about himself and his friends, we should not be surprised to find no reference to Martial by name in the Satires. Assuming that Juvenal, like Martial, remained in Rome during the eighties and nineties—I find the evidence for Juvenal's exile at this time or any time unconvincing—we may conclude that both were involved contemporaneously, if not alike, for about fifteen years in the literary activities of the city, Juvenal as a tyro, Martial as an established figure. Martial left Rome in 98 and returned to his native Spain, from which he addressed to Juvenal a last epigram (**12.18**). Juvenal's success, which came under Trajan and Hadrian, sprang from conditions considerably different from Martial's.

Though twenty years younger than Martial, then, Juvenal did know him during the nineties and shared the literary scene in Rome with him at a significant period of his own poetic development. So much for the biographical facts linking the two. Now for the facts provided by the poems. In Juvenal's earliest Book of Five Satires, four out of five have basic themes that appear frequently as the material of Martial's epigrams;[8] and the single exception, Satire 4, uses as the partial occasion of its drama an oversize turbot (*rhombus*), which is also a topos in Martial.[9] Satire 6, large enough to qualify by itself as Book II, surveys women's sexual proclivities; nobody needs to be reminded that Martial and his audience enjoyed the same subject. Book III, consisting of three Satires, was published probably early in the reign of Hadrian, some twenty years after Juvenal had last seen Martial. Nevertheless, Satire 7 describes the plight of poets and other practitioners of verbal arts in Rome, and Satire 9 toys with the world of male homosexuals: both topics occur over and over again in Martial. Finally, Satires 11 and 12 and the description

of old age in Satire 10, all from Book IV, and to a lesser extent parts of Satires 13 and 14 in Book V show continued preoccupation with material common to Martial. In short, there can be little doubt that between A.D. 110 and 130 Juvenal used topics and themes which had earlier won wide favor in the epigrams published by Martial between 85 and 101. It is a significant exercise to go systematically through Juvenal's Satires, especially the earlier ones, and point out line by line, passage by passage, what he shared with the epigrams of his Spanish friend.[10]

We have a combination of biographical and literary facts: the two poets were both in Rome and knew each other fairly well, and after Martial's death Juvenal wrote poems which repeatedly parallel in significant detail the epigrams of Martial. How can we interpret these facts so as to illuminate the relationship between the two? Modern preoccupation with this problem received major stimulus from an article published in 1888 by Henry Nettleship, who, while assessing Juvenal's achievement in general, took time to put forth a provocative explanation for the links between Martial and Juvenal, Epigrams and Satires.[11] According to him, Martial and Juvenal worked side by side in Rome during the nineties, but independently of each other, each drawing upon a common store of literary material then available in the city. And to make his thesis more plausible, Nettleship argued that the major portions of the Satires of Book I were composed, like the Epigrams, in the nineties.

Most scholars have rejected Nettleship's dating of the early Satires as well as his view of Juvenal's originality or independence. Thus, J. D. Duff, in the commentary which was first published in 1898, wrote: "The resemblance [between the two poets' themes] will not seem more than can be accounted for, if we believe that Juvenal, having already a thorough knowledge of Martial's epigrams, began to direct his satires against the same period and persons whom Martial had already riddled with his lighter artillery."[12] That same year, Harry Wilson printed his significant paper, which he had read in 1897 to the American Philological Association, on "The Literary Influence of Martial upon Juvenal." The title alone indicates that he stood with Duff against Nettleship on the question of independence.[13] Studying the mechanics of Martial's influence rigorously, Wilson argued that Juvenal used the typical techniques of *imitatio* normal for Latin poets; he knew Martial by heart, but did not simply copy him word for word. He either reused Martial's ideas in different words or used Martial's words in an altered context, to create Satires that were substantially different from the Epigrams.

The meticulous argument of Wilson and the general likelihood of his and Duff's assumptions that the older, successful poet influenced, but did not totally dominate, the younger have continued to prevail. There are, however, some questions which they did not face. Duff, for example, in stating that Juvenal dealt with the same period and persons as Martial, did not go on to explain the effect intended or achieved. What did the people and events of the eighties and nineties mean to Juvenal and his audience twenty to thirty years later? What was the point of being indignant over the dead past when Martial had treated it with his charming *lascivia*? By substituting heavy artillery for light (to keep Duff's image), was Juvenal moving farther away from reality or closer to the feelings of his audience? Wilson, too, left unexplained the fundamental literary connection between Juvenal's artful variations on Martial's wording and what he regarded as the evident difference between their respective styles and poetic purposes. If, as he wrote, "the high moral purpose and seriousness of the former [Juvenal] stand in sharp antithesis to the mocking triviality of the latter [Martial],"[14] one wonders about the range of Juvenal's *imitatio*. Assuming that we can distinguish the "high moral purpose" in the account of Persicus' arson from the "mocking triviality" of Tongilianus' arson in Martial, can we also say that this is a function of *imitatio*? Was Juvenal doing anything like Horace who used Lucretian language to comment on epic enthusiasm and on Epicurean exaggerations? That is, did Juvenal allude to the whole context of Martial and subtly differentiate his own attitude on all levels, or was he merely playing with Martial's words and, from quite another perspective, aiming at a moral purpose and seriousness to which the borrowings from Martial had no relevance?

Granted, then, that Juvenal did make use of Martial, both his words and his epigrammatic situations, the question remains: what was the extent of this use; what was its effect with the audience? It is not really an adequate answer to respond that Martial was a kind of satirist and so Juvenal drew from him what was naturally "satiric," for satire is so amorphous in form and manner (even without Martial) that turning Martial, for the purposes of argument, into a satirist says very little about how he might be utilized by Juvenal.[15] In theory it would be possible to argue that, because Juvenal regards Roman society with the dissatisfied eye of a wretched client and the literary situation in Rome with the unhappiness of a poet struggling for recognition, and because Martial earlier exhibited similar attitudes, Juvenal adopted his attitude from Martial. In fact, the shared viewpoints serve scholars rather to document the relative continuity of Roman conditions and the basis of the two poets' friendship: Juvenal is supposed to have felt the situation as personally as Martial.[16]

In more recent years, two scholars have offered more comprehensive answers to the problem of this relationship, directing attention as much to *how* the borrowings were made as to *what* was borrowed. Gilbert Highet, while discussing the broad tradition from which

Juvenal drew, commented on Martial's part in it as follows: "So many of Juvenal's jokes and satiric ideas and proper names and turns of phrase are adapted from Martial that the epigrams of Martial were clearly one of the chief influences that trained him to be a satirist. What he did was to take Martial's keen perception, his disillusioned but witty sense of contrast, his trick of epigram, and his peculiar blend of suave poetry and vulgar colloquialism, to clean them up, to give them a moral purpose, and to build them into poems of major length."[17] This seems promising, especially because it does not exploit the invidious contrast between Martial's "triviality" and Juvenal's "high seriousness," but gives full credit to the artistry of the Epigrams. Highet represents Juvenal as a skillful poet who engages himself creatively with the art of Martial at every level and extracts from it material to which he can give new shape and life. Unfortunately, in his analysis of the individual Satires, Highet did not attempt to work out this view of a Juvenal trained by Martial. His emphasis upon the satirist as an unhappy, hypersensitive person who has experienced profound personal suffering and upon the passionate personal truth of the Satires obscures any concern with the creative poet who saw merits in and exploited Martial's obvious assets.

It was in patent disagreement with Highet's emphasis that in 1962 H. A. Mason published his influential essay entitled: "Is Juvenal a Classic?"[18] In order to deny the crucial assumption of Highet and other biographical critics that Juvenal's Satires tell us the truth about himself and his period, Mason resorted to Martial. As he explained this tactic, "the key to Juvenal's art lies in the study of Martial. The two poets appeal to the same taste and presuppose the same habits in their listening and reading public."[19] Later, by way of conclusion, he imaginatively elaborated what he believed Juvenal presupposed in his public, wording it cleverly as if the satirist were making prefatory remarks to an edition of the Satires:

> Dear readers, you have enjoyed Martial; now come and see whether I cannot give extra point to his favorite topics by setting them, as it were, to a different tune: the declaimer's mode. But I assume you understand what Martial was doing when he confined his poems to the conventional jokes of polite society. You will know then that to enjoy us you must both suspend and apply your critical and moral sense. We are not called on in our art to give you *all* the facts (you know them as well as we) or to assume all the moral attitudes (we are not moral censors) but to take those that allow the maximum witty play of the mind. Prepare yourselves, therefore, dear readers, to find in my poems all the butts of Martial's epigrams, and in particular, the comically obscene situations you enjoy so much in the mime. You will see from my rewritings of Martial that I have my own notes, particularly the sarcastic and the mock-tragic and epic, and that by fitting my sections together I can exhibit more attitudes to the

same episode than you will find in any one of his epigrams.[20]

Mason offers the most detailed literary explanation of Martial's influence known to me, and he extends the range of this influence farther than any other interpreter: not only has Juvenal used his predecessor with great creativity but he also agrees with the basic attitude of Martial. In both poets wit is the main device for achieving effects: the essential manner of both is witty. So the answer to the question in Mason's title would be: Juvenal is a classic of wit.[21] Accordingly, "he was more interested in literature than social conditions and . . . he lacks any consistent standpoint or moral coherence. Indeed his whole art consists in opportunism and the surprise effects obtainable from deliberate inconsistency."[22] Whereas earlier commentators plunged into problems because they insisted on the basic difference in attitude and technique of Juvenal even when he was using Martial, Mason has eliminated that problem by insisting on the identity of the two poets' subjects, witty manners, and audiences. Juvenal has become Martial set to a slightly different tune.

There can be no question that Mason has at last properly emphasized one of the most important elements of Juvenal's art and most cleverly employed Martial to demonstrate his thesis. Wit *is* important in the Satires. However, in order to win his argument, he has claimed too much. He has, I believe, tended to overstress wit at the expense of other important factors of Juvenalian art and to force Juvenal too harshly into the mould of Martial. Aside from the fact that Juvenal himself had different origins from Martial and a personality of his own, it is evident that the eras of Trajan and Hadrian differed markedly from that of Domitian, and it seems dubious to posit an audience for Juvenal equipped with the "same taste" as Martial's. To limit one's attention, as Mason does, to verbal opportunism or manipulation of the Latin language is risky. To defend these limits by asserting that there is no sustained theme of significance in Juvenal's Satires, no engagement with genuine moral issues is to provoke a protest from those who read Juvenal otherwise. Martial may provide "the key to Juvenal's art" in a way quite different from what Mason believes: his work happens to be the most conveniently available to show how much Juvenal reshaped his literary heritage to fit his own purposes. In the remainder of this paper, I shall criticize Mason's thesis more fully, particularly by reference to Satire 3 and other Satires of Book I, in the hope of estimating more satisfactorily the function of Juvenalian wit and of defining its relation to the announced mood of indignation that characterizes the earlier Satires.

Now that I have sketched out the lines of controversy, I return to the passage of Satire 3 with which I began. I had posed the problem of the tone behind Juvenal's wit and suggested that, taken in isolation, the passage about the arsonist-profiteer might possibly be interpreted like the parallel epigram of Martial, as a cleverly reported joke of Roman society. That would be Mason's view of the passage and the entire Satire; he would add only that Juvenal's tune differed and that the satirist was able to accumulate more attitudes around the episode by reason of his broader scope. Nevertheless, according to Mason, Juvenal's audience responded here, as they were meant, primarily to the joke; all other effects in the passage are subordinate to that.

When we study this arson narrative in relation to its context, I believe, it becomes evident that Juvenal has drastically altered Martial (assuming that he did work here under some influence of Martial). Above all, he has shaped what was supposed to be only a joke so that it no longer is an end in itself, but has become subordinate to what must be called larger thematic purposes. First of all, take the matter of names. Martial called his arsonist Tongilianus. We can be sure that the name did not identify anyone, because Martial has fabricated this odd name.[23] Since the name possesses no automatic connotations, the narrative determines the identity of the arsonist. Probably Martial's audience was expected to substitute for this fantastic name the name of a real Roman or wealthy alien resident to whom scandal attributed arson. Calling him Tongilianus, Martial caught the alliteration and supported the light-hearted purposes of his wit. Juvenal, on the other hand, offers two names: Asturicus (212) and Persicus (221).[24] These names are meaningful in themselves: we are to think of remote Asturia in Spain and of Persia in the East, and then we imagine the nobility and wealth that could be won by Romans in these exotic spots.[25] We are not expected to play drawing-room games and guess the identity of Juvenal's arsonists: the names identify them as Romans from distinguished families.

Second, Juvenal has totally altered the narrative occasion and thereby changed our attitude toward the arsonist. Martial pictures himself, the irreverent Spaniard, striking up a conversation with Tongilianus, affecting to be sympathetic as the latter reports on his fire, then naughtily raising the question of arson at the end. In Satire 3, the speaker who recounts the episode is Umbricius, a character especially created by Juvenal for the poem.[26] He is not talking with the arsonist but with us, and he could never affect sympathy or amusement over this arson. Thus, the narrative has no real surprise, as Martial's does; it builds steadily toward its climax. For Umbricius, Asturicus and Persicus represent villains to whom he points with anger as he addresses each of us in the second person singular. The reasons for this anger, which are obvious from the fuller context (soon to be discussed) may be summarized in this way: he is a victim of the Rome which allows a distinguished Roman like Persicus to profit, not be executed, as a result of his criminal arson. The altered point of view and altered form of dialogue in turn decisively shape the wit here deployed.

Finally, Martial's totally independent joke, told for itself, has been subordinated by Juvenal to a larger context and thematic purposes. This case of arson is introduced in 212 in a conditional clause, to produce an antithesis to an actual instance of accidental fire, when the apartment of a poor man named Cordus was burned and all its miserable contents consumed (203-211). The list of people who react with horror at Asturicus' plight corresponds ironically to a heavily emphasized nobody (*nemo* in anaphora 211) who answered Cordus' need. The list of precious things contributed by "friends" to Asturicus corresponds to the list of diminutive, pathetically cherished possessions of Cordus which the fire destroyed (203-207). Whereas Umbricius summarizes Persicus' situation by saying that he recovered more and better things than he had before his planned fire, his pathetic summary of Cordus' plight dwells on the "nothing" he really possessed to begin with, all of which paltry "nothing" was lost without chance of replacement (*nil* rhetorically repeated 208-209). The antithesis rather than the verbal manipulation of the arson anecdote determines the ultimate effect of Juvenal's wit here. Cordus, the innocent, pathetic victim of a fire over which he had no control, decisively qualifies our attitude toward Persicus, profiteer from his act of arson. We can now conclude that Juvenal did not amplify Martial's anecdote with his lists of people sympathetic to Asturicus and of donors and donations merely to enhance his narrative with vivid details and so increase the final point. The expansions serve the antithesis, which in turn functions to express a pervasive theme about the injustice and un-Roman degeneracy controlling Rome. I think I can safely claim Martial never portrays a poor man as genuinely pathetic, never allows his audience to engage its emotions with problems of Roman justice.

Juvenal places the two contrasting stories about Cordus and the arsonists in a larger context that begins with Umbricius' question in 190:

quis timet aut timuit gelida Praeneste ruinam?

Beside Praeneste, Umbricius names three other charming towns of Latium or Southern Etruria, which implicitly offer pleasant, secure if humble homes in contrast with the Roman apartments that constantly threaten collapse. The contrast is worked out by a description of us (*nos urbem colimus* 193ff) fearfully sleeping when *ruina* is imminent (196). Then, the subject turns to fires, another aspect of urban residential danger, and "your" plight, anyone of "you" in the audience, as Umbricius suggests that outside Rome no fires occur at night, no sudden scares (197-198). He pictures "you" trapped on the top floor of a highly combustible apartment as fire races up the flimsy structure: "you" are

doomed, it appears, when he suddenly abandons the desperate scene to describe Cordus' troubles (198-202). Plainly, though, "you" and Cordus are alike victims of fire in contrast with the arsonists, except that "you" will not survive, whereas Cordus did escape with nothing and became a beggar. Having closed the antithesis with what now we would call savage wit about profitable arson, Umbricius returns to "you." He offers "you" a fine home—a place of safety from that menacing fire—for the price you now pay annually for your dark Roman garret, away from Rome in three typical towns of Latium (223ff). These three towns obviously balance the four names in 190ff. And the paragraph closes with an elaboration of the attractions of rusticity, both charming and witty, as "you" are invited to entertain the vision of a small plot of land which you yourself work, at last the master of something you can count on, if only a lone lizard. "You" seem to have a choice between death in Rome and secure life in the country, between losing your few possessions in Rome (where arsonists profit) or enjoying them undisturbed elsewhere, between victimization in Rome and honorable rustic independence. How can "you" hesitate? Umbricius, the angry speaker, is now about to abandon this corrupt city, and the whole trend of this paragraph is to persuade "you" to follow his example.

Juvenal, then, has re-worked the naughty wit of Martial's light epigram to voice anger and serve the needs of a thematic antithesis. And this revised joke about arson is not the only wit in the passage to be so shaped. Umbricius starts with hyperbole: *nos urbem colimus tenui tibicine fultam* (193); note the alliteration used to enhance the wit. The closest analogy to this—and not very close at that—Mayor found in witty Ovid, who described a modest farm house "standing by means of a prop" (*stantem tibicine villam, Fast.* 4.695). To give substance to his exaggeration, Umbricius goes on to describe how the agents of apartment owners criminally conceal the structural faults in a building, then "urge renters to sleep soundly in the face of imminent collapse" (*securos pendente iubet dormire ruina* 196). Sound sleep, used paradoxically here, might well remind Juvenal's audience of the way Horace idealized the condition of the simple countryman in terms of easy, peaceful slumber.[27] When the fire starts in "your" apartment, "you" learn of it by the shouts and bustle of "your" downstairs neighbor Ucalegon (199). In this instance, the wit inheres in the phrasing of the Latin and the choice of the name, which echo a passage from *Aeneid* 2.[28] Aeneas had a next-door neighbor in Troy, whose house was already afire when Aeneas awoke from his last sleep in his home, then rushed out to fight. The modern Ucalegon is an impoverished "son of Troy," and his neighbor, the modern Aeneas, is "you" in your garret, about to be burned unheroically to a cinder. Martial commonly uses metonymy with names of mythical heroes, but you would never find him using the trope in this thematic manner, to underline the degeneracy of Rome from the noble ideals of the *Aeneid*.

Umbricius shifts to Cordus, characterizing his few possessions by diminutives. "Cordus owned a bed that was too short for little Procula" (who was apparently a dwarf, 203). An old bookcase contained his tiny Greek texts (206); illiterate mice gnawed on the divine poetry of Greece (207):[29] *et divina opici rodebant carmina mures*. With this witty hexameter, shaped as a Golden Line, Juvenal concludes his detailed list of Cordus belongings. The mice and poetry, illiteracy and divinity, all linked by the pungent verb, establish the clever paradox, which contains both pathos and humor. While Cordus loses his precious diminutive library, Asturicus will be gaining one, expensive tomes plus bookshelves and ornamental busts. Umbricius then epitomizes Cordus' condition with a witty sequence on the word *nil / nihil*. Nothing was what Cordus really owned, and yet he lost all that nothing: the key word begins and ends the sentence (208-209). To make sure we react here in a way different from Martial's audience, Juvenal adds the adjective *infelix* and makes Cordus "poor, pathetic." He does what Vergil and Ovid frequently did to direct sympathy. Martial uses *infelix* to characterize people who *cause* unhappiness, not suffer it. Thus, in the Epigrams, only an ungenerous patron, an unfaithful wife, and a lion that has killed two children can be called *infelix*.[30]

After reworking Martial's epigram on arson, Umbricius returns nastily to "you" and starts: "If you can tear yourself away from the Circus" (*si potes avelli circensibus* 223), then goes on to offer "you" a pleasant home in a country town. The implication here, as on the other occasions when Juvenal uses this common motif, is that most Romans let themselves be lulled by the exciting spectacles of the Circus and Colosseum into quiescence about the indignities they were suffering.[31] Umbricius' attitude suggests a man of moral integrity: we find it exhibited by Cicero earlier and near Juvenal's time by Pliny.[32] Martial, on the other hand, wrote epigrams expressing in witty terms marvel and delight with the shows in the Colosseum. Umbricius resorts to wit to give a prejudiced picture of the garret "you" rent in Rome: *tenebras conducis* (225). Martial, as commentators note, describes an ill-lit public bath in terms of *tenebrae*, without, however, aiming at or achieving this typical Juvenalian pathos.[33] In the country, "you" can raise vegetables in your little garden, an idyllic scene which Umbricius punctuates wittily with a relative clause neatly worked into a complete hexameter: *unde epulum possis centum dare Pythagoreis* (229). Again, we are dealing with a joke that does not belong to Martial's repertoire and is not employed in Martial's manner. Juvenal also attaches pathos to the same joke in 15.173. Horace and Ovid handle differently the familiar jibe at the Pythagoreans and their foolish beans.[34] Finally, Umbricius brings the paragraph

to a close on the hyperbolical note of "becoming master of a lone lizard" (321). Commentators cite analogues in both Martial and Pliny for this figure of speech, but I dare say that a formula existed, learned in school, for this kind of expression.[35] What counts here is not the verbal parallel, but the special thematic way in which Juvenal uses the figure to support Umbricius' jaundiced view of Rome as a place where one securely owns nothing so long as one is afflicted with *paupertas*.[36]

We may now pause to draw some conclusions about how Juvenal uses wit in this section of Satire 3, before extending our analysis to other passages.

1. Juvenal obviously knew Martial's epigrams well, prized their wit and used it.

2. Juvenal also drew his wit from many other sources in his extensive literary tradition, not only from witty writers of earlier times such as Horace and Ovid, but also dead-serious epic poets like Vergil.

3. Wit saturates this passage: every two or three lines exhibit an example.

4. Juvenal uses a number of methods to introduce wit: (a) he brings a development to a neat close in a single hexameter, often in the form of a relative clause (229) or some surprising descriptive detail (207, 222); (b) he punctuates with hyberbole (231) or paradox (196); (c) he focuses attention on a single word in metonymy (193, 225) or a single resonant name (199, 205, 219, 221); (d) he manipulates a telling word like *nil / nihil* (208-209).[37]

5. Not only does each instance of wit enliven its lines, but it also serves the thematic purpose of the larger context.

6. The versatility of Juvenal's wit in respect of sources and mechanism, together with its crucial thematic functions, gives it a tone very remote from Martial's: it is either utterly angry or a blend of anger and humor, but never the naughty, basically tolerant *lascivia* which Martial rightly assigned to his *nugae*.

It seems to me that these conclusions place us somewhere between the positions occupied by Mason and Highet. Mason, conducting a polemical argument, tried to answer those like Highet who stress Juvenal's truth and moral sincerity, so he emphasized the factor of wit and depicted Juvenal as "a supreme manipulator of the Latin language."[38] This manipulator, according to him, negates the business of truth and moral fervor. However, his view of Juvenal's artistry is so confined as to be half-damning, for Mason feels obliged to deny the satirist any systematic themes and to insist on opportunism as Juvenal's dominant poetic strategy. Such a conception may, I think, arise from overemphasis of Martial's relevance. Although Mason rightly points out the common use of wit by Juvenal and Martial and frequently of the same witty situations, it does not follow that, because Martial's brief epigrams cannot develop themes and must limit themselves to mere verbal manipulation, Juvenal's broader scope must be similarly confined and represented as Martial set "to a different tune."

It is important to establish the fact of the special tonal and thematic qualities of Juvenalian wit, in opposition to Mason, and I shall first take another passage from this same Satire 3, then look at other Satires. We have seen what Juvenal did to Martial's slight arson joke in order to make it pulsate with indignation and sustain the theme of the poor native Roman victimized by a now-hostile Rome. Although the wit continued to act as a final point, it fitted the angry character and speech of Umbricius. Now let us look back to the beginning of Umbricius' tirade.

He rages first (21-57) because there is no place in Rome for the native honesty which conservative, rigidly moral Roman upbringing bred in him. He is always being pushed aside by men more willing to adapt to circumstances and stoop to unscrupulous actions. Such men, we might reasonably infer, are Italians. Then, however, Umbricius continues at greater length (58-125) by attacking the scoundrels who most flagrantly succeed in worming their way into the confidence of the rich: they are Greeks, Levantines, and other "sewage" from the East. Now, commentators often cite a short epigram of Martial in relation to these hundred lines of Juvenal. Like the arson joke, it can help us appreciate the special features of Juvenal's wit.

> vir bonus et pauper linguaque et pectore
>   verus,
>   quid tibi vis urbem qui, Fabiane, petis?
> qui nec leno potes nec comissator haberi
>   nec pavidos tristi voce citare reos
> nec potes uxorem cari corrumpere amici
>   nec potes algentes arrigere ad vetulas,
> vendere nec vanos circa Palatia fumos
>   plaudere nec Cano plaudere nec Glaphyro:
> unde miser vives? "homo certus, fidus amicus.
>   . . ."
>   hoc nihil est: numquam sic Philomelus eris.

(4.5)

Martial imagines himself meeting Fabianus, an Italian of the good old type (as the first line indicates) who is coming to Rome to live, and he expostulates with the newcomer. Martial is clearly not angry; he is wryly amused, sympathetic but cynical at the purpose of this incredibly naïve "nice guy." What Fabianus *cannot* do is far more important than the simple virtue he possesses; hence the long list (3-8). The point is made succinctly at the end: for all his Italian honesty, Fabianus is doomed to starve in Rome because he is not Greek. The name Philomelus connotes not only riches, but also the unscrupulous devices by which alone a poor man can achieve wealth in Rome, devices that come instinctively to Greeks, not honest Italians. By restricting his point to the bare name, however, Martial avoids anger or any deep feeling against Greeks, and he keeps our attention trained on Fabianus, a comic figure in his unrealistic expectations.

Although this epigram covers the general contents of Juvenal's hundred lines, it does not follow that Juvenal has merely elaborated Martial in his specially witty manner, opportunistically manipulating his language regardless of theme. Again, for example, he has drastically altered the dramatic situation, as he did with the arson joke. As Satire 3 opens, Juvenal encounters Umbricius at the Porta Capena on the edge of Rome, but Umbricius is leaving, not arriving. He is a native Roman, born on the Aventine and raised in Rome; he is not an enterprising Italian with stars in his eyes. Having lived some thirty-five to forty years in the city, increasingly unable to survive by natural honesty and equally unable to compromise his conservative Roman standards, Umbricius has desperately decided to abandon this hostile environment, with vague hopes of making a go of it in a lonely rural region south near Cumae. All we know about Fabianus is that he is not Roman, a good man riding the crest of vain hope before being plunged into the sobering, disappointing realities of Rome. Fabianus speaks only four words, which help to define his simple-mindedness but gain him no sympathy; whereas Juvenal quickly yields to Umbricius, who dominates the Satire with his angry speech denouncing the Rome which has forced him out of his very home. Thus, the basic theme assumes shape: Rome is no place for the genuine Roman (119), for it has expelled, virtually exiled him.[39] Compare the angry tone of Umbricius, apparently fully approved by the silent satirist, with the amused cynicism of Martial who, by himself dominating the epigram, keeps us coolly distant from such passions as might be generated by the situation. Remember, too, that Martial always keeps his audience aware that he himself speaks as neither Roman nor Italian, but as a Spanish visitor.

In line with our earlier conclusions, we find that Juvenal's verses are saturated with wit, employed to elaborate the pathos of Umbricius' defeat in Rome and to create strong animosity against his successful rivals, above all Greeks and Easterners. Thus, what Martial cleverly implied in a single name requires, because of Juvenal's important changes, nearly seventy lines.

Umbricius says that he leaves his native Rome to the unscrupulous entrepreneurs who profit from it. These people, who once eked out their existence as hired attendants at the arena, now have the ill-gotten wealth to stage gladiatorial shows there and give the verdict of death with public approval (*occidunt populariter* 37). Then, from the dignity of the arena they go home to contract for building public latrines! These are the kind of sports that Fortune exalts when it jests (40). Now what can Umbricius do in a Rome like that? He lists a series of evil acts he neither knows how to nor can perform (cf. Martial) and concludes sarcastically: I am spurned like a useless cripple (48). Hyperbole follows: who is a friend these days unless also an accomplice? After amplifying this charge, he moves with particularly sparkling wit against the Greeks.

We all remember Umbricius' exaggeration in calling Rome a Greek city (61), then angrily qualifying his statement with the assertion that the Syrian river Orontes has flown into the Tiber and swept along in its polluted waters a series of vicious types. His list (63-72) develops in a variety of witty impulses. To represent the ingenious adaptability of these intruders, he comes to a point with the incredible assertion: "Tell one to fly, and he will" (78). He protests against yielding priority to someone who came to Rome imported for sale like other Eastern products, plums and figs (83). These people are past masters in adulation, he continues (86). Although he might speak the same words, only a Greek would be believed (92). After all, Greeks are consummate actors. They play female parts so convincingly that—gratuitous obscenity—you would expect to find on examination that they have a woman's anatomy (96-97). They are a nation of actors (100). Then follows a list of adulatory acts, concluding with pointed vulgarity: Greeks can lavish praise for a belch or good aim in pissing (107). Umbricius continues with a list of household members who are subject to the Greeks' indiscriminate lust, and he saves for the end the most flagrant example: the aged grandmother who is laid (112). At this line, we reach a precise parallel with Martial's list (cf. line 6 of the cited epigram). Juvenal's obscenity makes a conclusive angry point, whereas Martial drops in his similar comment about old hags almost indifferently among a series of unordered acts, the last of which is the trivial one of applauding Greek musicians.

Picking out a few of the above examples of Juvenal's wit, Mason objects that the satirist "is out to make any point he can regardless of consistency."[40] But *are* these points indiscriminate and inconsistent? I do not think so. These hundred lines, dramatically shaped to produce quite different effects from the slight ones of Martial's epigram, give a consistent impression of continuous anger and of the personality of the angry speaker, and the techniques of wit—the choice sordid details, the hyperbole, the sweeping generalizations, the vivid rhetorical language—all fit the violent mood of this self-styled Roman and his outrageous view of un-Roman Rome.

The wit of Satire 3, then, functions differently from the characteristic wit of Martial: it is subordinated to the angry speech and indignant themes of the Satire; its jokes enhance individual lines without destroying the dominant thematic concerns of the larger context. The next problem is to determine how far these conclusions, valid for Satire 3, can be extended to other Satires. Mason seems not to recognize the difficulties involved in making generalizations about Juvenal's wit, for he applies his ideas equally to Satires 1, 3, 6, 9, 10, and 13. But just as there is a temporal gap between the audiences of Martial and those of Juvenal which might well presuppose a *change* in tastes, so at least twenty-five years separate Satires 1 or 3 and 13, and in those years we know from observation that Juvenal changed his methods, including those of wit.[41] The most obvious change occurs between Book II and Book III, as is indicated by the opening of Satire 7, large parts of Satire 8, and the entire cast of Satire 9. It is then methodologically unsound to equate the wit of the later Satires with that of Satires 1 through 6. Mason is particularly unsound because he *starts* his analysis of Juvenal's wit and initiates his argument for regarding Martial as the key to Juvenal's art by developing an admittedly brilliant, but misapplied, analysis of wit in Satire 9. Satire 9 indeed can be profitably likened to much of Martial. However, if we are treating Juvenal's wit with due consideration for his own development as a poet, we should be able to appreciate the differences between the manner of Satire 9 and that of the earlier Satires, and, if we do start with Satire 9 as akin to Martial, the soundest move to make next would be to consider the early poem on a similar subject: Satire 2. Then we would encounter, not Martial's wit, but the indignant, thematically relevant wit that, on the basis of our analysis of Satire 3, we should expect of Juvenal in Book I.

Satire 9 deals with a type familiar in Martial, and it gives him a name that occurs five times in Martial. We are introduced to one of those interesting "professionals" who hires himself out as both adulterer and satisfier of male homosexual desires. Naevolus' current employer requires his ambidextrous services for himself and for his wife.[42] To open the Satire, Juvenal uses a method reminiscent of Martial. Having bumped into Naevolus on the street (*occurras* 2), the satirist solicitously asks what is wrong, why Naevolus looks so badly. For about 25 lines he elaborates with seeming concern on his "friend's" condition, and only after this clever build-up does he surprise us by revealing the source of Naevolus' income: he is notorious throughout Rome as both *moechus* and *cinaedus*. This is precisely the tone of affected concern punctured by cynical realism that we met in the Tongilianus epigram and that can be found in numerous poems of Martial. Juvenal maintains that same tone of nonreproving realism to the end of the Satire, letting Naevolus dominate the conversation and voice his complaint in detail.

I hardly need to note that Naevolus bears little resemblance to Umbricius of Satire 3, and the satirist's mockery in Satire 9 differs radically from his sympathy in the earlier Satire. But it is interesting and important to recognize that in Book I Juvenal does not touch such a versatile character as the *moechus-cinaedus,* ideal for a Martial-like display of wit as it would be. When he encounters an adulterer or a homosexual in Book I, he exchanges no words of solicitous concern with them; the mere sight of them and the awareness of what they are sends him into paroxysms of rage. This is clear from Satire 1 where, claiming that what justifies his indignant satire is the variety of depraved people he meets in his beloved Rome, he cites as illustration the professional gigolo who ministers to the lust of rich hags (39ff), the husband who connives like a pander with the adulterer of his wife (55), the man who seduces his own daughter-in-law (77), and the adolescent who sets out on his affairs sporting his juvenile robe (*praetextatus adulter* 78), already corrupted.

Adultery is among the vices that stimulate indignation in Satire 1. Although Juvenal's vignettes are phrased cleverly and memorably, it is plain that he is not joking, like Martial, about the gigolo, husband-abetted adulterer, father-in-law, or juvenile adulterer. He leaves to Satire 6 more elaborate and lurid scenes that feature the adulteress, but his mood of indignation is essentially the same.[43] In Satire 2, he vents his rage on homosexuals without clouding the issue or attenuating the picture of corruption by amusingly combining *cinaedus* with *moechus.* Again, he expects us to picture him meeting people on the street, not conversing with them but erupting in anger as he realizes what they represent for Rome. "What Roman street," he asks, "is not crowded with perverts masquerading as strict moralists?" (*quis enim non vicus abundat tristibus obscenis?* 2.8-9). Even worse, as he strolls through the Forum and other public places, he must listen to these people orating piously against female adultery; for these are not just average perverts: they come from distinguished families and so exercise influence in Roman politics as Senators and Censors (29ff). Juvenal attacks them in two phases in Satire 2. First, he roars at the crypto-homosexuals who pose as Puritans; then, having stripped off their disguise, he pours his wrath on various homosexual acts which presumably are practised in secret by these same people, members of the "gay set" in Rome.

Martial treats these topics, as we would expect, with clever good humor. A favorite homosexual-joke in Rome exploited the unmistakable meaning of the verb *nubere:* to put on the marriage veil for another, that is, to marry. It must properly describe the act of a woman, a bride. Martial uses this topos in two epigrams published more than ten years apart, in each case to play with a situation that Juvenal in Satire 2 presents as outrageous. The first provides a useful contrast to the opening of the Satire:

> aspicis incomptis illum, Deciane, capillis,
> cuius et ipse times triste supercilium,
> qui loquitur Curios adsertoresque Camillos?
> nolito fronti credere: nupsit heri.

(1.24)

Martial points out to a companion a shaggy, severe-looking moralist who is apparently orating, denouncing contemporary corruption and citing the great virtuous Roman examples of the early Republic. The three lines of build-up are then suddenly broken by the surprise of 4: the "moralist" was married yesterday, to another man! Our amusement is not disturbed by complicated feelings about the pervert, for Martial has not identified his class.

Now compare the opening of Satire 2:

> ultra Sauromatas fugere hinc libet et glacialem
> Oceanum, quotiens aliquid de moribus audent
> qui Curios simulant et Bacchanalia vivunt . . .
> frontis nulla fides; quis enim non vicus
>   abundat
> tristibus obscenis? castigas turpia, cum sis
> inter Socraticos notissima fossa cinaedos?

(1-3, 8-10)

Juvenal is indignant from the first line, ready to leave Rome in disgust for the remotest spot beyond the limits of the Roman Empire, and he makes no witty surprise of his reason. Line 3 is memorable and frequently cited, but it is significantly different from Martial's line 3 and elicits a quite different response from the audience. Martial has a "moralist" talking of two virtuous old patriotic types, and this line forms part of his deceptive build-up to the surprise of line 4. Juvenal epitomizes in his two phrases, each occupying half the line, the outrageous paradox that provokes his indignation: people are pretending to be virtuous according to ancient Curio, but in fact living perversely. The same paradox is repeated neatly in *tristibus obscenis* and *Socraticos cinaedos.* Juvenal brands the pretense from the start, and he indicates, by the phrase about posing as a Curio, as well as by subsequent details, that he is dealing exclusively with the Roman upper classes, whose perversion gravely affects the whole character of Rome.[44]

Martial's second epigram starts from the surprise use of *nupsit,* develops the scene of marriage, then proceeds to an unexpected final question.

> barbatus rigido nupsit Callistratus Afro
> hac qua lege viro nubere virgo solet.
> praeluxere faces, velarunt flammea vultus,

nec tua defuerunt verba, Talasse, tibi.
dos etiam dicta est. nondum tibi, Roma,
    videtur

hoc satis? expectas numquid ut et pariat?

(12.42)

Martial constructs his first line brilliantly: the pair of initial adjectives, which imply that we have to do with a bearded moralist[45] and a stern Catonian personality, are startlingly related by the verb, upon which follow the pair of identifying names. Callistratus, who has grown a beard so as to masquerade as a Cynic, has married Afer, a man as seemingly stern as the proverbial *rigidi Catones* of Martial **10.19.**21. It has been a Roman ceremony, even though Callistratus has hardly been the usual *virgo*. So Martial apostrophizes Rome and asks her what she is waiting for, for Callistratus to have a baby? There is, I believe, some impatience behind the question, but the incredible hyperbole manipulated into the final word shows that Martial's emphasis is, as usual, on the joke. Callistratus appears a few epigrams earlier, also as a pervert, upon whom Martial comments with his typical cool amusement, without the slightest impatience.[46] Furthermore, in choosing a Greek name for Callistratus, Martial has weakened the force of the appeal to Rome: she is not being asked to punish one of her degenerate children, but to drive out a foreigner who is polluting the scene. After, who has a Roman name, receives little emphasis, and furthermore he plays the less disgraceful role in this marriage.

Juvenal breaks the elements of this epigram of Martial into two dramatic sequences involving "marriages" between males (2.117-142).[47] In the first (117-132), he gives a detailed description of the marriage-ceremony, then angrily apostrophizes Mars without using the special joke of Martial; in the second (132-142), he first listens to someone else eagerly represent the occasion as one of the "society weddings" of the season, then angrily denounces such corruption, consoling himself with the thought that at least children cannot be born from such unnatural unions. Juvenal's point is totally different from Martial's and entirely consistent with his stance in Satires 1 and 3 as an indignant Roman: Rome has become unmanned, and its once-heroic families now produce effeminates. The "bride" in 117ff is now not a Greek Callistratus but a Roman Gracchus, scion of one of Rome's most distinguished families. The groom, a nameless trumpeter, probably a Greek or Easterner, further establishes the disgraceful qualities of this "marriage." And it is not by chance that Juvenal apostrophizes Mars. As he constructs the scene, the bridal attire of Gracchus forms a sharp antithesis to the military setting of the ceremonies in honor of Mars in which he participated as a Salian priest (124-126). So how can Mars ignore the disgrace? In disgust, he tells Mars to quit his own Campus Martius, for, if he per-

mits this marriage, then he is no longer the warlike Roman Mars.

The second marriage involves no names, but every indication suggests that the "bride" again is a "man of distinction." The first three lines (132-135) are organized as a rapid conversation which conceals its point until the end, and we might well see in them some of the successful touches of Martial.

'officium cras
primo sole mihi peragendum in valle Quirini.'
quae causa officii? 'quid quaeris? nubit
    amicus
nec multos adhibet.'

(132-135)

Somebody starts talking to Juvenal about the important *officium* which he just *must* perform the very first thing in the morning. It sounds important, cast as it is in the traditional Roman terms of public responsibility. So Juvenal inquires about the *officium*. The social butterfly replies without the slightest shame that he has been invited to an exclusive wedding where a male friend will be the "bride." That ends the Martial-like sequence. Note the difference, however: the shocking point is placed in the mouth of a despicable member of the "gay set"; it is not the amused observation of the satirist. As a result, Juvenal is free to comment, and the remainder of the passage consists of savage denunciation, in typical Juvenalian manner, of this perversion that threatens Rome itself. Instead of producing the incredible fantasy of Martial to end his scene, he consoles himself with the thought that at least these vile marriages can produce no offspring, no matter how much a Gracchus wishes to hold his/her "husband." Thus, Satire 2 establishes the typical tactics of Juvenal's angry wit, whereas Satire 9 (which Mason wrongly employed to define the standard of Juvenalian wit) reflects a later stage in Juvenal's development, when he was moderating his indignant manner and experimenting with the cynical humor of Martial.

Up to this point, my effort has been to answer Mason by describing the angry wit of Juvenal's poetry and showing its thematic function in the early Satires. We are to accept the statement of the satirist in Satire 1 that he is indignant; we should be able to feel the same indignation coursing through Satire 2; and Umbricius substitutes for the indignant satirist in Satire 3.[48] The indignation determines the immediate effect of the wit; hence, it cannot possibly resemble the wit which Martial uses to support his *lascivia*. However, despite the consistency of Juvenal's angry wit, the response of the audience is neither indignation nor anger. At this point, then, I wish to turn to Juvenal's audience, that of his time and of our time, in order to explain how the consistently manifested Juvenalian *ira,* his famous *saeva indignatio,* achieved its ultimately pleasurable effect. I shall continue to use Satire 3 as my touchstone, because that is the masterpiece of Book I and because Mason has provided us a hypothesis concerning its ultimate impression that fits his view of Juvenal's wit, but, I believe, does not adequately account for the different sensitivities of Martial's and Juvenal's audiences.

Mason makes the following suggestions with regard to Satire 3: "I am inclined to suspect and certainly hope that there is a special point in the external structure and the general tone: that, in a word, Umbricius is not Martial, but Juvenal himself recalling in verse the recitations he had so often delivered in prose and laughing both at himself in that rôle and at the attempt by contemporary writers of solemn hexameters to take themselves seriously. The poem in that case would be a genuine and witty drama and a piece of literary not social criticism."[49] Mason has earlier argued for the similarity between Umbricius (or Juvenal) and Martial; I have been arguing against that interpretation. Now, he attempts to give Juvenal some special credit by suspecting and hoping that Juvenal himself functions through Umbricius, that the satirist mocks the style of prose recitations and solemn hexameters through the words of his character Umbricius. If so, Satire 3 would become witty drama and literary, not social, criticism. The audience would presumably recognize the literary mockery and so sit back and enjoy this Martial-like figure Umbricius.

Although I agree that Satire 3 did strike Juvenal's audience and should strike us as a witty drama, I believe that the mechanism of this drama and the actual impression it left (and leaves) is quite different from what Mason assumes. If I am correct in denying the close resemblance between Martial and Umbricius, then most of the details of Mason's hypothesis collapse. I should prefer to start from the observed differences between Martial and Umbricius (or Juvenal in the other Satires of Book I), from the evident fact that Juvenal subordinates wit to his announced mood of *indignatio.* Umbricius in Satire 3 and the satirist himself in the other Satires of Book I loudly declare their outrage over the degradation of Rome. It is my contention that these loud declarations in the form of Satires constitute self-consistent dramas, whose mood of rage is realistic enough to be accepted at face value. However, there is little doubt in my mind that Juvenal did not share the extremist ideas of his dramatic characters, Umbricius in 3 and "the satirist" elsewhere, and there is no doubt whatsoever that the sophisticated Roman audience repeatedly smiled and applauded at this superb display of "honest indignation." As I see it, then, in the interaction between Satire 3 and the Roman audience occurs the "dramatic effect." That effect depends upon the different personal experience of audience and Umbricius and the different attitudes that audience and indignant speakers draw from their experience of Rome. It is quite unnecessary to assume, as Mason does, that every indignant speaker is parodying somebody else and consequently that the dramatic participation of the audience is the merely supine experience of recognizing Martial smirking inside Umbricius.[50]

What I have in mind is that Juvenal devised angry satire in order to exploit the long moralistic tradition of Roman culture and to utilize the possibilities for ambivalence in the rôle of the indignant moralist. This is much more than literary criticism, although we are compelled to document this moralistic tradition by citing literature like Cato, Sallust, speeches in Livy, Seneca, Pliny the Elder, and others. Juvenal was involving his Roman audience with attitudes that were fundamental to their inherited and acquired idea of Rome. But since traditionalistic morality and the fierce appeal to it did not expire with Alaric's capture of Rome, since angry extremism is a phenomenon of all human experience, we should not be too distrustful of any inclination to react to Juvenalian indignation in the complicated way we react today to a speech in real life or, better still, in a work of literature or drama that waxes indignant and extremist over social and political issues.[51] When we and others are indignant, we know, we are often capable of superb touches of wit, which we mean angrily. The sweeping generalization, cleverly vicious character assassination, brilliant use of metonymy or obscenity to color the picture, hyperbole of all sorts—these and many other devices have long been recognized as features of angry speech. What we may say so tellingly in honest indignation does not necessarily strike our audience in the same simple manner; cooler listeners may register our indignation, but refuse to share it. Having so refused, they are open to other impressions, separate or combined: sympathy for our excitement, amusement at our hot language, condemnation of us as immature, irrational, or otherwise inadequate.

When a writer sets out to create an angry character for a drama, he relies on the complex response which people have to anger. We are never at ease with our own or others' anger, and yet anger is a basic passion. Formal drama regularly works with angry types or characters who express wrath on a particular occasion. It may be rash to risk the statement, but I would hazard the generalization that no good dramatist, no good drama, presents anger as an unqualified virtue. King Lear is one of the most magnificently angry characters in all tragedy, an angry father seething at the ingratitude of his daughters. Yet Shakespeare does not minimize the fact that Lear's fury springs from his own unwisdom and its consequences; the first outrage against innocent Cordelia betrays that. On the other hand, the anger of fathers in comedy, based as it is also on a foolish view of the behavior of children, is regularly represented as hilariously funny. Shakespeare could make tragedy or comedy out of the irate husband who feels he has been deceived.[52] The misanthrope can be presented for laughs or sober reflection. From the monumental wrath of Achilles, so magnificently staged for our sympathetic condemnation by Homer, to the various soldier types of Menander, Plautus, and Terence, the steps were not difficult for the dramatist. Anger lies at the disposal of the creative writer, ready to serve a comic or tragic view, and consequently any sophisticated audience would be prepared instinctively to respond intelligently, not with an identically sympathetic passion, to anger in drama or dramatic satire.

It is not necessary to dispute the facts alleged by Umbricius or the angry satirist. No doubt there was a case or two of arson committed by a man like Persicus; no doubt some Greeks were uncommonly successful in getting ahead in Rome; and Tacitus himself tells us that Nero was "married" to a male. What counts, however, is not the sporadic facts of moral degradation but the way an Umbricius reacts to them. When Juvenal recited Satire 3 to his first audience in Rome, it knew Umbricius' facts, but his indignation did not correspond to the attitude of sophisticated Romans to isolated episodes of vice. I imagine that, as Juvenal concluded, he smiled and bowed, was roundly applauded, and that, as the audience filed out to get a drink, conversation developed enthusiastically over this new literary sensation in Rome, not so much about the moral charges of Umbricius as about the interesting way Juvenal achieved so convincing a presentation of a moral extremist. How could comfortable men of distinction, politicians accustomed to inspect angry words closely, literary connoisseurs who were steeped in the dramatic traditions of anger, citizens of Rome in the relatively comfortable, uncontroversial reign of Trajan, how could they muster much sympathy or credulity for the extremist conclusions of Umbricius? Could anyone possibly imagine them deciding to abandon their wonderfully cosmopolitan and active Rome?

To fix even more clearly the Roman audience's reaction to Satire 3 by invoking our own reactions, let me attempt to modernize Satire 3 for the reader.[53] We are not dealing with an ancient analogue for our common flight to the suburbs, nor would we be able to reduplicate Umbricius with ease. Umbricius and his decision, after all, are extremist.[54] He is a man of the lower middle class who clings to the moribund Roman system of patronage and refuses to adapt to the new methods of earning a living. Yet he is well educated and cultured, and he voices the conservative creed of what today would be a family with a tradition (and usually affluent). Today we have no genuine counterpart to the talented Greeks and Orientals who replace this incompetent Roman. First, then, we must put together a modern Umbricius who is a composite of some contemporary disaffected types. From our Conservative Backlash, we might select a belligerent white

worker who angrily resists expansion of the union shops to include Blacks who might take his job; a scion of an old Eastern or Southern family which is losing its money because of inability to adjust to the times; and an inhabitant of an arch-conservative suburb who proudly proclaims the ideals of the John Birch Society. Now we have our modern Umbricius. The modernized scene should be the waterfront of San Diego, California, or some place comparable. Our "friend" is about to leave the United States forever. After he has denounced America with his raging half-truths, hyperbole, and blind prejudice, he will climb aboard a 50-foot sailboat, in which he has stowed his belongings, raise sail and set out heroically for an uninhabited island in the South Pacific! I hardly need to define our reactions to such extravagant behavior.

To conclude, wit is a vital element of Juvenalian satire, but it stands in a different relation to Juvenal's purposes than wit does to Martial's goals. In Martial, wit and *lascivia* operate in full agreement with each other; the verbal manipulation and the manner that Martial repeatedly professes have identical effects. The audience performs no complicated process when it hears or reads the Epigrams, for Martial does quite brilliantly exactly what he says he does.[55] Mason assumes that the wit of Juvenalian satire constantly undermines the announced mood of the speaker, who is quite apparently laughing at himself and literary seriousness; that would mean that individual passages in the Satires would operate generally in the manner of separate epigrams of Martial, the sudden final surprise dispelling an initially affected seriousness. His argument, however, as I have attempted to show, over-simplifies and hence falsifies the art of Juvenal. It tends to imply that wit is supreme in the Satires, that indignation is secondary, in fact, meretricious. If we read carefully the early Satires, the only ones which in fact proclaim *indignatio* or *ira* as their mood, and if we study the wit in context for its thematic and dramatic relevance, we discover that wit and anger operate, at the primary level, in full agreement with each other. That is, they produce a dramatically credible impression of a violently angry man who cannot distinguish between facts and his own extravagant reactions to them. However, this same angry wit functions at a second level with the audience, which can and must draw the distinctions that are not made in the Satires. Whereas Martial inclines us to like his witty picture of Rome, Juvenal inclines us by his extravagance to reject the distorted interpretation of what he claims is the real Rome. We enjoy the angry Satires, accordingly, by opposition to their wild anger; we treat Umbricius and the satirist who rage in the early Satires as dramatic characters whose indignation is part of the drama, not a requisite part of our response to the facts.

The contrast between the wit of Martial and Juvenal can be epitomized in their treatments of Rome's moralistic tradition. In the introduction to **Book I** of the **Epigrams**, Martial assumes an attitude that he maintains throughout **Book XII**. His poems are *ioci,* written with *lascivia verborum,* designed for an audience that enjoys the lusty humor of the Floralia. Therefore, he forbids Cato to enter his "theatre" in his conventional moral rôle; he may enter only as a "spectator," that is, prepared to enjoy himself. The short poem that concludes this Preface repeats the same ideas: where *licentia* is the mood, *Cato severus* has no place. **Book XI** announces a similar program in two poems. It rejects the severe brow of Cato and proclaims the wild deeds of the Saturnalian mood **(11.2)**; it also dismisses Cato's wife from its audience, because it intends to be naughtier than all other books (*nequior omnibus libellis* **11.15.**4). **Book X** has another variation: stiff Cato will be allowed to read the epigrams only if he has drunk well **(10.19.**21). For the poems of Martial, then, morality is ostensibly irrelevant. By contrast, Juvenal's indignation insists that morality is crucially relevant. The satirist repeatedly appeals to the venerable moralistic tradition of Rome, laments that it has fallen into disuse, and himself voices the anger of one who is out of touch with his own times. But whereas he takes himself seriously and denounces Roman vice with honest passion, the audience judges him to be a largely comic figure, full of irrelevancy. He is, in a sense, a Cato born 250 years too late. Thinking that his wit expresses the extreme extent of vice, he in fact rather exposes his own ridiculous extremism.[56] Nevertheless, correcting or laughing *at* moral extremism is not totally negating morality. Whereas Martial allows us to reject Cato and relax in witty amorality, laughing *with* him, Juvenal obliges us to achieve our amusement by adjusting to our moral awareness the extravagance of his Catonian speaker. The more complex operation of Juvenal's wit demands a more complex, less passive response from us in the audience.

Notes

[1] Legally speaking, arson was a capital crime. In Juvenal's time, it was punishable by deportation; under the Severans it merited execution. See *Dig.* 48.8.3.5.

[2] The standard biography of Martial still rests upon the researches of L. Friedlaender in his edition (Leipzig 1886). See R. Helm's article in *RE, M. Valerius Martialis.*

[3] What we now possess as Books X and XI constitutes a revised edition of poems many of which were written between 94 and 96; this second edition adds poems that refer flatteringly to Nerva and the first years of Trajan.

[4] For the fullest recent treatment of Juvenal's biography, Gilbert Highet's *Juvenal the Satirist* (Oxford 1954) is very valuable if used with discretion. See especially his chapters I through V. Two recent articles challenge the reliability of the evidence on which the biography conventionally depends. G. Brugnoli, "Vita Iuvenalis," *Studi urbinati* 37 (1963) 5-14, dates the transmitted *Vita* no earlier than the fourth century and argues that its standardized categories of information make the detail suspect. E. Flores, "Origini e ceto di Giovenale e loro riflessi nella problematica sociale delle satire," *Annali fac. Lett. & filos. Napoli* 10 (1962-1963) 51-80, sees reasons to assign the now-lost inscription of Aquinum to another, earlier Juvenal and to argue that the satirist did not own property in that area.

[5] See the chapters in R. Syme, *Tacitus* (Oxford 1958) 59ff on the early careers of Pliny and Tacitus under Domitian.

[6] The fact that Juvenal, Pliny, and Tacitus all agree in denigrating Domitian after the emperor's death can hardly be used as special evidence for Juvenal's sufferings from Domitian. Otherwise, we would be obliged to infer that Pliny and Tacitus had themselves suffered to a similar extent; and we know that to be untrue.

[7] See the prudent comments of Highet, pp. 11-12. For a less likely view, see the ingenious article of A. Michel, "La date des *Satires:* Juvénal, Héliodore et le tribun d'Arménie," *REL* 41 (1963) 315-327. He dates Book I after the accession of Hadrian in 118.

[8] In Satire 1, many of the vignettes of adulterers and adulteresses, gigolos, women who poison their husbands, women gladiators, etc., can be paralleled in Martial. Satire 2 deals with the crypto-homosexual who poses as a severe moralist and with his secret orgies. Parallels in Martial are common; see infra, pp. 24ff. I use Satire 3 throughout this article because of the many points it shares with Martial. Satire 5 scornfully portrays the *cliens* who, for a humiliating meal, allows himself to be "enslaved" and lose his *libertas* to an insulting *patronus.* Cf. Martial 4.40, 5.22, 5.44, 6.88, 9.100, 10.56.

[9] Cf. Martial 3.45.5 and especially 13.81.

[10] See the series of articles, based on his dissertation, by R. E. Colton in *CB* 39 (1963) 49-52 [on Satire 7 and Martial], 40 (1963) 1-4 [Sat. 4 and Martial], 41 (1964) 26-27 [Sat. 14], 41 (1965) 39, 41-45 [Sat. 11], *CJ* 61 (1965) 68-71 [Sat. 2], and *Traditio* 22 (1966) 403-419 [Sat. 3].

[11] "The Life and Poems of Juvenal," *JP* 16 (1888) 41-66, reprinted in his *Lectures and Essays* (Oxford 1895) 117-144.

[12] Duff. *D. Iunii Iuvenalis Saturae XIV,* p. xxii.

[13] Wilson, *AJP* 19 (1898) 193-209. Of less significance

is the almost contemporary article of G. Boissier, "Relations de Juvénal et de Martial," *Rev. Cours et Conferences* 7 (1899) 2.443-451. Boissier commented rather generally on similarities and differences between the two poets.

[14] Wilson, p. 193.

[15] C. W. Mendell, "Martial and the Satiric Epigram," *CP* 17 (1922) 1-20 points out that, between the time of Catullus and Martial, the epigram came under the influence of satire and so can in certain cases be called "satiric." J. W. Duff, *Roman Satire* (Berkeley 1936) 126ff devotes an entire chapter to Martial. See now also H. Szelest, "Martials satirische Epigramme und Horaz," *Das Altertum* 9 (1963) 27-37.

[16] Boissier (supra n. 13) commented on this in 1899. For more recent observations, see R. Marache, "Le revendication sociale chez Martial et Juvénal," *RCCM* 3 (1961) 30-67, and N. I. Barbu, "Les esclaves chez Martial et Juvénal," *Acta antiqua philippopolitana* (Sofia 1963) 67-74.

[17] Highet, p. 173.

[18] Mason, *Arion* 1:1 (1962) 8-44; 2 (1962) 39-79. This article is reprinted in *Essays on Roman Literature: Satire,* edited by Sullivan (London 1963) 93-176. Since that volume is more accessible and its numbering is easier to use, I shall consistently refer to its pagination.

[19] P. 96.

[20] P. 165. It is of course an exaggeration to claim that Juvenal treated *all* Martial's butts or to imply that *only* Martial's butts appear in the Satires. Where in Juvenal are the mocking portraits of writers who are jealous of or plagiarize him? Where are jokes on physical deformities and malfunctions as common as in Martial? It is equally strained to liken Juvenal's use of obscenity to Martial's. How frequently does one hear of pederasty in the Satires? Consider some of Martial's all too common terms like *cunnilingus, fellator, tribas, ficosus, masturbare:* one would have trouble locating more than a single Juvenalian reference to each of these five sexual interests. As I shall try to show, Juvenal was not dependent upon obscenity to the same extent as Martial and did not use it as Martial had done.

[21] See p. 107.

[22] *Ibid.*

[23] The name occurs only here and in 12.88.

[24] There is disagreement as to whether we are dealing with one person or two here. Some scholars believe that Persicus owned *domus Asturici,* Asturicus either

being a previous owner, perhaps builder of the house, or an ancestor. Others believe that Juvenal refers to two unrelated cases of arson, the hypothetical one involving Asturicus' house and a second one from which Persicus profited. See the next note.

[25] J. E. B. Mayor, *Thirteen Satires of Juvenal* (London 1889)[4], in his note on 3.212, says of Asturicus and Persicus: "names of conquering families." The two relevant entries in *RE* illustrate the disagreement mentioned in n. 24: on Asturicus, P. von Rohden wrote: "Beiname eines vornehmen Römers, Iuv. 3,212. Wohl willkürlich gewählt." On the other hand, Groag, after an extensive discussion of P. Fabius Persicus [Fabius # 120], consul A.D. 34, used this passage of Juvenal to justify a hypothetical Fabius Persicus Asturicus [Fabius # 121]. We know for sure of no Asturicus, but Persicus is well attested. Juvenal addresses a Persicus, presumably a quite different man and a friend, in 11.57.

[26] Umbricius is a rare name, too, but attested in Tacitus *Hist.* 1.27 and Pliny *N.H.* 10.19 as a noted *haruspex* in A.D. 69. See also *RE* s.v. Recently, Motto and Clark, *TAPA* 96 (1965) 275, have argued that "Umbricius is no historical figure contemporary to Juvenal," but that the name is chosen to refer to *umbra:* he therefore represents the shade of the deceased Rome.

[27] Cf. Horace *C.* 2.16.6 and 3.1.21, also *S.* 1.1.9-10.

[28] Juvenal's metrical unit *iam frivola transfert / Ucalegon* parodies *Aeneid* 2.311: *iam proximus ardet / Ucalegon.*

[29] Mason comments on this passage, p. 130.

[30] See Martial 2.46.9, 2.75.7, and 11.7.7.

[31] Juvenal alludes to the same point in 6.87, 10.81, and 11.53 and 197.

[32] See Cicero *Ad fam.* 7.1 and Pliny *Epist.* 9.6.

[33] Martial 2.14.12.

[34] Cf. Horace *S.* 2.6.63 and Ovid *Met.* 15.75ff.

[35] The formula would be something like this: a noun or verb expressing ownership would be combined with an objective genitive or accusative object, which would define the thing owned in a phrase consisting of *unus* and a noun in the diminutive or itself denoting something tiny and insignificant (e.g., *unius lacertae*).

[36] Note the way *vilicus* in 228 acquires entirely different connotations from those in 195.

[37] Aside from Mason, few scholars have appreciated Juvenal's wit and humor openly. But R. Marache,

"Rhétorique et humour chez Juvénal," *Hommages à Jean Bayet* (Brussels 1964) 474-478, without knowing Mason's work, makes some sensible comments on such devices as hyperbole.

[38] P. 176.

[39] I have analyzed Satire 3 in terms of this theme in "Studies in Book I of Juvenal," *YCS* 15 (1957) 55-68. See now Motto and Clark, "The Mythos of Juvenal 3," *TAPA* 96 (1965) 267-276.

[40] P. 128.

[41] See my article, "The Programs of Juvenal's Later Books," *CP* 57 (1962) 145-160.

[42] For similarly competent *cinaedi / adulteri,* see in Martial 10.40 and the jokes in 6.33, 11.45, 86, and 88 on the *paedico* who turns *fututor.*

[43] On Satire 6, see Mason pp. 135ff and my article "Juvenal 6: a Problem in Structure," *CP* 51 (1956) 73-94.

[44] By contrast, Naevolus, about whom he expresses tolerant amusement in Satire 9, is, like Martial's characters, no member of the aristocratic governing class. Juvenal calls him *vernam equitam* at 9.10.

[45] Beards were worn in Martial's time only as a protest and indicated adherence to a Cynic-Stoic form of life. Only with Hadrian did ordinary men begin to allow their beards to grow.

[46] See 12.35. In that poem, Martial assigns no beard to Callistratus because his joke aims at a different point. A man of the same name appears also in 5.13, 9.95, and 12.80. Martial also makes frequent use of the name of Afer: see 4.37 and 78, 6.77, 9.7 and 25, 10.84.

[47] J: Colin, "Juvénal et le mariage mystique de Gracchus," *Atti Tor* 90, (1955-1956) 114-216, claims that this marriage was a solemn act of ritual and that Juvenal, misunderstanding it, twisted it into an obscene orgy. However, the common evidence of Juvenal, Martial and Tacitus on such "marriages" gives no support to his hypothesis.

[48] On Satire 5, see n. 8, supra. Martial jokes about a poor man's loss of liberty as he cadges a meal; Juvenal uses the same situation to wax furious because of the Roman relevance.

[49] P. 135.

[50] I am here outlining a theory which I have developed at length in relation to conventional Roman views on anger in my monograph "Anger in Juvenal and Sen-

eca," *Calif. Publ. Class Phil.* 19 (1964) 127-196.

[51] Modern drama, especially on television, is beginning to develop angry types in the campus rebel, the Southern reactionary, and the nouveau-riche resident of the suburbs.

[52] Such dramas as the opera *I Pagliacci* and the ballet *Petrouschka* show further subtlety in their treatment of the angry lover. They deal with a clown who plays a cuckold in his stage role; but when this clown finds himself deceived in his real love, he becomes murderously furious.

[53] I am assuming my reader here is someone who has considerable experience of literature, and hence has the ability to back away and criticize what he reads or hears. I set no limits as to political or social sympathies.

[54] Cf. Molière's Oronte, whose misanthropy and final decision to abandon Paris for rustic solitude undoubtedly seemed more extremist and were easier for Molière, who took the part, to play for laughs in the late seventeenth century than they are today in modern revivals.

[55] I do not mean that Martial himself was so limited a character in his real life. But his Epigrams are fully consistent with their claim of *lascivia.*

[56] Laronia mockingly sneers at a hypocrite moralist in 2.40: *tertius e caelo cecidit Cato.* That alliterative irony could well be applied to the honest but extravagant moralist, too: he is something incredible, "out of this world."

Virginia M. Chaney (essay date 1971)

SOURCE: "Women, according to Martial," *The Classical Bulletin,* Vol. 48, No. 2, December, 1971, pp. 21-5.

[*In this essay, Chaney briefly surveys Martial's depiction of women—both those he admires and those whose features, vanity, or lack of virtue he disparages.*]

Martial frequently writes of women as types but his poems also deal with at least sixty-five women who are named and rather clearly described. Life itself is the theme of Martial, the life of the decadent Empire, and though he often writes in jest, he makes it quite clear in his preface that he respects all persons, even the lowest in status and character. "My page," says he, "smacks of humanity."

Women naturally were part of Martial's material. His subject matter was scandals, humors, fashions, follies, hypocrisies, Flavian types and eccentrics. He attained vividness by realistic detail. As Moses Hadas asserts, " . . . his total picture adds up to an indictment of social sham in all its manifestations." For such a type of writing, the epigram was a perfect vehicle and women the perfect foil. However, the Martial of the cutting epigram can love, with the simplest, most unsophisticated love, an innocent slave-child, Erotion, whom he immortalized in three poems (**5.34; 37; 10.61**). Erotion was a child beside whom "squirrels seemed clumsy." Simcox says of this aspect of Martial, one tenth of whose work may be called, even in our day, obscene: "He stands almost alone in Roman literature in his appreciation of mere girlhood; one of the most pathetic of his epitaphs is for a child of six who died of some face disease (**11.12**)."

Martial knows and can appreciate a good woman (**1.14; 4.13; 75**). He writes tenderly of the mutual affection which Calenus and Sulpicia preserved during the fifteen years of their married life, and dwells, tastefully for the age, upon the amorous ecstasies which were witnessed by their nuptial bed and by the lamp "copiously sprinkled with perfumes" (**10.38**). Little is known about this Sulpicia, a poetess of the time. She is mentioned by Ausonius and by Sidonius Apollinarius and a satirical poem on the expulsion by Domitian of the philosophers from Rome is commonly attributed to her. Paley ascribes to her the poems often contained in the editions of Tibullus.

Martial suggests (**10.35**) that all young wives who wish to please their husbands read Sulpicia—and all young husbands who wish to please their brides alone. "He who shall weigh well her poems will say no maid was so roguish, will say no maid was so modest." For fifteen years Sulpicia and Calenus enjoyed what Martial certainly considered to be wedded bliss. If given a choice, Calenus would have one day of his married life restored rather than "four spans of Pylean old age" (**10.38**).

Like other Roman authors, Martial was intrigued by the story of Arria the Elder, wife of Caecina Paetus. Arria's husband, involved in a conspiracy against the emperor, Claudius, A.D. 42, was ordered to kill himself. When he hesitated, Arria, who had refused to survive him, set him an example. No doubt such cases were exceptional. Perhaps in that decadent era courage was abnormally heightened and virtue itself began to suffer from an excess of stoicism. But side by side with Arria there are many cases of households tenderly united, of views quite simply pure and noble.

Other good women celebrated by Martial include: the wife of Stella the Poet; Aratulla, who presents an indirect plea for the recall of her brother from exile; Caesonia, wife of Canius Rufus, called "revered"; Marcella, who, supposedly, gave Martial a home in Spain that he might retire from the turbulent life of Rome; Polla, the wife of Lucan; Claudia Rufina, a refined lady of British birth; Portia, the heroic wife of Brutus; and Nigrina, who is a good wife because she is a happy wife.

In the corrupt period in which Martial lived, the marriage contracted for purely financial reasons was an everyday occurrence. In one of his epigrams (**11.23**), the poet poses as being willing to accept the hand of a rich old woman on the condition that they need never sleep together: *communis tecum nec mihi lectus erit* (**1.6**).

Consuls and praetors were crushed under the burden of the expenditure entailed by their honorable promotion, and Martial has invented the amusing anecdote of a young woman, Proculeia, who as soon as her husband was appointed to the praetorship announced her intention of divorcing him: "What, I ask, is the matter, Proculeia? . . . I will tell you: your husband was praetor . . . this is not divorce, Proculeia: it is good business" (**10.41**).

In **5.61**, Martial shows how the Roman matron, mistress of her own property in virtue of her *sine manu* status, was certain, thanks to the Julian laws, of recovering the bulk if not the whole of her dowry. Her husband was not free to administer the bulk if not the whole of her dowry. Her husband was not free to administer it in Italy without her consent, nor to mortgage it anywhere even with her agreement. Duly primed by her steward, who assisted her with advice and surrounded her with obsequious attention—this "curled spark" of a procurator whom we see always "clinging to the side" of Marianus' wife—the wealthy lady dispatched her business, made her dispositions, and issued her orders. Might this be called evidence of an early women's liberation movement?

This is the way Martial feels about the wealthy woman: "My turning down a wealthy match you say you think is a riddle? . . . Equality for man and wife can come no other way." And was Manilla (Maronilla) wealthy (**1.10**)? Gemellus is courting Manilla, and few understand why. What can he see in her? "It must be that she has T.B."

Other women with money are Phileros' seven wives, whose burials give him good return on his land; the wife of Aper, the sportsman, who transfixed her heart with a sharp arrow; Fabulla, rich and boastful; Galla, granting her favors for two gold pieces; and Secundilla, to whose husband, broken-hearted at her death, Martial says, "I cannot tell you how much I regret that this has happened to you."

Obviously, the women of Martial's day thought a great deal about their appearance. They were quite literally obsessed with their hair—its color and its arrangement.

Lalage found that her maid, Plecusa, had dressed her hair with an insecure pin, so that one curl had fallen out of place. "The crime Lalage avenged with the mirror in which she had observed it and Plecusa, smitten, fell because of those savage locks!" (2.66). Sometimes false hair was dyed blond with the *sapo* of Mainz obtained by blending goat's fat with beech ash (14.56). Gulla wears golden hair—and it is hers—Martial knows where she bought it.

Make-up, lavishly applied, was important to the Roman woman, especially to the matron. The matron's daytime face, which she made up on rising, made up again after her bath and did not unmake until after nightfall at the last moment before going to bed, causes Martial to say: "You lie stored away in a hundred caskets, and your face does not sleep with you!" (9.37).

Martial mentions teeth often, usually unpleasantly. "Four teeth, sweet Aelia, you had: one cough took two. Cough two took three and four." Aelia is then admonished to be happy, for she can lose no more teeth, regardless of her coughing.

Laecania and Thais have interesting teeth, too. "Thais has black, Laecania has snowy teeth. What is the reason? Laecania has bought ones, Thais her own" (5.43).

An extremely ugly poem (6.93) carries on the disagreeable picture of Thais by telling in great detail how bad she smells, ending, "When she has thought herself quite safe through a thousand tricks, when she has done everything, Thais smells like Thais." Probably Thais was unhealthy, since she is spoken of as being so thin she seems not to exist (10.101). Saufeia, too, is lectured on the importance of bathing (3.72), and so is Sellis (3.55).

Apparently, as in our own day, the woman of good proportions was admired, for Martial tells Flaccus (11.100) that he does not want a thin mistress, but not tallow, either. Evidently extreme height was not admired. To Claudia was addressed the sentiment:

> Summa Palatini poteras aequare colossi,
> Si fieres brevior, Claudia, sesquipede.

Lesbia (11.99) is so large that sitting down and rising are next to impossible for her—"your wretched clothes fetter you, Lesbia." The answer? "Lesbia, I advise you neither to get up nor sit down." Lydia, too, is extremely large (11.21). "Lydia is as widely developed as the rump of a bronze equestrian statue . . . as the aged breeches of a pauper Briton . . . this woman I am said to have embraced in a fishpond: I don't know; I think I embraced the fishpond itself."

Several of Martial's epigrams speak of a woman with one eye. Was the one-eyed person found frequently in the society of the Empire? Or was Martial simply using a disfigurement which does obviously detract from one's appearance?

> Philaenis weeps with just one eye.
>   Queer, is it not?
> You wish you knew the reason why?
>   That's all she's got.
>
>   (6.55)

Thais, too, is one-eyed; with grim humor, Martial writes: "Quintus loves Thais. What Thais? Thais the one-eyed. Thais is lacking one eye; Quintus is totally blind."

Lycoris combines several of the unattractive features often assigned by Martial to his women. She is very dark, even swarthy: "Black Lycoris has gone into the Tibur . . . While there, she believes, everything will become white" (4.62). She has black teeth, whose ivory she hopes, in vain, may be restored by the Tiburtine sun. Lycoris is old, too: Martial writes, "Lycoris seems to have a longer life than all her friends. I wish she liked my wife." And, finally, Lycoris is one-eyed, says the poet, "How well she sees with one eye!" (3.39).

Just as in our own day, women differed in their attitudes toward age; Gellia was an old woman, but called herself a girl. Martial called her shameless. Lesbia (10.39) tries to conceal her age, but the poet says she is fashioned of Promethean clay. Paula is described as man-hungry (1.74 and 10.5), but, worst of all, she is old (10.8).

Obviously, one of the basic problems of the Empire as Martial knew it was that of the frequency of divorce. Telesilla is a perfect example. Thirty days, or perhaps less, after Domitian had revised the Julian laws, "She is now marrying her tenth husband . . . by a more straightforward prostitute I am offended less" (6.7). Divorces follow so close on each other's heels that, as Martial says, "Marriage has become merely a form of legalized adultery. *Quae nubit totiens, non nubit: adultera lege est*" (6.7.5).

Over and over again the implication is made that husbands and wives commit foul play in order to marry again. Of Fabius and Chrestilla he writes (8.43): "Fabius buries his wives, Chrestilla her husbands, and each of them waves the funeral torch over a marriage bed. Match them, Venus; their end will be one funeral." And of Galla he says (9.78): "After the funerals of seven husbands Galla has married you, Picentinus. I think Galla wants to follow her husbands." (Both Galla and Picentinus were poisoners: see 7.43.)

It was not long before the presence of slaves introduced a seriously disturbing element into even legitimate households. Martial launches many a dart at home-keeping adulterers. He mocks the master who buys back the maid-servant mistress he cannot bear to do without (6.71); he makes merry over the great lady who has lost her heart to her hairdresser and having set him free pours an equestrian fortune into his lap (7.64); he attributes Marulla's many offsprings not to her husband Cinna but to Cinna's cook, his bailiff, his baker, his flutist, his wrestler, and his buffoon (6.39). No doubt these epigrams are aimed at the most crying scandals of the town. But the theme would have been less popular if scandals had been rarer, and the literature of the time gives us the impression that there must have been many Roman houses where the abusive dialogue which Martial's couplet presupposes might have taken place: "Your wife calls you an admirer of servant maids, and she herself is an admirer of litter bearers. You are a pair, Alauda." It is obvious that the abuses of slavery had introduced laxity of morals even into the houses where supplementary love affairs were taboo.

The type of woman free with her favors or granting them for money is often presented in the pages of Martial. He writes about the harlot who is over age, but who tries, rather unsuccessfully, to pursue her former life. Of Matrinia he says, "I am not able to love an old hag you ask, Matrinia? I am able, but you are dead, not just old." (Translation considerably cleaned up, but idea clear.) Marulla is obscene (10.55). So is Telesina, who gives herself to boys (2.49). Thais is one who draws the line at hardly any act (4.12; 4.50; 4.84).

In an echo of the style of Catullus, Martial rues the beauty of the girl whose character does not match her loveliness; of Catulla he says (7.53): "Most beautiful of all women who have been or are (*formosissima*), but vilest (*vilissima*) of all who have been or are, oh, how I could wish, Catulla, you could become less beautiful or more pure!"

Phyllis, a quite obscene woman, also a flirt, is typical of the clever woman described by Martial (10.81): when two had come to Phyllis early in the morning for carnal relations and each desired to enjoy her first, Phyllis promised that she would give herself equally to them, and did so: "That one held her foot, this one her robe." Caelia (11.75 and 7.30) is another tease, granting greater favors to slaves and to foreigners than to Romans.

The women of Martial have their foibles. Fabulla (8.79) has a failing perhaps not too unusual, after all. She is a lady who chooses her companion among the homely, that she may appear a beauty by comparison. Gellia has yet to learn that true grief is not ostentatious. When she is alone she does not weep for her dead father, but if anyone is present, her bidden tears flow. Martial assures Gellia that only that one who grieves without a witness truly grieves. There have always been those women who have adored titles, but whose plans have gone awry. To Gellia (5.17) Martial writes, "While you were telling us of your ancestors, and their ancestors, and the great names of your family, while you looked down on our equestrian order as a mean rank, and while you were asserting that you would marry no one who did not wear the broad border of the senator, you married . . . a porter."

It is Gellia, too, who believes that the consumption of the rabbit brings beauty to the eater. Says the poet, "When you send me a hare, Gellia, you say, 'You will be handsome for seven days, Marcus.' If you do not joke, if you speak truly, my light, you Gellia, have never eaten a hare!"

Philaenis (9.29) has died, apparently of old age. And what will be missed? Her tongue! Her tongue was louder than the noise in a thousand slave-marts, louder than a curly-headed troop of schoolboys, louder than the cries of a flock of cranes. Labulla (12.93), quite unfaithful to her husband (4.9), has discovered how to kiss her lover in the presence of her husband. She covers her dwarf fool with kisses; the lover then kisses the dwarf, and hands him back to the smiling lady. Says Martial, "How much bigger fool is the husband!"

Martial has much to say of the wife with unwifely attributes. One of the most cutting of his epigrams concerns the wife who equals her husband in bad disposition (8.35): "Seeing that you are like one another and a pair in your habits, vilest of wives, vilest of husbands, I wonder you don't agree!" Gellia (8.81) is a bad wife because her love belongs primarily to possessions. She does not swear by any gods or goddesses, but by her pearls: "These she hugs, these she kisses passionately, these she calls her brothers, these she calls her sisters, these *she loves more ardently than her two sons*. If by any chance the unhappy woman should lose them, she says she would not live even an hour . . ."

Martial wrote tenderly of a little girl, of the lovely woman Sulpicia, of the courageous Arria, but his sharp eye and clever epigram missed none of the vices and foibles of the women of his time.

Paul Plass (essay date 1985)

SOURCE: "An Aspect of Epigrammatic Wit in Martial and Tacitus," *Arethusa*, Vol. 18, No. 2, Fall, 1985, pp. 187-210.

[*In the following excerpt, Plass evaluates Martial's obscene epigrams in terms of Freud's commentary on the function and effectiveness of wit. Plass calls atten-*

tion to the way Martial manipulates syntax and word play to subvert codes of propriety, confound logic, and amuse his audience.]

I

In *De Amicitia* (37) Cicero mentions the following exchange between Laelius and Blossius on political loyalty:

L. Etiamne, si te in Capitolium faces ferre vellet?

B. Numquam voluisset id quidem, sed si voluisset, paruissem.

L. [Would you] actually [have done it], if he [Tiberius Gracchus] had wanted you to set fire to the Capitol?

B. He never would have wanted that, but if he had, I would have done it.

Laelius dismisses the reply as shocking *(nefaria)* without remarking on its most interesting aspect: Blossius' "yes" reflects the private code of friendship that was so powerful a factor in ancient ethics, but at the same time it is set against another, public code (Tiberius' "no"). The result is a statement with a slightly odd (as well as nefarious) sound to it. We await the answer with considerable interest, and when we hear what it is, its internal tension ("No . . . but yes") is sharp enough to be surprising. If we go beyond Laelius' shock we realize that the tension is due to subtle incoherence. We expect either unambiguous assertion of the public code ("He wouldn't have wanted that, and if he had, I wouldn't have done it") or unambiguous assertion of the private code ("He might have wanted that, and if so I would have done it"). Instead Blossius comes down between two stools, or rather sits on two at once: he asserts one code of morality on behalf of Tiberius, but he does not say "no" and promptly compromises the code on his own behalf by saying "yes."

Martial has an epigram **(IV.71)** which uses a somewhat similar pattern:

Quaero diu totam, Safroni Rufe, per urbem,
  si qua puella neget: nulla puella negat.
tamquam fas non sit, tamquam sit turpe
  negare,
    tamquam non liceat: nulla puella negat.
Casta igitur nulla est? Sunt castae mille. Quid
  ergo
    casta facit? Non dat, non tamen illa negat.

A. I've looked all over town for a woman who says "no," Rufus. There isn't any! It's as though it were illegal, indecent, improper: not one says "no"!

B. You mean there isn't a single chaste woman around?

A. Oh, no. There are thousands.

B. Well, what do they do?

A. They don't say "yes"—but they don't say "no" either.

In a companion piece **(IV.81)** he complains about a woman who has read his epigram and does say nothing but "no" to him, i.e., is chaste. In view of this, the point of the first poem seems to be that women are either promiscuous or coy, and the latter (those who don't say "yes" or "no") cynically straddle the issue by borrowing from the rules of both chastity and promiscuity. This is a witticism or joke because of the amusingly self-canceling sound of the last line. Blossius' reply is not amusing nor does anything suggest that Cicero thought of it even as epigrammatic; Laelius, at any rate, treats it as mere hypocrisy or outright political immorality. But it does have a "funny" sound; its structure is very similar to that of Martial's epigram and it could easily serve as a cynical political joke: "We wouldn't think of committing political crimes—unless we want to." Tacitus, in fact, uses just such bitter epigrammatic wit: "They call it a crime and—do it" (*Hist.* 3.25.3).

Epigram, joke, witticism, humor or striking remark are not easily distinguished, and what they often have in common is unexpected illogic of one sort or another. In outright joking the potential incoherence of "no . . . but yes" is simply given extreme form and becomes arresting nonsense. For example:

A. Is this the place where the Duke of Wellington spoke those words?

B. Yes, it's the place—but he never spoke the words.

A. I'm on a Chinese diet.

B. What's that?

A. You eat with—one chopstick.

The dialogue of the last joke is built around the contrast "[Yes,] you eat [but] with one chopstick" and illustrates nicely an essential feature of wit: "funniness," i.e., peculiarity which violates the code defining our expectation of what is reasonable. Dieting and starving are mutually exclusive, and since it is not possible to eat with one chopstick, the reply is logically incoherent. But it is also witty because its matter-of-fact verbal form is a façade concealing the incoherence. The façade is especially ingenious because the contrast between eating with two sticks and with one suggests something that is a natural part of dieting—reduction of intake. We instinctively think of a reduction by fifty percent; in fact, it is one hundred percent, and the joke is all the more effective because it also calls up the comic picture of someone trying to eat with one chopstick. Since conversation through question and answer is a basic way in which we express our sense of reality in dealing with others, the casually unreasonable reply is particularly startling (that is true of the Duke of Wellington joke as well). Moreover, ordinarily we instantly understand what others say and need not spend time in reflection. The brevity of the wit here exploits that fact: the illogic of the reply is obvious and stupid when spelled out, but when sprung suddenly it is superficially reasonable enough to create an odd kind of tension between sense and nonsense which is gratifying rather than annoying or pointless.

All of this brings us to Freud's reflections on wit. It is probably fair to say that of all of his proposals none matches the theory of wit in immediate appeal. It lends itself to empirical testing which is both easy and highly entertaining, as anyone who has read Freud's own collection of jokes knows. What is more, for all its sophistication it recommends itself to common sense, since it is plausible in light of familiar facts and not simply in light of theoretical considerations. There *is* something "funny" and "wrong" about jokes; indeed, the phrase "something funny" is in its peculiar ambivalence implicitly Freudian (Blossius' reply is not funny [amusing], but it is to Laelius a funny [strange] avowal of aggression).

I propose to use the theory in its most general form as a point of reference for the epigrammatic style of Martial and Tacitus, a style which is itself notably "witty" in as much as its precise metrical and linguistic forms are designed to give elegant point to the content. In the case of poetry, since much of the content was occasional or commonplace, epigrammatic wit depended largely on the skill with which writers could work within restrictions. The epigram could thus be an exercise more in form than in substance, and Latin was for this purpose an especially appropriate medium because its complex inflection combined with absence of the definite article naturally creates opportunity for play with words.

Freud's discussion of the nature of wit covers a wide area and touches on many points, but what is of interest for our purposes is the central thesis that he advances. In ordinary language we observe the rules of logic which reflect public standards of what is real and proper. Such standards prevent the aggressive, selfish pleasure principle from expressing itself in direct action and reducing society to a madhouse, but the pleasure principle can come out in a socially tolerable way under the guise of joking language, which is "funny" in the dual sense that, on the one hand, it expresses

improper ways of behaving and, on the other hand, does so through illogical ways of thinking and amusingly odd ways of talking. And all of this is usually deliberate; as Quintilian notes in his discussion of wit, things which are clever when said deliberately are stupid when they slip out (*Institutio* VI.III.23). We might compare the following inept effort at informed sympathy as a joke and as actual dialogue:

> An officer inspecting his infirmary sees a very sick man and asks what is wrong with him. 'He has typhus.' 'Ah, very bad, very bad. Had it myself—you either die or lose your mind.'

Public rules of one sort or another are always a factor in wit, as we can see from the fact that wit is notoriously risky because in some forms (sexual, ethnic, political) normally restrained factors may reach an offensively overt level. As one person's religion is another's superstition, so one person's joke is another's insult.

In general terms, then, social life depends on a variety of codes which establish expectations and thus permit us to relax our guard against surprise (e.g., surprise at learning that inspecting officers are either mad or dead; as we shall see, Tacitus does aim at surprising us with the realization that some emperors *were* mad). Conflict arises when codes and expectations are violated, and if we think of codes as embodiments of logic and patterns of sanity, violation may entail nothing less than a threat to our sense of reality. Language itself is one of the very deepest of codes depending on establishment and satisfaction of grammatical expectations. We can "feel" that after a plural subject a plural verb will shortly and properly come along, and we are satisfied when it does, much as we derive satisfaction from resolution of a musical sequence in accordance with a musical code. Verbal wit, then, creates pleasure through illogical, unexpected modes of thought and expression.

II

Martial's epigrams make up a corpus of wit which invites comparison with Freud's scheme. The most important aspect of their structure is, of course, literary, and that has often been studied in its own right, recently also with some reference to Freudian and other theories of wit.[1] Greek and Roman epigrammatists wrote poetry, not jokes, yet there is some value in setting literary factors aside to focus exclusively on the psychological structure of wit in order to see it from a special point of view—as an exercise in subverting codes. Freud distinguishes "tendentious" from "innocent" jokes and uses the former in particular to show that joking is analogous to dreaming.[2] Having made this point empirically by a running analysis of jokes, he moves on to his major psychological conclusion: like dreams, jokes release repressed tendentious (sexual, aggressive) material in disguised form. Martial's wit is clearly tendentious in this sense, and the most common violation of polite codes is the obscene joke. Obscene epigrams are, in fact, a major sub-form of ancient epigrammatic literature, and they will play a large role in our discussion. They are pertinent because their literary value often does not go beyond their formal wit, and they thus typify the importance of structure relative to content. The stock of obscenities is limited, and readers are not really interested in what they are but in how they work. Since translations of epigrams as poetry are usually unsuccessful because of the intricacy of language and meter, I will turn my examples from Martial into prose which follows as closely as possible familiar forms of jokes. Poetic form is lost, but the point of the epigram as well as its mechanism is preserved intact, and that is what we are interested in.

The effect of a joke, then, is determined in the first instance by the degree of its departure—ranging from subtle to gross—from a code. Excessively gross violation destroys wit because it is pointless as wit—it is simply an indecent or stupid remark. Absence of violation has the same effect: the remark simply deals with reality as it is. But a joke like "Why did the chicken cross the road?/ To get to the other side" seems not to violate any code, yet it is witty and illustrates an interesting point. Though wit involves violation of a social code, it has a social setting in so far as it is socially acceptable. In fact, it becomes a code itself, and its illogic is, in a sense, *not* unexpected since as a joke it signals us to expect the unexpected. One major signal of joking is the use of questions to set up mini-dialogues and thus elicit answers which lead to the joke; there is little wit in the *statement,* "The chicken crossed the road to get to the other side." Dozens of Martial's epigrams are cast in the form of brief dialogues given direction by leading questions. This formal aspect of wit is illustrated by the chicken joke; the question is, in effect, a set riddle whose answer, however, seems to be witless because it is mere information. But precisely by *not* being unexpected but banal the answer is, after all, unexpected. It is witty because it misses the point of the question in so far as such a question signals a joke. That is to say, the form of the wit *is* the wit, and this technique has been inelegantly but conveniently called "metajoking"—joking which disappoints expectation of wit as such.[3] We can also think of a metajoke as anti-climax or deflation, and ancient rhetorical theory recognized a technique of "suspension" followed either by anti-climax or by a climax that goes *beyond* what is expected (Quintilian, IX.II.22/23).

I am not aware of a true metajoke in Martial and suspect that in pure form it would not often have seemed witty to Greeks or Romans. But it is at least useful as an ideal type for considering some closely related Roman jokes. The principle "stupid question, stupid answer"[4] is illustrated by a witticism in Quintilian (VI.III.71): when a man coming out of a theater is asked whether he has been watching a play he replies, "No, I was playing ball in the orchestra." "Yes" would be mere information, "no" would be false. In so far as its content is odd the answer is not metawit; since it is unreasonable to play ball in the theater, the answer is not banal. On this score it is, if anything, a reverse metajoke: the question is banal, the answer odd, and Quintilian himself remarks that the answer "makes the question stupid." "Why did the chicken cross the road?" is clearly not stupid in the way it is stupid to ask what someone was doing in a theater. Yet both jokes are witty by not being "witty" in the ordinary sense because they are pointless exchanges. One of Martial's most famous epigrams has very much the same effect:

> **I.32** Non amo te, Sabidi, nec possum dicere quare:
>   hoc tantum possum dicere, non amo te.
>
> A. I don't like you, Sabidius.
>
> B. [Why is that?]
>
> A. I don't really know; all I can say is that—I don't like you.

We may see the point of this as a sober observation about the unaccountable chemistry of human relations. At the same time, it begins with a provocative remark, and its subsequent pointlessness allows us to detect the flavor of a true metajoke:

> A. Do you know why I don't like you, Sabidius?
>
> B. No, why?
>
> A. Don't ask *me.*

Here is a similar joke from Freud.[5]

> A. Life is a suspension bridge.
>
> B. Why is that?
>
> A. How should *I* know?

With these complications in mind we can turn to several other epigrams.

> **IV.65** Oculo Philaenis semper altero plorat.
>   quo fiat istud quaeritis modo? lusca est.
>
> A. Philaenis always cries from one eye.
>
> B. Oh? Why is that?
>
> A. She *has* only one eye.

The initial statement with its suggestion of medical oddity triggers the expectation that the answer will be witty. The wit, then, is the lack of wit; obviously, one-eyed persons cry from one eye, and our expectation is momentarily deflated. But only momentarily, for it is surprising that she has only one eye: the epigram in fact ridicules deformity, and so there is a point, though we reach it through a banal answer.

> **IV.43** Non dixi, Coracine, te cinaedum:
> non sum tam temerarius nec audax
> nec mendacia qui loquar libenter.
> si dixi, Coracine, te cinaedum,
> iratam mihi Pontiae lagonam,
> iratum calicem mihi Metili:
> iuro per Syrios tibi tumores,
> iuro per Berecyntios furores.
> Quid dixi tamen? Hoc leve et pusillum,
> quod notum est, quod et ipse non
>   negabis:
> dixi te, Coracine, cunnilingum.

A. I didn't call you a queer, Coracinus—I'm not that kind of person and I don't tell lies. I swear that I didn't call you a queer.

B. Well, what did you call me?

A. Nothing much, nothing you wouldn't say of yourself; you're a—cunt-licker.

This illustrates the other facet of "suspension": the climax by which expectation is outdone. We are led to expect not an insult but rather a soothing, anti-climactic disclaimer, and the joke is the provocative insolence. Two other epigrams play climax against anti-climax more subtly:

> **IX.4** Aureolis futui cum possit Galla duobus
> et plus quam futui, si totidem addideris,
> Aureolos a te cur accipit, Aeschyle, denos?
> non fellat tanti Galla. Quid ergo? Tacet.

A. Galla can be screwed for $50, and she'll do more than that for $100.

B. What do you get for $250?

A. For that she keeps her mouth shut.

> **XII.26** A latronibus esse te fututam
> dicis, Saenia: sed negant latrones.

Saenia, you say that robbers raped you; they say they didn't.

Here interplay invites a category error. In the first, some sort of climactically shameless sexual act turns out to be nothing more than Saenia's talk—but that is her greatest indecency; in the second, formal banality conceals climax when "we *didn't* rape her" is seen actually to be "we didn't *rape*," i.e., either "we did much worse" or "she went along willingly."

The joke at Coracinus' expense is a convenient place to start ranking Martial's epigrams in terms of codes. Its brutally blunt language is at the farthest remove from the code of ordinary decency, and as we have noted, violation may be so gross as not properly to be wit at all:

> **IV.50** Quid me, Thai, senem subinde dicis?
> nemo est, Thai, senex ad irrumandum.
> Why do you always call me old, Thais?
> Nobody is old—for sucking.

In the following epigrams impropriety is turned into genuine wit through a more subtle violation of expectation:

> **IV.56** Munera quod senibus viduisque ingentia
>   mittis,
> vis te munificum, Gargiliane, vocem?
> sordidius nihil est, nihil est te spurcius uno,
> qui potes insidias dona vocare tuas:
> sic avidis fallax indulget piscibus hamus,
> callida sic stultas decipit esca feras.
> quid sit largiri, quid sit donare docebo,
> si nescis: dona, Gargiliane, mihi.

A. It's disgusting, Gargilianus, the way you send gifts to flatter old men and widows. You call that a gift? It's nothing but a hook to catch fish.

B. How should I give gifts?

A. To—me.[6]

This is still fairly heavy-handed; impropriety can be more effectively veiled through (apparent) irrelevance:

> **X.8** Nubere Paula cupit nobis, ego ducere
>   Paulam
> nolo: anus est. Vellem, si magis esset anus.

Paula wants to marry me, but I won't have her because she's too old. I would, if she were—older.

Freud's example of this technique has an even more incoherent sound: "A wife is like an umbrella—sooner or later one takes a cab."[7] The initial sound of logical inconsequence masks and thereby turns improperly candid greed or lust into wit (the older she is, the sooner she will die and leave her money; marriage takes care of most sexual needs, but emergencies call for public means).

> **I.10** Petit Gemellus nuptias Maronillae

    et cupit et instat et precatur et donat.
      Adeone pulchra est? Immo foedius nil
est.
      Quid ergo in illa petitur et placet?
Tussit.

A. Gemellus is absolutely crazy about marrying Maronilla. He asks her all the time, sends gifts, begs, insists.

B. She's really pretty, eh?

A. Oh, no; ugly as Satan.

B. What does he like about her then?

A. Her cough.

The answer to the first question appears grossly illogical and sets up a puzzle resolved when we grasp the point of the second answer: a cough is a sign of consumption, of imminent death and of—inheritance. The violation of expectation is thus two-fold: the logical connection between "cough" and "money" is disguised and made to seem unreasonable; when we see that there is a connection, we also realize that it is improper.

We have noted that questions help channel a line of thought in the direction necessary to spring the joke. Freud discusses how a series of repeated statements can work in the same way by locking in a train of thought—making it "automatic"—so that critical resistance is lulled and the result is incongruity or unintended congruity.[8] In the following instance a violation of neutrality is wittily played out in a verbal lock-step:

In the Second World War an English bomber strays over Switzerland.

A. You are in Swiss airspace.

B. We know it.

A. If you don't leave immediately we will shoot.

B. We know it.

A. We're going to shoot.

B. We know it.

A. We're shooting.

B. You missed.

A. We know it.

The epigrams' rigid metrical pattern lends itself especially well to this kind of joke:

I.77 Pulchre valet Charinus et tamen pallet.
    parce bibit Charinus et tamen pallet.
    bene concoquit Charinus et tamen pallet.
    sole utitur Charinus et tamen pallet.
    tingit cutem Charinus et tamen pallet.
    cunnum Charinus lingit et tamen pallet.

    Charinus has good health—and yet is
pale.
    Charinus doesn't drink much—and yet is
pale.
    Charinus eats sensibly—and yet is pale.
    Charinus takes the sun—and yet is pale.
    Charinus uses cosmetics—and yet is
pale.
    Charinus licks cunt—and yet is pale.

II.33 Cur non basio te, Philaeni? calva es.
    cur non basio te, Philaeni? rufa es.
    cur non basio te, Philaeni? lusca es.
    haec qui basiat, o Philaeni, fellat.

Why don't I kiss you, Philaenis? You're bald.
Why don't I kiss you, Philaenis? You're red.
Why don't I kiss you, Philaenis? You're one-
eyed.
    Anyone who kisses that, Philaenis—
sucks.

In the last line Charinus is pale because he is effeminate or so shameless that he cannot blush; in the former case, paleness is incongruous within its line, though congruous in form and content with the other lines; in the latter case, it is congruous within its line, while the line itself, though congruous in form with the previous lines, is incongruous with their content. The Philaenis epigram is very close to riddle jokes ("What is bald, red and one-eyed?"), and we are carried by the hypnotic pattern (as we are in the first epigram) irresistibly into the (in)congruity of the answer, which depends on the sustained double entendre of a description that up to this point has been quite innocent.

XI.47 Omnia femineis quare dilecta catervis
    balnea devitat Lattara? Ne futuat.
Cur nec Pompeia lentus spatiatur in umbra
    nec petit Inachidos limina? Ne futuat.
Cur Lacedaemonio luteum ceromate corpus
    perfundit gelida Virgine? Ne futuat.
Cum sic feminei generis contagia vitet,
    cur lingit cunnum Lattara? Ne futuat.

Why does Lattara avoid the women at the
    public baths?
So as not to screw.
Why does he avoid the red-light district?
So as not to screw.
Why does he bathe in cold water?
So as not to screw.

Well, if he hates women so, why does he—
    lick cunt?
So as not to screw.

The last answer is incongruous with the earlier flow of thought: rejecting ordinary sexual activity turns out to be not a sign of chastity but of an abnormal practice, and the ambivalence is again set up by the fixed syntax which freezes expectation in order to betray it.

Before taking up the direct ambivalence of word play we can consider several other examples of syntactical ambivalence generated by a sudden shift in the emphasis of a statement.

In Nazi Germany Adolph Stinkfuss goes to the registrar's office and requests permission to change his name. The official takes his name down and agrees with a knowing laugh that a change is in order.

'Now, then,' he says, 'What new name do you want?'

'Moritz Stinkfuss.'

IV.84 Non est in populo nec urbe tota
    a se Thaida qui probet fututam,
    cum multi cupiant rogentque multi.
    Tam casta est, rogo, Thais? Immo fellat.

A. Nobody in town can claim to have screwed Thais, though they wish they could.

B. Is she really that chaste?

A. Oh no—she sucks.

XI.62 Lesbia se iurat gratis numquam esse
    fututam.
    Verum est. Cum futui vult, numerare solet.

Lesbia swears that she has never been screwed for free. And it's true—she always pays for it.

In one way or another these jokes initially misdirect our attention so that we grasp the statement at the wrong point only to have everything snap into place at the end. The effect is like that of two people speaking past each other.[9]

When the shift in how a sentence can be construed depends on a single word rather than on a broader instability in syntax the wit is double entendre.

V.47 Numquam se cenasse domi Philo iurat,
    et hoc est:
    non cenat, quotiens nemo vocavit eum.

Philo swears that he never dines at home. And it's true; when he's not invited out, he has nothing to eat at home.

XII.79 Donavi tibi multa quae rogasti;
    donavi tibi plura quam rogasti:
    non cessas tamen usque me rogare.
    Quisquis nil negat, Atticilla, fellat.

I gave you all you asked, I gave you more than you asked, but you always want more; a man who doesn't say "no" to anything, Atticilla—sucks.

XI.49 (50) Nulla est hora tibi qua non me,
    Phylli, furentem
    despolies: tanta calliditate rapis.
nunc plorat speculo fallax ancilla relicto,
    gemma vel a digito vel cadit aure lapis;
nunc furtiva lucri fieri bombycina possunt,
    profertur Cosmi nunc mihi siccus onyx;
amphora nunc petitur nigri cariosa Falerni,
    expiet ut somnos garrula saga tuos;
nunc ut emam grandemve lupum mullumve
    bilibrem,
    indixit cenam dives amica tibi.
Sit pudor et tandem veri respectus et aequi:
    nil tibi, Phylli, nego; nil mihi, Phylli, nega.

Phyllis, you've got a bottomless bag of tricks to fleece me—a lost ring to replace, an empty perfume bottle, some wine, a big dinner. Come on! Be fair! I don't deny you anything—don't you deny me anything.

The last two epigrams use different senses of "say no" or "deny"—mercenary and sexual—and the ambivalence is resolved abruptly in the former by the last word, which is primarily sexual ("to say no to nothing" suggests willingness to do anything) though also appropriate to the mercenary situation (never "to refuse the demands" of a greedy person is to be a "sucker" = "fool").[10] The joke about the parasite who dines at others' expense happens to work perfectly in English because "have to eat" = "eat/possess food."

Double entendre is, of course, easily the most common and in many ways most effective sexual joke because it adds to the forbidden sexual allusion the pleasure of blurring logic through equivocation and distorting language through verbal cleverness. Sexual double meaning is potentially present almost anywhere in language. In addition, the specifically sexual, alternative vocabulary which every language creates opens up an even wider range of word play (e.g., "Dick is a four-letter word"), and because one of the meanings is innocent, double entendre stays close to the public code.[11]

II.56 Gentibus in Libycis uxor tua, Galle,
    male audit

inmodicae foedo crimine avaritiae.
sed mera narrantur mendacia: non solet illa
accipere omnino. Quid solet ergo? Dare.

Gallus, in Libya your wife has a reputation for taking
[favors]. But it's all lies; she never takes [favors],
she—gives them.

III.79 Rem peragit nullam Sertorius, inchoat
omnes.

       hunc ego, cum futuit, non puto
perficere.

It's always 'go' on all sorts of projects with
Sertorius, but never 'come'—and that's true when
he screws, too.[12]

XII.20 Quare non habeat, Fabulle, quaeris
uxorem Themison? habet sororem.

Do you want to know why Themison doesn't have
a wife, Fabullus? He's got a sister [euphemism for
"mistress" with a hint at incest].

As a form of equivocation word play brings out the
subversion of logic and language in wit. The more
ingenious and complex the pun, the more dramatic the
confusion in reality, and we can end with one of
Martial's best:

II.17 Tonstrix Suburae faucibus sedet primis,
cruenta pendent qua flagella tortorum
Argique Letum multus obsidet sutor.
sed ista tonstrix, Ammiane, non tondet,
non tondet, inquam. Quid igitur facit?
Radit.

A. The lady barber who has a shop in the redlight
district doesn't give you a hair cut, Ammianus.

B. What does she do?

A. She gives you a shave.

The word for "shave" can also mean "clip" in the
sense of "rob" (cf. our "clip joint") as well as "skin"
in an obscene sense, and the triple entendre is the
more effective because the trigger word "shave" is on
the initial, innocent level a simple alternative to "hair
cut."[13]

Notes

[1] Burnikel 1980; Siedschlag 1977; cf. Richlin 1983.59
f. for the pertinence of Freud's theory to Roman humor
in general. I would like to thank my colleagues Barry
Powell and Martin Winkler for their suggestions.

[2] Freud 1905.90 ff.

[3] Marfurt 1977.44 (note 5); 89 for *Metawitz* and
Unsinnwitz, also discussed as "shaggy dog" jokes by
Stewart 1978.78 f. (Most of the modern jokes not
taken from Freud which I cite come from Marfurt).
Another example is the familiar "Have you heard the
latest joke?/ No/ Neither have I." Anti-climax (which
we will deal with shortly) is very clear in this instance, as it is in several other jokes in Freud (92):
"Not only did he disbelieve in ghosts, he was not
even frightened by them."

[4] Cf. Freud 1905.69: "Can you dye a horse blue? /
Yes, if he can stand boiling." Freud (57) also quotes
a proverb turned into a stupid statement: "Never to be
born would be the best thing for mortal men, but this
happens to scarcely one person in a hundred thousand."

[5] Freud 1905.139.

[6] V.32 is a less effective version of the same joke:
"Crispus didn't leave anything to his wife/ To whom
did he leave it?/ To himself."

[7] Freud 1905.110.

[8] Freud 1905.64 f. deals with automatism in jokes; for
a somewhat different type cf. Burnikel 1980.121.

[9] Cf. Freud 1905.70: Frederick the Great heard of a
preacher in Silesia who had the reputation of being in
contact with spirits. He sent for the man and received
him with the question, "You can conjure up spirits?"
The reply was, "At your Majesty's command. But
they won't come." (Hotspur makes the same joke in
Henry IV, part I, Act 3, Scene 1).

[10] For "suck" *(fello)* used as a general term of contempt or empty abuse as it is in English cf. Adams
1982.130 f.

[11] Cf. Freud 1905.100 for the social topography of
wit: "The greater the discrepancy between what is
given directly in the form of smut and what it necessarily calls up in the hearer, the more refined becomes the joke and the higher, too, it may venture to
climb into good society."

[12] The Latin is literally, "Sertorius finishes nothing,
begins everything/ I don't think he even finishes screw-
ing." *Perficere* ("finish") evidently has a specifically
sexual sense.

[13] Freud 1905.72 cites an epigram of Lessing based
on a Greek epigram also imitated by Martial and turned
into another exceptionally effective word play, which
in addition reverses the usual order of question/an-
swer to force the *hearer* to spring the joke: "Fabulla
swears that the hair she buys is her own—and she's

not really lying is she, Paulus?" (VI.12); cf. Burnikel 1980.52 f. . . .

Bibliography

Adams, J. N. 1982. *The Latin Sexual Vocabulary.* London. . . .

Burnikel. W. 1980. *Untersuchungen zur Struktur des Witzepigramms bei Lukillios und Martial.* Wiesbaden.

Freud, S. 1905. *Jokes and their Relation to the Unconscious.* Standard Edition, vol. VIII (1960). London.

Marfurt, B. 1977. *Textsorte Witz.* Tubingen. . . .

Siedschlag, E. 1977. *Zur Form von Martials Epigrammen.* Berlin.

Stewart, S. 1978. *Nonsense.* Baltimore and London.

N. M. Kay (essay date 1985)

SOURCE: An introduction to *Martial, Book XI,* Duckworth, 1985, pp. 14-18.

[*In the following excerpt, Kay provides a concise overview of Martial's literary legacy in Italy, England, France, and Spain.*]

. . . Martial was well known in late Antiquity: authors like Ausonius,[30] Sidonius Apollinaris,[31] and Luxorius[32] quoted from him and imitated him; the grammarians used him for illustrations;[33] and in the seventh century Isidore of Seville cites him some fourteen times, though twelve of these instances are from the *Xenia* and *Apophoreta*.[34] During the following years Martial continued to be known to Carolingian and other scholars, and, though some of their knowledge of him stems from the grammarians, Isidore and each other, some is independent of these sources; we find citations in Alcuin's pupils Hrabanus Maurus (776-856) and Theodulf (d. 821), and in Maurus' pupil Walahfrid Strabo (*c.* 809-49).[35] In the early Middle Ages Martial enjoyed popularity in England: the epigrammatist Godfrey of Winchester (*c.* 1050-1107)[36] produced good enough imitations to be confused with him in succeeding centuries; Henry of Huntingdon (d. 1154?)[37] used deliberate echoes of him in his small output; and John of Salisbury (*c.* 1115-80)[38] knew him better than anyone since Antiquity (his quotations include **11.56.**15f. and **11.104.**19f.). At a slightly later date we find Vincent of Beauvais (d. 1264) citing liberally from **Book XI** (e.g. **55.**3; **56.**1f.; **56.**15f.; **68.**1f.)[39] So from Antiquity to the Middle Ages there is no time at which Martial drops completely from sight; though never one of the most popular authors,[40] knowledge of him and interest in him was always somewhere maintained.

With the thirteenth century we come to the North Italian pre-humanists, in particular Lovato Lovati (d. 1309), Albertino Mussato (d. 1329), and Zambono di Andrea (d. 1315), all of whom were familiar with Martial; they heralded the great revival of learning of the humanists and a continuing concern with Martial in the period.[41] Petrarch and Boccaccio both allude to him,[42] though his importance and influence grew greater in the fifteenth century: a notable case in point was one of the great book collectors of the day, Giovanni Aurispa (*c.* 1369-1459); he was a friend of Antonio Beccadelli, whose collection of epigrams called *Hermaphroditus* (written *c.* 1425) caused a literary scandal. One of the poems (1.41) asks Aurispa to send a copy of Martial (which he did; it still exists); and the generally obscene tone of Beccadelli's work clearly shows the influence of Martial, though he had a voice of his own and produced epigrams far more lively and humorous than most neo-Latin poets and poetasters.[43] A single example must suffice, chosen for its similarity in subject to **11.21**:

> Ad Aurispam de Ursae Vulva (2.7)
>
>   ecquis erit, vir gnare, modus, ne
> vulva voracis
> Ursae testiculos sorbeat usque meos?
> ecquis erit, totum femur haec ne sugat hirudo,
> ne prorsus ventrem sugat ad usque meum?
> aut illam stringas quavis, Aurispa, medela,
> aut equidem cunno naufragor ipse suo.

In this same period Martial began to be read in Italian schools, which further boosted his popularity (some 110 manuscript copies of the time bear adequate witness)[44]—the placing of an author on school curricula often confirms a resurrection of his work or a deepening of interest in him. This also resulted in an increased output of imitations: many such neo-Latin pieces survive,[45] for the most part tediously uninteresting, but some, like those of Politian (1454-94) and Marullus (*c.* 1453-1500), well worthy of note.[46] Martial was one of the first authors to benefit from the advent of printing (first edition Rome 1470/1), and Calderinus' huge commentary, which is still of interest, appeared in 1474.[47]

This Italian work on Martial awakened interest in the rest of Europe: during the sixteenth century we find poets imitating and translating him for the first time in the vernacular. In France this begins in the 1530s with M.Scèves and the Lyons poets, Etienne Dolet, Nicolas de Bourbon and Gilbert Doucher;[48] Clement Marot wrote his epigrams in *c.* 1544, though they were not published until 1596—in them he draws much on Martial, but he often expands on the original to suit the social conditions of his day.[49] This is his version of **11.62,** '*De Macée*':

Macée me veult faire ecryore
Que requise est de marrite gent.
Tant plus viellist, plus a de gloire
Et jure comme ung vieulx sargent
Qu' on n'embrasse point son corps gent
Pour neant; et dit vray Macée:
Car toujours elle baille argent
Quant elle veult estre embrasée.[50]

Though the poets of the Pleiad knew Martial and produced some creditable copies of him,[51] they formulated
a policy of denigrating him in favour of Catullus: thus
of Ronsard's three translations (of **2.17; 3.46** and **9.73**),
the two latter were removed from later editions of his
poetry. Michel de Montaigne, very widely read in ancient literature, gives more than forty quotations of
Martial in his *Essays*—quotations which he sometimes
doctors to suit his own ends; in one essay he displays
a thorough acquaintance with the sexual material of
Book XI.[52] François de Maynard wrote the bulk of his
epigrams between 1615 and 1642, by virtue of which
he was labelled 'alter Gallico in orbe Martialis'; as a
riposte to the Venetian Andrea Navagero (1483-1529),
who had burned a copy of Martial each year, he had a
copy made for himself annually. Though he expands a
lot on the originals, he is by no means slavish in his
imitation and displays considerable innovation.[53]

Meanwhile the epigram was flourishing in England in
a century (*c.* 1550-1650) in which it reached a perfection which falls short of only Martial himself. Sir
Thomas More had published his epigrams in 1518, but
they rely heavily on the Greek Anthology and show
little familiarity with Martial.[54] One of the first English
translations of Martial, by Henry Howard, Earl of Surrey
(*c.* 1517-47), is also one of the best known and deservedly so:

My friend, the things that do attain
    The happy life be these, I find:
The riches left, not got with pain;
    The fruitful ground, the quiet mind . . . [55]

By 1550 Martial was being taught in the schools, and
the composition of epigrams in Latin was a daily chore
for many boys;[56] but the result was a rich crop of
imitators and translators towards the end of the century. Of these the most worth reading are Timothy
Kendall, George Turbevile, Edward Guilpin, Thomas
Bastard, Sir John Davies, John Weever and John
Harington.[57] A piece of Bastard's can stand as a motto
for them all (1.17):

Martiall, in sooth none should presume to
    write
Since time hath brought thy Epigrams to
    lighte:
For through our writing, thine so prais'de
    before

Have this obteinde, to be commended more:
    Yet to our selves although we winne no
    fame,
Wee please, which get our maister a good
    name.

But though they do indeed all owe much to Martial,
these poets at their best (debatably Davies and
Harington) provide their own witty turns of phrase and
describe or lampoon situations and people of their own
day to great effect. And they paved the way for the
epigrammatists who have made the most innovative
and durable use of Martial's legacy—Ben Jonson,
Robert Herrick and John Donne.[58] A contemporary of
theirs was the Welshman John Owen (*c.* 1560-1622),
whose Latin epigrams (about 1500 of them in ten books,
the vast majority being single elegiac distichs) gained
almost as much renown, and were translated and imitated almost as much as those of Martial.[59]

Much the same pattern is followed by the Spanish
vernacular epigram: the first sign of Martial's influence comes with the translation of *Sp.* **25b** by Garcilaso
de la Vega (*c.* 1501-36); the Sevillan Juan de Mal-
Lara (*c.* 1524-71) translated over thirty of Martial's
pieces, among them **11.32; 100** and **101;** best known
are Baltasar Gracian y Morales (1601-58),[60] who quoted
freely from Martial in his prose works, and Francisco
de Quevedo (1580-1645), who used Martial pointfully
in his own satirical verse,[61] as well as making some
straight translations.[62]

Thus in England, France and Spain the impulse from
Italy led to a flourishing of epigrammatic activity during the sixteenth and seventeenth centuries, especially
the years 1550-1650. In Germany that flourish began
rather later, the vernacular superseding the Latin epigram only after 1650, whereupon many minor poets[63]
addressed themselves to the task of imitating Martial:
none can be said to rise above the merely competent.[64]
As a sample here is G.P. Harsdörffer's (1607-58) version of **11.92**, *'An den Klügelmann'*:

Der fehlt Herr Klügling sehr, der dich
    schalhaftig nennt,
Du bist die Schalkheit selbst, wie männiglich
    bekennt.[65]

From the eighteenth century onwards there have been
many translators of Martial, both in prose and verse,
but none that have been anywhere near as successful
or entertaining as their predecessors[66] (the reason lies
in the fact that they have been for the most part translators pure and simple; they have not tried to adapt
Martial to their own style, idiom and climate as, for
example, Beccadelli, Jonson or Herrick did). To take
an example: one James Elphinston rendered all of
Martial into verse, but his fame rests on the ridicule
his efforts evoked from Burns:

O thou whom Poesy abhors,
Whom Prose has turned out of doors,
Heard'st thou yon groan?—proceed no further!
'Twas laurelled Martial calling, Murther! . . .

Notes

. . .[30] See G. Bernt, *Das lateinische Epigramm im Ubergang von der Spätantike zum frühen Mittelalter, Münchener beiträge zur Mediävistik und Renaissance Forschung* 2 (1968), p.46.

[31] ibid. p.95.

[32] ibid. p.108f.

[33] ibid. p.181: M. Manitius, *Philologus* 3 (1890), p.560f.

[34] Bernt, op.cit. p.181.

[35] ibid. p.183; 242n.27.

[36] See F. R. Hausmann, *M. in Italien, Studi Medievali* 17 (1976), p.173f.; F. J. C. Raby, *A History of Secular Latin Poetry in the Middle Ages*[2] (1957). 1.p.41.

[37] e.g. the reminiscence of 11.5.3 'difficile est opibus mores non tradere, Zeta' (T. Wright, *Satirical Poets of the Twelfth Century, Rerum Britannicarum Medii Aevi Scriptores* 59b (1872), 2.p.166).

[38] See Hausmann and Manitius locc.cit.

[39] ibid.

[40] e.g. his works are listed in only about a dozen medieval library catalogues: see Bernt, op.cit. p.178f.

[41] See Hausmann, op.cit. p.178f.; and passim, for humanist work on M.

[42] ibid. p.179f.; G. Martellotti, *RCCM* 2 (1960), p.388f.

[43] See Hausmann, op.cit. p.186f.

[44] ibid. p.191f.

[45] Some can be found in the anthologies of Ranutius Gherus (i.e. Jan Gruter): *Delitiae Poetarum Italorum; Gallorum;* and *Belgicorum.*

[46] See L. Bradner, *M & H* 8 (1954), p.62f.

[47] The first commentary on M. may have been that of the Englishman John Marrey (d.1407), but the authenticity of the work is doubted by F. R. Hausmann (*Catalogus Translationum et Commentariorum, Medieval and Renaissance Latin Translations and Commentaries,* ed. F. E. Cranz and P. O. Kristeller, 4 (1980), p.295).

[48] See K. H. Mehnert, *Sal Romanus und Esprit Français, Romanistiche Versuche und Vorarbeiten* 33 (1970), p.47f.

[49] ibid. p.55f.

[50] ed. C. A. Mayer (1970), no.174.

[51] For versions of 11.63 and 68 by de Baif, see E. T. Simon's complete translation of M. (1819), which includes versions by many French poets. It is interesting that 11.68 is the most popular piece for imitation in this book with eleven examples: how many, one wonders, go back to the original, and how many were redone from a French version?

[52] See D.Coleman, ap. R. R. Bolgar, *Classical Influences on European Culture A.D. 1500-1700* (1976), p.137f.

[53] See Mehnert, op.cit. p.106f.

[54] See H. H. Hudson, *The Epigram in the English Renaissance* (1947), p.29f.

[55] From M. 10.47.

[56] See Hudson, op.cit. p.147f.

[57] See T. K. Whipple, *M. and the English Epigram from Wyatt to Ben Jonson, Univ. of California Publications in Modern Philology* 10 (1925), passim.

[58] Pieces by Jonson and Herrick relevant to this book have been quoted in the appropriate places in the commentary. See further W. D. Briggs, *CPh* 11 (1916), p.169f.; *ModPh* 15 (1917/18), p.277f.; P. Nixon, *CPh* 5 (1910), p.189f. For more general works on the English Nachleben of M. see P. Nixon, *M. and the Modern Epigram* (1927); H. P. Dodd, *The Epigrammatists* (1876); and A. Amos, *M. and the Moderns* (1858).

[59] There is an edition of Owen's epigrams by J. R. C. Martyn (vol. 1, 1976; vol. 2, 1978); he quotes Ben Jonson's opinion of the man: 'a pure Pedantique Schoolmaster, sweeping his living from the posteriors of little children, having no thinge good in him, his Epigrammes being bare narration.'

[60] See A. A. Giulian, *M. and the Epigram in Spain in the Sixteenth and Seventeenth Centuries,* diss. Philadelphia (1930).

[61] See L. S. Lerner, *A & A* 23 (1977), p.122f.

[62] Edited by A. M. Arancon (1975).

[63] See R. Levy, *M. und die deutsche Epigrammatik des siebzehnten Jahrhunderts,* diss. Stuttgart (1903).

[64] Though (at a later date) Goethe's Venetian Epigrams are notable exceptions.

[65] Again it is interesting that most imitators made for the same over- worked epigrams in M.: in Book XI, for example, 56; 92; but esp. 67 were German favourites (see Levy, op.cit.).

[66] The reminiscences of M. in *Don Leon* are a welcome exception (see 11.104 intro.). Robert Louis Stevenson's versions of 11.18 and 56 (ed. Vailima, 8.p.575f.) are disappointingly drab.

T. P. Malnati (essay date 1988)

SOURCE: "Juvenal and Martial on Social Mobility," *The Classical Journal,* Vol. 83, No. 2, Dec. / Jan., 1988, pp. 133-41.

[*In the essay below, Malnati remarks on the different attitudes toward social mobility expressed by Martial (in eight epigrams from Book 5) and by Juvenal (in a passage from the third satire). He contends that although both poets are dealing here with the same issue—the law reserving the best seats in a theater for men of equestrian status—Juvenal's treatment reveals an aristocratic bias against upstarts in general, while the principal target of Martial's satire is social pretentiousness.*]

Suetonius notes that Domitian, with the powers granted him as censor, issued an edict which revived the *lex Roscia theatralis* (*Dom.* 8.3).[1] The law, which had been proposed by L. Roscius Otho in 67 B.C., reserved the first fourteen rows behind the orchestra in the theater for members of the equestrian order. The effect of Domitian's strict enforcement of this law provided Martial with the stimulus for the creation of a cycle of eight epigrams, the *lex Roscia* cycle of the fifth book: **8, 14, 23, 25, 27, 35, 38,** and **41.** Juvenal does not allow this topic of Martial's to remain unmentioned in his satires: he devotes several lines in the third satire to it. This gives us an excellent opportunity to compare and contrast the way the two poets handle the theme and to consider their attitudes to social mobility.[2]

The comparison between Martial's **V 8** and Juvenal 3. 153-59 has been made before. R. E. Colton believes that "both poets sneer at upstarts who have risen to equestrian status."[3] I suggest the opposite, that the two poets display widely differing attitudes on the subject of social mobility. Let us first consider the Juvenal passage:

"exeat," inquit,
"si pudor est, et de pulvino surgat equestri

cuius res legi non sufficit, et sedeant hic
lenonum pueri quocumque ex fornice nati;
hic plaudat nitidi praeconis filius inter
pinnirapi cultos iuvenes iuvenesque lanistae":
sic libitum vano, qui nos distinxit, Othoni.

(3. 153-59)

Colton writes that Juvenal's Umbricius complains that, while those who do not have the equestrian census are removed from the front rows, insult is added to injury by the ushers, who admit those who are not knights but possess the equestrian census: sons of auctioneers, of procurers, of gladiators and of gladiator trainers. Nowhere, however, does Juvenal suggest that these well-dressed sons of procurers *et al.* are not equestrians. The important word is in line 155, *legi.* Those without 400,000 sesterces are not entitled *by the law* to sit in the first fourteen rows. Those whom the seating attendant allows to sit in the equestrian area do have the required property qualification. Juvenal's real complaint is against the law which favors money. In line 159 the satirist inveighs against the proposer of the law which divides Roman citizens.

E. Courtney's analysis of Juvenal's position is certainly right: Juvenal perceives that money is breaking up "the traditional framework of society in that *fortuna mutat genus.*"[4] For the satirist it is reprehensible that an ex-barber could challenge *patricios omnes* with his wealth (*Sat.* 1. 24 f.). He is wholly indignant that a wealthy freedman does not give way in a client's queue to a praetor of a noble but impoverished family (*Sat.* 1. 102 f.). The satirist takes a very snobbish view and sneers at the parvenu for no other reason than that he is a parvenu.

For Juvenal social mobility is in itself a cause for indignation. Juvenal's attitude stems from an aristocratic ethos, an ethos which emphasizes the innate superiority of those of high birth. This might appear inconsistent with the way he reacts to the aristocracy of his day: *Stemmata Quid Faciunt?* Throughout the eighth satire he lambastes the aristocrats for their general corruption and degeneracy. One might think that Juvenal was promoting the ideal of meritocracy with his emphasis on *mores.* But Juvenal bases his judgement of the aristocracy on a higher set of criteria than he would apply to non-nobles. The fact that Juvenal is able to single out *novi homines,* such as Cicero and Marius, who were able to comply with the expectations set for and of the aristocracy, makes the aristocratic degeneracy all the more reprehensible. In this way Juvenal is making the point that the standards are not so high as to be unattainable. If the aristocrats fall short of this standard, this is no reflection on the standard.

In essence Juvenal is reproaching the aristocracy of his day for not displaying the proper *mores* to defend its position against the upstarts. His attack against the aristocracy is therefore wholly consistent with his contempt of the parvenu. From whichever perspective one approaches it, because of his adherence to an aristocratic ethos and for purely snobbish reasons, Juvenal is disturbed by and opposed to social mobility. Is this Martial's attitude? Let us consider the epigrams of the *lex Roscia* cycle.

> Edictum domini deique nostri,
> quo subsellia certiora fiunt
> et puros eques ordines recepit,
> dum laudat modo Phasis in theatro,
> Phasis purpureis ruber lacernis,
> et iactat tumido superbus ore:
> "Tandem commodius licet sedere,
> nunc est reddita dignitas equestris:
> turba non premimur, nec inquinamur."
> Haec et talia dum refert supinus,
> illas purpureas et adrogantes
> iussit surgere Leitus lacernas.

(V 8)

In the first epigram of the cycle Martial focuses on an individual named Phasis sitting among the first fourteen rows. Phasis praises the edict for keeping the equestrian order pure, and arrogantly denounces those below the rank of *eques*. He sits there dressed in a purple cloak. Purple was a mark of dignity. A purple border on a tunic signified membership in the senate and in the patrician and equestrian orders. Higher senatorial officials wore togas with a purple stripe woven into them. The purple serves to emphasize the dignified appearance that Phasis wishes to give. Martial, however, does not refer to stripes or borders in togas or tunics; it is Phasis' *lacerna* that the epigrammatist mentions. This becomes crucial to the subsequent surprise in the poem. The *lacerna* was a cloak that was worn originally over the toga in inclement weather. It later became popular as an all-weather cloak. Augustus took offence that its use was altering the traditional and unique dress of the Romans and prohibited anyone wearing it from entering the forum or the circus (Suet. *Aug.* 40.5). The toga over a tunic was the traditional dress of a Roman and conveniently marked out the individual's membership in a particular order. The *lacerna* does not fit into the scheme. Anyone could wear any color or design of *lacerna*.[5]

In epigram **V 8,** just as Phasis is lying back getting comfortable, the seating attendant, Leitus, "ordered that purple and arrogant cloak to get up." Martial saves the operative word of the surprise twist for last. The *lacerna* with which Phasis hoped to "cloak" his plebeian status fails him. Ironically, it is the cloak which marks him out as pretentious and facilitates his removal from the *pulvini equestres*. Phasis is not an equestrian and is, therefore, not permitted to sit in the first fourteen rows.

The only similarity between epigram **V 8** and Juvenal 3. 153-59, other than the obvious fact that both passages deal with the seating arrangements in the theater, is that there is a strict adherence to the law. The law stipulates that one must possess the equestrian census to be allowed to sit in the front rows. As mentioned above, Juvenal is upset that the law favors money. This does not worry Martial; for him the law is simply the law. The dandified Phasis is not like the well-dressed sons of gladiators who are allowed to sit in the first fourteen rows. Phasis might appear to resemble the *culti iuvenes,* but he is only a *would-be* parvenu. He does not have the required census and is therefore removed from his seat. Because he *pretends* to be an equestrian, he becomes the butt of Martial's humor. Juvenal does not focus on pretence. The satirist's indignation comes to the fore, and he even sympathises with those who are removed from the front rows. There is no sympathy in Martial's epigrams on Phasis' behalf, and there is no genuine parvenu here for Martial to sneer at.

In Juvenal the emphasis is on the fact that decent, wellborn Romans who do not have the equestrian census are replaced in the front rows by dandified upstarts. One of the epigrams of the *lex Roscia* cycle deals with an impoverished aristocrat:

> Ingenium studiumque tibi moresque genusque
> sunt equitis, fateor: cetera plebis habes.
> Bis septena tibi non sint subsellia tanti,
> ut sedeas viso pallidus Oceano.

(V 27)

The epigrammatist acknowledges the man's equestrian talent, eagerness, character and birth, yet all the rest is plebeian, that is to say, he does not have enough money to qualify for equestrian status. This is the type that Juvenal writes about, the type whose removal from the front rows makes the satirist so indignant. Martial again takes a straightforward, legalistic approach: this man does not have the required census and, therefore, neither is an equestrian nor is he allowed to sit in the front rows. Martial is not interested in any other criterion. Money is the only criterion that counts. In the punchline Martial casts doubt even on the other criteria to which this man lays claim. The very fact that the man tries to escape the usher's notice and turns pale in the process negates any claim to superior *mores*. Martial is not sympathetic to this man. As far as he is concerned, this type is just as much an impostor as the Phasis type. Martial's attitude remains different from Juvenal's.

There is an epigram in which Martial appears to speak up for a worthy Roman who is going to be expelled from the seat he has taken in the front rows:

"Quadringenta tibi non sunt, Chaerestrate.
  Surge,
    Leitus ecce venit. Sta, fuge, curre, late."
Ecquis, io, revocat discedentemque reducit?
  Ecquis, io, largas pandit amicus opes?
Quem chartis famaeque damus populisque
  loquendum?
  Quis Stygios non volt totus adire lacus?
Hoc, rogo, non melius quam rubro pulpita
  nimbo
    spargere et effuso permaduisse croco?
Quam non sensuro dare quadringenta caballo,
  aureus ut Scorpi nasus ubique micet?
O frustra locuples, o dissimulator amici,
  haec legis et laudas? Quae tibi fama perit!

(V 25)

As the poem begins, Chaerestratus is already seated and some individual informs him of the approach of Leitus. The very first words that this man utters are that Chaerestratus does not have the amount of money required to be an equestrian. The anonymous individual appears to display a great concern that Chaerestratus not endure the embarrassment of being removed from his seat. It is at this point that Martial cannot contain himself and cries out to ask if there is any "friend" who would convert his concern into hard cash and give Chaerestratus the amount he needs to qualify for equestrian status.

Martial intimates that Chaerestratus, like the unnamed plebeian in **V 27,** has a character and breeding worthy of recognition. Nevertheless, without sufficient funds he does not qualify for a seat in the *prima cavea.* in **V 25** a different point is added, that Chaerestratus' "friends" are only prepared to "mouth" their friendship. They display only mock concern. Even the reward of a glowing mention in Martial's epigrams does not stir the rich to part with any of their excessive wealth. In this epigram Chaerestratus fades into the background. His pretence is not the focus of attention. Rather Martial castigates those sitting around Chaerestratus who make the pretence to friendship. Although Martial does seem to sympathize with Chaerestratus, he does *not* suggest that he has a right to sit in the front rows. Martial's indignation does not stem from the enforcement of the law which favors money. Martial's indignation is created by the *pretended* concern of the rich who are more willing to spend lavish sums on a senseless horse than a comparatively modest amount on a worthy friend. One must note that Martial does not distinguish between the new-rich and the old-rich who are sitting around Chaerestratus, nor does he indicate whether Chaerestratus is an impoverished aristocrat or a would-be parvenu. Once again Martial is not sneering at the upstarts.

There is an epigram in which Martial rails against a man who is genuinely entitled to sit among the equestrians:

Spadone cum sis eviratior fluxo
et concubino mollior Celaenaeo
quem sectus ululat matris entheae Gallus,
theatra loqueris et gradus et edicta
trabeasque et Idus fibulasque censusque
et pumicata pauperes manu monstras.
Sedere in equitum liceat an tibi scamnis
videbo, Didyme; non licet maritorum.

(V 41)

The *eques* in question is named Didymus, and he is more unmanly than a frail eunuch, more effeminate than the male concubine, Attis. Nevertheless, this Didymus talks of theaters, the different levels, edicts, the cloak of the *equester ordo* and its distinctive clasp, the annual equestrian parade and the property qualification. All these are reserves of the equestrian order.[6] Didymus is stressing his right to sit in the first fourteen rows, but Martial has already set up the antithesis between his rank as an *eques* and his unmanliness. It is at this juncture that Didymus with an effeminate hand points at men of lesser means behind the equestrian rows. This puny man flaunts his economic superiority over the plebeians behind him. But in the penultimate line Martial prepares Didymus for a fall: *"Whether you are permitted to sit on the equestrian benches, I shall consider, Didymus."* Martial is baiting Didymus by seeming reluctant to grant him his "rightful" place among the equestrians at the theater. Then, in the last three words, *non licet maritorum,* Martial pounces on Didymus. Augustus decided to honor married men from among the plebeians with their own seating area at the theater (Suet. *Aug.* 44). But this seating area would have been in the *media cavea* behind the equestrians and along with the rest of the plebeians. It is apparently an inferior position to the one to which Didymus rightly has a claim. Martial presents a paradox. Didymus is allowed to sit in the best seats in the house, but he is not allowed to sit in the ones that are not so good. Didymus actually has the equestrian census; he is not pretending to be wealthy. However, it is a reflection on him that he cannot sit among the *mariti.* Martial does not ridicule Didymus because he has money. Nor does Martial intimate whether he is a parvenu or comes from a family of long-standing wealth. The joke does not rely on these particulars.

The next epigram, **V 38,** is similar in that it is addressed to a verified equestrian, but Martial introduces a new element:

Calliodorus habet censum (quis nescit?)
  equestrem,

Sexte, sed et fratrem Calliodorus habet.
"Quadringenta seca," qui dicis, [*suka merize*]:
uno credis equo posse sedere duos?
Quid cum fratre tibi, quid cum Polluce
    molesto?
    Non esset Pollux si tibi, Castor eras.
Unus cum sitis, duo, Calliodore, sedebis?
    Surge: [*soloikiosmon*], Calliodore, facis.
Aut imitare genus Ledae: cum fratre sedere
    non potes: alternis, Calliodore, sede.

                    (V 38)

The phrase *quis nescit* suggests that Calliodorus is the bombastic, pretentious type who boasts of and flaunts his wealth whenever he gets a chance. But Calliodorus has a brother who is not so fortunate and whom he insists on bringing to the theater. Martial's reaction to this is to ask if on *one* horse there can sit *two*. It would seem that Calliodorus' wealth is enough to enable only one person to qualify for equestrian status. In the fifth line Martial brings in a new idea. He compares Calliodorus and his brother to Castor and Pollux. The comparison is particularly apt. Castor and Pollux were brothers who shared one life and there is also the pun on *eques* insinuated in line six. Only one of the mythological brothers was an *eques*, a horse-rider.

In line seven Martial again changes the thrust of his attack. He points out the fraud by casting it under a different name, solecism. To translate it into English: "Although you two are one, you sit as two!" With this solecism Martial gets across the idea that what Calliodorus is doing is not correct.

The punchline is an unexpected one and even dulls the inherent wit of the solecism, but Martial has a point in doing so. It is the brother who sits wrongfully in the front rows; yet the poem is directed against Calliodorus. The brother is insignificant, and the poet leaves him unnamed. Why does Martial do this? The brother is not the prime mover of the fraud. Calliodorus wants his brother to accompany him so as to give the impression that he is more than just another parvenu. Now that he has "arrived," Calliodorus feels that he must pretend to be of an established family.

Most of the poems set in the theater are directed against those who pretend to be equestrians. The remaining epigrams of the cycle are in this category.

    Dum sibi redire de Patrensibus fundis
    ducena clamat coccinatus Euclides
    Corinthioque plura de suburbano
    longumque pulchra stemma repetit a Leda
    et suscitanti Leito reluctatur,
    equiti superbo nobili locupleti

cecidit repente magna de sinu clavis.
Numquam, Fabulle, nequior fuit clavis.

                    (V 35)

Martial places Euclides dressed in a dark red *lacerna* in the theater talking to Leitus. Euclides tells him of the income from his farms and suburban estates and of his noble background. Then the surprise turn: "suddenly out of the pocket of this arrogant, noble and rich equestrian fell a big key." A Roman of any account would be accompanied by a slave who would attend to such things as keys. As the key falls, all of Euclides' pretensions are deflated. Martial's build-up to this turn is superb.

To end the epigram, Martial works in a play on the word *nequior* as a description of the key itself. A key could be *nequam* for being faulty and not unlocking the door it was meant for. But this particular key is *nequior* because of its ability to unlock Euclides' secret. Furthermore, Martial may be working in a play on the name Euclides, *eu* + *kleio*: well locked. The incongruity of describing a key as faulty *because* of its ability to unlock the truth of Euclides' (well-locked) circumstances is cleverly snatched up by Martial and is used to round off the epigram.

    Herbarum fueras indutus, Basse, colores,
      iura theatralis dum siluere loci.
    Quae postquam placidi censoris cura renasci
      iussit et Oceanum certior audit eques,
    non nisi vel cocco madida vel murice tincta
      veste nites et te sic dare verba putas.
    Quadringentorum nullae sunt, Basse, lacernae
      aut meus ante omnis Cordus haberet equum.

                    (V 23)

Before Domitian revived the *lex Roscia* Bassus used to attend the theater dressed in green. Green was a color worn by women and effeminate males. After the edict, however, Bassus went to the theater dressed in scarlet or purple. Martial suggests that Bassus hoped to fool the seating attendant by appearing to be rich. Martial's punchline drives home the point: "No cloak is worth 400,000 sesterces." Like Phasis and Euclides, Bassus hoped to cloak his real status with expensive, pretentious clothing.

    Sedere primo solitus in gradu semper
    tunc, cum liceret occupare, Nanneius
    bis excitatus terque transtulit castra,
    et inter ipsas paene tertius sellas
    post Gaiumque Luciumque consedit.
    Illinc cucullo prospicit caput tectus
    oculoque ludos spectat indecens uno.
    Et hinc miser deiectus in viam transit,
    subsellioque semifultus extremo

et male receptus altero genu iactat
equiti sedere Leitoque se stare.

(V 14)

Twice, even three times, Nanneius is roused from his seat and is forced to "move camp." When he is forced into the aisle, he perches himself on the very edge of the last equestrian bench. To the equestrian sitting next to him he pretends to be sitting; to the usher he pretends to be standing.

There is no punchline nor is there any witticism in this epigram. For the humor Martial relies to a great extent on the very ludicrous nature of Nanneius' behavior. Here Martial approaches the kind of humor that is found in a scene from a Charlie Chaplin film. Martial describes a vaudeville character who, by adopting the ruse of half standing, half sitting, thinks he can outwit the seating attendant. His pretence, however, gains him nothing, for his removals would have been noticed by all the equestrians and plebeians whom he is trying to impress. He only succeeds in so far as the usher is concerned, and he is not an important individual in himself.

Now that the epigrams of the *lex Roscia* cycle have been considered, we can come to some conclusion about Martial's attitude to social mobility. Does Martial sneer at the upstarts in the same way as does Juvenal? Does Martial take a snobbish approach, attacking well-dressed sons of gladiators merely for being well-dressed sons of gladiators? No, Martial does not attack one who is genuine but a parvenu; he does *not* take a snobbish approach. In **V 8** Martial focuses on Phasis not because he is an upstart who, as Juvenal would think, does not *"really"* belong on the front rows; Phasis is the butt of Martial's humor because he *pretends* to be an equestrian. He ridicules Phasis for a reason, his pretence. Most of the epigrams in the cycle ridicule the Phasis type, the one who pretends to be rich, but is not. Into this category Martial places those with whom Juvenal sympathizes, people whose *mores* and *genus* the satirist believes ought to earn for them a place in the front rows, but who do not have the equestrian census.

Martial is not concerned in the slightest about one's birth.[7] It is not often that he gives his reader a clearcut indication as to whether he is dealing with a *libertus* or a *liber* of humble origin or an impoverished *generosus*. As far as Martial is concerned, no one without the equestrian census is permitted to sit in the first fourteen rows. Martial can and does make a parvenu the butt of his humor, but never does he ridicule an upstart merely for being an upstart. Martial attacks the parvenu when he makes the pretence to being something more than a rich man, such as when the upstart makes the pretence to high birth.[8]

Juvenal and Martial then do not share the same attitude to social mobility. Juvenal's position is clear: in accordance with an aristocratic ethos, he disapproves of it. For Martial social mobility is not a problem; it is not in itself a cause for indignation. This very fact is proof that Martial does not adhere to an aristocratic ethos. Martial does not appear interested in promoting aristocratic ideals; his main concern is to expose pretence.

Notes

[1] This paper derives from my dissertation, *The Nature of Martial's Humour: an examination of the mechanism of Martial's humour and its socio-political significance* (diss. Univ. of the Witwatersrand, Johannesburg, 1985).

[2] I am cautioned by J. P. Sullivan to define the term social mobility as it concerns Martial. I agree with Sullivan that Martial is a firm believer in the proper, respectful behavior of slaves and that he hates women who usurp the privileges of men, and particularly those women who cross class barriers to mate with household slaves. Women and slaves, however, are excluded from the free male citizenry. And social mobility does not refer to a civil servant ascending the *cursus*. It is rather something more basic, more like the sons of gladiators sitting *rightfully* in theater seats reserved for equestrians.

[3] See R. E. Colton, "Juvenal and Martial on the Equestrian Order," *CJ* 61 (1966) 157-59.

[4] See E. Courtney, *A Commentary on the Satires of Juvenal* (London 1980) 27. Horace expresses the same sentiment that is found in Juvenal: *Sat. II* 5.8. *Et genus et virtus nisi cum re vilior alga est.*

[5] The distinction between the *lacerna* and *toga* is made in two other epigrams: II 57 and V 26. There a certain Cordus used his magnificent cloak to obscure his impoverishment.

[6] The points listed are: Domitian's edict reviving the *lex Roscia,* the *trabea* and *fibula* worn by the equestrians in the annual parade of the equestrians held on the Ides of July and, finally, the property qualification for membership in the equestrian order.

[7] That is, in so far as he was not born into slavery.

[8] In a paper delivered at the *Conferencia sobre Marcial Calatayud* (May 1986), J. P. Sullivan expresses a very different opinion on the subject of Martial's attitude toward social mobility: "The satiric energy [of Martial] is stimulated by the shock he feels at the disregard of the conventional ordering of his ideal Roman society" (p. 25). "In the class-conscious world in which

Martial moves the stigma of lowly birth remains" (p. 19). (I would agree with this statement if to be born into slavery is what is meant.) And Sullivan particularly alerts us to the *cerdo* epigrams of book three: 16, 59 and 99 (pp. 18 f.). Sullivan would suggest that Martial conveys a resentment that the shoemaker usurps magisterial privilege by putting on games and spectacles and that this is evidence for concluding that Martial is basically a conservative social critic who disapproves of social mobility. But is there anything in the *cerdo* epigrams to suggest that Martial contradicts the impression he gives in the *lex Roscia* cycle? To test my analysis of the *lex Roscia* cycle in light of the *cerdo* epigrams one need only ask if Martial ridicules the shoemaker *merely for being a rich man and therefore an equestrian*? The answer is that he does not. In III 16 and 59 he ridicules the *cerdo* for producing gladiatorial shows. Then why does Martial say in III 99 that it is his *ars* and not his *vita* that he ridicules? The cobbler makes the *pretence* to being a civic leader: it was normal for games to be produced by officeholders. Hypocrisy and pretence are the objects of Martial's ridicule, not social mobility. The revelation of hypocrisy and pretence is the basis of the mechanism Martial employs to create his humor. Thus there is no inconsistency between the *lex Roscia* cycle and the *cerdo* epigrams. In both groups of epigrams Martial creates his humor through revealing or highlighting pretence, and he neither concerns himself with nor is bothered by social mobility.

J. P. Sullivan (essay date 1991)

SOURCE: "Humanity and Humour; Imagery and Wit" in *Martial: An Unexpected Classic,* Cambridge University Press, 1991, pp. 211-51.

[*In the following excerpt, Sullivan focuses on the poet's structural and technical artistry. Sullivan analyzes Martial's arrangement of epigrams within individual volumes, the variety of endings and metrical forms in his epigrams, his innovations in poetic diction and imagery, and the different kinds of humor Martial employs in his verses.*]

1. Evaluating Martial

It would be a bold critic who attempted to define authoritatively the nature of Martial's best poetry and explain precisely why he has been popular and acclaimed or neglected and patronised in different periods. The wild fluctuations of his reputation over the centuries will come as no surprise to those familiar with the dynamics of reader response to literature. Then again, he offers an easy target for feminist and cultural criticism in his misogyny and obscenity, and also, in his seemingly passive acceptance of Roman ideology, of autocracy, imperialism and social brutality, he is fair game for Bakhtinist critiques.

For all that he is an *important* poet, and a salutary preliminary to any evaluation would be to consider briefly what earlier critics have regarded as his main poetic achievements or virtues. The epigrammatist has been admired for his tenderness, his humour and his realism; for his innovative mastery of the Latin language, his extensive vocabulary and his brilliant gnomic dicta; for the technical expertise of his metrics, his vivid imagery and his skilful use of rhetorical devices; for his philosophy of life and his pedagogical value; for his devotion to his homeland (the *laudes Hispaniae*) and to the glories of imperial Rome; and also for his delight in paradox, unexpected turns of thought and, not least, his subtle irony and wit.

He has been damned, on the other hand, for his obscenity, for his adulation of his emperors from Titus to Trajan, his flattery of patrons, his bloodthirstiness, his lack of pity for the physically afflicted, his unconcealed hatred of women, his pederasty or his selective homophobia, his social snobbery against freedmen, his xenophobia, his obsession with money and gifts, his unjustifiably mendicant *persona,* his hypocrisy and envy and, not least, his poetic unevenness and frequent triviality.[1]

Critical reactions to his work have been correspondingly extreme: his books were burned as an annual sacrifice by Andrea Navigero but his poetic practice was made the basis of a whole theory of poetry by Baltasar Gracián and his followers.

Some of the favourable and unfavourable judgments are unassailable—his unevenness, for example, is admitted, despite the mock-modesty, by the poet himself **(1.16).** And obviously much of the later aversion to his work is due to social, moral and religious reactions that take no account of the historical conditions and the literary constraints (and liberties) under which Martial wrote. An additional factor, perhaps, is that modern readers are often uncomfortable with the satiric vein in literature. Satire, allegorical, ironic, witty or indignant, makes us uncomfortable, witness the unease apparent in critical discussions of Swift's work by writers as disparate as Dr Johnson and F. R. Leavis. Not that *all* satire is *au fond* negative: *saeva indignatio* may be prompted by principles and expressed in language as valid as that found in 'life-enhancing' novels or passionate lyric poems.

A fundamental question, often posed, is whether Martial *at his best* is a serious poet. What are the touchstones that the critic should apply to determine the answer?

A recent, plausibly argued claim for Martial's merits runs as follows:

. . . Martial at his greatest is *consonant* with the humanity presented where it moves us most deeply. One of these moments occurs when, faced with the dread facts of death, we find the values we place on human life enhanced, and we feel that a precious thing is gone when valued people die. Most readers would agree that such feelings are more intense when death has cut short the possibility of valued life in the 'taking off' of young people.[2]

The poem put forward to exemplify this is generally taken as one of Martial's finest:

> Hanc tibi, Fronto pater, genetrix Flaccilla, puellam
>   oscula commendo deliciasque meas,
> parvola ne nigras horrescat Erotion umbras
>   oraque Tartarei prodigiosa canis.
> Impletura fuit sextae modo frigora brumae,
>   vixisset totidem ni minus illa dies.
> Inter tam veteres ludat lasciva patronos
>   et nomen blaeso garriat ore meum.
> Mollia non rigidus caespes tegat ossa, nec illi,
>   terra, gravis fueris: non fuit illa tibi.
>
>   (5.34)

> Fronto, Father, Flacilla, Mother, extend
>   your protection from the Stygian shadows.
> The small Erotion (my household Iris)
>   has changed my house for yours. See that the hell-hound's
> horrid jaws don't scare her, who was no
>   more than six years old (less six days) on the
> Winter day she died. She'll play beside you
>   gossiping about me in child's language.
> Weigh lightly on her small bones, gentle earth,
>   as she, when living, lightly trod on you.
>
>   (Trs. Peter Whigham)

Unfortunately obituaries and epitaphs are not always good places to seek out personal feelings. Behind this moving poem there is a whole tradition of sepulchral epigram,[3] on which Martial must impose his individual touches. Similar epigrammatic traditions lie behind most of his work and only the Romantic yearning for poetic inspiration, pure and undefiled, and, be it added, quite impossible to attain, calls such skilful, and often felicitous, productions into question.

What then if it were objected that this elegy for Erotion is part of a diptych, the second part of which deliberately challenges us to reread and re-evaluate the original poem? It is certainly more elaborate:

> Puella senibus dulcior mihi cycnis,
>   agna Galaesi mollior Phalantini,

> cui nec lapillos praeferas Erythraeos,
> nec modo politum pecudis Indicae dentem
> nivesque primas liliumque non tactum;
> quae crine vicit Baetici gregis vellus
> Rhenique nodos aureamque nitelam;
> fragravit ore, quod rosarium Paesti,
> quod Atticarum prima mella cerarum,
> quod sucinorum rapta de manu glaeba;
> cui conparatus indecens erat pavo,
> inamabilis sciurus et frequens phoenix:
> adhuc recenti tepet Erotion busto,
> quam pessimorum lex amara fatorum
> sexta peregit hieme, nec tamen tota,
> nostros amores gaudiumque lususque—
> et esse tristem me meus vetat Paetus,
> pectusque pulsans pariter et comam vellens:
> 'Deflere non te vernulae pudet mortem?
> Ego coniugem' inquit 'extuli, et tamen vivo,
> notam, superbam, nobilem, locupletem.'
> Quid esse nostro fortius potest Paeto?
> Ducentiens accepit, et tamen vivit.
>
>   (5.37)

> My girl, sweeter voiced than slim-necked swans,
> fine against skin as Phalanthian fleece,
> smoother than blue-veined shell-hollow,
> fished from Lucrinian pools, for her, forget
> ivory new-gleaming, first snow, purest lily.
> Brighter her hair than golden wool,
> than knotted tresses of Rhine nymphs.
> Her breath the scent of summer rose, young
> honey fresh from Attic comb, amber
> snatched from palm, still warm. By her
> the peacock is a bawd, the squirrel
> malicious, phoenix commonplace.
> Warm she lies on a smouldering bier,
> Erotion, not quite six years old.
> Fate's bitter law snatched her from me.
> My love, my joy, delight gone all away.
> And my friend Paetus won't permit my tears.
> Beating his breast, tearing his hair, bellowing,
> 'Have you no shame to mourn a common slave?
> I've lost a wife,' he says, 'and yet I live,
> a woman well-known, well-born, well-endowed.'
> You deserve a medal, Paetus, for she left
> you twenty million, yet you live bereft.
>
>   (Trs. Helen Deutsch)

Here Martial, while rejecting his interlocutor's conservative posture on the status of even darling young slaves, has aroused at least some doubts in the reader: is this a subtle palinode? For although Paetus is crass and tasteless in his criticism, he successfully subverts the long exaggerated compliments with which the poem opens and makes us read Erotion's epitaph as a clever mixture of traditional motifs with the playful, sentimental imagery of the little girl stepping bravely past Cerberus and lisping Martial's name.

Yet given Martial's poetic techniques of cycles and ironic subversion, the two Erotion poems *do* have to be taken sylleptically. Self-contained though they are in one respect, they were intended to be read in conjunction, like the other cycles, or like Ovid's Cypassis diptych. Critics who have argued that each has a different aim and therefore different rules miss the larger intentions, for each *book* has its own aims and rules also.[4] The two poems interact to develop an ambiguity, which, if latent, is still pervasive in Martial's work. It may be used jocularly, as in the Quintus-Thais diptych (**3.8** and **11**), but it can also tinge apparently sincere poems. This quality ultimately enables the poet, in political palinodes such as **10.72**, which is a recantation of his flattery of the late emperor, to insinuate doubts in the constant reader's mind about whether Martial is *ever* serious about anything, even his relationships with his patrons. A constant problem for any writer who adopts irony and wit as a major poetic mode.

It is no long step from these lapidary intimations of mortality and life's evanescence to Martial's protreptic poems on the need to enjoy life while one can, to grow old gracefully, to accept one's place in the scheme of things, to cherish friendship, and to feel no fear of death when it must come. The underlying philosophy is a typical Roman version of Epicureanism, expressed best in his most famous and most translated poem '**On the Happy Life**'. The version presented here is the earliest and perhaps the best:[5]

> Vitam quae faciant beatiorem,
> iucundissime Martialis, haec sunt:
> res non parta labore, sed relicta;
> non ingratus ager, focus perennis;
> lis numquam, toga rara, mens quieta;
> vires ingenuae, salubre corpus;
> prudens simplicitas, pares amici;
> convictus facilis, sine arte mensa;
> nox non ebria, sed soluta curis;
> non tristis torus, et tamen pudicus;
> somnus, qui faciat breves tenebras:
> quod sis, esse velis nihilque malis;
> summum nec metuas diem nec optes.

(10.47)

> Martial, the things that do attain
> The happy life be these I find:
> The riches left, not got with pain,
> The fruitful ground, the quiet mind:
> The equal friend, no grudge, no strife,
> No charge of rule, no governance,
> Without disease the healthful life,

> The household of continuance,
> The mean diet, no delicate fare,
> True wisdom joined with simpleness,
> The night discharged of all care,
> Where wine the wit may not oppress,
> The faithful wife without debate,
> Such sleeps as may beguile the night,
> Content thyself with thine estate,
> Ne wish for death, ne fear his might.

(Trs. Henry Howard, Earl of Surrey)

Why the enormous popularity of this epigram? Part of the answer lies in the surface simplicity of the pregnant language in which Martial describes the simple life. But if the sentiments are scrutinised closely, there is more contained in them than the brief exposition of a Roman philosophical ideal, even though its emotive complexity is untainted by the ironic comments that conclude Horace's picture of the quiet life in the country (*Epode* 2).[6]

There are, in fact, certain nuances easily overlooked by the modern reader or the translator. At first sight, the poem is simply a manifesto of a cultivated Epicurean conformist: contentment with the easily available pleasures of the flesh: food, drink and sex, all in moderation; the avoidance of political and civic activities . . . ; the pleasures of friendship; and, finally, the unfearing acceptance of death. But there is a specifically Roman, indeed equestrian, tincture to this receipt for happiness in its emphasis on inherited property (not necessarily from one's own family); a strong central government and a stable social hierarchy from which friends of one's own class were to be chosen; and a protected environment in which physical strength is not required for any slavish exertions, since household servants will take care of one's modest wants.

Even Martial's choice of the word *torus* (bed), a common metonymy for married life, does not exclude the possibility of more transient unions or young slave lovers. (Translators invariably opt for the more respectable interpretation.) Certainly Epicurus had held . . . that he could not conceive of the Good, if he were to eliminate the pleasures of the belly and sex. He and his followers, including Lucretius, were, on the other hand, adamant against such violent passions as romantic love, jealousy, anger, emotional blindness, ambition and avarice, all of which upset the philosopher's spiritual equilibrium. . . .

In short, this depiction of the happy life has a tempered control that ensured its popularity, but it would be difficult to argue from it that Martial deepens our sense of the human condition in the way Virgil or Dante does. This is not to deny him a consistent moral philosophy given a pithy and cultivated expression, but there are undertones of doubt and layers of qualifications that make one reject claims that in these areas of human concern he says anything strikingly new or profound. These are not areas where ambiguity and irony are appropriate vehicles of a radical new vision.

2. Form, structure and metre

Martial's mastery of form and language has also been proposed as the undeniable hallmark of his best work. The forceful compression of his aphorisms; the controlled passion of his humorous invectives; his metrical variety and inventiveness; the innovative range of his poetic vocabulary; the originality and sensuousness of his imagery; and the multiplicity and ingenuity of his wit, have all, at one time or another, attracted admirers.

A brief survey of the grounds for some of these favourable judgements might conveniently begin with the formal aspects of Martial's *oeuvre,* primarily his *ordonnance* and his epigrammatic techniques.[7]

The beginning of a book was of considerable importance. Martial almost invariably opens with some variant of the conventional gesture of dedication. Four of them (II, VIII, IX and XII) have a long or short prose preface addressed to a named individual, the theme of which was often continued in a verse epigram. The dedicatee then generally became the subject or addressee of the early epigrams.

Book I and the *Xenia* and *Apophoreta* are exceptions; the general reader, or the world at large, is the recipient of the *apologia.* Martial was not yet ready by 86 to offer a book to Domitian directly, so in **1.4** the author speaks of the volume falling into the emperor's hands by chance. The second edition of **Book X,** for obvious reasons, is without a dedicatory address, which suggests that the first edition was directed to Domitian. **Book XI** was sent to Parthenius, obviously still influential, as he was chamberlain to the new emperor Nerva, whose advancement to the purple he had helped contrive. The lost anthology from **Books X** and **XI** was for Nerva. Although **Book XII**—or part of it—was sent to Rome with a long prefatory letter to Terentius Priscus, two of the poems **(12.8; 12.11)** point to special collections sent to Trajan and Parthenius.

Martial has several ways of opening his books, apart from addressing a friend, and this allows him to strike different notes. Following his model Catullus (*Cui dono lepidum novum libellum?* 1.1), Martial likes to address or refer to his book either in mock-modest tones (**II, III, V, VI, X, XI, XII, XIII**) or, less commonly, with open self-congratulation (**I, IX, VIII**). He may use more than one poem for the purpose: there are four such in **Book III.** In this way the poet can project onto the vain little book the pride, ambition and the need for protection that are really the author's in order to solicit, in a sophisticated way, the patronage he desires. Ovid liked to distance the author from the work in the same way.

The defence of poetic obscenity (e.g. **11.2**) is a variant of this. Such openings were part of his critical strategy for the re-evaluation of the epigrammatic genre. More striking is the political approach. Like Horace in the third book of the *Odes,* Martial will place a substantial block of three or more adulatory poems to Titus, Domitian or Nerva at or near the beginning of a volume (cf. ***Spec.,* IV, V, VI, VII, VIII, XI and XII**).

For the ending of a book, Martial appears to care rather less. **Books V, VI, IX** and **XII** close abruptly with epigrams that could have been at home anywhere in the earlier parts of these collections. **Book XII,** however, closes with a compliment to the powerful Instantius Rufus, just as **Books VII** and **VIII** concluded with deferential allusions to Domitian. These provide a ringing, if spurious, finality. The most favoured close is quietly self-reflective, addressing the general, or a particular, reader or even the book itself. The books were, after all, usually open-ended collections, to be added to as circumstances dictated; hence the disregard for rounding off the number of epigrams in most books.

Books X and **XI** offer a much better sense of an ending. The elaborate poem **10.104** serves as an indirect valedictory to an old Bilbilitan friend Flavus, who is returning to Spain. It incorporates an announcement of Martial's own intention of going back to Bilbilis. The imminent departure of the ship that the book is boarding creates a dramatic finale.

Within this framework, the main structuring device is the use of epigrammatic cycles, a traditional method of composition, utilised most effectively perhaps by Catullus. Examples of these cycles have been given already, and here one need only stress that they are rarely mechanical; their aim may be to deepen our perceptions of the subject, as with the poet's return to Spain **(10.13; 20; 37; 38; 96; 103; 104)**, or, more frequently, to subvert our initial responses, as in the case of Erotion.

This unifying principle is supplemented by two other honoured principles of arrangement: *variatio* and juxtaposition. Martial carefully—and often surprisingly—breaks the possible monotony of even the praises of the emperor by inserting lighter or more humorous material (cf. the preface to **Book VIII**). But the principle of *variatio* is carried imaginatively further than this. The lengths of the poems are varied, the metres mixed and the subjects change from serious to funny. The preponderance of satiric or moralising epigrams will be leavened by literary, epideictic or overtly autobiographical epigrams. But while this *modus operandi*

suits the main corpus of a book, the significant juxtaposition can be used not only for the heavy blocks
of imperial flattery and compliments to friends and
patrons, but also for satirical dialogue between epigrams (e.g. the Quintus-Lais epigrams of **3.8** and
3.11). By separating such antiphonal epigrams Martial can inject elements of both surprise and recognition.

Such relatively simple structural devices make the books
something more than *ad hoc* or *ad hominem* miscellanies. **Book XI** is a fair example of Martial's success.[8]
This book is given a theme, that of liberty, which is
presented on two levels, linked in the opening seven
poems. First there is the political freedom which the
new regime of Nerva inaugurates, and which fits also
with the acceptable licence of the Saturnalia and, by
implication, the obscene epigrams reflecting that freedom. Both are to be enjoyed under Nerva (*et licet et
sub te praeside, Nerva, libet*, **11.2.5**); only the immorality, the hypocrisy and the unacceptable licence taken
by matrons such as Paula, and supposedly encouraged
by the hypocritical Domitian, are no longer possible
(cf. **11.7.5**). The theme of Saturnalian and literary licence is repeated in a series of epigrams on the subject
(**11.15; 16; 17**). Its connection with the palace is reit-
erated in a self-justificatory epigram addressed to the
divine Augustus (**11.20**), quoting an obscene epigram
allegedly written by that emperor against Mark Antony's
wife Fulvia.

With the interrelation of political and literary freedom
established, the poet is emboldened to make greater
use than before of poetic obscenity. He may have had
a larger repository of this kind of thing, since social
and political factors dictated his selection of epigrams
for **Books VIII-X**. Structurally this material is presented in clusters (e.g. **21-3; 25-30; 60-4; 70-5**), which
are small enough not to become tedious. The less obscene satiric pieces are juxtaposed and varied in the
same way (e.g. **31-5; 37-9; 54-6; 82-4; 92-4**). The
pairing of complementary and contrasting epigrams may
be seen in **48** and **50** and **90-1**. The most obvious cycle
in the book revolves round Zoilus (**11.12; 30; 37; 54;
85; 92**). Addressees occur and recur, examples being
Flaccus, who is given, as usual, some of the more
sexually explicit material (**11.27; 100**).

The desirable presence of architectural symmetry, verbal and conceptual echoes and recurrent themes must,
in poetic volumes, be counterpointed by novelty, variety and surprise, even shock. In **Book XI**, with 108
poems, Martial's formal and material variety is consequently wide. Longer poems (those over fourteen lines)
and distichs are scattered judiciously through the work.
The subject-matter ranges from the political to the
autobiographical; the satirical topics are interspersed
with amatory and eulogistic verses, some epitaphs, an
invitation to dinner, a *soterion* (**11.36**) and a poem in

praise of Baiae, celebrating the poet's friendship with
Julius Martialis (**11.80**).

Book XI reveals the technical devices for structuring
poetic miscellanies to their best advantage, but some
comments on the other books may be in order. **Book
I** was characterised by its immense variety, once Martial had made his defence of epigram in the prefatory
epistle. It is not until **1.22** that the themes, such as the
hare and the lion, recur and the cyclic structuring is set
to work. Significantly, as a sort of advertisement for
himself, the long poem on Bilbilis (**1.49**) is made the
centre of the book—it is, in fact, the fiftieth epigram,
if the quatrain appended to the preface is included.

Book VIII is coloured by the fact that it is dedicated
to Domitian. It is devoid of the spicier sexual elements
that Martial had proclaimed almost essential to the
genre. Most of the epigrams reflect imperial policies
and achievements or larger current issues (not least
patronage for poets, **8.55**). Verses on private life vary
the potential monotony.

The harmonious and varied arrangement of the present
Book X may be due to Martial's careful re-editing.
After a low-key opening there is a striking conclusion.
The centre is occupied by **10.47** and **10.48**. The first,
Martial's most famous poem, on the happy life, is
followed, indeed illustrated, by an elaborate dinner
invitation to a simple meal for his best, or most distin-
guished, friends Flaccus, Stella and Cerialis.

For all Martial's efforts, however, the critic has to admit
that the structure of each of the books is, in various
ways, imperfect, at least by comparison with Horace's
Odes or Propertius' *Monobiblos*. Martial had to use
the poems available to him for each collection; he had
to select from the *libelli* sent to special friends and
patrons. The individual focus and practical constraints
of such compositions might militate against the general theme and structure of a particular book, yet they
could not be readily or—profitably—jettisoned.

It is of course to the individual poems that the reader
must turn to judge Martial's technical mastery of the
genre. This is not the place to enter into the details of
Martial's command of the rhetorical devices available
to him: anaphora, antithesis, anadiplosis or *reduplicatio*
(which he uses even more than Ovid with whom he
shares a predilection for the obsolescent epanadiplosis),
accumulatio, synathroesmus, amplificatio, chiasmus,
emphasis, *epiphora,* epanalepsis or *geminatio, redditio,
perspicuitas,* hyperbole, rhyme, the priamel—the list
could be extended indefinitely.[9]

Some features of his poetic craft, or his rhetorical tactics, stand out. There is, for instance, the noticeable
fondness for dramatic openings with deictic pronouns
and adjectives, often in rhetorical questions: *Crispulus*

iste quis est . . . ? Hic quem videtis . . . The aim again is vividness, to conjure up a scene before the reader's eyes. Equally effective is to *demand* the reader's attention, asking him or her to look, admire, observe, hear or accept. Peremptory imperatives of the 'Look, stranger, look!' kind or the equivalent interrogative forms are common: *aspice, aspicis? audi, lege* or *accipe, sume* (of gifts, particularly in the **Xenia** and **Apophoreta**). Sometimes Martial will present a question to begin a dialogue, a common and effective device in Greek epigram, which was popularised in Roman poetry by Catullus. It takes the form: 'Do you ask me (*quaeris*) why/what/where/how . . . ?'[10] A neat illustration of this (and of such figures as anadiplosis, chiasmus, anaphora, duplicatio and alliteration) is **1.57**:

> Qualem, Flacce, velim quaeris nolimve
>   puellam?
>   Nolo nimis facilem difficilemque nimis.
> Illud quod medium est atque inter utrumque
>   probamus:
>   nec volo quod cruciat, nec volo quod satiat.

> My taste in women, *Flaccus*? Give me one
> Neither too slow nor yet too quick to bed.
> For me, the middle sort: I've not the will
> To be Love's Martyr—nor his Glutton either.

(Trs. Peter Whigham)

To revert for a moment to 'realism', since that is an aspect of Martial's art often praised, and indeed put forward as a defence of his ethical neutrality as a 'mere observer'—Martial the nineteenth-century novelist, as it were. This too may be seen as a rhetorical mode, . . . where the author prides himself on the originality of his discussion). This is the ability to conjure up before the audience's very eyes events and people, scenes and objects (*sub oculis subiectio*), and arouse in that audience the appropriate, seemingly shared, emotions. (Quintilian in the succeeding section contrasts this sharply with the distancing effect of humour.)

Martial achieves this most commonly through his imagery, as we shall see later, but it should be observed here that his 'realism', which he shares with some ancient as well as modern novelists, is very often a 'denigration of the real' (to use Mary McCarthy's telling phrase).[11] Such realism goes hand in hand with the zest for particularity and specificity already observed.

Beyond this larger interest, critical admiration has focused also on the closure of the poems, specifically on the witty or otherwise impressive endings. A more balanced view of the structure of the individual epigrams is to be desired, since most discussion of it seems dominated, if unconsciously, by Lessing's famous remarks on the epigram.[12]

According to Lessing, the best sort of epigram, the true epigram, has a bipartite structure. In the first part a situation is set up, commonly in an objective or apparently neutral way, but one which arouses expectations. This is the *Erwartung,* the anticipation or 'set-up'.[13] The second, often shorter, more subjective part, then provides an *Aufschluss,* an explanation or personal, often witty, comment as a conclusion.

Lessing offered a genetic explanation of the epigram's development. The *Erwartung* was originally supplied by the building, grave, monument or object on which the epigram was inscribed as comment or explanation; later the comment or explanation becomes the *Aufschluss,* with the writer providing now a preliminary verbal *Erwartung.*

The epigram, in its later artistic development, freed now from its physical anchorage, had to fulfil by itself the two originally divided functions. It had to supply an imaginary object, as it were, and also the comment upon it. Its origins, which were rooted in the limited space for genuine inscriptions, still dictated economy and brevity, which in turn encouraged pointedness and then wit. Other short poetic pieces claiming to be epigrams consisted only of the *Erwartung* or the *Aufschluss.* These would not be true epigrams, but rather anecdotes or descriptions in the one case and maxims or statements in the other.

This analysis, or rather this persuasive definition, certainly does fit many epigrams, not only Martial's, but the whole tradition of which Martial became the paradigm. Certainly it fits most of Martial's satiric epigrams, particularly those which depend on the 'surprise endings'. . . . [14] Here the *Aufschluss* is often separately signalised in various ways and by various formal devices, such as a change in the person of the verb; by posing a direct or indirect question, the answer to which is the *Aufschluss;* by the use of an attention-grabbing address to a reader or to the subject of the epigram; or even by the poet himself coming forward to deliver his own opinion or some time-honoured verdict.

The problem is that Lessing's restrictive theory, quite apart from its underlying presuppositions of curiosity aroused and then satisfied, does not fit a large number of epigrams in the *Greek Anthology* and even in Martial's own corpus. Obvious counter-examples are the ecphrastic or expository epigrams, whose closures, however satisfying, would not qualify as *Aufschlusse.* And the theory does not fit even all satiric epigrams, since in *vituperationes,* which are often a long accumulation of insultingly hyperbolic descriptions, the last unit may be the strongest, but it may not be qualitatively different from those preceding it (cf. e.g. **3.93**). The closure may even be a separate joke or pun, which satisfactorily summarises, rather than explains, the description preceding it, as in the well-known epigram on Martial's tiny estate **(11.18).**

In such instances Lessing's *Erwartung* seems more important than the *Aufschluss;* it was for such reasons that Herder preferred the terms *Darstellung* and *Befriedigung* (roughly 'presentation' and 'release'). According to this 'romantic' theory, the latter was at the service of the former, providing just a point of view on the presentation, and not vice versa, as Lessing implied.

This view restores a unity to the poetic process; it pays more attention to the whole structure of the epigram, its openings, its rhetorical and thematic development, as well as its often striking closure. The completion, when strongly determined by the preceding structure, may then be reinforced by special closural devices characteristic of epigrams, such as 'point', puns, *sententiae* and even images.

Such a broader analysis confirms the perception of Martial's artistic diversity and counters the common notion that Martial only excels at paradoxical and witty epigrams, satirical in theme and rhetorical in treatment, with the main emphasis placed on the surprise ending. Once the restrictive view of the ideal epigram as bipartite in structure is abandoned as a tool of evaluation, an examination of what Martial actually does to structure his epigrams and to provide a satisfactory sense of an ending becomes more complex.

For the satiric epigrams it is true that Lessing's notion of *Aufschluss* is useful, once the social sources and psychological springs of Martial's pointed humour, surprise endings and puns are comprehended. In such epigrams the structure needs only to lead up logically, or at least rhetorically, to the surprise ending. Martial, however, does not always conclude an epigram with a paradox or a joke, even though this was regarded as his forte by later generations. To end an epigram on a gentler note frequent use is made of a *sententia,* the concise expression of what one hopes is a general truth or a just observation.[15]

Martial has contributed more than his share in inventing or adapting such *sententiae.* Obvious examples (mostly Epicurean in sentiment) are: *vivere bis vita est posse priore frui* (to be able to enjoy one's past life is like living twice, **10.23.**8); *non est vivere, sed valere vita* (life's not just living, but feeling well, **6.70.**15); *sera nimis vita est crastina, vive hodie* (life tomorrow comes too late, live today, **1.15.**12); *aestate pueri si valent, satis discunt* (if boys stay well in summer, they're learning enough, **10.62.**12); *cineri gloria sera venit* (glory comes too late to dead men, **1.25.**8); *non bene servo servitur amico* (it's no use being a slave to a friend who's a slave himself, **2.32.**7).[16]

Parallel to the coining of newly minted *sententiae* is the borrowing of an apt quotation from another poet, a proverb or popular saying, or even a Greek word or phrase. Recognition of the familiar here gives the reader the sense of a satisfactory ending. The technique is adopted by Horace and Petronius and such epigrammatists as Lucillius.[17] Martial, for example, adapts an otherwise unknown Ovidian quotation, after first quoting it (one assumes) correctly:

> 'Ride si sapis, o puella, ride'
> Paelignus, puto, dixerat poeta . . .
> Plora, si sapis, o puella, plora.

> **(2.41.**1-2, 23)

> 'Laugh, if you're wise, young lady, laugh!'
> The Paelignian poet, I think, said that . . .
> Cry, if you're wise, young lady, cry.

Elsewhere he uses a familiar Greek saying . . . to express his annoyance at having to fulfil his drunken promises.

A favoured form of ending for Martial, as for some Greek epigrammatists, is the dialectical resolution of paradoxes, supposed contradictions or contrasts or temporal changes (before-and-after, earlier-but-now). This might bring out the similarity between two different professions:

> Oplomachus nunc es, fueras opthalmicus ante.
> Fecisti medicus quod facis oplomachus.

> **(8.74)**

> You're a swordsman now; before you were an
>   oculist.
> Your sword does now what your scalpel did
>   before.

This is a neat example because the semi-chiastic anaphora and the assonance reinforce the point.[18]

Another form of an ending favoured by both the Greek epigrammatists and Martial is the reconciliation of two opposites or contrasting extremes by a compromise or a middle way. . . .[19] The most famous example occurs at **10.47.13:**

> summum nec metuas diem nec optes.
> Ne wish for Death ne fear his Might

> (Trs. Henry Howard)

Ending a poem with two stark alternatives, often in the form of commands, was an established epigram technique, to be found in Catullus (69ff.) and the *Priapea* (1.7f.), as well as in earlier Greek epigrammatists.

Martial's use of it may be seen in **1.103**.12 (cf. **1.91**; **7.54**.8; **8.54**.3f.). Here he is castigating a victim for living parsimoniously after receiving a large legacy; the poet resolves the paradox with this line:

> Aut vive aut decies, Scaevola, redde deis.
> Either enjoy life or give the gods back their
> million.

A parallel to this technique is to end an epigram with two opposing, even apparently contradictory, statements, which may involve a play upon two different meanings or connotations of a word. A straightforward example is:

> Digna tuo cur sis indignaque nomine dicam.
> Frigida es et nigra es: non es et es Chione.

(3.34)

> Why you deserve and don't deserve your
> name,
> I'll tell you. You're frigid and you're black.
> You are and you aren't Snow White.[20]

Sometimes the story of an event, generally presented objectively, is just capped with a witty or subjective comment,[21] which may be credited to someone other than the poet, as in **1.13** where Arria Paeta's courageous declaration replaces the author's expected praise for her bravery (cf. **1.42**). In **10.64**.6 a quotation from some obscene verses by Lucan substitutes for a defence of such writing by the epigrammatist himself.

Martial's metrical expertise, like his *doctrina* and technical skills, would not have been lost on his audience. The *ordonnance* of his first book, deploying *variatio* and the juxtaposition of verse forms to snare the reader's attention would set the pattern of his later collections.[22]

His elegiac epigrams follow the contemporary pattern of four to ten lines found also in the *Garlands of Meleager* and *Philip*. Interspersed are some fairly long hendecasyllabic poems and lengthy verses in other metres, including the elaborate *ecphrasis* on the environs of Bilbilis, which is modelled on Horace's second epode on the joys of country life, and written in an unusual combination of iambic trimeters and dimeters, as though to draw attention to itself.

Martial developed his own techniques for handling these metres, since his choice of verse forms was constrained to some degree by the epigram tradition. His distaste for the experimental metres of certain Hellenistic poets emerges in his defensiveness over the use of hexameters for epigram (**6.65**) and his vigorous protest against the critic who complains that he does not use such recherché forms as galliambics (**2.86**). He limits himself largely to the elegiac couplet in aggregates of one

to five distichs, to hendecasyllables, following Catullus, and, less frequently, to scazons. There is a scattering of other metres, eleven in all.

More significant are his divergences from his predecessors and from the established Augustan standards. In his elegiacs Martial abandons the standard Ovidian rule, to which Propertius gradually conformed, that the pentameter should generally end in a disyllable; he makes frequent use of three, four or five syllable words, and even six syllable words (e.g. *inimicitiae,* **5.20**.2).[23] Martial may have been developing a trend found in Ovid's later work or returning to the elegiac practice of Catullus. Ovid's mature work had established the disyllabic pentameter ending as the norm, but this diminishes the use of emphatic words at the close of the couplet. Martial often constructs his line in the Catullan pattern of

> sed pater ut gnatos diligit et generos.

Martial's endings therefore seem stronger than those Augustan practice favoured, particularly in his striking, if infrequent, use of monosyllabic words, and in his use of elision in the second half of the pentameter and spondees in the first. The unfettered practice of his Greek models may have played a part in this.

His hexameter endings generally follow the two dominant forms in ending with a disyllabic or trisyllabic word preceded by a disyllable, trisyllable or quadrisyllable. These endings account for most of his hexameter lines, but, like the Augustans, he occasionally saw the value of ending the verse with a strong polysyllabic name or adjective, eliminating the word division altogether. Examples are *amphitheatro, Caeciliane, Marcelliano, Pirithoumque, bardocucullo.* These are generally preceded by a dactylic fourth foot, as are his sparingly used double spondaic endings (e.g. *pendentia Mausolea*). A key to the hexameter, however, is the handling of caesura to break up the line. Here Martial follows the forms established by Ovid and avoids the experimentation of some of his contemporaries.

The commonest metrical form used after elegiacs, and interspersed carefully with them, is the phalaecean hendecasyllable. Martial is more rigid (or more stylised) than his model Catullus in disallowing the substitution of a spondee for a dactyl in the second foot; he invariably uses a spondee in the first foot instead of a trochee or iambus. This last struck the contemporary ear as harsh, to judge from the elder Pliny's comments (*NH* praef. 1), and moderns may miss the Catullan flexibility.[24] Similarly the lines are tighter in the later poet, who uses only one elision in every ten lines on average, as opposed to Catullus' one in every two. Martial is careful also to avoid the coincidence of word with foot, except for special effects such as in

Campus, porticus, umbra, Virgo, thermae

(5.20.9).

Usually he plays on the opposition of word accent and verse accent and manages to introduce a variety of caesuras, although again for special effects he will allow a short succession of identically placed caesuras as in **1.109**.1-4:

Issa est passere nequior Catulli,
Issa est purior osculo columbae,
Issa est blandior omnibus puellis,
Issa est carior Indicis lapillis.

Here the metrical repetition neatly reinforces the *accumulatio* and anaphora.

The next commonest metre in the epigrams is the scazon or choliambus. Martial follows the general Greek and Roman practice of allowing a spondee in the first or third foot or even in both, although never in the fifth, where Greek practice allowed it. Dactyls are common in the third and fifth. Anapaests are allowed only in the first foot, as in Babrius, but tribrachs are very common in the second, third and fourth feet, with two examples in the first foot. The caesura is almost invariably the penthemimeral caesura, mocked by Aristophanes as Euripides' metrical trademark, the hepthemimeral being generally limited to cases where a word ending occurs.

As regards less common metres, an uncomplicated and elegant iambic trimeter is used twice by itself (**6.12; 11.77**) and four more times in combination with the iambic dimeter (**1.49; 3.14; 9.77; 11.59**), a combination borrowed from Horace's first ten epodes. The dimeter is also used once in combination with a choriamb (**1.61**).

Continuous hexameters are used on four occasions by Martial: **2.73** and **7.98** are just single lines, and of the two remaining **1.53** is satiric and highly baroque in its style (e.g. v.5: *urbica Lingonicus Tyrianthina bardocucullus* and note *'fur es'* v.12). For using the metre at all, as in **6.64,** also satiric but running to thirty-two lines, Martial felt impelled to defend himself (**6.65**).

One solitary example of two lines of sotadic verse completes the tally (**3.29**). As in the only other surviving contemporary example (Petr. *Sat.* 23.3), the ditrochaeus is allowed only in the third and not the first and second foot. The choice of metre here seems dictated by the subject, the effeminate and frequently satirised freedman Zoilus.

3. Language and imagery

Martial's structural and technical virtuosity is paral-

leled by his linguistic resourcefulness, not only in terms of sheer vocabulary (4,582 words), but also in his striking innovations in poetic diction. He draws as freely as any epic writer on the inherited materials of the Roman literary tradition, prose and verse, as well as on contemporary writing both Greek and Latin, but his flexible form allows him liberties debarred to the practitioners of more elevated genres. Hence his free use of colloquialisms, vulgarisms, archaic quotation, foreign linguistic elements, such as Spanish place names, imported nouns such as *covinnus* and his not infrequent play on Greek expressions and proper names (e.g. Earinus, Palinurus and Hippodamus).

His ability to stretch and expand the language might impress us more if we could be sure how far the *hapax legomena,* the unique words in his corpus, are his own coinages and how far they are simply rare words which would be known, if not familiar, to his contemporary readers.[25] Certainly no other author of this period, except perhaps the elder Pliny, provides so many examples.

It is in this context, the context of a deliberate attempt to extend the boundaries of poetic discourse in Latin, that we must set his obscene language, where Martial goes to the limit among Latin writers of epigram, as we know it, in embracing the crudest non-euphemistic obscenities. Catullus runs him close, but a list of the words freely used in Martial's epigrams indicates that he uses more basic obscenities than his mentor.

Opinions about this aspect of Martial's language will differ widely. It is not a question that can be resolved in this study. For some it has been further evidence of Martial's immorality and unsuitability for acceptance as a classic; for others it will be grounds for claiming him as a supreme exponent of 'literary realism', or at least a pioneer in stretching the limits of acceptable art, while drawing on unconscious sources of wit and humour. As with satire as a whole, so with obscenity: a critical unease enters the debate. Perhaps for the English reader the key to understanding Martial is a just appreciation of Swift, just as the Spanish reader should look to Quevedo and the French to Rabelais.

Among the various ways Martial has of procuring a satisfactory closure to a poem, the presentation of an image or word-picture to convey the emotional import or value judgement should not be overlooked.[26] Obvious examples drawn from nature, everyday life, traditional occupations and food include

In steriles nolunt campos iuga ferre iuvenci:
pingue solum lassat, sed iuvat ipse labor.

(1.107.7-8)

Oxen balk at bearing the yoke in unfertile

fields:
rich soil is tiring, but the labour is a joy in
   itself.

(Here an allusion to writing poetry without adequate
patronage.) A more extended series of images is found
in this epigram:

Dulcia cum tantum scribas epigrammata
   semper
   et cerussata candidiora cute,
nullaque mica salis nec amari fellis in illis
   gutta sit, o demens, vis tamen illa legi!
Nec cibus ipse iuvat morsu fraudatus aceti,
   nec grata est facies, cui gelasinus abest.
Infanti melimela dato fatuasque mariscas:
   nam mihi, quae novit pungere, Chia sapit.

(7.25)

You always write only cloying epigrams, brighter
than whiteleaded skin, with no grain of salt nor a
drop of bitter gall in them, and yet you want them
read! But even food is no joy, robbed of the bite of
vinegar, and a face is dull without a dimple. Give
kids honey apples and boring fat figs: the Chian
kind is to my taste—they're tart.

Such examples, however, may serve as introduction to
a broader consideration of Martial's imagery and metaphor as a whole. It was this aspect of Martial's poetry
that so seduced the otherwise hostile Macaulay, who
was doubtless aware that for Aristotle the mastery of
metaphor was the pre-eminent token of the true poet.
. . .

It was to be expected that images, analogies and metaphors drawn from mythology would be kept to a minimum.[27] Only in connection with the imperial cult are
the comparisons drawn from myth truly functional, and
here Martial is the heir to a tradition of imperial flattery that goes back to Augustan times. Otherwise his
mythological allusions are merely variations for common ideas and expressions, often about poetic inspiration, aiming only to stimulate stock responses in his
audience and where metrically convenient. This rejection of myth as serious artistic material is deliberate
and is part of his marginalisation, so to speak, of
epic, lyric and tragedy. Not for Martial the exploita-
tion of the powerful latent symbolism of Greco-Roman mythology as visible in the writings of Virgil,
Horace, Ovid, Seneca and even Statius. Mythic allusions may be invoked humorously: to bolster a down-
to-earth demand for marital sodomy **(11.104)**, to express a critical position through arguments in the
mouth of the Muse **(8.3),** or to liken a hundred ways
of serving squash to the grisly banquet of Thyestes
(11.31), but these instances simply reinforce the principle.

Martial's imagery draws instead on familiar, sometimes
everyday sources, ranging from the refined to the most
sordid, hence his reputation for 'realism', discussed
earlier.

The polarities between which his lively imagination
moves are extreme. As was noticed in the conclusion
of chapter 5, there is a preponderant emphasis on sensual, sometimes exotic, imagery, invoking acute tactile
and olfactory associations, as may be seen in this evocative description of Diadumenus' kisses:

Quod spirat tenera malum mordente puella,
   quod de Corycio quae venit aura croco;
vinea quod primis floret cum cana racemis,
   gramina quod redolent, quae modo carpsit
   ovis;
quod myrtus, quod messor Arabs, quod sucina
   trita,
   pallidus Eoo ture quod ignis olet;
glaeba quod aestivo leviter cum spargitur
   imbre,
   quod madidas nardo passa corona comas:
hoc tua, saeve puer Diadumene, basia fragrant.
   Quid si tota dares illa sine invidia?

(3.65)

They smell of an apple bitten by a tender lass; of
the scent of Corycian saffron; of a vine blossoming
with the first bunches of white grapes; of fragrant
sheep-cropped grass; of the myrtle and the Arabian
harvester; of chafed amber; of the redolent pale
flame from eastern incense; of the earth after a light
sprinkle of summer rain; of a garland on tresses
dripping with spikenard: all these fragrances.
Diadumenus, cruel boy, are in your kisses. What
would they smell of, if you gave them without stint
or disdain.

The same insistent evocations recur in a poem on the
same topic of a boy's kisses, written almost a decade
later. This was singled out by A. E. Housman for especial praise: 'In all Martial there are no verses of
more choice and elegant refinement' (Housman *CP*
3.1167):

Lassa quod hesterni spirant opobalsama dracti,
   ultima quod curvo quae cadit aura croco;
poma quod hiberna maturescentia capsa,
   arbore quod verna luxuriosus ager;
de Palatinis dominae quod Serica prelis,
   sucina virginea quod regelata manu;
amphora quod nigri, sed longe, fracta Falerni,
   quod qui Sicanias detinet hortus apes;
quod Cosmi redolent alabastra focique
   deorum,
   quod modo divitibus lapsa corona comis:
singula quid dicam? non sunt satis; omnia
   misce:

hoc fragrant pueri basia mane mei.
Scire cupis nomen? si propter basia, dicam.
Iurasti: nimium scire, Sabine, cupis.

(11.8)

The breath of balm from last night's vial
    pressed;
    The effluence that falling saffron brings;
The scent of apples ripening in a chest;
    Or the rich foliage of a field in Spring;
Imperial silken robes from Palatine;
    Or amber, warming in a virgin's hand;
The far-off smell of spilt Falernian wine;
    A bee-loud garden in Sicilian land;
Odour, which spice and altar-incense send;
    Or wreath of flowerets from a rich brow
    drawn;
Why speak of these? Words fail. Their perfect
    blend
    Resemble my boy's kiss at early dawn.

You ask his name? Only to kiss him? Well!
You swear as much? Sabinus, I won't tell!

(Trs. Anthony Reid)

In stark contrast to these two poems addressed to young
boys is the Swiftian description of an old prostitute
Thais, who has already been the butt of shorter but
similar aspersions—on her bad morals and fittingly bad
teeth **(4.84; 5.43)**. The impact of the lines conveying
the images of sexual and physical corruption is reinforced by alliteration and other devices and culminates
in a rank paradox:

Tam male Thais olet quam non fullonis avari
    testa vetus media sed modo fracta via,
non ab amore recens hircus, non ora leonis,
    non detracta cani transtiberina cutis,
pullus abortivo nec cum putrescit in ovo,
    amphora corrupto nec vitiata garo.
Virus ut hoc alio fallax permutet odore,
    deposita quotiens balnea veste petit,
psilothro viret aut acida latet oblita creta
    aut tegitur pingui terque quaterque faba.
Cum bene se tutam per fraudes mille putavit.
    omnia cum fecit, Thaida Thais olet.

(6.93)

Worse than a fuller's tub doth Thais stink,
Broke in the streets and leaking through each
    chink;
Or lion's belch; or lustful, recking goats;
Or skin of dog that, dead, o' the bankside
    floats;
Or half-hatched chicken from broke rotten
    eggs;

Or tainted jars of stinking mackerel dregs.
This vile rank smell, with perfumes to
    disguise,
Whene'er she naked bathes, she doth devise.
She's with pomatum smudg'd or paint good
    store;
Or oil of bean flour varnished o'er and o'er.
A thousand ways she tries to make all well.
In vain. For still she doth of Thais smell.[28]

(Trs. Egerton MS 2982)

Yet another contrast may be seen in a biting lampoon
on Vacerra on moving day, where a more heartless
picture, this time of degraded poverty, is created by a
minute but descriptively coloured mosaic of sordid
household utensils:

Vidi, Vacerra, sarcinas tuas, vidi . . .
Ibat tripes grabatus et bipes mensa,
et cum lucerna corneoque cratere
matella curto rupta latere meiebat;
foco virenti suberat amphorae cervix;
fuisse gerres aut inutiles maenas
odor inpudicus urcei fatebatur,
qualis marinae vix sit aura piscinae.
Nec quadra deerat casei Tolosatis,
quadrima nigri nec corona pulei
calvaeque restes alioque cepisque,
nec plena turpi matris olla resina,
Summemmianae qua pilantur uxores . . .

(12.32.2, 11-22)

Vacerra, you and yours are now away . . .
A three-legg'd bed was first to greet the morn,
Then an oil-lamp, a mixing-bowl of horn,
Beside a table, with two legs gone missing;
A cracked old chamber-pot, that came out
    pissing;
Under a brazier, green with verdigris,
A wry-necked flagon lay dejectedly;
Then there were pilchards, salt-fish too, I
    think,
A jug betrayed them by the filthy stink,
A powerful smell that even recked beyond
The brackish water in a fishy pond.
What else? Cheese from Toulouse its presence
    told,
A blackened wreath of flea-bane, four years
    old,
And onion-ropes—but only ropes were left—
And garlic-strings—of garlic all bereft;
A pot of resin, from your mother's lair,
That Jezebels use to strip themselves of hair.

(Trs. Olive Pitt-Kethley)

In this last poem the connection of age and squalor is

once again thrown into relief. This might suggest that the correlation of the delicate imagery of perishable flowers and fleeting perfumes with beautiful young boys and of grosser analogies and similes (persistent stinks and so on) with older ruttish women is not simply sexual, but also a matter of contrasting the evanescence of youth with death and decay. The first is seen in the poem to Encolpus, who has vowed to sacrifice his hair to further his master's career: Martial prays:

> Quam primum longas, Phoebe, recide comas
>
> dum nulla teneri *sordent* lanugine voltus
> damque *decent* fusae *lactea* colla iubae.
>
> **(1.31**.4-7)

Cut his long locks, Apollo, as soon as may be, while his tender face is *soiled* by no down and while his flowing mane *looks well* on his *milky* neck.

Other examples are **4.7** and **10.42,** where facial down and growing old are again connected, and **10.90,** where a beard is connected with death (cf. **11.22**.7-8, etc.). Elsewhere, ugly images of disease (*atra* or *sceleratia lues*) are conjured up in connection with death, as in the description of Festus' suicide **(1.78)** and young Demetrius' early demise **(1.101**.6); cf. **11.91** on Canace (*horrida vultus   abstulit et in tenero sedit in ore lues*). The metaphorical connection of female sexuality and the infirmities of old age is most poignant in the short elegy on the ageing poet Mevius **(11.46).**

Descriptions like this surely hold up a very splintered mirror in which to reflect life. There is a preoccupation with the *particularity* of things, a sharpness of eye (and nose) for the charming or disgusting details appropriate to Martial's different aims. The images become even more forceful when coupled with his frequently blunt (or realistic) language in sexual matters and his willingness to use vulgar, down-to-earth expressions, as in his descriptions of the perverted Nanneius **(11.61)** and the decadent Zoilus **(3.82).**

In the poems just cited the emphasis on the senses of sight and particularly touch and smell in the generation of the imagery stands out, but auditory images are skilfully evoked in the description of the poet's noisy neighbourhood **(12.57)** and the luxurious estates of various friends (cf. e.g. **4.64).**

As might be expected, granted Martial's other preoccupations, the whole transactional nexus of giving and receiving presents, money, dinner, patronage provides a powerful source of imagery, replete with hyperbole or meiosis, as in the description of his tiny farm **(11.18)** or the insignificant cup presented him by Paulus **(8.33)** or the strange dinners he has been invited to **(1.43; 11.31; 12.48).**

His imagistic character sketches (*vituperationes*) of those who have supposedly offended or damaged him are especially ingenious. Examples are the attacks on the brutal barber Antiochus **(11.84)**; on the unknowns who foisted libellous verses on him (10.5) or presumed to castigate his publications **(6.64)**; and on a rude dinner guest **(7.20).** Equally elaborate are the descriptions of the client's life (cf. e.g. **5.22).**

Of particular help in the creation of Martial's contextual images was the metaphorical richness of Latin. The everyday roots of words could be exposed and manipulated by a writer with a feeling for such possibilities, particularly in word play. This was highly effective in sexual and related obscene areas, where the euphemisms and dead metaphors have their literal origins in the animal, vegetable and fruit kingdoms,[29] or in such basic human activities, aggressive and agricultural, as eating, cooking, beating, fighting, killing, cutting, digging, ploughing, sowing and grinding, to name just the most obvious. Of course most of this linguistic expertise and interest is at the service of larger issues, not least his persistent attempts to degrade female sexuality and to damn the gross style of living enjoyed by such freedmen as Zoilus.

4. Wit and humour

Finally the large question remains: Martial's wit and humour, the foundations of his high prestige in earlier centuries in Europe. His reputation then as one of the greatest Latin classics is enshrined in, for example, the verdict of Sir John Harington (1560-1612), perhaps the best of the English epigrammatists after Ben Jonson. Harington wrote in the *Metamorphoses of Ajax:* 'It is certain that of all poems, the Epigram is the plesawntest, and of all that writes Epigrams Martial is counted the wittiest.'

It is sometimes difficult for the post-Romantic sensibility to share Harington's enthusiasm for this aspect of Martial's genius.[30] But then Harington was writing when mannerism was the dominant style of European poetry, English metaphysical poetry being, in its idiosyncratic way, a vigorous branch of it.

There are other obstacles also. Martial's aggressive sexual humour, particularly in its selection of satiric targets, is hardly compatible with modern conventions— or indeed with some ancient conventions. Physical defects present just one instance.[31] Much of Martial's other joke material is nowadays offensive, particularly that concerning women, slaves, passive homoeroticism, prostitution and coital perversions. On the other hand, the stinginess of patrons, the social aberrancy of freedmen in a status-conscious milieu, while not repugnant to the modern reader in the same way, seem obsolete subjects for lively laughter.

Caesar Strabo, protagonist in the dialogue, is made to say in Cicero's *De oratore* (2.54.217) that a man with some wit can make a joke about anything except joking itself (*ego vero . . . omni de re facetius puto posse ab homine non inurbano quam de ipsis facetiis disputari*). Quintilian found himself baffled by the whole phenomenon of laughter, particularly as it could be stimulated by folly and even tickling: *unde autem concilietur risus et quibus ex locis peti soleat, difficillimum dicere* (*Inst.* 6.3.35; cf. 6.3.7).

Such cautions have to be borne in mind in attempting a sketch of the *techniques* Martial employs for arousing in his readers certain amused reactions. The effort, however, may yield not only further insights into Martial's poetic craftsmanship and rhetorical skills, but also perhaps into the nature of Roman wit and humour in general.[32]

Some general aspects of joking and witticisms may be disregarded as being of overly broad application to the present limited purposes. Obviously Martial takes advantage of the fact that even a mildly humorous story gains by being presented in verse, just as any joke gains in the telling by a skilled raconteur. The more artistic and sharp the verse (or the manner of telling) is, the greater the gain in our pleasure. The deployment of poetic and rhetorical devices superimpose a glitter on even mediocre material. Truisms and proverbs gain in the same way, when they are expressed in rhyme, or incorporate alliteration, assonance and brevity, although the neat expression of these also counted as 'wit' for theorists such as Harington and Baltasar Gracián.

Any long disquisition on the nature of humour itself and the multifariousness of its terminology[33] would be out of place here, but one may start with what is now a commonplace, but one highly relevant to many of Martial's satiric epigrams, that much humour is rooted in verbal aggression, which masks its hostility and defuses any explosive retaliation by invoking amusement or admiration in the audience. Martial takes great pains to stress the jocular light-heartedness of his work and his desire not to offend individuals.[34] But Quintilian points out, anticipating Freud, *a derisu non procul est risus* (*Inst.* 6.3.7) and Aristotle had already stated [*to skomna loidorema ti estin*] (*EN* 4.14.1128a). The socially explosive topics that Martial selects for the exercise of his satiric talents also tell a different story.[35]

It is another truism that most conscious humour, and almost all wit, relies on the element of surprise or unpredictability in different forms and to a greater or lesser degree. Just as language works by narrowing almost instantaneously the range of semantic and syntactic possibilities of each successive unit in a verbal sequence such as a sentence, so experience and the laws of reasoning both prepare us conceptually for a large, but still limited, range of progressions and endings to a story or conclusions to an argument. When this process is frustrated by linguistic ellipse, for example, or the logic is derailed, the result is incomprehensibility, nonsense or, with the appropriate circumstances, paradoxes, jokes, riddles or witticisms. Metaphor and analogy depend on a similar process: the implicit or explicit likeness presented can be appropriate, startling, puzzling, incongruous, disgusting, humorous, absurd, incomprehensible or, in poetic contexts, aesthetically impressive or frigid.

Why surprise . . . is so fundamental in the generation of laughter was explained by Aristotle in his discussion of metaphor and wit . . . (*Rhet.* 1412a). Being struck by the opposite of what one thought or expected, with or without the exclamation 'Of course! What a fool I was!' is the effect also of riddles, verbal coinages and other word play. Freud makes much of this element in jokes also, when he speaks of the pleasure derived from 'seeing' hidden similarities and differences.[36]

Before examining the phenomenon in its technical manifestations, one must allude briefly to Martial's readiness to go beyond surprise to achieve *shock* by the blatant use of obscenity,[37] often in conjunction with more innocuous rhetorical formulas. These obscene jokes are invariably 'tendentious' or aggressive, but they achieve their object of amusing the reader by their very flouting of social conventions. They allow the release, often under the merest pretext of wit, of forbidden emotions and repressed impulses. Of course the cleverer they are, the more uninhibited by shame our amusement becomes.[38]

In what follows, a somewhat heuristic classification of Martial's humorous techniques is adopted.[39] The divisions, although not entirely arbitrary, are not watertight, since allocating a joke to one or another may be open to interpretation and even disagreement, particularly as Martial often employs two or more techniques at once to produce the humorous reaction. The classifications proposed are:

> I Jokes based on an empirical observation which confounds commonsense expectations, generating paradoxes and incongruities

> II Jokes based on informal syllogistic reasoning which may end in conclusions which are seemingly valid, but are, on reflection, absurd, paradoxical or shocking, often because a superficial appearance of sense hides nonsense or illicit inferences

> III Humour based on various kinds of word play, such as puns

> IV Humour based on analogical metaphor or simile

or symbolic instances

V Humour dependent on various types of rhetorical *schemata* and tonalities, such as parody, hyperbole, rhyme, anaphora or irony

I. Surprise is most obviously the ingredient in the jokes and riddles that hinge on the [*para prosdokian*].[40] An elaborated paradox may be seen in the satiric epigram on Bassa (1.90), who seemed a Lucretia because she shunned the company of men, but who was actually a lesbian adulterer. Other human paradoxes are the individuals who claim to be poets but who do not write a line of verse or write only what is unreadable (cf. 3.9). A compliment to Domitian on his moral legislation ends in these lines (6.2.5-6):

> Nec spado iam nec moechus erit te praeside
>   quisquam:
>   at prius—o mores—et spado moechus erat.

> In your reign there will be no more eunuchs or adulterers: before—the immorality of it!—even a eunuch was an adulterer.

The strange contrast (cf. 1.30; 39) between the behaviour prompted by riches and that due to poverty is another fertile theme, often with sexual overtones (cf. 6.50; 9.88; 11.87). Comparisons between the poetic craft and the vulgar arts of the zither-player or charioteer with their inequitable pay differentials provoke a sour smile (3.4). Similarly the money spent on race horses is contrasted with more appropriate and charitable uses (5.25; 10.9). A neatly balanced set of antitheses purport to describe a paradoxical emotional state (5.83):

> Insequeris, fugio; fugis, insequor, haec mihi
>   mens est;
>   velle tuum nolo, Dindyme, nolle volo.

The upsetting of the reader's normal anticipations may be achieved without perverting logical argument. It can be done merely by the production of fresh evidence. The innkeeper's traditional habit of profitably watering wine is found reversed in Ravenna, where they cheat by simply serving it neat (cf. 1.56; 3.57; 9.98). There are similar reversals of expectation when the conduct of women who profess high ideals exemplifies the opposite (1.62; 5.17). Another example is the unexpected judgement on a dandy: *non bene olet qui semper bene olet* (He who always smells nice doesn't smell nice). The Romans, according to Cicero, believed that one should smell of nothing at all.

Obviously hypocrisy and pretence in general offer the requisite conditions for such surprise endings. The *Erwartung* or 'build-up' may then consist of a more or less elaborate description of the hypocrite's overt behaviour or public professions: this is then deflated without argument by the sudden revelation of the truth, but the *Aufschluss* purports to be empirical, not subjective. Martial's satiric observation and this mode of humour are highly compatible; hence the numerous examples of vice comically stripped of its disguises,[41] as in the epigram on Bassa (1.90). Martial can manage these effects on a small or large scale. If brevity be the soul of wit, the following is an excellent illustration.

> Pauper videri Cinna vult—et est pauper!
> Cinna wants to appear poor—in fact, he is!

More elaborate examples are in the short cycle of epigrams on a *cenipeta* (2.11; 14; 27): the deep mourning, the frenzied activity and the extreme sycophancy of Selius are prompted merely by his desire to be invited to dinner.

II. Somewhat more convoluted than these are the numerous jokes that depend on logical (or invalid) deductions of the types expounded in Aristotle's *Sophistici Elenchi* and perfectly familiar to Roman orators. They are humorous because the conclusion is more or less surprising or even shocking. So, for example, in 4.21 Segius says there are no gods; if there were gods, Segius would not be prosperous; in fact, he does prosper, so there are no gods and his existence proves it. An unholy, but logical conclusion. Gallus, in another example, is now convicted of long-standing incest with his stepmother: she continues to live with him after Gallus' father is dead (4.16). Lycoris has buried all her friends: I wish my wife were a friend of hers (4.24). Again a scandalously logical argument. More commonly such jokes involve *reductio ad absurdum,* anti-climax or bathos or what might be described as 'overkill'.[42] An epigram in which the climax goes *beyond* what would be anticipated is 4.43 on Coracinus, where Martial denies he called him a *cinaedus,* he said rather he was a *cunnilingus.* Even more elaborate are the attacks on Vetustilla and Zoilus (3.93; 82). In the first the old hag is shown to be so sexually insatiable that she'd need a torch up her (*intrare in istum sola fax potest cunnum,* 3.93.27). In the second, Zoilus' intolerably antisocial ostentation has to be tolerated because the traditional revenge of *irrumatio* is excluded. Why? *Fellat.* So he would enjoy it. Compare the apparently paradoxical logic in the sadist's refusal to beat the consenting masochist. In these epigrams hidden premisses are invoked.

The *derailment* of logic which is initially concealed by an apparently artless, almost reasonable, form of expression provides the opportunity for a variety of jokes.[43] The amusement is provoked when 'hidden nonsense is revealed as manifest nonsense', as in Wittgenstein's proposal for the dissolution of philosophical puzzles. Often the jokes are produced by setting up a logical chain of expectations which is dramatically uncoupled at its last link by an anticlimax or an incongruity, often in the form of a category mistake or a hyperbolic (and often obscene[44]) climax. A simple example is **10.8**:

> Nubere Paula cupit nobis, ego ducere Paulam
>   nolo: anus est. Vellem, si magis esset
>   anus.

Paula wants to marry the poet, but he is unwilling to accept the offer, since she's an old woman. He would, however, do so—if she were older. The reader had expected—if she were younger. The subtext is that Paula is undesirable but rich; although Martial would not mind waiting a short time for his inheritance, Paula has too many years left in her. And, unlike the hideous Maronilla pursued by Gemellus, she doesn't have an ominous cough **(1.10)**.

A more elaborate twist may be seen in **1.99**, where a generous poor man becomes unexpectedly miserly after receiving several large legacies (cf. **1.103**). Martial then uses the *reductio ad absurdum* for his imprecation:

> Optamus tibi millies, Calene.
> Hoc si contigerit, fame peribis.

> We pray you'll inherit a hundred million, Calenus: then you'll die of starvation.

Similar to these deformations of syllogistic reasoning is the misuse of analogical argument. For example, **10.102** depends on a tendentious analogy:

> Qua factus ratione sit requiris,
> qui numquam futuit, pater Philinus?
> Gaditanus, Avite, dicat istud,
> qui scribit nihil et tamen poeta est.

> You ask how Philinus can be father, when he's never fucked? Let the man from Cadiz explain that, Avitus: he writes nothing and yet he's a poet.

To claim to be a poet without proof may be pretentious, but it is in the realm of the conceivable; Philinus' paternity, however, is quite impossible and the analogy simultaneously discredits Gaditanus' claims.

A similar epigram **(1.72)** about a would-be poet who hopes plagiarism will get him the title follows the analogies of denture wearers and white lead on dark skin to conclude:

> Hac et tu ratione qua poeta es,
> calvus cum fueris, eris comatus.

> By the same reasoning that makes even you a poet, when you become bald, you'll be hairy.

A similar false analogy provides the point in **6.17**:

> Cinnam, Cinname, te iubes vocari.
> Non est hic, rogo, Cinna, barbarismus?
> Tu si Furius ante dictus esses,
> fur ista ratione dicereris.

> You demand you be called Cinna, Cinnamus. I ask you, isn't this a social error? If your name has previously been Robson, by that logic you'd be called Rob.

Cinna and Furius are both respectable names: *fur* is not.[45]

Under the heading of twisted logic may be classified also the *non sequitur,* most often found in the snappy retort, *Tu quoque.* Martial, for instance, is accused of writing bad verses; his response is, you don't write any at all **(1.110)**; his epigrams are too long; a mere distich, however, from Cosconius would be too long **(2.77;** cf. **6.65)**; his dress is shabby; well, at least it's paid for **(2.58)**. In forensic terms, this is distracting the jury from the issue.

Logic is defied in **4.69**: the rumours that Papylus' fine wine is lethal are rejected—and so is Papylus' invitation to have a drink. Here a premiss is accepted, but the appropriate conclusion is denied.

III. Particularly pervasive in Martial's *oeuvre* are the various forms of word play.[46] The most obvious is the simple pun (*calembour* or *Kalauer*) in the lexicographical sense of the use of one word or phrase to convey two different senses in the same context or the use of a homophone (or near homophone) with different meanings. Quite apart from our lack of 'inwardness with the living voice', punning has ceased to be a fashionable form of joking in comparatively recent times, if we except the work of James Joyce. It was not always so; James Boswell declared: 'A good pun may be admitted among the small excellencies of lively conversation.' Writers as different as Shakespeare and Thomas Hood made no apology for them. For the modern reader, however, to treat an accidental or external relationship, verbal or aural, as having *conceptual* significance is merely a poor joke.

Nevertheless philosophers and critics from Plato (particularly in the *Cratylus*), Aristotle (*Rhet.* 1400b), Lucretius and Varro to Freud and Derrida have regarded puns as valuable ways to ferret out 'truths' about the physical and psychological world in general and about literary texts in particular. It is against this intellectual background that the Greco-Roman fascination with homophones, homonyms and etymologies (true or false) must be set. Even Homer and heraclitus were aware of the linguistic possibilities in puns. The belief that words relate closely to things, indeed reflect their very essence, rather than being arbitrary symbols for them, was deep-rooted in ancient thinking. Varro certainly believed that there is *verum* in the *verbum* and his work is full of false speculative etymologies (*lucus a non lucendo, miles* from *milia* and the like). Names and nouns could illuminate the nature of things or reflect actual characteristics hidden in them.[47]

This is not to say that Martial is interested in such theories, but simply that the poet and his audience would attribute far greater significance to puns and word play in general than we would, and so they would be far more acceptable as a form of humour. One obvious type of punning is playing on the different significance of similar sounding words or parts of words. This often provides the point of a poem. Sometimes the play is bilingual, as in **5.35**, the case of the impostor Eucleides and the treacherous key, which reveals that he is a slave—*nequior clavis* puns on [*kleis*], Greek for key, although Martial must have known that the name derives from [*euklees*] (famous). Snow-White . . . is jeered at for her dark complexion and sexual frigidity **(3.34)**, the latter being then contrasted with the fieriness of Phlogis (derived from . . . 'fire'). A very artificial pun, combined with a defective anagram, provides a complex play on Paulinus/Palinurus, alluding to Aeneas' drowned helmsman and Paulinus' desire to micturate twice from a moving boat, incorrectly etymologising the name from [*paliu*] and [*ourein*] instead of [*ouros*], 'watcher'.

Real names could also be used for bantering word play, as in the case of Domitian's favourite Earinus **(9.13)**. Since [*earinos*] is the adjective for 'spring', which in Latin is *verna* (which also fortuitously, but here conveniently, means 'home-bred slave'), Martial can joke on the possibilities of other Greek seasonal names for such a slave, Oporinos (autumnal), Chimerinos (wintery), Therinos (summery).

Simpler plays are possible with Maternus by implying that he is effeminate **(1.96)**; Panaretus does not have all the virtues as the meaning of his Greek name might imply—he drinks too much **(6.89)**. Hermogenes is a real son of Hermes, god of thieves—he snitches napkins **(12.29)**. No wonder one Phileros is, as the literal meaning of his Greek name implies, fond of love— he's buried seven rich wives on his property **(10.43)**. Another Phileros has got through the besotted Galla's dowry **(2.34)**.

So even when not directly punning, Martial tries for allusive humour in chosen fictitious names that will fit, sometimes by contrast, the point of the epigram.[48] Historical connotations attached to a name may similarly reinforce, directly or indirectly, the thrust of the humour or satire. The literary technique is most obviously seen in Petronius, in Shakespeare or in Charles Dickens: we know what will be happening in Dotheboys

Hall or what behaviour to expect from Toby Belch or Mr Gradgrind. So the name Lesbia, with its Catullan reminiscences and its overtones of . . . (to fellate), is appropriate for one who practices fellation **(2.50)**, is an exhibitionist **(1.32)**, sexually aggressive **(6.23)** and an old hag **(10.39)** who has to pay for sex **(11.62)**. The historical connotations of Lais and Thais, the names of the great Greek courtesans, operate in the same symbolic way, as do such historical names as Sardanapallus or such mythical names as Hylas, Hyacinthus and Phoebus. Typical slave names also invite conceptual or literary word play (cf. Mistyllos/Taratalla, **1.50**).

Beyond plays on names, Martial looks to a wide variety of common words whose possible ambiguity in the right contexts encourages sexual innuendo or *double entendres* (Aristotle's and Quintilian's *emphasis*). A good example, whose subtlety is less likely to offend a modern sense of humour, is **4.39**, which is presented almost in the form of a riddle, a not uncommon technique of Martial's to build suspense before a climax:

> Argenti genus omne comparasti,
> et solus veteres Myronos artes,
> solus Praxitelus manum Scopaeque,
> solus Phidiaci toreuma caeli,
> solus Mentoreos habes labores.
> Nec desunt tibi vera Gratiana,
> nec quae Callaico linuntur auro,
> nec mensis anaglypta de paternis.
> argentum tamen inter omne miror
> quare non habeas, Charine, purum.

> You've collected all kinds of silver and only you have antique artworks by Myron, only you have the handiwork of Praxiteles and Scopas, only you have the curved reliefs of Phidias, only you the artistic pains of Mentor. And you don't lack genuine works by Gratius or Galician gold inlays or encrusted plate from ancestral tables. Yet among all this variety, Charinus, I'm surprised you don't have any *clean* silver.

Here Martial is feigning surprise that a rich connoisseur of wrought silver *objets d'art* and tableware has no *argentum purum* in his collection. The surface meaning of 'unadorned' yields the hidden suggestion that Charinus' propensity for oral sex leaves none of it untainted (*purus;* for this implication, cf. **3.75.5**; **6.50.6**; **6.66.5**; **11.61.14**; **14.70.2**).

Similar *double entendres* are generated by *soror/frater,* male or female siblings or lovers **(2.4)**; *ficus* (figs or haemorrhoids, **1.65**; **7.71**); *dare* (of innocent gifts or sexual favours, **2.49; 56; 7.30**); *irrumare* (of consensual oral sex or insulting humiliation as in **2.83; 4.17**). Martial is particularly fond of ambiguous possessives. Poems *I* write are *yours* if you buy them or recite them so badly that I disclaim them **(1.29; 1.38; 2.20)**; false teeth, false hair and such things are *yours* (implying natural), if you purchase them (**5.43; 6.12;** cf. **9.37; 12.23; 14.56**). But unvarnished and often frigid puns are found in such epigrams as **1.79** (different usages of *agere*); and sometimes the joke hinges only on the supposedly correct use or form of words (e.g. **2.3** *debere;* **1.65** *ficus/ficos*).

Somewhat more appealing are the pointed homophones (Fronto's *paronomasia*) found in such epigrams as **1.98** (*podagra/cheragra*). Although a whole epigram may be built around a favourite ambiguous word such as *purus,* sometimes a pun is used simply to terminate, more or less satisfactorily, an otherwise humorous poem. An example of this may be seen in Martial's fictive description of a tiny farm given him by Lupus, which, he claims, is no bigger than a window-box (**11.18**). The poem now generates a series of amusing meioses and comparisons (cf. IV below): it could be covered by a cricket's wing; it could be ravaged by an ant in a single day; a cucumber couldn't grow straight in it; a caterpillar would famish and a gnat would starve to death in it; a mushroom or a violet couldn't open in it; a mouse would be like the Calydonian Boar if it ravaged it; its harvest would scarcely fill a snail shell or make a nest for a swallow; its vintage fits into a nutshell; and a half-size Priapus, even without his sickle and phallus, would be too large for it. Obviously the joke could continue, but a crowning hyperbole (or meiosis) would be hard to find, so Martial resorts to a pun: Lupus should have given him a *prandium* instead of a *praedium,* a lunch instead of a ranch, a spree instead of a spread.

Under word play may be subsumed such jokes as that in **10.69,** where an incorrect and unexpected usage of a verb leads to the point:

> Custodes das, Polla, viro, non accipis ipsa.
> Hoc est uxorem ducere, Polla, virum.

The substitution of *ducere* for *nubere* implies that Polla 'wears the trousers' in the household, providing the point of the misogynistic joke. The idiom can be reversed to mock a macho homosexual (**1.24**).

IV. Martial's imagery has already been discussed, so the humorous metaphors, similes and symbolic instances that occur in the satiric epigrams need no more than a glance. These are well illustrated by the epigrams of witty and sustained invective against Vetustilla (**3.93**), Zoilus (**3.82**), the anonymous forger of his verses (**10.5**), Hedylus' cloak (**9.57**), Lydia (**11.21**) and Nanneius (**11.61**), and also by the ingenious string of belittling comparisons Martial uses to describe the pettiness of the gifts given him, a subject which invariably elicits his most pointed sallies. Worth recalling again are the epigrams on a gift of a tiny cup (**8.33**) and on the ridiculous size of his little farm (**11.18**). The hyperbole

of the imagery in such epigrams is put to deadly effect in the abuse aimed at the loose *cunnus* of the hapless Lydia (**11.21**) or the vile smell of Thais (**7.93**).

The imagery of Phaethon's fiery doom prompts several 'twists'. A bad poet should choose such a mythological subject—then appropriately burn his verses (**5.53**). An encaustic painting of Phaethon constitutes double jeopardy (**4.47**). A coarser visual image is conjured up by Philaenis' physical appearance (**2.33**): she is bald, red and one-eyed: the innuendo is easily grasped.

The kinetic images and imaginary instances used to describe Hermogenes' thieving propensities are particularly amusing: he is pictured as a deer sucking up frozen snakes and a rainbow catching the falling raindrops; if he can't steal a napkin, he'll steal a tablecloth, the awnings of the amphitheatre, the sails of a ship and the linen robes of Isis' priest (**12.28**).

V. Finally, there are the jokes or subsidiary aids to joking that depend essentially on 'the rediscovery of the familiar', in Freud's terminology.[49] Here the techniques used are metrical rhythms, repetition of words or phrases, modifications of familiar saws, allusion to quotations, historical or topical references, and such rhythmic devices and tropes as alliteration, rhyme, assonance, anaphora, *enumeratio, accumulatio* and others. The most ingenious example in English of the playful use of alliteration is Poulter's rhymes beginning

> An Austrian Army awfully arrayed
> Boldly by battery besieged Belgrade . . .

Martial's *tour de force* here is **5.24,** in which each line begins with the name of the gladiator Hermes; this is underscored by further alliteration within the lines. The repetition of a telling phrase or question is effectively deployed in **7.10,** where the rhetorical *Ole, quid ad te?* recurs four times; it is then reprised by four variations on *hoc ad te pertinet, Ole* in a crescendo of insults until the dismissive climax is reached. Similar to this are **1.77** (. . . *Charinus et tamen pallet*) and **11.47** (*ne futuat*).

A clever and untranslatable mixture of punning, assonance, rhyme, alliteration and anaphora together is offered in **12.39:**

> Odi te, quia bellus es, Sabelle.
> Res est putida bellus et Sabellus.
> Bellum denique malo quam Sabellum.
> Tabescas utinam, Sabelle belle.

Parody, which above all relies on the comfortable feeling of recognition and familiarity, is an infrequent humorous device in Martial. The most successful example (**2.41**) is based on perverting an untraceable or adapted line of Ovid's, *Ride si sapis, o puella, ride,*[50] by a series of amusingly sarcastic images into the advice, *Plora, si sapis, o puella, plora.*

The setting of proverbial saws in humorous or incongruous contexts provides a similar type of amusement, as in **1.27, 1.45.** In **11.90** the citation of Lucilius' famous epitaph on Metrophanes and a line ending of Ennius serves as a sardonic rebuke to the admirers of archaic poetry.

5. 'Willing to wound': Martial's poetic ambivalence

It would be unfair to Martial's achievement to leave his work on a technical note, although it was that wide-ranging technical expertise that inspired so many poets and critics in the sixteenth to the early eighteenth century to heights of emulation and adulation. Looking at his humour and wit in larger terms, the modern reader is disappointed by its datedness or appalled by its cruelty or obscenity, although the covert appeal of the 'black humour' in dead baby jokes, Lincoln jokes and indeed smoking-room stories in all their variety should make us suspicious of the latter reaction.

Nevertheless, it is significant that Martial's genius took that particular turn towards the line of wit and the satiric epigram. Now that we have some insight into the psychological workings of wit and humour, some speculations on the essence of Martial's art and the nature of his protean *oeuvre* may be ventured.

An interesting clue to his poetry is to be found in the younger Pliny's assessment of his character in the letter reporting his death (3.21). There Pliny, speaking both of his personality and his writings, as it were, refers to the combination in his verses of wit, malice and also the desire to please (*sal, fel* and *candor*). Nothing could better describe the impression left by a reading of the epigrams, the impression that is of a profound ambivalence that seems to spring from a divided spirit. William Empson once remarked that 'the machinations of ambiguity are among the very roots of poetry' and this suggests an interesting perspective from which to scrutinise Martial's writings—it will also partly account for the highly diverse reactions to them among critics and amateurs alike. Such a diagnosis of Martial as a poet of profound ambiguity may be confirmed by glancing briefly at the mixed feelings he shows towards his principal subjects: the imperial political structure; patronage; private life; and, not least, sexuality. Irony and wit are tempting, almost inevitable, modes for reflecting ambivalent feelings. Humour and ridicule help defuse the consequent anxieties. And it is no coincidence that Martial shows a particular sensitivity to the hypocrisy he detects in others.

Martial makes no bones about his dependence on the goodwill and generosity of patrons, but he is equally forthright about the flaws in the whole system and in individual benefactors. He professes his loyalty to the principate and its present incumbent, whoever he may be, but there is an undercurrent of complaints about the workings of the system as it affects poets such as himself, and he is quick to react to the overthrow of Domitian and his replacement by the new rulers, Nerva and Trajan. He clings to his hierarchical vision of Roman society, yet he accepts gratefully the favours of powerful imperial freedmen, even while rejecting the challenges presented by the cultural and economic evolution of the rest of the class to which they belong. He expresses intermittently through his epigrams a keen nostalgia for Spain and his home town, yet in his later years he evinces disquiet about his prospects on return and, in **Book XII,** bitter disillusion about his homecoming. His Epicurean ideals of the quiet life and contentment with little are undercut by his itemisation of how much that little entails and his patent desire for recognition, personal respect and the tangible, even expensive, proofs of that respect.

His attitudes towards women in general and in particular are especially ambivalent. He can simultaneously resent rich women as a class, while expressing admiration and gratitude to individual female patrons. He can denigrate their sexuality, while praising the virtue and restraint of certain historical and contemporary paragons, yet he would require in the ideal wife a scarcely attainable combination of outward respectability and private lasciviousness. The latter quality in the inhabitants of the *demi-monde* is at times derided and at times praised, even rewarded.

The same ambiguity will be found to pervade his homoerotic verses when the scarifying physical imagery used to depict mature female sexuality is abandoned for the fragrant language of the epigrams dedicated to young male slaves. Ecstatic praise for their fresh youthful bodies, however, is constantly soured by complaints of their waywardness and reluctance to reciprocate his affection. Critical of the abuse of power by other slave owners, he is not reluctant to exercise it in his own case against recalcitrance. His emphasis on purely physical charms is then belied by his keenly expressed desire for spontaneous affection from such favourites as Diadumenus, Dindymus, Telesphorus and Lygdus (cf. **5.83; 11.26; 12.71; 11.73**). The poignant epigram in the final book **(12.46)** seemed to Joseph Addison and others to be a notable and pithy summation of the ambiguity to be found in human relationships:

> Difficilis facilis, iucundus acerbus es idem:
>   nec tecum possum vivere, nec sine te.

> In all thy humours, whether grave or mellow,
> Thou'rt such a touchy, testy, pleasant fellow;
> Hast so much wit, and mirth, and spleen about
>   thee,

There is no living with thee, or without thee.

(Trs. Joseph Addison)

The *persona* presented then is of a poet who feels that he has been 'stung' by life: he reacts by 'stings'. 'Willing to wound, and yet afraid to strike' in Pope's words, he has to sharpen the weapons of wit and sarcasm as his only conceivable means of response to the world's duplicity and hypocrisy, in which he fears he sees his own reflected. . . .

Notes

[1] References for most of these judgments and the documentation for the swings in his reputation are given below in chapter 7.

[2] Mason (1988) 29, but see also the response by Sullivan (1989) 303.

[3] For a collection of examples, consult Lattimore (1942); Veyne (1964) 48; Tolkiehn (1967) 113. Other moving epitaphs by Martial for young people, men of distinction as well as slaves, are: 1.116 (for a friend's daughter); 6.28 (for Melior's slave boy); 7.96 (for a young slave of Bassus); 11.13 (for the mime Paris); 10.53 (for the charioteer Scorpus); 6.76 (for the praetorian Fuscus); 7.40 (on Etruscus' father); 10.70 (on Rabirius' parents); and 11.69 (on a dog).

[4] For this whole discussion, see Kenney (1964) 77, who defends the supposedly jarring collocation of the two poems against earlier objections by Lloyd (1953) 39.

[5] For a larger, but by no means complete, selection of English versions, see Sullivan (1986) 112; it was also popular in other literatures. Only the epigrams on Arria Paeta (1.13), of which Mrs Thrale made a collection of translations, and on Leander (*Spec.* 25), popular in the *siglo de oro,* cf. Moya del Baño (1967), run it close.

[6] There is, however, a debt to Horace here, and it is not the only one, since the identification of the happy man with the rural farmer is pervasive in Augustan literature (cf. e.g., Tibullus 1.1). It was a theme that enjoyed great popularity also in the Renaissance and in the seventeenth and eighteenth centuries. Then Martial's compact statement would be much elaborated and even Christianised; see Røstvig (1974) 291.

[7] A good recent study of Martial's structural conventions is Siedschlag (1977), which provides copious parallels to Martial's precedents in Greco-Roman epigram and elegy. Barwick (1932) 63 and (1947) 1 are still useful. Berends (1932) offers a general, overly schematic, discussion of the structuring of all twelve books.

[8] Here I follow the excellent analysis by Kay (1985) 5.

[9] The most comprehensive discussion of the influence of contemporary rhetoric on Martial is Barwick (1959) 3. On Martial's rhetorical techniques by comparison with his Greek models, see Pertsch (1911) 56. For the meanings of the rhetorical terms, see Dixon (1971) s.v., and for Martial's handling of these effects (and much more) Joepgen (1967) *passim*. Anadiplosis, verbal repetition, is used in one of his most famous epigrams (1.32): *Non amo te, Sabidi, nec possum dicere quare: hoc tantum possum dicere, non amo te. Accumulatio* is neatly used in the description of the happy life (10.47), and an amusing example of it, coupled with gross hyperbole, is Martial's description of his tiny farm (11.18). For *synathroesmus,* see Citroni (1975) *ad* 1.10.2; and for the priamel in Latin literature, exemplified in the opening epigram on the Colosseum in the *Liber de spectaculis,* see Race (1982).

[10] *Miraris* (do you wonder?) is similarly employed; see Weinreich (1926) 55. For examples of *quaeris,* see 2.38; 5.56; 6.67; 7.34; 8.12; 10.22; 11.19; 12.17; for *miraris,* see e.g. 5.73; 6.11; 7.18; 12.51. For all these various openings see Siedschlag (1977) 9.

[11] I have discussed this elsewhere in connection with Petronius, see Sullivan (1968) 104. For the less tendentious realism and *enargeia* of the Greek novelists, see Bartsch (1988) 8. For Martial's 'realism' and his fascination with concrete description, see Salemme (1976) 9. Similar is the characterisation of his work by Mehnert (1970) 19 'als Dokument der sozialen Verhältnisse'. Bohn (1860) in his preface speaks of 'his pictures of the manners and customs of Rome at that most interesting period, the commencement of the Christian era'.

[12] See, most conveniently, Lessing (1956) 7.425. For the genesis and significance of Lessing's views, which went well beyond those of J. C. Scaliger (1561) III *cap.* 126, who merely argued that 'pointedness' (*argutia*) was the soul of epigram rather than brevity; see ch. 7, p. 297; also Barwick (1959) 3 and Hutton (1935) 55. Objections to Lessing's views were offered early by Herder (1888) 337, who preferred the epigrams of the *Greek Anthology* to those for which Martial provided the paradigm. For later objections see Reitzenstein (1893) 103; Barwick (1959) 10; Citroni (1969) 219.

[13] To borrow a useful term from Smith (1968) 198. Other terms than Lessing's have been used such as *propositio-conclusio; expositio-conclusio; narratio-acumen; antecedens-consequens;* see Citroni (1969) 218 n.6. Smith describes the epigram portentously 'as a thematic sequence which reaches a point of maximal instability and then turns to the business of completing itself' (p. 199).

[14] As pointed out by Kay (1985) 7; Gerlach (1911) 5 had noticed the appropriateness of the analysis for Martial's 'surprise endings'.

[15] Barwick (1959) 104 sees this as one of the most important effects on Martial of the rhetorical style exemplified by the younger Seneca.

[16] Convenient collections can be found in Ker (1979) xii, West (1912), and de Sousa Pimentel (1991) 117.

[17] Hor. *Sat.* 1.2.120f.; Petr. *Sat.* 132.15; *AP* 9.572 (Lucillius); *AP* 12.1; 197 (Strato).

[18] Other examples are 1.11; 94; 4.34; 84; 7.75; 9.2; 8.20; 10.68; 11.35; 42; 12.97. *Reductio ad absurdum* is also an attractive closure (cf. 6.17), as is hyperbole, the introduction of a humorous exception or an unrelated factor; for other examples of these techniques, cf. *Spec.* 21; 3.12; 4.39; 8.35; 11.66; 12.54. The *quod non (sed)* construction achieves its effect by rejecting one explanation for another more amusing or satisfying one. Simple examples can be found in *Liber de spectaculis*: e.g. 6; 16; 17. Other, sometimes more elaborate, examples are 1.95; 2.11; 2.15; 6.48; 8.31; 9.62; 11.77; 12.89. See Siedschlag (1977) 29, 75 for detailed analysis.

[19] The . . . mean had been a Greek ethical principle since one of the Seven Sages came up with the concept of . . . (nothing in excess), after which Aristotle made it a fundamental part of his concept of virtue. Other examples in Martial are 2.36; 9.32; 11.100. Alternatively such contrast of two opposing aspects may be used to praise both or condemn one (e.g. 9.70). Sometimes present and past, mythological or real situations are simply juxtaposed as at 1.6.

[20] See also 8.20; 2.76; analogous jokes are found in 3.88; 90; 6.12.

[21] Instances are: *Spec.* 13; 14; 3.19; 4.18; 32; 6.15; 11.82. See also Laurens (1965) 323.

[22] For Martial's verse forms and metrical practice in general see Birt in Friedlaender (1886) 30, who proclaims it masterly, Giarratano (1908) and Holzberg (1988) 34; on the elegiacs, Platnauer (1948) 12; on the hendecasyllables, Ferguson (1970) 173; on the choliambics, Pelckmann (1908) s.v. Some metrically unusual practices to be found in his later books indicate that his inventive zest had not diminished. In Book XI the predominance of elegiacs (86 poems out of 108) is varied by sixteen hendecasyllabic epigrams (15%) and by four choliambic epigrams (4%). This corresponds roughly to the frequency in other books, except that two of the less common verse forms, iambic trimeters and a metre borrowed from Horace, are found in it (11.77; 11.59). Of the recognised 1,556 epigrams

of Martial, 1,235 are elegiac distichs (79%), 238 are hendecasyllables (15%) and 77 are choliambics (5%); hexameters of a very individual sort are used four times (1.53; 6.64; 2.73; 7.93); straight iambic senarii twice (6.12; 11.77); iambic senarius with iambic dimeter four times, a metre used in Horace's first ten epodes (1.49; 3.14; 9.77; 11.49); choliamb with dimeter once (1.61) and there is one example of sotadics (3.29). For a detailed statistical discussion of Martial's chosen metres and comparison with the usages of Catullus, Horace, the *Appendix Vergiliana* and the *Priapea*, see Moreno (1987) 267.

[23] For adverse comment on Ovidian usage, see Axelson (1958) 124, who cites in support Harrison (1943) 98. For further details, see Wilkinson (1948) 68.

[24] For the differences between Martial's and Catullus' practices in hendecasyllables, see Ferguson (1963) 3 and (1970) 173. Martial follows Catullus in one or two favoured arrangements of the hendecasyllabic line, such as noun and adjective placed at the beginning and end of the line (e.g. *argutis epigrammaton libellis*, 1.1.3) and balancing two related words in these positions (*praeconem facias vel architectum*, 5.56.11). Chiasmus is similarly frequent (e.g. *velox ingenio, decore felix*, 6.28.7; or *uxor pessima pessimus maritus*, 8.35.2). He differs from Catullus in avoiding endings of the *brevis lux, tacet nox* type, preferring a monosyllable before an unelided monosyllabic ending. although he uses few enough of these, none of them being strong or significant words, but rather weak monosyllables, such as pronouns and parts of the verbs *sum, fio* or *volo*. See Paukstadt (1876) 29.

[25] A good example of this problem may be found in 11.77: Vacerra sits around all day in public lavatories, not because he is dying to shit (*cacaturit*), but because he is dying to dine (*cenaturit*). The first desiderative form is authenticated only once elsewhere in Latin (*CIL* IV Suppl. 5242), but the second is most probably Martial's invention to produce an alliterative pun. Other examples from Book XI are *inevolutus* (unrolled), *dractum* (small flask), *botrus* (bunch of grapes) and *carnarius* (fond of flesh); see Kay (1985) *ad loc.;* also Huisentveld (1949) for his use of colloquial and vulgar expressions; for *hapax* usages, Fortuny Previ (1981-2) III; for Martial's use of Greek vocabulary, see Adamik (1975) 71; Fortuny Previ (1986) 73; on Spanish loan words, Dolç (1953) 27.

[26] See Barwick (1959) 43; Carrington (1972) 261. Other examples of such endings are: 7.42; 9.88; 99; 10.45; 59; 100; 11.100; 12.36. Their frequency increases in later books. Coincidentally some metrically unusual features are to be seen in his later books (IX-XII), e.g. the hexameter endings *dic aliquando* (104.6), *hircus habet cor* (11.84.17) and *apud me* (11.35.11; 52.1; 83.1; 12.17.9), which stand out because of their very rarity.

Both again point to increasing rather than diminishing poetic experimentation, and perhaps a rejection of conventional constraints and formal expectations, as with the increase in the number of obscene poems found in Book XI.

[27] A noticeable exception is in the political use made of Hercules (esp. 9.101; 64; 65), which accounts for an undue proportion of the references to Greek localities; see map 4, p. 177. For mythological themes in Martial, see Corsaro (1973) 171; Szelest (1974) 297.

[28] For similar denigratory uses of olfactory or tactile imagery against women, cf. 3.93, where images of rock predominate; 4.4, where smell is again evoked. Analogous but more expansive examples in Swift are 'The Lady's Dressing Room' (1730); 'A Beautiful Young Nymph Going to Bed' (1731); and 'Strephon and Chloe' (1731).

[29] Note, for example, the play Martial makes with 'fig' (*ficus*) in its various senses (1.65; 4.52; 7.72; 12.32); see Adams (1982) 138, who may be consulted for further illustrations of the linguistic areas Martial draws upon for his metaphors and images. See also Adamik (1981) 303, who counts three hundred or so similes in the *oeuvre*, a high proportion by comparison with other Latin poets. They often occur in clusters through the technique of *enumeratio*.

[30] See below (p. 278) for a general discussion of this enthusiasm.

[31] For example, although Aristotle says in Book II of the *Poetics* . . ., Plutarch would set limits on what physical defects were proper subjects for jokes (*Quaest. conviv.* 2.633b). Baldness was an acceptable butt; halitosis and blindness were not. Martial, like medieval and Renaissance humorists such as Thomas More, blithely ignores these limitations. Such humour, however, goes back to Homer's description of the gods' laughing at the limping of Hephaestus (*Il.* 18.411, 417).

[32] A valuable recent study of the political and ideological use of wit is Plass (1988). For earlier general discussions of Martial's humour, see Wölfflin (1887); McCartney (1919) 343; Gaertner (1956); Joepgen (1967); Kuppe (1967); Szelest (1981) 293; Burnikel (1980); Plass (1985) 187; and Malnati (1984).

[33] The best ancient discussions, to my mind, are the *Tractatus Coislinianus* and Arist. *Rhet.* 3.10.1411b-1413a (cf. *EN* 10.6.1176b; *Rhet.* 1.2.1371b; 2.3.1380b; 3.11.1411b). For a survey of Greek and Roman speculation on the subject, see Grant (1924). Some modern works by such authors as Freud (1960), Legman (1968) and Dundes (1987) have proved enlightening. The slippery complexity of the terms used in discussing humour is as patent in Greek and Latin as it is in English.

Moreover, the vocabulary for different aspects of the laughable changes with the passage of time and doubtless with changes in sensibility and aesthetic perceptions. One must settle for the recognition of 'family resemblances'. 'Wit', for example, has undergone considerable semantic change in the transition from Elizabethan to modern times. In most of Sir Richard Blackmore's *A Satire against Wit* (1699), the term is synonymous with obscenity and blasphemy; elsewhere in his writings he describes it as 'intellectual enameling' or 'a rich embroidery of flowers and figures'. Contrast this with Pope's definition, 'True Wit is Nature to Advantage dress'd: What oft was thought but ne'er so well express'd.' For changes in the concept in English, see Watson (1987) s.v.

[34] For a discussion of Martial's mock-modest stance see ch. 2 above. Even Pliny comments on Martial's desire to be friendly (*candor*). Aristotle's view that amusement and relaxation are necessary parts of life (*EN* 4.88.1128b) is not at odds with the thesis that humour is frequently hostile. . . . Again this is not the place to examine the various *motives* for deliberate humour: to increase one's sense of self-esteem, as Hobbes thought; to strike at one's enemies, deflate hierarchy, subvert authority or register social protest; to relax tension or conceal embarrassment; to amuse friends or company, or, paradoxically, sheer *Schadenfreude*.

[35] An analysis of the interconnection of Martial's social and erotic material, such as the decay of patronage, the disruptive excesses of the freedman class, the financial power and sexual corruption of women and the transgression at large of traditional boundaries is attempted in Sullivan (1987) 177.

[36] Allied to this, in certain other classes of joke, is 'recognition', the rediscovery of what is familiar rather than the discovery of what is new; here Freud (1960) 120 grudgingly gives credit to Aristotle for his theory that the pleasure of recognition is the basis for the enjoyment of art. . . .

[37] There must be little question by now that Martial uses more obscene words and allusions than any other known Roman poet; see again Adams (1982) 1-8 for a discussion of the general topic and *passim* for Martial's specific usages. The subject is only sketchily discussed by ancient theorists of rhetoric, since the orator is to be discouraged from . . . *obscenitas* and . . . *scurrilitas*, because of his need for a dignified *persona*. Aristotle had been very strict in discouraging a gentleman . . . from vulgarity. . . . Cf. Quint. *Inst.* 6.3.29: *dicacitas etiam scurrilis et scaenica huic personae alienissima est . . . obscenitas vero non a verbis tantum sed etiam a significatione;* cf. Cic. *Fam.* 2.1.5.

[38] See Freud (1960) 100. I pass over here Freud's view that a main unconscious motivation for telling 'dirty

jokes' is exhibitionism or the desire to expose oneself.

[39] More elaborate classifications are of course possible. I would single out for their ingenuity the classifications of Gracián in his *Agudeza y Ingenio* and, for brevity, Szelest (1981) 293. The categories adopted by Hofmann (1956-7) 433 are somewhat unfocused.

[40] Many of the epigrams describe *lusus naturae* and other strange events or appearances in nature. But few of these . . . are humorous or even interesting; in fact, they are often rather grim. The boy bitten by a snake hiding in the maw of a bronze statuary of a bear is a case in point. For further examples and some Greek precursors, see Szelest (1976) 251. Hairsbreadth escapes and startling deaths are also popular topics and often prompt a neat aphorism such as *in medio Tibure Sardinia est* (4.60.6).

[41] Malnati (1984) sees hypocrisy as the mainspring of Martial's humour. Examples of social hypocrisy are given in ch. 4 above, p. 159. Instances of sexual hypocrisy are especially numerous.

[42] Quintilian takes note of the last two of these (*Inst.* 9.2.22-3); they exemplify *sustentatio* or [*paradoxon*], depending on whether one looks at the *Erwartung* or the *Aufschluss*.

[43] It is a characteristic of Irish bulls ('If this letter offends you, please return it unopened'), of certain types of ethnic humour and, in the ancient world, of Abderite jokes as reported in the ancient collection *Philogelos;* cf. Baldwin (1983) 21. Plass (1988) 190 draws attention to Quintilian's remark: . . . *eadem quae si inprudentibus excidant stulta sunt, si simulamus venusta creduntur* (*Inst.* 6.3.23). The particular derailment of logic which consists in seizing on the wrong element in a complex proposition was singled out by William Hazlitt as an effective form of wit, which he described as 'diverting the chain of your adversary's argument abruptly and adroitly into another channel'. He instances 'the sarcastic reply of Porson, who hearing someone observe that "certain modern poets would be read and admired when Homer and Virgil were forgotten", made answer—"And not till then!" ' (See *Lectures on the English Comic Writers, Lecture I* (London 1819; repr. 1910) 17.) A more familiar instance is Robert Benchley's retort to a lady who pointed out to him that alcohol is a slow poison: 'Who's in a hurry?'

[44] As Plass (1988) 195 notes, citing 4.43; 50. Cf. also 2.73; 3.74; 4.84; 9.27; 12.79 for similar endings.

[45] This epigram is imitated more effectively by Johannes Burmeister in his *Martialis Renatus* (Luneburg 1618), to produce an anti-Papist joke turning on *Pontifex faex.*

[46] The standard discussion is Joepgen (1967); see also

Siedschlag (1977) 86. On puns the most comprehensive recent study is Redfern (1984), although this concentrates on French literature for examples. The importance of word play in general in Martial may be gauged from the frequency of its occurrence; cf. 1.20; 30; 41; 45; 47; 50; 65; 79; 81; 98; 100; 2.3; 7; 43; 67; 3.25; 34; 42; 67; 3.78; 4.9; 52; 5.26; 6.6; 17; 7.41; 57; 71; 8.16; 19; 22; 9.72; 95; 12.39. It is interesting that Martial uses this form of jocularity less and less as he grows older.

[47] See Snyder (1980) on the importance of word elements for Lucretius (e.g. the *ignis* in *lignis*); Ahl (1985) discusses their literary implications in Latin poetry, even suggesting that Roman poets might overlook the difference between diphthongs, long and short vowels, and aspirated and unaspirated words (p. 56); cf. 2.39.4.

[48] See further Giegengack (1969) 22.

[49] See Freud (1960) 120. On Martial's alliteration, see Adamik (1975b) 69; on ancient parody, Cèbe (1966).

[50] Discussed earlier. The closest analogies are *AA* 3.281ff., 3.513.

Abbreviations

. . . *AP Anthologia Palatina* . . .

CIL Corpus Inscriptionum Latinarum, ed. T. Mommsen *et al.,* (Berlin 1863-) . . .

Housman *CP The Collected Papers of A. E. Housman,* edd. J. Diggle and F. R. D. Goodyear (Cambridge 1972) . . .

Bibliography

. . . Adamik, Tamás (1975) 'The Function of Words of Greek Origin in the Poetry of Martial', *AUB* 7:71.

(1975b) 'Die Funktion der Alliteration bei Martial', *Ziva antika / Antiquité vivante* 25:69. . . .

(1981) 'Die Funktion der Vergleiche bei Martial', *Eos* 69:303.

Adams, J. N. (1982) 'Four Notes on the Latin Sexual Language: *CIL* IV. 8898, Persius 4.36, Martial 11.104.17, Petronius 21.2', *LCM* 7:86. . . .

Ahl, Frederic M. (1985) *Metaformations: Soundplay and Wordplay in Ovid and Other Classical Poets,* Ithaca, N.Y. . . .

Axelson, Berthil (1958) 'Der Mechanismus des Ovidischen Pentameterschlusses' in *Ovidiana,* ed. N. I. Herescu, Paris, p. 121. . . .

Baldwin, Barry (1983) *The Philogelos or Laughter-Lover,* Amsterdam. . . .

Bartsch, Shadi (1988) *Decoding the Greek Novel,* Princeton.

Barwick, Karl (1932) 'Zur Kompositionstechnik und Erklärung Martials', *Philologus* 87:63.

(1947) 'Catulls c. 68 und eine Kompositionsform der römischen Elegie und Epigrammatik', *Würz. Jahrbb.* 2:1.

(1959) *Martial und die Zeitgenössische Rhetorik, Ber. über die Verhandl. der Sachs. Akad. der Wiss. zu Leipzig, Phil.-Hist. Kl.,* 104:3. . . .

Berends, Herbert (1932) 'Die Anordnung in Martials Gedichtbüchern I-XII'. Diss. Jena. . . .

Bohn, Henry George, ed. (1860) *The Epigrams of Martial,* London. . . .

Burnikel, Walter (1980) *Untersuchungen zur Struktur des Witzepigramms bei Lukillius und Martial,* Wiesbaden. . . .

Carrington, A. G. (1972) 'Martial' in *Neronians and Flavians: Silver Latin* 1, ed. D. R. Dudley, London, p. 236. . . .

Cèbe, J. P. (1966) *La Caricature et la parodie dans le monde romain antique des origines à Juvenal,* Paris. . . .

Citroni, Mario (1969) 'La teoria Lessinghiana dell'epigramma e le interpretazione di Marziale', *Maia* 21:215.

(1975) *M. Valerii Martialis Epigrammaton Liber Primus,* Florence. . . .

Corsaro, F. (1973) 'Il mondo del mito negli Epigrammaton libri di Marziale' . . .

de Sousa Pimentel, M. C. de Castro-Maia (1991) 'Marcial moralizado: o risco da literatura fragmentária', *Euphros* 19:109. . . .

Dixon, P. (1971) *Handlist of Rhetorical Terms,* Chicago. . . .

Dolç y Dolç, Miguel (1953) *Hispania y Marcial, Contribución al Conocimento de la España Antigua,* Barcelona.

Dundes, Alan (1987) *Cracking Jokes - Studies of Sick Humour Cycles and Stereotypes,* Berkeley. . . .

Ferguson, John (1963) 'Catullus and Martial', *PACA* 6:3.

(1970) 'A Note on Catullus' Hendecasyllabics', *CP* 65:173. . . .

Fortuny Previ, Filomena (1981-2) 'Consideraciones sobre algunos *hapax* de Marcial', *Anales de la Universidad de Murcia* 40.1-2:111. . . .

Freud, Sigmund (1960) *Der Witz u. sein Verhältnis zum Umbewusstein,* Leipzig (1905) = *Jokes and their Relation to the Unconscious,* trs. James Strachey, London. . . .

Friedlaender, Ludwig (1886) *M. Valerii Martialis epigrammaton libri,* Leipzig. . . .

Gaertner, H. A. (1956) 'Beobachtungen zu den Formen des Witzes bei Martial' in *Festschrift Regenbogen,* Heidelberg, p. 53. . . .

Gerlach, O. (1911) 'De Martialis Figurae [*aprosdoketon*] quae vocatur usu', Diss. Jena. . . .

Giarratono, Caesar (1908) *De M. Val. Martialis re metrica,* Naples. . . .

Giegengack, J. M. (1969) 'Significant Names in Martial', Diss. Yale. . . .

Grant, Mary A. (1924) *The Ancient Rhetorical Theories of the Laughable,* Madison. . . .

Harrison, E. (1943) 'Latin Verse Composition and the Nasonian Code', *CR* 57:9. . . .

Herder, J. G. (1888) 'Anmerkungen über das griechische Epigramm', *Sämtliche Werke,* ed. B. Suphan, vol. 15, Berlin. . . .

Hofmann, Ruth (1956-7) 'Aufgliederung der Themen Martials', *Wiss. Zeitschr. der Karl-Marx Univ. Leipzig* 6:433. . . .

Holzberg, Niklas (1988) *Martial,* Heidelberg. . . .

Huisentveld, H. (1949) *De populaire elementen in de taal van M. Val. Martialis,* Nimwegen. . . .

Hutton, James (1935) *The Greek Anthology in Italy,* Ithaca, N.Y. (1946) *The Greek Anthology in France,* Ithaca, N.Y. . . .

Joepgen, Ursula (1967) 'Wortspiele bei Martial', Diss. Bonn. . . .

Kay, Nigel (1985) *Martial Book XI: A Commentary,* London. . . .

Kenney, E. J. (1964) 'Erotion again', *G&R* 11:77.

Ker, Walter C. A. (1968) *Martial, Epigrams*[2] 2 vols. (Loeb edn), London, Cambridge, Mass. (1st edn 1919, 1920). . . .

Kuppe, Eckart M. W. (1967) 'Sachwitz bei Martial', Diss. Bonn. . . .

Lattimore, Richmond (1942) *Themes in Greek and Latin Epitaphs,* Urbana, Ill.

Laurens, P. (1965) 'Martial et l'épigramme grecque du Ier siècle ap. J.-C.', *REL* 43:315. . . .

Legman, G. (1968) *The Rationale of the Dirty Joke,* New York. . . .

Lessing, Gottfried Ephraim (1956) 'Zerstreute Anmerkungen über das Epigramm und einige der vornehmsten Epigrammatisten' in *Lessings Werke,* ed. Kurt Wolfel, 1967, Frankfurt, Bd. 2.1:274. . . .

Lloyd, L. J. (1953) 'Erotion: a Note on Martial', *G&R* 22:39. . . .

Malnati, Thomas Peter (1984) 'The Nature of Martial's Humour', Diss. Witwatersrand, Johannesburg. . . .

Mason, H. A. (1988) 'Is Martial a Classic?', *The Cambridge Quarterly* 17:297. . . .

McCartney, E. S. (1919) 'Puns and Plays on Proper Names', *CJ* 14:343. . . .

Mehnert, K.-H. (1970) 'Sal romanus et esprit français. Studien zur Martialrezeption im Frankreich des 16. und 17. Jahrhunderts. Romanistische Versuche und Vorarbeiten', Diss. Bonn. . . .

Moreno, Jesús Luque (1987) 'Los versos del epigrama de Marcial', *Actas* 11:263. . . .

Moya de Baño, Francisca (1967) *El tema de Hero y Leandro en la literatura española,* Murcia. . . .

Paukstadt, R. (1876) 'De Martiale Catulli Imitatore', Diss. Halle. . . .

Pelckmann, J. (1908) 'Versus Choliambi apud Graecos et Romanos Historia', Diss. Greifswald. . . .

Pertsch, Erik (1911) 'De Valerio Martiale graecorum poetarum imitatore', Diss. Berlin. . . .

Plass, Paul (1985) 'An Aspect of Epigrammatic Wit in Martial and Tacitus', *Arethusa* 18:187. (1988) *Wit and the Writing of History,* Madison.

Platnauer, M. (1948) *Spicilegia Valeriana', G&R* 17:12. . . . (1951) *Latin Elegiac Verse,* Oxford.

Race, William H. (1982) *The Classical Priamel from Homer to Boethius,* Leiden.

Redfern, Walter (1984) *Puns,* Oxford. . . .

Reitzenstein, R. (1893) *Epigramm und Skolion. Ein Beitrag zur Geschichte der alexandrinischen Dichtung,* Giessen. . . .

Røstvig, Maren-Sophie (1974) 'The Ideal of the Happy Man' in *Literature and Western Civilization* IV, edd. D. Daiches and A. Thorlby, London, p. 291. . . .

Salemme, C. (1976) *Marziale e la 'poetica' degli oggetti. Struttura dell' epigramma di Marziale,* Naples. . . .

Siedschlag, Edgar (1977) *Zur Form von Martials Epigrammen,* Berlin. . . .

Smith, Barbara Herrstein (1968) *Poetic Closure, How Poems End,* London. . . .

Snyder, Jane M. (1980) *Puns and Poetry in Lucretius' 'De rerum natura',* Amsterdam. . . .

Sullivan, J. P. (1968) *The 'Satyricon' of Petronius: A Literary Study,* London and Bloomington, Indiana. . . .

(1986) 'Some Versions of Martial 10.47: The Happy Life', *CO* 63:112.

(1987) 'Martial's Satiric Epigrams' in *Homo Viator: Classical Essays for John Bramble,* edd. M. Whitby, Philip Hardie, Mary Whitby, Bristol, p. 259. . . .

(1989) 'Is Martial a Classic? A Reply', in *The Cambridge Quarterly* 18:303. . . .

Szelest, Hanna (1974) 'Domitian und Martial', *Eos* 62:105. . . .

(1976) 'Martials Epigramme auf merkwürdige Vorfälle', *Philologus* 120:251.

(1981) 'Humor bei Martial', *Eos* 69:293. . . .

Tolkiehn, Johannes (1969) 'Die inschriftliche Poesie der Römer' in Pfohl (1969) p. 113. . . .

Veyne, P. (1964) 'Martial, Virgile et quelques épitaphes', *REA* 66:48. . . .

Watson, E. A. (1987) *A Study of Selected English Critical Terms 1656-1800,* Oxford. . . .

Weinreich, Otto (1926) *Die Distichen des Catull,* Tübingen.

————. (1928) *Studien zu Martial: literarhistorische und religionsgeschichte Untersuchungen, Tüb. Beiträge zur Altertumswiss.* IV, Stuttgart. . . .

West, Alfred, S. (1912) *Wit and Wisdom from Martial Contained in 150 of his epigrams chosen and done into English with Introduction and Notes,* London. . .

Wilkinson, G. A. (1948) 'The Trisyllabic Ending of the Pentameter, its Treatment by Tibullus, Propertius and Martial', *CQ* 42:68. . . .

Wölfflin, Eduard (1887) 'Das Wortspiel im Lateinischen', *Sitzungsberichte der Königl. Bayer. Akad. der Wissenschaften* (philos. philol. u. histor. Classe) 2:187. . . .

John Garthwaite (essay date 1993)

SOURCE: "The Panegyrics of Domitan in Martial, Book 9," *Ramus,* Vol. 22, No. 1, 1993, pp. 78-102.

[In the essay that follows, Garthwaite focuses on Book 9, discerning a subtle thematic relationship between the epigrams praising the emperor Domitian, the verses dedicated to the young slave Earinus, and the poems dealing with patronage. Garthwaite concludes that the Earinus cycle represents an ironic commentary on Domitian's moral hypocrisy, and that the patronage epigrams suggest that imperial panegyrics are really nothing more than the poet's fulfillment of his part of the client-patron bargain.]

The rich diversity of Martial's *Epigrams* makes up, in Duff's words, 'one of the most extraordinary galleries of literary pictures, vignettes, miniatures, portraits, caricatures, sometimes almost thumbnail sketches' of the Classical Age.[1] Yet the books are by no means merely random or haphazard assortments. Like other Roman poets, Martial was attentive to the need to impose a sense of order and continuity on his published material.[2] Naturally the very number of poems, as well as their varied inspiration and often impromptu composition, would militate against any overall thematic coherence.[3] Moreover, Martial was also keen to exploit the inherent variety of the epigrammatic genre; thus, in the preface to **Book 8,** he says that he has interspersed more trivial and jocular material among his panegyrics of the emperor to prevent continuous eulogies from becoming tiresome to their recipient.

Such use of *variatio,* however, itself implies a concern for the arrangement and presentation of the collection.[4]

And there are other evident signs of order, particularly at the beginning of the books where we find dedications to Martial's most prominent patrons (starting with the emperor), along with the introduction of themes which will be elaborated later in the volume.[5] We also meet pairs of contrasting or complementary epigrams, either juxtaposed as with Martial's address to Domitian in **1.4** and the emperor's imagined sarcastic response in **1.5,** or slightly separated as with the epitaphs to Erotion (**5.34** and **5.37**). Sometimes a small group may be held together by a less obvious motif, as in variations on the theme of excessive drinking in **1.26-28.** Occasionally also, a pair of epigrams may frame and unify a much longer sequence. In **3.68,** for instance, Martial warns the respectable matrons among his readers of the blatantly phallic nature of the following poems; the subsequent series of obscene epigrams is then capped in **3.86** by a reminder to the same matrons of the earlier warning, and an invitation to read on. But perhaps the most frequent architectural devices of the books are the series, or cycles, of epigrams written as elaborations on a particular theme and spread intermittently throughout the volume. As Barwick has shown, these poems are placed in a deliberate order, both to create a logical progression within their series and to add a sense of unity to the book as a whole.[6]

Such forms of thematic arrangement, though relatively simple and intermittent, at least allow the possibility of more subtle and extensive interplays. Thus, for example, in his analysis of the ways Martial collected and published in the larger edition those epigrams written initially for individual patrons, White asks:[7]

By means of placement, or revision, or addition, were poems for patrons made to play upon one another? Were allusions created which would draw readers into a clearer knowledge of the patron and his relationship with the poet? Did the published book present patron-oriented material in any aspect which it would previously have lacked?

In fact, White goes on to doubt the likelihood of a positive answer to his queries. But in at least one instance, namely the panegyrics of Domitian spread throughout **Book 9,** the epigrams not only interact subtly with several other poems in the book but also assume, I believe, an altogether different significance when sewn into the larger context of the volume than they would have had as a self-contained booklet or *libellus* perhaps presented separately to the emperor.[8]

The Imperial Series

The cycle begins with the opening poem of **Book 9:**

> Dum Ianus hiemes, Domitianus autumnos,
> Augustus annis commodabit aestates,
> dum grande famuli nomen adseret Rheni

Germanicarum magna lux Kalendarum,
Tarpeia summi saxa dum patris stabunt,
dum voce supplex dumque ture placabit
matrona divae dulce Iuliae numen:
manebit altum Flaviae decus gentis
cum sole et astris cumque luce Romana.
invicta quidquid condidit manus, caeli est.

(9.1)

While Janus shall bestow winters on the years, Domitianus autumns, and Augustus summers; while the great day of Germanicus' Kalends shall claim the almighty name of the Rhine, now our captive; while the Tarpeian rock of the supreme father still stands; while the matron, with her devout prayers and offerings of incense, shall appease the gentle divinity of our sanctified Julia; then so long will the towering glory of the Flavian house endure, along with the sun, the stars and the light of Rome. Whatever this unconquered arm has founded belongs to heaven.

The poem introduces several imperial motifs: the birthday of Domitian signified by the renaming of October (the month of his birth) as Domitianus; the emperor's victories along the Rhine in honour of which he had renamed September (the month of his accession to the throne) with his own title Germanicus; the Capitoline temple of Jupiter, rebuilt by Domitian (and a topic to which Martial will return in **9.3**); and the imposing temple of the Flavian family (*altum Flaviae decus gentis*, 'the towering glory of the Flavian house', **9.1.8**), built on the emperor's birthplace and containing the ashes of (among others) his niece Julia.[9] The reference in the last line to the celestial nature (*caeli est*) of Domitian's building programme provides the bridge for the continuation of the imperial theme in **9.3**:

Quantum iam superis, Caesar, caeloque
     dedisti
     si repetas et si creditor esse velis,
grandis in aetherio licet auctio fiat Olympo
     coganturque dei vendere quidquid
     habent,
conturbabit Atlans, et non erit uncia tota,
     decidat tecum qua pater ipse deum.
pro Capitolinis quid enim tibi solvere
     templis,
     quid pro Tarpeiae frondis honore potest?
quid pro culminibus geminis matrona
     Tonantis?
     Pallada praetereo: res agit illa tuas.
quid loquar Alciden Phoebumque piosque
     Laconas?
     addita quid Latio Flavia templa polo?
expectes et sustineas, Auguste, necesse est:

nam tibi quod solvat non habet arca
     Iovis.

(9.3)

If you wanted to become a creditor, Caesar, and call in IOU's for all you have given to the gods and to heaven, then even if there were a giant auction in the celestial halls of Olympus, and the gods were forced to sell all their possessions, Atlas will still go broke and even the father of the gods will not have enough to settle up with you at ten cents in the dollar. For what can he possibly pay you for his Capitoline temples or for the honour of the Tarpeian oak-wreath? What can the Thunderer's wife pay you for her two temples? I'll forget about Minerva—she's your partner anyway. But what's the point of talking about Hercules and Phoebus and the pious Spartan twins; or about the Flavian shrine, the new addition to the Latin heaven? You will just have to hold on, Augustus; for Jupiter's money chest does not have enough to pay you back.

Implicit in this poem is the suggestion of Domitian's superiority to the Olympian gods, even to Jupiter himself.[10] This is measured in what might be considered rather crude and unflattering financial terms, and despite the ostensibly playful and light-hearted tone of the epigram, some of Martial's audience may have found an unpleasant irony in the notion that the emperor's building projects would exhaust even an Olympian vault, given the widespread (and apparently not altogether unfounded) fears at the time that they were, in fact, draining the public treasury.[11]

Both **9.1** and **9.3** are distinctly topical. The reference in the title Germanicus (**9.1.3f.**) to Domitian's military victories, for example, recalls the emperor's return in only the previous year from his latest Northern campaigns, honoured in a lengthy cycle in **Book 8**. And though many of the temples mentioned here date from various points in the reign, the celebration of the building programme in general seems to have been prompted by the recent opening of the Flavian shrine which frames the list of monuments at **9.1.6-8** and **9.3.12**.[12] Moreover, the publication of **Book 9** in A.D. 94 also coincided with the completion of a new temple for Hercules (cf. **9.64.2**) and with the celebration of the Capitoline contest (noted at **9.3.8**).[13]

The prominence of these epigrams at the beginning of the book, and the way they seem to itemise an imperial table of contents, suggests that they are programmatic. And this is borne out by the fact that their various themes are elaborated in a lengthy cycle of poems spread throughout the book.[14] In **9.20** Martial notes that the spot now covered by the marble and gold of the Flavian temple once witnessed the birth of Domitian; and again the poet implies the superiority of the emperor to Jupiter, adding that while the latter had only the rattling weapons of Cybele's eunuch priests to guard him in infancy, Domitian had the aegis and thunderbolt of the king of the gods himself. In still lighter vein, **9.34** pictures a rather tipsy Jupiter looking down enviously from heaven at the gleaming temple and tomb of the Flavians, and comparing it with the barrenness of his own rumoured burial place on Crete. **9.39** takes up the related topic of Domitian's birthday, also echoing **9.20.**7f. with the claim that this is the day on which Cybele would have wished to give birth to Jupiter (**9.39.**1f.). Martial adds that it is also the birthday of Caesonia, the wife of his friend Rufus, thus giving the latter double cause for celebration.

9.23 and **24** pick up the subject of the literary contests and Domitian's special relationship with Minerva, both noted earlier at **9.3.**8-10.[15] In **9.23** Martial prophesies that the poet Carus' Alban victory crown which now adorns a bust of the emperor will soon be joined by the winner's wreath from the Capitoline contest; and **9.24** compares the features of Domitian portrayed on the bust with the radiance of a kindly Jupiter, noting that such a likeness could only have been crafted by Minerva herself. Domitian's military victories are honoured once again in **9.31,** in which the sacrificial bird which Velius had sworn to offer on the safe return of his imperial commander is portrayed as not only offering itself willingly on the altar but also miraculously revealing silver coins in its mouth as it dies.

The indebtedness of Hercules to Domitian, noted at **9.3.**11, is elaborated in **9.64** and **65,** describing how the emperor has condescended to give his own features to a bust of Hercules in the latter's new temple. Domitian's superiority to the other gods, suggested earlier in the case of Jupiter, is now explicit; he is the 'greater Hercules' (*maiorem Alciden,* **9.64.**6) whose beauty, if only his lesser counterpart had possessed it, would have made him master, rather than slave, of the tyrannical Eurystheus (**9.65.**1-7). Similarly, an overt identification of Domitian with Jupiter is voiced in **9.91,** in which Martial humorously suggests that given the choice of dinner invitations from both the emperor and Jupiter, though heaven were closer than the palace, he would still be bound to his own earthly Jove (*me meus in terris Iuppiter ecce tenet,* 'see, my Jupiter holds me on earth', **9.91.**6).[16] The penultimate epigram of the cycle, **9.93,** retains this sympotic atmosphere, but with its emphasis on the name and titles of Domitian specifically recalls the format of the opening of **9.1;** Martial calls for a measure of wine for each letter of the name of the god Caesar (**9.93.**3f.), and a rose garland for each letter of the name of the ruler (Domitianus) who had founded the 'proud temple of

his sacred clan' (*sacrae nobile gentis opus,* **9.93.**6). Finally the poet asks his slave-boy for ten kisses to symbolise 'the name'—Germanicus—'which the god brought back from the Thracian world' (*nomen ab Odrysio quod deus orbe tulit,* **9.93.**8).

The final epigram of the cycle, **9.101,** is also the longest poem of the book; it continues the theme of **9.64** and **65** in comparing the labours of the lesser Hercules unfavourably with those of the greater, Domitian. Martial also recapitulates Domitian's services to Jupiter (**9.101.**14) and the Northern military triumphs which earned him the title Germanicus (*victor Hyperboreo nomen ab orbe tulit,* 'he brought back, as victor, a name from the Hyperborean world', **9.101.**20). The list concludes with what amounts to an index of the imperial themes of **Book 9:**

> templa deis, mores populis dedit, otia ferro,
> astra suis, caelo sidera, serta Iovi.

> **(9.101.**21f.)

He has given temples to the gods, morals to the people, peace to the sword, immortality to his family, stars to heaven, and victory wreaths to Jupiter.

As its length, position and contents show, this epigram was clearly written as the culmination of the series, intended as the epilogue of the imperial cycle and virtually of the book itself. Thus we can see that, despite their variety of theme and tone, and their seemingly random distribution throughout the book, the epigrams of this cycle are not simply an unplanned or unconnected assortment; rather, they follow a consistent scheme with a detailed, programmatic introduction (**9.1** and **9.3**), a systematic development, and concluding synopsis (**9.101**). One element of the conclusion, however, namely the theme of Domitian's moral leadership (*mores populis dedit,* 'he has given morals to the people', **9.101.**21), is missing from the two prefatory poems. But this, in fact, takes us back to another pair of epigrams, likewise placed at the beginning of the cycle and of the book:

> Tibi, summe Rheni domitor et parens orbis,
> pudice princeps, gratias agunt urbes;
> populos habebunt: parere iam scelus non est.
> non puer avari sectus arte mangonis
> virilitatis damna maeret ereptae,
> nec quam superbus computet stipem leno
> dat prostituto misera mater infanti.
> qui nec cubili fuerat ante te quondam,
> pudor esse per te coepit et lupanari.

> **(9.5)**

To you, mighty conqueror of the Rhine and parent of the world, prince of purity, the cities give thanks. Now they will have a populace; for giving birth is no longer a crime. No longer does any boy, mutilated by the greedy slave-dealer's well-practised knife, grieve for the destruction of his virility; nor does the impoverished mother give her prostituted infant the vile earnings for some arrogant pimp to count out. The decency which, before your reign, could not even be found in the marriage-bed, is now beginning to show itself even in the brothel.

Tamquam parva foret sexus iniuria nostri
    foedandos populo prostituisse mares,
iam cunae lenonis erat, ut ab ubere raptus
    sordida vagitu posceret aera puer:
immatura dabant infandas corpora poenas.
    non tulit Ausonius talia monstra pater,
idem qui teneris nuper succurrit ephebis,
    ne faceret steriles saeva libido viros.
dilexere prius pueri iuvenesque senesque,
    at nunc infantes te quoque, Caesar,
        amant.

(9.7)

As if it were a negligible injury to our sex to prostitute males to be defiled by the public—even the crib was not safe from the pimp; infant boys, torn from their mother's breast, would solicit sordid wages with piteous wailing. Immature bodies would suffer unspeakable outrage. The Ausonian father could not endure such dreadful horrors—just as he recently came to the aid of our growing youth, and stopped savage lust from inflicting sterility on men. Already boys, and men of all ages revered you. But now even infants love you, Caesar.

The initial description of Domitian as conqueror of the Rhine (*Rheni domitor,* **9.5**.1) provides a link with **9.1**. Moreover, the placement of **9.5** and **9.7** at the beginning of the book—clearly paired with **9.1** and **9.3**—as well as the summary of their theme in the conclusion at **9.101**.21, surely indicate that they too have a programmatic function, to introduce another set of poems in the imperial cycle, this time on Domitian's moral reforms. But further epigrams on this topic are neither as obvious nor, it seems, as numerous as those which develop from **9.1** and **9.3**.

We can point to **9.28** in which the comic actor Latinus insists that though his stage character is bawdy, his private life is pure, in keeping with the moral concerns of the emperor (*nec poteram gratus domino sine moribus esse,* 'I could not find favour with our master without moral principles', **9.28**.7). Similarly, **9.79** highlights the difference between the arrogance of the palace retinue of former emperors and the respectfulness and modesty of the present courtiers, who suppress their natural instincts to conform with the morals of their ruler:

nemo suos—haec est aulae natura potentis—
    sed domini mores Caesarianus habet.

(9.79.7f.)

No servant of Caesar retains his own manners, but—such is the spirit of the mighty palace—each holds true to those of his master.

At least these two poems indicate the programmatic nature of **9.5** and **9.7**, though it seems odd that such prominence in the introduction to what is otherwise a carefully schematised collection is given to a subject which apparently has a minor role in the remainder of the cycle. Moreover, Martial subsequently develops the theme of **9.5** and **9.7** with a significant alteration; for both **9.28** and **9.79** are concerned with the difference between appearance and reality (or expectation) in moral character, rather than with the actual censorial legislation outlined in the introduction—unlike the very specific connections between the prologue and elaboration of the rest of the cycle.

In **9.28** Latinus' public persona is debauched but his private life pure, while (in contrast) for the courtiers in **9.79** it is the propriety demanded in their public role that makes them suppress their natural instincts. In each case, admittedly, the criterion is the standard publicly required by the emperor. But as if to stress that appearances may be no less deceptive even among seemingly zealous and incorruptible moralists, Martial places immediately before **9.28** an epigram portraying a certain Chrestus, who also publicly advocates the highest moral standards and denounces contemporary vice with all the fervour of an old-time censor—while secretly performing fellatio on young boys. Clearly the two poems are deliberately juxtaposed, as shown by their strong verbal links in the references to the Curii (**9.27**.6 and **28**.4), the theatre (**9.27**.9 and **28**.5) and Cato (**9.27**.14 and **28**.3).

The theme of moral hypocrisy is, in fact, continued in **9.47** in which Pannychus preaches the teachings of Democritus and Zeno, and sports the shaggy beard of an old-fashioned Stoic, while being a notorious pathic. Similarly in **9.70** Caecilianus hypocritically rants at the immorality of the age, though it is his own morals, Martial concludes, that make the present times sordid. Thus, each of these three epigrams (**9.27, 47, 70**) presents an individual who poses as a watchdog of public morality whilst practising the very vices he condemns. Indeed, with their thematic and verbal interplays they seem to form a unified group which is no less consciously linked with the poems on Domitian's moral leadership.[17] Significantly also—and perhaps surprisingly, since it might be considered a common theme in Martial—this motif of hypocrisy and double standards in morality is voiced more often in **Book 9** than in any other.[18]

This paradoxical development from **9.5** and **9.7** of the subject of Domitian's curatorship of morals is further emphasised by the beginning, after only three epigrams (a total of ten lines), of another series of poems directly related to the emperor, though dedicated to Earinus (**9.11, 12, 13, 16, 17, 36**). Here indeed the topics of child prostitution and castration are echoed most strongly, for as we shall see, Martial stresses two features about Earinus: first, that he was Domitian's catamite and, second, that he had also suffered castration.[19] The relevance to **9.5** and **9.7** is clear—and striking; for this combination of poems seems to hint at precisely the same contrast between appearance and reality that Martial works into the theme of Domitian's moral leadership in the rest of **Book 9.**

The epigrams to Earinus were written to commemorate the dedication of clippings of the young slave's hair—marking his transition from boyhood—to the temple of Asclepius in his native Pergamum. Martial may have been asked (as we know had been the case with Statius) to compose some poems for the occasion;[20] hence a possibly uncontroversial explanation for their inclusion in **Book 9,** making their proximity to the epigrams on Domitian's moral edicts innocent, or at least unavoidable. But perhaps we should instead question the motivation for **9.5** and **9.7.** For in contrast to the topicality of the imperial motifs in **9.1** and **9.3,** the law against castration was over ten years old.[21] Granted, we can not know how recently Domitian had prohibited the prostitution of children, since no writer other than Martial bothers to mention it, though Suetonius, for example, provides an otherwise detailed discussion of the emperor's censorial legislation.[22] For Martial himself, Domitian's laws governing morality are a noticeably infrequent subject for panegyric, occurring elsewhere only at **6.2** and **6.4.** Arguably, then, his unusual interest in this topic in **Book 9** was actually prompted by its relevance to the figure of Earinus. Certainly, by including the final Earinus poem (**9.36**) in the imperial cycle of the book, Barwick also felt that the two series are consciously intertwined rather than fortuitously juxtaposed.[23] Nevertheless, his belief that these epigrams are unequivocally favourable to both Domitian and Earinus still prevails.[24]

The Earinus Epigrams

> Nomen cum violis rosisque natum,
> quo pars optima nominatur anni,
> Hyblam quod sapit Atticosque flores,
> quod nidos olet alitis superbae;

> nomen nectare dulcius beato,
> quo mallet Cybeles puer vocari
> et qui pocula temperat Tonanti,
> quod si Parrhasia sones in aula,
> respondent Veneres Cupidinesque;
> nomen nobile, molle, delicatum,
> versu dicere non rudi volebam;
> sed tu syllaba contumax rebellas.
> dicunt Eiarinon tamen poetae,
> sed Graeci quibus est nihil negatum
> et quos . . . ["*Ares*" *Ares*] decet sonare:
> nobis non licet esse tam disertis
> qui Musas colimus severiores.

(9.11)

> A name born with the violets and roses,
> by which the year's best part is called;
> a name that savours of Hybla and Attic
>   flowers,
> that bears the scent of the proud bird's nest;
> a name sweeter than the gods' own nectar,
> by which Cybele's boy, and he who
>   measures out drinks
> for the Thunderer would like to be called.
> If you utter his name in the royal palace,
> Venuses and Cupids make reply.
> A name so noble, soft and delicate
> that I wanted to express it
> in more than just a slipshod verse.
> But you—obstinate syllable—deny me.
> There are poets who say Eiarinos.
> But they are Greek and aren't bound by
>   convention.
> To them, 'Ares' sounds just as good
> with a long or short A.
> But we can't be quite so clever,
> for the Muses we worship are far less
>   flexible.

This first epigram of the series is teasing and allusive, refusing to identify its subject but repeatedly emphasising the name (*nomen,* 1,5,10; *nominatur,* 2), its derivation from springtime (1f.), and its resulting associations with vernal images of honey, fragrance and rebirth (3-6). One would naturally think of a name derived from the Latin *ver.* Not until Martial finally offers the metrically adapted form *Eiarinon* in line 13 do we realise we have been tricked as well as teased—for the name actually comes from the Greek *ear* (spring). But this initial insistence on a name which denotes a season is strikingly similar to the way in which the imperial cycle itself opens, with Martial's designation of autumn by the name Domitianus (**9.1**.1) and by the title Germanicus, claimed from 'the proud name of the enslaved Rhine' (*grande famuli nomen . . . Rheni,* **9.1.**3). As we have seen, the significance of the emperor's name and title will play a major role in the rest of the cycle, supplying the them of **9.93**, and being emphasised in the summation at **9.101.20**. Likewise, the name of Earinus as designator of springtime will continue to be emphasised, providing the main theme of the next two poems (**9.12** and **13**). An alert reader, however, may already have noticed a deliberate interlocking of the first Earinus poem and the imperial cycle. For in **9.1**, Martial mentions only three seasons—the winter denoted by Janus, the autumn by Domitianus (and Germanicus), the summer by Augustus (**9.1.1-4**). It is the subject of **9.11**, Earinus, the personification of springtime, who now supplies the fourth, and so completes the frame.

With this succinct illustration of Martial's schematic technique, we have as sure a sign as we can hope to find that the epigrams for Domitian are designed from their very outset also to incorporate the Earinus poems. As the author subtly implies, these are not two distinct cycles but a coherent and inseparable whole—though their intrinsic contradictions will surely make us begin to question the nature of the panegyrics and Martial's attitude to the emperor.

For the moment, however, let us follow the clues, as Martial supplies them, to the identity of the subject of **9.11**. It is a name, he continues, by which both Cybele's boy and Jupiter's cupbearer would prefer to be called (6-8), a name to which, if spoken in the palace, Venuses and Cupids respond (8f.). The analogy with Attis, who suffered emasculation as a result of Cybele's jealous love for him, strongly suggests that the subject of **9.11** is similarly a *castratus*. And Ganymede, Jupiter's young attendant and lover, is commonly used by Martial to typify attractive slave boys who serve the homosexual interests of their master.[25] In fact, we deduce from the next line that this particular slave belongs to the emperor. Thus, still without revealing the actual identity of his subject, Martial has focused our attention on what he considers to be the essential details about him—the derivation of his name from springtime, his emasculation, and his status as Domitian's young slave and lover. These features of the boy are then encapsulated in the description of the name as *nobile, molle, delicatum* ('noble, soft and delicate', 10)—terms applicable not only to springtime but also to one who gains nobility from an association with the emperor and who is, as the last two epithets suggest, an effeminate and catamite.[26] It seems as if the final revelation of the name, while providing an unexpected twist, is rather incidental.

The reference to Venuses and Cupids (**9.11.9**) who respond to the sound of Earinus' name obviously recalls the opening of Catullus 3, on the death of Lesbia's pet sparrow: *lugete o Veneres Cupidinesque* ('Mourn O Venuses and Cupids'). Martial's vague

respondent ('make reply') leaves unclear exactly what sort of response these deities make in Earinus' case. Perhaps we are to imagine that they simply repeat the name. But in the strong Catullan echo we do seem to hear a mournful reply, though this would hardly suit the ostensibly laudatory tone of the epigram. It has long been argued, of course, that the Catullan poem is itself ironic, involving a sexual joke in which *passer* ('sparrow') is used to signify 'penis'.[27] And in several epigrams in which Martial refers to Catullus' sparrow, the context does seem to invite, indeed even depend on, such an interpretation. In **11.6**, for example, Martial sets out to write light-hearted verse in keeping with the spirit of the Saturnalia (**11.6.1-4**); he calls on his slaveboy, Dindymus, first to mix powerful measures of wine such as Pythagoras (Nero's cup-bearer and lover) once prepared for his master, and then to 'give me kisses in Catullan profusion' (*da nunc basia, sed Catulliana,* **11.6.**14). In return, Martial 'will give you Catullus' sparrow' (*donabo tibi passerem Catulli,* **11.6.**16). Admittedly, the wine is requested for poetic, rather than erotic, stimulation (**11.6.**12f.); but the specific analogy with the notorious relationship of Pythagoras and Nero surely suggests that Martial also wants sexual favours from Dindymus.[28]

Moreover, at **7.14** Catullus' sparrow is mentioned in an explicitly phallic context: Martial's girlfriend has suffered the loss of 'her plaything and delight' (*lusus deliciasque suas,* **7.14.**2)—not such a loss as Lesbia once wept over when robbed of 'the naughty tricks of her sparrow' (*nequitiis passeris orba sui,* **7.14.**4), nor such as Stella's mistress mourned when deprived of her pet dove (**7.14.**5f.): his own girl, Martial claims, is not affected by such trifling losses. Rather, she has lost a slave-boy of barely twelve years old 'whose penis was not yet half a yard long'! (*mentula cui nondum sesquipedalis erat,* **7.14.**10). It has been suggested that 'the sexual exposé at the end of the epigram works only if something innocuous is intended in the earlier part'.[29] But this surely misses the point that the ostensibly ingenuous and sympathetic tone of the poem is a deliberately comic set-up, containing euphemistic *double entendres* which the punch-line suddenly makes grossly explicit. If Martial is also exploiting this ambiguity in his reference to Earinus, then there is an obvious, though cruel, irony in the idea of a mournful response to the name of this emasculated youth from those Venuses and Cupids who once lamented the demise of Lesbia's sparrow.

The following two epigrams which, along with **9.11**, make up the first segment of the Earinus cycle, again promote the symbolism of the name:

> Nomen habes teneri quod tempora nuncupat anni,

cum breve Cecropiae ver populantur
   apes:
nomen Acidalia meruit quod harundine
   pingi,
      quod Cytherea sua scribere gaudet acu.
nomen Erythraeis quod littera facta lapillis,
      gemma quod Heliadum pollice trita
      notet,
quod pinna scribente grues ad sidera tollant;
      quod decet in sola Caesaris esse domo.

(9.12)

You have a name that denotes the year's tender
season, when Athenian bees destroy the brief
springtime; a name that deserves to be coloured
by Venus' pen, that the Cytherean goddess happily
embroiders with her needle. A name marked out
by the letter made of Indian pearls, by the
Heliades' amber rubbed with the thumb. A name
that cranes should raise to the heavens, writing it
out with their wings. A name that properly belongs
only in Caesar's house.

Si daret autumnus mihi nomen, Oporinos
   essem,
      horrida si brumae sidera, Chimerinos;
dictus ab aestivo Therinos tibi mense
   vocarer:
      tempora cui nomen verna dedere, quis
      est?

(9.13)

If autumn were to give me my name,
   I would be Oporinos;
if it were winter's stormy sky,
   then I would be Chimerinos.
Were I named after summer's season,
   you would call me Therinos.
But the one named for springtime—
   who is he?

As in **9.11,** so in **9.12** the analogy between Earinus
and springtime is reciprocal; for just as the boy's
name denotes the season, so the terms used to describe spring itself are also depictive of Earinus.
Tener ('tender'), for example, used of the new year
at **9.12.1,** can also refer to young boys and, synony-
mously with *mollis* and *delicatus,* especially to effeminates.[30] But perhaps a more sombre and plain-
tive analogy emerges in the following line as Martial emphasises, not the beauty and fragrance of the
season, but the destruction of springtime by the
honey-bees. And in further variation, the apparent
reference to the V-shape of a pearl necklace
(**9.12.5f.**), and the mention of the letter formed by
the wings of cranes in flight (**9.12.7**), indicate that
Martial is now connecting Earinus with the Latin

ver as well as the Greek *ear.* Thus he may well be
envisaging possible Latin as well as Greek deriva-
tives for the name of this person called after the
'spring season' (*tempora verna,* **9.13.4**). In fact,
verna is especially suggestive since, besides being
the adjective 'vernal', it is also the noun 'houseboy'
or 'home-bred slave'. Again, this would aptly describe Earinus' status; but we should note, first, that
Martial occasionally uses *verna* in a derogatory sense,
and also that the term contradicts the earlier suggestion of the boy's nobility (*nomen nobile,* 'noble
name', **9.11.10**).[31]

The images of beauty, fragrance and fertility in **9.12,**
as in **9.11.1-5,** associate Earinus not simply with
springtime but especially with the erotic world of
lovers. Compare, for example, Martial's description
of his beloved little Erotion in **5.37,** an epigram aptly
termed 'a lover's address to his mistress rather than
a lament for a child'.[32] For Erotion was more desirable than Indian pearls, had breath as sweet as Attic
honey or amber rubbed in the palm, and was rarer
than the phoenix. The similarly sensuous portrayal
of Earinus perhaps befits one who is the emperor's
delicatus. But it might also be considered tactless to
dwell on the sexual nature of the relationship between this particular slave and master. Moreover,
we know by now that Earinus is a eunuch. Thus,
while these analogies with regeneration and the fertility of spring may harmonise with his name, they
are singularly inappropriate, if not cruelly sarcastic,
when applied to the person.

Not until **9.16** and **17,** and then only in passing,
does Martial reveal the occasion for which he has
composed the series:

Consilium formae speculum dulcisque
   capillos
      Pergameo posuit dona sacrata deo
ille puer tota domino gratissimus aula,
      nomine qui signat tempora verna suo.
felix quae tali censetur munere tellus!
      nec Ganymedeas mallet habere comas.

(9.16)

The mirror, planner of his beauty, and those tender
curls are offered in dedication to Pergamum's god
by the boy who of all the palace is dearest to his
master and whose name signifies springtime.
Blessed the land that is honoured by such a gift.
It would never prefer even the locks of Ganymede.

Latonae venerande nepos qui mitibus herbis
   Parcarum exoras pensa brevesque colos,
hos tibi laudatos domino, rata vota, capillos
   ille tuus Latia misit ab urbe puer;
addidit et nitidum sacratis crinibus orbem

quo felix facies iudice tuta fuit.
tu iuvenale decus serva, ne pulchrior ille
in longa fuerit quam breviore coma.

(9.17)

Latona's revered grandson whose magic herbs
gently prevail over the threads and short distaffs
of the Fates, to you that boy (your own *alumnus*)
has sent from the Latin city that gift he promised,
his hair so dearly prized by his master. To the
dedication of these curls he has added a gleaming
mirror whose reflection assured him that his happy
beauty was safe. Preserve his youthful radiance
so that he will not have been more beautiful with
long hair than he is now with short.

Here, then, the bare details: the dedication of some
clippings of hair, along with a mirror, to the temple
of Asclepius in Pergamum. Indeed, only in **9.16.**3f.
do we realise that this is a continuation of the Earinus
cycle, for the donor is the boy most pleasing in the
whole palace to his master, and one whose name
signifies springtime. The nobility which the young
slave gains from the emperor is reflected even in the
offering, since the land which receives it is 'fortunate' (*felix,* **9.16.**5) and would prefer it even to the
locks of Ganymede (**9.16.**6). The analogy hints not
so much at the superiority of Earinus to the heavenly cup-bearer, as at that of Domitian, the earthly
Jove, to Olympian Jupiter; it also serves to remind
us, however, of the pederastic nature of the relationship between the emperor and his attendant. Both
ideas will be elaborated in **9.36,** the final epigram of
the Earinus series.

In **9.17** Martial addresses Asclepius as the god whose
medicinal skills can offset the normally brief span
allotted by the Fates and so prolong human life; the
poet asks him to preserve Earinus' youthful beauty
so that he will be no less attractive with short hair
than he was with long. It is not an idle prayer, for
as we know from several of Martial's epigrams (including **9.36**), the cutting of a slave-boy's long curls
normally signified, along with his first beard, the
onset of manhood and so the end of his sexual relationship with his master.[33] As a eunuch, Earinus will,
of course, remain beardless. Nevertheless, the clip-
ping of the 'long hair so highly praised by his master' (*laudatos domino . . . capillos,* **9.17.**3) could
portend not only the loss of Earinus' childlike at-
tractiveness but also the end of his usefulness to the
emperor. Finally, we should note that *felix* typically
means not only 'fortunate' but also 'fertile' and 'productive';[34] thus, in its repeated use, first describing
the land that receives Earinus' gift (*felix . . . tellus,*
'fortunate the land', **9.16.**5), and then the beauty of
the boy himself (*felix facies,* 'fortunate appearance',
9.17.6), we may again detect an ironic contrast be-

tween the symbolic significance of Earinus' name
and the sterility of the person himself.

The last epigram of the series seems intended, with
its strong similarities to **9.34** (on the Flavian palace), to bind together the cycles to Earinus and
Domitian:

Viderat Ausonium posito modo crine
    ministrum
        Phryx puer, alterius gaudia nota Iovis:
'quod tuus ecce suo Caesar permisit ephebo
        tu permitte tuo, maxime rector,' ait.
'iam mihi prima latet longis lanugo capillis,
        iam tua me ridet Iuno vocatque virum.'
cui pater aetherius 'puer o dulcissime,' dixit
        'non ego quod poscis, res negat ipsa
    tibi:
Caesar habet noster similis tibi mille
    ministros
        tantaque sidereos vix capit aula mares;
at tibi si dederit vultus coma tonsa viriles,
        quis mihi qui nectar misceat alter erit?'

(9.36)

The Phrygian boy, well known pet of the other
Jupiter, had seen the Ausonian cupbearer with
his hair newly clipped.

'Almighty ruler,' he cries, 'look at what your
Caesar has allowed his young man to do. Give
yours the same right. Already the first fluff of a
beard lies hidden beneath my long curls. Even
now your Juno sneers at me and calls me a man.'

'My sweet young boy,' replied the heavenly father,
'it is not I, but circumstance, that prevents you.
Our Caesar has a thousand servants like you; his
palace, for all its size, can scarcely contain all
those dazzling young males. But if the cutting of
your hair should reveal the face of a man, who
else will I have to mix the nectar for me?'

Just as **9.34** pictures a rather inebriated Jupiter peer-
ing enviously down from the Olympian banquet at
the splendour of Domitian's Flavian temple, so **9.36**
depicts Ganymede looking down jealously from
heaven at the cutting of Earinus' long hair. Both
epigrams also have a similarly playful tone and a
conversational format culminating in a monologue
from Jupiter implicitly acknowledging his inferiority
to the emperor. Again it is noticeable, however, that
in each case Domitian's presumed superiority is based
on mundane, material considerations—on the gleaming Flavian tomb compared to the squalor of Jupiter's
supposed burial place (**9.34.**7f.), and the emperor's
thousand attendants compared to Jupiter's sole and
irreplaceable cupbearer (**9.36.**9-12). And is there not

also, perhaps, a comic incongruity in the image of the horde of handsome young Ganymedes packed into the palace of an emperor hailed only shortly before as 'prince of purity' (*pudice princeps,* **9.5.**2)?

The mythological scenario presented in this epigram seems altogether jocular, and might even be considered too inconsequential or frivolous to merit careful analysis. In comparing Domitian to Jupiter, and Earinus to Ganymede, Martial's aim seems to be flattery in an off-hand, light-hearted manner. Yet he also seems particularly keen to stress the variety, or even incompatibility, of possible perspectives in this supposedly guileless and uncontroversial analogy. At **9.36.**2, for example, Martial calls Jupiter the other, and so inferentially the inferior, Jove—reflecting, of course, his earlier claim of Domitian as the greater god. In contrast, Ganymede sees Jupiter as the supreme deity, addressing him as 'almighty ruler' (*maxime rector,* **9.36.**4). Similarly, Ganymede characterises himself (and Earinus) as an ephebe, a young man (**9.36.**3f.), though Jupiter insists on seeing him still as 'my sweet young boy' (*puer o dulcissime,* **9.36.**7). Moreover, though Ganymede equates himself initially with Earinus, his following words highlight, apparently unwittingly, an essential difference between them. For Juno, he adds, can already see the beginnings of a beard beneath his own long curls, and ridicules the man masquerading as a boy (**9.36.**5f.). Jupiter himself emphasises the fact in a further comparison. Domitian, he notes, has a thousand such attendants, a thousand handsome males (*sidereos . . . mares,* 'dazzling young males', **9.36.**10), all like Ganymede; the cutting of Ganymede's hair, he admits, is indeed likely to reveal the man beneath. The difference is unstated but cleverly stressed. For it is not simply his irreplaceability that prevents Ganymede from cutting his hair like Earinus, but the fact that Earinus is a eunuch—and Ganymede is not.

Jupiter, then, may provide a celestial parallel for his earthly counterpart's pederasty, but not for the castration of his young favourites. In spite of his rather desperate attempts to delay his cupbearer's adolescence, and his professed lack of a substitute, Jupiter has not resorted to the emasculation of Ganymede in order to prolong their sexual partnership. In contrast, the throngs of young *delicati* who, according to Martial, can scarcely be contained even in the vastness of Domitian's palace, would seem to relieve the emperor of even the practical necessity of having his slave boys castrated to gratify his sexual interests. In sum, the Earinus series closes with a sly subversion of the notion of Domitian's superiority to Jupiter and so contradicts a major premise of the imperial cycle. For now, by the ethical standards postulated by the emperor himself, Jupiter emerges as Domitian's moral superior.

Domitian's Patronage of Martial

Martial's ability and fame as a poet gave him, in his view, a greater claim to support from patrons than could be expected by other clients. For in return for their assistance, Martial could offer his benefactors celebrity and even immortality through his verse.[35] Granted, he often acknowledges the triviality of epigram compared to the loftier genres; yet he is also confident that his poetry will survive long after the monuments and tombs of the likes of Messala (significantly, the great Augustan patron of letters) have crumbled to dust (**8.3.**5-8; **10.2.**9-12).[36] Thus he can boast:

> gaudet honorato sed multus nomine lector,
>   cui victura meo munere fama datur.

>   (**5.15.**3f.)

Many a reader rejoices in the celebration of his name and the fame which will live after him, thanks to me.

But as Juvenal would later insist (*Sat.* 7.1-3), hopes for support of the arts lay increasingly with the emperor. So, in **5.19,** Martial asserts that in this age of selfishness it falls on Domitian to assume such a duty. For while the reign is unparalleled for the celebration of triumphs and the splendour of the city's buildings (**5.19.**5), the one significant blemish is the lack of personal patronage; for the poor still cultivate unrewarding friendships (**5.19.**8). There can be no finer quality in a monarch, the poet concludes, than for him to take on the mantle of patron (**5.19.**15). Significantly, however, Martial immediately follows this epigram with an assertion of bitter distaste for his own duties as a client (**5.20**). Here, he expresses his hatred of having to pay court in the halls of the mighty—a labour not of love or loyalty but of necessity which, far from providing him with the comforts and pleasures of life, actually deprives him of them (**5.20.**5-13).

A similar pairing occurs at **6.10** and **11,** in the first of which Martial complains that while the emperor presents great temples to Jupiter, he ignores the comparatively trivial requests of the poet (**6.10.**3f.). Again we note the contrast between the lavish expenditure on building projects and the utter lack of personal patronage. Martial concludes with the hope that silence may not mean refusal. The following epigram is addressed to Marcus, surely not coincidentally a self-indulgent, but stingy patron. The poet claims that the current lack of loyal servants, such as Pylades once was to Orestes, is caused by the absence of generous, fair-minded masters. While Marcus enjoys the finest food and clothing, but denies them to Martial, he still expects the poet to honour him

(6.11.5-8). But such loyalty cannot be gained by words alone—to gain this affection, the poet concludes, one must first buy it (*hoc non fit verbis, Marce; ut ameris, ama,* 'this doesn't come about by words, Marcus: to be loved you must love', 6.11.10). Again, the juxtaposing of related topics seems deliberate, and the blunt expression of the rather business-like obligation to pay for the poet's services seems to apply implicitly even to the emperor.

It is hardly surprising or accidental, then, that the eulogies of Domitian at the beginning of **Book 9** are closely followed by a material request from the poet (9.18). And appropriately, given the praise of the imperial building projects, Martial asks Domitian not for money but for the provision of a water supply for his house in Rome and his Nomentan farm.[37] He closes by promising that if his prayer is answered, he will honour the water 'as a Castalian spring or rain from Jupiter' (*Castalis haec [sc. unda] nobis aut Iovis imber erit,* 9.18.8). The analogies are highly suggestive, hinting clearly that the gift would, like the spring of the Muses, give Martial renewed poetic inspiration to repay his benefactor—specifically by celebrating him as the living Jove.

Yet, curiously, the following poem deals specifically with the insincerity of a client's praise of his master's buildings:

> Laudas balnea versibus trecentis
> cenantis bene Pontici, Sabelle.
> vis cenare, Sabelle, non lavari.

>   **(9.19)**

> You praise in full three hundred verses,
> Sabellus, Ponticus' bath house.
> He dines well, too.
> It's dinner you're after, not a bath.

This epigram is itself the last in a short series on the *cena* as an illustration of the pretences and realities of the client-patron relationship. In 9.9 Martial chastises Cantharus for his abusive behaviour even as a dinner guest, reminding him that he cannot indulge in both free speech and free food; the point seems to be that the man who is given his due forfeits the right to criticise. In 9.14, by contrast, he reveals that an unnamed client's apparent devotion to his patron is actually insincere; for it is the dinner table, with its expensive meat and fish, that he loves, not the patron himself (9.14.3). Martial concludes that he could buy such affection for himself if only he could provide equally fine fare. The subject of insincere clients is then repeated in the Sabellus epigram. But given the context, between Martial's petition to the emperor and promise of a verse tribute for its fulfilment (9.18) and his praise of Domitian's Flavian

temple (9.20), it is surely no coincidence that Sabellus is, like Martial, a poet—offering poetic tributes to a patron's building activities as a means of gaining support. And significantly, Sabellus' panegyric of the bath house, fulsome though it is, is prompted not by any admiration of the structure, or even ostensibly (especially in view of 9.14) of its builder, but entirely by the hope of material reward.

In sum, by a careful intertwining of poems and ideas, Martial seems to be suggesting to the astute reader a means of understanding the imperial panegyrics, not so much as expressions of sincere admiration and loyalty but, so to speak, as his down-payment in the transaction between patron and poet, from which he anticipates a return in the form of material support.

Whether Martial's plea for a private water supply was, in fact, ever granted, is still debated.[38] Certainly, he nowhere acknowledges receipt of it. But perhaps 9.22, the next poem to deal with Martial's request for support from a patron, provides a clue, or at least an indication of the poet's expectations. He addresses the wealthy (and possibly fictitious) Pastor who believes Martial's requests for money are prompted by the trite ambition to enjoy the luxuries of life, which the poet goes on to detail at some length (9.22.3-14). Noticeably, they are items which Martial typically represents as the indulgences of selfish patrons.[39] He swears, however, that he is interested in none of these. Rather, he desires wealth in order to 'bestow gifts and erect buildings' (*ut donem, Pastor, et aedificem,* 9.22.16)—at first glance a laudable aim to be, in contrast to the majority, a generous and public-spirited patron. But we may recall 4.67 in which a praetor turns down his long-time client's request for a gift of 100,000 sesterces with the plea that he is already committed to bestowing a much larger sum on Scorpus and Thallus—since the latter were famous charioteers the deceit is patent: the praetor is betting a fortune on the races. Similarly, 9.46 describes Gellius who devotes his whole life to petty building projects just so that he can say to any client who asks him for money, 'I'm building' (*aedifico,* 9.46.6). So Martial's promise at the end of 9.22 seems ironic rather than altruistic, mocking the rich who mask their selfishness with protestations of their generosity or of more pressing financial commitments. But more to the point, only in **Book 9** does Martial attribute 'building' to the wealthy as their excuse for failing to fulfil their patronal duties and support their clients—this in a volume dominated by the theme of Domitian's vast and hugely expensive building projects.

Apparently, then, on his own ironic though subtly voiced prediction, Martial held but little hope of remuneration for his imperial eulogies, among which he would surely also have counted those of **Book 8.** For in only the previous year he had dedicated that entire book to Domitian, devoting the highest proportion of epigrams in any volume to celebrating the regime. Here too he had included a prayer for support from the emperor **(8.24)** though again tinged with the expectation of refusal (*et si non dederis, Caesar, permitte rogari,* 'even if you don't grant it, Caesar, at least allow yourself to be asked', **8.24.**3). It has been suggested that, overall, Martial was not disappointed with the amount of reward from Domitian.[40] But actually, such remuneration seems to have become increasingly sparse—perhaps reflected in the fact that his published petitions to the emperor are often accompanied by either an open reminder of the lack of support thus far, or a strong attack on the stinginess and ingratitude of patrons in general.[41]

Might this not explain, at least in part, the sly interweaving of a carefully veiled, but bitingly sarcastic element among the eulogies of Domitian which the poet subsequently incorporated and published in **Book 9**? Remarkably, on the only other occasion when Martial celebrates Domitian's moral reforms **(6.2** and **4)** there is also, as I have argued elsewhere, a subtle indictment of the emperor's hypocrisy in this area **(6.3)**, likewise followed by a complaint about his refusal to support the poet, while spending lavishly on building projects **(6.10)**.[42] As we have seen, to those whom he celebrates in his verse Martial promises wide and undying renown. But there is an almost contractual obligation to repay the poet's gift; failure to do so is tantamount, in Martial's view, to dishonouring an agreement:

> Laudatus nostro quidam, Faustine, libello
> dissimulat, quasi nil debeat: imposuit.

(5.36)

> A certain man whom I praised in my book,
> Faustinus, pretends he owes me nothing.
> He has swindled me.

The surprise is that, however devious and unobtrusive his method, Martial does not shrink from binding even the emperor by the terms of this patron-poet contract, or from gaining poetic justice when the bargain is dishonoured.

Castrate the Patron

It might be argued that this analysis has created a new and unauthorised text from **Book 9,** namely by extracting and grouping together originally distinct poems. I would point out first, however, that in his dispersal of the various cycles throughout the volumes Martial clearly intends us to see connections

between often widely separated epigrams. Moreover, we should also allow the possibility of other structural devices, based not only on verbal and thematic interplays but on length and metre, operating alongside the series to Domitian and Earinus.[43] After all, Martial's professed aim was to blend variety with continuity. But what of **9.2**? Despite its prominent placement at the beginning of the volume, and between the first two epigrams to Domitian, it seems to have little relevance to the book overall and none whatsoever to the imperial poems that enclose it:

> Pauper amicitiae cum sis, Lupe, non es
>   amicae
>   et queritur de te mentula sola nihil.
> illa siligineis pinguescit adultera cunnis,
>   convivam pascit nigra farina tuum.
> incensura nives dominae Setina liquantur,
>   nos bibimus Corsi pulla venena cadi;
> empta tibi nox est fundis non tota paternis,
>   non sua desertus rura sodalis arat;
> splendet Erythraeis perlucida moecha lapillis,
>   ducitur addictus, te futuente, cliens;
> octo Syris suffulta datur lectica puellae,
>   nudum sandapilae pondus amicus erit.
> i nunc et miseros, Cybele, praecide
>   cinaedos:
>   haec erat, haec cultris mentula digna
>   tuis.

(9.2)

You are stingy to your friends, Lupus, but not to your mistress, and your prick alone has no cause for complaint about you. That adulteress of yours grows fat on cuntshaped cakes, while your guest gets a diet of black flour. Setine wines are decanted to set your mistress's ice ablaze; we drink the black poison of a Corsican keg. You sell off entire estates to buy one night—and not even a whole one; your abandoned retainer ploughs another man's fields. Your adulteress flashes and gleams with Indian pearls. But while you are fucking, your client is hauled off to bankruptcy court. Your girlfriend gets a sedan borne by eight Syrian slaves. Your friend will be a naked corpse—small burden—on a pauper's bier. Forget about castrating those wretched young queers of yours, Cybele—*this* was the prick worthy of your knife.

The poem involves the relationship between client and patron, with Lupus portrayed as a rich patron of gross self-indulgence at the expense of his needy dependant.[44] Indeed, his name seems to epitomise his selfishness and voracious (sexual) appetite.[45] He perhaps anticipates Pastor in **9.22**, in typifying those among the wealthy who spend a fortune on their own desires while denying their impoverished friends. In fact, there are both verbal and thematic parallels between the two poems, in the reference to the Setine region (**9.2**.5 and **22**.3), as well as in the depiction of expensive wine chilled with snow (**9.2**.5 and **22**.8), and finally in the reference to costly Syrian litter-bearers (**9.2**.11 and **22**.9). More noticeably, however, the portrayal of Lupus' mistress, gleaming with Indian pearls (*splendet Erythraeis perlucida moecha lapillis,* 'your adulteress flashes and gleams with Indian pearls', **9.2**.9) is echoed shortly afterwards in the description of Domitian's beloved Earinus, whose name is symbolised by these same Eastern jewels (*nomen Erythraeis quod littera facta lapillis,* 'a name marked out by the letter made of Indian pearls', **9.12**.5). Perhaps, then, **9.2** consciously anticipates at least two later epigrams. But may we not also detect a parallel, if only in hindsight, between the depiction of Lupus' selfish prodigality and the description, in the enclosing poems, of Domitian's huge expenditure on building projects?

Most striking, however, is the way the ending of **9.2** foreshadows another major element of the imperial series. For quite unexpectedly Martial addresses Cybele (**9.2**.13); there is no need, he insists, to castrate your wretched young acolytes—*this* was the prick (Lupus') most worthy of your knife. The anticipation of the topic of the castration edict in **9.5** and **9.7** is obvious. And as in these two epigrams, so in **9.2** Martial disavows the need to emasculate innocent children. Here, instead, it is the rich patron who deserves the knife, for his disgusting self-indulgence and a neglect which inflicts the direct hardship on his needy clients. Perhaps, after all, the placement of **9.2** is purposeful. For not only is its characterisation of Lupus, presented so conspicuously at the beginning of the book, analogous to that which lurks beneath the formal portrait of Domitian in the rest of the volume; is it not also possible that the fate which Lupus apparently richly deserves may equally embrace (in the poet's wicked fancy, at least) his even more prodigal and self-serving counterpart?

Notes

¹ J. Wight Duff, *A Literary History of Rome in the Silver Age* (London 1927), 501. For the text of Martial I follow W. M. Lindsay, *M. Val. Martialis Epigrammata* (Oxford 1902).

² For a recent discussion of the architecture of Hellenistic and Augustan poetry books see M. Santirocco, *Unity and Design in Horace's Odes* (Chapel Hill 1986), 313. For Martial cf. G. Erb, *Zu Komposition und Aufbau im ersten Buch Martials* (Frankfurt am Main 1981), and the useful survey by J. Sullivan, *Martial: The Unexpected Classic* (Cambridge 1991), 217-221.

³ As noted by N. Holzberg, *Martial* (Heidelberg 1988), 37.

⁴ For *variatio* as an ordering principle see Santirocco (n.2 above), 6-9.

⁵ Cf. the analysis of the programmatic opening of Book 11 by N. M. Kay, *Martial, Book 11: A Commentary* (London 1985), 5f. Also P. Howell, *A Commentary on Book 1 of the Epigrams of Martial* (London 1980), 11f.

⁶ K. Barwick, 'Zyklen bei Martial und in den kleinen Gedichten des Catull', *Philologus* 102 (1958), 284-318.

⁷ P. White, 'The Presentation and Dedication of the *Silvae* and the *Epigrams*', *JRS* 64 (1974), 50.

⁸ For Martial's offering of various *libelli,* each dedicated to an individual patron, prior to their compilation with other epigrams to form the larger volume, see White (n.7 above), 40ff.

⁹ For Domitian's birthday (October 24, A.D. 51), accession to the throne (September 14, A.D. 81) and renaming of both months see Suet. *Dom.* 1 and 13; for the Capitoline temple and the Flavian shrine see Suet. *Dom.* 1.1 and 5.1 and Statius, *Silv.* 4.3.16-18. For Julia's burial in the shrine see Suet. *Dom.* 17.3.

¹⁰ For the equation of Domitian with Jupiter in both Martial and Statius see K. Scott, *The Imperial Cult under the Flavians* (Stuttgart 1936), 133-139.

¹¹ On the long debate about whether Domitian's building projects actually ruined the treasury see P. M. Rogers, 'Domitian and the Finances of State', *Historia* 33 (1986), 60-78. My concern is not so much with the modern verdict but with the feelings of Martial's contemporaries; and here the judgements seem unambiguous. Suetonius (*Dom.* 12.1), for example, insists that the emperor was 'drained of money by the cost of his buildings and shows' (*exhaustus operum ac munerum impensis*), and relates that someone scrawled *ARCI* on one of Domitian's many arches, punning on the similarity between *arcus* ('arch') and the Greek *arkei* ('enough'). Plutarch (*Publ.* 15) describes Domitian's temple-building as a symptom not of piety but of sickness (*noson*), and compares his mania for building with Midas' insatiable craving for gold. Cf. also Pliny, *Pan.* 51.

¹² For an excellent survey of the chronology of Domitian's building projects see B. W. Jones, *The Emperor Domitian* (London 1992), 79-98. Martial (9.1) is the first to mention the Flavian shrine; for the dating of Book 9 to A.D. 94 see L. Friedlaender (ed.), *M. Val. Martialis Epigrammaton Libri* (Amsterdam 1961), 61. The shrine is also noted by Statius (*Silv.* 4.3.18) in A.D. 95 (for the date see F. Vollmer [ed.], *P. P. Statii Silvarum Libri* [Leipzig

1898], 8f.).[13] The Capitoline contest was revived in A.D. 86 and celebrated every four years thereafter (cf. *RE* 3.1528). For the topicality of the contest in the year of the publication of Book 9 cf. also 9.35.9f. and 9.40.

[14] My enumeration of the poems which constitute the imperial cycle in Book 9 differs from that suggested by Barwick (n.6 above), 287ff. He lists 1, 3, 5, 7, 18, 20, 34, 36, 39, 64, 65, 79, 83, 91, 93, 101; but this seems rather arbitrary, including, for example, the last epigram in a series dedicated to Earinus (9.36) while omitting its predecessors (9.11-13 and 16-17). Similarly, 9.23 and 24 are excluded even though they honour Domitian no less than Carus, the actual addressee. 9.31 is also omitted, despite addressing the emperor directly in the penultimate line. In contrast, 9.39 is included, though it does not address Domitian, and celebrates Martial's friend Rufus and his wife no less than the emperor. I prefer to base my analysis on thematic development rather than on the numerical schemes apparently favoured by Barwick.

[15] For Domitian's patronage of Minerva and the Alban games in her honour cf. Suet. *Dom.* 4.4.

[16] 9.83, on the splendour of Domitian's games, addresses the emperor directly and is thus also clearly part of the book's imperial cycle. Martial jokes that Rome owes a debt of thanks not only for the spectacles themselves but also for the fact that even those poets who are otherwise always giving recitations are now attending the games, and so giving everyone's ears a rest. The topic is not specifically introduced in 9.1 or 9.3, but the praise of Domitian's munificence and the wonders of the shows (here said to excel those of previous emperors, 83.2) obviously fits comfortably into the themes established by the introductory poems.

[17] Besides the links between 9.27 and 9.28 cf. also 9.27.7f. with 9.47.2f.; 9.27.9 with 9.70.1 and 5; 9.70.7-9 with 9.79.5f.

[18] On the presumed frequency of the topic see W. S. Anderson, '*Lascivia* vs. *Ira:* Martial and Juvenal', in *Essays on Roman Satire* (Princeton 1982), 367 n.8: 'Parallels in Martial are common.' But outside Book 9 cf. only 1.24; 1.96; 2.36; 7.58; 12.42.

[19] Admittedly, Martial does not say whether Earinus had been emasculated on Domitian's orders. Statius, however, reveals that the boy had suffered castration *after* his acquisition by the emperor and his arrival in the palace (*Silv.* 3.4.65ff.).

[20] Cf. Statius *Silv.* 3 pref.

[21] For the dating of the edict to A.D. 81-82 see A. Schoene (ed.), *Eusebi Chronicorum Canonum* vol.2 (Frankfurt 1967), 160f. Martial first mentions the law in 2.60 (published A.D. 85-86).

[22] *Dom.* 7-8. See also Dio 67.212, Statius *Silv.* 4.3.10ff.

[23] See n.14 above.

[24] E.g. Sullivan (n.2 above), 43 and 145.

[25] For Attis as a *castratus* cf. 5.41.2f.; 8.46.4. For Ganymede as an exemplar of the *delicatus* cf. 5.55; 2.43.13f.; 3.39; 10.98.1f.; 11.104.19f.

[26] Cf. 9.25.3 and 9.55.3 (*mollis*); 3.58.32 (*delicatus*).

[27] See G. Giangrande, 'Catullus' Lyrics on the *Passer*', *MPhL* 1 (1976), 137-146; Y. Nadeau, 'Catullus' Sparrow, Martial, Juvenal and Ovid', *Latomus* 43 (1984), 861-868; also Howell (n.5 above), 122ff., on the *passer Catulli* in Martial's poems to Stella. Against the argument see H. D. Jocelyn, 'On Some Unnecessarily Indecent Interpretations of Catullus 2 and 3', *Latomus* 43 (1982), 97-103. Other than the reference to Earinus, Martial uses *Veneres Cupidinesque* only in the epitaph for the actor Paris (11.13). In language evocative of Catullus' sparrow poem, Martial notes that the delight of the city, its playfulness and passion, and all the Venuses and Cupids are buried with Paris (11.13.3-6). The characterisation reflects, of course, the popularity and licentiousness of Roman farce in which Paris had been a leading player. But considering that Paris had been put to death for his adultery with Domitian's wife (cf. Suet. *Dom.* 3), we might also sense a sly sexual innuendo.

[28] For the 'marriage' of Nero and Pythagoras see Tacitus *Ann.* 15.37.

[29] R. A. Pitcher, '*Passer Catulli:* The Evidence of Martial', *Antichthon* 16 (1982), 100.

[30] E.g. 4.66.9; 9.25.9.

[31] E.g. 1.41.2; 6.29.1.

[32] L. J. Lloyd, 'Erotion: a Note on Martial', *G&R* 22 (1953), 40. Note also P. Watson, 'Erotion: *Puella Delicata?*', *CQ* 42 (1992), 257: 'To the reader approaching the poem (i.e. 5.37) for the first time, the language appears unequivocally erotic.' Compare the description of Erotion at 5.37.4 (more lovely than Indian pearls) with 9.12.5; 5.37.10 (smelling of Attic honey) with 9.11.3 and 9.12.2; 5.37.11 (smelling of amber) with 9.12.6; 5.37.13 (rarer than the phoenix) with 9.11.4.

[33] E.g. 1.31; 4.7; 5.48; 11.78.3f.; 12.18.24f.

[34] For the association of *felix* with Venus and fertility, see F. M. Ahl, *Lucan: An Introduction* (Ithaca 1976), 287ff.

[35] See the discussion by Sullivan (n.2 above), 117ff.

[36] For the epigrams as *nugae* (trifles) see e.g. 2.1.6; 4.10; 4.72.3. For an excellent account of Martial's assessment of the durability of his work see Sullivan (n.2 above), 56ff.

[37] Statius made a similar request of Domitian and was granted it (*Silv.* 3.1.61ff.).

[38] See R. Saller, *Personal Patronage under the Early Empire* (Cambridge 1982), 35. Martial's publication of the request but not of any subsequent thanks surely indicates that his plea was ignored, especially since he must have known of of Statius' public thanksgiving for the grant of a similar request. For another of Martial's petitions to Domitian, followed immediately by a public expression of gratitude for the granting of it cf. 2.91 and 92.

[39] Cf. 2.43; 6.11; 10.13; 10.98.

[40] Sullivan (n.2 above), 121. In contrast, H. Szelest, 'Domitian und Martial', *Eos* 62 (1974), 105ff., argues that Martial was bitter at the lack of imperial support. For further examinations of the forms and amounts of imperial and other patronage which Martial expected see R. Saller, 'Martial on Patronage and Literature', *CQ* 33 (1983), 246-257, and P. White, '*Amicitia* and the Profession of Poetry', *JRS* 68 (1978), 74-92.

[41] Apart from the petitions, already noted, at 2.91, 5.19, 6.10, 8.24 and 9.18, see also 6.87 for Martial's prayer for the gods and the emperor to give him what he wants if he has deserved it (followed by 6.88 in which a haughty patron denies the poet the dole for failing to salute him with due formality); also Martial's reminder to Domitian at 8.82 of the need to support his poets. Of these epigrams it is worth noting that only the earliest, 2.91, is followed by an acknowledgement of the granting of a request. Similarly, Statius notes at *Silv.* 4.1.63 the long hiatus in marks of recognition from the emperor.

[42] 'Martial, Book 6, on Domitian's Moral Censorship', *Prudentia* 22 (1990), 13-22.

[43] For example, I would suggest tentatively that 9.2 (on which, however, see further below) and 9.4 are linked by their explicit obscenity (n.b. *futuente*, 9.2.10; *futui*, 9.4.1 and 2) and by the fact that both concern payment for sex. Further, like 9.2, both 9.6 (on the disdainful refusal of a patron to acknowledge Martial's morning call) and 9.8 (on Bithynicus' omission from the will of

Fabius to whom he had given annual gifts) both involve the selfishness and arrogance of the wealthy. I would note also that 9.11-13 (on Earinus) are framed by two pairs of epigrams balanced in both length and theme—9.9 and 9.14 on contrasting attitudes of clients as dinner guests, and the misogynistic pair 9.10 and 9.15 about women as marriage partners.

[44] 9.2 is the model for Juvenal, *Sat.* 7.74-78 in which the rich miser Numitor (ironically described as down on his luck [*infelix*]) has no gifts for his client but plenty for his mistress. It is worth noting that the client here is a poet (7.78); see R. Colton, *Juvenal's Use of Martial's Epigrams* (Amsterdam 1991), 297f.

[45] In 5.56, 10.40 and 10.48, Lupus appears to be a real person and a friend of Martial. But the Lupus of 7.10 is deeply in debt, while in 11.55 he is a greedy legacy-hunter. In 11.108 he is a money-lender, and in 11.18 a wealthy patron who gives Martial a 'farm' smaller than a window-box.

Bruce W. Swann (essay date (1994)

SOURCE: "Martial's Catullus" in *Martial's Catullus*, Heorg Olms Verlag, 1994, pp. 33-46.

[*In the following excerpt, Swann calls attention to Martial's numerous references to Catullus, especially those allusions in which the younger poet names Catullus as his chief literary model.*]

Naming Catullus

. . . Martial names a 'Catullus' at least twenty-five times and, though there is doubt in five cases as to which 'Catullus' Martial meant, in twenty of the cases it is clear.[5] Six times the association is with Lesbia (**6.34**.7; **7.14**.3; **8.73**.8; **12.44**.5, **59**.3; **14.77**.1); five times it is with the word *passer* (twice at **1.7**.3-4; **1.109**.1; **4.14**.13; **11.6**.16); and twice it is with Verona (**10.103**.5; **14.195**.1). Three times Martial links Catullus with the epithet *doctus* (**7.99**.7; **14.100**.1, **152**.1), three times with Marsus (**pref. 1**; **2.71**.3; **5.5**.6), and once Martial simply compares himself to Catullus (**10.78**.16).[6] In these passages Martial consistently treats Catullus as a Roman poet, some of whose works were more well known than others, but a poet who, as Martial indicates, wrote epigrams just as he is doing. There is no indication that Martial considered Catullus as an extraordinary poet of love. He had loved a certain Lesbia to be sure in his poems, but other poets had loved in their poems as well, a fact which Martial does not hesitate to mention (Mart. **8.73**; **12.44**).

In several of the six cases in which Lesbia is mentioned, for example, she is simply Lesbia, *amica Catulli*

(**7.14**.3), who was in love *cum lepido . . . Catullo* (**12.44**.5), who was *dilecta Catullo* (**14.77**.1), or who *dictavit, docte Catulle, tibi* (**8.73**.8). In two other cases Lesbia is connected with the *basia* of Cat. 5 and 7. In **6.34** Martial speaks to Diadumenus and Diadumenus and concludes:

> nolo quot arguto dedit exorata Catullo
>   Lesbia: pauca cupit qui numerare potest.[7]

> I do not want as many as Lesbia when persuaded gave to eloquent Catullus—he wants few kisses who can count them.

The same tie with Lesbia and kisses occurs at **12.59**.1-3:

> Tantum dat tibi Roma basiorum
> post annos modo quindecim reverso
> quantum Lesbia non dedit Catullo.

> Rome is giving you just now returned after fifteen years, more kisses than Lesbia gave Catullus.

At **11.6**.14, one of the five poems which mention the *passer* of Catullus, the kisses are simply Catullan: *da nunc basia, sed Catulliana.* In other cases the connection is with the famous *passer* poems (**1.7**.3; **1.109**.1; **14.77**).[8] In three instances Martial links Catullus' name with Verona, his birthplace, (again in **1.7**; **10.103**.5; **14.195**), and in one case we assume that Catullus is intended (at **1.61**.1: *Verona docti syllabas amat vatis*). The association with Catullus is particularly significant at **10.103**. After thirty-four years away from his birthplace Martial was anticipating his return to Bilbilis. He tells the *municipes* that Verona would want Martial, by reason of his fame, to be called its own as much as it calls Catullus its own—and if they do not appreciate this fact, he can always return to Rome.[9]

> ecquid laeta iuvat vestri vos gloria vatis?
>   nam decus et nomen famaque vestra sumus,
> nec sua plus debet tenui Verona Catullo
>   meque velit dici non minus illa suum.
> Excipitis placida reducem si mente, venimus;
>   aspera si geritis corda, redire licet.

> (**10.103**.3-6, 11-12)

Does the happy renown of your poet please you? For I am your honor, reputation and renown, nor does Catullus' own Verona own more to its own fine poet and it would want me to be called its own no less. If you take me back gladly on my return, I am coming; if you bear me ill will, I can leave again.

Since this poem was written near the end of his career and his return to Bilbilis, Martial was not idly compar-

ing himself with whatever poet came to mind. Rather he was making a point that he was in fact comparable to Catullus in fame, contemporary popularity, and in the bond between poet and hometown. Martial made these comparisons with a poet who was famous for writing the sort of poems that he had written, and he expressed himself in terms that his readers could understand: the comparison was between Martial and Catullus, two writers of epigram. This was the view which Martial repeatedly emphasized (as will be seen below) both early and late within his career.

The epithet *doctus* is another means of identifying Catullus which Martial used, and it is one that is often noted. J. Ferguson has written that:

> Martial values Catullus first for his 'learning'. *Doctus,* contrary to what is sometimes said, is more than a stock epithet for a poet; it is peculiarly applied to Catullus, and marks him out as the leading poet of the neoteric school, which adapted Alexandrian poetry to Latin.[10]

It would be useful for the work at hand if Martial's use of *doctus* were another instance of his singling out Catullus vis-à-vis his own work. But after examining the passages where Martial uses *doctus* of Catullus, it is not immediately clear how Ferguson's view can be the case.[11] In **Book 14**, poems **100** and **152** were written for a *Panaca* and a *Gausapum quadratum* (a 'drinking vessel' and a 'woolen cloth'). In each case the reference is geographical in intent and was meant to identify the *terra docti Catulli.* At **8.73**.8, *docte Catulle* identifies Catullus as one of a number of poets who were inspired by a beloved someone. Each name bears an epithet or a descriptive noun. In line 7 it is *arguti . . . Tibulli.* Catullus elsewhere is also *argutus* (**6.34**.7). The epithets are not mutually exclusive. The intent of the poem is not a statement of literary criticism but Martial's request *da quod amem.*[12] Lastly, in the *doctoque Catullo* at **7.99**.7 Martial associates Catullus with Marsus and expresses the hope that he may be included in the company of these two. The poem which concludes **Book 7** offers Martial's suggestion to Crispinus that Martial *nec Marso nimium minor est doctoque Catullo.*[13] None of these examples seems to reveal Martial's concern with Catullus as "the leading poet of the neoteric school." In fact, it is difficult to see how *doctus* is in any way unique to Catullus when one also finds *docti Senecae* (**4.40**.2), *docti Pedonis* (**2.77**.5), *docti nota Neronis* (**8.70**.8), and *docto placeas Apollinari* [a literary critic] (**4.86**.3). The Muses were *doctae sorores* (**1.70**.15, **9.42**.3) and *doctas . . . Pieridas* (**10.58**.5-6). One also finds, among other things, *docta Neapolis* (**5.78**.14). Paukstadt was nearer the truth in claiming that Martial used *doctus* because Ovid had already done so (*Amores* 1.15.27) and that it was metrically convenient.

et si Martialis tam saepe epitheton *doctus* cum Catullo coniungit, non coniungit ea de causa, quod Catullum studiosum Graecarum litterarum praedicare voluit . . . sed quod paene constanter hoc adiectivum Catullo a prioribus poetis, qui eum citant, adtributum esse et facile in versum inire videbat.

                 (Paukstadt, 8-9)

And if Martial joined the epithet *doctus* with Catullus so often, he did not do so for the reason that he wanted to proclaim Catullus as learned in Greek literature . . . but because he saw that this adjective is almost constantly attributed to Catullus by the earlier poets who mention him and he saw that it was metrically convenient.

Paukstadt in fact continues this thought by pointing out Martial's disfavor for the only one of the longer poems that he mentions written *more Alexandrinorum:*

Carminum longiorum, quae Catullus more Alexandrinorum composuit, ad unum tantum adludit, ad Attin, cum dicat, talia carmina se non scribere. **II, 86,** 4. Nec dictat mihi luculentus Attis / Mollem debilitate Galliambon.

                 (p. 9)

He alludes to only one of the longer poems which Catullus wrote in the style of the Alexandrians, the *Attis,* when he says that he does not write such poems. *II, 86,* 4. Nor does the brilliant Attis instruct me to write in galliambics, soft with infirmity.

Where Martial associates Catullus with familiar images (Lesbia, *basia,* Verona, and the *doctus poeta*), he is clearly referring to Catullus, the poet. Martial's associations of Catullus with Marsus (and others) will be examined below. The twentieth example at **10.78.16** is one where Martial mentions Catullus without any epithet. He bids farewell to Macer (also mentioned in **5.28** and **10.18[17].**6), who is leaving to become governor in Dalmatia.[14] At the same time he speaks of his return to Spain and his desire to be considered by Macer as second to none but Catullus.

nos Celtas, Macer, et truces Hiberos
cum desiderio tui petemus.
sed quaecumque tamen feretur illinc
piscosi calamo Tagi notata,
Macrum pagina nostra nominabit:
sic inter veteres legar poetas,
nec multos mihi praeferas priores,
uno sed tibi sim minor Catullo.

               (10.78.9-16)

I will return to the Celts and fierce Hiberians with longing for you, Macer. But nevertheless, whatever page will be brought from there, written with a reed from the fish-filled Tagus, it will bear your name, Macer. So let me be read among the poets of old; nor should you prefer many earlier ones to me, but let me be a lesser poet to you than Catullus alone.

In these examples the pattern remains consistent. Martial treats Catullus as he treats other authors, and in terms that were familiar to the readers of epigram. Although Martial did not propose to imitate all that Catullus had written, he considered him a significant epigrammatist with whom he did not at all mind being compared. What Martial says about Catullus and his epigrams will next concern us.

Martial on Catullus and his poetry

Martial's affinity for Catullus is also prominent, as might be expected, in his statements about Catullus' poetry and the extent to which he made use, often a selective use, of Catullan material. These instances will now be examined. One of the earlier and more direct statements occurs in the Preface of **Book 1.** Martial addresses his readers and positions himself and his writings with respect to Catullus and others.

Spero me secutum in libellis meis tale temperamentum ut de illis queri non possit quisquis de se bene senserit, cum salva infimarum quoque personarum reverentia ludant; quae adeo antiquis auctoribus defuit ut nominibus non tantum veris abusi sint sed et magnis [. . .] lascivam verborum veritatem, id est epigrammaton linguam, excussarem, si meum esset exemplum: sic scribit Catullus, sic Marsus, sic Pedo, sic Gaetulicus, sic quicumque perlegitur.

I hope that I have used in my books such a tone that whoever thinks well of himself is not be able to complain about them, since they have their fun with a healthy respect even for lesser people. This respect was so lacking in earlier authors that they misused the names not only of the actual people but also those of important people [. . .] I would make an excuse for the lusty frankness of my vocabulary if I were setting the example—thus Catullus writes, and Marsus, Pedo, Gaetulicus, so anyone writes who is thoroughly read.

Martial is making two main points: "first he makes it absolutely clear that he is not going to attack real people; secondly, he defends himself against the charge of indecency."[15] As to writers who had attacked 'real people' Martial is, Howell continues, "presumably thinking of Naevius, of Lucilius . . . and above all, of Catullus."[16] Catullus' attacks on Mamurra and Julius Caesar (Cat. 29 and 57) are perhaps the most notable examples. Suetonius reports Catullus' reconciliation with Caesar (*Iul.* 73), but for Martial there may not have been the luxury of a second chance, so there is a distinct moderation in the hostility of the attack.[17] Catullus freely admits to his harsh iambic verses[18] while Martial goes out of his way to distance himself from direct attacks and to insist that, although *hominem pagina nostra sapit* (**10.4.**10), still *mea nec iuste quos odit pagina laesit* (**7.12.**3). After all, continues Martial,

> quid prodest, cupiant cum quidam nostra
>   videri,
>   si qua Lycambeo sanguine tela madent,
> vipereumque vomat nostro sub nomine virus,
>   qui Phoebi radios ferre diemque negat?
> ludimus innocui: scis hoc bene . . .

> (**7.12.**5-9)

What good is it, when certain people want them to seem to be mine, if any barbs are wet with Lycambes blood, and a man spits out his venom in my name who says he cannot bear sunshine and daylight? I am a harmless person at play, you know this well . . .

The reference to Archilochus in line 6 (*Lycambeo sanguine*) points to the sort of invective Martial wished to avoid, but at the same time it indicates how much a risk his poetry ran of being of being so classified.[19] It is perhaps not without significance to note that Gaetulicus, perhaps the poet whom Martial named (**Bk. 1 pref.**), wrote an epigram concerning the tomb of Archilochus.[20] The defence against charges of indecency also recalls Catullus:

> qui me ex versiculis meis putastis,
> quod sunt molliculi, parum pudicum.
> nam castum esse decet pium poetam
> ipsum, versiculos nihil necesse est.

> (16.3-6)

[Aurelius and Furus] you think me not sufficiently chaste because of my poems, the fact that they are sensual. It is all right for a responsible poet to be decent himself; in no way is it required that his poetry be.

Martial specifically refers to his own *lascivam verborum veritatem* as the *linguam epigrammaton*. He uses *lascivus* to describe both the eroticism within elegy as well as that within his own epigrams.[21] The latter usage occurs early in **Book 1.**

> qua Thymelen spectas derisoremque
>   Latinum,
>   illa fronte precor carmina nostra legas.
> innocuos censura potest permittere lusus:

> lasciva est nobis pagina, vita proba.

> (**1.4.**5-8)

I ask that you read our poems with that frame of mind with which you watch Thymele and the mime Latinus. The censor can allow harmless jests; my book is racy, my life clean.

This certainly suggests the thought of Cat. 16 and that of Ovid's *vita verecunda est, Musa iocosa mea*,[22] as does **11.15.**13, *mores non habet hic meos libellus.* Martial expresses the same idea in the preface to **Book 8** while explaining that this book will not have his usual playfulness.

> quamvis autem epigrammata a severissimis quoque et summae fortunae viris ita scripta sint ut mimicam verborum licentiam adfectasse videantur, ego tamen illis non permisi tam lascive loqui quam solent.

> Although epigrams have been written by the sternest men of the highest rank in such a way that they seem to have imitated the mime's loose language, nevertheless I have not permitted these to speak as lustily as they are accustomed.

Martial takes it for granted that readers realize that even these *severissimi viri* can write works that have the *mimicam verborum licentiam.*

Catullus et Alii

The writers with whom Martial associates Catullus are also indicative of his understanding of Catullus as an epigrammatist. We have just seen in the preface to **Book 1** how Martial cites the example of Catullus, Marsus, Pedo and Gaetulicus in an attempt to excuse his *lascivam verborum veritatem.* They, and anyone who is *perlegitur,* use the *epigrammaton linguam.*[23] Martial mentioned Gaetulicus only here,[24] but Albinovanus Pedo's name occurs again three times: twice coupled with Marsus (see below), and once (**10.20[19].**10) in referring to the *domus Pedonis* which was near Pliny's house, whither Martial was 'sending' Thalia with his book.[25] The references to Pedo which also include Marsus are more concerned with epigrams. At **2.77** Martial berates the writings of one Cosconius[26] who thinks Martial's epigrams are long.

> disce quod ignoras: Marsi doctique Pedonis
>   saepe duplex unum pagina tractat opus.
> non sunt longa quibus nihil est quod demere
>   possis,
>   sed tu, Cosconi, disticha longa facis.

> (**2.77.**5-8)

Learn what you do not know. Often a double page of learned Marsus and Pedo handles a single poem. Those things are not long from which there is nothing you can delete; but, Cosconius, you make distichs long.

The message is clear: the quality of the content matters more than any rules regarding the length of a work. That poem (epigram) which occupies even two pages is not long if it would suffer by any deletions. Cosconius, by this standard, cannot write a distich without its seeming long. Marsus and Pedo are the epigrammatists of choice here. Several years later, in **Book 5**, Martial again joins Catullus with Marsus and Pedo.

> sit locus et nostris aliqua tibi parte libellis,
>   qua Pedo, qua Marsus quaque Catullus
>   erit.
> ad Capitolini caelestia carmina belli
>   grande cothurnati pone Maronis opus.

> **(5.5**.5-8)

Let there be a place somewhere for my works, where Pedo, Marsus and Catullus will be. Place the splendid work of tragic Vergil next to the divine poems of the Capitoline war.

Martial is asking of Sextus, the *cultor facundus Palatinae Minervae* (the librarian of the collection in the temple of Minerva on the Palatine), a place for his works—a place with Pedo, Marsus and Catullus. Martial again associates all three writers with himself and his writings. In the preface to **Book 1** the connection among the poets is the *lascivam verborum veritatem* or the *epigrammaton linguam,* whereas here it is an actual shared location within the collection. Martial takes special pains to separate himself from the writers of epic. We can only assume that he likens his own writings to those with whom he would be filed. Later, in **Book 12** Martial established these two genres at the opposite ends of the literary spectrum.[27]

> Scribebamus epos; coepisti scribere: cessi,
>   aemula ne starent carmina nostra tuis.
>   . . . . .
> audemus saturas: Lucilius esse laboras.
>   ludo levis elegos: tu quoque ludis idem.
> quid minus esse potest? epigrammata fingere
>   coepi:
>   hinc etiam petitur iam mea palma tibi.

> **(12.94**.1-2, 7-10)

I began writing epics; you started to write them. I stopped so that my poems would not rival yours . . . I attempt satires; you work at being Lucilius.

I dabble in light elegies, you do the same. What can there be of less significance? I started writing epigrams; here too my victory is sought by you.

The same contrast between epic and epigram is found at the end of **8.55(56)**. In this case, Martial explores the connection between the great poets and their patron, Maecenas, and concludes by telling Flaccus that, with the right inducements, he would still be a Marsus, that is he would still write his epigrams:

> ergo ego Vergilius, si munera Maecenatis
>   des mihi? Vergilius non ero, Marsus ero.

> **(8.55[56]**.23-24)

So will I be a Vergil if you give me the incentives Maecenas gave? I will not be a Vergil, I will be a Marsus.

Martial expresses the epigrammatic connection between Catullus, Marsus (above p. 37, n. 13), and himself several other times. In **2.71** Martial addresses a Caecilianus and suggests that he would rather the poems of Caecilianus seem inferior to his own than that those of Marsus or Catullus should seem so.

> Candidius nihil est te, Caeciliane. Notavi,
>   si quando ex nostris disticha pauca lego,
> protinus aut Marsi recitas aut scripta Catulli.
>   hoc mihi das, tamquam deteriora legas,
> ut conlata magis placeant mea? Credimus
>   istud:
>   malo tamen recites, Caeciliane, tua.

Nothing is more frank than you, Caecilianus. I have noticed that, if ever I read a few lines of my poems, right away you answer with the works of Marsus and Catullus. Are you suggesting that my poems by comparison are more pleasing, as if you were reading worse things. I believe it; still, Caecilianus, I prefer you to read your own.

Martial is doubtless pleased to have his epigrams and those of Catullus and Marsus so closely associated, and to be favored by the comparison, but the point for the present work is that the association of the three as writers of epigram is taken for granted. The same idea occurs even more clearly stated at **7.99**. Martial suggests to Crispinus what he should say to Domitian should his poems be read at court.

> dicere de nobis ut lector candidus aude:
>   'Temporibus praestat non nihil iste tuis,
> nec Marso nimium minor est doctoque
>   Catullo.'
>   hoc satis est: ipsi cetera mando deo.

> **(7.99**.5-8)

Dare, as a forthright reader, to speak about me:
'This man confers not a little on your reign, nor
is he much less than Marsus and skilled Catullus.'
This is enough, the rest I resign to the divine
Domitian himself.

With more modesty Martial here adopts a position
second to Marsus and Catullus, but one that is *nec
nimium minor.* The literary figures with whom this
writer of epigrams here compares himself are Marsus
and Catullus; the figure who is a constant in all these
comparisons is Catullus.

Martial et Alii

However predominant the relation between Martial
and Catullus appears in these passages, one must
remember that Martial was also dependent upon a
number of other writers for material, and that he
mentioned many of them in his poems.[28] Vergil for
example is named as frequently as Catullus by Martial and verbal echoes of Vergil abound, but to
Martial Vergil is clearly *the* Roman poet.[29] He is
magnus Maro (**4.14**.14, **11.48**.1, **12.67**.5), *summus
Maro* (**12.3[4]**.1), and *aeternus Maro* (**11.52**.18). At
the same time Martial bemoans the recent neglect of
the resting place of Vergil's ashes (**11.50[49]**) and
the popularity of Ennius at the expense of Vergil
(**5.10**.7). Although Martial notes how Verona and
Mantua are equally fortunate in their bard (**14.195**)
and wishes that someone would play Maecenas to
him (**1.107**), he sets himself (and Catullus) apart from
Vergil in **5.5** as we have seen. Again, Martial is
addressing Sextus, who had access to Domitian as
secretary *a studiis* and who was also librarian of the
Palatine, and asks him for a place for his own
works—a place with Catullus and others. Vergil, on
the other hand, is placed with the *carmina belli* of
Domitian.[30] Therefore, while the reputations of Vergil
and Catullus are equally important to their cities of
origin and the impact of their work is a consistent
feature of Martial's epigrams, Martial is careful to
align himself in this epigram with Catullus and to
avoid the epic company of Vergil and Domitian.[31]

Now that it is clear to what extent Martial distanced
his own poems and those of Catullus from the works
of Vergil while continuing to make equal use of the
reputation of each poet, the significance of Martial's
references to Ovid may be viewed with more appreciation. Ovid, as Friedlaender emphatically observed,
was very important for Martial's elegiacs.[32] More
recently however the emphasis on the impact of Ovid
is somewhat diminished. After pointing out Martial's
indebtedness to Catullus, Kay remarks simply that
"of other literary figures Ovid may have written epigrams."[33] Whatever the count of other verbal echoes, Martial names Ovid in but five poems and alludes to him in one other (**8.73**). One reference is a

generic plural for "poets in Rome" (*Nasones
Vergiliosque vides* at **3.38**.10); the others involve
the *Metamorphoses* (**14.192**), Corinna and/or the
Paeligni (**1.61**.6; **5.10**.10; **8.73**.9-10; **12.44**.6). In none
of these cases does Martial refer to Ovid as a model
for his poetry as he refers to Catullus. Nor for that
matter does he set himself apart from Ovid as he
does from Vergil. While the number of verbal reminiscences which Zingerle and others have noted is
certainly not without significance for demonstrating
whom Martial had read and how often these authors
came to his mind (whether consciously or not), their
impact is not as direct on the reader, ancient or
modern, as is the impact of the passages already
cited by means of which Martial tells his reader what
he is doing. In the case of Catullus, Martial not only
borrows extensively from him but he also names him
as his model, whereas he declines to name Vergil
and Ovid as models however many times he names
them or makes use of their works. . . .

Notes

. . . [5] Wiseman, *Catullus and his World* (Cambridge
1985) 189, 192ff. discusses the possibility of the
identification of C. Valerius Catullus with Catullus
the mimographer (Mart. 5.30.3 and 12.83.4). The
occasions where Martial mentions an unknown
Catullus in a non-specific context are 6.69.1 and
12.73.1-2. In the first case martial addresses Catullus
and *tua Bassa,* in the second instance, again addressed to a Catullus, the reliability of a possible
inheritance is mentioned: *heredem tibi me, Catulle,
dicis. / non credam, nisi legero, Catulle*-not an uncommon theme or concern for Martial who frequently
deals with *captatio.* See Kay's note at 11.44, and
Mart. 2.40; 4.56; 5.39; 6.62, 63; 8.27; 9.8(9), 48;
11.44, 55, 67, 83; 12.40, 90.

[6] In some of these passages Martial may mention
more than one of these Catullan points of reference
(e.g., 1.7 has both the *passer* and Verona, and 7.99
both calls Catullus *doctus* and mentions Marsus), so
Martial may actually refer to Verona or use the epithet *doctus* more frequently than this listing would
indicate. The additional references will be apparent
in the examination of the passages which follows.

[7] *Basia* and Diadumenos also occur at Mart. 3.65.9;
5.46.1-3. The name is from a statue of Polykleitos
and "für ein Non plus ultra jugendlicher Schönheit
galt" (Friedlaender, 3.65.9).

[8] These three references occur early in the works of
Martial (Friedlaender I, pp. 50ff.). Two other references to a *passer Catulli* are later and more ambiguous. One, *sic forsan tener ausus est Catullus / magno
mittere Passerem Maroni* (4.14.13-14), uses *passer*
as a "Titel des Buchs des Catull" (Friedlaender, ad

loc.); the other, *donabo tibi Passerem Catulli* (11.6.16), offers "precise references . . . [which] are difficult to establish" (Kay, ad loc.). Kay suggests three interpretations: *passer* as (1) sparrow, (2) poems, or (3) *mentula,* and argues convincingly for the third. See also Howell, 1.7, and additional remarks there by Giangrande, who reopened this question in recent times in "Catullus' Lyrics on the *passer*," *Museum Philologum Londiniense* 1 (1976) 137-46 [=*Scripta minora Alexandrina* 4 (Amsterdam 1985) 487-96].

9 Much the same thought was expressed years earlier at 14.195, though in this case the relation is between Catullus and Vergil and the emphasis is on the similar 'size' of their fame as contrasted with the difference in size of their cities of origin: *tantum magna suo debet Verona Catullo, / quantum parva suo Mantua Vergilio* [As much as great Verona owes its Catullus, so little Mantua owes Vergil].

10 J. Ferguson, "Catullus and Martial," *PACA* 6 (1963) 7.

11 Newman, *RomC,* pp. 18-24 emphasizes Plautus' use of *doctus* as *callidus* and *malus,* then details Catullus' use of *doctus* and that of Lucretius and Cicero. He concludes (24) that Catullus "is *doctus* because he knows how to play on our feelings, because he has the dexterity in words that recalls a pantomime artist's nimbleness in the dance allied to the worldly wisdom of a courtier (better, a court jester) and the insight of a philosopher."

12 Martial's litany includes: Propertius/Cynthia, Gallus/Lycoris, Tibullus/Nemesis, Catullus/Lesbia, Ovid/Corinna, and Vergil/Alexis. Note that no particular attention is drawn to Catullus/Lesbia to differentiate them from any of the other pairs. This is also one case where Martial notes a difference between Catullus and himself. At 8.73.8 it was Lesbia who *dictavit, docte Catulle, tibi,* while Martial (12 pref.) attributes anything that pleases in his books to the fact that *dictavit auditor.*

13 Marsus, an Augustan writer of epigrams (a book entitled the *Cicuta*) and epic (an *Amazonis*), is grouped with Catullus and others as epigrammatists in the preface to Book 1 by Martial. A few fragments survive in C. Buechner, *Fragmenta poetarum Latinorum* (Leipzig 1982) 141-3; Schanz-Hosius, II, pp. 174-76. Crispinus was also mentioned by Juvenal at 1.27, 4.1ff., and 4.108 though of course Juvenal's treatment of him is far different. Martial was forced to deal with Crispinus directly, Juvenal was not. W. S. Anderson has "sketched out the lines of the controversy" of the relation between Martial and Juvenal in his "*Lascivia* vs. *ira:* Martial and Juvenal," *California Studies in Classical Antiquity* 3 (1970) 1-34

[=*Essays on Roman Satire* (Princeton 1982) 362-395].

14 Cf. Propertius 1.6, the farewell to a departing official. See *Menander Rhetor,* eds. D. A. Russell and N. G. Wilson (Oxford 1981) 126-9 for different kinds of the *propemptikon,* and F. Cairns, *Generic Composition in Greek and Roman Poetry* (Edinburgh 1972) 7-10, who examines this passage of Menander.

15 Howell, p. 96 includes Horace with Juvenal and Persius who "all feel obliged to apologise for not attacking real people (see E. J. Kenney, "The First Satire of Juvenal," *PCPhS* 8 (1962) 29-40 . . ." On the other hand Quintilian (*I.O.* 10.1 96) and Diomedes (Keil, *GL* I, 485, 11-17) count Horace among iambographers (cf. Newman, *RomC,* p. 46, n. 15). J. C. Bramble, *Persius and the Programmatic Satire* (Cambridge 1974) 196 allows Horace to have it both ways: "Horatian iambics are divided against themselves. At *Epod.* VI.13-14, Horace likens himself to the savage Archilochus . . . yet later, in the theoretical *Ep.* I.19-23ff., he follows Lucilius and Callimachus in disowning malevolence"; so too of the satires (198): "in *Sat.* II.1 he adopts an ambiguous stance, at one moment a pacifist, at another, an aggressor."

16 In "The Poet Cn. Naevius, P. Cornelius Scipio and Q. Caecilius Metellus," *Antichthon* 3 (1969) 32-47, H. D. Jocelyn reviewed the stories that "the poet Naevius had suffered police action of some kind for criticizing men of state," and found that "support is given to the view that they contain elements of truth" (33). For Lucilius, see W. Krenkel, *Lucilius Satiren* (Leiden 1970) I, pp. 22-23: "Freunde und Feinde."

17 M. Coffey, *Roman Satire* (London 1976) 98 refers to some of the hazards of the writer who either made or seemed to have made unwarranted statements about the emperor or others. While there is not "any justification for including Martial among the Roman satirists" (Coffey, p. 7), the hazards would have been the same.

18 Cat. 36.5, 40.2, 54.6 and frag. 3. While Quintilian admits that *iambus non sane a Romanis celebratus est ut proprium opus* and that it was *aliis quibusdam interpositus,* he does classify Catullus as one who had the *acerbitas* of the iambic (*I.O.* 10.1.96). Whether or not Horace was justified in claiming *Parios ego primus iambos / ostendi Latio* (*Ep.* 1.19.23-4) is a matter of some dispute. Catullus as *scriptor lyricus* was Jerome's statement (*Chronica* 150H). For other ancient passages mentioning Catullus in this light see Wiseman, *Catullus:* Appendices, esp. "V Iambics and Invective."

19 Friedlaender, 7.12: "wie hier klagt M. auch VII 72

X 3; 5; 33 darüber, dass unter seinem Namen giftige Schmähgedichte veröffentlicht wurden."

[20] *Anth. Pal.* 7.71. For estimonia on Lycambes, his daughters and Archilochus see M. L. West, *Iambi et elegi Graeci* I (Oxford 1971) 15.

[21] For elegy: *lascivus elegis an severus herois?* (3.20.6) and *Cynthia te vatem fecit, lascive Properti* (8.73.5). In 12.94 elegy and epigram are at the lower end of the scale of genres.

[22] Ovid *Tr.* 2.354. Some seventy lines later Ovid points out that Roman authors, as well as the Greeks, have had some less than serious things to say about love. *Romanus habet multa iocosa liber* (2.422). Among these Ovid includes *lascivus Catullus* who wrote not only of the *femina, cui falsum Lesbia nomen erat* (2.428), but of many other loves as well *in quibus ipse suum fassus adulterium est* (2.430). For Ovid the point that is worth making does not concern 'Lesbia', but the fact that Catullus revealed *suum adulterium,* though Catullus uses the word pejoratively of others (e.g., 66.84; 67.36; 78.6). Ovid's apparent lack of an appreciation for the 'romantic' forces which Lesbia unleashed in Catullus—forces which have, for some reason, only been rightly perceived in the last century—is shared by Martial and, as we hope to demonstrate, by many others.

[23] That is, indecent language and content "since the form of the epigram was so commonly used for erotic subjects" (Howell, p. 98). Recall Cat. 16.5-6.

[24] Cn. Cornelius Lentulus Gaetulicus (cos. 26 AD) was killed by Caligula; see Skutsch, *RE* IV (1900) 1384-86. Perhaps he is the author of nine epigrams in the *Greek Anthology,* one of which, 11.409, deals with a woman who drank too much. She is not unlike Martial's Phyllis who, on the morning after, renews her kisses in hopes of receiving more wine (12.65).

[25] Thalia, "die Muse des Epigramms" (Friedlaender, 4.8.12). At 7.17.4 she is *lascivae Thaliae* (cf. *lascivam veritatem* of the preface to Book 1). It is better not to disturb Pliny during the day, Martial says, wait until the carefree evening hours when his epigrams are more appropriate.

[26] Friedlaender, 2.77.1: "ob aber an eine wirkliche Person zu denken ist, erscheint zweifelhaft."

[27] A similar listing at 3.20 is not as orderly. In 12.94, says Coffey, p. 5, Martial "lists the genres in descending order of nobility (and size)."

[28] See for example Zingerle and E. Wagner.

[9] Vergil's name appears in 19 of Martial's poems with at least one indirect reference to him (8.73.9). Catullus appears in 17 poems, once in the preface to Book 1, and in four poems where the reference is not necessarily to Catullus Veronensis.

[30] Friedlaender, 5.5.1: "Sextus scheint hiernach das Amt *a studiis* bei Domitian bekleidet zu haben und zugleich Bibliothekar gewesen zu sein" (Sextus appears according to this to have occupied the position in charge of learning and to have been at the same time librarian); (v. 7): "Domitian hatte hiernach ein Gedicht über den Kampf um das Capitol im December 68, wobei er selbst in Gefahr gewesen war, verfasst." Or, was it an epic on the Gigantomachy (Newman, *RomC,* p. 79, n. 11)?

[31] This passage itself may be ascribed simply to Martial's delicate position in addressing Domitian, a position which would become still more precarious for Martial. Book 5 was published in the year 89, the year after which H. Szelest, "Domitian und Martial," *Eos* 62 (1974) 113 noted the change in Martial's approach to Domitian: "indessen finden wir in der früher, d. i. bis zum Jahre 90 entstandenen Büchern 17 von 23 Epigrammen, welche Äusserungen enthalten, die den Herrscher unwillig stimmen konnten, während nur 6 in den später veröffentlichten auftauchen." As for Vergil, the epic poet par excellence, Martial had also ascribed a less serious side to him in the *Apophoreta* (14.185).

[32] "Im elegischen Distichon schliesst sich M. zunächst an den grössten Meister dieser Form, Ovid, an. Ihm ist er in der Unerschöpflichkeit des Reichthums an Motiven und Wendungen, in der Fülle, Zierlichkeit und Glätte des Ausdrucks, in der Eleganz des Versbaus, auch in der Neigung zur Selbstwiederholung, sowohl der stofflichen als der formellen, verwandt" (Friedlaender I, p. 25). Zingerle's work, which Friedlaender notes, is perhaps, by virtue of its strengths, responsible for the emphatic nature of his remark.

[33] Kay, p. 13. Kay is circumspect in the commentary: "M. seems here to be borrowing from Ovid and distorting things" (11.29.8); "semicremata: only elsewhere in poetry at Ov. *Ibis* 632 . . . M. may have borrowed it from there" (11.54.2); "the line owes something to Ovid" (11.60.4).

Works Cited

Unless noted otherwise, citations of Catullus are from the text of W. Eisenhut (Leipzig 1983); those of Martial are from W. M. Lindsay (Oxford 1929).

ANRW Aufstieg und Niedergang der römischen Welt

CTC *Catalogus translationum et commentariorum*

PACA Proceedings of the African Classical Association

RE Real-Encyclopädie der klassischen Altertumswissenschaft

TAPA Transactions of the American Philological Association

Secondary Sources

Coffey, M. *Roman Satire* (London 1976)

Ferguson, J. "Catullus and Martial," *PACA* 6 (1963) 3-15

———. *Catullus* (Oxford 1988) [=*Greece and Rome: New Surveys in the Classics* 20]

Friedlaender L. *M. Valerii Martialis epigrammaton libri* (Leipzig 1886)

Howell, P. *A Commentary on Book One of the Epigrams of Martial* (London 1980)

Kay, N. M. *Martial Book XI: A Commentary* (New York 1985)

Newman, J. K. *Roman Catullus and the Modification of the Alexandrian Sensibility* (Hildesheim 1990)

Quinn, K. *Catullus: An Interpretation* (New York 1973)

Schanz, M. v. and C. HOSIUS. "C. Valerius Catullus," *Geschichte der römischen Literatur, erster Teil* (Munich 1927) 292-307

Sullivan, J. P. *Martial the unexpected classic* (Cambridge 1991)

Szelest, H. "Domitian und Martial," *Eos* 62 (1974) 105-114

Wagner, E. *De M. Valerio Martiale poetarum Augusteae aetatis imitatore* (Königsburg 1880)

Williams, G. *Tradition and Originality in Roman Poetry* (Oxford 1968)

Wiseman, T. P. *Catullus and his World: A Reappraisal* (Cambridge 1985)

Zingerle, A. *Martial's Ovid-Studien* (Innsbruck 1877)

FURTHER READING

Bellringer, A. R. "Martial, the Suburbanite." *Classical Journal* XXIII, No. 6 (March 1928): 425-35.

Claims that Martial was happiest at his small farm near Nomentum because it reminded him of his homeland.

Bramble, J. C. "Martial and Juvenal." In *The Cambridge History of Classical Literature*, Vol. 2, *Latin Literature*, edited by E. J. Kenney, pp. 597-623. Cambridge: Cambridge University Press, 1982.

Compares Juvenal with Martial, emphasizing the differences between them. In Bramble's judgment, although Juvenal recreates the Rome of Martial in his early satires, he attacks it with bitterness and hyperbole, challenging the traditional values that Martial treats with caution and respect.

Burriss, Eli Edward. "Martial and the Religion of His Day." *Classical Journal* XXI, No. 9 (June 1926): 679-80.

Looks briefly at references to religious beliefs and practices in Martial's epigrams.

Carrington, A. G. "Martial." In *Neronians and Flavians: Silver Latin I*, edited by D. R. Dudley, pp. 236-70. London: Routledge & Kegan Paul, 1972.

Calls attention to the skillful conjunction of style, content, and occasion in the best of Martial's verses. Carrington also stresses Martial's influence on writers as diverse as John Milton, Matthew Prior, George Orwell, and Ogden Nash.

Church, J. E., Jr., and J. C. Watson. "The Identity of the Mother in Martial VI. 3." *University of Nevada Studies* III, No. 1 (1911): 28-31.

Focuses on what epigram 6.3 may contribute to modern knowledge of the relationship between the emperor Domitian and Julia, his niece and mistress.

Colton, Robert E. "Juvenal and Martial on the Equestrian Order." *Classical Journal* 61, No. 4 (January 1966): 157-59.

Compares passages in which both Juvenal and Martial deride upstarts who have achieved equestrian status. Colton finds Martial's humor essentially light-hearted and Juvenal's acerbic.

———. *Juvenal's Use of Martial's Epigrams: A Study of Literary Influence*. Amsterdam, Adolf M. Hakkert, 1991, 775 p.

A detailed study of the impact of Martial's epigrams on Juvenal's satires.

Downs, Robert B. "Creator of the Epigram." In his *Famous Books: Ancient and Medieval*, pp. 217-20. New

York: Barnes & Noble, 1964.

A brief review of the literary and historical significance of Martial's work.

Duff, J. Wight. "Martial and Minor Flavian Poetry." In his *A Literary History of Rome in the Silver Age,* pp. 498-530. New York: Charles Scribner's Sons, 1927.

A comprehensive appraisal of Martial's work by the leading commentator on Martial in the first half of the twentieth century. The judgments Duff expresses here regarding Martial's preeminent stature as a writer of epigrams have been frequently cited—and generally endorsed—by later critics.

Duff, J. Wight. "Martial: The Epigram as Satire" in *Roman Satire: Its Outlook on Social Life*, University of California Press, 1936, pp. 126-46.

Duff discusses Martial's epigrams in the context of the tradition of Roman satire, particularly with regard to verse-forms and themes. Emphasizing Martial's originality and unusual powers of observation, he contends that Martial's indebtedness to other literary models is slight.

Giulian, Anthony A. *Martial and the Epigram in Spain in the Sixteenth and Seventeenth Centuries.* Publication of the Series in Romantic Languages and Literature, No. 22. Philadelphia: University of Pennsylvania, 1930, 117 p.

Prefatory remarks to Giulian's in-depth evaluation of Martial's influence on Spanish Renaissance literature.

Hawes, Adeline Belle. "A Spanish Poet in Rome." In her *Citizens of Long Ago: Essays on Life and Letters in the Roman Empire,* pp. 91-110. New York: Oxford University Press, 1934.

A romantic sketch of Martial's life and works that stresses his attachment to his native land.

Howell, Peter. Introduction to his *A Commentary on Book One of the Epigrams of Martial,* pp. 1-18. London: Athlone Press, 1980.

Reviews Martial's life and career, the ways in which he reshaped the form and content of the epigram, and his prodigious literary influence.

Leary, R. J. Introduction to *Martial Book XIV: The Apophoreta,* edited by T. J. Leary, pp. 1-28. London: Duckworth, 1996.

A detailed study of the *Apophoreta.* Leary furnishes background information on the celebration of Saturnalia, discusses the literary tradition of "catalogue" poems, and analyzes the arrangement of these epigrams by pairs and subject matter.

Marino, Peter A. "Woman: Poorly Inferior or Richly Superior?" *Classical Bulletin* 48, No. 2 (December 1971): 17-21.

Evaluates epigram 8.12—specifically, Martial's warning against marrying a rich woman—in the context of Roman laws and traditions concerning the legal status and permissible social conduct of married women.

Mason, H. A. "Is Martial a Classic?" *Cambridge Quarterly* 17, No. 4 (1988): 297-368.

Addresses the question of whether Martial was a "great" poet who, in his finest verses, spoke for all of humankind. Mason provides a close reading of scores of Martial's epigrams as he assesses the poet's tone and matter, his insight into the complexity of artistic composition, and his understanding of what constitutes a moral life.

Mendell, Clarence W. "Martial and the Satiric Epigram." *Classical Philology* XVII, No. 1 (January 1922): 1-20.

Examines the epigram in Roman literature before Martial and the lines of influence that shaped his development of the genre. Mendell asserts that Stoic satire profoundly affected the tone and subject matter of Martial's epigrams.

Nixon, Paul. "Martial." In his *Martial and the Modern Epigram,* pp. 31-51. New York: Longmans, Green, 1927.

An overview of Martial's life and works that defends him against the traditional charges of sycophancy and obscenity. Flattering one's patrons was standard practice then as now, Nixon points out, and Martial's pornographic verses represent only a minority of his epigrams.

Reeve, M. D. "Martial." In *Texts and Transmission: A Survey of the Latin Classics,* edited by L. D. Reynolds, pp. 239-44. Oxford: Clarendon Press, 1983.

A concise survey of the three basic groups of Martial manuscripts in French and Italian collections from the Middle Ages. Reeves considers whether the variants in these manuscript groups are evidence that Martial published different versions during his lifetime or whether the discrepancies represent revisions introduced during the process of transmission.

Sullivan, J. P. "Martial's Sexual Attitudes." *Philologus* 123, No. 2 (1979): 288-302.

Infers, from the picture the writer presents of himself in his poems, that Martial's sexual preference was active pederasty, and that he feared and resented sexually aggressive women. Sullivan contends that in both his choice of love objects and his bias against liberated women, Martial expressed conventional sexual values of his time.

———. Introduction to *Martial,* edited by J. P. Sullivan, pp. 1-66. New York: Garland, 1993.

A broad survey of Martial's reception and influence

from ancient times to the late twentieth-century. Sullivan focuses on Martial's many translators, imitators, and commentators, but he also traces the textual history of Martial's poems as well as the evolution of literary theory with respect to the form and function of the epigram.

Tanner, R. G. "Levels of Intent in Martial." In *Aufstieg und Neidergang der Römischen Welt,* edited by Hildegard Temporini and Wolfgang Haase. *Principat,* edited by Wolfgang Haase, 2624-77. Berlin: Walter de Gruyter, 1986.

Argues that Martial embedded several layers of meaning in the text of his epigrams. To test his hypothesis, Tanner analyzes the poet's use of different meters in relation to tone and content, his use of Stoic doctrine in Book 1, and the personalities of the people he satirized and to whom he addressed his poems.

Additional coverage of Martial's life and career is contained in the following sources published by Gale Group: *Dictionary of Literary Biography, Vol. 211*; *Poetry Criticism*, Vol. 10.

CLASSICAL AND MEDIEVAL LITERATURE CRITICISM

INDEXES

Literary Criticism Series
Cumulative Author Index

Literary Criticism Series
Cumulative Topic Index

CMLC Cumulative Nationality Index

CMLC Cumulative Title Index

CMLC Cumulative Critic Index

How to Use This Index

The main references

Calvino, Italo
1923–1985 .... CLC 5, 8, 11, 22, 33, 39,
73; SSC 3

list all author entries in the following Gale Literary Criticism series:

BLC = *Black Literature Criticism*
CLC = *Contemporary Literary Criticism*
CLR = *Children's Literature Review*
CMLC = *Classical and Medieval Literature Criticism*
DA = *DISCovering Authors*
DAB = *DISCovering Authors: British*
DAC = *DISCovering Authors: Canadian*
DAM = *DISCovering Authors: Modules*
    DRAM: *Dramatists Module*; *MST*: *Most-Studied Authors Module*;
    MULT: *Multicultural Authors Module*; *NOV*: *Novelists Module*;
    POET: *Poets Module*; *POP*: *Popular Fiction and Genre Authors Module*
DC = *Drama Criticism*
HLC = *Hispanic Literature Criticism*
LC = *Literature Criticism from 1400 to 1800*
NCLC = *Nineteenth-Century Literature Criticism*
PC = *Poetry Criticism*
SSC = *Short Story Criticism*
TCLC = *Twentieth-Century Literary Criticism*
WLC = *World Literature Criticism, 1500 to the Present*

The cross-references

See also CANR 23; CA 85-88;
   obituary CA116

list all author entries in the following Gale biographical and literary sources:

AAYA = *Authors & Artists for Young Adults*
AITN = *Authors in the News*
BEST = *Bestsellers*
BW = *Black Writers*
CA = *Contemporary Authors*
CAAS = *Contemporary Authors Autobiography Series*
CABS = *Contemporary Authors Bibliographical Series*
CANR = *Contemporary Authors New Revision Series*
CAP = *Contemporary Authors Permanent Series*
CDALB = *Concise Dictionary of American Literary Biography*
CDBLB = *Concise Dictionary of British Literary Biography*
DLB = *Dictionary of Literary Biography*
DLBD = *Dictionary of Literary Biography Documentary Series*
DLBY = *Dictionary of Literary Biography Yearbook*
HW = *Hispanic Writers*
JRDA = *Junior DISCovering Authors*
MAICYA = *Major Authors and Illustrators for Children and Young Adults*
MTCW = *Major 20th-Century Writers*
NNAL = *Native North American Literature*
SAAS = *Something about the Author Autobiography Series*
SATA = *Something about the Author*
YABC = *Yesterday's Authors of Books for Children*

Literary Criticism Series
Cumulative Author Index

20/1631
See Upward, Allen

A/C Cross
See Lawrence, T(homas) E(dward)

Abasiyanik, Sait Faik 1906-1954
See Sait Faik
See also CA 123

Abbey, Edward 1927-1989 **CLC 36, 59**
See also CA 45-48; 128; CANR 2, 41; MTCW 2

Abbott, Lee K(ittredge) 1947- **CLC 48**
See also CA 124; CANR 51; DLB 130

Abe, Kobo 1924-1993**CLC 8, 22, 53, 81; DAM NOV**
See also CA 65-68; 140; CANR 24, 60; DLB 182; MTCW 1, 2

Abelard, Peter c. 1079-c.1142 **CMLC 11**
See also DLB 115, 208

Abell, Kjeld 1901-1961 **CLC 15**
See also CA 111

Abish, Walter 1931- **CLC 22**
See also CA 101; CANR 37; DLB 130

Abrahams, Peter (Henry) 1919- **CLC 4**
See also BW 1; CA 57-60; CANR 26; DLB 117; MTCW 1, 2

Abrams, M(eyer) H(oward) 1912- **CLC 24**
See also CA 57-60; CANR 13, 33; DLB 67

Abse, Dannie 1923- **CLC 7, 29; DAB;DAM POET**
See also CA 53-56; CAAS 1; CANR 4, 46, 74; DLB 27; MTCW 1

Achebe, (Albert) Chinua(lumogu) 1930-**C L C 1, 3, 5, 7, 11, 26, 51, 75; BLC 1; DA; DAB; DAC; DAM MST, MULT, NOV;WLC**
See also AAYA 15; BW 2, 3; CA 1-4R; CANR 6, 26, 47; CLR 20; DLB 117; MAICYA; MTCW 1, 2; SATA 38, 40; SATA-Brief 38

Acker, Kathy 1948-1997 **CLC 45, 111**
See also CA 117; 122; 162; CANR 55

Ackroyd, Peter 1949- **CLC 34, 52**
See also CA 123; 127; CANR 51, 74; DLB 155; INT 127; MTCW 1

Acorn, Milton 1923- **CLC 15; DAC**
See also CA 103; DLB 53; INT 103

Adamov, Arthur 1908-1970 **CLC 4, 25; DAM DRAM**
See also CA 17-18; 25-28R; CAP 2; MTCW 1

Adams, Alice (Boyd) 1926-1999**CLC 6, 13, 46; SSC 24**
See also CA 81-84; 179; CANR 26, 53, 75; DLBY 86; INT CANR-26; MTCW 1, 2

Adams, Andy 1859-1935 **TCLC 56**
See also YABC 1

Adams, Brooks 1848-1927 **TCLC 80**
See also CA 123; DLB 47

Adams, Douglas (Noel) 1952- **CLC 27, 60; DAM POP**
See also AAYA 4; BEST 89:3; CA 106; CANR 34, 64; DLBY 83; JRDA; MTCW1

Adams, Francis 1862-1893 **NCLC 33**

Adams, Henry (Brooks) 1838-1918 **TCLC 4, 52; DA; DAB; DAC; DAM MST**
See also CA 104; 133; CANR 77; DLB 12, 47, 189; MTCW 1

Adams, Richard (George) 1920-**CLC 4, 5, 18; DAM NOV**
See also AAYA 16; AITN 1, 2; CA 49-52; CANR 3, 35; CLR 20; JRDA; MAICYA; MTCW 1, 2; SATA 7, 69

Adamson, Joy (-FriederikeVictoria) 1910-1980 **CLC 17**
See also CA 69-72; 93-96; CANR 22; MTCW 1; SATA 11; SATA-Obit 22

Adcock, Fleur 1934- **CLC 41**
See also CA 25-28R; CAAS 23; CANR 11, 34, 69; DLB 40

Addams, Charles (Samuel) 1912-1988**CLC 30**
See also CA 61-64; 126; CANR 12, 79

Addams, Jane 1860-1945 **TCLC 76**

Addison, Joseph 1672-1719 **LC 18**
See also CDBLB 1660-1789; DLB 101

Adler, Alfred (F.) 1870-1937 **TCLC 61**
See also CA 119; 159

Adler, C(arole) S(chwerdtfeger) 1932-**CLC 35**
See also AAYA 4; CA 89-92; CANR 19, 40; JRDA; MAICYA; SAAS 15; SATA 26, 63, 102

Adler, Renata 1938- **CLC 8, 31**
See also CA 49-52; CANR 5, 22, 52; MTCW 1

Ady, Endre 1877-1919 **TCLC 11**
See also CA 107

A. E. 1867-1935 **TCLC 3, 10**
See also Russell, George William

Aeschylus 525B.C.-456B.C. **CMLC 11; DA; DAB; DAC; DAM DRAM, MST; DC 8; WLCS**
See also DLB 176

Aesop 620(?)B.C.-564(?)B.C. **CMLC 24**
See also CLR 14; MAICYA; SATA 64

Affable Hawk
See MacCarthy, Sir(Charles Otto) Desmond

Africa, Ben
See Bosman, Herman Charles

Afton, Effie
See Harper, Frances Ellen Watkins

Agapida, Fray Antonio
See Irving, Washington

Agee, James (Rufus) 1909-1955 **TCLC 1, 19; DAM NOV**
See also AITN 1; CA 108; 148; CDALB 1941-1968; DLB 2, 26, 152; MTCW 1

Aghill, Gordon
See Silverberg, Robert

Agnon, S(hmuel) Y(osef Halevi) 1888-1970 **CLC 4, 8, 14; SSC 30**
See also CA 17-18; 25-28R; CANR 60; CAP 2; MTCW 1, 2

Agrippa von Nettesheim, Henry Cornelius 1486-1535 **LC 27**

Aguilera Malta, Demetrio 1909-1981
See also CA 111; 124; DAM MULT, NOV; DLB 145; HLCS 1; HW 1

Agustini, Delmira 1886-1914
See also CA 166; HLCS 1; HW 1, 2

Aherne, Owen
See Cassill, R(onald) V(erlin)

Ai 1947- **CLC 4, 14, 69**
See also CA 85-88; CAAS 13; CANR 70; DLB 120

Aickman, Robert (Fordyce) 1914-1981 **C L C 57**
See also CA 5-8R; CANR 3, 72

Aiken, Conrad (Potter) 1889-1973**CLC 1, 3, 5, 10, 52; DAM NOV, POET; PC 26; SSC 9**
See also CA 5-8R; 45-48; CANR 4, 60; CDALB 1929-1941; DLB 9, 45, 102; MTCW 1, 2; SATA 3, 30

Aiken, Joan (Delano) 1924- **CLC 35**
See also AAYA 1, 25; CA 9-12R; CANR 4, 23, 34, 64; CLR 1, 19; DLB 161; JRDA; MAICYA; MTCW 1; SAAS 1; SATA 2, 30, 73; SATA-Essay 109

Ainsworth, William Harrison 1805-1882 **NCLC 13**
See also DLB 21; SATA 24

Aitmatov, Chingiz (Torekulovich) 1928-**C L C 71**
See also CA 103; CANR 38; MTCW 1; SATA 56

Akers, Floyd
See Baum, L(yman) Frank

Akhmadulina, Bella Akhatovna 1937- **C L C 53; DAM POET**
See also CA 65-68

Akhmatova, Anna 1888-1966**CLC 11, 25, 64; DAM POET; PC 2**
See also CA 19-20; 25-28R; CANR 35; CAP 1; MTCW 1, 2

Aksakov, Sergei Timofeyvich 1791-1859 **NCLC 2**
See also DLB 198

Aksenov, Vassily
See Aksyonov, Vassily (Pavlovich)

Akst, Daniel 1956- **CLC 109**
See also CA 161

Aksyonov, Vassily (Pavlovich) 1932-**CLC 22, 37, 101**
See also CA 53-56; CANR 12, 48, 77

Akutagawa, Ryunosuke 1892-1927 **TCLC 16**
See also CA 117; 154

Alain 1868-1951 **TCLC 41**
See also CA 163

Alain-Fournier **TCLC 6**
See also Fournier, Henri Alban
See also DLB 65

Alarcon, Pedro Antonio de 1833-1891**NCLC 1**

Alas (y Urena), Leopoldo (Enrique Garcia) 1852-1901 **TCLC 29**
See also CA 113; 131; HW 1

Albee, Edward (Franklin III) 1928-**CLC 1, 2, 3, 5, 9, 11, 13, 25, 53, 86, 113; DA; DAB; DAC; DAM DRAM, MST; DC 11;WLC**
See also AITN 1; CA 5-8R; CABS 3; CANR 8, 54, 74; CDALB 1941-1968; DLB 7; INT CANR-8; MTCW 1, 2

Alberti, Rafael 1902- **CLC 7**

See also CA 85-88; CANR 81; DLB 108; HW 2

Albert the Great 1200(?)-1280 **CMLC 16**
See also DLB 115

Alcala-Galiano, Juan Valera y
See Valera y Alcala-Galiano, Juan

Alcott, Amos Bronson 1799-1888 **NCLC 1**
See also DLB 1

Alcott, Louisa May 1832-1888 **NCLC 6, 58; DA; DAB; DAC; DAM MST, NOV; SSC 27; WLC**
See also AAYA 20; CDALB 1865-1917; CLR 1, 38; DLB 1, 42, 79; DLBD 14; JRDA; MAICYA; SATA 100; YABC 1

Aldanov, M. A.
See Aldanov, Mark (Alexandrovich)

Aldanov, Mark (Alexandrovich) 1886(?)-1957 **TCLC 23**
See also CA 118

Aldington, Richard 1892-1962 **CLC 49**
See also CA 85-88; CANR 45; DLB 20, 36, 100, 149

Aldiss, Brian W(ilson) 1925- **CLC 5, 14, 40; DAM NOV**
See also CA 5-8R; CAAS 2; CANR 5, 28, 64; DLB 14; MTCW 1, 2; SATA 34

Alegria, Claribel 1924- **CLC 75; DAM MULT; HLCS 1; PC 26**
See also CA 131; CAAS 15; CANR 66; DLB 145; HW 1; MTCW 1

Alegria, Fernando 1918- **CLC 57**
See also CA 9-12R; CANR 5, 32, 72; HW 1, 2

Aleichem, Sholom **TCLC 1, 35; SSC 33**
See Rabinovitch, Sholem

Aleixandre, Vicente 1898-1984
See also CANR 81; HLCS 1; HW 2

Alepoudelis, Odysseus
See Elytis, Odysseus

Aleshkovsky, Joseph 1929-
See Aleshkovsky, Yuz
See also CA 121; 128

Aleshkovsky, Yuz **CLC 44**
See also Aleshkovsky, Joseph

Alexander, Lloyd (Chudley) 1924- **CLC 35**
See also AAYA 1, 27; CA 1-4R; CANR 1, 24, 38, 55; CLR 1, 5, 48; DLB 52; JRDA; MAICYA; MTCW 1; SAAS 19; SATA 3, 49, 81

Alexander, Meena 1951- **CLC 121**
See also CA 115; CANR 38, 70

Alexander, Samuel 1859-1938 **TCLC 77**

Alexie, Sherman (Joseph, Jr.) 1966- **CLC 96; DAM MULT**
See also AAYA 28; CA 138; CANR 65; DLB 175, 206; MTCW 1; NNAL

Alfau, Felipe 1902- **CLC 66**
See also CA 137

Alger, Horatio, Jr. 1832-1899 **NCLC 8**
See also DLB 42; SATA 16

Algren, Nelson 1909-1981 **CLC 4, 10, 33; SSC 33**
See also CA 13-16R; 103; CANR 20, 61; CDALB 1941-1968; DLB 9; DLBY 81, 82; MTCW 1, 2

Ali, Ahmed 1910- **CLC 69**
See also CA 25-28R; CANR 15, 34

Alighieri, Dante
See Dante

Allan, John B.
See Westlake, Donald E(dwin)

Allan, Sidney
See Hartmann, Sadakichi

Allan, Sydney

See Hartmann, Sadakichi

Allen, Edward 1948- **CLC 59**

Allen, Fred 1894-1956 **TCLC 87**

Allen, Paula Gunn 1939- **CLC 84; DAM MULT**
See also CA 112; 143; CANR 63; DLB 175; MTCW 1; NNAL

Allen, Roland
See Ayckbourn, Alan

Allen, Sarah A.
See Hopkins, Pauline Elizabeth

Allen, Sidney H.
See Hartmann, Sadakichi

Allen, Woody 1935- **CLC 16, 52; DAM POP**
See also AAYA 10; CA 33-36R; CANR 27, 38, 63; DLB 44; MTCW 1

Allende, Isabel 1942- **CLC 39, 57, 97; DAM MULT, NOV; HLC 1; WLCS**
See also AAYA 18; CA 125; 130; CANR 51, 74; DLB 145; HW 1, 2; INT 130; MTCW 1, 2

Alleyn, Ellen
See Rossetti, Christina (Georgina)

Allingham, Margery (Louise) 1904-1966 **CLC 19**
See also CA 5-8R; 25-28R; CANR 4, 58; DLB 77; MTCW 1, 2

Allingham, William 1824-1889 **NCLC 25**
See also DLB 35

Allison, Dorothy E. 1949- **CLC 78**
See also CA 140; CANR 66; MTCW 1

Allston, Washington 1779-1843 **NCLC 2**
See also DLB 1

Almedingen, E. M. **CLC 12**
See also Almedingen, Martha Edith von
See also SATA 3

Almedingen, Martha Edith von 1898-1971
See Almedingen, E. M.
See also CA 1-4R; CANR 1

Almodovar, Pedro 1949(?)- **CLC 114; HLCS 1**
See also CA 133; CANR 72; HW 2

Almqvist, Carl Jonas Love 1793-1866 **NCLC 42**

Alonso, Damaso 1898-1990 **CLC 14**
See also CA 110; 131; 130; CANR 72; DLB 108; HW 1, 2

Alov
See Gogol, Nikolai (Vasilyevich)

Alta 1942- **CLC 19**
See also CA 57-60

Alter, Robert B(ernard) 1935- **CLC 34**
See also CA 49-52; CANR 1, 47

Alther, Lisa 1944- **CLC 7, 41**
See also CA 65-68; CAAS 30; CANR 12, 30, 51; MTCW 1

Althusser, L.
See Althusser, Louis

Althusser, Louis 1918-1990 **CLC 106**
See also CA 131; 132

Altman, Robert 1925- **CLC 16, 116**
See also CA 73-76; CANR 43

Alurista 1949-
See Urista, Alberto H.
See also DLB 82; HLCS 1

Alvarez, A(lfred) 1929- **CLC 5, 13**
See also CA 1-4R; CANR 3, 33, 63; DLB 14, 40

Alvarez, Alejandro Rodriguez 1903-1965
See Casona, Alejandro
See also CA 131; 93-96; HW 1

Alvarez, Julia 1950- **CLC 93; HLCS 1**
See also AAYA 25; CA 147; CANR 69; MTCW 1

Alvaro, Corrado 1896-1956 **TCLC 60**

See also CA 163

Amado, Jorge 1912- **CLC 13, 40, 106; DAM MULT, NOV; HLC 1**
See also CA 77-80; CANR 35, 74; DLB 113; HW 2; MTCW 1, 2

Ambler, Eric 1909-1998 **CLC 4, 6, 9**
See also CA 9-12R; 171; CANR 7, 38, 74; DLB 77; MTCW 1, 2

Amichai, Yehuda 1924- **CLC 9, 22, 57, 116**
See also CA 85-88; CANR 46, 60; MTCW 1

Amichai, Yehudah
See Amichai, Yehuda

Amiel, Henri Frederic 1821-1881 **NCLC 4**

Amis, Kingsley (William) 1922-1995 **CLC 1, 2, 3, 5, 8, 13, 40, 44; DA; DAB; DAC; DAM MST, NOV**
See also AITN 2; CA 9-12R; 150; CANR 8, 28, 54; CDBLB 1945-1960; DLB 15, 27, 100, 139; DLBY 96; INT CANR-8; MTCW 1, 2

Amis, Martin (Louis) 1949- **CLC 4, 9, 38, 62, 101**
See also BEST 90:3; CA 65-68; CANR 8, 27, 54, 73; DLB 14, 194; INT CANR-27; MTCW 1

Ammons, A(rchie) R(andolph) 1926- **CLC 2, 3, 5, 8, 9, 25, 57, 108; DAM POET; PC 16**
See also AITN 1; CA 9-12R; CANR 6, 36, 51, 73; DLB 5, 165; MTCW 1, 2

Amo, Tauraatua i
See Adams, Henry (Brooks)

Amory, Thomas 1691(?)-1788 **LC 48**

Anand, Mulk Raj 1905- **CLC 23, 93; DAM NOV**
See also CA 65-68; CANR 32, 64; MTCW 1, 2

Anatol
See Schnitzler, Arthur

Anaximander c. 610B.C.-c. 546B.C. **CMLC 22**

Anaya, Rudolfo A(lfonso) 1937- **CLC 23; DAM MULT, NOV; HLC 1**
See also AAYA 20; CA 45-48; CAAS 4; CANR 1, 32, 51; DLB 82, 206; HW 1; MTCW 1, 2

Andersen, Hans Christian 1805-1875 **NCLC 7, 79; DA; DAB; DAC; DAM MST, POP; SSC 6; WLC**
See also CLR 6; MAICYA; SATA 100; YABC 1

Anderson, C. Farley
See Mencken, H(enry) L(ouis); Nathan, George Jean

Anderson, Jessica (Margaret) Queale 1916- **CLC 37**
See also CA 9-12R; CANR 4, 62

Anderson, Jon (Victor) 1940- **CLC 9; DAM POET**
See also CA 25-28R; CANR 20

Anderson, Lindsay (Gordon) 1923-1994 **CLC 20**
See also CA 125; 128; 146; CANR 77

Anderson, Maxwell 1888-1959 **TCLC 2; DAM DRAM**
See also CA 105; 152; DLB 7; MTCW 2

Anderson, Poul (William) 1926- **CLC 15**
See also AAYA 5; CA 1-4R; CAAS 2; CANR 2, 15, 34, 64; CLR 58; DLB 8; INT CANR-15; MTCW 1, 2; SATA 90; SATA-Brief 39; SATA-Essay 106

Anderson, Robert (Woodruff) 1917- **CLC 23; DAM DRAM**
See also AITN 1; CA 21-24R; CANR 32; DLB 7

Anderson, Sherwood 1876-1941 **TCLC 1, 10, 24; DA; DAB; DAC; DAM MST, NOV; SSC 1; WLC**

See also AAYA 30; CA 104; 121; CANR 61;
    CDALB 1917-1929; DLB 4, 9, 86; DLBD
    1; MTCW 1, 2
Andier, Pierre
    See Desnos, Robert
Andouard
    See Giraudoux, (Hippolyte) Jean
Andrade, Carlos Drummond de   CLC 18
    See also Drummond de Andrade, Carlos
Andrade, Mario de 1893-1945   TCLC 43
Andreae, Johann V(alentin) 1586-1654LC 32
    See also DLB 164
Andreas-Salome, Lou 1861-1937   TCLC 56
    See also CA 178; DLB 66
Andress, Lesley
    See Sanders, Lawrence
Andrewes, Lancelot 1555-1626   LC 5
    See also DLB 151, 172
Andrews, Cicily Fairfield
    See West, Rebecca
Andrews, Elton V.
    See Pohl, Frederik
Andreyev, Leonid (Nikolaevich) 1871-1919
    TCLC 3
    See also CA 104
Andric, Ivo 1892-1975   CLC 8
    See also CA 81-84; 57-60; CANR 43, 60; DLB
    147; MTCW 1
Androvar
    See Prado (Calvo), Pedro
Angelique, Pierre
    See Bataille, Georges
Angell, Roger 1920-   CLC 26
    See also CA 57-60; CANR 13, 44, 70; DLB 171,
    185
Angelou, Maya 1928-CLC 12, 35, 64, 77; BLC
    1; DA; DAB; DAC; DAM MST, MULT,
    POET, POP; WLCS
    See also AAYA 7, 20; BW 2, 3; CA 65-68;
    CANR 19, 42, 65; CDALBS; CLR 53; DLB
    38; MTCW 1, 2; SATA 49
Anna Comnena 1083-1153   CMLC 25
Annensky, Innokenty (Fyodorovich) 1856-1909
    TCLC 14
    See also CA 110; 155
Annunzio, Gabriele d'
    See D'Annunzio, Gabriele
Anodos
    See Coleridge, Mary E(lizabeth)
Anon, Charles Robert
    See Pessoa, Fernando (Antonio Nogueira)
Anouilh, Jean (Marie Lucien Pierre) 1910-1987
    CLC 1, 3, 8, 13, 40, 50; DAM DRAM; DC
    8
    See also CA 17-20R; 123; CANR 32; MTCW
    1, 2
Anthony, Florence
    See Ai
Anthony, John
    See Ciardi, John (Anthony)
Anthony, Peter
    See Shaffer, Anthony (Joshua); Shaffer, Peter
    (Levin)
Anthony, Piers 1934-   CLC 35;DAM POP
    See also AAYA 11; CA 21-24R; CANR 28, 56,
    73; DLB 8; MTCW 1, 2; SAAS 22; SATA 84
Anthony, Susan B(rownell) 1916-1991 T C L C
    84
    See also CA 89-92; 134
Antoine, Marc
    See Proust, (Valentin-Louis-George-Eugene-)
    Marcel
Antoninus, Brother

See Everson, William (Oliver)
Antonioni, Michelangelo 1912-   CLC 20
    See also CA 73-76; CANR 45, 77
Antschel, Paul 1920-1970
    See Celan, Paul
    See also CA 85-88; CANR 33, 61; MTCW 1
Anwar, Chairil 1922-1949   TCLC 22
    See also CA 121
Anzaldua, Gloria 1942-
    See also CA 175; DLB 122; HLCS 1
Apess, William 1798-1839(?)NCLC 73; DAM
    MULT
    See also DLB 175; NNAL
Apollinaire, Guillaume 1880-1918TCLC 3, 8,
    51; DAM POET; PC 7
    See also Kostrowitzki, Wilhelm Apollinaris de
    See also CA 152; MTCW 1
Appelfeld, Aharon 1932-   CLC 23, 47
    See also CA 112; 133
Apple, Max (Isaac) 1941-   CLC 9, 33
    See also CA 81-84; CANR 19, 54; DLB 130
Appleman, Philip (Dean) 1926-   CLC 51
    See also CA 13-16R; CAAS 18; CANR 6, 29,
    56
Appleton, Lawrence
    See Lovecraft, H(oward) P(hillips)
Apteryx
    See Eliot, T(homas) S(tearns)
Apuleius, (Lucius Madaurensis) 125(?)-175(?)
    CMLC 1
    See also DLB 211
Aquin, Hubert 1929-1977   CLC 15
    See also CA 105; DLB 53
Aquinas, Thomas 1224(?)-1274   CMLC 33
    See also DLB 115
Aragon, Louis 1897-1982   CLC 3, 22; DAM
    NOV, POET
    See also CA 69-72; 108; CANR 28, 71; DLB
    72; MTCW 1, 2
Arany, Janos 1817-1882   NCLC 34
Aranyos, Kakay
    See Mikszath, Kalman
Arbuthnot, John 1667-1735   LC 1
    See also DLB 101
Archer, Herbert Winslow
    See Mencken, H(enry) L(ouis)
Archer, Jeffrey (Howard) 1940-   CLC 28;
    DAM POP
    See also AAYA 16; BEST 89:3; CA 77-80;
    CANR 22, 52; INT CANR-22
Archer, Jules 1915-   CLC 12
    See also CA 9-12R; CANR 6, 69; SAAS 5;
    SATA 4, 85
Archer, Lee
    See Ellison, Harlan (Jay)
Arden, John 1930-CLC 6, 13, 15;DAM DRAM
    See also CA 13-16R; CAAS 4; CANR 31, 65,
    67; DLB 13; MTCW 1
Arenas, Reinaldo 1943-1990 CLC 41; DAM
    MULT; HLC 1
    See also CA 124; 128; 133; CANR 73; DLB
    145; HW 1; MTCW 1
Arendt, Hannah 1906-1975   CLC 66,98
    See also CA 17-20R; 61-64; CANR 26, 60;
    MTCW 1, 2
Aretino, Pietro 1492-1556   LC 12
Arghezi, Tudor 1880-1967   CLC 80
    See also Theodorescu, Ion N.
    See also CA 167
Arguedas, Jose Maria 1911-1969CLC 10, 18;
    HLCS 1
    See also CA 89-92; CANR 73; DLB 113; HW 1
Argueta, Manlio 1936-   CLC 31

See also CA 131; CANR 73; DLB 145; HW 1
Arias, Ron(ald Francis) 1941-
    See also CA 131; CANR 81; DAM MULT; DLB
    82; HLC 1; HW 1, 2; MTCW 2
Ariosto, Ludovico 1474-1533   LC 6
Aristides
    See Epstein, Joseph
Aristophanes 450B.C.-385B.C.CMLC 4; DA;
    DAB; DAC; DAM DRAM, MST; DC 2;
    WLCS
    See also DLB 176
Aristotle 384B.C.-322B.C.   CMLC 31; DA;
    DAB; DAC; DAM MST; WLCS
    See also DLB 176
Arlt, Roberto (Godofredo Christophersen)
    1900-1942TCLC 29; DAM MULT; HLC 1
    See also CA 123; 131; CANR 67; HW 1, 2
Armah, Ayi Kwei 1939-   CLC 5, 33; BLC 1;
    DAM MULT, POET
    See also BW 1; CA 61-64; CANR 21, 64; DLB
    117; MTCW 1
Armatrading, Joan 1950-   CLC 17
    See also CA 114
Arnette, Robert
    See Silverberg, Robert
Arnim, Achim von (Ludwig Joachim von
    Arnim) 1781-1831   NCLC 5; SSC 29
    See also DLB 90
Arnim, Bettina von 1785-1859   NCLC 38
    See also DLB 90
Arnold, Matthew 1822-1888NCLC 6, 29; DA;
    DAB; DAC; DAM MST, POET; PC 5;
    WLC
    See also CDBLB 1832-1890; DLB 32, 57
Arnold, Thomas 1795-1842   NCLC 18
    See also DLB 55
Arnow, Harriette (Louisa) Simpson 1908-1986
    CLC 2, 7, 18
    See also CA 9-12R; 118; CANR 14; DLB 6;
    MTCW 1, 2; SATA 42; SATA-Obit 47
Arouet, Francois-Marie
    See Voltaire
Arp, Hans
    See Arp, Jean
Arp, Jean 1887-1966   CLC 5
    See also CA 81-84; 25-28R; CANR 42, 77
Arrabal
    See Arrabal, Fernando
Arrabal, Fernando 1932-   CLC 2, 9, 18, 58
    See also CA 9-12R; CANR 15
Arreola, Juan Jose 1918-
    See also CA 113; 131; CANR 81; DAM MULT;
    DLB 113; HLC 1; HW 1, 2
Arrick, Fran   CLC 30
    See also Gaberman, Judie Angell
Artaud, Antonin (Marie Joseph) 1896-1948
    TCLC 3, 36; DAM DRAM
    See also CA 104; 149; MTCW 1
Arthur, Ruth M(abel) 1905-1979   CLC 12
    See also CA 9-12R; 85-88; CANR 4; SATA 7,
    26
Artsybashev, Mikhail (Petrovich) 1878-1927
    TCLC 31
    See also CA 170
Arundel, Honor (Morfydd) 1919-1973CLC 17
    See also CA 21-22; 41-44R; CAP 2; CLR 35;
    SATA 4; SATA-Obit 24
Arzner, Dorothy 1897-1979   CLC 98
Asch, Sholem 1880-1957   TCLC 3
    See also CA 105
Ash, Shalom
    See Asch, Sholem
Ashbery, John (Lawrence) 1927-CLC 2, 3, 4,

6, 9, 13, 15, 25, 41, 77; **DAM POET; PC 26**
See also CA 5-8R; CANR 9, 37, 66; DLB 5,
165; DLBY 81; INT CANR-9; MTCW 1, 2

Ashdown, Clifford
See Freeman, R(ichard) Austin

Ashe, Gordon
See Creasey, John

Ashton-Warner, Sylvia (Constance) 1908-1984
CLC 19
See also CA 69-72; 112; CANR 29; MTCW 1,
2

Asimov, Isaac 1920-1992 **CLC 1, 3, 9, 19, 26,
76, 92; DAM POP**
See also AAYA 13; BEST 90:2; CA 1-4R; 137;
CANR 2, 19, 36, 60; CLR 12; DLB 8; DLBY
92; INT CANR-19; JRDA; MAICYA;
MTCW 1, 2; SATA 1, 26, 74

Assis, Joaquim Maria Machado de
See Machado de Assis, Joaquim Maria

Astley, Thea (Beatrice May) 1925- **CLC 41**
See also CA 65-68; CANR 11, 43, 78

Aston, James
See White, T(erence) H(anbury)

Asturias, Miguel Angel 1899-1974 **CLC 3, 8,
13; DAM MULT, NOV; HLC 1**
See also CA 25-28; 49-52; CANR 32; CAP 2;
DLB 113; HW 1; MTCW 1, 2

Atares, Carlos Saura
See Saura (Atares), Carlos

Atheling, William
See Pound, Ezra (Weston Loomis)

Atheling, William, Jr.
See Blish, James (Benjamin)

Atherton, Gertrude (Franklin Horn) 1857-1948
TCLC 2
See also CA 104; 155; DLB 9, 78, 186

Atherton, Lucius
See Masters, Edgar Lee

Atkins, Jack
See Harris, Mark

Atkinson, Kate **CLC 99**
See also CA 166

Attaway, William (Alexander) 1911-1986 **CLC
92; BLC 1; DAM MULT**
See also BW 2, 3; CA 143; CANR 82; DLB 76

Atticus
See Fleming, Ian (Lancaster); Wilson, (Thomas)
Woodrow

Atwood, Margaret (Eleanor) 1939- **CLC 2, 3,
4, 8, 13, 15, 25, 44, 84; DA; DAB; DAC;
DAM MST, NOV, POET; PC 8; SSC 2;
WLC**
See also AAYA 12; BEST 89:2; CA 49-52;
CANR 3, 24, 33, 59; DLB 53; INT CANR-
24; MTCW 1, 2; SATA 50

Aubigny, Pierre d'
See Mencken, H(enry) L(ouis)

Aubin, Penelope 1685-1731(?) **LC 9**
See also DLB 39

Auchincloss, Louis (Stanton) 1917- **CLC 4, 6,
9, 18, 45; DAM NOV; SSC 22**
See also CA 1-4R; CANR 6, 29, 55; DLB 2;
DLBY 80; INT CANR-29; MTCW 1

Auden, W(ystan) H(ugh) 1907-1973 **CLC 1, 2,
3, 4, 6, 9, 11, 14, 43; DA; DAB; DAC; DAM
DRAM, MST, POET; PC 1; WLC**
See also AAYA 18; CA 9-12R; 45-48; CANR
5, 61; CDBLB 1914-1945; DLB 10, 20;
MTCW 1, 2

Audiberti, Jacques 1900-1965 **CLC 38; DAM
DRAM**
See also CA 25-28R

Audubon, John James 1785-1851 **NCLC 47**

Auel, Jean M(arie) 1936- **CLC 31, 107; DAM
POP**
See also AAYA 7; BEST 90:4; CA 103; CANR
21, 64; INT CANR-21; SATA 91

Auerbach, Erich 1892-1957 **TCLC 43**
See also CA 118; 155

Augier, Emile 1820-1889 **NCLC 31**
See also DLB 192

August, John
See De Voto, Bernard (Augustine)

Augustine 354-430 **CMLC 6; DA; DAB; DAC;
DAM MST; WLCS**
See also DLB 115

Aurelius
See Bourne, Randolph S(illiman)

Aurobindo, Sri
See Ghose, Aurabinda

Austen, Jane 1775-1817 **NCLC 1, 13, 19, 33,
51; DA; DAB; DAC; DAM MST, NOV;
WLC**
See also AAYA 19; CDBLB 1789-1832; DLB
116

Auster, Paul 1947- **CLC 47**
See also CA 69-72; CANR 23, 52, 75; MTCW
1

Austin, Frank
See Faust, Frederick (Schiller)

Austin, Mary (Hunter) 1868-1934 **TCLC 25**
See also CA 109; 178; DLB 9, 78, 206

Autran Dourado, Waldomiro Freitas 1926-
See Dourado, (Waldomiro Freitas) Autran
See also CA 179

Averroes 1126-1198 **CMLC 7**
See also DLB 115

Avicenna 980-1037 **CMLC 16**
See also DLB 115

Avison, Margaret 1918- **CLC 2, 4, 97; DAC;
DAM POET**
See also CA 17-20R; DLB 53; MTCW 1

Axton, David
See Koontz, Dean R(ay)

Ayckbourn, Alan 1939- **CLC 5, 8, 18, 33, 74;
DAB; DAM DRAM**
See also CA 21-24R; CANR 31, 59; DLB 13;
MTCW 1, 2

Aydy, Catherine
See Tennant, Emma (Christina)

Ayme, Marcel (Andre) 1902-1967 **CLC 11**
See also CA 89-92; CANR 67; CLR 25; DLB
72; SATA 91

Ayrton, Michael 1921-1975 **CLC 7**
See also CA 5-8R; 61-64; CANR 9, 21

Azorin **CLC 11**
See also Martinez Ruiz, Jose

Azuela, Mariano 1873-1952 **TCLC 3; DAM
MULT; HLC 1**
See also CA 104; 131; CANR 81; HW 1, 2;
MTCW 1, 2

Baastad, Babbis Friis
See Friis-Baastad, Babbis Ellinor

Bab
See Gilbert, W(illiam) S(chwenck)

Babbis, Eleanor
See Friis-Baastad, Babbis Ellinor

Babel, Isaac
See Babel, Isaak (Emmanuilovich)

Babel, Isaak (Emmanuilovich) 1894-1941(?)
TCLC 2, 13; SSC 16
See also CA 104; 155; MTCW 1

Babits, Mihaly 1883-1941 **TCLC 14**
See also CA 114

Babur 1483-1530 **LC 18**

Baca, Jimmy Santiago 1952-

See also CA 131; CANR 81; DAM MULT; DLB
122; HLC 1; HW 1, 2

Bacchelli, Riccardo 1891-1985 **CLC 19**
See also CA 29-32R; 117

Bach, Richard (David) 1936- **CLC 14; DAM
NOV, POP**
See also AITN 1; BEST 89:2; CA 9-12R; CANR
18; MTCW 1; SATA 13

Bachman, Richard
See King, Stephen (Edwin)

Bachmann, Ingeborg 1926-1973 **CLC 69**
See also CA 93-96; 45-48; CANR 69; DLB 85

Bacon, Francis 1561-1626 **LC 18, 32**
See also CDBLB Before 1660; DLB 151

Bacon, Roger 1214(?)-1292 **CMLC 14**
See also DLB 115

Bacovia, George **TCLC 24**
See also Vasiliu, Gheorghe

Badanes, Jerome 1937- **CLC 59**

Bagehot, Walter 1826-1877 **NCLC 10**
See also DLB 55

Bagnold, Enid 1889-1981 **CLC 25; DAM
DRAM**
See also CA 5-8R; 103; CANR 5, 40; DLB 13,
160, 191; MAICYA; SATA 1, 25

Bagritsky, Eduard 1895-1934 **TCLC 60**

Bagrjana, Elisaveta
See Belcheva, Elisaveta

Bagryana, Elisaveta 1893-1991 **CLC 10**
See also Belcheva, Elisaveta
See also CA 178; DLB 147

Bailey, Paul 1937- **CLC 45**
See also CA 21-24R; CANR 16, 62; DLB 14

Baillie, Joanna 1762-1851 **NCLC 71**
See also DLB 93

Bainbridge, Beryl (Margaret) 1933- **CLC 4, 5,
8, 10, 14, 18, 22, 62; DAM NOV**
See also CA 21-24R; CANR 24, 55, 75; DLB
14; MTCW 1, 2

Baker, Elliott 1922- **CLC 8**
See also CA 45-48; CANR 2, 63

Baker, Jean H. **TCLC 3, 10**
See also Russell, George William

Baker, Nicholson 1957- **CLC 61; DAM POP**
See also CA 135; CANR 63

Baker, Ray Stannard 1870-1946 **TCLC 47**
See also CA 118

Baker, Russell (Wayne) 1925- **CLC 31**
See also BEST 89:4; CA 57-60; CANR 11, 41,
59; MTCW 1, 2

Bakhtin, M.
See Bakhtin, Mikhail Mikhailovich

Bakhtin, M. M.
See Bakhtin, Mikhail Mikhailovich

Bakhtin, Mikhail
See Bakhtin, Mikhail Mikhailovich

Bakhtin, Mikhail Mikhailovich 1895-1975
CLC 83
See also CA 128; 113

Bakshi, Ralph 1938(?)- **CLC 26**
See also CA 112; 138

Bakunin, Mikhail (Alexandrovich) 1814-1876
NCLC 25, 58

Baldwin, James (Arthur) 1924-1987 **CLC 1, 2,
3, 4, 5, 8, 13, 15, 17, 42, 50, 67, 90; BLC 1;
DA; DAB; DAC; DAM MST, MULT, NOV,
POP; DC 1; SSC 10, 33; WLC**
See also AAYA 4; BW 1; CA 1-4R; 124; CABS
1; CANR 3, 24; CDALB 1941-1968; DLB
2, 7, 33; DLBY 87; MTCW 1, 2; SATA 9;
SATA-Obit 54

Ballard, J(ames) G(raham) 1930- **CLC 3, 6, 14,
36; DAM NOV, POP; SSC 1**

See also AAYA 3; CA 5-8R; CANR 15, 39, 65;
  DLB 14, 207; MTCW 1, 2; SATA 93
Balmont, Konstantin (Dmitriyevich) 1867-1943
  TCLC 11
  See also CA 109; 155
Baltausis, Vincas
  See Mikszath, Kalman
Balzac, Honore de 1799-1850 **NCLC 5, 35, 53;**
  **DA; DAB; DAC; DAM MST, NOV; SSC
  5; WLC**
  See also DLB 119
Bambara, Toni Cade 1939-1995 **CLC 19, 88;
  BLC 1; DA; DAC; DAM MST, MULT;
  SSC 35; WLCS**
  See also AAYA 5; BW 2, 3; CA 29-32R; 150;
  CANR 24, 49, 81; CDALBS; DLB 38;
  MTCW 1, 2
Bamdad, A.
  See Shamlu, Ahmad
Banat, D. R.
  See Bradbury, Ray (Douglas)
Bancroft, Laura
  See Baum, L(yman) Frank
Banim, John 1798-1842   **NCLC 13**
  See also DLB 116, 158, 159
Banim, Michael 1796-1874   **NCLC 13**
  See also DLB 158, 159
Banjo, The
  See Paterson, A(ndrew) B(arton)
Banks, Iain
  See Banks, Iain M(enzies)
Banks, Iain M(enzies) 1954-   **CLC 34**
  See also CA 123; 128; CANR 61; DLB 194;
  INT 128
Banks, Lynne Reid   **CLC 23**
  See also Reid Banks, Lynne
  See also AAYA 6
Banks, Russell 1940-   **CLC 37, 72**
  See also CA 65-68; CAAS 15; CANR 19, 52,
  73; DLB 130
Banville, John 1945-   **CLC 46, 118**
  See also CA 117; 128; DLB 14; INT 128
Banville, Theodore (Faullain) de 1832-1891
  NCLC 9
Baraka, Amiri 1934- **CLC 1, 2, 3, 5, 10, 14, 33,
  115; BLC 1; DA; DAC; DAM MST, MULT,
  POET, POP; DC 6; PC 4; WLCS**
  See also Jones, LeRoi
  See also BW 2, 3; CA 21-24R; CABS 3; CANR
  27, 38, 61; CDALB 1941-1968; DLB 5, 7,
  16, 38; DLBD 8; MTCW 1, 2
Barbauld, Anna Laetitia 1743-1825 **NCLC 50**
  See also DLB 107, 109, 142, 158
Barbellion, W. N. P.   **TCLC 24**
  See also Cummings, Bruce F(rederick)
Barbera, Jack (Vincent) 1945-   **CLC 44**
  See also CA 110; CANR 45
Barbey d'Aurevilly, Jules Amedee 1808-1889
  NCLC 1; SSC 17
  See also DLB 119
Barbour, John c. 1316-1395   **CMLC 33**
  See also DLB 146
Barbusse, Henri 1873-1935   **TCLC 5**
  See also CA 105; 154; DLB 65
Barclay, Bill
  See Moorcock, Michael (John)
Barclay, William Ewert
  See Moorcock, Michael (John)
Barea, Arturo 1897-1957   **TCLC 14**
  See also CA 111
Barfoot, Joan 1946-   **CLC 18**
  See also CA 105
Barham, Richard Harris 1788-1845 **NCLC 77**

See also DLB 159
Baring, Maurice 1874-1945   **TCLC 8**
  See also CA 105; 168; DLB 34
Baring-Gould, Sabine 1834-1924   **TCLC 88**
  See also DLB 156, 190
Barker, Clive 1952-   **CLC 52;DAM POP**
  See also AAYA 10; BEST 90:3; CA 121; 129;
  CANR 71; INT 129; MTCW 1, 2
Barker, George Granville 1913-1991 **CLC 8,
  48; DAM POET**
  See also CA 9-12R; 135; CANR 7, 38; DLB
  20; MTCW 1
Barker, Harley Granville
  See Granville-Barker, Harley
  See also DLB 10
Barker, Howard 1946-   **CLC 37**
  See also CA 102; DLB 13
Barker, Jane 1652-1732   **LC 42**
Barker, Pat(ricia) 1943-   **CLC 32, 94**
  See also CA 117; 122; CANR 50; INT 122
Barlach, Ernst 1870-1938   **TCLC 84**
  See also CA 178; DLB 56, 118
Barlow, Joel 1754-1812   **NCLC 23**
  See also DLB 37
Barnard, Mary (Ethel) 1909-   **CLC 48**
  See also CA 21-22; CAP 2
Barnes, Djuna 1892-1982 **CLC 3, 4, 8, 11, 29;
  SSC 3**
  See also CA 9-12R; 107; CANR 16, 55; DLB
  4, 9, 45; MTCW 1, 2
Barnes, Julian (Patrick) 1946- **CLC 42; DAB**
  See also CA 102; CANR 19, 54; DLB 194;
  DLBY 93; MTCW 1
Barnes, Peter 1931-   **CLC 5, 56**
  See also CA 65-68; CAAS 12; CANR 33, 34,
  64; DLB 13; MTCW 1
Barnes, William 1801-1886   **NCLC 75**
  See also DLB 32
Baroja (y Nessi), Pio 1872-1956 **TCLC 8; HLC
  1**
  See also CA 104
Baron, David
  See Pinter, Harold
Baron Corvo
  See Rolfe, Frederick (William Serafino Austin
    Lewis Mary)
Barondess, Sue K(aufman) 1926-1977 **CLC 8**
  See also Kaufman, Sue
  See also CA 1-4R; 69-72; CANR 1
Baron de Teive
  See Pessoa, Fernando (Antonio Nogueira)
Baroness Von S.
  See Zangwill, Israel
Barres, (Auguste-) Maurice 1862-1923 **TCLC
  47**
  See also CA 164; DLB 123
Barreto, Afonso Henrique de Lima
  See Lima Barreto, Afonso Henrique de
Barrett, (Roger) Syd 1946-   **CLC 35**
Barrett, William (Christopher) 1913-1992
  CLC 27
  See also CA 13-16R; 139; CANR 11, 67; INT
  CANR-11
Barrie, J(ames) M(atthew) 1860-1937 **TCLC
  2; DAB; DAM DRAM**
  See also CA 104; 136; CANR 77; CDBLB
  1890-1914; CLR 16; DLB 10, 141, 156;
  MAICYA; MTCW 1; SATA 100; YABC 1
Barrington, Michael
  See Moorcock, Michael (John)
Barrol, Grady
  See Bograd, Larry
Barry, Mike

See Malzberg, Barry N(athaniel)
Barry, Philip 1896-1949   **TCLC 11**
  See also CA 109; DLB 7
Bart, Andre Schwarz
  See Schwarz-Bart, Andre
Barth, John (Simmons) 1930- **CLC 1, 2, 3, 5, 7,
  9, 10, 14, 27, 51, 89; DAM NOV; SSC 10**
  See also AITN 1, 2; CA 1-4R; CABS 1; CANR
  5, 23, 49, 64; DLB 2; MTCW 1
Barthelme, Donald 1931-1989 **CLC 1, 2, 3, 5, 6,
  8, 13, 23, 46, 59, 115; DAM NOV; SSC 2**
  See also CA 21-24R; 129; CANR 20, 58; DLB
  2; DLBY 80, 89; MTCW 1, 2; SATA 7;
  SATA-Obit 62
Barthelme, Frederick 1943-   **CLC 36, 117**
  See also CA 114; 122; CANR 77; DLBY 85;
  INT 122
Barthes, Roland (Gerard) 1915-1980 **CLC 24,
  83**
  See also CA 130; 97-100; CANR 66; MTCW
  1, 2
Barzun, Jacques (Martin) 1907-   **CLC 51**
  See also CA 61-64; CANR 22
Bashevis, Isaac
  See Singer, Isaac Bashevis
Bashkirtseff, Marie 1859-1884   **NCLC 27**
Basho
  See Matsuo Basho
Basil of Caesaria c. 330-379   **CMLC 35**
Bass, Kingsley B., Jr.
  See Bullins, Ed
Bass, Rick 1958-   **CLC 79**
  See also CA 126; CANR 53; DLB 212
Bassani, Giorgio 1916-   **CLC 9**
  See also CA 65-68; CANR 33; DLB 128, 177;
  MTCW 1
Bastos, Augusto (Antonio) Roa
  See Roa Bastos, Augusto (Antonio)
Bataille, Georges 1897-1962   **CLC 29**
  See also CA 101; 89-92
Bates, H(erbert) E(rnest) 1905-1974 **CLC 46;
  DAB; DAM POP; SSC 10**
  See also CA 93-96; 45-48; CANR 34; DLB 162,
  191; MTCW 1, 2
Bauchart
  See Camus, Albert
Baudelaire, Charles 1821-1867 **NCLC 6, 29,
  55; DA; DAB; DAC; DAM MST, POET;
  PC 1; SSC 18; WLC**
Baudrillard, Jean 1929-   **CLC 60**
Baum, L(yman) Frank 1856-1919   **TCLC 7**
  See also CA 108; 133; CLR 15; DLB 22; JRDA;
  MAICYA; MTCW 1, 2; SATA 18, 100
Baum, Louis F.
  See Baum, L(yman) Frank
Baumbach, Jonathan 1933-   **CLC 6,23**
  See also CA 13-16R; CAAS 5; CANR 12, 66;
  DLBY 80; INT CANR-12; MTCW 1
Bausch, Richard (Carl) 1945-   **CLC 51**
  See also CA 101; CAAS 14; CANR 43, 61; DLB
  130
Baxter, Charles (Morley) 1947- **CLC 45, 78;
  DAM POP**
  See also CA 57-60; CANR 40, 64; DLB 130;
  MTCW 2
Baxter, George Owen
  See Faust, Frederick (Schiller)
Baxter, James K(eir) 1926-1972   **CLC 14**
  See also CA 77-80
Baxter, John
  See Hunt, E(verette) Howard, (Jr.)
Bayer, Sylvia
  See Glassco, John

Baynton, Barbara 1857-1929   **TCLC 57**

Beagle, Peter S(oyer) 1939-   **CLC 7,104**
> See also CA 9-12R; CANR 4, 51, 73; DLBY 80; INT CANR-4; MTCW 1; SATA 60

Bean, Normal
> See Burroughs, Edgar Rice

Beard, Charles A(ustin) 1874-1948 **TCLC 15**
> See also CA 115; DLB 17; SATA 18

Beardsley, Aubrey 1872-1898   **NCLC 6**

Beattie, Ann 1947-**CLC 8, 13, 18, 40, 63; DAM NOV, POP; SSC 11**
> See also BEST 90:2; CA 81-84; CANR 53, 73; DLBY 82; MTCW 1, 2

Beattie, James 1735-1803   **NCLC 25**
> See also DLB 109

Beauchamp, Kathleen Mansfield 1888-1923
> See Mansfield, Katherine
> See also CA 104; 134; DA; DAC; DAM MST; MTCW 2

Beaumarchais, Pierre-Augustin Caronde 1732-1799   **DC 4**
> See also DAM DRAM

Beaumont, Francis 1584(?)-1616**LC 33; DC 6**
> See also CDBLB Before 1660; DLB 58, 121

Beauvoir, Simone (Lucie Ernestine Marie Bertrand) de 1908-1986**CLC 1, 2, 4, 8, 14, 31, 44, 50, 71; DA; DAB; DAC; DAM MST, NOV; SSC 35; WLC**
> See also CA 9-12R; 118; CANR 28, 61; DLB 72; DLBY 86; MTCW 1, 2

Becker, Carl (Lotus) 1873-1945   **TCLC 63**
> See also CA 157; DLB 17

Becker, Jurek 1937-1997   **CLC 7, 19**
> See also CA 85-88; 157; CANR 60; DLB 75

Becker, Walter 1950-   **CLC 26**

Beckett, Samuel (Barclay) 1906-1989 **CLC 1, 2, 3, 4, 6, 9, 10, 11, 14, 18, 29, 57, 59, 83; DA; DAB; DAC; DAM DRAM, MST, NOV; SSC 16; WLC**
> See also CA 5-8R; 130; CANR 33, 61; CDBLB 1945-1960; DLB 13, 15; DLBY 90; MTCW 1, 2

Beckford, William 1760-1844   **NCLC 16**
> See also DLB 39

Beckman, Gunnel 1910-   **CLC 26**
> See also CA 33-36R; CANR 15; CLR 25; MAICYA; SAAS 9; SATA 6

Becque, Henri 1837-1899   **NCLC 3**
> See also DLB 192

Becquer, Gustavo Adolfo 1836-1870
> See also DAM MULT; HLCS 1

Beddoes, Thomas Lovell 1803-1849 **NCLC 3**
> See also DLB 96

Bede c. 673-735   **CMLC 20**
> See also DLB 146

Bedford, Donald F.
> See Fearing, Kenneth (Flexner)

Beecher, Catharine Esther 1800-1878 **NCLC 30**
> See also DLB 1

Beecher, John 1904-1980   **CLC 6**
> See also AITN 1; CA 5-8R; 105; CANR 8

Beer, Johann 1655-1700   **LC 5**
> See also DLB 168

Beer, Patricia 1924-   **CLC 58**
> See also CA 61-64; CANR 13, 46; DLB 40

Beerbohm, Max
> See Beerbohm, (Henry) Max(imilian)

Beerbohm, (Henry) Max(imilian) 1872-1956 **TCLC 1, 24**
> See also CA 104; 154; CANR 79; DLB 34, 100

Beer-Hofmann, Richard 1866-1945**TCLC 60**
> See also CA 160; DLB 81

Begiebing, Robert J(ohn) 1946-   **CLC 70**
> See also CA 122; CANR 40

Behan, Brendan 1923-1964 **CLC 1, 8, 11, 15, 79; DAM DRAM**
> See also CA 73-76; CANR 33; CDBLB 1945-1960; DLB 13; MTCW 1, 2

Behn, Aphra 1640(?)-1689 **LC 1, 30, 42; DA; DAB; DAC; DAM DRAM, MST, NOV, POET; DC 4; PC 13; WLC**
> See also DLB 39, 80, 131

Behrman, S(amuel) N(athaniel) 1893-1973 **CLC 40**
> See also CA 13-16; 45-48; CAP 1; DLB 7, 44

Belasco, David 1853-1931   **TCLC 3**
> See also CA 104; 168; DLB 7

Belcheva, Elisaveta 1893-   **CLC 10**
> See also Bagryana, Elisaveta

Beldone, Phil "Cheech"
> See Ellison, Harlan (Jay)

Beleno
> See Azuela, Mariano

Belinski, Vissarion Grigoryevich 1811-1848 **NCLC 5**
> See also DLB 198

Belitt, Ben 1911-   **CLC 22**
> See also CA 13-16R; CAAS 4; CANR 7, 77; DLB 5

Bell, Gertrude (Margaret Lowthian) 1868-1926 **TCLC 67**
> See also CA 167; DLB 174

Bell, J. Freeman
> See Zangwill, Israel

Bell, James Madison 1826-1902   **TCLC 43; BLC 1; DAM MULT**
> See also BW 1; CA 122; 124; DLB 50

Bell, Madison Smartt 1957-   **CLC 41, 102**
> See also CA 111; CANR 28, 54, 73; MTCW 1

Bell, Marvin (Hartley) 1937-**CLC 8, 31; DAM POET**
> See also CA 21-24R; CAAS 14; CANR 59; DLB 5; MTCW 1

Bell, W. L. D.
> See Mencken, H(enry) L(ouis)

Bellamy, Atwood C.
> See Mencken, H(enry) L(ouis)

Bellamy, Edward 1850-1898   **NCLC 4**
> See also DLB 12

Belli, Gioconda 1949-
> See also CA 152; HLCS 1

Bellin, Edward J.
> See Kuttner, Henry

Belloc, (Joseph) Hilaire (Pierre Sebastien Rene Swanton) 1870-1953 **TCLC 7, 18; DAM POET; PC 24**
> See also CA 106; 152; DLB 19, 100, 141, 174; MTCW 1; YABC 1

Belloc, Joseph Peter Rene Hilaire
> See Belloc, (Joseph) Hilaire (Pierre Sebastien Rene Swanton)

Belloc, Joseph Pierre Hilaire
> See Belloc, (Joseph) Hilaire (Pierre Sebastien Rene Swanton)

Belloc, M. A.
> See Lowndes, Marie Adelaide (Belloc)

Bellow, Saul 1915-**CLC 1, 2, 3, 6, 8, 10, 13, 15, 25, 33, 34, 63, 79; DA; DAB; DAC; DAM MST, NOV, POP; SSC 14; WLC**
> See also AITN 2; BEST 89:3; CA 5-8R; CABS 1; CANR 29, 53; CDALB 1941-1968; DLB 2, 28; DLBD 3; DLBY 82; MTCW 1, 2

Belser, Reimond Karel Maria de 1929-
> See Ruyslinck, Ward
> See also CA 152

Bely, Andrey   **TCLC 7; PC 11**
> See also Bugayev, Boris Nikolayevich
> See also MTCW 1

Belyi, Andrei
> See Bugayev, Boris Nikolayevich

Benary, Margot
> See Benary-Isbert, Margot

Benary-Isbert, Margot 1889-1979   **CLC 12**
> See also CA 5-8R; 89-92; CANR 4, 72; CLR 12; MAICYA; SATA 2; SATA-Obit 21

Benavente (y Martinez), Jacinto 1866-1954 **TCLC 3; DAM DRAM, MULT; HLCS 1**
> See also CA 106; 131; CANR 81; HW 1, 2; MTCW 1, 2

Benchley, Peter (Bradford) 1940- **CLC 4, 8; DAM NOV, POP**
> See also AAYA 14; AITN 2; CA 17-20R; CANR 12, 35, 66; MTCW 1, 2; SATA 3, 89

Benchley, Robert (Charles) 1889-1945 **TCLC 1, 55**
> See also CA 105; 153; DLB 11

Benda, Julien 1867-1956   **TCLC 60**
> See also CA 120; 154

Benedict, Ruth (Fulton) 1887-1948 **TCLC 60**
> See also CA 158

Benedict, Saint c. 480-c. 547   **CMLC 29**

Benedikt, Michael 1935-   **CLC 4, 14**
> See also CA 13-16R; CANR 7; DLB 5

Benet, Juan 1927-   **CLC 28**
> See also CA 143

Benet, Stephen Vincent 1898-1943 **TCLC 7; DAM POET; SSC 10**
> See also CA 104; 152; DLB 4, 48, 102; DLBY 97; MTCW 1; YABC 1

Benet, William Rose 1886-1950   **TCLC 28; DAM POET**
> See also CA 118; 152; DLB 45

Benford, Gregory (Albert) 1941-   **CLC 52**
> See also CA 69-72, 175; CAAE 175; CAAS 27; CANR 12, 24, 49; DLBY 82

Bengtsson, Frans (Gunnar) 1894-1954 **TCLC 48**
> See also CA 170

Benjamin, David
> See Slavitt, David R(ytman)

Benjamin, Lois
> See Gould, Lois

Benjamin, Walter 1892-1940   **TCLC 39**
> See also CA 164

Benn, Gottfried 1886-1956   **TCLC 3**
> See also CA 106; 153; DLB 56

Bennett, Alan 1934-**CLC 45, 77; DAB; DAM MST**
> See also CA 103; CANR 35, 55; MTCW 1, 2

Bennett, (Enoch) Arnold 1867-1931 **TCLC 5, 20**
> See also CA 106; 155; CDBLB 1890-1914; DLB 10, 34, 98, 135; MTCW 2

Bennett, Elizabeth
> See Mitchell, Margaret (Munnerlyn)

Bennett, George Harold 1930-
> See Bennett, Hal
> See also BW 1; CA 97-100

Bennett, Hal   **CLC 5**
> See also Bennett, George Harold
> See also DLB 33

Bennett, Jay 1912-   **CLC 35**
> See also AAYA 10; CA 69-72; CANR 11, 42, 79; JRDA; SAAS 4; SATA 41, 87; SATA-Brief 27

Bennett, Louise (Simone) 1919-**CLC 28; BLC 1; DAM MULT**
> See also BW 2, 3; CA 151; DLB 117

Benson, E(dward) F(rederic) 1867-1940
TCLC 27
See also CA 114; 157; DLB 135, 153

Benson, Jackson J. 1930-   CLC 34
See also CA 25-28R; DLB 111

Benson, Sally 1900-1972   CLC 17
See also CA 19-20; 37-40R; CAP 1; SATA 1,
35; SATA-Obit 27

Benson, Stella 1892-1933   TCLC 17
See also CA 117; 155; DLB 36, 162

Bentham, Jeremy 1748-1832   NCLC 38
See also DLB 107, 158

Bentley, E(dmund) C(lerihew) 1875-1956
TCLC 12
See also CA 108; DLB 70

Bentley, Eric (Russell) 1916-   CLC 24
See also CA 5-8R; CANR 6, 67; INT CANR-6

Beranger, Pierre Jean de 1780-1857NCLC 34

Berdyaev, Nicolas
See Berdyaev, Nikolai (Aleksandrovich)

Berdyaev, Nikolai (Aleksandrovich) 1874-1948
TCLC 67
See also CA 120; 157

Berdyayev, Nikolai (Aleksandrovich)
See Berdyaev, Nikolai (Aleksandrovich)

Berendt, John (Lawrence) 1939-   CLC 86
See also CA 146; CANR 75; MTCW 1

Beresford, J(ohn) D(avys) 1873-1947 TCLC
81
See also CA 112; 155; DLB 162, 178, 197

Bergelson, David 1884-1952   TCLC 81

Berger, Colonel
See Malraux, (Georges-)Andre

Berger, John (Peter) 1926-   CLC 2, 19
See also CA 81-84; CANR 51, 78; DLB 14, 207

Berger, Melvin H. 1927-   CLC 12
See also CA 5-8R; CANR 4; CLR 32; SAAS 2;
SATA 5, 88

Berger, Thomas (Louis) 1924-CLC 3, 5, 8, 11,
18, 38; DAM NOV
See also CA 1-4R; CANR 5, 28, 51; DLB 2;
DLBY 80; INT CANR-28; MTCW 1, 2

Bergman, (Ernst) Ingmar 1918- CLC 16, 72
See also CA 81-84; CANR 33, 70; MTCW 2

Bergson, Henri (-Louis) 1859-1941 TCLC 32
See also CA 164

Bergstein, Eleanor 1938-   CLC 4
See also CA 53-56; CANR 5

Berkoff, Steven 1937-   CLC 56
See also CA 104; CANR 72

Bermant, Chaim (Icyk) 1929-   CLC 40
See also CA 57-60; CANR 6, 31, 57

Bern, Victoria
See Fisher, M(ary) F(rances) K(ennedy)

Bernanos, (Paul Louis) Georges 1888-1948
TCLC 3
See also CA 104; 130; DLB 72

Bernard, April 1956-   CLC 59
See also CA 131

Berne, Victoria
See Fisher, M(ary) F(rances) K(ennedy)

Bernhard, Thomas 1931-1989 CLC 3, 32, 61
See also CA 85-88; 127; CANR 32, 57; DLB
85, 124; MTCW 1

Bernhardt, Sarah (Henriette Rosine) 1844-1923
TCLC 75
See also CA 157

Berriault, Gina 1926- CLC 54, 109; SSC 30
See also CA 116; 129; CANR 66; DLB 130

Berrigan, Daniel 1921-   CLC 4
See also CA 33-36R; CAAS 1; CANR 11, 43,
78; DLB 5

Berrigan, Edmund Joseph Michael, Jr. 1934-

1983
See Berrigan, Ted
See also CA 61-64; 110; CANR 14

Berrigan, Ted   CLC 37
See also Berrigan, Edmund Joseph Michael, Jr.
See also DLB 5, 169

Berry, Charles Edward Anderson 1931-
See Berry, Chuck
See also CA 115

Berry, Chuck   CLC 17
See also Berry, Charles Edward Anderson

Berry, Jonas
See Ashbery, John (Lawrence)

Berry, Wendell (Erdman) 1934- CLC 4, 6, 8,
27, 46; DAM POET
See also AITN 1; CA 73-76; CANR 50, 73; DLB
5, 6; MTCW 1

Berryman, John 1914-1972CLC 1, 2, 3, 4, 6, 8,
10, 13, 25, 62; DAM POET
See also CA 13-16; 33-36R; CABS 2; CANR
35; CAP 1; CDALB 1941-1968; DLB 48;
MTCW 1, 2

Bertolucci, Bernardo 1940-   CLC 16
See also CA 106

Berton, Pierre (Francis Demarigny) 1920-
CLC 104
See also CA 1-4R; CANR 2, 56; DLB 68; SATA
99

Bertrand, Aloysius 1807-1841   NCLC 31

Bertran de Born c. 1140-1215   CMLC 5

Besant, Annie (Wood) 1847-1933   TCLC 9
See also CA 105

Bessie, Alvah 1904-1985   CLC 23
See also CA 5-8R; 116; CANR 2, 80; DLB 26

Bethlen, T. D.
See Silverberg, Robert

Beti, Mongo   CLC 27; BLC 1; DAM MULT
See also Biyidi, Alexandre
See also CANR 79

Betjeman, John 1906-1984 CLC 2, 6, 10, 34,
43; DAB; DAM MST, POET
See also CA 9-12R; 112; CANR 33, 56; CDBLB
1945-1960; DLB 20; DLBY 84; MTCW 1,
2

Bettelheim, Bruno 1903-1990   CLC 79
See also CA 81-84; 131; CANR 23, 61; MTCW
1, 2

Betti, Ugo 1892-1953   TCLC 5
See also CA 104; 155

Betts, Doris (Waugh) 1932-   CLC 3, 6, 28
See also CA 13-16R; CANR 9, 66, 77; DLBY
82; INT CANR-9

Bevan, Alistair
See Roberts, Keith (John Kingston)

Bey, Pilaff
See Douglas, (George) Norman

Bialik, Chaim Nachman 1873-1934 TCLC 25
See also CA 170

Bickerstaff, Isaac
See Swift, Jonathan

Bidart, Frank 1939-   CLC 33
See also CA 140

Bienek, Horst 1930-   CLC 7, 11
See also CA 73-76; DLB 75

Bierce, Ambrose (Gwinett) 1842-1914(?)
TCLC 1, 7, 44; DA; DAC; DAM MST; SSC
9; WLC
See also CA 104; 139; CANR 78; CDALB
1865-1917; DLB 11, 12, 23, 71, 74, 186

Biggers, Earl Derr 1884-1933   TCLC 65
See also CA 108; 153

Billings, Josh
See Shaw, Henry Wheeler

Billington, (Lady) Rachel (Mary) 1942- C L C
43
See also AITN 2; CA 33-36R; CANR 44

Binyon, T(imothy) J(ohn) 1936-   CLC 34
See also CA 111; CANR 28

Bioy Casares, Adolfo 1914-1999CLC 4, 8, 13,
88; DAM MULT; HLC 1; SSC 17
See also CA 29-32R; 177; CANR 19, 43, 66;
DLB 113; HW 1, 2; MTCW 1, 2

Bird, Cordwainer
See Ellison, Harlan (Jay)

Bird, Robert Montgomery 1806-1854NCLC 1
See also DLB 202

Birkerts, Sven 1951-   CLC 116
See also CA 128; 133; 176; CAAS 29; INT 133

Birney, (Alfred) Earle 1904-1995CLC 1, 4, 6,
11; DAC; DAM MST, POET
See also CA 1-4R; CANR 5, 20; DLB 88;
MTCW 1

Biruni, al 973-1048(?)   CMLC 28

Bishop, Elizabeth 1911-1979 CLC 1, 4, 9, 13,
15, 32; DA; DAC; DAM MST, POET; PC
3
See also CA 5-8R; 89-92; CABS 2; CANR 26,
61; CDALB 1968-1988; DLB 5, 169;
MTCW 1, 2; SATA-Obit 24

Bishop, John 1935-   CLC 10
See also CA 105

Bissett, Bill 1939-   CLC 18; PC 14
See also CA 69-72; CAAS 19; CANR 15; DLB
53; MTCW 1

Bissoondath, Neil (Devindra) 1955-CLC 120;
DAC
See also CA 136

Bitov, Andrei (Georgievich) 1937-   CLC 57
See also CA 142

Biyidi, Alexandre 1932-
See Beti, Mongo
See also BW 1, 3; CA 114; 124; CANR 81;
MTCW 1, 2

Bjarme, Brynjolf
See Ibsen, Henrik (Johan)

Bjoernson, Bjoernstjerne (Martinius) 1832-
1910   TCLC 7, 37
See also CA 104

Black, Robert
See Holdstock, Robert P.

Blackburn, Paul 1926-1971   CLC 9, 43
See also CA 81-84; 33-36R; CANR 34; DLB
16; DLBY 81

Black Elk 1863-1950 TCLC 33;DAM MULT
See also CA 144; MTCW 1; NNAL

Black Hobart
See Sanders, (James) Ed(ward)

Blacklin, Malcolm
See Chambers, Aidan

Blackmore, R(ichard) D(oddridge) 1825-1900
TCLC 27
See also CA 120; DLB 18

Blackmur, R(ichard) P(almer) 1904-1965
CLC 2, 24
See also CA 11-12; 25-28R; CANR 71; CAP 1;
DLB 63

Black Tarantula
See Acker, Kathy

Blackwood, Algernon (Henry) 1869-1951
TCLC 5
See also CA 105; 150; DLB 153, 156, 178

Blackwood, Caroline 1931-1996CLC 6, 9, 100
See also CA 85-88; 151; CANR 32, 61, 65; DLB
14, 207; MTCW 1

Blade, Alexander
See Hamilton, Edmond; Silverberg, Robert

Blaga, Lucian 1895-1961 **CLC 75**
See also CA 157

Blair, Eric (Arthur) 1903-1950
See Orwell, George
See also CA 104; 132; DA; DAB; DAC; DAM
MST, NOV; MTCW 1, 2; SATA 29

Blair, Hugh 1718-1800 **NCLC 75**

Blais, Marie-Claire 1939-**CLC 2, 4, 6, 13, 22;
DAC; DAM MST**
See also CA 21-24R; CAAS 4; CANR 38, 75;
DLB 53; MTCW 1, 2

Blaise, Clark 1940- **CLC 29**
See also AITN 2; CA 53-56; CAAS 3; CANR
5, 66; DLB 53

Blake, Fairley
See De Voto, Bernard (Augustine)

Blake, Nicholas
See Day Lewis, C(ecil)
See also DLB 77

Blake, William 1757-1827 **NCLC 13, 37, 57;
DA; DAB; DAC; DAM MST, POET; PC
12; WLC**
See also CDBLB 1789-1832; CLR 52; DLB 93,
163; MAICYA; SATA 30

Blasco Ibanez, Vicente 1867-1928 **TCLC 12;
DAM NOV**
See also CA 110; 131; CANR 81; HW 1, 2;
MTCW 1

Blatty, William Peter 1928-**CLC 2;DAM POP**
See also CA 5-8R; CANR 9

Bleeck, Oliver
See Thomas, Ross (Elmore)

Blessing, Lee 1949- **CLC 54**

Blish, James (Benjamin) 1921-1975 **CLC 14**
See also CA 1-4R; 57-60; CANR 3; DLB 8;
MTCW 1; SATA 66

Bliss, Reginald
See Wells, H(erbert) G(eorge)

Blixen, Karen (Christentze Dinesen) 1885-1962
See Dinesen, Isak
See also CA 25-28; CANR 22, 50; CAP 2;
MTCW 1, 2; SATA 44

Bloch, Robert (Albert) 1917-1994 **CLC 33**
See also Fiske, Tarleton; Folke, Will; Hindin,
Nathan; Jarvis, E. K.; Kane, Wilson; Sheldon,
John; Young, Collier
See also AAYA 29; CA 179; 146; CAAE 179;
CAAS 20; CANR 5, 78; DLB 44; INT
CANR-5; MTCW 1; SATA 12; SATA-Obit
82

Blok, Alexander (Alexandrovich) 1880-1921
TCLC 5; PC 21
See also CA 104

Blom, Jan
See Breytenbach, Breyten

Bloom, Harold 1930- **CLC 24, 103**
See also CA 13-16R; CANR 39, 75; DLB 67;
MTCW 1

Bloomfield, Aurelius
See Bourne, Randolph S(illiman)

Blount, Roy (Alton), Jr. 1941- **CLC 38**
See also CA 53-56; CANR 10, 28, 61; INT
CANR-28; MTCW 1, 2

Bloy, Leon 1846-1917 **TCLC 22**
See also CA 121; DLB 123

Blume, Judy (Sussman) 1938- **CLC 12, 30;
DAM NOV, POP**
See also AAYA 3, 26; CA 29-32R; CANR 13,
37, 66; CLR 2, 15; DLB 52; JRDA;
MAICYA; MTCW 1, 2; SATA 2, 31, 79

Blunden, Edmund (Charles) 1896-1974 **C L C
2, 56**
See also CA 17-18; 45-48; CANR 54; CAP 2;

DLB 20, 100, 155; MTCW 1

Bly, Robert (Elwood) 1926-**CLC 1, 2, 5, 10, 15,
38; DAM POET**
See also CA 5-8R; CANR 41, 73; DLB 5;
MTCW 1, 2

Boas, Franz 1858-1942 **TCLC 56**
See also CA 115

Bobette
See Simenon, Georges (Jacques Christian)

Boccaccio, Giovanni 1313-1375 **CMLC 13;
SSC 10**

Bochco, Steven 1943- **CLC 35**
See also AAYA 11; CA 124; 138

Bodel, Jean 1167(?)-1210 **CMLC 28**

Bodenheim, Maxwell 1892-1954 **TCLC 44**
See also CA 110; DLB 9, 45

Bodker, Cecil 1927- **CLC 21**
See also CA 73-76; CANR 13, 44; CLR 23;
MAICYA; SATA 14

Boell, Heinrich (Theodor) 1917-1985 **CLC 2,
3, 6, 9, 11, 15, 27, 32, 72; DA; DAB; DAC;
DAM MST, NOV; SSC 23; WLC**
See also CA 21-24R; 116; CANR 24; DLB 69;
DLBY 85; MTCW 1, 2

Boerne, Alfred
See Doeblin, Alfred

Boethius 480(?)-524(?) **CMLC 15**
See also DLB 115

Boff, Leonardo (Genezio Darci) 1938-
See also CA 150; DAM MULT; HLC 1; HW 2

Bogan, Louise 1897-1970 **CLC 4, 39, 46, 93;
DAM POET; PC 12**
See also CA 73-76; 25-28R; CANR 33, 82; DLB
45, 169; MTCW 1, 2

Bogarde, Dirk 1921-1999 **CLC 19**
See also Van Den Bogarde, Derek Jules Gaspard
Ulric Niven
See also CA 179; DLB 14

Bogosian, Eric 1953- **CLC 45**
See also CA 138

Bograd, Larry 1953- **CLC 35**
See also CA 93-96; CANR 57; SAAS 21; SATA
33, 89

Boiardo, Matteo Maria 1441-1494 **LC 6**

Boileau-Despreaux, Nicolas 1636-1711 **LC 3**

Bojer, Johan 1872-1959 **TCLC 64**

Boland, Eavan (Aisling) 1944- **CLC 40, 67,
113; DAM POET**
See also CA 143; CANR 61; DLB 40; MTCW
2

Boll, Heinrich
See Boell, Heinrich (Theodor)

Bolt, Lee
See Faust, Frederick (Schiller)

Bolt, Robert (Oxton) 1924-1995**CLC 14; DAM
DRAM**
See also CA 17-20R; 147; CANR 35, 67; DLB
13; MTCW 1

Bombal, Maria Luisa 1910-1980
See also CA 127; CANR 72; HLCS 1; HW 1

Bombet, Louis-Alexandre-Cesar
See Stendhal

Bomkauf
See Kaufman, Bob (Garnell)

Bonaventura **NCLC 35**
See also DLB 90

Bond, Edward 1934- **CLC 4, 6, 13, 23; DAM
DRAM**
See also CA 25-28R; CANR 38, 67; DLB 13;
MTCW 1

Bonham, Frank 1914-1989 **CLC 12**
See also AAYA 1; CA 9-12R; CANR 4, 36;
JRDA; MAICYA; SAAS 3; SATA 1, 49;

SATA-Obit 62

Bonnefoy, Yves 1923- **CLC 9, 15, 58; DAM
MST, POET**
See also CA 85-88; CANR 33, 75; MTCW 1, 2

Bontemps, Arna(ud Wendell) 1902-1973**C L C
1, 18; BLC 1; DAM MULT, NOV, POET**
See also BW 1; CA 1-4R; 41-44R; CANR 4,
35; CLR 6; DLB 48, 51; JRDA; MAICYA;
MTCW 1, 2; SATA 2, 44; SATA-Obit 24

Booth, Martin 1944- **CLC 13**
See also CA 93-96; CAAS 2

Booth, Philip 1925- **CLC 23**
See also CA 5-8R; CANR 5; DLBY 82

Booth, Wayne C(layson) 1921- **CLC 24**
See also CA 1-4R; CAAS 5; CANR 3, 43; DLB
67

Borchert, Wolfgang 1921-1947 **TCLC 5**
See also CA 104; DLB 69, 124

Borel, Petrus 1809-1859 **NCLC 41**

Borges, Jorge Luis 1899-1986**CLC 1, 2, 3, 4, 6,
8, 9, 10, 13, 19, 44, 48, 83; DA; DAB; DAC;
DAM MST, MULT; HLC 1; PC 22; SSC
4; WLC**
See also AAYA 26; CA 21-24R; CANR 19, 33,
75; DLB 113; DLBY 86; HW 1, 2; MTCW
1, 2

Borowski, Tadeusz 1922-1951 **TCLC 9**
See also CA 106; 154

Borrow, George (Henry) 1803-1881 **NCLC 9**
See also DLB 21, 55, 166

Bosch (Gavino), Juan 1909-
See also CA 151; DAM MST, MULT; DLB 145;
HLCS 1; HW 1, 2

Bosman, Herman Charles 1905-1951 **T C L C
49**
See also Malan, Herman
See also CA 160

Bosschere, Jean de 1878(?)-1953 **TCLC 19**
See also CA 115

Boswell, James 1740-1795**LC 4, 50; DA; DAB;
DAC; DAM MST; WLC**
See also CDBLB 1660-1789; DLB 104, 142

Bottoms, David 1949- **CLC 53**
See also CA 105; CANR 22; DLB 120; DLBY
83

Boucicault, Dion 1820-1890 **NCLC 41**

Boucolon, Maryse 1937(?)-
See Conde, Maryse
See also BW 3; CA 110; CANR 30, 53, 76

Bourget, Paul (Charles Joseph) 1852-1935
TCLC 12
See also CA 107; DLB 123

Bourjaily, Vance (Nye) 1922- **CLC 8, 62**
'See also CA 1-4R; CAAS 1; CANR 2, 72; DLB
2, 143

Bourne, Randolph S(illiman) 1886-1918
TCLC 16
See also CA 117; 155; DLB 63

Bova, Ben(jamin William) 1932- **CLC 45**
See also AAYA 16; CA 5-8R; CAAS 18; CANR
11, 56; CLR 3; DLBY 81; INT CANR-11;
MAICYA; MTCW 1; SATA 6, 68

Bowen, Elizabeth (Dorothea Cole) 1899-1973
**CLC 1, 3, 6, 11, 15, 22, 118; DAM NOV;
SSC 3, 28**
See also CA 17-18; 41-44R; CANR 35; CAP 2;
CDBLB 1945-1960; DLB 15, 162; MTCW
1, 2

Bowering, George 1935- **CLC 15, 47**
See also CA 21-24R; CAAS 16; CANR 10; DLB
53

Bowering, Marilyn R(uthe) 1949- **CLC 32**
See also CA 101; CANR 49

Bowers, Edgar 1924- **CLC 9**
See also CA 5-8R; CANR 24; DLB 5
Bowie, David **CLC 17**
See also Jones, David Robert
Bowles, Jane (Sydney) 1917-1973 **CLC 3, 68**
See also CA 19-20; 41-44R; CAP 2
Bowles, Paul (Frederick) 1910- **CLC 1, 2, 19, 53; SSC 3**
See also CA 1-4R; CAAS 1; CANR 1, 19, 50, 75; DLB 5, 6; MTCW 1, 2
Box, Edgar
See Vidal, Gore
Boyd, Nancy
See Millay, Edna St. Vincent
Boyd, William 1952- **CLC 28, 53, 70**
See also CA 114; 120; CANR 51, 71
Boyle, Kay 1902-1992 **CLC 1, 5, 19, 58, 121; SSC 5**
See also CA 13-16R; 140; CAAS 1; CANR 29, 61; DLB 4, 9, 48, 86; DLBY 93; MTCW 1, 2
Boyle, Mark
See Kienzle, William X(avier)
Boyle, Patrick 1905-1982 **CLC 19**
See also CA 127
Boyle, T. C. 1948-
See Boyle, T(homas) Coraghessan
Boyle, T(homas) Coraghessan 1948- **CLC 36, 55, 90; DAM POP; SSC 16**
See also BEST 90:4; CA 120; CANR 44, 76; DLBY 86; MTCW 2
Boz
See Dickens, Charles (John Huffam)
Brackenridge, Hugh Henry 1748-1816 **NCLC 7**
See also DLB 11, 37
Bradbury, Edward P.
See Moorcock, Michael (John)
See also MTCW 2
Bradbury, Malcolm (Stanley) 1932- **CLC 32, 61; DAM NOV**
See also CA 1-4R; CANR 1, 33; DLB 14, 207; MTCW 1, 2
Bradbury, Ray (Douglas) 1920- **CLC 1, 3, 10, 15, 42, 98; DA; DAB; DAC; DAM MST, NOV, POP; SSC 29; WLC**
See also AAYA 15; AITN 1, 2; CA 1-4R; CANR 2, 30, 75; CDALB 1968-1988; DLB 2, 8; MTCW 1, 2; SATA 11, 64
Bradford, Gamaliel 1863-1932 **TCLC 36**
See also CA 160; DLB 17
Bradley, David (Henry), Jr. 1950- **CLC 23, 118; BLC 1; DAM MULT**
See also BW 1, 3; CA 104; CANR 26, 81; DLB 33
Bradley, John Ed(mund, Jr.) 1958- **CLC 55**
See also CA 139
Bradley, Marion Zimmer 1930- **CLC 30; DAM POP**
See also AAYA 9; CA 57-60; CAAS 10; CANR 7, 31, 51, 75; DLB 8; MTCW 1, 2; SATA 90
Bradstreet, Anne 1612(?)-1672 **LC 4, 30; DA; DAC; DAM MST, POET; PC 10**
See also CDALB 1640-1865; DLB 24
Brady, Joan 1939- **CLC 86**
See also CA 141
Bragg, Melvyn 1939- **CLC 10**
See also BEST 89:3; CA 57-60; CANR 10, 48; DLB 14
Brahe, Tycho 1546-1601 **LC 45**
Braine, John (Gerard) 1922-1986 **CLC 1, 3, 41**
See also CA 1-4R; 120; CANR 1, 33; CDBLB 1945-1960; DLB 15; DLBY 86; MTCW 1

Bramah, Ernest 1868-1942 **TCLC 72**
See also CA 156; DLB 70
Brammer, William 1930(?)-1978 **CLC 31**
See also CA 77-80
Brancati, Vitaliano 1907-1954 **TCLC 12**
See also CA 109
Brancato, Robin F(idler) 1936- **CLC 35**
See also AAYA 9; CA 69-72; CANR 11, 45; CLR 32; JRDA; SAAS 9; SATA 97
Brand, Max
See Faust, Frederick (Schiller)
Brand, Millen 1906-1980 **CLC 7**
See also CA 21-24R; 97-100; CANR 72
Branden, Barbara **CLC 44**
See also CA 148
Brandes, Georg (Morris Cohen) 1842-1927 **TCLC 10**
See also CA 105
Brandys, Kazimierz 1916- **CLC 62**
Branley, Franklyn M(ansfield) 1915- **CLC 21**
See also CA 33-36R; CANR 14, 39; CLR 13; MAICYA; SAAS 16; SATA 4, 68
Brathwaite, Edward (Kamau) 1930- **CLC 11; BLCS; DAM POET**
See also BW 2, 3; CA 25-28R; CANR 11, 26, 47; DLB 125
Brautigan, Richard (Gary) 1935-1984 **CLC 1, 3, 5, 9, 12, 34, 42; DAM NOV**
See also CA 53-56; 113; CANR 34; DLB 2, 5, 206; DLBY 80, 84; MTCW 1; SATA 56
Brave Bird, Mary 1953-
See Crow Dog, Mary (Ellen)
See also NNAL
Braverman, Kate 1950- **CLC 67**
See also CA 89-92
Brecht, (Eugen) Bertolt (Friedrich) 1898-1956 **TCLC 1, 6, 13, 35; DA; DAB; DAC; DAM DRAM, MST; DC 3; WLC**
See also CA 104; 133; CANR 62; DLB 56, 124; MTCW 1, 2
Brecht, Eugen Berthold Friedrich
See Brecht, (Eugen) Bertolt (Friedrich)
Bremer, Fredrika 1801-1865 **NCLC 11**
Brennan, Christopher John 1870-1932 **TCLC 17**
See also CA 117
Brennan, Maeve 1917-1993 **CLC 5**
See also CA 81-84; CANR 72
Brent, Linda
See Jacobs, Harriet A(nn)
Brentano, Clemens (Maria) 1778-1842 **NCLC 1**
See also DLB 90
Brent of Bin Bin
See Franklin, (Stella Maria Sarah) Miles (Lampe)
Brenton, Howard 1942- **CLC 31**
See also CA 69-72; CANR 33, 67; DLB 13; MTCW 1
Breslin, James 1930-1996
See Breslin, Jimmy
See also CA 73-76; CANR 31, 75; DAM NOV; MTCW 1, 2
Breslin, Jimmy **CLC 4, 43**
See also Breslin, James
See also AITN 1; DLB 185; MTCW 2
Bresson, Robert 1901- **CLC 16**
See also CA 110; CANR 49
Breton, Andre 1896-1966 **CLC 2, 9, 15, 54; PC 15**
See also CA 19-20; 25-28R; CANR 40, 60; CAP 2; DLB 65; MTCW 1, 2
Breytenbach, Breyten 1939(?)- **CLC 23, 37;**

DAM POET
See also CA 113; 129; CANR 61
Bridgers, Sue Ellen 1942- **CLC 26**
See also AAYA 8; CA 65-68; CANR 11, 36; CLR 18; DLB 52; JRDA; MAICYA; SAAS 1; SATA 22, 90; SATA-Essay 109
Bridges, Robert (Seymour) 1844-1930 **TCLC 1; DAM POET**
See also CA 104; 152; CDBLB 1890-1914; DLB 19, 98
Bridie, James **TCLC 3**
See also Mavor, Osborne Henry
See also DLB 10
Brin, David 1950- **CLC 34**
See also AAYA 21; CA 102; CANR 24, 70; INT CANR-24; SATA 65
Brink, Andre (Philippus) 1935- **CLC 18, 36, 106**
See also CA 104; CANR 39, 62; INT 103; MTCW 1, 2
Brinsmead, H(esba) F(ay) 1922- **CLC 21**
See also CA 21-24R; CANR 10; CLR 47; MAICYA; SAAS 5; SATA 18, 78
Brittain, Vera (Mary) 1893(?)-1970 **CLC 23**
See also CA 13-16; 25-28R; CANR 58; CAP 1; DLB 191; MTCW 1, 2
Broch, Hermann 1886-1951 **TCLC 20**
See also CA 117; DLB 85, 124
Brock, Rose
See Hansen, Joseph
Brodkey, Harold (Roy) 1930-1996 **CLC 56**
See also CA 111; 151; CANR 71; DLB 130
Brodskii, Iosif
See Brodsky, Joseph
Brodsky, Iosif Alexandrovich 1940-1996
See Brodsky, Joseph
See also AITN 1; CA 41-44R; 151; CANR 37; DAM POET; MTCW 1, 2
Brodsky, Joseph 1940-1996 **CLC 4, 6, 13, 36, 100; PC 9**
See also Brodskii, Iosif; Brodsky, Iosif Alexandrovich
See also MTCW 1
Brodsky, Michael (Mark) 1948- **CLC 19**
See also CA 102; CANR 18, 41, 58
Bromell, Henry 1947- **CLC 5**
See also CA 53-56; CANR 9
Bromfield, Louis (Brucker) 1896-1956 **TCLC 11**
See also CA 107; 155; DLB 4, 9, 86
Broner, E(sther) M(asserman) 1930- **CLC 19**
See also CA 17-20R; CANR 8, 25, 72; DLB 28
Bronk, William (M.) 1918-1999 **CLC 10**
See also CA 89-92; 177; CANR 23; DLB 165
Bronstein, Lev Davidovich
See Trotsky, Leon
Bronte, Anne 1820-1849 **NCLC 71**
See also DLB 21, 199
Bronte, Charlotte 1816-1855 **NCLC 3, 8, 33, 58; DA; DAB; DAC; DAM MST, NOV; WLC**
See also AAYA 17; CDBLB 1832-1890; DLB 21, 159, 199
Bronte, Emily (Jane) 1818-1848 **NCLC 16, 35; DA; DAB; DAC; DAM MST, NOV, POET; PC 8; WLC**
See also AAYA 17; CDBLB 1832-1890; DLB 21, 32, 199
Brooke, Frances 1724-1789 **LC 6, 48**
See also DLB 39, 99
Brooke, Henry 1703(?)-1783 **LC 1**
See also DLB 39
Brooke, Rupert (Chawner) 1887-1915 **TCLC**

2, 7; DA; DAB; DAC; DAM MST, POET; PC 24; WLC
  See also CA 104; 132; CANR 61; CDBLB 1914-1945; DLB 19; MTCW 1, 2
Brooke-Haven, P.
  See Wodehouse, P(elham) G(renville)
Brooke-Rose, Christine 1926(?)- **CLC 40**
  See also CA 13-16R; CANR 58; DLB 14
Brookner, Anita 1928- **CLC 32, 34, 51; DAB; DAM POP**
  See also CA 114; 120; CANR 37, 56; DLB 194; DLBY 87; MTCW 1, 2
Brooks, Cleanth 1906-1994 **CLC 24, 86, 110**
  See also CA 17-20R; 145; CANR 33, 35; DLB 63; DLBY 94; INT CANR-35; MTCW 1, 2
Brooks, George
  See Baum, L(yman) Frank
Brooks, Gwendolyn 1917- **CLC 1, 2, 4, 5, 15, 49; BLC 1; DA; DAC; DAM MST, MULT, POET; PC 7; WLC**
  See also AAYA 20; AITN 1; BW 2, 3; CA 1-4R; CANR 1, 27, 52, 75; CDALB 1941-1968; CLR 27; DLB 5, 76, 165; MTCW 1, 2; SATA 6
Brooks, Mel   **CLC 12**
  See also Kaminsky, Melvin
  See also AAYA 13; DLB 26
Brooks, Peter 1938-   **CLC 34**
  See also CA 45-48; CANR 1
Brooks, Van Wyck 1886-1963   **CLC 29**
  See also CA 1-4R; CANR 6; DLB 45, 63, 103
Brophy, Brigid (Antonia) 1929-1995 **CLC 6, 11, 29, 105**
  See also CA 5-8R; 149; CAAS 4; CANR 25, 53; DLB 14; MTCW 1, 2
Brosman, Catharine Savage 1934-   **CLC 9**
  See also CA 61-64; CANR 21, 46
Brossard, Nicole 1943-   **CLC 115**
  See also CA 122; CAAS 16; DLB 53
Brother Antoninus
  See Everson, William (Oliver)
The Brothers Quay
  See Quay, Stephen; Quay, Timothy
Broughton, T(homas) Alan 1936-   **CLC 19**
  See also CA 45-48; CANR 2, 23, 48
Broumas, Olga 1949-   **CLC 10, 73**
  See also CA 85-88; CANR 20, 69
Brown, Alan 1950-   **CLC 99**
  See also CA 156
Brown, Charles Brockden 1771-1810 **NCLC 22, 74**
  See also CDALB 1640-1865; DLB 37, 59, 73
Brown, Christy 1932-1981   **CLC 63**
  See also CA 105; 104; CANR 72; DLB 14
Brown, Claude 1937- **CLC 30; BLC 1; DAM MULT**
  See also AAYA 7; BW 1, 3; CA 73-76; CANR 81
Brown, Dee (Alexander) 1908- **CLC 18, 47; DAM POP**
  See also AAYA 30; CA 13-16R; CAAS 6; CANR 11, 45, 60; DLBY 80; MTCW 1, 2; SATA 5
Brown, George
  See Wertmueller, Lina
Brown, George Douglas 1869-1902 **TCLC 28**
  See also CA 162
Brown, George Mackay 1921-1996 **CLC 5, 48, 100**
  See also CA 21-24R; 151; CAAS 6; CANR 12, 37, 67; DLB 14, 27, 139; MTCW 1; SATA 35
Brown, (William) Larry 1951-   **CLC 73**

See also CA 130; 134; INT 133
Brown, Moses
  See Barrett, William (Christopher)
Brown, Rita Mae 1944- **CLC 18, 43, 79; DAM NOV, POP**
  See also CA 45-48; CANR 2, 11, 35, 62; INT CANR-11; MTCW 1, 2
Brown, Roderick (Langmere) Haig-
  See Haig-Brown, Roderick (Langmere)
Brown, Rosellen 1939-   **CLC 32**
  See also CA 77-80; CAAS 10; CANR 14, 44
Brown, Sterling Allen 1901-1989 **CLC 1, 23, 59; BLC 1; DAM MULT, POET**
  See also BW 1, 3; CA 85-88; 127; CANR 26; DLB 48, 51, 63; MTCW 1, 2
Brown, Will
  See Ainsworth, William Harrison
Brown, William Wells 1813-1884 **NCLC 2; BLC 1; DAM MULT; DC 1**
  See also DLB 3, 50
Browne, (Clyde) Jackson 1948(?)- **CLC 21**
  See also CA 120
Browning, Elizabeth Barrett 1806-1861 **NCLC 1, 16, 61, 66; DA; DAB; DAC; DAM MST, POET; PC 6; WLC**
  See also CDBLB 1832-1890; DLB 32, 199
Browning, Robert 1812-1889 **NCLC 19, 79; DA; DAB; DAC; DAM MST, POET; PC 2; WLCS**
  See also CDBLB 1832-1890; DLB 32, 163; YABC 1
Browning, Tod 1882-1962   **CLC 16**
  See also CA 141; 117
Brownson, Orestes Augustus 1803-1876 **NCLC 50**
  See also DLB 1, 59, 73
Bruccoli, Matthew J(oseph) 1931- **CLC 34**
  See also CA 9-12R; CANR 7; DLB 103
Bruce, Lenny   **CLC 21**
  See also Schneider, Leonard Alfred
Bruin, John
  See Brutus, Dennis
Brulard, Henri
  See Stendhal
Brulls, Christian
  See Simenon, Georges (Jacques Christian)
Brunner, John (Kilian Houston) 1934-1995 **CLC 8, 10; DAM POP**
  See also CA 1-4R; 149; CAAS 8; CANR 2, 37; MTCW 1, 2
Bruno, Giordano 1548-1600   **LC 27**
Brutus, Dennis 1924- **CLC 43; BLC 1; DAM MULT, POET; PC 24**
  See also BW 2, 3; CA 49-52; CAAS 14; CANR 2, 27, 42, 81; DLB 117
Bryan, C(ourtlandt) D(ixon) B(arnes) 1936- **CLC 29**
  See also CA 73-76; CANR 13, 68; DLB 185; INT CANR-13
Bryan, Michael
  See Moore, Brian
Bryant, William Cullen 1794-1878 **NCLC 6, 46; DA; DAB; DAC; DAM MST, POET; PC 20**
  See also CDALB 1640-1865; DLB 3, 43, 59, 189
Bryusov, Valery Yakovlevich 1873-1924 **TCLC 10**
  See also CA 107; 155
Buchan, John 1875-1940 **TCLC 41; DAB; DAM POP**
  See also CA 108; 145; DLB 34, 70, 156; MTCW 1; YABC 2

Buchanan, George 1506-1582   **LC 4**
  See also DLB 152
Buchheim, Lothar-Guenther 1918-   **CLC 6**
  See also CA 85-88
Buchner, (Karl) Georg 1813-1837 **NCLC 26**
Buchwald, Art(hur) 1925-   **CLC 33**
  See also AITN 1; CA 5-8R; CANR 21, 67; MTCW 1, 2; SATA 10
Buck, Pearl S(ydenstricker) 1892-1973 **CLC 7, 11, 18; DA; DAB; DAC; DAM MST, NOV**
  See also AITN 1; CA 1-4R; 41-44R; CANR 1, 34; CDALBS; DLB 9, 102; MTCW 1, 2; SATA 1, 25
Buckler, Ernest 1908-1984 **CLC 13; DAC; DAM MST**
  See also CA 11-12; 114; CAP 1; DLB 68; SATA 47
Buckley, Vincent (Thomas) 1925-1988 **CLC 57**
  See also CA 101
Buckley, William F(rank), Jr. 1925- **CLC 7, 18, 37; DAM POP**
  See also AITN 1; CA 1-4R; CANR 1, 24, 53; DLB 137; DLBY 80; INT CANR-24; MTCW 1, 2
Buechner, (Carl) Frederick 1926- **CLC 2, 4, 6, 9; DAM NOV**
  See also CA 13-16R; CANR 11, 39, 64; DLBY 80; INT CANR-11; MTCW 1, 2
Buell, John (Edward) 1927-   **CLC 10**
  See also CA 1-4R; CANR 71; DLB 53
Buero Vallejo, Antonio 1916-   **CLC 15, 46**
  See also CA 106; CANR 24, 49, 75; HW 1; MTCW 1, 2
Bufalino, Gesualdo 1920(?)-   **CLC 74**
  See also DLB 196
Bugayev, Boris Nikolayevich 1880-1934 **TCLC 7; PC 11**
  See also Bely, Andrey
  See also CA 104; 165; MTCW 1
Bukowski, Charles 1920-1994 **CLC 2, 5, 9, 41, 82, 108; DAM NOV, POET; PC 18**
  See also CA 17-20R; 144; CANR 40, 62; DLB 5, 130, 169; MTCW 1, 2
Bulgakov, Mikhail (Afanas'evich) 1891-1940 **TCLC 2, 16; DAM DRAM, NOV; SSC 18**
  See also CA 105; 152
Bulgya, Alexander Alexandrovich 1901-1956 **TCLC 53**
  See also Fadeyev, Alexander
  See also CA 117
Bullins, Ed 1935- **CLC 1, 5, 7; BLC 1; DAM DRAM, MULT; DC 6**
  See also BW 2, 3; CA 49-52; CAAS 16; CANR 24, 46, 73; DLB 7, 38; MTCW 1, 2
Bulwer-Lytton, Edward (George Earle Lytton) 1803-1873 **NCLC 1, 45**
  See also DLB 21
Bunin, Ivan Alexeyevich 1870-1953 **TCLC 6; SSC 5**
  See also CA 104
Bunting, Basil 1900-1985 **CLC 10, 39, 47; DAM POET**
  See also CA 53-56; 115; CANR 7; DLB 20
Bunuel, Luis 1900-1983 **CLC 16, 80; DAM MULT; HLC 1**
  See also CA 101; 110; CANR 32, 77; HW 1
Bunyan, John 1628-1688 **LC 4; DA; DAB; DAC; DAM MST; WLC**
  See also CDBLB 1660-1789; DLB 39
Burckhardt, Jacob (Christoph) 1818-1897 **NCLC 49**
Burford, Eleanor
  See Hibbert, Eleanor Alice Burford

Burgess, AnthonyCLC 1, 2, 4, 5, 8, 10, 13, 15, 22, 40, 62, 81, 94; DAB
    See also Wilson, John (Anthony) Burgess
    See also AAYA 25; AITN 1; CDBLB 1960 to Present; DLB 14, 194; DLBY 98; MTCW 1

Burke, Edmund 1729(?)-1797 LC 7, 36; DA; DAB; DAC; DAM MST; WLC
    See also DLB 104

Burke, Kenneth (Duva) 1897-1993 CLC 2, 24
    See also CA 5-8R; 143; CANR 39, 74; DLB 45, 63; MTCW 1, 2

Burke, Leda
    See Garnett, David

Burke, Ralph
    See Silverberg, Robert

Burke, Thomas 1886-1945   TCLC 63
    See also CA 113; 155; DLB 197

Burney, Fanny 1752-1840   NCLC 12, 54
    See also DLB 39

Burns, Robert 1759-1796 LC 3, 29, 40; DA; DAB; DAC; DAM MST, POET; PC 6; WLC
    See also CDBLB 1789-1832; DLB 109

Burns, Tex
    See L'Amour, Louis (Dearborn)

Burnshaw, Stanley 1906-   CLC 3, 13,44
    See also CA 9-12R; DLB 48; DLBY 97

Burr, Anne 1937-   CLC 6
    See also CA 25-28R

Burroughs, Edgar Rice 1875-1950 TCLC 2, 32; DAM NOV
    See also AAYA 11; CA 104; 132; DLB 8; MTCW 1, 2; SATA 41

Burroughs, William S(eward) 1914-1997CLC 1, 2, 5, 15, 22, 42, 75, 109; DA; DAB; DAC; DAM MST, NOV, POP; WLC
    See also AITN 2; CA 9-12R; 160; CANR 20, 52; DLB 2, 8, 16, 152; DLBY 81, 97; MTCW 1, 2

Burton, Sir Richard F(rancis) 1821-1890 NCLC 42
    See also DLB 55, 166, 184

Busch, Frederick 1941-   CLC 7, 10, 18, 47
    See also CA 33-36R; CAAS 1; CANR 45, 73; DLB 6

Bush, Ronald 1946-   CLC 34
    See also CA 136

Bustos, F(rancisco)
    See Borges, Jorge Luis

Bustos Domecq, H(onorio)
    See Bioy Casares, Adolfo; Borges, Jorge Luis

Butler, Octavia E(stelle) 1947- CLC 38, 121; BLCS; DAM MULT, POP
    See also AAYA 18; BW 2, 3; CA 73-76; CANR 12, 24, 38, 73; DLB 33; MTCW 1, 2; SATA 84

Butler, Robert Olen (Jr.) 1945-CLC 81; DAM POP
    See also CA 112; CANR 66; DLB 173; INT 112; MTCW 1

Butler, Samuel 1612-1680   LC 16, 43
    See also DLB 101, 126

Butler, Samuel 1835-1902 TCLC 1, 33; DA; DAB; DAC; DAM MST, NOV; WLC
    See also CA 143; CDBLB 1890-1914; DLB 18, 57, 174

Butler, Walter C.
    See Faust, Frederick (Schiller)

Butor, Michel (Marie Francois) 1926-CLC 1, 3, 8, 11, 15
    See also CA 9-12R; CANR 33, 66; DLB 83; MTCW 1, 2

Butts, Mary 1892(?)-1937   TCLC 77

See also CA 148

Buzo, Alexander (John) 1944-   CLC 61
    See also CA 97-100; CANR 17, 39, 69

Buzzati, Dino 1906-1972   CLC 36
    See also CA 160; 33-36R; DLB 177

Byars, Betsy (Cromer) 1928-   CLC 35
    See also AAYA 19; CA 33-36R; CANR 18, 36, 57; CLR 1, 16; DLB 52; INT CANR-18; JRDA; MAICYA; MTCW 1; SAAS 1; SATA 4, 46, 80; SATA-Essay 108

Byatt, A(ntonia) S(usan Drabble) 1936- C L C 19, 65; DAM NOV, POP
    See also CA 13-16R; CANR 13, 33, 50, 75; DLB 14, 194; MTCW 1, 2

Byrne, David 1952-   CLC 26
    See also CA 127

Byrne, John Keyes 1926-
    See Leonard, Hugh
    See also CA 102; CANR 78; INT 102

Byron, George Gordon (Noel) 1788-1824 NCLC 2, 12; DA; DAB; DAC; DAM MST, POET; PC 16; WLC
    See also CDBLB 1789-1832; DLB 96, 110

Byron, Robert 1905-1941   TCLC 67
    See also CA 160; DLB 195

C. 3. 3.
    See Wilde, Oscar

Caballero, Fernan 1796-1877   NCLC 10

Cabell, Branch
    See Cabell, James Branch

Cabell, James Branch 1879-1958   TCLC 6
    See also CA 105; 152; DLB 9, 78; MTCW 1

Cable, George Washington 1844-1925 T C L C 4; SSC 4
    See also CA 104; 155; DLB 12, 74; DLBD 13

Cabral de Melo Neto, Joao 1920-   CLC 76; DAM MULT
    See also CA 151

Cabrera Infante, G(uillermo) 1929-CLC 5, 25, 45, 120; DAM MULT; HLC 1
    See also CA 85-88; CANR 29, 65; DLB 113; HW 1, 2; MTCW 1, 2

Cade, Toni
    See Bambara, Toni Cade

Cadmus and Harmonia
    See Buchan, John

Caedmon fl. 658-680   CMLC 7
    See also DLB 146

Caeiro, Alberto
    See Pessoa, Fernando (Antonio Nogueira)

Cage, John (Milton, Jr.) 1912-1992   CLC 41
    See also CA 13-16R; 169; CANR 9, 78; DLB 193; INT CANR-9

Cahan, Abraham 1860-1951   TCLC 71
    See also CA 108; 154; DLB 9, 25, 28

Cain, G.
    See Cabrera Infante, G(uillermo)

Cain, Guillermo
    See Cabrera Infante, G(uillermo)

Cain, James M(allahan) 1892-1977CLC 3, 11, 28
    See also AITN 1; CA 17-20R; 73-76; CANR 8, 34, 61; MTCW 1

Caine, Mark
    See Raphael, Frederic (Michael)

Calasso, Roberto 1941-   CLC 81
    See also CA 143

Calderon de la Barca, Pedro 1600-1681   L C 23; DC 3; HLCS 1

Caldwell, Erskine (Preston) 1903-1987CLC 1, 8, 14, 50, 60; DAM NOV; SSC 19
    See also AITN 1; CA 1-4R; 121; CAAS 1; CANR 2, 33; DLB 9, 86; MTCW 1, 2

Caldwell, (Janet Miriam) Taylor (Holland) 1900-1985CLC 2, 28, 39; DAM NOV, POP
    See also CA 5-8R; 116; CANR 5; DLBD 17

Calhoun, John Caldwell 1782-1850NCLC 15
    See also DLB 3

Calisher, Hortense 1911-CLC 2, 4, 8, 38; DAM NOV; SSC 15
    See also CA 1-4R; CANR 1, 22, 67; DLB 2; INT CANR-22; MTCW 1, 2

Callaghan, Morley Edward 1903-1990CLC 3, 14, 41, 65; DAC; DAM MST
    See also CA 9-12R; 132; CANR 33, 73; DLB 68; MTCW 1, 2

Callimachus c. 305B.C.-c.240B.C. CMLC 18
    See also DLB 176

Calvin, John 1509-1564   LC 37

Calvino, Italo 1923-1985CLC 5, 8, 11, 22, 33, 39, 73; DAM NOV; SSC 3
    See also CA 85-88; 116; CANR 23, 61; DLB 196; MTCW 1, 2

Cameron, Carey 1952-   CLC 59
    See also CA 135

Cameron, Peter 1959-   CLC 44
    See also CA 125; CANR 50

Camoens, Luis Vaz de 1524(?)-1580
    See also HLCS 1

Camoes, Luis de 1524(?)-1580
    See also HLCS 1

Campana, Dino 1885-1932   TCLC 20
    See also CA 117; DLB 114

Campanella, Tommaso 1568-1639   LC 32

Campbell, John W(ood, Jr.) 1910-1971 C L C 32
    See also CA 21-22; 29-32R; CANR 34; CAP 2; DLB 8; MTCW 1

Campbell, Joseph 1904-1987   CLC 69
    See also AAYA 3; BEST 89:2; CA 1-4R; 124; CANR 3, 28, 61; MTCW 1, 2

Campbell, Maria 1940-   CLC 85; DAC
    See also CA 102; CANR 54; NNAL

Campbell, (John) Ramsey 1946-CLC 42; SSC 19
    See also CA 57-60; CANR 7; INT CANR-7

Campbell, (Ignatius) Roy (Dunnachie) 1901-1957   TCLC 5
    See also CA 104; 155; DLB 20; MTCW 2

Campbell, Thomas 1777-1844   NCLC 19
    See also DLB 93; 144

Campbell, Wilfred   TCLC 9
    See also Campbell, William

Campbell, William 1858(?)-1918
    See Campbell, Wilfred
    See also CA 106; DLB 92

Campion, Jane   CLC 95
    See also CA 138

Campos, Alvaro de
    See Pessoa, Fernando (Antonio Nogueira)

Camus, Albert 1913-1960CLC 1, 2, 4, 9, 11, 14, 32, 63, 69; DA; DAB; DAC; DAM DRAM, MST, NOV; DC 2; SSC 9;WLC
    See also CA 89-92; DLB 72; MTCW 1, 2

Canby, Vincent 1924-   CLC 13
    See also CA 81-84

Cancale
    See Desnos, Robert

Canetti, Elias 1905-1994CLC 3, 14, 25, 75, 86
    See also CA 21-24R; 146; CANR 23, 61, 79; DLB 85, 124; MTCW 1, 2

Canfield, Dorothea F.
    See Fisher, Dorothy (Frances) Canfield

Canfield, Dorothea Frances
    See Fisher, Dorothy (Frances) Canfield

Canfield, Dorothy

See Fisher, Dorothy (Frances) Canfield

Canin, Ethan 1960-   **CLC 55**
See also CA 131; 135

Cannon, Curt
See Hunter, Evan

Cao, Lan 1961-   **CLC 109**
See also CA 165

Cape, Judith
See Page, P(atricia) K(athleen)

Capek, Karel 1890-1938   **TCLC 6, 37; DA;
DAB; DAC; DAM DRAM, MST, NOV; DC
1; WLC**
See also CA 104; 140; MTCW 1

Capote, Truman 1924-1984 **CLC 1, 3, 8, 13, 19,
34, 38, 58; DA; DAB; DAC; DAM MST,
NOV, POP; SSC 2; WLC**
See also CA 5-8R; 113; CANR 18, 62; CDALB
1941-1968; DLB 2, 185; DLBY 80, 84;
MTCW 1, 2; SATA 91

Capra, Frank 1897-1991   **CLC 16**
See also CA 61-64; 135

Caputo, Philip 1941-   **CLC 32**
See also CA 73-76; CANR 40

Caragiale, Ion Luca 1852-1912   **TCLC 76**
See also CA 157

Card, Orson Scott 1951- **CLC 44, 47, 50; DAM
POP**
See also AAYA 11; CA 102; CANR 27, 47, 73;
INT CANR-27; MTCW 1, 2; SATA 83

Cardenal, Ernesto 1925-   **CLC·31; DAM
MULT, POET; HLC 1; PC 22**
See also CA 49-52; CANR 2, 32, 66; HW 1, 2;
MTCW 1, 2

Cardozo, Benjamin N(athan) 1870-1938
TCLC 65
See also CA 117; 164

Carducci, Giosue (Alessandro Giuseppe) 1835-
1907   **TCLC 32**
See also CA 163

Carew, Thomas 1595(?)-1640   **LC 13**
See also DLB 126

Carey, Ernestine Gilbreth 1908-   **CLC 17**
See also CA 5-8R; CANR 71; SATA 2

Carey, Peter 1943-   **CLC 40, 55, 96**
See also CA 123; 127; CANR 53, 76; INT 127;
MTCW 1, 2; SATA 94

Carleton, William 1794-1869   **NCLC 3**
See also DLB 159

Carlisle, Henry (Coffin) 1926-   **CLC 33**
See also CA 13-16R; CANR 15

Carlsen, Chris
See Holdstock, Robert P.

Carlson, Ron(ald F.) 1947-   **CLC 54**
See also CA 105; CANR 27

Carlyle, Thomas 1795-1881   **NCLC 70; DA;
DAB; DAC; DAM MST**
See also CDBLB 1789-1832; DLB 55; 144

Carman, (William) Bliss 1861-1929 **TCLC 7;
DAC**
See also CA 104; 152; DLB 92

Carnegie, Dale 1888-1955   **TCLC 53**

Carossa, Hans 1878-1956   **TCLC 48**
See also CA 170; DLB 66

Carpenter, Don(ald Richard) 1931-1995 **C L C
41**
See also CA 45-48; 149; CANR 1, 71

Carpenter, Edward 1844-1929   **TCLC 88**
See also CA 163

Carpentier (y Valmont), Alejo 1904-1980 **CLC
8, 11, 38, 110; DAM MULT; HLC 1; SSC
35**
See also CA 65-68; 97-100; CANR 11, 70; DLB
113; HW 1, 2

Carr, Caleb 1955(?)-   **CLC 86**
See also CA 147; CANR 73

Carr, Emily 1871-1945   **TCLC 32**
See also CA 159; DLB 68

Carr, John Dickson 1906-1977   **CLC 3**
See also Fairbairn, Roger
See also CA 49-52; 69-72; CANR 3, 33, 60;
MTCW 1, 2

Carr, Philippa
See Hibbert, Eleanor Alice Burford

Carr, Virginia Spencer 1929-   **CLC 34**
See also CA 61-64; DLB 111

Carrere, Emmanuel 1957-   **CLC 89**

Carrier, Roch 1937- **CLC 13, 78; DAC; DAM
MST**
See also CA 130; CANR 61; DLB 53; SATA
105

Carroll, James P. 1943(?)-   **CLC 38**
See also CA 81-84; CANR 73; MTCW 1

Carroll, Jim 1951-   **CLC 35**
See also AAYA 17; CA 45-48; CANR 42

Carroll, Lewis   **NCLC 2, 53; PC 18; WLC**
See also Dodgson, Charles Lutwidge
See also CDBLB 1832-1890; CLR 2, 18; DLB
18, 163, 178; DLBY 98; JRDA

Carroll, Paul Vincent 1900-1968   **CLC 10**
See also CA 9-12R; 25-28R; DLB 10

Carruth, Hayden 1921- **CLC 4, 7, 10, 18, 84;
PC 10**
See also CA 9-12R; CANR 4, 38, 59; DLB 5,
165; INT CANR-4; MTCW 1, 2; SATA 47

Carson, Rachel Louise 1907-1964   **CLC 71;
DAM POP**
See also CA 77-80; CANR 35; MTCW 1, 2;
SATA 23

Carter, Angela (Olive) 1940-1992 **CLC 5, 41,
76; SSC 13**
See also CA 53-56; 136; CANR 12, 36, 61; DLB
14, 207; MTCW 1, 2; SATA 66; SATA-Obit
70

Carter, Nick
See Smith, Martin Cruz

Carver, Raymond 1938-1988 **CLC 22, 36, 53,
55; DAM NOV; SSC 8**
See also CA 33-36R; 126; CANR 17, 34, 61;
DLB 130; DLBY 84, 88; MTCW 1, 2

Cary, Elizabeth, Lady Falkland 1585-1639
LC 30

Cary, (Arthur) Joyce (Lunel) 1888-1957
TCLC 1, 29
See also CA 104; 164; CDBLB 1914-1945;
DLB 15, 100; MTCW 2

Casanova de Seingalt, Giovanni Jacopo 1725-
1798   **LC 13**

Casares, Adolfo Bioy
See Bioy Casares, Adolfo

Casely-Hayford, J(oseph) E(phraim) 1866-1930
TCLC 24; BLC 1; DAM MULT
See also BW 2; CA 123; 152

Casey, John (Dudley) 1939-   **CLC 59**
See also BEST 90:2; CA 69-72; CANR 23

Casey, Michael 1947-   **CLC 2**
See also CA 65-68; DLB 5

Casey, Patrick
See Thurman, Wallace (Henry)

Casey, Warren (Peter) 1935-1988   **CLC 12**
See also CA 101; 127; INT 101

Casona, Alejandro   **CLC 49**
See also Alvarez, Alejandro Rodriguez

Cassavetes, John 1929-1989   **CLC 20**
See also CA 85-88; 127; CANR 82

Cassian, Nina 1924-   **PC 17**

Cassill, R(onald) V(erlin) 1919-   **CLC 4, 23**

See also CA 9-12R; CAAS 1; CANR 7, 45; DLB
6

Cassirer, Ernst 1874-1945   **TCLC 61**
See also CA 157

Cassity, (Allen) Turner 1929-   **CLC 6, 42**
See also CA 17-20R; CAAS 8; CANR 11; DLB
105

Castaneda, Carlos (Cesar Aranha) 1931(?)-
1998   **CLC 12, 119**
See also CA 25-28R; CANR 32, 66; HW 1;
MTCW 1

Castedo, Elena 1937-   **CLC 65**
See also CA 132

Castedo-Ellerman, Elena
See Castedo, Elena

Castellanos, Rosario 1925-1974 **CLC 66; DAM
MULT; HLC 1**
See also CA 131; 53-56; CANR 58; DLB 113;
HW 1; MTCW 1

Castelvetro, Lodovico 1505-1571   **LC 12**

Castiglione, Baldassare 1478-1529   **LC 12**

Castle, Robert
See Hamilton, Edmond

Castro (Ruz), Fidel 1926(?)-
See also CA 110; 129; CANR 81; DAM MULT;
HLC 1; HW 2

Castro, Guillen de 1569-1631   **LC 19**

Castro, Rosalia de 1837-1885   **NCLC 3, 78;
DAM MULT**

Cather, Willa
See Cather, Willa Sibert

Cather, Willa Sibert 1873-1947 **TCLC 1, 11,
31; DA; DAB; DAC; DAM MST, NOV;
SSC 2; WLC**
See also AAYA 24; CA 104; 128; CDALB 1865-
1917; DLB 9, 54, 78; DLBD 1; MTCW 1, 2;
SATA 30

Catherine, Saint 1347-1380   **CMLC 27**

Cato, Marcus Porcius 234B.C.-149B.C.
CMLC 21
See also DLB 211

Catton, (Charles) Bruce 1899-1978   **CLC 35**
See also AITN 1; CA 5-8R; 81-84; CANR 7,
74; DLB 17; SATA 2; SATA-Obit 24

Catullus c. 84B.C.-c. 54B.C.   **CMLC 18**
See also DLB 211

Cauldwell, Frank
See King, Francis (Henry)

Caunitz, William J. 1933-1996   **CLC 34**
See also BEST 89:3; CA 125; 130; 152; CANR
73; INT 130

Causley, Charles (Stanley) 1917-   **CLC 7**
See also CA 9-12R; CANR 5, 35; CLR 30; DLB
27; MTCW 1; SATA 3, 66

Caute, (John) David 1936- **CLC 29; DAM NOV**
See also CA 1-4R; CAAS 4; CANR 1, 33, 64;
DLB 14

Cavafy, C(onstantine) P(eter) 1863-1933
TCLC 2, 7; DAM POET
See also Kavafis, Konstantinos Petrou
See also CA 148; MTCW 1

Cavallo, Evelyn
See Spark, Muriel (Sarah)

Cavanna, Betty   **CLC 12**
See also Harrison, Elizabeth Cavanna
See also JRDA; MAICYA; SAAS 4; SATA 1,
30

Cavendish, Margaret Lucas 1623-1673 **LC 30**
See also DLB 131

Caxton, William 1421(?)-1491(?)   **LC 17**
See also DLB 170

Cayer, D. M.
See Duffy, Maureen

Author Index

Cayrol, Jean 1911-   **CLC 11**
    See also CA 89-92; DLB 83
Cela, Camilo Jose 1916-   **CLC 4, 13, 59, 122;**
    DAM MULT; HLC 1
    See also BEST 90:2; CA 21-24R; CAAS 10;
    CANR 21, 32, 76; DLBY 89; HW 1; MTCW
    1, 2
Celan, Paul   **CLC 10, 19, 53, 82; PC 10**
    See also Antschel, Paul
    See also DLB 69
Celine, Louis-Ferdinand CLC 1, 3, 4, 7, 9, 15,
    47
    See also Destouches, Louis-Ferdinand
    See also DLB 72
Cellini, Benvenuto 1500-1571   **LC 7**
Cendrars, Blaise 1887-1961   **CLC 18, 106**
    See also Sauser-Hall, Frederic
Cernuda (y Bidon), Luis 1902-1963 **CLC 54;**
    DAM POET
    See also CA 131; 89-92; DLB 134; HW 1
Cervantes, Lorna Dee 1954-
    See also CA 131; CANR 80; DLB 82; HLCS 1;
    HW 1
Cervantes (Saavedra), Miguel de 1547-1616
    LC 6, 23; DA; DAB; DAC; DAM MST,
    NOV; SSC 12; WLC
Cesaire, Aime (Fernand) 1913- **CLC 19, 32,**
    112; BLC 1; DAM MULT, POET; PC 25
    See also BW 2, 3; CA 65-68; CANR 24, 43,
    81; MTCW 1, 2
Chabon, Michael 1963-   **CLC 55**
    See also CA 139; CANR 57
Chabrol, Claude 1930-   **CLC 16**
    See also CA 110
Challans, Mary 1905-1983
    See Renault, Mary
    See also CA 81-84; 111; CANR 74; MTCW 2;
    SATA 23; SATA-Obit 36
Challis, George
    See Faust, Frederick (Schiller)
Chambers, Aidan 1934-   **CLC 35**
    See also AAYA 27; CA 25-28R; CANR 12, 31,
    58; JRDA; MAICYA; SAAS 12; SATA 1, 69,
    108
Chambers, James 1948-
    See Cliff, Jimmy
    See also CA 124
Chambers, Jessie
    See Lawrence, D(avid) H(erbert Richards)
Chambers, Robert W(illiam) 1865-1933
    TCLC 41
    See also CA 165; DLB 202; SATA 107
Chandler, Raymond (Thornton) 1888-1959
    TCLC 1, 7; SSC 23
    See also AAYA 25; CA 104; 129; CANR
    60;CDALB 1929-1941; DLBD 6; MTCW 1,
    2
Chang, Eileen 1920-1995   **SSC 28**
    See also CA 166
Chang, Jung 1952-   **CLC 71**
    See also CA 142
Chang Ai-Ling
    See Chang, Eileen
Channing, William Ellery 1780-1842 **NCLC**
    17
    See also DLB 1, 59
Chao, Patricia 1955-   **CLC 119**
    See also CA 163
Chaplin, Charles Spencer 1889-1977 **CLC 16**
    See also Chaplin, Charlie
    See also CA 81-84; 73-76
Chaplin, Charlie
    See Chaplin, Charles Spencer

    See also DLB 44
Chapman, George 1559(?)-1634 **LC 22; DAM**
    DRAM
    See also DLB 62, 121
Chapman, Graham 1941-1989   **CLC 21**
    See Monty Python
    See also CA 116; 129; CANR 35
Chapman, John Jay 1862-1933   **TCLC 7**
    See also CA 104
Chapman, Lee
    See Bradley, Marion Zimmer
Chapman, Walker
    See Silverberg, Robert
Chappell, Fred (Davis) 1936-   **CLC 40, 78**
    See also CA 5-8R; CAAS 4; CANR 8, 33, 67;
    DLB 6, 105
Char, Rene(-Emile) 1907-1988 **CLC 9, 11, 14,**
    55; DAM POET
    See also CA 13-16R; 124; CANR 32; MTCW
    1, 2
Charby, Jay
    See Ellison, Harlan (Jay)
Chardin, Pierre Teilhard de
    See Teilhard de Chardin, (Marie Joseph) Pierre
Charles I 1600-1649   **LC 13**
Charriere, Isabelle de 1740-1805   **NCLC 66**
Charyn, Jerome 1937-   **CLC 5, 8, 18**
    See also CA 5-8R; CAAS 1; CANR 7, 61;
    DLBY 83; MTCW 1
Chase, Mary (Coyle) 1907-1981   **DC 1**
    See also CA 77-80; 105; SATA 17; SATA-Obit
    29
Chase, Mary Ellen 1887-1973   **CLC 2**
    See also CA 13-16; 41-44R; CAP 1; SATA 10
Chase, Nicholas
    See Hyde, Anthony
Chateaubriand, Francois Renede 1768-1848
    NCLC 3
    See also DLB 119
Chatterje, Sarat Chandra 1876-1936(?)
    See Chatterji, Saratchandra
    See also CA 109
Chatterji, Bankim Chandra 1838-1894 **NCLC**
    19
Chatterji, Saratchandra   **TCLC 13**
    See also Chatterje, Sarat Chandra
Chatterton, Thomas 1752-1770 **LC 3;DAM**
    POET
    See also DLB 109
Chatwin, (Charles) Bruce 1940-1989 **CLC 28,**
    57, 59; DAM POP
    See also AAYA 4; BEST 90:1; CA 85-88; 127;
    DLB 194, 204
Chaucer, Daniel
    See Ford, Ford Madox
Chaucer, Geoffrey 1340(?)-1400 **LC 17; DA;**
    DAB; DAC; DAM MST, POET; PC 19;
    WLCS
    See also CDBLB Before 1660; DLB 146
Chavez, Denise (Elia) 1948-
    See also CA 131; CANR 56, 81; DAM MULT;
    DLB 122; HLC 1; HW 1, 2; MTCW 2
Chaviaras, Strates 1935-
    See Haviaras, Stratis
    See also CA 105
Chayefsky, Paddy   **CLC 23**
    See also Chayefsky, Sidney
    See also DLB 7, 44; DLBY 81
Chayefsky, Sidney 1923-1981
    See Chayefsky, Paddy
    See also CA 9-12R; 104; CANR 18; DAM
    DRAM
Chedid, Andree 1920-   **CLC 47**

    See also CA 145
Cheever, John 1912-1982 **CLC 3, 7, 8, 11, 15,**
    25, 64; DA; DAB; DAC; DAM MST, NOV,
    POP; SSC 1; WLC
    See also CA 5-8R; 106; CABS 1; CANR 5, 27,
    76; CDALB 1941-1968; DLB 2, 102; DLBY
    80, 82; INT CANR-5; MTCW 1, 2
Cheever, Susan 1943-   **CLC 18, 48**
    See also CA 103; CANR 27, 51; DLBY 82; INT
    CANR-27
Chekhonte, Antosha
    See Chekhov, Anton (Pavlovich)
Chekhov, Anton (Pavlovich) 1860-1904 **TCLC**
    3, 10, 31, 55, 96; DA; DAB; DAC; DAM
    DRAM, MST; DC 9; SSC 2, 28;WLC
    See also CA 104; 124; SATA 90
Chernyshevsky, Nikolay Gavrilovich 1828-1889
    NCLC 1
Cherry, Carolyn Janice 1942-
    See Cherryh, C. J.
    See also CA 65-68; CANR 10
Cherryh, C. J.   **CLC 35**
    See also Cherry, Carolyn Janice
    See also AAYA 24; DLBY 80; SATA 93
Chesnutt, Charles W(addell) 1858-1932
    TCLC 5, 39; BLC 1; DAM MULT; SSC 7
    See also BW 1, 3; CA 106; 125; CANR 76; DLB
    12, 50, 78; MTCW 1, 2
Chester, Alfred 1929(?)-1971   **CLC 49**
    See also CA 33-36R; DLB 130
Chesterton, G(ilbert) K(eith) 1874-1936
    TCLC 1, 6, 64; DAM NOV,POET; SSC 1
    See also CA 104; 132; CANR 73; CDBLB
    1914-1945; DLB 10, 19, 34, 70, 98, 149,
    178; MTCW 1, 2; SATA 27
Chiang, Pin-chin 1904-1986
    See Ding Ling
    See also CA 118
Ch'ien Chung-shu 1910-   **CLC 22**
    See also CA 130; CANR 73; MTCW 1, 2
Child, L. Maria
    See Child, Lydia Maria
Child, Lydia Maria 1802-1880   **NCLC 6, 73**
    See also DLB 1, 74; SATA 67
Child, Mrs.
    See Child, Lydia Maria
Child, Philip 1898-1978   **CLC 19, 68**
    See also CA 13-14; CAP 1; SATA 47
Childers, (Robert) Erskine 1870-1922 **T C L C**
    65
    See also CA 113; 153; DLB 70
Childress, Alice 1920-1994 **CLC 12, 15, 86, 96;**
    BLC 1; DAM DRAM, MULT, NOV; DC 4
    See also AAYA 8; BW 2, 3; CA 45-48; 146;
    CANR 3, 27, 50, 74; CLR 14; DLB 7, 38;
    JRDA; MAICYA; MTCW 1, 2; SATA 7, 48,
    81
Chin, Frank (Chew, Jr.) 1940-   **DC 7**
    See also CA 33-36R; CANR 71; DAM MULT;
    DLB 206
Chislett, (Margaret) Anne 1943-   **CLC 34**
    See also CA 151
Chitty, Thomas Willes 1926-   **CLC 11**
    See also Hinde, Thomas
    See also CA 5-8R
Chivers, Thomas Holley 1809-1858 **NCLC 49**
    See also DLB 3
Choi, Susan   **CLC 119**
Chomette, Rene Lucien 1898-1981
    See Clair, Rene
    See also CA 103
Chopin, Kate TCLC 5, 14; DA; DAB; SSC 8;
    WLCS

See also Chopin, Katherine
See also CDALB 1865-1917; DLB 12, 78

Chopin, Katherine 1851-1904
See Chopin, Kate
See also CA 104; 122; DAC; DAM MST, NOV

Chretien de Troyes c. 12th cent.- **CMLC 10**
See also DLB 208

Christie
See Ichikawa, Kon

Christie, Agatha (Mary Clarissa) 1890-1976
CLC 1, 6, 8, 12, 39, 48, 110; DAB; DAC;
DAM NOV
See also AAYA 9; AITN 1, 2; CA 17-20R; 61-64; CANR 10, 37; CDBLB 1914-1945; DLB 13, 77; MTCW 1, 2; SATA 36

Christie, (Ann) Philippa
See Pearce, Philippa
See also CA 5-8R; CANR 4

Christine de Pizan 1365(?)-1431(?) **LC 9**
See also DLB 208

Chubb, Elmer
See Masters, Edgar Lee

Chulkov, Mikhail Dmitrievich 1743-1792 **LC 2**
See also DLB 150

Churchill, Caryl 1938- **CLC 31, 55; DC 5**
See also CA 102; CANR 22, 46; DLB 13; MTCW 1

Churchill, Charles 1731-1764 **LC 3**
See also DLB 109

Chute, Carolyn 1947- **CLC 39**
See also CA 123

Ciardi, John (Anthony) 1916-1986 **CLC 10, 40, 44; DAM POET**
See also CA 5-8R; 118; CAAS 2; CANR 5, 33; CLR 19; DLB 5; DLBY 86; INT CANR-5; MAICYA; MTCW 1, 2; SAAS 26; SATA 1, 65; SATA-Obit 46

Cicero, Marcus Tullius 106B.C.-43B.C.
CMLC 3
See also DLB 211

Cimino, Michael 1943- **CLC 16**
See also CA 105

Cioran, E(mil) M. 1911-1995 **CLC 64**
See also CA 25-28R; 149

Cisneros, Sandra 1954- **CLC 69, 118; DAM MULT; HLC 1; SSC 32**
See also AAYA 9; CA 131; CANR 64; DLB 122, 152; HW 1, 2; MTCW 2

Cixous, Helene 1937- **CLC 92**
See also CA 126; CANR 55; DLB 83; MTCW 1, 2

Clair, Rene **CLC 20**
See also Chomette, Rene Lucien

Clampitt, Amy 1920-1994 **CLC 32; PC 19**
See also CA 110; 146; CANR 29, 79; DLB 105

Clancy, Thomas L., Jr. 1947-
See Clancy, Tom
See also CA 125; 131; CANR 62; INT 131; MTCW 1, 2

Clancy, Tom **CLC 45, 112; DAM NOV, POP**
See Clancy, Thomas L., Jr.
See also AAYA 9; BEST 89:1, 90:1; MTCW 2

Clare, John 1793-1864 **NCLC 9; DAB; DAM POET; PC 23**
See also DLB 55, 96

Clarin
See Alas (y Urena), Leopoldo (Enrique Garcia)

Clark, Al C.
See Goines, Donald

Clark, (Robert) Brian 1932- **CLC 29**
See also CA 41-44R; CANR 67

Clark, Curt
See Westlake, Donald E(dwin)

Clark, Eleanor 1913-1996 **CLC 5, 19**
See also CA 9-12R; 151; CANR 41; DLB 6

Clark, J. P.
See Clark, John Pepper
See also DLB 117

Clark, John Pepper 1935- **CLC 38; BLC 1; DAM DRAM, MULT; DC 5**
See also Clark, J. P.
See also BW 1; CA 65-68; CANR 16, 72; MTCW 1

Clark, M. R.
See Clark, Mavis Thorpe

Clark, Mavis Thorpe 1909- **CLC 12**
See also CA 57-60; CANR 8, 37; CLR 30; MAICYA; SAAS 5; SATA 8, 74

Clark, Walter Van Tilburg 1909-1971 **CLC 28**
See also CA 9-12R; 33-36R; CANR 63; DLB 9, 206; SATA 8

Clark Bekederemo, J(ohnson) P(epper)
See Clark, John Pepper

Clarke, Arthur C(harles) 1917- **CLC 1, 4, 13, 18, 35; DAM POP; SSC 3**
See also AAYA 4; CA 1-4R; CANR 2, 28, 55, 74; JRDA; MAICYA; MTCW 1, 2; SATA 13, 70

Clarke, Austin 1896-1974 **CLC 6, 9; DAM POET**
See also CA 29-32; 49-52; CAP 2; DLB 10, 20

Clarke, Austin C(hesterfield) 1934- **CLC 8, 53; BLC 1; DAC; DAM MULT**
See also BW 1; CA 25-28R; CAAS 16; CANR 14, 32, 68; DLB 53, 125

Clarke, Gillian 1937- **CLC 61**
See also CA 106; DLB 40

Clarke, Marcus (Andrew Hislop) 1846-1881
NCLC 19

Clarke, Shirley 1925- **CLC 16**

Clash, The
See Headon, (Nicky) Topper; Jones, Mick; Simonon, Paul; Strummer, Joe

Claudel, Paul (Louis Charles Marie) 1868-1955
TCLC 2, 10
See also CA 104; 165; DLB 192

Claudius, Matthias 1740-1815 **NCLC 75**
See also DLB 97

Clavell, James (du Maresq) 1925-1994 **CLC 6, 25, 87; DAM NOV, POP**
See also CA 25-28R; 146; CANR 26, 48; MTCW 1, 2

Cleaver, (Leroy) Eldridge 1935-1998 **CLC 30, 119; BLC 1; DAM MULT**
See also BW 1, 3; CA 21-24R; 167; CANR 16, 75; MTCW 2

Cleese, John (Marwood) 1939- **CLC 21**
See also Monty Python
See also CA 112; 116; CANR 35; MTCW 1

Cleishbotham, Jebediah
See Scott, Walter

Cleland, John 1710-1789 **LC 2, 48**
See also DLB 39

Clemens, Samuel Langhorne 1835-1910
See Twain, Mark
See also CA 104; 135; CDALB 1865-1917; DA; DAB; DAC; DAM MST, NOV; DLB 11, 12, 23, 64, 74, 186, 189; JRDA; MAICYA; SATA 100; YABC 2

Cleophil
See Congreve, William

Clerihew, E.
See Bentley, E(dmund) C(lerihew)

Clerk, N. W.
See Lewis, C(live) S(taples)

Cliff, Jimmy **CLC 21**

See also Chambers, James

Cliff, Michelle 1946- **CLC 120; BLCS**
See also BW 2; CA 116; CANR 39, 72; DLB 157

Clifton, (Thelma) Lucille 1936- **CLC 19, 66; BLC 1; DAM MULT, POET; PC 17**
See also BW 2, 3; CA 49-52; CANR 2, 24, 42, 76; CLR 5; DLB 5, 41; MAICYA; MTCW 1, 2; SATA 20, 69

Clinton, Dirk
See Silverberg, Robert

Clough, Arthur Hugh 1819-1861 **NCLC 27**
See also DLB 32

Clutha, Janet Paterson Frame 1924-
See Frame, Janet
See also CA 1-4R; CANR 2, 36, 76; MTCW 1, 2

Clyne, Terence
See Blatty, William Peter

Cobalt, Martin
See Mayne, William (James Carter)

Cobb, Irvin S(hrewsbury) 1876-1944 **TCLC 77**
See also CA 175; DLB 11, 25, 86

Cobbett, William 1763-1835 **NCLC 49**
See also DLB 43, 107, 158

Coburn, D(onald) L(ee) 1938- **CLC 10**
See also CA 89-92

Cocteau, Jean (Maurice Eugene Clement) 1889-1963 **CLC 1, 8, 15, 16, 43; DA; DAB; DAC; DAM DRAM, MST, NOV; WLC**
See also CA 25-28; CANR 40; CAP 2; DLB 65; MTCW 1, 2

Codrescu, Andrei 1946- **CLC 46, 121; DAM POET**
See also CA 33-36R; CAAS 19; CANR 13, 34, 53, 76; MTCW 2

Coe, Max
See Bourne, Randolph S(illiman)

Coe, Tucker
See Westlake, Donald E(dwin)

Coen, Ethan 1958- **CLC 108**
See also CA 126

Coen, Joel 1955- **CLC 108**
See also CA 126

The Coen Brothers
See Coen, Ethan; Coen, Joel

Coetzee, J(ohn) M(ichael) 1940- **CLC 23, 33, 66, 117; DAM NOV**
See also CA 77-80; CANR 41, 54, 74; MTCW 1, 2

Coffey, Brian
See Koontz, Dean R(ay)

Coffin, Robert P(eter) Tristram 1892-1955
TCLC 95
See also CA 123; 169; DLB 45

Cohan, George M(ichael) 1878-1942 **TCLC 60**
See also CA 157

Cohen, Arthur A(llen) 1928-1986 **CLC 7, 31**
See also CA 1-4R; 120; CANR 1, 17, 42; DLB 28

Cohen, Leonard (Norman) 1934- **CLC 3, 38; DAC; DAM MST**
See also CA 21-24R; CANR 14, 69; DLB 53; MTCW 1

Cohen, Matt 1942- **CLC 19; DAC**
See also CA 61-64; CAAS 18; CANR 40; DLB 53

Cohen-Solal, Annie 19(?)- **CLC 50**

Colegate, Isabel 1931- **CLC 36**
See also CA 17-20R; CANR 8, 22, 74; DLB 14; INT CANR-22; MTCW 1

Coleman, Emmett

See Reed, Ishmael

Coleridge, M. E.
See Coleridge, Mary E(lizabeth)

Coleridge, Mary E(lizabeth) 1861-1907**TCLC 73**
See also CA 116; 166; DLB 19, 98

Coleridge, Samuel Taylor 1772-1834**NCLC 9, 54; DA; DAB; DAC; DAM MST, POET; PC 11; WLC**
See also CDBLB 1789-1832; DLB 93, 107

Coleridge, Sara 1802-1852 **NCLC 31**
See also DLB 199

Coles, Don 1928- **CLC 46**
See also CA 115; CANR 38

Coles, Robert (Martin) 1929- **CLC 108**
See also CA 45-48; CANR 3, 32, 66, 70; INT CANR-32; SATA 23

Colette, (Sidonie-Gabrielle) 1873-1954**TCLC 1, 5, 16; DAM NOV; SSC 10**
See also CA 104; 131; DLB 65; MTCW 1, 2

Collett, (Jacobine) Camilla (Wergeland) 1813-1895 **NCLC 22**

Collier, Christopher 1930- **CLC 30**
See also AAYA 13; CA 33-36R; CANR 13, 33; JRDA; MAICYA; SATA 16, 70

Collier, James L(incoln) 1928-**CLC 30; DAM POP**
See also AAYA 13; CA 9-12R; CANR 4, 33, 60; CLR 3; JRDA; MAICYA; SAAS 21; SATA 8, 70

Collier, Jeremy 1650-1726 **LC 6**

Collier, John 1901-1980 **SSC 19**
See also CA 65-68; 97-100; CANR 10; DLB 77

Collingwood, R(obin) G(eorge) 1889(?)-1943 **TCLC 67**
See also CA 117; 155

Collins, Hunt
See Hunter, Evan

Collins, Linda 1931- **CLC 44**
See also CA 125

Collins, (William) Wilkie 1824-1889**NCLC 1, 18**
See also CDBLB 1832-1890; DLB 18, 70, 159

Collins, William 1721-1759 **LC 4, 40; DAM POET**
See also DLB 109

Collodi, Carlo 1826-1890 **NCLC 54**
See also Lorenzini, Carlo
See also CLR 5

Colman, George 1732-1794
See Glassco, John

Colt, Winchester Remington
See Hubbard, L(afayette) Ron(ald)

Colter, Cyrus 1910- **CLC 58**
See also BW 1; CA 65-68; CANR 10, 66; DLB 33

Colton, James
See Hansen, Joseph

Colum, Padraic 1881-1972 **CLC 28**
See also CA 73-76; 33-36R; CANR 35; CLR 36; MAICYA; MTCW 1; SATA 15

Colvin, James
See Moorcock, Michael (John)

Colwin, Laurie (E.) 1944-1992**CLC 5, 13, 23, 84**
See also CA 89-92; 139; CANR 20, 46; DLBY 80; MTCW 1

Comfort, Alex(ander) 1920-**CLC 7;DAM POP**
See also CA 1-4R; CANR 1, 45; MTCW 1

Comfort, Montgomery
See Campbell, (John) Ramsey

Compton-Burnett, I(vy) 1884(?)-1969 **CLC 1,**

3, 10, 15, 34; DAM NOV
See also CA 1-4R; 25-28R; CANR 4; DLB 36; MTCW 1

Comstock, Anthony 1844-1915 **TCLC 13**
See also CA 110; 169

Comte, Auguste 1798-1857 **NCLC 54**

Conan Doyle, Arthur
See Doyle, Arthur Conan

Conde (Abellan), Carmen 1901-
See also CA 177; DLB 108; HLCS 1; HW 2

Conde, Maryse 1937- **CLC 52, 92; BLCS; DAM MULT**
See also Boucolon, Maryse
See also BW 2; MTCW 1

Condillac, Etienne Bonnot de 1714-1780 **LC 26**

Condon, Richard (Thomas) 1915-1996**CLC 4, 6, 8, 10, 45, 100; DAM NOV**
See also BEST 90:3; CA 1-4R; 151; CAAS 1; CANR 2, 23; INT CANR-23; MTCW 1, 2

Confucius 551B.C.-479B.C. **CMLC 19; DA; DAB; DAC; DAM MST; WLCS**

Congreve, William 1670-1729 **LC 5, 21; DA; DAB; DAC; DAM DRAM, MST, POET; DC 2; WLC**
See also CDBLB 1660-1789; DLB 39, 84

Connell, Evan S(helby), Jr. 1924-**CLC 4, 6, 45; DAM NOV**
See also AAYA 7; CA 1-4R; CAAS 2; CANR 2, 39, 76; DLB 2; DLBY 81; MTCW 1, 2

Connelly, Marc(us Cook) 1890-1980 **CLC 7**
See also CA 85-88; 102; CANR 30; DLB 7; DLBY 80; SATA-Obit 25

Connor, Ralph **TCLC 31**
See also Gordon, Charles William
See also DLB 92

Conrad, Joseph 1857-1924**TCLC 1, 6, 13, 25, 43, 57; DA; DAB; DAC; DAM MST, NOV; SSC 9; WLC**
See also AAYA 26; CA 104; 131; CANR 60; CDBLB 1890-1914; DLB 10, 34, 98, 156; MTCW 1, 2; SATA 27

Conrad, Robert Arnold
See Hart, Moss

Conroy, Pat
See Conroy, (Donald) Pat(rick)
See also MTCW 2

Conroy, (Donald) Pat(rick) 1945-**CLC 30, 74; DAM NOV, POP**
See also Conroy, Pat
See also AAYA 8; AITN 1; CA 85-88; CANR 24, 53; DLB 6; MTCW 1

Constant (de Rebecque), (Henri) Benjamin 1767-1830 **NCLC 6**
See also DLB 119

Conybeare, Charles Augustus
See Eliot, T(homas) S(tearns)

Cook, Michael 1933- **CLC 58**
See also CA 93-96; CANR 68; DLB 53

Cook, Robin 1940- **CLC 14;DAM POP**
See also BEST 90:2; CA 108; 111; CANR 41; INT 111

Cook, Roy
See Silverberg, Robert

Cooke, Elizabeth 1948- **CLC 55**
See also CA 129

Cooke, John Esten 1830-1886 **NCLC 5**
See also DLB 3

Cooke, John Estes
See Baum, L(yman) Frank

Cooke, M. E.
See Creasey, John

Cooke, Margaret

See Creasey, John

Cook-Lynn, Elizabeth 1930- **CLC 93;DAM MULT**
See also CA 133; DLB 175; NNAL

Cooney, Ray **CLC 62**

Cooper, Douglas 1960- **CLC 86**

Cooper, Henry St. John
See Creasey, John

Cooper, J(oan) California (?)-**CLC 56; DAM MULT**
See also AAYA 12; BW 1; CA 125; CANR 55; DLB 212

Cooper, James Fenimore 1789-1851**NCLC 1, 27, 54**
See also AAYA 22; CDALB 1640-1865; DLB 3; SATA 19

Coover, Robert (Lowell) 1932- **CLC 3, 7, 15, 32, 46, 87; DAM NOV; SSC 15**
See also CA 45-48; CANR 3, 37, 58; DLB 2; DLBY 81; MTCW 1, 2

Copeland, Stewart (Armstrong) 1952-**CLC 26**

Copernicus, Nicolaus 1473-1543 **LC 45**

Coppard, A(lfred) E(dgar) 1878-1957 **TCLC 5; SSC 21**
See also CA 114; 167; DLB 162; YABC 1

Coppee, Francois 1842-1908 **TCLC 25**
See also CA 170

Coppola, Francis Ford 1939- **CLC 16**
See also CA 77-80; CANR 40, 78; DLB 44

Corbiere, Tristan 1845-1875 **NCLC 43**

Corcoran, Barbara 1911- **CLC 17**
See also AAYA 14; CA 21-24R; CAAS 2; CANR 11, 28, 48; CLR 50; DLB 52; JRDA; SAAS 20; SATA 3, 77

Cordelier, Maurice
See Giraudoux, (Hippolyte) Jean

Corelli, Marie 1855-1924 **TCLC 51**
See also Mackay, Mary
See also DLB 34, 156

Corman, Cid 1924- **CLC 9**
See also Corman, Sidney
See also CAAS 2; DLB 5, 193

Corman, Sidney 1924-
See Corman, Cid
See also CA 85-88; CANR 44; DAM POET

Cormier, Robert (Edmund) 1925-**CLC 12, 30; DA; DAB; DAC; DAM MST, NOV**
See also AAYA 3, 19; CA 1-4R; CANR 5, 23, 76; CDALB 1968-1988; CLR 12, 55; DLB 52; INT CANR-23; JRDA; MAICYA; MTCW 1, 2; SATA 10, 45, 83

Corn, Alfred (DeWitt, III) 1943- **CLC 33**
See also CA 179; CAAE 179; CAAS 25; CANR 44; DLB 120; DLBY 80

Corneille, Pierre 1606-1684 **LC 28; DAB; DAM MST**

Cornwell, David (John Moore) 1931- **CLC 9, 15; DAM POP**
See also le Carre, John
See also CA 5-8R; CANR 13, 33, 59; MTCW 1, 2

Corso, (Nunzio) Gregory 1930- **CLC 1, 11**
See also CA 5-8R; CANR 41, 76; DLB 5, 16; MTCW 1

Cortazar, Julio 1914-1984**CLC 2, 3, 5, 10, 13, 15, 33, 34, 92; DAM MULT, NOV; HLC 1; SSC 7**
See also CA 21-24R; CANR 12, 32, 81; DLB 113; HW 1, 2; MTCW 1, 2

Cortes, Hernan 1484-1547 **LC 31**

Corvinus, Jakob
See Raabe, Wilhelm (Karl)

Corwin, Cecil

See Kornbluth, C(yril) M.

Cosic, Dobrica 1921-   **CLC 14**
    See also CA 122; 138; DLB 181

Costain, Thomas B(ertram) 1885-1965 **C L C 30**
    See also CA 5-8R; 25-28R; DLB 9

Costantini, Humberto 1924(?)-1987 **CLC 49**
    See also CA 131; 122; HW 1

Costello, Elvis 1955-   **CLC 21**

Costenoble, Philostene
    See Ghelderode, Michel de

Cotes, Cecil V.
    See Duncan, Sara Jeannette

Cotter, Joseph Seamon Sr. 1861-1949 **T C L C 28; BLC 1; DAM MULT**
    See also BW 1; CA 124; DLB 50

Couch, Arthur Thomas Quiller
    See Quiller-Couch, SirArthur (Thomas)

Coulton, James
    See Hansen, Joseph

Couperus, Louis (Marie Anne) 1863-1923 **TCLC 15**
    See also CA 115

Coupland, Douglas 1961-**CLC 85; DAC; DAM POP**
    See also CA 142; CANR 57

Court, Wesli
    See Turco, Lewis (Putnam)

Courtenay, Bryce 1933-   **CLC 59**
    See also CA 138

Courtney, Robert
    See Ellison, Harlan (Jay)

Cousteau,Jacques-Yves 1910-1997 **CLC 30**
    See also CA 65-68; 159; CANR 15, 67; MTCW 1; SATA 38, 98

Coventry, Francis 1725-1754   **LC 46**

Cowan, Peter (Walkinshaw) 1914-   **SSC 28**
    See also CA 21-24R; CANR 9, 25, 50

Coward, Noel (Peirce) 1899-1973**CLC 1, 9, 29, 51; DAM DRAM**
    See also AITN 1; CA 17-18; 41-44R; CANR 35; CAP 2; CDBLB 1914-1945; DLB 10; MTCW 1, 2

Cowley, Abraham 1618-1667   **LC 43**
    See also DLB 131, 151

Cowley, Malcolm 1898-1989   **CLC 39**
    See also CA 5-8R; 128; CANR 3, 55; DLB 4, 48; DLBY 81, 89; MTCW 1, 2

Cowper, William 1731-1800   **NCLC 8;DAM POET**
    See also DLB 104, 109

Cox, William Trevor 1928-   **CLC 9, 14, 71; DAM NOV**
    See also Trevor, William
    See also CA 9-12R; CANR 4, 37, 55, 76; DLB 14; INT CANR-37; MTCW 1, 2

Coyne, P. J.
    See Masters, Hilary

Cozzens, James Gould 1903-1978**CLC 1, 4, 11, 92**
    See also CA 9-12R; 81-84; CANR 19; CDALB 1941-1968; DLB 9; DLBD 2; DLBY 84, 97; MTCW 1, 2

Crabbe, George 1754-1832   **NCLC 26**
    See also DLB 93

Craddock, Charles Egbert
    See Murfree, Mary Noailles

Craig, A. A.
    See Anderson, Poul (William)

Craik, Dinah Maria (Mulock) 1826-1887 **NCLC 38**
    See also DLB 35, 163; MAICYA; SATA 34

Cram, Ralph Adams 1863-1942   **TCLC 45**

See also CA 160

Crane, (Harold) Hart 1899-1932 **TCLC 2, 5, 80; DA; DAB; DAC; DAM MST, POET; PC 3; WLC**
    See also CA 104; 127; CDALB 1917-1929; DLB 4, 48; MTCW 1, 2

Crane, R(onald) S(almon) 1886-1967**CLC 27**
    See also CA 85-88; DLB 63

Crane, Stephen (Townley) 1871-1900 **T C L C 11, 17, 32; DA; DAB; DAC; DAM MST, NOV, POET; SSC 7; WLC**
    See also AAYA 21; CA 109; 140; CDALB 1865-1917; DLB 12, 54, 78; YABC 2

Cranshaw, Stanley
    See Fisher, Dorothy (Frances) Canfield

Crase, Douglas 1944-   **CLC 58**
    See also CA 106

Crashaw, Richard 1612(?)-1649   **LC 24**
    See also DLB 126

Craven, Margaret 1901-1980   **CLC 17;DAC**
    See also CA 103

Crawford, F(rancis) Marion 1854-1909**TCLC 10**
    See also CA 107; 168; DLB 71

Crawford, Isabella Valancy 1850-1887**N C L C 12**
    See also DLB 92

Crayon, Geoffrey
    See Irving, Washington

Creasey, John 1908-1973   **CLC 11**
    See also CA 5-8R; 41-44R; CANR 8, 59; DLB 77; MTCW 1

Crebillon, Claude Prosper Jolyot de (fils) 1707-1777   **LC 1, 28**

Credo
    See Creasey, John

Credo, Alvaro J. de
    See Prado (Calvo), Pedro

Creeley, Robert (White) 1926-**CLC 1, 2, 4, 8, 11, 15, 36, 78; DAM POET**
    See also CA 1-4R; CAAS 10; CANR 23, 43; DLB 5, 16, 169; DLBD 17; MTCW 1, 2

Crews, Harry (Eugene) 1935- **CLC 6, 23, 49**
    See also AITN 1; CA 25-28R; CANR 20, 57; DLB 6, 143, 185; MTCW 1, 2

Crichton, (John) Michael 1942-**CLC 2, 6, 54, 90; DAM NOV, POP**
    See also AAYA 10; AITN 2; CA 25-28R; CANR 13, 40, 54, 76; DLBY 81; INT CANR-13; JRDA; MTCW 1, 2; SATA 9, 88

Crispin, Edmund   **CLC 22**
    See Montgomery, (Robert) Bruce
    See also DLB 87

Cristofer, Michael 1945(?)-   **CLC 28; DAM DRAM**
    See also CA 110; 152; DLB 7

Croce, Benedetto 1866-1952   **TCLC 37**
    See also CA 120; 155

Crockett, David 1786-1836   **NCLC 8**
    See also DLB 3, 11

Crockett, Davy
    See Crockett, David

Crofts, Freeman Wills 1879-1957   **TCLC 55**
    See also CA 115; DLB 77

Croker, John Wilson 1780-1857   **NCLC 10**
    See also DLB 110

Crommelynck, Fernand 1885-1970   **CLC 75**
    See also CA 89-92

Cromwell, Oliver 1599-1658   **LC 43**

Cronin, A(rchibald) J(oseph) 1896-1981**C L C 32**
    See also CA 1-4R; 102; CANR 5; DLB 191; SATA 47; SATA-Obit 25

Cross, Amanda
    See Heilbrun, Carolyn G(old)

Crothers, Rachel 1878(?)-1958   **TCLC 19**
    See also CA 113; DLB 7

Croves, Hal
    See Traven, B.

Crow Dog, Mary (Ellen) (?)-   **CLC 93**
    See also Brave Bird, Mary
    See also CA 154

Crowfield, Christopher
    See Stowe, Harriet (Elizabeth) Beecher

Crowley, Aleister   **TCLC 7**
    See also Crowley, Edward Alexander

Crowley, Edward Alexander 1875-1947
    See Crowley, Aleister
    See also CA 104

Crowley, John 1942-   **CLC 57**
    See also CA 61-64; CANR 43; DLBY 82; SATA 65

Crud
    See Crumb, R(obert)

Crumarums
    See Crumb, R(obert)

Crumb, R(obert) 1943-   **CLC 17**
    See also CA 106

Crumbum
    See Crumb, R(obert)

Crumski
    See Crumb, R(obert)

Crum the Bum
    See Crumb, R(obert)

Crunk
    See Crumb, R(obert)

Crustt
    See Crumb, R(obert)

Cruz, Victor Hernandez 1949-
    See also BW 2; CA 65-68; CAAS 17; CANR 14, 32, 74; DAM MULT, POET; DLB 41; HLC 1; HW 1, 2; MTCW 1

Cryer, Gretchen (Kiger) 1935-   **CLC 21**
    See also CA 114; 123

Csath, Geza 1887-1919   **TCLC 13**
    See also CA 111

Cudlip, David R(ockwell) 1933-   **CLC 34**
    See also CA 177

Cullen, Countee 1903-1946**TCLC 4, 37; BLC 1; DA; DAC; DAM MST, MULT, POET; PC 20; WLCS**
    See also BW 1; CA 108; 124; CDALB 1917-1929; DLB 4, 48, 51; MTCW 1, 2; SATA 18

Cum, R.
    See Crumb, R(obert)

Cummings, Bruce F(rederick) 1889-1919
    See Barbellion, W. N. P.
    See also CA 123

Cummings, E(dward) E(stlin) 1894-1962**CLC 1, 3, 8, 12, 15, 68; DA; DAB; DAC; DAM MST, POET; PC 5; WLC**
    See also CA 73-76; CANR 31; CDALB 1929-1941; DLB 4, 48; MTCW 1, 2

Cunha, Euclides (Rodrigues Pimenta) da 1866-1909   **TCLC 24**
    See also CA 123

Cunningham, E. V.
    See Fast, Howard (Melvin)

Cunningham, J(ames) V(incent) 1911-1985 **CLC 3, 31**
    See also CA 1-4R; 115; CANR 1, 72; DLB 5

Cunningham, Julia(Woolfolk) 1916- **CLC 12**
    See also CA 9-12R; CANR 4, 19, 36; JRDA; MAICYA; SAAS 2; SATA 1, 26

Cunningham, Michael 1952-   **CLC 34**
    See also CA 136

Cunninghame Graham, R(obert) B(ontine)
1852-1936 **TCLC 19**
See also Graham, R(obert) B(ontine)
Cunninghame
See also CA 119; DLB 98
Currie, Ellen 19(?)- **CLC 44**
Curtin, Philip
See Lowndes, Marie Adelaide (Belloc)
Curtis, Price
See Ellison, Harlan (Jay)
Cutrate, Joe
See Spiegelman, Art
Cynewulf c. 770-c. 840 **CMLC 23**
Czaczkes, Shmuel Yosef
See Agnon, S(hmuel) Y(osef Halevi)
Dabrowska, Maria (Szumska) 1889-1965**CLC 15**
See also CA 106
Dabydeen, David 1955- **CLC 34**
See also BW 1; CA 125; CANR 56
Dacey, Philip 1939- **CLC 51**
See also CA 37-40R; CAAS 17; CANR 14, 32, 64; DLB 105
Dagerman, Stig (Halvard) 1923-1954 **TCLC 17**
See also CA 117; 155
Dahl, Roald 1916-1990**CLC 1, 6, 18, 79; DAB; DAC; DAM MST, NOV, POP**
See also AAYA 15; CA 1-4R; 133; CANR 6, 32, 37, 62; CLR 1, 7, 41; DLB 139; JRDA; MAICYA; MTCW 1, 2; SATA 1, 26, 73; SATA-Obit 65
Dahlberg, Edward 1900-1977 **CLC 1, 7, 14**
See also CA 9-12R; 69-72; CANR 31, 62; DLB 48; MTCW 1
Daitch, Susan 1954- **CLC 103**
See also CA 161
Dale, Colin **TCLC 18**
See also Lawrence, T(homas) E(dward)
Dale, George E.
See Asimov, Isaac
Dalton, Roque 1935-1975
See also HLCS 1; HW 2
Daly, Elizabeth 1878-1967 **CLC 52**
See also CA 23-24; 25-28R; CANR 60; CAP 2
Daly, Maureen 1921- **CLC 17**
See also AAYA 5; CANR 37; JRDA; MAICYA; SAAS 1; SATA 2
Damas, Leon-Gontran 1912-1978 **CLC 84**
See also BW 1; CA 125; 73-76
Dana, Richard Henry Sr. 1787-1879**NCLC 53**
Daniel, Samuel 1562(?)-1619 **LC 24**
See also DLB 62
Daniels, Brett
See Adler, Renata
Dannay, Frederic 1905-1982 **CLC 11;DAM POP**
See also Queen, Ellery
See also CA 1-4R; 107; CANR 1, 39; DLB 137; MTCW 1
D'Annunzio, Gabriele 1863-1938**TCLC 6, 40**
See also CA 104; 155
Danois, N. le
See Gourmont, Remy (-Marie-Charles) de
Dante 1265-1321 **CMLC 3, 18; DA; DAB; DAC; DAM MST, POET; PC 21; WLCS**
d'Antibes, Germain
See Simenon, Georges (Jacques Christian)
Danticat, Edwidge 1969- **CLC 94**
See also AAYA 29; CA 152; CANR 73; MTCW 1
Danvers, Dennis 1947- **CLC 70**
Danziger, Paula 1944- **CLC 21**

See also AAYA 4; CA 112; 115; CANR 37; CLR 20; JRDA; MAICYA; SATA 36, 63, 102; SATA-Brief 30
Da Ponte, Lorenzo 1749-1838 **NCLC 50**
Dario, Ruben 1867-1916 **TCLC 4; DAM MULT; HLC 1; PC 15**
See also CA 131; CANR 81; HW 1, 2; MTCW 1, 2
Darley, George 1795-1846 **NCLC 2**
See also DLB 96
Darrow, Clarence (Seward) 1857-1938**TCLC 81**
See also CA 164
Darwin, Charles 1809-1882 **NCLC 57**
See also DLB 57, 166
Daryush, Elizabeth 1887-1977 **CLC 6, 19**
See also CA 49-52; CANR 3, 81; DLB 20
Dasgupta, Surendranath 1887-1952**TCLC 81**
See also CA 157
Dashwood, Edmee Elizabeth Monica de la Pasture 1890-1943
See Delafield, E. M.
See also CA 119; 154
Daudet, (Louis Marie) Alphonse 1840-1897 **NCLC 1**
See also DLB 123
Daumal, Rene 1908-1944 **TCLC 14**
See also CA 114
Davenant, William 1606-1668 **LC 13**
See also DLB 58, 126
Davenport, Guy (Mattison, Jr.) 1927-**CLC 6, 14, 38; SSC 16**
See also CA 33-36R; CANR 23, 73; DLB 130
Davidson, Avram (James) 1923-1993
See Queen, Ellery
See also CA 101; 171; CANR 26; DLB 8
Davidson, Donald (Grady) 1893-1968**CLC 2, 13, 19**
See also CA 5-8R; 25-28R; CANR 4; DLB 45
Davidson, Hugh
See Hamilton, Edmond
Davidson, John 1857-1909 **TCLC 24**
See also CA 118; DLB 19
Davidson, Sara 1943- **CLC 9**
See also CA 81-84; CANR 44, 68; DLB 185
Davie, Donald (Alfred) 1922-1995 **CLC 5, 8, 10, 31**
See also CA 1-4R; 149; CAAS 3; CANR 1, 44; DLB 27; MTCW 1
Davies, Ray(mond Douglas) 1944- **CLC 21**
See also CA 116; 146
Davies, Rhys 1901-1978 **CLC 23**
See also CA 9-12R; 81-84; CANR 4; DLB 139, 191
Davies, (William) Robertson 1913-1995 **CLC 2, 7, 13, 25, 42, 75, 91; DA; DAB; DAC; DAM MST, NOV, POP; WLC**
See also BEST 89:2; CA 33-36R; 150; CANR 17, 42; DLB 68; INT CANR-17; MTCW 1, 2
Davies, W(illiam) H(enry) 1871-1940**TCLC 5**
See also CA 104; 179; DLB 19, 174
Davies, Walter C.
See Kornbluth, C(yril) M.
Davis, Angela (Yvonne) 1944- **CLC 77; DAM MULT**
See also BW 2, 3; CA 57-60; CANR 10, 81
Davis, B. Lynch
See Bioy Casares, Adolfo; Borges, Jorge Luis
Davis, B. Lynch
See Bioy Casares, Adolfo
Davis, Harold Lenoir 1894-1960 **CLC 49**
See also CA 178; 89-92; DLB 9, 206

Davis, Rebecca (Blaine) Harding 1831-1910 **TCLC 6**
See also CA 104; 179; DLB 74
Davis, Richard Harding 1864-1916 **TCLC 24**
See also CA 114; DLB 12, 23, 78, 79, 189; DLBD 13
Davison, Frank Dalby 1893-1970 **CLC 15**
See also CA 116
Davison, Lawrence H.
See Lawrence, D(avid) H(erbert Richards)
Davison, Peter (Hubert) 1928- **CLC 28**
See also CA 9-12R; CAAS 4; CANR 3, 43; DLB 5
Davys, Mary 1674-1732 **LC 1, 46**
See also DLB 39
Dawson, Fielding 1930- **CLC 6**
See also CA 85-88; DLB 130
Dawson, Peter
See Faust, Frederick (Schiller)
Day, Clarence (Shepard, Jr.) 1874-1935 **TCLC 25**
See also CA 108; DLB 11
Day, Thomas 1748-1789 **LC 1**
See also DLB 39; YABC 1
Day Lewis, C(ecil) 1904-1972 **CLC 1, 6, 10; DAM POET; PC 11**
See also Blake, Nicholas
See also CA 13-16; 33-36R; CANR 34; CAP 1; DLB 15, 20; MTCW 1, 2
Dazai Osamu 1909-1948 **TCLC 11**
See also Tsushima, Shuji
See also CA 164; DLB 182
de Andrade, Carlos Drummond 1892-1945
See Drummond de Andrade, Carlos
Deane, Norman
See Creasey, John
Deane, Seamus (Francis) 1940- **CLC 122**
See also CA 118; CANR 42
de Beauvoir, Simone (Lucie Ernestine Marie Bertrand)
See Beauvoir, Simone (Lucie Ernestine Marie Bertrand) de
de Beer, P.
See Bosman, Herman Charles
de Brissac, Malcolm
See Dickinson, Peter (Malcolm)
de Chardin, Pierre Teilhard
See Teilhard de Chardin, (Marie Joseph) Pierre
Dee, John 1527-1608 **LC 20**
Deer, Sandra 1940- **CLC 45**
De Ferrari, Gabriella 1941- **CLC 65**
See also CA 146
Defoe, Daniel 1660(?)-1731 **LC 1, 42; DA; DAB; DAC; DAM MST, NOV; WLC**
See also AAYA 27; CDBLB 1660-1789; DLB 39, 95, 101; JRDA; MAICYA; SATA 22
de Gourmont, Remy(-Marie-Charles)
See Gourmont, Remy (-Marie-Charles) de
de Hartog, Jan 1914- **CLC 19**
See also CA 1-4R; CANR 1
de Hostos, E. M.
See Hostos (y Bonilla), Eugenio Maria de
de Hostos, Eugenio M.
See Hostos (y Bonilla), Eugenio Maria de
Deighton, Len **CLC 4, 7, 22, 46**
See also Deighton, Leonard Cyril
See also AAYA 6; BEST 89:2; CDBLB 1960 to Present; DLB 87
Deighton, Leonard Cyril 1929-
See Deighton, Len
See also CA 9-12R; CANR 19, 33, 68; DAM NOV, POP; MTCW 1, 2
Dekker, Thomas 1572(?)-1632 **LC 22;DAM**

DRAM
See also CDBLB Before 1660; DLB 62, 172

Delafield, E. M. 1890-1943   **TCLC 61**
See also Dashwood, Edmee Elizabeth Monica de la Pasture
See also DLB 34

de la Mare, Walter (John) 1873-1956**TCLC 4, 53; DAB; DAC; DAM MST, POET; SSC 14; WLC**
See also CA 163; CDBLB 1914-1945; CLR 23; DLB 162; MTCW 1; SATA 16

Delaney, Franey
See O'Hara, John (Henry)

Delaney, Shelagh 1939-**CLC 29;DAM DRAM**
See also CA 17-20R; CANR 30, 67; CDBLB 1960 to Present; DLB 13; MTCW 1

Delany, Mary (Granville Pendarves) 1700-1788 **LC 12**

Delany, Samuel R(ay, Jr.) 1942-**CLC 8, 14, 38; BLC 1; DAM MULT**
See also AAYA 24; BW 2, 3; CA 81-84; CANR 27, 43; DLB 8, 33; MTCW 1, 2

De La Ramee, (Marie) Louise 1839-1908
See Ouida
See also SATA 20

de la Roche, Mazo 1879-1961   **CLC 14**
See also CA 85-88; CANR 30; DLB 68; SATA 64

De La Salle, Innocent
See Hartmann, Sadakichi

Delbanco, Nicholas (Franklin) 1942- **CLC 6, 13**
See also CA 17-20R; CAAS 2; CANR 29, 55; DLB 6

del Castillo, Michel 1933-   **CLC 38**
See also CA 109; CANR 77

Deledda, Grazia(Cosima) 1875(?)-1936**TCLC 23**
See also CA 123

Delgado, Abelardo B(arrientos) 1931-
See also CA 131; CAAS 15; DAM MST, MULT; DLB 82; HLC 1; HW 1, 2

Delibes, Miguel   **CLC 8, 18**
See also Delibes Setien, Miguel

Delibes Setien, Miguel 1920-
See Delibes, Miguel
See also CA 45-48; CANR 1, 32; HW 1; MTCW 1

DeLillo, Don 1936- **CLC 8, 10, 13, 27, 39, 54, 76; DAM NOV, POP**
See also BEST 89:1; CA 81-84; CANR 21, 76; DLB 6, 173; MTCW 1, 2

de Lisser, H. G.
See De Lisser, H(erbert) G(eorge)
See also DLB 117

De Lisser, H(erbert) G(eorge) 1878-1944 **TCLC 12**
See also de Lisser, H. G.
See also BW 2; CA 109; 152

Deloney, Thomas 1560(?)-1600   **LC 41**
See also DLB 167

Deloria, Vine (Victor), Jr. 1933-**CLC 21, 122; DAM MULT**
See also CA 53-56; CANR 5, 20, 48; DLB 175; MTCW 1; NNAL; SATA 21

Del Vecchio, John M(ichael) 1947-   **CLC 29**
See also CA 110; DLBD 9

de Man, Paul (Adolph Michel) 1919-1983 **CLC 55**
See also CA 128; 111; CANR 61; DLB 67; MTCW 1, 2

De Marinis, Rick 1934-   **CLC 54**
See also CA 57-60; CAAS 24; CANR 9, 25, 50

Dembry, R. Emmet
See Murfree, Mary Noailles

Demby, William 1922-**CLC 53; BLC 1; DAM MULT**
See also BW 1, 3; CA 81-84; CANR 81; DLB 33

de Menton, Francisco
See Chin, Frank (Chew, Jr.)

Demetrius of Phalerum c. 307B.C.-**CMLC 34**

Demijohn, Thom
See Disch, Thomas M(ichael)

de Molina, Tirso 1580-1648
See also HLCS 2

de Montherlant, Henry (Milon)
See Montherlant, Henry (Milon) de

Demosthenes 384B.C.-322B.C.   **CMLC 13**
See also DLB 1É76

de Natale, Francine
See Malzberg, Barry N(athaniel)

Denby, Edwin (Orr) 1903-1983   **CLC 48**
See also CA 138; 110

Denis, Julio
See Cortazar, Julio

Denmark, Harrison
See Zelazny, Roger (Joseph)

Dennis, John 1658-1734   **LC 11**
See also DLB 101

Dennis, Nigel (Forbes) 1912-1989   **CLC 8**
See also CA 25-28R; 129; DLB 13, 15; MTCW 1

Dent, Lester 1904(?)-1959   **TCLC 72**
See also CA 112; 161

De Palma, Brian (Russell) 1940-   **CLC 20**
See also CA 109

De Quincey, Thomas 1785-1859   **NCLC 4**
See also CDBLB 1789-1832; DLB 110; 144

Deren, Eleanora 1908(?)-1961
See Deren, Maya
See also CA 111

Deren, Maya 1917-1961   **CLC 16, 102**
See also Deren, Eleanora

Derleth, August (William) 1909-1971**CLC 31**
See also CA 1-4R; 29-32R; CANR 4; DLB 9; DLBD 17; SATA 5

Der Nister 1884-1950   **TCLC 56**

de Routisie, Albert
See Aragon, Louis

Derrida, Jacques 1930-   **CLC 24, 87**
See also CA 124; 127; CANR 76; MTCW 1

Derry Down Derry
See Lear, Edward

Dersonnes, Jacques
See Simenon, Georges (Jacques Christian)

Desai, Anita 1937-**CLC 19, 37, 97; DAB; DAM NOV**
See also CA 81-84; CANR 33, 53; MTCW 1, 2; SATA 63

Desai, Kiran 1971-   **CLC 119**
See also CA 171

de Saint-Luc, Jean
See Glassco, John

de Saint Roman, Arnaud
See Aragon, Louis

Descartes, Rene 1596-1650   **LC 20, 35**

De Sica, Vittorio 1901(?)-1974   **CLC 20**
See also CA 117

Desnos, Robert 1900-1945   **TCLC 22**
See also CA 121; 151

Destouches, Louis-Ferdinand 1894-1961**CLC 9, 15**
See also Celine, Louis-Ferdinand
See also CA 85-88; CANR 28; MTCW 1

de Tolignac, Gaston

See Griffith, D(avid Lewelyn) W(ark)

Deutsch, Babette 1895-1982   **CLC 18**
See also CA 1-4R; 108; CANR 4, 79; DLB 45; SATA 1; SATA-Obit 33

Devenant, William 1606-1649   **LC 13**

Devkota, Laxmiprasad 1909-1959 **TCLC 23**
See also CA 123

De Voto, Bernard (Augustine) 1897-1955 **TCLC 29**
See also CA 113; 160; DLB 9

De Vries, Peter 1910-1993 **CLC 1, 2, 3, 7, 10, 28, 46; DAM NOV**
See also CA 17-20R; 142; CANR 41; DLB 6; DLBY 82; MTCW 1, 2

Dewey, John 1859-1952   **TCLC 95**
See also CA 114; 170

Dexter, John
See Bradley, Marion Zimmer

Dexter, Martin
See Faust, Frederick (Schiller)

Dexter, Pete 1943-   **CLC 34, 55;DAM POP**
See also BEST 89:2; CA 127; 131; INT 131; MTCW 1

Diamano, Silmang
See Senghor, Leopold Sedar

Diamond, Neil 1941-   **CLC 30**
See also CA 108

Diaz del Castillo, Bernal 1496-1584   **LC 31; HLCS 1**

di Bassetto, Corno
See Shaw, George Bernard

Dick, Philip K(indred) 1928-1982**CLC 10, 30, 72; DAM NOV, POP**
See also AAYA 24; CA 49-52; 106; CANR 2, 16; DLB 8; MTCW 1, 2

Dickens, Charles (John Huffam) 1812-1870 **NCLC 3, 8, 18, 26, 37, 50; DA; DAB; DAC; DAM MST, NOV; SSC 17; WLC**
See also AAYA 23; CDBLB 1832-1890; DLB 21, 55, 70, 159, 166; JRDA; MAICYA; SATA 15

Dickey, James (Lafayette) 1923-1997 **CLC 1, 2, 4, 7, 10, 15, 47, 109; DAM NOV, POET, POP**
See also AITN 1, 2; CA 9-12R; 156; CABS 2; CANR 10, 48, 61; CDALB 1968-1988; DLB 5, 193; DLBD 7; DLBY 82, 93, 96, 97, 98; INT CANR-10; MTCW 1, 2

Dickey, William 1928-1994   **CLC 3, 28**
See also CA 9-12R; 145; CANR 24, 79; DLB 5

Dickinson, Charles 1951-   **CLC 49**
See also CA 128

Dickinson, Emily (Elizabeth) 1830-1886 **NCLC 21, 77; DA; DAB; DAC; DAM MST, POET; PC 1; WLC**
See also AAYA 22; CDALB 1865-1917; DLB 1; SATA 29

Dickinson, Peter (Malcolm) 1927-**CLC 12, 35**
See also AAYA 9; CA 41-44R; CANR 31, 58; CLR 29; DLB 87, 161; JRDA; MAICYA; SATA 5, 62, 95

Dickson, Carr
See Carr, John Dickson

Dickson, Carter
See Carr, John Dickson

Diderot, Denis 1713-1784   **LC 26**

Didion, Joan 1934-**CLC 1, 3, 8, 14, 32; DAM NOV**
See also AITN 1; CA 5-8R; CANR 14, 52, 76; CDALB 1968-1988; DLB 2, 173, 185; DLBY 81, 86; MTCW 1, 2

Dietrich, Robert
See Hunt, E(verette) Howard, (Jr.)

Difusa, Pati
See Almodovar, Pedro
Dillard, Annie 1945- **CLC 9, 60, 115; DAM NOV**
See also AAYA 6; CA 49-52; CANR 3, 43, 62; DLBY 80; MTCW 1, 2; SATA 10
Dillard, R(ichard) H(enry) W(ilde) 1937- **CLC 5**
See also CA 21-24R; CAAS 7; CANR 10; DLB 5
Dillon, Eilis 1920-1994 **CLC 17**
See also CA 9-12R; 147; CAAS 3; CANR 4, 38, 78; CLR 26; MAICYA; SATA 2, 74; SATA-Essay 105; SATA-Obit 83
Dimont, Penelope
See Mortimer, Penelope (Ruth)
Dinesen, Isak **CLC 10, 29, 95; SSC 7**
See also Blixen, Karen (Christentze Dinesen)
See also MTCW 1
Ding Ling **CLC 68**
See also Chiang, Pin-chin
Diphusa, Patty
See Almodovar, Pedro
Disch, Thomas M(ichael) 1940- **CLC 7, 36**
See also AAYA 17; CA 21-24R; CAAS 4; CANR 17, 36, 54; CLR 18; DLB 8; MAICYA; MTCW 1, 2; SAAS 15; SATA 92
Disch, Tom
See Disch, Thomas M(ichael)
d'Isly, Georges
See Simenon, Georges (Jacques Christian)
Disraeli, Benjamin 1804-1881 **NCLC 2, 39, 79**
See also DLB 21, 55
Ditcum, Steve
See Crumb, R(obert)
Dixon, Paige
See Corcoran, Barbara
Dixon, Stephen 1936- **CLC 52; SSC 16**
See also CA 89-92; CANR 17, 40, 54; DLB 130
Doak, Annie
See Dillard, Annie
Dobell, Sydney Thompson 1824-1874 **NCLC 43**
See also DLB 32
Doblin, Alfred **TCLC 13**
See also Doeblin, Alfred
Dobrolyubov, Nikolai Alexandrovich 1836-1861 **NCLC 5**
Dobson, Austin 1840-1921 **TCLC 79**
See also DLB 35; 144
Dobyns, Stephen 1941- **CLC 37**
See also CA 45-48; CANR 2, 18
Doctorow, E(dgar) L(aurence) 1931- **CLC 6, 11, 15, 18, 37, 44, 65, 113; DAM NOV, POP**
See also AAYA 22; AITN 2; BEST 89:3; CA 45-48; CANR 2, 33, 51, 76; CDALB 1968-1988; DLB 2, 28, 173; DLBY 80; MTCW 1, 2
Dodgson, Charles Lutwidge 1832-1898
See Carroll, Lewis
See also CLR 2; DA; DAB; DAC; DAM MST, NOV, POET; MAICYA; SATA 100; YABC 2
Dodson, Owen (Vincent) 1914-1983 **CLC 79; BLC 1; DAM MULT**
See also BW 1; CA 65-68; 110; CANR 24; DLB 76
Doeblin, Alfred 1878-1957 **TCLC 13**
See also Doblin, Alfred
See also CA 110; 141; DLB 66
Doerr, Harriet 1910- **CLC 34**
See also CA 117; 122; CANR 47; INT 122
Domecq, H(onorio Bustos)
See Bioy Casares, Adolfo

Domecq, H(onorio) Bustos
See Bioy Casares, Adolfo; Borges, Jorge Luis
Domini, Rey
See Lorde, Audre (Geraldine)
Dominique
See Proust, (Valentin-Louis-George-Eugene-) Marcel
Don, A
See Stephen, Sir Leslie
Donaldson, Stephen R. 1947- **CLC 46; DAM POP**
See also CA 89-92; CANR 13, 55; INT CANR-13
Donleavy, J(ames) P(atrick) 1926- **CLC 1, 4, 6, 10, 45**
See also AITN 2; CA 9-12R; CANR 24, 49, 62, 80; DLB 6, 173; INT CANR-24; MTCW 1, 2
Donne, John 1572-1631 **LC 10, 24; DA; DAB; DAC; DAM MST, POET; PC 1; WLC**
See also CDBLB Before 1660; DLB 121, 151
Donnell, David 1939(?)- **CLC 34**
Donoghue, P. S.
See Hunt, E(verette) Howard, (Jr.)
Donoso (Yanez), Jose 1924-1996 **CLC 4, 8, 11, 32, 99; DAM MULT; HLC 1; SSC 34**
See also CA 81-84; 155; CANR 32, 73; DLB 113; HW 1, 2; MTCW 1, 2
Donovan, John 1928-1992 **CLC 35**
See also AAYA 20; CA 97-100; 137; CLR 3; MAICYA; SATA 72; SATA-Brief 29
Don Roberto
See Cunninghame Graham, R(obert) B(ontine)
Doolittle, Hilda 1886-1961 **CLC 3, 8, 14, 31, 34, 73; DA; DAC; DAM MST, POET; PC 5; WLC**
See also H. D.
See also CA 97-100; CANR 35; DLB 4, 45; MTCW 1, 2
Dorfman, Ariel 1942- **CLC 48, 77; DAM MULT; HLC 1**
See also CA 124; 130; CANR 67, 70; HW 1, 2; INT 130
Dorn, Edward (Merton) 1929- **CLC 10, 18**
See also CA 93-96; CANR 42, 79; DLB 5; INT 93-96
Dorris, Michael (Anthony) 1945-1997 **CLC 109; DAM MULT, NOV**
See also AAYA 20; BEST 90:1; CA 102; 157; CANR 19, 46, 75; CLR 58; DLB 175; MTCW 2; NNAL; SATA 75; SATA-Obit 94
Dorris, Michael A.
See Dorris, Michael (Anthony)
Dorsan, Luc
See Simenon, Georges (Jacques Christian)
Dorsange, Jean
See Simenon, Georges (Jacques Christian)
Dos Passos, John (Roderigo) 1896-1970 **CLC 1, 4, 8, 11, 15, 25, 34, 82; DA; DAB; DAC; DAM MST, NOV; WLC**
See also CA 1-4R; 29-32R; CANR 3; CDALB 1929-1941; DLB 4, 9; DLBD 1, 15; DLBY 96; MTCW 1, 2
Dossage, Jean
See Simenon, Georges (Jacques Christian)
Dostoevsky, Fedor Mikhailovich 1821-1881 **NCLC 2, 7, 21, 33, 43; DA; DAB; DAC; DAM MST, NOV; SSC 2, 33; WLC**
Doughty, Charles M(ontagu) 1843-1926 **TCLC 27**
See also CA 115; 178; DLB 19, 57, 174
Douglas, Ellen **CLC 73**
See also Haxton, Josephine Ayres; Williamson,

Ellen Douglas
Douglas, Gavin 1475(?)-1522 **LC 20**
See also DLB 132
Douglas, George
See Brown, George Douglas
Douglas, Keith (Castellain) 1920-1944 **TCLC 40**
See also CA 160; DLB 27
Douglas, Leonard
See Bradbury, Ray (Douglas)
Douglas, Michael
See Crichton, (John) Michael
Douglas, (George) Norman 1868-1952 **TCLC 68**
See also CA 119; 157; DLB 34, 195
Douglas, William
See Brown, George Douglas
Douglass, Frederick 1817(?)-1895 **NCLC 7, 55; BLC 1; DA; DAC; DAM MST, MULT; WLC**
See also CDALB 1640-1865; DLB 1, 43, 50, 79; SATA 29
Dourado, (Waldomiro Freitas) Autran 1926- **CLC 23, 60**
See also Autran Dourado, Waldomiro Freitas
See also CA 179; CANR 34, 81; DLB 145; HW 2
Dourado, Waldomiro Autran 1926-
See Dourado, (Waldomiro Freitas) Autran
See also CA 179
Dove, Rita (Frances) 1952- **CLC 50, 81; BLCS; DAM MULT, POET; PC 6**
See also BW 2; CA 109; CAAS 19; CANR 27, 42, 68, 76; CDALBS; DLB 120; MTCW 1
Doveglion
See Villa, Jose Garcia
Dowell, Coleman 1925-1985 **CLC 60**
See also CA 25-28R; 117; CANR 10; DLB 130
Dowson, Ernest (Christopher) 1867-1900 **TCLC 4**
See also CA 105; 150; DLB 19, 135
Doyle, A. Conan
See Doyle, Arthur Conan
Doyle, Arthur Conan 1859-1930 **TCLC 7; DA; DAB; DAC; DAM MST, NOV; SSC 12; WLC**
See also AAYA 14; CA 104; 122; CDBLB 1890-1914; DLB 18, 70, 156, 178; MTCW 1, 2; SATA 24
Doyle, Conan
See Doyle, Arthur Conan
Doyle, John
See Graves, Robert (von Ranke)
Doyle, Roddy 1958(?)- **CLC 81**
See also AAYA 14; CA 143; CANR 73; DLB 194
Doyle, Sir A. Conan
See Doyle, Arthur Conan
Doyle, Sir Arthur Conan
See Doyle, Arthur Conan
Dr. A
See Asimov, Isaac; Silverstein, Alvin
Drabble, Margaret 1939- **CLC 2, 3, 5, 8, 10, 22, 53; DAB; DAC; DAM MST, NOV, POP**
See also CA 13-16R; CANR 18, 35, 63; CDBLB 1960 to Present; DLB 14, 155; MTCW 1, 2; SATA 48
Drapier, M. B.
See Swift, Jonathan
Drayham, James
See Mencken, H(enry) L(ouis)
Drayton, Michael 1563-1631 **LC 8; DAM POET**

See also DLB 121
Dreadstone, Carl
See Campbell, (John) Ramsey
Dreiser, Theodore (Herman Albert) 1871-1945
**TCLC 10, 18, 35, 83; DA; DAC; DAM
MST, NOV; SSC 30; WLC**
See also CA 106; 132; CDALB 1865-1917;
DLB 9, 12, 102, 137; DLBD 1; MTCW 1, 2
Drexler, Rosalyn 1926-   **CLC 2, 6**
See also CA 81-84; CANR 68
Dreyer, Carl Theodor 1889-1968   **CLC 16**
See also CA 116
Drieu la Rochelle, Pierre(-Eugene) 1893-1945
TCLC 21
See also CA 117; DLB 72
Drinkwater, John 1882-1937   **TCLC 57**
See also CA 109; 149; DLB 10, 19, 149
Drop Shot
See Cable, George Washington
Droste-Hulshoff, Annette Freiinvon 1797-1848
NCLC 3
See also DLB 133
Drummond, Walter
See Silverberg, Robert
Drummond, William Henry 1854-1907 **TCLC
25**
See also CA 160; DLB 92
Drummond de Andrade, Carlos 1902-1987
CLC 18
See also Andrade, Carlos Drummond de
See also CA 132; 123
Drury, Allen (Stuart) 1918-1998   **CLC 37**
See also CA 57-60; 170; CANR 18, 52; INT
CANR-18
Dryden, John 1631-1700**LC 3, 21; DA; DAB;
DAC; DAM DRAM, MST, POET; DC 3;
PC 25;WLC**
See also CDBLB 1660-1789; DLB 80, 101, 131
Duberman, Martin (Bauml) 1930-   **CLC 8**
See also CA 1-4R; CANR 2, 63
Dubie, Norman (Evans) 1945-   **CLC 36**
See also CA 69-72; CANR 12; DLB 120
Du Bois, W(illiam) E(dward) B(urghardt) 1868-
1963   **CLC 1, 2, 13, 64, 96; BLC 1; DA;
DAC; DAM MST, MULT, NOV; WLC**
See also BW 1, 3; CA 85-88; CANR 34, 82;
CDALB 1865-1917; DLB 47, 50, 91; MTCW
1, 2; SATA 42
Dubus, Andre 1936-1999**CLC 13, 36, 97; SSC
15**
See also CA 21-24R; 177; CANR 17; DLB 130;
INT CANR-17
Duca Minimo
See D'Annunzio, Gabriele
Ducharme, Rejean 1941-   **CLC 74**
See also CA 165; DLB 60
Duclos, Charles Pinot 1704-1772   **LC 1**
Dudek, Louis 1918-   **CLC 11, 19**
See also CA 45-48; CAAS 14; CANR 1; DLB
88
Duerrenmatt, Friedrich 1921-1990 **CLC 1, 4,
8, 11, 15, 43, 102; DAM DRAM**
See also CA 17-20R; CANR 33; DLB 69, 124;
MTCW 1, 2
Duffy, Bruce 1953(?)-   **CLC 50**
See also CA 172
Duffy, Maureen 1933-   **CLC 37**
See also CA 25-28R; CANR 33, 68; DLB 14;
MTCW 1
Dugan, Alan 1923-   **CLC 2, 6**
See also CA 81-84; DLB 5
du Gard, Roger Martin
See Martin du Gard, Roger

Duhamel, Georges 1884-1966   **CLC 8**
See also CA 81-84; 25-28R; CANR 35; DLB
65; MTCW 1
Dujardin, Edouard (Emile Louis) 1861-1949
TCLC 13
See also CA 109; DLB 123
Dulles, John Foster 1888-1959   **TCLC 72**
See also CA 115; 149
Dumas, Alexandre (pere)
See Dumas, Alexandre (Davy de la Pailleterie)
Dumas, Alexandre (Davy de la Pailleterie)
1802-1870   **NCLC 11; DA; DAB; DAC;
DAM MST, NOV; WLC**
See also DLB 119, 192; SATA 18
Dumas, Alexandre (fils) 1824-1895**NCLC 71;
DC 1**
See also AAYA 22; DLB 192
Dumas, Claudine
See Malzberg, Barry N(athaniel)
Dumas, Henry L. 1934-1968   **CLC 6, 62**
See also BW 1; CA 85-88; DLB 41
du Maurier, Daphne 1907-1989**CLC 6, 11, 59;
DAB; DAC; DAM MST, POP; SSC 18**
See also CA 5-8R; 128; CANR 6, 55; DLB 191;
MTCW 1, 2; SATA 27; SATA-Obit 60
Dunbar, Paul Laurence 1872-1906   **TCLC 2,
12; BLC 1; DA; DAC; DAM MST, MULT,
POET; PC 5; SSC 8; WLC**
See also BW 1, 3; CA 104; 124; CANR 79;
CDALB 1865-1917; DLB 50, 54, 78; SATA
34
Dunbar,William 1460(?)-1530(?)   **LC 20**
See also DLB 132, 146
Duncan, Dora Angela
See Duncan, Isadora
Duncan, Isadora 1877(?)-1927   **TCLC 68**
See also CA 118; 149
Duncan, Lois 1934-   **CLC 26**
See also AAYA 4; CA 1-4R; CANR 2, 23, 36;
CLR 29; JRDA; MAICYA; SAAS 2; SATA
1, 36, 75
Duncan, Robert (Edward) 1919-1988 **CLC 1,
2, 4, 7, 15, 41, 55; DAM POET; PC 2**
See also CA 9-12R; 124; CANR 28, 62; DLB
5, 16, 193; MTCW 1, 2
Duncan, Sara Jeannette 1861-1922 **TCLC 60**
See also CA 157; DLB 92
Dunlap, William 1766-1839   **NCLC 2**
See also DLB 30, 37, 59
Dunn, Douglas (Eaglesham) 1942- **CLC 6, 40**
See also CA 45-48; CANR 2, 33; DLB 40;
MTCW 1
Dunn, Katherine (Karen) 1945-   **CLC 71**
See also CA 33-36R; CANR 72; MTCW 1
Dunn, Stephen 1939-   **CLC 36**
See also CA 33-36R; CANR 12, 48, 53; DLB
105
Dunne, Finley Peter 1867-1936   **TCLC 28**
See also CA 108; 178; DLB 11, 23
Dunne, John Gregory 1932-   **CLC 28**
See also CA 25-28R; CANR 14, 50; DLBY 80
Dunsany, Edward John Moreton Drax Plunkett
1878-1957
See Dunsany, Lord
See also CA 104; 148; DLB 10; MTCW 1
Dunsany, Lord   **TCLC 2, 59**
See also Dunsany, Edward John Moreton Drax
Plunkett
See also DLB 77, 153, 156
du Perry, Jean
See Simenon, Georges (Jacques Christian)
Durang, Christopher (Ferdinand) 1949-**C L C
27, 38**

See also CA 105; CANR 50, 76; MTCW 1
Duras, Marguerite 1914-1996**CLC 3, 6, 11, 20,
34, 40, 68, 100**
See also CA 25-28R; 151; CANR 50; DLB 83;
MTCW 1, 2
Durban, (Rosa) Pam 1947-   **CLC 39**
See also CA 123
Durcan, Paul 1944- **CLC 43, 70;DAM POET**
See also CA 134
Durkheim, Emile 1858-1917   **TCLC 55**
Durrell, Lawrence (George) 1912-1990 **C L C
1, 4, 6, 8, 13, 27, 41; DAM NOV**
See also CA 9-12R; 132; CANR 40, 77;CDBLB
1945-1960; DLB 15, 27, 204; DLBY 90;
MTCW 1, 2
Durrenmatt, Friedrich
See Duerrenmatt, Friedrich
Dutt, Toru 1856-1877   **NCLC 29**
Dwight, Timothy 1752-1817   **NCLC 13**
See also DLB 37
Dworkin, Andrea 1946-   **CLC 43**
See also CA 77-80; CAAS 21; CANR 16, 39,
76; INT CANR-16; MTCW 1, 2
Dwyer, Deanna
See Koontz, Dean R(ay)
Dwyer, K. R.
See Koontz, Dean R(ay)
Dwyer, Thomas A. 1923-   **CLC 114**
See also CA 115
Dye, Richard
See De Voto, Bernard (Augustine)
Dylan, Bob 1941-   **CLC 3, 4, 6, 12, 77**
See also CA 41-44R; DLB 16
E. V. L.
See Lucas, E(dward) V(errall)
Eagleton, Terence (Francis) 1943-
See Eagleton, Terry
See also CA 57-60; CANR 7, 23, 68; MTCW 1,
2
Eagleton, Terry   **CLC 63**
See also Eagleton, Terence (Francis)
See also MTCW 1
Early, Jack
See Scoppettone, Sandra
East, Michael
See West, Morris L(anglo)
Eastaway, Edward
See Thomas, (Philip) Edward
Eastlake, William (Derry) 1917-1997 **CLC 8**
See also CA 5-8R; 158; CAAS 1; CANR 5, 63;
DLB 6, 206; INT CANR-5
Eastman, Charles A(lexander) 1858-1939
TCLC 55; DAM MULT
See also CA 179; DLB 175; NNAL; YABC 1
Eberhart, Richard (Ghormley) 1904-**CLC 3,
11, 19, 56; DAM POET**
See also CA 1-4R; CANR 2; CDALB 1941-
1968; DLB 48; MTCW 1
Eberstadt, Fernanda 1960-   **CLC 39**
See also CA 136; CANR 69
Echegaray (y Eizaguirre), Jose (Maria Waldo)
1832-1916   **TCLC 4; HLCS 1**
See also CA 104; CANR 32; HW 1; MTCW 1
Echeverria, (Jose) Esteban (Antonino) 1805-
1851   **NCLC 18**
Echo
See Proust, (Valentin-Louis-George-Eugene-)
Marcel
Eckert, Allan W. 1931-   **CLC 17**
See also AAYA 18; CA 13-16R; CANR 14, 45;
INT CANR-14; SAAS 21; SATA 29, 91;
SATA-Brief 27
Eckhart, Meister 1260(?)-1328(?)   **CMLC 9**

See also DLB 115
Eckmar, F. R.
See de Hartog, Jan
Eco, Umberto 1932- **CLC 28, 60; DAM NOV,
POP**
See also BEST 90:1; CA 77-80; CANR 12, 33,
55; DLB 196; MTCW 1, 2
Eddison, E(ric) R(ucker) 1882-1945**TCLC 15**
See also CA 109; 156
Eddy, Mary (Ann Morse) Baker 1821-1910
TCLC 71
See also CA 113; 174
Edel, (Joseph) Leon 1907-1997   **CLC 29, 34**
See also CA 1-4R; 161; CANR 1, 22; DLB 103;
INT CANR-22
Eden, Emily 1797-1869   **NCLC 10**
Edgar, David 1948-   **CLC 42;DAM DRAM**
See also CA 57-60; CANR 12, 61; DLB 13;
MTCW 1
Edgerton, Clyde (Carlyle) 1944-   **CLC 39**
See also AAYA 17; CA 118; 134; CANR 64;
INT 134
Edgeworth, Maria 1768-1849   **NCLC 1,51**
See also DLB 116, 159, 163; SATA 21
Edison, Thomas 1847-1931   **TCLC 96**
Edmonds, Paul
See Kuttner, Henry
Edmonds, Walter D(umaux) 1903-1998 **C L C
35**
See also CA 5-8R; CANR 2; DLB 9; MAICYA;
SAAS 4; SATA 1, 27; SATA-Obit 99
Edmondson, Wallace
See Ellison, Harlan (Jay)
Edson, Russell   **CLC 13**
See also CA 33-36R
Edwards, Bronwen Elizabeth
See Rose, Wendy
Edwards, G(erald) B(asil) 1899-1976**CLC 25**
See also CA 110
Edwards, Gus 1939-   **CLC 43**
See also CA 108; INT 108
Edwards, Jonathan 1703-1758   **LC 7; DA;
DAC; DAM MST**
See also DLB 24
Efron, Marina Ivanovna Tsvetaeva
See Tsvetaeva (Efron), Marina (Ivanovna)
Ehle, John (Marsden, Jr.) 1925-   **CLC 27**
See also CA 9-12R
Ehrenbourg, Ilya (Grigoryevich)
See Ehrenburg, Ilya (Grigoryevich)
Ehrenburg, Ilya (Grigoryevich) 1891-1967
CLC 18, 34, 62
See also CA 102; 25-28R
Ehrenburg, Ilyo (Grigoryevich)
See Ehrenburg, Ilya (Grigoryevich)
Ehrenreich, Barbara 1941-   **CLC 110**
See also BEST 90:4; CA 73-76; CANR 16, 37,
62; MTCW 1, 2
Eich, Guenter 1907-1972   **CLC 15**
See also CA 111; 93-96; DLB 69, 124
Eichendorff, Joseph Freiherrvon 1788-1857
NCLC 8
See also DLB 90
Eigner, Larry   **CLC 9**
See also Eigner, Laurence (Joel)
See also CAAS 23; DLB 5
Eigner, Laurence (Joel) 1927-1996
See Eigner, Larry
See also CA 9-12R; 151; CANR 6; DLB 193
Einstein, Albert 1879-1955   **TCLC 65**
See also CA 121; 133; MTCW 1, 2
Eiseley, Loren Corey 1907-1977   **CLC 7**
See also AAYA 5; CA 1-4R; 73-76; CANR 6;

DLBD 17
Eisenstadt, Jill 1963-   **CLC 50**
See also CA 140
Eisenstein, Sergei (Mikhailovich) 1898-1948
TCLC 57
See also CA 114; 149
Eisner, Simon
See Kornbluth, C(yril) M.
Ekeloef, (Bengt) Gunnar 1907-1968 **CLC 27;
DAM POET; PC 23**
See also CA 123; 25-28R
Ekelof, (Bengt) Gunnar
See Ekeloef, (Bengt) Gunnar
Ekelund, Vilhelm 1880-1949   **TCLC 75**
Ekwensi, C. O. D.
See Ekwensi, Cyprian (Odiatu Duaka)
Ekwensi, Cyprian (Odiatu Duaka) 1921-**CLC
4; BLC 1; DAM MULT**
See also BW 2, 3; CA 29-32R; CANR 18, 42,
74; DLB 117; MTCW 1, 2; SATA 66
Elaine   **TCLC 18**
See also Leverson, Ada
El Crummo
See Crumb, R(obert)
Elder, Lonne III 1931-1996   **DC 8**
See also BLC 1; BW 1, 3; CA 81-84; 152;
CANR 25; DAM MULT; DLB 7, 38, 44
Elia
See Lamb, Charles
Eliade, Mircea 1907-1986   **CLC 19**
See also CA 65-68; 119; CANR 30, 62; MTCW
1
Eliot, A. D.
See Jewett, (Theodora) Sarah Orne
Eliot, Alice
See Jewett, (Theodora) Sarah Orne
Eliot, Dan
See Silverberg, Robert
Eliot, George 1819-1880 **NCLC 4, 13, 23, 41,
49; DA; DAB; DAC; DAM MST, NOV; PC
20; WLC**
See also CDBLB 1832-1890; DLB 21, 35, 55
Eliot, John 1604-1690   **LC 5**
See also DLB 24
Eliot, T(homas) S(tearns) 1888-1965**CLC 1, 2,
3, 6, 9, 10, 13, 15, 24, 34, 41, 55, 57, 113;
DA; DAB; DAC; DAM DRAM, MST,
POET; PC 5; WLC**
See also AAYA 28; CA 5-8R; 25-28R; CANR
41;CDALB 1929-1941; DLB 7, 10, 45, 63;
DLBY 88; MTCW 1, 2
Elizabeth 1866-1941   **TCLC 41**
Elkin, Stanley L(awrence) 1930-1995 **CLC 4,
6, 9, 14, 27, 51, 91; DAM NOV, POP; SSC
12**
See also CA 9-12R; 148; CANR 8, 46; DLB 2,
28; DLBY 80; INT CANR-8; MTCW 1, 2
Elledge, Scott   **CLC 34**
Elliot, Don
See Silverberg, Robert
Elliott, Don
See Silverberg, Robert
Elliott, George P(aul) 1918-1980   **CLC 2**
See also CA 1-4R; 97-100; CANR 2
Elliott, Janice 1931-   **CLC 47**
See also CA 13-16R; CANR 8, 29; DLB 14
Elliott, Sumner Locke 1917-1991   **CLC 38**
See also CA 5-8R; 134; CANR 2, 21
Elliott, William
See Bradbury, Ray (Douglas)
Ellis, A. E.   **CLC 7**
Ellis, Alice Thomas   **CLC 40**
See also Haycraft, Anna

See also DLB 194; MTCW 1
Ellis, Bret Easton 1964-**CLC 39, 71, 117; DAM
POP**
See also AAYA 2; CA 118; 123; CANR 51, 74;
INT 123; MTCW 1
Ellis, (Henry) Havelock 1859-1939 **TCLC 14**
See also CA 109; 169; DLB 190
Ellis, Landon
See Ellison, Harlan (Jay)
Ellis, Trey 1962-   **CLC 55**
See also CA 146
Ellison, Harlan (Jay) 1934-   **CLC 1, 13, 42;
DAM POP; SSC 14**
See also Jarvis, E. K.
See also AAYA 29; CA 5-8R; CANR 5, 46; DLB
8; INT CANR-5; MTCW 1, 2
Ellison, Ralph (Waldo) 1914-1994 **CLC 1, 3,
11, 54, 86, 114; BLC 1; DA; DAB; DAC;
DAM MST, MULT, NOV; SSC 26;WLC**
See also AAYA 19; BW 1, 3; CA 9-12R; 145;
CANR 24, 53; CDALB 1941-1968; DLB 2,
76; DLBY 94; MTCW 1, 2
Ellmann, Lucy (Elizabeth) 1956-   **CLC 61**
See also CA 128
Ellmann, Richard (David) 1918-1987**CLC 50**
See also BEST 89:2; CA 1-4R; 122; CANR 2,
28, 61; DLB 103; DLBY 87; MTCW 1, 2
Elman, Richard (Martin) 1934-1997 **CLC 19**
See also CA 17-20R; 163; CAAS 3; CANR 47
Elron
See Hubbard, L(afayette) Ron(ald)
Eluard, Paul   **TCLC 7, 41**
See also Grindel, Eugene
Elyot, Sir Thomas 1490(?)-1546   **LC 11**
Elytis, Odysseus 1911-1996 **CLC 15, 49, 100;
DAM POET; PC 21**
See also CA 102; 151; MTCW 1, 2
Emecheta, (Florence Onye) Buchi 1944-**C L C
14, 48; BLC 2; DAM MULT**
See also BW 2, 3; CA 81-84; CANR 27, 81;
DLB 117; MTCW 1, 2; SATA 66
Emerson, Mary Moody 1774-1863 **NCLC 66**
Emerson, Ralph Waldo 1803-1882 **NCLC 1,
38; DA; DAB; DAC; DAM MST, POET;
PC 18; WLC**
See also CDALB 1640-1865; DLB 1, 59, 73
Eminescu, Mihail 1850-1889   **NCLC 33**
Empson, William 1906-1984**CLC 3, 8, 19, 33,
34**
See also CA 17-20R; 112; CANR 31, 61; DLB
20; MTCW 1, 2
Enchi, Fumiko (Ueda) 1905-1986   **CLC 31**
See also CA 129; 121; DLB 182
Ende, Michael (Andreas Helmuth) 1929-1995
CLC 31
See also CA 118; 124; 149; CANR 36; CLR
14; DLB 75; MAICYA; SATA 61; SATA-
Brief 42; SATA-Obit 86
Endo, Shusaku 1923-1996 **CLC 7, 14, 19, 54,
99; DAM NOV**
See also CA 29-32R; 153; CANR 21, 54; DLB
182; MTCW 1, 2
Engel, Marian 1933-1985   **CLC 36**
See also CA 25-28R; CANR 12; DLB 53; INT
CANR-12
Engelhardt, Frederick
See Hubbard, L(afayette) Ron(ald)
Enright, D(ennis) J(oseph) 1920-**CLC 4, 8, 31**
See also CA 1-4R; CANR 1, 42; DLB 27; SATA
25
Enzensberger, Hans Magnus 1929- **CLC 43**
See also CA 116; 119
Ephron, Nora 1941-   **CLC 17, 31**

See also AITN 2; CA 65-68; CANR 12, 39
Epicurus 341B.C.-270B.C.   **CMLC 21**
See also DLB 176
Epsilon
See Betjeman, John
Epstein, Daniel Mark 1948-   **CLC 7**
See also CA 49-52; CANR 2, 53
Epstein, Jacob 1956-   **CLC 19**
See also CA 114
Epstein, Jean 1897-1953   **TCLC 92**
Epstein, Joseph 1937-   **CLC 39**
See also CA 112; 119; CANR 50, 65
Epstein, Leslie 1938-   **CLC 27**
See also CA 73-76; CAAS 12; CANR 23, 69
Equiano, Olaudah 1745(?)-1797 **LC 16; BLC
2; DAM MULT**
See also DLB 37, 50
ER   **TCLC 33**
See also CA 160; DLB 85
Erasmus, Desiderius 1469(?)-1536   **LC 16**
Erdman, Paul E(mil) 1932-   **CLC 25**
See also AITN 1; CA 61-64; CANR 13, 43
Erdrich, Louise 1954-**CLC 39, 54, 120; DAM
MULT, NOV, POP**
See also AAYA 10; BEST 89:1; CA 114; CANR
41, 62; CDALBS; DLB 152, 175, 206;
MTCW 1; NNAL; SATA 94
Erenburg, Ilya (Grigoryevich)
See Ehrenburg, Ilya (Grigoryevich)
Erickson, Stephen Michael 1950-
See Erickson, Steve
See also CA 129
Erickson, Steve 1950-   **CLC 64**
See also Erickson, Stephen Michael
See also CANR 60, 68
Ericson, Walter
See Fast, Howard (Melvin)
Eriksson, Buntel
See Bergman, (Ernst) Ingmar
Ernaux, Annie 1940-   **CLC 88**
See also CA 147
Erskine, John 1879-1951   **TCLC 84**
See also CA 112; 159; DLB 9, 102
Eschenbach, Wolfram von
See Wolfram von Eschenbach
Eseki, Bruno
See Mphahlele, Ezekiel
Esenin, Sergei (Alexandrovich) 1895-1925
TCLC 4
See also CA 104
Eshleman, Clayton 1935-   **CLC 7**
See also CA 33-36R; CAAS 6; DLB 5
Espriella, Don Manuel Alvarez
See Southey, Robert
Espriu, Salvador 1913-1985   **CLC 9**
See also CA 154; 115; DLB 134
Espronceda, Jose de 1808-1842   **NCLC 39**
Esquivel, Laura 1951(?)-
See also AAYA 29; CA 143; CANR 68; HLCS
1; MTCW 1
Esse, James
See Stephens, James
Esterbrook, Tom
See Hubbard, L(afayette) Ron(ald)
Estleman, Loren D. 1952-**CLC 48; DAM NOV,
POP**
See also AAYA 27; CA 85-88; CANR 27, 74;
INT CANR-27; MTCW 1, 2
Euclid 306B.C.-283B.C.   **CMLC 25**
Eugenides, Jeffrey 1960(?)-   **CLC 81**
See also CA 144
Euripides c. 485B.C.-406B.C.**CMLC 23; DA;
DAB; DAC; DAM DRAM, MST; DC 4;**

WLCS
See also DLB 176
Evan, Evin
See Faust, Frederick (Schiller)
Evans, Caradoc 1878-1945   **TCLC 85**
Evans, Evan
See Faust, Frederick (Schiller)
Evans, Marian
See Eliot, George
Evans, Mary Ann
See Eliot, George
Evarts, Esther
See Benson, Sally
Everett, Percival L. 1956-   **CLC 57**
See also BW 2; CA 129
Everson, R(onald) G(ilmour) 1903-   **CLC 27**
See also CA 17-20R; DLB 88
Everson, William (Oliver) 1912-1994 **CLC 1,
5, 14**
See also CA 9-12R; 145; CANR 20; DLB 212;
MTCW 1
Evtushenko, Evgenii Aleksandrovich
See Yevtushenko, Yevgeny (Alexandrovich)
Ewart, Gavin (Buchanan) 1916-1995**CLC 13,
46**
See also CA 89-92; 150; CANR 17, 46; DLB
40; MTCW 1
Ewers, Hanns Heinz 1871-1943   **TCLC 12**
See also CA 109; 149
Ewing, Frederick R.
See Sturgeon, Theodore (Hamilton)
Exley, Frederick (Earl) 1929-1992 **CLC 6, 11**
See also AITN 2; CA 81-84; 138; DLB 143;
DLBY 81
Eynhardt, Guillermo
See Quiroga, Horacio (Sylvestre)
Ezekiel, Nissim 1924-   **CLC 61**
See also CA 61-64
Ezekiel, Tish O'Dowd 1943-   **CLC 34**
See also CA 129
Fadeyev, A.
See Bulgya, Alexander Alexandrovich
Fadeyev, Alexander   **TCLC 53**
See also Bulgya, Alexander Alexandrovich
Fagen, Donald 1948-   **CLC 26**
Fainzilberg, Ilya Arnoldovich 1897-1937
See Ilf, Ilya
See also CA 120; 165
Fair, Ronald L. 1932-   **CLC 18**
See also BW 1; CA 69-72; CANR 25; DLB 33
Fairbairn, Roger
See Carr, John Dickson
Fairbairns, Zoe (Ann) 1948-   **CLC 32**
See also CA 103; CANR 21
Falco, Gian
See Papini, Giovanni
Falconer, James
See Kirkup, James
Falconer, Kenneth
See Kornbluth, C(yril) M.
Falkland, Samuel
See Heijermans, Herman
Fallaci, Oriana 1930-   **CLC 11, 110**
See also CA 77-80; CANR 15, 58; MTCW 1
Faludy, George 1913-   **CLC 42**
See also CA 21-24R
Faludy, Gyoergy
See Faludy, George
Fanon, Frantz 1925-1961   **CLC 74; BLC 2;
DAM MULT**
See also BW 1; CA 116; 89-92
Fanshawe, Ann 1625-1680   **LC 11**
Fante, John (Thomas) 1911-1983   **CLC 60**

See also CA 69-72; 109; CANR 23; DLB 130;
DLBY 83
Farah, Nuruddin 1945-**CLC 53; BLC 2; DAM
MULT**
See also BW 2, 3; CA 106; CANR 81; DLB
125
Fargue, Leon-Paul 1876(?)-1947   **TCLC 11**
See also CA 109
Farigoule, Louis
See Romains, Jules
Farina, Richard 1936(?)-1966   **CLC 9**
See also CA 81-84; 25-28R
Farley, Walter (Lorimer) 1915-1989 **CLC 17**
See also CA 17-20R; CANR 8, 29; DLB 22;
JRDA; MAICYA; SATA 2, 43
Farmer, Philip Jose 1918-   **CLC 1, 19**
See also AAYA 28; CA 1-4R; CANR 4, 35; DLB
8; MTCW 1; SATA 93
Farquhar, George 1677-1707   **LC 21;DAM
DRAM**
See also DLB 84
Farrell, J(ames) G(ordon) 1935-1979 **CLC 6**
See also CA 73-76; 89-92; CANR 36; DLB 14;
MTCW 1
Farrell, James T(homas) 1904-1979**CLC 1, 4,
8, 11, 66; SSC 28**
See also CA 5-8R; 89-92; CANR 9, 61; DLB 4,
9, 86; DLBD 2; MTCW 1, 2
Farren, Richard J.
See Betjeman, John
Farren, Richard M.
See Betjeman, John
Fassbinder, Rainer Werner 1946-1982**CLC 20**
See also CA 93-96; 106; CANR 31
Fast, Howard (Melvin) 1914-   **CLC 23; DAM
NOV**
See also AAYA 16; CA 1-4R; CAAS 18; CANR
1, 33, 54, 75; DLB 9; INT CANR-33; MTCW
1; SATA 7; SATA-Essay 107
Faulcon, Robert
See Holdstock, Robert P.
Faulkner, William (Cuthbert) 1897-1962**CLC
1, 3, 6, 8, 9, 11, 14, 18, 28, 52, 68; DA; DAB;
DAC; DAM MST, NOV; SSC 1, 35; WLC**
See also AAYA 7; CA 81-84; CANR 33;
CDALB 1929-1941; DLB 9, 11, 44, 102;
DLBD 2; DLBY 86, 97; MTCW 1, 2
Fauset, Jessie Redmon 1884(?)-1961**CLC 19,
54; BLC 2; DAM MULT**
See also BW 1; CA 109; DLB 51
Faust, Frederick (Schiller) 1892-1944(?)
TCLC 49; DAM POP
See also CA 108; 152
Faust, Irvin 1924-   **CLC 8**
See also CA 33-36R; CANR 28, 67; DLB 2,
28; DLBY 80
Fawkes, Guy
See Benchley, Robert (Charles)
Fearing, Kenneth (Flexner) 1902-1961 **C L C
51**
See also CA 93-96; CANR 59; DLB 9
Fecamps, Elise
See Creasey, John
Federman, Raymond 1928-   **CLC 6,47**
See also CA 17-20R; CAAS 8; CANR 10, 43;
DLBY 80
Federspiel, J(uerg) F. 1931-   **CLC 42**
See also CA 146
Feiffer, Jules (Ralph) 1929-   **CLC 2, 8, 64;
DAM DRAM**
See also AAYA 3; CA 17-20R; CANR 30, 59;
DLB 7, 44; INT CANR-30; MTCW 1; SATA
8, 61

Feige, Hermann Albert Otto Maximilian
See Traven, B.

Feinberg, David B. 1956-1994   **CLC 59**
See also CA 135; 147

Feinstein, Elaine 1930-   **CLC 36**
See also CA 69-72; CAAS 1; CANR 31, 68;
DLB 14, 40; MTCW 1

Feldman, Irving (Mordecai) 1928-   **CLC 7**
See also CA 1-4R; CANR 1; DLB 169

Felix-Tchicaya, Gerald
See Tchicaya, Gerald Felix

Fellini, Federico 1920-1993   **CLC 16, 85**
See also CA 65-68; 143; CANR 33

Felsen, Henry Gregor 1916-   **CLC 17**
See also CA 1-4R; CANR 1; SAAS 2; SATA 1

Fenno, Jack
See Calisher, Hortense

Fenollosa, Ernest (Francisco) 1853-1908
TCLC 91

Fenton, James Martin 1949-   **CLC 32**
See also CA 102; DLB 40

Ferber, Edna 1887-1968   **CLC 18, 93**
See also AITN 1; CA 5-8R; 25-28R; CANR 68;
DLB 9, 28, 86; MTCW 1, 2; SATA 7

Ferguson, Helen
See Kavan, Anna

Ferguson, Samuel 1810-1886   **NCLC 33**
See also DLB 32

Fergusson, Robert 1750-1774   **LC 29**
See also DLB 109

Ferling, Lawrence
See Ferlinghetti, Lawrence (Monsanto)

Ferlinghetti, Lawrence (Monsanto) 1919(?)-
CLC 2, 6, 10, 27, 111; DAM POET; PC 1
See also CA 5-8R; CANR 3, 41, 73; CDALB
1941-1968; DLB 5, 16; MTCW 1, 2

Fernandez, Vicente Garcia Huidobro
See Huidobro Fernandez, Vicente Garcia

Ferre, Rosario 1942-
See also CA 131; CANR 55, 81; DLB 145;
HLCS 1; HW 1, 2; MTCW 1

Ferrer, Gabriel (Francisco Victor) Miro
See Miro (Ferrer), Gabriel (Francisco Victor)

Ferrier, Susan (Edmonstone) 1782-1854
NCLC 8
See also DLB 116

Ferrigno, Robert 1948(?)-   **CLC 65**
See also CA 140

Ferron, Jacques 1921-1985   **CLC 94; DAC**
See also CA 117; 129; DLB 60

Feuchtwanger, Lion 1884-1958   **TCLC 3**
See also CA 104; DLB 66

Feuillet, Octave 1821-1890   **NCLC 45**
See also DLB 192

Feydeau, Georges (Leon Jules Marie) 1862-
1921   **TCLC 22; DAM DRAM**
See also CA 113; 152; DLB 192

Fichte, Johann Gottlieb 1762-1814 **NCLC 62**
See also DLB 90

Ficino, Marsilio 1433-1499   **LC 12**

Fiedeler, Hans
See Doeblin, Alfred

Fiedler, Leslie A(aron) 1917-   **CLC 4, 13, 24**
See also CA 9-12R; CANR 7, 63; DLB 28, 67;
MTCW 1, 2

Field, Andrew 1938-   **CLC 44**
See also CA 97-100; CANR 25

Field, Eugene 1850-1895   **NCLC 3**
See also DLB 23, 42, 140; DLBD 13; MAICYA;
SATA 16

Field, Gans T.
See Wellman, Manly Wade

Field, Michael 1915-1971   **TCLC 43**

See also CA 29-32R
Field, Peter
See Hobson, Laura Z(ametkin)

Fielding, Henry 1707-1754   **LC 1, 46; DA;
DAB; DAC; DAM DRAM, MST, NOV;
WLC**
See also CDBLB 1660-1789; DLB 39, 84, 101

Fielding, Sarah 1710-1768   **LC 1, 44**
See also DLB 39

Fields, W. C. 1880-1946   **TCLC 80**
See also DLB 44

Fierstein, Harvey (Forbes) 1954-   **CLC 33;
DAM DRAM, POP**
See also CA 123; 129

Figes, Eva 1932-   **CLC 31**
See also CA 53-56; CANR 4, 44; DLB 14

Finch, Anne 1661-1720   **LC 3; PC 21**
See also DLB 95

Finch, Robert (Duer Claydon) 1900- **CLC 18**
See also CA 57-60; CANR 9, 24, 49; DLB 88

Findley, Timothy 1930- **CLC 27, 102; DAC;
DAM MST**
See also CA 25-28R; CANR 12, 42, 69; DLB
53

Fink, William
See Mencken, H(enry) L(ouis)

Firbank, Louis 1942-
See Reed, Lou
See also CA 117

Firbank, (Arthur Annesley) Ronald 1886-1926
TCLC 1
See also CA 104; 177; DLB 36

Fisher, Dorothy (Frances) Canfield 1879-1958
TCLC 87
See also CA 114; 136; CANR 80; DLB 9, 102;
MAICYA; YABC 1

Fisher, M(ary) F(rances) K(ennedy) 1908-1992
CLC 76, 87
See also CA 77-80; 138; CANR 44; MTCW 1

Fisher, Roy 1930-   **CLC 25**
See also CA 81-84; CAAS 10; CANR 16; DLB
40

Fisher, Rudolph 1897-1934 **TCLC 11; BLC 2;
DAM MULT; SSC 25**
See also BW 1, 3; CA 107; 124; CANR 80; DLB
51, 102

Fisher, Vardis (Alvero) 1895-1968   **CLC 7**
See also CA 5-8R; 25-28R; CANR 68; DLB 9,
206

Fiske, Tarleton 1917-1994
See Bloch, Robert (Albert)
See also CA 179; CAAE 179

Fitch, Clarke
See Sinclair, Upton (Beall)

Fitch, John IV
See Cormier, Robert (Edmund)

Fitzgerald, Captain Hugh
See Baum, L(yman) Frank

FitzGerald, Edward 1809-1883   **NCLC 9**
See also DLB 32

Fitzgerald, F(rancis) Scott (Key) 1896-1940
**TCLC 1, 6, 14, 28, 55; DA; DAB; DAC;
DAM MST, NOV; SSC 6, 31; WLC**
See also AAYA 24; AITN 1; CA 110; 123;
CDALB 1917-1929; DLB 4, 9, 86; DLBD 1,
15, 16; DLBY 81, 96; MTCW 1, 2

Fitzgerald, Penelope 1916-   **CLC 19, 51, 61**
See also CA 85-88; CAAS 10; CANR 56; DLB
14, 194; MTCW 2

Fitzgerald, Robert (Stuart) 1910-1985 **CLC 39**
See also CA 1-4R; 114; CANR 1; DLBY 80

FitzGerald, Robert D(avid) 1902-1987 **CLC 19**
See also CA 17-20R

Fitzgerald, Zelda (Sayre) 1900-1948 **TCLC 52**
See also CA 117; 126; DLBY 84

Flanagan, Thomas (James Bonner) 1923-
CLC 25, 52
See also CA 108; CANR 55; DLBY 80; INT
108; MTCW 1

Flaubert, Gustave 1821-1880 **NCLC 2, 10, 19,
62, 66; DA; DAB; DAC; DAM MST, NOV;
SSC 11; WLC**
See also DLB 119

Flecker, Herman Elroy
See Flecker, (Herman) James Elroy

Flecker, (Herman) James Elroy 1884-1915
TCLC 43
See also CA 109; 150; DLB 10, 19

Fleming, Ian (Lancaster) 1908-1964   **CLC 3,
30; DAM POP**
See also AAYA 26; CA 5-8R; CANR
59; CDBLB 1945-1960; DLB 87, 201;
MTCW 1, 2; SATA 9

Fleming, Thomas (James) 1927-   **CLC 37**
See also CA 5-8R; CANR 10; INT CANR-10;
SATA 8

Fletcher, John 1579-1625   **LC 33; DC 6**
See also CDBLB Before 1660; DLB 58

Fletcher, John Gould 1886-1950   **TCLC 35**
See also CA 107; 167; DLB 4, 45

Fleur, Paul
See Pohl, Frederik

Flooglebuckle, Al
See Spiegelman, Art

Flying Officer X
See Bates, H(erbert) E(rnest)

Fo, Dario 1926- **CLC 32, 109; DAM DRAM;
DC 10**
See also CA 116; 128; CANR 68; DLBY 97;
MTCW 1, 2

Fogarty, Jonathan Titulescu Esq.
See Farrell, James T(homas)

Folke, Will 1917-1994
See Bloch, Robert (Albert); Bloch, Robert
(Albert)
See also CA 179; CAAE 179

Follett, Ken(neth Martin) 1949-   **CLC 18;
DAM NOV, POP**
See also AAYA 6; BEST 89:4; CA 81-84; CANR
13, 33, 54; DLB 87; DLBY 81; INT CANR-
33; MTCW 1

Fontane, Theodor 1819-1898   **NCLC 26**
See also DLB 129

Foote, Horton 1916- **CLC 51, 91; DAM DRAM**
See also CA 73-76; CANR 34, 51; DLB 26; INT
CANR-34

Foote, Shelby 1916- **CLC 75; DAM NOV, POP**
See also CA 5-8R; CANR 3, 45, 74; DLB 2,
17; MTCW 2

Forbes, Esther 1891-1967   **CLC 12**
See also AAYA 17; CA 13-14; 25-28R; CAP 1;
CLR 27; DLB 22; JRDA; MAICYA; SATA
2, 100

Forche, Carolyn (Louise) 1950- **CLC 25, 83,
86; DAM POET; PC 10**
See also CA 109; 117; CANR 50, 74; DLB 5,
193; INT 117; MTCW 1

Ford, Elbur
See Hibbert, Eleanor Alice Burford

Ford, Ford Madox 1873-1939 **TCLC 1, 15, 39,
57; DAM NOV**
See also CA 104; 132; CANR 74; CDBLB
1914-1945; DLB 162; MTCW 1, 2

Ford, Henry 1863-1947   **TCLC 73**
See also CA 115; 148

Ford, John 1586-(?)   **DC 8**

See also CDBLB Before 1660; DAM DRAM; DLB 58

Ford, John 1895-1973 **CLC 16**
See also CA 45-48

Ford, Richard 1944- **CLC 46, 99**
See also CA 69-72; CANR 11, 47; MTCW 1

Ford, Webster
See Masters, Edgar Lee

Foreman, Richard 1937- **CLC 50**
See also CA 65-68; CANR 32, 63

Forester, C(ecil) S(cott) 1899-1966 **CLC 35**
See also CA 73-76; 25-28R; DLB 191; SATA 13

Forez
See Mauriac, Francois (Charles)

Forman, James Douglas 1932- **CLC 21**
See also AAYA 17; CA 9-12R; CANR 4, 19, 42; JRDA; MAICYA; SATA 8, 70

Fornes, Maria Irene 1930-**CLC 39, 61; DC 10; HLCS 1**
See also CA 25-28R; CANR 28, 81; DLB 7; HW 1, 2; INT CANR-28; MTCW 1

Forrest, Leon (Richard) 1937-1997 **CLC 4; BLCS**
See also BW 2; CA 89-92; 162; CAAS 7; CANR 25, 52; DLB 33

Forster, E(dward) M(organ) 1879-1970 **C L C 1, 2, 3, 4, 9, 10, 13, 15, 22, 45, 77; DA; DAB; DAC; DAM MST, NOV; SSC 27;WLC**
See also AAYA 2; CA 13-14; 25-28R; CANR 45; CAP 1; CDBLB 1914-1945; DLB 34, 98, 162, 178, 195; DLBD 10; MTCW 1, 2; SATA 57

Forster, John 1812-1876 **NCLC 11**
See also DLB 144, 184

Forsyth, Frederick 1938- **CLC 2, 5, 36; DAM NOV, POP**
See also BEST 89:4; CA 85-88; CANR 38, 62; DLB 87; MTCW 1, 2

Forten, Charlotte L. **TCLC 16; BLC 2**
See also Grimke, Charlotte L(ottie) Forten
See also DLB 50

Foscolo, Ugo 1778-1827 **NCLC 8**

Fosse, Bob **CLC 20**
See also Fosse, Robert Louis

Fosse, Robert Louis 1927-1987
See Fosse, Bob
See also CA 110; 123

Foster, Stephen Collins 1826-1864 **NCLC 26**

Foucault, Michel 1926-1984 **CLC 31, 34, 69**
See also CA 105; 113; CANR 34; MTCW 1, 2

Fouque, Friedrich (Heinrich Karl) de la Motte 1777-1843 **NCLC 2**
See also DLB 90

Fourier, Charles 1772-1837 **NCLC 51**

Fournier, Henri Alban 1886-1914
See Alain-Fournier
See also CA 104

Fournier, Pierre 1916- **CLC 11**
See also Gascar, Pierre
See also CA 89-92; CANR 16, 40

Fowles, John (Philip) 1926-**CLC 1, 2, 3, 4, 6, 9, 10, 15, 33, 87; DAB; DAC; DAM MST; SSC 33**
See also CA 5-8R; CANR 25, 71; CDBLB 1960 to Present; DLB 14, 139, 207; MTCW 1, 2; SATA 22

Fox, Paula 1923- **CLC 2, 8, 121**
See also AAYA 3; CA 73-76; CANR 20, 36, 62; CLR 1, 44; DLB 52; JRDA; MAICYA; MTCW 1; SATA 17, 60

Fox, William Price (Jr.) 1926- **CLC 22**
See also CA 17-20R; CAAS 19; CANR 11; DLB

2; DLBY 81

Foxe, John 1516(?)-1587 **LC 14**
See also DLB 132

Frame, Janet 1924-**CLC 2, 3, 6, 22, 66, 96; SSC 29**
See also Clutha, Janet Paterson Frame

France, Anatole **TCLC 9**
See also Thibault, Jacques Anatole Francois
See also DLB 123; MTCW 1

Francis, Claude 19(?)- **CLC 50**

Francis, Dick 1920-**CLC 2, 22, 42, 102; DAM POP**
See also AAYA 5, 21; BEST 89:3; CA 5-8R; CANR 9, 42, 68; CDBLB 1960 to Present; DLB 87; INT CANR-9; MTCW 1, 2

Francis, Robert (Churchill) 1901-1987 **C L C 15**
See also CA 1-4R; 123; CANR 1

Frank, Anne(lies Marie) 1929-1945**TCLC 17; DA; DAB; DAC; DAM MST; WLC**
See also AAYA 12; CA 113; 133; CANR 68; MTCW 1, 2; SATA 87; SATA-Brief 42

Frank, Bruno 1887-1945 **TCLC 81**
See also DLB 118

Frank, Elizabeth 1945- **CLC 39**
See also CA 121; 126; CANR 78; INT 126

Frankl, Viktor E(mil) 1905-1997 **CLC 93**
See also CA 65-68; 161

Franklin, Benjamin
See Hasek, Jaroslav (Matej Frantisek)

Franklin, Benjamin 1706-1790 **LC 25; DA; DAB; DAC; DAM MST; WLCS**
See also CDALB 1640-1865; DLB 24, 43, 73

Franklin, (Stella Maria Sarah) Miles (Lampe) 1879-1954 **TCLC 7**
See also CA 104; 164

Fraser, (Lady) Antonia (Pakenham) 1932- **CLC 32, 107**
See also CA 85-88; CANR 44, 65; MTCW 1, 2; SATA-Brief 32

Fraser, George MacDonald 1925- **CLC 7**
See also CA 45-48; CANR 2, 48, 74; MTCW 1

Fraser, Sylvia 1935- **CLC 64**
See also CA 45-48; CANR 1, 16, 60

Frayn, Michael 1933-**CLC 3, 7, 31, 47; DAM DRAM, NOV**
See also CA 5-8R; CANR 30, 69; DLB 13, 14, 194; MTCW 1, 2

Fraze, Candida (Merrill) 1945- **CLC 50**
See also CA 126

Frazer, J(ames) G(eorge) 1854-1941**TCLC 32**
See also CA 118

Frazer, Robert Caine
See Creasey, John

Frazer, Sir James George
See Frazer, J(ames) G(eorge)

Frazier, Charles 1950- **CLC 109**
See also CA 161

Frazier, Ian 1951- **CLC 46**
See also CA 130; CANR 54

Frederic, Harold 1856-1898 **NCLC 10**
See also DLB 12, 23; DLBD 13

Frederick, John
See Faust, Frederick (Schiller)

Frederick the Great 1712-1786 **LC 14**

Fredro, Aleksander 1793-1876 **NCLC 8**

Freeling, Nicolas 1927- **CLC 38**
See also CA 49-52; CAAS 12; CANR 1, 17, 50; DLB 87

Freeman, Douglas Southall 1886-1953 **T C L C 11**
See also CA 109; DLB 17; DLBD 17

Freeman, Judith 1946- **CLC 55**

See also CA 148

Freeman, Mary Eleanor Wilkins 1852-1930 **TCLC 9; SSC 1**
See also CA 106; 177; DLB 12, 78

Freeman, R(ichard) Austin 1862-1943 **T C L C 21**
See also CA 113; DLB 70

French, Albert 1943- **CLC 86**
See also BW 3; CA 167

French, Marilyn 1929-**CLC 10, 18, 60; DAM DRAM, NOV, POP**
See also CA 69-72; CANR 3, 31; INT CANR-31; MTCW 1, 2

French, Paul
See Asimov, Isaac

Freneau, Philip Morin 1752-1832 **NCLC 1**
See also DLB 37, 43

Freud, Sigmund 1856-1939 **TCLC 52**
See also CA 115; 133; CANR 69; MTCW 1, 2

Friedan, Betty (Naomi) 1921- **CLC 74**
See also CA 65-68; CANR 18, 45, 74; MTCW 1, 2

Friedlander, Saul 1932- **CLC 90**
See also CA 117; 130; CANR 72

Friedman, B(ernard) H(arper) 1926- **CLC 7**
See also CA 1-4R; CANR 3, 48

Friedman, Bruce Jay 1930- **CLC 3, 5, 56**
See also CA 9-12R; CANR 25, 52; DLB 2, 28; INT CANR-25

Friel, Brian 1929- **CLC 5, 42, 59, 115; DC 8**
See also CA 21-24R; CANR 33, 69; DLB 13; MTCW 1

Friis-Baastad, Babbis Ellinor 1921-1970**C L C 12**
See also CA 17-20R; 134; SATA 7

Frisch, Max (Rudolf) 1911-1991**CLC 3, 9, 14, 18, 32, 44; DAM DRAM, NOV**
See also CA 85-88; 134; CANR 32, 74; DLB 69, 124; MTCW 1, 2

Fromentin, Eugene (Samuel Auguste) 1820-1876 **NCLC 10**
See also DLB 123

Frost, Frederick
See Faust, Frederick (Schiller)

Frost, Robert (Lee) 1874-1963**CLC 1, 3, 4, 9, 10, 13, 15, 26, 34, 44; DA; DAB; DAC; DAM MST, POET; PC 1; WLC**
See also AAYA 21; CA 89-92; CANR 33; CDALB 1917-1929; DLB 54; DLBD 7; MTCW 1, 2; SATA 14

Froude, James Anthony 1818-1894 **NCLC 43**
See also DLB 18, 57, 144

Froy, Herald
See Waterhouse, Keith (Spencer)

Fry, Christopher 1907- **CLC 2, 10, 14; DAM DRAM**
See also CA 17-20R; CAAS 23; CANR 9, 30, 74; DLB 13; MTCW 1, 2; SATA 66

Frye, (Herman) Northrop 1912-1991**CLC 24, 70**
See also CA 5-8R; 133; CANR 8, 37; DLB 67, 68; MTCW 1, 2

Fuchs, Daniel 1909-1993 **CLC 8, 22**
See also CA 81-84; 142; CAAS 5; CANR 40; DLB 9, 26, 28; DLBY 93

Fuchs, Daniel 1934- **CLC 34**
See also CA 37-40R; CANR 14, 48

Fuentes, Carlos 1928-**CLC 3, 8, 10, 13, 22, 41, 60, 113; DA; DAB; DAC; DAM MST, MULT, NOV; HLC 1; SSC 24;WLC**
See also AAYA 4; AITN 2; CA 69-72; CANR 10, 32, 68; DLB 113; HW 1, 2; MTCW 1, 2

Fuentes, Gregorio Lopez y

See Lopez y Fuentes, Gregorio
Fuertes, Gloria 1918- **PC 27**
See also CA 178; DLB 108; HW 2
Fugard, (Harold) Athol 1932-**CLC 5, 9, 14, 25, 40, 80; DAM DRAM; DC 3**
See also AAYA 17; CA 85-88; CANR 32, 54; MTCW 1
Fugard, Sheila 1932- **CLC 48**
See also CA 125
Fuller, Charles (H., Jr.) 1939-**CLC 25; BLC 2; DAM DRAM, MULT; DC 1**
See also BW 2; CA 108; 112; DLB 38; INT 112; MTCW 1
Fuller, John (Leopold) 1937- **CLC 62**
See also CA 21-24R; CANR 9, 44; DLB 40
Fuller, Margaret **NCLC 5, 50**
See also Ossoli, Sarah Margaret (Fuller marchesa d')
Fuller, Roy (Broadbent) 1912-1991**CLC 4, 28**
See also CA 5-8R; 135; CAAS 10; CANR 53; DLB 15, 20; SATA 87
Fulton, Alice 1952- **CLC 52**
See also CA 116; CANR 57; DLB 193
Furphy, Joseph 1843-1912 **TCLC 25**
See also CA 163
Fussell, Paul 1924- **CLC 74**
See also BEST 90:1; CA 17-20R; CANR 8, 21, 35, 69; INT CANR-21; MTCW 1, 2
Futabatei, Shimei 1864-1909 **TCLC 44**
See also CA 162; DLB 180
Futrelle, Jacques 1875-1912 **TCLC 19**
See also CA 113; 155
Gaboriau, Emile 1835-1873 **NCLC 14**
Gadda, Carlo Emilio 1893-1973 **CLC 11**
See also CA 89-92; DLB 177
Gaddis, William 1922-1998**CLC 1, 3, 6, 8, 10, 19, 43, 86**
See also CA 17-20R; 172; CANR 21, 48; DLB 2; MTCW 1, 2
Gage, Walter
See Inge, William (Motter)
Gaines, Ernest J(ames) 1933- **CLC 3, 11, 18, 86; BLC 2; DAM MULT**
See also AAYA 18; AITN 1; BW 2, 3; CA 9-12R; CANR 6, 24, 42, 75; CDALB 1968-1988; DLB 2, 33, 152; DLBY 80; MTCW 1, 2; SATA 86
Gaitskill, Mary 1954- **CLC 69**
See also CA 128; CANR 61
Galdos, Benito Perez
See Perez Galdos, Benito
Gale, Zona 1874-1938 **TCLC 7;DAM DRAM**
See also CA 105; 153; DLB 9, 78
Galeano, Eduardo (Hughes) 1940- **CLC 72; HLCS 1**
See also CA 29-32R; CANR 13, 32; HW 1
Galiano, Juan Valera y Alcala
See Valera y Alcala-Galiano, Juan
Galilei, Galileo 1546-1642 **LC 45**
Gallagher, Tess 1943- **CLC 18, 63; DAM POET; PC 9**
See also CA 106; DLB 212
Gallant, Mavis 1922- **CLC 7, 18, 38; DAC; DAM MST; SSC 5**
See also CA 69-72; CANR 29, 69; DLB 53; MTCW 1, 2
Gallant, Roy A(rthur) 1924- **CLC 17**
See also CA 5-8R; CANR 4, 29, 54; CLR 30; MAICYA; SATA 4, 68
Gallico, Paul (William) 1897-1976 **CLC 2**
See also AITN 1; CA 5-8R; 69-72; CANR 23; DLB 9, 171; MAICYA; SATA 13
Gallo, Max Louis 1932- **CLC 95**

See also CA 85-88
Gallois, Lucien
See Desnos, Robert
Gallup, Ralph
See Whitemore, Hugh (John)
Galsworthy, John 1867-1933**TCLC 1, 45; DA; DAB; DAC; DAM DRAM, MST, NOV; SSC 22; WLC**
See also CA 104; 141; CANR 75; CDBLB 1890-1914; DLB 10, 34, 98, 162; DLBD 16; MTCW 1
Galt, John 1779-1839 **NCLC 1**
See also DLB 99, 116, 159
Galvin, James 1951- **CLC 38**
See also CA 108; CANR 26
Gamboa, Federico 1864-1939 **TCLC 36**
See also CA 167; HW 2
Gandhi, M. K.
See Gandhi, Mohandas Karamchand
Gandhi, Mahatma
See Gandhi, Mohandas Karamchand
Gandhi, Mohandas Karamchand 1869-1948 **TCLC 59; DAM MULT**
See also CA 121; 132; MTCW 1, 2
Gann, Ernest Kellogg 1910-1991 **CLC 23**
See also AITN 1; CA 1-4R; 136; CANR 1
Garcia, Cristina 1958- **CLC 76**
See also CA 141; CANR 73; HW 2
Garcia Lorca, Federico 1898-1936**TCLC 1, 7, 49; DA; DAB; DAC; DAM DRAM, MST, MULT, POET; DC 2; HLC 2; PC 3; WLC**
See also CA 104; 131; CANR 81; DLB 108; HW 1, 2; MTCW 1, 2
Garcia Marquez, Gabriel (Jose) 1928-**CLC 2, 3, 8, 10, 15, 27, 47, 55, 68; DA; DAB; DAC; DAM MST, MULT, NOV, POP; HLC 1; SSC 8; WLC**
See also AAYA 3; BEST 89:1, 90:4; CA 33-36R; CANR 10, 28, 50, 75, 82; DLB 113; HW 1, 2; MTCW 1, 2
Garcilaso de la Vega, El Inca 1503-1536
See also HLCS 1
Gard, Janice
See Latham, Jean Lee
Gard, Roger Martin du
See Martin du Gard, Roger
Gardam, Jane 1928- **CLC 43**
See also CA 49-52; CANR 2, 18, 33, 54; CLR 12; DLB 14, 161; MAICYA; MTCW 1; SAAS 9; SATA 39, 76; SATA-Brief 28
Gardner, Herb(ert) 1934- **CLC 44**
See also CA 149
Gardner, John (Champlin), Jr. 1933-1982 **CLC 2, 3, 5, 7, 8, 10, 18, 28, 34; DAM NOV, POP; SSC 7**
See also AITN 1; CA 65-68; 107; CANR 33, 73; CDALBS; DLB 2; DLBY 82; MTCW 1; SATA 40; SATA-Obit 31
Gardner, John (Edmund) 1926-**CLC 30; DAM POP**
See also CA 103; CANR 15, 69; MTCW 1
Gardner, Miriam
See Bradley, Marion Zimmer
Gardner, Noel
See Kuttner, Henry
Gardons, S. S.
See Snodgrass, W(illiam) D(e Witt)
Garfield, Leon 1921-1996 **CLC 12**
See also AAYA 8; CA 17-20R; 152; CANR 38, 41, 78; CLR 21; DLB 161; JRDA; MAICYA; SATA 1, 32, 76; SATA-Obit 90
Garland, (Hannibal) Hamlin 1860-1940 **TCLC 3; SSC 18**

See also CA 104; DLB 12, 71, 78, 186
Garneau, (Hector de) Saint-Denys 1912-1943 **TCLC 13**
See also CA 111; DLB 88
Garner, Alan 1934-**CLC 17; DAB;DAM POP**
See also AAYA 18; CA 73-76, 178; CAAE 178; CANR 15, 64; CLR 20; DLB 161; MAICYA; MTCW 1, 2; SATA 18, 69; SATA-Essay 108
Garner, Hugh 1913-1979 **CLC 13**
See also CA 69-72; CANR 31; DLB 68
Garnett, David 1892-1981 **CLC 3**
See also CA 5-8R; 103; CANR 17, 79; DLB 34; MTCW 2
Garos, Stephanie
See Katz, Steve
Garrett, George (Palmer) 1929-**CLC 3, 11, 51; SSC 30**
See also CA 1-4R; CAAS 5; CANR 1, 42, 67; DLB 2, 5, 130, 152; DLBY 83
Garrick, David 1717-1779**LC 15;DAM DRAM**
See also DLB 84
Garrigue, Jean 1914-1972 **CLC 2, 8**
See also CA 5-8R; 37-40R; CANR 20
Garrison, Frederick
See Sinclair, Upton (Beall)
Garro, Elena 1920(?)-1998
See also CA 131; 169; DLB 145; HLCS 1; HW 1
Garth, Will
See Hamilton, Edmond; Kuttner, Henry
Garvey, Marcus (Moziah, Jr.) 1887-1940 **TCLC 41; BLC 2; DAM MULT**
See also BW 1; CA 120; 124; CANR 79
Gary, Romain **CLC 25**
See also Kacew, Romain
See also DLB 83
Gascar, Pierre **CLC 11**
See also Fournier, Pierre
Gascoyne, David (Emery) 1916- **CLC 45**
See also CA 65-68; CANR 10, 28, 54; DLB 20; MTCW 1
Gaskell, Elizabeth Cleghorn 1810-1865**NCLC 70; DAB; DAM MST; SSC 25**
See also CDBLB 1832-1890; DLB 21, 144, 159
Gass, William H(oward) 1924-**CLC 1, 2, 8, 11, 15, 39; SSC 12**
See also CA 17-20R; CANR 30, 71; DLB 2; MTCW 1, 2
Gasset, Jose Ortega y
See Ortega y Gasset, Jose
Gates, Henry Louis, Jr. 1950-**CLC 65; BLCS; DAM MULT**
See also BW 2, 3; CA 109; CANR 25, 53, 75; DLB 67; MTCW 1
Gautier, Theophile 1811-1872 **NCLC 1, 59; DAM POET; PC 18; SSC 20**
See also DLB 119
Gawsworth, John
See Bates, H(erbert) E(rnest)
Gay, John 1685-1732 **LC 49;DAM DRAM**
See also DLB 84, 95
Gay, Oliver
See Gogarty, Oliver St. John
Gaye, Marvin (Penze) 1939-1984 **CLC 26**
See also CA 112
Gebler, Carlo (Ernest) 1954- **CLC 39**
See also CA 119; 133
Gee, Maggie (Mary) 1948- **CLC 57**
See also CA 130; DLB 207
Gee, Maurice (Gough) 1931- **CLC 29**
See also CA 97-100; CANR 67; CLR 56; SATA 46, 101
Gelbart, Larry (Simon) 1923- **CLC 21, 61**

See also CA 73-76; CANR 45

Gelber, Jack 1932-   **CLC 1, 6, 14, 79**
See also CA 1-4R; CANR 2; DLB 7

Gellhorn, Martha (Ellis) 1908-1998 **CLC 14, 60**
See also CA 77-80; 164; CANR 44; DLBY 82, 98

Genet, Jean 1910-1986**CLC 1, 2, 5, 10, 14, 44, 46; DAM DRAM**
See also CA 13-16R; CANR 18; DLB 72; DLBY 86; MTCW 1, 2

Gent, Peter 1942-   **CLC 29**
See also AITN 1; CA 89-92; DLBY 82

Gentile, Giovanni 1875-1944   **TCLC 96**
See also CA 119

Gentlewoman in New England, A
See Bradstreet, Anne

Gentlewoman in Those Parts, A
See Bradstreet, Anne

George, Jean Craighead 1919-   **CLC 35**
See also AAYA 8; CA 5-8R; CANR 25; CLR 1; DLB 52; JRDA; MAICYA; SATA 2, 68

George, Stefan (Anton) 1868-1933**TCLC 2, 14**
See also CA 104

Georges, Georges Martin
See Simenon, Georges (Jacques Christian)

Gerhardi, William Alexander
See Gerhardie, William Alexander

Gerhardie, William Alexander 1895-1977 **CLC 5**
See also CA 25-28R; 73-76; CANR 18; DLB 36

Gerstler, Amy 1956-   **CLC 70**
See also CA 146

Gertler, T.   **CLC 34**
See also CA 116; 121; INT 121

Ghalib   **NCLC 39, 78**
See also Ghalib, Hsadullah Khan

Ghalib, Hsadullah Khan 1797-1869
See Ghalib
See also DAM POET

Ghelderode, Michel de 1898-1962**CLC 6, 11; DAM DRAM**
See also CA 85-88; CANR 40, 77

Ghiselin, Brewster 1903-   **CLC 23**
See also CA 13-16R; CAAS 10; CANR 13

Ghose, Aurabinda 1872-1950   **TCLC 63**
See also CA 163

Ghose, Zulfikar 1935-   **CLC 42**
See also CA 65-68; CANR 67

Ghosh, Amitav 1956-   **CLC 44**
See also CA 147; CANR 80

Giacosa, Giuseppe 1847-1906   **TCLC 7**
See also CA 104

Gibb, Lee
See Waterhouse, Keith (Spencer)

Gibbon, Lewis Grassic   **TCLC 4**
See also Mitchell, James Leslie

Gibbons, Kaye 1960- **CLC 50, 88;DAM POP**
See also CA 151; CANR 75; MTCW 1

Gibran, Kahlil 1883-1931 **TCLC 1, 9; DAM POET, POP; PC 9**
See also CA 104; 150; MTCW 2

Gibran, Khalil
See Gibran, Kahlil

Gibson, William 1914- **CLC 23; DA; DAB; DAC; DAM DRAM, MST**
See also CA 9-12R; CANR 9, 42, 75; DLB 7; MTCW 1; SATA 66

Gibson, William (Ford) 1948- **CLC 39, 63; DAM POP**
See also AAYA 12; CA 126; 133; CANR 52; MTCW 1

Gide, Andre (Paul Guillaume) 1869-1951 **TCLC 5, 12, 36; DA; DAB; DAC; DAM MST, NOV; SSC 13; WLC**
See also CA 104; 124; DLB 65; MTCW 1, 2

Gifford, Barry (Colby) 1946-   **CLC 34**
See also CA 65-68; CANR 9, 30, 40

Gilbert, Frank
See De Voto, Bernard (Augustine)

Gilbert, W(illiam) S(chwenck) 1836-1911 **TCLC 3; DAM DRAM, POET**
See also CA 104; 173; SATA 36

Gilbreth, Frank B., Jr. 1911-   **CLC 17**
See also CA 9-12R; SATA 2

Gilchrist, Ellen 1935-**CLC 34, 48; DAM POP; SSC 14**
See also CA 113; 116; CANR 41, 61; DLB 130; MTCW 1, 2

Giles, Molly 1942-   **CLC 39**
See also CA 126

Gill, Eric 1882-1940   **TCLC 85**

Gill, Patrick
See Creasey, John

Gilliam, Terry (Vance) 1940-   **CLC 21**
See also Monty Python
See also AAYA 19; CA 108; 113; CANR 35; INT 113

Gillian, Jerry
See Gilliam, Terry (Vance)

Gilliatt, Penelope (Ann Douglass) 1932-1993 **CLC 2, 10, 13, 53**
See also AITN 2; CA 13-16R; 141; CANR 49; DLB 14

Gilman, Charlotte (Anna) Perkins (Stetson) 1860-1935   **TCLC 9, 37; SSC 13**
See also CA 106; 150; MTCW 1

Gilmour, David 1949-   **CLC 35**
See also CA 138, 147

Gilpin, William 1724-1804   **NCLC 30**

Gilray, J. D.
See Mencken, H(enry) L(ouis)

Gilroy, Frank D(aniel) 1925-   **CLC 2**
See also CA 81-84; CANR 32, 64; DLB 7

Gilstrap, John 1957(?)-   **CLC 99**
See also CA 160

Ginsberg, Allen 1926-1997**CLC 1, 2, 3, 4, 6, 13, 36, 69, 109; DA; DAB; DAC; DAM MST, POET; PC 4; WLC**
See also AITN 1; CA 1-4R; 157; CANR 2, 41, 63; CDALB 1941-1968; DLB 5, 16, 169; MTCW 1, 2

Ginzburg, Natalia 1916-1991**CLC 5, 11, 54, 70**
See also CA 85-88; 135; CANR 33; DLB 177; MTCW 1, 2

Giono, Jean 1895-1970   **CLC 4, 11**
See also CA 45-48; 29-32R; CANR 2, 35; DLB 72; MTCW 1

Giovanni, Nikki 1943- **CLC 2, 4, 19, 64, 117; BLC 2; DA; DAB; DAC; DAM MST, MULT, POET; PC 19; WLCS**
See also AAYA 22; AITN 1; BW 2, 3; CA 29-32R; CAAS 6; CANR 18, 41, 60; CDALBS; CLR 6; DLB 5, 41; INT CANR-18; MAICYA; MTCW 1, 2; SATA 24, 107

Giovene, Andrea 1904-   **CLC 7**
See also CA 85-88

Gippius, Zinaida (Nikolayevna) 1869-1945
See Hippius, Zinaida
See also CA 106

Giraudoux, (Hippolyte) Jean 1882-1944 **TCLC 2, 7; DAM DRAM**
See also CA 104; DLB 65

Gironella, Jose Maria 1917-   **CLC 11**
See also CA 101

Gissing, George (Robert) 1857-1903**TCLC 3, 24, 47**
See also CA 105; 167; DLB 18, 135, 184

Giurlani, Aldo
See Palazzeschi, Aldo

Gladkov, Fyodor (Vasilyevich) 1883-1958 **TCLC 27**
See also CA 170

Glanville, Brian (Lester) 1931-   **CLC 6**
See also CA 5-8R; CAAS 9; CANR 3, 70; DLB 15, 139; SATA 42

Glasgow, Ellen (Anderson Gholson) 1873-1945 **TCLC 2, 7; SSC 34**
See also CA 104; 164; DLB 9, 12; MTCW 2

Glaspell, Susan 1882(?)-1948**TCLC 55; DC 10**
See also CA 110; 154; DLB 7, 9, 78; YABC 2

Glassco, John 1909-1981   **CLC 9**
See also CA 13-16R; 102; CANR 15; DLB 68

Glasscock, Amnesia
See Steinbeck, John (Ernst)

Glasser, Ronald J. 1940(?)-   **CLC 37**

Glassman, Joyce
See Johnson, Joyce

Glendinning, Victoria 1937-   **CLC 50**
See also CA 120; 127; CANR 59; DLB 155

Glissant, Edouard 1928- **CLC 10, 68; DAM MULT**
See also CA 153

Gloag, Julian 1930-   **CLC 40**
See also AITN 1; CA 65-68; CANR 10, 70

Glowacki, Aleksander
See Prus, Boleslaw

Gluck, Louise (Elisabeth) 1943-**CLC 7, 22, 44, 81; DAM POET; PC 16**
See also CA 33-36R; CANR 40, 69; DLB 5; MTCW 2

Glyn, Elinor 1864-1943   **TCLC 72**
See also DLB 153

Gobineau, Joseph Arthur (Comte) de 1816-1882   **NCLC 17**
See also DLB 123

Godard, Jean-Luc 1930-   **CLC 20**
See also CA 93-96

Godden, (Margaret) Rumer 1907-1998 **C L C 53**
See also AAYA 6; CA 5-8R; 172; CANR 4, 27, 36, 55, 80; CLR 20; DLB 161; MAICYA; SAAS 12; SATA 3, 36; SATA-Obit 109

Godoy Alcayaga, Lucila 1889-1957
See Mistral, Gabriela
See also BW 2; CA 104; 131; CANR 81; DAM MULT; HW 1, 2; MTCW 1, 2

Godwin, Gail (Kathleen) 1937- **CLC 5, 8, 22, 31, 69; DAM POP**
See also CA 29-32R; CANR 15, 43, 69; DLB 6; INT CANR-15; MTCW 1, 2

Godwin, William 1756-1836   **NCLC 14**
See also CDBLB 1789-1832; DLB 39, 104, 142, 158, 163

Goebbels, Josef
See Goebbels, (Paul) Joseph

Goebbels, (Paul) Joseph 1897-1945 **TCLC 68**
See also CA 115; 148

Goebbels, Joseph Paul
See Goebbels, (Paul) Joseph

Goethe, Johann Wolfgang von 1749-1832 **NCLC 4, 22, 34; DA; DAB; DAC; DAM DRAM, MST, POET; PC 5; WLC**
See also DLB 94

Gogarty, Oliver St. John 1878-1957**TCLC 15**
See also CA 109; 150; DLB 15, 19

Gogol, Nikolai (Vasilyevich) 1809-1852**NCLC 5, 15, 31; DA; DAB; DAC; DAM DRAM,**

MST; DC 1; SSC 4, 29; WLC
See also DLB 198

Goines, Donald 1937(?)-1974 **CLC 80; BLC 2; DAM MULT, POP**
See also AITN 1; BW 1, 3; CA 124; 114; CANR 82; DLB 33

Gold, Herbert 1924-   **CLC 4, 7, 14, 42**
See also CA 9-12R; CANR 17, 45; DLB 2; DLBY 81

Goldbarth, Albert 1948-   **CLC 5, 38**
See also CA 53-56; CANR 6, 40; DLB 120

Goldberg, Anatol 1910-1982   **CLC 34**
See also CA 131; 117

Goldemberg, Isaac 1945-   **CLC 52**
See also CA 69-72; CAAS 12; CANR 11, 32; HW 1

Golding, William (Gerald) 1911-1993 **CLC 1, 2, 3, 8, 10, 17, 27, 58, 81; DA; DAB; DAC; DAM MST, NOV; WLC**
See also AAYA 5; CA 5-8R; 141; CANR 13, 33, 54; CDBLB 1945-1960; DLB 15, 100; MTCW 1, 2

Goldman, Emma 1869-1940   **TCLC 13**
See also CA 110; 150

Goldman, Francisco 1954-   **CLC 76**
See also CA 162

Goldman, William (W.) 1931-   **CLC 1, 48**
See also CA 9-12R; CANR 29, 69; DLB 44

Goldmann, Lucien 1913-1970   **CLC 24**
See also CA 25-28; CAP 2

Goldoni, Carlo 1707-1793 **LC 4; DAM DRAM**

Goldsberry, Steven 1949-   **CLC 34**
See also CA 131

Goldsmith, Oliver 1728-1774 **LC 2, 48; DA; DAB; DAC; DAM DRAM, MST, NOV, POET; DC 8; WLC**
See also CDBLB 1660-1789; DLB 39, 89, 104, 109, 142; SATA 26

Goldsmith, Peter
See Priestley, J(ohn) B(oynton)

Gombrowicz, Witold 1904-1969 **CLC 4, 7, 11, 49; DAM DRAM**
See also CA 19-20; 25-28R; CAP 2

Gomez de la Serna, Ramon 1888-1963 **CLC 9**
See also CA 153; 116; CANR 79; HW 1, 2

Goncharov, Ivan Alexandrovich 1812-1891 **NCLC 1, 63**

Goncourt, Edmond (Louis Antoine Huot) de 1822-1896   **NCLC 7**
See also DLB 123

Goncourt, Jules (Alfred Huot) de 1830-1870 **NCLC 7**
See also DLB 123

Gontier, Fernande 19(?)-   **CLC 50**

Gonzalez Martinez, Enrique 1871-1952 **TCLC 72**
See also CA 166; CANR 81; HW 1, 2

Goodman, Paul 1911-1972   **CLC 1, 2, 4, 7**
See also CA 19-20; 37-40R; CANR 34; CAP 2; DLB 130; MTCW 1

Gordimer, Nadine 1923- **CLC 3, 5, 7, 10, 18, 33, 51, 70; DA; DAB; DAC; DAM MST, NOV; SSC 17; WLCS**
See also CA 5-8R; CANR 3, 28, 56; INT CANR-28; MTCW 1, 2

Gordon, Adam Lindsay 1833-1870 **NCLC 21**

Gordon, Caroline 1895-1981 **CLC 6, 13, 29, 83; SSC 15**
See also CA 11-12; 103; CANR 36; CAP 1; DLB 4, 9, 102; DLBD 17; DLBY 81; MTCW 1, 2

Gordon, Charles William 1860-1937
See Connor, Ralph

See also CA 109

Gordon, Mary (Catherine) 1949- **CLC 13, 22**
See also CA 102; CANR 44; DLB 6; DLBY 81; INT 102; MTCW 1

Gordon, N. J.
See Bosman, Herman Charles

Gordon, Sol 1923-   **CLC 26**
See also CA 53-56; CANR 4; SATA 11

Gordone, Charles 1925-1995 **CLC 1, 4; DAM DRAM; DC 8**
See also BW 1, 3; CA 93-96; 150; CANR 55; DLB 7; INT 93-96; MTCW 1

Gore, Catherine 1800-1861   **NCLC 65**
See also DLB 116

Gorenko, Anna Andreevna
See Akhmatova, Anna

Gorky, Maxim 1868-1936 **TCLC 8; DAB; SSC 28; WLC**
See also Peshkov, Alexei Maximovich
See also MTCW 2

Goryan, Sirak
See Saroyan, William

Gosse, Edmund (William) 1849-1928 **TCLC 28**
See also CA 117; DLB 57, 144, 184

Gotlieb, Phyllis Fay (Bloom) 1926-   **CLC 18**
See also CA 13-16R; CANR 7; DLB 88

Gottesman, S. D.
See Kornbluth, C(yril) M.; Pohl, Frederik

Gottfried von Strassburg fl. c.1210- **CMLC 10**
See also DLB 138

Gould, Lois   **CLC 4, 10**
See also CA 77-80; CANR 29; MTCW 1

Gourmont, Remy (-Marie-Charles) de 1858-1915   **TCLC 17**
See also CA 109; 150; MTCW 2

Govier, Katherine 1948-   **CLC 51**
See also CA 101; CANR 18, 40

Goyen, (Charles) William 1915-1983 **CLC 5, 8, 14, 40**
See also AITN 2; CA 5-8R; 110; CANR 6, 71; DLB 2; DLBY 83; INT CANR-6

Goytisolo, Juan 1931-   **CLC 5, 10, 23; DAM MULT; HLC 1**
See also CA 85-88; CANR 32, 61; HW 1, 2; MTCW 1, 2

Gozzano, Guido 1883-1916   **PC 10**
See also CA 154; DLB 114

Gozzi, (Conte) Carlo 1720-1806 **NCLC 23**

Grabbe, Christian Dietrich 1801-1836 **NCLC 2**
See also DLB 133

Grace, Patricia Frances 1937-   **CLC 56**
See also CA 176

Gracian y Morales, Baltasar 1601-1658 **LC 15**

Gracq, Julien   **CLC 11, 48**
See also Poirier, Louis
See also DLB 83

Grade, Chaim 1910-1982   **CLC 10**
See also CA 93-96; 107

Graduate of Oxford, A
See Ruskin, John

Grafton, Garth
See Duncan, Sara Jeannette

Graham, John
See Phillips, David Graham

Graham, Jorie 1951-   **CLC 48, 118**
See also CA 111; CANR 63; DLB 120

Graham, R(obert) B(ontine) Cunninghame
See Cunninghame Graham, R(obert) B(ontine)
See also DLB 98, 135, 174

Graham, Robert
See Haldeman, Joe (William)

Graham, Tom

See Lewis, (Harry) Sinclair

Graham, W(illiam) S(ydney) 1918-1986 **CLC 29**
See also CA 73-76; 118; DLB 20

Graham, Winston (Mawdsley) 1910- **CLC 23**
See also CA 49-52; CANR 2, 22, 45, 66; DLB 77

Grahame, Kenneth 1859-1932 **TCLC 64; DAB**
See also CA 108; 136; CANR 80; CLR 5; DLB 34, 141, 178; MAICYA; MTCW 2; SATA 100; YABC 1

Granovsky, Timofei Nikolaevich 1813-1855 **NCLC 75**
See also DLB 198

Grant, Skeeter
See Spiegelman, Art

Granville-Barker, Harley 1877-1946 **TCLC 2; DAM DRAM**
See also Barker, Harley Granville
See also CA 104

Grass, Guenter (Wilhelm) 1927- **CLC 1, 2, 4, 6, 11, 15, 22, 32, 49, 88; DA; DAB; DAC; DAM MST, NOV; WLC**
See also CA 13-16R; CANR 20, 75; DLB 75, 124; MTCW 1, 2

Gratton, Thomas
See Hulme, T(homas) E(rnest)

Grau, Shirley Ann 1929-   **CLC 4, 9; SSC 15**
See also CA 89-92; CANR 22, 69; DLB 2; INT CANR-22; MTCW 1

Gravel, Fern
See Hall, James Norman

Graver, Elizabeth 1964-   **CLC 70**
See also CA 135; CANR 71

Graves, Richard Perceval 1945-   **CLC 44**
See also CA 65-68; CANR 9, 26, 51

Graves, Robert (von Ranke) 1895-1985 **CLC 1, 2, 6, 11, 39, 44, 45; DAB; DAC; DAM MST, POET; PC 6**
See also CA 5-8R; 117; CANR 5, 36; CDBLB 1914-1945; DLB 20, 100, 191; DLBD 18; DLBY 85; MTCW 1, 2; SATA 45

Graves, Valerie
See Bradley, Marion Zimmer

Gray, Alasdair (James) 1934-   **CLC 41**
See also CA 126; CANR 47, 69; DLB 194; INT 126; MTCW 1, 2

Gray, Amlin 1946-   **CLC 29**
See also CA 138

Gray, Francine du Plessix 1930-   **CLC 22; DAM NOV**
See also BEST 90:3; CA 61-64; CAAS 2; CANR 11, 33, 75, 81; INT CANR-11; MTCW 1, 2

Gray, John (Henry) 1866-1934   **TCLC 19**
See also CA 119; 162

Gray, Simon (James Holliday) 1936- **CLC 9, 14, 36**
See also AITN 1; CA 21-24R; CAAS 3; CANR 32, 69; DLB 13; MTCW 1

Gray, Spalding 1941- **CLC 49, 112; DAM POP; DC 7**
See also CA 128; CANR 74; MTCW 2

Gray, Thomas 1716-1771 **LC 4, 40; DA; DAB; DAC; DAM MST; PC 2; WLC**
See also CDBLB 1660-1789; DLB 109

Grayson, David
See Baker, Ray Stannard

Grayson, Richard (A.) 1951-   **CLC 38**
See also CA 85-88; CANR 14, 31, 57

Greeley, Andrew M(oran) 1928-   **CLC 28; DAM POP**
See also CA 5-8R; CAAS 7; CANR 7, 43, 69;

MTCW 1, 2
Green, Anna Katharine 1846-1935 **TCLC 63**
See also CA 112; 159; DLB 202
Green, Brian
See Card, Orson Scott
Green, Hannah
See Greenberg, Joanne (Goldenberg)
Green, Hannah 1927(?)-1996 **CLC 3**
See also CA 73-76; CANR 59
Green, Henry 1905-1973 **CLC 2, 13, 97**
See also Yorke, Henry Vincent
See also CA 175; DLB 15
Green, Julian (Hartridge) 1900-1998
See Green, Julien
See also CA 21-24R; 169; CANR 33; DLB 4,
72; MTCW 1
Green, Julien **CLC 3, 11, 77**
See also Green, Julian (Hartridge)
See also MTCW 2
Green, Paul (Eliot) 1894-1981 **CLC 25; DAM
DRAM**
See also AITN 1; CA 5-8R; 103; CANR 3; DLB
7, 9; DLBY 81
Greenberg, Ivan 1908-1973
See Rahv, Philip
See also CA 85-88
Greenberg, Joanne (Goldenberg) 1932- **C L C
7, 30**
See also AAYA 12; CA 5-8R; CANR 14, 32,
69; SATA 25
Greenberg, Richard 1959(?)- **CLC 57**
See also CA 138
Greene, Bette 1934- **CLC 30**
See also AAYA 7; CA 53-56; CANR 4; CLR 2;
JRDA; MAICYA; SAAS 16; SATA 8, 102
Greene, Gael **CLC 8**
See also CA 13-16R; CANR 10
Greene, Graham (Henry) 1904-1991 **CLC 1, 3,
6, 9, 14, 18, 27, 37, 70, 72; DA; DAB; DAC;
DAM MST, NOV; SSC 29; WLC**
See also AITN 2; CA 13-16R; 133; CANR 35,
61; CDBLB 1945-1960; DLB 13, 15, 77,
100, 162, 201, 204; DLBY 91; MTCW 1, 2;
SATA 20
Greene, Robert 1558-1592 **LC 41**
See also DLB 62, 167
Greer, Richard
See Silverberg, Robert
Gregor, Arthur 1923- **CLC 9**
See also CA 25-28R; CAAS 10; CANR 11;
SATA 36
Gregor, Lee
See Pohl, Frederik
Gregory, Isabella Augusta (Persse) 1852-1932
TCLC 1
See also CA 104; DLB 10
Gregory, J. Dennis
See Williams, John A(lfred)
Grendon, Stephen
See Derleth, August (William)
Grenville, Kate 1950- **CLC 61**
See also CA 118; CANR 53
Grenville, Pelham
See Wodehouse, P(elham) G(renville)
Greve, Felix Paul (Berthold Friedrich) 1879-
1948
See Grove, Frederick Philip
See also CA 104; 141; 175; CANR 79; DAC;
DAM MST
Grey, Zane 1872-1939 **TCLC 6;DAM POP**
See also CA 104; 132; DLB 212; MTCW 1, 2
Grieg, (Johan) Nordahl (Brun) 1902-1943
TCLC 10

See also CA 107
Grieve, C(hristopher) M(urray) 1892-1978
CLC 11, 19; DAM POET
See also MacDiarmid, Hugh; Pteleon
See also CA 5-8R; 85-88; CANR 33; MTCW 1
Griffin, Gerald 1803-1840 **NCLC 7**
See also DLB 159
Griffin, John Howard 1920-1980 **CLC 68**
See also AITN 1; CA 1-4R; 101; CANR 2
Griffin, Peter 1942- **CLC 39**
See also CA 136
Griffith, D(avid Lewelyn) W(ark) 1875(?)-1948
TCLC 68
See also CA 119; 150; CANR 80
Griffith, Lawrence
See Griffith, D(avid Lewelyn) W(ark)
Griffiths, Trevor 1935- **CLC 13, 52**
See also CA 97-100; CANR 45; DLB 13
Griggs, Sutton Elbert 1872-1930(?) **TCLC 77**
See also CA 123; DLB 50
Grigson, Geoffrey (Edward Harvey) 1905-1985
CLC 7, 39
See also CA 25-28R; 118; CANR 20, 33; DLB
27; MTCW 1, 2
Grillparzer, Franz 1791-1872 **NCLC 1**
See also DLB 133
Grimble, Reverend Charles James
See Eliot, T(homas) S(tearns)
Grimke, Charlotte L(ottie) Forten 1837(?)-1914
See Forten, Charlotte L.
See also BW 1; CA 117; 124; DAM MULT,
POET
Grimm, Jacob Ludwig Karl 1785-1863 **NCLC
3, 77**
See also DLB 90; MAICYA; SATA 22
Grimm, Wilhelm Karl 1786-1859 **NCLC 3, 77**
See also DLB 90; MAICYA; SATA 22
Grimmelshausen, Johann Jakob Christoffel von
1621-1676 **LC 6**
See also DLB 168
Grindel, Eugene 1895-1952
See Eluard, Paul
See also CA 104
Grisham, John 1955- **CLC 84;DAM POP**
See also AAYA 14; CA 138; CANR 47, 69;
MTCW 2
Grossman, David 1954- **CLC 67**
See also CA 138
Grossman, Vasily (Semenovich) 1905-1964
CLC 41
See also CA 124; 130; MTCW 1
Grove, Frederick Philip **TCLC 4**
See also Greve, Felix Paul (Berthold Friedrich)
See also DLB 92
Grubb
See Crumb, R(obert)
Grumbach, Doris (Isaac) 1918- **CLC 13, 22, 64**
See also CA 5-8R; CAAS 2; CANR 9, 42, 70;
INT CANR-9; MTCW 2
Grundtvig, Nicolai Frederik Severin 1783-1872
NCLC 1
Grunge
See Crumb, R(obert)
Grunwald, Lisa 1959- . **CLC 44**
See also CA 120
Guare, John 1938- **CLC 8, 14, 29, 67; DAM
DRAM**
See also CA 73-76; CANR 21, 69; DLB 7;
MTCW 1, 2
Gudjonsson, Halldor Kiljan 1902-1998
See Laxness, Halldor
See also CA 103; 164
Guenter, Erich

See Eich, Guenter
Guest, Barbara 1920- **CLC 34**
See also CA 25-28R; CANR 11, 44; DLB 5,
193
Guest, Edgar A(lbert) 1881-1959 **TCLC 95**
See also CA 112; 168
Guest, Judith (Ann) 1936- **CLC 8, 30; DAM
NOV, POP**
See also AAYA 7; CA 77-80; CANR 15, 75;
INT CANR-15; MTCW 1, 2
Guevara, Che **CLC 87; HLC 1**
See also Guevara (Serna), Ernesto
Guevara (Serna), Ernesto 1928-1967 **CLC 87;
DAM MULT; HLC 1**
See also Guevara, Che
See also CA 127; 111; CANR 56; HW 1
Guicciardini, Francesco 1483-1540 **LC 49**
Guild, Nicholas M. 1944- **CLC 33**
See also CA 93-96
Guillemin, Jacques
See Sartre, Jean-Paul
Guillen, Jorge 1893-1984 **CLC 11; DAM
MULT, POET; HLCS 1**
See also CA 89-92; 112; DLB 108; HW 1
Guillen, Nicolas (Cristobal) 1902-1989 **C L C
48, 79; BLC 2; DAM MST, MULT, POET;
HLC 1; PC 23**
See also BW 2; CA 116; 125; 129; HW 1
Guillevic, (Eugene) 1907- **CLC 33**
See also CA 93-96
Guillois
See Desnos, Robert
Guillois, Valentin
See Desnos, Robert
Guimaraes Rosa, Joao 1908-1967
See also CA 175; HLCS 2
Guiney, Louise Imogen 1861-1920 **TCLC 41**
See also CA 160; DLB 54
Guiraldes, Ricardo (Guillermo) 1886-1927
TCLC 39
See also CA 131; HW 1; MTCW 1
Gumilev, Nikolai (Stepanovich) 1886-1921
TCLC 60
See also CA 165
Gunesekera, Romesh 1954- **CLC 91**
See also CA 159
Gunn, Bill **CLC 5**
See also Gunn, William Harrison
See also DLB 38
Gunn, Thom(son William) 1929- **CLC 3, 6, 18,
32, 81; DAM POET; PC 26**
See also CA 17-20R; CANR 9, 33; CDBLB
1960 to Present; DLB 27; INT CANR-33;
MTCW 1
Gunn, William Harrison 1934(?)-1989
See Gunn, Bill
See also AITN 1; BW 1, 3; CA 13-16R; 128;
CANR 12, 25, 76
Gunnars, Kristjana 1948- **CLC 69**
See also CA 113; DLB 60
Gurdjieff, G(eorgei) I(vanovich) 1877(?)-1949
TCLC 71
See also CA 157
Gurganus, Allan 1947- **CLC 70;DAM POP**
See also BEST 90:1; CA 135
Gurney, A(lbert) R(amsdell), Jr. 1930- **C L C
32, 50, 54; DAM DRAM**
See also CA 77-80; CANR 32, 64
Gurney, Ivor (Bertie) 1890-1937 **TCLC 33**
See also CA 167
Gurney, Peter
See Gurney, A(lbert) R(amsdell), Jr.
Guro, Elena 1877-1913 **TCLC 56**

Gustafson, James M(oody) 1925-   **CLC 100**
    See also CA 25-28R; CANR 37
Gustafson, Ralph (Barker) 1909-   **CLC 36**
    See also CA 21-24R; CANR 8, 45; DLB 88
Gut, Gom
    See Simenon, Georges (Jacques Christian)
Guterson, David 1956-   **CLC 91**
    See also CA 132; CANR 73; MTCW 2
Guthrie, A(lfred) B(ertram), Jr. 1901-1991
    CLC 23
    See also CA 57-60; 134; CANR 24; DLB 212;
    SATA 62; SATA-Obit 67
Guthrie, Isobel
    See Grieve, C(hristopher) M(urray)
Guthrie, Woodrow Wilson 1912-1967
    See Guthrie, Woody
    See also CA 113; 93-96
Guthrie, Woody   **CLC 35**
    See also Guthrie, Woodrow Wilson
Gutierrez Najera, Manuel 1859-1895
    See also HLCS 2
Guy, Rosa (Cuthbert) 1928-   **CLC 26**
    See also AAYA 4; BW 2; CA 17-20R; CANR
    14, 34; CLR 13; DLB 33; JRDA; MAICYA;
    SATA 14, 62
Gwendolyn
    See Bennett, (Enoch) Arnold
H. D.   **CLC 3, 8, 14, 31, 34, 73; PC 5**
    See also Doolittle, Hilda
H. de V.
    See Buchan, John
Haavikko, Paavo Juhani 1931-   **CLC 18, 34**
    See also CA 106
Habbema, Koos
    See Heijermans, Herman
Habermas, Juergen 1929-   **CLC 104**
    See also CA 109
Habermas, Jurgen
    See Habermas, Juergen
Hacker, Marilyn 1942-   **CLC 5, 9, 23, 72, 91;**
    DAM POET
    See also CA 77-80; CANR 68; DLB 120
Haeckel, Ernst Heinrich (Philipp August) 1834-
    1919   **TCLC 83**
    See also CA 157
Hafiz c. 1326-1389   **CMLC 34**
Hafiz c. 1326-1389(?)   **CMLC 34**
Haggard, H(enry) Rider 1856-1925 **TCLC 11**
    See also CA 108; 148; DLB 70, 156, 174, 178;
    MTCW 2; SATA 16
Hagiosy, L.
    See Larbaud, Valery (Nicolas)
Hagiwara Sakutaro 1886-1942 **TCLC 60; PC
    18**
Haig, Fenil
    See Ford, Ford Madox
Haig-Brown, Roderick (Langmere) 1908-1976
    CLC 21
    See also CA 5-8R; 69-72; CANR 4, 38; CLR
    31; DLB 88; MAICYA; SATA 12
Hailey, Arthur 1920- **CLC 5; DAM NOV, POP**
    See also AITN 2; BEST 90:3; CA 1-4R; CANR
    2, 36, 75; DLB 88; DLBY 82; MTCW 1, 2
Hailey, Elizabeth Forsythe 1938-   **CLC 40**
    See also CA 93-96; CAAS 1; CANR 15, 48;
    INT CANR-15
Haines, John (Meade) 1924-   **CLC 58**
    See also CA 17-20R; CANR 13, 34; DLB 212
Hakluyt, Richard 1552-1616   **LC 31**
Haldeman, Joe (William) 1943-   **CLC 61**
    See also CA 53-56; CAAS 25; CANR 6, 70,
    72; DLB 8; INT CANR-6
Hale, Sarah Josepha (Buell) 1788-1879 **NCLC
75**
    See also DLB 1, 42, 73
Haley, Alex(ander Murray Palmer) 1921-1992
    **CLC 8, 12, 76; BLC 2; DA; DAB; DAC;
    DAM MST, MULT, POP**
    See also AAYA 26; BW 2, 3; CA 77-80; 136;
    CANR 61; CDALBS; DLB 38; MTCW 1, 2
Haliburton, Thomas Chandler 1796-1865
    NCLC 15
    See also DLB 11, 99
Hall, Donald (Andrew, Jr.) 1928- **CLC 1, 13,
    37, 59; DAM POET**
    See also CA 5-8R; CAAS 7; CANR 2, 44, 64;
    DLB 5; MTCW 1; SATA 23, 97
Hall, Frederic Sauser
    See Sauser-Hall, Frederic
Hall, James
    See Kuttner, Henry
Hall, James Norman 1887-1951   **TCLC 23**
    See also CA 123; 173; SATA 21
Hall, Radclyffe
    See Hall, (Marguerite) Radclyffe
    See also MTCW 2
Hall, (Marguerite) Radclyffe 1886-1943
    TCLC 12
    See also CA 110; 150; DLB 191
Hall, Rodney 1935-   **CLC 51**
    See also CA 109; CANR 69
Halleck, Fitz-Greene 1790-1867   **NCLC 47**
    See also DLB 3
Halliday, Michael
    See Creasey, John
Halpern, Daniel 1945-   **CLC 14**
    See also CA 33-36R
Hamburger, Michael (Peter Leopold) 1924-
    CLC 5, 14
    See also CA 5-8R; CAAS 4; CANR 2, 47; DLB
    27
Hamill, Pete 1935-   **CLC 10**
    See also CA 25-28R; CANR 18, 71
Hamilton, Alexander 1755(?)-1804 **NCLC 49**
    See also DLB 37
Hamilton, Clive
    See Lewis, C(live) S(taples)
Hamilton, Edmond 1904-1977   **CLC 1**
    See also CA 1-4R; CANR 3; DLB 8
Hamilton, Eugene (Jacob) Lee
    See Lee-Hamilton, Eugene (Jacob)
Hamilton, Franklin
    See Silverberg, Robert
Hamilton, Gail
    See Corcoran, Barbara
Hamilton, Mollie
    See Kaye, M(ary) M(argaret)
Hamilton, (Anthony Walter) Patrick 1904-1962
    CLC 51
    See also CA 176; 113; DLB 191
Hamilton, Virginia 1936-   **CLC 26; DAM
    MULT**
    See also AAYA 2, 21; BW 2, 3; CA 25-28R;
    CANR 20, 37, 73; CLR 1, 11, 40; DLB 33,
    52; INT CANR-20; JRDA; MAICYA;
    MTCW 1, 2; SATA 4, 56, 79
Hammett, (Samuel) Dashiell 1894-1961 **C L C
    3, 5, 10, 19, 47; SSC 17**
    See also AITN 1; CA 81-84; CANR 42; CDALB
    1929-1941; DLBD 6; DLBY 96; MTCW 1,
    2
Hammon, Jupiter 1711(?)-1800(?)   **NCLC 5;
    BLC 2; DAM MULT, POET; PC 16**
    See also DLB 31, 50
Hammond, Keith
    See Kuttner, Henry
Hamner, Earl (Henry), Jr. 1923-   **CLC 12**
    See also AITN 2; CA 73-76; DLB 6
Hampton, Christopher (James) 1946- **CLC 4**
    See also CA 25-28R; DLB 13; MTCW 1
Hamsun, Knut   **TCLC 2, 14, 49**
    See also Pedersen, Knut
Handke, Peter 1942- **CLC 5, 8, 10, 15, 38; DAM
    DRAM, NOV**
    See also CA 77-80; CANR 33, 75; DLB 85, 124;
    MTCW 1, 2
Hanley, James 1901-1985   **CLC 3, 5, 8, 13**
    See also CA 73-76; 117; CANR 36; DLB 191;
    MTCW 1
Hannah, Barry 1942-   **CLC 23, 38, 90**
    See also CA 108; 110; CANR 43, 68; DLB 6;
    INT 110; MTCW 1
Hannon, Ezra
    See Hunter, Evan
Hansberry, Lorraine (Vivian) 1930-1965 **CLC
    17, 62; BLC 2; DA; DAB; DAC; DAM
    DRAM, MST, MULT; DC 2**
    See also AAYA 25; BW 1, 3; CA 109; 25-28R;
    CABS 3; CANR 58; CDALB 1941-1968;
    DLB 7, 38; MTCW 1, 2
Hansen, Joseph 1923-   **CLC 38**
    See also CA 29-32R; CAAS 17; CANR 16, 44,
    66; INT CANR-16
Hansen, Martin A(lfred) 1909-1955 **TCLC 32**
    See also CA 167
Hanson, Kenneth O(stlin) 1922-   **CLC 13**
    See also CA 53-56; CANR 7
Hardwick, Elizabeth (Bruce) 1916- **CLC 13;
    DAM NOV**
    See also CA 5-8R; CANR 3, 32, 70; DLB 6;
    MTCW 1, 2
Hardy, Thomas 1840-1928 **TCLC 4, 10, 18, 32,
    48, 53, 72; DA; DAB; DAC; DAM MST,
    NOV, POET; PC 8; SSC 2; WLC**
    See also CA 104; 123; CDBLB 1890-1914;
    DLB 18, 19, 135; MTCW 1, 2
Hare, David 1947-   **CLC 29, 58**
    See also CA 97-100; CANR 39; DLB 13;
    MTCW 1
Harewood, John
    See Van Druten, John (William)
Harford, Henry
    See Hudson, W(illiam) H(enry)
Hargrave, Leonie
    See Disch, Thomas M(ichael)
Harjo, Joy 1951- **CLC 83; DAM MULT; PC 27**
    See also CA 114; CANR 35, 67; DLB 120, 175;
    MTCW 2; NNAL
Harlan, Louis R(udolph) 1922-   **CLC 34**
    See also CA 21-24R; CANR 25, 55, 80
Harling, Robert 1951(?)-   **CLC 53**
    See also CA 147
Harmon, William (Ruth) 1938-   **CLC 38**
    See also CA 33-36R; CANR 14, 32, 35; SATA
    65
Harper, F. E. W.
    See Harper, Frances Ellen Watkins
Harper, Frances E. W.
    See Harper, Frances Ellen Watkins
Harper, Frances E. Watkins
    See Harper, Frances Ellen Watkins
Harper, Frances Ellen
    See Harper, Frances Ellen Watkins
Harper, Frances Ellen Watkins 1825-1911
    **TCLC 14; BLC 2; DAM MULT, POET;
    PC 21**
    See also BW 1, 3; CA 111; 125; CANR 79; DLB
    50
Harper, Michael S(teven) 1938-   **CLC 7, 22**

See also BW 1; CA 33-36R; CANR 24; DLB 41

Harper, Mrs. F. E. W.
See Harper, Frances Ellen Watkins

Harris, Christie (Lucy) Irwin 1907- **CLC 12**
See also CA 5-8R; CANR 6; CLR 47; DLB 88; JRDA; MAICYA; SAAS 10; SATA 6, 74

Harris, Frank 1856-1931 **TCLC 24**
See also CA 109; 150; CANR 80; DLB 156, 197

Harris, George Washington 1814-1869 **NCLC 23**
See also DLB 3, 11

Harris, Joel Chandler 1848-1908 **TCLC 2; SSC 19**
See also CA 104; 137; CANR 80; CLR 49; DLB 11, 23, 42, 78, 91; MAICYA; SATA 100; YABC 1

Harris, John (Wyndham Parkes Lucas) Beynon 1903-1969
See Wyndham, John
See also CA 102; 89-92

Harris, MacDonald **CLC 9**
See also Heiney, Donald (William)

Harris, Mark 1922- **CLC 19**
See also CA 5-8R; CAAS 3; CANR 2, 55; DLB 2; DLBY 80

Harris, (Theodore) Wilson 1921- **CLC 25**
See also BW 2, 3; CA 65-68; CAAS 16; CANR 11, 27, 69; DLB 117; MTCW 1

Harrison, Elizabeth Cavanna 1909-
See Cavanna, Betty
See also CA 9-12R; CANR 6, 27

Harrison, Harry (Max) 1925- **CLC 42**
See also CA 1-4R; CANR 5, 21; DLB 8; SATA 4

Harrison, James (Thomas) 1937- **CLC 6, 14, 33, 66; SSC 19**
See also CA 13-16R; CANR 8, 51, 79; DLBY 82; INT CANR-8

Harrison, Jim
See Harrison, James (Thomas)

Harrison, Kathryn 1961- **CLC 70**
See also CA 144; CANR 68

Harrison, Tony 1937- **CLC 43**
See also CA 65-68; CANR 44; DLB 40; MTCW 1

Harriss, Will(ard Irvin) 1922- **CLC 34**
See also CA 111

Harson, Sley
See Ellison, Harlan (Jay)

Hart, Ellis
See Ellison, Harlan (Jay)

Hart, Josephine 1942(?)- **CLC 70; DAM POP**
See also CA 138; CANR 70

Hart, Moss 1904-1961 **CLC 66; DAM DRAM**
See also CA 109; 89-92; DLB 7

Harte, (Francis) Bret(t) 1836(?)-1902 **TCLC 1, 25; DA; DAC; DAM MST; SSC 8; WLC**
See also CA 104; 140; CANR 80; CDALB 1865-1917; DLB 12, 64, 74, 79, 186; SATA 26

Hartley, L(eslie) P(oles) 1895-1972 **CLC 2, 22**
See also CA 45-48; 37-40R; CANR 33; DLB 15, 139; MTCW 1, 2

Hartman, Geoffrey H. 1929- **CLC 27**
See also CA 117; 125; CANR 79; DLB 67

Hartmann, Sadakichi 1867-1944 **TCLC 73**
See also CA 157; DLB 54

Hartmann von Aue c. 1160-c.1205 **CMLC 15**
See also DLB 138

Hartmann von Aue 1170-1210 **CMLC 15**

Haruf, Kent 1943- **CLC 34**

See also CA 149

Harwood, Ronald 1934- **CLC 32; DAM DRAM, MST**
See also CA 1-4R; CANR 4, 55; DLB 13

Hasegawa Tatsunosuke
See Futabatei, Shimei

Hasek, Jaroslav (Matej Frantisek) 1883-1923 **TCLC 4**
See also CA 104; 129; MTCW 1, 2

Hass, Robert 1941- **CLC 18, 39, 99; PC 16**
See also CA 111; CANR 30, 50, 71; DLB 105, 206; SATA 94

Hastings, Hudson
See Kuttner, Henry

Hastings, Selina **CLC 44**

Hathorne, John 1641-1717 **LC 38**

Hatteras, Amelia
See Mencken, H(enry) L(ouis)

Hatteras, Owen **TCLC 18**
See also Mencken, H(enry) L(ouis); Nathan, George Jean

Hauptmann, Gerhart (Johann Robert) 1862-1946 **TCLC 4; DAM DRAM**
See also CA 104; 153; DLB 66, 118

Havel, Vaclav 1936- **CLC 25, 58, 65; DAM DRAM; DC 6**
See also CA 104; CANR 36, 63; MTCW 1, 2

Haviaras, Stratis **CLC 33**
See also Chaviaras, Strates

Hawes, Stephen 1475(?)-1523(?) **LC 17**
See also DLB 132

Hawkes, John (Clendennin Burne, Jr.) 1925-1998 **CLC 1, 2, 3, 4, 7, 9, 14, 15, 27, 49**
See also CA 1-4R; 167; CANR 2, 47, 64; DLB 2, 7; DLBY 80, 98; MTCW 1, 2

Hawking, S. W.
See Hawking, Stephen W(illiam)

Hawking, Stephen W(illiam) 1942- **CLC 63, 105**
See also AAYA 13; BEST 89:1; CA 126; 129; CANR 48; MTCW 2

Hawkins, Anthony Hope
See Hope, Anthony

Hawthorne, Julian 1846-1934 **TCLC 25**
See also CA 165

Hawthorne, Nathaniel 1804-1864 **NCLC 39; DA; DAB; DAC; DAM MST, NOV; SSC 3, 29; WLC**
See also AAYA 18; CDALB 1640-1865; DLB 1, 74; YABC 2

Haxton, Josephine Ayres 1921-
See Douglas, Ellen
See also CA 115; CANR 41

Hayaseca y Eizaguirre, Jorge
See Echegaray (y Eizaguirre), Jose (Maria Waldo)

Hayashi, Fumiko 1904-1951 **TCLC 27**
See also CA 161; DLB 180

Haycraft, Anna
See Ellis, Alice Thomas
See also CA 122; MTCW 2

Hayden, Robert E(arl) 1913-1980 **CLC 5, 9, 14, 37; BLC 2; DA; DAC; DAM MST, MULT, POET; PC 6**
See also BW 1, 3; CA 69-72; 97-100; CABS 2; CANR 24, 75, 82; CDALB 1941-1968; DLB 5, 76; MTCW 1, 2; SATA 19; SATA-Obit 26

Hayford, J(oseph) E(phraim) Casely
See Casely-Hayford, J(oseph) E(phraim)

Hayman, Ronald 1932- **CLC 44**
See also CA 25-28R; CANR 18, 50; DLB 155

Haywood, Eliza (Fowler) 1693(?)-1756 **LC 1, 44**

See also DLB 39

Hazlitt, William 1778-1830 **NCLC 29**
See also DLB 110, 158

Hazzard, Shirley 1931- **CLC 18**
See also CA 9-12R; CANR 4, 70; DLBY 82; MTCW 1

Head, Bessie 1937-1986 **CLC 25, 67; BLC 2; DAM MULT**
See also BW 2, 3; CA 29-32R; 119; CANR 25, 82; DLB 117; MTCW 1, 2

Headon, (Nicky) Topper 1956(?)- **CLC 30**

Heaney, Seamus (Justin) 1939- **CLC 5, 7, 14, 25, 37, 74, 91; DAB; DAM POET; PC 18; WLCS**
See also CA 85-88; CANR 25, 48, 75; CDBLB 1960 to Present; DLB 40; DLBY 95; MTCW 1, 2

Hearn, (Patricio) Lafcadio (Tessima Carlos) 1850-1904 **TCLC 9**
See also CA 105; 166; DLB 12, 78, 189

Hearne, Vicki 1946- **CLC 56**
See also CA 139

Hearon, Shelby 1931- **CLC 63**
See also AITN 2; CA 25-28R; CANR 18, 48

Heat-Moon, William Least **CLC 29**
See also Trogdon, William (Lewis)
See also AAYA 9

Hebbel, Friedrich 1813-1863 **NCLC 43; DAM DRAM**
See also DLB 129

Hebert, Anne 1916- **CLC 4, 13, 29; DAC; DAM MST, POET**
See also CA 85-88; CANR 69; DLB 68; MTCW 1, 2

Hecht, Anthony (Evan) 1923- **CLC 8, 13, 19; DAM POET**
See also CA 9-12R; CANR 6; DLB 5, 169

Hecht, Ben 1894-1964 **CLC 8**
See also CA 85-88; DLB 7, 9, 25, 26, 28, 86

Hedayat, Sadeq 1903-1951 **TCLC 21**
See also CA 120

Hegel, Georg Wilhelm Friedrich 1770-1831 **NCLC 46**
See also DLB 90

Heidegger, Martin 1889-1976 **CLC 24**
See also CA 81-84; 65-68; CANR 34; MTCW 1, 2

Heidenstam, (Carl Gustaf) Vernervon 1859-1940 **TCLC 5**
See also CA 104

Heifner, Jack 1946- **CLC 11**
See also CA 105; CANR 47

Heijermans, Herman 1864-1924 **TCLC 24**
See also CA 123

Heilbrun, Carolyn G(old) 1926- **CLC 25**
See also CA 45-48; CANR 1, 28, 58

Heine, Heinrich 1797-1856 **NCLC 4, 54; PC 25**
See also DLB 90

Heinemann, Larry (Curtiss) 1944- **CLC 50**
See also CA 110; CAAS 21; CANR 31, 81; DLBD 9; INT CANR-31

Heiney, Donald (William) 1921-1993
See Harris, MacDonald
See also CA 1-4R; 142; CANR 3, 58

Heinlein, Robert A(nson) 1907-1988 **CLC 1, 3, 8, 14, 26, 55; DAM POP**
See also AAYA 17; CA 1-4R; 125; CANR 1, 20, 53; DLB 8; JRDA; MAICYA; MTCW 1, 2; SATA 9, 69; SATA-Obit 56

Helforth, John
See Doolittle, Hilda

Hellenhofferu, Vojtech Kapristian z
See Hasek, Jaroslav (Matej Frantisek)

Heller, Joseph 1923-**CLC 1, 3, 5, 8, 11, 36, 63; DA; DAB; DAC; DAM MST, NOV, POP; WLC**
See also AAYA 24; AITN 1; CA 5-8R; CABS 1; CANR 8, 42, 66; DLB 2, 28; DLBY 80; INT CANR-8; MTCW 1, 2

Hellman, Lillian (Florence) 1906-1984**CLC 2, 4, 8, 14, 18, 34, 44, 52; DAM DRAM; DC 1**
See also AITN 1, 2; CA 13-16R; 112; CANR 33; DLB 7; DLBY 84; MTCW 1, 2

Helprin, Mark 1947-**CLC 7, 10, 22, 32; DAM NOV, POP**
See also CA 81-84; CANR 47, 64; CDALBS; DLBY 85; MTCW 1, 2

Helvetius, Claude-Adrien 1715-1771   **LC 26**

Helyar, Jane Penelope Josephine 1933-
See Poole, Josephine
See also CA 21-24R; CANR 10, 26; SATA 82

Hemans, Felicia 1793-1835   **NCLC 71**
See also DLB 96

Hemingway, Ernest (Miller) 1899-1961 **C L C 1, 3, 6, 8, 10, 13, 19, 30, 34, 39, 41, 44, 50, 61, 80; DA; DAB; DAC; DAM MST, NOV; SSC 1, 25; WLC**
See also AAYA 19; CA 77-80; CANR 34; CDALB 1917-1929; DLB 4, 9, 102, 210; DLBD 1, 15, 16; DLBY 81, 87, 96, 98; MTCW 1, 2

Hempel, Amy 1951-   **CLC 39**
See also CA 118; 137; CANR 70; MTCW 2

Henderson, F. C.
See Mencken, H(enry) L(ouis)

Henderson, Sylvia
See Ashton-Warner, Sylvia (Constance)

Henderson, Zenna (Chlarson) 1917-1983**S S C 29**
See also CA 1-4R; 133; CANR 1; DLB 8; SATA 5

Henkin, Joshua   **CLC 119**
See also CA 161

Henley, Beth   **CLC 23; DC 6**
See also Henley, Elizabeth Becker
See also CABS 3; DLBY 86

Henley, Elizabeth Becker 1952-
See Henley, Beth
See also CA 107; CANR 32, 73; DAM DRAM, MST; MTCW 1, 2

Henley, William Ernest 1849-1903   **TCLC 8**
See also CA 105; DLB 19

Hennissart, Martha
See Lathen, Emma
See also CA 85-88; CANR 64

Henry, O.   **TCLC 1, 19; SSC 5; WLC**
See also Porter, William Sydney

Henry, Patrick 1736-1799   **LC 25**

Henryson, Robert 1430(?)-1506(?)   **LC 20**
See also DLB 146

Henry VIII 1491-1547   **LC 10**
See also DLB 132

Henschke, Alfred
See Klabund

Hentoff, Nat(han Irving) 1925-   **CLC 26**
See also AAYA 4; CA 1-4R; CAAS 6; CANR 5, 25, 77; CLR 1, 52; INT CANR-25; JRDA; MAICYA; SATA 42, 69; SATA-Brief 27

Heppenstall, (John) Rayner 1911-1981 **C L C 10**
See also CA 1-4R; 103; CANR 29

Heraclitus c. 540B.C.-c.450B.C.   **CMLC 22**
See also DLB 176

Herbert, Frank (Patrick) 1920-1986 **CLC 12, 23, 35, 44, 85; DAM POP**
See also AAYA 21; CA 53-56; 118; CANR 5,

43; CDALBS; DLB 8; INT CANR-5; MTCW 1, 2; SATA 9, 37; SATA-Obit 47

Herbert, George 1593-1633   **LC 24; DAB; DAM POET; PC 4**
See also CDBLB Before 1660; DLB 126

Herbert, Zbigniew 1924-1998   **CLC 9, 43; DAM POET**
See also CA 89-92; 169; CANR 36, 74; MTCW 1

Herbst, Josephine (Frey) 1897-1969 **CLC 34**
See also CA 5-8R; 25-28R; DLB 9

Heredia, Jose Maria 1803-1839
See also HLCS 2

Hergesheimer, Joseph 1880-1954   **TCLC 11**
See also CA 109; DLB 102, 9

Herlihy, James Leo 1927-1993   **CLC 6**
See also CA 1-4R; 143; CANR 2

Hermogenes fl. c. 175-   **CMLC 6**

Hernandez, Jose 1834-1886   **NCLC 17**

Herodotus c.484B.C.-429B.C.   **CMLC 17**
See also DLB 176

Herrick, Robert 1591-1674**LC 13; DA; DAB; DAC; DAM MST, POP; PC 9**
See also DLB 126

Herring, Guilles
See Somerville, Edith

Herriot, James 1916-1995**CLC 12;DAM POP**
See also Wight, James Alfred
See also AAYA 1; CA 148; CANR 40; MTCW 2; SATA 86

Herrmann, Dorothy 1941-   **CLC 44**
See also CA 107

Herrmann, Taffy
See Herrmann, Dorothy

Hersey, John (Richard) 1914-1993**CLC 1, 2, 7, 9, 40, 81, 97; DAM POP**
See also AAYA 29; CA 17-20R; 140; CANR 33; CDALBS; DLB 6, 185; MTCW 1, 2; SATA 25; SATA-Obit 76

Herzen, Aleksandr Ivanovich 1812-1870 **NCLC 10, 61**

Herzl, Theodor 1860-1904   **TCLC 36**
See also CA 168

Herzog, Werner 1942-   **CLC 16**
See also CA 89-92

Hesiod c. 8th cent. B.C.-   **CMLC 5**
See also DLB 176

Hesse, Hermann 1877-1962**CLC 1, 2, 3, 6, 11, 17, 25, 69; DA; DAB; DAC; DAM MST, NOV; SSC 9; WLC**
See also CA 17-18; CAP 2; DLB 66; MTCW 1, 2; SATA 50

Hewes, Cady
See De Voto, Bernard (Augustine)

Heyen, William 1940-   **CLC 13, 18**
See also CA 33-36R; CAAS 9; DLB 5

Heyerdahl, Thor 1914-   **CLC 26**
See also CA 5-8R; CANR 5, 22, 66, 73; MTCW 1, 2; SATA 2, 52

Heym, Georg (Theodor Franz Arthur) 1887-1912   **TCLC 9**
See also CA 106

Heym, Stefan 1913-   **CLC 41**
See also CA 9-12R; CANR 4; DLB 69

Heyse, Paul (Johann Ludwig von) 1830-1914 **TCLC 8**
See also CA 104; DLB 129

Heyward, (Edwin) DuBose 1885-1940 **T C L C 59**
See also CA 108; 157; DLB 7, 9, 45; SATA 21

Hibbert, Eleanor Alice Burford 1906-1993 **CLC 7; DAM POP**
See also BEST 90:4; CA 17-20R; 140; CANR

9, 28, 59; MTCW 2; SATA 2; SATA-Obit 74

Hichens, Robert (Smythe) 1864-1950 **T C L C 64**
See also CA 162; DLB 153

Higgins, George V(incent) 1939-**CLC 4, 7, 10, 18**
See also CA 77-80; CAAS 5; CANR 17, 51; DLB 2; DLBY 81, 98; INT CANR-17; MTCW 1

Higginson, Thomas Wentworth 1823-1911 **TCLC 36**
See also CA 162; DLB 1, 64

Highet, Helen
See MacInnes, Helen (Clark)

Highsmith, (Mary) Patricia 1921-1995**CLC 2, 4, 14, 42, 102; DAM NOV, POP**
See also CA 1-4R; 147; CANR 1, 20, 48, 62; MTCW 1, 2

Highwater, Jamake (Mamake) 1942(?)- **C L C 12**
See also AAYA 7; CA 65-68; CAAS 7; CANR 10, 34; CLR 17; DLB 52; DLBY 85; JRDA; MAICYA; SATA 32, 69; SATA-Brief 30

Highway, Tomson 1951-**CLC 92; DAC;DAM MULT**
See also CA 151; CANR 75; MTCW 2; NNAL

Higuchi, Ichiyo 1872-1896   **NCLC 49**

Hijuelos, Oscar 1951- **CLC 65; DAM MULT, POP; HLC 1**
See also AAYA 25; BEST 90:1; CA 123; CANR 50, 75; DLB 145; HW 1, 2; MTCW 2

Hikmet, Nazim 1902(?)-1963   **CLC 40**
See also CA 141; 93-96

Hildegard von Bingen 1098-1179   **CMLC 20**
See also DLB 148

Hildesheimer, Wolfgang 1916-1991   **CLC 49**
See also CA 101; 135; DLB 69, 124

Hill, Geoffrey (William) 1932- **CLC 5, 8, 18, 45; DAM POET**
See also CA 81-84; CANR 21; CDBLB 1960 to Present; DLB 40; MTCW 1

Hill, George Roy 1921-   **CLC 26**
See also CA 110; 122

Hill, John
See Koontz, Dean R(ay)

Hill, Susan (Elizabeth) 1942- **CLC 4, 113; DAB; DAM MST, NOV**
See also CA 33-36R; CANR 29, 69; DLB 14, 139; MTCW 1

Hillerman, Tony 1925-   **CLC 62;DAM POP**
See also AAYA 6; BEST 89:1; CA 29-32R; CANR 21, 42, 65; DLB 206; SATA 6

Hillesum, Etty 1914-1943   **TCLC 49**
See also CA 137

Hilliard, Noel (Harvey) 1929-   **CLC 15**
See also CA 9-12R; CANR 7, 69

Hillis, Rick 1956-   **CLC 66**
See also CA 134

Hilton, James 1900-1954   **TCLC 21**
See also CA 108; 169; DLB 34, 77; SATA 34

Himes, Chester (Bomar) 1909-1984**CLC 2, 4, 7, 18, 58, 108; BLC 2; DAM MULT**
See also BW 2; CA 25-28R; 114; CANR 22; DLB 2, 76, 143; MTCW 1, 2

Hinde, Thomas   **CLC 6, 11**
See also Chitty, Thomas Willes

Hindin, Nathan 1917-1994
See Bloch, Robert (Albert)
See also CA 179; CAAE 179

Hine, (William) Daryl 1936-   **CLC 15**
See also CA 1-4R; CAAS 15; CANR 1, 20; DLB 60

Hinkson, Katharine Tynan

See Tynan, Katharine

Hinojosa(-Smith), Rolando (R.) 1929-
See Hinojosa-Smith, Rolando
See also CA 131; CAAS 16; CANR 62; DAM
MULT; DLB 82; HLC 1; HW 1, 2; MTCW 2

Hinojosa-Smith, Rolando 1929-
See Hinojosa(-Smith), Rolando (R.)
See also CAAS 16; HLC 1; MTCW 2

Hinton, S(usan) E(loise) 1950- **CLC 30, 111;**
DA; DAB; DAC; DAM MST, NOV
See also AAYA 2; CA 81-84; CANR 32, 62;
CDALBS; CLR 3, 23; JRDA; MAICYA;
MTCW 1, 2; SATA 19, 58

Hippius, Zinaida **TCLC 9**
See also Gippius, Zinaida (Nikolayevna)

Hiraoka, Kimitake 1925-1970
See Mishima, Yukio
See also CA 97-100; 29-32R; DAM DRAM;
MTCW 1, 2

Hirsch, E(ric) D(onald),Jr. 1928- **CLC 79**
See also CA 25-28R; CANR 27, 51; DLB 67;
INT CANR-27; MTCW 1

Hirsch, Edward 1950- **CLC 31, 50**
See also CA 104; CANR 20, 42; DLB 120

Hitchcock, Alfred (Joseph) 1899-1980**CLC 16**
See also AAYA 22; CA 159; 97-100; SATA 27;
SATA-Obit 24

Hitler, Adolf 1889-1945 **TCLC 53**
See also CA 117; 147

Hoagland, Edward 1932- **CLC 28**
See also CA 1-4R; CANR 2, 31, 57; DLB 6;
SATA 51

Hoban, Russell (Conwell) 1925- **CLC 7, 25;**
DAM NOV
See also CA 5-8R; CANR 23, 37, 66; CLR 3;
DLB 52; MAICYA; MTCW 1, 2; SATA 1,
40, 78

Hobbes, Thomas 1588-1679 **LC 36**
See also DLB 151

Hobbs, Perry
See Blackmur, R(ichard) P(almer)

Hobson, Laura Z(ametkin) 1900-1986**CLC 7,**
25
See also CA 17-20R; 118; CANR 55; DLB 28;
SATA 52

Hochhuth, Rolf 1931- **CLC 4, 11, 18; DAM**
DRAM
See also CA 5-8R; CANR 33, 75; DLB 124;
MTCW 1, 2

Hochman, Sandra 1936- **CLC 3, 8**
See also CA 5-8R; DLB 5

Hochwaelder, Fritz 1911-1986**CLC 36; DAM**
DRAM
See also CA 29-32R; 120; CANR 42; MTCW 1

Hochwalder, Fritz
See Hochwaelder, Fritz

Hocking, Mary (Eunice) 1921- **CLC 13**
See also CA 101; CANR 18, 40

Hodgins, Jack 1938- **CLC 23**
See also CA 93-96; DLB 60

Hodgson, William Hope 1877(?)-1918 **T C L C**
13
See also CA 111; 164; DLB 70, 153, 156, 178;
MTCW 2

Hoeg, Peter 1957- **CLC 95**
See also CA 151; CANR 75; MTCW 2

Hoffman, Alice 1952- **CLC 51;DAM NOV**
See also CA 77-80; CANR 34, 66; MTCW 1, 2

Hoffman, Daniel (Gerard) 1923-**CLC 6, 13, 23**
See also CA 1-4R; CANR 4; DLB 5

Hoffman, Stanley 1944- **CLC 5**
See also CA 77-80

Hoffman, William M(oses) 1939- **CLC 40**

See also CA 57-60; CANR 11, 71

Hoffmann, E(rnst) T(heodor) A(madeus) 1776-
1822 **NCLC 2; SSC 13**
See also DLB 90; SATA 27

Hofmann, Gert 1931- **CLC 54**
See also CA 128

Hofmannsthal, Hugo von 1874-1929**TCLC 11;**
DAM DRAM; DC 4
See also CA 106; 153; DLB 81, 118

Hogan, Linda 1947- **CLC 73;DAM MULT**
See also CA 120; CANR 45, 73; DLB 175;
NNAL

Hogarth, Charles
See Creasey, John

Hogarth, Emmett
See Polonsky, Abraham (Lincoln)

Hogg, James 1770-1835 **NCLC 4**
See also DLB 93, 116, 159

Holbach, Paul Henri Thiry Baron 1723-1789
LC 14

Holberg, Ludvig 1684-1754 **LC 6**

Holden, Ursula 1921- **CLC 18**
See also CA 101; CAAS 8; CANR 22

Holderlin, (Johann Christian) Friedrich 1770-
1843 **NCLC 16; PC 4**

Holdstock, Robert
See Holdstock, Robert P.

Holdstock, Robert P. 1948- **CLC 39**
See also CA 131; CANR 81

Holland, Isabelle 1920- **CLC 21**
See also AAYA 11; CA 21-24R; CANR 10, 25,
47; CLR 57; JRDA; MAICYA; SATA 8, 70;
SATA-Essay 103

Holland, Marcus
See Caldwell, (Janet Miriam) Taylor (Holland)

Hollander, John 1929- **CLC 2, 5, 8, 14**
See also CA 1-4R; CANR 1, 52; DLB 5; SATA
13

Hollander, Paul
See Silverberg, Robert

Holleran, Andrew 1943(?)- **CLC 38**
See also CA 144

Hollinghurst, Alan 1954- **CLC 55, 91**
See also CA 114; DLB 207

Hollis, Jim
See Summers, Hollis (Spurgeon, Jr.)

Holly, Buddy 1936-1959 **TCLC 65**

Holmes, Gordon
See Shiel, M(atthew) P(hipps)

Holmes, John
See Souster, (Holmes) Raymond

Holmes, John Clellon 1926-1988 **CLC 56**
See also CA 9-12R; 125; CANR 4; DLB 16

Holmes, Oliver Wendell, Jr. 1841-1935**TCLC**
77
See also CA 114

Holmes, Oliver Wendell 1809-1894 **NCLC 14**
See also CDALB 1640-1865; DLB 1, 189;
SATA 34

Holmes, Raymond
See Souster, (Holmes) Raymond

Holt, Victoria
See Hibbert, Eleanor Alice Burford

Holub, Miroslav 1923-1998 **CLC 4**
See also CA 21-24R; 169; CANR 10

Homer c. 8th cent. B.C.- **CMLC 1, 16; DA;**
DAB; DAC; DAM MST, POET; PC 23;
WLCS
See also DLB 176

Hongo, Garrett Kaoru 1951- **PC 23**
See also CA 133; CAAS 22; DLB 120

Honig, Edwin 1919- **CLC 33**
See also CA 5-8R; CAAS 8; CANR 4, 45; DLB

5

Hood, Hugh (John Blagdon) 1928-**CLC 15, 28**
See also CA 49-52; CAAS 17; CANR 1, 33;
DLB 53

Hood, Thomas 1799-1845 **NCLC 16**
See also DLB 96

Hooker, (Peter) Jeremy 1941- **CLC 43**
See also CA 77-80; CANR 22; DLB 40

hooks, bell **CLC 94; BLCS**
See also Watkins, Gloria
See also MTCW 2

Hope, A(lec) D(erwent) 1907- **CLC 3, 51**
See also CA 21-24R; CANR 33, 74; MTCW 1,
2

Hope, Anthony 1863-1933 **TCLC 83**
See also CA 157; DLB 153, 156

Hope, Brian
See Creasey, John

Hope, Christopher (David Tully) 1944- **C L C**
52
See also CA 106; CANR 47; SATA 62

Hopkins, Gerard Manley 1844-1889 **N C L C**
17; DA; DAB; DAC; DAM MST, POET;
PC 15; WLC
See also CDBLB 1890-1914; DLB 35, 57

Hopkins, John (Richard) 1931-1998 **CLC 4**
See also CA 85-88; 169

Hopkins, Pauline Elizabeth 1859-1930**T C L C**
28; BLC 2; DAM MULT
See also BW 2, 3; CA 141; CANR 82; DLB 50

Hopkinson, Francis 1737-1791 **LC 25**
See also DLB 31

Hopley-Woolrich, Cornell George 1903-1968
See Woolrich, Cornell
See also CA 13-14; CANR 58; CAP 1; MTCW
2

Horatio
See Proust, (Valentin-Louis-George-Eugene-)
Marcel

Horgan, Paul (George Vincent O'Shaughnessy)
1903-1995 **CLC 9, 53;DAM NOV**
See also CA 13-16R; 147; CANR 9, 35; DLB
212; DLBY 85; INT CANR-9; MTCW 1, 2;
SATA 13; SATA-Obit 84

Horn, Peter
See Kuttner, Henry

Hornem, Horace Esq.
See Byron, George Gordon (Noel)

Horney, Karen (Clementine Theodore
Danielsen) 1885-1952 **TCLC 71**
See also CA 114; 165

Hornung, E(rnest) W(illiam) 1866-1921
TCLC 59
See also CA 108; 160; DLB 70

Horovitz, Israel (Arthur) 1939-**CLC 56; DAM**
DRAM
See also CA 33-36R; CANR 46, 59; DLB 7

Horvath, Odon von
See Horvath, Oedoen von
See also DLB 85, 124

Horvath, Oedoen von 1901-1938 **TCLC 45**
See also Horvath, Odon von
See also CA 118

Horwitz, Julius 1920-1986 **CLC 14**
See also CA 9-12R; 119; CANR 12

Hospital, Janette Turner 1942- **CLC 42**
See also CA 108; CANR 48

Hostos, E. M. de
See Hostos (y Bonilla), Eugenio Maria de

Hostos, Eugenio M. de
See Hostos (y Bonilla), Eugenio Maria de

Hostos, Eugenio Maria
See Hostos (y Bonilla), Eugenio Maria de

Hostos (y Bonilla), Eugenio Mariade 1839-1903
   TCLC 24
   See also CA 123; 131; HW 1
Houdini
   See Lovecraft, H(oward) P(hillips)
Hougan, Carolyn 1943-   **CLC 34**
   See also CA 139
Household, Geoffrey (Edward West) 1900-1988
   CLC 11
   See also CA 77-80; 126; CANR 58; DLB 87;
   SATA 14; SATA-Obit 59
Housman, A(lfred) E(dward) 1859-1936
   **TCLC 1, 10; DA; DAB; DAC; DAM MST,
   POET; PC 2; WLCS**
   See also CA 104; 125; DLB 19; MTCW 1, 2
Housman, Laurence 1865-1959   **TCLC 7**
   See also CA 106; 155; DLB 10; SATA 25
Howard, Elizabeth Jane 1923-   **CLC 7, 29**
   See also CA 5-8R; CANR 8, 62
Howard, Maureen 1930-   **CLC 5, 14, 46**
   See also CA 53-56; CANR 31, 75; DLBY 83;
   INT CANR-31; MTCW 1, 2
Howard, Richard 1929-   **CLC 7, 10, 47**
   See also AITN 1; CA 85-88; CANR 25, 80; DLB
   5; INT CANR-25
Howard, Robert E(rvin) 1906-1936 **TCLC 8**
   See also CA 105; 157
Howard, Warren F.
   See Pohl, Frederik
Howe, Fanny (Quincy) 1940-   **CLC 47**
   See also CA 117; CAAS 27; CANR 70; SATA-
   Brief 52
Howe, Irving 1920-1993   **CLC 85**
   See also CA 9-12R; 141; CANR 21, 50; DLB
   67; MTCW 1, 2
Howe, Julia Ward 1819-1910   **TCLC 21**
   See also CA 117; DLB 1, 189
Howe, Susan 1937-   **CLC 72**
   See also CA 160; DLB 120
Howe, Tina 1937-   **CLC 48**
   See also CA 109
Howell, James 1594(?)-1666   **LC 13**
   See also DLB 151
Howells, W. D.
   See Howells, William Dean
Howells, William D.
   See Howells, William Dean
Howells, William Dean 1837-1920 **TCLC 7, 17,
   41**
   See also CA 104; 134; CDALB 1865-1917;
   DLB 12, 64, 74, 79, 189; MTCW 2
Howes, Barbara 1914-1996   **CLC 15**
   See also CA 9-12R; 151; CAAS 3; CANR 53;
   SATA 5
Hrabal, Bohumil 1914-1997   **CLC 13, 67**
   See also CA 106; 156; CAAS 12; CANR 57
Hroswitha of Gandersheim c. 935-c.1002
   CMLC 29
   See also DLB 148
Hsun, Lu
   See Lu Hsun
Hubbard, L(afayette) Ron(ald) 1911-1986
   CLC 43; DAM POP
   See also CA 77-80; 118; CANR 52; MTCW 2
Huch, Ricarda (Octavia) 1864-1947 **TCLC 13**
   See also CA 111; DLB 66
Huddle, David 1942-   **CLC 49**
   See also CA 57-60; CAAS 20; DLB 130
Hudson, Jeffrey
   See Crichton, (John) Michael
Hudson, W(illiam) H(enry) 1841-1922 **T C L C
   29**
   See also CA 115; DLB 98, 153, 174; SATA 35

Hueffer, Ford Madox
   See Ford, Ford Madox
Hughart, Barry 1934-   **CLC 39**
   See also CA 137
Hughes, Colin
   See Creasey, John
Hughes, David (John) 1930-   **CLC 48**
   See also CA 116; 129; DLB 14
Hughes, Edward James
   See Hughes, Ted
   See also DAM MST, POET
Hughes, (James) Langston 1902-1967 **CLC 1,
   5, 10, 15, 35, 44, 108; BLC 2; DA; DAB;
   DAC; DAM DRAM, MST, MULT, POET;
   DC 3; PC 1; SSC 6; WLC**
   See also AAYA 12; BW 1, 3; CA 1-4R; 25-28R;
   CANR 1, 34, 82; CDALB 1929-1941; CLR
   17; DLB 4, 7, 48, 51, 86; JRDA; MAICYA;
   MTCW 1, 2; SATA 4, 33
Hughes, Richard (Arthur Warren) 1900-1976
   CLC 1, 11; DAM NOV
   See also CA 5-8R; 65-68; CANR 4; DLB 15,
   161; MTCW 1; SATA 8; SATA-Obit 25
Hughes, Ted 1930-1998   **CLC 2, 4, 9, 14, 37,
   119; DAB; DAC; PC 7**
   See also Hughes, Edward James
   See also CA 1-4R; 171; CANR 1, 33, 66; CLR
   3; DLB 40, 161; MAICYA; MTCW 1, 2;
   SATA 49; SATA-Brief 27; SATA-Obit 107
Hugo, Richard F(ranklin) 1923-1982 **CLC 6,
   18, 32; DAM POET**
   See also CA 49-52; 108; CANR 3; DLB 5, 206
Hugo, Victor (Marie) 1802-1885 **NCLC 3, 10,
   21; DA; DAB; DAC; DAM DRAM, MST,
   NOV, POET; PC 17; WLC**
   See also AAYA 28; DLB 119, 192; SATA 47
Huidobro, Vicente
   See Huidobro Fernandez, Vicente Garcia
Huidobro Fernandez, Vicente Garcia 1893-
   1948   **TCLC 31**
   See also CA 131; HW 1
Hulme, Keri 1947-   **CLC 39**
   See also CA 125; CANR 69; INT 125
Hulme, T(homas) E(rnest) 1883-1917 **T C L C
   21**
   See also CA 117; DLB 19
Hume, David 1711-1776   **LC 7**
   See also DLB 104
Humphrey, William 1924-1997   **CLC 45**
   See also CA 77-80; 160; CANR 68; DLB 212
Humphreys, Emyr Owen 1919-   **CLC 47**
   See also CA 5-8R; CANR 3, 24; DLB 15
Humphreys, Josephine 1945-   **CLC 34, 57**
   See also CA 121; 127; INT 127
Huneker, James Gibbons 1857-1921 **TCLC 65**
   See also DLB 71
Hungerford, Pixie
   See Brinsmead, H(esba) F(ay)
Hunt, E(verette) Howard, (Jr.) 1918- **CLC 3**
   See also AITN 1; CA 45-48; CANR 2, 47
Hunt, Kyle
   See Creasey, John
Hunt, (James Henry) Leigh 1784-1859 **N C L C
   1, 70; DAM POET**
   See also DLB 96, 110, 144
Hunt, Marsha 1946-   **CLC 70**
   See also BW 2, 3; CA 143; CANR 79
Hunt, Violet 1866(?)-1942   **TCLC 53**
   See also DLB 162, 197
Hunter, E. Waldo
   See Sturgeon, Theodore (Hamilton)
Hunter, Evan 1926-   **CLC 11, 31; DAM POP**
   See also CA 5-8R; CANR 5, 38, 62; DLBY 82;

   INT CANR-5; MTCW 1; SATA 25
Hunter, Kristin (Eggleston) 1931-   **CLC 35**
   See also AITN 1; BW 1; CA 13-16R; CANR
   13; CLR 3; DLB 33; INT CANR-13;
   MAICYA; SAAS 10; SATA 12
Hunter, Mary
   See Austin, Mary (Hunter)
Hunter, Mollie 1922-   **CLC 21**
   See also McIlwraith, Maureen Mollie Hunter
   See also AAYA 13; CANR 37, 78; CLR 25; DLB
   161; JRDA; MAICYA; SAAS 7; SATA 54,
   106
Hunter, Robert (?)-1734   **LC 7**
Hurston, Zora Neale 1903-1960 **CLC 7, 30, 61;
   BLC 2; DA; DAC; DAM MST, MULT,
   NOV; SSC 4; WLCS**
   See also AAYA 15; BW 1, 3; CA 85-88; CANR
   61; CDALBS; DLB 51, 86; MTCW 1, 2
Huston, John (Marcellus) 1906-1987 **CLC 20**
   See also CA 73-76; 123; CANR 34; DLB 26
Hustvedt, Siri 1955-   **CLC 76**
   See also CA 137
Hutten, Ulrich von 1488-1523   **LC 16**
   See also DLB 179
Huxley, Aldous (Leonard) 1894-1963 **CLC 1,
   3, 4, 5, 8, 11, 18, 35, 79; DA; DAB; DAC;
   DAM MST, NOV; WLC**
   See also AAYA 11; CA 85-88; CANR 44;
   CDBLB 1914-1945; DLB 36, 100, 162, 195;
   MTCW 1, 2; SATA 63
Huxley, T(homas) H(enry) 1825-1895 **N C L C
   67**
   See also DLB 57
Huysmans, Joris-Karl 1848-1907 **TCLC 7, 69**
   See also CA 104; 165; DLB 123
Hwang, David Henry 1957-   **CLC 55; DAM
   DRAM; DC 4**
   See also CA 127; 132; CANR 76; DLB 212;
   INT 132; MTCW 2
Hyde, Anthony 1946-   **CLC 42**
   See also CA 136
Hyde, Margaret O(ldroyd) 1917-   **CLC 21**
   See also CA 1-4R; CANR 1, 36; CLR 23; JRDA;
   MAICYA; SAAS 8; SATA 1, 42, 76
Hynes, James 1956(?)-   **CLC 65**
   See also CA 164
Hypatia c. 370-415   **CMLC 35**
Ian, Janis 1951-   **CLC 21**
   See also CA 105
Ibanez, Vicente Blasco
   See Blasco Ibanez, Vicente
Ibarbourou, Juana de 1895-1979
   See also HLCS 2; HW 1
Ibarguengoitia, Jorge 1928-1983   **CLC 37**
   See also CA 124; 113; HW 1
Ibsen, Henrik (Johan) 1828-1906 **TCLC 2, 8,
   16, 37, 52; DA; DAB; DAC; DAM DRAM,
   MST; DC 2; WLC**
   See also CA 104; 141
Ibuse, Masuji 1898-1993   **CLC 22**
   See also CA 127; 141; DLB 180
Ichikawa, Kon 1915-   **CLC 20**
   See also CA 121
Idle, Eric 1943-   **CLC 21**
   See also Monty Python
   See also CA 116; CANR 35
Ignatow, David 1914-1997 **CLC 4, 7, 14, 40**
   See also CA 9-12R; 162; CAAS 3; CANR 31,
   57; DLB 5
Ignotus
   See Strachey, (Giles) Lytton
Ihimaera, Witi 1944-   **CLC 46**
   See also CA 77-80

Ilf, Ilya   **TCLC 21**
   See also Fainzilberg, Ilya Arnoldovich
Illyes, Gyula 1902-1983   **PC 16**
   See also CA 114; 109
Immermann, Karl (Lebrecht) 1796-1840
   NCLC 4, 49
   See also DLB 133
Ince, Thomas H. 1882-1924   **TCLC 89**
Inchbald, Elizabeth 1753-1821   **NCLC 62**
   See also DLB 39, 89
Inclan, Ramon (Maria) del Valle
   See Valle-Inclan, Ramon (Maria) del
Infante, G(uillermo) Cabrera
   See Cabrera Infante, G(uillermo)
Ingalls, Rachel (Holmes) 1940-   **CLC 42**
   See also CA 123; 127
Ingamells, Reginald Charles
   See Ingamells, Rex
Ingamells, Rex 1913-1955   **TCLC 35**
   See also CA 167
Inge, William (Motter) 1913-1973 **CLC 1, 8,**
   19; DAM DRAM
   See also CA 9-12R; CDALB 1941-1968; DLB
   7; MTCW 1, 2
Ingelow, Jean 1820-1897   **NCLC 39**
   See also DLB 35, 163; SATA 33
Ingram, Willis J.
   See Harris, Mark
Innaurato, Albert (F.) 1948(?)-   **CLC 21, 60**
   See also CA 115; 122; CANR 78; INT 122
Innes, Michael
   See Stewart, J(ohn) I(nnes) M(ackintosh)
Innis, Harold Adams 1894-1952   **TCLC 77**
   See also DLB 88
Ionesco, Eugene 1909-1994**CLC 1, 4, 6, 9, 11,**
   15, 41, 86; DA; DAB; DAC; DAM DRAM,
   MST; WLC
   See also CA 9-12R; 144; CANR 55; MTCW 1,
   2; SATA 7; SATA-Obit 79
Iqbal, Muhammad 1873-1938   **TCLC 28**
Ireland, Patrick
   See O'Doherty, Brian
Iron, Ralph
   See Schreiner, Olive (Emilie Albertina)
Irving, John (Winslow) 1942-**CLC 13, 23, 38,**
   112; DAM NOV, POP
   See also AAYA 8; BEST 89:3; CA 25-28R;
   CANR 28, 73; DLB 6; DLBY 82; MTCW 1,
   2
Irving, Washington 1783-1859   **NCLC 2, 19;**
   DA; DAB; DAC; DAM MST; SSC 2; WLC
   See also CDALB 1640-1865; DLB 3, 11, 30,
   59, 73, 74, 186; YABC 2
Irwin, P. K.
   See Page, P(atricia) K(athleen)
Isaacs, Jorge Ricardo 1837-1895   **NCLC 70**
Isaacs, Susan 1943-   **CLC 32;DAM POP**
   See also BEST 89:1; CA 89-92; CANR 20, 41,
   65; INT CANR-20; MTCW 1, 2
Isherwood, Christopher (William Bradshaw)
   1904-1986   **CLC 1, 9, 11, 14, 44; DAM**
   DRAM, NOV
   See also CA 13-16R; 117; CANR 35; DLB 15,
   195; DLBY 86; MTCW 1, 2
Ishiguro, Kazuo 1954-   **CLC 27, 56, 59, 110;**
   DAM NOV
   See also BEST 90:2; CA 120; CANR 49; DLB
   194; MTCW 1, 2
Ishikawa, Hakuhin
   See Ishikawa, Takuboku
Ishikawa, Takuboku 1886(?)-1912 **TCLC 15;**
   DAM POET; PC 10
   See also CA 113; 153

Iskander, Fazil 1929-   **CLC 47**
   See also CA 102
Isler, Alan (David) 1934-   **CLC 91**
   See also CA 156
Ivan IV 1530-1584   **LC 17**
Ivanov, Vyacheslav Ivanovich 1866-1949
   TCLC 33
   See also CA 122
Ivask, Ivar Vidrik 1927-1992   **CLC 14**
   See also CA 37-40R; 139; CANR 24
Ives, Morgan
   See Bradley, Marion Zimmer
Izumi Shikibu c. 973-c. 1034   **CMLC 33**
J. R. S.
   See Gogarty, Oliver St. John
Jabran, Kahlil
   See Gibran, Kahlil
Jabran, Khalil
   See Gibran, Kahlil
Jackson, Daniel
   See Wingrove, David (John)
Jackson, Jesse 1908-1983   **CLC 12**
   See also BW 1; CA 25-28R; 109; CANR 27;
   CLR 28; MAICYA; SATA 2, 29; SATA-Obit
   48
Jackson, Laura (Riding) 1901-1991
   See Riding, Laura
   See also CA 65-68; 135; CANR 28; DLB 48
Jackson, Sam
   See Trumbo, Dalton
Jackson, Sara
   See Wingrove, David (John)
Jackson, Shirley 1919-1965   **CLC 11, 60, 87;**
   DA; DAC; DAM MST; SSC 9; WLC
   See also AAYA 9; CA 1-4R; 25-28R; CANR 4,
   52; CDALB 1941-1968; DLB 6; MTCW 2;
   SATA 2
Jacob, (Cyprien-)Max 1876-1944   **TCLC 6**
   See also CA 104
Jacobs, Harriet A(nn) 1813(?)-1897**NCLC 67**
Jacobs, Jim 1942-   **CLC 12**
   See also CA 97-100; INT 97-100
Jacobs, W(illiam) W(ymark) 1863-1943
   TCLC 22
   See also CA 121; 167; DLB 135
Jacobsen, Jens Peter 1847-1885   **NCLC 34**
Jacobsen, Josephine 1908-   **CLC 48,102**
   See also CA 33-36R; CAAS 18; CANR 23, 48
Jacobson, Dan 1929-   **CLC 4, 14**
   See also CA 1-4R; CANR 2, 25, 66; DLB 14,
   207; MTCW 1
Jacqueline
   See Carpentier (y Valmont), Alejo
Jagger, Mick 1944-   **CLC 17**
Jahiz, al- c. 780-c. 869   **CMLC 25**
Jakes, John (William) 1932- **CLC 29; DAM**
   NOV, POP
   See also BEST 89:4; CA 57-60; CANR 10, 43,
   66; DLBY 83; INT CANR-10; MTCW 1, 2;
   SATA 62
James, Andrew
   See Kirkup, James
James, C(yril) L(ionel) R(obert) 1901-1989
   CLC 33; BLCS
   See also BW 2; CA 117; 125; 128; CANR 62;
   DLB 125; MTCW 1
James, Daniel (Lewis) 1911-1988
   See Santiago, Danny
   See also CA 174; 125
James, Dynely
   See Mayne, William (James Carter)
James, Henry Sr. 1811-1882   **NCLC 53**
James, Henry 1843-1916 **TCLC 2, 11, 24, 40,**

   47, 64; **DA; DAB; DAC; DAM MST, NOV;**
   SSC 8, 32; WLC
   See also CA 104; 132; CDALB 1865-1917;
   DLB 12, 71, 74, 189; DLBD 13; MTCW 1,
   2
James, M. R.
   See James, Montague (Rhodes)
   See also DLB 156
James, Montague (Rhodes) 1862-1936 **T C L C**
   6; SSC 16
   See also CA 104; DLB 201
James, P. D. 1920-   **CLC 18, 46, 122**
   See also White, Phyllis Dorothy James
   See also BEST 90:2; CDBLB 1960 to Present;
   DLB 87; DLBD 17
James, Philip
   See Moorcock, Michael (John)
James, William 1842-1910   **TCLC 15, 32**
   See also CA 109
James I 1394-1437   **LC 20**
Jameson, Anna 1794-1860   **NCLC 43**
   See also DLB 99, 166
Jami, Nur al-Din 'Abd al-Rahman 1414-1492
   LC 9
Jammes, Francis 1868-1938   **TCLC 75**
Jandl, Ernst 1925-   **CLC 34**
Janowitz, Tama 1957-   **CLC 43;DAM POP**
   See also CA 106; CANR 52
Japrisot, Sebastien 1931-   **CLC 90**
Jarrell, Randall 1914-1965**CLC 1, 2, 6, 9, 13,**
   49; DAM POET
   See also CA 5-8R; 25-28R; CABS 2; CANR 6,
   34; CDALB 1941-1968; CLR 6; DLB 48, 52;
   MAICYA; MTCW 1, 2; SATA 7
Jarry, Alfred 1873-1907   **TCLC 2, 14; DAM**
   DRAM; SSC 20
   See also CA 104; 153; DLB 192
Jarvis, E. K. 1917-1994
   See Bloch, Robert (Albert)
   See also CA 179; CAAE 179
Jeake, Samuel, Jr.
   See Aiken, Conrad (Potter)
Jean Paul 1763-1825   **NCLC 7**
Jefferies, (John) Richard 1848-1887**NCLC 47**
   See also DLB 98, 141; SATA 16
Jeffers, (John) Robinson 1887-1962**CLC 2, 3,**
   11, 15, 54; DA; DAC; DAM MST, POET;
   PC 17; WLC
   See also CA 85-88; CANR 35; CDALB 1917-
   1929; DLB 45, 212; MTCW 1, 2
Jefferson, Janet
   See Mencken, H(enry) L(ouis)
Jefferson, Thomas 1743-1826   **NCLC 11**
   See also CDALB 1640-1865; DLB 31
Jeffrey, Francis 1773-1850   **NCLC 33**
   See also DLB 107
Jelakowitch, Ivan
   See Heijermans, Herman
Jellicoe, (Patricia) Ann 1927-   **CLC 27**
   See also CA 85-88; DLB 13
Jen, Gish   **CLC 70**
   See also Jen, Lillian
Jen, Lillian 1956(?)-
   See Jen, Gish
   See also CA 135
Jenkins, (John) Robin 1912-   **CLC 52**
   See also CA 1-4R; CANR 1; DLB 14
Jennings, Elizabeth (Joan) 1926- **CLC 5, 14**
   See also CA 61-64; CAAS 5; CANR 8, 39, 66;
   DLB 27; MTCW 1; SATA 66
Jennings, Waylon 1937-   **CLC 21**
Jensen, Johannes V. 1873-1950   **TCLC 41**
   See also CA 170

Jensen, Laura (Linnea) 1948-   **CLC 37**
    See also CA 103
Jerome, Jerome K(lapka) 1859-1927**TCLC 23**
    See also CA 119; 177; DLB 10, 34, 135
Jerrold, Douglas William 1803-1857**NCLC 2**
    See also DLB 158, 159
Jewett, (Theodora) Sarah Orne 1849-1909
    TCLC 1, 22; SSC 6
    See also CA 108; 127; CANR 71; DLB 12, 74;
    SATA 15
Jewsbury, Geraldine (Endsor) 1812-1880
    NCLC 22
    See also DLB 21
Jhabvala, Ruth Prawer 1927-**CLC 4, 8, 29, 94;**
    DAB; DAM NOV
    See also CA 1-4R; CANR 2, 29, 51, 74; DLB
    139, 194; INT CANR-29; MTCW 1, 2
Jibran, Kahlil
    See Gibran, Kahlil
Jibran, Khalil
    See Gibran, Kahlil
Jiles, Paulette 1943-   **CLC 13, 58**
    See also CA 101; CANR 70
Jimenez (Mantecon), Juan Ramon 1881-1958
    TCLC 4; DAM MULT, POET; HLC 1; PC
    7
    See also CA 104; 131; CANR 74; DLB 134;
    HW 1; MTCW 1, 2
Jimenez, Ramon
    See Jimenez (Mantecon), Juan Ramon
Jimenez Mantecon, Juan
    See Jimenez (Mantecon), Juan Ramon
Jin, Ha 1956-   **CLC 109**
    See also CA 152
Joel, Billy   **CLC 26**
    See also Joel, William Martin
Joel, William Martin 1949-
    See Joel, Billy
    See also CA 108
John, Saint 7th cent. -   **CMLC 27**
John of the Cross, St. 1542-1591   **LC 18**
Johnson, B(ryan) S(tanley William) 1933-1973
    CLC 6, 9
    See also CA 9-12R; 53-56; CANR 9; DLB 14,
    40
Johnson, Benj. F. of Boo
    See Riley, James Whitcomb
Johnson, Benjamin F. of Boo
    See Riley, James Whitcomb
Johnson, Charles (Richard) 1948-**CLC 7, 51,**
    65; BLC 2; DAM MULT
    See also BW 2, 3; CA 116; CAAS 18; CANR
    42, 66, 82; DLB 33; MTCW 2
Johnson, Denis 1949-   **CLC 52**
    See also CA 117; 121; CANR 71; DLB 120
Johnson, Diane 1934-   **CLC 5, 13, 48**
    See also CA 41-44R; CANR 17, 40, 62; DLBY
    80; INT CANR-17; MTCW 1
Johnson, Eyvind (Olof Verner) 1900-1976
    CLC 14
    See also CA 73-76; 69-72; CANR 34
Johnson, J. R.
    See James, C(yril) L(ionel) R(obert)
Johnson, James Weldon 1871-1938 **TCLC 3,**
    19; BLC 2; DAM MULT, POET; PC 24
    See also BW 1, 3; CA 104; 125; CANR 82;
    CDALB 1917-1929; CLR 32; DLB 51;
    MTCW 1, 2; SATA 31
Johnson, Joyce 1935-   **CLC 58**
    See also CA 125; 129
Johnson, Judith (Emlyn) 1936- **CLC 7, 15**
    See also CA 25-28R, 153; CANR 34
Johnson, Lionel (Pigot) 1867-1902 **TCLC 19**

See also CA 117; DLB 19
Johnson, Marguerite (Annie)
    See Angelou, Maya
Johnson, Mel
    See Malzberg, Barry N(athaniel)
Johnson, Pamela Hansford 1912-1981**CLC 1,**
    7, 27
    See also CA 1-4R; 104; CANR 2, 28; DLB 15;
    MTCW 1, 2
Johnson, Robert 1911(?)-1938   **TCLC 69**
    See also BW 3; CA 174
Johnson, Samuel 1709-1784 **LC 15, 52; DA;**
    DAB; DAC; DAM MST; WLC
    See also CDBLB 1660-1789; DLB 39, 95, 104,
    142
Johnson, Uwe 1934-1984   **CLC 5, 10, 15, 40**
    See also CA 1-4R; 112; CANR 1, 39; DLB 75;
    MTCW 1
Johnston, George (Benson) 1913-   **CLC 51**
    See also CA 1-4R; CANR 5, 20; DLB 88
Johnston, Jennifer 1930-   **CLC 7**
    See also CA 85-88; DLB 14
Jolley, (Monica) Elizabeth 1923-**CLC 46; SSC**
    19
    See also CA 127; CAAS 13; CANR 59
Jones, Arthur Llewellyn 1863-1947
    See Machen, Arthur
    See also CA 104
Jones, D(ouglas) G(ordon) 1929-   **CLC 10**
    See also CA 29-32R; CANR 13; DLB 53
Jones, David (Michael) 1895-1974**CLC 2, 4, 7,**
    13, 42
    See also CA 9-12R; 53-56; CANR 28; CDBLB
    1945-1960; DLB 20, 100; MTCW 1
Jones, David Robert 1947-
    See Bowie, David
    See also CA 103
Jones, Diana Wynne 1934-   **CLC 26**
    See also AAYA 12; CA 49-52; CANR 4, 26,
    56; CLR 23; DLB 161; JRDA; MAICYA;
    SAAS 7; SATA 9, 70, 108
Jones, Edward P. 1950-   **CLC 76**
    See also BW 2, 3; CA 142; CANR 79
Jones, Gayl 1949-   **CLC 6, 9; BLC 2; DAM**
    MULT
    See also BW 2, 3; CA 77-80; CANR 27, 66;
    DLB 33; MTCW 1, 2
Jones, James 1921-1977   **CLC 1, 3, 10, 39**
    See also AITN 1, 2; CA 1-4R; 69-72; CANR 6;
    DLB 2, 143; DLBD 17; DLBY 98; MTCW 1
Jones, John J.
    See Lovecraft, H(oward) P(hillips)
Jones, LeRoi   **CLC 1, 2, 3, 5, 10, 14**
    See also Baraka, Amiri
    See also MTCW 2
Jones, Louis B. 1953-   **CLC 65**
    See also CA 141; CANR 73
Jones, Madison (Percy, Jr.) 1925-   **CLC 4**
    See also CA 13-16R; CAAS 11; CANR 7, 54;
    DLB 152
Jones, Mervyn 1922-   **CLC 10, 52**
    See also CA 45-48; CAAS 5; CANR 1; MTCW
    1
Jones, Mick 1956(?)-   **CLC 30**
Jones, Nettie (Pearl) 1941-   **CLC 34**
    See also BW 2; CA 137; CAAS 20
Jones, Preston 1936-1979   **CLC 10**
    See also CA 73-76; 89-92; DLB 7
Jones, Robert F(rancis) 1934-   **CLC 7**
    See also CA 49-52; CANR 2, 61
Jones, Rod 1953-   **CLC 50**
    See also CA 128
Jones, Terence Graham Parry 1942- **CLC 21**

See also Jones, Terry; Monty Python
    See also CA 112; 116; CANR 35; INT 116
Jones, Terry
    See Jones, Terence Graham Parry
    See also SATA 67; SATA-Brief 51
Jones, Thom 1945(?)-   **CLC 81**
    See also CA 157
Jong, Erica 1942-   **CLC 4, 6, 8, 18, 83; DAM**
    NOV, POP
    See also AITN 1; BEST 90:2; CA 73-76; CANR
    26, 52, 75; DLB 2, 5, 28, 152; INT CANR-
    26; MTCW 1, 2
Jonson, Ben(jamin) 1572(?)-1637   **LC 6, 33;**
    DA; DAB; DAC; DAM DRAM, MST,
    POET; DC 4; PC 17; WLC
    See also CDBLB Before 1660; DLB 62, 121
Jordan, June 1936-**CLC 5, 11, 23, 114; BLCS;**
    DAM MULT, POET
    See also AAYA 2; BW 2, 3; CA 33-36R; CANR
    25, 70; CLR 10; DLB 38; MAICYA; MTCW
    1; SATA 4
Jordan, Neil (Patrick) 1950-   **CLC 110**
    See also CA 124; 130; CANR 54; INT 130
Jordan, Pat(rick M.) 1941-   **CLC 37**
    See also CA 33-36R
Jorgensen, Ivar
    See Ellison, Harlan (Jay)
Jorgenson, Ivar
    See Silverberg, Robert
Josephus, Flavius c. 37-100   **CMLC 13**
Josipovici, Gabriel 1940-   **CLC 6, 43**
    See also CA 37-40R; CAAS 8; CANR 47; DLB
    14
Joubert, Joseph 1754-1824   **NCLC 9**
Jouve, Pierre Jean 1887-1976   **CLC 47**
    See also CA 65-68
Jovine, Francesco 1902-1950   **TCLC 79**
Joyce, James (Augustine Aloysius) 1882-1941
    TCLC 3, 8, 16, 35, 52; DA;DAB; DAC;
    DAM MST, NOV, POET; PC 22; SSC 3,
    26; WLC
    See also CA 104; 126; CDBLB 1914-1945;
    DLB 10, 19, 36, 162; MTCW 1, 2
Jozsef, Attila 1905-1937   **TCLC 22**
    See also CA 116
Juana Ines de la Cruz 1651(?)-1695   **LC 5;**
    HLCS 1; PC 24
Judd, Cyril
    See Kornbluth, C(yril) M.; Pohl, Frederik
Julian of Norwich 1342(?)-1416(?) **LC 6, 52**
    See also DLB 146
Junger, Sebastian 1962-   **CLC 109**
    See also AAYA 28; CA 165
Juniper, Alex
    See Hospital, Janette Turner
Junius
    See Luxemburg, Rosa
Just, Ward (Swift) 1935-   **CLC 4, 27**
    See also CA 25-28R; CANR 32; INT CANR-
    32
Justice, Donald (Rodney) 1925-   **CLC 6, 19,**
    102; DAM POET
    See also CA 5-8R; CANR 26, 54, 74; DLBY
    83; INT CANR-26; MTCW 2
Juvenal c. 60-c. 13   **CMLC 8**
    See also Juvenalis, Decimus Junius
    See also DLB 211
Juvenalis, Decimus Junius 55(?)-c. 127(?)
    See Juvenal
Juvenis
    See Bourne, Randolph S(illiman)
Kacew, Romain 1914-1980
    See Gary, Romain

See also CA 108; 102
Kadare, Ismail 1936- **CLC 52**
See also CA 161
Kadohata, Cynthia **CLC 59, 122**
See also CA 140
Kafka, Franz 1883-1924**TCLC 2, 6, 13, 29, 47, 53; DA; DAB; DAC; DAM MST, NOV; SSC 5, 29, 35; WLC**
See also CA 105; 126; DLB 81; MTCW 1, 2
Kahanovitsch, Pinkhes
See Der Nister
Kahn, Roger 1927- **CLC 30**
See also CA 25-28R; CANR 44, 69; DLB 171; SATA 37
Kain, Saul
See Sassoon, Siegfried (Lorraine)
Kaiser, Georg 1878-1945 **TCLC 9**
See also CA 106; DLB 124
Kaletski, Alexander 1946- **CLC 39**
See also CA 118; 143
Kalidasa fl. c. 400- **CMLC 9; PC 22**
Kallman, Chester (Simon) 1921-1975 **CLC 2**
See also CA 45-48; 53-56; CANR 3
Kaminsky, Melvin 1926-
See Brooks, Mel
See also CA 65-68; CANR 16
Kaminsky, Stuart M(elvin) 1934- **CLC 59**
See also CA 73-76; CANR 29, 53
Kandinsky, Wassily 1866-1944 **TCLC 92**
See also CA 118; 155
Kane, Francis
See Robbins, Harold
Kane, Paul
See Simon, Paul (Frederick)
Kane, Wilson 1917-1994
See Bloch, Robert (Albert)
See also CA 179; CAAE 179
Kanin, Garson 1912-1999 **CLC 22**
See also AITN 1; CA 5-8R; 177; CANR 7, 78; DLB 7
Kaniuk, Yoram 1930- **CLC 19**
See also CA 134
Kant, Immanuel 1724-1804 **NCLC 27, 67**
See also DLB 94
Kantor, MacKinlay 1904-1977 **CLC 7**
See also CA 61-64; 73-76; CANR 60, 63; DLB 9, 102; MTCW 2
Kaplan, David Michael 1946- **CLC 50**
Kaplan, James 1951- **CLC 59**
See also CA 135
Karageorge, Michael
See Anderson, Poul (William)
Karamzin, Nikolai Mikhailovich 1766-1826 **NCLC 3**
See also DLB 150
Karapanou, Margarita 1946- **CLC 13**
See also CA 101
Karinthy, Frigyes 1887-1938 **TCLC 47**
See also CA 170
Karl, Frederick R(obert) 1927- **CLC 34**
See also CA 5-8R; CANR 3, 44
Kastel, Warren
See Silverberg, Robert
Kataev, Evgeny Petrovich 1903-1942
See Petrov, Evgeny
See also CA 120
Kataphusin
See Ruskin, John
Katz, Steve 1935- **CLC 47**
See also CA 25-28R; CAAS 14, 64; CANR 12; DLBY 83
Kauffman, Janet 1945- **CLC 42**
See also CA 117; CANR 43; DLBY 86

Kaufman, Bob (Garnell) 1925-1986 **CLC 49**
See also BW 1; CA 41-44R; 118; CANR 22; DLB 16, 41
Kaufman, George S. 1889-1961**CLC 38; DAM DRAM**
See also CA 108; 93-96; DLB 7; INT 108; MTCW 2
Kaufman, Sue **CLC 3, 8**
See also Barondess, Sue K(aufman)
Kavafis, Konstantinos Petrou 1863-1933
See Cavafy, C(onstantine) P(eter)
See also CA 104
Kavan, Anna 1901-1968 **CLC 5, 13, 82**
See also CA 5-8R; CANR 6, 57; MTCW 1
Kavanagh, Dan
See Barnes, Julian (Patrick)
Kavanagh, Julie 1952- **CLC 119**
See also CA 163
Kavanagh, Patrick (Joseph) 1904-1967 **CLC 22**
See also CA 123; 25-28R; DLB 15, 20; MTCW 1
Kawabata, Yasunari 1899-1972 **CLC 2, 5, 9, 18, 107; DAM MULT; SSC 17**
See also CA 93-96; 33-36R; DLB 180; MTCW 2
Kaye, M(ary) M(argaret) 1909- **CLC 28**
See also CA 89-92; CANR 24, 60; MTCW 1, 2; SATA 62
Kaye, Mollie
See Kaye, M(ary) M(argaret)
Kaye-Smith, Sheila 1887-1956 **TCLC 20**
See also CA 118; DLB 36
Kaymor, Patrice Maguilene
See Senghor, Leopold Sedar
Kazan, Elia 1909- **CLC 6, 16, 63**
See also CA 21-24R; CANR 32, 78
Kazantzakis, Nikos 1883(?)-1957 **TCLC 2, 5, 33**
See also CA 105; 132; MTCW 1, 2
Kazin, Alfred 1915-1998 **CLC 34, 38, 119**
See also CA 1-4R; CAAS 7; CANR 1, 45, 79; DLB 67
Keane, Mary Nesta (Skrine) 1904-1996
See Keane, Molly
See also CA 108; 114; 151
Keane, Molly **CLC 31**
See also Keane, Mary Nesta (Skrine)
See also INT 114
Keates, Jonathan 1946(?)- **CLC 34**
See also CA 163
Keaton, Buster 1895-1966 **CLC 20**
Keats, John 1795-1821**NCLC 8, 73; DA; DAB; DAC; DAM MST, POET; PC 1; WLC**
See also CDBLB 1789-1832; DLB 96, 110
Keene, Donald 1922- **CLC 34**
See also CA 1-4R; CANR 5
Keillor, Garrison **CLC 40, 115**
See also Keillor, Gary (Edward)
See also AAYA 2; BEST 89:3; DLBY 87; SATA 58
Keillor, Gary (Edward) 1942-
See Keillor, Garrison
See also CA 111; 117; CANR 36, 59; DAM POP; MTCW 1, 2
Keith, Michael
See Hubbard, L(afayette) Ron(ald)
Keller, Gottfried 1819-1890 **NCLC 2; SSC 26**
See also DLB 129
Keller, Nora Okja **CLC 109**
Kellerman, Jonathan 1949- **CLC 44;DAM POP**
See also BEST 90:1; CA 106; CANR 29, 51;

INT CANR-29
Kelley, William Melvin 1937- **CLC 22**
See also BW 1; CA 77-80; CANR 27; DLB 33
Kellogg, Marjorie 1922- **CLC 2**
See also CA 81-84
Kellow, Kathleen
See Hibbert, Eleanor Alice Burford
Kelly, M(ilton) T(erry) 1947- **CLC 55**
See also CA 97-100; CAAS 22; CANR 19, 43
Kelman, James 1946- **CLC 58, 86**
See also CA 148; DLB 194
Kemal, Yashar 1923- **CLC 14, 29**
See also CA 89-92; CANR 44
Kemble, Fanny 1809-1893 **NCLC 18**
See also DLB 32
Kemelman, Harry 1908-1996 **CLC 2**
See also AITN 1; CA 9-12R; 155; CANR 6, 71; DLB 28
Kempe, Margery 1373(?)-1440(?) **LC 6**
See also DLB 146
Kempis, Thomas a 1380-1471 **LC 11**
Kendall, Henry 1839-1882 **NCLC 12**
Keneally, Thomas (Michael) 1935- CLC 5, 8, 10, 14, 19, 27, 43, 117; DAM NOV**
See also CA 85-88; CANR 10, 50, 74; MTCW 1, 2
Kennedy, Adrienne (Lita) 1931-**CLC 66; BLC 2; DAM MULT; DC 5**
See also BW 2, 3; CA 103; CAAS 20; CABS 3; CANR 26, 53, 82; DLB 38
Kennedy, John Pendleton 1795-1870**NCLC 2**
See also DLB 3
Kennedy, Joseph Charles 1929-
See Kennedy, X. J.
See also CA 1-4R; CANR 4, 30, 40; SATA 14, 86
Kennedy, William 1928- **CLC 6, 28, 34, 53; DAM NOV**
See also AAYA 1; CA 85-88; CANR 14, 31, 76; DLB 143; DLBY 85; INT CANR-31; MTCW 1, 2; SATA 57
Kennedy, X. J. **CLC 8, 42**
See also Kennedy, Joseph Charles
See also CAAS 9; CLR 27; DLB 5; SAAS 22
Kenny, Maurice (Francis) 1929- **CLC 87; DAM MULT**
See also CA 144; CAAS 22; DLB 175; NNAL
Kent, Kelvin
See Kuttner, Henry
Kenton, Maxwell
See Southern, Terry
Kenyon, Robert O.
See Kuttner, Henry
Kepler, Johannes 1571-1630 **LC 45**
Kerouac, Jack **CLC 1, 2, 3, 5, 14, 29, 61**
See also Kerouac, Jean-Louis Lebris de
See also AAYA 25; CDALB 1941-1968; DLB 2, 16; DLBD 3; DLBY 95; MTCW 2
Kerouac, Jean-Louis Lebris de 1922-1969
See Kerouac, Jack
See also AITN 1; CA 5-8R; 25-28R; CANR 26, 54; DA; DAB; DAC; DAM MST, NOV, POET; POP; MTCW 1, 2; WLC
Kerr, Jean 1923- **CLC 22**
See also CA 5-8R; CANR 7; INT CANR-7
Kerr, M. E. **CLC 12, 35**
See also Meaker, Marijane (Agnes)
See also AAYA 2, 23; CLR 29; SAAS 1
Kerr, Robert **CLC 55**
Kerrigan, (Thomas) Anthony 1918-**CLC 4, 6**
See also CA 49-52; CAAS 11; CANR 4
Kerry, Lois
See Duncan, Lois

Kesey, Ken (Elton) 1935- **CLC 1, 3, 6, 11, 46, 64; DA; DAB; DAC; DAM MST, NOV, POP; WLC**

See also AAYA 25; CA 1-4R; CANR 22, 38, 66; CDALB 1968-1988; DLB 2, 16, 206; MTCW 1, 2; SATA 66

Kesselring, Joseph (Otto) 1902-1967**CLC 45; DAM DRAM, MST**

See also CA 150

Kessler, Jascha (Frederick) 1929- **CLC 4**

See also CA 17-20R; CANR 8, 48

Kettelkamp, Larry (Dale) 1933- **CLC 12**

See also CA 29-32R; CANR 16; SAAS 3; SATA 2

Key, Ellen 1849-1926 **TCLC 65**

Keyber, Conny

See Fielding, Henry

Keyes, Daniel 1927-**CLC 80; DA; DAC; DAM MST, NOV**

See also AAYA 23; CA 17-20R; CANR 10, 26, 54, 74; MTCW 2; SATA 37

Keynes, John Maynard 1883-1946 **TCLC 64**

See also CA 114; 162, 163; DLBD 10; MTCW 2

Khanshendel, Chiron

See Rose, Wendy

Khayyam, Omar 1048-1131 **CMLC 11; DAM POET; PC 8**

Kherdian, David 1931- **CLC 6, 9**

See also CA 21-24R; CAAS 2; CANR 39, 78; CLR 24; JRDA; MAICYA; SATA 16, 74

Khlebnikov, Velimir **TCLC 20**

See also Khlebnikov, Viktor Vladimirovich

Khlebnikov, Viktor Vladimirovich 1885-1922

See Khlebnikov, Velimir

See also CA 117

Khodasevich, Vladislav (Felitsianovich) 1886-1939 **TCLC 15**

See also CA 115

Kielland, Alexander Lange 1849-1906 **TCLC 5**

See also CA 104

Kiely, Benedict 1919- **CLC 23, 43**

See also CA 1-4R; CANR 2; DLB 15

Kienzle, William X(avier) 1928- **CLC 25; DAM POP**

See also CA 93-96; CAAS 1; CANR 9, 31, 59; INT CANR-31; MTCW 1, 2

Kierkegaard, Soren 1813-1855 **NCLC 34, 78**

Kieslowski, Krzysztof 1941-1996 **CLC 120**

See also CA 147; 151

Killens, John Oliver 1916-1987 **CLC 10**

See also BW 2; CA 77-80; 123; CAAS 2; CANR 26; DLB 33

Killigrew, Anne 1660-1685 **LC 4**

See also DLB 131

Kim

See Simenon, Georges (Jacques Christian)

Kincaid, Jamaica 1949- **CLC 43, 68; BLC 2; DAM MULT, NOV**

See also AAYA 13; BW 2, 3; CA 125; CANR 47, 59; CDALBS; DLB 157; MTCW 2

King, Francis (Henry) 1923-**CLC 8, 53; DAM NOV**

See also CA 1-4R; CANR 1, 33; DLB 15, 139; MTCW 1

King, Kennedy

See Brown, George Douglas

King, Martin Luther, Jr. 1929-1968 **CLC 83; BLC 2; DA; DAB; DAC; DAM MST, MULT; WLCS**

See also BW 2, 3; CA 25-28; CANR 27, 44; CAP 2; MTCW 1, 2; SATA 14

King, Stephen (Edwin) 1947-**CLC 12, 26, 37, 61, 113; DAM NOV, POP; SSC 17**

See also AAYA 1, 17; BEST 90:1; CA 61-64; CANR 1, 30, 52, 76; DLB 143; DLBY 80; JRDA; MTCW 1, 2; SATA 9, 55

King, Steve

See King, Stephen (Edwin)

King, Thomas 1943- **CLC 89; DAC;DAM MULT**

See also CA 144; DLB 175; NNAL; SATA 96

Kingman, Lee **CLC 17**

See also Natti, (Mary) Lee

See also SAAS 3; SATA 1, 67

Kingsley, Charles 1819-1875 **NCLC 35**

See also DLB 21, 32, 163, 190; YABC 2

Kingsley, Sidney 1906-1995 **CLC 44**

See also CA 85-88; 147; DLB 7

Kingsolver, Barbara 1955-**CLC 55, 81; DAM POP**

See also AAYA 15; CA 129; 134; CANR 60; CDALBS; DLB 206; INT 134; MTCW 2

Kingston, Maxine (Ting Ting) Hong 1940- **CLC 12, 19, 58, 121; DAM MULT, NOV; WLCS**

See also AAYA 8; CA 69-72; CANR 13, 38, 74; CDALBS; DLB 173, 212; DLBY 80; INT CANR-13; MTCW 1, 2; SATA 53

Kinnell, Galway 1927- **CLC 1, 2, 3, 5, 13, 29; PC 26**

See also CA 9-12R; CANR 10, 34, 66; DLB 5; DLBY 87; INT CANR-34; MTCW 1, 2

Kinsella, Thomas 1928- **CLC 4, 19**

See also CA 17-20R; CANR 15; DLB 27; MTCW 1, 2

Kinsella, W(illiam) P(atrick) 1935- **CLC 27, 43; DAC; DAM NOV, POP**

See also AAYA 7; CA 97-100; CAAS 7; CANR 21, 35, 66, 75; INT CANR-21; MTCW 1, 2

Kinsey, Alfred C(harles) 1894-1956**TCLC 91**

See also CA 115; 170; MTCW 2

Kipling, (Joseph) Rudyard 1865-1936 **TCLC 8, 17; DA; DAB; DAC; DAM MST, POET; PC 3; SSC 5; WLC**

See also CA 105; 120; CANR 33; CDBLB 1890-1914; CLR 39; DLB 19, 34, 141, 156; MAICYA; MTCW 1, 2; SATA 100; YABC 2

Kirkup, James 1918- **CLC 1**

See also CA 1-4R; CAAS 4; CANR 2; DLB 27; SATA 12

Kirkwood, James 1930(?)-1989 **CLC 9**

See also AITN 2; CA 1-4R; 128; CANR 6, 40

Kirshner, Sidney

See Kingsley, Sidney

Kis, Danilo 1935-1989 **CLC 57**

See also CA 109; 118; 129; CANR 61; DLB 181; MTCW 1

Kivi, Aleksis 1834-1872 **NCLC 30**

Kizer, Carolyn (Ashley) 1925-**CLC 15, 39, 80; DAM POET**

See also CA 65-68; CAAS 5; CANR 24, 70; DLB 5, 169; MTCW 2

Klabund 1890-1928 **TCLC 44**

See also CA 162; DLB 66

Klappert, Peter 1942- **CLC 57**

See also CA 33-36R; DLB 5

Klein, A(braham) M(oses) 1909-1972**CLC 19; DAB; DAC; DAM MST**

See also CA 101; 37-40R; DLB 68

Klein, Norma 1938-1989 **CLC 30**

See also AAYA 2; CA 41-44R; 128; CANR 15, 37; CLR 2, 19; INT CANR-15; JRDA; MAICYA; SAAS 1; SATA 7, 57

Klein, T(heodore) E(ibon) D(onald) 1947-

CLC 34

See also CA 119; CANR 44, 75

Kleist, Heinrich von 1777-1811 **NCLC 2, 37; DAM DRAM; SSC 22**

See also DLB 90

Klima, Ivan 1931- **CLC 56;DAM NOV**

See also CA 25-28R; CANR 17, 50

Klimentov, Andrei Platonovich 1899-1951

See Platonov, Andrei

See also CA 108

Klinger, Friedrich Maximilianvon 1752-1831 **NCLC 1**

See also DLB 94

Klingsor the Magician

See Hartmann, Sadakichi

Klopstock, Friedrich Gottlieb 1724-1803 **NCLC 11**

See also DLB 97

Knapp, Caroline 1959- **CLC 99**

See also CA 154

Knebel, Fletcher 1911-1993 **CLC 14**

See also AITN 1; CA 1-4R; 140; CAAS 3; CANR 1, 36; SATA 36; SATA-Obit 75

Knickerbocker, Diedrich

See Irving, Washington

Knight, Etheridge 1931-1991**CLC 40; BLC 2; DAM POET; PC 14**

See also BW 1, 3; CA 21-24R; 133; CANR 23, 82; DLB 41; MTCW 2

Knight, Sarah Kemble 1666-1727 **LC 7**

See also DLB 24, 200

Knister, Raymond 1899-1932 **TCLC 56**

See also DLB 68

Knowles, John 1926- **CLC 1, 4, 10, 26; DA; DAC; DAM MST, NOV**

See also AAYA 10; CA 17-20R; CANR 40, 74, 76; CDALB 1968-1988; DLB 6; MTCW 1, 2; SATA 8, 89

Knox, Calvin M.

See Silverberg, Robert

Knox, John c. 1505-1572 **LC 37**

See also DLB 132

Knye, Cassandra

See Disch, Thomas M(ichael)

Koch, C(hristopher) J(ohn) 1932- **CLC 42**

See also CA 127

Koch, Christopher

See Koch, C(hristopher) J(ohn)

Koch, Kenneth 1925- **CLC 5, 8, 44;DAM POET**

See also CA 1-4R; CANR 6, 36, 57; DLB 5; INT CANR-36; MTCW 2; SATA 65

Kochanowski, Jan 1530-1584 **LC 10**

Kock, Charles Paul de 1794-1871 **NCLC 16**

Koda Shigeyuki 1867-1947

See Rohan, Koda

See also CA 121

Koestler, Arthur 1905-1983**CLC 1, 3, 6, 8, 15, 33**

See also CA 1-4R; 109; CANR 1, 33; CDBLB 1945-1960; DLBY 83; MTCW 1, 2

Kogawa, Joy Nozomi 1935- **CLC 78; DAC; DAM MST, MULT**

See also CA 101; CANR 19, 62; MTCW 2; SATA 99

Kohout, Pavel 1928- **CLC 13**

See also CA 45-48; CANR 3

Koizumi, Yakumo

See Hearn, (Patricio) Lafcadio (Tessima Carlos)

Kolmar, Gertrud 1894-1943 **TCLC 40**

See also CA 167

Komunyakaa, Yusef 1947-**CLC 86, 94; BLCS**

See also CA 147; DLB 120

Konrad, George
See Konrad, Gyoergy
Konrad, Gyoergy 1933-   **CLC 4, 10, 73**
See also CA 85-88
Konwicki, Tadeusz 1926- **CLC 8, 28, 54, 117**
See also CA 101; CAAS 9; CANR 39, 59;
MTCW 1
Koontz, Dean R(ay) 1945-   **CLC 78; DAM
NOV, POP**
See also AAYA 9; BEST 89:3, 90:2; CA 108;
CANR 19, 36, 52; MTCW 1; SATA 92
Kopernik, Mikolaj
See Copernicus, Nicolaus
Kopit, Arthur (Lee) 1937-**CLC 1, 18, 33; DAM
DRAM**
See also AITN 1; CA 81-84; CABS 3; DLB 7;
MTCW 1
Kops, Bernard 1926-   **CLC 4**
See also CA 5-8R; DLB 13
Kornbluth, C(yril) M. 1923-1958   **TCLC 8**
See also CA 105; 160; DLB 8
Korolenko, V. G.
See Korolenko, Vladimir Galaktionovich
Korolenko, Vladimir
See Korolenko, Vladimir Galaktionovich
Korolenko, Vladimir G.
See Korolenko, Vladimir Galaktionovich
Korolenko, Vladimir Galaktionovich 1853-
1921   **TCLC 22**
See also CA 121
Korzybski, Alfred (Habdank Skarbek) 1879-
1950   **TCLC 61**
See also CA 123; 160
Kosinski, Jerzy (Nikodem) 1933-1991**CLC 1,
2, 3, 6, 10, 15, 53, 70; DAM NOV**
See also CA 17-20R; 134; CANR 9, 46; DLB
2; DLBY 82; MTCW 1, 2
Kostelanetz, Richard (Cory) 1940- **CLC 28**
See also CA 13-16R; CAAS 8; CANR 38, 77
Kostrowitzki, Wilhelm Apollinaris de 1880-
1918
See Apollinaire, Guillaume
See also CA 104
Kotlowitz, Robert 1924-   **CLC 4**
See also CA 33-36R; CANR 36
Kotzebue, August (Friedrich Ferdinand) von
1761-1819   **NCLC 25**
See also DLB 94
Kotzwinkle, William 1938-   **CLC 5, 14, 35**
See also CA 45-48; CANR 3, 44; CLR 6; DLB
173; MAICYA; SATA 24, 70
Kowna, Stancy
See Szymborska, Wislawa
Kozol, Jonathan 1936-   **CLC 17**
See also CA 61-64; CANR 16, 45
Kozoll, Michael 1940(?)-   **CLC 35**
Kramer, Kathryn 19(?)-   **CLC 34**
Kramer, Larry 1935-**CLC 42; DAM POP; DC
8**
See also CA 124; 126; CANR 60
Krasicki, Ignacy 1735-1801   **NCLC 8**
Krasinski, Zygmunt 1812-1859   **NCLC 4**
Kraus, Karl 1874-1936   **TCLC 5**
See also CA 104; DLB 118
Kreve (Mickevicius), Vincas 1882-1954**TCLC
27**
See also CA 170
Kristeva, Julia 1941-   **CLC 77**
See also CA 154
Kristofferson, Kris 1936-   **CLC 26**
See also CA 104
Krizanc, John 1956-   **CLC 57**
Krleza, Miroslav 1893-1981   **CLC 8,114**

See also CA 97-100; 105; CANR 50; DLB 147
Kroetsch, Robert 1927- **CLC 5, 23, 57; DAC;
DAM POET**
See also CA 17-20R; CANR 8, 38; DLB 53;
MTCW 1
Kroetz, Franz
See Kroetz, Franz Xaver
Kroetz, Franz Xaver 1946-   **CLC 41**
See also CA 130
Kroker, Arthur (W.) 1945-   **CLC 77**
See also CA 161
Kropotkin, Peter (Aleksieevich) 1842-1921
TCLC 36
See also CA 119
Krotkov, Yuri 1917-   **CLC 19**
See also CA 102
Krumb
See Crumb, R(obert)
Krumgold, Joseph (Quincy) 1908-1980 **C L C
12**
See also CA 9-12R; 101; CANR 7; MAICYA;
SATA 1, 48; SATA-Obit 23
Krumwitz
See Crumb, R(obert)
Krutch, Joseph Wood 1893-1970   **CLC 24**
See also CA 1-4R; 25-28R; CANR 4; DLB 63,
206
Krutzch, Gus
See Eliot, T(homas) S(tearns)
Krylov, Ivan Andreevich 1768(?)-1844**N C L C
1**
See also DLB 150
Kubin, Alfred (Leopold Isidor) 1877-1959
TCLC 23
See also CA 112; 149; DLB 81
Kubrick, Stanley 1928-1999   **CLC 16**
See also AAYA 30; CA 81-84; 177; CANR 33;
DLB 26
Kumin, Maxine (Winokur) 1925- **CLC 5, 13,
28; DAM POET; PC 15**
See also AITN 2; CA 1-4R; CAAS 8; CANR 1,
21, 69; DLB 5; MTCW 1, 2; SATA 12
Kundera, Milan 1929- **CLC 4, 9, 19, 32, 68,
115; DAM NOV; SSC 24**
See also AAYA 2; CA 85-88; CANR 19, 52,
74; MTCW 1, 2
Kunene, Mazisi (Raymond) 1930-   **CLC 85**
See also BW 1, 3; CA 125; CANR 81; DLB
117
Kunitz, Stanley (Jasspon) 1905-**CLC 6, 11, 14;
PC 19**
See also CA 41-44R; CANR 26, 57; DLB 48;
INT CANR-26; MTCW 1, 2
Kunze, Reiner 1933-   **CLC 10**
See also CA 93-96; DLB 75
Kuprin, Aleksandr Ivanovich 1870-1938
TCLC 5
See also CA 104
Kureishi, Hanif 1954(?)-   **CLC 64**
See also CA 139; DLB 194
Kurosawa, Akira 1910-1998   **CLC 16, 119;
DAM MULT**
See also AAYA 11; CA 101; 170; CANR 46
Kushner, Tony 1957(?)-**CLC 81; DAM DRAM;
DC 10**
See also CA 144; CANR 74; MTCW 2
Kuttner, Henry 1915-1958   **TCLC 10**
See also Vance, Jack
See also CA 107; 157; DLB 8
Kuzma, Greg 1944-   **CLC 7**
See also CA 33-36R; CANR 70
Kuzmin, Mikhail 1872(?)-1936   **TCLC 40**
See also CA 170

Kyd, Thomas 1558-1594**LC 22; DAM DRAM;
DC 3**
See also DLB 62
Kyprianos, Iossif
See Samarakis, Antonis
La Bruyere, Jean de 1645-1696   **LC 17**
Lacan, Jacques (Marie Emile) 1901-1981
CLC 75
See also CA 121; 104
Laclos, Pierre Ambroise Francois Choderlos de
1741-1803   **NCLC 4**
La Colere, Francois
See Aragon, Louis
Lacolere, Francois
See Aragon, Louis
La Deshabilleuse
See Simenon, Georges (Jacques Christian)
Lady Gregory
See Gregory, Isabella Augusta (Persse)
Lady of Quality, A
See Bagnold, Enid
**La Fayette, Marie (Madelaine Pioche de la
Vergne Comtes** 1634-1693   **LC 2**
Lafayette, Rene
See Hubbard, L(afayette) Ron(ald)
Laforgue, Jules 1860-1887**NCLC 5, 53; PC 14;
SSC 20**
Lagerkvist, Paer (Fabian) 1891-1974 **CLC 7,
10, 13, 54; DAM DRAM, NOV**
See also Lagerkvist, Par
See also CA 85-88; 49-52; MTCW 1, 2
Lagerkvist, Par   **SSC 12**
See also Lagerkvist, Paer (Fabian)
See also MTCW 2
Lagerloef, Selma (Ottiliana Lovisa) 1858-1940
TCLC 4, 36
See also Lagerlof, Selma (Ottiliana Lovisa)
See also CA 108; MTCW 2; SATA 15
Lagerlof, Selma (Ottiliana Lovisa)
See Lagerloef, Selma (Ottiliana Lovisa)
See also CLR 7; SATA 15
La Guma, (Justin) Alex(ander) 1925-1985
CLC 19; BLCS; DAM NOV
See also BW 1, 3; CA 49-52; 118; CANR 25,
81; DLB 117; MTCW 1, 2
Laidlaw, A. K.
See Grieve, C(hristopher) M(urray)
Lainez, Manuel Mujica
See Mujica Lainez, Manuel
See also HW 1
Laing, R(onald)D(avid) 1927-1989   **CLC 95**
See also CA 107; 129; CANR 34; MTCW 1
Lamartine, Alphonse (Marie Louis Prat) de
1790-1869**NCLC 11; DAM POET; PC 16**
Lamb, Charles 1775-1834   **NCLC 10; DA;
DAB; DAC; DAM MST; WLC**
See also CDBLB 1789-1832; DLB 93, 107, 163;
SATA 17
Lamb, Lady Caroline 1785-1828   **NCLC 38**
See also DLB 116
Lamming, George (William) 1927- **CLC 2, 4,
66; BLC 2; DAM MULT**
See also BW 2, 3; CA 85-88; CANR 26, 76;
DLB 125; MTCW 1, 2
L'Amour, Louis (Dearborn) 1908-1988 **C L C
25, 55; DAM NOV, POP**
See also AAYA 16; AITN 2; BEST 89:2; CA 1-
4R; 125; CANR 3, 25, 40; DLB 206; DLBY
80; MTCW 1, 2
Lampedusa, Giuseppe (Tomasi) di 1896-1957
TCLC 13
See also Tomasi di Lampedusa, Giuseppe
See also CA 164; DLB 177; MTCW 2

Lampman, Archibald 1861-1899 **NCLC 25**
See also DLB 92

Lancaster, Bruce 1896-1963 **CLC 36**
See also CA 9-10; CANR 70; CAP 1; SATA 9

Lanchester, John **CLC 99**

Landau, Mark Alexandrovich
See Aldanov, Mark (Alexandrovich)

Landau-Aldanov, Mark Alexandrovich
See Aldanov, Mark (Alexandrovich)

Landis, Jerry
See Simon, Paul (Frederick)

Landis, John 1950- **CLC 26**
See also CA 112; 122

Landolfi, Tommaso 1908-1979 **CLC 11, 49**
See also CA 127; 117; DLB 177

Landon, Letitia Elizabeth 1802-1838 **NCLC 15**
See also DLB 96

Landor, Walter Savage 1775-1864 **NCLC 14**
See also DLB 93, 107

Landwirth, Heinz 1927-
See Lind, Jakov
See also CA 9-12R; CANR 7

Lane, Patrick 1939- **CLC 25; DAM POET**
See also CA 97-100; CANR 54; DLB 53; INT 97-100

Lang, Andrew 1844-1912 **TCLC 16**
See also CA 114; 137; DLB 98, 141, 184; MAICYA; SATA 16

Lang, Fritz 1890-1976 **CLC 20, 103**
See also CA 77-80; 69-72; CANR 30

Lange, John
See Crichton, (John) Michael

Langer, Elinor 1939- **CLC 34**
See also CA 121

Langland, William 1330(?)-1400(?) **LC 19; DA; DAB; DAC; DAM MST, POET**
See also DLB 146

Langstaff, Launcelot
See Irving, Washington

Lanier, Sidney 1842-1881 **NCLC 6; DAM POET**
See also DLB 64; DLBD 13; MAICYA; SATA 18

Lanyer, Aemilia 1569-1645 **LC 10, 30**
See also DLB 121

Lao-Tzu
See Lao Tzu

Lao Tzu fl. 6th cent. B.C.- **CMLC 7**

Lapine, James (Elliot) 1949- **CLC 39**
See also CA 123; 130; CANR 54; INT 130

Larbaud, Valery (Nicolas) 1881-1957 **TCLC 9**
See also CA 106; 152

Lardner, Ring
See Lardner, Ring(gold) W(ilmer)

Lardner, Ring W., Jr.
See Lardner, Ring(gold) W(ilmer)

Lardner, Ring(gold) W(ilmer) 1885-1933 **TCLC 2, 14; SSC 32**
See also CA 104; 131; CDALB 1917-1929; DLB 11, 25, 86; DLBD 16; MTCW 1, 2

Laredo, Betty
See Codrescu, Andrei

Larkin, Maia
See Wojciechowska, Maia (Teresa)

Larkin, Philip (Arthur) 1922-1985 **CLC 3, 5, 8, 9, 13, 18, 33, 39, 64; DAB; DAM MST, POET; PC 21**
See also CA 5-8R; 117; CANR 24, 62; CDBLB 1960 to Present; DLB 27; MTCW 1, 2

Larra (y Sanchez de Castro), Mariano Josede 1809-1837 **NCLC 17**

Larsen, Eric 1941- **CLC 55**

See also CA 132

Larsen, Nella 1891-1964 **CLC 37; BLC 2; DAM MULT**
See also BW 1; CA 125; DLB 51

Larson, Charles R(aymond) 1938- **CLC 31**
See also CA 53-56; CANR 4

Larson, Jonathan 1961-1996 **CLC 99**
See also AAYA 28; CA 156

Las Casas, Bartolome de 1474-1566 **LC 31**

Lasch, Christopher 1932-1994 **CLC 102**
See also CA 73-76; 144; CANR 25; MTCW 1, 2

Lasker-Schueler, Else 1869-1945 **TCLC 57**
See also DLB 66, 124

Laski, Harold 1893-1950 **TCLC 79**

Latham, Jean Lee 1902-1995 **CLC 12**
See also AITN 1; CA 5-8R; CANR 7; CLR 50; MAICYA; SATA 2, 68

Latham, Mavis
See Clark, Mavis Thorpe

Lathen, Emma **CLC 2**
See also Hennissart, Martha; Latsis, Mary J(ane)

Lathrop, Francis
See Leiber, Fritz (Reuter, Jr.)

Latsis, Mary J(ane) 1927(?)-1997
See Lathen, Emma
See also CA 85-88; 162

Lattimore, Richmond (Alexander) 1906-1984 **CLC 3**
See also CA 1-4R; 112; CANR 1

Laughlin, James 1914-1997 **CLC 49**
See also CA 21-24R; 162; CAAS 22; CANR 9, 47; DLB 48; DLBY 96, 97

Laurence, (Jean) Margaret (Wemyss) 1926-1987 **CLC 3, 6, 13, 50, 62; DAC; DAM MST; SSC 7**
See also CA 5-8R; 121; CANR 33; DLB 53; MTCW 1, 2; SATA-Obit 50

Laurent, Antoine 1952- **CLC 50**

Lauscher, Hermann
See Hesse, Hermann

Lautreamont, Comte de 1846-1870 **NCLC 12; SSC 14**

Laverty, Donald
See Blish, James (Benjamin)

Lavin, Mary 1912-1996 **CLC 4, 18, 99; SSC 4**
See also CA 9-12R; 151; CANR 33; DLB 15; MTCW 1

Lavond, Paul Dennis
See Kornbluth, C(yril) M.; Pohl, Frederik

Lawler, Raymond Evenor 1922- **CLC 58**
See also CA 103

Lawrence, D(avid) H(erbert Richards) 1885-1930 **TCLC 2, 9, 16, 33, 48, 61, 93; DA; DAB; DAC; DAM MST, NOV, POET; SSC 4, 19; WLC**
See also CA 104; 121; CDBLB 1914-1945; DLB 10, 19, 36, 98, 162, 195; MTCW 1, 2

Lawrence, T(homas) E(dward) 1888-1935 **TCLC 18**
See also Dale, Colin
See also CA 115; 167; DLB 195

Lawrence of Arabia
See Lawrence, T(homas) E(dward)

Lawson, Henry (Archibald Hertzberg) 1867-1922 **TCLC 27; SSC 18**
See also CA 120

Lawton, Dennis
See Faust, Frederick (Schiller)

Laxness, Halldor **CLC 25**
See also Gudjonsson, Halldor Kiljan

Layamon fl. c. 1200- **CMLC 10**
See also DLB 146

Laye, Camara 1928-1980 **CLC 4, 38; BLC 2; DAM MULT**
See also BW 1; CA 85-88; 97-100; CANR 25; MTCW 1, 2

Layton, Irving (Peter) 1912- **CLC 2, 15; DAC; DAM MST, POET**
See also CA 1-4R; CANR 2, 33, 43, 66; DLB 88; MTCW 1, 2

Lazarus, Emma 1849-1887 **NCLC 8**

Lazarus, Felix
See Cable, George Washington

Lazarus, Henry
See Slavitt, David R(ytman)

Lea, Joan
See Neufeld, John (Arthur)

Leacock, Stephen (Butler) 1869-1944 **TCLC 2; DAC; DAM MST**
See also CA 104; 141; CANR 80; DLB 92; MTCW 2

Lear, Edward 1812-1888 **NCLC 3**
See also CLR 1; DLB 32, 163, 166; MAICYA; SATA 18, 100

Lear, Norman (Milton) 1922- **CLC 12**
See also CA 73-76

Leautaud, Paul 1872-1956 **TCLC 83**
See also DLB 65

Leavis, F(rank) R(aymond) 1895-1978 **CLC 24**
See also CA 21-24R; 77-80; CANR 44; MTCW 1, 2

Leavitt, David 1961- **CLC 34; DAM POP**
See also CA 116; 122; CANR 50, 62; DLB 130; INT 122; MTCW 2

Leblanc, Maurice (Marie Emile) 1864-1941 **TCLC 49**
See also CA 110

Lebowitz, Fran(ces Ann) 1951(?)- **CLC 11, 36**
See also CA 81-84; CANR 14, 60, 70; INT CANR-14; MTCW 1

Lebrecht, Peter
See Tieck, (Johann) Ludwig

le Carre, John **CLC 3, 5, 9, 15, 28**
See also Cornwell, David (John Moore)
See also BEST 89:4; CDBLB 1960 to Present; DLB 87; MTCW 2

Le Clezio, J(ean) M(arie) G(ustave) 1940- **CLC 31**
See also CA 116; 128; DLB 83

Leconte de Lisle, Charles-Marie-Rene 1818-1894 **NCLC 29**

Le Coq, Monsieur
See Simenon, Georges (Jacques Christian)

Leduc, Violette 1907-1972 **CLC 22**
See also CA 13-14; 33-36R; CANR 69; CAP 1

Ledwidge, Francis 1887(?)-1917 **TCLC 23**
See also CA 123; DLB 20

Lee, Andrea 1953- **CLC 36; BLC 2; DAM MULT**
See also BW 1, 3; CA 125; CANR 82

Lee, Andrew
See Auchincloss, Louis (Stanton)

Lee, Chang-rae 1965- **CLC 91**
See also CA 148

Lee, Don L. **CLC 2**
See also Madhubuti, Haki R.

Lee, George W(ashington) 1894-1976 **CLC 52; BLC 2; DAM MULT**
See also BW 1; CA 125; DLB 51

Lee, (Nelle) Harper 1926- **CLC 12, 60; DA; DAB; DAC; DAM MST, NOV; WLC**
See also AAYA 13; CA 13-16R; CANR 51; CDALB 1941-1968; DLB 6; MTCW 1, 2; SATA 11

Lee, Helen Elaine 1959(?)- **CLC 86**

See also CA 148

Lee, Julian
See Latham, Jean Lee

Lee, Larry
See Lee, Lawrence

Lee, Laurie 1914-1997 **CLC 90; DAB; DAM POP**
See also CA 77-80; 158; CANR 33, 73; DLB 27; MTCW 1

Lee, Lawrence 1941-1990 **CLC 34**
See also CA 131; CANR 43

Lee, Li-Young 1957- **PC 24**
See also CA 153; DLB 165

Lee, Manfred B(ennington) 1905-1971**CLC 11**
See also Queen, Ellery
See also CA 1-4R; 29-32R; CANR 2; DLB 137

Lee, Shelton Jackson 1957(?)- **CLC 105; BLCS; DAM MULT**
See also Lee, Spike
See also BW 2, 3; CA 125; CANR 42

Lee, Spike
See Lee, Shelton Jackson
See also AAYA 4, 29

Lee, Stan 1922- **CLC 17**
See also AAYA 5; CA 108; 111; INT 111

Lee, Tanith 1947- **CLC 46**
See also AAYA 15; CA 37-40R; CANR 53; SATA 8, 88

Lee, Vernon **TCLC 5; SSC 33**
See also Paget, Violet
See also DLB 57, 153, 156, 174, 178

Lee, William
See Burroughs, William S(eward)

Lee, Willy
See Burroughs, William S(eward)

Lee-Hamilton, Eugene (Jacob) 1845-1907 **TCLC 22**
See also CA 117

Leet, Judith 1935- **CLC 11**

Le Fanu, Joseph Sheridan 1814-1873**NCLC 9, 58; DAM POP; SSC 14**
See also DLB 21, 70, 159, 178

Leffland, Ella 1931- **CLC 19**
See also CA 29-32R; CANR 35, 78, 82; DLBY 84; INT CANR-35; SATA 65

Leger, Alexis
See Leger, (Marie-Rene Auguste) Alexis Saint-Leger

Leger, (Marie-Rene Auguste) Alexis Saint-Leger 1887-1975 **CLC 4, 11, 46; DAM POET; PC 23**
See also CA 13-16R; 61-64; CANR 43; MTCW 1

Leger, Saintleger
See Leger, (Marie-Rene Auguste) Alexis Saint-Leger

Le Guin, Ursula K(roeber) 1929- **CLC 8, 13, 22, 45, 71; DAB; DAC; DAM MST, POP; SSC 12**
See also AAYA 9, 27; AITN 1; CA 21-24R; CANR 9, 32, 52, 74; CDALB 1968-1988; CLR 3, 28; DLB 8, 52; INT CANR-32; JRDA; MAICYA; MTCW 1, 2; SATA 4, 52, 99

Lehmann, Rosamond (Nina) 1901-1990**CLC 5**
See also CA 77-80; 131; CANR 8, 73; DLB 15; MTCW 2

Leiber, Fritz (Reuter,Jr.) 1910-1992 **CLC 25**
See also CA 45-48; 139; CANR 2, 40; DLB 8; MTCW 1, 2; SATA 45; SATA-Obit 73

Leibniz, Gottfried Wilhelm von 1646-1716**LC 35**
See also DLB 168

Leimbach, Martha 1963-
See Leimbach, Marti
See also CA 130

Leimbach, Marti **CLC 65**
See also Leimbach, Martha

Leino, Eino **TCLC 24**
See also Loennbohm, Armas Eino Leopold

Leiris, Michel (Julien) 1901-1990 **CLC 61**
See also CA 119; 128; 132

Leithauser, Brad 1953- **CLC 27**
See also CA 107; CANR 27, 81; DLB 120

Lelchuk, Alan 1938- **CLC 5**
See also CA 45-48; CAAS 20; CANR 1, 70

Lem, Stanislaw 1921- **CLC 8, 15, 40**
See also CA 105; CAAS 1; CANR 32; MTCW 1

Lemann, Nancy 1956- **CLC 39**
See also CA 118; 136

Lemonnier, (Antoine Louis) Camille 1844-1913 **TCLC 22**
See also CA 121

Lenau, Nikolaus 1802-1850 **NCLC 16**

L'Engle, Madeleine (Camp Franklin) 1918- **CLC 12; DAM POP**
See also AAYA 28; AITN 2; CA 1-4R; CANR 3, 21, 39, 66; CLR 1, 14, 57; DLB 52; JRDA; MAICYA; MTCW 1, 2; SAAS 15; SATA 1, 27, 75

Lengyel, Jozsef 1896-1975 **CLC 7**
See also CA 85-88; 57-60; CANR 71

Lenin 1870-1924
See Lenin, V. I.
See also CA 121; 168

Lenin, V. I. **TCLC 67**
See also Lenin

Lennon, John (Ono) 1940-1980 **CLC 12, 35**
See also CA 102

Lennox, Charlotte Ramsay 1729(?)-1804 **NCLC 23**
See also DLB 39

Lentricchia, Frank (Jr.) 1940- **CLC 34**
See also CA 25-28R; CANR 19

Lenz, Siegfried 1926- **CLC 27;SSC 33**
See also CA 89-92; CANR 80; DLB 75

Leonard, Elmore (John, Jr.) 1925-**CLC 28, 34, 71, 120; DAM POP**
See also AAYA 22; AITN 1; BEST 89:1, 90:4; CA 81-84; CANR 12, 28, 53, 76; DLB 173; INT CANR-28; MTCW 1, 2

Leonard, Hugh **CLC 19**
See also Byrne, John Keyes
See also DLB 13

Leonov, Leonid (Maximovich) 1899-1994 **CLC 92; DAM NOV**
See also CA 129; CANR 74, 76; MTCW 1, 2

Leopardi, (Conte) Giacomo 1798-1837**NCLC 22**

Le Reveler
See Artaud, Antonin (Marie Joseph)

Lerman, Eleanor 1952- **CLC 9**
See also CA 85-88; CANR 69

Lerman, Rhoda 1936- **CLC 56**
See also CA 49-52; CANR 70

Lermontov, Mikhail Yuryevich 1814-1841 **NCLC 47; PC 18**
See also DLB 205

Leroux, Gaston 1868-1927 **TCLC 25**
See also CA 108; 136; CANR 69; SATA 65

Lesage, Alain-Rene 1668-1747 **LC 2, 28**

Leskov, Nikolai (Semyonovich) 1831-1895 **NCLC 25; SSC 34**

Lessing, Doris (May) 1919-**CLC 1, 2, 3, 6, 10, 15, 22, 40, 94; DA; DAB; DAC; DAM MST, NOV; SSC 6; WLCS**
See also CA 9-12R; CAAS 14; CANR 33, 54, 76; CDBLB 1960 to Present; DLB 15, 139; DLBY 85; MTCW 1, 2

Lessing, Gotthold Ephraim 1729-1781 **LC 8**
See also DLB 97

Lester, Richard 1932- **CLC 20**

Lever, Charles (James) 1806-1872 **NCLC 23**
See also DLB 21

Leverson, Ada 1865(?)-1936(?) **TCLC 18**
See also Elaine
See also CA 117; DLB 153

Levertov, Denise 1923-1997**CLC 1, 2, 3, 5, 8, 15, 28, 66; DAM POET; PC 11**
See also CA 1-4R, 178; 163; CAAE 178; CAAS 19; CANR 3, 29, 50; CDALBS; DLB 5, 165; INT CANR-29; MTCW 1, 2

Levi, Jonathan **CLC 76**

Levi, Peter (Chad Tigar) 1931- **CLC 41**
See also CA 5-8R; CANR 34, 80; DLB 40

Levi, Primo 1919-1987 **CLC 37, 50;SSC 12**
See also CA 13-16R; 122; CANR 12, 33, 61, 70; DLB 177; MTCW 1, 2

Levin, Ira 1929- **CLC 3, 6; DAM POP**
See also CA 21-24R; CANR 17, 44, 74; MTCW 1, 2; SATA 66

Levin, Meyer 1905-1981 **CLC 7; DAM POP**
See also AITN 1; CA 9-12R; 104; CANR 15; DLB 9, 28; DLBY 81; SATA 21; SATA-Obit 27

Levine, Norman 1924- **CLC 54**
See also CA 73-76; CAAS 23; CANR 14, 70; DLB 88

Levine, Philip 1928-**CLC 2, 4, 5, 9, 14, 33, 118; DAM POET; PC 22**
See also CA 9-12R; CANR 9, 37, 52; DLB 5

Levinson, Deirdre 1931- **CLC 49**
See also CA 73-76; CANR 70

Levi-Strauss, Claude 1908- **CLC 38**
See also CA 1-4R; CANR 6, 32, 57; MTCW 1, 2

Levitin, Sonia (Wolff) 1934- **CLC 17**
See also AAYA 13; CA 29-32R; CANR 14, 32, 79; CLR 53; JRDA; MAICYA; SAAS 2; SATA 4, 68

Levon, O. U.
See Kesey, Ken (Elton)

Levy, Amy 1861-1889 **NCLC 59**
See also DLB 156

Lewes, George Henry 1817-1878 **NCLC 25**
See also DLB 55, 144

Lewis, Alun 1915-1944 **TCLC 3**
See also CA 104; DLB 20, 162

Lewis, C. Day
See Day Lewis, C(ecil)

Lewis, C(live) S(taples) 1898-1963**CLC 1, 3, 6, 14, 27; DA; DAB; DAC; DAM MST, NOV, POP; WLC**
See also AAYA 3; CA 81-84; CANR 33, 71; CDBLB 1945-1960; CLR 3, 27; DLB 15, 100, 160; JRDA; MAICYA; MTCW 1, 2; SATA 13, 100

Lewis, Janet 1899-1998 **CLC 41**
See also Winters, Janet Lewis
See also CA 9-12R; 172; CANR 29, 63; CAP 1; DLBY 87

Lewis, Matthew Gregory 1775-1818**NCLC 11, 62**
See also DLB 39, 158, 178

Lewis, (Harry) Sinclair 1885-1951 **TCLC 4, 13, 23, 39; DA; DAB; DAC; DAM MST, NOV; WLC**
See also CA 104; 133;CDALB 1917-1929; DLB

Author Index

9, 102; DLBD 1; MTCW 1, 2

Lewis, (Percy) Wyndham 1882(?)-1957**TCLC 2, 9; SSC 34**
See also CA 104; 157; DLB 15; MTCW 2

Lewisohn, Ludwig 1883-1955   **TCLC 19**
See also CA 107; DLB 4, 9, 28, 102

Lewton, Val 1904-1951   **TCLC 76**

Leyner, Mark 1956-   **CLC 92**
See also CA 110; CANR 28, 53; MTCW 2

Lezama Lima, Jose 1910-1976**CLC 4, 10, 101; DAM MULT; HLCS 2**
See also CA 77-80; CANR 71; DLB 113; HW 1, 2

L'Heureux, John (Clarke) 1934-   **CLC 52**
See also CA 13-16R; CANR 23, 45

Liddell, C. H.
See Kuttner, Henry

Lie, Jonas (Lauritz Idemil) 1833-1908(?) **TCLC 5**
See also CA 115

Lieber, Joel 1937-1971   **CLC 6**
See also CA 73-76; 29-32R

Lieber, Stanley Martin
See Lee, Stan

Lieberman, Laurence (James) 1935- **CLC 4, 36**
See also CA 17-20R; CANR 8, 36

Lieh Tzu fl. 7th cent. B.C.-5th cent. B.C. **CMLC 27**

Lieksman, Anders
See Haavikko, Paavo Juhani

Li Fei-kan 1904-
See Pa Chin
See also CA 105

Lifton, Robert Jay 1926-   **CLC 67**
See also CA 17-20R; CANR 27, 78; INT CANR-27; SATA 66

Lightfoot, Gordon 1938-   **CLC 26**
See also CA 109

Lightman, Alan P(aige) 1948-   **CLC 81**
See also CA 141; CANR 63

Ligotti, Thomas (Robert) 1953-**CLC 44; SSC 16**
See also CA 123; CANR 49

Li Ho 791-817   **PC 13**

Liliencron, (Friedrich Adolf Axel) Detlevvon 1844-1909   **TCLC 18**
See also CA 117

Lilly, William 1602-1681   **LC 27**

Lima, Jose Lezama
See Lezama Lima, Jose

Lima Barreto, Afonso Henriquede 1881-1922 **TCLC 23**
See also CA 117

Limonov, Edward 1944-   **CLC 67**
See also CA 137

Lin, Frank
See Atherton, Gertrude (Franklin Horn)

Lincoln, Abraham 1809-1865   **NCLC 18**

Lind, Jakov   **CLC 1, 2, 4, 27, 82**
See also Landwirth, Heinz
See also CAAS 4

Lindbergh, Anne (Spencer) Morrow 1906-**CLC 82; DAM NOV**
See also CA 17-20R; CANR 16, 73; MTCW 1, 2; SATA 33

Lindsay, David 1878-1945   **TCLC 15**
See also CA 113

Lindsay, (Nicholas) Vachel 1879-1931 **TCLC 17; DA; DAC; DAM MST, POET; PC 23; WLC**
See also CA 114; 135; CANR 79; CDALB 1865-1917; DLB 54; SATA 40

Linke-Poot
See Doeblin, Alfred

Linney, Romulus 1930-   **CLC 51**
See also CA 1-4R; CANR 40, 44, 79

Linton, Eliza Lynn 1822-1898   **NCLC 41**
See also DLB 18

Li Po 701-763   **CMLC 2**

Lipsius, Justus 1547-1606   **LC 16**

Lipsyte, Robert (Michael) 1938-**CLC 21; DA; DAC; DAM MST, NOV**
See also AAYA 7; CA 17-20R; CANR 8, 57; CLR 23; JRDA; MAICYA; SATA 5, 68

Lish, Gordon (Jay) 1934-   **CLC 45;SSC 18**
See also CA 113; 117; CANR 79; DLB 130; INT 117

Lispector, Clarice 1925(?)-1977   **CLC 43; HLCS 2; SSC 34**
See also CA 139; 116; CANR 71; DLB 113; HW 2

Littell, Robert 1935(?)-   **CLC 42**
See also CA 109; 112; CANR 64

Little, Malcolm 1925-1965
See Malcolm X
See also BW 1, 3; CA 125; 111; CANR 82; DA; DAB; DAC; DAM MST, MULT; MTCW 1, 2

Littlewit, Humphrey Gent.
See Lovecraft, H(oward) P(hillips)

Litwos
See Sienkiewicz, Henryk (Adam Alexander Pius)

Liu, E 1857-1909   **TCLC 15**
See also CA 115

Lively, Penelope (Margaret) 1933- **CLC 32, 50; DAM NOV**
See also CA 41-44R; CANR 29, 67, 79; CLR 7; DLB 14, 161, 207; JRDA; MAICYA; MTCW 1, 2; SATA 7, 60, 101

Livesay, Dorothy (Kathleen) 1909-**CLC 4, 15, 79; DAC; DAM MST, POET**
See also AITN 2; CA 25-28R; CAAS 8; CANR 36, 67; DLB 68; MTCW 1

Livy c. 59B.C.-c. 17   **CMLC 11**
See also DLB 211

Lizardi, Jose Joaquin Fernandez de 1776-1827 **NCLC 30**

Llewellyn, Richard
See Llewellyn Lloyd, Richard Dafydd Vivian
See also DLB 15

Llewellyn Lloyd, Richard Dafydd Vivian 1906-1983   **CLC 7, 80**
See also Llewellyn, Richard
See also CA 53-56; 111; CANR 7, 71; SATA 11; SATA-Obit 37

Llosa, (Jorge) Mario (Pedro) Vargas
See Vargas Llosa, (Jorge) Mario (Pedro)

Lloyd, Manda
See Mander, (Mary) Jane

Lloyd Webber, Andrew 1948-
See Webber, Andrew Lloyd
See also AAYA 1; CA 116; 149; DAM DRAM; SATA 56

Llull, Ramon c. 1235-c. 1316   **CMLC 12**

Lobb, Ebenezer
See Upward, Allen

Locke, Alain (Le Roy) 1886-1954 **TCLC 43; BLCS**
See also BW 1, 3; CA 106; 124; CANR 79; DLB 51

Locke, John 1632-1704   **LC 7, 35**
See also DLB 101

Locke-Elliott, Sumner
See Elliott, Sumner Locke

Lockhart, John Gibson 1794-1854 **NCLC 6**
See also DLB 110, 116, 144

Lodge, David (John) 1935-**CLC 36;DAM POP**
See also BEST 90:1; CA 17-20R; CANR 19, 53; DLB 14, 194; INT CANR-19; MTCW 1, 2

Lodge, Thomas 1558-1625   **LC 41**

Lodge, Thomas 1558-1625   **LC 41**
See also DLB 172

Loennbohm, Armas Eino Leopold 1878-1926
See Leino, Eino
See also CA 123

Loewinsohn, Ron(ald William) 1937-**CLC 52**
See also CA 25-28R; CANR 71

Logan, Jake
See Smith, Martin Cruz

Logan, John (Burton) 1923-1987   **CLC 5**
See also CA 77-80; 124; CANR 45; DLB 5

Lo Kuan-chung 1330(?)-1400(?)   **LC 12**

Lombard, Nap
See Johnson, Pamela Hansford

London, Jack **TCLC 9, 15, 39; SSC 4; WLC**
See also London, John Griffith
See also AAYA 13; AITN 2; CDALB 1865-1917; DLB 8, 12, 78, 212; SATA 18

London, John Griffith 1876-1916
See London, Jack
See also CA 110; 119; CANR 73; DA; DAB; DAC; DAM MST, NOV; JRDA; MAICYA; MTCW 1, 2

Long, Emmett
See Leonard, Elmore (John, Jr.)

Longbaugh, Harry
See Goldman, William (W.)

Longfellow, Henry Wadsworth 1807-1882 **NCLC 2, 45; DA; DAB; DAC; DAM MST, POET; WLCS**
See also CDALB 1640-1865; DLB 1, 59; SATA 19

Longinus c. 1st cent. -   **CMLC 27**
See also DLB 176

Longley, Michael 1939-   **CLC 29**
See also CA 102; DLB 40

Longus fl. c. 2nd cent. -   **CMLC 7**

Longway, A. Hugh
See Lang, Andrew

Lonnrot, Elias 1802-1884   **NCLC 53**

Lopate, Phillip 1943-   **CLC 29**
See also CA 97-100; DLBY 80; INT 97-100

Lopez Portillo (y Pacheco), Jose 1920-**CLC 46**
See also CA 129; HW 1

Lopez y Fuentes, Gregorio 1897(?)-1966**CLC 32**
See also CA 131; HW 1

Lorca, Federico Garcia
See Garcia Lorca, Federico

Lord, Bette Bao 1938-   **CLC 23**
See also BEST 90:3; CA 107; CANR 41, 79; INT 107; SATA 58

Lord Auch
See Bataille, Georges

Lord Byron
See Byron, George Gordon (Noel)

Lorde, Audre (Geraldine) 1934-1992**CLC 18, 71; BLC 2; DAM MULT, POET; PC 12**
See also BW 1, 3; CA 25-28R; 142; CANR 16, 26, 46, 82; DLB 41; MTCW 1, 2

Lord Houghton
See Milnes, Richard Monckton

Lord Jeffrey
See Jeffrey, Francis

Lorenzini, Carlo 1826-1890
See Collodi, Carlo

See also MAICYA; SATA 29, 100
Lorenzo, Heberto Padilla
See Padilla (Lorenzo), Heberto
Loris
See Hofmannsthal, Hugo von
Loti, Pierre   **TCLC 11**
See also Viaud, (Louis Marie) Julien
See also DLB 123
Lou, Henri
See Andreas-Salome, Lou
Louie, David Wong 1954-   **CLC 70**
See also CA 139
Louis, Father M.
See Merton, Thomas
Lovecraft, H(oward) P(hillips) 1890-1937
    TCLC 4, 22; DAM POP; SSC 3
See also AAYA 14; CA 104; 133; MTCW 1, 2
Lovelace, Earl 1935-   **CLC 51**
See also BW 2; CA 77-80; CANR 41, 72; DLB
125; MTCW 1
Lovelace, Richard 1618-1657   **LC 24**
See also DLB 131
Lowell, Amy 1874-1925   **TCLC 1, 8; DAM
POET; PC 13**
See also CA 104; 151; DLB 54, 140; MTCW 2
Lowell, James Russell 1819-1891   **NCLC 2**
See also CDALB 1640-1865; DLB 1, 11, 64,
79, 189
Lowell, Robert (Traill Spence, Jr.) 1917-1977
    **CLC 1, 2, 3, 4, 5, 8, 9, 11, 15, 37; DA; DAB;
DAC; DAM MST, NOV; PC 3;WLC**
See also CA 9-12R; 73-76; CABS 2; CANR 26,
60; CDALBS; DLB 5, 169;MTCW 1, 2
Lowenthal, Michael (Francis) 1969-**CLC 119**
See also CA 150
Lowndes, Marie Adelaide (Belloc) 1868-1947
    TCLC 12
See also CA 107; DLB 70
Lowry, (Clarence) Malcolm 1909-1957**T C L C
6, 40; SSC 31**
See also CA 105; 131; CANR 62; CDBLB
1945-1960; DLB 15; MTCW 1, 2
Lowry, Mina Gertrude 1882-1966
See Loy, Mina
See also CA 113
Loxsmith, John
See Brunner, John (Kilian Houston)
Loy, Mina   **CLC 28; DAM POET; PC 16**
See also Lowry, Mina Gertrude
See also DLB 4, 54
Loyson-Bridet
See Schwob, Marcel (Mayer Andre)
Lucan 39-65   **CMLC 33**
See also DLB 211
Lucas, Craig 1951-   **CLC 64**
See also CA 137; CANR 71
Lucas, E(dward) V(errall) 1868-1938 **T C L C
73**
See also CA 176; DLB 98, 149, 153; SATA 20
Lucas, George 1944-   **CLC 16**
See also AAYA 1, 23; CA 77-80; CANR 30;
SATA 56
Lucas, Hans
See Godard, Jean-Luc
Lucas, Victoria
See Plath, Sylvia
Lucian c. 120-c. 180   **CMLC 32**
See also DLB 176
Ludlam, Charles 1943-1987   **CLC 46,50**
See also CA 85-88; 122; CANR 72
Ludlum, Robert 1927-**CLC 22, 43; DAM NOV,
POP**
See also AAYA 10; BEST 89:1, 90:3; CA 33-

36R; CANR 25, 41, 68; DLBY 82; MTCW
1, 2
Ludwig, Ken   **CLC 60**
Ludwig, Otto 1813-1865   **NCLC 4**
See also DLB 129
Lugones, Leopoldo 1874-1938   **TCLC 15;
HLCS 2**
See also CA 116; 131; HW 1
Lu Hsun 1881-1936   **TCLC 3; SSC 20**
See also Shu-Jen, Chou
Lukacs, George   **CLC 24**
See also Lukacs, Gyorgy (Szegeny von)
Lukacs, Gyorgy (Szegeny von) 1885-1971
See Lukacs, George
See also CA 101; 29-32R; CANR 62; MTCW 2
Luke, Peter (Ambrose Cyprian) 1919-1995
    CLC 38
See also CA 81-84; 147; CANR 72; DLB 13
Lunar, Dennis
See Mungo, Raymond
Lurie, Alison 1926-   **CLC 4, 5, 18, 39**
See also CA 1-4R; CANR 2, 17, 50; DLB 2;
MTCW 1; SATA 46
Lustig, Arnost 1926-   **CLC 56**
See also AAYA 3; CA 69-72; CANR 47; SATA
56
Luther, Martin 1483-1546   **LC 9, 37**
See also DLB 179
Luxemburg, Rosa 1870(?)-1919   **TCLC 63**
See also CA 118
Luzi, Mario 1914-   **CLC 13**
See also CA 61-64; CANR 9, 70; DLB 128
Lyly, John 1554(?)-1606**LC 41; DAM DRAM;
DC 7**
See also DLB 62, 167
L'Ymagier
See Gourmont, Remy (-Marie-Charles) de
Lynch, B. Suarez
See Bioy Casares, Adolfo; Borges, Jorge Luis
Lynch, B. Suarez
See Bioy Casares, Adolfo
Lynch, David (K.) 1946-   **CLC 66**
See also CA 124; 129
Lynch, James
See Andreyev, Leonid (Nikolaevich)
Lynch Davis, B.
See Bioy Casares, Adolfo; Borges, Jorge Luis
Lyndsay, Sir David 1490-1555   **LC 20**
Lynn, Kenneth S(chuyler) 1923-   **CLC 50**
See also CA 1-4R; CANR 3, 27, 65
Lynx
See West, Rebecca
Lyons, Marcus
See Blish, James (Benjamin)
Lyre, Pinchbeck
See Sassoon, Siegfried (Lorraine)
Lytle, Andrew (Nelson) 1902-1995   **CLC 22**
See also CA 9-12R; 150; CANR 70; DLB 6;
DLBY 95
Lyttelton, George 1709-1773   **LC 10**
Maas, Peter 1929-   **CLC 29**
See also CA 93-96; INT 93-96; MTCW 2
Macaulay, Rose 1881-1958   **TCLC 7, 44**
See also CA 104; DLB 36
Macaulay, Thomas Babington 1800-1859
    NCLC 42
See also CDBLB 1832-1890; DLB 32, 55
MacBeth, George (Mann) 1932-1992**CLC 2, 5,
9**
See also CA 25-28R; 136; CANR 61, 66; DLB
40; MTCW 1; SATA 4; SATA-Obit 70
MacCaig, Norman (Alexander) 1910-**CLC 36;
DAB; DAM POET**

See also CA 9-12R; CANR 3, 34; DLB 27
MacCarthy, Sir (Charles Otto) Desmond 1877-
1952   **TCLC 36**
See also CA 167
MacDiarmid, HughCLC 2, 4, 11, 19, 63; PC 9
See also Grieve, C(hristopher) M(urray)
See also CDBLB 1945-1960; DLB 20
MacDonald, Anson
See Heinlein, Robert A(nson)
Macdonald, Cynthia 1928-   **CLC 13, 19**
See also CA 49-52; CANR 4, 44; DLB 105
MacDonald, George 1824-1905   **TCLC 9**
See also CA 106; 137; CANR 80; DLB 18, 163,
178; MAICYA; SATA 33, 100
Macdonald, John
See Millar, Kenneth
MacDonald, John D(ann) 1916-1986 **CLC 3,
27, 44; DAM NOV, POP**
See also CA 1-4R; 121; CANR 1, 19, 60; DLB
8; DLBY 86; MTCW 1, 2
Macdonald, John Ross
See Millar, Kenneth
Macdonald, Ross   **CLC 1, 2, 3, 14, 34, 41**
See also Millar, Kenneth
See also DLBD 6
MacDougal, John
See Blish, James (Benjamin)
MacEwen, Gwendolyn (Margaret) 1941-1987
    CLC 13, 55
See also CA 9-12R; 124; CANR 7, 22; DLB
53; SATA 50; SATA-Obit 55
Macha, Karel Hynek 1810-1846   **NCLC 46**
Machado (y Ruiz), Antonio 1875-1939**T C L C
3**
See also CA 104; 174; DLB 108; HW 2
Machado de Assis, Joaquim Maria 1839-1908
    TCLC 10; BLC 2; HLCS 2; SSC 24
See also CA 107; 153
Machen, Arthur   **TCLC 4; SSC 20**
See also Jones, Arthur Llewellyn
See also DLB 36, 156, 178
Machiavelli, Niccolo 1469-1527**LC 8, 36; DA;
DAB; DAC; DAM MST; WLCS**
MacInnes, Colin 1914-1976   **CLC 4, 23**
See also CA 69-72; 65-68; CANR 21; DLB 14;
MTCW 1, 2
MacInnes, Helen (Clark) 1907-1985 **CLC 27,
39; DAM POP**
See also CA 1-4R; 117; CANR 1, 28, 58; DLB
87; MTCW 1, 2; SATA 22; SATA-Obit 44
Mackenzie, Compton (Edward Montague)
1883-1972   **CLC 18**
See also CA 21-22; 37-40R; CAP 2; DLB 34,
100
Mackenzie, Henry 1745-1831   **NCLC 41**
See also DLB 39
Mackintosh, Elizabeth 1896(?)-1952
See Tey, Josephine
See also CA 110
MacLaren, James
See Grieve, C(hristopher) M(urray)
Mac Laverty, Bernard 1942-   **CLC 31**
See also CA 116; 118; CANR 43; INT 118
MacLean, Alistair (Stuart) 1922(?)-1987**C L C
3, 13, 50, 63; DAM POP**
See also CA 57-60; 121; CANR 28, 61; MTCW
1; SATA 23; SATA-Obit 50
Maclean, Norman (Fitzroy) 1902-1990   **C L C
78; DAM POP; SSC 13**
See also CA 102; 132; CANR 49; DLB 206
MacLeish, Archibald 1892-1982**CLC 3, 8, 14,
68; DAM POET**
See also CA 9-12R; 106; CANR 33, 63;

CDALBS; DLB 4, 7, 45; DLBY 82; MTCW 1, 2

MacLennan, (John) Hugh 1907-1990 **CLC 2, 14, 92; DAC; DAM MST**
See also CA 5-8R; 142; CANR 33; DLB 68; MTCW 1, 2

MacLeod, Alistair 1936-**CLC 56; DAC; DAM MST**
See also CA 123; DLB 60; MTCW 2

Macleod, Fiona
See Sharp, William

MacNeice, (Frederick) Louis 1907-1963 **C L C 1, 4, 10, 53; DAB; DAM POET**
See also CA 85-88; CANR 61; DLB 10, 20; MTCW 1, 2

MacNeill, Dand
See Fraser, George MacDonald

Macpherson, James 1736-1796 **LC 29**
See also Ossian
See also DLB 109

Macpherson, (Jean) Jay 1931- **CLC 14**
See also CA 5-8R; DLB 53

MacShane, Frank 1927- **CLC 39**
See also CA 9-12R; CANR 3, 33; DLB 111

Macumber, Mari
See Sandoz, Mari(e Susette)

Madach, Imre 1823-1864 **NCLC 19**

Madden, (Jerry) David 1933- **CLC 5, 15**
See also CA 1-4R; CAAS 3; CANR 4, 45; DLB 6; MTCW 1

Maddern, Al(an)
See Ellison, Harlan (Jay)

Madhubuti, Haki R. 1942-**CLC 6, 73; BLC 2; DAM MULT, POET; PC 5**
See also Lee, Don L.
See also BW 2, 3; CA 73-76; CANR 24, 51, 73; DLB 5, 41; DLBD 8; MTCW 2

Maepenn, Hugh
See Kuttner, Henry

Maepenn, K. H.
See Kuttner, Henry

Maeterlinck, Maurice 1862-1949 **TCLC 3; DAM DRAM**
See also CA 104; 136; CANR 80; DLB 192; SATA 66

Maginn, William 1794-1842 **NCLC 8**
See also DLB 110, 159

Mahapatra, Jayanta 1928- **CLC 33;DAM MULT**
See also CA 73-76; CAAS 9; CANR 15, 33, 66

Mahfouz, Naguib (Abdel Aziz Al-Sabilgi) 1911(?)-
See Mahfuz, Najib
See also BEST 89:2; CA 128; CANR 55; DAM NOV; MTCW 1, 2

Mahfuz, Najib **CLC 52, 55**
See also Mahfouz, Naguib (Abdel Aziz Al-Sabilgi)
See also DLBY 88

Mahon, Derek 1941- **CLC 27**
See also CA 113; 128; DLB 40

Mailer, Norman 1923-**CLC 1, 2, 3, 4, 5, 8, 11, 14, 28, 39, 74, 111; DA; DAB; DAC; DAM MST, NOV, POP**
See also AITN 2; CA 9-12R; CABS 1; CANR 28, 74, 77; CDALB 1968-1988; DLB 2, 16, 28, 185; DLBD 3; DLBY 80, 83; MTCW 1, 2

Maillet, Antonine 1929- **CLC 54, 118; DAC**
See also CA 115; 120; CANR 46, 74, 77; DLB 60; INT 120; MTCW 2

Mais, Roger 1905-1955 **TCLC 8**
See also BW 1, 3; CA 105; 124; CANR 82; DLB 125; MTCW 1

Maistre, Joseph de 1753-1821 **NCLC 37**

Maitland, Frederic 1850-1906 **TCLC 65**

Maitland, Sara (Louise) 1950- **CLC 49**
See also CA 69-72; CANR 13, 59

Major, Clarence 1936-**CLC 3, 19, 48; BLC 2; DAM MULT**
See also BW 2, 3; CA 21-24R; CAAS 6; CANR 13, 25, 53, 82; DLB 33

Major, Kevin (Gerald) 1949- **CLC 26; DAC**
See also AAYA 16; CA 97-100; CANR 21, 38; CLR 11; DLB 60; INT CANR-21; JRDA; MAICYA; SATA 32, 82

Maki, James
See Ozu, Yasujiro

Malabaila, Damiano
See Levi, Primo

Malamud, Bernard 1914-1986**CLC 1, 2, 3, 5, 8, 9, 11, 18, 27, 44, 78, 85;DA; DAB; DAC; DAM MST, NOV, POP; SSC 15;WLC**
See also AAYA 16; CA 5-8R; 118; CABS 1; CANR 28, 62; CDALB 1941-1968; DLB 2, 28, 152; DLBY 80, 86; MTCW 1, 2

Malan, Herman
See Bosman, Herman Charles; Bosman, Herman Charles

Malaparte, Curzio 1898-1957 **TCLC 52**

Malcolm, Dan
See Silverberg, Robert

Malcolm X **CLC 82, 117; BLC 2; WLCS**
See also Little, Malcolm

Malherbe, Francois de 1555-1628 **LC 5**

Mallarme, Stephane 1842-1898 **NCLC 4, 41; DAM POET; PC 4**

Mallet-Joris, Francoise 1930- **CLC 11**
See also CA 65-68; CANR 17; DLB 83

Malley, Ern
See McAuley, James Phillip

Mallowan, Agatha Christie
See Christie, Agatha (Mary Clarissa)

Maloff, Saul 1922- **CLC 5**
See also CA 33-36R

Malone, Louis
See MacNeice, (Frederick) Louis

Malone, Michael (Christopher) 1942-**CLC 43**
See also CA 77-80; CANR 14, 32, 57

Malory, (Sir) Thomas 1410(?)-1471(?)**LC 11; DA; DAB; DAC; DAM MST; WLCS**
See also CDBLB Before 1660; DLB 146; SATA 59; SATA-Brief 33

Malouf, (George Joseph) David 1934-**CLC 28, 86**
See also CA 124; CANR 50, 76; MTCW 2

Malraux, (Georges-)Andre 1901-1976**CLC 1, 4, 9, 13, 15, 57; DAM NOV**
See also CA 21-22; 69-72; CANR 34, 58; CAP 2; DLB 72; MTCW 1, 2

Malzberg, Barry N(athaniel) 1939- **CLC 7**
See also CA 61-64; CAAS 4; CANR 16; DLB 8

Mamet, David (Alan) 1947-**CLC 9, 15, 34, 46, 91; DAM DRAM; DC 4**
See also AAYA 3; CA 81-84; CABS 3; CANR 15, 41, 67, 72; DLB 7; MTCW 1, 2

Mamoulian, Rouben (Zachary) 1897-1987 **CLC 16**
See also CA 25-28R; 124

Mandelstam, Osip (Emilievich) 1891(?)-1938(?) **TCLC 2, 6; PC 14**
See also CA 104; 150; MTCW 2

Mander, (Mary) Jane 1877-1949 **TCLC 31**
See also CA 162

Mandeville, John fl. 1350- **CMLC 19**
See also DLB 146

Mandiargues, Andre Pieyre de **CLC 41**
See also Pieyre de Mandiargues, Andre
See also DLB 83

Mandrake, Ethel Belle
See Thurman, Wallace (Henry)

Mangan, James Clarence 1803-1849**NCLC 27**

Maniere, J.-E.
See Giraudoux, (Hippolyte) Jean

Mankiewicz, Herman (Jacob) 1897-1953 **TCLC 85**
See also CA 120; 169; DLB 26

Manley, (Mary) Delariviere 1672(?)-1724 **L C 1, 42**
See also DLB 39, 80

Mann, Abel
See Creasey, John

Mann, Emily 1952- **DC 7**
See also CA 130; CANR 55

Mann, (Luiz) Heinrich 1871-1950 **TCLC 9**
See also CA 106; 164; DLB 66, 118

Mann, (Paul) Thomas 1875-1955 **TCLC 2, 8, 14, 21, 35, 44, 60; DA; DAB; DAC; DAM MST, NOV; SSC 5; WLC**
See also CA 104; 128; DLB 66; MTCW 1, 2

Mannheim, Karl 1893-1947 **TCLC 65**

Manning, David
See Faust, Frederick (Schiller)

Manning, Frederic 1887(?)-1935 **TCLC 25**
See also CA 124

Manning, Olivia 1915-1980 **CLC 5, 19**
See also CA 5-8R; 101; CANR 29; MTCW 1

Mano, D. Keith 1942- **CLC 2, 10**
See also CA 25-28R; CAAS 6; CANR 26, 57; DLB 6

Mansfield, KatherineTCLC 2, 8, 39; DAB; SSC 9, 23; WLC
See also Beauchamp, Kathleen Mansfield
See also DLB 162

Manso, Peter 1940- **CLC 39**
See also CA 29-32R; CANR 44

Mantecon, Juan Jimenez
See Jimenez (Mantecon), Juan Ramon

Manton, Peter
See Creasey, John

Man Without a Spleen, A
See Chekhov, Anton (Pavlovich)

Manzoni, Alessandro 1785-1873 **NCLC 29**

Map, Walter 1140-1209 **CMLC 32**

Mapu, Abraham (ben Jekutiel) 1808-1867 **NCLC 18**

Mara, Sally
See Queneau, Raymond

Marat, Jean Paul 1743-1793 **LC 10**

Marcel, Gabriel Honore 1889-1973 **CLC 15**
See also CA 102; 45-48; MTCW 1, 2

March, William 1893-1954 **TCLC 96**

Marchbanks, Samuel
See Davies, (William) Robertson

Marchi, Giacomo
See Bassani, Giorgio

Margulies, Donald **CLC 76**

Marie de France c. 12th cent. - **CMLC 8; PC 22**
See also DLB 208

Marie de l'Incarnation 1599-1672 **LC 10**

Marier, Captain Victor
See Griffith, D(avid Lewelyn) W(ark)

Mariner, Scott
See Pohl, Frederik

Marinetti, Filippo Tommaso 1876-1944**TCLC 10**
See also CA 107; DLB 114

Marivaux, Pierre Carlet de Chamblain de 1688-

1763 **LC 4; DC 7**
Markandaya, Kamala **CLC 8, 38**
See also Taylor, Kamala (Purnaiya)
Markfield, Wallace 1926- **CLC 8**
See also CA 69-72; CAAS 3; DLB 2, 28
Markham, Edwin 1852-1940 **TCLC 47**
See also CA 160; DLB 54, 186
Markham, Robert
See Amis, Kingsley (William)
Marks, J
See Highwater, Jamake (Mamake)
Marks-Highwater, J
See Highwater, Jamake (Mamake)
Markson, David M(errill) 1927- **CLC 67**
See also CA 49-52; CANR 1
Marley, Bob **CLC 17**
See also Marley, Robert Nesta
Marley, Robert Nesta 1945-1981
See Marley, Bob
See also CA 107; 103
Marlowe, Christopher 1564-1593 **LC 22, 47;**
DA; DAB; DAC; DAM DRAM, MST; DC
1; WLC
See also CDBLB Before 1660; DLB 62
Marlowe, Stephen 1928-
See Queen, Ellery
See also CA 13-16R; CANR 6, 55
Marmontel, Jean-Francois 1723-1799 **LC 2**
Marquand, John P(hillips) 1893-1960 **CLC 2,**
10
See also CA 85-88; CANR 73; DLB 9, 102;
MTCW 2
Marques, Rene 1919-1979 **CLC 96; DAM**
MULT; HLC 2
See also CA 97-100; 85-88; CANR 78; DLB
113; HW 1, 2
Marquez, Gabriel (Jose) Garcia
See Garcia Marquez, Gabriel (Jose)
Marquis, Don(ald Robert Perry) 1878-1937
TCLC 7
See also CA 104; 166; DLB 11, 25
Marric, J. J.
See Creasey, John
Marryat, Frederick 1792-1848 **NCLC 3**
See also DLB 21, 163
Marsden, James
See Creasey, John
Marsh, (Edith) Ngaio 1899-1982 **CLC 7, 53;**
DAM POP
See also CA 9-12R; CANR 6, 58; DLB 77;
MTCW 1, 2
Marshall, Garry 1934- **CLC 17**
See also AAYA 3; CA 111; SATA 60
Marshall, Paule 1929- **CLC 27, 72; BLC 3;**
DAM MULT; SSC 3
See also BW 2, 3; CA 77-80; CANR 25, 73;
DLB 157; MTCW 1, 2
Marshallik
See Zangwill, Israel
Marsten, Richard
See Hunter, Evan
Marston, John 1576-1634 **LC 33; DAM DRAM**
See also DLB 58, 172
Martha, Henry
See Harris, Mark
Marti (y Perez), Jose (Julian) 1853-1895
NCLC 63; DAM MULT; HLC 2
See also HW 2
Martial c. 40-c. 104 **CMLC 35; PC 10**
See also DLB 211
Martin, Ken
See Hubbard, L(afayette) Ron(ald)
Martin, Richard

See Creasey, John
Martin, Steve 1945- **CLC 30**
See also CA 97-100; CANR 30; MTCW 1
Martin, Valerie 1948- **CLC 89**
See also BEST 90:2; CA 85-88; CANR 49
Martin, Violet Florence 1862-1915 **TCLC 51**
Martin, Webber
See Silverberg, Robert
Martindale, Patrick Victor
See White, Patrick (Victor Martindale)
Martin du Gard, Roger 1881-1958 **TCLC 24**
See also CA 118; DLB 65
Martineau, Harriet 1802-1876 **NCLC 26**
See also DLB 21, 55, 159, 163, 166, 190; YABC
2
Martines, Julia
See O'Faolain, Julia
Martinez, Enrique Gonzalez
See Gonzalez Martinez, Enrique
Martinez, Jacinto Benavente y
See Benavente (y Martinez), Jacinto
Martinez Ruiz, Jose 1873-1967
See Azorin; Ruiz, Jose Martinez
See also CA 93-96; HW 1
Martinez Sierra, Gregorio 1881-1947 **TCLC 6**
See also CA 115
Martinez Sierra, Maria (de la O'Le Jarraga)
1874-1974 **TCLC 6**
See also CA 115
Martinsen, Martin
See Follett, Ken(neth Martin)
Martinson, Harry (Edmund) 1904-1978 **CLC**
14
See also CA 77-80; CANR 34
Marut, Ret
See Traven, B.
Marut, Robert
See Traven, B.
Marvell, Andrew 1621-1678 **LC 4, 43; DA;**
DAB; DAC; DAM MST, POET; PC 10;
WLC
See also CDBLB 1660-1789; DLB 131
Marx, Karl (Heinrich) 1818-1883 **NCLC 17**
See also DLB 129
Masaoka Shiki **TCLC 18**
See also Masaoka Tsunenori
Masaoka Tsunenori 1867-1902
See Masaoka Shiki
See also CA 117
Masefield, John (Edward) 1878-1967 **CLC 11,**
47; DAM POET
See also CA 19-20; 25-28R; CANR 33; CAP 2;
CDBLB 1890-1914; DLB 10, 19, 153, 160;
MTCW 1, 2; SATA 19
Maso, Carole 19(?)- **CLC 44**
See also CA 170
Mason, Bobbie Ann 1940- **CLC 28, 43, 82; SSC**
4
See also AAYA 5; CA 53-56; CANR 11, 31,
58; CDALBS; DLB 173; DLBY 87; INT
CANR-31; MTCW 1, 2
Mason, Ernst
See Pohl, Frederik
Mason, Lee W.
See Malzberg, Barry N(athaniel)
Mason, Nick 1945- **CLC 35**
Mason, Tally
See Derleth, August (William)
Mass, William
See Gibson, William
Master Lao
See Lao Tzu
Masters, Edgar Lee 1868-1950 **TCLC 2, 25;**

DA; DAC; DAM MST, POET; PC 1;
WLCS
See also CA 104; 133; CDALB 1865-1917; DLB
54; MTCW 1, 2
Masters, Hilary 1928- **CLC 48**
See also CA 25-28R; CANR 13, 47
Mastrosimone, William 19(?)- **CLC 36**
Mathe, Albert
See Camus, Albert
Mather, Cotton 1663-1728 **LC 38**
See also CDALB 1640-1865; DLB 24, 30, 140
Mather, Increase 1639-1723 **LC 38**
See also DLB 24
Matheson, Richard Burton 1926- **CLC 37**
See also CA 97-100; DLB 8, 44; INT 97-100
Mathews, Harry 1930- **CLC 6, 52**
See also CA 21-24R; CAAS 6; CANR 18, 40
Mathews, John Joseph 1894-1979 **CLC 84;**
DAM MULT
See also CA 19-20; 142; CANR 45; CAP 2;
DLB 175; NNAL
Mathias, Roland (Glyn) 1915- **CLC 45**
See also CA 97-100; CANR 19, 41; DLB 27
Matsuo Basho 1644-1694 **PC 3**
See also DAM POET
Mattheson, Rodney
See Creasey, John
Matthews, Brander 1852-1929 **TCLC 95**
See also DLB 71, 78; DLBD 13
Matthews, Greg 1949- **CLC 45**
See also CA 135
Matthews, William (Procter, III) 1942-1997
CLC 40
See also CA 29-32R; 162; CAAS 18; CANR
12, 57; DLB 5
Matthias, John (Edward) 1941- **CLC 9**
See also CA 33-36R; CANR 56
Matthiessen, Peter 1927- **CLC 5, 7, 11, 32, 64;**
DAM NOV
See also AAYA 6; BEST 90:4; CA 9-12R;
CANR 21, 50, 73; DLB 6, 173; MTCW 1, 2;
SATA 27
Maturin, Charles Robert 1780(?)-1824 **NCLC**
6
See also DLB 178
Matute (Ausejo), Ana Maria 1925- **CLC 11**
See also CA 89-92; MTCW 1
Maugham, W. S.
See Maugham, W(illiam) Somerset
Maugham, W(illiam) Somerset 1874-1965
CLC 1, 11, 15, 67, 93; DA; DAB; DAC;
DAM DRAM, MST, NOV; SSC 8; WLC
See also CA 5-8R; 25-28R; CANR 40; CDBLB
1914-1945; DLB 10, 36, 77, 100, 162, 195;
MTCW 1, 2; SATA 54
Maugham, William Somerset
See Maugham, W(illiam) Somerset
Maupassant, (Henri Rene Albert) Guy de 1850-
1893 **NCLC 1, 42; DA; DAB; DAC; DAM**
MST; SSC 1; WLC
See also DLB 123
Maupin, Armistead 1944- **CLC 95; DAM POP**
See also CA 125; 130; CANR 58; INT 130;
MTCW 2
Maurhut, Richard
See Traven, B.
Mauriac, Claude 1914-1996 **CLC 9**
See also CA 89-92; 152; DLB 83
Mauriac, Francois (Charles) 1885-1970 **CLC**
4, 9, 56; SSC 24
See also CA 25-28; CAP 2; DLB 65; MTCW 1,
2
Mavor, Osborne Henry 1888-1951

See Bridie, James
See also CA 104

Maxwell, William (Keepers, Jr.) 1908-**CLC 19**
See also CA 93-96; CANR 54; DLBY 80; INT
93-96

May, Elaine 1932- **CLC 16**
See also CA 124; 142; DLB 44

Mayakovski, Vladimir (Vladimirovich) 1893-
1930 **TCLC 4, 18**
See also CA 104; 158; MTCW 2

Mayhew, Henry 1812-1887 **NCLC 31**
See also DLB 18, 55, 190

Mayle, Peter 1939(?)- **CLC 89**
See also CA 139; CANR 64

Maynard, Joyce 1953- **CLC 23**
See also CA 111; 129; CANR 64

Mayne, William (James Carter) 1928-**CLC 12**
See also AAYA 20; CA 9-12R; CANR 37, 80;
CLR 25; JRDA; MAICYA; SAAS 11; SATA
6, 68

Mayo, Jim
See L'Amour, Louis (Dearborn)

Maysles, Albert 1926- **CLC 16**
See also CA 29-32R

Maysles, David 1932- **CLC 16**

Mazer, Norma Fox 1931- **CLC 26**
See also AAYA 5; CA 69-72; CANR 12, 32,
66; CLR 23; JRDA; MAICYA; SAAS 1;
SATA 24, 67, 105

Mazzini, Guiseppe 1805-1872 **NCLC 34**

McAuley, James Phillip 1917-1976 **CLC 45**
See also CA 97-100

McBain, Ed
See Hunter, Evan

McBrien, William Augustine 1930- **CLC 44**
See also CA 107

McCaffrey, Anne (Inez) 1926-**CLC 17; DAM
NOV, POP**
See also AAYA 6; AITN 2; BEST 89:2; CA 25-
28R; CANR 15, 35, 55; CLR 49; DLB 8;
JRDA; MAICYA; MTCW 1, 2; SAAS 11;
SATA 8, 70

McCall, Nathan 1955(?)- **CLC 86**
See also BW 3; CA 146

McCann, Arthur
See Campbell, John W(ood, Jr.)

McCann, Edson
See Pohl, Frederik

McCarthy, Charles, Jr. 1933-
See McCarthy, Cormac
See also CANR 42, 69; DAM POP; MTCW 2

McCarthy, Cormac 1933- **CLC 4, 57, 59, 101**
See also McCarthy, Charles, Jr.
See also DLB 6, 143; MTCW 2

McCarthy, Mary (Therese) 1912-1989**CLC 1,
3, 5, 14, 24, 39, 59; SSC 24**
See also CA 5-8R; 129; CANR 16, 50, 64; DLB
2; DLBY 81; INT CANR-16; MTCW 1, 2

McCartney, (James) Paul 1942- **CLC 12, 35**
See also CA 146

McCauley, Stephen (D.) 1955- **CLC 50**
See also CA 141

McClure, Michael (Thomas) 1932-**CLC 6, 10**
See also CA 21-24R; CANR 17, 46, 77; DLB
16

McCorkle, Jill (Collins) 1958- **CLC 51**
See also CA 121; DLBY 87

McCourt, Frank 1930- **CLC 109**
See also CA 157

McCourt, James 1941- **CLC 5**
See also CA 57-60

McCourt, Malachy 1932- **CLC 119**

McCoy, Horace(Stanley) 1897-1955**TCLC 28**·

See also CA 108; 155; DLB 9

McCrae, John 1872-1918 **TCLC 12**
See also CA 109; DLB 92

McCreigh, James
See Pohl, Frederik

McCullers, (Lula) Carson (Smith) 1917-1967
**CLC 1, 4, 10, 12, 48, 100; DA; DAB; DAC;
DAM MST, NOV; SSC 9, 24;WLC**
See also AAYA 21; CA 5-8R; 25-28R; CABS
1, 3; CANR 18; CDALB 1941-1968; DLB
2, 7, 173; MTCW 1, 2; SATA 27

McCulloch, John Tyler
See Burroughs, Edgar Rice

McCullough, Colleen 1938(?)- **CLC 27, 107;
DAM NOV, POP**
See also CA 81-84; CANR 17, 46, 67; MTCW
1, 2

McDermott, Alice 1953- **CLC 90**
See also CA 109; CANR 40

McElroy, Joseph 1930- **CLC 5, 47**
See also CA 17-20R

McEwan, Ian (Russell) 1948- **CLC 13, 66;
DAM NOV**
See also BEST 90:4; CA 61-64; CANR 14, 41,
69; DLB 14, 194; MTCW 1, 2

McFadden, David 1940- **CLC 48**
See also CA 104; DLB 60; INT 104

McFarland, Dennis 1950- **CLC 65**
See also CA 165

McGahern, John 1934- **CLC 5, 9, 48;SSC 17**
See also CA 17-20R; CANR 29, 68; DLB 14;
MTCW 1

McGinley, Patrick (Anthony) 1937- **CLC 41**
See also CA 120; 127; CANR 56; INT 127

McGinley, Phyllis 1905-1978 **CLC 14**
See also CA 9-12R; 77-80; CANR 19; DLB 11,
48; SATA 2, 44; SATA-Obit 24

McGinniss, Joe 1942- **CLC 32**
See also AITN 2; BEST 89:2; CA 25-28R;
CANR 26, 70; DLB 185; INT CANR-26

McGivern, Maureen Daly
See Daly, Maureen

McGrath, Patrick 1950- **CLC 55**
See also CA 136; CANR 65

McGrath, Thomas (Matthew) 1916-1990**CLC
28, 59; DAM POET**
See also CA 9-12R; 132; CANR 6, 33; MTCW
1; SATA 41; SATA-Obit 66

McGuane, Thomas (Francis III) 1939-**CLC 3,
7, 18, 45**
See also AITN 2; CA 49-52; CANR 5, 24, 49;
DLB 2, 212; DLBY 80; INT CANR-24;
MTCW 1

McGuckian, Medbh 1950- **CLC 48; DAM
POET; PC 27**
See also CA 143; DLB 40

McHale, Tom 1942(?)-1982 **CLC 3, 5**
See also AITN 1; CA 77-80; 106

McIlvanney, William 1936- **CLC 42**
See also CA 25-28R; CANR 61; DLB 14, 207

McIlwraith, Maureen Mollie Hunter
See Hunter, Mollie
See also SATA 2

McInerney, Jay 1955-**CLC 34, 112;DAM POP**
See also AAYA 18; CA 116; 123; CANR 45,
68; INT 123; MTCW 2

McIntyre, Vonda N(eel) 1948- **CLC 18**
See also CA 81-84; CANR 17, 34, 69; MTCW
1

McKay, ClaudeTCLC 7, 41; BLC 3; DAB;PC
2
See also McKay, Festus Claudius
See also DLB 4, 45, 51, 117

McKay, Festus Claudius 1889-1948
See McKay, Claude
See also BW 1, 3; CA 104; 124; CANR 73; DA;
DAC; DAM MST, MULT, NOV, POET;
MTCW 1, 2; WLC

McKuen, Rod 1933- **CLC 1, 3**
See also AITN 1; CA 41-44R; CANR 40

McLoughlin, R. B.
See Mencken, H(enry) L(ouis)

McLuhan, (Herbert) Marshall 1911-1980
CLC 37, 83
See also CA 9-12R; 102; CANR 12, 34, 61;
DLB 88; INT CANR-12; MTCW 1, 2

McMillan, Terry (L.) 1951-**CLC 50, 61, 112;
BLCS; DAM MULT, NOV, POP**
See also AAYA 21; BW 2, 3; CA 140; CANR
60; MTCW 2

McMurtry, Larry (Jeff) 1936-**CLC 2, 3, 7, 11,
27, 44; DAM NOV, POP**
See also AAYA 15; AITN 2; BEST 89:2; CA 5-
8R; CANR 19, 43, 64; CDALB 1968-1988;
DLB 2, 143; DLBY 80, 87; MTCW 1, 2

McNally, T. M. 1961- **CLC 82**

McNally, Terrence 1939- **CLC 4, 7, 41, 91;
DAM DRAM**
See also CA 45-48; CANR 2, 56; DLB 7;
MTCW 2

McNamer, Deirdre 1950- **CLC 70**

McNeal, Tom **CLC 119**

McNeile, Herman Cyril 1888-1937
See Sapper
See also DLB 77

McNickle, (William) D'Arcy 1904-1977 **C L C
89; DAM MULT**
See also CA 9-12R; 85-88; CANR 5, 45; DLB
175, 212; NNAL; SATA-Obit 22

McPhee, John (Angus) 1931- **CLC 36**
See also BEST 90:1; CA 65-68; CANR 20, 46,
64, 69; DLB 185; MTCW 1, 2

McPherson, James Alan 1943- **CLC 19, 77;
BLCS**
See also BW 1, 3; CA 25-28R; CAAS 17;
CANR 24, 74; DLB 38; MTCW 1, 2

McPherson, William (Alexander) 1933- **C L C
34**
See also CA 69-72; CANR 28; INT CANR-28

Mead, George Herbert 1873-1958 **TCLC 89**

Mead, Margaret 1901-1978 **CLC 37**
See also AITN 1; CA 1-4R; 81-84; CANR 4;
MTCW 1, 2; SATA-Obit 20

Meaker, Marijane (Agnes) 1927-
See Kerr, M. E.
See also CA 107; CANR 37, 63; INT 107;
JRDA; MAICYA; MTCW 1; SATA 20,61, 99

Medoff, Mark (Howard) 1940- **CLC 6, 23;
DAM DRAM**
See also AITN 1; CA 53-56; CANR 5; DLB 7;
INT CANR-5

Medvedev, P. N.
See Bakhtin, Mikhail Mikhailovich

Meged, Aharon
See Megged, Aharon

Meged, Aron
See Megged, Aharon

Megged, Aharon 1920- **CLC 9**
See also CA 49-52; CAAS 13; CANR 1

Mehta, Ved (Parkash) 1934- **CLC 37**
See also CA 1-4R; CANR 2, 23, 69; MTCW 1

Melanter
See Blackmore, R(ichard) D(oddridge)

Melies, Georges 1861-1938 **TCLC 81**

Melikow, Loris
See Hofmannsthal, Hugo von

Melmoth, Sebastian
See Wilde, Oscar
Meltzer, Milton 1915-   **CLC 26**
See also AAYA 8; CA 13-16R; CANR 38; CLR
13; DLB 61; JRDA; MAICYA; SAAS 1;
SATA 1, 50, 80
Melville, Herman 1819-1891**NCLC 3, 12, 29,
45, 49; DA; DAB; DAC; DAM MST, NOV;
SSC 1, 17; WLC**
See also AAYA 25; CDALB 1640-1865; DLB
3, 74; SATA 59
Menander c. 342B.C.-c. 292B.C.   **CMLC 9;
DAM DRAM; DC 3**
See also DLB 176
Menchu, Rigoberta 1959-
See also HLCS 2
Menchu, Rigoberta 1959-
See also CA 175; HLCS 2
Mencken, H(enry) L(ouis) 1880-1956 **TCLC
13**
See also CA 105; 125; CDALB 1917-1929;
DLB 11, 29, 63, 137; MTCW 1, 2
Mendelsohn, Jane 1965(?)-   **CLC 99**
See also CA 154
Mercer, David 1928-1980**CLC 5;DAM DRAM**
See also CA 9-12R; 102; CANR 23; DLB 13;
MTCW 1
Merchant, Paul
See Ellison, Harlan (Jay)
Meredith, George 1828-1909   **TCLC 17, 43;
DAM POET**
See also CA 117; 153; CANR 80; CDBLB 1832-
1890; DLB 18, 35, 57, 159
Meredith, William (Morris) 1919-**CLC 4, 13,
22, 55; DAM POET**
See also CA 9-12R; CAAS 14; CANR 6, 40;
DLB 5
Merezhkovsky, Dmitry Sergeyevich 1865-1941
TCLC 29
See also CA 169
Merimee, Prosper 1803-1870**NCLC 6,65; SSC
7**
See also DLB 119, 192
Merkin, Daphne 1954-   **CLC 44**
See also CA 123
Merlin, Arthur
See Blish, James (Benjamin)
Merrill; James (Ingram) 1926-1995**CLC 2, 3,
6, 8, 13, 18, 34, 91; DAM POET**
See also CA 13-16R; 147; CANR 10, 49, 63;
DLB 5, 165; DLBY 85; INT CANR-10;
MTCW 1, 2
Merriman, Alex
See Silverberg, Robert
Merriman, Brian 1747-1805   **NCLC 70**
Merritt, E. B.
See Waddington, Miriam
Merton, Thomas 1915-1968 **CLC 1, 3, 11, 34,
83; PC 10**
See also CA 5-8R; 25-28R; CANR 22, 53; DLB
48; DLBY 81; MTCW 1, 2
Merwin, W(illiam) S(tanley) 1927- **CLC 1, 2,
3, 5, 8, 13, 18, 45, 88; DAM POET**
See also CA 13-16R; CANR 15, 51; DLB 5,
169; INT CANR-15; MTCW 1, 2
Metcalf, John 1938-   **CLC 37**
See also CA 113; DLB 60
Metcalf, Suzanne
See Baum, L(yman) Frank
Mew, Charlotte (Mary) 1870-1928   **TCLC 8**
See also CA 105; DLB 19, 135
Mewshaw, Michael 1943-   **CLC 9**
See also CA 53-56; CANR 7, 47; DLBY 80

Meyer, June
See Jordan, June
Meyer, Lynn
See Slavitt, David R(ytman)
Meyer-Meyrink, Gustav 1868-1932
See Meyrink, Gustav
See also CA 117
Meyers, Jeffrey 1939-   **CLC 39**
See also CA 73-76; CANR 54; DLB 111
Meynell, Alice (Christina Gertrude Thompson)
1847-1922   **TCLC 6**
See also CA 104; 177; DLB 19, 98
Meyrink, Gustav   **TCLC 21**
See also Meyer-Meyrink, Gustav
See also DLB 81
Michaels, Leonard 1933- **CLC 6, 25;SSC 16**
See also CA 61-64; CANR 21, 62; DLB 130;
MTCW 1
Michaux, Henri 1899-1984   **CLC 8, 19**
See also CA 85-88; 114
Micheaux, Oscar (Devereaux) 1884-1951
TCLC 76
See also BW 3; CA 174; DLB 50
Michelangelo 1475-1564   **LC 12**
Michelet, Jules 1798-1874   **NCLC 31**
Michels, Robert 1876-1936   **TCLC 88**
Michener, James A(lbert) 1907(?)-1997 **C L C
1, 5, 11, 29, 60, 109; DAM NOV, POP**
See also AAYA 27; AITN 1; BEST 90:1; CA 5-
8R; 161; CANR 21, 45, 68; DLB 6; MTCW
1, 2
Mickiewicz, Adam 1798-1855   **NCLC 3**
Middleton,Christopher 1926-   **CLC 13**
See also CA 13-16R; CANR 29, 54; DLB 40
Middleton, Richard (Barham) 1882-1911
TCLC 56
See also DLB 156
Middleton, Stanley 1919-   **CLC 7, 38**
See also CA 25-28R; CAAS 23; CANR 21, 46,
81; DLB 14
Middleton, Thomas 1580-1627 **LC 33; DAM
DRAM, MST; DC 5**
See also DLB 58
Migueis, Jose Rodrigues 1901-   **CLC 10**
Mikszath, Kalman 1847-1910   **TCLC 31**
See also CA 170
Miles, Jack   **CLC 100**
Miles, Josephine (Louise) 1911-1985**CLC 1, 2,
14, 34, 39; DAM POET**
See also CA 1-4R; 116; CANR 2, 55; DLB 48
Militant
See Sandburg, Carl (August)
Mill, John Stuart 1806-1873   **NCLC 11, 58**
See also CDBLB 1832-1890; DLB 55, 190
Millar, Kenneth 1915-1983**CLC 14;DAM POP**
See also Macdonald, Ross
See also CA 9-12R; 110; CANR 16, 63; DLB
2; DLBD 6; DLBY 83; MTCW 1, 2
Millay, E. Vincent
See Millay, Edna St. Vincent
Millay, Edna St. Vincent 1892-1950 **TCLC 4,
49; DA; DAB; DAC; DAM MST, POET;
PC 6; WLCS**
See also CA 104; 130; CDALB 1917-1929;
DLB 45; MTCW 1, 2
Miller, Arthur 1915-**CLC 1, 2, 6, 10, 15, 26, 47,
78; DA; DAB; DAC; DAM DRAM, MST;
DC 1; WLC**
See also AAYA 15; AITN 1; CA 1-4R; CABS
3; CANR 2, 30, 54, 76; CDALB 1941-1968;
DLB 7; MTCW 1, 2
Miller, Henry (Valentine) 1891-1980**CLC 1, 2,
4, 9, 14, 43, 84; DA; DAB; DAC; DAM**

MST, NOV; WLC
See also CA 9-12R; 97-100; CANR 33, 64;
CDALB 1929-1941; DLB 4, 9; DLBY 80;
MTCW 1, 2
Miller, Jason 1939(?)-   **CLC 2**
See also AITN 1; CA 73-76; DLB 7
Miller, Sue 1943-   **CLC 44;DAM POP**
See also BEST 90:3; CA 139; CANR 59; DLB
143
Miller, Walter M(ichael, Jr.) 1923-**CLC 4, 30**
See also CA 85-88; DLB 8
Millett, Kate 1934-   **CLC 67**
See also AITN 1; CA 73-76; CANR 32, 53, 76;
MTCW 1, 2
Millhauser, Steven (Lewis) 1943-**CLC 21, 54,
109**
See also CA 110; 111; CANR 63; DLB 2; INT
111; MTCW 2
Millin, Sarah Gertrude 1889-1968 **CLC 49**
See also CA 102; 93-96
Milne, A(lan) A(lexander) 1882-1956**TCLC 6,
88; DAB; DAC; DAM MST**
See also CA 104; 133; CLR 1, 26; DLB 10, 77,
100, 160; MAICYA; MTCW 1, 2; SATA 100;
YABC 1
Milner, Ron(ald) 1938-**CLC 56; BLC 3; DAM
MULT**
See also AITN 1; BW 1; CA 73-76; CANR 24,
81; DLB 38; MTCW 1
Milnes, Richard Monckton 1809-1885 **N C L C
61**
See also DLB 32, 184
Milosz, Czeslaw 1911- **CLC 5, 11, 22, 31, 56,
82; DAM MST, POET; PC 8; WLCS**
See also CA 81-84; CANR 23, 51; MTCW 1, 2
Milton, John 1608-1674 **LC 9, 43; DA; DAB;
DAC; DAM MST, POET; PC 19; WLC**
See also CDBLB 1660-1789; DLB 131, 151
Min, Anchee 1957-   **CLC 86**
See also CA 146
Minehaha, Cornelius
See Wedekind, (Benjamin) Frank(lin)
Miner, Valerie 1947-   **CLC 40**
See also CA 97-100; CANR 59
Minimo, Duca
See D'Annunzio, Gabriele
Minot, Susan 1956-   **CLC 44**
See also CA 134
Minus, Ed 1938-   **CLC 39**
Miranda, Javier
See Bioy Casares, Adolfo
Miranda, Javier
See Bioy Casares, Adolfo
Mirbeau, Octave 1848-1917   **TCLC 55**
See also DLB 123, 192
Miro (Ferrer), Gabriel (Francisco Victor) 1879-
1930   **TCLC 5**
See also CA 104
Mishima, Yukio 1925-1970**CLC 2, 4, 6, 9, 27;
DC 1; SSC 4**
See also Hiraoka, Kimitake
See also DLB 182; MTCW 2
Mistral, Frederic 1830-1914   **TCLC 51**
See also CA 122
Mistral, Gabriela   **TCLC 2; HLC 2**
See also Godoy Alcayaga, Lucila
See also MTCW 2
Mistry, Rohinton 1952-   **CLC 71; DAC**
See also CA 141
Mitchell, Clyde
See Ellison, Harlan (Jay); Silverberg, Robert
Mitchell, James Leslie 1901-1935
See Gibbon, Lewis Grassic

See also CA 104; DLB 15
Mitchell, Joni 1943- **CLC 12**
See also CA 112
Mitchell, Joseph (Quincy) 1908-1996**CLC 98**
See also CA 77-80; 152; CANR 69; DLB 185;
DLBY 96
Mitchell, Margaret (Munnerlyn) 1900-1949
TCLC 11; DAM NOV, POP
See also AAYA 23; CA 109; 125; CANR 55;
CDALBS; DLB 9; MTCW 1, 2
Mitchell, Peggy
See Mitchell, Margaret (Munnerlyn)
Mitchell, S(ilas) Weir 1829-1914 **TCLC 36**
See also CA 165; DLB 202
Mitchell, W(illiam) O(rmond) 1914-1998**CLC
25; DAC; DAM MST**
See also CA 77-80; 165; CANR 15, 43; DLB
88
Mitchell, William 1879-1936 **TCLC 81**
Mitford, Mary Russell 1787-1855 **NCLC 4**
See also DLB 110, 116
Mitford, Nancy 1904-1973 **CLC 44**
See also CA 9-12R; DLB 191
Miyamoto, (Chujo) Yuriko 1899-1951 **TCLC
37**
See also CA 170, 174; DLB 180
Miyazawa, Kenji 1896-1933 **TCLC 76**
See also CA 157
Mizoguchi, Kenji 1898-1956 **TCLC 72**
See also CA 167
Mo, Timothy (Peter) 1950(?)- **CLC 46**
See also CA 117; DLB 194; MTCW 1
Modarressi, Taghi (M.) 1931- **CLC 44**
See also CA 121; 134; INT 134
Modiano, Patrick (Jean) 1945- **CLC 18**
See also CA 85-88; CANR 17, 40; DLB 83
Moerck, Paal
See Roelvaag, O(le) E(dvart)
Mofolo, Thomas (Mokopu) 1875(?)-1948
TCLC 22; BLC 3; DAM MULT
See also CA 121; 153; MTCW 2
Mohr, Nicholasa 1938-**CLC 12; DAM MULT;
HLC 2**
See also AAYA 8; CA 49-52; CANR 1, 32, 64;
CLR 22; DLB 145; HW 1, 2; JRDA; SAAS
8; SATA 8, 97
Mojtabai, A(nn) G(race) 1938- **CLC 5, 9, 15,
29**
See also CA 85-88
Moliere 1622-1673**LC 10, 28; DA; DAB; DAC;
DAM DRAM, MST; WLC**
Molin, Charles
See Mayne, William (James Carter)
Molnar, Ferenc 1878-1952 **TCLC 20;DAM
DRAM**
See also CA 109; 153
Momaday, N(avarre) Scott 1934- **CLC 2, 19,
85, 95; DA; DAB; DAC; DAM MST,
MULT, NOV, POP; PC 25; WLCS**
See also AAYA 11; CA 25-28R; CANR 14, 34,
68; CDALBS; DLB 143, 175; INT CANR-
14; MTCW 1, 2; NNAL; SATA 48; SATA-
Brief 30
Monette, Paul 1945-1995 **CLC 82**
See also CA 139; 147
Monroe, Harriet 1860-1936 **TCLC 12**
See also CA 109; DLB 54, 91
Monroe, Lyle
See Heinlein, Robert A(nson)
Montagu, Elizabeth 1720-1800 **NCLC 7**
Montagu, Mary (Pierrepont) Wortley 1689-
1762 **LC 9; PC 16**
See also DLB 95, 101

Montagu, W. H.
See Coleridge, Samuel Taylor
Montague, John (Patrick) 1929- **CLC 13, 46**
See also CA 9-12R; CANR 9, 69; DLB 40;
MTCW 1
Montaigne, Michel (Eyquem) de 1533-1592
LC 8; DA; DAB; DAC; DAM MST; WLC
Montale, Eugenio 1896-1981**CLC 7, 9, 18; PC
13**
See also CA 17-20R; 104; CANR 30; DLB 114;
MTCW 1
Montesquieu, Charles-Louis de Secondat 1689-
1755 **LC 7**
Montgomery, (Robert) Bruce 1921-1978
See Crispin, Edmund
See also CA 104
Montgomery, L(ucy) M(aud) 1874-1942
TCLC 51; DAC; DAM MST
See also AAYA 12; CA 108; 137; CLR 8; DLB
92; DLBD 14; JRDA; MAICYA; MTCW 2;
SATA 100; YABC 1
Montgomery, Marion H., Jr. 1925- **CLC 7**
See also AITN 1; CA 1-4R; CANR 3, 48; DLB
6
Montgomery, Max
See Davenport, Guy (Mattison, Jr.)
Montherlant, Henry (Milon) de 1896-1972
CLC 8, 19; DAM DRAM
See also CA 85-88; 37-40R; DLB 72; MTCW
1
Monty Python
See Chapman, Graham; Cleese, John
(Marwood); Gilliam, Terry (Vance); Idle,
Eric; Jones, Terence Graham Parry; Palin,
Michael (Edward)
See also AAYA 7
Moodie, Susanna (Strickland) 1803-1885
NCLC 14
See also DLB 99
Mooney, Edward 1951-
See Mooney, Ted
See also CA 130
Mooney, Ted **CLC 25**
See also Mooney, Edward
Moorcock, Michael (John) 1939-**CLC 5, 27, 58**
See Bradbury, Edward P.
See also AAYA 26; CA 45-48; CAAS 5; CANR
2, 17, 38, 64; DLB 14; MTCW 1, 2; SATA
93
Moore, Brian 1921-1999**CLC 1, 3, 5, 7, 8, 19,
32, 90; DAB; DAC; DAM MST**
See also CA 1-4R; 174; CANR 1, 25, 42, 63;
MTCW 1, 2
Moore, Edward
See Muir, Edwin
Moore, G. E. 1873-1958 **TCLC 89**
Moore, George Augustus 1852-1933**TCLC 7;
SSC 19**
See also CA 104; 177; DLB 10, 18, 57, 135
Moore, Lorrie **CLC 39, 45, 68**
See also Moore, Marie Lorena
Moore, Marianne (Craig) 1887-1972**CLC 1, 2,
4, 8, 10, 13, 19, 47; DA; DAB; DAC; DAM
MST, POET; PC 4; WLCS**
See also CA 1-4R; 33-36R; CANR 3, 61;
CDALB 1929-1941; DLB 45; DLBD 7;
MTCW 1, 2; SATA 20
Moore, Marie Lorena 1957-
See Moore, Lorrie
See also CA 116; CANR 39
Moore, Thomas 1779-1852 **NCLC 6**
See also DLB 96, 144
Mora, Pat(ricia) 1942-

See also CA 129; CANR 57, 81; CLR 58; DAM
MULT; DLB 209; HLC 2; HW 1, 2; SATA
92
Morand, Paul 1888-1976 **CLC 41;SSC 22**
See also CA 69-72; DLB 65
Morante, Elsa 1918-1985 **CLC 8, 47**
See also CA 85-88; 117; CANR 35; DLB 177;
MTCW 1, 2
Moravia, Alberto 1907-1990**CLC 2, 7, 11, 27,
46; SSC 26**
See also Pincherle, Alberto
See also DLB 177; MTCW 2
More, Hannah 1745-1833 **NCLC 27**
See also DLB 107, 109, 116, 158
More, Henry 1614-1687 **LC 9**
See also DLB 126
More, Sir Thomas 1478-1535 **LC 10, 32**
Moreas, Jean **TCLC 18**
See also Papadiamantopoulos, Johannes
Morgan, Berry 1919- **CLC 6**
See also CA 49-52; DLB 6
Morgan, Claire
See Highsmith, (Mary) Patricia
Morgan, Edwin (George) 1920- **CLC 31**
See also CA 5-8R; CANR 3, 43; DLB 27
Morgan, (George) Frederick 1922- **CLC 23**
See also CA 17-20R; CANR 21
Morgan, Harriet
See Mencken, H(enry) L(ouis)
Morgan, Jane
See Cooper, James Fenimore
Morgan, Janet 1945- **CLC 39**
See also CA 65-68
Morgan, Lady 1776(?)-1859 **NCLC 29**
See also DLB 116, 158
Morgan, Robin (Evonne) 1941- **CLC 2**
See also CA 69-72; CANR 29, 68; MTCW 1;
SATA 80
Morgan, Scott
See Kuttner, Henry
Morgan, Seth 1949(?)-1990 **CLC 65**
See also CA 132
Morgenstern, Christian 1871-1914 **TCLC 8**
See also CA 105
Morgenstern, S.
See Goldman, William (W.)
Moricz, Zsigmond 1879-1942 **TCLC 33**
See also CA 165
Morike, Eduard (Friedrich) 1804-1875**NCLC
10**
See also DLB 133
Moritz, Karl Philipp 1756-1793 **LC 2**
See also DLB 94
Morland, Peter Henry
See Faust, Frederick (Schiller)
Morley, Christopher (Darlington) 1890-1957
TCLC 87
See also CA 112; DLB 9
Morren, Theophil
See Hofmannsthal, Hugo von
Morris, Bill 1952- **CLC 76**
Morris, Julian
See West, Morris L(anglo)
Morris, Steveland Judkins 1950(?)-
See Wonder, Stevie
See also CA 111
Morris, William 1834-1896 **NCLC 4**
See also CDBLB 1832-1890; DLB 18, 35, 57,
156, 178, 184
Morris, Wright 1910-1998**CLC 1, 3, 7, 18, 37**
See also CA 9-12R; 167; CANR 21, 81; DLB
2, 206; DLBY 81; MTCW 1, 2
Morrison, Arthur 1863-1945 **TCLC 72**

See also CA 120; 157; DLB 70, 135, 197
Morrison, Chloe Anthony Wofford
See Morrison, Toni
Morrison, James Douglas 1943-1971
See Morrison, Jim
See also CA 73-76; CANR 40
Morrison, Jim   **CLC 17**
See also Morrison, James Douglas
Morrison, Toni 1931-CLC 4, 10, 22, 55, 81, 87;
    BLC 3; DA; DAB; DAC; DAM MST,
    MULT, NOV, POP
See also AAYA 1, 22; BW 2, 3; CA 29-32R;
    CANR 27, 42, 67; CDALB 1968-1988; DLB
    6, 33, 143; DLBY 81; MTCW 1, 2; SATA 57
Morrison, Van 1945-   **CLC 21**
See also CA 116; 168
Morrissy, Mary 1958-   **CLC 99**
Mortimer, John (Clifford) 1923- CLC 28, 43;
    DAM DRAM, POP
See also CA 13-16R; CANR 21, 69; CDBLB
    1960 to Present; DLB 13; INT CANR-21;
    MTCW 1, 2
Mortimer, Penelope (Ruth) 1918-   **CLC 5**
See also CA 57-60; CANR 45
Morton, Anthony
See Creasey, John
Mosca, Gaetano 1858-1941   **TCLC 75**
Mosher, Howard Frank 1943-   **CLC 62**
See also CA 139; CANR 65
Mosley, Nicholas 1923-   **CLC 43, 70**
See also CA 69-72; CANR 41, 60; DLB 14, 207
Mosley, Walter 1952- CLC 97; BLCS; DAM
    MULT, POP
See also AAYA 17; BW 2; CA 142; CANR 57;
    MTCW 2
Moss, Howard 1922-1987 CLC 7, 14, 45, 50;
    DAM POET
See also CA 1-4R; 123; CANR 1, 44; DLB 5
Mossgiel, Rab
See Burns, Robert
Motion, Andrew (Peter) 1952-   **CLC 47**
See also CA 146; DLB 40
Motley, Willard (Francis) 1909-1965 CLC 18
See also BW 1; CA 117; 106; DLB 76, 143
Motoori, Norinaga 1730-1801   **NCLC 45**
Mott, Michael (Charles Alston) 1930-CLC 15,
    34
See also CA 5-8R; CAAS 7; CANR 7, 29
Mountain Wolf Woman 1884-1960   **CLC 92**
See also CA 144; NNAL
Moure, Erin 1955-   **CLC 88**
See also CA 113; DLB 60
Mowat, Farley (McGill) 1921-CLC 26; DAC;
    DAM MST
See also AAYA 1; CA 1-4R; CANR 4, 24, 42,
    68; CLR 20; DLB 68; INT CANR-24; JRDA;
    MAICYA; MTCW 1, 2; SATA 3, 55
Mowatt, Anna Cora 1819-1870   **NCLC 74**
Moyers, Bill 1934-   **CLC 74**
See also AITN 2; CA 61-64; CANR 31, 52
Mphahlele, Es'kia
See Mphahlele, Ezekiel
See also DLB 125
Mphahlele, Ezekiel 1919-   CLC 25; BLC 3;
    DAM MULT
See Mphahlele, Es'kia
See also BW 2, 3; CA 81-84; CANR 26, 76;
    MTCW 2
Mqhayi, S(amuel) E(dward) K(rune Loliwe)
    1875-1945TCLC 25; BLC 3;DAM MULT
See also CA 153
Mrozek, Slawomir 1930-   **CLC 3, 13**
See also CA 13-16R; CAAS 10; CANR 29;

MTCW 1
Mrs. Belloc-Lowndes
See Lowndes, Marie Adelaide (Belloc)
Mtwa, Percy (?)-   **CLC 47**
Mueller, Lisel 1924-   **CLC 13, 51**
See also CA 93-96; DLB 105
Muir, Edwin 1887-1959   **TCLC 2, 87**
See also CA 104; DLB 20, 100, 191
Muir, John 1838-1914   **TCLC 28**
See also CA 165; DLB 186
Mujica Lainez, Manuel 1910-1984   **CLC 31**
See Lainez, Manuel Mujica
See also CA 81-84; 112; CANR 32; HW 1
Mukherjee, Bharati 1940-CLC 53, 115; DAM
    NOV
See also BEST 89:2; CA 107; CANR 45, 72;
    DLB 60; MTCW 1, 2
Muldoon, Paul 1951-CLC 32, 72;DAM POET
See also CA 113; 129; CANR 52; DLB 40; INT
    129
Mulisch, Harry 1927-   **CLC 42**
See also CA 9-12R; CANR 6, 26, 56
Mull, Martin 1943-   **CLC 17**
See also CA 105
Muller, Wilhelm   **NCLC 73**
Mulock, Dinah Maria
See Craik, Dinah Maria (Mulock)
Munford, Robert 1737(?)-1783   **LC 5**
See also DLB 31
Mungo, Raymond 1946-   **CLC 72**
See also CA 49-52; CANR 2
Munro, Alice 1931-   CLC 6, 10, 19, 50, 95;
    DAC; DAM MST, NOV; SSC 3; WLCS
See also AITN 2; CA 33-36R; CANR 33, 53,
    75; DLB 53; MTCW 1, 2; SATA 29
Munro, H(ector) H(ugh) 1870-1916
See Saki
See also CA 104; 130; CDBLB 1890-1914; DA;
    DAB; DAC; DAM MST, NOV; DLB 34, 162;
    MTCW 1, 2; WLC
Murdoch, (Jean) Iris 1919-CLC 1, 2, 3, 4, 6, 8,
    11, 15, 22, 31, 51; DAB; DAC; DAM MST,
    NOV
See also CA 13-16R; CANR 8, 43, 68; CDBLB
    1960 to Present; DLB 14, 194; INT CANR-
    8; MTCW 1, 2
Murfree, Mary Noailles 1850-1922   **SSC 22**
See also CA 122; 176; DLB 12, 74
Murnau, Friedrich Wilhelm
See Plumpe, Friedrich Wilhelm
Murphy, Richard 1927-   **CLC 41**
See also CA 29-32R; DLB 40
Murphy, Sylvia 1937-   **CLC 34**
See also CA 121
Murphy, Thomas (Bernard) 1935-   **CLC 51**
See also CA 101
Murray, Albert L. 1916-   **CLC 73**
See also BW 2; CA 49-52; CANR 26, 52, 78;
    DLB 38
Murray, Judith Sargent 1751-1820 NCLC 63
See also DLB 37, 200
Murray, Les(lie) A(llan) 1938-CLC 40; DAM
    POET
See also CA 21-24R; CANR 11, 27, 56
Murry, J. Middleton
See Murry, John Middleton
Murry, John Middleton 1889-1957 TCLC 16
See also CA 118; DLB 149
Musgrave, Susan 1951-   **CLC 13, 54**
See also CA 69-72; CANR 45
Musil, Robert (Edler von) 1880-1942 T C L C
    12, 68; SSC 18
See also CA 109; CANR 55; DLB 81, 124;

MTCW 2
Muske, Carol 1945-   **CLC 90**
See also Muske-Dukes, Carol (Anne)
Muske-Dukes, Carol (Anne) 1945-
See Muske, Carol
See also CA 65-68; CANR 32, 70
Musset, (Louis Charles) Alfred de 1810-1857
    NCLC 7
See also DLB 192
Mussolini, Benito (Amilcare Andrea) 1883-1945
    TCLC 96
See also CA 116
My Brother's Brother
See Chekhov, Anton (Pavlovich)
Myers, L(eopold) H(amilton) 1881-1944
    TCLC 59
See also CA 157; DLB 15
Myers, Walter Dean 1937-   CLC 35; BLC 3;
    DAM MULT, NOV
See also AAYA 4, 23; BW 2; CA 33-36R;
    CANR 20, 42, 67; CLR 4, 16, 35; DLB 33;
    INT CANR-20; JRDA; MAICYA; MTCW 2;
    SAAS 2; SATA 41, 71, 109; SATA-Brief 27
Myers, Walter M.
See Myers, Walter Dean
Myles, Symon
See Follett, Ken(neth Martin)
Nabokov, Vladimir (Vladimirovich) 1899-1977
    CLC 1, 2, 3, 6, 8, 11, 15, 23, 44, 46, 64;
    DA; DAB; DAC; DAM MST, NOV; SSC
    11; WLC
See also CA 5-8R; 69-72; CANR 20; CDALB
    1941-1968; DLB 2; DLBD 3; DLBY 80, 91;
    MTCW 1, 2
Nagai Kafu 1879-1959   **TCLC 51**
See also Nagai Sokichi
See also DLB 180
Nagai Sokichi 1879-1959
See Nagai Kafu
See also CA 117
Nagy, Laszlo 1925-1978   **CLC 7**
See also CA 129; 112
Naidu, Sarojini 1879-1943   **TCLC 80**
Naipaul, Shiva(dhar Srinivasa) 1945-1985
    CLC 32, 39; DAM NOV
See also CA 110; 112; 116; CANR 33; DLB
    157; DLBY 85; MTCW 1, 2
Naipaul, V(idiadhar) S(urajprasad) 1932-
    CLC 4, 7, 9, 13, 18, 37, 105; DAB; DAC;
    DAM MST, NOV
See also CA 1-4R; CANR 1, 33, 51; CDBLB
    1960 to Present; DLB 125, 204, 206; DLBY
    85; MTCW 1, 2
Nakos, Lilika 1899(?)-   **CLC 29**
Narayan, R(asipuram) K(rishnaswami) 1906-
    CLC 7, 28, 47, 121; DAM NOV; SSC 25
See also CA 81-84; CANR 33, 61; MTCW 1,
    2; SATA 62
Nash, (Frediric) Ogden 1902-1971   CLC 23;
    DAM POET; PC 21
See also CA 13-14; 29-32R; CANR 34, 61; CAP
    1; DLB 11; MAICYA; MTCW 1,2; SATA 2,
    46
Nashe, Thomas 1567-1601(?)   **LC 41**
See also DLB 167
Nashe, Thomas 1567-1601   **LC 41**
Nathan, Daniel
See Dannay, Frederic
Nathan, George Jean 1882-1958   **TCLC 18**
See also Hatteras, Owen
See also CA 114; 169; DLB 137
Natsume, Kinnosuke 1867-1916
See Natsume, Soseki

See also CA 104

Natsume, Soseki 1867-1916 **TCLC 2, 10**
See also Natsume, Kinnosuke
See also DLB 180

Natti, (Mary) Lee 1919-
See Kingman, Lee
See also CA 5-8R; CANR 2

Naylor, Gloria 1950-**CLC 28, 52; BLC 3; DA; DAC; DAM MST, MULT, NOV, POP; WLCS**
See also AAYA 6; BW 2, 3; CA 107; CANR 27, 51, 74; DLB 173; MTCW 1, 2

Neihardt, John Gneisenau 1881-1973**CLC 32**
See also CA 13-14; CANR 65; CAP 1; DLB 9, 54

Nekrasov, Nikolai Alekseevich 1821-1878
NCLC 11

Nelligan, Emile 1879-1941 **TCLC 14**
See also CA 114; DLB 92

Nelson, Willie 1933- **CLC 17**
See also CA 107

Nemerov, Howard (Stanley) 1920-1991**CLC 2, 6, 9, 36; DAM POET; PC 24**
See also CA 1-4R; 134; CABS 2; CANR 1, 27, 53; DLB 5, 6; DLBY 83; INT CANR-27; MTCW 1, 2

Neruda, Pablo 1904-1973**CLC 1, 2, 5, 7, 9, 28, 62; DA; DAB; DAC; DAM MST, MULT, POET; HLC 2; PC 4; WLC**
See also CA 19-20; 45-48; CAP 2; HW 1; MTCW 1, 2

Nerval, Gerard de 1808-1855**NCLC 1, 67; PC 13; SSC 18**

Nervo, (Jose) Amado (Ruiz de) 1870-1919
TCLC 11; HLCS 2
See also CA 109; 131; HW 1

Nessi, Pio Baroja y
See Baroja (y Nessi), Pio

Nestroy, Johann 1801-1862 **NCLC 42**
See also DLB 133

Netterville, Luke
See O'Grady, Standish (James)

Neufeld, John (Arthur) 1938- **CLC 17**
See also AAYA 11; CA 25-28R; CANR 11, 37, 56; CLR 52; MAICYA; SAAS 3; SATA 6, 81

Neville, Emily Cheney 1919- **CLC 12**
See also CA 5-8R; CANR 3, 37; JRDA; MAICYA; SAAS 2; SATA 1

Newbound, Bernard Slade 1930-
See Slade, Bernard
See also CA 81-84; CANR 49; DAM DRAM

Newby, P(ercy) H(oward) 1918-1997 **CLC 2, 13; DAM NOV**
See also CA 5-8R; 161; CANR 32, 67; DLB 15; MTCW 1

Newlove, Donald 1928- **CLC 6**
See also CA 29-32R; CANR 25

Newlove, John (Herbert) 1938- **CLC 14**
See also CA 21-24R; CANR 9, 25

Newman, Charles 1938- **CLC 2, 8**
See also CA 21-24R

Newman, Edwin (Harold) 1919- **CLC 14**
See also AITN 1; CA 69-72; CANR 5

Newman, John Henry 1801-1890 **NCLC 38**
See also DLB 18, 32, 55

Newton, (Sir)Isaac 1642-1727 **LC 35, 52**

Newton, Suzanne 1936- **CLC 35**
See also CA 41-44R; CANR 14; JRDA; SATA 5, 77

Nexo, Martin Andersen 1869-1954 **TCLC 43**

Nezval, Vitezslav 1900-1958 **TCLC 44**
See also CA 123

Ng, Fae Myenne 1957(?)- **CLC 81**
See also CA 146

Ngema, Mbongeni 1955- **CLC 57**
See also BW 2; CA 143

Ngugi, James T(hiong'o) **CLC 3, 7, 13**
See also Ngugi wa Thiong'o

Ngugi wa Thiong'o 1938- **CLC 36; BLC 3; DAM MULT, NOV**
See also Ngugi, James T(hiong'o)
See also BW 2; CA 81-84; CANR 27, 58; DLB 125; MTCW 1, 2

Nichol, B(arrie) P(hillip) 1944-1988 **CLC 18**
See also CA 53-56; DLB 53; SATA 66

Nichols, John (Treadwell) 1940- **CLC 38**
See also CA 9-12R; CAAS 2; CANR 6, 70; DLBY 82

Nichols, Leigh
See Koontz, Dean R(ay)

Nichols, Peter (Richard) 1927- **CLC 5, 36, 65**
See also CA 104; CANR 33; DLB 13; MTCW 1

Nicolas, F. R. E.
See Freeling, Nicolas

Niedecker, Lorine 1903-1970 **CLC 10, 42; DAM POET**
See also CA 25-28; CAP 2; DLB 48

Nietzsche, Friedrich (Wilhelm) 1844-1900
TCLC 10, 18, 55
See also CA 107; 121; DLB 129

Nievo, Ippolito 1831-1861 **NCLC 22**

Nightingale, Anne Redmon 1943-
See Redmon, Anne
See also CA 103

Nightingale, Florence 1820-1910 **TCLC 85**
See also DLB 166

Nik. T. O.
See Annensky, Innokenty (Fyodorovich)

Nin, Anais 1903-1977 **CLC 1, 4, 8, 11, 14, 60; DAM NOV, POP; SSC 10**
See also AITN 2; CA 13-16R; 69-72; CANR 22, 53; DLB 2, 4, 152; MTCW 1, 2

Nishida, Kitaro 1870-1945 **TCLC 83**

Nishiwaki, Junzaburo 1894-1982 **PC 15**
See also CA 107

Nissenson, Hugh 1933- **CLC 4, 9**
See also CA 17-20R; CANR 27; DLB 28

Niven, Larry **CLC 8**
See also Niven, Laurence Van Cott
See also AAYA 27; DLB 8

Niven, Laurence Van Cott 1938-
See Niven, Larry
See also CA 21-24R; CAAS 12; CANR 14, 44, 66; DAM POP; MTCW 1, 2; SATA 95

Nixon, Agnes Eckhardt 1927- **CLC 21**
See also CA 110

Nizan, Paul 1905-1940 **TCLC 40**
See also CA 161; DLB 72

Nkosi, Lewis 1936- **CLC 45; BLC 3; DAM MULT**
See also BW 1, 3; CA 65-68; CANR 27, 81; DLB 157

Nodier, (Jean) Charles (Emmanuel) 1780-1844
NCLC 19
See also DLB 119

Noguchi, Yone 1875-1947 **TCLC 80**

Nolan, Christopher 1965- **CLC 58**
See also CA 111

Noon, Jeff 1957- **CLC 91**
See also CA 148

Norden, Charles
See Durrell, Lawrence (George)

Nordhoff, Charles (Bernard) 1887-1947
TCLC 23

See also CA 108; DLB 9; SATA 23

Norfolk, Lawrence 1963- **CLC 76**
See also CA 144

Norman, Marsha 1947-**CLC 28; DAM DRAM; DC 8**
See also CA 105; CABS 3; CANR 41; DLBY 84

Normyx
See Douglas, (George) Norman

Norris, Frank 1870-1902 **SSC 28**
See also Norris, (Benjamin) Frank(lin, Jr.)
See also CDALB 1865-1917; DLB 12, 71, 186

Norris, (Benjamin) Frank(lin, Jr.) 1870-1902
TCLC 24
See also Norris, Frank
See also CA 110; 160

Norris, Leslie 1921- **CLC 14**
See also CA 11-12; CANR 14; CAP 1; DLB 27

North, Andrew
See Norton, Andre

North, Anthony
See Koontz, Dean R(ay)

North, Captain George
See Stevenson, Robert Louis (Balfour)

North, Milou
See Erdrich, Louise

Northrup, B. A.
See Hubbard, L(afayette) Ron(ald)

North Staffs
See Hulme, T(homas) E(rnest)

Norton, Alice Mary
See Norton, Andre
See also MAICYA; SATA 1, 43

Norton, Andre 1912- **CLC 12**
See also Norton, Alice Mary
See also AAYA 14; CA 1-4R; CANR 68; CLR 50; DLB 8, 52; JRDA; MTCW 1; SATA 91

Norton, Caroline 1808-1877 **NCLC 47**
See also DLB 21, 159, 199

Norway, Nevil Shute 1899-1960
See Shute, Nevil
See also CA 102; 93-96; MTCW 2

Norwid, Cyprian Kamil 1821-1883 **NCLC 17**

Nosille, Nabrah
See Ellison, Harlan (Jay)

Nossack, Hans Erich 1901-1978 **CLC 6**
See also CA 93-96; 85-88; DLB 69

Nostradamus 1503-1566 **LC 27**

Nosu, Chuji
See Ozu, Yasujiro

Notenburg, Eleanora (Genrikhovna) von
See Guro, Elena

Nova, Craig 1945- **CLC 7, 31**
See also CA 45-48; CANR 2, 53

Novak, Joseph
See Kosinski, Jerzy (Nikodem)

Novalis 1772-1801 **NCLC 13**
See also DLB 90

Novis, Emile
See Weil, Simone (Adolphine)

Nowlan, Alden (Albert) 1933-1983 **CLC 15; DAC; DAM MST**
See also CA 9-12R; CANR 5; DLB 53

Noyes, Alfred 1880-1958 **TCLC 7;PC 27**
See also CA 104; DLB 20

Nunn, Kem **CLC 34**
See also CA 159

Nye, Robert 1939- **CLC 13, 42;DAM NOV**
See also CA 33-36R; CANR 29, 67; DLB 14; MTCW 1; SATA 6

Nyro, Laura 1947- **CLC 17**

Oates, Joyce Carol 1938-**CLC 1, 2, 3, 6, 9, 11, 15, 19, 33, 52, 108; DA; DAB; DAC; DAM**

MST, NOV, POP; SSC 6;WLC
See also AAYA 15; AITN 1; BEST 89:2; CA 5-8R; CANR 25, 45, 74; CDALB 1968-1988; DLB 2, 5, 130; DLBY 81; INT CANR-25; MTCW 1, 2

O'Brien, Darcy 1939-1998   CLC 11
See also CA 21-24R; 167; CANR 8, 59

O'Brien, E. G.
See Clarke, Arthur C(harles)

O'Brien, Edna 1936- CLC 3, 5, 8, 13, 36, 65, 116; DAM NOV; SSC 10
See also CA 1-4R; CANR 6, 41, 65; CDBLB 1960 to Present; DLB 14; MTCW 1, 2

O'Brien, Fitz-James 1828-1862   NCLC 21
See also DLB 74

O'Brien, Flann   CLC 1, 4, 5, 7, 10, 47
See also O Nuallain, Brian

O'Brien, Richard 1942-   CLC 17
See also CA 124

O'Brien, (William) Tim(othy) 1946- CLC 7, 19, 40, 103; DAM POP
See also AAYA 16; CA 85-88; CANR 40, 58; CDALBS; DLB 152; DLBD 9; DLBY 80; MTCW 2

Obstfelder, Sigbjoern 1866-1900   TCLC 23
See also CA 123

O'Casey, Sean 1880-1964 CLC 1, 5, 9, 11, 15, 88; DAB; DAC; DAM DRAM, MST; WLCS
See also CA 89-92; CANR 62;CDBLB 1914-1945; DLB 10; MTCW 1, 2

O'Cathasaigh, Sean
See O'Casey, Sean

Ochs, Phil 1940-1976   CLC 17
See also CA 65-68

O'Connor, Edwin (Greene) 1918-1968CLC 14
See also CA 93-96; 25-28R

O'Connor, (Mary) Flannery 1925-1964 C L C 1, 2, 3, 6, 10, 13, 15, 21, 66, 104; DA; DAB; DAC; DAM MST, NOV; SSC 1, 23;WLC
See also AAYA 7; CA 1-4R; CANR 3, 41; CDALB 1941-1968; DLB 2, 152; DLBD 12; DLBY 80; MTCW 1, 2

O'Connor, Frank   CLC 23; SSC 5
See also O'Donovan, Michael John
See also DLB 162

O'Dell, Scott 1898-1989   CLC 30
See also AAYA 3; CA 61-64; 129; CANR 12, 30; CLR 1, 16; DLB 52; JRDA; MAICYA; SATA 12, 60

Odets, Clifford 1906-1963CLC 2, 28, 98; DAM DRAM; DC 6
See also CA 85-88; CANR 62; DLB 7, 26; MTCW 1, 2

O'Doherty, Brian 1934-   CLC 76
See also CA 105

O'Donnell, K. M.
See Malzberg, Barry N(athaniel)

O'Donnell, Lawrence
See Kuttner, Henry

O'Donovan, Michael John 1903-1966CLC 14
See also O'Connor, Frank
See also CA 93-96

Oe, Kenzaburo 1935- CLC 10, 36, 86; DAM NOV; SSC 20
See also CA 97-100; CANR 36, 50, 74; DLB 182; DLBY 94; MTCW 1, 2

O'Faolain, Julia 1932-   CLC 6, 19, 47, 108
See also CA 81-84; CAAS 2; CANR 12, 61; DLB 14; MTCW 1

O'Faolain, Sean 1900-1991 CLC 1, 7, 14, 32, 70; SSC 13
See also CA 61-64; 134; CANR 12, 66; DLB

15, 162; MTCW 1, 2

O'Flaherty, Liam 1896-1984CLC 5, 34; SSC 6
See also CA 101; 113; CANR 35; DLB 36, 162; DLBY 84; MTCW 1, 2

Ogilvy, Gavin
See Barrie, J(ames) M(atthew)

O'Grady, Standish (James) 1846-1928 T C L C 5
See also CA 104; 157

O'Grady, Timothy 1951-   CLC 59
See also CA 138

O'Hara, Frank 1926-1966 CLC 2, 5, 13, 78; DAM POET
See also CA 9-12R; 25-28R; CANR 33; DLB 5, 16, 193; MTCW 1, 2

O'Hara, John (Henry) 1905-1970CLC 1, 2, 3, 6, 11, 42; DAM NOV; SSC 15
See also CA 5-8R; 25-28R; CANR 31, 60; CDALB 1929-1941; DLB 9, 86; DLBD 2; MTCW 1, 2

O Hehir, Diana 1922-   CLC 41
See also CA 93-96

Ohiyesa 1858-1939
See Eastman, Charles A(lexander)
See also CA 179

Okigbo, Christopher (Ifenayichukwu) 1932-1967 CLC 25, 84; BLC 3; DAM MULT, POET; PC 7
See also BW 1, 3; CA 77-80; CANR 74; DLB 125; MTCW 1, 2

Okri, Ben 1959-   CLC 87
See also BW 2, 3; CA 130; 138; CANR 65; DLB 157; INT 138; MTCW 2

Olds, Sharon 1942- CLC 32, 39, 85; DAM POET; PC 22
See also CA 101; CANR 18, 41, 66; DLB 120; MTCW 2

Oldstyle, Jonathan
See Irving, Washington

Olesha, Yuri (Karlovich) 1899-1960   CLC 8
See also CA 85-88

Oliphant, Laurence 1829(?)-1888   NCLC 47
See also DLB 18, 166

Oliphant, Margaret (Oliphant Wilson) 1828-1897   NCLC 11, 61; SSC 25
See also DLB 18, 159, 190

Oliver, Mary 1935-   CLC 19, 34, 98
See also CA 21-24R; CANR 9, 43; DLB 5, 193

Olivier, Laurence (Kerr) 1907-1989 CLC 20
See also CA 111; 150; 129

Olsen, Tillie 1912-CLC 4, 13, 114; DA; DAB; DAC; DAM MST; SSC 11
See also CA 1-4R; CANR 1, 43, 74; CDALBS; DLB 28, 206; DLBY 80; MTCW 1, 2

Olson, Charles (John) 1910-1970CLC 1, 2, 5, 6, 9, 11, 29; DAM POET; PC 19
See also CA 13-16; 25-28R; CABS 2; CANR 35, 61; CAP 1; DLB 5, 16, 193; MTCW 1, 2

Olson, Toby 1937-   CLC 28
See also CA 65-68; CANR 9, 31

Olyesha, Yuri
See Olesha, Yuri (Karlovich)

Ondaatje, (Philip) Michael 1943-CLC 14, 29, 51, 76; DAB; DAC; DAM MST
See also CA 77-80; CANR 42, 74; DLB 60; MTCW 2·

Oneal, Elizabeth 1934-
See Oneal, Zibby
See also CA 106; CANR 28; MAICYA; SATA 30, 82

Oneal, Zibby   CLC 30
See also Oneal, Elizabeth
See also AAYA 5; CLR 13; JRDA

O'Neill, Eugene (Gladstone) 1888-1953TCLC 1, 6, 27, 49; DA; DAB; DAC; DAM DRAM, MST; WLC
See also AITN 1; CA 110; 132; CDALB 1929-1941; DLB 7; MTCW 1, 2

Onetti, Juan Carlos 1909-1994   CLC 7, 10; DAM MULT, NOV; HLCS 2;SSC 23
See also CA 85-88; 145; CANR 32, 63; DLB 113; HW 1, 2; MTCW 1, 2

O Nuallain, Brian 1911-1966
See O'Brien, Flann
See also CA 21-22; 25-28R; CAP 2

Ophuls, Max 1902-1957   TCLC 79
See also CA 113

Opie, Amelia 1769-1853   NCLC 65
See also DLB 116, 159

Oppen, George 1908-1984   CLC 7, 13,34
See also CA 13-16R; 113; CANR 8, 82; DLB 5, 165

Oppenheim, E(dward) Phillips 1866-1946 TCLC 45
See also CA 111; DLB 70

Opuls, Max
See Ophuls, Max

Origen c. 185-c. 254   CMLC 19

Orlovitz, Gil 1918-1973   CLC 22
See also CA 77-80; 45-48; DLB 2, 5

Orris
See Ingelow, Jean

Ortega y Gasset, Jose 1883-1955   TCLC 9; DAM MULT; HLC 2
See also CA 106; 130; HW 1, 2; MTCW 1, 2

Ortese, Anna Maria 1914-   CLC 89
See also DLB 177

Ortiz, Simon J(oseph) 1941- CLC 45; DAM MULT, POET; PC 17
See also CA 134; CANR 69; DLB 120, 175; NNAL

Orton, Joe   CLC 4, 13, 43; DC 3
See also Orton, John Kingsley
See also CDBLB 1960 to Present; DLB 13; MTCW 2

Orton, John Kingsley 1933-1967
See Orton, Joe
See also CA 85-88; CANR 35, 66; DAM DRAM; MTCW 1, 2

Orwell, George TCLC 2, 6, 15, 31, 51; DAB; WLC
See also Blair, Eric (Arthur)
See also CDBLB 1945-1960; DLB 15, 98, 195

Osborne, David
See Silverberg, Robert

Osborne, George
See Silverberg, Robert

Osborne, John (James) 1929-1994CLC 1, 2, 5, 11, 45; DA; DAB; DAC; DAM DRAM, MST; WLC
See also CA 13-16R; 147; CANR 21, 56; CDBLB 1945-1960; DLB 13; MTCW 1, 2

Osborne, Lawrence 1958-   CLC 50

Osbourne, Lloyd 1868-1947   TCLC 93

Oshima, Nagisa 1932-   CLC 20
See also CA 116; 121; CANR 78

Oskison, John Milton 1874-1947 TCLC 35; DAM MULT
See also CA 144; DLB 175; NNAL

Ossian c. 3rd cent. -   CMLC 28
See also Macpherson, James

Ossoli, Sarah Margaret (Fuller marchesa d') 1810-1850
See Fuller, Margaret
See also SATA 25

Ostrovsky, Alexander 1823-1886NCLC 30, 57

Otero, Blas de 1916-1979   **CLC 11**
   See also CA 89-92; DLB 134
Otto, Rudolf 1869-1937   **TCLC 85**
Otto, Whitney 1955-   **CLC 70**
   See also CA 140
Ouida   **TCLC 43**
   See also De La Ramee, (Marie) Louise
   See also DLB 18, 156
Ousmane, Sembene 1923-   **CLC 66; BLC 3**
   See also BW 1, 3; CA 117; 125; CANR 81;
      MTCW 1
Ovid 43B.C.-17 **CMLC 7; DAM POET; PC 2**
   See also DLB 211
Owen, Hugh
   See Faust, Frederick (Schiller)
Owen, Wilfred (Edward Salter) 1893-1918
      TCLC 5, 27; DA; DAB; DAC; DAM MST,
      POET; PC 19; WLC
   See also CA 104; 141; CDBLB 1914-1945;
      DLB 20; MTCW 2
Owens, Rochelle 1936-   **CLC 8**
   See also CA 17-20R; CAAS 2; CANR 39
Oz, Amos 1939-**CLC 5, 8, 11, 27, 33, 54; DAM**
      NOV
   See also CA 53-56; CANR 27, 47, 65; MTCW
      1, 2
Ozick, Cynthia 1928- **CLC 3, 7, 28, 62; DAM**
      NOV, POP; SSC 15
   See also BEST 90:1; CA 17-20R; CANR 23,
      58; DLB 28, 152; DLBY 82; INT CANR-
      23; MTCW 1, 2
Ozu, Yasujiro 1903-1963   **CLC 16**
   See also CA 112
Pacheco, C.
   See Pessoa, Fernando (Antonio Nogueira)
Pacheco, Jose Emilio 1939-
   See also CA 111; 131; CANR 65; DAM MULT;
      HLC 2; HW 1, 2
Pa Chin   **CLC 18**
   See also Li Fei-kan
Pack, Robert 1929-   **CLC 13**
   See also CA 1-4R; CANR 3, 44, 82; DLB 5
Padgett, Lewis
   See Kuttner, Henry
Padilla (Lorenzo), Heberto 1932-   **CLC 38**
   See also AITN 1; CA 123; 131; HW 1
Page, Jimmy 1944-   **CLC 12**
Page, Louise 1955-   **CLC 40**
   See also CA 140; CANR 76
Page, P(atricia) K(athleen) 1916- **CLC 7, 18;**
      DAC; DAM MST; PC 12
   See also CA 53-56; CANR 4, 22, 65; DLB 68;
      MTCW 1
Page, Thomas Nelson 1853-1922   **SSC 23**
   See also CA 118; 177; DLB 12, 78; DLBD 13
Pagels, Elaine Hiesey 1943-   **CLC 104**
   See also CA 45-48; CANR 2, 24, 51
Paget, Violet 1856-1935
   See Lee, Vernon
   See also CA 104; 166
Paget-Lowe, Henry
   See Lovecraft, H(oward) P(hillips)
Paglia, Camille (Anna) 1947-   **CLC 68**
   See also CA 140; CANR 72; MTCW 2
Paige, Richard
   See Koontz, Dean R(ay)
Paine, Thomas 1737-1809   **NCLC 62**
   See also CDALB 1640-1865; DLB 31, 43, 73,
      158
Pakenham, Antonia
   See Fraser, (Lady) Antonia (Pakenham)
Palamas, Kostes 1859-1943   **TCLC 5**
   See also CA 105

Palazzeschi, Aldo 1885-1974   **CLC 11**
   See also CA 89-92; 53-56; DLB 114
Pales Matos, Luis 1898-1959
   See also HLCS 2; HW 1
Paley, Grace 1922- **CLC 4, 6, 37; DAM POP;**
      SSC 8
   See also CA 25-28R; CANR 13, 46, 74; DLB
      28; INT CANR-13; MTCW 1, 2
Palin, Michael (Edward) 1943-   **CLC 21**
   See also Monty Python
   See also CA 107; CANR 35; SATA 67
Palliser, Charles 1947-   **CLC 65**
   See also CA 136; CANR 76
Palma, Ricardo 1833-1919   **TCLC 29**
   See also CA 168
Pancake, Breece Dexter 1952-1979
   See Pancake, Breece D'J
   See also CA 123; 109
Pancake, Breece D'J   **CLC 29**
   See also Pancake, Breece Dexter
   See also DLB 130
Panko, Rudy
   See Gogol, Nikolai (Vasilyevich)
Papadiamantis, Alexandros 1851-1911**TCLC**
      29
   See also CA 168
Papadiamantopoulos, Johannes 1856-1910
   See Moreas, Jean
   See also CA 117
Papini, Giovanni 1881-1956   **TCLC 22**
   See also CA 121
Paracelsus 1493-1541   **LC 14**
   See also DLB 179
Parasol, Peter
   See Stevens, Wallace
Pardo Bazan, Emilia 1851-1921   **SSC 30**
Pareto, Vilfredo 1848-1923   **TCLC 69**
   See also CA 175
Parfenie, Maria
   See Codrescu, Andrei
Parini, Jay (Lee) 1948-   **CLC 54**
   See also CA 97-100; CAAS 16; CANR 32
Park, Jordan
   See Kornbluth, C(yril) M.; Pohl, Frederik
Park, Robert E(zra) 1864-1944   **TCLC 73**
   See also CA 122; 165
Parker, Bert
   See Ellison, Harlan (Jay)
Parker, Dorothy (Rothschild) 1893-1967**CLC**
      15, 68; DAM POET; SSC 2
   See also CA 19-20; 25-28R; CAP 2; DLB 11,
      45, 86; MTCW 1, 2
Parker, Robert B(rown) 1932-**CLC 27; DAM**
      NOV, POP
   See also AAYA 28; BEST 89:4; CA 49-52;
      CANR 1, 26, 52; INT CANR-26; MTCW 1
Parkin, Frank 1940-   **CLC 43**
   See also CA 147
Parkman, Francis, Jr. 1823-1893   **NCLC 12**
   See also DLB 1, 30, 186
Parks, Gordon (Alexander Buchanan) 1912-
      CLC 1, 16; BLC 3; DAM MULT
   See also AITN 2; BW 2, 3; CA 41-44R; CANR
      26, 66; DLB 33; MTCW 2; SATA 8, 108
Parmenides c. 515B.C.-c.450B.C.   **CMLC 22**
   See also DLB 176
Parnell, Thomas 1679-1718   **LC 3**
   See also DLB 94
Parra, Nicanor 1914-   **CLC 2, 102; DAM**
      MULT; HLC 2
   See also CA 85-88; CANR 32; HW 1; MTCW
      1
Parra Sanojo, Ana Teresa de la 1890-1936

   See also HLCS 2
Parrish, Mary Frances
   See Fisher, M(ary) F(rances) K(ennedy)
Parson
   See Coleridge, Samuel Taylor
Parson Lot
   See Kingsley, Charles
Partridge, Anthony
   See Oppenheim, E(dward) Phillips
Pascal, Blaise 1623-1662   **LC 35**
Pascoli, Giovanni 1855-1912   **TCLC 45**
   See also CA 170
Pasolini, Pier Paolo 1922-1975   **CLC 20, 37,**
      106; PC 17
   See also CA 93-96; 61-64; CANR 63; DLB 128,
      177; MTCW 1
Pasquini
   See Silone, Ignazio
Pastan, Linda (Olenik) 1932- **CLC 27; DAM**
      POET
   See also CA 61-64; CANR 18, 40, 61; DLB 5
Pasternak, Boris (Leonidovich) 1890-1960
      CLC 7, 10, 18, 63; DA; DAB; DAC; DAM
      MST, NOV, POET; PC 6; SSC 31;WLC
   See also CA 127; 116; MTCW 1, 2
Patchen, Kenneth 1911-1972   **CLC 1, 2, 18;**
      DAM POET
   See also CA 1-4R; 33-36R; CANR 3, 35; DLB
      16, 48; MTCW 1
Pater, Walter (Horatio) 1839-1894   **NCLC 7**
   See also CDBLB 1832-1890; DLB 57, 156
Paterson, A(ndrew) B(arton) 1864-1941
      TCLC 32
   See also CA 155; SATA 97
Paterson, Katherine (Womeldorf) 1932-**CLC**
      12, 30
   See also AAYA 1; CA 21-24R; CANR 28, 59;
      CLR 7, 50; DLB 52; JRDA; MAICYA;
      MTCW 1; SATA 13, 53, 92
Patmore, Coventry Kersey Dighton 1823-1896
      NCLC 9
   See also DLB 35, 98
Paton, Alan (Stewart) 1903-1988 **CLC 4, 10,**
      25, 55, 106; DA; DAB; DAC; DAM MST,
      NOV; WLC
   See also AAYA 26; CA 13-16; 125; CANR 22;
      CAP 1; DLBD 17; MTCW 1, 2; SATA 11;
      SATA-Obit 56
Paton Walsh, Gillian 1937-
   See Walsh, Jill Paton
   See also CANR 38; JRDA; MAICYA; SAAS 3;
      SATA 4, 72, 109
Patton, George S. 1885-1945   **TCLC 79**
Paulding, James Kirke 1778-1860   **NCLC 2**
   See also DLB 3, 59, 74
Paulin, Thomas Neilson 1949-
   See Paulin, Tom
   See also CA 123; 128
Paulin, Tom   **CLC 37**
   See also Paulin, Thomas Neilson
   See also DLB 40
Paustovsky, Konstantin (Georgievich) 1892-
      1968   **CLC 40**
   See also CA 93-96; 25-28R
Pavese, Cesare 1908-1950   **TCLC 3; PC 13;**
      SSC 19
   See also CA 104; 169; DLB 128, 177
Pavic, Milorad 1929-   **CLC 60**
   See also CA 136; DLB 181
Pavlov, Ivan Petrovich 1849-1936   **TCLC 91**
   See also CA 118
Payne, Alan
   See Jakes, John (William)

Paz, Gil
See Lugones, Leopoldo
Paz, Octavio 1914-1998CLC **3, 4, 6, 10, 19, 51,**
65, 119; DA; DAB; DAC; DAM MST,
MULT, POET; HLC 2; PC 1;WLC
See also CA 73-76; 165; CANR 32, 65; DLBY
90, 98; HW 1, 2; MTCW 1, 2
p'Bitek, Okot 1931-1982 **CLC 96; BLC 3;**
DAM MULT
See also BW 2, 3; CA 124; 107; CANR 82; DLB
125; MTCW 1, 2
Peacock, Molly 1947- **CLC 60**
See also CA 103; CAAS 21; CANR 52; DLB
120
Peacock, Thomas Love 1785-1866 **NCLC 22**
See also DLB 96, 116
Peake, Mervyn 1911-1968 **CLC 7, 54**
See also CA 5-8R; 25-28R; CANR 3; DLB 15,
160; MTCW 1; SATA 23
Pearce, Philippa **CLC 21**
See also Christie, (Ann) Philippa
See also CLR 9; DLB 161; MAICYA; SATA 1,
67
Pearl, Eric
See Elman, Richard (Martin)
Pearson, T(homas) R(eid) 1956- **CLC 39**
See also CA 120; 130; INT 130
Peck, Dale 1967- **CLC 81**
See also CA 146; CANR 72
Peck, John 1941- **CLC 3**
See also CA 49-52; CANR 3
Peck, Richard (Wayne) 1934- **CLC 21**
See also AAYA 1, 24; CA 85-88; CANR 19,
38; CLR 15; INT CANR-19; JRDA;
MAICYA; SAAS 2; SATA 18, 55, 97
Peck, Robert Newton 1928- **CLC 17; DA;**
DAC; DAM MST
See also AAYA 3; CA 81-84; CANR 31, 63;
CLR 45; JRDA; MAICYA; SAAS 1; SATA
21, 62; SATA-Essay 108
Peckinpah, (David) Sam(uel) 1925-1984 C L C
20
See also CA 109; 114; CANR 82
Pedersen, Knut 1859-1952
See Hamsun, Knut
See also CA 104; 119; CANR 63; MTCW 1, 2
Peeslake, Gaffer
See Durrell, Lawrence (George)
Peguy, Charles Pierre 1873-1914 **TCLC 10**
See also CA 107
Peirce, Charles Sanders 1839-1914 **TCLC 81**
Pellicer, Carlos 1900(?)-1977
See also CA 153; 69-72; HLCS 2; HW 1
Pena, Ramon del Valle y
See Valle-Inclan, Ramon (Maria) del
Pendennis, Arthur Esquir
See Thackeray, William Makepeace
Penn, William 1644-1718 **LC 25**
See also DLB 24
PEPECE
See Prado (Calvo), Pedro
Pepys, Samuel 1633-1703 **LC 11; DA; DAB;**
DAC; DAM MST; WLC
See also CDBLB 1660-1789; DLB 101
Percy, Walker 1916-1990CLC **2, 3, 6, 8, 14, 18,**
47, 65; DAM NOV, POP
See also CA 1-4R; 131; CANR 1, 23, 64; DLB
2; DLBY 80, 90; MTCW 1, 2
Percy, William Alexander 1885-1942TCLC **84**
See also CA 163; MTCW 2
Perec, Georges 1936-1982 **CLC 56, 116**
See also CA 141; DLB 83
Pereda (y Sanchez de Porrua), Jose Mariade

1833-1906 **TCLC 16**
See also CA 117
Pereda y Porrua, Jose Maria de
See Pereda (y Sanchez de Porrua), Jose Maria
de
Peregoy, George Weems
See Mencken, H(enry) L(ouis)
Perelman, S(idney) J(oseph) 1904-1979 C L C
3, 5, 9, 15, 23, 44, 49; DAM DRAM; SSC
32
See also AITN 1, 2; CA 73-76; 89-92; CANR
18; DLB 11, 44; MTCW 1, 2
Peret, Benjamin 1899-1959 **TCLC 20**
See also CA 117
Peretz, Isaac Loeb 1851(?)-1915 **TCLC 16;**
SSC 26
See also CA 109
Peretz, Yitzhkok Leibush
See Peretz, Isaac Loeb
Perez Galdos, Benito 1843-1920 **TCLC 27;**
HLCS 2
See also CA 125; 153; HW 1
Peri Rossi, Cristina 1941-
See also CA 131; CANR 59, 81; DLB 145;
HLCS 2; HW 1, 2
Perrault, Charles 1628-1703 **LC 3, 52**
See also MAICYA; SATA 25
Perry, Brighton
See Sherwood, Robert E(mmet)
Perse, St.-John
See Leger, (Marie-Rene Auguste) Alexis Saint-
Leger
Perutz, Leo(pold) 1882-1957 **TCLC 60**
See also CA 147; DLB 81
Peseenz, Tulio F.
See Lopez y Fuentes, Gregorio
Pesetsky, Bette 1932- **CLC 28**
See also CA 133; DLB 130
Peshkov, Alexei Maximovich 1868-1936
See Gorky, Maxim
See also CA 105; 141; DA; DAC; DAM DRAM,
MST, NOV; MTCW 2
Pessoa, Fernando (Antonio Nogueira) 1888-
1935TCLC **27; DAM MULT; HLC 2; PC**
20
See also CA 125
Peterkin, Julia Mood 1880-1961 **CLC 31**
See also CA 102; DLB 9
Peters, Joan K(aren) 1945- **CLC 39**
See also CA 158
Peters, Robert L(ouis) 1924- **CLC 7**
See also CA 13-16R; CAAS 8; DLB 105
Petofi, Sandor 1823-1849 **NCLC 21**
Petrakis, Harry Mark 1923- **CLC 3**
See also CA 9-12R; CANR 4, 30
Petrarch 1304-1374 CMLC **20; DAM POET;**
PC 8
Petronius c. 20-66 **CMLC 34**
See also DLB 211
Petrov, Evgeny **TCLC 21**
See also Kataev, Evgeny Petrovich
Petry, Ann (Lane) 1908-1997 **CLC 1, 7, 18**
See also BW 1, 3; CA 5-8R; 157; CAAS 6;
CANR 4, 46; CLR 12; DLB 76; JRDA;
MAICYA; MTCW 1; SATA 5; SATA-Obit 94
Petursson, Halligrimur 1614-1674 **LC 8**
Peychinovich
See Vazov, Ivan (Minchov)
Phaedrus c. 18B.C.-c. 50 **CMLC 25**
See also DLB 211
Philips, Katherine 1632-1664 **LC 30**
See also DLB 131
Philipson, Morris H. 1926- **CLC 53**

See also CA 1-4R; CANR 4
Phillips, Caryl 1958- **CLC 96; BLCS; DAM**
MULT
See also BW 2; CA 141; CANR 63; DLB 157;
MTCW 2
Phillips, David Graham 1867-1911 **TCLC 44**
See also CA 108; 176; DLB 9, 12
Phillips, Jack
See Sandburg, Carl (August)
Phillips, Jayne Anne 1952-CLC **15, 33; SSC 16**
See also CA 101; CANR 24, 50; DLBY 80; INT
CANR-24; MTCW 1, 2
Phillips, Richard
See Dick, Philip K(indred)
Phillips, Robert (Schaeffer) 1938- **CLC 28**
See also CA 17-20R; CAAS 13; CANR 8; DLB
105
Phillips, Ward
See Lovecraft, H(oward) P(hillips)
Piccolo, Lucio 1901-1969 **CLC 13**
See also CA 97-100; DLB 114
Pickthall, Marjorie L(owry) C(hristie) 1883-
1922 **TCLC 21**
See also CA 107; DLB 92
Pico della Mirandola, Giovanni 1463-1494LC
15
Piercy, Marge 1936- CLC **3, 6, 14, 18, 27, 62**
See also CA 21-24R; CAAS 1; CANR 13, 43,
66; DLB 120; MTCW 1, 2
Piers, Robert
See Anthony, Piers
Pieyre de Mandiargues, Andre 1909-1991
See Mandiargues, Andre Pieyre de
See also CA 103; 136; CANR 22, 82
Pilnyak, Boris **TCLC 23**
See also Vogau, Boris Andreyevich
Pincherle, Alberto 1907-1990 **CLC 11, 18;**
DAM NOV
See also Moravia, Alberto
See also CA 25-28R; 132; CANR 33, 63;
MTCW 1
Pinckney, Darryl 1953- **CLC 76**
See also BW 2, 3; CA 143; CANR 79
Pindar 518B.C.-446B.C. **CMLC 12;PC 19**
See also DLB 176
Pineda, Cecile 1942- **CLC 39**
See also CA 118
Pinero, Arthur Wing 1855-1934 **TCLC 32;**
DAM DRAM
See also CA 110; 153; DLB 10
Pinero, Miguel (Antonio Gomez) 1946-1988
CLC 4, 55
See also CA 61-64; 125; CANR 29; HW 1
Pinget, Robert 1919-1997 **CLC 7, 13, 37**
See also CA 85-88; 160; DLB 83
Pink Floyd
See Barrett, (Roger) Syd; Gilmour, David; Ma-
son, Nick; Waters, Roger; Wright, Rick
Pinkney, Edward 1802-1828 **NCLC 31**
Pinkwater, Daniel Manus 1941- **CLC 35**
See also Pinkwater, Manus
See also AAYA 1; CA 29-32R; CANR 12, 38;
CLR 4; JRDA; MAICYA; SAAS 3; SATA 46,
76
Pinkwater, Manus
See Pinkwater, Daniel Manus
See also SATA 8
Pinsky, Robert 1940- CLC **9, 19, 38, 94, 121;**
DAM POET; PC 27
See also CA 29-32R; CAAS 4; CANR 58;
DLBY 82, 98; MTCW 2
Pinta, Harold
See Pinter, Harold

Pinter, Harold 1930-CLC **1, 3, 6, 9, 11, 15, 27, 58, 73; DA; DAB; DAC; DAM DRAM, MST; WLC**
See also CA 5-8R; CANR 33, 65; CDBLB 1960 to Present; DLB 13; MTCW 1, 2

Piozzi, Hester Lynch (Thrale) 1741-1821 **NCLC 57**
See also DLB 104, 142

Pirandello, Luigi 1867-1936TCLC **4, 29; DA; DAB; DAC; DAM DRAM, MST; DC 5; SSC 22; WLC**
See also CA 104; 153; MTCW 2

Pirsig, Robert M(aynard) 1928-CLC **4, 6, 73; DAM POP**
See also CA 53-56; CANR 42, 74; MTCW 1, 2; SATA 39

Pisarev, Dmitry Ivanovich 1840-1868 **N C L C 25**

Pix, Mary (Griffith) 1666-1709   **LC 8**
See also DLB 80

Pixerecourt, (Rene Charles) Guilbertde 1773-1844   **NCLC 39**
See also DLB 192

Plaatje, Sol(omon) T(shekisho) 1876-1932 **TCLC 73; BLCS**
See also BW 2, 3; CA 141; CANR 79

Plaidy, Jean
See Hibbert, Eleanor Alice Burford

Planche, James Robinson 1796-1880NCLC **42**

Plant, Robert 1948-   **CLC 12**

Plante, David (Robert) 1940- CLC **7, 23, 38; DAM NOV**
See also CA 37-40R; CANR 12, 36, 58, 82; DLBY 83; INT CANR-12; MTCW 1

Plath, Sylvia 1932-1963 CLC **1, 2, 3, 5, 9, 11, 14, 17, 50, 51, 62, 111; DA; DAB; DAC; DAM MST, POET; PC 1; WLC**
See also AAYA 13; CA 19-20; CANR 34; CAP 2; CDALB 1941-1968; DLB 5, 6, 152; MTCW 1, 2; SATA 96

Plato 428(?)B.C.-348(?)B.C.   **CMLC 8; DA; DAB; DAC; DAM MST; WLCS**
See also DLB 176

Platonov, Andrei   **TCLC 14**
See also Klimentov, Andrei Platonovich

Platt, Kin 1911-   **CLC 26**
See also AAYA 11; CA 17-20R; CANR 11; JRDA; SAAS 17; SATA 21, 86

Plautus c. 251B.C.-184B.C. **CMLC 24; DC 6**
See also DLB 211

Plick et Plock
See Simenon, Georges (Jacques Christian)

Plimpton, George (Ames) 1927-   **CLC 36**
See also AITN 1; CA 21-24R; CANR 32, 70; DLB 185; MTCW 1, 2; SATA 10

Pliny the Elder c. 23-79   **CMLC 23**
See also DLB 211

Plomer, William Charles Franklin 1903-1973 **CLC 4, 8**
See also CA 21-22; CANR 34; CAP 2; DLB 20, 162, 191; MTCW 1; SATA 24

Plowman, Piers
See Kavanagh, Patrick (Joseph)

Plum, J.
See Wodehouse, P(elham) G(renville)

Plumly, Stanley (Ross) 1939-   **CLC 33**
See also CA 108; 110; DLB 5, 193; INT 110

Plumpe, Friedrich Wilhelm 1888-1931T C L C 53
See also CA 112

Po Chu-i 772-846   **CMLC 24**

Poe, Edgar Allan 1809-1849 NCLC **1, 16, 55, 78; DA; DAB; DAC; DAM MST, POET;**

PC **1; SSC 34; WLC**
See also AAYA 14; CDALB 1640-1865; DLB 3, 59, 73, 74; SATA 23

Poet of Titchfield Street, The
See Pound, Ezra (Weston Loomis)

Pohl, Frederik 1919-   **CLC 18; SSC 25**
See also AAYA 24; CA 61-64; CAAS 1; CANR 11, 37, 81; DLB 8; INT CANR-11; MTCW 1, 2; SATA 24

Poirier, Louis 1910-
See Gracq, Julien
See also CA 122; 126

Poitier, Sidney 1927-   **CLC 26**
See also BW 1; CA 117

Polanski, Roman 1933-   **CLC 16**
See also CA 77-80

Poliakoff, Stephen 1952-   **CLC 38**
See also CA 106; DLB 13

Police, The
See Copeland, Stewart (Armstrong); Summers, Andrew James; Sumner, Gordon Matthew

Polidori, John William 1795-1821 **NCLC 51**
See also DLB 116

Pollitt, Katha 1949-   **CLC 28, 122**
See also CA 120; 122; CANR 66; MTCW 1, 2

Pollock, (Mary) Sharon 1936-CLC **50; DAC; DAM DRAM, MST**
See also CA 141; DLB 60

Polo, Marco 1254-1324   **CMLC 15**

Polonsky, Abraham (Lincoln) 1910- CLC **92**
See also CA 104; DLB 26; INT 104

Polybius c. 200B.C.-c.118B.C.   **CMLC 17**
See also DLB 176

Pomerance, Bernard 1940-   **CLC 13;DAM DRAM**
See also CA 101; CANR 49

Ponge, Francis (Jean Gaston Alfred) 1899-1988 **CLC 6, 18; DAM POET**
See also CA 85-88; 126; CANR 40

Poniatowska, Elena 1933-
See also CA 101; CANR 32, 66; DAM MULT; DLB 113; HLC 2; HW 1, 2

Pontoppidan, Henrik 1857-1943   **TCLC 29**
See also CA 170

Poole, Josephine   **CLC 17**
See also Helyar, Jane Penelope Josephine
See also SAAS 2; SATA 5

Popa, Vasko 1922-1991   **CLC 19**
See also CA 112; 148; DLB 181

Pope, Alexander 1688-1744 LC **3; DA; DAB; DAC; DAM MST, POET; PC 26; WLC**
See also CDBLB 1660-1789; DLB 95, 101

Porter, Connie (Rose) 1959(?)-   **CLC 70**
See also BW 2, 3; CA 142; SATA 81

Porter, Gene(va Grace) Stratton 1863(?)-1924 **TCLC 21**
See also CA 112

Porter, Katherine Anne 1890-1980CLC **1,3,7, 10, 13, 15, 27, 101; DA; DAB; DAC; DAM MST, NOV; SSC 4, 31**
See also AITN 2; CA 1-4R; 101; CANR 1, 65; CDALBS; DLB 4, 9, 102; DLBD 12; DLBY 80; MTCW 1, 2; SATA 39; SATA-Obit 23

Porter, Peter (Neville Frederick) 1929-CLC **5, 13, 33**
See also CA 85-88; DLB 40

Porter, William Sydney 1862-1910
See Henry, O.
See also CA 104; 131; CDALB 1865-1917; DA; DAB; DAC; DAM MST; DLB 12, 78, 79; MTCW 1, 2; YABC 2

Portillo (y Pacheco), Jose Lopez
See Lopez Portillo (y Pacheco), Jose

Portillo Trambley, Estela 1927-1998
See also CANR 32; DAM MULT; DLB 209; HLC 2; HW 1

Post, Melville Davisson 1869-1930 **TCLC 39**
See also CA 110

Potok, Chaim 1929-   CLC **2, 7, 14, 26, 112; DAM NOV**
See also AAYA 15; AITN 1, 2; CA 17-20R; CANR 19, 35, 64; DLB 28, 152; INTCANR-19; MTCW 1, 2; SATA 33, 106

Potter, (Helen) Beatrix 1866-1943
See Webb, (Martha) Beatrice (Potter)
See also MAICYA; MTCW 2

Potter, Dennis (Christopher George) 1935-1994 **CLC 58, 86**
See also CA 107; 145; CANR 33, 61; MTCW 1

Pound, Ezra (Weston Loomis) 1885-1972CLC **1, 2, 3, 4, 5, 7, 10, 13, 18, 34, 48, 50, 112; DA; DAB; DAC; DAM MST, POET; PC 4; WLC**
See also CA 5-8R; 37-40R; CANR 40; CDALB 1917-1929; DLB 4, 45, 63; DLBD 15; MTCW 1, 2

Povod, Reinaldo 1959-1994   **CLC 44**
See also CA 136; 146

Powell, Adam Clayton, Jr. 1908-1972CLC **89; BLC 3; DAM MULT**
See also BW 1, 3; CA 102; 33-36R

Powell, Anthony (Dymoke) 1905-CLC **1, 3, 7, 9, 10, 31**
See also CA 1-4R; CANR 1, 32, 62; CDBLB 1945-1960; DLB 15; MTCW 1, 2

Powell, Dawn 1897-1965   **CLC 66**
See also CA 5-8R; DLBY 97

Powell, Padgett 1952-   **CLC 34**
See also CA 126; CANR 63

Power, Susan 1961-   **CLC 91**

Powers, J(ames) F(arl) 1917-CLC **1, 4, 8, 57; SSC 4**
See also CA 1-4R; CANR 2, 61; DLB 130; MTCW 1

Powers, John J(ames) 1945-
See Powers, John R.
See also CA 69-72

Powers, John R.   **CLC 66**
See also Powers, John J(ames)

Powers, Richard (S.) 1957-   **CLC 93**
See also CA 148; CANR 80

Pownall, David 1938-   **CLC 10**
See also CA 89-92; CAAS 18; CANR 49; DLB 14

Powys, John Cowper 1872-1963CLC **7, 9, 15, 46**
See also CA 85-88; DLB 15; MTCW 1, 2

Powys, T(heodore) F(rancis) 1875-1953 **TCLC 9**
See also CA 106; DLB 36, 162

Prado (Calvo), Pedro 1886-1952   **TCLC 75**
See also CA 131; HW 1

Prager, Emily 1952-   **CLC 56**

Pratt, E(dwin) J(ohn) 1883(?)-1964 CLC **19; DAC; DAM POET**
See also CA 141; 93-96; CANR 77; DLB 92

Premchand   **TCLC 21**
See also Srivastava, Dhanpat Rai

Preussler, Otfried 1923-   **CLC 17**
See also CA 77-80; SATA 24

Prevert, Jacques (Henri Marie) 1900-1977 **CLC 15**
See also CA 77-80; 69-72; CANR 29, 61; MTCW 1; SATA-Obit 30

Prevost, Abbe (Antoine Francois) 1697-1763 **LC 1**

Price, (Edward) Reynolds 1933-CLC 3, 6, 13, 43, 50, 63; DAM NOV; SSC 22
See also CA 1-4R; CANR 1, 37, 57; DLB 2; INT CANR-37
Price, Richard 1949- CLC 6, 12
See also CA 49-52; CANR 3; DLBY 81
Prichard, Katharine Susannah 1883-1969 CLC 46
See also CA 11-12; CANR 33; CAP 1; MTCW 1; SATA 66
Priestley, J(ohn) B(oynton) 1894-1984CLC 2, 5, 9, 34; DAM DRAM, NOV
See also CA 9-12R; 113; CANR 33;CDBLB 1914-1945; DLB 10, 34, 77, 100, 139; DLBY 84; MTCW 1, 2
Prince 1958(?)- CLC 35
Prince, F(rank) T(empleton) 1912- CLC 22
See also CA 101; CANR 43, 79; DLB 20
Prince Kropotkin
See Kropotkin, Peter (Alekseieevich)
Prior, Matthew 1664-1721 LC 4
See also DLB 95
Prishvin, Mikhail 1873-1954 TCLC 75
Pritchard, William H(arrison) 1932- CLC 34
See also CA 65-68; CANR 23; DLB 111
Pritchett, V(ictor) S(awdon) 1900-1997 CLC 5, 13, 15, 41; DAM NOV; SSC 14
See also CA 61-64; 157; CANR 31, 63; DLB 15, 139; MTCW 1, 2
Private 19022
See Manning, Frederic
Probst, Mark 1925- CLC 59
See also CA 130
Prokosch, Frederic 1908-1989 CLC 4, 48
See also CA 73-76; 128; CANR 82; DLB 48; MTCW 2
Propertius, Sextus c. 50B.C.-c.16B.C. CMLC 32
See also DLB 211
Prophet, The
See Dreiser, Theodore (Herman Albert)
Prose, Francine 1947- CLC 45
See also CA 109; 112; CANR 46; SATA 101
Proudhon
See Cunha, Euclides (Rodrigues Pimenta) da
Proulx, Annie
See Proulx, E(dna) Annie
Proulx, E(dna) Annie 1935- CLC 81;DAM POP
See also CA 145; CANR 65; MTCW 2
Proust, (Valentin-Louis-George-Eugene-) Marcel 1871-1922 TCLC 7, 13, 33; DA; DAB; DAC; DAM MST, NOV; WLC
See also CA 104; 120; DLB 65; MTCW 1, 2
Prowler, Harley
See Masters, Edgar Lee
Prus, Boleslaw 1845-1912 TCLC 48
Pryor, Richard (Franklin Lenox Thomas) 1940- CLC 26
See also CA 122; 152
Przybyszewski, Stanislaw 1868-1927TCLC 36
See also CA 160; DLB 66
Pteleon
See Grieve, C(hristopher) M(urray)
See also DAM POET
Puckett, Lute
See Masters, Edgar Lee
Puig, Manuel 1932-1990CLC 3, 5, 10, 28, 65; DAM MULT; HLC 2
See also CA 45-48; CANR 2, 32, 63; DLB 113; HW 1, 2; MTCW 1, 2
Pulitzer, Joseph 1847-1911 TCLC 76
See also CA 114; DLB 23

Purdy, A(lfred) W(ellington) 1918- CLC 3, 6, 14, 50; DAC; DAM MST, POET
See also CA 81-84; CAAS 17; CANR 42, 66; DLB 88
Purdy, James (Amos) 1923- CLC 2, 4, 10, 28, 52
See also CA 33-36R; CAAS 1; CANR 19, 51; DLB 2; INT CANR-19; MTCW 1
Pure, Simon
See Swinnerton, Frank Arthur
Pushkin, Alexander (Sergeyevich) 1799-1837 NCLC 3, 27; DA; DAB; DAC; DAM DRAM, MST, POET; PC 10; SSC 27;WLC
See also DLB 205; SATA 61
P'u Sung-ling 1640-1715 LC 49; SSC 31
Putnam, Arthur Lee
See Alger, Horatio, Jr.
Puzo, Mario 1920-1999 CLC 1, 2, 6, 36, 107; DAM NOV, POP
See also CA 65-68; CANR 4, 42, 65; DLB 6; MTCW 1, 2
Pygge, Edward
See Barnes, Julian (Patrick)
Pyle, Ernest Taylor 1900-1945
See Pyle, Ernie
See also CA 115; 160
Pyle, Ernie 1900-1945 TCLC 75
See Pyle, Ernest Taylor
See also DLB 29; MTCW 2
Pyle, Howard 1853-1911 TCLC 81
See also CA 109; 137; CLR 22; DLB 42, 188; DLBD 13; MAICYA; SATA 16, 100
Pym, Barbara (Mary Crampton) 1913-1980 CLC 13, 19, 37, 111
See also CA 13-14; 97-100; CANR 13, 34; CAP 1; DLB 14, 207; DLBY 87; MTCW 1, 2
Pynchon, Thomas (Ruggles, Jr.) 1937-CLC 2, 3, 6, 9, 11, 18, 33, 62, 72; DA; DAB; DAC; DAM MST, NOV, POP; SSC 14;WLC
See also BEST 90:2; CA 17-20R; CANR 22, 46, 73; DLB 2, 173; MTCW 1, 2
Pythagoras c. 570B.C.-c.500B.C. CMLC 22
See also DLB 176
Q
See Quiller-Couch, SirArthur (Thomas)
Qian Zhongshu
See Ch'ien Chung-shu
Qroll
See Dagerman, Stig (Halvard)
Quarrington, Paul (Lewis) 1953- CLC 65
See also CA 129; CANR 62
Quasimodo, Salvatore 1901-1968 CLC 10
See also CA 13-16; 25-28R; CAP 1; DLB 114; MTCW 1
Quay, Stephen 1947- CLC 95
Quay, Timothy 1947- CLC 95
Queen, Ellery CLC 3, 11
See also Dannay, Frederic; Davidson, Avram (James); Lee, Manfred B(ennington); Marlowe, Stephen; Sturgeon, Theodore (Hamilton); Vance, John Holbrook
Queen, Ellery, Jr.
See Dannay, Frederic; Lee, Manfred B(ennington)
Queneau, Raymond 1903-1976 CLC 2, 5, 10, 42
See also CA 77-80; 69-72; CANR 32; DLB 72; MTCW 1, 2
Quevedo, Francisco de 1580-1645 LC 23
Quiller-Couch, Sir Arthur(Thomas) 1863-1944 TCLC 53
See also CA 118; 166; DLB 135, 153, 190
Quin, Ann (Marie) 1936-1973 CLC 6

See also CA 9-12R; 45-48; DLB 14
Quinn, Martin
See Smith, Martin Cruz
Quinn, Peter 1947- CLC 91
Quinn, Simon
See Smith, Martin Cruz
Quintana, Leroy V. 1944-
See also CA 131; CANR 65; DAM MULT; DLB 82; HLC 2; HW 1, 2
Quiroga, Horacio (Sylvestre) 1878-1937 TCLC 20; DAM MULT; HLC 2
See also CA 117; 131; HW 1; MTCW 1
Quoirez, Francoise 1935- CLC 9
See Sagan, Francoise
See also CA 49-52; CANR 6, 39, 73; MTCW 1, 2
Raabe, Wilhelm (Karl) 1831-1910 TCLC 45
See also CA 167; DLB 129
Rabe, David (William) 1940- CLC 4, 8, 33; DAM DRAM
See also CA 85-88; CABS 3; CANR 59; DLB 7
Rabelais, Francois 1483-1553LC 5; DA; DAB; DAC; DAM MST; WLC
Rabinovitch, Sholem 1859-1916
See Aleichem, Sholom
See also CA 104
Rabinyan, Dorit 1972- CLC 119
See also CA 170
Rachilde 1860-1953 TCLC 67
See also DLB 123, 192
Racine, Jean 1639-1699 LC 28; DAB; DAM MST
Radcliffe, Ann (Ward) 1764-1823NCLC 6, 55
See also DLB 39, 178
Radiguet, Raymond 1903-1923 TCLC 29
See also CA 162; DLB 65
Radnoti, Miklos 1909-1944 TCLC 16
See also CA 118
Rado, James 1939- CLC 17
See also CA 105
Radvanyi, Netty 1900-1983
See Seghers, Anna
See also CA 85-88; 110; CANR 82
Rae, Ben
See Griffiths, Trevor
Raeburn, John (Hay) 1941- CLC 34
See also CA 57-60
Ragni, Gerome 1942-1991 CLC 17
See also CA 105; 134
Rahv, Philip 1908-1973 CLC 24
See also Greenberg, Ivan
See also DLB 137
Raimund, Ferdinand Jakob 1790-1836NCLC 69
See also DLB 90
Raine, Craig 1944- CLC 32, 103
See also CA 108; CANR 29, 51; DLB 40
Raine, Kathleen (Jessie) 1908- CLC 7, 45
See also CA 85-88; CANR 46; DLB 20; MTCW 1
Rainis, Janis 1865-1929 TCLC 29
See also CA 170
Rakosi, Carl 1903- CLC 47
See also Rawley, Callman
See also CAAS 5; DLB 193
Raleigh, Richard
See Lovecraft, H(oward) P(hillips)
Raleigh, Sir Walter 1554(?)-1618 LC 31, 39
See also CDBLB Before 1660; DLB 172
Rallentando, H. P.
See Sayers, Dorothy L(eigh)
Ramal, Walter
See de la Mare, Walter (John)

Ramana Maharshi 1879-1950 **TCLC 84**
Ramoacn y Cajal, Santiago 1852-1934 **T C L C 93**
Ramon, Juan
See Jimenez (Mantecon), Juan Ramon
Ramos, Graciliano 1892-1953 **TCLC 32**
See also CA 167; HW 2
Rampersad, Arnold 1941- **CLC 44**
See also BW 2, 3; CA 127; 133; CANR 81; DLB 111; INT 133
Rampling, Anne
See Rice, Anne
Ramsay, Allan 1684(?)-1758 **LC 29**
See also DLB 95
Ramuz, Charles-Ferdinand 1878-1947 **T C L C 33**
See also CA 165
Rand, Ayn 1905-1982 **CLC 3, 30, 44, 79; DA; DAC; DAM MST, NOV, POP; WLC**
See also AAYA 10; CA 13-16R; 105; CANR 27, 73; CDALBS; MTCW 1, 2
Randall, Dudley (Felker) 1914- **CLC 1; BLC 3; DAM MULT**
See also BW 1, 3; CA 25-28R; CANR 23, 82; DLB 41
Randall, Robert
See Silverberg, Robert
Ranger, Ken
See Creasey, John
Ransom, John Crowe 1888-1974 **CLC 2, 4, 5, 11, 24; DAM POET**
See also CA 5-8R; 49-52; CANR 6, 34; CDALBS; DLB 45, 63; MTCW 1, 2
Rao, Raja 1909- **CLC 25, 56; DAM NOV**
See also CA 73-76; CANR 51; MTCW 1, 2
Raphael, Frederic (Michael) 1931- **CLC 2, 14**
See also CA 1-4R; CANR 1; DLB 14
Ratcliffe, James P.
See Mencken, H(enry) L(ouis)
Rathbone, Julian 1935- **CLC 41**
See also CA 101; CANR 34, 73
Rattigan, Terence (Mervyn) 1911-1977 **CLC 7; DAM DRAM**
See also CA 85-88; 73-76; CDBLB 1945-1960; DLB 13; MTCW 1, 2
Ratushinskaya, Irina 1954- **CLC 54**
See also CA 129; CANR 68
Raven, Simon (Arthur Noel) 1927- **CLC 14**
See also CA 81-84
Ravenna, Michael
See Welty, Eudora
Rawley, Callman 1903-
See Rakosi, Carl
See also CA 21-24R; CANR 12, 32
Rawlings, Marjorie Kinnan 1896-1953 **TCLC 4**
See also AAYA 20; CA 104; 137; CANR 74; DLB 9, 22, 102; DLBD 17; JRDA; MAICYA; MTCW 2; SATA 100; YABC 1
Ray, Satyajit 1921-1992 **CLC 16, 76; DAM MULT**
See also CA 114; 137
Read, Herbert Edward 1893-1968 **CLC 4**
See also CA 85-88; 25-28R; DLB 20, 149
Read, Piers Paul 1941- **CLC 4, 10, 25**
See also CA 21-24R; CANR 38; DLB 14; SATA 21
Reade, Charles 1814-1884 **NCLC 2, 74**
See also DLB 21
Reade, Hamish
See Gray, Simon (James Holliday)
Reading, Peter 1946- **CLC 47**
See also CA 103; CANR 46; DLB 40

Reaney, James 1926- **CLC 13; DAC; DAM MST**
See also CA 41-44R; CAAS 15; CANR 42; DLB 68; SATA 43
Rebreanu, Liviu 1885-1944 **TCLC 28**
See also CA 165
Rechy, John (Francisco) 1934- **CLC 1, 7, 14, 18, 107; DAM MULT; HLC 2**
See also CA 5-8R; CAAS 4; CANR 6, 32, 64; DLB 122; DLBY 82; HW 1, 2; INT CANR-6
Redcam, Tom 1870-1933 **TCLC 25**
Reddin, Keith **CLC 67**
Redgrove, Peter (William) 1932- **CLC 6, 41**
See also CA 1-4R; CANR 3, 39, 77; DLB 40
Redmon, Anne **CLC 22**
See also Nightingale, Anne Redmon
See also DLBY 86
Reed, Eliot
See Ambler, Eric
Reed, Ishmael 1938- **CLC 2, 3, 5, 6, 13, 32, 60; BLC 3; DAM MULT**
See also BW 2, 3; CA 21-24R; CANR 25, 48, 74; DLB 2, 5, 33, 169; DLBD 8; MTCW 1, 2
Reed, John (Silas) 1887-1920 **TCLC 9**
See also CA 106
Reed, Lou **CLC 21**
See also Firbank, Louis
Reeve, Clara 1729-1807 **NCLC 19**
See also DLB 39
Reich, Wilhelm 1897-1957 **TCLC 57**
Reid, Christopher (John) 1949- **CLC 33**
See also CA 140; DLB 40
Reid, Desmond
See Moorcock, Michael (John)
Reid Banks, Lynne 1929-
See Banks, Lynne Reid
See also CA 1-4R; CANR 6, 22, 38; CLR 24; JRDA; MAICYA; SATA 22, 75
Reilly, William K.
See Creasey, John
Reiner, Max
See Caldwell, (Janet Miriam) Taylor (Holland)
Reis, Ricardo
See Pessoa, Fernando (Antonio Nogueira)
Remarque, Erich Maria 1898-1970 **CLC 21; DA; DAB; DAC; DAM MST, NOV**
See also AAYA 27; CA 77-80; 29-32R; DLB 56; MTCW 1, 2
Remington, Frederic 1861-1909 **TCLC 89**
See also CA 108; 169; DLB 12, 186, 188; SATA 41
Remizov, A.
See Remizov, Aleksei (Mikhailovich)
Remizov, A. M.
See Remizov, Aleksei (Mikhailovich)
Remizov, Aleksei (Mikhailovich) 1877-1957 **TCLC 27**
See also CA 125; 133
Renan, Joseph Ernest 1823-1892 **NCLC 26**
Renard, Jules 1864-1910 **TCLC 17**
See also CA 117
Renault, Mary **CLC 3, 11, 17**
See also Challans, Mary
See also DLBY 83; MTCW 2
Rendell, Ruth (Barbara) 1930- **CLC 28, 48; DAM POP**
See also Vine, Barbara
See also CA 109; CANR 32, 52, 74; DLB 87; INT CANR-32; MTCW 1, 2
Renoir, Jean 1894-1979 **CLC 20**
See also CA 129; 85-88

Resnais, Alain 1922- **CLC 16**
Reverdy, Pierre 1889-1960 **CLC 53**
See also CA 97-100; 89-92
Rexroth, Kenneth 1905-1982 **CLC 1, 2, 6, 11, 22, 49, 112; DAM POET; PC 20**
See also CA 5-8R; 107; CANR 14, 34, 63; CDALB 1941-1968; DLB 16, 48, 165, 212; DLBY 82; INT CANR-14; MTCW 1, 2
Reyes, Alfonso 1889-1959 **TCLC 33; HLCS 2**
See also CA 131; HW 1
Reyes y Basoalto, Ricardo Eliecer Neftali
See Neruda, Pablo
Reymont, Wladyslaw (Stanislaw) 1868(?)-1925 **TCLC 5**
See also CA 104
Reynolds, Jonathan 1942- **CLC 6, 38**
See also CA 65-68; CANR 28
Reynolds, Joshua 1723-1792 **LC 15**
See also DLB 104
Reynolds, Michael Shane 1937- **CLC 44**
See also CA 65-68; CANR 9
Reznikoff, Charles 1894-1976 **CLC 9**
See also CA 33-36; 61-64; CAP 2; DLB 28, 45
Rezzori (d'Arezzo), Gregorvon 1914-1998 **CLC 25**
See also CA 122; 136; 167
Rhine, Richard
See Silverstein, Alvin
Rhodes, Eugene Manlove 1869-1934 **TCLC 53**
Rhodius, Apollonius c. 3rd cent.B.C.- **C M L C 28**
See also DLB 176
R'hoone
See Balzac, Honore de
Rhys, Jean 1890(?)-1979 **CLC 2, 4, 6, 14, 19, 51; DAM NOV; SSC 21**
See also CA 25-28R; 85-88; CANR 35, 62; CDBLB 1945-1960; DLB 36, 117, 162; MTCW 1, 2
Ribeiro, Darcy 1922-1997 **CLC 34**
See also CA 33-36R; 156
Ribeiro, Joao Ubaldo (Osorio Pimentel) 1941- **CLC 10, 67**
See also CA 81-84
Ribman, Ronald (Burt) 1932- **CLC 7**
See also CA 21-24R; CANR 46, 80
Ricci, Nino 1959- **CLC 70**
See also CA 137
Rice, Anne 1941- **CLC 41; DAM POP**
See also AAYA 9; BEST 89:2; CA 65-68; CANR 12, 36, 53, 74; MTCW 2
Rice, Elmer (Leopold) 1892-1967 **CLC 7, 49; DAM DRAM**
See also CA 21-22; 25-28R; CAP 2; DLB 4, 7; MTCW 1, 2
Rice, Tim(othy Miles Bindon) 1944- **CLC 21**
See also CA 103; CANR 46
Rich, Adrienne (Cecile) 1929- **CLC 3, 6, 7, 11, 18, 36, 73, 76; DAM POET; PC 5**
See also CA 9-12R; CANR 20, 53, 74; CDALBS; DLB 5, 67; MTCW 1, 2
Rich, Barbara
See Graves, Robert (von Ranke)
Rich, Robert
See Trumbo, Dalton
Richard, Keith **CLC 17**
See also Richards, Keith
Richards, David Adams 1950- **CLC 59; DAC**
See also CA 93-96; CANR 60; DLB 53
Richards, I(vor) A(rmstrong) 1893-1979 **C L C 14, 24**
See also CA 41-44R; 89-92; CANR 34, 74; DLB 27; MTCW 2

Richards, Keith 1943-
See Richard, Keith
See also CA 107; CANR 77
Richardson, Anne
See Roiphe, Anne (Richardson)
Richardson, Dorothy Miller 1873-1957**TCLC
3**
See also CA 104; DLB 36
Richardson, Ethel Florence (Lindesay) 1870-
1946
See Richardson, Henry Handel
See also CA 105
Richardson, Henry Handel **TCLC 4**
See Richardson, Ethel Florence (Lindesay)
See also DLB 197
Richardson, John 1796-1852 **NCLC 55; DAC**
See also DLB 99
Richardson, Samuel 1689-1761**LC 1, 44; DA;
DAB; DAC; DAM MST, NOV; WLC**
See also CDBLB 1660-1789; DLB 39
Richler, Mordecai 1931-**CLC 3, 5, 9, 13, 18, 46,
70; DAC; DAM MST, NOV**
See also AITN 1; CA 65-68; CANR 31, 62; CLR
17; DLB 53; MAICYA; MTCW 1, 2; SATA
44, 98; SATA-Brief 27
Richter, Conrad (Michael) 1890-1968**CLC 30**
See also AAYA 21; CA 5-8R; 25-28R; CANR
23; DLB 9, 212; MTCW 1, 2; SATA 3
Ricostranza, Tom
See Ellis, Trey
Riddell, Charlotte 1832-1906 **TCLC 40**
See also CA 165; DLB 156
Ridgway, Keith 1965- **CLC 119**
See also CA 172
Riding, Laura **CLC 3, 7**
See also Jackson, Laura (Riding)
Riefenstahl, Berta Helene Amalia 1902-
See Riefenstahl, Leni
See also CA 108
Riefenstahl, Leni **CLC 16**
See also Riefenstahl, Berta Helene Amalia
Riffe, Ernest
See Bergman, (Ernst) Ingmar
Riggs, (Rolla) Lynn 1899-1954 **TCLC 56;
DAM MULT**
See also CA 144; DLB 175; NNAL
Riis, Jacob A(ugust) 1849-1914 **TCLC 80**
See also CA 113; 168; DLB 23
Riley, James Whitcomb 1849-1916**TCLC 51;
DAM POET**
See also CA 118; 137; MAICYA; SATA 17
Riley, Tex
See Creasey, John
Rilke, Rainer Maria 1875-1926**TCLC 1, 6, 19;
DAM POET; PC 2**
See also CA 104; 132; CANR 62; DLB 81;
MTCW 1, 2
Rimbaud, (Jean Nicolas) Arthur 1854-1891
**NCLC 4, 35; DA; DAB; DAC; DAM MST,
POET; PC 3; WLC**
Rinehart, Mary Roberts 1876-1958**TCLC 52**
See also CA 108; 166
Ringmaster, The
See Mencken, H(enry) L(ouis)
Ringwood, Gwen(dolyn Margaret) Pharis
1910-1984 **CLC 48**
See also CA 148; 112; DLB 88
Rio, Michel 19(?)- **CLC 43**
Ritsos, Giannes
See Ritsos, Yannis
Ritsos, Yannis 1909-1990 **CLC 6, 13, 31**
See also CA 77-80; 133; CANR 39, 61; MTCW
1

Ritter, Erika 1948(?)- **CLC 52**
Rivera, Jose Eustasio 1889-1928 **TCLC 35**
See also CA 162; HW 1, 2
Rivera, Tomas 1935-1984
See also CA 49-52; CANR 32; DLB 82; HLCS
2; HW 1
Rivers, Conrad Kent 1933-1968 **CLC 1**
See also BW 1; CA 85-88; DLB 41
Rivers, Elfrida
See Bradley, Marion Zimmer
Riverside, John
See Heinlein, Robert A(nson)
Rizal, Jose 1861-1896 **NCLC 27**
Roa Bastos, Augusto (Antonio) 1917-**CLC 45;
DAM MULT; HLC 2**
See also CA 131; DLB 113; HW 1
Robbe-Grillet, Alain 1922-**CLC 1, 2, 4, 6, 8, 10,
14, 43**
See also CA 9-12R; CANR 33, 65; DLB 83;
MTCW 1, 2
Robbins, Harold 1916-1997**CLC 5; DAM NOV**
See also CA 73-76; 162; CANR 26, 54; MTCW
1, 2
Robbins, Thomas Eugene 1936-
See Robbins, Tom
See also CA 81-84; CANR 29, 59; DAM NOV,
POP; MTCW 1, 2
Robbins, Tom **CLC 9, 32, 64**
See also Robbins, Thomas Eugene
See also BEST 90:3; DLBY 80; MTCW 2
Robbins, Trina 1938- **CLC 21**
See also CA 128
Roberts, Charles G(eorge) D(ouglas) 1860-1943
TCLC 8
See also CA 105; CLR 33; DLB 92; SATA 88;
SATA-Brief 29
Roberts, Elizabeth Madox 1886-1941 **TCLC
68**
See also CA 111; 166; DLB 9, 54, 102; SATA
33; SATA-Brief 27
Roberts, Kate 1891-1985 **CLC 15**
See also CA 107; 116
Roberts, Keith (John Kingston) 1935-**CLC 14**
See also CA 25-28R; CANR 46
Roberts, Kenneth (Lewis) 1885-1957**TCLC 23**
See also CA 109; DLB 9
Roberts, Michele (B.) 1949- **CLC 48**
See also CA 115; CANR 58
Robertson, Ellis
See Ellison, Harlan (Jay); Silverberg, Robert
Robertson, Thomas William 1829-1871**NCLC
35; DAM DRAM**
Robeson, Kenneth
See Dent, Lester
Robinson, Edwin Arlington 1869-1935**TCLC
5; DA; DAC; DAM MST, POET; PC 1**
See also CA 104; 133; CDALB 1865-1917;
DLB 54; MTCW 1, 2
Robinson, Henry Crabb 1775-1867**NCLC 15**
See also DLB 107
Robinson, Jill 1936- **CLC 10**
See also CA 102; INT 102
Robinson, Kim Stanley 1952- **CLC 34**
See also AAYA 26; CA 126; SATA 109
Robinson, Lloyd
See Silverberg, Robert
Robinson, Marilynne 1944- **CLC 25**
See also CA 116; CANR 80; DLB 206
Robinson, Smokey **CLC 21**
See also Robinson, William, Jr.
Robinson, William, Jr. 1940-
See Robinson, Smokey
See also CA 116

Robison, Mary 1949- **CLC 42, 98**
See also CA 113; 116; DLB 130; INT 116
Rod, Edouard 1857-1910 **TCLC 52**
Roddenberry, Eugene Wesley 1921-1991
See Roddenberry, Gene
See also CA 110; 135; CANR 37; SATA 45;
SATA-Obit 69
Roddenberry, Gene **CLC 17**
See Roddenberry, Eugene Wesley
See also AAYA 5; SATA-Obit 69
Rodgers, Mary 1931- **CLC 12**
See also CA 49-52; CANR 8, 55; CLR 20; INT
CANR-8; JRDA; MAICYA; SATA 8
Rodgers, W(illiam) R(obert) 1909-1969**CLC 7**
See also CA 85-88; DLB 20
Rodman, Eric
See Silverberg, Robert
Rodman, Howard 1920(?)-1985 **CLC 65**
See also CA 118
Rodman, Maia
See Wojciechowska, Maia (Teresa)
Rodo, Jose Enrique 1872(?)-1917
See also CA 178; HLCS 2; HW 2
Rodriguez, Claudio 1934- **CLC 10**
See also DLB 134
Rodriguez, Richard 1944-
See also CA 110; CANR 66; DAM MULT; DLB
82; HLC 2; HW 1, 2
Roelvaag, O(le) E(dvart) 1876-1931**TCLC 17**
See also CA 117; 171; DLB 9
Roethke, Theodore (Huebner) 1908-1963**CLC
1, 3, 8, 11, 19, 46, 101; DAM POET; PC 15**
See also CA 81-84; CABS 2; CDALB 1941-
1968; DLB 5, 206; MTCW 1, 2
Rogers, Samuel 1763-1855 **NCLC 69**
See also DLB 93
Rogers, Thomas Hunton 1927- **CLC 57**
See also CA 89-92; INT 89-92
Rogers, Will(iam Penn Adair) 1879-1935
TCLC 8, 71; DAM MULT
See also CA 105; 144; DLB 11; MTCW 2;
NNAL
Rogin, Gilbert 1929- **CLC 18**
See also CA 65-68; CANR 15
Rohan, Koda **TCLC 22**
See also Koda Shigeyuki
Rohlfs, Anna Katharine Green
See Green, Anna Katharine
Rohmer, Eric **CLC 16**
See also Scherer, Jean-Marie Maurice
Rohmer, Sax **TCLC 28**
See also Ward, Arthur Henry Sarsfield
See also DLB 70
Roiphe, Anne (Richardson) 1935- **CLC 3, 9**
See also CA 89-92; CANR 45, 73; DLBY 80;
INT 89-92
Rojas, Fernando de 1465-1541**LC 23; HLCS 1**
Rojas, Gonzalo 1917-
See also HLCS 2; HW 2
Rojas, Gonzalo 1917-
See also CA 178; HLCS 2
Rolfe, Frederick (William Serafino Austin
Lewis Mary) 1860-1913 **TCLC 12**
See also CA 107; DLB 34, 156
Rolland, Romain 1866-1944 **TCLC 23**
See also CA 118; DLB 65
Rolle, Richard c. 1300-c.1349 **CMLC 21**
See also DLB 146
Rolvaag, O(le) E(dvart)
See Roelvaag, O(le) E(dvart)
Romain Arnaud, Saint
See Aragon, Louis
Romains, Jules 1885-1972 **CLC 7**

See also CA 85-88; CANR 34; DLB 65; MTCW 1

Romero, Jose Ruben 1890-1952   **TCLC 14**
See also CA 114; 131; HW 1

Ronsard, Pierre de 1524-1585   **LC 6; PC 11**

Rooke, Leon 1934-   **CLC 25, 34; DAM POP**
See also CA 25-28R; CANR 23, 53

Roosevelt, Franklin Delano 1882-1945 **TCLC 93**
See also CA 116; 173

Roosevelt, Theodore 1858-1919   **TCLC 69**
See also CA 115; 170; DLB 47, 186

Roper, William 1498-1578   **LC 10**

Roquelaure, A. N.
See Rice, Anne

Rosa, Joao Guimaraes 1908-1967   **CLC 23; HLCS 1**
See also CA 89-92; DLB 113

Rose, Wendy 1948- **CLC 85; DAM MULT; PC 13**
See also CA 53-56; CANR 5, 51; DLB 175; NNAL; SATA 12

Rosen, R. D.
See Rosen, Richard (Dean)

Rosen, Richard (Dean) 1949-   **CLC 39**
See also CA 77-80; CANR 62; INT CANR-30

Rosenberg, Isaac 1890-1918   **TCLC 12**
See also CA 107; DLB 20

Rosenblatt, Joe   **CLC 15**
See Rosenblatt, Joseph

Rosenblatt, Joseph 1933-
See Rosenblatt, Joe
See also CA 89-92; INT 89-92

Rosenfeld, Samuel
See Tzara, Tristan

Rosenstock, Sami
See Tzara, Tristan

Rosenstock, Samuel
See Tzara, Tristan

Rosenthal, M(acha) L(ouis) 1917-1996   **CLC 28**
See also CA 1-4R; 152; CAAS 6; CANR 4, 51; DLB 5; SATA 59

Ross, Barnaby
See Dannay, Frederic

Ross, Bernard L.
See Follett, Ken(neth Martin)

Ross, J. H.
See Lawrence, T(homas) E(dward)

Ross, John Hume
See Lawrence, T(homas) E(dward)

Ross, Martin
See Martin, Violet Florence
See also DLB 135

Ross, (James) Sinclair 1908-1996   **CLC 13; DAC; DAM MST; SSC 24**
See also CA 73-76; CANR 81; DLB 88

Rossetti, Christina (Georgina) 1830-1894   **NCLC 2, 50, 66; DA; DAB; DAC; DAM MST, POET; PC 7; WLC**
See also DLB 35, 163; MAICYA; SATA 20

Rossetti, Dante Gabriel 1828-1882   **NCLC 4, 77; DA; DAB; DAC; DAM MST, POET; WLC**
See also CDBLB 1832-1890; DLB 35

Rossner, Judith (Perelman) 1935- **CLC 6, 9, 29**
See also AITN 2; BEST 90:3; CA 17-20R; CANR 18, 51, 73; DLB 6; INT CANR-18; MTCW 1, 2

Rostand, Edmond (Eugene Alexis) 1868-1918   **TCLC 6, 37; DA; DAB; DAC; DAM DRAM, MST; DC 10**
See also CA 104; 126; DLB 192; MTCW 1

Roth, Henry 1906-1995   **CLC 2, 6, 11, 104**
See also CA 11-12; 149; CANR 38, 63; CAP 1; DLB 28; MTCW 1, 2

Roth, Philip (Milton) 1933- **CLC 1, 2, 3, 4, 6, 9, 15, 22, 31, 47, 66, 86, 119; DA; DAB; DAC; DAM MST, NOV, POP; SSC 26; WLC**
See also BEST 90:3; CA 1-4R; CANR 1, 22, 36, 55; CDALB 1968-1988; DLB 2, 28, 173; DLBY 82; MTCW 1, 2

Rothenberg, Jerome 1931-   **CLC 6, 57**
See also CA 45-48; CANR 1; DLB 5, 193

Roumain, Jacques (Jean Baptiste) 1907-1944   **TCLC 19; BLC 3; DAM MULT**
See also BW 1; CA 117; 125

Rourke, Constance (Mayfield) 1885-1941   **TCLC 12**
See also CA 107; YABC 1

Rousseau, Jean-Baptiste 1671-1741   **LC 9**

Rousseau, Jean-Jacques 1712-1778 **LC 14, 36; DA; DAB; DAC; DAM MST; WLC**

Roussel, Raymond 1877-1933   **TCLC 20**
See also CA 117

Rovit, Earl (Herbert) 1927-   **CLC 7**
See also CA 5-8R; CANR 12

Rowe, Elizabeth Singer 1674-1737   **LC 44**
See also DLB 39, 95

Rowe, Nicholas 1674-1718   **LC 8**
See also DLB 84

Rowley, Ames Dorrance
See Lovecraft, H(oward) P(hillips)

Rowson, Susanna Haswell 1762(?)-1824   **NCLC 5, 69**
See also DLB 37, 200

Roy, Arundhati 1960(?)-   **CLC 109**
See also CA 163; DLBY 97

Roy, Gabrielle 1909-1983 **CLC 10, 14; DAB; DAC; DAM MST**
See also CA 53-56; 110; CANR 5, 61; DLB 68; MTCW 1; SATA 104

Royko, Mike 1932-1997   **CLC 109**
See also CA 89-92; 157; CANR 26

Rozewicz, Tadeusz 1921-   **CLC 9, 23; DAM POET**
See also CA 108; CANR 36, 66; MTCW 1, 2

Ruark, Gibbons 1941-   **CLC 3**
See also CA 33-36R; CAAS 23; CANR 14, 31, 57; DLB 120

Rubens, Bernice (Ruth) 1923-   **CLC 19, 31**
See also CA 25-28R; CANR 33, 65; DLB 14, 207; MTCW 1

Rubin, Harold
See Robbins, Harold

Rudkin, (James) David 1936-   **CLC 14**
See also CA 89-92; DLB 13

Rudnik, Raphael 1933-   **CLC 7**
See also CA 29-32R

Ruffian, M.
See Hasek, Jaroslav (Matej Frantisek)

Ruiz, Jose Martinez   **CLC 11**
See also Martinez Ruiz, Jose

Rukeyser, Muriel 1913-1980 **CLC 6, 10, 15, 27; DAM POET; PC 12**
See also CA 5-8R; 93-96; CANR 26, 60; DLB 48; MTCW 1, 2; SATA-Obit 22

Rule, Jane (Vance) 1931-   **CLC 27**
See also CA 25-28R; CAAS 18; CANR 12; DLB 60

Rulfo, Juan 1918-1986   **CLC 8, 80; DAM MULT; HLC 2; SSC 25**
See also CA 85-88; 118; CANR 26; DLB 113; HW 1, 2; MTCW 1, 2

Rumi, Jalal al-Din 1297-1373   **CMLC 20**

Runeberg, Johan 1804-1877   **NCLC 41**

Runyon, (Alfred) Damon 1884(?)-1946 **TCLC 10**
See also CA 107; 165; DLB 11, 86, 171; MTCW 2

Rush, Norman 1933-   **CLC 44**
See also CA 121; 126; INT 126

Rushdie, (Ahmed) Salman 1947- **CLC 23, 31, 55, 100; DAB; DAC; DAM MST, NOV, POP; WLCS**
See also BEST 89:3; CA 108; 111; CANR 33, 56; DLB 194; INT 111; MTCW 1, 2

Rushforth, Peter (Scott) 1945-   **CLC 19**
See also CA 101

Ruskin, John 1819-1900   **TCLC 63**
See also CA 114; 129; CDBLB 1832-1890; DLB 55, 163, 190; SATA 24

Russ, Joanna 1937-   **CLC 15**
See also CANR 11, 31, 65; DLB 8; MTCW 1

Russell, George William 1867-1935
See Baker, Jean H.
See also CA 104; 153; CDBLB 1890-1914; DAM POET

Russell, (Henry) Ken(neth Alfred) 1927- **CLC 16**
See also CA 105

Russell, William Martin 1947-   **CLC 60**
See also CA 164

Rutherford, Mark   **TCLC 25**
See also White, William Hale
See also DLB 18

Ruyslinck, Ward 1929-   **CLC 14**
See also Belser, Reimond Karel Maria de

Ryan, Cornelius (John) 1920-1974   **CLC 7**
See also CA 69-72; 53-56; CANR 38

Ryan, Michael 1946-   **CLC 65**
See also CA 49-52; DLBY 82

Ryan, Tim
See Dent, Lester

Rybakov, Anatoli (Naumovich) 1911-1998   **CLC 23, 53**
See also CA 126; 135; 172; SATA 79; SATA-Obit 108

Ryder, Jonathan
See Ludlum, Robert

Ryga, George 1932-1987 **CLC 14; DAC; DAM MST**
See also CA 101; 124; CANR 43; DLB 60

S. H.
See Hartmann, Sadakichi

S. S.
See Sassoon, Siegfried (Lorraine)

Saba, Umberto 1883-1957   **TCLC 33**
See also CA 144; CANR 79; DLB 114

Sabatini, Rafael 1875-1950   **TCLC 47**
See also CA 162

Sabato, Ernesto (R.) 1911- **CLC 10, 23; DAM MULT; HLC 2**
See also CA 97-100; CANR 32, 65; DLB 145; HW 1, 2; MTCW 1, 2

Sa-Carniero, Mario de 1890-1916 **TCLC 83**

Sacastru, Martin
See Bioy Casares, Adolfo

Sacastru, Martin
See Bioy Casares, Adolfo

Sacher-Masoch, Leopold von 1836(?)-1895   **NCLC 31**

Sachs, Marilyn (Stickle) 1927-   **CLC 35**
See also AAYA 2; CA 17-20R; CANR 13, 47; CLR 2; JRDA; MAICYA; SAAS 2; SATA 3, 68

Sachs, Nelly 1891-1970   **CLC 14, 98**
See also CA 17-18; 25-28R; CAP 2; MTCW 2

Sackler, Howard (Oliver) 1929-1982 **CLC 14**

See also CA 61-64; 108; CANR 30; DLB 7

Sacks, Oliver (Wolf) 1933-   **CLC 67**
See also CA 53-56; CANR 28, 50, 76; INT
CANR-28; MTCW 1, 2

Sadakichi
See Hartmann, Sadakichi

Sade, Donatien Alphonse Francois, Comte de
1740-1814   **NCLC 47**

Sadoff, Ira 1945-   **CLC 9**
See also CA 53-56; CANR 5, 21; DLB 120

Saetone
See Camus, Albert

Safire, William 1929-   **CLC 10**
See also CA 17-20R; CANR 31, 54

Sagan, Carl (Edward) 1934-1996 **CLC 30, 112**
See also AAYA 2; CA 25-28R; 155; CANR 11,
36, 74; MTCW 1, 2; SATA 58; SATA-Obit
94

Sagan, Francoise   **CLC 3, 6, 9, 17, 36**
See also Quoirez, Francoise
See also DLB 83; MTCW 2

Sahgal, Nayantara (Pandit) 1927-   **CLC 41**
See also CA 9-12R; CANR 11

Saint, H(arry) F. 1941-   **CLC 50**
See also CA 127

St. Aubin de Teran, Lisa 1953-
See Teran, Lisa St. Aubin de
See also CA 118; 126; INT 126

Saint Birgitta of Sweden c. 1303-1373 **C M L C**
24

Sainte-Beuve, Charles Augustin 1804-1869
NCLC 5

Saint-Exupery, Antoine (Jean Baptiste Marie
Roger) de 1900-1944 **TCLC 2, 56; DAM**
NOV;WLC
See also CA 108; 132; CLR 10; DLB 72;
MAICYA; MTCW 1, 2; SATA 20

St. John, David
See Hunt, E(verette) Howard, (Jr.)

Saint-John Perse
See Leger, (Marie-Rene Auguste) Alexis Saint-
Leger

Saintsbury, George (Edward Bateman) 1845-
1933   **TCLC 31**
See also CA 160; DLB 57, 149

Sait Faik   **TCLC 23**
See also Abasiyanik, Sait Faik

Saki   **TCLC 3; SSC 12**
See also Munro, H(ector) H(ugh)
See also MTCW 2

Sala, George Augustus   **NCLC 46**

Salama, Hannu 1936-   **CLC 18**

Salamanca, J(ack) R(ichard) 1922- **CLC 4, 15**
See also CA 25-28R

Salas, Floyd Francis 1931-
See also CA 119; CAAS 27; CANR 44, 75;
DAM MULT; DLB 82; HLC 2; HW 1, 2;
MTCW 2

Sale, J. Kirkpatrick
See Sale, Kirkpatrick

Sale, Kirkpatrick 1937-   **CLC 68**
See also CA 13-16R; CANR 10

Salinas, Luis Omar 1937-   **CLC 90; DAM**
MULT; HLC 2
See also CA 131; CANR 81; DLB 82; HW 1, 2

Salinas (y Serrano), Pedro 1891(?)-1951
TCLC 17
See also CA 117; DLB 134

Salinger, J(erome) D(avid) 1919- **CLC 1, 3, 8,**
12, 55, 56; DA; DAB; DAC; DAM MST,
NOV, POP; SSC 2, 28; WLC
See also AAYA 2; CA 5-8R; CANR 39; CDALB
1941-1968; CLR 18; DLB 2, 102, 173;

MAICYA; MTCW 1, 2; SATA 67

Salisbury, John
See Caute, (John) David

Salter, James 1925-   **CLC 7, 52, 59**
See also CA 73-76; DLB 130

Saltus, Edgar (Everton) 1855-1921   **TCLC 8**
See also CA 105; DLB 202

Saltykov, Mikhail Evgrafovich 1826-1889
NCLC 16

Samarakis, Antonis 1919-   **CLC 5**
See also CA 25-28R; CAAS 16; CANR 36

Sanchez, Florencio 1875-1910   **TCLC 37**
See also CA 153; HW 1

Sanchez, Luis Rafael 1936-   **CLC 23**
See also CA 128; DLB 145; HW 1

Sanchez, Sonia 1934-   **CLC 5, 116; BLC 3;**
DAM MULT; PC 9
See also BW 2, 3; CA 33-36R; CANR 24, 49,
74; CLR 18; DLB 41; DLBD 8;MAICYA;
MTCW 1, 2; SATA 22

Sand, George 1804-1876 **NCLC 2, 42, 57; DA;**
DAB; DAC; DAM MST, NOV; WLC
See also DLB 119, 192

Sandburg, Carl (August) 1878-1967 **CLC 1, 4,**
10, 15, 35; DA; DAB; DAC; DAM MST,
POET; PC 2; WLC
See also AAYA 24; CA 5-8R; 25-28R; CANR
35; CDALB 1865-1917; DLB 17, 54;
MAICYA; MTCW 1, 2; SATA 8

Sandburg, Charles
See Sandburg, Carl (August)

Sandburg, Charles A.
See Sandburg, Carl (August)

Sanders, (James) Ed(ward) 1939-   **CLC 53;**
DAM POET
See also CA 13-16R; CAAS 21; CANR 13, 44,
78; DLB 16

Sanders, Lawrence 1920-1998 **CLC 41; DAM**
POP
See also BEST 89:4; CA 81-84; 165; CANR
33, 62; MTCW 1

Sanders, Noah
See Blount, Roy (Alton), Jr.

Sanders, Winston P.
See Anderson, Poul (William)

Sandoz, Mari(e Susette) 1896-1966   **CLC 28**
See also CA 1-4R; 25-28R; CANR 17, 64; DLB
9, 212; MTCW 1, 2; SATA 5

Saner, Reg(inald Anthony) 1931-   **CLC 9**
See also CA 65-68

Sankara 788-820   **CMLC 32**

Sannazaro, Jacopo 1456(?)-1530   **LC 8**

Sansom, William 1912-1976 **CLC 2, 6; DAM**
NOV; SSC 21
See also CA 5-8R; 65-68; CANR 42; DLB 139;
MTCW 1

Santayana, George 1863-1952   **TCLC 40**
See also CA 115; DLB 54, 71; DLBD 13

Santiago, Danny   **CLC 33**
See also James, Daniel (Lewis)
See also DLB 122

Santmyer, Helen Hoover 1895-1986 **CLC 33**
See also CA 1-4R; 118; CANR 15, 33; DLBY
84; MTCW 1

Santoka, Taneda 1882-1940   **TCLC 72**

Santos, Bienvenido N(uqui) 1911-1996 **C L C**
22; DAM MULT
See also CA 101; 151; CANR 19, 46

Sapper   **TCLC 44**
See also McNeile, Herman Cyril

Sapphire
See Sapphire, Brenda

Sapphire, Brenda 1950-   **CLC 99**

Sappho fl. 6th cent. B.C.-   **CMLC 3; DAM**
POET; PC 5
See also DLB 176

Saramago, Jose 1922-   **CLC 119;HLCS 1**
See also CA 153

Sarduy, Severo 1937-1993 **CLC 6, 97; HLCS 1**
See also CA 89-92; 142; CANR 58, 81; DLB
113; HW 1, 2

Sargeson, Frank 1903-1982   **CLC 31**
See also CA 25-28R; 106; CANR 38, 79

Sarmiento, Domingo Faustino 1811-1888
See also HLCS 2

Sarmiento, Felix Ruben Garcia
See Dario, Ruben

Saro-Wiwa, Ken(ule Beeson) 1941-1995 **C L C**
114
See also BW 2; CA 142; 150; CANR 60; DLB
157

Saroyan, William 1908-1981 **CLC 1, 8, 10, 29,**
34, 56; DA; DAB; DAC; DAM DRAM,
MST, NOV; SSC 21; WLC
See also CA 5-8R; 103; CANR 30; CDALBS;
DLB 7, 9, 86; DLBY 81; MTCW 1, 2; SATA
23; SATA-Obit 24

Sarraute, Nathalie 1900- **CLC 1, 2, 4, 8, 10, 31,**
80
See also CA 9-12R; CANR 23, 66; DLB 83;
MTCW 1, 2

Sarton, (Eleanor) May 1912-1995 **CLC 4, 14,**
49, 91; DAM POET
See also CA 1-4R; 149; CANR 1, 34, 55; DLB
48; DLBY 81; INT CANR-34; MTCW 1, 2;
SATA 36; SATA-Obit 86

Sartre, Jean-Paul 1905-1980 **CLC 1, 4, 7, 9, 13,**
18, 24, 44, 50, 52; DA; DAB; DAC; DAM
DRAM, MST, NOV; DC 3; SSC 32; WLC
See also CA 9-12R; 97-100; CANR 21; DLB
72; MTCW 1, 2

Sassoon, Siegfried (Lorraine) 1886-1967 **C L C**
36; DAB; DAM MST, NOV, POET; PC 12
See also CA 104; 25-28R; CANR 36; DLB 20,
191; DLBD 18; MTCW 1, 2

Satterfield, Charles
See Pohl, Frederik

Saul, John (W. III) 1942- **CLC 46; DAM NOV,**
POP
See also AAYA 10; BEST 90:4; CA 81-84;
CANR 16, 40, 81; SATA 98

Saunders, Caleb
See Heinlein, Robert A(nson)

Saura (Atares), Carlos 1932-   **CLC 20**
See also CA 114; 131; CANR 79; HW 1

Sauser-Hall, Frederic 1887-1961   **CLC 18**
See also Cendrars, Blaise
See also CA 102; 93-96; CANR 36, 62; MTCW
1

Saussure, Ferdinand de 1857-1913 **TCLC 49**

Savage, Catharine
See Brosman, Catharine Savage

Savage, Thomas 1915-   **CLC 40**
See also CA 126; 132; CAAS 15; INT 132

Savan, Glenn 19(?)-   **CLC 50**

Sayers, Dorothy L(eigh) 1893-1957 **TCLC 2,**
15; DAM POP
See also CA 104; 119; CANR 60; CDBLB 1914-
1945; DLB 10, 36, 77, 100; MTCW 1, 2

Sayers, Valerie 1952-   **CLC 50, 122**
See also CA 134; CANR 61

Sayles, John (Thomas) 1950-   **CLC 7, 10, 14**
See also CA 57-60; CANR 41; DLB 44

Scammell, Michael 1935-   **CLC 34**
See also CA 156

Scannell, Vernon 1922-   **CLC 49**

See also CA 5-8R; CANR 8, 24, 57; DLB 27;
SATA 59

Scarlett, Susan
See Streatfeild, (Mary) Noel

Scarron
See Mikszath, Kalman

Schaeffer, Susan Fromberg 1941- **CLC 6, 11, 22**
See also CA 49-52; CANR 18, 65; DLB 28;
MTCW 1, 2; SATA 22

Schary, Jill
See Robinson, Jill

Schell, Jonathan 1943-　　　　　**CLC 35**
See also CA 73-76; CANR 12

Schelling, Friedrich Wilhelm Josephvon 1775-
1854　　　　　　　　　　　　**NCLC 30**
See also DLB 90

Schendel, Arthur van 1874-1946　**TCLC 56**

Scherer, Jean-Marie Maurice 1920-
See Rohmer, Eric
See also CA 110

Schevill, James (Erwin) 1920-　　　**CLC 7**
See also CA 5-8R; CAAS 12

Schiller, Friedrich 1759-1805　**NCLC 39, 69;
DAM DRAM**
See also DLB 94

Schisgal, Murray (Joseph) 1926-　　　**CLC 6**
See also CA 21-24R; CANR 48

Schlee, Ann 1934-　　　　　　　　**CLC 35**
See also CA 101; CANR 29; SATA 44; SATA-
Brief 36

Schlegel, August Wilhelmvon 1767-1845
NCLC 15
See also DLB 94

Schlegel, Friedrich 1772-1829　　**NCLC 45**
See also DLB 90

Schlegel, Johann Elias (von) 1719(?)-1749**L C
5**

Schlesinger, Arthur M(eier), Jr. 1917-**CLC 84**
See also AITN 1; CA 1-4R; CANR 1, 28, 58;
DLB 17; INT CANR-28; MTCW 1, 2; SATA
61

Schmidt, Arno (Otto) 1914-1979　　**CLC 56**
See also CA 128; 109; DLB 69

Schmitz, Aron Hector 1861-1928
See Svevo, Italo
See also CA 104; 122; MTCW 1

Schnackenberg, Gjertrud 1953-　　　**CLC 40**
See also CA 116; DLB 120

Schneider, Leonard Alfred 1925-1966
See Bruce, Lenny
See also CA 89-92

Schnitzler, Arthur 1862-1931**TCLC 4; SSC 15**
See also CA 104; DLB 81, 118

Schoenberg, Arnold 1874-1951　　**TCLC 75**
See also CA 109

Schonberg, Arnold
See Schoenberg, Arnold

Schopenhauer, Arthur 1788-1860　**NCLC 51**
See also DLB 90

Schor, Sandra (M.) 1932(?)-1990　　**CLC 65**
See also CA 132

Schorer, Mark 1908-1977　　　　　　**CLC 9**
See also CA 5-8R; 73-76; CANR 7; DLB 103

Schrader, Paul (Joseph) 1946-　　　**CLC 26**
See also CA 37-40R; CANR 41; DLB 44

Schreiner, Olive (Emilie Albertina) 1855-1920
TCLC 9
See also CA 105; 154; DLB 18, 156, 190

Schulberg, Budd (Wilson) 1914-　**CLC 7, 48**
See also CA 25-28R; CANR 19; DLB 6, 26,
28; DLBY 81

Schulz, Bruno 1892-1942**TCLC 5, 51; SSC 13**

See also CA 115; 123; MTCW 2

Schulz, Charles M(onroe) 1922-　　**CLC 12**
See also CA 9-12R; CANR 6; INT CANR-6;
SATA 10

Schumacher, E(rnst) F(riedrich) 1911-1977
CLC 80
See also CA 81-84; 73-76; CANR 34

Schuyler, James Marcus 1923-1991**CLC 5, 23;
DAM POET**
See also CA 101; 134; DLB 5, 169; INT 101

Schwartz, Delmore (David) 1913-1966**CLC 2,
4, 10, 45, 87; PC 8**
See also CA 17-18; 25-28R; CANR 35; CAP 2;
DLB 28, 48; MTCW 1, 2

Schwartz, Ernst
See Ozu, Yasujiro

Schwartz, John Burnham 1965-　　　**CLC 59**
See also CA 132

Schwartz, Lynne Sharon 1939-　　　**CLC 31**
See also CA 103; CANR 44; MTCW 2

Schwartz, Muriel A.
See Eliot, T(homas) S(tearns)

Schwarz-Bart, Andre 1928-　　　　**CLC 2, 4**
See also CA 89-92

Schwarz-Bart, Simone 1938-　　**CLC 7; BLCS**
See also BW 2; CA 97-100

**Schwitters, Kurt (Hermann Edward Karl
Julius)** 1887-1948　　　　　　**TCLC 95**
See also CA 158

Schwob, Marcel (Mayer Andre) 1867-1905
TCLC 20
See also CA 117; 168; DLB 123

Sciascia, Leonardo 1921-1989　**CLC 8, 9, 41**
See also CA 85-88; 130; CANR 35; DLB 177;
MTCW 1

Scoppettone, Sandra 1936-　　　　　**CLC 26**
See also AAYA 11; CA 5-8R; CANR 41, 73;
SATA 9, 92

Scorsese, Martin 1942-　　　　　**CLC 20, 89**
See also CA 110; 114; CANR 46

Scotland, Jay
See Jakes, John (William)

Scott, Duncan Campbell 1862-1947 **TCLC 6;
DAC**
See also CA 104; 153; DLB 92

Scott, Evelyn 1893-1963　　　　　　**CLC 43**
See also CA 104; 112; CANR 64; DLB 9, 48

Scott, F(rancis) R(eginald) 1899-1985**CLC 22**
See also CA 101; 114; DLB 88; INT 101

Scott, Frank
See Scott, F(rancis) R(eginald)

Scott, Joanna 1960-　　　　　　　　**CLC 50**
See also CA 126; CANR 53

Scott, Paul (Mark) 1920-1978　　**CLC 9, 60**
See also CA 81-84; 77-80; CANR 33; DLB 14,
207; MTCW 1

Scott, Sarah 1723-1795　　　　　　　**LC 44**
See also DLB 39

Scott, Walter 1771-1832　**NCLC 15, 69; DA;
DAB; DAC; DAM MST, NOV, POET; PC
13; SSC 32; WLC**
See also AAYA 22; CDBLB 1789-1832; DLB
93, 107, 116, 144, 159; YABC 2

Scribe, (Augustin) Eugene 1791-1861 **NCLC
16; DAM DRAM; DC 5**
See also DLB 192

Scrum, R.
See Crumb, R(obert)

Scudery, Madeleine de 1607-1701　　　**LC 2**

Scum
See Crumb, R(obert)

Scumbag, Little Bobby
See Crumb, R(obert)

Seabrook, John
See Hubbard, L(afayette) Ron(ald)

Sealy, I. Allan 1951-　　　　　　　**CLC 55**

Search, Alexander
See Pessoa, Fernando (Antonio Nogueira)

Sebastian, Lee
See Silverberg, Robert

Sebastian Owl
See Thompson, Hunter S(tockton)

Sebestyen, Ouida 1924-　　　　　　**CLC 30**
See also AAYA 8; CA 107; CANR 40; CLR 17;
JRDA; MAICYA; SAAS 10; SATA 39

Secundus, H. Scriblerus
See Fielding, Henry

Sedges, John
See Buck, Pearl S(ydenstricker)

Sedgwick, Catharine Maria 1789-1867**NCLC
19**
See also DLB 1, 74

Seelye, John (Douglas) 1931-　　　　　**CLC 7**
See also CA 97-100; CANR 70; INT 97-100

Seferiades, Giorgos Stylianou 1900-1971
See Seferis, George
See also CA 5-8R; 33-36R; CANR 5, 36;
MTCW 1

Seferis, George　　　　　　　　　**CLC 5, 11**
See also Seferiades, Giorgos Stylianou

Segal, Erich (Wolf) 1937-　**CLC 3, 10; DAM
POP**
See also BEST 89:1; CA 25-28R; CANR 20,
36, 65; DLBY 86; INT CANR-20; MTCW 1

Seger, Bob 1945-　　　　　　　　　**CLC 35**

Seghers, Anna　　　　　　　　　　　**CLC 7**
See also Radvanyi, Netty
See also DLB 69

Seidel, Frederick (Lewis) 1936-　　　**CLC 18**
See also CA 13-16R; CANR 8; DLBY 84

Seifert, Jaroslav 1901-1986　**CLC 34, 44, 93**
See also CA 127; MTCW 1, 2

Sei Shonagon c. 966-1017(?)　　　　**CMLC 6**

Sejour, Victor 1817-1874　　　　　　**DC 10**
See also DLB 50

Sejour Marcou et Ferrand, Juan Victor
See Sejour, Victor

Selby, Hubert, Jr. 1928-**CLC 1, 2, 4, 8; SSC 20**
See also CA 13-16R; CANR 33; DLB 2

Selzer, Richard 1928-　　　　　　　**CLC 74**
See also CA 65-68; CANR 14

Sembene, Ousmane
See Ousmane, Sembene

Senancour, Etienne Pivert de 1770-1846
NCLC 16
See also DLB 119

Sender, Ramon (Jose) 1902-1982**CLC 8; DAM
MULT; HLC 2**
See also CA 5-8R; 105; CANR 8; HW 1;
MTCW 1

Seneca, Lucius Annaeus c. 1-c. 65　**CMLC 6;
DAM DRAM; DC 5**
See also DLB 211

Senghor, Leopold Sedar 1906- **CLC 54; BLC
3; DAM MULT, POET; PC 25**
See also BW 2; CA 116; 125; CANR 47, 74;
MTCW 1, 2

Senna, Danzy 1970-　　　　　　　**CLC 119**
See also CA 169

Serling, (Edward) Rod(man) 1924-1975 **C L C
30**
See also AAYA 14; AITN 1; CA 162; 57-60;
DLB 26

Serna, Ramon Gomez de la
See Gomez de la Serna, Ramon

Serpieres

See Guillevic, (Eugene)
Service, Robert
See Service, Robert W(illiam)
See also DAB; DLB 92
Service, Robert W(illiam) 1874(?)-1958**TCLC 15; DA; DAC; DAM MST, POET; WLC**
See also Service, Robert
See also CA 115; 140; SATA 20
Seth, Vikram 1952- **CLC 43, 90;DAM MULT**
See also CA 121; 127; CANR 50, 74; DLB 120; INT 127; MTCW 2
Seton, Cynthia Propper 1926-1982 **CLC 27**
See also CA 5-8R; 108; CANR 7
Seton, Ernest (Evan) Thompson 1860-1946 **TCLC 31**
See also CA 109; CLR 59; DLB 92; DLBD 13; JRDA; SATA 18
Seton-Thompson, Ernest
See Seton, Ernest (Evan) Thompson
Settle, Mary Lee 1918- **CLC 19, 61**
See also CA 89-92; CAAS 1; CANR 44; DLB 6; INT 89-92
Seuphor, Michel
See Arp, Jean
Sevigne, Marie (de Rabutin-Chantal) Marquise de 1626-1696 **LC 11**
Sewall, Samuel 1652-1730 **LC 38**
See also DLB 24
Sexton, Anne (Harvey) 1928-1974**CLC 2, 4, 6, 8, 10, 15, 53; DA; DAB; DAC; DAM MST, POET; PC 2; WLC**
See also CA 1-4R; 53-56; CABS 2; CANR 3, 36; CDALB 1941-1968; DLB 5, 169; MTCW 1, 2; SATA 10
Shaara, Jeff 1952- **CLC 119**
See also CA 163
Shaara, Michael (Joseph, Jr.) 1929-1988**CLC 15; DAM POP**
See also AITN 1; CA 102; 125; CANR 52; DLBY 83
Shackleton, C. C.
See Aldiss, Brian W(ilson)
Shacochis, Bob **CLC 39**
See also Shacochis, Robert G.
Shacochis, Robert G. 1951-
See Shacochis, Bob
See also CA 119; 124; INT 124
Shaffer, Anthony (Joshua) 1926- **CLC 19; DAM DRAM**
See also CA 110; 116; DLB 13
Shaffer, Peter (Levin) 1926-**CLC 5, 14, 18, 37, 60; DAB; DAM DRAM, MST; DC 7**
See also CA 25-28R; CANR 25, 47, 74; CDBLB 1960 to Present; DLB 13; MTCW 1, 2
Shakey, Bernard
See Young, Neil
Shalamov, Varlam (Tikhonovich) 1907(?)-1982 **CLC 18**
See also CA 129; 105
Shamlu, Ahmad 1925- **CLC 10**
Shammas, Anton 1951- **CLC 55**
Shange, Ntozake 1948-**CLC 8, 25, 38, 74; BLC 3; DAM DRAM, MULT; DC 3**
See also AAYA 9; BW 2; CA 85-88; CABS 3; CANR 27, 48, 74; DLB 38; MTCW 1, 2
Shanley, John Patrick 1950- **CLC 75**
See also CA 128; 133
Shapcott, Thomas W(illiam) 1935- **CLC 38**
See also CA 69-72; CANR 49
Shapiro, Jane **CLC 76**
Shapiro, Karl (Jay) 1913-**CLC 4, 8, 15, 53; PC 25**
See also CA 1-4R; CAAS 6; CANR 1, 36, 66;

DLB 48; MTCW 1, 2
Sharp, William 1855-1905 **TCLC 39**
See also CA 160; DLB 156
Sharpe, Thomas Ridley 1928-
See Sharpe, Tom
See also CA 114; 122; INT 122
Sharpe, Tom **CLC 36**
See also Sharpe, Thomas Ridley
See also DLB 14
Shaw, Bernard **TCLC 45**
See also Shaw, George Bernard
See also BW 1; MTCW 2
Shaw, G. Bernard
See Shaw, George Bernard
Shaw, George Bernard 1856-1950**TCLC 3, 9, 21; DA; DAB; DAC; DAM DRAM, MST; WLC**
See also Shaw, Bernard
See also CA 104; 128; CDBLB 1914-1945; DLB 10, 57, 190; MTCW 1, 2
Shaw, Henry Wheeler 1818-1885 **NCLC 15**
See also DLB 11
Shaw, Irwin 1913-1984 **CLC 7, 23, 34; DAM DRAM, POP**
See also AITN 1; CA 13-16R; 112; CANR 21; CDALB 1941-1968; DLB 6, 102; DLBY 84; MTCW 1, 21
Shaw, Robert 1927-1978 **CLC 5**
See also AITN 1; CA 1-4R; 81-84; CANR 4; DLB 13, 14
Shaw, T. E.
See Lawrence, T(homas) E(dward)
Shawn, Wallace 1943- **CLC 41**
See also CA 112
Shea, Lisa 1953- **CLC 86**
See also CA 147
Sheed, Wilfrid (John Joseph) 1930-**CLC 2, 4, 10, 53**
See also CA 65-68; CANR 30, 66; DLB 6; MTCW 1, 2
Sheldon, Alice Hastings Bradley 1915(?)-1987
See Tiptree, James, Jr.
See also CA 108; 122; CANR 34; INT 108; MTCW 1
Sheldon, John 1917-1994
See Bloch, Robert (Albert)
See also CA 179; CAAE 179
Shelley, Mary Wollstonecraft (Godwin) 1797-1851**NCLC 14, 59; DA; DAB; DAC; DAM MST, NOV; WLC**
See also AAYA 20; CDBLB 1789-1832; DLB 110, 116, 159, 178; SATA 29
Shelley, Percy Bysshe 1792-1822 **NCLC 18; DA; DAB; DAC; DAM MST, POET; PC 14; WLC**
See also CDBLB 1789-1832; DLB 96, 110, 158
Shepard, Jim 1956- **CLC 36**
See also CA 137; CANR 59; SATA 90
Shepard, Lucius 1947- **CLC 34**
See also CA 128; 141; CANR 81
Shepard, Sam 1943-**CLC 4, 6, 17, 34, 41, 44; DAM DRAM; DC 5**
See also AAYA 1; CA 69-72; CABS 3; CANR 22; DLB 7, 212; MTCW 1, 2
Shepherd, Michael
See Ludlum, Robert
Sherburne, Zoa (Lillian Morin) 1912-1995 **CLC 30**
See also AAYA 13; CA 1-4R; 176; CANR 3, 37; MAICYA; SAAS 18; SATA 3
Sheridan, Frances 1724-1766 **LC 7**
See also DLB 39, 84
Sheridan, Richard Brinsley 1751-1816**N C L C**

5; **DA; DAB; DAC; DAM DRAM, MST; DC 1; WLC**
See also CDBLB 1660-1789; DLB 89
Sherman, Jonathan Marc **CLC 55**
Sherman, Martin 1941(?)- **CLC 19**
See also CA 116; 123
Sherwin, Judith Johnson
See Johnson, Judith (Emlyn)
Sherwood, Frances 1940- **CLC 81**
See also CA 146
Sherwood, Robert E(mmet) 1896-1955**T C L C 3; DAM DRAM**
See also CA 104; 153; DLB 7, 26
Shestov, Lev 1866-1938 **TCLC 56**
Shevchenko, Taras 1814-1861 **NCLC 54**
Shiel, M(atthew) P(hipps) 1865-1947**TCLC 8**
See also Holmes, Gordon
See also CA 106; 160; DLB 153; MTCW 2
Shields, Carol 1935- **CLC 91, 113;DAC**
See also CA 81-84; CANR 51, 74; MTCW 2
Shields, David 1956- **CLC 97**
See also CA 124; CANR 48
Shiga, Naoya 1883-1971 **CLC 33;SSC 23**
See also CA 101; 33-36R; DLB 180
Shikibu, Murasaki c. 978-c. 1014 **CMLC 1**
Shilts, Randy 1951-1994 **CLC 85**
See also AAYA 19; CA 115; 127; 144; CANR 45; INT 127; MTCW 2
Shimazaki, Haruki 1872-1943
See Shimazaki Toson
See also CA 105; 134
Shimazaki Toson 1872-1943 **TCLC 5**
See also Shimazaki, Haruki
See also DLB 180
Sholokhov, Mikhail (Aleksandrovich) 1905-1984 **CLC 7, 15**
See also CA 101; 112; MTCW 1, 2; SATA-Obit 36
Shone, Patric
See Hanley, James
Shreve, Susan Richards 1939- **CLC 23**
See also CA 49-52; CAAS 5; CANR 5, 38, 69; MAICYA; SATA 46, 95; SATA-Brief 41
Shue, Larry 1946-1985**CLC 52;DAM DRAM**
See also CA 145; 117
Shu-Jen, Chou 1881-1936
See Lu Hsun
See also CA 104
Shulman, Alix Kates 1932- **CLC 2,10**
See also CA 29-32R; CANR 43; SATA 7
Shuster, Joe 1914- **CLC 21**
Shute, Nevil **CLC 30**
See also Norway, Nevil Shute
See also MTCW 2
Shuttle, Penelope (Diane) 1947- **CLC 7**
See also CA 93-96; CANR 39; DLB 14, 40
Sidney, Mary 1561-1621 **LC 19, 39**
Sidney, Sir Philip 1554-1586 **LC 19, 39; DA; DAB; DAC; DAM MST, POET**
See also CDBLB Before 1660; DLB 167
Siegel, Jerome 1914-1996 **CLC 21**
See also CA 116; 169; 151
Siegel, Jerry
See Siegel, Jerome
Sienkiewicz, Henryk (Adam Alexander Pius) 1846-1916 **TCLC 3**
See also CA 104; 134
Sierra, Gregorio Martinez
See Martinez Sierra, Gregorio
Sierra, Maria (de la O'LeJarraga) Martinez
See Martinez Sierra, Maria (de la O'LeJarraga)
Sigal, Clancy 1926- **CLC 7**
See also CA 1-4R

Sigourney, Lydia Howard (Huntley) 1791-1865
   NCLC **21**
   See also DLB 1, 42, 73

Siguenza y Gongora, Carlos de 1645-1700L C
   8; HLCS 2

Sigurjonsson, Johann 1880-1919   **TCLC 27**
   See also CA 170

Sikelianos, Angelos 1884-1951   **TCLC 39**

Silkin, Jon 1930-   **CLC 2, 6, 43**
   See also CA 5-8R; CAAS 5; DLB 27

Silko, Leslie (Marmon) 1948-CLC 23, 74, 114;
   DA; DAC; DAM MST, MULT, POP;
   WLCS
   See also AAYA 14; CA 115; 122; CANR 45,
   65; DLB 143, 175; MTCW 2; NNAL

Sillanpaa, Frans Eemil   **CLC 19**
   See also CA 129; 93-96; MTCW 1

Sillitoe, Alan 1928-   **CLC 1, 3, 6, 10, 19, 57**
   See also AITN 1; CA 9-12R; CAAS 2; CANR
   8, 26, 55; CDBLB 1960 to Present; DLB 14,
   139; MTCW 1, 2; SATA 61

Silone, Ignazio 1900-1978   **CLC 4**
   See also CA 25-28; 81-84; CANR 34; CAP 2;
   MTCW 1

Silver, Joan Micklin 1935-   **CLC 20**
   See also CA 114; 121; INT 121

Silver, Nicholas
   See Faust, Frederick (Schiller)

Silverberg, Robert 1935- CLC 7;DAM POP
   See also Jarvis, E. K.
   See also AAYA 24; CA 1-4R; CAAS 3; CANR
   1, 20, 36; CLR 59; DLB 8; INT CANR-20;
   MAICYA; MTCW 1, 2; SATA 13, 91; SATA-
   Essay 104

Silverstein, Alvin 1933-   **CLC 17**
   See also CA 49-52; CANR 2; CLR 25; JRDA;
   MAICYA; SATA 8, 69

Silverstein, Virginia B(arbara Opshelor) 1937-
   CLC 17
   See also CA 49-52; CANR 2; CLR 25; JRDA;
   MAICYA; SATA 8, 69

Sim, Georges
   See Simenon, Georges (Jacques Christian)

Simak, Clifford D(onald) 1904-1988CLC 1, 55
   See also CA 1-4R; 125; CANR 1, 35; DLB 8;
   MTCW 1; SATA-Obit 56

Simenon, Georges (Jacques Christian) 1903-
   1989   **CLC 1, 2, 3, 8, 18, 47; DAM POP**
   See also CA 85-88; 129; CANR 35; DLB 72;
   DLBY 89; MTCW 1, 2

Simic, Charles 1938-   **CLC 6, 9, 22, 49, 68;**
   DAM POET
   See also CA 29-32R; CAAS 4; CANR 12, 33,
   52, 61; DLB 105; MTCW 2

Simmel, Georg 1858-1918   **TCLC 64**
   See also CA 157

Simmons, Charles (Paul) 1924-   **CLC 57**
   See also CA 89-92; INT 89-92

Simmons, Dan 1948-   **CLC 44;DAM POP**
   See also AAYA 16; CA 138; CANR 53, 81

Simmons, James (Stewart Alexander) 1933-
   CLC 43
   See also CA 105; CAAS 21; DLB 40

Simms, William Gilmore 1806-1870 NCLC **3**
   See also DLB 3, 30, 59, 73

Simon, Carly 1945-   **CLC 26**
   See also CA 105

Simon, Claude 1913-1984   **CLC 4, 9, 15, 39;**
   DAM NOV
   See also CA 89-92; CANR 33; DLB 83; MTCW
   1

Simon, (Marvin) Neil 1927-CLC 6, 11, 31, 39,
   70; DAM DRAM

   See also AITN 1; CA 21-24R; CANR 26, 54;
   DLB 7; MTCW 1, 2

Simon, Paul (Frederick) 1941(?)-   **CLC 17**
   See also CA 116; 153

Simonon, Paul 1956(?)-   **CLC 30**

Simpson, Harriette
   See Arnow, Harriette (Louisa) Simpson

Simpson, Louis (Aston Marantz) 1923-CLC 4,
   7, 9, 32; DAM POET
   See also CA 1-4R; CAAS 4; CANR 1, 61; DLB
   5; MTCW 1, 2

Simpson, Mona (Elizabeth) 1957-   **CLC 44**
   See also CA 122; 135; CANR 68

Simpson, N(orman) F(rederick) 1919-CLC 29
   See also CA 13-16R; DLB 13

Sinclair, Andrew (Annandale) 1935- CLC 2,
   14
   See also CA 9-12R; CAAS 5; CANR 14, 38;
   DLB 14; MTCW 1

Sinclair, Emil
   See Hesse, Hermann

Sinclair, Iain 1943-   **CLC 76**
   See also CA 132; CANR 81

Sinclair, Iain MacGregor
   See Sinclair, Iain

Sinclair, Irene
   See Griffith, D(avid Lewelyn) W(ark)

Sinclair, Mary Amelia St. Clair 1865(?)-1946
   See Sinclair, May
   See also CA 104

Sinclair, May 1863-1946   **TCLC 3, 11**
   See also Sinclair, Mary Amelia St. Clair
   See also CA 166; DLB 36, 135

Sinclair, Roy
   See Griffith, D(avid Lewelyn) W(ark)

Sinclair, Upton (Beall) 1878-1968 CLC 1, 11,
   15, 63; DA; DAB; DAC; DAM MST, NOV;
   WLC
   See also CA 5-8R; 25-28R; CANR 7; CDALB
   1929-1941; DLB 9; INT CANR-7; MTCW
   1, 2; SATA 9

Singer, Isaac
   See Singer, Isaac Bashevis

Singer, Isaac Bashevis 1904-1991CLC 1, 3, 6,
   9, 11, 15, 23, 38, 69, 111; DA; DAB; DAC;
   DAM MST, NOV; SSC 3; WLC
   See also AITN 1, 2; CA 1-4R; 134; CANR 1,
   39; CDALB 1941-1968; CLR 1; DLB 6, 28,
   52; DLBY 91; JRDA; MAICYA; MTCW 1,
   2; SATA 3, 27; SATA-Obit 68

Singer, Israel Joshua 1893-1944   **TCLC 33**
   See also CA 169

Singh, Khushwant 1915-   **CLC 11**
   See also CA 9-12R; CAAS 9; CANR 6

Singleton, Ann
   See Benedict, Ruth (Fulton)

Sinjohn, John
   See Galsworthy, John

Sinyavsky, Andrei (Donatevich) 1925-1997
   CLC 8
   See also CA 85-88; 159

Sirin, V.
   See Nabokov, Vladimir (Vladimirovich)

Sissman, L(ouis) E(dward) 1928-1976CLC 9,
   18
   See also CA 21-24R; 65-68; CANR 13; DLB 5

Sisson, C(harles) H(ubert) 1914-   **CLC 8**
   See also CA 1-4R; CAAS 3; CANR 3, 48; DLB
   27

Sitwell, Dame Edith 1887-1964 CLC 2, 9, 67;
   DAM POET; PC 3
   See also CA 9-12R; CANR 35; CDBLB 1945-
   1960; DLB 20; MTCW 1, 2

Siwaarmill, H. P.
   See Sharp, William

Sjoewall, Maj 1935-   **CLC 7**
   See also CA 65-68; CANR 73

Sjowall, Maj
   See Sjoewall, Maj

Skelton, John 1463-1529   **PC 25**

Skelton, Robin 1925-1997   **CLC 13**
   See also AITN 2; CA 5-8R; 160; CAAS 5;
   CANR 28; DLB 27, 53

Skolimowski, Jerzy 1938-   **CLC 20**
   See also CA 128

Skram, Amalie (Bertha) 1847-1905 TCLC 25
   See also CA 165

Skvorecky, Josef (Vaclav) 1924-   **CLC 15, 39,**
   69; DAC; DAM NOV
   See also CA 61-64; CAAS 1; CANR 10, 34,
   63; MTCW 1, 2

Slade, Bernard   **CLC 11, 46**
   See also Newbound, Bernard Slade
   See also CAAS 9; DLB 53

Slaughter, Carolyn 1946-   **CLC 56**
   See also CA 85-88

Slaughter, Frank G(ill) 1908-   **CLC 29**
   See also AITN 2; CA 5-8R; CANR 5; INT
   CANR-5

Slavitt, David R(ytman) 1935-   CLC 5, 14
   See also CA 21-24R; CAAS 3; CANR 41; DLB
   5, 6

Slesinger, Tess 1905-1945   **TCLC 10**
   See also CA 107; DLB 102

Slessor, Kenneth 1901-1971   **CLC 14**
   See also CA 102; 89-92

Slowacki, Juliusz 1809-1849   **NCLC 15**

Smart, Christopher 1722-1771   LC 3; **DAM**
   POET; PC 13
   See also DLB 109

Smart, Elizabeth 1913-1986   **CLC 54**
   See also CA 81-84; 118; DLB 88

Smiley, Jane (Graves) 1949-CLC 53, 76; DAM
   POP
   See also CA 104; CANR 30, 50, 74; INT CANR-
   30

Smith, A(rthur) J(ames) M(arshall) 1902-1980
   CLC 15; DAC
   See also CA 1-4R; 102; CANR 4; DLB 88

Smith, Adam 1723-1790   **LC 36**
   See also DLB 104

Smith, Alexander 1829-1867   **NCLC 59**
   See also DLB 32, 55

Smith, Anna Deavere 1950-   **CLC 86**
   See also CA 133

Smith, Betty (Wehner) 1896-1972   **CLC 19**
   See also CA 5-8R; 33-36R; DLBY 82; SATA 6

Smith, Charlotte (Turner) 1749-1806 N C L C
   23
   See also DLB 39, 109

Smith, Clark Ashton 1893-1961   **CLC 43**
   See also CA 143; CANR 81; MTCW 2

Smith, Dave   **CLC 22, 42**
   See also Smith, David (Jeddie)
   See also CAAS 7; DLB 5

Smith, David (Jeddie) 1942-
   See Smith, Dave
   See also CA 49-52; CANR 1, 59; DAM POET

Smith, Florence Margaret 1902-1971
   See Smith, Stevie
   See also CA 17-18; 29-32R; CANR 35; CAP 2;
   DAM POET; MTCW 1, 2

Smith, Iain Crichton 1928-1998   **CLC 64**
   See also CA 21-24R; 171; DLB 40, 139

Smith, John 1580(?)-1631   **LC 9**
   See also DLB 24, 30

Smith, Johnston
   See Crane, Stephen (Townley)
Smith, Joseph, Jr. 1805-1844   **NCLC 53**
Smith, Lee 1944-   **CLC 25, 73**
   See also CA 114; 119; CANR 46; DLB 143;
   DLBY 83; INT 119
Smith, Martin
   See Smith, Martin Cruz
Smith, Martin Cruz 1942-   **CLC 25; DAM**
   MULT, POP
   See also BEST 89:4; CA 85-88; CANR 6, 23,
   43, 65; INT CANR-23; MTCW 2; NNAL
Smith, Mary-Ann Tirone 1944-   **CLC 39**
   See also CA 118; 136
Smith, Patti 1946-   **CLC 12**
   See also CA 93-96; CANR 63
Smith, Pauline (Urmson) 1882-1959**TCLC 25**
Smith, Rosamond
   See Oates, Joyce Carol
Smith, Sheila Kaye
   See Kaye-Smith, Sheila
Smith, Stevie   **CLC 3, 8, 25, 44; PC 12**
   See also Smith, Florence Margaret
   See also DLB 20; MTCW 2
Smith, Wilbur (Addison) 1933-   **CLC 33**
   See also CA 13-16R; CANR 7, 46, 66; MTCW
   1, 2
Smith, William Jay 1918-   **CLC 6**
   See also CA 5-8R; CANR 44; DLB 5; MAICYA;
   SAAS 22; SATA 2, 68
Smith, Woodrow Wilson
   See Kuttner, Henry
Smolenskin, Peretz 1842-1885   **NCLC 30**
Smollett, Tobias (George) 1721-1771**LC 2, 46**
   See also CDBLB 1660-1789; DLB 39, 104
Snodgrass, W(illiam) D(e Witt) 1926-**CLC 2,**
   6, 10, 18, 68; DAM POET
   See also CA 1-4R; CANR 6, 36, 65; DLB 5;
   MTCW 1, 2
Snow, C(harles) P(ercy) 1905-1980 **CLC 1, 4,**
   6, 9, 13, 19; DAM NOV
   See also CA 5-8R; 101; CANR 28; CDBLB
   1945-1960; DLB 15, 77; DLBD 17; MTCW
   1, 2
Snow, Frances Compton
   See Adams, Henry (Brooks)
Snyder, Gary (Sherman) 1930-**CLC 1, 2, 5, 9,**
   32, 120; DAM POET; PC 21
   See also CA 17-20R; CANR 30, 60; DLB 5,
   16, 165, 212; MTCW 2
Snyder, Zilpha Keatley 1927-   **CLC 17**
   See also AAYA 15; CA 9-12R; CANR 38; CLR
   31; JRDA; MAICYA; SAAS 2; SATA 1, 28,
   75
Soares, Bernardo
   See Pessoa, Fernando (Antonio Nogueira)
Sobh, A.
   See Shamlu, Ahmad
Sobol, Joshua   **CLC 60**
Socrates 469B.C.-399B.C.   **CMLC 27**
Soderberg, Hjalmar 1869-1941   **TCLC 39**
Sodergran, Edith (Irene)
   See Soedergran, Edith (Irene)
Soedergran, Edith (Irene) 1892-1923 **T C L C**
   31
Softly, Edgar
   See Lovecraft, H(oward) P(hillips)
Softly, Edward
   See Lovecraft, H(oward) P(hillips)
Sokolov, Raymond 1941-   **CLC 7**
   See also CA 85-88
Solo, Jay
   See Ellison, Harlan (Jay)

Sologub, Fyodor   **TCLC 9**
   See also Teternikov, Fyodor Kuzmich
Solomons, Ikey Esquir
   See Thackeray, William Makepeace
Solomos, Dionysios 1798-1857   **NCLC 15**
Solwoska, Mara
   See French, Marilyn
Solzhenitsyn, Aleksandr I(sayevich) 1918-
   CLC 1, 2, 4, 7, 9, 10, 18, 26, 34, 78; DA;
   DAB; DAC; DAM MST, NOV; SSC
   32;WLC
   See also AITN 1; CA 69-72; CANR 40, 65;
   MTCW 1, 2
Somers, Jane
   See Lessing, Doris (May)
Somerville, Edith 1858-1949   **TCLC 51**
   See also DLB 135
Somerville & Ross
   See Martin, Violet Florence; Somerville, Edith
Sommer, Scott 1951-   **CLC 25**
   See also CA 106
Sondheim, Stephen (Joshua) 1930- **CLC 30,**
   39; DAM DRAM
   See also AAYA 11; CA 103; CANR 47, 68
Song, Cathy 1955-   **PC 21**
   See also CA 154; DLB 169
Sontag, Susan 1933-**CLC 1, 2, 10, 13, 31, 105;**
   DAM POP
   See also CA 17-20R; CANR 25, 51, 74; DLB
   2, 67; MTCW 1, 2
Sophocles 496(?)B.C.-406(?)B.C.   **CMLC 2;**
   DA; DAB; DAC; DAM DRAM, MST; DC
   1; WLCS
   See also DLB 176
Sordello 1189-1269   **CMLC 15**
Sorel, Georges 1847-1922   **TCLC 91**
   See also CA 118
Sorel, Julia
   See Drexler, Rosalyn
Sorrentino, Gilbert 1929-**CLC 3, 7, 14, 22, 40**
   See also CA 77-80; CANR 14, 33; DLB 5, 173;
   DLBY 80; INT CANR-14
Soto, Gary 1952-   **CLC 32, 80; DAM MULT;**
   HLC 2
   See also AAYA 10; CA 119; 125; CANR 50,
   74; CLR 38; DLB 82; HW 1, 2; INT 125;
   JRDA; MTCW 2; SATA 80
Soupault, Philippe 1897-1990   **CLC 68**
   See also CA 116; 147; 131
Souster, (Holmes) Raymond 1921-**CLC 5, 14;**
   DAC; DAM POET
   See also CA 13-16R; CAAS 14; CANR 13, 29,
   53; DLB 88; SATA 63
Southern, Terry 1924(?)-1995   **CLC 7**
   See also CA 1-4R; 150; CANR 1, 55; DLB 2
Southey, Robert 1774-1843   **NCLC 8**
   See also DLB 93, 107, 142; SATA 54
Southworth, Emma Dorothy Eliza Nevitte
   1819-1899   **NCLC 26**
Souza, Ernest
   See Scott, Evelyn
Soyinka, Wole 1934-**CLC 3, 5, 14, 36, 44; BLC**
   3; DA; DAB; DAC; DAM DRAM, MST,
   MULT; DC 2; WLC
   See also BW 2, 3; CA 13-16R; CANR 27, 39,
   82; DLB 125; MTCW 1, 2
Spackman, W(illiam) M(ode) 1905-1990**C L C**
   46
   See also CA 81-84; 132
Spacks, Barry (Bernard) 1931-   **CLC 14**
   See also CA 154; CANR 33; DLB 105
Spanidou, Irini 1946-   **CLC 44**
Spark, Muriel (Sarah) 1918-**CLC 2, 3, 5, 8, 13,**

   18, 40, 94; DAB; DAC; DAM MST, NOV;
   SSC 10
   See also CA 5-8R; CANR 12, 36, 76; CDBLB
   1945-1960; DLB 15, 139; INT CANR-12;
   MTCW 1, 2
Spaulding, Douglas
   See Bradbury, Ray (Douglas)
Spaulding, Leonard
   See Bradbury, Ray (Douglas)
Spence, J. A. D.
   See Eliot, T(homas) S(tearns)
Spencer, Elizabeth 1921-   .   **CLC 22**
   See also CA 13-16R; CANR 32, 65; DLB 6;
   MTCW 1; SATA 14
Spencer, Leonard G.
   See Silverberg, Robert
Spencer, Scott 1945-   **CLC 30**
   See also CA 113; CANR 51; DLBY 86
Spender, Stephen (Harold) 1909-1995**CLC 1,**
   2, 5, 10, 41, 91; DAM POET
   See also CA 9-12R; 149; CANR 31, 54; CDBLB
   1945-1960; DLB 20; MTCW 1, 2
Spengler, Oswald (Arnold Gottfried) 1880-1936
   TCLC 25
   See also CA 118
Spenser, Edmund 1552(?)-1599**LC 5, 39; DA;**
   DAB; DAC; DAM MST, POET; PC 8;
   WLC
   See also CDBLB Before 1660; DLB 167
Spicer, Jack 1925-1965 **CLC 8, 18, 72; DAM**
   POET
   See also CA 85-88; DLB 5, 16, 193
Spiegelman, Art 1948-   **CLC 76**
   See also AAYA 10; CA 125; CANR 41, 55, 74;
   MTCW 2; SATA 109
Spielberg, Peter 1929-   **CLC 6**
   See also CA 5-8R; CANR 4, 48; DLBY 81
Spielberg, Steven 1947-   **CLC 20**
   See also AAYA 8, 24; CA 77-80; CANR 32;
   SATA 32
Spillane, Frank Morrison 1918-
   See Spillane, Mickey
   See also CA 25-28R; CANR 28, 63; MTCW 1,
   2; SATA 66
Spillane, Mickey   **CLC 3, 13**
   See also Spillane, Frank Morrison
   See also MTCW 2
Spinoza, Benedictus de 1632-1677   **LC 9**
Spinrad, Norman (Richard) 1940-   **CLC 46**
   See also CA 37-40R; CAAS 19; CANR 20; DLB
   8; INT CANR-20
Spitteler, Carl (Friedrich Georg) 1845-1924
   TCLC 12
   See also CA 109; DLB 129
Spivack, Kathleen (Romola Drucker) 1938-
   CLC 6
   See also CA 49-52
Spoto, Donald 1941-   **CLC 39**
   See also CA 65-68; CANR 11, 57
Springsteen, Bruce (F.) 1949-   **CLC 17**
   See also CA 111
Spurling, Hilary 1940-   **CLC 34**
   See also CA 104; CANR 25, 52
Spyker, John Howland
   See Elman, Richard (Martin)
Squires, (James) Radcliffe 1917-1993**CLC 51**
   See also CA 1-4R; 140; CANR 6, 21
Srivastava, Dhanpat Rai 1880(?)-1936
   See Premchand
   See also CA 118
Stacy, Donald
   See Pohl, Frederik
Stael, Germaine de 1766-1817

See Stael-Holstein, Anne Louise Germaine Necker Baronn
See also DLB 119

Stael-Holstein, Anne Louise Germaine Necker Baronn 1766-1817 **NCLC 3**
See also Stael, Germaine de
See also DLB 192

Stafford, Jean 1915-1979 **CLC 4, 7, 19, 68; SSC 26**
See also CA 1-4R; 85-88; CANR 3, 65; DLB 2, 173; MTCW 1, 2; SATA-Obit 22

Stafford, William (Edgar) 1914-1993 **CLC 4, 7, 29; DAM POET**
See also CA 5-8R; 142; CAAS 3; CANR 5, 22; DLB 5, 206; INT CANR-22

Stagnelius, Eric Johan 1793-1823 **NCLC 61**

Staines, Trevor
See Brunner, John (Kilian Houston)

Stairs, Gordon
See Austin, Mary (Hunter)

Stairs, Gordon
See Austin, Mary (Hunter)

Stalin, Joseph 1879-1953 **TCLC 92**

Stannard, Martin 1947- **CLC 44**
See also CA 142; DLB 155

Stanton, Elizabeth Cady 1815-1902 **TCLC 73**
See also CA 171; DLB 79

Stanton, Maura 1946- **CLC 9**
See also CA 89-92; CANR 15; DLB 120

Stanton, Schuyler
See Baum, L(yman) Frank

Stapledon, (William) Olaf 1886-1950 **TCLC 22**
See also CA 111; 162; DLB 15

Starbuck, George (Edwin) 1931-1996 **CLC 53; DAM POET**
See also CA 21-24R; 153; CANR 23

Stark, Richard
See Westlake, Donald E(dwin)

Staunton, Schuyler
See Baum, L(yman) Frank

Stead, Christina (Ellen) 1902-1983 **CLC 2, 5, 8, 32, 80**
See also CA 13-16R; 109; CANR 33, 40; MTCW 1, 2

Stead, William Thomas 1849-1912 **TCLC 48**
See also CA 167

Steele, Richard 1672-1729 **LC 18**
See also CDBLB 1660-1789; DLB 84, 101

Steele, Timothy (Reid) 1948- **CLC 45**
See also CA 93-96; CANR 16, 50; DLB 120

Steffens, (Joseph) Lincoln 1866-1936 **TCLC 20**
See also CA 117

Stegner, Wallace (Earle) 1909-1993 **CLC 9, 49, 81; DAM NOV; SSC 27**
See also AITN 1; BEST 90:3; CA 1-4R; 141; CAAS 9; CANR 1, 21, 46; DLB 9, 206; DLBY 93; MTCW 1, 2

Stein, Gertrude 1874-1946 **TCLC 1, 6, 28, 48; DA; DAB; DAC; DAM MST, NOV, POET; PC 18; WLC**
See also CA 104; 132; CDALB 1917-1929; DLB 4, 54, 86; DLBD 15; MTCW 1, 2

Steinbeck, John (Ernst) 1902-1968 **CLC 1, 5, 9, 13, 21, 34, 45, 75; DA; DAB; DAC; DAM DRAM, MST, NOV; SSC 11; WLC**
See also AAYA 12; CA 1-4R; 25-28R; CANR 1, 35; CDALB 1929-1941; DLB 7, 9, 212; DLBD 2; MTCW 1, 2; SATA 9

Steinem, Gloria 1934- **CLC 63**
See also CA 53-56; CANR 28, 51; MTCW 1, 2

Steiner, George 1929- **CLC 24; DAM NOV**

See also CA 73-76; CANR 31, 67; DLB 67; MTCW 1, 2; SATA 62

Steiner, K. Leslie
See Delany, Samuel R(ay, Jr.)

Steiner, Rudolf 1861-1925 **TCLC 13**
See also CA 107

Stendhal 1783-1842 **NCLC 23, 46; DA; DAB; DAC; DAM MST, NOV; SSC 27; WLC**
See also DLB 119

Stephen, Adeline Virginia
See Woolf, (Adeline) Virginia

Stephen, Sir Leslie 1832-1904 **TCLC 23**
See also CA 123; DLB 57, 144, 190

Stephen, Sir Leslie
See Stephen, Sir Leslie

Stephen, Virginia
See Woolf, (Adeline) Virginia

Stephens, James 1882(?)-1950 **TCLC 4**
See also CA 104; DLB 19, 153, 162

Stephens, Reed
See Donaldson, Stephen R.

Steptoe, Lydia
See Barnes, Djuna

Sterchi, Beat 1949- **CLC 65**

Sterling, Brett
See Bradbury, Ray (Douglas); Hamilton, Edmond

Sterling, Bruce 1954- **CLC 72**
See also CA 119; CANR 44

Sterling, George 1869-1926 **TCLC 20**
See also CA 117; 165; DLB 54

Stern, Gerald 1925- **CLC 40, 100**
See also CA 81-84; CANR 28; DLB 105

Stern, Richard (Gustave) 1928- **CLC 4, 39**
See also CA 1-4R; CANR 1, 25, 52; DLBY 87; INT CANR-25

Sternberg, Josef von 1894-1969 **CLC 20**
See also CA 81-84

Sterne, Laurence 1713-1768 **LC 2, 48; DA; DAB; DAC; DAM MST, NOV; WLC**
See also CDBLB 1660-1789; DLB 39

Sternheim, (William Adolf) Carl 1878-1942 **TCLC 8**
See also CA 105; DLB 56, 118

Stevens, Mark 1951- **CLC 34**
See also CA 122

Stevens, Wallace 1879-1955 **TCLC 3, 12, 45; DA; DAB; DAC; DAM MST, POET; PC 6; WLC**
See also CA 104; 124; CDALB 1929-1941; DLB 54; MTCW 1, 2

Stevenson, Anne (Katharine) 1933- **CLC 7, 33**
See also CA 17-20R; CAAS 9; CANR 9, 33; DLB 40; MTCW 1

Stevenson, Robert Louis (Balfour) 1850-1894 **NCLC 5, 14, 63; DA; DAB; DAC; DAM MST, NOV; SSC 11; WLC**
See also AAYA 24; CDBLB 1890-1914; CLR 10, 11; DLB 18, 57, 141, 156, 174; DLBD 13; JRDA; MAICYA; SATA 100; YABC 2

Stewart, J(ohn) I(nnes) M(ackintosh) 1906-1994 **CLC 7, 14, 32**
See also CA 85-88; 147; CAAS 3; CANR 47; MTCW 1, 2

Stewart, Mary (Florence Elinor) 1916- **CLC 7, 35, 117; DAB**
See also AAYA 29; CA 1-4R; CANR 1, 59; SATA 12

Stewart, Mary Rainbow
See Stewart, Mary (Florence Elinor)

Stifle, June
See Campbell, Maria

Stifter, Adalbert 1805-1868 **NCLC 41; SSC 28**

See also DLB 133

Still, James 1906- **CLC 49**
See also CA 65-68; CAAS 17; CANR 10, 26; DLB 9; SATA 29

Sting 1951-
See Sumner, Gordon Matthew
See also CA 167

Stirling, Arthur
See Sinclair, Upton (Beall)

Stitt, Milan 1941- **CLC 29**
See also CA 69-72

Stockton, Francis Richard 1834-1902
See Stockton, Frank R.
See also CA 108; 137; MAICYA; SATA 44

Stockton, Frank R. **TCLC 47**
See also Stockton, Francis Richard
See also DLB 42, 74; DLBD 13; SATA-Brief 32

Stoddard, Charles
See Kuttner, Henry

Stoker, Abraham 1847-1912
See Stoker, Bram
See also CA 105; 150; DA; DAC; DAM MST, NOV; SATA 29

Stoker, Bram 1847-1912 **TCLC 8; DAB; WLC**
See also Stoker, Abraham
See also AAYA 23; CDBLB 1890-1914; DLB 36, 70, 178

Stolz, Mary (Slattery) 1920- **CLC 12**
See also AAYA 8; AITN 1; CA 5-8R; CANR 13, 41; JRDA; MAICYA; SAAS 3; SATA 10, 71

Stone, Irving 1903-1989 **CLC 7; DAM POP**
See also AITN 1; CA 1-4R; 129; CAAS 3; CANR 1, 23; INT CANR-23; MTCW 1, 2; SATA 3; SATA-Obit 64

Stone, Oliver (William) 1946- **CLC 73**
See also AAYA 15; CA 110; CANR 55

Stone, Robert (Anthony) 1937- **CLC 5, 23, 42**
See also CA 85-88; CANR 23, 66; DLB 152; INT CANR-23; MTCW 1

Stone, Zachary
See Follett, Ken(neth Martin)

Stoppard, Tom 1937- **CLC 1, 3, 4, 5, 8, 15, 29, 34, 63, 91; DA; DAB; DAC; DAM DRAM, MST; DC 6; WLC**
See also CA 81-84; CANR 39, 67; CDBLB 1960 to Present; DLB 13; DLBY 85; MTCW 1, 2

Storey, David (Malcolm) 1933- **CLC 2, 4, 5, 8; DAM DRAM**
See also CA 81-84; CANR 36; DLB 13, 14, 207; MTCW 1

Storm, Hyemeyohsts 1935- **CLC 3; DAM MULT**
See also CA 81-84; CANR 45; NNAL

Storm, Theodor 1817-1888 **SSC 27**

Storm, (Hans) Theodor (Woldsen) 1817-1888 **NCLC 1; SSC 27**
See also DLB 129

Storni, Alfonsina 1892-1938 **TCLC 5; DAM MULT; HLC 2**
See also CA 104; 131; HW 1

Stoughton, William 1631-1701 **LC 38**
See also DLB 24

Stout, Rex (Todhunter) 1886-1975 **CLC 3**
See also AITN 2; CA 61-64; CANR 71

Stow, (Julian) Randolph 1935- **CLC 23, 48**
See also CA 13-16R; CANR 33; MTCW 1

Stowe, Harriet (Elizabeth) Beecher 1811-1896 **NCLC 3, 50; DA; DAB; DAC; DAM MST, NOV; WLC**
See also CDALB 1865-1917; DLB 1, 12, 42,

74, 189; JRDA; MAICYA; YABC 1

Strachey, (Giles) Lytton 1880-1932 **TCLC 12**
See also CA 110; 178; DLB 149; DLBD 10;
MTCW 2

Strand, Mark 1934- **CLC 6, 18, 41, 71; DAM
POET**
See also CA 21-24R; CANR 40, 65; DLB 5;
SATA 41

Straub, Peter (Francis) 1943- **CLC 28, 107;
DAM POP**
See also BEST 89:1; CA 85-88; CANR 28, 65;
DLBY 84; MTCW 1, 2

Strauss, Botho 1944- **CLC 22**
See also CA 157; DLB 124

Streatfeild, (Mary) Noel 1895(?)-1986 **CLC 21**
See also CA 81-84; 120; CANR 31; CLR 17;
DLB 160; MAICYA; SATA 20; SATA-Obit
48

Stribling, T(homas) S(igismund) 1881-1965
CLC 23
See also CA 107; DLB 9

Strindberg, (Johan) August 1849-1912 **TCLC
1, 8, 21, 47; DA; DAB; DAC; DAM DRAM,
MST; WLC**
See also CA 104; 135; MTCW 2

Stringer, Arthur 1874-1950 **TCLC 37**
See also CA 161; DLB 92

Stringer, David
See Roberts, Keith (John Kingston)

Stroheim, Erich von 1885-1957 **TCLC 71**

Strugatskii, Arkadii (Natanovich) 1925-1991
CLC 27
See also CA 106; 135

Strugatskii, Boris (Natanovich) 1933- **CLC 27**
See also CA 106

Strummer, Joe 1953(?)- **CLC 30**

Strunk, William, Jr. 1869-1946 **TCLC 92**
See also CA 118; 164

Stryk, Lucien 1924- **PC 27**
See also CA 13-16R; CANR 10, 28, 55

Stuart, Don A.
See Campbell, John W(ood, Jr.)

Stuart, Ian
See MacLean, Alistair (Stuart)

Stuart, Jesse (Hilton) 1906-1984 **CLC 1, 8, 11,
14, 34; SSC 31**
See also CA 5-8R; 112; CANR 31; DLB 9, 48,
102; DLBY 84; SATA 2; SATA-Obit 36

Sturgeon, Theodore (Hamilton) 1918-1985
CLC 22, 39
See also Queen, Ellery
See also CA 81-84; 116; CANR 32; DLB 8;
DLBY 85; MTCW 1, 2

Sturges, Preston 1898-1959 **TCLC 48**
See also CA 114; 149; DLB 26

Styron, William 1925- **CLC 1, 3, 5, 11, 15, 60;
DAM NOV, POP; SSC 25**
See also BEST 90:4; CA 5-8R; CANR 6, 33,
74; CDALB 1968-1988; DLB 2, 143; DLBY
80; INT CANR-6; MTCW 1, 2

Su, Chien 1884-1918
See Su Man-shu
See also CA 123

Suarez Lynch, B.
See Bioy Casares, Adolfo; Borges, Jorge Luis

Suassuna, Ariano Vilar 1927-
See also CA 178; HLCS 1; HW 2

Suckow, Ruth 1892-1960 **SSC 18**
See also CA 113; DLB 9, 102

Sudermann, Hermann 1857-1928 **TCLC 15**
See also CA 107; DLB 118

Sue, Eugene 1804-1857 **NCLC 1**
See also DLB 119

Sueskind, Patrick 1949- **CLC 44**
See also Suskind, Patrick

Sukenick, Ronald 1932- **CLC 3, 4, 6, 48**
See also CA 25-28R; CAAS 8; CANR 32; DLB
173; DLBY 81

Suknaski, Andrew 1942- **CLC 19**
See also CA 101; DLB 53

Sullivan, Vernon
See Vian, Boris

Sully Prudhomme 1839-1907 **TCLC 31**

Su Man-shu **TCLC 24**
See also Su, Chien

Summerforest, Ivy B.
See Kirkup, James

Summers, Andrew James 1942- **CLC 26**

Summers, Andy
See Summers, Andrew James

Summers, Hollis (Spurgeon, Jr.) 1916- **CLC 10**
See also CA 5-8R; CANR 3; DLB 6

**Summers, (Alphonsus Joseph-Mary Augustus)
Montague** 1880-1948 **TCLC 16**
See also CA 118; 163

Sumner, Gordon Matthew **CLC 26**
See also Sting

Surtees, Robert Smith 1803-1864 **NCLC 14**
See also DLB 21

Susann, Jacqueline 1921-1974 **CLC 3**
See also AITN 1; CA 65-68; 53-56; MTCW 1,
2

Su Shih 1036-1101 **CMLC 15**

Suskind, Patrick
See Sueskind, Patrick
See also CA 145

Sutcliff, Rosemary 1920-1992 **CLC 26; DAB;
DAC; DAM MST, POP**
See also AAYA 10; CA 5-8R; 139; CANR 37;
CLR 1, 37; JRDA; MAICYA; SATA 6, 44,
78; SATA-Obit 73

Sutro, Alfred 1863-1933 **TCLC 6**
See also CA 105; DLB 10

Sutton, Henry
See Slavitt, David R(ytman)

Svevo, Italo 1861-1928 **TCLC 2, 35; SSC 25**
See also Schmitz, Aron Hector

Swados, Elizabeth (A.) 1951- **CLC 12**
See also CA 97-100; CANR 49; INT 97-100

Swados, Harvey 1920-1972 **CLC 5**
See also CA 5-8R; 37-40R; CANR 6; DLB 2

Swan, Gladys 1934- **CLC 69**
See also CA 101; CANR 17, 39

Swarthout, Glendon (Fred) 1918-1992 **CLC 35**
See also CA 1-4R; 139; CANR 1, 47; SATA 26

Sweet, Sarah C.
See Jewett, (Theodora) Sarah Orne

Swenson, May 1919-1989 **CLC 4, 14, 61, 106;
DA; DAB; DAC; DAM MST, POET; PC
14**
See also CA 5-8R; 130; CANR 36, 61; DLB 5;
MTCW 1, 2; SATA 15

Swift, Augustus
See Lovecraft, H(oward) P(hillips)

Swift, Graham (Colin) 1949- **CLC 41, 88**
See also CA 117; 122; CANR 46, 71; DLB 194;
MTCW 2

Swift, Jonathan 1667-1745 **LC 1, 42; DA;
DAB; DAC; DAM MST, NOV, POET; PC
9; WLC**
See also CDBLB 1660-1789; CLR 53; DLB 39,
95, 101; SATA 19

Swinburne, Algernon Charles 1837-1909
**TCLC 8, 36; DA; DAB; DAC; DAM MST,
POET; PC 24; WLC**
See also CA 105; 140; CDBLB 1832-1890;
DLB 35, 57

Swinfen, Ann **CLC 34**

Swinnerton, Frank Arthur 1884-1982 **CLC 31**
See also CA 108; DLB 34

Swithen, John
See King, Stephen (Edwin)

Sylvia
See Ashton-Warner, Sylvia (Constance)

Symmes, Robert Edward
See Duncan, Robert (Edward)

Symonds, John Addington 1840-1893 **NCLC
34**
See also DLB 57, 144

Symons, Arthur 1865-1945 **TCLC 11**
See also CA 107; DLB 19, 57, 149

Symons, Julian (Gustave) 1912-1994 **CLC 2,
14, 32**
See also CA 49-52; 147; CAAS 3; CANR 3,
33, 59; DLB 87, 155; DLBY 92; MTCW 1

Synge, (Edmund) J(ohn) M(illington) 1871-
1909 **TCLC 6, 37; DAM DRAM; DC 2**
See also CA 104; 141; CDBLB 1890-1914;
DLB 10, 19

Syruc, J.
See Milosz, Czeslaw

Szirtes, George 1948- **CLC 46**
See also CA 109; CANR 27, 61

Szymborska, Wislawa 1923- **CLC 99**
See also CA 154; DLBY 96; MTCW 2

T. O., Nik
See Annensky, Innokenty (Fyodorovich)

Tabori, George 1914- **CLC 19**
See also CA 49-52; CANR 4, 69

Tagore, Rabindranath 1861-1941 **TCLC 3, 53;
DAM DRAM, POET; PC 8**
See also CA 104; 120; MTCW 1, 2

Taine, Hippolyte Adolphe 1828-1893 **NCLC
15**

Talese, Gay 1932- **CLC 37**
See also AITN 1; CA 1-4R; CANR 9, 58; DLB
185; INT CANR-9; MTCW 1, 2

Tallent, Elizabeth (Ann) 1954- **CLC 45**
See also CA 117; CANR 72; DLB 130

Tally, Ted 1952- **CLC 42**
See also CA 120; 124; INT 124

Talvik, Heiti 1904-1947 **TCLC 87**

Tamayo y Baus, Manuel 1829-1898 **NCLC 1**

Tammsaare, A(nton) H(ansen) 1878-1940
TCLC 27
See also CA 164

Tam'si, Tchicaya U
See Tchicaya, Gerald Felix

Tan, Amy (Ruth) 1952- **CLC 59, 120; DAM
MULT, NOV, POP**
See also AAYA 9; BEST 89:3; CA 136; CANR
54; CDALBS; DLB 173; MTCW 2; SATA
75

Tandem, Felix
See Spitteler, Carl (Friedrich Georg)

Tanizaki, Jun'ichiro 1886-1965 **CLC 8, 14, 28;
SSC 21**
See also CA 93-96; 25-28R; DLB 180; MTCW
2

Tanner, William
See Amis, Kingsley (William)

Tao Lao
See Storni, Alfonsina

Tarassoff, Lev
See Troyat, Henri

Tarbell, Ida M(inerva) 1857-1944 **TCLC 40**
See also CA 122; DLB 47

Tarkington, (Newton) Booth 1869-1946 **TCLC
9**

See also CA 110; 143; DLB 9, 102; MTCW 2; SATA 17

Tarkovsky, Andrei (Arsenyevich) 1932-1986 **CLC 75**
See also CA 127

Tartt, Donna 1964(?)- **CLC 76**
See also CA 142

Tasso, Torquato 1544-1595 **LC 5**

Tate, (John Orley) Allen 1899-1979**CLC 2, 4, 6, 9, 11, 14, 24**
See also CA 5-8R; 85-88; CANR 32; DLB 4, 45, 63; DLBD 17; MTCW 1, 2

Tate, Ellalice
See Hibbert, Eleanor Alice Burford

Tate, James (Vincent) 1943- **CLC 2, 6, 25**
See also CA 21-24R; CANR 29, 57; DLB 5, 169

Tavel, Ronald 1940- **CLC 6**
See also CA 21-24R; CANR 33

Taylor, C(ecil) P(hilip) 1929-1981 **CLC 27**
See also CA 25-28R; 105; CANR 47

Taylor, Edward 1642(?)-1729 **LC 11; DA; DAB; DAC; DAM MST, POET**
See also DLB 24

Taylor, Eleanor Ross 1920- **CLC 5**
See also CA 81-84; CANR 70

Taylor, Elizabeth 1912-1975 **CLC 2, 4, 29**
See also CA 13-16R; CANR 9, 70; DLB 139; MTCW 1; SATA 13

Taylor, Frederick Winslow 1856-1915 **TCLC 76**

Taylor, Henry (Splawn) 1942- **CLC 44**
See also CA 33-36R; CAAS 7; CANR 31; DLB 5

Taylor, Kamala (Purnaiya) 1924-
See Markandaya, Kamala
See also CA 77-80

Taylor, Mildred D. **CLC 21**
See also AAYA 10; BW 1; CA 85-88; CANR 25; CLR 9, 59; DLB 52; JRDA; MAICYA; SAAS 5; SATA 15, 70

Taylor, Peter (Hillsman) 1917-1994**CLC 1, 4, 18, 37, 44, 50, 71; SSC 10**
See also CA 13-16R; 147; CANR 9, 50; DLBY 81, 94; INT CANR-9; MTCW 1, 2

Taylor, Robert Lewis 1912-1998 **CLC 14**
See also CA 1-4R; 170; CANR 3, 64; SATA 10

Tchekhov, Anton
See Chekhov, Anton (Pavlovich)

Tchicaya, Gerald Felix 1931-1988 **CLC 101**
See also CA 129; 125; CANR 81

Tchicaya U Tam'si
See Tchicaya, Gerald Felix

Teasdale, Sara 1884-1933 **TCLC 4**
See also CA 104; 163; DLB 45; SATA 32

Tegner, Esaias 1782-1846 **NCLC 2**

Teilhard de Chardin, (Marie Joseph) Pierre 1881-1955 **TCLC 9**
See also CA 105

Temple, Ann
See Mortimer, Penelope (Ruth)

Tennant, Emma (Christina) 1937-**CLC 13, 52**
See also CA 65-68; CAAS 9; CANR 10, 38, 59; DLB 14

Tenneshaw, S. M.
See Silverberg, Robert

Tennyson, Alfred 1809-1892 **NCLC 30, 65; DA; DAB; DAC; DAM MST, POET; PC 6; WLC**
See also CDBLB 1832-1890; DLB 32

Teran, Lisa St. Aubin de **CLC 36**
See also St. Aubin de Teran, Lisa

Terence c. 184B.C.-c. 159B.C.**CMLC 14; DC 7**

See also DLB 211

Teresa de Jesus, St. 1515-1582 **LC 18**

Terkel, Louis 1912-
See Terkel, Studs
See also CA 57-60; CANR 18, 45, 67; MTCW 1, 2

Terkel, Studs **CLC 38**
See also Terkel, Louis
See also AITN 1; MTCW 2

Terry, C. V.
See Slaughter, Frank G(ill)

Terry, Megan 1932- **CLC 19**
See also CA 77-80; CABS 3; CANR 43; DLB 7

Tertullian c. 155-c. 245 **CMLC 29**

Tertz, Abram
See Sinyavsky, Andrei (Donatevich)

Tesich, Steve 1943(?)-1996 **CLC 40, 69**
See also CA 105; 152; DLBY 83

Tesla, Nikola 1856-1943 **TCLC 88**

Teternikov, Fyodor Kuzmich 1863-1927
See Sologub, Fyodor
See also CA 104

Tevis, Walter 1928-1984 **CLC 42**
See also CA 113

Tey, Josephine **TCLC 14**
See also Mackintosh,Elizabeth
See also DLB 77

Thackeray, William Makepeace 1811-1863 **NCLC 5, 14, 22, 43; DA; DAB; DAC; DAM MST, NOV; WLC**
See also CDBLB 1832-1890; DLB 21, 55, 159, 163; SATA 23

Thakura, Ravindranatha
See Tagore, Rabindranath

Tharoor, Shashi 1956- **CLC 70**
See also CA 141

Thelwell, Michael Miles 1939- **CLC 22**
See also BW 2; CA 101

Theobald, Lewis, Jr.
See Lovecraft, H(oward) P(hillips)

Theodorescu, Ion N. 1880-1967
See Arghezi, Tudor
See also CA 116

Theriault, Yves 1915-1983 **CLC 79; DAC; DAM MST**
See also CA 102; DLB 88

Theroux, Alexander (Louis) 1939- **CLC 2, 25**
See also CA 85-88; CANR 20, 63

Theroux, Paul (Edward) 1941- **CLC 5, 8, 11, 15, 28, 46; DAM POP**
See also AAYA 28; BEST 89:4; CA 33-36R; CANR 20, 45, 74; CDALBS; DLB 2; MTCW 1, 2; SATA 44, 109

Thesen, Sharon 1946- **CLC 56**
See also CA 163

Thevenin, Denis
See Duhamel, Georges

Thibault, Jacques Anatole Francois 1844-1924
See France, Anatole
See also CA 106; 127; DAM NOV; MTCW 1, 2

Thiele, Colin (Milton) 1920- **CLC 17**
See also CA 29-32R; CANR 12, 28, 53; CLR 27; MAICYA; SAAS 2; SATA 14, 72

Thomas, Audrey (Callahan) 1935-**CLC 7, 13, 37, 107; SSC 20**
See also AITN 2; CA 21-24R; CAAS 19; CANR 36, 58; DLB 60; MTCW 1

Thomas, D(onald) M(ichael) 1935- **CLC 13, 22, 31**
See also CA 61-64; CAAS 11; CANR 17, 45, 75; CDBLB 1960 to Present; DLB 40, 207; INT CANR-17; MTCW 1, 2

Thomas, Dylan (Marlais) 1914-1953**TCLC 1, 8, 45; DA; DAB; DAC; DAM DRAM, MST, POET; PC 2; SSC 3; WLC**
See also CA 104; 120; CANR 65; CDBLB 1945-1960; DLB 13, 20, 139; MTCW 1, 2; SATA 60

Thomas, (Philip) Edward 1878-1917 **TCLC 10; DAM POET**
See also CA 106; 153; DLB 98

Thomas, Joyce Carol 1938- **CLC 35**
See also AAYA 12; BW 2, 3; CA 113; 116; CANR 48; CLR 19; DLB 33; INT 116; JRDA; MAICYA; MTCW 1, 2; SAAS 7; SATA 40, 78

Thomas, Lewis 1913-1993 **CLC 35**
See also CA 85-88; 143; CANR 38, 60; MTCW 1, 2

Thomas, M. Carey 1857-1935 **TCLC 89**

Thomas, Paul
See Mann, (Paul) Thomas

Thomas, Piri 1928- **CLC 17;HLCS 2**
See also CA 73-76; HW 1

Thomas, R(onald) S(tuart) 1913- **CLC 6, 13, 48; DAB; DAM POET**
See also CA 89-92; CAAS 4; CANR 30; CDBLB 1960 to Present; DLB 27; MTCW 1

Thomas, Ross (Elmore) 1926-1995 **CLC 39**
See also CA 33-36R; 150; CANR 22, 63

Thompson, Francis Clegg
See Mencken, H(enry) L(ouis)

Thompson, Francis Joseph 1859-1907**TCLC 4**
See also CA 104; CDBLB 1890-1914; DLB 19

Thompson, Hunter S(tockton) 1939- **CLC 9, 17, 40, 104; DAM POP**
See also BEST 89:1; CA 17-20R; CANR 23, 46, 74, 77; DLB 185; MTCW 1, 2

Thompson, James Myers
See Thompson, Jim (Myers)

Thompson, Jim(Myers) 1906-1977(?)**CLC 69**
See also CA 140

Thompson, Judith **CLC 39**

Thomson, James 1700-1748 **LC 16, 29, 40; DAM POET**
See also DLB 95

Thomson, James 1834-1882 **NCLC 18;DAM POET**
See also DLB 35

Thoreau, Henry David 1817-1862**NCLC 7, 21, 61; DA; DAB; DAC; DAM MST; WLC**
See also CDALB 1640-1865; DLB 1

Thornton, Hall
See Silverberg, Robert

Thucydides c.455B.C.-399B.C. **CMLC 17**
See also DLB 176

Thurber, James (Grover) 1894-1961 **CLC 5, 11, 25; DA; DAB; DAC; DAM DRAM, MST, NOV; SSC 1**
See also CA 73-76; CANR 17, 39; CDALB 1929-1941; DLB 4, 11, 22, 102; MAICYA; MTCW 1, 2; SATA 13

Thurman, Wallace (Henry) 1902-1934**TCLC 6; BLC 3; DAM MULT**
See also BW 1, 3; CA 104; 124; CANR 81; DLB 51

Ticheburn, Cheviot
See Ainsworth, William Harrison

Tieck, (Johann) Ludwig 1773-1853 **NCLC 5, 46; SSC 31**
See also DLB 90

Tiger, Derry
See Ellison, Harlan (Jay)

Tilghman, Christopher 1948(?)- **CLC 65**
See also CA 159

Tillinghast, Richard(Williford) 1940-**CLC 29**
See also CA 29-32R; CAAS 23; CANR 26, 51

Timrod, Henry 1828-1867　　　　**NCLC 25**
See also DLB 3

Tindall, Gillian(Elizabeth) 1938-　　**CLC 7**
See also CA 21-24R; CANR 11, 65

Tiptree, James, Jr. 　　　　**CLC 48, 50**
See also Sheldon, Alice Hastings Bradley
See also DLB 8

Titmarsh, Michael Angelo
See Thackeray, William Makepeace

**Tocqueville, Alexis (Charles Henri Maurice
Clerel, Comte) de** 1805-1859
　　　　　　　　　NCLC 7, 63

Tolkien, J(ohn) R(onald) R(euel) 1892-1973
　　　　**CLC 1, 2, 3, 8, 12, 38; DA; DAB; DAC;
DAM MST, NOV, POP; WLC**
See also AAYA 10; AITN 1; CA 17-18; 45-48;
CANR 36; CAP 2; CDBLB 1914-1945; CLR
56; DLB 15, 160; JRDA; MAICYA; MTCW
1, 2; SATA 2, 32, 100; SATA-Obit 24

Toller, Ernst 1893-1939　　　　**TCLC 10**
See also CA 107; DLB 124

Tolson, M. B.
See Tolson, Melvin B(eaunorus)

Tolson, Melvin B(eaunorus) 1898(?)-1966
　　　　CLC 36, 105; BLC 3; DAM MULT, POET
See also BW 1, 3; CA 124; 89-92; CANR 80;
DLB 48, 76

Tolstoi, Aleksei Nikolaevich
See Tolstoy, Alexey Nikolaevich

Tolstoy, Alexey Nikolaevich 1882-1945**T C L C
18**
See also CA 107; 158

Tolstoy, Count Leo
See Tolstoy, Leo (Nikolaevich)

Tolstoy, Leo (Nikolaevich) 1828-1910**TCLC 4,
11, 17, 28, 44, 79; DA; DAB; DAC; DAM
MST, NOV; SSC 9, 30; WLC**
See also CA 104; 123; SATA 26

Tomasi di Lampedusa, Giuseppe 1896-1957
See Lampedusa, Giuseppe (Tomasi) di
See also CA 111

Tomlin, Lily 　　　　　　**CLC 17**
See also Tomlin, Mary Jean

Tomlin, Mary Jean 1939(?)-
See Tomlin, Lily
See also CA 117

Tomlinson, (Alfred) Charles 1927-**CLC 2, 4, 6,
13, 45; DAM POET; PC 17**
See also CA 5-8R; CANR 33; DLB 40

Tomlinson, H(enry) M(ajor) 1873-1958**TCLC
71**
See also CA 118; 161; DLB 36, 100, 195

Tonson, Jacob
See Bennett, (Enoch) Arnold

Toole, John Kennedy 1937-1969　**CLC 19, 64**
See also CA 104; DLBY 81; MTCW 2

Toomer, Jean 1894-1967**CLC 1, 4, 13, 22; BLC
3; DAM MULT; PC 7; SSC 1; WLCS**
See also BW 1; CA 85-88; CDALB 1917-1929;
DLB 45, 51; MTCW 1, 2

Torley, Luke
See Blish, James (Benjamin)

Tornimparte, Alessandra
See Ginzburg, Natalia

Torre, Raoul della
See Mencken, H(enry) L(ouis)

Torrey, E(dwin) Fuller 1937-　　**CLC 34**
See also CA 119; CANR 71

Torsvan, Ben Traven
See Traven, B.

Torsvan, Benno Traven

See Traven, B.

Torsvan, Berick Traven
See Traven, B.

Torsvan, Berwick Traven
See Traven, B.

Torsvan, Bruno Traven
See Traven, B.

Torsvan, Traven
See Traven, B.

Tournier, Michel (Edouard) 1924-**CLC 6, 23,
36, 95**
See also CA 49-52; CANR 3, 36, 74; DLB 83;
MTCW 1, 2; SATA 23

Tournimparte, Alessandra
See Ginzburg, Natalia

Towers, Ivar
See Kornbluth, C(yril) M.

Towne, Robert (Burton) 1936(?)-　　**CLC 87**
See also CA 108; DLB 44

Townsend, Sue 　　　　　　**CLC 61**
See also Townsend, Susan Elaine
See also AAYA 28; SATA 55, 93; SATA-Brief
48

Townsend, Susan Elaine 1946-
See Townsend, Sue
See also CA 119; 127; CANR 65; DAB; DAC;
DAM MST

Townshend, Peter (Dennis Blandford) 1945-
　　　　CLC 17, 42
See also CA 107

Tozzi, Federigo 1883-1920　　　　**TCLC 31**
See also CA 160

Traill, Catharine Parr 1802-1899　**NCLC 31**
See also DLB 99

Trakl, Georg 1887-1914　　　　**TCLC 5;PC 20**
See also CA 104; 165; MTCW 2

Transtroemer, Tomas (Goesta) 1931-**CLC 52,
65; DAM POET**
See also CA 117; 129; CAAS 17

Transtromer, Tomas Gosta
See Transtroemer, Tomas (Goesta)

Traven, B. (?)-1969　　　　**CLC 8, 11**
See also CA 19-20; 25-28R; CAP 2; DLB 9,
56; MTCW 1

Treitel, Jonathan 1959-　　　　**CLC 70**

Tremain, Rose 1943-　　　　**CLC 42**
See also CA 97-100; CANR 44; DLB 14

Tremblay, Michel 1942-　**CLC 29, 102; DAC;
DAM MST**
See also CA 116; 128; DLB 60; MTCW 1, 2

Trevanian 　　　　　　**CLC 29**
See also Whitaker, Rod(ney)

Trevor, Glen
See Hilton, James

Trevor, William 1928-**CLC 7, 9, 14, 25, 71, 116;
SSC 21**
See also Cox, William Trevor
See also DLB 14, 139; MTCW 2

Trifonov, Yuri (Valentinovich) 1925-1981
　　　　CLC 45
See also CA 126; 103; MTCW 1

Trilling, Lionel 1905-1975　　**CLC 9, 11, 24**
See also CA 9-12R; 61-64; CANR 10; DLB 28,
63; INT CANR-10; MTCW 1, 2

Trimball, W. H.
See Mencken, H(enry) L(ouis)

Tristan
See Gomez de la Serna, Ramon

Tristram
See Housman, A(lfred) E(dward)

Trogdon, William (Lewis) 1939-
See Heat-Moon, William Least
See also CA 115; 119; CANR 47; INT 119

Trollope, Anthony 1815-1882**NCLC 6, 33; DA;
DAB; DAC; DAM MST, NOV; SSC 28;
WLC**
See also CDBLB 1832-1890; DLB 21, 57, 159;
SATA 22

Trollope, Frances 1779-1863　　　**NCLC 30**
See also DLB 21, 166

Trotsky, Leon 1879-1940　　　　**TCLC 22**
See also CA 118; 167

Trotter (Cockburn), Catharine 1679-1749**L C
8**
See also DLB 84

Trout, Kilgore
See Farmer, Philip Jose

Trow, George W. S. 1943-　　　　**CLC 52**
See also CA 126

Troyat, Henri 1911-　　　　　　**CLC 23**
See also CA 45-48; CANR 2, 33, 67; MTCW 1

Trudeau, G(arretson) B(eekman) 1948-
See Trudeau, Garry B.
See also CA 81-84; CANR 31; SATA 35

Trudeau, Garry B. 　　　　　　**CLC 12**
See also Trudeau, G(arretson) B(eekman)
See also AAYA 10; AITN 2

Truffaut, Francois 1932-1984　**CLC 20, 101**
See also CA 81-84; 113; CANR 34

Trumbo, Dalton 1905-1976　　　　**CLC 19**
See also CA 21-24R; 69-72; CANR 10; DLB
26

Trumbull, John 1750-1831　　　**NCLC 30**
See also DLB 31

Trundlett, Helen B.
See Eliot, T(homas) S(tearns)

Tryon, Thomas 1926-1991　**CLC 3, 11;DAM
POP**
See also AITN 1; CA 29-32R; 135; CANR 32,
77; MTCW 1

Tryon, Tom
See Tryon, Thomas

Ts'ao Hsueh-ch'in 1715(?)-1763　　　**LC 1**

Tsushima, Shuji 1909-1948
See Dazai Osamu
See also CA 107

Tsvetaeva (Efron), Marina (Ivanovna) 1892-
1941　　　　**TCLC 7, 35; PC 14**
See also CA 104; 128; CANR 73; MTCW 1, 2

Tuck, Lily 1938-　　　　　　**CLC 70**
See also CA 139

Tu Fu 712-770　　　　　　　　**PC 9**
See also DAM MULT

Tunis, John R(oberts) 1889-1975　　**CLC 12**
See also CA 61-64; CANR 62; DLB 22, 171;
JRDA; MAICYA; SATA 37; SATA-Brief 30

Tuohy, Frank 　　　　　　**CLC 37**
See also Tuohy, John Francis
See also DLB 14, 139

Tuohy, John Francis 1925-1999
See Tuohy, Frank
See also CA 5-8R; 178; CANR 3, 47

Turco, Lewis (Putnam) 1934-　　**CLC 11, 63**
See also CA 13-16R; CAAS 22; CANR 24, 51;
DLBY 84

Turgenev, Ivan 1818-1883　　　**NCLC 21; DA;
DAB; DAC; DAM MST, NOV; DC 7; SSC
7; WLC**

Turgot, Anne-Robert-Jacques 1727-1781　**L C
26**

Turner, Frederick 1943-　　　　**CLC 48**
See also CA 73-76; CAAS 10; CANR 12, 30,
56; DLB 40

Tutu, Desmond M(pilo) 1931-**CLC 80; BLC 3;
DAM MULT**
See also BW 1, 3; CA 125; CANR 67, 81

Tutuola, Amos 1920-1997 **CLC 5, 14, 29; BLC 3; DAM MULT**
See also BW 2, 3; CA 9-12R; 159; CANR 27, 66; DLB 125; MTCW 1, 2

Twain, Mark **TCLC 6, 12, 19, 36, 48, 59; SSC 34; WLC**
See also Clemens, Samuel Langhorne
See also AAYA 20; CLR 58; DLB 11, 12, 23, 64, 74

Tyler, Anne 1941- **CLC 7, 11, 18, 28, 44, 59, 103; DAM NOV, POP**
See also AAYA 18; BEST 89:1; CA 9-12R; CANR 11, 33, 53; CDALBS; DLB 6, 143; DLBY 82; MTCW 1, 2; SATA 7, 90

Tyler, Royall 1757-1826 **NCLC 3**
See also DLB 37

Tynan, Katharine 1861-1931 **TCLC 3**
See also CA 104; 167; DLB 153

Tyutchev, Fyodor 1803-1873 **NCLC 34**

Tzara, Tristan 1896-1963 **CLC 47; DAM POET; PC 27**
See also CA 153; 89-92; MTCW 2

Uhry, Alfred 1936- **CLC 55; DAM DRAM, POP**
See also CA 127; 133; INT 133

Ulf, Haerved
See Strindberg, (Johan) August

Ulf, Harved
See Strindberg, (Johan) August

Ulibarri, Sabine R(eyes) 1919- **CLC 83; DAM MULT; HLCS 2**
See also CA 131; CANR 81; DLB 82; HW 1, 2

Unamuno (y Jugo), Miguel de 1864-1936 **TCLC 2, 9; DAM MULT, NOV; HLC 2; SSC 11**
See also CA 104; 131; CANR 81; DLB 108; HW 1, 2; MTCW 1, 2

Undercliffe, Errol
See Campbell, (John) Ramsey

Underwood, Miles
See Glassco, John

Undset, Sigrid 1882-1949 **TCLC 3; DA; DAB; DAC; DAM MST, NOV; WLC**
See also CA 104; 129; MTCW 1, 2

Ungaretti, Giuseppe 1888-1970 **CLC 7, 11, 15**
See also CA 19-20; 25-28R; CAP 2; DLB 114

Unger, Douglas 1952- **CLC 34**
See also CA 130

Unsworth, Barry (Forster) 1930- **CLC 76**
See also CA 25-28R; CANR 30, 54; DLB 194

Updike, John (Hoyer) 1932- **CLC 1, 2, 3, 5, 7, 9, 13, 15, 23, 34, 43, 70; DA; DAB; DAC; DAM MST, NOV, POET, POP; SSC 13, 27; WLC**
See also CA 1-4R; CABS 1; CANR 4, 33, 51; CDALB 1968-1988; DLB 2, 5, 143; DLBD 3; DLBY 80, 82, 97; MTCW 1, 2

Upshaw, Margaret Mitchell
See Mitchell, Margaret (Munnerlyn)

Upton, Mark
See Sanders, Lawrence

Upward, Allen 1863-1926 **TCLC 85**
See also CA 117; DLB 36

Urdang, Constance (Henriette) 1922- **CLC 47**
See also CA 21-24R; CANR 9, 24

Uriel, Henry
See Faust, Frederick (Schiller)

Uris, Leon (Marcus) 1924- **CLC 7, 32; DAM NOV, POP**
See also AITN 1, 2; BEST 89:2; CA 1-4R; CANR 1, 40, 65; MTCW 1, 2; SATA 49

Urista, Alberto H. 1947-
See Alurista

See also CA 45-48; CANR 2, 32; HLCS 1; HW 1

Urmuz
See Codrescu, Andrei

Urquhart, Jane 1949- **CLC 90; DAC**
See also CA 113; CANR 32, 68

Usigli, Rodolfo 1905-1979
See also CA 131; HLCS 1; HW 1

Ustinov, Peter (Alexander) 1921- **CLC 1**
See also AITN 1; CA 13-16R; CANR 25, 51; DLB 13; MTCW 2

U Tam'si, Gerald Felix Tchicaya
See Tchicaya, Gerald Felix

U Tam'si, Tchicaya
See Tchicaya, Gerald Felix

Vachss, Andrew (Henry) 1942- **CLC 106**
See also CA 118; CANR 44

Vachss, Andrew H.
See Vachss, Andrew (Henry)

Vaculik, Ludvik 1926- **CLC 7**
See also CA 53-56; CANR 72

Vaihinger, Hans 1852-1933 **TCLC 71**
See also CA 116; 166

Valdez, Luis (Miguel) 1940- **CLC 84; DAM MULT; DC 10; HLC 2**
See also CA 101; CANR 32, 81; DLB 122; HW 1

Valenzuela, Luisa 1938- **CLC 31, 104; DAM MULT; HLCS 2; SSC 14**
See also CA 101; CANR 32, 65; DLB 113; HW 1, 2

Valera y Alcala-Galiano, Juan 1824-1905 **TCLC 10**
See also CA 106

Valery, (Ambroise) Paul (Toussaint Jules) 1871-1945 **TCLC 4, 15; DAM POET; PC 9**
See also CA 104; 122; MTCW 1, 2

Valle-Inclan, Ramon (Maria) del 1866-1936 **TCLC 5; DAM MULT; HLC 2**
See also CA 106; 153; CANR 80; DLB 134; HW 2

Vallejo, Antonio Buero
See Buero Vallejo, Antonio

Vallejo, Cesar (Abraham) 1892-1938 **TCLC 3, 56; DAM MULT; HLC 2**
See also CA 105; 153; HW 1

Valles, Jules 1832-1885 **NCLC 71**
See also DLB 123

Vallette, Marguerite Eymery
See Rachilde

Valle Y Pena, Ramon del
See Valle-Inclan, Ramon (Maria) del

Van Ash, Cay 1918- **CLC 34**

Vanbrugh, Sir John 1664-1726 **LC 21; DAM DRAM**
See also DLB 80

Van Campen, Karl
See Campbell, John W(ood, Jr.)

Vance, Gerald
See Silverberg, Robert

Vance, Jack **CLC 35**
See also Kuttner, Henry; Vance, John Holbrook
See also DLB 8

Vance, John Holbrook 1916-
See Queen, Ellery; Vance, Jack
See also CA 29-32R; CANR 17, 65; MTCW 1

Van Den Bogarde, Derek Jules Gaspard Ulric Niven 1921-1999
See Bogarde, Dirk
See also CA 77-80; 179

Vandenburgh, Jane **CLC 59**
See also CA 168

Vanderhaeghe, Guy 1951- **CLC 41**

See also CA 113; CANR 72

van der Post, Laurens (Jan) 1906-1996 **CLC 5**
See also CA 5-8R; 155; CANR 35; DLB 204

van de Wetering, Janwillem 1931- **CLC 47**
See also CA 49-52; CANR 4, 62

Van Dine, S. S. **TCLC 23**
See also Wright, Willard Huntington

Van Doren, Carl (Clinton) 1885-1950 **TCLC 18**
See also CA 111; 168

Van Doren, Mark 1894-1972 **CLC 6, 10**
See also CA 1-4R; 37-40R; CANR 3; DLB 45; MTCW 1, 2

Van Druten, John (William) 1901-1957 **TCLC 2**
See also CA 104; 161; DLB 10

Van Duyn, Mona (Jane) 1921- **CLC 3, 7, 63, 116; DAM POET**
See also CA 9-12R; CANR 7, 38, 60; DLB 5

Van Dyne, Edith
See Baum, L(yman) Frank

van Itallie, Jean-Claude 1936- **CLC 3**
See also CA 45-48; CAAS 2; CANR 1, 48; DLB 7

van Ostaijen, Paul 1896-1928 **TCLC 33**
See also CA 163

Van Peebles, Melvin 1932- **CLC 2, 20; DAM MULT**
See also BW 2, 3; CA 85-88; CANR 27, 67, 82

Vansittart, Peter 1920- **CLC 42**
See also CA 1-4R; CANR 3, 49

Van Vechten, Carl 1880-1964 **CLC 33**
See also CA 89-92; DLB 4, 9, 51

Van Vogt, A(lfred) E(lton) 1912- **CLC 1**
See also CA 21-24R; CANR 28; DLB 8; SATA 14

Varda, Agnes 1928- **CLC 16**
See also CA 116; 122

Vargas Llosa, (Jorge) Mario (Pedro) 1936- **CLC 3, 6, 9, 10, 15, 31, 42, 85; DA; DAB; DAC; DAM MST, MULT, NOV; HLC 2**
See also CA 73-76; CANR 18, 32, 42, 67; DLB 145; HW 1, 2; MTCW 1, 2

Vasiliu, Gheorghe 1881-1957
See Bacovia, George
See also CA 123

Vassa, Gustavus
See Equiano, Olaudah

Vassilikos, Vassilis 1933- **CLC 4, 8**
See also CA 81-84; CANR 75

Vaughan, Henry 1621-1695 **LC 27**
See also DLB 131

Vaughn, Stephanie **CLC 62**

Vazov, Ivan (Minchov) 1850-1921 **TCLC 25**
See also CA 121; 167; DLB 147

Veblen, Thorstein B(unde) 1857-1929 **TCLC 31**
See also CA 115; 165

Vega, Lope de 1562-1635 **LC 23; HLCS 2**

Venison, Alfred
See Pound, Ezra (Weston Loomis)

Verdi, Marie de
See Mencken, H(enry) L(ouis)

Verdu, Matilde
See Cela, Camilo Jose

Verga, Giovanni (Carmelo) 1840-1922 **TCLC 3; SSC 21**
See also CA 104; 123

Vergil 70B.C.-19B.C. **CMLC 9; DA; DAB; DAC; DAM MST, POET; PC 12; WLCS**
See also Virgil

Verhaeren, Emile (Adolphe Gustave) 1855-1916 **TCLC 12**

See also CA 109

Verlaine, Paul (Marie) 1844-1896 **NCLC 2, 51;**
  DAM POET; PC 2

Verne, Jules (Gabriel) 1828-1905 **TCLC 6, 52**
  See also AAYA 16; CA 110; 131; DLB 123;
  JRDA; MAICYA; SATA 21

Very, Jones 1813-1880 **NCLC 9**
  See also DLB 1

Vesaas, Tarjei 1897-1970 **CLC 48**
  See also CA 29-32R

Vialis, Gaston
  See Simenon, Georges (Jacques Christian)

Vian, Boris 1920-1959 **TCLC 9**
  See also CA 106; 164; DLB 72; MTCW 2

Viaud, (Louis Marie) Julien 1850-1923
  See Loti, Pierre
  See also CA 107

Vicar, Henry
  See Felsen, Henry Gregor

Vicker, Angus
  See Felsen, Henry Gregor

Vidal, Gore 1925- **CLC 2, 4, 6, 8, 10, 22, 33, 72;**
  DAM NOV, POP
  See also AITN 1; BEST 90:2; CA 5-8R; CANR
  13, 45, 65; CDALBS; DLB 6, 152; INT
  CANR-13; MTCW 1, 2

Viereck, Peter (Robert Edwin) 1916- **CLC 4;**
  PC 27
  See also CA 1-4R; CANR 1, 47; DLB 5

Vigny, Alfred (Victor) de 1797-1863 **NCLC 7;**
  DAM POET; PC 26
  See also DLB 119, 192

Vilakazi, Benedict Wallet 1906-1947 **TCLC 37**
  See also CA 168

Villa, Jose Garcia 1904-1997 **PC 22**
  See also CA 25-28R; CANR 12

Villarreal, Jose Antonio 1924-
  See also CA 133; DAM MULT; DLB 82; HLC
  2; HW 1

Villaurrutia, Xavier 1903-1950 **TCLC 80**
  See also HW 1

**Villiers de l'Isle Adam, Jean Marie Mathias
  Philippe Auguste, Comte de** 1838-1889
  NCLC 3; SSC 14
  See also DLB 123

Villon, Francois 1431-1463(?) **PC 13**
  See also DLB 208

Vinci, Leonardo da 1452-1519 **LC 12**

Vine, Barbara **CLC 50**
  See also Rendell, Ruth(Barbara)
  See also BEST 90:4

Vinge, Joan (Carol) D(ennison) 1948- **CLC 30;**
  SSC 24
  See also CA 93-96; CANR 72; SATA 36

Violis, G.
  See Simenon, Georges (Jacques Christian)

Viramontes, Helena Maria 1954-
  See also CA 159; DLB 122; HLCS 2; HW 2

Virgil 70B.C.-19B.C.
  See Vergil
  See also DLB 211

Visconti, Luchino 1906-1976 **CLC 16**
  See also CA 81-84; 65-68; CANR 39

Vittorini, Elio 1908-1966 **CLC 6, 9, 14**
  See also CA 133; 25-28R

Vivekananda, Swami 1863-1902 **TCLC 88**

Vizenor, Gerald Robert 1934- **CLC 103; DAM
  MULT**
  See also CA 13-16R; CAAS 22; CANR 5, 21,
  44, 67; DLB 175; MTCW 2; NNAL

Vizinczey, Stephen 1933- **CLC 40**
  See also CA 128; INT 128

Vliet, R(ussell) G(ordon) 1929-1984 **CLC 22**

See also CA 37-40R; 112; CANR 18

Vogau, Boris Andreyevich 1894-1937(?)
  See Pilnyak, Boris
  See also CA 123

Vogel, Paula A(nne) 1951- **CLC 76**
  See also CA 108

Voigt, Cynthia 1942- **CLC 30**
  See also AAYA 3, 30; CA 106; CANR 18, 37,
  40; CLR 13, 48; INT CANR-18; JRDA;
  MAICYA; SATA 48, 79; SATA-Brief 33

Voigt, Ellen Bryant 1943- **CLC 54**
  See also CA 69-72; CANR 11, 29, 55; DLB 120

Voinovich, Vladimir (Nikolaevich) 1932- **CLC
  10, 49**
  See also CA 81-84; CAAS 12; CANR 33, 67;
  MTCW 1

Vollmann, William T. 1959- **CLC 89; DAM
  NOV, POP**
  See also CA 134; CANR 67; MTCW 2

Voloshinov, V. N.
  See Bakhtin, Mikhail Mikhailovich

Voltaire 1694-1778 **LC 14; DA; DAB; DAC;
  DAM DRAM, MST; SSC 12; WLC**

von Aschendrof, Baron Ignatz
  See Ford, Ford Madox

von Daeniken, Erich 1935- **CLC 30**
  See also AITN 1; CA 37-40R; CANR 17, 44

von Daniken, Erich
  See von Daeniken, Erich

von Heidenstam, (Carl Gustaf) Verner
  See Heidenstam, (Carl Gustaf) Verner von

von Heyse, Paul (Johann Ludwig)
  See Heyse, Paul (Johann Ludwig von)

von Hofmannsthal, Hugo
  See Hofmannsthal, Hugo von

von Horvath, Odon
  See Horvath, Oedoen von

von Horvath, Oedoen
  See Horvath, Oedoen von

von Liliencron, (Friedrich Adolf Axel) Detlev
  See Liliencron, (Friedrich Adolf Axel) Detlev
  von

Vonnegut, Kurt, Jr. 1922- **CLC 1, 2, 3, 4, 5, 8,
  12, 22, 40, 60, 111; DA; DAB; DAC; DAM
  MST, NOV, POP; SSC 8; WLC**
  See also AAYA 6; AITN 1; BEST 90:4; CA 1-
  4R; CANR 1, 25, 49, 75; CDALB 1968-
  1988; DLB 2, 8, 152; DLBD 3; DLBY 80;
  MTCW 1, 2

Von Rachen, Kurt
  See Hubbard, L(afayette) Ron(ald)

von Rezzori (d'Arezzo), Gregor
  See Rezzori (d'Arezzo), Gregor von

von Sternberg, Josef
  See Sternberg, Josef von

Vorster, Gordon 1924- **CLC 34**
  See also CA 133

Vosce, Trudie
  See Ozick, Cynthia

Voznesensky, Andrei (Andreievich) 1933-
  CLC 1, 15, 57; DAM POET
  See also CA 89-92; CANR 37; MTCW 1

Waddington, Miriam 1917- **CLC 28**
  See also CA 21-24R; CANR 12, 30; DLB 68

Wagman, Fredrica 1937- **CLC 7**
  See also CA 97-100; INT 97-100

Wagner, Linda W.
  See Wagner-Martin, Linda (C.)

Wagner, Linda Welshimer
  See Wagner-Martin, Linda (C.)

Wagner, Richard 1813-1883 **NCLC 9**
  See also DLB 129

Wagner-Martin, Linda (C.) 1936- **CLC 50**

See also CA 159

Wagoner, David (Russell) 1926- **CLC 3, 5, 15**
  See also CA 1-4R; CAAS 3; CANR 2, 71; DLB
  5; SATA 14

Wah, Fred(erick James) 1939- **CLC 44**
  See also CA 107; 141; DLB 60

Wahloo, Per 1926-1975 **CLC 7**
  See also CA 61-64; CANR 73

Wahloo, Peter
  See Wahloo, Per

Wain, John (Barrington) 1925-1994 **CLC 2,
  11, 15, 46**
  See also CA 5-8R; 145; CAAS 4; CANR 23,
  54; CDBLB 1960 to Present; DLB 15, 27,
  139, 155; MTCW 1, 2

Wajda, Andrzej 1926- **CLC 16**
  See also CA 102

Wakefield, Dan 1932- **CLC 7**
  See also CA 21-24R; CAAS 7

Wakoski, Diane 1937- **CLC 2, 4, 7, 9, 11, 40;
  DAM POET; PC 15**
  See also CA 13-16R; CAAS 1; CANR 9, 60;
  DLB 5; INT CANR-9; MTCW 2

Wakoski-Sherbell, Diane
  See Wakoski, Diane

Walcott, Derek (Alton) 1930- **CLC 2, 4, 9, 14,
  25, 42, 67, 76; BLC 3; DAB; DAC; DAM
  MST, MULT, POET; DC 7**
  See also BW 2; CA 89-92; CANR 26, 47, 75,
  80; DLB 117; DLBY 81; MTCW 1, 2

Waldman, Anne (Lesley) 1945- **CLC 7**
  See also CA 37-40R; CAAS 17; CANR 34, 69;
  DLB 16

Waldo, E. Hunter
  See Sturgeon, Theodore (Hamilton)

Waldo, Edward Hamilton
  See Sturgeon, Theodore (Hamilton)

Walker, Alice (Malsenior) 1944- **CLC 5, 6, 9,
  19, 27, 46, 58, 103; BLC 3; DA; DAB;
  DAC; DAM MST, MULT, NOV, POET,
  POP; SSC 5; WLCS**
  See also AAYA 3; BEST 89:4; BW 2, 3; CA
  37-40R; CANR 9, 27, 49, 66, 82; CDALB
  1968-1988; DLB 6, 33, 143; INT CANR-27;
  MTCW 1, 2; SATA 31

Walker, David Harry 1911-1992 **CLC 14**
  See also CA 1-4R; 137; CANR 1; SATA 8;
  SATA-Obit 71

Walker, Edward Joseph 1934-
  See Walker, Ted
  See also CA 21-24R; CANR 12, 28, 53

Walker, George F. 1947- **CLC 44, 61; DAB;
  DAC; DAM MST**
  See also CA 103; CANR 21, 43, 59; DLB 60

Walker, Joseph A. 1935- **CLC 19; DAM
  DRAM, MST**
  See also BW 1, 3; CA 89-92; CANR 26; DLB
  38

Walker, Margaret (Abigail) 1915-1998 **CLC 1,
  6; BLC; DAM MULT; PC 20**
  See also BW 2, 3; CA 73-76; 172; CANR 26,
  54, 76; DLB 76, 152; MTCW 1, 2

Walker, Ted **CLC 13**
  See also Walker, Edward Joseph
  See also DLB 40

Wallace, David Foster 1962- **CLC 50, 114**
  See also CA 132; CANR 59; MTCW 2

Wallace, Dexter
  See Masters, Edgar Lee

Wallace, (Richard Horatio) Edgar 1875-1932
  TCLC 57
  See also CA 115; DLB 70

Wallace, Irving 1916-1990 **CLC 7, 13; DAM**

NOV, POP
See also AITN 1; CA 1-4R; 132; CAAS 1; CANR 1, 27; INT CANR-27; MTCW 1, 2

Wallant, Edward Lewis 1926-1962 **CLC 5, 10**
See also CA 1-4R; CANR 22; DLB 2, 28, 143; MTCW 1, 2

Wallas, Graham 1858-1932 **TCLC 91**

Walley, Byron
See Card, Orson Scott

Walpole, Horace 1717-1797 **LC 49**
See also DLB 39, 104

Walpole, Hugh (Seymour) 1884-1941 **TCLC 5**
See also CA 104; 165; DLB 34; MTCW 2

Walser, Martin 1927- **CLC 27**
See also CA 57-60; CANR 8, 46; DLB 75, 124

Walser, Robert 1878-1956 **TCLC 18;SSC 20**
See also CA 118; 165; DLB 66

Walsh, Jill Paton **CLC 35**
See also Paton Walsh, Gillian
See also AAYA 11; CLR 2; DLB 161; SAAS 3

Walter, William Christian
See Andersen, Hans Christian

Wambaugh, Joseph (Aloysius, Jr.) 1937-**CLC 3, 18; DAM NOV, POP**
See also AITN 1; BEST 89:3; CA 33-36R; CANR 42, 65; DLB 6; DLBY 83; MTCW 1, 2

Wang Wei 699(?)-761(?) **PC 18**

Ward, Arthur Henry Sarsfield 1883-1959
See Rohmer, Sax
See also CA 108; 173

Ward, Douglas Turner 1930- **CLC 19**
See also BW 1; CA 81-84; CANR 27; DLB 7, 38

Ward, E. D.
See Lucas, E(dward) V(errall)

Ward, Mary Augusta
See Ward, Mrs. Humphry

Ward, Mrs. Humphry 1851-1920 **TCLC 55**
See also DLB 18

Ward, Peter
See Faust, Frederick (Schiller)

Warhol, Andy 1928(?)-1987 **CLC 20**
See also AAYA 12; BEST 89:4; CA 89-92; 121; CANR 34

Warner, Francis (Robert le Plastrier) 1937- **CLC 14**
See also CA 53-56; CANR 11

Warner, Marina 1946- **CLC 59**
See also CA 65-68; CANR 21, 55; DLB 194

Warner, Rex (Ernest) 1905-1986 **CLC 45**
See also CA 89-92; 119; DLB 15

Warner, Susan (Bogert) 1819-1885 **NCLC 31**
See also DLB 3, 42

Warner, Sylvia (Constance) Ashton
See Ashton-Warner, Sylvia (Constance)

Warner, Sylvia Townsend 1893-1978 **CLC 7, 19; SSC 23**
See also CA 61-64; 77-80; CANR 16, 60; DLB 34, 139; MTCW 1, 2

Warren, Mercy Otis 1728-1814 **NCLC 13**
See also DLB 31, 200

Warren, Robert Penn 1905-1989 **CLC 1, 4, 6, 8, 10, 13, 18, 39, 53, 59; DA; DAB; DAC; DAM MST, NOV, POET; SSC 4;WLC**
See also AITN 1; CA 13-16R; 129; CANR 10, 47;CDALB 1968-1988; DLB 2, 48, 152; DLBY 80, 89; INT CANR-10; MTCW 1, 2; SATA 46; SATA-Obit 63

Warshofsky, Isaac
See Singer, Isaac Bashevis

Warton, Thomas 1728-1790 **LC 15;DAM POET**

See also DLB 104, 109

Waruk, Kona
See Harris, (Theodore) Wilson

Warung, Price 1855-1911 **TCLC 45**

Warwick, Jarvis
See Garner, Hugh

Washington, Alex
See Harris, Mark

Washington, Booker T(aliaferro) 1856-1915 **TCLC 10; BLC 3; DAM MULT**
See also BW 1; CA 114; 125; SATA 28

Washington, George 1732-1799 **LC 25**
See also DLB 31

Wassermann, (Karl) Jakob 1873-1934 **T C L C 6**
See also CA 104; 163; DLB 66

Wasserstein, Wendy 1950- **CLC 32, 59, 90; DAM DRAM; DC 4**
See also CA 121; 129; CABS 3; CANR 53, 75; INT 129; MTCW 2; SATA 94

Waterhouse, Keith (Spencer) 1929- **CLC 47**
See also CA 5-8R; CANR 38, 67; DLB 13, 15; MTCW 1, 2

Waters, Frank (Joseph) 1902-1995 **CLC 88**
See also CA 5-8R; 149; CAAS 13; CANR 3, 18, 63; DLB 212; DLBY 86

Waters, Roger 1944- **CLC 35**

Watkins, Frances Ellen
See Harper, Frances Ellen Watkins

Watkins, Gerrold
See Malzberg, Barry N(athaniel)

Watkins, Gloria 1955(?)-
See hooks, bell
See also BW 2; CA 143; MTCW 2

Watkins, Paul 1964- **CLC 55**
See also CA 132; CANR 62

Watkins, Vernon Phillips 1906-1967 **CLC 43**
See also CA 9-10; 25-28R; CAP 1; DLB 20

Watson, Irving S.
See Mencken, H(enry) L(ouis)

Watson, John H.
See Farmer, Philip Jose

Watson, Richard F.
See Silverberg, Robert

Waugh, Auberon (Alexander) 1939- **CLC 7**
See also CA 45-48; CANR 6, 22; DLB 14, 194

Waugh, Evelyn (Arthur St. John) 1903-1966 **CLC 1, 3, 8, 13, 19, 27, 44, 107; DA; DAB; DAC; DAM MST, NOV, POP; WLC**
See also CA 85-88; 25-28R; CANR 22; CDBLB 1914-1945; DLB 15, 162, 195; MTCW 1, 2

Waugh, Harriet 1944- **CLC 6**
See also CA 85-88; CANR 22

Ways, C. R.
See Blount, Roy (Alton), Jr.

Waystaff, Simon
See Swift, Jonathan

Webb, (Martha) Beatrice (Potter) 1858-1943 **TCLC 22**
See also Potter, (Helen) Beatrix
See also CA 117; DLB 190

Webb; Charles (Richard) 1939- **CLC 7**
See also CA 25-28R

Webb, James H(enry), Jr. 1946- **CLC 22**
See also CA 81-84

Webb, Mary (Gladys Meredith) 1881-1927 **TCLC 24**
See also CA 123; DLB 34

Webb, Mrs. Sidney
See Webb, (Martha) Beatrice (Potter)

Webb, Phyllis 1927- **CLC 18**
See also CA 104; CANR 23; DLB 53

Webb, Sidney (James) 1859-1947 **TCLC 22**

See also CA 117; 163; DLB 190

Webber, Andrew Lloyd **CLC 21**
See also Lloyd Webber, Andrew

Weber, Lenora Mattingly 1895-1971 **CLC 12**
See also CA 19-20; 29-32R; CAP 1; SATA 2; SATA-Obit 26

Weber, Max 1864-1920 **TCLC 69**
See also CA 109

Webster, John 1579(?)-1634(?) **LC 33; DA; DAB; DAC; DAM DRAM, MST; DC 2; WLC**
See also CDBLB Before 1660; DLB 58

Webster, Noah 1758-1843 **NCLC 30**
See also DLB 1, 37, 42, 43, 73

Wedekind, (Benjamin) Frank(lin) 1864-1918 **TCLC 7; DAM DRAM**
See also CA 104; 153; DLB 118

Weidman, Jerome 1913-1998 **CLC 7**
See also AITN 2; CA 1-4R; 171; CANR 1; DLB 28

Weil, Simone (Adolphine) 1909-1943 **TCLC 23**
See also CA 117; 159; MTCW 2

Weininger, Otto 1880-1903 **TCLC 84**

Weinstein, Nathan
See West, Nathanael

Weinstein, Nathan von Wallenstein
See West, Nathanael

Weir, Peter (Lindsay) 1944- **CLC 20**
See also CA 113; 123

Weiss, Peter (Ulrich) 1916-1982 **CLC 3, 15, 51; DAM DRAM**
See also CA 45-48; 106; CANR 3; DLB 69, 124

Weiss, Theodore (Russell) 1916- **CLC 3, 8, 14**
See also CA 9-12R; CAAS 2; CANR 46; DLB 5

Welch, (Maurice) Denton 1915-1948 **TCLC 22**
See also CA 121; 148

Welch, James 1940- **CLC 6, 14, 52; DAM MULT, POP**
See also CA 85-88; CANR 42, 66; DLB 175; NNAL

Weldon, Fay 1931-**CLC 6, 9, 11, 19, 36, 59, 122; DAM POP**
See also CA 21-24R; CANR 16, 46, 63; CDBLB 1960 to Present; DLB 14, 194; INT CANR-16; MTCW 1, 2

Wellek, Rene 1903-1995 **CLC 28**
See also CA 5-8R; 150; CAAS 7; CANR 8; DLB 63; INT CANR-8

Weller, Michael 1942- **CLC 10, 53**
See also CA 85-88

Weller, Paul 1958- **CLC 26**

Wellershoff, Dieter 1925- **CLC 46**
See also CA 89-92; CANR 16, 37

Welles, (George) Orson 1915-1985 **CLC 20, 80**
See also CA 93-96; 117

Wellman, John McDowell 1945-
See Wellman, Mac
See also CA 166

Wellman, Mac 1945- **CLC 65**
See also Wellman, John McDowell; Wellman, John McDowell

Wellman, Manly Wade 1903-1986 **CLC 49**
See also CA 1-4R; 118; CANR 6, 16, 44; SATA 6; SATA-Obit 47

Wells, Carolyn 1869(?)-1942 **TCLC 35**
See also CA 113; DLB 11

Wells, H(erbert) G(eorge) 1866-1946**TCLC 6, 12, 19; DA; DAB; DAC; DAM MST, NOV; SSC 6; WLC**
See also AAYA 18; CA 110; 121; CDBLB 1914-1945; DLB 34, 70, 156, 178; MTCW 1, 2; SATA 20

Wells, Rosemary 1943-   **CLC 12**
  See also AAYA 13; CA 85-88; CANR 48; CLR
    16; MAICYA; SAAS 1; SATA 18, 69
Wen I-to 1899-1946   **TCLC 28**
Wentworth, Robert
  See Hamilton, Edmond
Werfel, Franz (Viktor) 1890-1945   **TCLC 8**
  See also CA 104; 161; DLB 81, 124
Wergeland, Henrik Arnold 1808-1845 **N C L C
    5**
Wersba, Barbara 1932-   **CLC 30**
  See also AAYA 2, 30; CA 29-32R; CANR 16,
    38; CLR 3; DLB 52; JRDA; MAICYA; SAAS
    2; SATA 1, 58; SATA-Essay 103
Wertmueller, Lina 1928-   **CLC 16**
  See also CA 97-100; CANR 39, 78
Wescott, Glenway 1901-1987 **CLC 13; SSC 35**
  See also CA 13-16R; 121; CANR 23, 70; DLB
    4, 9, 102
Wesker, Arnold 1932-   **CLC 3, 5, 42; DAB;
    DAM DRAM**
  See also CA 1-4R; CAAS 7; CANR 1, 33;
    CDBLB 1960 to Present; DLB 13; MTCW 1
Wesley, Richard (Errol) 1945-   **CLC 7**
  See also BW 1; CA 57-60; CANR 27; DLB 38
Wessel, Johan Herman 1742-1785   **LC 7**
West, Anthony (Panther) 1914-1987 **CLC 50**
  See also CA 45-48; 124; CANR 3, 19; DLB 15
West, C. P.
  See Wodehouse, P(elham) G(renville)
West, (Mary) Jessamyn 1902-1984 **CLC 7, 17**
  See also CA 9-12R; 112; CANR 27; DLB 6;
    DLBY 84; MTCW 1, 2; SATA-Obit 37
West, Morris L(anglo) 1916-   **CLC 6, 33**
  See also CA 5-8R; CANR 24, 49, 64; MTCW
    1, 2
West, Nathanael 1903-1940 **TCLC 1, 14, 44;
    SSC 16**
  See also CA 104; 125; CDALB 1929-1941;
    DLB 4, 9, 28; MTCW 1, 2
West, Owen
  See Koontz, Dean R(ay)
West, Paul 1930-   **CLC 7, 14, 96**
  See also CA 13-16R; CAAS 7; CANR 22, 53,
    76; DLB 14; INT CANR-22; MTCW 2
West, Rebecca 1892-1983   **CLC 7, 9, 31, 50**
  See also CA 5-8R; 109; CANR 19; DLB 36;
    DLBY 83; MTCW 1, 2
Westall, Robert (Atkinson) 1929-1993 **CLC 17**
  See also AAYA 12; CA 69-72; 141; CANR 18,
    68; CLR 13; JRDA; MAICYA; SAAS 2;
    SATA 23, 69; SATA-Obit 75
Westermarck, Edward 1862-1939   **TCLC 87**
Westlake, Donald E(dwin) 1933- **CLC 7, 33;
    DAM POP**
  See also CA 17-20R; CAAS 13; CANR 16, 44,
    65; INT CANR-16; MTCW 2
Westmacott, Mary
  See Christie, Agatha (Mary Clarissa)
Weston, Allen
  See Norton, Andre
Wetcheek, J. L.
  See Feuchtwanger, Lion
Wetering, Janwillem van de
  See van de Wetering, Janwillem
Wetherald, Agnes Ethelwyn 1857-1940 **T C L C
    81**

See also DLB 99
Wetherell, Elizabeth
  See Warner, Susan (Bogert)
Whale, James 1889-1957   **TCLC 63**
Whalen, Philip 1923-   **CLC 6, 29**
  See also CA 9-12R; CANR 5, 39; DLB 16
Wharton, Edith (Newbold Jones) 1862-1937
    **TCLC 3, 9, 27, 53; DA; DAB; DAC; DAM
    MST, NOV; SSC 6; WLC**
  See also AAYA 25; CA 104; 132; CDALB 1865-
    1917; DLB 4, 9, 12, 78, 189; DLBD 13;
    MTCW 1, 2
Wharton, James
  See Mencken, H(enry) L(ouis)
Wharton, William (a pseudonym) CLC 18, 37
  See also CA 93-96; DLBY 80; INT 93-96
Wheatley (Peters), Phillis 1754(?)-1784 **LC 3,
    50; BLC 3; DA; DAC; DAMMST, MULT,
    POET; PC 3; WLC**
  See also CDALB 1640-1865; DLB 31, 50
Wheelock, John Hall 1886-1978   **CLC 14**
  See also CA 13-16R; 77-80; CANR 14; DLB
    45
White, E(lwyn) B(rooks) 1899-1985 **CLC 10,
    34, 39; DAM POP**
  See also AITN 2; CA 13-16R; 116; CANR 16,
    37; CDALBS; CLR 1, 21; DLB 11, 22;
    MAICYA; MTCW 1, 2; SATA 2, 29, 100;
    SATA-Obit 44
White, Edmund (Valentine III) 1940- **CLC 27,
    110; DAM POP**
  See also AAYA 7; CA 45-48; CANR 3, 19, 36,
    62; MTCW 1, 2
White, Patrick (Victor Martindale) 1912-1990
    CLC 3, 4, 5, 7, 9, 18, 65, 69
  See also CA 81-84; 132; CANR 43; MTCW 1
White, Phyllis Dorothy James 1920-
  See James, P. D.
  See also CA 21-24R; CANR 17, 43, 65; DAM
    POP; MTCW 1, 2
White, T(erence)H(anbury) 1906-1964 **C L C
    30**
  See also AAYA 22; CA 73-76; CANR 37; DLB
    160; JRDA; MAICYA; SATA 12
White, Terence deVere 1912-1994   **CLC 49**
  See also CA 49-52; 145; CANR 3
White, Walter
  See White, Walter F(rancis)
  See also BLC; DAM MULT
White, Walter F(rancis) 1893-1955 **TCLC 15**
  See also White, Walter
  See also BW 1; CA 115; 124; DLB 51
White, William Hale 1831-1913
  See Rutherford, Mark
  See also CA 121
Whitehead, E(dward) A(nthony) 1933- **CLC 5**
  See also CA 65-68; CANR 58
Whitemore, Hugh (John) 1936-   **CLC 37**
  See also CA 132; CANR 77; INT 132
Whitman, Sarah Helen (Power) 1803-1878
    NCLC 19
  See also DLB 1
Whitman, Walt(er) 1819-1892 **NCLC 4, 31;
    DA; DAB; DAC; DAM MST, POET; PC
    3; WLC**
  See also CDALB 1640-1865; DLB 3, 64; SATA
    20
Whitney, Phyllis A(yame) 1903-   **CLC 42;
    DAM POP**
  See also AITN 2; BEST 90:3; CA 1-4R; CANR
    3, 25, 38, 60; CLR 59; JRDA; MAICYA;
    MTCW 2; SATA 1, 30
Whittemore, (Edward) Reed (Jr.) 1919- **CLC 4**

See also CA 9-12R; CAAS 8; CANR 4; DLB 5
Whittier, John Greenleaf 1807-1892 **NCLC 8,
    59**
  See also DLB 1
Whittlebot, Hernia
  See Coward, Noel (Peirce)
Wicker, Thomas Grey 1926-
  See Wicker, Tom
  See also CA 65-68; CANR 21, 46
Wicker, Tom   **CLC 7**
  See also Wicker, Thomas Grey
Wideman, John Edgar 1941- **CLC 5, 34, 36, 67,
    122; BLC 3; DAM MULT**
  See also BW 2, 3; CA 85-88; CANR 14, 42,
    67; DLB 33, 143; MTCW 2
Wiebe, Rudy (Henry) 1934-   **CLC 6, 11, 14;
    DAC; DAM MST**
  See also CA 37-40R; CANR 42, 67; DLB 60
Wieland, Christoph Martin 1733-1813 **N C L C
    17**
  See also DLB 97
Wiene, Robert 1881-1938   **TCLC 56**
Wieners, John 1934-   **CLC 7**
  See also CA 13-16R; DLB 16
Wiesel, Elie(zer) 1928- **CLC 3, 5, 11, 37; DA;
    DAB; DAC; DAM MST, NOV; WLCS**
  See also AAYA 7; AITN 1; CA 5-8R; CAAS 4;
    CANR 8, 40, 65; CDALBS; DLB 83; DLBY
    87; INT CANR-8; MTCW 1, 2; SATA 56
Wiggins, Marianne 1947-   **CLC 57**
  See also BEST 89:3; CA 130; CANR 60
Wight, James Alfred 1916-1995
  See Herriot, James
  See also CA 77-80; SATA 55; SATA-Brief 44
Wilbur, Richard (Purdy) 1921- **CLC 3, 6, 9, 14,
    53, 110; DA; DAB; DAC; DAM MST,
    POET**
  See also CA 1-4R; CABS 2; CANR 2, 29, 76;
    CDALBS; DLB 5, 169; INT CANR-29;
    MTCW 1, 2; SATA 9, 108
Wild, Peter 1940-   **CLC 14**
  See also CA 37-40R; DLB 5
Wilde, Oscar 1854(?)-1900 **TCLC 1, 8, 23, 41;
    DA; DAB; DAC; DAM DRAM, MST,
    NOV; SSC 11; WLC**
  See also CA 104; 119; CDBLB 1890-1914;
    DLB 10, 19, 34, 57, 141, 156, 190; SATA 24
Wilder, Billy   **CLC 20**
  See also Wilder, Samuel
  See also DLB 26
Wilder, Samuel 1906-
  See Wilder, Billy
  See also CA 89-92
Wilder, Thornton (Niven) 1897-1975 **CLC 1, 5,
    6, 10, 15, 35, 82; DA; DAB; DAC; DAM
    DRAM, MST, NOV; DC 1; WLC**
  See also AAYA 29; AITN 2; CA 13-16R; 61-
    64; CANR 40; CDALBS; DLB 4, 7, 9; DLBY
    97; MTCW 1, 2
Wilding, Michael 1942-   **CLC 73**
  See also CA 104; CANR 24, 49
Wiley, Richard 1944-   **CLC 44**
  See also CA 121; 129; CANR 71
Wilhelm, Kate   **CLC 7**
  See also Wilhelm, KatieGertrude
  See also AAYA 20; CAAS 5; DLB 8; INT
    CANR-17
Wilhelm, Katie Gertrude 1928-
  See Wilhelm, Kate
  See also CA 37-40R; CANR 17, 36, 60; MTCW
    1
Wilkins, Mary
  See Freeman, Mary Eleanor Wilkins

Willard, Nancy 1936-　　　　　**CLC 7, 37**
　See also CA 89-92; CANR 10, 39, 68; CLR 5;
　　DLB 5, 52; MAICYA; MTCW 1; SATA 37,
　　71; SATA-Brief 30
William of Ockham 1285-1347　　**CMLC 32**
Williams, Ben Ames 1889-1953　　**TCLC 89**
　See also DLB 102
Williams, C(harles) K(enneth) 1936-**CLC 33,
　56; DAM POET**
　See also CA 37-40R; CAAS 26; CANR 57; DLB
　　5
Williams, Charles
　See Collier, James L(incoln)
Williams, Charles (Walter Stansby) 1886-1945
　　TCLC 1, 11
　See also CA 104; 163; DLB 100, 153
Williams, (George) Emlyn 1905-1987**CLC 15;
　DAM DRAM**
　See also CA 104; 123; CANR 36; DLB 10, 77;
　　MTCW 1
Williams, Hank 1923-1953　　　**TCLC 81**
Williams, Hugo 1942-　　　　　**CLC 42**
　See also CA 17-20R; CANR 45; DLB 40
Williams, J. Walker
　See Wodehouse, P(elham) G(renville)
Williams, John A(lfred) 1925-**CLC 5, 13; BLC
　3; DAM MULT**
　See also BW 2, 3; CA 53-56; CAAS 3; CANR
　　6, 26, 51; DLB 2, 33; INT CANR-6
Williams, Jonathan (Chamberlain) 1929-
　　CLC 13
　See also CA 9-12R; CAAS 12; CANR 8; DLB
　　5
Williams, Joy 1944-　　　　　**CLC 31**
　See also CA 41-44R; CANR 22, 48
Williams, Norman 1952-　　　　**CLC 39**
　See also CA 118
Williams, Sherley Anne 1944-**CLC 89; BLC 3;
　DAM MULT, POET**
　See also BW 2, 3; CA 73-76; CANR 25, 82;
　　DLB 41; INT CANR-25; SATA 78
Williams, Shirley
　See Williams, Sherley Anne
Williams, Tennessee 1911-1983**CLC 1, 2, 5, 7,
　8, 11, 15, 19, 30, 39, 45, 71, 111; DA; DAB;
　DAC; DAM DRAM, MST; DC 4;WLC**
　See also AITN 1, 2; CA 5-8R; 108; CABS 3;
　　CANR 31; CDALB 1941-1968; DLB7;
　　DLBD 4; DLBY 83; MTCW 1, 2
Williams, Thomas (Alonzo) 1926-1990**CLC 14**
　See also CA 1-4R; 132; CANR 2
Williams, William C.
　See Williams, William Carlos
Williams, William Carlos 1883-1963**CLC 1, 2,
　5, 9, 13, 22, 42, 67; DA; DAB; DAC; DAM
　MST, POET; PC 7; SSC 31**
　See also CA 89-92; CANR 34; CDALB 1917-
　　1929; DLB 4, 16, 54, 86; MTCW 1, 2
Williamson, David (Keith) 1942-　　**CLC 56**
　See also CA 103; CANR 41
Williamson, Ellen Douglas 1905-1984
　See Douglas, Ellen
　See also CA 17-20R; 114; CANR 39
Williamson, Jack　　　　　　　**CLC 29**
　See also Williamson, John Stewart
　See also CAAS 8; DLB 8
Williamson, John Stewart 1908-
　See Williamson, Jack
　See also CA 17-20R; CANR 23, 70
Willie, Frederick
　See Lovecraft, H(oward) P(hillips)
Willingham, Calder (Baynard, Jr.) 1922-1995
　　CLC 5, 51

　See also CA 5-8R; 147; CANR 3; DLB 2, 44;
　　MTCW 1
Willis, Charles
　See Clarke, Arthur C(harles)
Willis, Fingal O'Flahertie
　See Wilde, Oscar
Willy
　See Colette, (Sidonie-Gabrielle)
Willy, Colette
　See Colette, (Sidonie-Gabrielle)
Wilson, A(ndrew) N(orman) 1950-　　**CLC 33**
　See also CA 112; 122; DLB 14, 155, 194;
　　MTCW 2
Wilson, Angus (Frank Johnstone) 1913-1991
　　CLC 2, 3, 5, 25, 34; SSC 21
　See also CA 5-8R; 134; CANR 21; DLB 15,
　　139, 155; MTCW 1, 2
Wilson, August 1945-　　**CLC 39, 50, 63, 118;
　BLC 3; DA; DAB; DAC; DAM DRAM,
　-MST, MULT; DC 2; WLCS**
　See also AAYA 16; BW 2, 3; CA 115; 122;
　　CANR 42, 54, 76; MTCW 1, 2
Wilson, Brian 1942-　　　　　**CLC 12**
Wilson, Colin 1931-　　　　　**CLC 3, 14**
　See also CA 1-4R; CAAS 5; CANR 1, 22, 33,
　　77; DLB 14, 194; MTCW 1
Wilson, Dirk
　See Pohl, Frederik
Wilson, Edmund 1895-1972**CLC 1, 2, 3, 8, 24**
　See also CA 1-4R; 37-40R; CANR 1, 46; DLB
　　63; MTCW 1, 2
Wilson, Ethel Davis (Bryant) 1888(?)-1980
　　CLC 13; DAC; DAM POET
　See also CA 102; DLB 68; MTCW 1
Wilson, John 1785-1854　　　　**NCLC 5**
Wilson, John (Anthony) Burgess 1917-1993
　See Burgess, Anthony
　See also CA 1-4R; 143; CANR 2, 46; DAC;
　　DAM NOV; MTCW 1, 2
Wilson, Lanford 1937-　**CLC 7, 14, 36; DAM
　DRAM**
　See also CA 17-20R; CABS 3; CANR 45; DLB
　　7
Wilson, Robert M. 1944-　　　　**CLC 7, 9**
　See also CA 49-52; CANR 2, 41; MTCW 1
Wilson, Robert McLiam 1964-　　**CLC 59**
　See also CA 132
Wilson, Sloan 1920-　　　　　**CLC 32**
　See also CA 1-4R; CANR 1, 44
Wilson, Snoo 1948-　　　　　**CLC 33**
　See also CA 69-72
Wilson, William S(mith) 1932-　　**CLC 49**
　See also CA 81-84
Wilson, (Thomas) Woodrow 1856-1924**T C L C
　79**
　See also CA 166; DLB 47
Winchilsea, Anne (Kingsmill) Finch Counte
　　1661-1720
　See Finch, Anne
Windham, Basil
　See Wodehouse, P(elham) G(renville)
Wingrove, David (John) 1954-　　**CLC 68**
　See also CA 133
Winnemucca, Sarah 1844-1891　　**NCLC 79**
Winstanley, Gerrard 1609-1676　　**LC 52**
Wintergreen, Jane
　See Duncan, Sara Jeannette
Winters, Janet Lewis　　　　　　**CLC 41**
　See also Lewis, Janet
　See also DLBY 87
Winters, (Arthur) Yvor 1900-1968　**CLC 4, 8,
　32**
　See also CA 11-12; 25-28R; CAP 1; DLB 48;

　　MTCW 1
Winterson, Jeanette 1959-**CLC 64;DAM POP**
　See also CA 136; CANR 58; DLB 207; MTCW
　　2
Winthrop, John 1588-1649　　　　**LC 31**
　See also DLB 24, 30
Wirth, Louis 1897-1952　　　　**TCLC 92**
Wiseman, Frederick 1930-　　　　**CLC 20**
　See also CA 159
Wister, Owen 1860-1938　　　　**TCLC 21**
　See also CA 108; 162; DLB 9, 78, 186; SATA
　　62
Witkacy
　See Witkiewicz, Stanislaw Ignacy
Witkiewicz, Stanislaw Ignacy 1885-1939
　　TCLC 8
　See also CA 105; 162
Wittgenstein, Ludwig (Josef Johann) 1889-1951
　　TCLC 59
　See also CA 113; 164; MTCW 2
Wittig, Monique 1935(?)-　　　　**CLC 22**
　See also CA 116; 135; DLB 83
Wittlin, Jozef 1896-1976　　　　**CLC 25**
　See also CA 49-52; 65-68; CANR 3
Wodehouse, P(elham) G(renville) 1881-1975
　　**CLC 1, 2, 5, 10, 22; DAB; DAC; DAM
　NOV; SSC 2**
　See also AITN 2; CA 45-48; 57-60; CANR 3,
　　33; CDBLB 1914-1945; DLB 34, 162;
　　MTCW 1, 2; SATA 22
Woiwode, L.
　See Woiwode, Larry (Alfred)
Woiwode, Larry (Alfred) 1941-　　**CLC 6, 10**
　See also CA 73-76; CANR 16; DLB 6; INT
　　CANR-16
Wojciechowska, Maia (Teresa) 1927-**CLC 26**
　See also AAYA 8; CA 9-12R; CANR 4, 41; CLR
　　1; JRDA; MAICYA; SAAS 1; SATA 1, 28,
　　83; SATA-Essay 104
Wolf, Christa 1929-　　　　　**CLC 14, 29, 58**
　See also CA 85-88; CANR 45; DLB 75; MTCW
　　1
Wolfe, Gene (Rodman) 1931-　**CLC 25;DAM
　POP**
　See also CA 57-60; CAAS 9; CANR 6, 32, 60;
　　DLB 8; MTCW 2
Wolfe, George C. 1954-　　　**CLC 49; BLCS**
　See also CA 149
Wolfe, Thomas (Clayton) 1900-1938**TCLC 4,
　13, 29, 61; DA; DAB; DAC; DAM MST,
　NOV; SSC 33; WLC**
　See also CA 104; 132; CDALB 1929-1941;
　　DLB 9, 102; DLBD 2, 16; DLBY 85, 97;
　　MTCW 1, 2
Wolfe, Thomas Kennerly, Jr. 1930-
　See Wolfe, Tom
　See also CA 13-16R; CANR 9, 33, 70; DAM
　　POP; DLB 185; INT CANR-9; MTCW 1, 2
Wolfe, Tom　　　　　**CLC 1, 2, 9, 15, 35, 51**
　See also Wolfe, Thomas Kennerly, Jr.
　See also AAYA 8; AITN 2; BEST 89:1; DLB
　　152
Wolff, Geoffrey (Ansell) 1937-　　**CLC 41**
　See also CA 29-32R; CANR 29, 43, 78
Wolff, Sonia
　See Levitin, Sonia (Wolff)
Wolff, Tobias (Jonathan Ansell) 1945-　**C L C
　39, 64**
　See also AAYA 16; BEST 90:2; CA 114; 117;
　　CAAS 22; CANR 54, 76; DLB 130; INT 117;
　　MTCW 2
Wolfram von Eschenbach c. 1170-c. 1220
　　CMLC 5

See also DLB 138

Wolitzer, Hilma 1930- **CLC 17**
See also CA 65-68; CANR 18, 40; INT CANR-18; SATA 31

Wollstonecraft, Mary 1759-1797 **LC 5, 50**
See also CDBLB 1789-1832; DLB 39, 104, 158

Wonder, Stevie **CLC 12**
See also Morris, Steveland Judkins

Wong, Jade Snow 1922- **CLC 17**
See also CA 109

Woodberry, George Edward 1855-1930
TCLC 73
See also CA 165; DLB 71, 103

Woodcott, Keith
See Brunner, John (Kilian Houston)

Woodruff, Robert W.
See Mencken, H(enry) L(ouis)

Woolf, (Adeline) Virginia 1882-1941**TCLC 1,**
5, 20, 43, 56; DA; DAB; DAC; DAM MST,
NOV; SSC 7; WLC
See also Woolf, Virginia Adeline
See also CA 104; 130; CANR 64; CDBLB
1914-1945; DLB 36, 100, 162; DLBD 10;
MTCW 1

Woolf, Virginia Adeline
See Woolf, (Adeline) Virginia
See also MTCW 2

Woollcott, Alexander (Humphreys) 1887-1943
TCLC 5
See also CA 105; 161; DLB 29

Woolrich,Cornell 1903-1968 **CLC 77**
See also Hopley-Woolrich, Cornell George

Wordsworth, Dorothy 1771-1855 **NCLC 25**
See also DLB 107

Wordsworth, William 1770-1850 **NCLC 12,**
38; DA; DAB; DAC; DAM MST, POET;
PC 4; WLC
See also CDBLB 1789-1832; DLB 93, 107

Wouk, Herman 1915-**CLC 1, 9, 38; DAM NOV,**
POP
See also CA 5-8R; CANR 6, 33, 67; CDALBS;
DLBY 82; INT CANR-6; MTCW 1, 2

Wright, Charles (Penzel, Jr.) 1935-**CLC 6, 13,**
28, 119
See also CA 29-32R; CAAS 7; CANR 23, 36,
62; DLB 165; DLBY 82; MTCW 1, 2

Wright, Charles Stevenson 1932- **CLC 49;**
BLC 3; DAM MULT, POET
See also BW 1; CA 9-12R; CANR 26; DLB 33

Wright, Frances 1795-1852 **NCLC 74**
See also DLB 73

Wright, Frank Lloyd 1867-1959 **TCLC 95**
See also CA 174

Wright, Jack R.
See Harris, Mark

Wright, James (Arlington) 1927-1980**CLC 3,**
5, 10, 28; DAM POET
See also AITN 2; CA 49-52; 97-100; CANR 4,
34, 64; CDALBS; DLB 5, 169; MTCW 1, 2

Wright, Judith (Arandell) 1915- **CLC 11, 53;**
PC 14
See also CA 13-16R; CANR 31, 76; MTCW 1,
2; SATA 14

Wright, L(auraii) R. 1939- **CLC 44**
See also CA 138

Wright, Richard (Nathaniel) 1908-1960 **C L C**
1, 3, 4, 9, 14, 21, 48, 74; BLC 3; DA; DAB;
DAC; DAM MST, MULT, NOV; SSC 2;
WLC
See also AAYA 5; BW 1; CA 108; CANR
64;CDALB 1929-1941; DLB 76, 102; DLBD
2; MTCW 1, 2

Wright, Richard B(ruce) 1937- **CLC 6**

See also CA 85-88; DLB 53

Wright, Rick 1945- **CLC 35**

Wright, Rowland
See Wells, Carolyn

Wright, Stephen 1946- **CLC 33**

Wright, Willard Huntington 1888-1939
See Van Dine, S. S.
See also CA 115; DLBD 16

Wright, William 1930- **CLC 44**
See also CA 53-56; CANR 7, 23

Wroth, Lady Mary 1587-1653(?) **LC 30**
See also DLB 121

Wu Ch'eng-en 1500(?)-1582(?) **LC 7**

Wu Ching-tzu 1701-1754 **LC 2**

Wurlitzer, Rudolph 1938(?)- **CLC 2, 4, 15**
See also CA 85-88; DLB 173

Wyatt, Thomas c. 1503-1542 **PC 27**
See also DLB 132

Wycherley, William 1641-1715**LC 8, 21; DAM**
DRAM
See also CDBLB 1660-1789; DLB 80

Wylie, Elinor (Morton Hoyt) 1885-1928
TCLC 8; PC 23
See also CA 105; 162; DLB 9, 45

Wylie, Philip (Gordon) 1902-1971 **CLC 43**
See also CA 21-22; 33-36R; CAP 2; DLB 9

Wyndham, John **CLC 19**
See also Harris, John (Wyndham Parkes Lucas)
Beynon

Wyss, Johann David Von 1743-1818**NCLC 10**
See also JRDA; MAICYA; SATA 29; SATA-
Brief 27

Xenophon c. 430B.C.-c.354B.C. **CMLC 17**
See also DLB 176

Yakumo Koizumi
See Hearn, (Patricio) Lafcadio (Tessima Carlos)

Yamamoto, Hisaye 1921-**SSC 34; DAM MULT**

Yanez, Jose Donoso
See Donoso (Yanez), Jose

Yanovsky, Basile S.
See Yanovsky, V(assily) S(emenovich)

Yanovsky, V(assily) S(emenovich) 1906-1989
CLC 2, 18
See also CA 97-100; 129

Yates, Richard 1926-1992 **CLC 7, 8, 23**
See also CA 5-8R; 139; CANR 10, 43; DLB 2;
DLBY 81, 92; INT CANR-10

Yeats, W. B.
See Yeats, William Butler

Yeats, William Butler 1865-1939**TCLC 1, 11,**
18, 31, 93; DA; DAB; DAC; DAM DRAM,
MST, POET; PC 20; WLC
See also CA 104; 127; CANR 45; CDBLB
1890-1914; DLB 10, 19, 98, 156; MTCW 1,
2

Yehoshua, A(braham) B. 1936- **CLC 13, 31**
See also CA 33-36R; CANR 43

Yep, Laurence Michael 1948- **CLC 35**
See also AAYA 5; CA 49-52; CANR 1, 46; CLR
3, 17, 54; DLB 52; JRDA; MAICYA; SATA
7, 69

Yerby, Frank G(arvin) 1916-1991 **CLC 1, 7,**
22; BLC 3; DAM MULT
See also BW 1, 3; CA 9-12R; 136; CANR 16,
52; DLB 76; INT CANR-16; MTCW 1

Yesenin, Sergei Alexandrovich
See Esenin, Sergei (Alexandrovich)

Yevtushenko, Yevgeny (Alexandrovich) 1933-
CLC 1, 3, 13, 26, 51; DAM POET
See also CA 81-84; CANR 33, 54; MTCW 1

Yezierska, Anzia 1885(?)-1970 **CLC 46**
See also CA 126; 89-92; DLB 28; MTCW 1

Yglesias, Helen 1915- **CLC 7, 22**

See also CA 37-40R; CAAS 20; CANR 15, 65;
INT CANR-15; MTCW 1

Yokomitsu Riichi 1898-1947 **TCLC 47**
See also CA 170

Yonge, Charlotte(Mary) 1823-1901 **TCLC 48**
See also CA 109; 163; DLB 18, 163; SATA 17

York, Jeremy
See Creasey, John

York, Simon
See Heinlein, Robert A(nson)

Yorke, Henry Vincent 1905-1974 **CLC 13**
See also Green, Henry
See also CA 85-88; 49-52

Yosano Akiko 1878-1942 **TCLC 59;PC 11**
See also CA 161

Yoshimoto, Banana **CLC 84**
See also Yoshimoto, Mahoko

Yoshimoto, Mahoko 1964-
See Yoshimoto, Banana
See also CA 144

Young, Al(bert James) 1939-**CLC 19; BLC 3;**
DAM MULT
See also BW 2, 3; CA 29-32R; CANR 26, 65;
DLB 33

Young, Andrew(John) 1885-1971 **CLC 5**
See also CA 5-8R; CANR 7, 29

Young, Collier 1917-1994
See Bloch, Robert (Albert)
See also CA 179; CAAE 179

Young, Edward 1683-1765 **LC 3, 40**
See also DLB 95

Young, Marguerite(Vivian) 1909-1995**CLC 82**
See also CA 13-16; 150; CAP 1

Young, Neil 1945- **CLC 17**
See also CA 110

Young Bear, Ray A. 1950- **CLC 94;DAM**
MULT
See also CA 146; DLB 175; NNAL

Yourcenar, Marguerite 1903-1987**CLC 19, 38,**
50, 87; DAM NOV
See also CA 69-72; CANR 23, 60; DLB 72;
DLBY 88; MTCW 1, 2

Yurick, Sol 1925- **CLC 6**
See also CA 13-16R; CANR 25

Zabolotsky, NikolaiAlekseevich 1903-1958
TCLC 52
See also CA 116; 164

Zagajewski, Adam **PC 27**

Zamiatin, Yevgeni
See Zamyatin, Evgeny Ivanovich

Zamora, Bernice (B. Ortiz) 1938- **CLC 89;**
DAM MULT; HLC 2
See also CA 151; CANR 80; DLB 82; HW 1, 2

Zamyatin, Evgeny Ivanovich 1884-1937
TCLC 8, 37
See also CA 105; 166

Zangwill, Israel 1864-1926 **TCLC 16**
See also CA 109; 167; DLB 10, 135, 197

Zappa, Francis Vincent, Jr. 1940-1993
See Zappa, Frank
See also CA 108; 143; CANR 57

Zappa, Frank **CLC 17**
See also Zappa, Francis Vincent, Jr.

Zaturenska, Marya 1902-1982 **CLC 6,11**
See also CA 13-16R; 105; CANR 22

Zeami 1363-1443 **DC 7**

Zelazny, Roger(Joseph) 1937-1995 **CLC 21**
See also AAYA 7; CA 21-24R; 148; CANR 26,
60; DLB 8; MTCW 1, 2; SATA57;SATA-
Brief 39

Zhdanov, AndreiAlexandrovich 1896-1948
TCLC 18
See also CA 117; 167

Zhukovsky, Vasily(Andreevich) 1783-1852
NCLC 35
See also DLB 205
Ziegenhagen, Eric **CLC 55**
Zimmer, Jill Schary
See Robinson, Jill
Zimmerman, Robert
See Dylan, Bob
Zindel, Paul 1936-**CLC 6, 26; DA; DAB; DAC;**
DAM DRAM, MST, NOV; DC 5
See also AAYA 2; CA 73-76; CANR 31, 65;
CDALBS; CLR 3, 45; DLB 7, 52; JRDA;
MAICYA; MTCW 1, 2; SATA 16, 58, 102
Zinov'Ev, A. A.
See Zinoviev, Alexander (Aleksandrovich)
Zinoviev, Alexander(Aleksandrovich) 1922-
CLC 19
See also CA 116; 133; CAAS 10
Zoilus
See Lovecraft, H(oward) P(hillips)
Zola, Emile (Edouard Charles Antoine) 1840-
1902**TCLC 1, 6, 21, 41; DA; DAB; DAC;**
DAM MST, NOV; WLC
See also CA 104; 138; DLB 123
Zoline, Pamela 1941- **CLC 62**
See also CA 161
Zorrilla y Moral, Jose 1817-1893 **NCLC 6**
Zoshchenko, Mikhail (Mikhailovich) 1895-1958
TCLC 15; SSC 15
See also CA 115; 160
Zuckmayer, Carl 1896-1977 **CLC 18**
See also CA 69-72; DLB 56, 124
Zuk, Georges
See Skelton, Robin
Zukofsky, Louis 1904-1978**CLC 1, 2, 4, 7, 11,**
18; DAM POET; PC 11
See also CA 9-12R; 77-80; CANR 39; DLB 5,
165; MTCW 1
Zweig, Paul 1935-1984 **CLC 34, 42**
See also CA 85-88; 113
Zweig, Stefan 1881-1942 **TCLC 17**
See also CA 112; 170; DLB 81, 118
Zwingli, Huldreich 1484-1531 **LC 37**
See also DLB 179

Literary Criticism Series
Cumulative Topic Index

This index lists all topic entries in Gale's *Classical and Medieval Literature Criticism, Contemporary Literary Criticism, Literature Criticism from 1400 to 1800, Nineteenth-Century Literature Criticism,* and *Twentieth-Century Literary Criticism.*

Age of Johnson LC 15: 1-87
Johnson's London, 3-15
aesthetics of neoclassicism, 15-36
"age of prose and reason," 36-45
clubmen and bluestockings, 45-56
printing technology, 56-62
periodicals: "a map of busy life," 62-74
transition, 74-86

Age of Spenser LC 39: 1-70
Overviews, 2-21
Literary Style, 22-34
Poets and the Crown, 34-70

AIDS in Literature CLC 81: 365-416

Alcohol and Literature TCLC 70: 1-58
overview, 2-8
fiction, 8-48
poetry and drama, 48-58

American Abolitionism NCLC 44: 1-73
overviews, 2-26
abolitionist ideals, 26-46
the literature of abolitionism, 46-72

American Autobiography TCLC 86: 1-115
overviews, 3-36
American authors and autobiography, 36-82
African-American autobiography, 82-114

American Black Humor Fiction TCLC 54: 1-85
characteristics of black humor, 2-13
origins and development, 13-38
black humor distinguished from related literary trends, 38-60
black humor and society, 60-75
black humor reconsidered, 75-83

American Civil War in Literature NCLC 32: 1-109
overviews, 2-20
regional perspectives, 20-54

fiction popular during the war, 54-79
the historical novel, 79-108

American Frontier in Literature NCLC 28: 1-103
definitions, 2-12
development, 12-17
nonfiction writing about the frontier, 17-30
frontier fiction, 30-45
frontier protagonists, 45-66
portrayals of Native Americans, 66-86
feminist readings, 86-98
twentieth-century reaction against frontier literature, 98-100

American Humor Writing NCLC 52: 1-59
overviews, 2-12
the Old Southwest, 12-42
broader impacts, 42-5
women humorists, 45-58

***American Mercury,* The TCLC 74: 1-80**

American Popular Song, Golden Age of TCLC 42: 1-49
background and major figures, 2-34
the lyrics of popular songs, 34-47

American Proletarian Literature TCLC 54: 86-175
overviews, 87-95
American proletarian literature and the American Communist Party, 95-111
ideology and literary merit, 111-7
novels, 117-36
Gastonia, 136-48
drama, 148-54
journalism, 154-9
proletarian literature in the United States, 159-74

American Romanticism NCLC 44: 74-138
overviews, 74-84
sociopolitical influences, 84-104
Romanticism and the American frontier,

104-15
thematic concerns, 115-37

American Western Literature TCLC 46: 1-100
definition and development of American Western literature, 2-7
characteristics of the Western novel, 8-23
Westerns as history and fiction, 23-34
critical reception of American Western literature, 34-41
the Western hero, 41-73
women in Western fiction, 73-91
later Western fiction, 91-9

Art and Literature TCLC 54: 176-248
overviews, 176-93
definitions, 193-219
influence of visual arts on literature, 219-31
spatial form in literature, 231-47

Arthurian Literature CMLC 10: 1-127
historical context and literary beginnings, 2-27
development of the legend through Malory, 27-64
development of the legend from Malory to the Victorian Age, 65-81
themes and motifs, 81-95
principal characters, 95-125

Arthurian Revival NCLC 36: 1-77
overviews, 2-12
Tennyson and his influence, 12-43
other leading figures, 43-73
the Arthurian legend in the visual arts, 73-6

Australian Literature TCLC 50: 1-94
origins and development, 2-21
characteristics of Australian literature, 21-33
historical and critical perspectives, 33-41
poetry, 41-58

fiction, 58-76
drama, 76-82
Aboriginal literature, 82-91

Beat Generation, Literature of the TCLC 42: 50-102
overviews, 51-9
the Beat generation as a social phenomenon, 59-62
development, 62-5
Beat literature, 66-96
influence, 97-100

The Bell Curve Controversy CLC 91: 281-330

Bildungsroman in Nineteenth-Century Literature NCLC 20: 92-168
surveys, 93-113
in Germany, 113-40
in England, 140-56
female *Bildungsroman,* 156-67

Bloomsbury Group TCLC 34: 1-73
history and major figures, 2-13
definitions, 13-7
influences, 17-27
thought, 27-40
prose, 40-52
and literary criticism, 52-4
political ideals, 54-61
response to, 61-71

The Blues in Literature TCLC 82: 1-71

Bly, Robert, *Iron John: A Book about Men and Men's Work* **CLC 70: 414-62**

The Book of J CLC 65: 289-311

Buddhism and Literature TCLC 70: 59-164
eastern literature, 60-113
western literature, 113-63

Businessman in American Literature TCLC 26: 1-48
portrayal of the businessman, 1-32
themes and techniques in business fiction, 32-47

Catholicism in Nineteenth-Century American Literature NCLC 64: 1-58
overviews, 3-14
polemical literature, 14-46
Catholicism in literature, 47-57

Celtic Mythology CMLC 26: 1-111
overviews, 2-22
Celtic myth as literature and history, 22-

48
Celtic religion: Druids and divinities, 48-80
Fionn MacCuhaill and the Fenian cycle, 80-111

Celtic Twilight
See Irish Literary Renaissance

Chartist Movement and Literature, The NCLC 60: 1-84
overview: nineteenth-century working-class fiction, 2-19
Chartist fiction and poetry, 19-73
the Chartist press, 73-84

Children's Literature, Nineteenth-Century NCLC 52: 60-135
overviews, 61-72
moral tales, 72-89
fairy tales and fantasy, 90-119
making men/making women, 119-34

The City and Literature TCLC 90: 1-124
Overviews, 2-9
The City in American Literature, 9-86
The City in European Literature, 86-124

Civic Critics, Russian NCLC 20: 402-46
principal figures and background, 402-9
and Russian Nihilism, 410-6
aesthetic and critical views, 416-45

The Cockney School NCLC 68: 1-64
overview, 2-7
Blackwood's Magazine and the contemporary critical response, 7-24
the political and social import of the Cockneys and their critics, 24-63

Colonial America: The Intellectual Background LC 25: 1-98
overviews, 2-17
philosophy and politics, 17-31
early religious influences in Colonial America, 31-60
consequences of the Revolution, 60-78
religious influences in post-revolutionary America, 78-87
colonial literary genres, 87-97

Colonialism in Victorian English Literature NCLC 56: 1-77
overviews, 2-34
colonialism and gender, 34-51
monsters and the occult, 51-76

Columbus, Christopher, Books on the Quincentennial of His Arrival in the New World CLC 70: 329-60

Comic Books TCLC 66: 1-139
historical and critical perspectives, 2-48
superheroes, 48-67
underground comix, 67-88
comic books and society, 88-122
adult comics and graphic novels, 122-36

Connecticut Wits NCLC 48: 1-95
general overviews, 2-40
major works, 40-76
intellectual context, 76-95

Crime in Literature TCLC 54: 249-307
evolution of the criminal figure in literature, 250-61
crime and society, 261-77
literary perspectives on crime and punishment, 277-88
writings by criminals, 288-306

Czechoslovakian Literature of the Twentieth Century TCLC 42: 103-96
through World War II, 104-35
de-Stalinization, the Prague Spring, and contemporary literature, 135-72
Slovak literature, 172-85
Czech science fiction, 185-93

Dadaism TCLC 46: 101-71
background and major figures, 102-16
definitions, 116-26
manifestos and commentary by Dadaists, 126-40
theater and film, 140-58
nature and characteristics of Dadaist writing, 158-70

Darwinism and Literature NCLC 32: 110-206
background, 110-31
direct responses to Darwin, 131-71
collateral effects of Darwinism, 171-205

Death in Nineteenth-Century British Literature NCLC 68: 65-142
overviews, 66-92
responses to death, 92-102
feminist perspectives, 103-17
striving for immortality, 117-41

Death in Literature TCLC 78:1-183
fiction, 2-115
poetry, 115-46
drama, 146-81

de Man, Paul, Wartime Journalism of CLC 55: 382-424

Detective Fiction, Nineteenth-Century NCLC 36: 78-148

origins of the genre, 79-100
history of nineteenth-century detective
fiction, 101-33
significance of nineteenth-century
detective fiction, 133-46

**Detective Fiction, Twentieth-Century
TCLC 38: 1-96**
genesis and history of the detective
story, 3-22
defining detective fiction, 22-32
evolution and varieties, 32-77
the appeal of detective fiction, 77-90

**Disease and Literature TCLC 66: 140-
283**
overviews, 141-65
disease in nineteenth-century literature,
165-81
tuberculosis and literature, 181-94
women and disease in literature, 194-
221
plague literature, 221-53
AIDS in literature, 253-82

**The Double in Nineteenth-Century
Literature NCLC 40: 1-95**
genesis and development of the theme,
2-15
the double and Romanticism, 16-27
sociological views, 27-52
psychological interpretations, 52-87
philosophical considerations, 87-95

Dramatic Realism NCLC 44: 139-202
overviews, 140-50
origins and definitions, 150-66
impact and influence, 166-93
realist drama and tragedy, 193-201

Drugs and Literature TCLC 78: 184-282
overviews, 185-201
pre-twentieth-century literature, 201-42
twentieth-century literature, 242-82

Eastern Mythology CMLC 26: 112-92
heroes and kings, 113-51
cross-cultural perspective, 151-69
relations to history and society, 169-
92

**Electronic "Books": Hypertext and
Hyperfiction CLC 86: 367-404**
books vs. CD-ROMS, 367-76
hypertext and hyperfiction, 376-95
implications for publishing, libraries,
and the public, 395-403

**Eliot, T. S., Centenary of Birth CLC 55:
345-75**

Elizabethan Drama LC 22: 140-240
origins and influences, 142-67
characteristics and conventions, 167-83
theatrical production, 184-200
histories, 200-12
comedy, 213-20
tragedy, 220-30

Elizabethan Prose Fiction LC 41: 1-70
overviews, 1-15
origins and influences, 15-43
style and structure, 43-69

The Encyclopedists LC 26: 172-253
overviews, 173-210
intellectual background, 210-32
views on esthetics, 232-41
views on women, 241-52

**English Caroline Literature LC 13: 221-
307**
background, 222-41
evolution and varieties, 241-62
the Cavalier mode, 262-75
court and society, 275-91
politics and religion, 291-306

**English Decadent Literature of the 1890s
NCLC 28: 104-200**
fin de siècle: the Decadent period, 105-
19
definitions, 120-37
major figures: "the tragic generation,"
137-50
French literature and English literary
Decadence, 150-7
themes, 157-61
poetry, 161-82
periodicals, 182-96

English Essay, Rise of the LC 18: 238-308
definitions and origins, 236-54
influence on the essay, 254-69
historical background, 269-78
the essay in the seventeenth century,
279-93
the essay in the eighteenth century, 293-
307

**English Mystery Cycle Dramas LC 34: 1-
88**
overviews, 1-27
the nature of dramatic performances, 27-
42
the medieval worldview and the mystery
cycles, 43-67
the doctrine of repentance and the
mystery cycles, 67-76
the fall from grace in the mystery cycles,
76-88

**English Revolution, Literature of the LC
43: 1-58**
overviews, 2-24
pamphlets of the English Revolution,
24-38
political Sermons of the English
Revolution, 38-48
poetry of the English Revolution, 48-
57

**English Romantic Hellenism NCLC 68:
143-250**
overviews, 144-69
historical development of English
Romantic Hellenism, 169-91
inflience of Greek mythology on the
Romantics, 191-229
influence of Greek literature, art, and
culture on the Romantics, 229-50

**English Romantic Poetry NCLC 28: 201-
327**
overviews and reputation, 202-37
major subjects and themes, 237-67
forms of Romantic poetry, 267-78
politics, society, and Romantic poetry,
278-99
philosophy, religion, and Romantic
poetry, 299-324

Espionage Literature TCLC 50: 95-159
overviews, 96-113
espionage fiction/formula fiction, 113-
26
spies in fact and fiction, 126-38
the female spy, 138-44
social and psychological perspectives,
144-58

**European Romanticism NCLC 36: 149-
284**
definitions, 149-77
origins of the movement, 177-82
Romantic theory, 182-200
themes and techniques, 200-23
Romanticism in Germany, 223-39
Romanticism in France, 240-61
Romanticism in Italy, 261-4
Romanticism in Spain, 264-8
impact and legacy, 268-82

**Existentialism and Literature TCLC 42:
197-268**
overviews and definitions, 198-209
history and influences, 209-19
Existentialism critiqued and defended,
220-35
philosophical and religious perspectives,
235-41
Existentialist fiction and drama, 241-67

Topic Index

Familiar Essay NCLC 48: 96-211
  definitions and origins, 97-130
  overview of the genre, 130-43
  elements of form and style, 143-59
  elements of content, 159-73
  the Cockneys: Hazlitt, Lamb, and Hunt,
    173-91
  status of the genre, 191-210

The Faust Legend LC 47: 1-117

Fear in Literature TCLC 74: 81-258
  overviews, 81
  pre-twentieth-century literature, 123
  twentieth-century literature, 182

Feminism in the 1990s: Commentary on Works by Naomi Wolf, Susan Faludi, and Camille Paglia CLC 76: 377-415

Feminist Criticism in 1990 CLC 65: 312-60

Fifteenth-Century English Literature LC 17: 248-334
  background, 249-72
  poetry, 272-315
  drama, 315-23
  prose, 323-33

Film and Literature TCLC 38: 97-226
  overviews, 97-119
  film and theater, 119-34
  film and the novel, 134-45
  the art of the screenplay, 145-66
  genre literature/genre film, 167-79
  the writer and the film industry, 179-90
  authors on film adaptations of their
    works, 190-200
  fiction into film: comparative essays,
    200-23

Finance and Money as Represented in Nineteenth-Century Literature NCLC 76: 1-69
  historical perspectives, 2-20
  the image of money, 20-37
  the dangers of money, 37-50
  women and money, 50-69

Folklore and Literature TCLC 86: 116-293
  overviews, 118-144
  Native American literature, 144-67
  African-American literature, 167-238
  Folklore and the American West, 238-57
  Modern and postmodern literature, 257-91

French Drama in the Age of Louis XIV LC 28: 94-185
  overview, 95-127
  tragedy, 127-46
  comedy, 146-66
  tragicomedy, 166-84

French Enlightenment LC 14: 81-145
  the question of definition, 82-9
  Le siècle des lumières, 89-94
  women and the salons, 94-105
  censorship, 105-15
  the philosophy of reason, 115-31
  influence and legacy, 131-44

French Realism NCLC 52: 136-216
  origins and definitions, 137-70
  issues and influence, 170-98
  realism and representation, 198-215

French Revolution and English Literature NCLC 40: 96-195
  history and theory, 96-123
  romantic poetry, 123-50
  the novel, 150-81
  drama, 181-92
  children's literature, 192-5

Futurism, Italian TCLC 42: 269-354
  principles and formative influences,
    271-9
  manifestos, 279-88
  literature, 288-303
  theater, 303-19
  art, 320-30
  music, 330-6
  architecture, 336-9
  and politics, 339-46
  reputation and significance, 346-51

**Gaelic Revival
See Irish Literary Renaissance**

Gates, Henry Louis, Jr., and African-American Literary Criticism CLC 65: 361-405

Gay and Lesbian Literature CLC 76: 416-39

German Exile Literature TCLC 30: 1-58
  the writer and the Nazi state, 1-10
  definition of, 10-4
  life in exile, 14-32
  surveys, 32-50
  Austrian literature in exile, 50-2
  German publishing in the United States,
    52-7

German Expressionism TCLC 34: 74-160
  history and major figures, 76-85
  aesthetic theories, 85-109
  drama, 109-26
  poetry, 126-38
  film, 138-42
  painting, 142-7
  music, 147-53
  and politics, 153-8

***Glasnost* and Contemporary Soviet Literature CLC 59: 355-97**

Gothic Novel NCLC 28: 328-402
  development and major works, 328-34
  definitions, 334-50
  themes and techniques, 350-78
  in America, 378-85
  in Scotland, 385-91
  influence and legacy, 391-400

Graphic Narratives CLC 86: 405-32
  history and overviews, 406-21
  the "Classics Illustrated" series, 421-2
  reviews of recent works, 422-32

Greek Historiography CMLC 17: 1-49

Greek Mythology CMLC-26 193-320
  overviews, 194-209
  origins and development of Greek
    mythology, 209-29
  cosmogonies and divinities in Greek
    mythology, 229-54
  heroes and heroines in Greek mythol-
    ogy, 254-80
  women in Greek mythology, 280-320

Harlem Renaissance TCLC 26: 49-125
  principal issues and figures, 50-67
  the literature and its audience, 67-74
  theme and technique in poetry, fiction,
    and drama, 74-115
  and American society, 115-21
  achievement and influence, 121-2

Havel, Václav, Playwright and President CLC 65: 406-63

Historical Fiction, Nineteenth-Century NCLC 48: 212-307
  definitions and characteristics, 213-36
  Victorian historical fiction, 236-65
  American historical fiction, 265-88
  realism in historical fiction, 288-306

Holocaust and the Atomic Bomb: Fifty Years Later CLC 91: 331-82
  the Holocaust remembered, 333-52
  Anne Frank revisited, 352-62
  the atomic bomb and American memory,
    362-81

Holocaust Denial Literature TCLC 58: 1-110
  overviews, 1-30
  Robert Faurisson and Noam Chomsky,
    30-52
  Holocaust denial literature in America,
    52-71
  library access to Holocaust denial
    literature, 72-5
  the authenticity of Anne Frank's diary,
    76-90
  David Irving and the "normalization" of
    Hitler, 90-109

Holocaust, Literature of the TCLC 42:
355-450
  historical overview, 357-61
  critical overview, 361-70
  diaries and memoirs, 370-95
  novels and short stories, 395-425
  poetry, 425-41
  drama, 441-8

Homosexuality in Nineteenth-Century
Literature NCLC 56: 78-182
  defining homosexuality, 80-111
  Greek love, 111-44
  trial and danger, 144-81

Hungarian Literature of the Twentieth
Century TCLC 26: 126-88
  surveys of, 126-47
  Nyugat and early twentieth-century
    literature, 147-56
  mid-century literature, 156-68
  and politics, 168-78
  since the 1956 revolt, 178-87

Hysteria in Nineteenth-Century Literature
NCLC 64: 59-184
  the history of hysteria, 60-75
  the gender of hysteria, 75-103
  hysteria and women's narratives, 103-57
  hysteria in nineteenth-century poetry,
    157-83

Imagism TCLC 74: 259-454
  history and development, 260
  major figures, 288
  sources and influences, 352
  Imagism and other movements, 397
  influence and legacy, 431

Incest in Nineteenth-Century American
Literature NCLC 76: 70-141
  overview, 71-88
  the concern for social order, 88-117
  authority and authorship, 117-40

Indian Literature in English TCLC 54:
308-406
  overview, 309-13
  origins and major figures, 313-25
  the Indo-English novel, 325-55
  Indo-English poetry, 355-67
  Indo-English drama, 367-72
  critical perspectives on Indo-English
    literature, 372-80
  modern Indo-English literature, 380-9
  Indo-English authors on their work,
    389-404

Industrial Revolution in Literature, The
NCLC 56: 183-273
  historical and cultural perspectives, 184-
    201
  contemporary reactions to the machine,
    201-21
  themes and symbols in literature, 221-
    73

The Irish Famine as Represented in
Nineteenth-Century Literature NCLC 64:
185-261
  overviews, 187-98
  historical background, 198-212
  famine novels, 212-34
  famine poetry, 234-44
  famine letters and eye-witness accounts,
    245-61

Irish Literary Renaissance TCLC 46:
172-287
  overview, 173-83
  development and major figures, 184-202
  influence of Irish folklore and mythol-
    ogy, 202-22
  Irish poetry, 222-34
  Irish drama and the Abbey Theatre, 234-
    56
  Irish fiction, 256-86

Irish Nationalism and Literature NCLC
44: 203-73
  the Celtic element in literature, 203-
    19
  anti-Irish sentiment and the Celtic
    response, 219-34
  literary ideals in Ireland, 234-45
  literary expressions, 245-73

The Irish Novel NCLC 80: 1-130
  overviews, 3-9
  principal figures, 9-22
  peasant and middle class Irish novelists,
    22-76
  aristocratic Irish and Anglo-Irish
    novelists, 76-129

Italian Futurism
See Futurism, Italian

Italian Humanism LC 12: 205-77
  origins and early development, 206-18
  revival of classical letters, 218-23
  humanism and other philosophies, 224-
    39
  humanisms and humanists, 239-46
  the plastic arts, 246-57
  achievement and significance, 258-76

Italian Romanticism NCLC 60: 85-145
  origins and overviews, 86-101
  Italian Romantic theory, 101-25
  the language of Romanticism, 125-45

Jacobean Drama LC 33: 1-37
  the Jacobean worldview: an era of
    transition, 2-14
  the moral vision of Jacobean drama, 14-
    22
  Jacobean tragedy, 22-3
  the Jacobean masque, 23-36

Jewish-American Fiction TCLC 62: 1-
181
  overviews, 2-24
  major figures, 24-48
  Jewish writers and American life, 48-78
  Jewish characters in American fiction,
    78-108
  themes in Jewish-American fiction, 108-
    43
  Jewish-American women writers, 143-
    59
  the Holocaust and Jewish-American
    fiction, 159-81

Knickerbocker Group, The NCLC 56:
274-341
  overviews, 276-314
  Knickerbocker periodicals, 314-26
  writers and artists, 326-40

Lake Poets, The NCLC 52: 217-304
  characteristics of the Lake Poets and
    their works, 218-27
  literary influences and collaborations,
    227-66
  defining and developing Romantic
    ideals, 266-84
  embracing Conservatism, 284-303

Larkin, Philip, Controversy CLC 81:
417-64

Latin American Literature, Twentieth-
Century TCLC 58: 111-98
  historical and critical perspectives, 112-
    36
  the novel, 136-45
  the short story, 145-9

drama, 149-60
poetry, 160-7
the writer and society, 167-86
Native Americans in Latin American
   literature, 186-97

**Literature and Millenial Lists CLC 119:
431-67**
criticism, 434-67
introduction, 431-33
The Modern Library list, 433
The Waterstone list, 438-439

**Madness in Nineteenth-Century Litera-
ture NCLC76: 142-284**
overview, 143-54
autobiography, 154-68
poetry, 168-215
fiction, 215-83

**Madness in Twentieth-Century Literature
TCLC 50: 160-225**
overviews, 161-71
madness and the creative process, 171-
   86
suicide, 186-91
madness in American literature, 191-207
madness in German literature, 207-13
madness and feminist artists, 213-24

Memoirs of Trauma CLC 109: 419-466
overview, 420
criticism, 429

Metaphysical Poets LC 24: 356-439
early definitions, 358-67
surveys and overviews, 367-92
cultural and social influences, 392-406
stylistic and thematic variations, 407-38

Modern Essay, The TCLC 58: 199-273
overview, 200-7
the essay in the early twentieth century,
   207-19
characteristics of the modern essay, 219-
   32
modern essayists, 232-45
the essay as a literary genre, 245-73

**Modern Japanese Literature TCLC 66:
284-389**
poetry, 285-305
drama, 305-29
fiction, 329-61
western influences, 361-87

Modernism TCLC 70: 165-275
definitions, 166-184
Modernism and earlier influences, 184-
   200

stylistic and thematic traits, 200-229
poetry and drama, 229-242
redefining Modernism, 242-275

**Muckraking Movement in American
Journalism TCLC 34: 161-242**
development, principles, and major
   figures, 162-70
publications, 170-9
social and political ideas, 179-86
targets, 186-208
fiction, 208-19
decline, 219-29
impact and accomplishments, 229-40

**Multiculturalism in Literature and
Education CLC 70: 361-413**

**Music and Modern Literature TCLC 62:
182-329**
overviews, 182-211
musical form/literary form, 211-32
music in literature, 232-50
the influence of music on literature,
   250-73
literature and popular music, 273-303
jazz and poetry, 303-28

**Native American Literature CLC 76:
440-76**

**Natural School, Russian NCLC 24: 205-
40**
history and characteristics, 205-25
contemporary criticism, 225-40

Naturalism NCLC 36: 285-382
definitions and theories, 286-305
critical debates on Naturalism, 305-16
Naturalism in theater, 316-32
European Naturalism, 332-61
American Naturalism, 361-72
the legacy of Naturalism, 372-81

Negritude TCLC 50: 226-361
origins and evolution, 227-56
definitions, 256-91
Negritude in literature, 291-343
Negritude reconsidered, 343-58

New Criticism TCLC 34: 243-318
development and ideas, 244-70
debate and defense, 270-99
influence and legacy, 299-315

**The New World in Renaissance Literature
LC 31: 1-51**
overview, 1-18
utopia vs. terror, 18-31
explorers and Native Americans, 31-51

**New York Intellectuals and *Partisan
Review* TCLC 30: 117-98**
development and major figures, 118-28
influence of Judaism, 128-39
Partisan Review, 139-57
literary philosophy and practice, 157-75
political philosophy, 175-87
achievement and significance, 187-97

***The New Yorker* TCLC 58: 274-357**
overviews, 274-95
major figures, 295-304
New Yorker style, 304-33
fiction, journalism, and humor at *The
   New Yorker,* 333-48
the new *New Yorker,* 348-56

Newgate Novel NCLC 24: 166-204
development of Newgate literature, 166-
   73
Newgate Calendar, 173-7
Newgate fiction, 177-95
Newgate drama, 195-204

**Nigerian Literature of the Twentieth
Century TCLC 30: 199-265**
surveys of, 199-227
English language and African life, 227-
   45
politics and the Nigerian writer, 245-54
Nigerian writers and society, 255-62

**Nineteenth-Century Captivity Narratives
NCLC 80:131-218**
overview, 132-37
the political significance of captivity
   narratives, 137-67
images of gender, 167-96
moral instruction, 197-217

**Nineteenth-Century Native American
Autobiography NCLC 64: 262-389**
overview, 263-8
problems of authorship, 268-81
the evolution of Native American
   autobiography, 281-304
political issues, 304-15
gender and autobiography, 316-62
autobiographical works during the turn
   of the century, 362-88

Norse Mythology CMLC-26: 321-85
history and mythological tradition, 322-
   44
Eddic poetry, 344-74
Norse mythology and other traditions,
   374-85

Northern Humanism LC 16: 281-356
background, 282-305

precursor of the Reformation, 305-14
the Brethren of the Common Life, the
   Devotio Moderna, and education,
   314-40
the impact of printing, 340-56

Novel of Manners, The NCLC 56: 342-96
social and political order, 343-53
domestic order, 353-73
depictions of gender, 373-83
the American novel of manners, 383-95

**Nuclear Literature: Writings and
Criticism in the Nuclear Age TCLC 46:
288-390**
overviews, 290-301
fiction, 301-35
poetry, 335-8
nuclear war in Russo-Japanese literature, 338-55
nuclear war and women writers, 355-67
the nuclear referent and literary
   criticism, 367-88

**Occultism in Modern Literature TCLC
50: 362-406**
influence of occultism on literature,
   363-72
occultism, literature, and society, 372-
   87
fiction, 387-96
drama, 396-405

**Opium and the Nineteenth-Century
Literary Imagination NCLC 20: 250-301**
original sources, 250-62
historical background, 262-71
and literary society, 271-9
and literary creativity, 279-300

The Oxford Movement NCLC 72: 1-197
overviews, 2-24
background, 24-59
and education, 59-69
religious responses, 69-128
literary aspects, 128-178
political implications, 178-196

**The Parnassian Movement NCLC 72:
198-241**
overviews, 199-231
and epic form, 231-38
and positivism, 238-41

**Periodicals, Nineteenth-Century British
NCLC 24: 100-65**
overviews, 100-30
in the Romantic Age, 130-41
in the Victorian era, 142-54
and the reviewer, 154-64

**Plath, Sylvia, and the Nature of Biography
CLC 86: 433-62**
the nature of biography, 433-52
reviews of *The Silent Woman,* 452-61

**Political Theory from the 15th to the 18th
Century LC 36: 1-55**
Overview, 1-26
Natural Law, 26-42
Empiricism, 42-55

Polish Romanticism NCLC 52: 305-71
overviews, 306-26
major figures, 326-40
Polish Romantic drama, 340-62
influences, 362-71

Popular Literature TCLC 70: 279-382
overviews, 280-324
"formula" fiction, 324-336
readers of popular literature, 336-351
evolution of popular literature, 351-382

**The Portrayal of Jews in Nineteenth-
Century English Literature NCLC 72:
242-368**
overviews, 244-77
Anglo-Jewish novels, 277-303
depictions by non-Jewish writers, 303-
   44
Hebraism versus Hellenism, 344-67

Postmodernism TCLC 90:125-307
Overview, 126-166
Criticism , 166-224
Fiction, 224-282
Poetry, 282-300
Drama, 300-307

**Pre-Raphaelite Movement NCLC 20:
302-401**
overview, 302-4
genesis, 304-12
Germ and *Oxford and Cambridge
   Magazine,* 312-20
Robert Buchanan and the "Fleshly
   School of Poetry," 320-31
satires and parodies, 331-4
surveys, 334-51
aesthetics, 351-75
sister arts of poetry and painting, 375-
   94
influence, 394-9

Preromanticism LC 40: 1-56
overviews, 2-14
defining the period, 14-23
new directions in poetry and prose, 23-
   45
the focus on the self, 45-56

Presocratic Philosophy CMLC 22: 1-56
overviews, 3-24
the Ionians and the Pythagoreans, 25-35
Heraclitus, the Eleatics, and the
   Atomists, 36-47
the Sophists, 47-55

**Protestant Reformation, Literature of the
LC 37: 1-83**
overviews, 1-49
humanism and scholasticism, 49-69
the reformation and literature, 69-82

**Psychoanalysis and Literature TCLC 38:
227-338**
overviews, 227-46
Freud on literature, 246-51
psychoanalytic views of the literary
   process, 251-61
psychoanalytic theories of response to
   literature, 261-88
psychoanalysis and literary criticism,
   288-312
psychoanalysis as literature/literature as
   psychoanalysis, 313-34

Rap Music CLC 76: 477-50

**Renaissance Natural Philosophy LC 27:
201-87**
cosmology, 201-28
astrology, 228-54
magic, 254-86

Restoration Drama LC 21: 184-275
general overviews, 185-230
Jeremy Collier stage controversy, 230-9
other critical interpretations, 240-75

**Revising the Literary Canon CLC 81:
465-509**

Robin Hood, Legend of LC 19: 205-58
origins and development of the Robin
   Hood legend, 206-20
representations of Robin Hood, 220-44
Robin Hood as hero, 244-56

**Rushdie, Salman, *Satanic Verses* Contro-
versy CLC 55 214-63; 59: 404-56**

Russian Nihilism NCLC 28: 403-47
definitions and overviews, 404-17
women and Nihilism, 417-27
literature as reform: the Civic Critics,
   427-33
Nihilism and the Russian novel:
   Turgenev and Dostoevsky, 433-47

Russian Thaw TCLC 26: 189-247

Topic Index

literary history of the period, 190-206
theoretical debate of socialist realism,
    206-11
Novy Mir, 211-7
Literary Moscow, 217-24
Pasternak, *Zhivago,* and the Nobel
    Prize, 224-7
poetry of liberation, 228-31
Brodsky trial and the end of the Thaw,
    231-6
achievement and influence, 236-46

Salem Witch Trials LC-38: 1-145
    overviews, 2-30
    historical background, 30-65
    judicial background, 65-78
    the search for causes, 78-115
    the role of women in the trials, 115-44

**Salinger, J. D., Controversy Surrounding
In Search of J. D. Salinger CLC 55: 325-
44**

**Science and Modern Literature TCLC
90: 308-419**
    Overviews, 295-333
    Fiction, 333-395
    Poetry, 395-405
    Drama, 405-419

**Science Fiction, Nineteenth-Century
NCLC 24: 241-306**
    background, 242-50
    definitions of the genre, 251-6
    representative works and writers, 256-
        75
    themes and conventions, 276-305

Scottish Chaucerians LC 20: 363-412

**Scottish Poetry, Eighteenth-Century LC
29: 95-167**
    overviews, 96-114
    the Scottish Augustans, 114-28
    the Scots Vernacular Revival, 132-63
    Scottish poetry after Burns, 163-6

Sea in Literature, The TCLC 82: 72-191
    drama, 73-79
    poetry, 79-119
    fiction, 119-191

Sensation Novel, The NCLC 80: 219-330
    overviews, 221-46
    principal figures, 246-62
    nineteenth-century reaction, 262-91
    feminist criticism, 291-329

**Sentimental Novel, The NCLC 60: 146-
245**

overviews, 147-58
the politics of domestic fiction, 158-79
a literature of resistance and repression,
    179-212
the reception of sentimental fiction, 213-
    44

Sex and Literature TCLC 82: 192-434
    overviews, 193-216
    drama, 216-263
    poetry, 263-287
    fiction, 287-431

**Sherlock Holmes Centenary TCLC 26:
248-310**
    Doyle's life and the composition of the
        Holmes stories, 248-59
    life and character of Holmes, 259-78
    method, 278-9
    Holmes and the Victorian world, 279-92
    Sherlockian scholarship, 292-301
    Doyle and the development of the
        detective story, 301-7
    Holmes's continuing popularity, 307-9

Slave Narratives, American NCLC 20: 1-91
    background, 2-9
    overviews, 9-24
    contemporary responses, 24-7
    language, theme, and technique, 27-70
    historical authenticity, 70-5
    antecedents, 75-83
    role in development of Black American
        literature, 83-8

**Spanish Civil War Literature TCLC 26:
311-85**
    topics in, 312-33
    British and American literature, 333-59
    French literature, 359-62
    Spanish literature, 362-73
    German literature, 373-5
    political idealism and war literature,
        375-83

**Spanish Golden Age Literature LC 23:
262-332**
    overviews, 263-81
    verse drama, 281-304
    prose fiction, 304-19
    lyric poetry, 319-31

**Spasmodic School of Poetry NCLC 24:
307-52**
    history and major figures, 307-21
    the Spasmodics on poetry, 321-7
    Firmilian and critical disfavor, 327-
        39
    theme and technique, 339-47
    influence, 347-51

Sports in Literature TCLC 86: 294-445
    overviews, 295-324
    major writers and works, 324-402
    sports, literature, and social issues, 402-
        45

**Steinbeck, John, Fiftieth Anniversary of
The Grapes of Wrath CLC 59: 311-54**

Sturm und Drang NCLC 40: 196-276
    definitions, 197-238
    poetry and poetics, 238-58
    drama, 258-75

**Supernatural Fiction in the Nineteenth
Century NCLC 32: 207-87**
    major figures and influences, 208-35
    the Victorian ghost story, 236-54
    the influence of science and occultism,
        254-66
    supernatural fiction and society, 266-86

**Supernatural Fiction, Modern TCLC 30:
59-116**
    evolution and varieties, 60-74
    "decline" of the ghost story, 74-86
    as a literary genre, 86-92
    technique, 92-101
    nature and appeal, 101-15

Surrealism TCLC 30: 334-406
    history and formative influences, 335-43
    manifestos, 343-54
    philosophic, aesthetic, and political
        principles, 354-75
    poetry, 375-81
    novel, 381-6
    drama, 386-92
    film, 392-8
    painting and sculpture, 398-403
    achievement, 403-5

Symbolism, Russian TCLC 30: 266-333
    doctrines and major figures, 267-92
    theories, 293-8
    and French Symbolism, 298-310
    themes in poetry, 310-4
    theater, 314-20
    and the fine arts, 320-32

**Symbolist Movement, French NCLC 20:
169-249**
    background and characteristics, 170-86
    principles, 186-91
    attacked and defended, 191-7
    influences and predecessors, 197-211
    and Decadence, 211-6
    theater, 216-26
    prose, 226-33
    decline and influence, 233-47

Television and Literature TCLC 78: 283-426

television and literacy, 283-98
reading vs. watching, 298-341
adaptations, 341-62
literary genres and television, 362-90
television genres and literature, 390-410
children's literature/children's television, 410-25

Theater of the Absurd TCLC 38: 339-415

"The Theater of the Absurd," 340-7
major plays and playwrights, 347-58
and the concept of the absurd, 358-86
theatrical techniques, 386-94
predecessors of, 394-402
influence of, 402-13

Tin Pan Alley
See American Popular Song, Golden Age of

Transcendentalism, American NCLC 24: 1-99

overviews, 3-23
contemporary documents, 23-41
theological aspects of, 42-52
and social issues, 52-74
literature of, 74-96

Travel Writing in the Nineteenth Century NCLC 44: 274-392

the European grand tour, 275-303
the Orient, 303-47
North America, 347-91

Travel Writing in the Twentieth Century TCLC 30: 407-56

conventions and traditions, 407-27
and fiction writing, 427-43
comparative essays on travel writers, 443-54

True-Crime Literature CLC 99: 333-433

history and analysis, 334-407
reviews of true-crime publications, 407-23
writing instruction, 424-29
author profiles, 429-33

***Ulysses* and the Process of Textual Reconstruction TCLC 26: 386-416**

evaluations of the new *Ulysses,* 386-94
editorial principles and procedures, 394-401
theoretical issues, 401-16

Utopian Literature, Nineteenth-Century NCLC 24: 353-473

definitions, 354-74

overviews, 374-88
theory, 388-408
communities, 409-26
fiction, 426-53
women and fiction, 454-71

Utopian Literature, Renaissance LC-32: 1-63

overviews, 2-25
classical background, 25-33
utopia and the social contract, 33-9
origins in mythology, 39-48
utopia and the Renaissance country house, 48-52
influence of millenarianism, 52-62

Vampire in Literature TCLC 46: 391-454

origins and evolution, 392-412
social and psychological perspectives, 413-44
vampire fiction and science fiction, 445-53

Victorian Autobiography NCLC 40: 277-363

development and major characteristics, 278-88
themes and techniques, 289-313
the autobiographical tendency in Victorian prose and poetry, 313-47
Victorian women's autobiographies, 347-62

Victorian Fantasy Literature NCLC 60: 246-384

overviews, 247-91
major figures, 292-366
women in Victorian fantasy literature, 366-83

Victorian Hellenism NCLC 68: 251-376

overviews, 252-78
the meanings of Hellenism, 278-335
the literary influence, 335-75

Victorian Novel NCLC 32: 288-454

development and major characteristics, 290-310
themes and techniques, 310-58
social criticism in the Victorian novel, 359-97
urban and rural life in the Victorian novel, 397-406
women in the Victorian novel, 406-25
Mudie's Circulating Library, 425-34
the late-Victorian novel, 434-51

Vietnam War in Literature and Film CLC 91: 383-437

overview, 384-8

prose, 388-412
film and drama, 412-24
poetry, 424-35

Vorticism TCLC 62: 330-426

Wyndham Lewis and Vorticism, 330-8
characteristics and principles of Vorticism, 338-65
Lewis and Pound, 365-82
Vorticist writing, 382-416
Vorticist painting, 416-26

Well-Made Play, The NCLC 80: 331-370

overviews, 332-45
Scribe's style, 345-56
the influence of the well-made play, 356-69

Women's Autobiography, Nineteenth Century NCLC 76: 285-368

overviews, 287-300
autobiographies concerned with religious and political issues, 300-15
autobiographies by women of color, 315-38
autobiographies by women pioneers, 338-51
autobiographies by women of letters, 351-68

Women's Diaries, Nineteenth-Century NCLC 48: 308-54

overview, 308-13
diary as history, 314-25
sociology of diaries, 325-34
diaries as psychological scholarship, 334-43
diary as autobiography, 343-8
diary as literature, 348-53

Women Writers, Seventeenth-Century LC 30: 2-58

overview, 2-15
women and education, 15-9
women and autobiography, 19-31
women's diaries, 31-9
early feminists, 39-58

World War I Literature TCLC 34: 392-486

overview, 393-403
English, 403-27
German, 427-50
American, 450-66
French, 466-74
and modern history, 474-82

Yellow Journalism NCLC 36: 383-456

overviews, 384-96
major figures, 396-413

Young Playwrights Festival
    1988—CLC 55: 376-81
    1989—CLC 59: 398-403
    1990—CLC 65: 444-8

CMLC Cumulative Nationality Index

ARABIC
Alf Layla wa-Layla (The Arabian Nights) 2
Averroes 7
Avicenna 16
Al-Biruni 28
Al-Jahiz 25
The *Koran* 23

BABYLONIAN
Epic of Gilgamesh 3

CATALAN
Ramon Llull 12

CHINESE
Confucius 19
Lao Tzu 7
Lieh Tzu 27
Li Po 2
Po Chu-i 24
Su Shih 15

ENGLISH
The Alliterative *Morte Arthure* 10
Anglo-Saxon Chronicle 4
Roger Bacon 14
Bede 20
Beowulf 1
Bevis of Hampton 35
Caedmon 7
Cynewulf 23
The Dream of the Rood 14
Havelok the Dane 34
Layamon 10
John Mandeville 19
Walter Map 32
William of Ockham 32

Pearl 19
Richard Rolle 21
Sir Gawain and the Green Knight 2

FINNISH
Kalevala 6

FRENCH
Peter Abelard 11
Jean Bodel 28
Chanson de Roland (The Song of Roland) 1
Chretien de Troyes 10
Marie de France 8
Ordo Representacionis Ade (Mystery of Adam) 4
Le Roman de la Rose (The Romance of the Rose) 8

GERMAN
Albert the Great 16
Gottfried von Strassburg 10
Hartmann von Aue 15
Hildegard von Bingen 20
Hroswitha of Gandersheim 29
Meister Eckhart 9
Das Nibelungenlied 12
Wolfram von Eschenbach 5

GREEK
Aeschylus 11
Aesop 24
Anaximander 22
Anna Comnena 25
Aristophanes 4
Aristotle 31
Basil of Cesarea 35
Callimachus 18

Demetrius 34
Demosthenes 13
Epicurus 21
Euclid 25
Euripides 23
Heraclitus 22
Hermogenes 6
Herodotus 17
Hesiod 5
Hypatia 35
Iliad (Homer) 1
Longus 7
Lucian 32
Menander 9
Odyssey (Homer) 16
Origen 19
Parmenides 22
Pindar 12
Plato 8
Polybius 17
Pythagoras 22
Apollonius Rhodius 28
Sappho 3
Sophocles 2
Thucydides 17
Xenophon 17

HEBREW
The Book of Job 14
Flavius Josephus 13
Song of Songs 18
Tehillim (The Book of Psalms) 4
Torah 30

ICELANDIC
Hrafnkels saga Freysgoda (Hrafnkel's Saga) 2
Njals saga 13

INDIAN
  Bhagavad Gita **12**
  Kalidasa **9**
  Mahabharata **5**
  Sankara **32**

IRISH
  Ossian **28**
  Tain Bo Cualnge **30**

ITALIAN
  Thomas Aquinas **33**
  St. Benedict **29**
  Giovanni Boccaccio **13**
  St. Catherine **27**
  Inferno (Dante) **3**
  Petrarch **20**
  Marco Polo **15**
  Sordello **15**
  Vita Nuova (Dante) **18**

JAPANESE
  Izumi Shikibu **33**
  Kojiki **21**
  Kokinshu **29**
  Lady Murasaki (*Genji monogatori* [*The
    Tale of Genji*]) **1**
  Sei Shonagon **6**

PERSIAN
  Hafiz **34**
  Omar Khayyam **11**
  Jalal al-Din Rumi **20**

PROVENCAL
  Betran de Born **5**

ROMAN
  Aeneid (Vergil) **9**
  Apuleius **1**
  St. Augustine **6**
  Boethius **15**
  Marcus Porcius Cato **21**
  Catullus **18**
  Marcus Tullius Cicero **3**
  Eutropius **30**
  St. Jerome **30**
  Juvenal **8**
  Livy **11**
  Longinus **27**
  Lucan **33**
  Martial **35**
  Ovid **7**
  Petronius **34**
  Phaedrus **25**
  Plautus **24**
  Pliny the Elder **23**
  Sextus Propertius **32**
  Lucius Annaeus Seneca **6**
  Terence **14**
  Tertullian **29**

RUSSIAN
  Slovo o polku Igoreve (*The Igor Tale*) **1**

SCOTTISH
  John Barbour **33**

SPANISH
  Poema de mio Cid (*Poem of the Cid*) **4**
  Razón de amor **16**

SWEDISH
  St. Birgitta **24**

TURKISH
  Kitab-i-dedem Qorkut (*Book of Dede
    Korkut*) **8**

WELSH
  Mabinogion **9**

CMLC Cumulative Title Index

Ab urbe condita libri (Livy) **11**:310-86
"Abdallah-the-Hunter" **2**:63
"Abdallah-the-Mariner" **2**:42, 63
Abhijñana-sakuntala (Kalidasa) **9**:82, 86-7, 89-97, 100-02, 108-13, 127, 130-34, 136-39
"Aboulhusn ed Duraj and the Leper" **2**:40
About Gods (Cicero)
  See *De natura deorum*
About the Burning of the City (Lucan)
  See *De Incendio Urbu*
Abraham (Hroswitha of Gandersheim) **29**:101-03, 112, 115, 119, 139, 147-48, 163, 174, 176, 178, 189, 192, 198
"Abu Kasem's Slippers" **2**:32-5
Academics (Cicero) **3**:193,202
The Academics; or, A History and Defense of the Beliefs of the New Academy (Cicero)
  See *Academics*
Acharnae (Aristophanes) **4**:44, 62, 69, 76, 87, 94, 97-99, 105-06, 108-10, 113, 123-28, 131-33, 135, 137, 142-43, 149, 151-52, 157, 159-60, 162-63, 165-66
The Acharnians (Aristophanes)
  See *Acharnae*
The Acharnians (Euripides) **23**:175
Acontius (Callimachus) **18**:7-9, 42, 43
Ad Atticum (Cicero) **3**:186-87, 200
Ad Brutum (Cicero) **3**:200
Ad familiares (Cicero) **3**:200
Ad filium (Cato) **21**:28, 39, 46, 48-9
Ad helviam matrem de consolatione (Seneca) **6**:382, 410
Ad Leptinem (Demosthenes)
  See *Against Leptines*
Ad Marciam (Seneca) **6**:382
Ad Martyras (Tertullian)
  See *To the Martyrs*
Ad Nationes (Tertullian)
  See *To the Heathen*

Ad P. Lentulum (Cicero) **3**:186
Ad Polybium de consolatione (Seneca) **6**:382
Ad Q. fratrem (Cicero) **3**:200
Ad Quosdam Sapientes Huius Libri Fautores (Hroswitha of Gandersheim) **29**:100
Ad Scapulam (Tertullian)
  See *To Scapula*
Ad Simplicium (Augustine) **6**:9
Ad Uxorem (Tertullian)
  See *To His Wife*
Adam
  See *Ordo Representacionis Ade*
Addictus (Lucian) **32**:15
Address to Polla (Lucan) **33**:422
Address to the Heathen (Tertullian)
  See *To the Heathen*
Adelphi (Terence)
  See *Adelphoe*
Adelphoe (Terence) **14**:301, 303-04, 306-07, 309, 313-14, 316, 320-21, 332-37, 339-40, 347-49, 352, 357-60, 362-66, 368, 370-71, 374-77, 381, 383-85, 387, 394, 397
Adelphoi (Menander) **9**:270
"Advaita Vedanta" (Sankara) **32**:332, 342, 344
Adversus Helvidium (Jerome) **30**:108, 131
Adversus Hermogenem (Tertullian)
  See *Against Hermogenes*
Adversus Iovinianum (Jerome)
  See *Adversus Jovinianum*
Adversus Jovinianum (Jerome) **30**:57, 76, 108, 131
Adversus Marcionem (Tertullian)
  See *Against Marcion*
Adversus Rufin (Jerome) **30**:118, 120-21
Adversus Valentinians (Tertullian)
  See *Against the Valentiniams*
The Aeneid (Vergil) **9**:294-447
Aeolus (Euripides) **23**:117, 203
Aesopia (Aesop)

  See *Aesop's Fables*
Aesop's Fables (Aesop) **24**:4-5, 12, 14-15, 17-18, 32-33, 44, 56, 63-65, 70, 74, 77, 82-83
De aeternitate mundi (Aquinas) **33**:108
Africa (Petrarch) **20**:212, 214, 226, 235-39, 245, 251, 260, 308, 326-27, 333
"After Being Separated for a Long Time" (Li Po) **2**:132
Against Androtion (Demosthenes) **13**:148-9, 156, 163-4, 169, 171, 184
Against Aphobus (Demosthenes) **13**:163, 184
Against Apion (Josephus)
  See *Contra Apionem*
Against Aristocrates (Demosthenes) **13**:148, 156-8, 164, 169, 189
Against Aristogiton (Demosthenes) **13**:149
Against Callicles (Demosthenes) **13**:168
Against Catilina (Cicero)
  See *In Catilinam*
Against Conon (Demosthenes) **13**:144
Against Eratosthenes (Demosthenes) **13**:179
"Against Eunomius" (Basil of Caesaria) **35**:87, 120
Against Hermogenes (Tertullian) **29**:311-12, 362, 368, 371, 373
Against Jovinian (Jerome)
  See *Adversus Jovinianum*
Against Leptines (Demosthenes) **13**:137, 148-51, 156, 163-4, 169-71, 197
Against Marcion (Tertullian) **29**:311-12, 316, 329-30, 362-64, 366, 371-73, 384
Against Medias (Demosthenes)
  See *Against Midias*
Against Midias (Demosthenes) **13**:140, 149, 165, 169
Against Neaera (Demosthenes) **13**:169
Against Onetor (Demosthenes) **13**:163, 168, 184
Against Praxeas (Tertullian) **29**:311-12, 371-72
Against Praxiphanes (Callimachus) **18**:36-7, 48

Against Superstitions (Seneca) **6**:330, 342

Against the Academicians (Augustine)
    See *Contra academicos*

Against the Gentiles (Josephus)
    See *Contra Apionem*

Against the Greeks (Josephus)
    See *Contra Apionem*

Against the Jews (Tertullian) **29**:311-12

Against the Megarians (Epicurus) **21**:165

Against the Physicists (Epicurus) **21**:165

Against the Valentiniams (Tertullian) **29**:311-12, 330, 372

Against Theophrastus (Epicurus) **21**:71, 165

Against Timocrates (Demosthenes) **13**:146-8, 156, 163-4, 169

Agamemnon (Aeschylus) **11**:85-6, 101-02, 104-05, 107-08, 110-11, 113, 116-20, 126, 128, 132-34, 136, 138-42, 148, 150-55, 158, 162-63, 165, 167, 171, 175-76, 179-82, 184-85, 187, 190-91, 194-97, 200-07, 217, 220-22

Agamemnon (Seneca) **6**:339, 343, 363, 366-69, 377-81, 389, 407, 409, 414, 417, 431-32, 440, 442, 447

Agesilaus (Xenophon) **17**:329, 330, 331, 339, 340, 349, 350, 352, 353, 354, 355, 359, 362, 374

Agnes (Hroswitha of Gandersheim) **29**:123

De agricultura (Cato) **21**:17, 26-30, 39, 41-50, 54-7

Ahwal al-Nafs (Avicenna) **16**:166

"Ailas e que'm miey huelh" (Sordello) **15**:367

Aitia (Callimachus) **18**:6-9, 11, 18, 22-4, 30, 32, 34-8, 42, 44, 48-50, 53, 62-4, 68

Aitnaiai (Aeschylus) **11**:217

Akharnes (Aristophanes)
    See *Acharnae*

"Al poco giorno e al gan cerchio d'ombra" (Petrarch) **20**:283

"Alâ Ed-Dîn Abu Esh-Shamât" **2**:43

Alcestis (Euripides) **23**:113-14, 121-24, 127, 129-31, 150, 156-60, 162, 171-74, 177, 180, 185, 188, 207

De Alchimia (Albert the Great)
    See *Libellus de Alchimia*

Alcibiades (Plato)
    See *Alcibiades I*

Alcibiades I (Plato) **8**:218, 305-06, 311, 356

Alcibiades II (Plato) **8**:250, 305, 311

Alcibiades Major (Plato)
    See *Alcibiades I*

Alcmaeon at Corinth (Euripides) **23**:173, 176

Alexander (Euripides) **23**:176

Alexander the False Prophet (Lucian) **32**:10, 15, 35, 38, 45-46, 58

The Alexiad (Anna Comnena) **25**:1-86

Alexias (Anna Comnena)
    See *The Alexiad*

Alf Layla wa-Layla **2**:1-73

"Ali and the Kurd Sharper" **2**:40

"Ali Baba and the Forty Thieves" **2**:1-2, 23, 45, 49

"Alî Shâr" **2**:43

"Ali Sher and Zumurrud" **2**:114

"Ali the Son of Bakkar and Shems-en-Nahar" **2**:14

al-Isharat wa al-Tanbiha (Avicenna) 169, 171

Alku Kalevala
    See *Kalevala*

"Alladin and the Wonderful Lamp" **2**:1-2, 8, 21, 23-24, 72

Allegoria mitologica (Boccaccio) **13**:63-4

"Alliterative *Morte Arthure*"
    See *Morte Arthure "Alliterative"*

Al-Nubl wa l-tannabbal wa-dhamm al-kibr **25**:332

Al-Qanun al Masudu (Biruni)
    See *Kitab al-Qanun al Mas'udi fi'l-Hay'a wan-nujim*

Al-Risalah fi Nafy al-tashbih **25**:329

Al-Saidana (Biruni)
    See *Kiib al-Sydanah*

al-Tacliqat (Avicenna) **16**:167

Al-Tahdid (Biruni)
    See *Kitab Tahdid Nihayat al-Amakin*

Al-Tanbih 'Ala Sina'at al Tamwih (Biruni) **28**:155

Ameto (Boccaccio) **13**:9, 18, 23, 27-8, 30, 32-3, 44-5, 48, 61

De amicitia (Cicero) **3**:193, 195, 202

"Amor, tu vedi ben che quesra donna" (Petrarch) **20**:283

Amores (Ovid) **7**:292-93, 295-97, 299, 305, 323, 326, 329, 336, 343, 346-49, 353, 355-56, 376-79, 388, 390, 393, 396, 398, 413, 417, 419-21, 423, 426-27, 436, 441, 444

Amorosa visione (Boccaccio) **13**:18, 27-8, 32-3, 68, 72, 87

Amphitruo (Plautus) **24**:170-72, 175-78, 184, 199

Amphitryon (Plautus)
    See *Amphitruo*

Anabasis (Xenophon) **17**:322, 324, 326, 327, 328, 330, 339, 340, 341, 342, 348, 349, 354, 357, 358, 359, 360, 361, 362, 364, 365, 366, 372, 374

Anacharsis (Lucian) **32**:17, 25, 39

Analects (Confucius)
    See *Lun Yu*

Analysis of the Analects (Su Shih) **15**:407

Analytics (Aristotle) **31**:64, 86

Ancient History of the Jews (Josephus)
    See *Antiquitates Judaicae*

Ancient Poems (Confucius)
    See *Shih Ching*

Andria (Terence) **14**:302-08, 311-13, 315-17, 331, 333-35, 337-41, 344-45, 347-49, 352, 355-356, 358, 363-65, 369-70, 383-85, 389-90, 392-93

"Androcles and the Lion" (Aesop) **24**:58

Andromache (Euripides) **23**:114, 121-22, 125, 127-30, 174, 182-83, 185, 189, 207

Andromeda (Euripides) **23**:120, 174, 182

Androtion (Demosthenes)
    See *Against Androtion*

Anger (Menander)
    See *Orge*

Anglo-Saxon Chronicle **4**:1-33

De anima (Albert the Great) **16**:7, 61, 106, 109, 113, 115

De Anima (Aristotle) **31**:65, 86-87, 274-75, 305, 327, 337, 358-66, 370, 374, 379

De anima (Avicenna) **16**:176

De anima (Tertullian)
    See *On the Soul*

De animalibus (Albert the Great) **16**:18, 21, 35-7, 61, 64, 82-3, 103, 107, 110

Animals (Albert the Great)
    See *De animalibus*

Annals of Lu (Confucius)
    See *Ch'un Ch'iu*

Annapurna-stotra (Sankara) **32**:390

"Answering a Layman's Question" (Li Po) **2**:140

"The Ant and the Fly" (Aesop) **24**:36

Antigone (Sophocles) **2**:289, 296, 299-301, 303-04, 306-09, 311, 314-15, 318-20, 324-25, 327, 331, 334-35, 338-40, 342-43, 345, 349-55, 360, 366, 368, 377-78, 380-83, 393-97,

417-19, 423, 426-28

Antiope (Euripides) 117, 192

Antiquitates Judaicae (Josephus) **13**:199-207, 211-3, 215-8, 220, 224, 226-35, 239, 242, 247-51, 256-65, 268-71, 286, 291-2, 294-7, 299-300, 302, 305, 308-9, 311-3, 315-20

Antiquities of the Jews (Josephus)
    See *Antiquitates Judaicae*

"Aphrodite Ode" (Sappho)
    See "Ode to Aphrodite"

Apion Answered (Josephus)
    See *Contra Apionem*

Apionem (Josephus)
    See *Contra Apionem*

Apocalypse (Hroswitha of Gandersheim) **29**:183

Apocalypse (Rolle) **21**:351

Apocolocyntosis Divi Claudii (Seneca) **6**:244, 374, 382-84

Apologeticum (Tertullian)
    See *Apology*

Apologeticus (Tertullian)
    See *Apology*

Apologia (Plato) **8**:250, 260, 277, 306, 357

Apologia sive oratoria de magia (Apuleius) **1**:7-8, 10, 12-13, 20, 23, 26, 33-4

Apologia Socratis (Xenophon)
    See *Apology*

Apology (Apuleius)
    See *Apologia sive oratoria de magia*

Apology (Plato)
    See *Apologia*

Apology (Tertullian) **29**:310, 311, 312, 329, 330, 334, 338, 346-349, 367, 384

Apology (Xenophon) **17**:342, 343, 369-71

Apology for 'On Salaried Posts' (Lucian) **32**:39

Apology of Origen (Origen) **19**:188-89, 199

Apomnemoneumata (Xenophon)
    See *Memorabilia*

Apophoreta (Martial) **35**:303-04, 331, 364, 375, 377

Apophthegmata (Cato) **21**:22, 41, 54

Apotheosis of Arsinoe (Callimachus)
    See *Deification of Arsinoe*

"The Apples of Paradise" **2**:40

The Arabian Nights
    See *Alf Layla wa-Layla*

The Arabian Nights' Entertainments
    See *Alf Layla wa-Layla*

The Arbitrants (Menander)
    See *Epitrepontes*

The Arbitration (Menander)
    See *Epitrepontes*

Arbor scientiae (Llull) **12**:108-11, 115, 125

El arbre de filosofia d'amor (Llull)
    See *The Tree of the Philosophy of Love*

Arbre de Sciencia (Llull)
    See *Arbor scientiae*

Archias (Cicero) **3**:198-99, 210

Argo (Aeschylus) **11**:124

Argonautica (Rhodius) **28**:2-27, 29-110

Argonautika (Rhodius)
    See *Argonautica*

Arithmetic (Boethius)
    See *De Arithmetica*

De Arithmetica (Boethius) **15**:63, 69, 86

Der arme Heinrich (Hartmann von Aue) **15**:148-54, 164, 191, 194, 205-07, 209, 220, 224, 241-44, 244-49

"Arrius and His Aitches" (Catullus)
    See "Poem 84"

"Arriving at Principles" (Po Chu-i) **24**:311

Ars Amandi (Ovid)
    See *Ars amatoria*

Ars amatoria (Ovid) 7:281-83, 292-98, 304-06, 309-10, 326, 329, 331, 342-47, 349, 353, 377-79, 386-87, 396-98, 401-02, 404, 412-13, 416-19, 421-23, 426, 430, 435-43, 446

Ars brevis (Llull) 12:106-07, 109, 133

Ars demonstrativa (Llull) 12:105-06, 110, 117, 134

Ars generalis (Llull) 12:104, 107-08

Ars generalis ultima (Llull) 12:114-16, 128

Ars inventiva (Llull) 12:97, 109, 114-15, 120, 128, 132

Ars magna (Llull) 12:93-4, 104, 111, 132

Art of Contemplation (Llull) 12:125, 129

Art of Finding Truth (Llull)
   See *Ars inventiva*

Art of Love (Ovid)
   See *Ars amatoria*

Art of Rhetoric (Hermogenes) 6:186

De arte metrica (Bede) 20:42, 93, 120

Ascensio (Hroswitha of Gandersheim) 29:123

The Ascension of our Lord (Hroswitha of Gandersheim) 29:136

"Asceticon" (Basil of Caesaria) 35:91, 92

"The Ash Tree" (Marie de France)
   See "Le Fraisne"

Asinaria (Plautus) 24:170-73, 175, 218, 220-21, 233, 235, 240, 244, 248-49, 263-64, 270-71, 273

Asinus aureus (Apuleius) 1:6-9, 11-12, 14-18, 20, 22-23, 26, 32, 37-38, 46-50

Aspis (Menander) 9:253-58, 260-61, 263, 265, 267-70, 276-77

"Ass in the Lion's skin" (Aesop) 24:43

Assembly of Women (Aristophanes)
   See *Ekklesiazousai*

"At Kuo Hsiang-cheng's When I was Drunk I Painted" (Su Shih) 15:402

"At the Serpentine Moved by Autumn" (Po Chu-i) 24:338

Athamas (Aeschylus) 11:122

Atomic Films (Epicurus) 21:73

Atoms and Space (Epicurus) 21:73

"Atretan deu ben chantar finamen" (Sordello) 15:362-63, 368

"*Attis*" (Catullus)
   See "*Poem 63*"

"*Atys*" (Catullus)
   See "*Poem 63*"

Auge (Euripides) 23:203

"Augustinus" (Petrarch) 20:286-87

Aulularia (Plautus) 24:171-73, 175-76, 178-79, 181, 184, 218, 258

Authorized Doctrines (Epicurus)
   See *Principal Doctrines*

Autolycus (Euripides) 23:173

"Autumn Banks Song" (Li Po) 2:161, 164

"Autumn Day" (Po Chu-i) 24:335

"Autumn Evening" (Po Chu-i) 24:336, 339

"Autumn Feelings" (Po Chu-i) 24:336

"Autumn Hibiscus" (Po Chu-i) 24:337

"Autumn Moon" (Po Chu-i) 24:336

The Babylonians (Aristophanes) 4:99, 126, 159, 163, 165

Bacchae (Euripides) 23:103-04, 108, 110, 114, 120, 122, 124-26, 131, 136-38, 140, 142-44, 146-50, 153, 171, 173-76, 186, 189, 204-07, 212, 219-22

Bacchanals (Euripides)
   See *Bacchae*

The Bacchants (Euripides)
   See *Bacchae*

Bacchides (Plautus) 24:170-73, 175, 180, 184, 186, 190-91, 193, 196, 229-34, 236, 239-40,
244, 248, 256, 264, 269-70, 272-73, 276-79, 281, 283-85

The Bacchis Sisters (Plautus)
   See *Bacchides*

Bad Temper (Menander)
   See *Orge*

"Baghach Khan Son of Dirse Khan" 8:104

"Bamsi Beyrek of the Grey Horse"
   See "Bamsi-Beyrek"

"Bamsi-Beyrek" 8:98, 103, 108-09

The Banquet (Lucian) 32:43-44, 46, 49

The Banqueters (Aristophanes) 4:37, 100, 163

De Baptismo (Tertullian)
   See *On Baptism*

"The Barber's Sixth Brother" 2:21

Basilius (Hroswitha of Gandersheim) 29:123, 136, 183, 185

Batrakhoi (Aristophanes) 4:44-5, 61-3, 69. 79. 86-90, 94. 98. 102. 105-6. 110-11. 120-21. 123-24, 127, 129-30, 133, 135, 137-38, 140, 145-46. 148, 150, 154, 156, 159, 161-63, 165

"The Battle of Brunanburh" 4:4, 7, 9, 13-15, 17-19, 27-30

"The battle of Lora" (Ossian) 28:303

"The Battle of Maldon" 4:2-9, 11-15, 25-7, 29-31

"Battle to the South of the City" (Li Po) 2:132

Bayan madhahib al-Shiah 25:329

"Beginning of Autumn: A Poem to Send to Tzu-yu" (Su Shih) 15:414

"Bel m'es ab motz legiers a far" (Sordello) 15:361-62

De Bello Civili (Lucan)
   See *Civil War*

Bellum Civile (Lucan)
   See *Civil War*

Bellum Judaicum (Josephus) 13:201-5, 209, 211-20, 222, 224, 229-30, 232-5, 239, 241-56, 263-73, 275-301, 303-8, 310-2, 314-5, 317-20

"Bending Bamboos of Yun-tang Valley" (Su Shih) 15:382, 386

Benedictus (Eckhart)
   See *Book of Divine Consolation*

Beowulf 1:53-159

"Berenice's Lock of Hair" (Catullus)
   See "*Poem 66*"

Bhagavad Gita 12:1-90

Bhagavadgita 5:187, 196-99, 216-19, 223, 226, 228, 235-38, 242-43, 246, 248, 250, 269, 272, 275

Bhagavadgita-bhasya (Sankara) 32:362, 390

Bhagavat Gita
   See *Bhagavadgita*

Bhagavatpada (Sankara) 32:389

Bhagavatpujyapada (Sankara) 32:389

Bhaja Govindam (Sankara) 32:356

Bhaja-govinda-stotra (Sankara) 32:390

Bharata
   See *Mahabharata*

Bidayat al-mujtahid (Averroes) 7:37, 41, 43

Big Epitome (Epicurus) 21:154

The Birds (Aristophanes)
   See *Ornithes*

The Birth of Kumara (Kalidasa)
   See *Kumarasambhava*

The Birth of the Prince (Kalidasa)
   See *Kumarasambhava*

The Birth of the War-God (Kalidasa)
   See *Kumarasambhava*

"Bisclavret" (Marie de France) 8:114, 121-23, 131, 134, 147-48, 154, 158, 161-66, 171, 181

"Bitterness on the Stairs of Jade" (Li Po) 2:144,
160

Black Sea Letters (Ovid)
   See *Epistulae ex Ponto*

"The Blacksmith Who Could Handle Fire" 2:40

Blanquerna (Llull) 12:93-5, 97, 106-07, 112, 122-24, 126, 129, 133

Boasting Match over Maids and Youths
   See *Kitab Mufakharat al-jawari wa l-ghilman*

Boasting-Match between Girls and Boys
   See *Kitab Mufakharat al-jawari wa l-ghilman*

The boke maad of Rycharde hampole hetemyte to an ankeresse (Rolle) 21:274

Bone-Collectors (Aeschylus) 11:124

De bono (Albert the Great) 16:44-7, 49-50, 53-4, 65-7, 69, 71-2, 74-7, 79-81

The Book of Animals
   See *Kitab al-Hayawan*

The Book of Beasts
   See *Kitab al-Hayawan*

Book of Changes (Confucius)
   See *I Ching*

Book of Chaos (Llull) 12:129

Book of Contemplation of God (Llull) 12:95-8, 100-03, 109, 113-14, 120-23, 125-28, 132

Book of Dede Korkut
   See *Kitabi-i Dedem Qorkut*

Book of Divine Consolation (Eckhart) 9:35-6, 40, 42, 56-7, 70-6

Book of Divine Works (Hildegard von Bingen)
   See *Liber divinorum Operum*

Book of Doctrine for Boys (Llull) 12:97

Book of Eloquence and Clear Expression
   See *Kitab al-Bayan wa l'Tabyin*

The Book of Eloquence and Exposition
   See *Kitab al-Bayan wa l'Tabyin*

The Book of General Knowledge (Biruni) 28:176

Book of Godly Comfort (Eckhart)
   See *Book of Divine Consolation*

Book of Grandfather Qorkut
   See *Kitabi-i Dedem Qorkut*

Book of Hebrew Names (Jerome)
   See *Onomasticum*

Book of Historical Documents (Confucius)
   See *Shu Ching*

Book of History (Confucius)
   See *Shu Ching*

The Book of Instruction in the Elements of the Art of Astrology (Biruni) 28:130, 139, 142

The Book of Job 14:117-214

The Book of Korkut
   See *Kitabi-i Dedem Qorkut*

Book of Lieh Tzu (Lieh Tzu)
   See *The Treatise of the Transecendent Master of the Void*

Book of Life's Merits (Hildegard von Bingen)
   See *Liber vitae meritorum*

The Book of Marco Polo (Polo)
   See *The Travels of Marco Polo the Venetian*

Book of Minerals (Albert the Great)
   See *Liber mineralium*

The Book of Misers
   See *Kitab al-Bukhala*

Book of Music (Confucius)
   See *Yueh*

The Book of My Grandfather Korkut
   See *Kitabi-i Dedem Qorkut*

Book of Odes (Confucius)
   See *Shih Ching*

Book of Poetry (Confucius)
   See *Shih Ching*

The Book of Psalms
   See *Tehillim*

The Book of Purgatory (Marie de France)

See *L'Espurgatoire Saint Patrice*
Book of Questions (Saint Birgitta of Sweden) **24**:130-31
Book of Rites (Confucius)
See *Li Chi*
Book of Rituals (Confucius)
See *Li Chi*
Book of Simple Medicine (Hildegard von Bingen) **20**:167
The Book of Singing Slave-Girls
See *Kitab al-Qiyan*
Book of Songs (Confucius)
See *Shih Ching*
Book of Tao (Lao Tzu)
See *Tao te Ching*
Book of the Ascent and Descent of the Mind (Llull)
See *Liber de ascensu et descensu intellectus*
Book of the Beasts (Llull) **12**:133-34
The Book of the Five Wise Men (Llull) **12**:125
Book of the Friend and the Beloved (Llull)
See *Book of the Lover and the Beloved*
Book of the Gentile and the Three Wise Men (Llull) **12**:113, 118, 125-26
Book of the Lover and the Beloved (Llull) **12**:93-4, 101, 122-23, 125-29, 131-33
Book of the Order of Chivalry (Llull)
See *Libre del orde de cavalleria*
Book of the Principles and Grades of Medicine (Llull)
See *Liber principiorum medicinae*
Book of the Tartar and the Christian (Llull) **12**:125
The Book of the Thousand Nights and One Night
See *Alf Layla wa-Layla*
The Book of the Uthmaniyya
See *Kitab al-Uthmaniyya*
Book of Wonders (Llull) **12**:134
Book on the Sites and Names of Hebrew Places (Jerome) **30**:88
The Bookes of the Golden Asse (Apuleius)
See *Asinus aureus*
Books of Rites and Ancient Ceremonies and of Institutions (Confucius)
See *Li Chi*
Braggart Warrior (Plautus)
See *Miles Glorious*
Brahma-sutra-bhasya (Sankara) **32**:304-05, 309, 328-30, 333, 337, 342-43, 358, 362, 388-92
Brennu-Njáls Saga
See *Njáls saga*
Breviarium ab Urbe Condita (Eutropius) **30**:1-48
Brhadaranyaka Upanisad (Sankara) **32**:304-05, 307-10, 328, 330, 354, 358, 384
Brief Art of Finding Truth (Llull)
See *Ars brevis*
"Bring in the Wine" (Li Po) **2**:159
Brothers (Menander)
See *Adelphoi*
The Brothers (Terence)
See *Adelphoe*
The Bruce (Barbour) **33**:143-252
"Brunanburh"
See "The Battle of Brunanburh"
Brus, Brut (Barbour)
See *The Bruce*
Brut (Layamon) **10**:311-21, 326-29, 333, 335-38, 341, 343-50, 353, 355-60, 362, 364, 370-71
Brutus (Cicero)
See *De claris oratoribus*
Brutus: On Famous Orators (Cicero)
See *De claris oratoribus*

Brutus; or the illustrious Orators (Cicero)
See *De claris oratoribus*
Bucolicum carmen (Petrarch) **20**:327
"Butterfly and Wasp" (Aesop) **24**:36
"Buying Rice" (Su Shih) **15**:416
"By the Passes" (Li Po) **2**:160
"Byrhtnoth's Death"
See "The Battle of Maldon"
Cabiri (Aeschylus) **11**:124
Caccia di Diana (Boccaccio) **13**:62-3, 65, 67-74, 94-102
De Caelo (Aquinas) **33**:85, 87-88, 97
De Caelo (Aristotle) **31**:69, 86, 356, 394
De caelo et mundo (Albert the Great) **16**:7, 18, 22, 61
"Calhon and Colvala" (Ossian) **28**:311
"Calhon and Cuhona" (Ossian) **28**:303
Calimachus (Hroswitha of Gandersheim) **29**:101-03, 113, 115, 119, 137, 139, 142, 162, 174-75, 180, 198
"Camaralzaman and Badoura" **2**:36, 42-3, 50
Canon (Avicenna) **16**:171-80
The Canon (Epicurus) **21**:73, 119, 130, 153-54, 165
Canonice (Epicurus) **21**:130
Cant de Ramon (Llull) **12**:122
Cantar de mio Cid
See *Poema de mio Cid*
Canticum amoris (Rolle) **21**:353, 368, 376
"Cantus amoris" (Rolle) **21**:368, 370-71, 374-75
"Canzone IV" (Petrarch) **20**:257
Canzoniere (Petrarch) **20**:205, 215-17, 226, 236-37, 239-53, 257, 269, 271-84, 293-97, 299-303, 305, 307, 311-12, 314-20, 323, 327-28, 331-35
Capita Philosophica (John) **27**:43
Captives (Plautus)
See *Captivi*
Captivi (Plautus) **24**:170-72, 175, 179-82, 189, 272
Carmen bucolicum (Petrarch) **20**:237
Carmen de gestis Oddonis (Hroswitha of Gandersheim)
See *Gallicanus*
Carmen de moribus (Cato) **21**:22, 28, 40, 46-50, 54-5
Carthaginian (Plautus)
See *Poenulus*
De casibus virorum illustrium (Boccaccio) **13**:33, 38, 45-7, 52, 66
Casina (Plautus) **24**:170-73, 175, 183, 208, 214-17, 219, 229-33, 235-36, 239, 257, 272-73
Casket (Plautus)
See *Cistellaria*
Catachtonion (Lucan) **33**:422
Cataplus (Lucian) **32**:8, 27
Catechism (Epicurus) **21**:124, 126-27
De catechizandis rudibus (Augustine) **6**:93
Categories (Aristotle) **31**:18-23, 44, 46-47, 50-51, 86, 304-07, 309, 311-12, 316-22
Catilinarians (Cicero)
See *In Catilinam*
Cato maior (Cicero)
See *De senectute*
Cato the Elder: On Old Age (Cicero)
See *De senectute*
Catoptrica (Euclid)
See *Catoptrics*
Catoptrics (Euclid) **25**:1-86
The Cattle-Raid of Cooley
See *Tain Bo Cualnge*
"Catullus's Yacht" (Catullus)
See "Poem 4"

Causae et Curae (Hildegard von Bingen) **20**:154, 158, 182-83
De causis elementorum (Albert the Great)
See *De causis et proprietatibus elementorum et planetarum*
De causis et procreatione un'iversi (Albert the Great) **16**:7
De causis et proprietatibus elementorum et planetarum (Albert the Great) **16**:7, 9, 56, 61, 83, 99
De Celestibus (Bacon)
See *De Coelestibus*
Censure of the Conduct of Secretaries **25**:324
Cent Noms de Déu (Llull)
See *Hundred Names of God*
Cerberus (Pindar)
See *Descent of Heracles into the Underworld*
"Le Chaitivel" (Marie de France) **8**:120-21, 130-31, 133-34, 138, 143-44, 147, 151-52, 156, 162, 164-65, 169-70, 182, 186-89
La Chanson de Roland **1**:160-267
Chanson des Saisnes: (Bodel) **28**:250-51, 266
Charioteer (Menander) **9**:214
"Charite and Tlepolemus" (Apuleius) **1**:40
Charmides (Plato) **8**:255, 263-65, 286, 306, 310, 314, 349, 356
Charon, or The Inspectors (Lucian) **32**:17, 35-36, 47
Charrette (Chretien de Troyes)
See *Lancelot*
Cheat Him Twice (Menander)
See *Dis Exapaton*
Le Chevalier à l'épée (Chretien de Troyes) **10**:232
Le Chevalier au Lion (Chretien de Troyes)
See *Yvain*
Le Chevalier de la Charrette (Chretien de Troyes)
See *Lancelot*
"Chevrefoil" (Marie de France) **8**:116, 120-21, 130-31, 133-34, 137, 139, 147-48, 150, 158-59, 161, 163-65, 170, 179, 182-84, 189
"Chiare fresche e dolci acque" (Petrarch) **20**:300
"Chievrefueil" (Marie de France)
See "Chevrefoil"
Chionia and Hirena (Hroswitha of Gandersheim) **29**:182
Choephori (Aeschylus)
See *Libation Bearers*
Choephoroe (Aeschylus)
See *Libation Bearers*
Christ (Cynewulf) **23**:3-6, 11, 14-18, 20-21, 30-32, 34, 42, 49-50, 54, 81-83, 86
"Christ and Satan" (Caedmon) **7**:84, 91-3, 102-03
Christian Theology (Abelard) **11**:9, 10, 11, 12, 14, 16, 17, 21, 26, 51-3, 64, 65
Chronicle
See *Anglo-Saxon Chronicle*
Chronicle (Jerome) **30**:107
The Chronology of Ancient Nations (Biruni) **28**:113-15, 122, 136, 139-20, 142, 146, 149, 153, 167-69, 171-72, 176-77, 180
Chrysippus (Euripides) **23**:117
ch'uch'iu (Confucius)
See *Ch'un Ch'iu*
Ch'un Ch'iu (Confucius) **19**:29, 31, 35, 38, 42, 46, 50, 84-85
Cimone (Boccaccio) **13**:28
Circe (Aeschylus) **11**:124
Cistellaria (Plautus) **24**:170-73, 218, 233, 235, 239, 258-60
"The City Mouse and the Country Mouse" (Marie de France) **8**:190

"City of Brass" 2:2, 23-4, 40, 51-3
The City of God (Augustine)
    See *De civitate Dei*
"The City of Irem" 2:40
Civil War (Lucan) 33:335-427
De civitate Dei (Augustine) 6:4, 10-11, 21-22,
    29, 43, 54, 57-8, 60, 66-8, 83, 90-1, 105-08,
    122-23, 142
De civitate Dei (Petrarch) 20:288
*The Claims of Superiority of the Blacks over the
    Whites* 25:324
De claris mulieribus (Boccaccio) 13:33, 38, 45-
    7, 52, 55-8, 66, 97-8
De claris oratoribus (Cicero) 3:193, 201-02, 206-
    09, 218, 259, 261, 263, 288
Classes of Singers
    See *Fi Tabaqat al-mughannin*
Classic of History (Confucius)
    See *Shu Ching*
Classic of Poetry (Confucius)
    See *Shih Ching*
"Clear Autumn Sky" (Po Chu-i) 24:337
Cligés (Chretien de Troyes) 10:133, 138-44, 147,
    149, 159-61, 163-64, 166-69, 171-75, 178-
    79, 183, 190-95, 198, 204-05, 207-08, 210,
    215, 218, 222-25, 229-30, 232-39
"Climbing to the Old Graves East of the Village"
    (Po Chu-i) 24:345
Clitophon (Plato) 8:218, 305, 311
The Clock (Lucian) 32:48, 63
The Cloud-Messenger (Kalidasa)
    See *Meghaduta*
The Clouds (Aristophanes)
    See *Nephelai*
"The Cock and the Fox" (Aesop) 24:19, 66
"The Cock and the Pearl" (Aesop) 24:43
"Cock and the Precious Stone" (Aesop) 24:9
De Coelestibus (Bacon) 14:47
Collatio laureationis (Petrarch) 20:326
Collations (Eckhart)
    See *Rede der Unterscheidungen*
Coma Berenices (Callimachus)
    See *Lock of Berenice*
Comedia delle ninfe fiorentine (Boccaccio)
    13:63-5, 97
Comedy of Asses (Plautus)
    See *Asinaria*
The Commandment of Love to God (Rolle)
    21:314, 316, 363, 383-86
Commentaries (Bede) 20:61
Commentaries on Aristotle (Aquinas) 33:13, 43,
    108
Commentaries on Aristotle (Aquinas) 33:95
Commentaries on Isaiah (Origen) 19:188
Commentaries on Scripture (Rolle) 21:278, 328
Commentaries on the Sentences (Albert the Great)
    See *Commentary on the Book of the Sentences*
Commentarii (Xenophon)
    See *Memorabilia*
Commentarioli in Psalmos (Jerome) 30:89
Commentarius in Ezechiel (Jerome) 30:67
Commentarius in Micheam (Jerome) 30:67
*Commentarius quo medetu filio, servis,
    familiaribus* (Cato) 21:21
Commentary on Apollonius Pergaeus Conics
    (Hypatia)
    See *On the Comics of Apollonius*
*Commentary on Aristotle's De Generatione et de
    Coruptione* (Averroes) 7:30
Commentary on Aristotle's Nichomachean Ethics
    (Averroes) 7:43
Commentary on Artistotle's Meteorology (Albert
    the Great) 16:97

Commentary on Bhagavadgita (Sankara)
    See *Bhagavadgita-bhasya*
Commentary on Book I of the Sentences (Aquinas)
    See *Commentaries on Aristotle*
Commentary on Brahmasutra (Sankara)
    See *Brahma-sutra-bhasya*
Commentary on Brhadaranyaka (Sankara)
    See *Brhadaranyaka Upanisad*
Commentary on Daniel (Jerome) 30:60, 107, 113,
    117
Commentary on Ecclesiastes (Jerome) 30:86, 119
Commentary on Ephesians (Jerome) 30:56-57,
    119
Commentary on Ezechiel 42:13f (Jerome) 30:92,
    119, 121
Commentary on Galatians (Jerome) 30:56, 59,
    108, 111, 119
Commentary on Genesis (Origen) 19:186, 201,
    246
Commentary on III de Anima (Averroes) 7:24
Commentary on Isaias (Jerome) 30:112-113, 121
Commentary on Jeremiah (Jerome) 30:67
Commentary on Osee (Jerome) 30:99
Commentary on Plato's Republic (Averroes)
    7:30, 38, 40-3
Commentary on St. John (Origen) 19:186-88,
    209, 247, 257, 260, 262-63
Commentary on St Luke (Albert the Great) 16:29
Commentary on St. Matthews's Gospel (Jerome)
    30:88
Commentary on the Book of the Sentences (Albert
    the Great) 16:6-7, 14, 16, 26, 31, 44, 66,
    68, 76, 86, 93-4
Commentary on the Divine Names (Albert the
    Great) 16:28-9
Commentary on the Epistle to the Galatians
    (Jerome)
    See *Commentary on Galatians*
Commentary on the Gospel according to Matthew
    (Origen) 19:187, 240, 246
Commentary on the Perihermenias (William of
    Ockham) 32:210
Commentary on the Prophet Daniel (Jerome)
    See *Commentary on Daniel*
Commentary on the Psalms (Origen) 19:202
*Commentary on the Psalms and Canticles of the
    Old Testament* (Rolle) 21:273, 279, 284,
    294, 362
Commentary on the Sentences (William of
    Ockham) 32:209-10
Commentary on the Sentences of Peter Lombard
    (Albert the Great)
    See *Commentary on the Book of the Sentences*
Commentary on the Song of Songs (Origen)
    19:210, 212, 240, 255-62
Commentary on Zacharias (Jerome) 30:99
The Commonplace Book of Sei Shonagon (Sei
    Shonagon)
    See *Makura no soshi*
Communia Mathematica (Bacon) 14:15, 46, 80
Communium Naturalium (Bacon) 14:15, 48, 80,
    100, 104-05
Compendium artis demonstrativae (Llull)
    See *Ars demonstrativa*
Compendium of Philosophy (Bacon)
    See *Compendium Studii Philosophiae*
Compendium of Roman History (Eutropius)
    See *Breviarium ab Urbe Condita*
Compendium of the Logic of al-ghazzali (Llull)
    12:113-14, 116, 126, 128, 132
Compendium of the Study of Philosophy (Bacon)
    See *Compendium Studii Philosophiae*
Compendium on Precious Stones (Biruni) 28:115,

    132, 134-36, 155, 176-77
Compendium Studii Philosophiae (Bacon) 14:8-
    9, 28-31, 36-37, 42, 45, 50, 68-69, 100-01,
    105
Compendium Studii Theologiae (Bacon) 14:9,
    15, 22, 25, 42, 45, 50, 64
Compendium theologiae (Aquinas) 33:120
Compotus naturalium (Bacon) 14:63
"Concerning a Certain Hermit" (Map) 32:78
Concerning Contempt for the World (Petrarch)
    20:221
Concerning Famous Women (Boccaccio)
    See *De claris mulieribus*
"Concerning King Herla" (Map) 32:79
Concerning Rhetoric (Aristotle)
    See *Gryllus*
Concerning the Antiquities of the Jews (Josephus)
    See *Antiquitates Judaicae*
Concerning the Capture (Josephus)
    See *Bellum Judaicum*
Concerning the Jewish War (Josephus)
    See *Bellum Judaicum*
"Concerning the Origin of the Carthusians" (Map)
    32:78
"Concerning the Undiscriminating Piety of Welsh-
    men" (Map) 32:80
"Conclusio Praedictae Epistolae" (Map) 32:
Condemnation of Sodomites
    See *Dhamm al-liwat*
Confessions (Augustine) 6:4, 8, 14, 16, 19, 21-4,
    29, 34, 41, 44, 46, 52-6, 60, 63-9, 72, 78,
    84, 92, 96-8, 100-04, 110-13, 116-20, 122,
    126-29, 131-33, 136-38, 140-42, 146, 149
"Confronting The Wine" (Po Chu-i) 24:359
Les Congés: (Bodel) 28:195, 266
Conica (Euclid)
    See *Conics*
Conics (Euclid) 25:1-86, 97, 108
"Conloch and Cuhona" (Ossian) 28:311
Connection by Marriage (Menander)
    See *Samia*
Consolatio (Boethius)
    See *De consolatione philosophiae*
Consolation (Cicero)
    See *Consolationes*
The Consolation of Philosophy (Boethius)
    See *The Consolation of Philosophy*
De consolatione philosophiae (Boethius) 3, 4,
    9, 10-15, 15-23, 24, 31, 33, 37-43, 43-47,
    47-53, 53-58, 58-69, 69-79, 87, 88, 88-97,
    97-124, 125-26, 128-32, 134-45
Consolationes (Cicero) 3:227
The Consonants of Law (Lucian) 32:39
De constantia (Seneca) 6:382
Constitution of Sparta (Xenophon) 17:326, 334,
    341, 348, 349
De consulatu suo (Cicero) 3:198
Conte de la Charrette (Chretien de Troyes)
    See *Lancelot*
Conte du Graal (Chretien de Troyes)
    See *Perceval*
De contemptu mundi (Petrarch) 20:213
Li Contes del Graal (Chretien de Troyes)
    See *Perceval*
Contest for the Arms (Aeschylus) 11:125
Contra academicos (Augustine) 6:5, 46, 65, 68,
    90
Contra amatores mundi (Rolle) 21:332, 381, 398
Contra Apionem (Josephus) 13:207-8, 211-2,
    214, 219-20, 225-39, 247, 250, 253, 256,
    259-60, 262-3, 268, 270, 272, 279, 281, 296,
    301-2, 306-8, 312-3, 315, 317-20
Contra Celsum (Origen) 19:211, 217, 225-27,

Title Index

249

Contra epistolum Manichaei (Augustine) **6**:9

"Contra Eunomium" (Basil of Caesaria)
See "Against Eunomius"

Contra Eutychen et Nestorium (Boethius) **15**:86, 125-6, 128, 130, 132-3, 135-6, 138

"Conversation in the Mountains" (Li Po) **2**:144

A Conversation of Origen with Heracleides (Origen) **19**:233

Conversion of Thais (Hroswitha of Gandersheim)
See *Paphnutius*

Convivium (Lucian) **32**:10

Corbaccio (Boccaccio) **13**:9, 37, 67, 70-1, 73-4, 88-94

De Corona (Cicero) **3**:267

De Corona militis (Tertullian) **29**:333-34, 338, 346-49, 373

De correptione et gratia (Augustine) **6**:9-10, 89

"Corricthura" (Ossian) **28**:303-04

De Coruna (Demosthenes)
See *On the Crown*

Counsels on Discernment (Eckhart) **9**:69

Court Gossip (Map)
See *De Nugis Curialium*

"Courtyard Pines" (Po Chu-i) **24**:341

"Covala" (Ossian) **28**:311

Cratylus (Plato) **8**:306, 336, 361

Cresphontes (Euripides) **23**:207

Critias (Plato) **8**:232, 259, 261, 306, 311

Crito (Plato) **8**:282

"Croma" (Ossian) **28**:303

"Crossing at Seven Li Shallows" (Su Shih) **15**:396-97

"The Crow Instructing His Child" (Marie de France) **8**:194

Crown Speech (Demosthenes)
See *On the Crown*

"Crying Over Old Friends, Then Sending (the Poem) to Yüan the Ninth" (Po Chu-i) **24**:354

The Cualnge Cattle-raid
See *Tain Bo Cualnge*

Cupid and Psyche (Apuleius) **1**:22, 26, 40-2

Curculio (Plautus) **24**:170-73, 175-76, 183, 193, 196-97, 199, 217, 258, 260, 262-63

Cursus S. Benedicti (Benedict, Saint) **29**:26-9

The Cyclops (Euripides) **23**:131-32

Cynegeticus (Xenophon) **17**:350, 375

The Cynic (Lucian) **32**:33, 35

Cynthia Monobiblos (Propertius) **32**:222-24, 232, 235-36, 239, 255, 292-93

Cyropaedia (Xenophon) **17**:318-22, 323, 326, 327, 329-31, 335, 337, 340, 341, 343, 348, 349, 350, 351-52, 361-68, 372, 375, 376-85

Daitaleis (Aristophanes) **4**:62

Daksina-murti-stotra (Sankara) **32**:390

Danaides (Aeschylus) **11**:88, 119, 158, 160, 167, 179, 183, 192

The Dance (Lucian) **32**:35, 39, 60, 62

Danesh Namesh (Avicenna) **16**:150

"Daniel" (Caedmon) **7**:84, 87, 89-90

Daphnephorica (Pindar) **12**:321

Daphnis (Longus)
See *Daphnis and Chloe*

Daphnis and Chloe (Longus) **7**;214-76

"Darthula" (Ossian) **28**:303

Data (Euclid) **25**:1-86, 92-3, 97, 104, 110, 113, 191, 208, 264

Daughter of Pelias (Euripides) **23**:173

Daughters of Danäus (Aeschylus)
See *Danaides*

Daughters of Phorcus (Aeschylus) **11**:124

Daughters of Phorkys (Aeschylus)

See *Daughters of Phorcus*

De beneficiis (Seneca) **6**:344, 348, 374, 381-83

De brevitate vitae (Seneca) **6**:344, 382

De clementia (Seneca) **6**:344, 374, 381-82, 397, 399, 401-02, 408

De clementia I (Seneca) **6**:399

De clementia II (Seneca) **6**:399

De ira (Seneca) **6**:344, 347, 382, 385, 411, 424, 436-37

De otio (Seneca) **6**:382

De providentia (Seneca) **6**:374, 381

De vita beata (Seneca) **6**:382, 412

De Dea Syria (Lucian)
See *The Syrian Goddess*

The Dead Come to Life, or, The Fisherman The Fisherman (Lucian) **32**:10, 32, 35, 37, 48—51, 63, 65

"The Death of Edward the Confessor" **4**:13

"The Death of Enkidu" **3**:336

"The Death of Gilgamesh" **3**:333, 336-37, 349

Decameron (Boccaccio) **13**:3-28, 30-8, 42-3, 45, 47-52, 55-7, 59-65, 67, 71-2, 74-5, 82-4, 86, 88-91, 94, 114-8, 122-31

"Decaying-Sick and Devoid of Interest I Then Sing of my Feelings" (Po Chu-i) **24**:343

Decisive Treatise (Averroes)
See *Fasl al-maqal*

Dede Korkut
See *Kitabi-i Dedem Qorkut*

Dede Korkut nameh
See *Kitabi-i Dedem Qorkut*

"The Defence of Walled Towns" (Sordello) **15**:330, 344

Defense (Plato)
See *Apologia*

Defense (Xenophon)
See *Apology*

Deification of Arsinoe (Callimachus) **18**:34, 39, 60

Demonax (Lucian) **32**:8

Descent of Heracles into the Underworld (Pindar) **12**:321

Descent of the Gods (Hesiod)
See *Theogony*

Desconort (Llull) **12**:108, 120, 122

Destructio destructionis philosophorum (Averroes)
See *Tahafut al-tahafut*

Destructio Destructionum (Averroes)
See *Tahafut al-tahafut*

Destruction of the Destruction (Averroes)
See *Tahafut al-tahafut*

"Deus Amanz" (Marie de France)
See "Les Dous Amanz"

"The Devout Prince" **2**:40

Devyaparadha-ksamapana-stotra (Sankara) **32**:390

Dhamm al-kuttab **25**:333

Dhamm al-liwat **25**:333

Dialectica (Abelard) **11**:62, 64, 66

De dialectica (Augustine) **6**:133-36, 138

Dialectica (John)
See *Capita Philosophica*

Dialogi (Seneca) **6**:374, 381-82, 410, 413

Dialogue) (Catherine)
See *Il Dialogo*

Dialogue against the Luciferians (Jerome) **30**:105

Dialogue between a Christian and a Jew (Abelard)
See *Dialogue between a Philosopher, a Jew and A Christian*

Dialogue between a Philosopher, a Jew and A Christian (Abelard) **11**:4, 11, 21, 24, 51-53, 67

A Dialogue between a Saracen and a Christian (John)
See *Disputatio Saraceni et Christiani*

Dialogue contra Pelagianos (Jerome) **30**:118, 135

Dialogue of the Philosopher with a Jew and a Christian (Abelard)
See *Dialogue between a Philosopher, a Jew and A Christian*

Dialogue of Trismegistus (Apuleius) **1**:17

Dialogues (Seneca)
See *Dialogi*

Dialogues of the Courtesans (Lucian) **32**:7, 33, 39-40

Dialogues of the Dead (Lucian) **32**:7-8, 33, 47, 51, 54-55

Dialogues of the Gods (Lucian) **32**:7, 33, 39-40

Dialogues of the Sea Gods (Lucian) **32**:39-40

Dialogues on the Supreme Good, the End of All Moral Action (Cicero)
See *De finibus*

Dialogus (William of Ockham) **32**:183-84, 197-99, 201-03

Diana's Hunt (Boccaccio)
See *Caccia di Diana*

Diary of Izumi Shikibu Nikki (Izumi Shikibu)
See *Izumi Shikibu nikki*

Dictyluci (Aeschylus)
See *Net-Draggers*

"Dido" (Ovid) **7**:312

Dionysius (Hroswitha of Gandersheim) **29**:123

"Dirge for Blacatz" (Sordello)
See "Planher vuelh en Blacatz"

Dis Exapaton (Menander) **9**:258, 270

Disceptatio Christiani et Saraceni (John) **27**:

"Discourse on Dragon and Tiger (Lead and Mercury)" (Su Shih) **15**:400

"Discourse on Literature" (Su Shih) **15**:420

"Discourse to the Young" (Basil of Caesaria) **35**:11, 75

"Discussing Marriage" (Po Chu-i) **24**:300

Disowned (Lucian) **32**:39

Disputatio Saraceni et Christiani (John) **27**:57

Disputation (Llull) **12**:119

Disputed Questions (Aquinas) **33**:31, 43, 95, 109-10, 114-15

Dissuasio Valerii ad Ruffinum philosophum ne uxorem ducat (Map)
See *Valerius ad Rufiniam de non ducenda Uxore*

Distinction and Exposition
See *Kitab al-Bayan wa l'Tabyin*

The Distinction between Enmity and Envy
See *Fi Fasl ma bayn al-adawah wa l-hasad*

Dithyrambs (Pindar) **12**:320, 355

Divan-i Hafiz (Hafiz)
See *Diwan-i Hafiz*

Divine Song
See *Bhagavad Gita*

Division of the Canon (Euclid)
See *Sectio Canonis*

De Divisione Nomine (Aquinas) **33**:85, 89, 94, 96

Divisions (Boethius) **15**:27, 29-30

The Divisions of Oratory (Cicero)
See *Partiones oratoriae*

Diwan-i Hafiz (Hafiz) **34**:59, 64, 66-67, 69-70, 74, 78, 90, 93-112, 128

Diwan-i shams-i tabrizi (Rumi) **20**:352-53, 371-72

De doctrina Christiana (Augustine) **6**:69, 81-2,

85, 92-4, 111, 113, 126, 133-36, 138

Doctrina pueril (Llull) **12**:104-05, 107, 121

"The Doe and Her Fawn" (Marie de France) **8**:193-94

"The Dog and the Meat" (Aesop) **24**:42

"Dog and the Wolf" (Aesop) **24**:6, 19

De domo (Cicero) **3**:269

"Dompna meillz qu om pot pensar" (Sordello) **15**:361

"Donna mi vene" (Petrarch) **20**:273

"Una donna piu bella" (Petrarch) **20**:241

De dono perseverantiae (Augustine) **6**:10

A Double Deceit (Menander)
See *Dis Exapaton*

The Double Indictment (Lucian) **32**:32, 48, 51, 63-65

The Dour Man (Menander)
See *Dyskolos*

"Les Dous Amanz" (Marie de France) **8**:116-17, 121, 131, 133-34, 136-39, 147, 153-54, 156, 162-65, 181, 187

The Downward Journey (Lucian) **32**:47, 51, 55

"A Draught of Sesamum" (Su Shih) **15**:383, 391

Dream (Cicero)
See *Somnium Scipionis*

Dream of Scipio (Cicero)
See *Somnium Scipionis*

The Dream of the Rood **14**:215-294

The Dream, or Lucan's Career (Lucian) **32**:9, 17, 32

"Dreams of the Sky-land" (Li Po) **2**:134

Drinkers and Drinks
See *Fil-Sharib wa l-mashrub*

"Drinking Alone by Moonlight" (Li Po) **2**:132, 143, 163

Drunkenness (Menander) **9**:248

Dulcitius (Hroswitha of Gandersheim) **29**:01, 110-11, 15, 118, 126, 139, 150, 158, 162, 174-75, 191, 198, 200

"A Dung-Beetle" (Marie de France)
See "A Wolf and a Dung-Beetle"

Duties (Cicero)
See *De officiis*

Dvadasa-manjarika-stotra (Sankara) **32**:390

The Dynasty of Raghu (Kalidasa)
See *Raghuvamsa*

Dyskolos (Menander) **9**:231-33, 235-41, 243-52, 257, 260-65, 269-70, 272-77, 279-84, 286-87

"Eagle and the Beetle" (Aesop) **24**:35

"The Eagle and the Fox" (Aesop) **24**:43

"Early Spring in the Creek" (Po Chu-i) **24**:339

Earnestness and Jesting
See *Fi l-Jidd wa 'l-bazl*

"The Ebony Horse" **2**:51

Ecclesiazusae (Aristophanes)
See *Ekklesiazousai*

"Ecloga I" (Petrarch) **20**:263

The Education of Cyrus (Xenophon)
See *Cyropaedia*

Ego dormio (Rolle) **21**:294, 336-37, 356-57, 359-61, 363, 367-69, 371-75, 389, 396

Ego dormio et cor meum vigilat (Rolle)
See *Ego dormio*

Egyptians (Aeschylus) **11**:88, 160, 179

Eight Questions (Bede) **20**:121

"Eight Sights of Feng-hsiang" (Su Shih) **15**:410

Eighth Isthmian (Pindar)
See *Isthmian 8*

Eighth Olympian (Pindar)
See *Olympian 8*

Eighth Pythian (Pindar)
See *Pythian 8*

"Eighty some paces" (Su Shih) **15**:398

Eirene (Aristophanes) **4**:44-5, 60-2, 78, 87, 93, 108-09, 124-26, 132-33, 138, 142-44, 148-49, 153-54, 160, 162-63. 165-68

Ekklesiazousai (Aristophanes) **4**:44, 60-62, 65, 68, 78, 87, 94, 110, 124-26, 128-29, 147, 149-50, 152, 155-56, 161-62, 166, 168-77, 179-80

Electra (Euripides) **23**:110, 114, 122-24, 131, 175-76, 186, 189, 206-07, 215, 222

Electra (Sophocles)
See *Elektra*

electricments of Geometry (Euclid)
See *Elements*

Elegia di Constanza (Boccaccio) **13**:62-4, 73

Elegia di madonna Fiammetta (Boccaccio)
See *Fiammetta*

Elegies (Ovid)
See *Tristia*

Elegies of Gloom (Ovid)
See *Tristia*

Elektra (Sophocles) **2**:289, 293, 300, 314-15, 319-22, 324, 326-27, 331, 335, 338-40, 347, 349, 351, 353-54, 357-58, 368, 380, 384-85, 395-96, 417-18, 421

Elementary Exercises (Hermogenes)
See *Progymnasmata*

Elements (Euclid) **25**:1-86, 90, 92-4, 96-8, 101-05, 107, 110-18, 132-42, 144, 149, 162-79, 180-99, 200-01, 205-06, 208, 211-17, 220-45, 249, 254, 261-62, 264

Elements of Music (Euclid) **25**:1-86, 90, 99, 110, 208, 211, 213, 215

Elen (Cynewulf) **23**:5-6, 9, 14-18, 21-23, 28, 30-32, 42, 44, 46, 71, 81-83, 86, 93

Eleusinians (Aeschylus) **11**:192

Eleventh Nemean (Pindar)
See *Nemean 11*

Eleventh Olympian (Pindar)
See *Olympian 11*

Eleventh Pythian (Pindar)
See *Pythian 11*

"Eliduc" (Marie de France) **8**:114, 118, 121, 129-30, 133, 135, 140, 144-45, 147-49, 152, 158, 160-61, 164-66, 170, 182

Embassy (Demosthenes)
See *On the Misconduct of the Embassy*

Emendatio peccatoris (Rolle) **21**:295

Emendatio vitae (Rolle) **21**:278, 303, 307, 310-11, 313-14, 320, 329, 335, 341-42, 344-45, 347-48, 351-52, 369, 386, 389, 392-95, 397-98

"An Emperor and his Ape" (Marie de France) **8**:175

"Emril Son of Beyril" **8**:105

Enarration on Psalm 90 (Augustine) **6**:111

Enarration on Psalm 136 (Augustine) **6**:116

Enarrationes in psalmos (Augustine) **6**:83

Enchiridion ad laurentium (Augustine) **6**:9, 21, 68

Encomia (Pindar) **12**:320-21, 357, 363-64

Encomion on Sosibius (Callimachus) **18**:43

Encomium (Pindar)
See *Encomia*

Encomium nominis Ihesu (Rolle) **21**:389

Ends (Epicurus) **21**:124

English Translation and Commentary on the Psalter (Rolle) **21**:278-80, 284, 294, 309, 332, 351

Enid (Chretien de Troyes)
See *Erec et Enide*

Ensegnamen d'Onor (Sordello) **15**:331-32, 354, 256, 270, 376-76

The Envier and the Envied
See *Fi l-Hasid wa l-mahsud*

Epic of Gilgamesh **3**:301-75

Epicleros (Menander) **9**:203

Epidicus (Plautus) **24**:170-73, 175, 183, 196, 219, 271

Epigram C (Martial) **35**:376, 410

Epigram CIV (Martial) **35**:330

Epigram CLII (Martial) **35**:410

Epigram I (Martial) **35**:258-59, 262-63, 266, 273-74, 276-77, 279-80, 282, 285-87, 290-98, 302-14, 316, 322, 326-27, 330, 332-34, 347, 351, 354-55, 359, 361, 372, 375, 376-81, 383, 385-386-389, 396, 409-414

Epigram II (Martial) **35**:255, 274, 276-77, 280-82, 285-86, 288, 292-93, 296-97, 302-04, 306-07, 309-10, 316, 324, 326, 328-34, 355-56, 361, 363, 365, 378-380, 385-389, 409-410, 413

Epigram III (Martial) **35**:263, 266, 274-76, 279, 285-87, 292, 295-97, 302, 304, 306, 308-10, 315, 321-22, 326, 328-33, 338-39, 355, 363, 365, 374, 376, 378-381, 385-388, 396, 414

Epigram IV (Martial) **35**:261, 266, 276, 279-80, 286, 302-04, 306-10, 315, 332-34, 345, 355-57, 360, 362, 382-383, 385-388, 405, 409-410, 413

Epigram IX (Martial) 263, 267, 275, 279, 281-82, 287-88, 291, 293, 295-98, 302-04, 306-07, 310, 312-13, 315-16, 322, 324, 326, 328-32, 334-36, 356, 360, 365, 380, 385, 387-388, 397-405-406, 410

Epigram L (Martial) **35**:376

Epigram LIV (Martial) 376

Epigram LIX (Martial) **5**:409

Epigram LX (Martial) **35**:376

Epigram LXX (Martial) **35**:376

Epigram V (Martial) **35**:260, 262, 265, 272, 278-80, 285, 288, 291-92, 294, 296-98, 302-07, 309-11, 314, 322-25, 327-34, 354-56, 362, 373, 379-380, 382-383, 385, 387-388, 390, 396, 402, 404, 406, 409-414

Epigram VI (Martial) **35**:274, 276, 278-79, 281, 285-87, 291-93, 296, 298, 302-04, 306-10, 312-13, 315, 321, 324-25, 330-32, 355-56, 378-380, 382-383, 385-388, 400, 404-405, 409-410

Epigram VII (Martial) 258, 264-66, 273, 276, 279-82, 286-88, 291, 291, 293, 295-98, 302-04, 306-08, 310-12, 320-21, 323-24, 326, 329, 331-32, 340, 356, 379-381, 383, 388, 401, 409-411, 413

Epigram VIII (Martial) 264-67, 273-74, 276, 279-81, 286, 288, 291-93, 295, 297-98, 302-04, 306-07, 309-11, 315, 322, 324-26, 329-34, 355-56, 367-368, 371, 376, 378-379, 381, 383, 388, 404-405, 409-413, 414

Epigram X (Martial) 255, 258, 260-61, 267, 273-74, 278-79, 281, 293-98, 304, 306-13, 315-16, 322, 325-28, 330-35, 348, 351, 354-56, 360, 374-76, 387, 379, 383, 385-387, 404, 409-410-412

Epigram XC (Martial) **35**:376

Epigram XCII (Martial) **35**:376

Epigram XI (Martial) **35**:255, 276, 278-79, 281, 291, 296-98, 304, 306-08, 310, 313, 315-16, 326, 331-34, 351, 354-56, 361-62, 364-65, 374-376, 378, 380-382, 383, 385, 388-90, 401, 404, 409, 412-413

Epigram XII (Martial) **35**:259-60, 264, 272, 276-78, 280, 286, 288, 291-92, 295-98, 303, 308-12, 329-31, 348, 351, 356, 360, 362-63, 375, 382-83, 387-390, 409, 412-414

Epigram XIII (Martial) 295-96, 326, 331
Epigram XIV (Martial) 279-80, 291, 296, 307, 310, 326, 329, 332, 355, 367, 371,388, 409, 413-414
Epigram XLI (Martial) **35**:367, 369
Epigram XLIX (Martial) **35**:331
Epigram XLXIII (Martial) **35**:376
Epigram XV (Martial) **35**:331
Epigram XXCII (Martial) **35**:376
Epigram XXCV (Martial) **35**:376
Epigram XXI (Martial) **35**:376
Epigram XXIII (Martial) **35**:329, 367, 370
Epigram XXV (Martial) **35**:367-369, 376
Epigram XXVII (Martial) 329, 367-369
Epigram XXVIII (Martial) **35**:399
Epigram XXX (Martial) **35**:376
Epigram XXXI (Martial) **35**:376
Epigram XXXV (Martial) **35**:367, 370
Epigram XXXVII (Martial) **35**:376
Epigram XXXVIII (Martial) **35**:329, 367, 370
Epigrammata (Martial) **35**:396
Epigrammaton libri (Martial)
    See *Epigrammata*
Epigrams (Callimachus) **18**:18, 25, 32, 34-8, 48
Epigrams (Martial)
    See *Epigrammata*
Epinicia (Pindar) **12**:320-22
Epinomis (Plato) **8**:248, 305-06, 311
"Episode of Nala"
    See *Nalopakhyana*
Epist. 14 (Jerome) **30**:116
Epist. 21 (Jerome) **30**:118, 121
Epist. 22 (Jerome) **30**:118
Epist. 33 (Jerome) **30**:118, 135
Epist. 45 (Jerome) **30**:128
Epist. 46 (Jerome) **30**:129-30
Epist. 52 (Jerome) **30**:117, 120
Epist. 53 (Jerome) **30**:118, 120, 130, 136
Epist. 58 (Jerome) **30**:130
Epist. 60 (Jerome) **30**:120
Epist. 70 (Jerome) **30**:121
Epist. 74 (Jerome) **30**:117
Epist. 98 (Jerome) **30**:117
Epist. 107 (Jerome) **30**:120
Epistle (Rolle) **21**:299
Epistle 1 (Basil of Caesaria) **53**:20, 21, 44, 49
Epistle 2 (Basil of Caesaria) **35**:10, 22
Epistle 3 (Basil of Caesaria) **35**:9, 49
Epistle 4 (Basil of Caesaria) **35**:44, 49
Epistle 5 (Basil of Caesaria) **35**:16, 44
Epistle 14 (Basil of Caesaria) **35**:9, 21, 49
Epistle 18 (Basil of Caesaria) **35**:41, 90
Epistle 19 (Basil of Caesaria) **35**:38
Epistle 20 (Basil of Caesaria) **35**:38
Epistle 21 (Basil of Caesaria) **35**:42, 49
Epistle 25 (Basil of Caesaria) **35**:30
Epistle 26 (Basil of Caesaria) **35**:15
Epistle 27 (Basil of Caesaria) **35**:28, 39
Epistle 28 (Basil of Caesaria) **35**:12
Epistle 30 (Basil of Caesaria) **35**:15, 42
Epistle 31 (Basil of Caesaria) **35**:41
Epistle 36 (Basil of Caesaria) **35**:40
Epistle 39 (Basil of Caesaria) **35**:22, 49
Epistle 40 (Basil of Caesaria) **35**:20, 23
Epistle 41 (Basil of Caesaria) **35**:20, 23
Epistle 42 (Basil of Caesaria) **35**:16, 38
Epistle 47 (Basil of Caesaria) **35**:24
Epistle XLVII (Seneca) **6**:384
Epistle 48 (Basil of Caesaria) **35**:25, 33, 39
Epistle 49 (Basil of Caesaria) **35**:37
Epistle 51 (Basil of Caesaria) **35**:22
Epistle 53 (Basil of Caesaria) **35**:38, 57
Epistle 54 (Basil of Caesaria) **35**:27, 38, 41

Epistle 55 (Basil of Caesaria) **35**:27
Epistle 56 (Basil of Caesaria) **35**:44
Epistle 58 (Basil of Caesaria) **35**:25
Epistle 59 (Basil of Caesaria) **35**:25, 44
Epistle 60 (Basil of Caesaria) **35**:25, 44
Epistle 66 (Basil of Caesaria) **35**:31
Epistle 68 (Basil of Caesaria) **35**:26
Epistle 69 (Basil of Caesaria) **35**:31
Epistle 70 (Basil of Caesaria) **35**:31
Epistle 71 (Basil of Caesaria) **35**:30
Epistle 72 (Basil of Caesaria) **35**:40
Epistle 73 (Basil of Caesaria) **35**:40, 44
Epistle 74 (Basil of Caesaria) **35**:14, 28, 49
Epistle 75 (Basil of Caesaria) **35**:28
Epistle 76 (Basil of Caesaria) **35**:28
Epistle 80 (Basil of Caesaria) **35**:31
Epistle 81 (Basil of Caesaria) **35**:27
Epistle 83 (Basil of Caesaria) **35**:31
Epistle 84 (Basil of Caesaria) **35**:29
Epistle 92 (Basil of Caesaria) **35**:31
Epistle 93 (Basil of Caesaria) **35**:31
Epistle 94 (Basil of Caesaria) **35**:14, 26
Epistle 97 (Basil of Caesaria) **35**:28
Epistle 98 (Basil of Caesaria) **35**:25, 28, 29
Epistle 99 (Basil of Caesaria) **35**:27
Epistle 104 (Basil of Caesaria) **35**:27
Epistle 106 (Basil of Caesaria) **35**:11
Epistle 110 (Basil of Caesaria) **35**:27, 40
Epistle 111 (Basil of Caesaria) **35**:27
Epistle 112 (Basil of Caesaria) **35**:49
Epistle 122 (Basil of Caesaria) **35**:28
Epistle 125 (Basil of Caesaria) **35**:30
Epistle 128 (Basil of Caesaria) **35**:26, 30
Epistle 130 (Basil of Caesaria) **35**:30
Epistle 133 (Basil of Caesaria) **35**:49
Epistle 135 (Basil of Caesaria) **35**:42
Epistle 136 (Basil of Caesaria) **35**:28
Epistle 138 (Basil of Caesaria) **35**:28
Epistle 141 (Basil of Caesaria) **35**:25
Epistle 155 (Basil of Caesaria) **35**:54
Epistle 157 (Basil of Caesaria) **35**:52
Epistle 160 (Basil of Caesaria) **35**:27, 38
Epistle 160 (Basil of Caesaria) **35**:27
Epistle 170 (Basil of Caesaria) **35**:27
Epistle 171 (Basil of Caesaria) **35**:27
Epistle 173 (Basil of Caesaria) **35**:6
Epistle 189 (Basil of Caesaria) **35**:37
Epistle 190 (Basil of Caesaria) **35**:45
Epistle 191 (Basil of Caesaria) **35**:39, 44
Epistle 195 (Basil of Caesaria) **35**:38
Epistle 198 (Basil of Caesaria) **35**:28, 38, 39
Epistle 202 (Basil of Caesaria) **35**:28
Epistle 203 (Basil of Caesaria) **35**:30
Epistle 204 (Basil of Caesaria) **35**:30
Epistle 207 (Basil of Caesaria) **35**:22, 28, 30
Epistle 210 (Basil of Caesaria) **35**:20, 30
Epistle 215 (Basil of Caesaria) **35**:32, 38, 39
Epistle 222 (Basil of Caesaria) **35**:9
Epistle 223 (Basil of Caesaria) **35**:21, 30
Epistle 224 (Basil of Caesaria) **35**:30
Epistle 225 (Basil of Caesaria) **35**:30
Epistle 226 (Basil of Caesaria) **35**:30
Epistle 231 (Basil of Caesaria) **35**:31
Epistle 237 (Basil of Caesaria) **35**:38
Epistle 239 (Basil of Caesaria) **35**:32, 49
Epistle 242 (Basil of Caesaria) **35**:32, 42
Epistle 243 (Basil of Caesaria) **35**:32
Epistle 244 (Basil of Caesaria) **35**:26, 30
Epistle 251 (Basil of Caesaria) **35**:26
Epistle 252 (Basil of Caesaria) **35**:53
Epistle 259 (Basil of Caesaria) **35**:28
Epistle 263 (Basil of Caesaria) **35**:32
Epistle 266 (Basil of Caesaria) **35**:32

Epistle 268 (Basil of Caesaria) **35**:33
Epistle 270 (Basil of Caesaria) **35**:37
Epistle 271 (Basil of Caesaria) **35**:42
Epistle 276 (Basil of Caesaria) **35**:15
Epistle 278 (Basil of Caesaria) **35**:278
Epistle 279 (Basil of Caesaria) **35**:279
Epistle 280 (Basil of Caesaria) **35**:27
Epistle 281 (Basil of Caesaria) **35**:27
Epistle 282 (Basil of Caesaria) **35**:25, 53
Epistle 283 (Basil of Caesaria) **35**:15
Epistle 290 (Basil of Caesaria) **35**:49
Epistle 291 (Basil of Caesaria) **35**:49
Epistle 298 (Basil of Caesaria) **35**:17
Epistle 299 (Basil of Caesaria) **35**:11
Epistle 301 (Basil of Caesaria) **35**:17
Epistle 326 (Basil of Caesaria) **35**:16
Epistle 335 (Basil of Caesaria) **35**:20
Epistle 336 (Basil of Caesaria) **35**:20, 21
Epistle 337 (Basil of Caesaria) **35**:20
Epistle 338 (Basil of Caesaria) **35**:20, 33
Epistle 339 (Basil of Caesaria) **35**:20, 49
Epistle 358 (Basil of Caesaria) **35**:20
Epistle ad P. Lentulum (Cicero)
    See *Ad P. Lentulum*
Epistle for the Next World and This on Manners, Managing Men and Social Relations
    See *Risalat al-Maad wa l-maash fi l-adab watabir al-nas wa-muamalatihim*
""*Epistle of the Same to certain Learned Patrons of this Book*"" (Hroswitha of Gandersheim) **29**:123, 138
Epistle Valerii (Map)
    See *Valerius ad Rufiniam de non ducenda Uxore*
Epistles (Ovid)
    See *Heroides*
Epistles (Plato) **8**:305, 311
Epistles (Seneca)
    See *Epistulae morales*
Epistles 6 (Basil of Caesaria) **35**:17
Epistles 8 (Basil of Caesaria) **35**:10, 22, 44, 49
Epistolæ Heroidum (Ovid)
    See *Heroides*
Epistola de secretis operibus naturae (Bacon) **14**:64
""*Epistola Eiusdem ad Quasdam Sapientes Huius Libri Fautores*"" (Charles)
    See ""*Epistle of the Same to certain Learned Patrons of this Book*""
Epistola fratris Rogerii Baconis de secretis operibus naturae et de nullitate magiae (Bacon) **14**:44
Epistolae familiares (Petrarch) **20**:237, 266-68, 288-90, 294, 296-97, 303-05, 308, 314, 318, 320, 326, 331, 333
Epistolae rerum familiarium (Petrarch) **20**:256-57, 261
Epistolae seniles (Petrarch) **20**:266, 296, 323, 326, 331
Epistolario (Catherine) **27**:19, 20, 21, 23, 24, 25, 26, 28, 30, 31, 34
Epistole metrice (Petrarch) **20**:327, 333
Epistul ad Eustochium (Jerome) **30**:67
Epistulae ex Ponto (Ovid) **7**:323, 343, 344, 347, 378, 398, 423, 426
Epistulae morales (Seneca) **6**:347, 352-53, 374-75, 381-83, 410-11, 417
Epitaphium Sanctae Paulae (Jerome) **30**:82-85, 92
"*Epithalamium of Peleus and Thetis*" (Catullus)
    See "*Poem 64*"
Epitrepontes (Menander) **9**:203, 207-09, 211-13, 215-18, 223-24, 227, 230, 232, 238-44, 246-

47, 249-52, 260, 269-71, 278, 281
Eptiaphios (Demosthenes) **13**:166
"Equitan" (Marie de France) **8**:114, 121, 123, 131-32, 134, 136, 143, 147, 149-50, 157, 159, 162-65, 171, 175, 182
"Er encontra'l temps de mai" (Sordello) **15**:363
Erec (Hartmann von Aue) **15**:158, 164-65, 176, 183, 185, 188-96, 196-202, 207-13, 218-23, 228-41, 244
Erec and Enid (Chretien de Troyes)
 See *Erec et Enide*
Erec et Enide (Chretien de Troyes) **10**:132-33, 139, 141-43, 146-48, 159-61, 163, 165-67, 169, 171-73, 178, 183-89, 191-93, 195, 197, 200-01, 204-10, 218-19, 223-26, 229-39
Erechtheus (Euripides) **23**:104, 173, 207
Erga (Hesiod)
 See *Works and Days*
Erotic Adventures (Ovid)
 See *Amores*
"Esaiam" (Basil of Caesaria) **35**:23
Esope (Marie de France)
 See *The Fables*
Esposizioni (Boccaccio) **13**:62, 67
Espurgatoire (Marie de France)
 See *L'Espurgatoire Saint Patrice*
L'Espurgatoire Saint Patrice (Marie de France) **8**:114-15, 128, 146, 159-61, 173-77
Essays in Portraiture (Lucian) **32**:39
Essays in Portraiture Defended (Lucian) **32**:39
Ethica seu Scito te ipsum (Abelard)
 See *Scito Te Ipsum*
Ethics (Abelard)
 See *Scito Te Ipsum*
Ethics (Aquinas) **33**:89
De Eucharistico Sacramento (Albert the Great) **16**:42
Eudemian Ethics (Aristotle) **31**:64, 66-67, 71-72, 77, 81, 88, 266, 330
Eudemus (Aristotle) **31**:66, 68, 228, 252, 354-56
"Eulogy on Paula" (Jerome)
 See *Epitaphium Sanctae Paulae*
Eumenides (Aeschylus) **11**:85-7, 92, 96, 100, 102, 105, 107, 114, 116-17, 119, 132, 134-35, 137-38, 140, 143, 150, 152-53, 155-57, 162, 165-66, 172, 178-79, 180-85, 191-92, 194, 197-98, 204-05, 207, 216, 218, 222, 225
The Eunich (Lucian) **32**:25, 43-46, 48
Eunuch (Terence)
 See *Eunuchus*
Eunuchus (Terence) **14**:299, 303-08, 311-15, 317-18, 321, 330-33, 335, 337, 340, 342-43, 345-49, 352-54, 357-58, 364-66, 369-71, 383-84, 387
Euthydemus (Plato) **8**:218, 250, 265-66, 306, 314, 357, 361
Euthyphro (Plato)
 See *Euthyphron*
Euthyphron (Plato) **8**:263, 286, 306
Evast and Blanquerna (Llull)
 See *Blanquerna*
"Evening Rain" (Po Chu-i) **24**:336, 339
Ex Ponto (Ovid)
 See *Epistulae ex Ponto*
Exemplaria Adamantii (Origen) **19**:192
"Exhortation" (Rolle) **21**:367, 369, 375
Exhortation to Chastity (Tertullian) **29**:312-16, 318, 367
De exhortatione castitatis (Tertullian)
 See *Exhortation to Chastity*
"Exile's Letter" (Li Po) **2**:140
"Exodus" (Caedmon) **7**:83-4, 87, 89-90, 93, 104
Expositio epistolae ad Galatas (Augustine) **6**:10

Expositio in Epist. ad Romanos (Abelard) **11**:10, 12, 53
An Exposition of the Different Kinds of Shi'ism
 See *Bayan madhahib al-Shiah*
An Exposition of the Methods of Argument Concerning the Doctrine of the Faith and a Determination of Doubts and Misleading Innovations Brought into the Faith (Averroes)
 See *Kitab al-kashf 'an manahij al-adilla fi 'aqa'id al-milla, wa ta'rif ma waqa'a fiha bihasb at-ta'wil min ash-shibah al-muzigha wal-bida 'al-mudilla*
Exposition of the Psalms (Rolle)
 See *Commentary on the Psalms and Canticles of the Old Testament*
Expositions on the Gospel according to John (Origen)
 See *Commentary on St. John*
Extravagantes (Saint Birgitta of Sweden) **24**:107, 131-32, 134, 136, 158-64
Exxlesisastical History of the English People (Bede)
 See *Historia ecclesiastica gentis Anglorum*
The Fables (Marie de France) **8**:115, 128, 146, 160-61, 171-75, 179
"Facing Wine" (Po Chu-i) **24**:346
Fada'il al-Atrak
 See *Kitab Manaqib al-Turkwa-ammat jund al-khilafah*
Fadl Hashim ala Abd Shams **25**:329
The Fall and Conversion of Mary (Hroswitha of Gandersheim)
 See *Abraham*
The Fall and Conversion of Theophilus (Hroswitha of Gandersheim) **29**:108, 136
"Fall of Angels" (Caedmon)
 See "Lament of the Fallen Angels"
De Falsa Legatione (Demosthenes)
 See *On the Misconduct of the Embassy*
Fang Chi (Confucius) **19**:20
"A Farmer and a River" (Aesop) **24**:18
Fasl (Averroes)
 See *Fasl al-maqal*
Fasl al-maqal (Averroes) **7**:39, 41-4, 69-72
Fasti (Ovid) **7**:284, 286, 292-93, 323-27, 330, 335, 343-46, 362-65, 377, 389, 401-03, 413-19, 424-35, 444
De Fastis (Ovid)
 See *Fasti*
Fates of the Apostles (Cynewulf) **23**:5-6, 14-18, 23, 41-42, 44, 46, 77-81, 83
"The Father and His Sons" (Aesop) **24**:66
Felix (Llull) **12**:105-07, 109, 123, 125, 133-34
Felix or The Book of Marvels (Llull)
 See *Felix*
"The Ferryman and the Hermit" **2**:40
Fi Bani Umayyah
 See *Risalah fi l-Nabitah*
Fi Dhammm al-zaman **25**:331
Fi Fasl ma bayn al-adawah wa l-hasad **25**:323, 332
Fi fihrist kutub Muhammad ibn Zakariyya' al-Razi (Biruni) **28**:176
Fi l-Balaghah wa l-ijaz **25**:331
Fi l-Hasid wa l-mahsud **25**:332
Fi l-Ishq wa l-nisa **25**:333
Fi l-Jidd wa 'l-bazl **25**:322, 324, 332
Fi l-wukala wa-muwakkilin **25**:332
Fi Madh alnabidh **25**:330
Fi Madh al-tujjar wa-dhamm amal al-sultan **25**:333
Fi Mawt Abi Harb al-Saffar **25**:331

Fi sayr sahmay as-sa'adah wa-lghayb (Biruni) **28**:151
Fi Sinnat al-quwwad **25**:331
Fi Tabaqat al-mughannin **25**:333
Fi Tafdil-al-bafn ala l-zahr **25**:322, 324, 333
Fiammetta (Boccaccio) **13**:7, 29-30, 32-3, 63, 67, 88, 97
De fide catholica (Boethius) **15**:9, 24, 3, 43, 52, 57, 62, 67
De Fide Orthodoxa (John) **27**:43, 48, 49, 51, 57, 67, 69
Fifth Isthmian (Pindar)
 See *Isthmian 5*
Fifth Nemean (Pindar)
 See *Nemean 5*
"Fighting to the South of the City" (Li Po) **2**:132
Fihi ma fihi (Rumi) **20**:371
Fil-Abbasiyyah
 See *Kitab al-Abbasiyya*
Filocolo (Boccaccio) **13**:23, 32-3, 44-5, 61-5, 102-3, 105, 112, 114-22
Filocopo (Boccaccio) **13**:9, 26-8, 30
Filostrato (Boccaccio) **13**:9, 29, 32-3, 62-3, 65, 87-8, 102-3, 106, 110, 112
Fil-Sharib wa l-mashrub **25**:330
Fingal (Ossian) **28**:283-85, 296, 299, 301, 303, 305, 311, 314, 326, 328-29, 334-35, 337-44, 348, 351, 353, 359-61, 364, 367, 371, 373-74, 378-79, 382-83
De finibus (Cicero) **3**:193, 202, 260, 288
"Finis Epistolae Praemissae" (Map) **32**:81
"Fir Tree and Bramble" (Aesop) **24**:36
Fire of Love (Rolle)
 See *Fire of Love*
"The First Birthday of Golden Bells" (Po Chu-i) **24**:352
First Isthmian (Pindar)
 See *Isthmian 1*
First Nemean (Pindar)
 See *Nemean 1*
First Olympian (Pindar)
 See *Olympian 1*
First Olynthiac (Demosthenes)
 See *Olynthiac 1*
First Oration (John) **27**:85
First Philippic (Cicero)
 See *Philippics*
First Philippic (Demosthenes)
 See *Philippic 1*
First Pythian (Pindar)
 See *Pythian 1*
"The Fisherman and the Genie" **2**:45, 53-5, 68
The Fisherman's Art (Ovid)
 See *Halieutica*
Five Books of Moses
 See *Torah*
The Flatterer (Menander)
 See *Kolax*
"The Flies and the Honey-pot" (Aesop) **24**:58
Florida (Apuleius)
 See *Floridium*
Floridium (Apuleius) **1**:7, 12, 23-4
"Flower-non-Flower" (Po Chu-i) **24**:338
"Following the Rhymes of Chiang Hui shi" (Su Shih) **15**:414, 416
For Cluentius (Cicero)
 See *Pro Cluentio*
For Marcus Caelius (Cicero)
 See *Pro Caelio*
For Megalopolis (Demosthenes) **13**:137, 148, 156-7, 159, 164, 197
For Phormio (Demosthenes) **13**:184
For Quinctius (Cicero)

See *Pro Quinctio*

For the Liberty of the Rhodians (Demosthenes)
   See *For the Rhodians*

For the Megalopolitans (Demosthenes)
   See *For Megalopolis*

For the Rhodians (Demosthenes)   **13**:137, 148,
   156-7, 159, 164, 171

"Forbidden Palace Moon" (Po Chu-i)   **24**:339

The Form of Living (Rolle)   **21**:294, 299-300, 307,
   314-15, 317, 327, 332, 335, 345, 347-48,
   351-52, 356, 359, 362, 367-69, 371-72, 375,
   381, 386, 393-94

The Form of Perfect Living (Rolle)
   See *The Form of Living*

Foundation of Alexandria (Rhodius)   **28**:27

Foundation of Kaunos (Rhodius)   **28**:27, 29

Foundation of Naucratis (Rhodius)   **28**:27

Foundation of Rhodes (Rhodius)   **28**:27

Fount of Knowledge (John)
   See *Sources of Knowledge*

The Four Branches of the Mabinogi
   See *Pedeir Keinc y Mabinogi*

"The Four Sorrows" (Marie de France)
   See "Le Chaitivel"

Fourteenth Olympian (Pindar)
   See *Olympian 14*

Fourth Nemean (Pindar)
   See *Nemean 4*

Fourth Philippic (Demosthenes)
   See *Philippic IV*

Fourth Pythian (Pindar)
   See *Pythian 4*

"The Fox and the Bear" (Marie de France)   **8**:190

"The Fox and the Crow" (Aesop)   **24**:43, 58, 60-
   62

"The Fox and the Grapes" (Aesop)   **24**:43

"The Fox and the Stork" (Aesop)   **24**:61

*Fragments of Ancient Poetry collected in the High-
   lands of Scotland* (Ossian)   **28**:296, 302, 304,
   333, 339, 351-52, 359-60, 366, 378

"Fragrant Hearth Peak" (Po Chu-i)   **24**:357

"Le Fraisse" (Marie de France)   **8**:114, 116, 121,
   131, 133-34, 136, 138, 140, 147, 152-53,
   159-60, 162-63, 165-66, 181

Free Choice of the Will (Augustine)
   See *De libero arbitrio voluntatis*

Free Will (Augustine)
   See *De libero arbitrio voluntatis*

"Fresne" (Marie de France)
   See "Le Fraisne"

The Friars (Aristophanes)   **4**:100

"A Friend Visits at Night" (Po Chu-i)   **24**:322

The Frogs (Aristophanes)
   See *Batrakhoi*

"Frolicking to the Temple of Truth Realized" (Po
   Chu-i)   **24**:331-32

De Fuga in persecutione (Tertullian)
   See *On Flight in Persecution*

Fugitivi (Lucian)
   See *The Runaways*

Furens (Seneca)
   See *Hercules furens*

Furies (Aeschylus)
   See *Eumenides*

Furious Hercules (Seneca)
   See *Hercules furens*

Galatia (Callimachus)   **18**:34

Gallicanus (Hroswitha of Gandersheim)   **29**:101,
   103-04, 110, 115, 117-18, 120-21, 126-27,
   137-38, 146-48, 150, 161-62

Gallicianm Psalter (Jerome)   **30**:79

Gallus (Lucian)   **32**:8, 17, 24-25, 28

"Ganem, Son to Abou Ayoub, and Known by the

Surname of Love's Slave"   **2**:14, 36, 38

Gangapstotra (Sankara)   **32**:390

Gastly Gladnesse (Rolle)   **21**:367

Gauvain (Chretien de Troyes)
   See *Perceval*

Genealogia deorum gentilium (Boccaccio)   **13**:33,
   38, 41, 43-4, 52-4, 62, 66, 96, 98, 103

Genealogies of the Gentile Gods (Boccaccio)
   See *Genealogia deorum gentilium*

Genealogies of the Pagan Gods (Boccaccio)
   See *Genealogia deorum gentilium*

De genealogiis deorum (Boccaccio)
   See *Genealogia deorum gentilium*

Genealogy of the Gods (Boccaccio)
   See *Genealogia deorum gentilium*

Generation of Animals (Aristotle)
   See *De Generatione Animalium*

De Generatione Animalium (Aristotle)   **31**:65-66,
   86, 328, 332-53, 374

De generatione et corruptione (Albert the Great)
   16:7, 61

De Generatione et Corruptione (Aquinas)   **33**:88

De Generatione et Corruptione (Aristotle)   **31**:86,
   312, 325, 329

De genesi ad litteram (Augustine)   **6**:9, 137, 139

De Genesi ad litteram imperfectum (Augustine)
   6:137

De Genesi adversus Manichaeos (Augustine)
   6:137

"Genesis" (Caedmon)   **7**:78-9, 82-9, 91-4, 104

"Genesis A" (Caedmon)   **7**:84-90

"Genesis B" (Caedmon)   **7**:85-6, 91, 93

Genesis of the Gods (Hesiod)
   See *Theogony*

Genji Monogatari (Shikibu)   **1**:413-76

Georgos (Menander)   **9**:250

Gertadés (Aristophanes)   **4**:102, 105

Gerusalemme liberata (Petrarch)   **20**:214

Gesta Ottonis (Hroswitha of Gandersheim)
   29:108, 122-24, 134, 140, 153, 156-58, 183,
   190

Gilgamesh
   See *Epic of Gilgamesh*

"Gilgamesh and the Agga of Kish"   **3**:336

"Gilgamesh and the Bull of Heaven"   **3**:337, 349

"Gilgamesh and the Huluppu Tree"   **3**:326, 337,
   349, 362

"Gilgamesh and the Land of the Living"   **3**:325,
   332-33, 336-37, 349

"Gilgamesh, Enkidu and the Nether World"
   See "Gilgamesh and the Huluppu Tree"

Gilgamesh Epic
   See *Epic of Gilgamesh*

Gilgamish
   See *Epic of Gilgamesh*

"Giovene donna" (Petrarch)   **20**:299, 305

The Girl from Andros (Terence)
   See *Andria*

The Girl from Samos (Menander)
   See *Samia*

The Girl Who Gets Her Hair Cut Short(Menander)
   See *Perikeiromene*

The Girl with Shorn Hair (Menander)
   See *Perikeiromene*

Gita
   See *Bhagavadgita*

Gita
   See *Bhagavad Gita*

Glaucus of Potniae (Aeschylus)
   See *Glaucus Potnieus*

Glaucus Potnieus (Aeschylus)   **11**:159, 179

"The Gnat and the Bull" (Aesop)   **24**:37

"Goat's Leaf" (Marie de France)

See "Chevrefoil"

The Golden Ass (Apuleius)
   See *Asinus aureus*

Gongolf (Hroswitha of Gandersheim)
   See *Gongolfus*

Gongolfus (Hroswitha of Gandersheim)   **29**:123,
   182

Gorgias (Plato)   **8**:217, 233, 235, 239, 247-48,
   255, 264, 266-68, 270, 274, 283, 285-87,
   306, 322

Gout (Lucian)   **32**:41

"Gradually Aging" (Po Chu-i)   **24**:348

"The Grasshopper and the Ant" (Aesop)   **24**:43,
   67, 69

De gratia et libero arbitrio (Augustine)   **6**:89,
   118, 122

"Great Asceticon" (Basil of Caesaria)   **35**:91, 93

Great Epic
   See *Mahabharata*

Gregorius (Hartmann von Aue)   **15**:164, 171-75,
   175-83, 194, 207, 213-18, 218

Grumpy (Menander)
   See *Dyskolos*

Gryllus (Aristotle)   **31**:227-38

"Guigemar" (Marie de France)
   See "Lay of Guigemar"

"Guildeluec and Gualadun" (Marie de France)
   See "Eliduc"

Guillaume d'Angleterre (Chretien de Troyes)
   10:137, 139, 142-43, 183, 218, 225, 232

"Guingamor" (Marie de France)   **8**:122-23, 126-
   28, 131

Gulnare of the Sea   **2**:14, 23

Gurvastakam (Sankara)   **32**:390

De Haersibus (John)   **27**:57, 67, 74

"*Hair of Berenice*" (Catullus)
   See "*Poem 66*"

Halieticon/On Fishing (Ovid)
   See *Halieutica*

Halieutica (Ovid)   **7**:328-29

"Hard Roads to Shu" (Li Po)   **2**:131-32, 145, 158,
   166

"Hardships of Travel" (Li Po)   **2**:139

"The Hare and the Tortoise" (Aesop)   **24**:37, 42,
   66-67

The Harpist (Menander)   **9**:288

"Harrowing of Hell" (Caedmon)   **7**:79, 91-2

Hated (Menander)
   See *Misoumenos*

Haunted House (Plautus)
   See *Mostellaria*

Havelok the Dane   **34**:144-247

"The Hawk and the Owl" (Marie de France)
   8:192, 194

Hazar Afsana
   See *Alf Layla wa-Layla*

He Clips Her Hair (Menander)
   See *Perikeiromene*

Healing (Avicenna)
   See *Kitab al-Shifa*

"Hearing Wild Geese" (Po Chu-i)   **24**:376

"Heart At Ease" (Po Chu-i)   **24**:325-26

Heautontimoreumenos (Terence)   **14**:299, 302-
   04, 306-07, 309, 311, 313-14, 316-18, 332-
   35, 337-38, 345, 347, 349, 352, 358-59,
   363-66, 381, 383-84, 386-87

Heautontimorumenus (Menander)   **9**:243, 269

"The Heavy Taxes" (Po Chu-i)   **24**:294

Hebraic Questions on Genesis (Jerome)
   See *Liber Hebraicarum Quaestionum in
   Genesim*

Hebrew Questions on Genesis (Jerome)
   See *Liber Hebraicarum Quaestionum in*

Genesim
Hecabe (Euripides)
  See *Hecuba*
Hecale (Callimachus) **18**:9, 18, 35, 38-42, 50, 52-3, 60-2
Hecuba (Euripides) **23**:112, 119, 121, 123-24, 129-30, 173-75, 182-85, 207, 213
Hecyra (Terence) **14**:299, 301-08, 311-13, 317-20, 325, 329, 332-36, 340, 342-44, 347-49, 352-53, 356-58, 364-65, 368, 383-84, 386, 389, 398
Helen (Euripides) **23**:114, 122, 124, 126-27, 132, 174-78, 187-91, 206-07, 222
Heliades (Aeschylus) **11**:211
Hell (Dante)
  See *Inferno*
Hellenica (Xenophon) **17**:328, 329, 330, 339, 342, 344, 346, 347, 348, 349, 350, 352, 359, 368, 371-76, 378
"Heng-chiang Lyrics" (Li Po) **2**:161
Heracleidae (Euripides) **23**:111-12, 119, 124-28, 131-32, 182, 184-86, 189, 206-7
Heracles (Euripides) **23**:114, 122, 174-77, 186-88, 194-95, 204-07, 213, 220-22
Heracles Furens (Euripides) **23**:122-24, 126-27, 129, 174, 205
Heracles Mad (Euripides)
  See *Heracles Furens*
Heracles's Children (Euripides)
  See *Heracles Furens*
Herakles Mad (Euripides)
  See *Heracles Furens*
"The Herb Gatherer" (Po Chu-i) **24**:294
Hercules furens (Seneca) **6**:340, 342-43, 363, 366, 369-70, 372-73, 379-81, 402-03, 405, 413, 415-17, 422-23, 431-32, 440-41, 446
Hercules oetaeus (Seneca) **6**:342-44, 363, 366, 370, 377, 379, 381, 414, 417-18, 423, 431-32, 446
Hercules on Oeta (Seneca)
  See *Hercules oetaeus*
Hermontimus (Lucian) **32**:10, 17, 32, 35, 43-44
Hero (Menander) **9**:207, 211, 217, 246, 252
Heroides (Ovid) **7**:291-93, 296-97, 299-301, 303, 310-13, 316-19, 321, 329-36, 343-44, 346-47, 355, 376-83, 388, 417, 419-20, 425, 444
Heroines (Ovid)
  See *Heroides*
"Hexaemeron" (Basil of Caesaria) **35**:48, 77, 79
Hexapla (Origen) **19**:184, 191-93
Hiero (Xenophon) **17**:327, 331-36, 365, 374, 375
Hija Muhammmed b. al-Jahm al-Barmaki **25**:331
Hikayet-i Oguzname-i Kazan Beg ve Gayri
  See *Kitabi-i Dedem Qorkut*
Hiketides (Aeschylus)
  See *Suppliants*
Hipparchus (Plato) **8**:305, 311
Hippeis (Aristophanes) **4**:38, 43, 46, 60, 62-3, 65, 74, 94, 98-9, 101, 114-15, 126-28, 132, 143, 146, 148, 152, 162-63, 167
Hippias (Lucian) **32**:39
Hippias maior (Plato) **8**:270, 305-06
Hippias Major (Plato)
  See *Hippias maior*
Hippias Minor (Plato) **8**:306
Hippolytus (Euripides) **23**:104, 113, 118-19, 121-26, 171, 173, 175-76, 180-82, 185, 195-97, 201-05, 207
Histoire naturelle (Pliny the Elder)
  See *Historia naturalis*
Historia (Lucian)
  See *True History*
Historia abbetum (Bede) **20**:29, 38, 49, 57, 72-

3, 75, 85, 89
Historia Animalium (Aristotle) **31**:64-65, 327, 332, 339, 373
Historia Calamitatum (Abelard) **11**:24, 28, 32, 33, 40, 45, 48, 51, 52, 55, 57-59, 61, 63-66
Historia ecclesiastica gentis Anglorum (Bede) **20**:4, 6, 10-11, 14, 18-19, 26-32, 34-5, 38-40, 46-57, 61-3, 67-86, 89, 92-3, 98-101, 103, 106, 117, 119, 121-22
Historia naturalis (Pliny the Elder) **23**:317-77
Historical Records (Confucius)
  See *Shih Chi*
Histories (Polybius) **17**:148-207
History (Anna Comnena)
  See *The Alexiad*
History (Herodotus) **17**:49-147
History of Animals (Aristotle)
  See *Historia Animalium*
History of My Troubles (Abelard)
  See *Historia Calamitatum*
The History of Rome from Its Foundation (Livy)
  See *Ab urbe condita libri*
History of the Abbots (Bede)
  See *Historia abbetum*
History of the House of Aragon (Sordello)
  See *Los progres e avansaments dei Res d'Aragon*
History of the Jewish War (Josephus)
  See *Bellum Judaicum*
History of the Peloponnesian War (Thucydides) **17**:208-315
History of the War (Thucydides)
  See *History of the Peloponnesian War*
Hiyal al-lusas **25**:332
Hiyal al-mukaddin **25**:332
Homesickness **25**:324
Homilies (Bede) **20**:3, 7-8
"Homilies on the Hexaemeron" (Basil of Caesaria) **35**:65
"Homily of Psalm 29" (Basil of Caesaria) **35**:88
Homily on Exodus (Origen) **19**:260
"Homily on Psalm 28" (Basil of Caesaria) **35**:89
"Homily on Psalm 33" (Basil of Caesaria) **35**:89
"Homily on Psalm 44" (Basil of Caesaria) **35**:89
"Homily on Psalm 45 and 59" (Basil of Caesaria) **35**:89
"Homily on Psalm 48" (Basil of Caesaria) **35**:88
"Homily on Psalm 59" (Basil of Caesaria) **35**:89
"Homily on the Ending of the Four Thousand" (Bede) **20**:8
"Homily on the Eve of the Resurrection" (Bede) **20**:5
Homily on the Song of Songs (Origen) **19**:255-56, 258, 262, 268
"The Honeysuckle" (Marie de France)
  See "Chevrefoil"
Hortensius (Cicero) **3**:178, 242, 288
"How Basat Killed Goggle-eye" **8**:103, 108-09
"How Could Solomon and Achaz beget children while still mere boys themselves?"(Jerome) **30**:89
How History Should Be Written (Lucian)
  See *How to Write History*
"How Prince Urez Son of Prince Kazan was Taken Prisoner" **8**:103
"How Salur Kazan's House was Pillaged"
  See "The Plunder of the Home of Salur-Kazan"
"How the Outer Oghuz Rebelled Against the Inner Oghuz and How Beyrek Died" **8**:103
How to Write History (Lucian) **32**:4, 43
Hrafnkatla
  See *Hrafnkel's saga Freysgodi*
Hrafnkel's Saga

See *Hrafnkel's saga Freysgodi*
Hrafnkel's saga Freysgodi **2**:74-129
Hrotsvithae Opera (Hroswitha of Gandersheim)
  See *Opera*
"Hsiang-yang Song" (Li Po) **2**:161
Humash
  See *Torah*
Hundred Names of God (Llull) **12**:122, 125
"Hundred Pace Rapids" (Su Shih) **15**:410
"Hymn" (Caedmon) **7**:84-5, 93-7, 100-01, 103-13
Hymn (Pindar) **12**:355-56
Hymn I (Callimachus) **18**:3-6, 23, 28-31, 34, 39
Hymn II (Callimachus) **18**:11, 28-31, 33-8, 40, 44, 52
Hymn III (Callimachus) **18**:10-11, 24, 28-9, 33, 39, 42-3, 50-1, 56-8
Hymn IV (Callimachus) **18**:10-11, 24, 28-32, 34, 39, 51, 58-9
"Hymn to Aphrodite" (Sappho)
  See "Ode to Aphrodite"
Hymn to Apollo (Callimachus)
  See *Hymn II*
Hymn to Artemis (Callimachus)
  See *Hymn III*
Hymn to Athena Bath of Pallas (Callimachus)
  See *Hymn V*
Hymn to Delos (Callimachus)
  See *Hymn IV*
Hymn to Demeter (Callimachus)
  See *Hymn VI*
"Hymn to the Virgin" (Petrarch) **20**:217
Hymn to Zeus (Callimachus)
  See *Hymn I*
Hymn to Zeus (Pindar) **12**:276-78, 320
Hymn V (Callimachus) **18**:9, 11, 30-2, 35-6, 38-9, 52
Hymn VI (Callimachus) **18**:11-15, 28-9, 31-2, 34-6, 38-9, 52, 58
Hymns (Callimachus) **18**:28, 38, 50, 53, 62
Hymns to the Gods (Pindar) **12**:320
Hypobolimaeus (Menander) **9**:203
Hyporcemata (Pindar) **12**:320-21, 355-57, 364
Hyporcheme (Pindar)
  See *Hyporcemata*
Hyppolytus (Seneca) **6**:340, 342, 363, 373
Hypsipyle (Aeschylus) **11**:124
Hypsipyle (Euripides) **23**:114, 126
I. 3 (Pindar)
  See *Isthmian 3*
I. 4 (Pindar)
  See *Isthmian 4*
I Ching (Confucius) **19**:16, 38, 48, 50, 68, 71
"I have left my post in Hsu-chou" (Su Shih) **15**:412
"I shâk El-Mausili with the Merchant" **2**:43
"I' vo pensando" (Petrarch) **20**:273, 301
Iambi (Callimachus) **18**:9, 24, 34-8, 42, 49, 53, 55-6, 58
Ibis (Callimachus) **18**:11, 37, 62-4
Ibis (Ovid) **7**:327-28, 444
Icaromennipus, or Beyond the Clouds (Lucian) **32**:16, 33, 35-36, 47-48, 50-52, 59, 61-62
Ichneutai (Sophocles) **2**:289, 338, 388, 408
De ideis (Hermogenes)
  See *On Types of Style*
De Idololatria (Tertullian)
  See *On Idolatry*
De ieiunio (Tertullian)
  See *On Fasting*
Ifrad al-maqal fi amr al-dalal (Biruni) **28**:177
The Ignorant Book-collector (Lucian) **32**:43, 45
De ignorantia (Petrarch) **20**:258, 286-90

Title Index

I-king (Confucius)
See *I Ching*
Il Dialogo (Catherine) **27**:3, 4, 7, 13, 14, 15, 16, 19, 20, 21, 31
Il Dialogo della Ddivina Provvidenza ovvero Libro della Divina Dottrina (Catherine)
See *Il Dialogo*
Iliacon (Lucan) **33**:422
Iliad (Homer) **1**:268-412
Iliads (Homer)
See *Iliad*
Ilias (Homer)
See *Iliad*
De immortalitate animae (Augustine) **6**:68
In Catilinam (Cicero) **3**:193, 196, 198, 268, 270
In Collation (Eckhart)
See *Rede der Unterscheidungen*
In Daniel (Jerome)
See *Commentary on Daniel*
In Earnest and in Jest
See *Fi l-Jidd wa 'l-bazl*
In Ecclesiastes (Jerome)
See *Commentary on Ecclesiastes*
In enigmatibus (Bacon) **14**:62
In Ephesians (Jerome)
See *Commentary on Ephesians*
In Ezechielem (Montgomery)
See *Commentary on Ezechiel 42:13f*
In Galatians (Jerome)
See *Commentary on Galatians*
In Hab. (Jerome) **30**:119
In Mich. (Jerome) **30**:119
In Pisonem (Cicero) **3**:269, 284
In Praise of Date-Wine
See *Fi Madh alnabidh*
In Praise of my Country (Lucian) **32**:39
In Praise of Nero (Lucan)
See *Laudes Neronis*
"In Quest of the Tao in An-Ling, I Met Kai Huan Who Fashioned for Me a Register of the Realized Ones; (This Poem) Left Behind As a Present When About to Depart" (Li Po) **2**:175
"In the Midst of Illness a Friend Visits Me" (Po Chu-i) **24**:348
In topica Ciceronis (Boethius) **15**:7, 26, 54-5, 62, 74, 95
In Vatinium (Cicero) **3**:223
De incendio amoris (Rolle)
See *De incendio amoris*
De Incendio Urbu (Lucan) **33**:422
Incendium amoris (Rolle) **21**:275, 284, 294, 303, 307, 310-13, 316, 319, 321, 328, 331-34, 336-39, 342-49, 352-54, 356, 359, 361, 367-68, 372-73, 383-86, 389-99
De Incessu Animalium (Aristotle) **31**:65, 332
India (Biruni) **28**:114-16, 118, 120-22, 129-30, 139-43, 145-46, 149-53, 157, 161, 167-72, 176-78
Indica (Biruni)
See *India*
Inferno (Dante) **3**:1-169
'Ingredientibus' (Abelard)
See *Logica 'Ingredientibus'*
The Innocent Mother-in-Law (Terence)
See *Hecyra*
"Inscription for Six one Spring" (Su Shih) **15**:399
"Inscription for the Lotus Clepsydra at Hsu-chou" (Su Shih) **15**:399,409
De Insomniis (Aristotle) **31**:66
De Institutione Musica (Boethius)
See *In topica Ciceronis*
Instruction in Honor (Sordello)

See *Ensegnamen d'Onor*
The Intellect (Albert the Great)
See *De intellectu et intelligibili*
De intellectu et intelligibili (Albert the Great) **16**:61, 112, 116, 118
De interpretatione (Abelard) **11**:63
De interpretatione (Aristotle) **31**:4, 64, 86, 305-07, 311
"Interrogations" (Basil of Caesaria) **35**:91
Introductio (Abelard) **11**:10
An Introduction to Categorical Syllogisms (Boethius) **15**:27, 29
Introduction to the Elements of Astrology (Biruni)
See *The Book of Instruction in the Elements of the Art of Astrology*
Invecativae contra medicum (Petrarch) **20**:263, 266, 288-89
Invectiva in quedam ignarum dialectices (Abelard) **11**:67
Invectivae against the One Who Criticized Italy (Petrarch) **20**:258
Invective against the Doctor of Medicine (Petrarch)
See *Invecativae contra medicum*
Invective on His Own Ignorance and That of Many Other (Petrarch)
See *De ignorantia*
De inventione (Cicero) **3**:182, 193, 201, 206, 216, 218-19, 244, 258-60, 263
De inventione (Hermogenes)
See *On Invention*
"Io son ventu al punto de la rota" (Petrarch) **20**:283
Ion (Euripides) **23**:104, 110, 114, 122, 124-27, 129, 131-32, 137-45, 147, 153, 174-78, 180, 182, 187-91
Ion (Plato) **8**:305-06, 331
Iphigeneia (Euripides) **23**:178, 187-89, 191
Iphigeneia in Tauris (Euripides)
See *Iphigenia among the Taurians*
Iphigenia (Aeschylus) **11**:125
Iphigenia among the Tauri (Euripides)
See *Iphigenia among the Taurians*
Iphigenia among the Taurians (Euripides) **23**:114, 116, 119, 122-27, 132, 174-75, 183, 207, 213, 220, 222
Iphigenia at Aulis (Euripides) **23**:110, 114, 119, 121, 124-25, 127, 129-30, 132, 173-76, 196, 204, 206-07, 220-22
Iphigenia at Tauris (Euripides)
See *Iphigenia among the Taurians*
Iphigenia in Tauris (Euripides)
See *Iphigenia among the Taurians*
Isaiam (Jerome)
See *Commentary on Isaias*
Isharat wa al-Tanbihat (Avicenna) **16**:150
Isth. 9 (Pindar)
See *Isthmian 9*
Isthm. VII (Pindar)
See *Isthmian 7*
Isthmian 1 (Pindar) **12**:271, 319, 344, 352, 355-56, 365-66, 369, 378, 383-84
Isthmian 2 (Pindar) **12**:312-13, 319, 352-53, 362-63, 383
Isthmian 3 (Pindar) **12**:295, 306, 313, 356, 365-66
Isthmian 4 (Pindar) **12**:288, 295, 301, 312, 353, 356, 365, 367, 371, 376, 378, 380, 383
Isthmian 5 (Pindar) **12**:273, 278, 288, 306-07, 310, 323, 337, 357-58, 370, 378
Isthmian 6 (Pindar) **12**:319, 325-26, 354, 357-58, 366, 370, 377-79, 382-83
Isthmian 7 (Pindar) **12**:263, 270, 306-07, 326,

356, 362, 365-67, 383
Isthmian 8 (Pindar) **12**:271-73, 319, 325, 355-58, 382-83
Isthmian 9 (Pindar) **12**:357
Isthmian Odes (Pindar) **12**:321, 353, 357
Eunuchus#it2 (Lucian)
See *The Eunich*
Itala (Jerome) **30**:79-80
"Italia mia" (Petrarch) **20**:239, 241, 245, 280
Iudicium Deorum (Lucian) **32**:7
De iuventute et senectute (Albert the Great) **16**:90
Iwein (Hartmann von Aue) **15**:154-63, 164-71, 176, 183-96, 202-06, 233, 244-45
Ixion (Broughton) **11**:122
Izumi Shikibu kashu (Izumi Shikibu) **33**:303-304, 307
Izumi Shikibu nikki (Izumi Shikibu) **33**:261, 326
Izumi Shikibu seishu (Izumi Shikibu) **33**:277-78
Izumi Shikibu shu (Izumi Shikibu) **33**:274
"The Jackdaw and the Doves" (Aesop) **24**:22
"Jaefer and the Old Bedouin" **2**:40
"Jaudar" **2**:42
Jawabat fi-imamah **25**:329
Jaya
See *Mahabharata*
Jeu d'Adam
See *Ordo Representacionis Ade*
Le Jeu de Saint Nicholas: (Bodel) **28**:191, 193-96, 198-200, 202-03, 211-16, 218, 220, 224-26, 230, 235, 237, 239-42, 246-61, 264, 266, 270, 272
Jeu de Saint Nicolas (Bodel)
See *Le Jeu de Saint Nicholas:*
Jewish Antiquities (Josephus)
See *Antiquitates Judaicae*
Jewish War (Josephus)
See *Bellum Judaicum*
Job
See *The Book of Job*
Judica (Rolle) **21**:394
Judica me Deus (Rolle) **21**:351, 390-92, 394-95
Juliana (Cynewulf) **23**:3, 6, 9, 14-16, 18, 21, 31, 42-44, 46, 66-69, 72-73, 80-81, 83
"Kafour the Eunuch" **2**:40
Kalevala **6**:206-88
Kalewala
See *Kalevala*
"Kan Turali Son of Kanli Koja" **8**:103, 108-09
Kataplous (Lucian)
See *Cataplus*
Kaupina-pancakam (Sankara) **32**:390
Ke Orazioni (Catherine) **27**:18, 19, 20, 21
Kedeia (Menander)
See *Samia*
Keeping Secrets and Holding the Tongue
See *Kitab Kitman al-sirr wa-hifz al-lisan*
Kena Upanisad (Sankara) **32**:372
"Khalifeh the Fisherman" **2**:14, 40
Kindly Ones (Aeschylus)
See *Eumenides*
King Mark and Iseut the Fair (Chretien de Troyes) **10**:139, 218
King Oedipus (Sophocles)
See *Oedipous Tyrannos*
Kitab Akhlaq al-wuzaraa (Biruni) **25**:331
Kitab al Âthâru'l-Baqiah (Biruni)
See *The Chronology of Ancient Nations*
Kitab al-Abbasiyya **25**:272-73, 329
Kitab al-Akhbar wa-kayfa tasihh **25**:330
Kitab al-Amsar wa-ajaib al-baldan **25**:330
Kitab al-Ansar **25**:328
Kitab al-Âthâr al-Baqiyah 'an al-Qurun al-Khaliyah (Biruni)

See *The Chronology of Ancient Nations*
Kitab al-Bayan wa l'Tabyin **25**:269, 271, 293, 314, 316, 319, 323, 328, 331, 333
Kitab al-Bukhala **25**:292-300, 308, 323, 328, 331-33
Kitab al-Bursan wa l-urjan wa l-umyan wa l-hulan **25**:294, 328, 331
Kitab al-Hayawan **25**:269, 272, 293-294, 314, 319, 323, 328, 330-31, 333
Kitab al-Jamahir fir ma'rifat al-Jawahir (Biruni)
See *Compendium on Precious Stones*
Kitab al-kashf 'an manahij al-adilla (Averroes)
See *Kitab al-kashf 'an manahij al-adilla fi 'aqa'id al-milla,wa ta'rif ma waqa'a fiha bi-hasb at-ta'wil min ash-shibah al-muzigha wal-bida 'al-mudilla*
Kitab al-kashf 'an manahij al-adilla fi 'aqa'id al-milla,wa ta'rif ma waqa'a fiha bi-hasb at-ta'wil min ash-shibah al-muzigha wal-bida 'al-mudilla (Averroes) **7**:37-43, 45, 69-70
Kitab al-Masail wa l-jawabat fi l-marifah **25**:330
Kitab al-Najat (Avicenna) **16**:147, 150, 162
Kitab al-Qanun al Mas'udi fi 'l-Hay'a w-an-nujim (Biruni) **28**:
Kitab al-Qawl fi l-bighal **25**:330
Kitab al-Qiyan **25**:294, 328, 332-33
Kitab al-Shamil fi 'l-mawjudat al-mahususah wa 'l-ma'qulah (Biruni)
See *The Book of General Knowledge*
Kitab al-Shifa (Avicenna) **16**:136-37, 147, 150, 157-58, 162-64
Kitab al-Tafhim (Biruni) **28**:116, 156, 176-77
Kitab al-tahqiq ma lil hind min maqbula lil-'qaql aw mardhula (Biruni)
See *India*
Kitab al-Tarbi wa l-Tadwir **25**:323, 328, 330
Kitab al-Uthmaniyya **25**:271-74, 276-78, 294, 328
Kitab Atimat al-Arab **25**:331
Kitab Batanjal (Biruni) **28**:150-51, 167-68, 171
Kitab Fakhr al-Sudan ala l-Bidan **25**:298, 330-31
Kitab fi ista'ab al-wujuh fi san'at alasturlab (Biruni)
See *The Book of Instruction in the Elements of the Art of Astrology*
Kitab fi'l-tawassut bain Aristutali wa Jalinu fi'l-muharrik al-awwal (Biruni) **28**:176
Kitab Hujaj al-nubuwwah **25**:330
Kitab Istihqaq al-imamah **25**:329
Kitab Khalq al-Quran **25**:330
Kitab Kitman al-sirr wa-hifz al-lisan **25**:323, 332
Kitab Manaqib al-Turkwa-ammat jund al-khilafah **25**:280-83, 286, 324, 329
Kitab Mufakharat al-jawari wa l-ghilman **25**:322, 324, 333
Kitab Samkhya (Biruni) **28**:150-51
Kitab Tahdid Nihayat al-Amakin (Biruni) **28**:115, 129, 176-78
Kitab Taswib Ali fi takhim al-hakamayn **25**:329
Kitab Wujub al-Imama **25**:273
Kitabi Qorqut
See *Kitabi-i Dedem Qorkut*
Kitabi-i Dedem Qorkut **8**:95-110
Kiib al-Sydanah (Biruni) **28**:115, 128, 156, 176
"The Kite and the Jay" (Marie de France) **8**:194
The Knight of the Cart (Chretien de Troyes)
See *Lancelot*
The Knight with the Lion (Chretien de Troyes)
See *Yvain*
The Knight with the Sword (Chretien de Troyes)
See *Le Chevalier à l'épée*
The Knights (Aristophanes)

See *Hippeis*
Know the Ways of God (Hildegard von Bingen)
See *Scivias*
Know Thyself (Abelard)
See *Scito Te Ipsum*
Kojiki **21**:217-68
Kokinshu **29**:206, 208-11, 214-17, 221-25, 227-29, 231, 236, 245-46, 248-52, 259-61, 266, 268, 270, 273-75, 280, 283, 287-90, 292-94, 297, 299, 303-04
Kolax (Menander) **9**:213, 269
The Koran **23**:230-316
Kulliyyat (Averroes) **7**:66
Kumarasambhava (Kalidasa) **9**:82-6, 89-90, 95-6, 102, 107, 114-15, 118-19, 125, 128-29
Laberinto d'amore (Boccaccio) **13**:16
Lacedaemoniorum respublica (Xenophon)
See *Constitution of Sparta*
Laches (Plato) **8**:263-65, 286, 306, 356
Ladies Lunching Together (Menander)
See *Synaristosai*
The Lady of Andros (Terence)
See *Andria*
"The Lady of the Highest Prime" **2**:174
Laelius (Cicero)
See *De amicitia*
Laelius: On Friendship (Cicero)
See *De amicitia*
"Lai des Deuz Amanz" (Marie de France)
See "Les Dous Amanz"
Lais (Marie de France) 114-15, 130, 141, 146, 150, 157-62, 167, 172-73, 175, 177, 179-81, 184-85, 187-89, 195
Laïus (Aeschylus) **11**:122, 124, 159, 174
Lam'at (Biruni) **28**:115
"The Lamb and the Goat" (Marie de France) **8**:192
"Lament Everlasting" (Po Chu-i) **24**:292-93, 318, 331, 356-57, 362
"Lament for Blacas" (Sordello)
See "Planher vuelh en Blacatz"
"Lament for Lord Blacatz" (Sordello)
See "Planher vuelh en Blacatz"
"Lament of the Fallen Angels" (Caedmon) **7**:91, 93
Lancelot (Chretien de Troyes) **10**:133-39, 141-44, 147-49, 157, 159-63, 165-67, 169, 171-74, 176, 178-81, 183, 189-90, 195-98, 200, 208-10, 214-16, 218, 222-26, 228-30, 232-40
"Lanval" (Marie de France) **8**:122-23, 125, 127-28, 130-31, 133, 140-47, 149, 154, 156, 158, 161-64, 166, 169-70
"Laostic" (Marie de France)
See "Laüstic"
Lao-tzu (Lao Tzu)
See *Tao te Ching*
"Late Autumn Evening" (Po Chu-i) **24**:338
Latin Psalter (Rolle) **21**:351
Laudes Neronis (Lucan) **33**:422
"Laüstic" (Marie de France) **8**:114, 120, 129, 131-34, 136-39, 144-45, 147-48, 153, 158-59, 161-66, 170, 181, 188
The Law (Cicero)
See *De legibus*
Laws (Cicero)
See *De legibus*
Laws (Plato) **8**:207, 217-18, 147, 249-50, 258-59, 261-62, 265-68, 279, 282-83, 305-06, 311, 318, 325, 328, 345-46, 362-64
"Lay le Freyne" (Marie de France)
See "Le Fraisne"
"Lay of Guigemar" (Marie de France) **8**:114-17,

122-23, 125, 127-28, 130-31, 133-35, 140, 145-49, 152-53, 161-67, 170, 172, 177-79, 181, 184, 188-89
Lay of the Nibelungen
See *Book of Chaos*
Lay of the Nibelungs
See *Book of Chaos*
Lays (Marie de France)
See *Lais*
Leading Doctrines (Epicurus)
See *Principal Doctrines*
De lege agraria (Cicero) **3**:268
Legends of the Saints (Barbour) **33**:156
Leges (Plato)
See *Laws*
De legibus (Cicero) **3**:177, 194, 201, 211, 214-15, 221, 249-51, 256-57, 276-77, 296-98
The lepers, the Lame, the Blind, and the Cross-Eyed
See *Kitab al-Bursan wa l-urjan wa l-umyan wa l-hulan*
Leptinea (Demosthenes)
See *Against Leptines*
Leptines (Demosthenes)
See *Against Leptines*
Lesbian Pastorals (Longus)
See *Daphnis and Chloe*
The Lesbian Pastorals of Daphnis and Chloe (Longus)
See *Daphnis and Chloe*
Lesser Hippias (Plato)
See *Hippias Minor*
Lesson of Honour (Sordello)
See *Ensegnamen d'Onor*
Letter 33 (Jerome)
See *Epist. 33*
Letter 43 (Jerome) **30**:129, 136
Letter 44 (Jerome) **30**:129
Letter 46 (Jerome)
See *Epist. 46*
Letter 53 (Jerome)
See *Epist. 53*
Letter CVII (Jerome)
See *Epitaphium Sanctae Paulae*
"Letter in Answer to Hsieh Min-shihn" (Su Shih) **15**:420
Letter L (Jerome) **30**:76
Letter on the Secret Works of Art and the Nullity of Magic (Bacon)
See *Epistola fratris Rogerii Baconis de secretis operibus naturae et de nullitate magiae*
Letter to Egbert (Bede) **20**:69-71, 92
"Letter to Han Ching-chou" (Li Po) **2**:169-73
Letter to Herodotus (Epicurus) **21**:73, 130-31, 165, 167-68, 170-75, 179-81, 188, 205, 207
Letter to Menoeceus (Epicurus) **21**:147-48, 161, 165, 176, 178, 182, 184-87
"Letter to Posterity" (Petrarch) **20**:237-40, 242, 246
Letter to Pythocles (Epicurus) **21**:118, 121, 164-65, 167, 169
"Letter to the Chief Administrator of Anchou, P'ei" (Li Po) **2**:170
"Letter Written on Behalf of Longevity Mountain in Answer to the Proclamation of Meng Shao-fu" (Li Po) **2**:172
Letter XLIX (Jerome) **30**:80
Letter XXII (Jerome) **30**:77
La Lettere (Catherine)
See *Epistolario*
"Letters" (Basil of Caesaria) **35**:56
Letters (Epicurus) **21**:73
Letters (Jerome) **30**:72-80, 121

Letters (Ovid)
   See *Heroides*
Letters (Seneca)
   See *Epistulae morales*
Letters from Campania (Lucan) **33**:422
Letters from the Black Sea (Ovid)
   See *Epistulae ex Ponto*
Letters of Heloise and Abelard (Abelard) **11**:55-6
Letters of the Heroines (Ovid)
   See *Heroides*
Letters to Atticus (Cicero)
   See *Ad Atticum*
Letters to Friends (Cicero)
   See *Ad familiares*
Letters to Lucilius (Seneca)
   See *Epistulae morales*
"Letting the Intellect Go and Experiencing Pure Ignorance" (Eckhart) **9**:24
Lexiphanes (Lucian) **32**:13-14, 16, 26, 38, 40, 42
Li (Confucius)
   See *Li Chi*
Li Chi (Confucius) **19**:11, 20-21, 26-28, 35-36, 38, 40, 46, 69
Li Jeus de Saint Nicolai (Bodel)
   See *Le Jeu de Saint Nicholas:*
Li ki (Confucius)
   See *Li Chi*
Libation Bearers (Aeschylus) **11**:85, 87-8, 102, 104-05, 107, 116, 118-19, 131, 138, 140, 151, 153-54, 159, 162-64, 181, 184-85, 191, 193-95, 202, 205-07, 211, 217, 223
Libation-Pourers (Aeschylus)
   See *Libation Bearers*
Libellus de Alchimia (Albert the Great) **16**:65
Liber celestis imperatoris ad reges (Saint Birgitta of Sweden) **24**:101-02, 107
Liber celestis revelacionum (Saint Birgitta of Sweden) **24**:92, 94-96, 101
Liber contemplationis (Llull) **12**:104
Liber de amore Dei contra amatores mundi (Rolle) **21**:275, 391
Liber de ascensu et descensu intellectus (Llull) **12**:107. 111
Liber de lumine (Llull) **12**:110
Liber de retardatione accidentium senectutis (Bacon) **14**:64
Liber de sancta virginitate (Augustine) **6**:38
Liber divinorum Operum (Hildegard von Bingen) **20**:132-33, 135-39, 145, 152-55, 161-63, 174-75, 180
Liber epigrammatum (Bede) **20**:121
Liber Hebraicarum Quaestionum in Genesim (Jerome) **30**:88, 93, 111, 119
Liber Hymnorum (Abelard) **11**:45
Liber mineralium (Albert the Great) **16**:55, 62-4, 97, 100-02
Liber Positionum (Eckhart) **9**:56
Liber praedicationis contra Iudaeos (Llull) **12**:117
Liber principiorum medicinae (Llull) **12**:107
Liber Questionum (Saint Birgitta of Sweden) **24**:90
Liber Spectaculorum (Martial) **35**:254, 303-04, 326, 330-31, 365
Liber vitae meritorum (Hildegard von Bingen) **20**:132-33, 152-53, 161-62, 175
De libero arbitrio voluntatis (Augustine) **6**:5, 9-10, 68, 102, 117-18, 149
Liberum arbitrium voluntatis (Augustine)
   See *De libero arbitrio voluntatis*
Libre d'amic e Amat (Llull)

   See *Book of the Lover and the Beloved*
Libre de meravelles (Llull)
   See *Felix*
Libre del orde de cavalleria (Llull) **12**:104, 107
Libri quoestionum epistolicarum (Cato) **21**:22
Libro della Divina Dottrina (Catherine)
   See *Il Dialogo*
Life (Josephus)
   See *Vita*
Life and Afterlife
   See *Kitab Wujub al-Imama*
Life of Dante (Boccaccio)
   See *Vita di Dante*
Life of Malchus (Jerome)
   See *Vita Malchi monachi captivi*
Life of Paul (Jerome)
   See *Vita Pauli*
Life of St. Cuthbert (Bede)
   See *Vita sancti Cuthberti*
Liki (Confucius)
   See *Li Chi*
"The Lion and the Mouse" (Aesop) **24**:63, 66
Literary Collection (Po Chu-i)
   See *Wen-chi*
Little Epitome (Epicurus) **21**:75, 154
Lives of the Abbots (Bede)
   See *Historia abbetum*
The Living Flame (Rolle) **21**:312
Le Livre de l'Espurgatorie (Marie de France)
   See *L'Espurgatoire Saint Patrice*
Le Livre de Marco Polo (Polo)
   See *The Travels of Marco Polo the Venetian*
Lock of Berenice (Callimachus) **18**:15-17, 30, 35, 43, 59, 61, 63-4
Locri (Menander) **9**:203
Logica 'Ingredientibus' (Abelard) **11**:63, 64, 66
Logica 'Nostrorum' (Abelard) **11**:62, 64, 66
Logical Treatises (Albert the Great) **16**:4
"The Lonely Wife" (Li Po) **2**:132
Long Commentary on the Metaphysics (Averroes)
   See *Tafsir ma ba'd al-tabi'ah*
"Longer Questions" (Basil of Caesaria) **35**:91
"Longer Rule 7" (Basil of Caesaria) **35**:92
"Longer Rules" (Basil of Caesaria) **35**:73, 97
Longer Work (Bacon)
   See *Opus Majus*
Lord's Song
   See *Bhagavadgita*
The Lord's Song
   See *Bhagavad Gita*
Love-Poems (Ovid)
   See *Amores*
The Lover of Lies (Lucian) **32**:15-26, 28, 33, 43-47
"The Lovers of the Benou Udreh" **2**:40
"A Lu Mountain Song for the Palace Censor Empty-Boat Lu" (Li Po) **2**:152, 164
De Luctu (Lucian) **32**:7
Lun Yu (Confucius) **19**:10-11, 17-23, 26, 28-33, 35-36, 38-42, 48-50, 68-69, 72-76, 78-85, 88-89, 95-101
"Lute Song" (Po Chu-i) **24**:292, 331, 357
"Lying Sick during the Cold Food Festival" (Po Chu-i) **24**:347
Lykourgeia (Aeschylus) **11**:192
Lysis (Plato) **8**:254, 264-66, 306, 314
Lysistrata (Aristophanes) **4**:44, 60-2, 65, 68, 88, 93-94, 107-10, 113, 123-26, 133, 142, 144-45, 151, 153-56, 160, 163, 166, 169-75
The Mabinogion
   See *Pedeir Keinc y Mabinogi*
Mad Hercules (Seneca)
   See *Hercules furens*

"The Mad Lover" **2**:40
"The Magic Horse" **2**:49
De magistro (Augustine) **6**:126, 133-36, 138
Magnificat (Rolle) **21**:351
Mahabharata **5**:177-287
The Maid of Andros (Terence)
   See *Andria*
"Maid of Craca" (Ossian) **28**:305
Makura no soshi (Sei Shonagon) **6**:291-96, 299-309, 311-26
Makura Zoshi (Sei Shonagon)
   See *Makura no soshi*
Malavika and Agnimitra(Kalidasa)
   See *Malavikagnimitra*
Malavikagnimitra (Kalidasa) **9**:82, 85, 90, 96-7, 99-102, 126, 128, 131-33, 137-38
"Maldon"
   See "The Battle of Maldon"
"Malvina's Dream" (Ossian) **28**:303
The Man from Sikyon (Menander)
   See *Sikyonios*
"The Man of Yemen and His Six Slave Girls" **2**:40
The Man She Hated (Menander)
   See *Misoumenos*
"The Man Who Never Laughed Again" **2**:40
The Man Who Punished Himself (Menander)
   See *Heautontimorumenus*
Manahij (Averroes)
   See *Kitab al-kashf 'an manahij al-adilla fi 'aqa'id al-milla,wa ta'rif ma waqa'a fihabi-hasb at-ta'wil min ash-shibah al-muzigha wal-bida 'al-mudilla*
Mandeville's Travels (Mandeville) **19**:107-80
Mandukya Upanisad (Sankara) **32**:362
Manilian (Cicero)
   See *Pro Lege Manilia*
Maqalah fi sifat asbab al0sukhunat al-mawjudah fi'l-'alam wa ikhtilaf fusul al-sanah (Biruni) **28**:176
Maqalah fi'l-bahth 'an al-athar al-'ulwiyah (Biruni) **28**:176
Marco Polo (Polo)
   See *The Travels of Marco Polo the Venetian*
Marco Polo's Travels (Polo)
   See *The Travels of Marco Polo the Venetian*
Maria (Hroswitha of Gandersheim) **29**:123, 136, 182-82, 185
Mariale (Albert the Great) **16**:42
Marius (Cicero) **3**:198
Marriage of Arsinoe (Callimachus) **18**:34
Martyrology (Bede) **20**:61
Mary the Niece of Abraham (Hroswitha of Gandersheim)
   See *Abraham*
Masnavi (Rumi)
   See *Mathnawi*
Masters of the Frying Pan (Aristophanes) **4**:167
Mathnavi (Rumi)
   See *Mathnawi*
Mathnawi (Rumi) **20**:338-40, 342, 352-54, 356, 365-67, 371, 373-74, 376-83, 385-88
Matsuibon (Izumi Shikibu) **33**:278
Medea (Euripides) **23**:103-04, 113, 119, 121-23, 127-29, 132, 171, 173-77, 180-82, 185, 193-95, 201-04, 207, 218
Medea (Lucan) **33**:422
Medea (Ovid) **7**:286, 297, 336, 346-47, 376, 420, 425, 444-45
Medea (Seneca) **6**:336, 344-45, 363, 366, 371, 373, 377-81, 404-10, 413-18, 426-27, 432-33, 436, 441
Medicamina Faciei (Ovid) **7**:346

Meditacio de passione Christi (Rolle) **21**:307, 357, 368, 374

Meditation B (Rolle) **21**:393

Meditation on the Passion (Rolle)
See *Meditacio de passione Christi*

Megalopolis (Demosthenes)
See *For Megalopolis*

Meghaduta (Kalidasa) **9**:89-90, 92, 95, 102, 107, 113, 115, 125-26, 129

Meister Eckhart: The Essential Sermons, Commentaries, Treatises, and Defense (Eckhart) **9**:67

Melos amoris (Rolle) **21**:283, 287-92, 311, 352-56, 369, 381-82, 386, 389-90, 399

Melum contemplativorum (Rolle)
See *Melos amoris*

Memoirs (Xenophon)
See *Memorabilia*

Memorabilia (Xenophon) **17**:329, 331, 335, 337, 340, 341, 342, 343, 344, 345, 349, 362, 374, 375

De Memoria (Aristotle) **31**:65-66

De memoria et reminiscentia (Albert the Great) **16**:61, 110

"A Memorial of Self-Introduction Written for Assistant Director of the Censorate Sung" (Li Po) **2**:173-74

Menaechmi (Plautus) **24**:170-72, 175, 181, 184, 212, 220, 230, 240

Mendicants' Tricks
See *Hiyal al-mukaddin*

Mending of Life (Rolle)
See *Mending of Life*

Menexenus (Plato) **8**:305-07

Mennipus, or, a Necromantic Experiment (Lucian) **32**:8, 10-11, 36, 47-52, 56, 59-63

Mennipus, or The Descent into Hades (Lucian)
See *Mennipus or, a Necromantic Experiment*

Meno (Plato) **8**:206, 218, 250, 264, 283-85, 305-07, 311, 320-22, 328, 356-57, 362

Menon (Plato)
See *Meno*

Mercator (Plautus) **24**:170-73, 175, 220-21, 233, 236, 256, 263

De Mercede Conductis (Lucian) **32**:10

Merchant (Plautus)
See *Mercator*

De Meretr. (Lucian) **32**:16-17, 26

The Merits of the Turks and of the Caliphal Army ihn General
See *Kitab Manaqib al-Turkwa-ammat jund al-khilafah*

Metamorphoses (Apuleius) **1**:3, 7-8, 12-13, 15, 17-24, 26-27, 29-37, 39-43, 45

Metamorphoses (Ovid) **7**:286, 291-92, 298-99, 304-05, 314-16, 322, 324-36, 335-44, 346, 349, 357, 361-63, 365, 368-77, 379, 383-93, 395-96, 398-402, 404, 412-18, 430-32, 434-35, 438, 443-46

Metamorphosis (Ovid)
See *Metamorphoses*

Metaphysica (Aquinas) **33**:88, 90-91

Metaphysics (Aristotle) **31**:4-6, 8, 10-13, 19, 23-55, 57, 59, 65-66, 68-69, 74-75, 86-87, 254, 275, 284, 292, 296, 304-05, 309, 312, 316, 321-22, 338, 344-45, 347, 356, 359, 372-73, 376, 379, 381, 384, 386, 392

Metaphysics (Avicenna) **16**:159-60, 164

Meteora (Albert the Great)
See *De meteoris*

De meteoris (Albert the Great) **16**:7, 36, 55, 61

Meteororum (Albert the Great)
See *De meteoris*

De methodo vehementiae (Hermogenes)
See *On the Method of Deinotes*

De metrica arte (Bede)
See *De arte metrica*

Metrodorus (Epicurus) **21**:119

Metropolises and Geographical Curiosities
See *Kitab al-Amsar wa-ajaib al-baldan*

Middle Commentary on Porphyry's Isagoge and on Aristotle's Categoriae (Averroes) **7**:67

Midiana (Demosthenes)
See *Against Midias*

Miles Glorious (Plautus) **24**:170-71, 173, 175, 184-86, 192-93, 196-97, 200, 206, 230-31, 233, 236, 270-72

"The Milk-woman and Her Pail" (Aesop) **24**:66-67

"The Miller His Son and Their Ass" (Aesop) **24**:66-68

"Milun" (Marie de France) **8**:121, 128, 131-34, 147-50, 159, 162-66, 170, 175, 182, 187

Mineralia (Albert the Great)
See *Liber mineralium*

De Mineralibus (Albert the Great) **16**:18, 35, 61

The Minor Epitome (Epicurus)
See *Little Epitome*

Minos (Plato)
See *Meno*

Mirror of Future Times (Hildegard von Bingen)
See *Pentachronon*

Misoumenos (Menander) **9**:258, 260, 269-70, 276, 287

The Mistaken Critic (Lucian)
See *The Would-Be Critic*

"Misty Yangtze" (Su Shih) **15**:397

"Modern Music in the Yen Ho Palace" (Su Shih) **15**:385

"The Monkey and Her Baby" (Marie de France) **8**:191

"The Monkey King" (Marie de France) **8**:191

"Monk's Catechism of Morals and Obligations" (Basil of Caesaria) **35**:47

Monobiblos (Propertius)
See *Cynthia Monobiblos*

De Monogamia (Tertullian)
See *On Monogamy*

De montibus (Boccaccio) **13**:33, 38, 52

Moral Epistles (Seneca)
See *Epistulae morales*

"Moralia" (Basil of Caesaria) **35**:11, 71, 77, 87, 93, 94, 96

"Morals" (Basil of Caesaria)
See "Moralia"

Morte Arthure "Alliterative" **10**:375-436

De morte et vita (Albert the Great) **16**:61

Mostellaria (Plautus) **24**:170-71, 173, 175, 186, 208, 220, 247, 263, 271

The Mother-in-Law (Terence)
See *Hecyra*

De motibus animalium (Albert the Great) **16**:61

De Motu Animalium (Aristotle) **31**:65, 86, 332, 339, 356

"A Mouse and a Frog" (Marie de France) **8**:174

"Moved by Autumn at the Serpentine" (Po Chu-i) **24**:338

Movement of Animals (Albert the Great) **5**:

Movement of Animals (Aristotle)
See *De Motu Animalium*

"Moving to Lin-kao Pavilion" (Su Shih) **15**:410

La Mule sans frein (Chretien de Troyes) **10**:178-79, 232

Multiplication of Species (Bacon)
See *Tractatus de Mulitiplicatione Specierum*

De Multiplicatione Specierum (Bacon)

See *Tractatus de Mulitiplicatione Specierum*

De mundo (Apuleius) **1**:12, 24

Murasaki Shikibu nikki (Shikibu) **1**:457

Music (Boethius)
See *In topica Ciceronis*

Music (Confucius)
See *Yueh*

De musica (Augustine) **6**:33, 68, 73, 133-34

De Musica (Boethius)
See *In topica Ciceronis*

"The Muslim Champion and the Christian Damsel" **2**:27

"My Body" (Po Chu-i) **24**:350

"My Trip in a Dream to the Lady of Heaven Mountain" (Li Po) **2**:150

Myrmidons (Aeschylus) **11**:101, 125, 193

Mystère d'Adam
See *Ordo Representacionis Ade*

Mystery of Adam
See *Ordo Representacionis Ade*

Mystical Theology (Albert the Great) **16**:29, 119

N. 4 (Pindar)
See *Nemean 4*

N. 6 (Pindar)
See *Nemean 6*

N. 7 (Pindar)
See *Nemean 7*

N. 9 (Pindar)
See *Nemean 9*

"Nala and Damayanti"
See *Nalopakhyana*

Nalopakhyana **5**:188, 206

De Natura Deorum (Aristotle) **31**:69

De natura deorum (Cicero) **3**:182, 202, 243, 248, 255-56, 268, 278, 279, 287

De natura et gratia (Augustine) **6**:9-10

De natura et origine animae (Albert the Great) **16**:112

De natura locorum (Albert the Great) **16**:7, 22, 61

Natural History (Pliny the Elder)
See *Historia naturalis*

Natural Questions (Seneca)
See *Naturales quaestiones*

Naturales quaestiones (Seneca) **6**:344, 348-49, 374, 381, 383, 387, 410-11

The Nature of Love (Rolle) **21**:367-69, 374-75

The Nature of Places (Albert the Great)
See *De natura locorum*

The Necessity of the Imamate
See *Kitab Istihqaq al-imamah*

Nekyomanteia (Lucian) **32**:27-28

"Nel dolce tempo de la prima etade" (Petrarch) **20**:281-82

Nem. IV (Pindar)
See *Nemean 4*

Nem. VIII (Pindar)
See *Nemean 8*

Nemea (Aeschylus) **11**:192

Nemean 1 (Pindar) **12**:270, 347-48, 364-65, 378

Nemean 2 (Pindar) **12**:313, 359-60, 362, 378

Nemean 3 (Pindar) **12**:264, 268, 322, 357-58, 365, 369-70, 374, 378, 382-84

Nemean 4 (Pindar) **12**:264, 271, 299-301, 303, 321, 330, 353-54, 357-58, 362, 367, 371, 378, 382-83

Nemean V (Pindar)
See *Nemean 5*

Nemean 5 (Pindar) **12**:267, 269-70, 272, 304, 307, 309, 311, 325, 357-58, 360, 366, 371, 378-80, 382-84

Nemean 6 (Pindar) **12**:267, 269, 271, 273, 302, 304-05, 323, 357-60, 365, 368, 370, 378

Title Index

Nemean 7 (Pindar) **12**:276, 288, 299-300, 309, 311, 319, 357-59, 361, 365, 367, 376, 378-79, 383

Nemean 8 (Pindar) **12**:263, 269, 288, 309, 311, 323, 326, 357-59, 362, 365, 367, 371, 376, 379, 382-83

Nemean 9 (Pindar) **12**:296, 307, 321, 353, 364-65, 370, 378, 382

Nemean 10 (Pindar) **12**:270, 274, 321, 348, 353, 355, 362, 365, 368-69

Nemean 11 (Pindar) **12**:272, 315-16, 321, 365-67, 378

Nemean Odes (Pindar) **12**:353

Nephelai (Aristophanes) **4**:37, 42, 44-5, 50, 53-4, 58-9, 61-7, 87, 89, 98, 100, 102, 105-06, 110-11, 124-26, 130-32, 137, 143-44, 146, 148, 150, 152-53, 159-60, 162-63, 165-66, 168

Nereïds (Aeschylus) **11**:125

Net Drawers (Aeschylus)
    See *Net-Draggers*

Net-Draggers (Aeschylus) **11**:124, 152

New Kalevala
    See *Kalevala*

New Life (Dante)
    See *La vita nuova*

New Songs (Po Chu-i) **24**:294

Nibelung Lay
    See *Book of Chaos*

Der Nibelunge Nôt
    See *Book of Chaos*

Nibelungen Lay
    See *Book of Chaos*

Nibelungen Noth
    See *Book of Chaos*

Nibelungen Song
    See *Book of Chaos*

Das Nibelungenlied **12**:136-255

Nibelungen's Need
    See *Book of Chaos*

Nicomachean Ethics (Aristotle) **31**:6, 64, 66-67, 69, 71-99, 261, 265-66, 268, 272, 274-77, 289, 370, 376

Niece of the Hermit of Abraham (Hroswitha of Gandersheim)
    See *Abraham*

"Night Snow" (Po Chu-i) **24**:340

"The Nightingale" (Marie de France)
    See "Laüstic"

Nigrinus (Lucian) **32**:10, 17-18, 23, 32-33, 35-37

Nine Books of the Subtleties of Different Kinds of Creatures (Hildegard von Bingen)
    See *Subtilitates naturarum diversarum creaturarum*

Ninfale d'Ameto (Boccaccio)
    See *Ameto*

Ninfale fiesolano (Boccaccio) **13**:28, 32, 63

Ninth Nemean (Pindar)
    See *Nemean 9*

Ninth Paean (Pindar)
    See *Paean 9*

Ninth Pythian (Pindar)
    See *Pythian 9*

Niobe (Aeschylus) **11**:167, 193

Niobe (Sophocles) **2**:348

Nirvanapstatkam (Sankara) **32**:390

Njála
    See *Njáls saga*

Njáls saga **13**:322-77

"The Nobleman" (Eckhart) **9**:56-7

Nomothetes (Menander) **9**:203

"Non a tanti animali" (Petrarch) **20**:299

"Non fur ma' Giove" (Petrarch) **20**:241

"North Garden" (Po Chu-i) **24**:337

'Nostrorum' (Abelard)
    See *Logica 'Nostrorum'*

"Not Going Out of the Gate" (Po Chu-i)
    See "Not Leaving The Gates"

"Not Leaving The Gates" (Po Chu-i) **24**:356, 377

Notes for Public Speaking (Hermogenes) **6**:158

"Notice of Hall of Thought" (Su Shih) **15**:399, 403

De notitia caelestium (Bacon) **14**:62

Nourishment (Albert the Great)
    See *De nutrimento et nutribili*

Novelle (Boccaccio) **13**:13, 15-6

Novelliere (Boccaccio) **13**:22

Nugae (Map)
    See *De Nugis Curialium*

De Nugis Curialium (Map) **32**:70, 77, 82-86, 89-90, 100-08, 113-17, 120-22

"*Nuptuals of Peleus and Thetis*" (Catullus)
    See "*Poem 64*"

"Nur-Ed-Din and Shems-Ed-Din" **2**:42

"The Nurse and the Wolf" (Aesop) **24**:43

De nutrimento et nutribili (Albert the Great) **16**:61

O. 1 (Pindar)
    See *Olympian 1*

O. 7 (Pindar)
    See *Olympian 7*

O. 8 (Pindar)
    See *Olympian 8*

O. 9 (Pindar)
    See *Olympian 9*

O. 14 (Pindar)
    See *Olympian 14*

Octavia (Seneca) **6**:336, 342-43, 366, 374-75, 379-81, 389

De octo viridiariis (Rolle) **21**:295

"Ode to a Beloved Woman" (Sappho)
    See "Ode to Anactoria"

"Ode to Anactoria" (Sappho) **3**:380, 386-87, 396, 416, 436

"Ode to Aphrodite" (Sappho) **3**:381, 385-86, 440

"Ode to Vaucluse" (Petrarch) **20**:228

"Ode to Venus" (Sappho)
    See "Ode to Aphrodite"

Odysseis (Homer)
    See *Odyssey*

Odysses (Homer)
    See *Odyssey*

Odyssey (Homer) **1**:287, 293, 310, 312, 315-17, 319-20, 329, 338, 354, 362-63, 369-72, 375, 379, 388, 396-97, 400, 407-08; **16**:185, 192-94, 198-200, 202-08, 210-11, 216-17, 219-20, 222, 232-35, 237-39, 243-62, 264-66, 269-79, 282-83, 285-89, 292-301, 303-05, 307-08, 310-23, 333

Oeconomicus (Xenophon) **17**:323, 326, 345, 374, 375

Oedipous epi Kolonoi (Sophocles) **2**:289, 292, 296, 298, 300-01, 303-05, 312, 314-16, 318-19, 321, 325, 330, 335-36, 338-39, 342, 345-46, 349-52, 362-63, 367-70, 377, 388, 392, 398, 416-19, 421, 425-28

Oedipous Tyrannos (Sophocles) **2**:288-89, 292, 296, 300, 304-05, 309-10, 312-16, 319-21, 324-24, 337-40, 343-45, 347, 349-51, 353, 355-57, 359-62, 369-78, 382, 384, 387, 389-92, 394, 409-10, 415-21, 423-29

Oedipus (Aeschylus) **11**:122, 124, 138, 159-60

Oedipus (Seneca) **6**:343-44, 366, 369, 373, 379-81, 388-89, 413, 415, 417, 420-22, 428, 432

Oedipus (Sophocles)

    See *Oedipous Tyrannos*

Oedipus at Colonos (Sophocles)
    See *Oedipous epi Kolonoi*

Oedipus Coloneus (Sophocles)
    See *Oedipous epi Kolonoi*

Oedipus in Colonos (Sophocles)
    See *Oedipous epi Kolonoi*

Oedipus Rex (Sophocles)
    See *Oedipous Tyrannos*

Oedipus the King (Sophocles)
    See *Oedipous Tyrannos*

"Oenone" (Ovid) **7**:311

Oetaeus (Seneca)
    See *Hercules oetaeus*

Of Delight in God (Rolle) **21**:343

Of Love and Women
    See *Fi l-Ishq wa l-nisa*

Of Natural and Moral Philosophy (Apuleius) **1**:12-13

Of Stewards and Those Who Appoint Them
    See *Fi l-wukala wa-muwakkilin*

Of the Abbasids
    See *Kitab al-Abbasiyya*

Of the Virtues of the Holy Name of Jesus (Rolle) **21**:324

Offices (Cicero)
    See *De officiis*

De officiis (Cicero) **3**:192-93, 196, 202-03, 214, 221, 228-29, 242, 245, 254-57, 288-89, 296-98

Ol. IX (Pindar)
    See *Olympian 9*

Ol. XI (Pindar)
    See *Olympian 11*

Old Cantankerous (Menander)
    See *Dyskolos*

Old Kalevala
    See *Kalevala*

"Old Love Is Best" (Sappho) **3**:396

"An Old Man of Tu-ling" (Po Chu-i) **24**:294, 299

"The Old Man with the Broken Arm" (Po Chu-i) **24**:294

"Old Peasant of Tu Lin" (Po Chu-i)
    See "An Old Man of Tu-ling"

"Olden Airs" (Li Po) **2**:178

Olympian 1 (Pindar) **12**:263, 269, 295, 298-99, 301, 304-05, 307, 309, 319, 322, 334, 349, 354, 363, 367, 371-72, 377-81, 383

Olympian 2 (Pindar) **12**:264, 271, 293, 298, 304, 319, 321, 351, 358, 363, 365, 367, 379, 383

Olympian 3 (Pindar) **12**:266, 312, 319, 353, 363, 368-69, 378, 383-84

Olympian 4 (Pindar) **12**:321, 354, 362-63, 365, 378, 380, 383

Olympian 5 (Pindar) **12**:321, 353, 363, 365, 370, 377-79, 382-83

Olympian 6 (Pindar) **12**:264, 267, 313, 353, 355, 364, 369, 378-84

Olympian VII (Pindar)
    See *Olympian 7*

Olympian 7 (Pindar) **12**:264, 267, 296, 298, 308-09, 313, 320, 348, 353, 362, 369, 372, 374, 378, 380, 382-83

Olympian 8 (Pindar) **12**:269, 289, 302, 326, 357, 359, 365, 369, 378-80, 382-83

Olympian 9 (Pindar) **12**:289, 300, 352, 355, 365-66, 368, 370, 372, 378, 381-84

Olympian 10 (Pindar) **12**:272, 304, 309, 322, 352-53, 365-67, 378-79

Olympian 11 (Pindar) **12**:264, 344, 352-53, 380

Olympian 12 (Pindar) **12**:309, 343

Olympian 13 (Pindar) **12**:304, 320, 322, 338, 348,

353, 355-56, 362, 378, 380, 383-84
Olympian 14 (Pindar) **12**:294-95, 297, 301, 323, 325, 348, 352, 378, 383
Olympian Odes 1 (Pindar)
  See *Olympian 1*
Olynthiac I (Demosthenes) **13**:145, 148-9, 166, 171, 197
Olynthiac II (Demosthenes) **13**:148, 151, 171, 180, 197
Olynthiac III (Demosthenes) **13**:144, 146, 148-9, 151, 165, 171
Olynthiacs (Demosthenes) **13**:138, 143, 149-51, 165, 169, 183, 189
"On a Picture Screen" (Li Po) **2**:136
"On Anactoria" (Sappho)
  See "Ode to Anactoria"
On Ancient Medicine (Thucydides) **17**:253
On Anger (Seneca)
  See *De ira*
On Animals (Albert the Great)
  See *De animalibus*
On Armaments (Demosthenes) **13**:158
On Baptism (Tertullian) **29**:311-12, 377
"On Bathing" (Po Chu-i) **24**:346
On Charity (Rolle) **21**:300
On Choice and Aversion (Epicurus)
  See *On Choice and Avoidance*
On Choice and Avoidance (Epicurus) **21**:73, 75, 124, 165
On Christian Doctrine (Augustine)
  See *De doctrina Christiana*
On Clemency (Seneca)
  See *De clementia*
On Consolation (Seneca) **6**:344
On Divination (Cicero)
  See *De divinatione*
On Division (Boethius)
  See *Divisions*
On Divisions (Euclid) **25**:1-86, 90, 93, 104, 110
On Divisions (of figures) (Euclid)
  See *On Divisions*
On Dreams (Aristotle) **31**:366
On Duties (Cicero)
  See *De officiis*
"On Eloquence" (Petrarch) **20**:290
On Fasting (Tertullian) **29**:312, 325
On First Principles (Origen)
  See *De Principiis*
"On First Seeing A White Hair" (Po Chu-i) **24**:344
On Flight in Persecution (Tertullian) **29**:312, 316, 333-34, 338
On Forms (Hermogenes)
  See *On Types of Style*
On Free Will (Augustine)
  See *De libero arbitrio voluntatis*
On Friendship (Cicero)
  See *De amicitia*
On Funerals (Lucian) **32**:43, 45
On Gentleness (Seneca) **6**:423
On Giving and Receiving Favours (Seneca)
  See *De beneficiis*
On Glory (Cicero) **3**:177
On Good Deeds (Seneca) **6**:427
On Grace (Rolle) **21**:299-300
On Grace and Free Will (Augustine)
  See *De gratia et libero arbitrio*
On Halonnesus (Demosthenes) **13**:165
On His Consulship (Cicero)
  See *De consulatu suo*
On Holiness (Epicurus) **21**:142
On Household Economy (Xenophon)
  See *Oeconomicus*

On Ideas (Hermogenes)
  See *On Types of Style*
On Idolatry (Tertullian) **29**:311-12, 334, 338, 346-49, 370, 373
On Invention (Cicero)
  See *De inventione*
On Invention (Hermogenes) **6**:170-72, 185-86, 188, 191, 198-202
On Justice and the Other Virtues (Epicurus) **21**:73, 154
On Keeping Secrets and Guarding One's Tongue
  See *Kitab Kitman al-sirr wa-hifz al-lisan*
On Kingdom (Epicurus) **21**:109
On Laws (Cicero)
  See *De legibus*
"On Leisure and Solitude" (Petrarch) **20**:286
On Lives (Epicurus) **21**:73-5, 124, 165
On Love (Epicurus) **21**:73
On Martyrdom (Origen) **19**:187
On Mercy (Seneca)
  See *De clementia*
On Method (Hermogenes)
  See *On the Method of Deinotes*
On Misconduct of Ambassadors (Demosthenes)
  See *On the Misconduct of the Embassy*
On Modesty (Tertullian) **29**:311-12, 319-25, 327, 337
On Monogamy (Tertullian) **29**:312-16, 318, 325, 363, 369, 373-74
On Music (Epicurus) **21**:73
On Nature (Epicurus) **21**:72-4, 164-65, 168, 170-71, 201-02, 204
"On Nourishing Life" (Su Shih) **15**:401
On Old Age (Cicero)
  See *De senectute*
"On Oracles" (Petrarch) **20**:286
On Order (Augustine)
  See *De ordine*
On Orthography (Bede)
  See *De orthographia*
On Patience (Tertullian) **29**:311-12
On Peace of Mind (Seneca)
  See *De tranquillitate animi*
On Physics (Epicurus) **21**:122, 154
On Piety (Epicurus) **21**:154
On Power (Aquinas) **33**:95-97
On Prayer (Tertullian) **29**:311-12
On Prescription of Heretics (Tertullian) **29**:311-12, 332, 335, 360, 363, 366, 368, 370, 376
On Providence (Seneca)
  See *De providentia*
On Qualities of Style (Hermogenes)
  See *On Types of Style*
On Repentence (Tertullian) **29**:311-12, 319-23, 325, 362, 380-81
On Sacrafices (Lucian) **32**:7, 43, 45, 47
On Salaried Posts in Great Houses (Lucian) **32**:33, 35, 43
On Shows (Tertullian) **29**:312, 338, 373
On Sleep and Waking (Albert the Great) **16**:16
On Staseis (Hermogenes)
  See *On Stases*
On Stases (Hermogenes) **6**:158, 170-74, 185-86, 191, 196, 198-202
"On Study and Learning" (Petrarch) **20**:286-87
On Style (Demetrius of Phalerum) **34**:1-43
"On Taking Leave of Tzu-yu at Ying-chou: Two Poems" (Su Shih) **15**:411
On the Activity of God (Hildegard von Bingen)
  See *Liber divinorum Operum*
On the Adornment of Women (Tertullian) **29**:311
On the Affairs in the Chersonese (Demosthenes)
  See *On the Chersonese*

"On the Ages of the World" (Bede) **20**:7
On the Astronomical Cannon of Diophantus (Hypatia) **35**:221
On the Best Kind of Orators (Cicero)
  See *De optimo genere oratorum*
On the Blessed Life (Cicero)
  See *Tusculan Disputations*
On the Categoric Syllogism (Apuleius) **1**:12-13
On the Categorical Syllogism (Boethius) **15**:27
On the Catholic Faith (Boethius)
  See *De fide catholica*
On the Causes and Properties of the Elements and of the Planets (Albert the Great)
  See *De causis et proprietatibus elementorum et planetarum*
On the Chaplet (Tertullian) **29**:311-12
On the Chersonese (Demosthenes) **13**:138, 146, 148-9, 152, 161, 166, 193, 195
On the Chief Good and Evil (Cicero)
  See *De finibus*
On the Christian Struggle (Augustine) **6**:21
On the City of God (Augustine)
  See *De civitate Dei*
On the Cloak (Tertullian) **29**:312, 329, 347
On the Comics of Apollonius (Hypatia) **35**:221, 223
On the Computation of Time (Bede)
  See *De temporum ratione*
On the Criterion (Epicurus)
  See *The Canon*
On the Crown (Demosthenes) **13**:139, 143, 145, 147-52, 162, 166, 172-5, 179, 183-4, 189, 191-5, 197
On the Dance (Lucian)
  See *The Dance*
On the Death of Peregrinus The Passing Peregrinus (Lucian) **32**:8, 14-15, 38, 45-46, 58
On the Difference between Enmity and Envy
  See *Fi Fasl ma bayn al-adawah wa l-hasad*
On the Divine Unity and Trinity (Abelard)
  See *Theologia 'Summi boni'*
On the Dress of Women (Tertullian) **29**:312
On the End or Telos (Epicurus) **21**:154
On the False Embassy (Demosthenes)
  See *On the Misconduct of the Embassy*
On the Figures and Tropes of the Holy Scripture (Bede)
  See *De schematibus et tropis sacrae scripturae*
On the Flesh of Christ (Tertullian) **29**:311-12
"On the Forty-two Stations of the Isrealites in the Desert" (Jerome) **30**:89
On the Fraudulent Embassy (Demosthenes)
  See *On the Misconduct of the Embassy*
On the Freedom of Rhodes (Demosthenes)
  See *For the Rhodians*
On the Goal (Epicurus) **21**:165
On the God of Socrates (Apuleius) **1**:4, 7, 12-13, 23, 32
On the Gods (Epicurus) **21**:73, 154
On the Greatest Degree of Good and Evil (Cicero)
  See *De finibus*
"On the Happ Life" (Martial)
  See "Vitam quae faciunt beatiorem"
On the Happy Life (Seneca)
  See *De vita beata*
On the Heaven (Aristotle)
  See *De Caelo*
On the Hypothetical Syllogism (Boethius) **15**:9, 27,
"On the Judgment Rendered by Solomon" (Jerome) **30**:89
On the Kinds of Life (Epicurus) **21**:141

On the Lacedaemonian Polity (Xenophon)
  See *Constitution of Sparta*
On the Measurements of Time (Bede)
  See *De temporibus*
On the Method of Deinotes (Hermogenes) **6**:158, 188, 191, 202
On the Method of Force (Hermogenes)
  See *On the Method of Deinotes*
On the Misconduct of the Embassy (Demosthenes) **13**:138, 147-9, 165, 168, 172, 183-4, 189, 194-5
On the Moral End (Epicurus) **21**:118
On the Nature of Gods (Cicero)
  See *De natura deorum*
On the Nature of Good (Augustine) **6**:9
On the Nature of Things (Bede) **20**:44
On the Orator (Cicero)
  See *De oratore*
On the Pattern for Rhetorical Effectiveness (Hermogenes) **6**:170
On the Peace (Demosthenes) **13**:138, 148-9, 159-60, 165
"On the Red Cliff" (Su Shih)
  See "Rhymeprose on the Red Cliff"
On the Reorganization (Demosthenes) **13**:165
"On the Restoration of the Examination System" (Su Shih) **15**:385
On the Resurrection (Origen) **19**:186
On the Resurrection (Tertullian)
  See *On the Resurrection of the Flesh*
On the Resurrection of the Flesh (Tertullian) **29**:311-12, 363, 368, 371-72
On the Rhodians (Demosthenes)
  See *For the Rhodians*
"On the Right Way to Make a Translation" (Jerome) **30**:89, 97
On the Science of Moral Habits (Avicenna) **16**:164
On the Shortness of Life (Seneca)
  See *De brevitate vitae*
On the Soul (Aristotle)
  See *Eudemus*
On the Soul (Avicenna) **16**:164
On the Soul (Tertullian) **29**:311-12, 330, 334
On the State (Cicero)
  See *De republica*
"On the Study of Sacred Scripture" (Jerome) **30**:89
On the Sublime (Longinus)
  See *Peri Hysos*
On the Superiority of the Belly to the Back
  See *Fi Tafdil-al-bafn ala l-zahr*
On the Symmories (Demosthenes) **13**:145, 148, 159, 163-4, 171, 197
On the Treaties with Alexander (Demosthenes) **13**:166
On the Trinity (Augustine)
  See *De Trinitate*
On the Trinity (Boethius)
  See *On the Trinity*
"On the twelfth night" (Su Shih) **15**:398
On the Unity of the Intellect: against Averroes (Augustine) **16**:57
On the Universe (Apuleius)
  See *De mundo*
On the Usefulness of Mathematics (Bacon)
  See *De utilitate mathematicae*
"On the Vestiments of the High Priest" (Jerome) **30**:89
On the Vices Contracted in the Study of Theology (Bacon) **14**:92
On the Virtues of the Turk
  See *Kitab Manaqib al-Turkwa-ammat jund al-*

khilafah
On Times (Bede)
  See *De temporibus*
On Types of Style (Hermogenes) **6**:158, 170, 185-92, 196, 200-02, 204
On Veiling Virgins (Tertullian) **29**:311-12, 377
On Vision (Epicurus) **21**:73
"On Wisdom" (Petrarch) **20**:286
One the Art of Metre (Bede)
  See *De arte metrica*
Onomasticum (Jerome) **30**:88, 111
Onos (Lucian) **32**:23-28
Opera (Hroswitha of Gandersheim) **29**:121, 140
Opera omnia (Euclid) **25**:1-86, 212
Optica (Euclid)
  See *Optics*
Optica, Liber de visu (Euclid)
  See *Optics*
Optics (Bacon) **14**:20
Optics (Biruni) **28**:130
Optics (Euclid) **25**:1-86, 90, 98, 110, 148-62, 199-205, 231, 261-62, 264
De Optimo (Cicero)
  See *De optimo genere oratorum*
De optimo genere dicendi (Cicero) **3**:188, 193, 199, 201, 217-18, 259-63, 288
De Optimo Genere Interpretandi (Jerome) **30**:56
De optimo genere oratorum (Cicero) **3**:201, 261
Opus imperfectum contra Julianum (Augustine) **6**:149
Opus Maius (Bacon)
  See *Opus Majus*
Opus Majus (Bacon) **14**:3-5, 7-8, 15, 18, 20, 22-23, 29-31, 34-35, 37, 40, 42, 47, 49-50, 53-54, 59, 61-65, 68-70, 73, 76-77, 80, 82, 84, 86, 92-94, 100, 102, 106-15
Opus Minus (Bacon) **14**:15, 18-20, 29, 40, 48, 52, 54, 62-63, 66-68, 80, 100, 102-03
Opus nonaginta duierum (William of Ockham) **32**:199
Opus Prophetale (Jerome) **30**:89
Opus Sermonum (Eckhart) **9**:57
Opus Tertium (Bacon) **14**:15, 19-21, 29-30, 40, 47-48, 52, 54, 58-59, 62-63, 65, 67-68, 80, 83, 86, 100-05, 108
Opus Tripartitum (Eckhart) **9**:55
De oratione (Tertullian) **29**:374
The Orator (Cicero)
  See *De optimo genere dicendi*
Orator ad M. Brutum (Cicero)
  See *De optimo genere dicendi*
The Orator: To Marcus Brutus (Cicero)
  See *De optimo genere dicendi*
De oratore (Cicero) **3**:186, 193, 200-01, 207-11, 217-18, 227, 246, 258-59, 261, 263, 270, 288
De oratore ad filium (Cato) **21**:21
Ordinatio (William of Ockham) **32**:138, 145
De ordine (Augustine) **6**:5, 102
Ordo Representacionis Ade **4**:182-221
Ordo virtutum (Hildegard von Bingen) **20**:153-54, 176
Orestea (Aeschylus)
  See *Oresteia*
Oresteia (Aeschylus) **11**:77, 100-01, 105-06, 109, 117-19, 123, 128, 130, 132-34, 136-40, 153-56, 158-59, 160, 162-63, 167-68, 180, 184, 190-91, 193-95, 197-99, 206, 209, 211, 217-19, 222-23
Orestes (Aeschylus) **11**:134
Orestes (Euripides) **23**:119, 121, 123-25, 173, 175-76, 186, 189, 203, 206
Organon (Aristotle) **31**:86, 260, 318
Orge (Menander) **9**:244, 248, 250, 284

Origines (Cato) **21**:3, 20-1, 23-4, 26-7, 29, 39, 41, 47, 49, 54-6
De originibus (Cato) **21**:20
Origins (Cato)
  See *Origines*
Ornithes (Aristophanes) **4**:44-6, 58, 62-7, 87, 93-6. 100. 110, 114, 124-26. 131-33, 135, 142, 144, 146-49, 155, 159-61, 165-66, 168
Orpheus (Lucan) **33**:422
De orthographia (Bede) **20**:42
De otio religiosorum (Petrarch) **20**:213, 263
Our Daily Life (Rolle) **21**:299
Our Daily Work (Rolle) **21**:300-01, 307
P. 1 (Pindar)
  See *Pythian 1*
P. 2 (Pindar)
  See *Pythian 2*
P. 3 (Pindar)
  See *Pythian 3*
P. 4 (Pindar)
  See *Pythian 4*
P. 5 (Pindar)
  See *Pythian 5*
P. 6 (Pindar)
  See *Pythian 6*
P. 8 (Pindar)
  See *Pythian 8*
"A Pact With My Heart" (Po Chu-i) **24**:315
"Padre del ciel" (Petrarch) **20**:257
Paean 1 (Pindar) **12**:355
Paean 2 (Pindar) **12**:321, 351, 360-61
Paean 4 (Pindar) **12**:352, 382
Paean 5 (Pindar) **12**:359
Paean 6 (Pindar) **12**:271, 300, 358-59
Paean 8 (Pindar) **12**:
Paean 9 (Pindar) **12**:266, 308-09, 356
Paean for Ceos (Pindar) **12**:318
Paean for the Abderites (Pindar)
  See *Paean 2*
Paeans (Pindar) **12**:318, 320-21, 352
Pafnutius (Hroswitha of Gandersheim)
  See *Paphnutius*
The Pageant of Seasons
  See *Rtusamhara*
"The Palace of the Grotto of Mists" (Sordello) **15**:391
De Pallio (Tertullian)
  See *On the Cloak*
Panegyris Oddonum (Hroswitha of Gandersheim)
  See *Gesta Ottonis*
Paphnutius (Hroswitha of Gandersheim) **29**:102-03, 112, 115, 119-20, 122, 126, 139, 145-46, 148-50, 163, 174, 176, 178, 180, 183, 198-99, 201
Paraphrase (Caedmon)
  See "Genesis"
Paraphrase of Genesis (Caedmon)
  See "Genesis"
The Parasite (Lucian) **32**:33, 41-42
A Parasite's Brain to the Rescue (Terence)
  See *Phormio*
Parisian Questions and Prologues (Eckhart) **9**:69
The Parliament of the Gods (Lucian) **32**:47-48, 50
Parliament of Women (Aristophanes)
  See *Ekklesiazousai*
Parmenides (Plato) **8**:232, 234, 240, 258-60, 264, 282, 293, 306, 310, 317, 320, 328, 333-34, 338, 340-41, 361, 364
Partheneia (Pindar) **12**:320-21, 351, 356
De Partibus Animalium (Aristotle) **31**:65-66, 69, 74, 86, 328, 332, 339, 356
"The Parting" (Li Po) **2**:138

"A Parting Banquet for the Collator Shu-yün at the Hsieh T'iao Lodge in Hsüan-chou" (Li Po) **2**:163

Partiones oratoriae (Cicero) **3**:201, 218, 259-60, 263

Partitiones (Cicero)
  See *Partiones oratoriae*

Parts of Animals (Aristotle)
  See *De Partibus Animalium*

Parva Naturalia (Aristotle) **31**:65, 68, 86, 358-59

Parzival (Wolfram von Eschenbach) **5**:293-94, 296-302, 304-05, 307-10, 312, 314-17, 320-23, 325-26, 333-45, 347, 350-54, 357-58, 360, 362, 366, 369-71, 373, 376, 380-83, 385-86, 390-92, 395-96, 400-01, 403-04, 409, 411, 416-17, 419-23, 425, 429-32

Pasiphae (Euripides) **23**:203

"Passing the Huai" (Su Shih) **15**:413

The Passion of the Holy Maidens (Hroswitha of Gandersheim) **29**:180

The Pastorals of Daphnis and Chloe (Longus)
  See *Daphnis and Chloe*

Patrologia Graeca (Origen) **19**:231

"The Pavilion of Flying Cranes" (Su Shih) **15**:382

"The Pavilion to Glad Rain" (Su Shih) **15**:382

Peace (Aristophanes)
  See *Eirene*

The Peace (Demosthenes)
  See *On the Peace*

"Peacock and Crane" (Aesop) **24**:36

Pearl **19**:275-407

"A Peasant and a Dung-Beetle" (Marie de France) **8**:174

"The Peasant Who Saw His Wife with Her Lover" (Marie de France) **8**:190

Pedeir Keinc y Mabinogi **9**:144-98

"*Peleus and Thetis*" (Catullus)
  See "*Poem 64*"

Peliades (Euripides) **23**:116

Penelope (Aeschylus) **11**:124

Pentachronon (Hildegard von Bingen) **20**:163

Pentateuch
  See *Torah*

Perception (Epicurus) **21**:73

Perceval (Chretien de Troyes) **10**:133, 137, 139, 143, 145-46, 150, 157, 159, 161-66, 169, 178-79, 183, 189-90, 195-96, 199, 206-09, 216-20, 223-26, 228-40

Perceval le Gallois (Chretien de Troyes)
  See *Perceval*

Percevax le viel (Chretien de Troyes)
  See *Perceval*

"Perchance: Two Poems" (Po Chu-i) **24**:343

Peregrinus (Lucian)
  See *On the Death of Peregrinus The Passing Peregrinus*

Peri hermeneias (Apuleius) **1**:24

Peri Hysos (Longinus) **27**:122-204

Perikeiromene (Menander) **9**:207, 210-11, 213, 215, 217, 221, 223, 225, 228, 230, 232, 238-39, 246-48, 250-52, 260, 267, 269-71, 276-77, 281, 288

Perisan Lyrics (Hafiz) **34**:57

Perr Archon (Origen)
  See *De Principiis*

Persa (Plautus) **24**:170-73, 175, 187, 219, 220-21, 247, 262, 269

Persae (Aeschylus)
  See *Persians*

Persian (Plautus)
  See *Persa*

Persian Song (Hafiz) **34**:57, 60, 63-64, 67

Persians (Aeschylus) **11**:77, 85, 88, 96, 102, 112-13, 117-18, 121, 127, 133-35, 139, 151-53, 156, 158-60, 179, 181-84, 191, 193-95, 198, 200, 202-03, 205, 211, 215-20

Perspective (Bacon)
  See *De Scientia Perspectiva*

Phaedo (Plato) **8**:204-07, 209, 233, 235-36, 239, 261, 268, 305-07, 312, 320, 322-25, 328, 331, 340-41, 358, 361-62

Phaedra (Seneca) **6**:341, 366, 368-70, 377, 379-81, 389, 403-06, 413-16, 418, 424-26, 432, 448

Phaedrus (Plato) **8**:205, 210, 220, 230, 232-33, 241, 244, 254-55, 259, 262, 264-66, 270, 275, 283, 299, 306-07, 317, 322-25, 331, 334, 355, 359, 362, 364

Phaenomena (Euclid) **25**:1-86, 97-8, 108, 144, 168, 258-66

Phalaris I (Lucian) **32**:39

Phalaris II (Lucian) **32**:39

Pharsalia (Lucan)
  See *Civil War*

Philebus (Plato) **8**:248, 260, 264-68, 270, 306, 310, 333, 341, 361, 363-64

Philippic I (Demosthenes) **13**:137, 148-9, 152, 165, 171, 183, 190-2, 195, 197

Philippic II (Demosthenes) **13**:138, 148-9, 151, 160, 165, 172

Philippic III (Demosthenes) **13**:138, 143-5, 148, 161, 166, 172, 177, 180, 192-3, 195

Philippic IV (Demosthenes) **13**:162, 166

Philippics (Cicero) **3**:192-93, 196, 198-99, 229-30, 253, 268, 271-73

Philippics (Demosthenes) **13**:139, 142-3, 149-52, 158, 161-2, 172, 174, 180, 183, 189

"Philocalia" (Basil of Caesaria) **35**:21

Philoctetes (Aeschylus) **11**:125, 140

Philoctetes at Troy (Sophocles) **2**:341

Philoktetes (Sophocles) **2**:289, 294-95, 302-05, 314, 316, 318, 320, 325, 338, 341, 346, 352-54, 357, 367-68, 377, 385-87, 397-408, 415-16, 419, 426

Philomena (Chretien de Troyes) **10**:137

Philoseudes (Lucian)
  See *The Lover of Lies*

Philosopher (Plato) **8**:259

Philosophers for Sale (Lucian) **32**:35, 47-51, 63

De Philosophia (Aristotle) **31**:66, 68-69, 354, 356

Philosophical Topics (John)
  See *Capita Philosophica*

Philosophies for Sale (Lucian)
  See *Philosophers for Sale*

Phineus (Aeschylus) **11**:159, 174

The Phoenician Women (Euripides) **23**:112, 121, 124-25, 189, 206-07, 219-21

The Phoenician Women (Seneca)
  See *Phoenissae*

Phoenissae (Euripides)
  See *The Phoenician Women*

Phoenissae (Seneca) **6**:363, 366, 379-80, 402, 413, 421, 432, 437

"Phoenix Song" (Li Po) **2**:152

Phormio (Terence) **14**:303, 306-07, 311, 313-18, 320, 333, 335, 340, 341, 347-49, 352-53, 356-57, 364, 376-80, 383-85, 389-90

Phrixus (Euripides) **23**:207

Phychostasia (Aeschylus)
  See *Weighing of Souls*

"Phyllis" (Ovid) **7**:311

Physica (Albert the Great) **16**:4, 36, 61

Physica (Hildegard von Bingen) **20**:154

Physicorum (Albert the Great) **16**:36

Physics (Albert the Great)
  See *Physica*

Physics (Aquinas) **33**:94

Physics (Aristotle) **31**:8-9, 11-13, 52, 57, 66, 69, 86-87, 275, 304, 309, 312, 322, 338-39, 345, 347, 359, 361, 375-87, 387-96

The Pillow Book of Sei Shonagon (Sei Shonagon)
  See *Makura no soshi*

Pillow Sketches (Sei Shonagon)
  See *Makura no soshi*

Pinakes (Callimachus) **18**:38, 45-8, 62-4, 68-70

"Pine Wine of the Middle Mountains" (Su Shih) **15**:382

"The Pious Black Slave" **2**:40

Piscator (Lucian)
  See *The Dead Come to Life, or, The Fisherman The Fisherman*

Planctus (Abelard) **11**:55, 68

"Planher vuelh en Blacatz" (Sordello) **15**:332, 337, 343, 365, 375, 377

"Planting Flowers at the Eastern Slope" (Po Chu-i) **24**:340

De Plantis (Albert the Great) **16**:18

Plants (Albert the Great)
  See *De vegetabilibus*

"Playfully Enjoying the Chrysanthemums at East Garden" (Po Chu-i) **24**:327

"Playing with Pine and Bamboo" (Po Chu-i) **24**:342

Plays (Hroswitha of Gandersheim)
  See *The Plays of Hroswitha*

The Plays of Hroswitha (Hroswitha of Gandersheim) **29**:107, 137, 200-01

Ploutos (Aristophanes) **4**:44, 46, 62, 67, 76, 90, 94, 111, 115, 124-26, 147-48, 153, 161, 165-68, 174-75, 177-80

"The Plunder of the Home of Salur-Kazan" **8**:97, 103, 109

Plutus (Aristophanes)
  See *Ploutos*

Podagra (Lucian) **32**:26

"Poem 1" (Catullus) **18**:104, 108, 110-11, 117, 122-23, 130-32, 150, 167-78, 185-93

"Poem 2" (Catullus) **18**:116, 161, 178, 187-93, 196

"Poem 3" (Catullus) **18**:166, 174, 178, 187-88

"Poem 4" (Catullus) **18**:108, 117, 167, 180, 187-88

"Poem 5" (Catullus) **18**:102, 137-38, 141, 159, 166, 179, 186, 188, 196-97

"Poem 6" (Catullus) **18**:99, 106, 122, 125-27, 129-30, 133, 138, 188, 195-96

"Poem 7" (Catullus) **18**:102, 108, 118, 137-38, 140, 150, 160-61, 166, 181, 186, 188, 196-97

"Poem 8" (Catullus) **18**:138, 153, 160-61, 166, 188, 192

"Poem 9" (Catullus) **18**:121, 128, 186, 188

"Poem 10" (Catullus) **18**:99, 107, 122-26, 129-30, 188

"Poem 11" (Catullus) **18**:99, 116, 119, 126, 133, 162, 166-67, 179, 181-82, 185, 187-88, 192, 194

"Poem 12" (Catullus) **18**:122, 181, 188

"Poem 13" (Catullus) **18**:102, 109, 127, 180, 186

"Poem 14" (Catullus) **18**:99-101, 166, 186, 188

"Poem 14b" (Catullus) **18**:122, 193

"Poem 15" (Catullus) **18**:119, 133-34, 188-90, 193-95, 197

"Poem 16" (Catullus) **18**:119, 132, 134, 137, 167, 186, 188-90, 193-97

"Poem 17" (Catullus) **18**:122, 129-30, 181

"Poem 18" (Catullus) **18**:127

"Poem 18" (Filderman) **18**:127

"Poem 21" (Catullus) **18**:119, 134, 181, 188

"Poem 22" (Catullus) **18**:100-01, 145

"Poem 23" (Catullus) **18**:99, 119, 133-34, 181, 188

"Poem 24" (Catullus) **18**:99, 132, 134, 188

"Poem 25" (Catullus) **18**:132-33, 166

"Poem 26" (Catullus) **18**:99, 119, 134, 188

"Poem 28" (Catullus) **18**:99, 121, 132, 188

"Poem 29" (Catullus) **18**:99, 118, 144, 166, 181, 187-88

"Poem 30" (Catullus) **18**:99, 125, 169, 171

"Poem 31" (Catullus) **18**:103, 117, 146, 166-67, 186-88

"Poem 32" (Catullus) **18**:115, 122-23, 130, 133, 137-38, 146, 181

"Poem 33" (Catullus) **18**:122, 132-33, 146

"Poem 34" (Catullus) **18**:110-11, 166-67, 176, 181-82

"Poem 35" (Catullus) **18**:93, 99-102, 122, 128, 130, 147, 167, 186

"Poem 36" (Catullus) **18**:100-01, 121, 127, 145, 167, 186

"Poem 37" (Catullus) **18**:118-20, 133

"Poem 38" (Catullus) **18**:99, 181

"Poem 39" (Catullus) **18**:106, 118-19, 131, 133

"Poem 41" (Catullus) **18**:122, 129-30, 146

"Poem 42" (Catullus) **18**:131, 187

"Poem 43" (Catullus) **18**:118, 122-23, 130, 177, 188

"Poem 44" (Catullus) **18**:166

"Poem 45" (Catullus) **18**:122, 126, 130, 166, 181, 188

"Poem 46" (Catullus) **18**:132, 177, 181, 187-88

"Poem 47" (Catullus) **18**:99, 121, 181

"Poem 48" (Catullus) **18**:132, 137-38, 181, 186, 188

"Poem 49" (Catullus) **18**:145, 167, 179, 182

"Poem 50" (Catullus) **18**:99-101, 103, 109, 139, 188-89, 192-93

"Poem 51" (Catullus) **18**:111, 115, 143, 146, 169, 176, 179, 182, 186, 188

"Poem 52" (Catullus) **18**:118, 121, 188

"Poem 53" (Catullus) **18**:139, 188

"Poem 54" (Catullus) **18**:122, 144, 167, 186

"Poem 55" (Catullus) **18**:99, 122, 127, 130, 166, 186, 188

"Poem 56" (Catullus) **18**:99, 109, 130-32, 134, 188

"Poem 57" (Catullus) **18**:132, 144, 188

"Poem 58" (Catullus) **18**:118-19, 133, 179, 182

"Poem 58b" (Catullus) **18**:99, 122, 186

"Poem 59" (Catullus) **18**:99, 130

"Poem 60" (Catullus) **18**:104, 110-11, 117, 123, 130-32, 150, 171, 185-89

"Poem 61" (Catullus) **18**:110-11, 114, 117, 123, 145, 166, 168, 182, 185, 188

"Poem 62" (Catullus) **18**:111, 117, 123, 142, 167-68, 182

"Poem 63" (Catullus) **18**:78, 80, 105, 107-08, 111, 115-17, 123, 135-36, 145, 166, 168, 170, 172, 174, 182-83, 185

"Poem 64" (Catullus) **18**:77-78, 99-101, 104-05, 107-08, 110-11, 113-14, 117, 136, 143, 155, 167-69, 174-75, 177, 183, 189

"Poem 65" (Catullus) **18**:86, 88, 90, 100-01, 110-11, 115-16, 123, 166, 176, 184

"Poem 66" (Catullus) **18**:78, 80, 88-90, 108, 111, 115-16, 123, 166, 176

"Poem 67" (Catullus) **18**:88, 90, 111, 123, 1399, 184

"Poem 68" (Catullus) **18**:74, 84, 86-88, 90, 100-02, 104, 110-11, 113-14, 116, 145, 149, 155, 162, 166-69, 171-72, 175-77, 179-80, 182-85

"Poem 68a" (Catullus) **18**:169

"Poem 69" (Catullus) **18**:78, 104, 117-18, 122, 130, 132, 138, 150, 186-88

"Poem 70" (Catullus) **18**:118, 155, 157, 171, 180

"Poem 71" (Catullus) **18**:118, 122, 132-33, 188-89

"Poem 72" (Catullus) **18**:115, 118, 156-57, 180, 189

"Poem 74" (Catullus) **18**:122-23, 132

"Poem 75" (Catullus) **18**:87, 152, 154, 157

"Poem 76" (Catullus) **18**:86-87, 138-39, 153-56, 158, 161, 171, 175, 177, 180, 183, 189

"Poem 77" (Catullus) **18**:118, 188

"Poem 78" (Catullus) **18**:110, 122, 131-32

"Poem 79" (Catullus) **18**:147

"Poem 80" (Catullus) **18**:133, 185

"Poem 81" (Catullus) **18**:132

"Poem 82" (Catullus) **18**:132

"Poem 84" (Catullus) **18**:81, 117, 139, 185, 188

"Poem 85" (Catullus) **18**:87, 116, 129, 152, 171, 186

"Poem 86" (Catullus) **18**:118, 122-23, 130

"Poem 87" (Catullus) **18**:156-59, 161

"Poem 88" (Catullus) **18**:122, 132, 182

"Poem 89" (Catullus) **18**:132

"Poem 90" (Catullus) **18**:122, 132

"Poem 91" (Catullus) **18**:118, 122-23, 132

"Poem 92" (Catullus) **18**:186

"Poem 93" (Catullus) **18**:185

"Poem 94" (Catullus) **18**:122

"Poem 95" (Catullus) **18**:99-101, 145, 167, 176, 188-89

"Poem 96" (Catullus) **18**:146, 186, 188

"Poem 97" (Catullus) **18**:116, 122, 131-34

"Poem 99" (Catullus) **18**:102, 138

"Poem 100" (Catullus) **18**:118, 122, 132-33, 186

"Poem 101" (Catullus) **18**:146, 185-86, 189

"Poem 102" (Catullus) **18**:186

"Poem 103" (Catullus) **18**:123

"Poem 104" (Catullus) **18**:184

"Poem 106" (Catullus) **18**:133

"Poem 107" (Catullus) **18**:186

"Poem 109" (Catullus) **18**:149, 180, 186

"Poem 110" (Catullus) **18**:123, 131

"Poem 111" (Catullus) **18**:123, 132

"Poem 113" (Catullus) **18**:123, 131, 187-88

"Poem 116" (Catullus) **18**:100-01, 104, 117, 130, 132, 138, 150, 186-87

Poema de mio Cid **4**:222-341

Poems from the Divan of Hafiz (Hafiz)
    See *Diwan-i Hafiz*

The Poems of Shemseddin Mohammed Hafiz of Shiraz (Hafiz)
    See *Diwan-i Hafiz*

Poenulus (Plautus) **24**:170-73, 175, 186, 196, 219, 240, 247, 258

Poetics (Aristotle) **31**:87, 101-219, 222, 366-67, 269, 291, 304-07

"Poignant Grief During a Sunny Spring" (Li Po) **2**:132

Politica (Aristotle)
    See *Politics*

Politics (Aristotle) **31**:61-63, 66-69, 72, 87, 230, 261, 266, 355-56, 371-73

Politicus (Aristotle)
    See *Politics*

Politicus (Plato)
    See *Politikos*

Politikos (Plato) **8**:249, 258-60, 282, 306, 310, 333-34, 349, 359, 361

Polydectes (Aeschylus) **11**:124-25, 193

Pontius Glaucus (Cicero) **3**:198

Porisms (Euclid) **25**:1-86, 94-7, 105-8, 110, 120

"The Porter and the Ladies" **2**:47

Po-shih wen-chi (Po Chu-i)
    See *Po-shih wen-chi*

Possessed Woman (Menander) **9**:211

Posterior Analytics (Aquinas) **33**:94-95, 110

"Posteritati" (Petrarch) **20**:326

Posteritati (Boccaccio) **13**:66

"Postscript to the Calligraphy of the Six T'ang Masters" (Su Shih) **15**:421

"Postscript to the Paintings of P'u Yung-sheng" (Su Shih) **15**:420

Pot of Gold (Plautus)
    See *Aulularia*

De Potentia (Aquinas)
    See *On Power*

Practical Oratory (Hermogenes) **6**:204

De praedestinatione sanctorum (Augustine) **6**:89

Praef. in lib. Paral. juxta LXX (Jerome) **30**:96

Praef. in Pent. (Jerome) **30**:97

Praefatio (Hroswitha of Gandersheim) **29**:116-17, 119

De Praescriptione Haereticorum (Tertullian)
    See *On Prescription of Heretics*

"Predictae Epistolae" (Map)
    See *"Conclusio Praedictae Epistolae"*

Prefatio (Hroswitha of Gandersheim)
    See *Praefatio*

"The Pregnant Hound" (Marie de France) **8**:190

Priestess (Menander) **9**:214

Primordia (Hroswitha of Gandersheim) **29**:123-24, 133, 140, 142, 172, 194

Primordia Caenobii Gandeshemensis (Hroswitha of Gandersheim)
    See *Primordia*

"Prince Ahmed and the Fairy Pari Banou" **2**:36, 49

Principal Doctrines (Epicurus) **21**:73, 154, 161, 164-65, 167, 175, 184, 187-88, 205

De Principiis (Origen) **19**:186, 199, 201, 203, 205, 209, 225, 227, 235-36, 246, 248, 258, 261, 263, 265

De principiis motus processivi (Albert the Great) **16**:61

Principles of Music (Boethius)
    See *In topica Ciceronis*

Prior Analytics (Aristotle) **31**:66, 86-87, 242, 267, 280, 313-16, 322, 333

Pro Archia (Cicero)
    See *Archias*

Pro Balbo (Cicero) **3**:271

Pro Caecina (Cicero) **3**:214

Pro Caelio (Cicero) **3**:176, 197-99, 269-70

Pro Cluentio (Cicero) **3**:197-99, 214, 267-68

Pro Lege Manilia (Cicero) **3**:198-99

Pro Ligario (Cicero) **3**:272

Pro Marcello (Cicero) **3**:198-99, 271-72

Pro Milone (Cicero) **3**:198-99, 270-71

Pro Murena (Cicero) **3**:198, 203

Pro Plancio (Cicero) **3**:198

Pro Quinctio (Cicero) **3**:264

Pro Roscio Amerino (Cicero) **3**:198, 265-66

Pro Roscio comoedo (Cicero) **3**:265

Pro se de magia liber (Apuleius)
    See *Apologia sive oratoria de magia*

Pro Sestio (Cicero) **3**:198, 269, 298

Problems (Epicurus) **21**:73-4, 188

Processional Hymns (Pindar)
    See *Prosodia*

A Professor of Public Speaking (Lucian) **32**:13-14, 26, 38, 43, 46

Los progres e avansaments dei Res d'Aragon (Sordello) **15**:330, 338, 344

The Progress and Power of the Kings of Arragon (Sordello)
　　See *Los progres e avansaments dei Res d'Aragon*

Progymnasmata (Hermogenes) **6**:162, 170, 185, 191, 198, 202

"Prologue" (Map) **32**:80-81

Prologus (William of Ockham) **32**:138-40

"Prologus Galeatus" (Jerome) **30**:71

Prometheia (Aeschylus)
　　See *Prometheus Bound*

Prometheus (Aeschylus)
　　See *Prometheus Bound*

Prometheus Bound (Aeschylus) **11**:88, 98-9, 101-02, 105-06, 109-10, 113, 118-19, 123, 128-29, 135-37, 140, 143, 148, 151-55, 157, 166-67, 175, 179, 181, 183, 193-95, 197, 200, 208-09, 217, 219

Prometheus Delivered (Aeschylus)
　　See *Prometheus Unbound*

Prometheus the Fire Bringer (Aeschylus)
　　See *Prometheus the Firebearer*

Prometheus the Firebearer (Aeschylus) **11**:88, 159, 179

Prometheus the Firekindler (Aeschylus) **11**:167, 175

Prometheus Unbound (Aeschylus) **11**:88, 90, 106, 123, 136, 175, 179

Prometheus Vinctus (Aeschylus)
　　See *Prometheus Bound*

Proofs of Prophethood
　　See *Kitab Hujaj al-nubuwwah*

Properties of the Elements (Albert the Great)
　　See *De causis et proprietatibus elementorum et planetarum*

Prose Treatises (Rolle) **21**:278

Prosecution of Aristocrates (Demosthenes)
　　See *Against Aristocrates*

Prosodia (Pindar) **12**:320-21

Proteus (Aeschylus) **11**:162

Protogoras (Plato) **8**:219, 232, 247-48, 253-54, 266-68, 283-84, 305-07, 310, 347

Proto-Kalevala
　　See *Kalevala*

Protreptious (Aristotle) **31**:66, 68, 230, 354-56

De provinciis consularibus (Cicero) **3**:215, 271

Psalm 1 **4**:387, 390, 402, 417, 427, 434, 442, 450

Psalm 2 **4**:355, 357, 364-65, 368, 384, 447, 450

Psalm 3 **4**:359, 379, 386, 389, 432-33, 439, 446, 448

Psalm 4 **4**:364, 390, 426, 438, 448

Psalm 5 **4**:359, 383, 389, 390, 406, 438, 448

Psalm 6 **4**:359, 370, 373, 387, 390, 418, 432-33, 438, 448

Psalm 7 **4**:359, 426, 446, 448

Psalm 8 **4**:357, 361, 368, 373, 385, 390, 395-96, 398, 419, 434, 439, 441, 448, 453

Psalm 9 **4**:359, 364, 405, 432, 440, 450

Psalm 10 **4**:359, 364, 379, 450

Psalm 11 **4**:59, 364, 366, 389, 448

Psalm 12 **4**:426, 453, 455

Psalm 13 **4**:359, 432, 434, 448

Psalm 14 **4**:359, 364, 370, 378-79, 416, 426, 434

Psalm 15 **4**:357, 367-68, 377, 383, 450

Psalm 16 **4**:364, 368, 379, 434

Psalm 17 **4**:359, 364, 387, 391, 426, 448

Psalm 18 **4**:359, 364, 372, 382, 384, 388-89, 406, 443, 445-47, 449, 454

Psalm 19 **4**:345, 354, 359, 368, 380, 384, 388, 395, 397, 426, 441-42, 450

Psalm 20 **4**:345, 357, 365, 368, 373, 384, 388

Psalm 21 **4**:357, 359, 368, 384, 440

Psalm 22 **4**:359, 364-66, 368, 373, 382-83, 386-87, 389-90, 392, 419, 427, 434, 448, 450-51

Psalm 23 **4**:356, 377, 386, 389, 392, 417, 427, 434, 448

Psalm 24 **4**:345, 357, 373, 375, 378, 380, 383, 406-07, 450

Psalm 25 **4**:359, 390, 394, 402, 432, 449

Psalm 26 **4**:359, 364, 376, 378, 382, 387, 391, 406, 426, 448

Psalm 27 **4**:359, 373, 376, 378, 382, 389-90, 404-06, 432, 434, 441, 448

Psalm 28 **4**:359, 373, 383, 385, 407, 440

Psalm 29 **4**:345, 357, 368, 379-80, 384, 395, 401, 434, 439, 441

Psalm 30 **4**:359, 377, 394, 434, 455

Psalm 31 **4**:365, 402, 431-33

Psalm 32 **4**:359, 387, 390, 433-34

Psalm 33 **4**:359, 371, 381, 427, 434, 440-41, 446, 449

Psalm 34 **4**:346, 359, 381, 388, 426, 434, 449

Psalm 35 **4**:350, 359, 378, 382, 434

Psalm 36 **4**:359, 368, 427

Psalm 37 **4**:346, 359, 370, 382, 387, 402, 434

Psalm 38 **4**:383, 390, 392, 433, 448

Psalm 39 **4**:359, 433, 455

Psalm 40 **4**:381-82, 386, 389, 393, 433-34, 440, 449-50

Psalm 41 **4**:350, 359, 368, 439

Psalm 42 **4**:347, 368, 377-78, 380, 383, 386, 405, 407, 432, 451

Psalm 43 **4**:368, 377-78, 405, 440

Psalm 44 **4**:359, 381, 385, 387, 394, 413, 432

Psalm 45 **4**:357, 365, 368, 384, 440, 443, 450

Psalm 46 **4**:354, 385, 401

Psalm 47 **4**:345, 357, 381, 389, 405, 434, 438, 440

Psalm 48 **4**:357, 389, 407-08, 453

Psalm 49 **4**:359, 370, 434, 442

Psalm 50 **4**:357, 362, 364, 370, 384, 387, 395, 405, 434, 440

Psalm 51 **4**:364, 373, 375, 383, 385, 387, 406-07, 426-28, 431-32, 434, 446

Psalm 52 **4**:359, 446

Psalm 53 **4**:389

Psalm 54 **4**:446, 448, 450

Psalm 55 **4**:350, 448

Psalm 56 **4**:446, 450

Psalm 57 **4**:372, 405, 433, 441, 446, 448-49

Psalm 59 **4**:359, 446, 450

Psalm 60 **4**:359, 368, 381, 387, 446, 449

Psalm 61 **4**:357, 359, 368, 385, 442

Psalm 62 **4**:354, 359, 401

Psalm 63 **4**:359, 368, 378, 385, 405-06

Psalm 64 **4**:359

Psalm 65 **4**:359, 405, 407, 434

Psalm 66 **4**:359, 381-82, 387, 389, 406, 413, 434, 441, 450

Psalm 67 **4**:357

Psalm 68 **4**:357, 369, 372-73, 377, 395, 404, 406-08, 440-42, 450, 453

Psalm 69 **4**:351, 359, 365, 382, 386, 394, 427, 432-33, 441, 448, 450

Psalm 70 **4**:433, 449

Psalm 71 **4**:359

Psalm 72 **4**:345, 365, 373, 384, 421, 439

Psalm 73 **4**:347, 362, 364, 387, 389, 434

Psalm 74 **4**:381, 385, 432

Psalm 76 **4**:357, 362, 400-01

Psalm 77 **4**:354, 440

Psalm 78 **4**:362, 369, 393, 442, 447

Psalm 79 **4**:381, 385, 432, 434

Psalm 80 **4**:369, 381, 385

Psalm 81 **4**:395, 401, 405, 407, 434, 438, 440, 442

Psalm 82 **4**:370, 385

Psalm 83 **4**:385

Psalm 84 **4**:368, 378, 385, 405-06

Psalm 85 **4**:359, 385, 387, 450

Psalm 86 **4**:359, 389, 406, 434, 440

Psalm 87 **4**:357, 368, 373, 408

Psalm 88 **4**:359, 382-83, 386, 432-34, 437, 440, 443, 454

Psalm 89 **4**:368, 381, 384-85, 401, 447

Psalm 90 **4**:356, 368, 374, 377, 389, 411, 434, 440

Psalm 91 **4**:359, 368, 377, 434, 452

Psalm 92 **4**:377, 379

Psalm 93 **4**:353, 369, 409, 434, 450

Psalm 94 **4**:353, 359, 378-79, 381, 386, 391, 451

Psalm 95 **4**:380, 440, 442, 446

Psalm 96 **4**:357, 381, 389, 421, 434, 445, 449

Psalm 97 **4**:353, 387, 405, 434, 454

Psalm 98 **4**:381, 441

Psalm 99 **4**:357, 441

Psalm 100 **4**:380-81, 383, 434, 442

Psalm 101 **4**:357, 384

Psalm 102 **4**:373-74, 382, 440, 448, 450

Psalm 103 **4**:359, 364, 368, 377-78, 381, 385, 387, 390, 427, 434, 449

Psalm 104 **4**:368, 379, 381, 385, 387, 393, 395, 398, 414-16, 434, 441

Psalm 105 **4**:345, 353, 369, 381, 385, 401, 442, 445, 449

Psalm 106 **4**:345, 369, 383, 390, 401, 439, 445, 449

Psalm 107 **4**:345, 377, 383, 450, 453

Psalm 108 **4**:368, 449-50

Psalm 109 **4**:359, 386, 391, 434

Psalm 110 **4**:357, 365-66, 368, 384

Psalm 111 **4**:357, 449

Psalm 112 **4**:434, 449

Psalm 113 **4**:357, 369, 382, 434, 441

Psalm 114 **4**:345, 353, 357, 368, 427, 434

Psalm 115 **4**:359, 443, 449

Psalm 116 **4**:359, 382, 390, 408

Psalm 117 **4**:434

Psalm 118 **4**:345, 347, 359, 369, 377, 383, 406-08, 413, 439, 442, 450

Psalm 119 **4**:359, 367, 376, 390, 393-94, 428, 434, 442, 449-50

Psalm 120 **4**:350, 357, 368, 450, 455

Psalm 121 **4**:368, 373, 387, 418, 452

Psalm 122 **4**:345, 375, 395, 439, 447

Psalm 123 **4**:386

Psalm 124 **4**:434

Psalm 125 **4**:395

Psalm 126 **4**:345, 358, 379, 385, 387

Psalm 127 **4**:357, 373

Psalm 128 **4**:387

Psalm 129 **4**:353, 357, 382

Psalm 130 **4**:386, 434, 440

Psalm 131 **4**:359, 386, 434

Psalm 132 **4**:359, 368, 373, 384, 386, 406, 447

Psalm 133 **4**:356, 392, 428, 434

Psalm 134 **4**:368, 378, 380, 407, 450

Psalm 135 **4**:434, 439, 449-50

Psalm 136 **4**:352, 368, 383

Psalm 137 **4**:358, 393-94, 418, 422, 434, 446

Psalm 138 **4**:359, 382, 450

Psalm 139 **4**:359, 364, 366, 378-79, 393, 411,

437
Psalm 140 **4**:359
Psalm 142 **4**:359, 446
Psalm 143 **4**:434, 455
Psalm 144 **4**:374, 377, 384, 443, 447, 449
Psalm 145 **4**:359, 434, 449
Psalm 146 **4**:369, 391, 434
Psalm 147 **4**:391, 397, 434
Psalm 148 **4**:398, 434, 441
Psalm 149 **4**:372, 385, 391, 434, 440
Psalm 150 **4**:357, 369, 405, 421, 434, 438, 441, 443, 450
Psalm Book
   See *Tehillim*
Psalms
   See *Tehillim*
"Psalms of David"
   See *Tehillim*
Psalter
   See *Tehillim*
Pseudologista (Lucian) **32**:13-14, 26
Pseudolus (Plautus) **24**:170-71, 173, 175, 179-81, 183, 196, 208, 243, 263-64, 271, 278
Pseudoria (Euclid) **25**:1-86, 90, 94, 104
Psophodes (Menander) **9**:203
Psterior Analytics (Aristotle) **31**:242, 267, 292, 314-15, 318-21, 327
Psychology (Avicenna) **16**:166-68
De pudicitia (Tertullian)
   See *On Modesty*
Purgatorio (Petrarch) **20**:216
Purgatory (Marie de France)
   See *L'Espurgatoire Saint Patrice*
The Purgatory of St. Patrick (Marie de France)
   See *L'Espurgatoire Saint Patrice*
The Purpose of Life (Epicurus) **21**:72-3, 75
Pyth. III (Pindar)
   See *Pythian 3*
Pyth. X (Pindar)
   See *Pythian 10*
Pyth XI (Pindar)
   See *Pythian 11*
Pythian XII (Pindar)
   See *Pythian 12*
Pythian 1 (Pindar) **12**:260, 267, 273, 295-96, 298-99, 304-05, 309, 319, 323, 335, 338, 347, 349, 354, 356-57, 359, 361, 364, 366-67, 376, 378-80, 382-84
Pythian 2 (Pindar) **12**:269, 274, 298, 302, 306-07, 317, 319, 352, 355, 360, 364, 366, 378-81, 383-84
Pythian 3 (Pindar) **12**:264, 270, 278, 298-99, 306, 313, 340, 346, 354, 364-65, 367, 369, 376, 378-80, 382-83
Pythian 4 (Pindar) **12**:272, 296, 298-99, 304-05, 312, 320-22, 326, 343, 354, 375-79, 382
Pythian 5 (Pindar) **12**:271, 296-97, 307, 317, 320, 353, 357, 376-80, 382
Pythian 6 (Pindar) **12**:267, 273, 296, 319, 337, 353-54, 363-64, 377, 379
Pythian 7 (Pindar) **12**:317, 325, 353, 359, 361-62, 383
Pythian 8 (Pindar) **12**:272, 288, 297, 300, 304, 309, 314, 320, 323, 326, 337-38, 349, 356, 359-60, 362, 365, 378-80, 382-84
Pythian 9 (Pindar) **12**:264, 283, 313, 320, 322, 356, 366, 368-69, 372
Pythian 10 (Pindar) **12**:263, 270, 303, 312-13, 318, 322, 325, 334, 337, 343, 357, 365-66, 371, 377-79, 383-84
Pythian 11 (Pindar) **12**:263, 270, 274, 322, 326, 347, 352-53, 356, 365-66, 379, 382, 384
Pythian XII (Pindar)
   See *Pythian 12*
Pythian 12 (Pindar) **12**:271, 319, 353, 363, 367

Pythian Odes 10 (Pindar)
   See *Pythian 10*
Qasim al-surur wa'ayn al-hayat (Biruni) **28**:176
Quaestiones disputatas de veritate (Aquinas)
   See *Disputed Questions*
Quaestiones evangeliorum (Augustine) **6**:68, 94
Quaestiones Naturales (Seneca)
   See *Naturales quaestiones*
Quaestiones super libros i-vi Physicorum Aristotelis (Bacon) **14**:49, 66
Quaestiones super octos libros Physicorum (William of Ockham) **32**:145, 150
De quantitate animae (Augustine) **6**:68
"Quatre Dols" (Marie de France)
   See *"Le Chaitivel"*
Quatuor oraciones (Saint Birgitta of Sweden) **24**:93, 97, 101, 158
Queen Arsinoe (Callimachus) **18**:5-6
"Quel c'ha nostra natura in se piu degno" (Petrarch) **20**:333
Questio Quodlibetis (Aquinas)
   See *Quodlibets*
Questions and Answers on the Subject of Knowledge
   See *Kitab al-Masail wa l-jawabat fi l-marifah*
Questions of Truth (Aquinas) **33**:56, 60
Questions on Aristotle (Bacon)
   See *Quaestiones super libros i-vi Physicorum Aristotelis*
Questions on Aristotle's Physics (Bacon)
   See *Quaestiones super libros i-vi Physicorum Aristotelis*
Questions on Genesis (Jerome) **30**:56
Questions on Genesis (Jerome)
   See *Liber Hebraicarum Quaestionum in Genesim*
Quodlibeta (William of Ockham) **32**:131, 138-41, 165, 206
Quodlibets (Aquinas) **33**:31, 33, 43, 93, 95
The Qur'an
   See *The Koran*
Raghuvamsa (Kalidasa) **9**:82, 84-5, 89-91, 102, 115, 118-19, 121, 125-26, 138
"Raising a Cup of Wine to Query the Moon" (Li Po) **2**:166
"The Rajah's Diamond" **2**:36
Ransom of Hector (Aeschylus) **11**:125, 193
The Rape of the Locks (Menander)
   See *Perikeiromene*
"The Rat and the Frog" (Aesop) **24**:44
Razón de amor **16**:336-376
Razón de amor con los denuestos del agua y el vino
   See *Razón de amor*
Rbaiyyat (Khayyam)
   See *Rubáiyát*
De re militari (Cato) **21**:40, 47-8
De re rustica (Cato)
   See *De re rustica*
"Ready for a Drink" (Li Po) **2**:166
Real and Assumed Superiority and a Condemnation of Arrogance
   See *Al-Nubl wa l-tannabbal wa-dhamm al-kibr*
De Rebus Metallicis (Albert the Great) **16**:18
Record of Rites (Confucius)
   See *Li Chi*
Records of Ancient Matters
   See *Kojiki*
"The Red Cliff" (Su Shih)
   See *"Rhymeprose on the Red Cliff"*
Rede der Unterscheidungen (Eckhart) **9**:35, 42
"Refrain of the Great Song" (Po Chu-i) **24**:349
Refutation (John) **27**:57

"Reg. Br." (Basil of Caesaria) **35**:96
"Reg. Resp." (Basil of Caesaria) **35**:22
De Regismine Principum (Aquinas) **33**:22-25, 27
Regula (Benedict, Saint)
   See *Rule of St. Benedict*
"Regulae" (Basil of Caesaria) **35**:16, 22
"Rejoicing at Elder Brother Ch'en's Arrival" (Po Chu-i) **24**:322
Religion (Epicurus) **21**:73
Remedia Amoris (Ovid) **7**:344-46, 353, 377, 379, 398, 429, 440, 444
Remedia studii (Bacon) **14**:62
Remedies of Love (Ovid)
   See *Remedia Amoris*
De remediis utriusque fortunae (Petrarch) **20**:213-14, 261-62, 290-91, 308, 312, 326
"Remembering Golden Bells (Who Died at Three)" (Po Chu-i) **24**:352
Renderings from the Dewan of Khwaja Shamsu'ddin Mahamad Hafiz Shirazi (Hafiz)
   See *Diwan-i Hafiz*
Replies Concerning the Imamate
   See *Jawabat fi-imamah*
Reportatio (William of Ockham) **32**:138-39, 209
The Republic (Cicero)
   See *De republica*
Republic (Plato) **8**:206, 211, 217, 219, 223, 225-28, 232-33, 236, 239, 241, 243-44, 246, 248-50, 252-53, 255, 259-61, 263-68, 270, 276-83, 285, 287, 290-92, 294, 299, 305-06, 308-11, 313, 317, 322, 324-25, 328-29, 331, 339-48, 352, 357-58, 363-64
De republica (Cicero) **3**:177-78, 194, 200-01, 211-12, 214, 221, 225-26, 232, 244, 249-51, 254, 256-57, 285, 288, 296-98
De rerum generatione ex elementis (Bacon) **14**:62
Rerum memorandarum libri (Petrarch) **20**:256, 286-87, 290
Rerum vulgarium fragmenta (Petrarch)
   See *Canzoniere*
De Resurrectione (Albert the Great) **16**:118, 125
De resurrectione mortuorum (Tertullian)
   See *On the Resurrection of the Flesh*
Retractiones (Augustine) **6**:9, 32, 116
"Returning Late and Feeling Sad" (Po Chu-i) **24**:354
"Returning to the Fields" (Po Chu-i) **24**:326
Revelation concerning Purgatory (Rolle) **21**:299
Revelationes (Saint Birgitta of Sweden) **24**:97, 125-26, 134, 156-64
Revelationes extravagantes (Saint Birgitta of Sweden) **24**:92-93, 95-97, 158
Revelations Celestes (Saint Birgitta of Sweden) **24**:90
Reysen und Wenderschafften duch des Gelobte Land (Mandeville)
   See *Mandeville's Travels*
"Rhapsody of Remorse" (Li Po) **2**:169
Rhesus (Euripides) **23**:121, 123-25, 173
Rhetoric (Aristotle) **31**:87, 98, 220-301, 305-06, 355-56
Rhetoric (Epicurus) **21**:119
Rhetorica (Cicero)
   See *De inventione*
Rhetorum Praeceptor (Lucian)
   See *A Professor of Public Speaking*
"Rhymeprose on the Red Cliff" (Su Shih) **15**:382, 385, 398, 419, 421-24
Rime (Petrarch)
   See *Canzoniere*
Rime disperse (Petrarch) **20**:327, 333-34
Rime in vitae e morte Madonna Laura (Petrarch)

20:214, 217, 249
Rime sparse (Petrarch)
    See *Canzoniere*
Risalah fi Fadilat sinaat al-kalem **25**:330
Risalah fi l-Nabitah **25**:329
Risalah ila Ahmad b. Abi Daud yukhbiruh fiha bi-Kitab al Futya **25**:329
Risalat al-Adwiyyah (Avicenna) **16**:147
Risalat al-Maad wa l-maash fi l-adab watabir al-nas wa-muamalatihim **25**:332
Risalat al-Qiyan
    See *Kitab al-Qiyan*
Rituals (Confucius)
    See *Li Chi*
Rivals (Plato) **8**:305, 311
Riyadat al-fikr wa'l-'aql (Biruni) **28**:176
Robbers' Tricks
    See *Hiyal al-lusas*
"Rock of Yen-yu" (Su Shih) **15**:387
"De Rollone et eius uxore" (Map) **32**:122
Roman
    See *Le Roman de la Rose*
The Roman Calendar (Ovid)
    See *Fasti*
Le Roman de la Rose **8**:374-453
Roman Psalter (Jerome) **30**:79
The Romance
    See *Le Roman de la Rose*
The Romance of the Rose
    See *Le Roman de la Rose*
Romanz de la Rose
    See *Le Roman de la Rose*
Rood
    See *The Dream of the Rood*
Rope (Plautus)
    See *Rudens*
Rosciana (Cicero)
    See *Pro Roscio Amerino*
Rose
    See *Le Roman de la Rose*
"Rose and Nightingale" (Hafiz) **34**:
"Rose in Bloom" **2**:23
Rtusamhara (Kalidasa) **9**:89-90, 103-05, 107
Ruba'iyat (Khayyam)
    See *Rubáiyát*
Rubáiyát (Khayyam) **11**:228-309
Ruba'iyat (Rumi) **20**:352-53, 371
Rudens (Plautus) **24**:170-73, 175-77, 181, 183, 187-89, 233, 240, 257-59
Rule for Monks (Benedict, Saint)
    See *Rule of St. Benedict*
Rule of St. Benedict (Benedict, Saint) **29**:7-21, 23-26, 28-39, 43, 52, 54-60, 64, 67-80, 82, 84-85, 88, 90-91
The Runaways (Lucian) **32**:8, 14, 16, 24-25, 48-49
Rycharde Rolle Hermyte of Hampull in his contemplacyons of the drede and loue of god (Rolle) **21**:278
Sacra parallela (John) **27**:48
Sacred Treatises (Boethius)
    See *Theological Tractates*
De Sacrificiis (Lucian)
    See *On Sacrifices*
De Sacrificio Missae (Albert the Great) **16**:42
"Saif El-Mulûk" **2**:43
Sakuntala (Kalidasa)
    See *Abhijñana-sakuntala*
Salticae Fabulae (Lucan) **33**:422
"A Salutation of Jesus" (Rolle) **21**:367, 372
Samia (Menander) **9**:205-06, 211, 213, 215, 217, 220-21, 224, 238, 246, 249, 252-53, 255, 257-61, 264, 269-72, 275-78, 281, 287-88

The Samian Woman (Menander)
    See *Samia*
Sarva-darsana-siddhantasangraha (Sankara) **32**:390
Satira (Petronius)
    See *Satyricon*
Satirarium libri (Petronius)
    See *Satyricon*
"Satire Agaimst Three Disinherited Lords" (Sordello) **15**:276
Satires (Juvenal) **8**:7, 14, 19, 22, 27-8, 59-60, 66, 68-9, 73-8
Satiricon (Petronius)
    See *Satyricon*
Satiricum (Petronius)
    See *Satyricon*
Saturicon (Petronius)
    See *Satyricon*
Saturnalia (Lucan) **33**:422
Saturnalia (Lucian) **32**:8, 15, 18, 48
Satyra (Petronius)
    See *Satyricon*
Satyrici libri (Petronius)
    See *Satyricon*
Satyricon (Petronius) **34**:248-427
"Saying Farewell to the Children at Nanling as I Leave for the Capital" (Li Po) **2**:174
"The Scavenger and the Noble Lady" **2**:40
De schematibus et tropis sacrae scripturae (Bede) **20**:42,93
Schionatulander (Wolfram von Eschenbach)
    See *Titurel*
Scientia (Aquinas) **33**:114
De scientia experimentali (Bacon) **14**:5, 80
De Scientia Perspectiva (Bacon) **14**:20, 47
Scipio's Dream (Cicero)
    See *Somnium Scipionis*
Scite Teipsum (Abelard)
    See *Scito Te Ipsum*
Scito Te Ipsum (Abelard) **11**:5, 10, 12, 16, 20, 24, 49, 51, 53, 54, 57, 68
Scivias (Hildegard von Bingen) **20**:132-33, 135-37, 143, 153, 161-63, 168, 172-75, 178, 182-86
Scorpiace (Tertullian) **29**:312, 329-30, 332, 334-38
Scripta Super Sententias (Albert the Great)
    See *Commentary on the Book of the Sentences*
Scriptum Principale (Bacon) **14**:15
The Seasons (Kalidasa)
    See *Rtusamhara*
Second Alcibiades (Plato)
    See *Alcibiades II*
Second Olympian (Pindar)
    See *Olympian 2*
Second Olynthiac (Demosthenes)
    See *Olynthiac II*
Second Philippic (Cicero)
    See *Philippics*
Second Philippic (Demosthenes)
    See *Philippic II*
Second Pythian (Pindar)
    See *Pythian 2*
De secreto conflictu curarum mearum (Petrarch) **20**:318
Secretum (Petrarch) **20**:212, 214, 243-44, 246, 250, 258, 261-63, 266, 272, 279, 287, 290, 294, 299, 303, 323, 326-27
Sectio Canonis (Euclid) **25**:1-86, 99, 110, 205-20, 245-258
"Seeing Off the Spring" (Po Chu-i) **24**:347
"Seeing off Wei Wan, Recluse of Wang-wu Mountain, on His Trip Home" (Li Po) **2**:168

"Segrek Son of Ushun Koja" **8**:103
Sei Shonagon ga Makura-no-Soshi (Sei Shonagon)
    See *Makura no soshi*
Sei Shonagon's Pillow Book (Sei Shonagon)
    See *Makura no soshi*
Seishu (Izumi Shikibu)
    See *Izumi Shikibu seishu*
"Seizure" (Sappho)
    See "Ode to Anactoria"
Select Apophthegums (Epicurus) **21**:122
Select Odes (Hafiz) **34**:56
Self-Punishment (Terence)
    See *Heautontimoreumenos*
"Self-Realization" (Po Chu-i) **24**:346
The Self-Tormentor (Terence)
    See *Heautontimoreumenos*
De senectute (Cicero) **3**:193, 195, 202, 204, 227, 231, 288
"Senh' En Sordel mandamen" (Sordello) **15**:362
De Sensu (Aristotle) **31**:65, 332, 359
De sensu et sensato (Albert the Great) **16**:61, 106, 110
Sentences (Albert the Great)
    See *Commentary on the Book of the Sentences*
Sentences (William of Ockham)
    See *Commentary on the Sentences*
Septem (Aeschylus)
    See *Seven against Thebes*
Sermo angelicus (Saint Birgitta of Sweden) **24**:101, 129, 158
Sermon on St. John the Baptist (Abelard) **11**:66
Seven against Thebes (Aeschylus) **11**:77, 83-5, 88, 96, 102-03, 107, 111, 113, 117, 119, 124, 127, 133-35, 137-39, 142, 151-54, 156, 159, 167, 173, 179, 181, 184, 194, 200, 205, 207, 217
Seven before Thebes (Aeschylus)
    See *Seven against Thebes*
Seventh Epistle (Plato)
    See *Seventh Letter*
Seventh Isthmian (Pindar)
    See *Isthmian 7*
Seventh Letter (Plato) **8**:222, 305-06, 334, 338-41, 349
Seventh Nemean (Pindar)
    See *Nemean 7*
The Sham Eunich (Terence)
    See *Eunuchus*
Shearing of Glycera (Menander)
    See *Perikeiromene*
"The Shepherd's Boy and the Wolf" (Aesop) **24**:66
The Shield (Menander)
    See *Aspis*
Shield of Heracles (Hesiod)
    See *Shield of Herakles*
Shield of Herakles (Hesiod) **5**:74, 82-83, 118, 174
Shih (Confucius)
    See *Shih Ching*
Shih Chi (Confucius) **19**:21, 84
Shih Ching (Confucius) **19**:6, 19, 21, 29, 31, 34-35, 38-39, 46, 51
Shih King (Confucius)
    See *Shih Ching*
Shinkombon (Izumi Shikibu) **33**:278
The Ship (Lucian) **32**:43-44, 47-48
Shorn Lady (Menander)
    See *Perikeiromene*
Short Treatise in Praise of Dante (Boccaccio)
    See *Trattatello in lode di Dante*
"Shorter Interrogation" (Basil of Caesaria) **35**:96
The Short-Haired Lass (Menander)

Title Index

See *Perikeiromene*
Shoulder Bite (Chretien de Troyes) **10**:232
Shu (Confucius)
 See *Shu Ching*
Shu Ching (Confucius) **19**:6, 9, 19-20, 28, 34-35, 38, 46, 67
Shu King (Confucius)
 See *Shu Ching*
"Si co'l malaus ge no se sap gardar" (Sordello) **15**:363
Sic et Non (Abelard) **11**:4, 7, 9, 10, 14, 16, 21, 24, 27, 31, 48, 66
"Sighing over Mr Ch'ang" (Po Chu-i) **24**:353
"Sighing over White Hairs neath the Cherry Blossoms" (Po Chu-i) **24**:361
"Sighs over Getting Old" (Po Chu-i) **24**:345
"Signor mio caro" (Petrarch) **20**:334
The Sikyonian (Menander)
 See *Sikyonios*
Sikyonios (Menander) **9**:260, 269-70, 278, 288
Silvae (Lucan) **33**:422
De sinderesi (Albert the Great) **16**:49
"Singing Alone in the Mountains" (Po Chu-i) **24**:330
"Singing of Indolence" (Po Chu-i) **24**:310
Sir Gawain and The Green Knight **2**:181-287
"*Sirmio*" (Catullus)
 See "*Poem 31*"
Sisyphus (Aeschylus) **11**:123
Sivanamlyastakam (Sankara) **32**:390
Sivanandalahari (Sankara) **32**:390
Sivaparadha-ksamapana-stotra (Sankara) **32**:390
Sixth Isthmian (Pindar)
 See *Isthmian 6*
Sixth Nemean (Pindar)
 See *Nemean 6*
Sixth Olympian (Pindar)
 See *Olympian 6*
Sixth Paean (Pindar)
 See *Paean 6*
Sixth Pythian (Pindar)
 See *Pythian 6*
Slander (Lucian) **32**:39
"Sleeper Awakened" **2**:20
"Sleeping at Noon" (Po Chu-i) **24**:340
A Slip of the Tongue in Greeting (Lucian) **32**:39
Slovo o polku Igoreve **1**:477-530
"Small Asceticon" (Basil of Caesaria) **35**:91
"Snake and the Crab" (Aesop) **24**:23
"The Snow of Southern Ch'in" (Po Chu-i) **24**:358
Soliloquia (Augustine) **6**:53, 62, 68-9, 90, 126
Soliloquies (Augustine)
 See *Soliloquia*
Soliloquy (Abelard) **11**:67
Somnium (Lucian)
 See *The Dream, or Lucan's Career*
Somnium Scipionis (Cicero) **3**:181, 200, 211, 289, 293-95
De somno et vigilia (Albert the Great) **16**:7, 61, 110
"Song Before Drinking" (Li Po) **2**:140
"Song of Ch'ang-kan" (Li Po) **2**:144
The Song of Ivor's Campaign
 See *Slovo o polku Igoreve*
"A Song of Love-Longing to Jesus" (Rolle) **21**:367-69, 374
"Song of Lu-shan" (Li Po) **2**:144
"Song of Maldon"
 See "The Battle of Maldon"
The Song of Roland
 See *La Chanson de Roland*
Song of Songs **18**:199-316
"Song of the Cranes" (Su Shih) **15**:382

"Song of the Heavenly Horse" (Li Po) **2**:144-156
Song of the Lord
 See *Bhagavadgita*
Song of the Lord
 See *Bhagavad Gita*
"A Song of the Love of Jesus" (Rolle) **21**:367, 369, 372
"Song of the Roosting Crows" (Li Po) **2**:140, 157-58
"Song of the Stone Drums" (Su Shih) **15**:410
Song of Troy (Lucan)
 See *Iliacon*
"Song of Unending Sorrow" (Po Chu-i)
 See "Lament Everlasting"
Songs for a Chorus of Maidens (Pindar)
 See *Partheneia*
Songs for Dancing (Pindar)
 See *Hyporcemata*
"Songs of Ch'in" (Po Chu-i) **24**:293, 295, 299, 301
"Songs of the Marches" (Li Po) **2**:132
Sonnets from Hafiz and Other Verses (Hafiz) **34**:67
Sophist (Plato) **8**:258-60, 282, 306, 309-10, 321-22, 333-34, 338, 359, 361
Sophistici Elenchi (Aristotle) **31**:66, 242
Sophistics (Aristotle)
 See *Sophistici Elenchi*
Soul Conductors (Aeschylus)
 See *Spirit-Raisers*
Sources of Knowledge (John) **27**:43, 50, 57, 67
"A Southern Lake in Late Autumn" (Po Chu-i) **24**:337
"De Sp. Sancto" (Basil of Caesaria) **35**:21, 31, 94, 97, 110
"Sparrow Song" (Li Po) **2**:138
Spectacula (Martial)
 See *Liber Spectaculorum*
De Spectaculis (Tertullian)
 See *On Shows*
Spectaculorum Liber (Martial)
 See *Liber Spectaculorum*
De Speculis (Euclid) **25**:1-86, 200
Speech Is Better than Silence
 See *Tafdil al-nutq ala l-samt*
Sphekes (Aristophanes) **4**:44-5, 62, 65, 67, 93-4, 110, 125-26, 130-31, 134, 144, 149, 152, 154, 159, 162, 165-66
Sphinx (Aeschylus) **11**:159
Spirit-Raisers (Aeschylus) **11**:124
De Spiritu et Anima (Albert the Great) **16**:128
De spiritu et respiratione (Albert the Great) **16**:61
"De Spiritu Sancto" (Basil of Caesaria)
 See "De Sp. Sancto"
De Spiritus Creatur (Aquinas) **33**:95
"Spirto gentil" (Petrarch) **20**:241
Spring and Autumn (Confucius)
 See *Ch'un Ch'iu*
Spring and Autumn Annals (Confucius)
 See *Ch'un Ch'iu*
The Square and the Circle
 See *Kitab al-Tarbi wa l-Tadwir*
The Square and the Round
 See *Kitab al-Tarbi wa l-Tadwir*
St. Benedict's Rule (Benedict, Saint)
 See *Rule of St. Benedict*
St. Patrick's Purgatory (Marie de France)
 See *L'Espurgatoire Saint Patrice*
State (Cicero)
 See *De republica*
"Statement of Resolutions after Being Drunk on a Spring Day" (Li Po) **2**:132

Statesman (Plato)
 See *Politikos*
De statibus (Hermogenes)
 See *On Stases*
The Stewartis Orygynalle (Barbour) **33**:156, 159
Stichus (Plautus) **24**:170-72, 175, 233, 239, 247
"Stomach and Feet" (Aesop) **24**:36
"The Story of Bamsi Beyrek"
 See "Bamsi-Beyrek"
"The Story of Basat Who Killed Depegöz"
 See "How Basat Killed Goggle-eye"
"The Story of Basat Who Kills the One-Eyed Giant"
 See "How Basat Killed Goggle-eye"
The Story of Burnt Njal
 See *Njáls saga*
Story of Calamities (Abelard)
 See *Historia Calamitatum*
"The Story of Deli Dumril"
 See "Wild Dumril Son of Dukha Koja"
"The Story of Emrem" **8**:108
Story of His Misfortunes (Abelard)
 See *Historia Calamitatum*
The Story of Igor's Campaign
 See *Slovo o polku Igoreve*
"The Story of Kan Turali"
 See "Kan Turali Son of Kanli Koja"
"The Story of Ma'aruf" **2**:39
"The Story of the Captivity of Salur Kazan" **8**:108
The Story of the Grail (Chretien de Troyes)
 See *Perceval*
"The Story of the House of SalurKazan"
 See "The Plunder of the Home of Salur-Kazan"
The Story of the Oghuzname—the Oghuz
 See *Kitabi-i Dedem Qorkut*
Stromata (Origen)
 See *Stromateis*
Stromateis (Origen) **19**:186, 201, 203, 205, 215
Subtilitates naturarum diversarum creaturarum (Hildegard von Bingen) **20**:153, 183
Sum of Techology (Aquinas)
 See *Summa Theologica*
Summa contra Gentiles (Aquinas) **33**:10, 37, 108, 110, 114, 119-20
Summa de Bono (Albert the Great) **16**:31
Summa de creaturis (Albert the Great) **16**:26, 31, 42, 86, 103, 107-08, 112
Summa de homine (Albert the Great) **16**:31, 112-13
"Summa Juris" (Sordello) **15**:338
Summa logicae (William of Ockham) **32**:130, 134, 146, 152-53, 155-56, 162, 206, 209
Summa of Theology (Aquinas)
 See *Summa Theologica*
Summa Theologiae (Albert the Great)
 See *Summa Theologica*
Summa Theologica (Albert the Great) **16**:7, 14, 16, 26, 28, 30, 32, 36, 39, 42, 93-4, 104, 108-11, 121
Summa Theologica (Aquinas) **33**:20, 26, 31, 36-37, 43, 48, 52, 56-60, 62, 92-96, 100-16, 119-36
Summa Totius Logicae (William of Ockham) **32**:182
Super apocalypsim (Rolle) **21**:390, 394, 396-97
Super canticum canticorum (Rolle) **21**:393, 396-97
Super lectiones mortuorum (Rolle) **21**:389, 392
Super Oratione Dominica (Eckhart) **9**:42
Super orationem dominicam (Rolle) **21**:389
Super psalmum vicesimum (Rolle) **21**:390, 393
Super symbolum apostolorum (Rolle) **21**:389
Super symbolum S. Anthanasii (Rolle) **21**:389

Super threnos Ieremiae (Rolle) **21**:389-90
*The Superiority of the House of Hashim to That of
    Abd Shams*
    See *Fadl Hashim ala Abd Shams*
The Superstitious Man (Menander) **9**:214
Suppliant Maidens (Aeschylus)
    See *Suppliants*
Suppliant Women (Aeschylus)
    See *Suppliants*
The Suppliant Women (Euripides) **23**:110-12,
    123, 125-28, 174-76, 182, 184-85, 206, 209
Suppliants (Aeschylus) **11**:88, 101-02, 108, 110-
    11, 116-18, 123, 127, 133-40, 148, 150, 152-
    53, 156, 158-60, 175, 178-79, 180-81,
    183-84, 190-91, 193-95, 198, 201, 205, 207-
    09, 211, 216-17
Suppliants (Euripides)
    See *The Suppliant Women*
Supplices (Aeschylus)
    See *Suppliants*
Surface-Loci (Euclid) **25**:1-86, 97-8, 108
"The Swallow and the Other Birds" (Marie de
    France) **8**:174
Symmories (Demosthenes)
    See *On the Symmories*
Symphonia (Hildegard von Bingen) **20**:153
Symposium (Epicurus) **21**:70, 73-4
Symposium (Plato) **8**:210, 234-35, 254-55, 259,
    265-66, 270, 280, 283, 305-07, 310, 317,
    330-31, 355-56, 358-59, 361, 363-69
Symposium (Xenophon) **17**:345, 346
Synaristosai (Menander) **9**:270
The Syrian Goddess (Lucian) **32**:25-27, 40-41
"The Szechwan Road" (Li Po) **2**:138
De tabernaculo (Bede) **20**:89
Tactics (Polybius) **17**:168
Tafdil al-nutq ala l-samt **25**:332
Tafsir ma ba'd al-tabi'ah (Averroes) **7**:64-5, 67
Tahafut (Averroes)
    See *Tahafut al-tahafut*
Tahafut al-tahafut (Averroes) **7**:16, 21, 24-6, 30,
    42, 68, 71
Tahafut at-tahafut (Averroes)
    See *Tahafut al-tahafut*
Tain Bo Cuailnge
    See *Tain Bo Cualnge*
Tain Bo Cualnge **30**:145-240
Taittiriya Upanisads (Sankara) **32**:336, 342, 358,
    359, 362
The Tale of Genji (Shikibu)
    See *Genji Monogatari*
The Tale of Igor's Campaign
    See *Slovo o polku Igoreve*
Talkhis (Averroes) **7**:63-5
Talks of Instruction (Eckhart) **9**:56-7
"De Tantalo" (Map) **32**:122
Tao te Ching (Lao Tzu) **7**:116-213
Tao-teh ching (Lao Tzu)
    See *Tao te Ching*
The Teachings of Honor (Sordello)
    See *Ensegnamen d'Onor*
Tehillim **4**:342-456
Telephus (Euripides) **23**:158, 174, 182
Temora (Ossian) **28**:286, 303, 305, 308-09, 311,
    321, 326, 328-29, 334-35, 337-38, 348, 351,
    359-61, 364, 367, 371-72, 378-80
"Temple Inscription for Han Wen-kung at Ch'ao-
    chou" (Su Shih) **15**:399
De temporibus (Bede) **20**:34, 43-4, 49, 66, 75,
    78, 121
De temporibus meis (Cicero) **3**:198
De temporum ratione (Bede) **20**:34, 49, 66, 75,
    78, 91, 93, 120-21

"The Temptation" (Caedmon) **7**;91
Tenth Nemean (Pindar)
    See *Nemean 10*
Tenth Olympian (Pindar)
    See *Olympian 10*
Tenth Pythian (Pindar)
    See *Pythian 10*
Tereus (Sophocles) **2**:348
De termino Paschali (Bacon) **14**:63
"The Terraced Road of the Two-Edged Sword
    Mountains" (Li Po) **2**:132
Teseida (Boccaccio) **13**:9, 29, 32-3, 44-5, 62,
    65, 87, 102-14
Testimony of the Soul (Tertullian) **29**:312
Tetrapla (Origen) **19**:184
Thais (Menander) **9**:237
"That God is not the author of evil" (Basil of
    Caesaria) **35**:77
Theaetetus (Plato) **8**:221-22, 254-55, 259, 264,
    284, 306, 309-10, 321, 361
Theages (Plato) **8**:305, 311
Thebais (Seneca) **6**:339, 342-43
Theogony (Hesiod) **5**:70-5, 77-9, 83, 86-7, 92-6,
    99-100, 102-05, 108-10, 113-18, 121-23,
    128-30, 134-35, 137, 140-43, 145-50, 159-
    68, 170, 173-74
Theologia Christiana (Abelard)
    See *Christian Theology*
Theologia 'Scholiarum' (Abelard) **11**:53, 66
Theologia 'Summi boni' (Abelard) **11**:10, 24, 65,
    66
Theological Tractates (Boethius) **15**:24, 31-33
Theological Treatises (Boethius)
    See *Theological Tractates*
Theology (Abelard)
    See *Christian Theology*
Theophilus (Hroswitha of Gandersheim) **29**:123,
    183
"Thesaurus Thesaurum" (Sordello) **15**:329, 338,
    377
Thesmophoriazusae (Aristophanes) **4**:44, 60-63,
    67-68, 94, 105-06, 110, 113, 116, 124-26,
    130, 137, 145, 150, 152, 155, 161, 163, 175
Third Nemean (Pindar)
    See *Nemean 3*
Third Olympian (Pindar)
    See *Olympian 3*
Third Olynthiac (Demosthenes)
    See *Olynthiac III*
Third Philippic (Demosthenes)
    See *Philippic III*
Third Pythian (Pindar)
    See *Pythian 3*
Thirteenth Olympian (Pindar)
    See *Olympian 13*
The Thousand and One Nights
    See *Alf Layla wa-Layla*
Thracian Women (Aeschylus) **11**:125
The thre Arrows in the Dome (Rolle) **21**:275
Three Bob Day (Plautus)
    See *Trinummus*
"The Three Calenders, Sons of Kings, and the Five
    Ladies of Baghdad" **2**:16, 49, 51, 72
Threnoi (Pindar) **12**:320
"Thy Joy Be in the Love of Jesus" (Rolle) **21**:367-
    69, 374
Thyestes (Seneca) **6**:339-40, 342-43, 366, 368,
    377-81, 389-91, 393, 400, 402-04, 406-10,
    414-15, 418, 426, 428-29, 431-32, 441, 444-
    45
"T'ien Mountain Ascended in a Dream" (Li Po)
    2:144, 164, 166
Timaeus (Plato) **8**:209, 211, 222, 232, 241, 244,

    255, 259-61, 265, 306, 310-11, 317-18, 320,
    323, 325, 328, 332, 341, 349, 351-53, 361-
    63
Timocrates (Epicurus) **21**:119
Timon (Lucian) **32**:17, 48, 50
Titurel (Wolfram von Eschenbach) **5**:301-02,
    314, 317, 323, 325-26, 335, 359, 386, 390-
    91, 429-32
"To a Beautiful Woman on the Road" (Li Po)
    2:144
To His Wife (Tertullian) **29**:312-17
"To Li Yung" (Li Po) **2**:169
To one who said 'You're a Promethius in words
    (Lucian) **32**:32
To Scapula (Tertullian) **29**:311-12, 329-30, 334-
    35
To the Heathen (Tertullian) **29**:310, 312, 329,
    334, 363
To the Martyrs (Tertullian) **29**:311, 312, 338
"To Wang Lun" (Li Po) **2**:143
"To Wei Liang-tsai, Prefect of Chiang-hsia—Writ-
    ten on My Exile to Yen-Lang bythe Grace
    of the Emperor after the Uprising to Express
    Thoughts Arising from Memories of Past
    Travels" (Li Po) **2**:168
Topica (Cicero)
    See *Topica: To Gaius Trebatius*
Topica: To Gaius Trebatius (Cicero) **3**:201, 259-
    60, 263
De topicis differentiis (Boethius) **15**:7, 27, 29,
    88, 129, 131, 136
Topics (Aristotle) **31**:51, 86, 238, 240, 242, 280,
    291, 293, 304-05, 307-09, 312, 317, 320
Topics (Aristotle) **31**:51, 86, 238, 240, 242, 280,
    291, 293, 304-05, 307-09, 312, 317, 320
Topics (Boethius)
    See *De topicis differentiis*
Torah **30**:241-390
"The Tower of Tranquillity" (Su Shih) **15**:383
"The Town Mouse and the Country Mouse"
    (Aesop) **24**:66, 68
Toxaris (Lucian) **32**:22-24, 26, 28, 39
Trachiniae (Sophocles)
    See *The Trakhiniai*
The Trachinian Women (Sophocles)
    See *The Trakhiniai*
Trachinians (Sophocles)
    See *The Trakhiniai*
The Trackers (Sophocles)
    See *Ichneutai*
Tractates (Boethius)
    See *Theological Tractates*
Tractatus de astronomia (Llull) **12**:103-10
Tractatus de Mulitiplicatione Specierum (Bacon)
    14:20, 47, 62-63, 80
Tractatus de natura boni (Albert the Great) **16**:31,
    66, 72-3, 75, 80
Tractatus expositorius enigmatus alchemiae (Ba-
    con) **14**:63-64
Tractatus novus de astronomia (Llull) **12**:110
The Trakhiniai (Sophocles) **2**:289, 294, 296, 300,
    302, 315, 319-20, 322, 324, 338-39, 343-45,
    349-51, 353, 358, 377, 379, 382, 415-16,
    418-19, 422-23
De tranquillitate animi (Seneca) **6**:344, 382, 393
The Transformation of Lucius Apuleius Madeura
    (Apuleius)
    See *Asinus aureus*
The Transformation/Transformations (Ovid)
    See *Metamorphoses*
The Transformations (Apuleius)
    See *Metamorphoses*
Trattatello in lode di Dante (Boccaccio) **13**:51,

101
Travels (Mandeville)
  See *Mandeville's Travels*
Travels of John Mandeville (Mandeville)
  See *Mandeville's Travels*
The Travels of Marco Polo the Venetian (Polo)
  15:251-320
The Treatise of the Transecendent Master of the Void (Lieh Tzu) **27**:92-121
Treatise on the Demons (Origen) **19**:203
Tree of Science (Llull)
  See *Arbor scientiae*
The Tree of the Philosophy of Love (Llull) **12**:122, 131-32
"Le Tresor" (Sordello) **15**:339
"Tress of Berenice" (Catullus)
  See *"Poem 66"*
Trifles of the Court (Map)
  See *De Nugis Curialium*
"Trimalchio's Dinner" (Petronius) **34**:252-53
De Trinitate (Aquinas) **33**:93
De Trinitate (Augustine) **6**:21, 27, 62, 68, 70, 77, 85-7, 90-1, 116, 119-21, 138-40
De trinitate (Boethius) **15**:31-2, 43, 56, 59, 79, 86, 95, 125-30, 136, 141
Trinummus (Plautus) **24**:170-73, 186, 189, 208, 218, 257, 259
Trionfi (Petrarch) **20**:214, 240, 272-73, 307, 327, 335
Trionfo del tempo (Petrarch) **20**:295
Trionfo della morte (Petrarch) **20**:215
Trionfo dell'Eternita (Petrarch) **20**:294, 298
Trip to the Underworld (Lucan)
  See *Catachtonion*
Tristan (Chretien de Troyes)
  See *King Mark and Iseut the Fair*
Tristan and Iseult
  See *Tristan und Isolde*
Tristan and Isolde
  See *Tristan und Isolde*
Tristan und Isolde (Gottfried von Strassburg) **10**:247-48, 250, 254-60, 263-64, 267-68, 274-79, 282-83, 298, 300-01, 303-06
Tristan und Isolt
  See *Tristan und Isolde*
Tristia (Ovid) **7**:291, 293-94, 300, 306, 320-23, 332, 341, 343, 346-47, 349, 376-78, 392, 398, 426, 430, 435, 446
Tristibus (Ovid)
  See *Tristia*
Triumphs (Petrarch)
  See *Trionfi*
Triumphus cupidinis (Petrarch) **20**:334
Troades (Euripides)
  See *Trojan Women*
Troades (Seneca) **6**:340, 342-43, 363, 366-70, 375-80, 389, 413, 415, 425, 428-29, 431-32
Troas (Seneca)
  See *Troades*
Trojan Women (Euripides) **23**:110-11, 121-27, 129-30, 174-77, 182, 184, 201-02, 204-05
The Trojan Women (Seneca)
  See *Troades*
Troy Book (Barbour) **33**:156, 158
Truculentus (Plautus) **24**:170-73, 186, 190, 192-93, 195-96, 198, 200, 216, 218, 220-21, 229-31, 242-43, 272-73
True Discourse of Celsus the Epicurean (Origen) **19**:189
True History (Lucian) **32**:4-7, 15-16, 22-24, 26-28, 32-33, 37-38, 41-42
A True Story (Lucian)
  See *True History*

Tusculan Disputations (Cicero) **3**:177, 183, 193, 196, 202, 211, 242, 255, 274, 287
Tusculans (Cicero)
  See *Tusculan Disputations*
Twelfth Olympian (Pindar)
  See *Olympian 12*
Twelfth Pythian (Pindar)
  See *Pythian 12*
Twin Menaechmi (Plautus)
  See *Menaechmi*
Two Bacchides (Plautus)
  See *Bacchides*
"The Two Jealous Sisters" **2**:45
"The Two Lovers" (Marie de France)
  See "Les Dous Amanz"
"The Two Rats" (Aesop) **24**:19
"The Two Wolves" (Marie de France) **8**:192
The Tyrannicide (Lucian) **32**:39
Tzu Ssu Tzu (Confucius) **19**:20
The Unbridled Mule (Chretien de Troyes)
  See *La Mule sans frein*
Unfinished Work Against Julian (Augustine)
  See *Opus imperfectum contra Julianum*
"The Unfortunate One" (Marie de France)
  See "Le Chaitivel"
de Unitate et Trinitate Divina (Abelard)
  See *Theologia 'Summi boni'*
De unitate Intellectus (Aquinas) **33**:108
Upadesasahasri (Sankara) **32**:358-59, 363, 391
Upadesasahasri, gadyabandha (Sankara) **32**:360
"Upon His Returning Home to Pei-hai, I Respectfully Offer a Farewell Banquet to Reverend Master Kao Ju-Kuei, Gentleman of the Tao after He Transmitted to Me a Register of the Way" (Li Po) **2**:177
Urmuzdyar wa mihryar (Biruni) **28**:176
Urvasi Won by Valor (Kalidasa)
  See *Vikramorvasiya*
De utilitate grammaticae (Bacon) **14**:46, 64
De utilitate mathematicae (Bacon) **14**:5
Uusi Kalevala
  See *Kalevala*
Valerius ad Rufiniam de non ducenda Uxore (Map) **32**:70, 83, 86, 105-06, 114, 116
Valiant Woman (Albert the Great) **16**:29
Vanha Kalevala
  See *Kalevala*
Vatican Fragments (Epicurus) **21**:161
De vegetabilibus (Albert the Great) **16**:20, 36-7, 61, 64
De vera religione (Augustine) **6**:68
Verae Historiae (Lucian)
  See *True History*
"Vergine bella" (Petrarch) **20**:241
De Veritate (Aquinas)
  See *Disputed Questions*
Verrines (Cicero) **3**:196-99, 202, 267, 268, 286
Version from Hafiz (Hafiz) **34**:62
Vetus Romana (Jerome) **30**:80
Victoria Berenices (Callimachus)
  See *Lock of Berenice*
Vikramorvasiya (Kalidasa) **9**:82, 86-8, 90-1, 96-7, 99-100, 102, 125, 131-34, 136-39
"The Village of Chu-Ch'en" (Po Chu-i) **24**:351
Vindication of Ali's Resort to Arbitration
  See *Kitab Taswib Ali fi takhim al-hakamayn*
"Vinse hanibal" (Petrarch) **20**:333
De Virginibus Velandis (Tertullian)
  See *On Veiling Virgins*
De Viris Illustribus (Jerome) **30**:56, 67, 110, 117
De viris illustribus (Petrarch) **20**:237, 256, 260
The Virtues of the Turks
  See *Kitab Manaqib al-Turk wa-ammat jund al-*

khilafah
Vision of St. John (Hroswitha of Gandersheim) **29**:123
"Visit to Gold Mountain Temple" (Su Shih) **15**:410
Visnu-sat-padi (Sankara) **32**:390
De Visu (Euclid)
  See *Optics*
Vita (Hildegard von Bingen) **20**:143, 147-49, 152-54, 167, 176
Vita (Josephus) **13**:217, 220, 222, 235, 239, 249, 253, 255, 263, 265, 268, 270-2, 302, 305, 307-8, 311, 316-8
De vita activa contemplativa (Rolle) **21**:273
Vita di Dante (Boccaccio) **13**:53-4
Vita Hilarionis (Jerome) **30**:109
Vita Malchi monachi captivi (Jerome) **30**:80-82, 104, 109, 133
La vita nuova (Dante) **18**:317-84
Vita Pauli (Jerome) **30**:119, 132
Vita sancti Cuthberti (Bede) **20**:38, 62, 66-7, 71-2, 75, 81, 83
De vita solitaria (Petrarch) **20**:213, 259-60, 287, 290
Vitae patrum (Jerome) **30**:108-09
"Vitam quae faciunt beatiorem" (Martial) **35**:374
Vitarium Auctio (Map) **32**:10, 17, 25
"Vogliami sprona" (Petrarch) **20**:241
De vulgari eloquentia (Boccaccio) **13**:65
Vulgate (Jerome) **30**:55-56, 71-72, 79-80, 85-86, 93-94
"Waking from Drunkenness on a Spring Day" (Li Po) **2**:141
War (Josephus)
  See *Bellum Judaicum*
Wars of the Jews (Josephus)
  See *Bellum Judaicum*
"Was Melchisedech an ordinary mortal or was he an apparition of the Holy Ghost?" (Jerome) **30**:89
The Wasps (Aristophanes)
  See *Sphekes*
"Watching a Wheat Harvest" (Po Chu-i) **24**:294
"Watching Children Play" (Po Chu-i) **24**:351
The Way and Its Nature (Lao Tzu)
  See *Tao te Ching*
Wealth (Aristophanes)
  See *Ploutos*
"Weeping at Night over Li I-tao" (Po Chu-i) **24**:355
"Weeping over Li the Third" (Po Chu-i) **24**:353
"Weeping over Wang Chih-fu" (Po Chu-i) **24**:354
Weighing of Souls (Aeschylus) **11**:123-24, 193
Wen-chi (Po Chu-i) **24**:355-57, 360-61, 377
"The Werewolf" (Marie de France)
  See "Bisclavret"
"When Wilt Thou Come to Comfort Me?" (Rolle) **21**:316
"White Hairs" (Po Chu-i) **24**:344
"White-Haired Person of Shang-yang (Lamenting Her Unwed Solitude)" (Po Chu-i) **24**:297
"Wild Deer" (Hafiz) **34**:77-78
"Wild Dumril Son of Dukha Koja" **8**:104, 108-09
Willehalm (Wolfram von Eschenbach) **5**:293, 296, 298-302, 309-14, 317, 322-23, 326, 335-37, 343, 350-53, 357-62, 366, 373, 383, 386, 396-97, 399-400, 420, 429, 431
Willehalm von Oranse (Wolfram von Eschenbach)
  See *Willehalm*
William of England (Chretien de Troyes)
  See *Guillaume d'Angleterre*
"The Wind and the Sun" (Aesop) **24**:64, 66

"The Window of Bamboos" (Po Chu-i) **24**:342

"Wine Will Be Served" (Li Po) **2**:143

"Winter and Spring" (Aesop) **24**:36

"The Wisdom of Dede Korkut" **8**:103, 107

"A Wolf and a Dung-Beetle" (Marie de France) **8**:174-75

"Wolf and Lamb" (Aesop) **24**:13, 42-43

"The Wolf and the Crane" (Aesop) **24**:13, 58

"The Wolf and the Kid" (Marie de France) **8**:193

"The Wolf and the Sow" (Marie de France) **8**:190

"A Wolf as King of the Beasts" (Marie de France) **8**:175

"The Wolf in Sheep's Clothing" (Aesop) **24**:43

"The Wolves and the Dogs" (Aesop) **24**:82

"A Woman and Her Hen" (Marie de France) **8**:171

The Woman from Andros (Terence)
    See *Andria*

The Woman from Samos (Menander)
    See *Samia*

Woman of Leucas (Menander) **9**:211

Woman of Thessaly (Menander) **9**:214

Women at the Thesmophoria (Aristophanes)
    See *Thesmophoriazusae*

Women in Assembly (Aristophanes)
    See *Ekklesiazousai*

Women in Parliament (Aristophanes)
    See *Ekklesiazousai*

Women Keeping the Festival of the Thesmophoria (Aristophanes)
    See *Thesmophoriazusae*

The Women of Phoenicia (Euripides) **23**:173, 175

Women of Salamis (Aeschylus) **11**:125

The Women of Troy (Euripides)
    See *Trojan Women*

The Women's Assembly (Aristophanes)
    See *Ekklesiazousai*

A Women's Lunch-Party (Menander)
    See *Synaristosai*

"A Woodcutter and Hermes" (Aesop) **24**:18

"the Words of a Funeral Dirge" (Po Chu-i) **24**:355

Works (Hesiod)
    See *Works and Days*

Works (Po Chu-i)
    See *Works*

Works and Days (Hesiod) **5**:70, 72-4, 75-7, 79-84, 86-101, 103-05, 108, 110-11, 114-16, 121-27, 129-51, 153, 156, 160-63, 167-68, 170-74

Works of Ossian (Ossian) **28**:334

The Would-Be Critic (Lucian) **32**:45-46, 63

"The Wretched One" (Marie de France)
    See "Le Chaitivel"

"The Wrong Box" **2**:36

Xantriae (Aeschylus) **11**:124

Xenia (Martial) **35**:303-04, 331, 364, 375, 377

"Yearning" (Li Po) **2**:159-60

"Year's End" (Po Chu-i) **24**:350

Yes and No (Abelard)
    See *Sic et Non*

Yi (Confucius)
    See *I Ching*

"Yigenek Son of Kazilak Koja" **8**:104

Yi-king (Confucius)
    See *I Ching*

Yogasutra-bhasya-vivirana (Sankara) **32**:359

"Yonec" (Marie de France) **8**:114, 116-17, 121-23, 127-28, 131, 134, 139-40, 142, 144-45, 147, 149, 154, 161-65, 170, 181

"The Young King of the Black Isles" **2**:72

"The Young Man from Baghdad" **2**:43

Yueh (Confucius) **19**:35, 38

Yvain (Chretien de Troyes) **10**:131, 133-34, 136, 138-39, 141, 143-47, 149, 157, 159-69, 171, 173, 182-90, 194-97, 199, 206, 208, 210, 215-16, 218-21, 223, 225-26, 229-32, 234-35, 237-39

"De Yxione" (Map) **32**:122

Zeus Cathechized (Lucian) **32**:48, 50-51, 53

Zeus Rants (Lucian) **32**:40, 47-50, 55

Zokashu (Izumi Shikibu) **33**:278

Title Index

CMLC Cumulative Critic Index

Abbott, Frank Frost
Petronius **34**:254, 256, 261

Abu'l-'Addus, Yusuf
Al-Jahiz **25**:314

'Abdul Hakim, Khalifa
Rumi, Jalal al-Din **20**:345

Abe Akio
Sei Shonagon **6**:299

Abusch, Tzvi
Epic of Gilgamesh **3**:365

Adams, Charles Darwin
Demoshenes **13**:148

Adams, Henry
The Song of Roland **1**:166

Adams, Marilyn McCord
William of Ockham **32**:138, 188

Adcock, F. E.
Thucydides **17**:288

Addison, Joseph
Aeneid **9**:310
Iliad **1**:282
Ovid **7**:292
Sappho **3**:379
Sophocles **2**:293

Adler, Mortimer J.
Plato **8**:342

Adlington, William

Apuleius **1**:6

Ahl, Frederick M.
Lucan **33**:379

Ahmad, S. Maqbul
Al-Biruni **28**:123

Aiken, Conrad
Murasaki, Lady **1**:423

Aili, Hans
St. Birgitta **24**:97

Albert, S.M.
Albert the Great **16**:33

Alford, John A.
Rolle, Richard **21**:378

Alic, Margaret
Hypatia **35**:222

Alighieri, Dante
Aeneid **9**:297
Bertran de Born **5**:4
Seneca, Lucius Annaeus **6**:331
Sordello **15**:323

Ali-Shah, Omar
Khayyam **11**:288

Allen, Archibald W.
Livy **11**:334

Allen, Harold J.
Presocratic philosophy **22**:42

Allen, Hope Emily
Rolle, Richard **21**:308

Allen, Philip Schuyler
Petronius **34**:285

Allen, Richard F.
Njals saga **13**:358
Sankara **32**:312

Allen, Walter, Jr.
Martial **35**:328

Allinson, Francis G.
Menander **9**:204

Allison, Rev. William T.
The Book of Psalms **4**:371

Al-Nadim
Arabian Nights **2**:3

Alphonso-Karkala, John B.
Kalevala **6**:259

Alter, Robert
The Book of Psalms **4**:451
Song of Songs **18**:283

Ambivius, Lucius
Terence **14**:302

Ames, Roger T.
Confucius **19**:88

Amis, Kingsley
Beowulf **1**:112

Anacker, Robert
Chretien de Troyes **10**:144

Anderson, David
St. John **27**:83

Anderson, Earl R.
Cynewulf **23**:86

Anderson, George K.
Beowulf **1**:98
The Dream of the Rood **14**:245

Anderson, Graham
Lucian **32**:13, 22

Anderson, J. K.
Xenophon **17**:342

Anderson, William S.
Juvenal **8**:59
Martial **35**:338
Plautus **24**:255

Andersson, Theodore M.
Hrafnkel's Saga **2**:103

Annas, Julia
Epicurus **21**:201

Anthes, Rudolf
Eastern Mythology **26**:113

Apuleius, Lucius
Apuleius **1**:3

Aquinas, St. Thomas
Augustine, St. **6**:5

Averroes **7**:3
Plato **8**:217

Arberry, A. J.
Hafiz **34**:52
Rumi, Jalal al-Din **20**:364

Archibald, Katherine
Aquinas, St. Thomas **33**:20

Arendt, Hannah
Augustine, St. **6**:116

Aristophanes
Aeschylus **11**:73

Aristotle
Aeschylus **11**:73
Greek Historiography **17**:13
Hesiod **5**:69
Iliad **1**:273
Plato **8**:202
Sophocles **2**:291

Armstrong, A. H.
Presocratic philosophy **22**:29

Arnhart, Larry
Rhetoric **31**:264

Arnold, E. Vernon
Seneca, Lucius Annaeus **6**:362

Arnold, Edwin
Hesiod **5**:71
Iliad **1**:308
Odyssey **16**:208
Sappho **3**:384

Arnold, Mary
Poem of the Cid **4**:226

Arnold, Matthew
Aeneid **9**:316
Aristophanes **4**:54
Iliad **1**:300
Mabinogion **9**:146
Ossian **28**:293
The Song of Roland **1**:162
Sophocles **2**:311

Arnott, Geoffrey
Menander **9**:261

Arnott, W. G.
Menander **9**:253

Arnould, E. J.
Rolle, Richard **21**:350

Arnstein, Adolf
Meister Eckhart **9**:4

Arrowsmith, William
Aristophanes **4**:131

'Arudi, Nizami-i-
Avicenna **16**:147

Ascham, Roger
Cicero, Marcus Tullius **3**:186

Ashe, Geoffrey

Arthurian Legend 10:2

Asquith, Herbert Henry
Demosthenes **13**:135

Astin, Alan E.
Cato, Marcus Porcius **21**:38

Aston, W. G.
Murasaki, Lady **1**:416
Sei Shonagon **6**:291

Athanasius
The Book of Psalms **4**:344

Atkins, J. W. H.
Aristophanes **4**:104
Longinus **27**:136

Atkinson, James C.
Mystery of Adam **4**:207

Auden, W. H.
Iliad **1**:347
Njals saga **13**:330

Auerbach, Erich
Augustine, St. **6**:79
Inferno **3**:72, 95
Mystery of Adam **4**:193
Odyssey **16**:221
Poem of the Cid **4**:251

Augustine, St.
Apuleius **1**:4
Augustine, St. **6**:4
Cicero, Marcus Tullius **3**:177
Epicurus **21**:79
Plato **8**:208
Seneca, Lucius Annaeus **6**:330

Aurobindo, Sri
Bhagavad Gita **12**:32

Austerlitz, Robert
Kalevala **6**:255

Austin, Scott
Parmenides **22**:242

Averroes
Plato **8**:212

Avery, Peter
Khayyam **11**:297

Axtell, Harold
Pliny the Elder **23**:318

Ayscough, Florence
Li Po **2**:132

Bachofen, J. J.
Aeschylus **11**:92
Sappho **3**:382

Bacon, Francis
Plato **8**:219

Bader, Jonathan
Sankara **32**:358

Bagley, F. R. C.

Khayyam **11**:283

Bagnani, Gilbert
Petronius **34**:308

Bailey, Cyril
Epicurus **21**:130

Baker, Donald C.
Beowulf **1**:154

Baldwin, Barry
Lucian **32**:7

Baldwin, Charles Sears
Sir Gawain and the Green Knight
2:186
Poetics **31**:123
Rhetoric **31**:221

Baldwin, Spurgeon W., Jr.
Aesop **24**:29

Baljon, J. M. S.
The *Koran* **23**:274

Bamberger, Bernard J.
Torah **30**:297

Banks, Mary Macleod
Morte Arthure **10**:377

Barani, Syed Hasan
Al-Biruni **28**:112

Barber, Richard
Sir Gawain and the Green Knight
2:215

Barbera, Andre
Euclid **25**:205

Barbi, Michele
Inferno **3**:87

Barfield, Owen
Bhagavad Gita **12**:71
The Book of Psalms **4**:392

Bargen, Doris G.
Murasaki, Lady **1**:467

Baricelli, Jean-Pierre
Kalevala **6**:280

Barker, E. Phillips
Seneca, Lucius Annaeus **6**:375

Barker, William
Xenophon **17**:318

Barnes, Geraldine
Bevis of Hampton **35**:197

Barnes, Jonathan
Pythagoras **22**:319

Barney, Stephen A.
Romance of the Rose **8**:435

Barnstone, Willis
Llull, Ramon **12**:126
Sappho **3**:435

Barolini, Teodolinda
Sordello **15**:368

Baroody, Wilson G.
Torah **30**:321

Barr, William
Juvenal **8**:86

Barron, W. R. J.
Havelok **34**:227
Layamon **10**:360
Sir Gawain and the Green Knight
2:261

Barth, John
Arabian Nights **2**:43

Basgoz, Ilhan
Book of Dede Korkut **8**:108

Basore, John W.
Seneca, Lucius Annaeus **6**:374

Bassett, Samuel Eliot
Iliad **1**:329
Odyssey **16**:214

Basthiaensen, A. A. R.
Tertullian **29**:360

Bate, A. K.
Map, Walter **32**:95

Bates, William Nickerson
Euripides **23**:115
Sophocles **2**:336

Batts, Michael S.
Gottfried von Strassburg **10**:293
Hartmann von Aue **15**:183

Bausani, Alessandro
Hafiz **34**:78

Bayerschmidt, Carl F.
Njals saga **13**:326
Wolfram von Eschenbach **5**:311

Beagon, Mary
Pliny the Elder **23**:363

Beare, W.
Terence **14**:343

Beaufret, Jean
Heraclitus **22**:147

Becher, Anne G.
Phaedrus **25**:386

Beck, Roger
Petronius **34**:396

Bede
Cædmon **7**:77

Beer, Frances
Hildegard von Bingen **20**:175

Bell, Alexander
Havelok **34**:165

Bell, Aubrey F. G.
Poem of the Cid **4**:251

Bell, David N.
St. Benedict of Nursia **29**:48

Bell, Richard
The *Koran* **23**:239, 267

Bennett, James O'Donnell
Arabian Nights **2**:27

Bennett, Josephine Waters
Mandeville, Sir John **19**:117

Benson, Eugene
Sordello **15**:33

Benson, Larry D.
Morte Arthure **10**:386
Sir Gawain and the Green Knight
2:227

Bentwich, Norman
Josephus, Flavius **13**:199

Berggren, J. L.
Euclid **25**:258

Bergin, Thomas G.
Boccaccio, Giovanni **13**:74

Berkeley, George
Plato **8**:221

Berns, Laurence
Poetics **31**:159

Berry, Francis
Sir Gawain and the Green Knight
2:194

Berthoud, J. A.
Inferno **3**:116

Bespaloff, Rachel
Iliad **1**:343

Besserman, Lawrence
Sir Gawain and the Green Knight
2:280

Bettelheim, Bruno
Arabian Nights **2**:53

Beye, Charles Rowan
Apollonius Rhodius **28**:46
Hesiod **5**:131

Bigg, Charles
Origen **19**:189

Bilde, Per
Josephus, Flavius **13**:302

Billson, Charles J.
Kalevala **6**:233

Bird, H. W.
Eutropius **30**:30, 33, 38, 43

Bishop, Ian
Pearl **19**:339

Bittinger, J. B.
The Book of Psalms **4**:363

Bixby, James T.
Kalevala **6**:217
Lao Tzu **7**:118

Blackham, H. J.
Aesop **24**:79

Blair, Hugh
Iliad **1**:289
Ossian **28**:276
Sophocles **2**:296

Blair, Peter Hunter
Bede **20**:74

Blamires, David
Wolfram von Eschenbach **5**:342

Blanchette, Oliva
Aquinas, St. Thomas **33**:84

Bloch, R. Howard
The Song of Roland **1**:240

Blomfield, Joan
Beowulf **1**:85

Blondel, Maurice
Augustine, St. **6**:28

Bloomfield, Morton W.
Sir Gawain and the Green Knight
2:214

Blount, Margaret
Aesop **24**:40

Blow, Susan E.
Inferno **3**:42

Bluestine, Carolyn
Poem of the Cid **4**:309

Blum, Rudolf
Callimachus **18**:62

Boatner, Janet W.
The Song of Roland **1**:211

Boccaccio, Giovanni
Boccaccio, Giovanni **13**:3, 17
Inferno **3**:4

Bohner, Philotheus
William of Ockham **32**:128, 133

Boissier, Gaston
Martial **35**:251

Bollard, J. K.
Mabinogion **9**:176

Bolotin, David
Science **31**:387

Bolton, W. F.
Hrafnkel's Saga **2**:106

Bonjour, Adrien
Beowulf **1**:105

Bonnard, Andre
Sappho **3**:424

Bonner, Anthony
Llull, Ramon **12**:133

Bonner, Gerald
Bede **20**:86

Boren, James L.
Morte Arthure **10**:415

Borges, Jorge Luis
Anglo-Saxon Chronicle **4**:21
Arabian Nights **2**:29, 37, 67
Inferno **3**:141
Layamon **10**:327

Bosley, Keith
Kalevala **6**:283

Bostock, J. Knight
Hartmann von Aue **15**:163

Botta, Anne C. Lynch
Arabian Nights **2**:8
Cicero, Marcus Tullius **3**:192

Bourke, Vernon J.
Aquinas, St. Thomas **33**:41

Bovie, Palmer
Propertius, Sextus **32**:264

Bowen, Charles
Tain Bo Cualnge **30**:150

Bowen, Edwin W.
Petronius **34**:249

Bowra, C. M.
Aeneid **9**:358
Aeschylus **11**:178
Aristophanes **4**:140
Epic of Gilgamesh **3**:313
Iliad **1**:321
Pindar **12**:323
Poem of the Cid **4**:259
Sappho **3**:398, 399
Sophocles **2**:342

Bowring, Richard
Murasaki, Lady **1**:457

Braddock, Joseph
Sappho **3**:438

Braden, Gordon
Seneca, Lucius Annaeus **6**:399

Branca, Vittore
Boccaccio, Giovanni **13**:62

Branham, R. Bracht
Lucian **32**:57

Branston, Brian
Nonarse Mythology **26**:322

Brentano, Franz
Aristotelian Philosophy **31**:4

Bowen, Alan C.

Euclid 25:245

Bowra, C.M.
Odyssey **16**:292
Sordello **15**:353

Bramley, H. R.
Rolle, Richard **21**:276

Branch, M. A.
Kalevala **6**:267

Brandes, Georg
The Igor Tale **1**:478
Iliad **1**:317

Brandon, S. G. F.
Epic of Gilgamesh **3**:314

Brault, Gerard J.
The Song of Roland **1**:256

Braun, Richard E.
Juvenal **8**:67

Brennan, Gerald
Poem of the Cid **4**:256

Brett, G. S.
Poetics **31**:113

Breuer, Mordechai
Torah **30**:346

Brewer, Derek
Sir Gawain and the Green Knight
2:241, 270

Brewer, J. S.
Bacon, Roger **14**:6

Bridges, John Henry
Bacon, Roger **14**:14

Brinton, Alan
Rhetoric **31**:271

Briscoe, J.
Livy **11**:375

Brockelmann, Carl
The *Koran* **23**:254

Brodeur, Arthur Gilchrist
Beowulf **1**:112

Bromwich, Rachel
Arthurian Legend **10**:49
Mabinogion **9**:171

Brooke, Christopher
Abelard **11**:28

Brooke, Stopford A.
Beowulf **1**:63
Cynewulf **23**:2
The Dream of the Rood **14**:216

Broshi, Magen
Josephus, Flavius **13**:271

Brothers, A. J.
Terence **14**:385

Critic Index

Brower, Robert H.
Kokinshu **29**:227

Brown, Carleton F.
Pearl **19**:278

Brown, George Hardin
Bede **20**:114

Brown, Norman O.
Hesiod **5**:109

Brown, J. T. T.
Barbour, John **33**:156

Brown, Peter
Augustine, St. **6**:100
Origen **19**:264

Browne, Rev. G. F.
Bede **20**:3

Browning, R.
Anna Comnena **25**:43

Browning, Robert
Aristophanes **4**:55

Bruce, James Douglas
Arthurian Legend **10**:120

Brueggemann, Walter
The Book of Psalms **4**:434

Bruere, Richard
Lucan **33**:358
Pliny the Elder **23**:333

Bruford, Alan
Tain Bo Cualnge **30**:224

Bryant, Nigel
Chretien de Troyes **10**:216

Bryant, William Cullen
Iliad **1**:306

Bryce, Derek
Lieh Tzu **27**:120

Brzezinski, Monica
The Dream of the Rood **14**:288

Buber, Martin
The Book of Job **14**:206
The Book of Psalms **4**:401

Buck, Philo M., Jr.
Aristophanes **4**:86
Inferno **3**:83
Mahabharata **5**:220

Buckler, Georgina
Anna Comnena **25**:9

Burgel, J. Christoph
Hafiz **34**:112

Burn, Andrew Robert
Sappho **3**:430

Burnet, John
Anaximander **22**:58, 60

Burnett, Anne Pippin
Pindar **12**:377
Sappho **3**:481

Burrow, J. A.
The Dream of the Rood **14**:238
Sir Gawain and the Green Knight
2:235, 277

Burshatin, Israel
Poem of the Cid **4**:329

Burton, Richard F.
Arabian Nights **2**:13, 15

Bury, J. B.
Polybius **17**:155
Socrates **27**:287
Xenophon **17**:328

Bussanich, John
Hesiod **5**:163

Butler, Cuthbert
St. Benedict of Nursia **29**:3

Butler, H. E.
Martial **35**:253

Butler, Samuel
Iliad **1**:311
Odyssey **16**:200, 221

Butterworth, Charles E.
Avicenna **16**:163

Buttimore, R. A.
Propertius, Sextus **32**:295

Buxton, Richard
Greek Mythology **26**:244

Byron, Lord
Aeneid **9**:385

Cabaniss, J. Allen
Petronius **34**:322

Cadell, Jessie E.
Khayyam **11**:243

Cadiou, Rene
Origen **19**:197

Caesar, Julius
Terence **14**:326

Cairns, Huntington
Cicero, Marcus Tullius **3**:237

Caldwell, Richard
Greek Mythology **26**:219

Calin, William C.
Mystery of Adam **4**:200

Calvin, John
The Book of Job **14**:118
The Book of Psalms **4**:349
Seneca, Lucius Annaeus **6**:332

Campbell, James
Bede **20**:48, 63

Campbell, Joseph
Arabian Nights **2**:39
Epic of Gilgamesh **3**:319
Mahabharata **5**:238

Campbell, Lewis
Aeschylus **11**:108
Sophocles **2**:313

Campbell, Mary B.
Mandeville, Sir John **19**:161
Polo, Marco **15**:311

Camps, W. A.
Propertius, Sextus **32**:260

Cantarino, Vicente
Averroes **7**:47

Canter, H. V.
Livy **11**:321

Canuteson, John
The Dream of the Rood **14**:276

Carlyle, John A.
Inferno **3**:19

Carlyle, Thomas
Inferno **3**:12
Das Nibelungenlied **12**:138

Carne-Ross, D. S.
Pindar **12**:367

Carpenter, Frederick I.
Ossian **28**:327

Cassell, Anthony K.
Boccaccio, Giovanni **13**:94
Inferno **3**:151

Cassirer, Ernst
Augustine, St. **6**:52, 77

Cather, Willa
Sappho **3**:388

Catullus, Gaius Valerius
Cicero, Marcus Tullius **3**:174

Cawley, Frank Stanton
Hrafnkel's Saga **2**:83

Caxton, William
Arthurian Legend **10**:27

Ceadel, E. B.
Kokinshu **29**:221

Chadwick, Rev. H.
Origen **19**:225

Chadwick, Henry
Boethius **15**:53, 58
Origen **19**:214

Chamberlain, Basil Hall
Kojiki **21**:217

Chambers, E. K.
Mystery of Adam **4**:184

Chambers, R. W.
Bede **20**:23
Beowulf **1**:74

Chan, Wing-tsit
Confucius **19**:48, 67

Chandler, Richard E.
Poem of the Cid **4**:266

Chaney, Virginia M.
Martial **35**:353

Chapman, George
Iliad **1**:276
Odyssey **16**:184

Charlesworth, Martin Percival
Josephus, Flavius **13**:220

Charleton, Walter
Epicurus **21**:90

Chateaubriand, Viscount de
Augustine, St. **6**:11
Inferno **3**:7

Chaucer, Geoffrey
Inferno **3**:5

Chaytor, H. J.
Bertran de Born **5**:21
Sordello **15**:332

Chen, Ellen Marie
Lao Tzu **7**:176

Chen, Kwei
Po Chu-i **24**:292

Chen, Yu-Shih
Su Shih **15**:417

Ch'en Shou-yi
Li Po **2**:142

Chenu, M.-D.
Aquinas, St. Thomas **33**:30

Cherniss, H. F.
Presocratic Philosophy **22**:3

Cherniss, Michael D.
Romance of the Rose **8**:431

Chesterton, G. K.
Aesop **24**:16
Aquinas, St. Thomas **33**:3
Arabian Nights **2**:18
The Book of Job **14**:188
The Song of Roland **1**:174

Chittick, William C.
The Koran **23**:309

Chretien de Troyes
Chretien de Troyes **10**:131, 141,
160

Christine de Pizan
Romance of the Rose **8**:376

Christoph, Siegfried Richard

Wolfram von Eschenbach **5**:386, 409

Chroust, Anton-Hermann
Rhetoric **31**:227

Chuangtse
Lao Tzu **7**:117

Cicero, Marcus Tullius
Cato, Marcus Porcius **21**:3
Epicurus **21**:61
Plato **8**:205
Terence **14**:305

Cizevskij, Dmitrij
The Igor Tale **1**:501

Clark, Cyril Drummond Le Gros
Su Shih **15**:381, 385

Clark, David W.
William of Ockham **32**:174

Clark, Donald Lemen
Hermogenes **6**:161

Clark, George
Aesop **24**:44

Clark, James M.
Meister Eckhart **9**:45, 54

Clark, John
Poem of the Cid **4**:230

Clark, S. L.
Hartmann von Aue **15**:228

Clarke, H. Butler
Poem of the Cid **4**:229

Clarke, Howard W.
Odyssey **16**:279

Clauss, James J.
Apollonius Rhodius **28**:71

Cleary, Thomas
The *Koran* **23**:305

Clerk, Archibald
Ossian **28**:294

Clifton-Everest, J. M.
Hartmann von Aue **15**:202

Cline, Ruth Harwood
Chretien de Troyes **10**:195

Closs, August
Gottfried von Strassburg **10**:255

Cochrane, Charles Norris
Thucydides **17**:243

Coffin, Harrison Cadwallader
St. Jerome **30**: 66

Cohen, Shaye J. D.
Josephus, Flavius **13**:263, 273

Col, Pierre

Romance of the Rose **8**:380

Coleman, T. W.
Rolle, Richard **21**:323

Coleridge, H. N.
Hesiod **5**:70

Coleridge, Samuel Taylor
Arabian Nights **2**:4
Aristophanes **4**:47
Inferno **3**:10
Pindar **12**:260
Poem of the Cid **4**:224

Colgrave, Bertram
Bede **20**:8, 82

Colish, Marcia L.
Augustine, St. **6**:123

Colledge, Edmund
Meister Eckhart **9**:68

Collinder, Bjorn
Kalevala **6**:247

Collins, Christopher
Longus **7**:251

Colton, Arthur W.
Map, Walter **32**:76

Colum, Padraic
Arabian Nights **2**:26
Mabinogion **9**:165

Comfort, W. W.
Chretien de Troyes **10**:137

Comparetti, Domenico
Kalevala **6**:219

Comper, Frances M. M.
Rolle, Richard **21**:310

Conant, Martha Pike
Arabian Nights **2**:20

Condren, Edward I.
Hrafnkel's Saga **2**:112

Congdon, Kirby
Aesop **24**:39

Congreve, William
Pindar **12**:259

Connor, W. Robert
Thucydides **17**:307

Cons, Louis
Aesop **24**:18

Conte, Gian Biagio
Cato, Marcus Porcius **21**:54

Conybeare, John Josias
Beowulf **1**:55

Cook, Albert S.
Cynewulf **23**:27
Ovid **7**:412

Poem of the Cid **4**:270
Sophocles **2**:404

Cook, Charles W.
Epic of Gilgamesh **3**:352

Cook, Robert G.
Chretien de Troyes **10**:183

Cooper, Arthur
Li Po **2**:145

Cooper, Lane
Poetics **31**:120

Copleston, Frederick C.
Abelard **11**:14
Averroes **7**:16

Copleston, Reginald S.
Aeschylus **11**:95

Copley, Frank O.
Livy **11**:363
Terence **14**:349

Corcoran, Thomas H.
Seneca, Lucius Annaeus **6**:436

Cornford, Francis Macdonald
Aristophanes **4**:78
Plato **8**:272
Thucydides **17**:235

Cornwallis, William
Seneca, Lucius Annaeus **6**:334

Cosman, Madeleine Pelner
Gottfried von Strassburg **10**:292

Costa, C. D. N.
Seneca, Lucius Annaeus **6**:413

Coulter, Cornelia C.
Hroswitha of Gandersheim **29**:99

Courthope, W. J.
Beowulf **1**:59

Courtney, W. L.
Sappho **3**:394

Cowell, Edward Byles
Khayyam **11**:230

Cowley, Abraham
The Book of Psalms **4**:351
Pindar **12**:258

Crabbe, Anna
Boethius **15**:69

Cracroft, Bernard
Arabian Nights **2**:9

Craigie, W. A.
Barbour, John **33**:142
Hrafnkel's Saga **2**:78

Crane, Susan
Bevis of Hampton **35**:191

Cranston, Edwin A.

Izumi, Shikibu **33**:264
Izumi, Shikibu **33**:303
Kokinshu **29**:295

Crawford, John Martin
Kalevala **6**:214

Crawford, S. J.
Cædmon **7**:92

Creek, Herbert L.
Bevis of Hampton **35**:150

Creekmore, Hubert
Juvenal **8**:64

Creel, H. G.
Lieh Tzu **27**:98

Crem, Theresa M.
Rhetoric **31**:238

Croce, Benedetto
Inferno **3**:58
Plato **8**:269
Terence **14**:326

Croiset, Maurice
Aristophanes **4**:70

Crombie, A. C.
Bacon, Roger **14**:79

Cross, R. Nicol
Socrates **27**:229

Crossley-Holland, Kevin
Norse Mythology **26**:337

Crump, M. Marjorie
Ovid **7**:314

Crusemann, Frank
Torah **30**:356

Cruttwell, Charles Thomas
Cato, Marcus Porcius **21**:22

Cumming, William Patterson
St. Birgitta **24**:89

Cummings, Hubertis M.
Boccaccio, Giovanni **13**:87

Cunliffe, John W.
Seneca, Lucius Annaeus **6**:339

Cunningham, Stanley B.
Albert the Great **16**:43, 65

Curley III, Thomas F.
Boethius **15**:97

Curran, Leo C.
Propertius, Sextus **32**:270

Currie, H. MacL.
Phaedrus **25**:366

Curtius, Ernst Robert
Aeneid **9**:345, 376
Augustine, St. **6**:56
Hermogenes **6**:158

Critic Index

Inferno 3:98

Dahlberg, Charles
Romance of the Rose 8:414

Dall, Caroline H.
Sordello 15:328

D'Alton, Rev. J. F.
Cicero, Marcus Tullius 3:207

Dalven, Rae
Anna Comnena 25:58

Damon, S. Foster
Marie de France 8:120

Dandekar, R. N.
Mahabharata 5:227

Dane, Joseph A.
Bodel, Jean 28:247, 249
Mystery of Adam 4:216

Danielou, Jean
Origen 19:206

Darrow, Clarence
Khayyam 11:274

Dashti, Ali
Khayyam 11:280

Davenport, Guy
Sappho 3:471

Davenport, W. A.
Sir Gawain and the Green Knight 2:273

David, E.
Aristophanes 4:174

Davidson, A. B.
The Book of Job 14:138

Davidson, Herbert A.
Avicenna 16:147

Davidson, Thomas
Sappho 3:388

Davies, James
Catullus 18:73

Davis, J. Cary
Poem of the Cid 4:260

Davis, Scott
Kalevala 6:278

Davis, Thomas X.
St. Benedict of Nursia 29:68

Dawson, Christopher
Bacon, Roger 14:65

De Boer, T. J.
Averroes 7:7

De Chasca, Edmund
Poem of the Cid 4:295

De la Mare, Walter
Arabian Nights 2:35

De Ley, Margo
Razon de Amor 16:347

De Quincey, Thomas
Arabian Nights 2:8
Herodotus 17:54
Iliad 1:294
Odyssey 16:197
Sophocles 2:309

De Sanctis, Francesco
Boccaccio, Giovanni 13:17
Inferno 3:23, 31

De Vere, Aubrey
Poem of the Cid 4:229
The Song of Roland 1:163

De Vericour, Professor
Poem of the Cid 4:225

De Vogel, C. J.
Pythagoras 22:288

De Vogüé, Adalbert
St. Benedict of Nursia 29:85

Dean, Christopher
Arthurian Legend 10:65
Morte Arthure 10:431

Deferrari, Roy J.
Basil of Caesaria 35:46

Demetillo, Ricaredo
Murasaki, Lady 1:429

Den Boer, W.
Eutropius 30:2
Thucydides 17:302

DeWitt, Norman Wentworth
Epicurus 21:144

Devereux, Daniel T.
Aristotelian Philosophy 31:79

Deyermond, A. D.
Poem of the Cid 4:289

Diamond, Robert E.
The Dream of the Rood 14:236

Diederich, Mary Dorothea
St. Jerome 30:82

Dill, Samuel
Juvenal 8:26
Seneca, Lucius Annaeus 6:345

Dimler, G. Richard
Wolfram von Eschenbach 5:344

Dinshaw, Carolyn L.
Bodel, Jean 28:239

Dinsmore, Charles Allen
Iliad 1:326

Dionysius of Halicarnassus

Sappho 3:379
Thucydides 17:209
Xenophon 17:329

Disraeli, Issac
Beowulf 1:56

Dobson, J. F.
Demosthenes 13:141

Dodds, E. R.
Augustine, St. 6:21

Dodsley, Robert
Aesop 24:8

Dole, Nathan Haskell
Petrarch 20:229

Donner, Morton
Sir Gawain and the Green Knight 2:224

Donohoe, Joseph I., Jr.
The Song of Roland 1:228

Donovan, Mortimer J.
Marie de France 8:145

Doolittle, Hilda
Sappho 3:432

Dorfman, Eugene
Poem of the Cid 4:271

Doumas C.
Apollonius Rhodius 28:29

Dover, K. J.
Aristophanes 4:147, 159
Demosthenes 13:185

Draper, John W.
Poetics 31:102

Driberg, J. H.
Aesop 24:19

Dronke, Peter
Abelard 11:39
Hildegard von Bingen 20:143
Hroswitha of Gandersheim 29:178

Dryden, John
Aeneid 9:300
Apuleius 1:7
Iliad 1:282
Juvenal 8:5
Ovid 7:291
Pindar 12:258

Dubs, Homer H.
Socrates 27:269

Ducharme, Leonard
Albert the Great 16:86

Duckett, Eleanor Shipley
Bede 20:42
Boethius 15:23

Duckworth, George E.
St. Jerome 30:80

Terence 14:337

Duclow, Donald F.
Meister Eckhart 9:70

Duff, J. Wight
Cicero, Marcus Tullius 3:197
Juvenal 8:34
Livy 11:336
Martial 35:302
Phaedrus 25:337
Terence 14:305

Duff, Mountstuart E. Grant
Polybius 17:152

Duggan, Joseph J.
Poem of the Cid 4:312

Dumezil, Georges
Mahabharata 5:254

Duncan, Douglas
Lucian 32:31

Dunlop, John
Cato, Marcus Porcius 21:17

Dunn, Charles W.
Romance of the Rose 8;417

Dunn, Joseph
Tain Bo Cualnge 30:146

Dunne, M.A.
Sordello 15:339

Durling, Robert M.
Petrarch 20:270

Dzielska, Maria
Hypatia 35:226

Earle, John
Beowulf 1:57

Easton, Stewart C.
Bacon, Roger 14:73

Eaton, John H.
The Book of Psalms 4:438

Ebenstein, William
Cicero, Marcus Tullius 3:251

Ebin, Lois A.
Barbour, John 33:189

Echard, Lawrence
Terence 14:297

Eckermann, Johann Peter
Longus 7:217
Sophocles 2:303

Eckhart, Meister
Meister Eckhart 9:24

Eckstein, A. M.
Polybius 17:192

Edel, Abraham
Aristotelian Philosophy 31:55

Edgerton, Franklin
Kalidasa **9**:113

Edgren, A. Hjalmar
Kalidasa **9**:87

Edinger, Edward F.
Greek Mythology **26**:241

Edmonds, J. M.
Longus **7**:220

Edwards, Bateman
Aesop **24**:20

Ehrenberg, Victor
Aristophanes **4**:117

Eide, Elling O.
Li Po **2**:149

Einarsson, Stefan
Hrafnkel's Saga **2**:97

Eliade, Mircea
Bhagavad Gita **12**:74
Epic of Gilgamesh **3**:341
Mahabharata **5**:235

Eliot, George
Sophocles **2**:311

Eliot, T. S.
Aeneid **9**:380
Inferno **3**:67
Pindar **12**:265
Seneca, Lucius Annaeus **6**:371

Ellis, Roger
St. Birgitta **24**:89

Elwell-Sutton, L. P.
Khayyam **11**:304

Elyot, Thomas
Ovid **7**:286

Embree, Ainslee T.
Al-Biruni **28**:159

Emerson, Oliver Farrar
Beowulf **1**:68

Emerson, Ralph Waldo
The Book of Psalms **4**:360
Plato **8**:235
Socrates **27**:211

Engelhardt, George J.
Sir Gawain and the Green Knight
2:204

Enright, D. J.
Murasaki, Lady **1**:447
Sei Shonagon **6**:301

Erasmus, Desiderius
Cicero, Marcus Tullius **3**:184
St. Jerome **30**:51
Seneca, Lucius Annaeus **6**:332

Erickson, Keith V.
Rhetoric **31**:256

Eskenazi, Tamara Cohn
Torah **30**:329

Eusebius
Josephus, Flavius **13**:219
Origen **19**:183

Eustathios
Iliad **1**:274

Evans, J. A. S.
Herodotus **17**:109, 132

Evelyn-White, Hugh G.
Hesiod **5**:83

Everett, Dorothy
Layamon **10**:329
Morte Arthure **10**:378
Pearl **19**:321
Sir Gawain and the Green Knight
2:197

Eves, Howard
Euclid **25**:131

Ewert, Alfred
Marie de France **8**:129

Faber, Ernst
Confucius **19**:12

Falk, Marcia
Song of Songs **18**:297

Fant, Maureen B.
Sappho **3**:481

Fantham, Elaine
Cato, Marcus Porcius **21**:57
Lucan **33**:392

Farnell, Ida
Sordello **15**:330

Faris, Wendy B.
Arabian Nights **2**:69

Farnell, Ida
Bertran de Born **5**:18

Farnham, Willard
Boccaccio, Giovanni **13**:62

Farrington, Benjamin
Epicurus **21**:159

Fauriel, C. C.
Bertran de Born **5**:10

Faust, Diana M.
Marie de France **8**:185

Fedotov, George P.
The Igor Tale **1**:491

Fedwick, Paul Jonathan
Basil of Caesaria **35**:86

Feldman, Louis H.
Josephus, Flavius **13**:256

Felson-Rubin, Nancy

Odyssey **16**:321

Feng, Kuan
Lao Tzu **7**:155

Fennell, John
The Igor Tale **1**:521

Ferejohn, Michael T.
Science **31**:315

Ferguson, John
Euripides **23**:172
Juvenal **8**:84
Sophocles **2**:408

Ferguson, Margaret W.
Augustine, St. **6**:109

Fergusson, Francis
Sophocles **2**:359

Ferrante, Joan
Marie de France **8**:158

Festugiere, Andre-Jean
Apuleius **1**:24
Epicurus **21**:138

Ficino, Marsilio
Plato **8**:217

Fideler, David R.
Pythagoras **22**:331

Field, P. J. C.
Sir Gawain and the Green Knight
2:258

Fielding, Henry
Aristophanes **4**:41

Finlayson, John
Morte Arthure **10**:391

Finley, John H., Jr.
Pindar **12**:287
Thucydides **17**:251

Finley, M. I.
Greek Historiography **17**:13, 26
Odyssey **16**:253
Xenophon **17**:368

Fiore, Silvestro
Epic of Gilgamesh **3**:325

Fitch, George Hamlin
Arabian Nights **2**:22

Fite, Warner
Plato **8**:280

FitzGerald, Edward
Khayyam **11**:233

Fitzgerald, William
Catullus **18**:189

Flaccus, Statylius
Sophocles **2**:292

Fleming, John V.

The Dream of the Rood **14**:245

Fletcher, Jefferson Butler
Inferno **3**:56

Fogelqvist, Ingvar
St. Birgitta **24**:139

Foley, Helene P.
Aristophanes **4**:169
Euripides **23**:205

Forbes, J. T.
Socrates **27**:225

Ford, J. D. M.
Poem of the Cid **4**:233

Forehand, Walter E.
Terence **14**:381

Fornara, Charles W.
Herodotus **17**:96

Forster, E. M.
Arabian Nights **2**:26

Foscolo, Ugo
Boccaccio, Giovanni **13**:13
Petrarch **20**:194

Fowles, John
Marie de France **8**:157

Fowlie, Wallace
Inferno **3**:144

Fox, Denton
Njals saga **13**:339

Fox, Margaret Mary
Basil of Caesaria **35**:51

France, John
Anna Comnena **25**:51, 77

Frank, Grace
Bodel, Jean **28**:191
Mystery of Adam **4**:191, 197

Frank, Tenney
Cicero, Marcus Tullius **3**:211

Frankel, Hermann
Hesiod **5**:99
Ovid **7**:319
Sappho **3**:418

Frankforter, A. Daniel
Hroswitha of Gandersheim **29**
:159, 172

Frappier, Jean
Chretien de Troyes **10**:160

Freccero, John
Inferno **3**:145

Fredericks, S. C.
Juvenal **8**:79

Fremantle, William Henry
St. Jerome **30**:56

Critic Index

Frese, Delores Warwick
Anglo-Saxon Chronicle **4**:27

Freud, Sigmund
Sophocles **2**:313

Frey, John A.
Marie de France **8**:132

Friberg, Eino
Kalevala **6**:275, 278

Friedlander, Ludwig
Juvenal **8**:20

Friedlander, Paul
Plato **8**:355

Friedrich, Paul
Sappho **3**:457

Friedrich, Rainer
Odyssey **16**:330

Fromm, Erich
The Book of Psalms **4**:416

Fronto, Marcus Cornelius
Cicero, Marcus Tullius **3**:176

Fry, Paul H.
Longinus **27**:180

Frye, Northrop
Aristophanes **4**:130
The Book of Job **14**:189

Fu, Charles Wei-hsun
Lao Tzu **7**:167

Fuller, B. A. G.
Anaximander **22**:59
Heraclitus **22**:116
Parmenides **22**:206
Pythagoras **22**:269

Fung Yu-lan
Confucius **19**:37
Lao Tzu **7**:126

Gadamer, Hans-Georg
Plato **8**:333

Gadd, C. J.
Eastern Mythology **26**:169

Galinsky, G. Karl
Ovid **7**:383

Ganim, John M.
Havelok **34**:218

Gantz, Jeffrey
Celtic Mythology **26**:5
Mabinogion **9**:159, 186

Garci-Gomez, Miguel
Poem of the Cid **4**:335

Gardner, Edmund G.
St. Catherine **27**:3

Gardner, John

Epic of Gilgamesh **3**:340
Morte Arthure **10**:399
Pearl **19**:327
Sir Gawain and the Green Knight
2:233

Garner, John Leslie
Khayyam **11**:262

Garthwaite, John
Martial **35**:396

Gaselee, S(tephen)
Apuleius **1**:17

Gasquet, Cardinal
St. Benedict of Nursia **29**:11

Gassner, John
Terence **14**:339

Gayley, Charles Mills
Mystery of Adam **4**:186

Geddes, J., Jr.
The Song of Roland **1**:169

Gellius, Aulus
Cicero, Marcus Tullius **3**:176

Gentrup, William F.
Torah **30**:321

Geoffrey of Monmouth
Arthurian Legend **10**:18

Gerhardt, Mia I.
Arabian Nights **2**:42

Gero, Stephen
Tertullian **29**:344

Gerow, Edwin
Kalidasa **9**:130

Ghazoul, Ferial Jabouri
Arabian Nights **2**:61

Gibb, H. A. R.
Arabian Nights **2**:28
The *Koran* **23**:258

Gibbon, Edward
Augustine, St. **6**:10
Boethius **15**:2
Hypatia **35**:205

Gibbs, J.
Apuleius **1**:13

Gibbs, Marion E.
Wolfram von Eshcenbach **5**:347,
429

Gifford, William
Juvenal **8**:6

Gilder, Rosamond
Hroswitha of Gandersheim **29**:105

Giles, Lionel
Lieh Tzu **27**:93

Gill, Christopher
Petronius **34**:388

Gillies, Marshall M.
Apollonius Rhodius **28**:9

Gilson, Etienne
Abelard **11**:17
Aquinas, St. Thomas **33**:7
Augustine, St. **6**:44
Averroes **7**:18, 26
Bacon, Roger **14**:86
Meister Eckhart **9**:42, 60

Gilula, Dwora
Terence **14**:389

Girard, Rene
The Book of Job **14**:191
Sophocles **2**:408

Gladdon, Samuel Lyndon
Hildegard von Bingen **20**:182

Gladstone, W. E.
Iliad **1**:297

Glover, T. R.
Herodotus **17**:67

Glunz, Michael
Hafiz **34**:128

Gnagy, Allan S.
Anaximander **22**:99

Godolphin, F. R. B.
Propertius, Sextus **32**:254

Godwin, William
Poem of the Cid **4**:225

Goethe, Johann Wolfgang von
Kalidasa **9**:130
Longus **7**:217
Menander **9**:227
Sophocles **2**:303

Goldberg, Harriet
Razon de Amor **16**:360

Goldberg, Sander M.
Menander **9**:276
Terence **14**:372

Goldin, Frederick
The Song of Roland **1**:251

Golding, Arthur
Ovid **7**:287

Goldsmith, Margaret E.
Beowulf **1**:134

Gollancz, I.
Sir Gawain and the Green Knight
2:186

Gollancz, Israel
Pearl **19**:286

Goller, Karl Heinz
Morte Arthure **10**:418

Gombrowicz, Witold
Inferno **3**:131

Gomez-Lobo, Alfonso
Socrates **27**:382

Gomme, A. W.
Menander **9**:259
Thucydides **17**:261

Gomperz, Heinrich
Heraclitus **22**:126

Good, Edwin M.
The Book of Job **14**:206

Goodell, Thomas Dwight
Aeschylus **11**:112

Goodheart, Eugene
The Book of Job **14**:171

Goodrich, Norma Lorre
Arthurian Legend **10**:100, 108

Goodspeed, Edgar J.
Tertullian **29**:310

Goodyear, F. R. D.
Phaedrus **25**:365

Goold, G. P.
Catullus **18**:166
Demetrius **34**:27

Gordis, Robert
The Book of Job **14**:175

Gordon, E. V.
Hrafnkel's Saga **2**:86

Gosse, Edmund
Beowulf **1**:73

Gottfried von Strassburg
Gottfried von Strassburg **10**:246,
249, 258
Wolfram von Eschenbach **5**:291

Gradon, Pamela
Beowulf **1**:138

Graham, A. C.
Lieh Tzu **27**:108

Grahn, Judy
Sappho **3**:494

Grane, Leifn
Abelard **11**:25

Granrud, John E.
Cicero, Marcus Tullius **3**:205

Gransden, Antonia
Anglo-Saxon Chronicle **4**:21

Grant, Michael
Aeschylus **11**:175
Apuleius **1**:26
Cicero, Marcus Tullius **3**:285, 291
Josephus, Flavius **13**:240
Livy **11**:367

Ovid **7**:405
Polybius **17**:176
Thucycdides **17**:296

Graves, Robert
Aeneid **9**:394
Apuleius **1**:20
Iliad **1**:361
Menander **9**:236
Terence **14**:341

Gray, Cecile Crovatt Gay
Tain Bo Cualnge **30**:159

Gray, Vivienne
Xenophon **17**:371

Gray, V. J.
Xenophon **17**:369

Gray, Wallace
Iliad **1**:405

Grayson, Christopher
Xenophon **17**:346

Green, D. H.
Hartmann von Aue **15**:206
Wolfram von Eschenbach **5**:391

Green, Peter
Apollonius Rhodius **28**:102
Juvenal **8**:68
Ovid **7**:419
Sappho **3**:438

Green, William H.
Torah **30**:242
Greenberg, Moshe
The Book of Job **14**:196

Greene, Thomas
Aeneid **9**:399

Greenfield, Concetta Carestia
Petrarch **20**:265

Greenfield, Stanley B.
Beowulf **1**:119
Cynewulf **23**:39
The Dream of the Rood **14**:243

Greenwood, Thomas
Albert the Great **16**:17

Gregory, Eileen
Sappho **3**:495

Grene, David
Aeschylus **11**:220
Herodotus **17**:113
Thucydides **17**:280

Grierson, Herbert J. C.
Beowulf **1**:90

Grieve, Patricia E.
Razon de Amor **16**:364

Griffin, Jasper
Iliad **1**:392
Odyssey **16**:304

Grigson, Geoffrey
Sei Shonagon **6**:300

Grimm, Charles
Chretien de Troyes **10**:141

Grobman, Neil R.
Ossian **28**:349

Groden, Suzy Q.
Sappho **3**:436

Groos, Arthur
Wolfram von Eschenbach **5**:423

Grossman, Judith
Arabian Nights **2**:57

Grossvogel, Steven
Boccaccio, Giovanni **13**:114

Grube, G. M. A.
Aristophanes **4**:136
Cicero, Marcus Tullius **3**:258
Demetrius **34**:1, 38
Petronius **34**:332

Gruffydd, W. J.
Mabinogion **9**:159

Grundy, G. B.
Thucydides **17**:268

Grunmann-Gaudet, Minnette
The Song of Roland **1**:248

Guardini, Romano
Augustine, St. **6**:95
The Book of Psalms **4**:414

Guarino, Guido A.
Boccaccio, Giovanni **13**:52

Gudzy, N. K.
The Igor Tale **1**:485

Gulley, Norman
Socrates **27**:303
Poetics **31**:174

Gunderloch, Anja
Ossian **28**:377

Gunkel, Hermann
The Book of Psalms **4**:379

Gunn, Alan M. F.
Romance of the Rose **8**:402

Guthrie, W. K. C.
Anaximander **22**:68
Plato **8**:321, 360
Presocratic philosophy **22**:19, 32
Pythagoras **22**:275
Socrates **27**:320

Habel, Norman C.
Torah **30**: 281

Hackett, Jeremiah M. G.
Bacon, Roger **14**:99, 110

Hadas, Moses

Aeschylus **11**:150
Apuleius **1**:23
Aristophanes **4**:121
Cato, Marcus Porcius **21**:27
Hesiod **5**:98
Juvenal **8**:45
Petronius **34**:293
Plato **8**:304
Sappho **3**:417
Seneca, Lucius Annaeus **6**:378, 385

Haden, James
Socrates **27**:348

Hagendahl, Harald
St. Jerome **30**:116

Hagg, Tomas
Longus **7**:262

Haight, Anne Lyon
Hroswitha of Gandersheim **29**:132

Haight, Elizabeth Hazelton
Apuleius **1**:18
Lucian **32**:4

Haines, C. R.
Sappho **3**:397

Hainsworth, Peter
Petrarch **20**:324

Haley, Lucille
Ovid **7**:310

Hall, David L.
Confucius **19**:88

Hallam, Henry
Bacon, Roger **14**:16
Poem of the Cid **4**:225

Hallberg, Peter
Hrafnkel's Saga **2**:124
Njals saga **13**:339

Hallett, Judith P.
Sappho **3**:465

Halleux, Pierre
Hrafnkel's Saga **2**:99, 102

Halliwell, Stephen
Poetics **31**:187

Halverson, John
Beowulf **1**:131
Havelok **34**:195

Hamilton, Edith
Aeschylus **11**:128
Aristophanes **4**:109
Sophocles **2**:328
Terence **14**:322

Hammett, Peter E.
St. Benedict of Nursia **29**:76

Hamori, Andras
Arabian Nights **2**:51

Menander **9**:243, 276

Hanford, James Holly
Razon de Amor **16**:337

Hanning, Robert
Havelok **34**:168
Marie de France **8**:158

Hansen, William F.
Greek Mythology **26**:202

Hanson, John Arthur
Plautus **24**:191

Hanson-Smith, Elizabeth
Mabinogion **9**:192

Haraszti, Zoltan
Mandeville, Sir John **19**:113

Hardie, W. F. R.
Aristotelian Philosophy **31**:79

Hardison, O. B., Jr.
Mystery of Adam **4**:203

Hardy, E. G.
Juvenal **8**:17

Hardy, Lucy
Boccaccio, Giovanni **13**:30

Harris, Charles
Kalidasa **9**:81

Harris, Joseph
Norse Mythology **26**:366

Harrison, Ann Tukey
The Song of Roland **1**:261

Harrison, Robert
The Song of Roland **1**:220

Harsh, Philip Whaley
Menander **9**:216
Plautus **24**:174

Hart, Henry H.
Polo, Marco **15**:309

Hart, Thomas R.
Poem of the Cid **4**:306

Hartley, L. P.
Murasaki, Lady **1**:422

Hartmann, Louis N.
St. Jerome **30**:85

Hastings, R.
Boccaccio, Giovanni **13**:59

Hatto, A. T.
Gottfried von Strassburg **10**:259
Das Nibelungenlied **12**:194

Havelock, Eric A.
Catullus **18**:91
Hesiod **5**:111, 150
Iliad **1**:382, 386

Hay, John
Khayyam **11**: 261

Haymes, Edward R.
Das Nibelungenlied **12**: 244

Headstrom, Birger R.
Boccaccio, Giovanni **13**:35

Hearn, Lafcadio
Khayyam **11**:258

Heath, Sir Thomas
Euclid **25**:92, 101

Hegel, G. W. F.
Aristophanes **4**:46
The Book of Job **14**:157
Inferno **3**:12
Plato **8**:225
Sophocles **2**:297

Heidegger, Martin
Plato **8**:295
Sophocles **2**:376

Heidel, Alexander
Epic of Gilgamesh **3**:310

Heine, Heinrich
Bertran de Born **5**:10

Heinemann, Frederik J.
Hrafnkel's Saga **2**:120, 123

Heinen, Anton
Al-Biruni **28**:125

Heiserman, Arthur
Apuleius **1**:46
Longus **7**:254
Xenophon **17**:351

Henderson, John
Phaedrus **25**:355

Heninger, S. K., Jr.
Pythagoras **22**:301

Herder, Johann Gottfried von
The Book of Psalms **4**:355
Kalidasa **9**:102

Herington, John
Aeschylus **11**:210

Hermann, Frankel
Pindar **12**:305

Herodotus
Hesiod **5**:68

Herrick, Marvin Theodore
Poetics **31**:135

Herriott, J. Homer
Polo, Marco **15**:289

Hesse, Hermann
Arabian Nights **2**:28
Boccaccio, Giovanni **13**:32

Hewlett, Maurice

Hesiod **5**:83

Heyman, Harald E.
Havelok **34**:152

Hibbard, Laura A.
Bevis of Hampton **35**:171

Hickes, George
Cædmon **7**:78

Hieatt, Constance
The Song of Roland **1**:209

Higgins, W. E.
Xenophon **17**:352

Highet, Gilbert
Arabian Nights **2**:41
Beowulf **1**:97
Cicero, Marcus Tullius **3**:232, 241
The Dream of the Rood **14**:243
Juvenal **8**:40, 45
Pindar **12**:279
Romance of the Rose **8**:399

Hillebrandt, A.
Kalidasa **9**:95

Hillgarth, J. N.
Llull, Ramon **12**:112

Hillman, Michael Craig
Hafiz **34**:86

Hilpisch, Stephanus
St. Benedict of Nursia **29**:23

Hinton, James
Map, Walter **32**:87

Hirakawa, Sukehiro
Po Chu-i **24**:375

Hiroko, Odagiri
Izumi, Shikibu **33**:328

Hirsch, S. A.
Bacon, Roger **14**:23

Hirsch, Steven W.
Xenophon **17**:361

Hisamatsu, Sen'ichi
Sei Shonagon **6**:292

Hobbes, Thomas
Odyssey **16**:189
Thucydides **17**:214

Hodge, R. I. V.
Propertius, Sextus **32**:295

Hodgson, Geraldine E.
Rolle, Richard **21**:298

Holderlin, Friedrich
Sophocles **2**:297

Hole, Richard
Arabian Nights **2**:4

Hollander, Lee M.

Njals saga **13**:326
Norse Mythology **26**:344

Hollander, Robert
Boccaccio, Giovanni **13**:67, 88
Vita Nuova **18**:362

Hollister, C. Warren
Anglo-Saxon Chronicle **4**:19

Holmes, Urban T., Jr.
Chretien de Troyes **10**:150

Holyday, Barten
Juvenal **8**:4

Homann, Holger
Das Nibelungenlied **12**:239

Honko, Lauri
Kalevala **6**:271

Hooper, William Davis
Cato, Marcus Porcius **21**:26

Hopkins, E. Washburn
Mahabharata **5**:192

Horowitz, Irving L.
Averroes **7**:28

Horstman, C.
Rolle, Richard **21**:282

Horton, Christine
Bodel, Jean **28**:224

Hough, Lynn Harold
The Book of Psalms **4**:388

Hourani, George F.
Averroes **7**:36

House, Humphrey
Poetics **31**:147, 152

Housman, Laurence
Khayyam **11**:278

Howard, Donald R.
Sir Gawain and the Green Knight
2:221

Howe, Nicholas Phillies
Pliny the Elder **23**:347

Howells, W. D.
Ossian **28**:317

Howes, Robert C.
The Igor Tale **1**:517

Hoyt, Prentiss C.
Bevis of Hampton **35**:146

Hroswitha, Abess
Terence **14**:349

Hsu, Sung-peng
Lao Tzu **7**:182, 190

Huang Kuo-pin

Li Po **2**:164

Hubbard, Elbert
Hypatia **35**:206

Hueffer, Francis
Bertran de Born **5**:12

Hugel, Baron Friedrich von
Meister Eckhart **9**:27

Hughes, L.
St. Jerome **30**:71

Hugill, William Meredith
Aristophanes **4**:107

Hugo, Victor
Inferno **3**:22

Huizinga, Johan
Abelard **11**:6

Hulbert, James R.
Beowulf **1**:90

Hull, Denison Bingham
Iliad **1**:398

Hume, David
Cicero, Marcus Tullius **3**:188

Humphries, Rolfe
Juvenal **8**:58

Hunt, H. A. K.
Cicero, Marcus Tullius **3**:253

Hunt, J. William
Aeneid **9**:433

Hunt, Tony
Bodel, Jean **28**:221

Hunter, R. L.
Apollonius Rhodius **28**:27

Hunter, Richard
Apollonius Rhodius **28**:60

Huppe, Bernard F.
Augustine, St. **6**:92
Cædmon **7**:105
The Dream of the Rood **14**:278

Hussey, Edward
Anaximander **22**:83
Heraclitus **22**:136, 181
Parmenides **22**:223

Hutchins, William M.
Al-Jahiz **25**:321

Hutson, Arthur E.
Das Nibelungenlied **12**:162

Hutton, Richard Holt
Khayyam **11**:271

Huxley, Aldous
Bhagavad Gita **12**:54
Meister Eckhart **9**:68
Sappho **3**:398

Ildephonse, Cardinal Schuster
St. Benedict of Nursia **29**:25

Ing, Paul Tan Chee
Lao Tzu **7**:164

Ingalls, Daniel H. H.
Kalidasa **9**:122
Sankara **32**:304

Inge, William Ralph
Meister Eckhart **9**:25

Iqbal, Afzal
Rumi, Jalal al-Din **20**:353

Irani, K. D.
Eastern Mythology **26**:163

Irving, Edward B., Jr.
Beowulf **1**:123
The Dream of the Rood **14**:283

Irwin, Terence
Epicurus **21**:192
Aristotelian Philosophy **31**:85

Isayeva, Natalia
Sankara **32**:382

Isenberg, M.
The Igor Tale **1**:515

Isherwood, Christopher
Bhagavad Gita **12**:54

Isidore of Seville
Plato **8**:211

Ivanhoe, Philip J.
Confucius **19**:95

Ivry, Alfred L.
Averroes **7**:52

Jack, George B.
Havelok **34**:213

Jackson, F. J. Foakes
Anna Comnena **25**:36
Josephus, Flavius **13**:226

Jackson, Holbrook
Khayyam **11**:264

Jackson, W. H.
Hartmann von Aue **15**:188

Jackson, W. T. H.
Chretien de Troyes **10**:218
Gottfried von Strassburg **10**:267,
285, 302

Jacob, Alfred
Razon de Amor **16**:340

Jacobs, Joseph
Aesop **24**:12
Longus **7**:217

Jacobsen, Thorkild
Epic of Gilgamesh **3**:342

Jacobson, Howard
Ovid **7**:378

Jaeger, C. Stephen
Gottfried von Strassburg **10**:298,
303

Jaeger, Werner
Aeschylus **11**:133
Aristophanes **4**:96
Demosthenes **13**:152
Hesiod **5**:91
Odyssey **16**:209
Plato **8**:281
Sappho **3**:413
Sophocles **2**:331

Jakobson, Roman
The Igor Tale **1**:499

James, Montague Rhodes
Map, Walter **32**:82, 91

Janeira, Armando Martins
Sei Shonagon **6**:302

Jansen, John F.
Tertullian **29**:366

Jansen, J. J. G.
The *Koran* **23**:287

Janson, Tore
Cato, Marcus Porcius **21**:29

Jaspers, Karl
Augustine, St. **6**:69
Lao Tzu **7**:139
Plato **8**:312

Jastrow, Morris, Jr.
The Book of Job **14**:150
Epic of Gilgamesh **3**:303

Jebb, Richard C.
Euripides **23**:100
Hesiod **5**:77
Sophocles **2**:322
Thucydides **17**:215

Jeffery, Arthur
The *Koran* **23**:249

Jenkins, John I.
Aquinas, St. Thomas **33**:107

Jenkins, T. Atkinson
The Song of Roland **1**:175

Jenkyns, Richard
Sappho **3**:479

Jevons, Frank Byron
Herodotus **17**:59
Thucydides **17**:226

John, Ivor B.
Mabinogion **9**:148

John of Salisbury
Augustine, St. **6**:4
Plato **8**:211

John Paul II
Aquinas, St. Thomas **33**:46

Johnson, Ann S.
Anglo-Saxon Chronicle **4**:17

Johnson, Leslie Peter
Wolfram von Eschenbach **5**:373

Johnson, Samuel
Aeneid **9**:316

Johnson, Sidney M.
Wolfram von Eschenbach **5**:429

Johnson, Skuli
Martial **35**:311

Johnson, W. R.
Aeneid **9**:439
Lucan **33**:400
Ovid **7**:401
Sappho **3**:476
Propertius, Sextus **32**:277

Johnston, F. R.
St. Birgitta **24**:113

Jones, Charles W.
Bede **20**:35

Jones, Francis L.
Martial **35**:299

Jones, George Fenwick
The Song of Roland **1**:194

Jones, Gwyn
Beowulf **1**:144
Hrafnkel's Saga **2**:84
Mabinogion **9**:167, 174
Njals saga **13**:323

Jones, Martin H.
Wolfram von Eschenbach **5**:354

Jones, Rufus M.
Meister Eckhart **9**:40

Jones, Thomas
Arthurian Legend **10**:18
Mabinogion **9**:167

Jones, W. Lewis
Layamon **10**:319

Jordan, William J.
Rhetoric **31**:248

Jump, John D.
Pindar **12**:327

Jung, C. G.
Meister Eckhart **9**:30

Juvenal
Cicero, Marcus Tullius **3**:175

Kafka, Franz
Odyssey **16**:208

Kahn, Charles H.
Anaximander **22**:91

Heraclitus **22**:154
Pythagoras **22**:308

Kant, Immanuel
Plato **8**:223

Kato, Shuichi
Murasaki, Lady **1**:450
Sei Shonagon **6**:304

Kay, N. M.
Martial **35**:364

Kazmi, S. Hasan Askari
Al-Biruni **28**:183

Keene, Donald
Murasaki, Lady **1**:432

Keith, A. Berriedale
Kalidasa **9**:96

Kelly, Patricia
Tain Bo Cualnge **30**: 197

Kelsey, W. Michael
Eastern Mythology **26**:151

Kemp-Welch, Alice
Marie de France **8**:114

Kendall, Willmoore
Cicero, Marcus Tullius **3**:274

Kennedy, Charles W.
Beowulf **1**:89
Cædmon **7**:84
Cynewulf **23**:13
The Dream of the Rood **14**:227

Kennedy, George A.
Demosthenes **13**:167
Hermogenes **6**:184, 194
Ovid **7**:376

Kenney, E. J.
Ovid **7**:345, 443

Kent, Roland G.
Plautus **24**:170

Ker, W. P.
Anglo-Saxon Chronicle **4**:2
Beowulf **1**:59, 64
Boccaccio, Giovanni **13**:42
Chretien de Troyes **10**:131
The Dream of the Rood **14**:229
The Song of Roland **1**:164

Kerenyi, C.
Greek Mythology **26**:280
Kalevala **6**:241

Kerferd, G. B.
Presocratic philosophy **22**:47

Khallikan, Ibn
Al-Jahiz **25**:269

Kibler, William W.
Chretien de Troyes **10**:231

Kibre, Pearl

Albert the Great **16**:97

Kieckhefer, Richard
Meister Eckhart **9**:66

Kierkegaard, Søren
Aristophanes **4**:48
The Book of Job **14**:125
Plato **8**:232
Sophocles **2**:305

King, James Roy
Rumi, Jalal al-Din **20**:382

King, K. C.
Hartmann von Aue **15**:171

Kinghorn, A. M.
Barbour, John **33**:182

Kirk, G. S.
Epic of Gilgamesh **3**:331
Greek Mythology **26**:229, 254
Heraclitus **22**:132
Iliad **1**:371
Odyssey **16**:273
Parmenides **22**:234
Presocratic philosophy **22**:16

Kirkby, Helen
Boethius **15**:79

Kirkham, Victoria
Boccaccio, Giovanni **13**:94

Kirkwood, G. M.
Sappho **3**:445
Sophocles **2**:377

Kitto, H. D. F.
Aeschylus **11**:137
Odyssey **16**:287
Sophocles **2**:393

Klaeber, Friederich
Beowulf **1**:69

Klein, Karen Wilk
Bertran de Born **5**:35

Kleiner, Sighard
St. Benedict of Nursia **29**:34

Kleiner, Yu. A.
Cædmon **7**:111

Klemp, P. J.
Vita Nuova **18**:367

Knapp, Charles
Aeneid **9**:341

Knapp, Peggy Ann
Sir Gawain and the Green Knight
2:268

Knight, Douglas
Torah **30**:301

Knight, Virginia
Apollonius Rhodius **28**:78

Knight, W. F. Jackson

Ovid **7**:340

Knoche, Ulrich
Juvenal **8**:56

Knorr, William C.
Euclid **25**:220

Knowles, Dom David
Rolle, Richard **21**:302

Knowlton, Sister Mary Arthur
Rolle, Richard **21**:366

Knox, Bernard M. W.
Aeschylus **11**:183
Euripides **23**:200
Sophocles **2**:371, 397

Kobayashi, Ichiro
Kokinshu **29**:206

Koht, Halvdan
Hrafnkel's Saga **2**:82

Kolbing, Eugen
Bevis of Hampton **35**:140

Konishi, Jin'ichi
Kokinshu **29**:208
Murasaki, Lady **1**:471
Sei Shonagon **6**:322

Konstan, David
Menander **9**:282
Terence **14**:376

Korte, Alfred
Callimachus **18**:3

Kotanski, Wieslaw
Kojiki **21**:260

Kott, Jan
Sophocles **2**:410

Koyre, Alexandre
Plato **8**:284

Kraft, Kent T.
Cicero, Marcus Tullius **3**:293

Kratz, Dennis M.
Hroswitha of Gandersheim **29**:153

Kratz, Henry
Hrafnkel's Saga **2**:126
Wolfram von Eschenbach **5**:365

Kraus, Franklin B.
Martial **35**:308

Krishnamoorthy, K.
Kalidasa **9**:114

Kristeller, Paul Oskar
Augustine, St. **6**:64
Plato **8**:326

Krohn, Julius
Kalevala **6**:216

Kroll, Paul W.

Li Po **2**:174

Kupfer, Joseph
Bacon, Roger **14**:95

Kustas, George L.
Hermogenes **6**:175, 178

Laborde, E. D.
Anglo-Saxon Chronicle **4**:7

Lacey, W. K.
Cicero, Marcus Tullius **3**:281

Lactantius, Lucius Caelius Firmianus
Cicero, Marcus Tullius **3**:177

Lacy, Norris J.
Chretien de Troyes **10**:169

Laertius, Diogenes
Epicurus **21**:72

Lagercrantz, Olof
Inferno **3**:134

Laidlaw, W. A.
Cicero, Marcus Tullius **3**:252

Laistner, M. L. W.
Livy **11**:325

Lamberton, Robert
Hesiod **5**:170

Landor, Walter Savage
Seneca, Lucius Annaeus **6**:337

Lang, Andrew
Kalevala **6**:212, 230
Khayyam **11**:266
Layamon **10**:317
Odyssey **16**:204

Lange, Lynda
Science **31**:324

Lanham, Richard A.
Ovid **7**:395

Larbaud, Valery
St. Jerome **30**:79

Lassner, Jacob
Al-Jahiz **25**:280

Lateiner, Donald
Herodotus **17**:126

Latham, Ronald
Polo, Marco **15**:298

Lattimore, Richmond
Herodotus **17**:83
Iliad **1**:344

Lau, D. C.
Lao Tzu **7**:147

Lawrence Bruce B.
Al-Biruni **28**:148, 166

Lawrence, William Witherle
Beowulf **1**:75

Lawton, W. C.
Hesiod **5**:79

Layamon
Layamon **10**:311, 314

Leach, Anna
Arabian Nights **2**:16

Leaman, Oliver
Averroes **7**:66

Le Bossu, Rene
Aeneid **9**:298
Iliad **1**:278
Odyssey **16**:187

Lecky, W. E. H.
Bacon, Roger **14**:11

Lee, Alvin A.
Beowulf **1**:140

Lee, Guy
Catullus **18**:185

Leech, Kenneth
Llull, Ramon **12**:124

Leff, Gordon
Abelard **11**:22
Augustine, St. **6**:88

Lefkowitz, Mary R.
Apollonius Rhodius **28**:17
Sappho **3**:481

Le Gentil, Pierre
The Song of Roland **1**:203

Legge, James
Confucius **19**:3

Legouis, Emile
Layamon **10**:319

Leibniz, Gottfried Wilhelm
Augustine, St. **6**:8
Averroes **7**:5
Plato **8**:220

Leiter, Louis H.
The Dream of the Rood **14**:256

Lemke, Walter H., Jr.
Bodel, Jean **28**:218

Leon, Harry J.
Cicero, Marcus Tullius **3**:218

Leonard, William Ellery
Socrates **27**:232

Lerer, Seth
Boethius **15**:124

Le Saint, William P.
Tertullian **29**:313, 319

Lesky, Albin

Aeschylus **11**:158, 190
Demosthenes **13**:162
Hesiod **5**:112
Odyssey **16**:304
Pindar **12**:317
Sophocles **2**:378

Lessing, Gotthold Ephraim
Martial **35**:249
Sophocles **2**:294

Letts, Malcolm
Mandeville, Sir John **19**:108

Lever, Katherine
Aristophanes **4**:123
Menander **9**:227, 233

Levy, G. R.
Epic of Gilgamesh **3**:313

Levy, Howard S.
Po Chu-i **24**:296

Lewis, C. S.
Aeneid **9**:364
Apuleius **1**:32
Beowulf **1**:87
Boethius **15**:43
The Book of Psalms **4**:403
Chretien de Troyes **10**:147
Layamon **10**:343
Romance of the Rose **8**:387
Sir Gawain and the Green Knight **2**:221

Lewis, George Cornewall
Thucydides **17**:243

Levy, Reuben
Avicenna **16**:180

Lewis, Geoffrey
Book of Dede Korkut **8**:103

Lewis, Rev. Gerrard
Poem of the Cid **4**:228

Liebeschuetz, W.
Boethius **15**:47
Livy **11**:357

Likhachov, Dmitry
The Igor Tale **1**:523

Lindberg, David C.
Bacon, Roger **14**:106
Euclid **25**:148

Lindsay, Jack
Bertran de Born **5**:55
Longus **7**:229

Lindsay, Thomas B.
Juvenal **8**:17

Littell, Robert
Murasaki, Lady **1**:419

Littleton, C. Scott
Eastern Mythology **26**:121

Liu Wu-chi

Confucius **19**:42
Li Po **2**:143

Livy
Livy **11**:311
Cato, Marcus Porcius **21**:4

Lloyd, G. E. R.
Presocratic philosophy **22**:36
Science **31**:311, 331

Lloyd-Jones, Hugh
Aeschylus **11**:168
Menander **9**:231
Odyssey **16**:321
Pindar **12**:342

Locke, John
Aesop **24**:4

Lodge, Thomas
Seneca, Lucius Annaeus **6**:335

Lofmark, Carl
Wolfram von Eschenbach **5**:358

Long, A. A.
Epicurus **21**:163

Long, J. Bruce
Mahabharata **5**:270

Longfellow, Henry Wadsworth
Beowulf **1**:57
Inferno **3**:23

Longinus
Aeschylus **11**:83
Cicero, Marcus Tullius **3**:174
Odyssey **16**:192
Plato **8**:206
Sappho **3**:379
Sophocles **2**:292

Longus
Longus **7**:216

Lonnrot, Elias
Kalevala **6**:208, 210

Loomis, Roger Sherman
Arthurian Legend **10**:57, 90, 110
Layamon **10**:341

Lord, Albert B.
Iliad **1**:363
Odyssey **16**:259˙

Lord Byron
Martial **35**:251

Lord, Catherine
Poetics **31**:168

Louth, Andrew
Origen **19**:254

Loux, Michael J.
William of Ockham **32**:152

Lowe, J. C. B.
Plautus **24**:238

Lowell, Amy
Izumi, Shikibu **33**:258
Murasaki, Lady **1**:417

Lowth, Robert
The Book of Psalms **4**:352
Song of Songs **18**:238

Lucas, F. L.
Epic of Gilgamesh **3**:309
Li Po **2**:135
Seneca, Lucius Annaeus **6**:363

Luck, Georg
Ovid **7**:346

Luke, J. Tracy
Epic of Gilgamesh **3**:343

Luscombe, D. E.
Abelard **11**:48, 61

Lu-shih, Lin
Lao Tzu **7**:155

Luther, Martin
The Book of Psalms **4**:347
Cicero, Marcus Tullius **3**:185
Song of Songs **18**:230

Luttrell, Claude
Chretien de Troyes **10**:195

Lyne, R. O. A. M.
Catullus **18**:148

Lyons, Deborah
Greek Mythology **26**:265

Macaulay, Thomas Babbington
Catullus **18**:99
Martial **35**:251
Greek Historiography **17**:2
Ovid **7**:292

MacCana, Proinsias
Celtic Mythology **26**:2, 68

MacCulloch, John Arnott
Norse Mythology **26**:327

Macdonell, Arthur A.
Mahabharata **5**:185

McInerny, Ralph
Aquinas, St. Thomas **33**:60

Mackail, J. W.
Aeneid **9**:327
Cato, Marcus Porcius **21**:25
Iliad **1**:315
Odyssey **16**:243
Sappho **3**:389
Seneca, Lucius Annaeus **6**:344
Sophocles **2**:317
Terence **14**:302

MacKay, L. A.
Apuleius **1**:32

MacKillop, James
Celtic Mythology **26**:96

Macrae-Gibson, O. D.
The Dream of the Rood **14**:278

Macrobius, Ambrosius Theodosius
Aeneid **9**:294
Apuleius **1**:3
Cicero, Marcus Tullius **3**:178

Maeterlinck, Maurice
Arabian Nights **2**:17

Magnus, Albertus
Albert the Great **16**:65

Magnus, Leonard A.
The Igor Tale **1**:480

Magnusson, Magnus
Njals saga **13**:332

Magoun, Francis Peabody, Jr.
Cædmon **7**:101
Kalevala **6**:246

Mahaffey, John Pentland
Xeonophon **17**:322

Maier, John
Epic of Gilgamesh **3**:354

Mainster, Phoebe A.
Barbour, John **33**:223

Mair, Victor H.
Li Po **2**:168

Maki, J. M.
Murasaki, Lady **1**:426

Makin, Peter
Bertran de Born **5**:56
Sordello **15**:360

Mallery, Richard D.
Polo, Marco **15**:295

Malnati, T. P.
Martial **35**:367

Malone, Kemp
Beowulf **1**:92
Cædmon **7**:109

Malory, Sir Thomas
Arthurian Legend **10**:44

Malti-Douglas, Fedwa
Al-Jahiz **25**:292

Malvern, Marjorie M.
Marie de France **8**:171

Mandal, Paresh Chandra
Kalidasa **9**:137

Mandelstam, Osip
Inferno **3**:74

Manilius
Menander **9**:214

Mann, Cameron
Arabian Nights **2**:19

Critic Index

Manning, Susan
Ossian **28**:352

Marble, Annie Russell
Petrarch **20**:225

March, Andrew L.
Su Shih **15**:395

Margesson, Helen P.
Polo, Marco **15**:273

Marie de France
Marie de France **8**:113

Maritain, Jacques
Augustine, St. **6**:24
Inferno **3**:101

Markman, Alan M.
Sir Gawain and the Green Knight
2:209

Marks, Claude
Bertran de Born **5**:48

Marmura, Michael
Avicenna **16**:165

Marotta, Joseph
Wolfram von Eschenbach **5**:396

Marquardt, Patricia
Hesiod **5**:161

Marrou, Henri
Augustine, St. **6**:60

Marsh, George P.
Polo, Marco **15**:269

Marshall, F. W.
Bodel, Jean **28**:198

Marti, Berthe M.
Lucan **33**:347

Martin, Charles
Catullus **18**:138

Martin, Christopher
Ovid **7**:430

Martin, R. H.
Terence **14**:354

Mascaro, Juan
Bhagavad Gita **12**:57

Masih, Y.
Sankara **32**:351

Mason, Herbert
Epic of Gilgamesh **3**:336

Masters, Edgar Lee
Li Po **2**:137

Matter, E. Ann
Song of Songs **18**:306

Matthews, Caitlín
Mabinogion **9**:186

Matthews, William
Morte Arthure **10**:380

Maurer, Armand
William of Ockham **32**:164

Maxwell, Herbert
Bacon, Roger **14**:14
Barbour, John **33**:154

May, Rollo
Inferno **3**:154

Mayer, Frederick
Bacon, Roger **14**:69

Mayer, J. P.
Cicero, Marcus Tullius **3**:220

Maynadier, Howard
Arthurian Legend **10**:115

Mays, James Luther
The Book of Psalms **4**:443

McCabe, Mary Margaret
Rhetoric **31**:280

McCallum, J. Ramsay
Abelard **11**:10

McCann, Justin
St. Benedict of Nursia **29**:29

McConnell, Winder
Hartmann von Aue **15**:241

McCoy, Patricia
Das Nibelungenlied **12**:162

McCulloh, William E.
Longus **7**:242

McCullough, Helen Craig
Kokinshu **29**:258

McDiarmid, Matthew P.
Barbour, John **33**:213

McDonald, William C.
Hartmann von Aue **15**:244

McGiffert, Arthur Cushman
St. John **27**:42

McGrade, Arthur Stephen
William of Ockham **32**:180

McGregor, James H.
Boccaccio, Giovanni **13**:102

McGuire, Michael D.
Meister Eckhart **9**:60

McKay, K. J.
Callimachus **18**:28

McKeon, Richard
Cicero, Marcus Tullius **3**:241

McKeown, J. C.
Ovid **7**:424

McKenzie, Kenneth
Vita Nuova **18**:325

McKim, Anne M.
Barbour, John **33**:205
Barbour, John **33**:230

McKirahan, Richard D., Jr.
Anaximander **22**:106
Parmenides **22**:252
Pythagoras **22**:350

McLeish, Kenneth
Catullus **18**:144

McNamee, Maurice B., S. J.
Beowulf **1**:116

McNary, Sarah F.
Beowulf **1**:58

Meagher, Robert Emmet
Greek Mythology **26**:300

Meaney, Audrey L.
Anglo-Saxon Chronicle **4**:31

Megas, Georgios A.
Aesop **24**:23

Mehl, Dieter
Bevis of Hampton **35**:177
Havelok **34**:190

Meisami, Julie Scott
Hafiz **34**:135

Mendell, Clarence W.
Petronius **34**:270
Seneca, Lucius Annaeus **6**:375

Menocal, Maria Rosa
Vita Nuova **18**:372

Menon, Yakeshava
Sankara **32**:312

Merchant, Frank Ivan
Seneca, Lucius Annaeus **6**:357

Meredith, George
Aristophanes **4**:56
Menander **9**:243
Terence **14**:303

Merimee, Ernest
Poem of the Cid **4**:246

Merrill, John Ernest
St. John **27**:50

Merriman, James Douglas
Arthurian Legend **10**:35

Merton, Thomas
Meister Eckhart **9**:58

Mew, James
Arabian Nights **2**:11

Meyendorff, John
St. John **27**:56

Meyers, Carol
Song of Songs **18**:292

Michael, Ian
Poem of the Cid **4**:291

Michelangelo
Inferno **3**:6

Michener, Richard L.
Chretien de Troyes **10**:171

Mickel, Emanuel J., Jr.
Marie de France **8**:150

Mill, J. S.
Plato **8**:247

Miller, Barbara Stoler
Bhagavad Gita **12**:85

Miller, Frank Justus
Seneca, Lucius Annaeus **6**:362

Miller, Norma
Menander **9**:284

Miller, Patrick D., Jr.
The Book of Psalms **4**:430, 448

Miller, William
Anna Comnena **25**:2

Mills, M.
Havelok **34**:177

Milman, Henry Hart
Inferno **3**:22
St. Jerome **30**:55

Milton, John
The Book of Psalms **4**:351

Miner, Earl
Izumi, Shikibu **33**:299
Kokinshu **29**:227

Mirel, Barbara
Aesop **24**:59

Mirsky, Prince D. S.
The Igor Tale **1**:484

Mitchell, John D.
Kalidasa **9**:108

Mittelstadt, Michael C.
Longus **7**:238

Molinaro, Ursule
Hypatia **35**:225

Momigliano, Arnaldo
Greek Historiography **17**:36
Polybius **17**:185
Xenophon **17**:336

Mommsen, Theodor E.
Cicero, Marcus Tullius **3**:189
Petrarch **20**:236
Terence **14**:304

Monahan, Michael

Sappho 3:397

Monk, Samuel H.
Longinus 27:154

Montaigne, Michel de
Cicero, Marcus Tullius 3:187
Iliad 1:275
Seneca, Lucius Annaeus 6:333
Terence 14:362

Montgomery, Thomas
Poem of the Cid 4:331

Mookerjee, Arun Kumar
Mahabharata 5:276

Moon, Harold
Poem of the Cid 4:267

Mooney, George W.
Apollonius Rhodius 28:2

Moore, George
Longus 7:223

Moore, Olin H.
Bertran de Born 5:29

Moorman, Charles
Iliad 1:376
Mabinogion 9:195
Das Nibelungenlied 12:223
Pearl 19:314
The Song of Roland 1:231

Moorman, Frederic W.
Sir Gawain and the Green Knight
2:184

Moravcsik, J. M. E.
Science 31:303

Morgan, Bayard Quincy
Wolfram von Eschenbach 5:307

Morgan, Wendy
Mystery of Adam 4:211

Morghen, Raffaello
Inferno 3:121

Morley, Henry
Layamon 10:312

Morrall, J. B.
Cicero, Marcus Tullius 3:295

Morris, George S.
Bacon, Roger 14:13

Morris, Ivan
Murasaki, Lady 1:434, 438
Sei Shonagon 6:303

Morris, Mark
Sei Shonagon 6:307

Morris, Richard
Pearl 19:277

Morris, Rosemary
Arthurian Legend 10:95

Morris, William
Arthurian Legend 10:81

Morrison, Madison
Lao Tzu 7:203

Mortimer, Raymond
Murasaki, Lady 1:417, 423

Moseley, C.W.R.D.
Mandeville, Sir John 19:148

Motto, Anna Lydia
Seneca, Lucius Annaeus 6:384,
411

Moulton, Carroll
Menander 9:272

Moulton, Richard G.
Arabian Nights 2:22
The Book of Psalms 4:366

Mowatt, D. G.
Das Nibelungenlied 12:177, 220

Mowinckel, Sigmund
The Book of Psalms 4:405

Mudrick, Marvin
Marie de France 8:166

Mueller, Ian
Euclid 25:162

Mueller, Werner A.
Das Nibelungenlied 12:179

Muir, Edwin
Odyssey 16:287

Muir, Lynette R.
Mystery of Adam 4:204

Mullally, Evelyn
Chretien de Troyes 10:229

Muller, Herbert J.
Aeschylus 11:152

Murakami, Fuminobu
Kojiki 21:264

Murasaki, Lady
Sei Shonagon 6:291

Murdoch, Iris
Plato 8:362

Mure, G. R. G.
Aristotelian Philosophy 31:61

Murnaghan, Sheila
Odyssey 16:310

Murphy, Francis X.
Petrarch 20:255
St. Jerome 30:104

Murphy, Mabel Gant
Aeneid 9:330

Murray, Gilbert

Aeschylus 11:144
Demosthenes 13:137
Iliad 1:312
Ovid 7:303
Pindar 12:303
Sophocles 2:340

Murray, Oswyn
Herodotus 17:102

Murray, Thomas Chalmers
The Book of Psalms 4:361

Murry, J. Middleton
Beowulf 1:69

Musa, Mark
Vita Nuova 18:355

Muscatine, Charles
Romance of the Rose 8:407

Musurillo, Herbert
Juvenal 8:61
Petronius 34:330

Myerowitz, Molly
Ovid 7:435

Nabokov, Vladimir
The Igor Tale 1:504

Nadeau, Ray
Hermogenes 6:170

Nadvi, Syed H. H.
Al-Biruni 28:132

Nakosteen, Mehdi
Khayyam 11:295

Nasr, Seyyed Hossein
Al-Biruni 28:175

Naumann, Hans
Wolfram von Eschenbach 5:304

Navia, Luis E.
Socrates 27:374

Needler, George Henry
Das Nibelungenlied 12:153

Nehamas, Alexander
Plato 8:364

Nelson, Deborah
Chretien de Troyes 10:199

Nelson, Leonard
Socrates 27:241

Nepaulsingh, Colbert I.
Razon de Amor 16:366

Nethercut, William R.
Apuleius 1:38

Neugebauer, O.
Euclid 25:141

Newbold, William Romaine
Bacon, Roger 14:37

Newby, P. H.
Arabian Nights 2:38

Newman, Barbara J.
Hildegard von Bingen 20:161, 172

Newman, John Henry Cardinal
Cicero, Marcus Tullius 3:188, 191

Newsom, Carroll V.
Euclid 25:131

Newstead, Helaine
Map, Walter 32:92

Nichols, James R.
Murasaki, Lady 1:442

Nichols, Marianna da Vinci
Hroswitha of Gandersheim 29:142

Nichols, Stephen G., Jr.
The Song of Roland 1:189

Nicholson, Reynold A.
Rumi, Jalal al-Din 20:352

Niebuhr, H. Richard
Augustine, St. 6:56

Nietzsche, Friedrich
Aeschylus 11:98
Aristophanes 4:57
Inferno 3:46
Plato 8:251
Sophocles 2:312

Niles, John D.
Beowulf 1:150

Nilsson, Martin P.
Greek Mythology 26:209

Nisbet, R. G. M.
Cicero, Marcus Tullius 3:263

Nisetich, Frank J.
Pindar 12:335

Nissen, Christopher
Boccaccio, Giovanni 13:122

Noble, Peter S.
Chretien de Troyes 10:210

Noffke, Suzanne
St. Catherine 27:12

Nohrnberg, James
Inferno 3:139

Nordal, Sigurður
Hrafnkel's Saga 2:91

Norinaga, Motoori
Murasaki, Lady 1:415

Normore, Calvin G.
William of Ockham 32:205

Northcott, Kenneth J.
Wolfram von Eschenbach 5:403

Critic Index

Norton, Charles Eliot
Khayyam **11**:236
Vita Nuova **18**:318

Norwood, Frances
Apuleius **1**:26

Norwood, Gilbert
Aeschylus **11**:116
Aristophanes **4**:92
Menander **9**:205
Pindar **12**:266
Terence **14**:309, 315

Nothnagle, John T.
Chretien de Troyes **10**:157

Nutt, Alfred
Wolfram von Eschenbach **5**:299

Nyberg, Lars
Apollonius Rhodius **28**:34

Nyberg, Tore
St. Birgitta **24**:122

Nyland, Waino
Kalevala **6**:238

Obata, Shigeyoshi
Li Po **2**:133

Obrist, Barbara
St. Birgitta **24**:106

Obuchowski, Mary Dejong
Murasaki, Lady **1**:444

Ó Cathasaigh, Tomás
Celtic Mythology **26**:40
Tain Bo Cualnge **30**: 214

O'Cleirigh, P.M.
Origen **19**:234

Odenkirchen, Carl V.
Mystery of Adam **4**:205

Ogilvy, J. D. A.
Beowulf **1**:154

Oinas, Felix J.
Kalevala **6**:254

Oldfather, W. A.
Cicero, Marcus Tullius **3**:206

Olschki, Leonardo
Polo, Marco **15**:293

Olson, Elder
Longinus **27**:165

O'Meara, Thomas Franklin
Aquinas, St. Thomas **33**:119

Oppenheim, A. Leo
Epic of Gilgamesh **3**:321

O'Rahilly, Thomas F.
Celtic Mythology **26**:28

Origen

Song of Songs **18**:200

Ormsby, John
Poem of the Cid **4**:226

Osborn, Eric
Basil of Caesaria **35**:69
Tertullian **29**:381

Osen, Lynn M.
Hypatia **35**:219

Osgood, Charles G.
Boccaccio, Giovanni **13**:37

Osterud, Svein
Hesiod **5**:145

Otis, Brooks
Aeneid **9**:429
Ovid **7**:356

Otter, Monika
Map, Walter **32**:117

Otto, Rudolph
Meister Eckhart **9**:35

Ovid
Ovid **7**:281

Owen, D. D. R.
Chretien de Troyes **10**:173
The Song of Roland **1**:191, 236

Owen, S. G.
Juvenal **8**:25

Owen, Stephen
Li Po **2**:156

Owens, Joseph
Aristotelian Philosophy **31**:23

Owens, William M.
Plautus **24**:276

Packer, Mark
Poetics **31**:180

Paden, William D., Jr.
Bertran de Born **5**:51, 61

Padula, Vincenzo
Propertius, Sextus **32**:218

Page, Denys
Odyssey **16**:300
Sappho **3**:430

Pagels, Elaine
Augustine, St. **6**:140

Palgrave, Francis T.
Ovid **7**:299
Sappho **3**:386

Palsson, Hermann
Hrafnkel's Saga **2**:108

Palumbo, Donald
Arabian Nights **2**:71

Pancoast, Henry S.
Layamon **10**:314

Pandiri, Thalia A.
Longus **7**:265

Pandit, R. S.
Kalidasa **9**:103

Papini, Giovanni
Augustine, St. **6**:37

Pappas, Nickolas
Socrates **27**:368

Park, Katharine
Albert the Great **16**:112

Parker, Douglass
Terence **14**:352

Parry, Adam
Aeneid **9**:421

Parry, Kenneth
St. John **27**:85

Parshall, Linda B.
Wolfram von Eschenbach **5**:378

Patch, Howard R.
Boethius **15**:15
The Dream of the Rood **14**:218

Pater, Walter
Apuleius **1**:14
Plato **8**:252

Paterson, John
The Book of Psalms **4**:395

Paton, Lucy Allen
Layamon **10**:315

Patrick, Mary Mills
Sappho **3**:393

Patten, Faith H.
The Dream of the Rood **14**:268

Patterson, Annabel M.
Hermogenes **6**:178

Patton, John H.
Meister Eckhart **9**:60

Paul, Herbert
Cicero, Marcus Tullius **3**:194

Payne, F. Anne
Lucian **32**:50

Payne, John
Arabian Nights **2**:12
Hafiz **34**:45

Pearson, C. H.
Juvenal **8**:11

Pearson, Karl
Meister Eckhart **9**:9

Pearson, Lionel

Demosthenes **13**:182

Pease, Arthur Stanley
St. Jerome **30**:57

Pease, Samuel James
Xenophon **17**:329

Peck, Russell A.
Morte Arthure **10**:406

Peers, E. Allison
Llull, Ramon **12**:92, 95

Pei, Mario A.
The Song of Roland **1**:178

Pekarik, Andrew
Murasaki, Lady **1**:460

Pellat, Charles
Al-Jahiz **25**:326

Pence, Mary Elizabeth
St. Jerome **30**: 72

Penwill, J. L.
Apuleius **1**:42

Penzer, N. M.
Polo, Marco **15**:276

Pepler, Conrad
Rolle, Richard **21**:330

Perkins, Agnes
Aesop **24**:56

Perrier, Joseph Louis
Bertran de Born **5**:24

Perry, Ben Edwin
Aesop **24**:32
Apuleius **1**:34
Petronius **34**:277
Phaedrus **25**:347

Perry, George G.
Rolle, Richard **21**:272

Perry, Henry Ten Eyck
Menander **9**:214
Terence **14**:333

Perse, St.-John
Inferno **3**:131

Peters, F. E.
Al-Biruni **28**:138

Petersen, David L.
Torah **30**:339

Petrarch, Francesco
Augustine, St. **6**:7
Boccaccio, Giovanni **13**:4
Cicero, Marcus Tullius **3**:181, 182

Petronio, Giuseppe
Boccaccio, Giovanni **13**:47

Pfeiffer, Rudolf
Callimachus **18**:43

Pflieger, Pat
Aesop **24**:66

Philippides, Marios
Longus **7**:260

Philostratus
Hermogenes **6**:158

Pickering, Charles J.
Khayyam **11**:249
Avicenna **16**:156

Pickering, F. P.
Hartmann von Aue **15**:218

Pidal, Ramon Menendez
Poem of the Cid **4**:234

Pinkerton, Percy E.
Wolfram von Eschenbach **5**:293

Piramus, Denis
Marie de France **8**:113

Plass, Paul
Martial **35**:357

Plato
Aristophanes **4**:38
Iliad **1**:270
Plato **8**:200

Pliny the Younger
Martial **35**:248

Plumptre, E. H.
Bacon, Roger **14**:10

Plutarch
Aeschylus **11**:84
Aristophanes **4**:40
Cato, Marcus Porcius **21**:4
Demosthenes **13**:148, 163, 185
Epicurus **21**:70
Herodotus **17**:50
Menander **9**:203
Sappho **3**:379

Poag, James F.
Wolfram von Eschenbach **5**:400

Podlecki, Anthony J.
Pindar **12**:351
Sappho **3**:491

Poe, Joe Park
Seneca, Lucius Annaeus **6**:389

Poggioli, Renato
The Igor Tale **1**:507
Inferno **3**:123

Polomé, Edgar C.
Norse Mythology **26**:353

Polybius
Greek Historiography **17**:25

Pomeroy, Sarah B.
Aristophanes **4**:155

Pope, Alexander

Aeneid **9**:313, 358
Iliad **1**:284
Odyssey **16**:192

Pope, John C.
Cædmon **7**:110

Pope, Marvin H.
The Book of Job **14**:181
Song of Songs **18**:266

Popper, K. R.
Plato **8**:348

Portalie, Eugene
Augustine, St. **6**:17

Porter, Jean
Aquinas, St. Thomas **33**:65

Portor, Laura Spencer
Arabian Nights **2**:23

Poschl, Viktor
Aeneid **9**:377

Post, Chandler Rathfon
Razon de Amor **16**:338

Post, L. A.
Menander **9**:218

Pound, Ezra
Bertran de Born **5**:22
Inferno **3**:99
Odyssey **16**:279
Poem of the Cid **4**:232
The Song of Roland **1**:173
Sordello **15**:347

Powell, F. York
Hrafnkel's Saga **2**:76

Power, Eileen
Polo, Marco **15**:291

Powys, John Cowper
Iliad **1**:358
Inferno **3**:88

Powys, Llewelyn
Khayyam **11**:275

Prabhavananda, Swami
Bhagavad Gita **12**:54

Pratt, Norman T.
Seneca, Lucius Annaeus **6**:429

Preston, Keith
Martial **35**:277
Petronius **34**:266

Prescott, Henry W.
Aeneid **9**:335

Press, Alan R.
Bertran de Born **5**:48

Pretor, Alfred
Xenophon **17**:322

Price, Arnold H.

Das Nibelungenlied **12**:164

Price, John Valdimir
Ossian **28**:359

Priest, George Madison
Wolfram von Eschenbach **5**:301

Priest, John F.
Aesop **24**:73

Pritchett, V. S.
Murasaki, Lady **1**:452
Poem of the Cid **4**:263, 264

Proclus Diadochus
Euclid **25**:89
Plato **8**:209

Prothero, Rowland E.
The Book of Psalms **4**:373

Proust, Marcel
Arabian Nights **2**:25

Prowett, C. G.
Apuleius **1**:13

Pruyser, Paul W.
Epic of Gilgamesh **3**:343

Pseudo-Longinus
Demosthenes **13**:134, 175

Puette, William J.
Murasaki, Lady **1**:463

Puhvel, Jaan
Celtic Mythology **26**:13
Eastern Mythology **26**:179

Purdon, Liam O.
Barbour, John **33**:245

Purser, Louis C.
Ovid **7**:299

Putnam, Edward Kirby
Havelok **34**:145

Putnam, Michael C. J.
Aeneid **9**:428

Quasimodo, Salvatore
Inferno **3**:113
Sappho **3**:435

Qudsi, Obaidullah
Al-Biruni **28**:143

Quennell, Peter
Apuleius **1**:22

Quiller-Couch, Sir Arthur
Beowulf **1**:67

Quinn, Kenneth
Aeneid **9**:408
Catullus **18**:99, 116

Quinones, Ricardo J.
Inferno **3**:140

Quintilian
Aeneid **9**:294
Aristophanes **4**:40
Hesiod **5**:69
Menander **9**:203
Ovid **7**:286
Seneca, Lucius Annaeus **6**:403

Rabin, Chaim
Song of Songs **18**:259

Radhakrishnan, Sarvepalli
Bhagavad Gita **12**:14
Mahabharata **5**:195

Radice, Betty
Abelard **11**:56
Terence **14**:363

Radner, Joan N.
Tain Bo Cualnge **30**: 187

Rahman, Fazlur
Avicenna **16**:134

Raleigh, Walter
Boccaccio, Giovanni **13**:32

Ralphs, Sheila
Inferno **3**:135

Ramanuja
Bhagavad Gita **12**:3

Rambachan, Anantanand
Sankara **32**:365

Ramsay, G. G.
Juvenal **8**:38

Ramsay, W. M.
Basil of Caesaria **35**:34

Rand, Edward Kennard
Aeneid **9**:350
Boethius **15**:4
Cicero, Marcus Tullius **3**:210, 231

Randall, Dale B. J.
Sir Gawain and the Green Knight
2:212

Rankin, David
Tertullian **29**:379

Rankin, H. D.
Petronius **34**:350

Raphael, Frederic
Catullus **18**:144

Rapin, Rene
Iliad **1**:276

Rascoe, Burton
Apuleius **1**:17
Boccaccio, Giovanni **13**:42

Raven, J. E.
Presocratic philosophy **22**:16
Parmenides **22**:234

Rawlinson, Henry

Polo, Marco **15**:267

Raybin, David
Bodel, Jean **28**:264

Reckford, Kenneth J.
Menander **9**:238

Rees, D. A.
Science **31**:353

Regan, Mariann Sanders
Petrarch **20**:293

Rehder, Robert M.
Rumi, Jalal al-Din **20**:367

Reid, Margaret J. C.
Arthurian Legend **10**:44, 62

Reinhardt, Karl
Sophocles **2**:351

Reinstein, P. Gila
Aesop **24**:52

Reiss, Edmund
Boethius **15**:88

Rehder, Von R. M.
Hafiz **34**:92

Rejak, Tessa
Josephus, Flavius **13**:278

Renan, Ernest
The Book of Job **14**:170
Mabinogion **9**:144

Renard, John
Rumi, Jalal al-Din **20**:389

Renoir, Alain
The Song of Roland **1**:199

Rexroth, Kenneth
Abelard **11**:55
Apuleius **1**:37
Beowulf **1**:118
Bhagavad Gita **12**:73
Epic of Gilgamesh **3**:323
Kalevala **6**:252
Mahabharata **5**:242
Murasaki, Lady **1**:441

Rhodes, Jim
Pearl **19**:393

Rhys, John
Mabinogion **9**:147

Rice, Robert C.
Cynewulf **23**:77

Richards, Herbert
Aristophanes **4**:75

Richardson, Professor
Ossian **28**:291

Richardson, Samuel
Aesop **24**:4

Richardson, T. Wade
Petronius **34**:406

Richey, Margaret Fitzgerald
Gottfried von Strassburg **10**:274
Wolfram von Eschenbach **5**:309, 323

Rickert, Edith
Marie de France **8**:113

Rider, Jeff
Layamon **10**:355

Riegel, Jeffrey K.
Confucius **19**:78

Rigg, A. G.
Map, Walter **32**:113

Riha, T.
The Igor Tale **1**:515

Rimmer, J. Thomas
Sei Shonagon **6**:325

Rist, J. M.
Demetrius **34**:34
Hypatia **35**:213

Roberts, Deborah H.
Poetics **31**:206

Roberts, W. Rhys
Longinus **27**:131

Robertson, Howard S.
Bodel, Jean **28**:211

Robinson, Christopher
Lucian **32**:39

Robinson, David Moore
Sappho **3**:396

Robinson, Fred C.
Beowulf **1**:153

Robinson, H. Wheeler
The Book of Psalms **4**:377

Roche, Paul
Sappho **3**:434

Roche, Thomas P., Jr.
Petrarch **20**:247

Rogers, A.K.
Socrates **27**:258

Romilly, Jacqueline de
Aeschylus **11**:192
Hesiod **5**:158

Rorty, Richard
Aristotelian Philosophy **31**:43

Rose, H. J.
Aristophanes **4**:103
Greek Mythology **26**:194

Rosenmeyer, Thomas G.
Aeschylus **11**:196
Euripides **23**:135, 154

Rosenthal, Joel T.
Bede **20**:98

Ross, David
Aristotelian Philosophy **31**:63

Ross, E. Denison
Polo, Marco **15**:284

Rossetti, Dante Gabriel
Vita Nuova **18**:324

Rossi, Paolo
Llull, Ramon **12**:109

Rostovtzeff, Mikhail
Aristophanes **4**:79

Rousseau, Philip
Basil of Caesaria **35**:109

Routh, James
Beowulf **1**:64

Rowley, H. H.
Song of Songs **18**:246

Roy, S.S.
Sankara **32**:319

Royce, Josiah
The Book of Job **14**:130
Meister Eckhart **9**:14

Rubin, David Lee
Phaedrus **25**:376

Ruskin, John
Inferno **3**:14, 19, 21

Russell, Bertrand
Abelard **11**:9
Augustine, St. **6**:53
Averroes **7**:15
Avicenna **16**:171
Bacon, Roger **14**:68
Plato **8**:290
Parmenides **22**:221

Russell, D. A.
Hermogenes **6**:192

Rutherford, Ward
Celtic Mythology **26**:56

Ryder, Arthur W.
Kalidasa **9**:87

Ryder, Frank G.
Das Nibelungenlied **12**:187

Ryder, K. C.
Plautus **24**:233

Sabra, A. I.
Averroes **7**:62
Avicenna **16**:156

Sachiko, Murata
The *Koran* **23**:309

Sachs, Joe
Science **31**:375

Sacker, Hughes
Hartmann von Aue **15**:154
Das Nibelungenlied **12**:220
Wolfram von Eschenbach **5**:336

Sahas, Daniel J.
St. John **27**:67

Sahlin, Claire
St. Birgitta **24**:156

Saint Palaye, Jean Bapstiste de La Curne de
Bertran de Born **5**:4

Saintsbury, George
Aristophanes **4**:69
Longinus **27**:123
Longus **7**:221
Ossian **28**:325

Saklatvala, Beram
Arthurian Legend **10**:13

Sale, George
The *Koran* **23**:232

Salinas, Pedro
Poem of the Cid **4**:247

Salus, Peter H.
Norse Mythology **26**:348

Samuel, Maurice
The Book of Psalms **4**:425

Sandars, N. K.
Epic of Gilgamesh **3**:315

Sandbach, F. H.
Aristophanes **4**:156
Menander **9**:259, 268
Terence **14**:367

Sanford, Eva Matthews
Lucan **33**:343

Sankovitch, Tilde A.
Bertran de Born **5**:61
Marie de France **8**:177

Sansom, George
Sei Shonagon **6**:294

Santayana, George
Inferno **3**:54
Plato **8**:257

Sarasin, Jean Francois
Epicurus **21**:80

Sargeant, Winthrop
Bhagavad Gita **12**:79

Sarna, Nahum A.
The Book of Psalms **4**:421

Sarton, George
Bacon, Roger **14**:61
Euclid **25**:130

Sasson, Jack M.
Epic of Gilgamesh **3**:336

Saunders, A. N. W.
Demosthenes **13**:175

Savage, Henry Littleton
Sir Gawain and the Green Knight
2:206

Sayers, Dorothy L.
The Song of Roland **1**:183

Scartazzini, G. A.
Inferno **3**:39

Schach, Paul
Njals saga **13**:374

Schein, Seth L.
Iliad **1**:399

Schelling, Friedrich Wilhelm Joseph von
Inferno **3**:8

Scheps, Walter
Barbour, John **33**:202

Scherer, W.
Gottfried von Strassburg **10**:248
Wolfram von Eschenbach **5**:295

Schirmer, Walter F.
Layamon **10**:336

Schlauch, Margaret
The Dream of the Rood **14**:223

Schlegel, August Wilhelm
Aeschylus **11**:84
Aristophanes **4**:42
Seneca, Lucius Annaeus **6**:336
Sophocles **2**:299

Schlegel, Frederich
Wolfram von Eschenbach **5**:293

Schleiermacher, Friedrich Ernst Daniel
Plato **8**:228

Schmeling, Gareth
Petronius **34**:348

Schnyder, Hans
Sir Gawain and the Green Knight
2:217

Schoenberner, Franz
Das Nibelungenlied **12**:169

Schofield, Malcom
Heraclitus **22**:193
Parmenides **22**:234

Schopenhauer, Arthur
Meister Eckhart **9**:45
Plato **8**:244

Schotter, Anne Howland
Pearl **19**:365

Schreckenberg, Heinz
Josephus, Flavius **13**:299

Schroeder, Bethany A.
Bodel, Jean **28**:216

Schroeder, Eric
Hafiz **34**:69

Schroeder, Peter R.
Hroswitha of Gandersheim **29**:197

Schucking, Levin L.
Beowulf **1**:78

Schulman, Alan R.
Eastern Mythology **26**:140

Schwartz, Kessel
Poem of the Cid **4**:266

Schwertner, Thomas M.
Albert the Great **16**:19

Scodel, Ruth
Sophocles **2**:426

Scott, John A.
Socrates **27**:276

Scott, Karen
St. Catherine **27**:23

Scragg, D. G.
Anglo-Saxon Chronicle **4**:25

Scullard, H. H.
Cato, Marcus Porcius **21**:31

Sealey, Rapha l
Kalevala **6**:245

Sedgefield, Walter John
Anglo-Saxon Chronicle **4**:3

Sedgwick, Henry Dwight
Petrarch **20**:219

Segal, Charles
Pindar **12**:375
Sappho **3**:442
Seneca, Lucius Annaeus **6**:447
Sophocles **2**:423

Segal, Erich
Plautus **24**:207

Sei Shonagon
Sei Shonagon **6**:289

Seidenberg, A.
Euclid **25**:179

Seidensticker, Edward
Murasaki, Lady **1**:455

Selincourt, Aubrey de
Greek Historiography **17**:20
Herodotus **17**:90

Sellar, W. Y.
Aeneid **9**:318
Ovid **7**:293
Propertius, Sextus **32**:222

Sellars, Wilfrid
Aristotelian Philosophy **31**:18

Sehmsdorf, Henning K.
Norse Mythology **26**:374

Semple, W. H.
Martial **35**:319

Seneca, Lucius Annaeus, the Elder
Aeneid **9**:294
Ovid **7**:285

Senack, Christine M.
Science **31**:369

Serafini-Sauli, Judith Powers
Boccaccio, Giovanni **13**:84

Setala, E. N.
Kalevala **6**:235

Sewall, Richard B.
The Book of Job **14**:165
Sophocles **2**:388

Sewter, E. R. A.
Anna Comnena **25**:49

Seymour, M. C.
Mandeville, Sir John **19**:128

Shaftesbury, Anthony Earl of
Seneca, Lucius Annaeus **6**:335

Shaw, J. E.
Vita Nuova **18**:331

Shaw, James R.
Albert the Great **16**:81

Shedd, Gordon M.
Sir Gawain and the Green Knight
2:245

Sheldon-Williams, I. P.
Basil of Caesaria **35**:64

Shelley, Percy Bysshe
Aeschylus **11**:89

Shenoy, Anasuya R.
Mahabharata **5**:247

Shepard, G.
Cædmon **7**:97

Sheppard, J. T.
Aeschylus **11**:126
Euripides **23**:107

Sherley-Price, Leo
Bede **20**:60

Shippey, T. A.
Beowulf **1**:146

Shirazi, J. K. M.
Khayyam **11**:268

Shklar, Judith N.
Hesiod **5**:128

Shorey, Paul
Plato **8**:262

Showerman, Grant
Cicero, Marcus Tullius **3**:203

Shumway, Daniel Bussier
Gottfried von Strassburg **10**:250

Shutt, R. J. H.
Josephus, Flavius **13**:235, 267

Sidney, Sir Philip
The Book of Psalms **4**:351
Xenophon **17**:351

Sighart, Joachim
Albert the Great **16**:3

Sigurdsson, Gísli
Norse Mythology **26**:380

Sikes, E. E.
Aeneid **9**:329
Lucan **33**:335

Simmons, Merle E.
Poem of the Cid **4**:310

Simonides
Sophocles **2**:290

Singer, Carl S.
Das Nibelungenlied **12**:211

Singer, Charles
Hildegard von Bingen **20**:131

Singleton, Charles S.
Inferno **3**:102
Vita Nuova **18**:339

Singleton, Mack
Poem of the Cid **4**:254

Sipe, A. W. Richard
St. Benedict of Nursia **29**:71

Siraisi, Nancy G.
Avicenna **16**:171

Sisam, Kenneth
Beowulf **1**:121

Sismondi, J. C. L. Simonde de
Bertran de Born **5**:8

Sjoestedt, Marie-Louise
Celtic Mythology **26**:48

Skinner, John V.
Meister Eckhart **9**:54

Slater, Anne Saxon
Hrafnkel's Saga **2**:104

Slater, Niall W.
Petronius **34**:417

Small, Stuart G. P.
Catullus **18**:167

Smart, J. S.

Ossian **28**:318

Smertenko, Johan J.
Li Po **2**:135

Smiley, Charles N.
Hesiod **5**:85

Smith, Adam
Sophocles **2**:293

Smith, Colin
Poem of the Cid **4**:277, 316

Smith, Huston
Meister Eckhart **9**:66

Smith, J. C.
Beowulf **1**:90

Smith, J. M. Powis
The Book of Psalms **4**:375

Smith, Justin H.
Bertran de Born **5**:18

Smith, Kirby Flower
Martial **35**:270

Smith, Morton
Josephus, Flavius **13**:290

Smith, Robert W.
Origen **19**:230

Smyth, Herbert Weir
Aeschylus **11**:120
Sappho **3**:434

Smythe, Barbara
Bertran de Born **5**:23

Snavely, Guy
Aesop **24**:14

Snell, Bruno
Aristophanes **4**:120
Callimachus **18**:21
Pindar **12**:275
Sappho **3**:417

Solomos, Alexis
Aristophanes **4**:153

Solmsen, Friedrich
Propertius, Sextus **32**:256

Sonstroem, David
Khayyam **11**:292

Sørensen, Villy
Seneca, Lucius Annaeus **6**:418

Soulen, Richard N.
Song of Songs **18**:256

Southern, R. W.
Abelard **11**:33
Bede **20**:46

Spaeth, John W., Jr.
Martial **35**:289, 294

Spearing, A. C.
Pearl **19**:349
Sir Gawain and the Green Knight **2**:248

Spector, Sheila A.
Bevis of Hampton **35**:183

Speirs, John
Sir Gawain and the Green Knight **2**:188

Spence, Sarah
Aeneid **9**:442

Spender, Stephen
Sophocles **2**:427

Spenser, Edmund
Arthurian Legend **10**:61

Spiegel, Harriet
Marie de France **8**:189

Sponsler, Lucy A.
Poem of the Cid **4**:293

Sprague, Rosemary
Hroswitha of Gandersheim **29**:115

Spretnak, Charlene
Greek Mythology **26**:294

Springer, Otto
Wolfram von Eschenbach **5**:321

St. Bernard of Clairvaux
Song of Songs **18**:217

St. Gregory of Nyssa
Song of Songs **18**:212

Stablein, Patricia H.
Bertran de Born **5**:61

Stace, W. T.
Epicurus **21**:128

Staines, David
Chretien de Troyes **10**:218
Havelok **34**:200

Staley, Lynn
Pearl **19**:371

Stanbury, Sarah
Pearl **19**:379

Stanford, W. B.
Odyssey **16**:247
Sappho **3**:415

Stanton, Elizabeth Cady
Song of Songs **18**:245

Stapylton, Robert
Juvenal **8**:3

Starkie, Walter
Poem of the Cid **4**:252

Ste. Croix, G. E. M. de

Thucydides **17**:296

Steele, R. B.
Livy **11**:315

Steele, Robert
Bacon, Roger **14**:45

Stehle, Eva
Sappho **3**:469

Steiner, George
Iliad **1**:368

Steiner, Grundy
Pliny the Elder **23**:328

Steiner, Rudolf
Bhagavad Gita **12**:7

Stendhal
Arabian Nights **2**:6

Steneck, Nicholas H.
Albert the Great **16**:103

Stenton, F. M.
Bede **20**:34

Stephens, Anna Cox
Kalevala **6**:228

Stephens, J. N.
Bede **20**:106

Stephens, Wade C.
Ovid **7**:337

Stephenson, William E.
Apuleius **1**:29

Stevens, John
Marie de France **8**:137

Stevenson, James A.C.
Barbour, John **33**:213

Stewart, Douglas J.
Hesiod **5**:118, 124

Stinton, T. C. W.
Phaedrus **25**:363

Stone, Brian
Arthurian Legend **10**:85

Stone, Charles J.
Mahabharata **5**:179

Stone, Edward Noble
Mystery of Adam **4**:190

Strachan-Davidson, J. L.
Polybius **17**:150

Strahan, James
The Book of Job **14**:144

Strauss, Leo
Xenophon **17**:331

Studer, Paul
Mystery of Adam **4**:186

Stump, Eleonore
Aquinas, St. Thomas **33**:69
The Book of Job **14**:138

Sueltzer, Alexa
Torah **30**:253

Suetonius
Terence **14**:339

Suhm, P. A.
Njals saga **13**:330

Sukthankar, V. S.
Mahabharata **5**:225

Sullivan, J. P.
Martial **35**:372
Petronius **34**:323, 336
Propertius, Sextus **32**:281

Sumer, Faruk
Book of Dede Korkut **8**:98

Suso, Henry
Meister Eckhart **9**:7, 8

Sutton, Dana Ferrin
Aristophanes **4**:162
Terence **14**:393

Suzuki, Daisetz Teitaro
Lieh Tzu **27**:95
Meister Eckhart **9**:49

Sveinsson, Einar Ólafur
Njals saga **13**:347

Swann, Bruce W.
Martial **35**:409

Swanton, Michael
Layamon **10**:350

Swinburne, Algernon Charles
Aristophanes **4**:57
Sappho **3**:392

Syme, Ronald
Cicero, Marcus Tullius **3**:222

Symonds, John Addington
Aeschylus **11**:99
Aristophanes **4**:58
Boccaccio, Giovanni **13**:26
Hesiod **5**:74
Pindar **12**:261
Sappho **3**:385

Symons, Arthur
Augustine, St. **6**:16

Syrianus
Hermogenes **6**:158

Taber, John A.
Sankara **32**:327

Tagore, Rabindranath
Kalidasa **9**:92

Taine, H. A.
The Song of Roland **1**:162

TaMaKH, R. Abraham b. Isaac ha-Levi
Song of Songs **18**:226

Tambling, Jeremy
Inferno **3**:158

Tate, Allen
Inferno **3**:112

Tatlock, John S. P.
Layamon **10**:318, 349

Tatum, James
Plautus **24**:229

Taylor, A. E.
Epicurus **21**:116
Socrates **27**:293

Taylor, Beverly
Arthurian Legend **10**:74

Taylor, Henry Osborn
Bacon, Roger **14**:16
Inferno **3**:55
Wolfram von Eschenbach **5**:302

Taylor, Mary-Agnes
Aesop **24**:68

Taylor, Paul B.
Norse Mythology **26**:348

Taylor, Thomas
Apuleius **1**:12

Ten Brink, Bernard
Cædmon **7**:80

Tennyson, Alfred Lord
Aeneid **9**:317
Arabian Nights **2**:6
Arthurian Legend **10**:64, 90

Terrien, Samuel
The Book of Job **14**:162

Tessitore, Aristide
Aristotelian Philosophy **31**:88

Thackeray, H. St. John
Josephus, Flavius **13**:206

Theisen, Jerome
St. Benedict of Nursia **29**:80

Theisen, Wilfred
Euclid **25**:198

Thierry, Augustin
Bertran de Born **5**:9

Thomas, Calvin
Gottfried von Strassburg **10**:254
Das Nibelungenlied **12**:160

Thomas, R. George
Hrafnkel's Saga **2**:116

Thomas, R. S. D.
Euclid **25**:258

Thompson, Lynette
Lucan **33**:374

Thompson, Maurice
Sappho **3**:386

Thompson, Raymond H.
Chretien de Troyes **10**:197

Thompson, Wesley E.
Polybius **17**:198

Thomson, Derick S.
Ossian **28**:337

Thoreau, Henry D.
Aeschylus **11**:91
Iliad **1**:296

Thorndike, Lynn
Albert the Great **16**:7
Bacon, Roger **14**:48

Thornley, George
Longus **7**:216

Thorpe, Benjamin
Cædmon **7**:78

Thorpe, Lewis
Map, Walter **32**:104

Thucydides
Herodotus **17**:90

Ticknor, George
Poem of the Cid **4**:228

Tierney, Brian
William of Ockham **32**:195

Tigay, Jeffrey H.
Epic of Gilgamesh **3**:349

Tillyard, E. M. W.
Aeneid **9**:384
Beowulf **1**:111
Boccaccio, Giovanni **13**:43
Herodotus **17**:77
Iliad **1**:348
Odyssey **16**:243
The Song of Roland **1**:180

Timothy, H. B.
Tertullian **29**:353

Tobin, Frank J.
Hartmann von Aue **15**:213, 223

Todd, F. A.
Petronius **34**:297

Todorov, Tzvetan
Arabian Nights **2**:44, 48

Tolkien, J. R. R.
Anglo-Saxon Chronicle **4**:11
Beowulf **1**:80
Sir Gawain and the Green Knight **2**:201

Tolman, Albert H.
Kalevala **6**:231

Tolstoy, Leo
Odyssey **16**:253

Topsfield, L. T.
Chretien de Troyes **10**:201

Torjesen, Karen Jo
Tertullian **29**:375

Tornay, Stephen Chak
Averroes **7**:10

Toy, C. H.
The Book of Job **14**:138

Toynbee, Arnold J.
Greek Historiography **17**:5

Trace, Jacqueline
Barbour, John **33**:176

Tracy, H. L.
Aeschylus **11**:147

Trapp, Joseph
Terence **14**:385

Tress, Daryl McGowan
Science **31**:337

Trevelyan, G. Otto
Ovid **7**:292

Trever, Albert Augustus
Hesiod **5**:88

Trible, Phyllis
Song of Songs **18**:275

Trigg, Joseph W.
Origen **19**:245

Trinkaus, Charles
Petrarch **20**:284

Trollope, Anthony
Cicero, Marcus Tullius **3**:192

Trypanis, C. A.
Sappho **3**:474

Tsanoff, Radoslav
Augustine, St. **6**:41

Tu Fu
Li Po **2**:132

Tugwell, Simon
Albert the Great **16**:115

Turbervile, George
Ovid **7**:290

Turner, Eric G.
Menander **9**:257

Turner, Paul
Longus **7**:235

Turunen, Aimo
Kalevala **6**:258

Turville-Petre, Thorlac
Havelok **34**:240

Twomey, Michael W.
Morte Arthure **10**:425

Tyrwhitt, Thomas
Layamon **10**:311

Uhland, Johann
Bertran de Born **5**:10

Uitti, Karl D.
Chretien de Troyes **10**:190
Romance of the Rose **8**:446
The Song of Roland **1**:243

Urwin, Kenneth
Mystery of Adam **4**:191

Usher, Stephen
Greek Historiography **17**:23

Uysal, Ahmet E.
Book of Dede Korkut **8**:98

Vaidya, C. V.
Mahabharata **5**:189

Valency, Maurice
Vita Nuova **18**:349

Valla, Lorenzo
Cato, Marcus Porcius **21**:4
Epicurus **21**:79

Van Antwerp, Margaret
Razon de Amor **16**:353

Van Buitenen, J. A. B.
Mahabharata **5**:267

Van Buskirk, William R.
Lao Tzu **7**:119

Van Doren, Mark
Aeneid **9**:366
The Book of Psalms **4**:425
Iliad **1**:336
Murasaki, Lady **1**:420
Odyssey **16**:231

Van Nooten, Barend A.
Mahabharata **5**:249

Vance, Eugene
The Song of Roland **1**:214

van Hamel, A. G.
Celtic Mythology **26**:80

Vannovsky, Alexander
Kojiki **21**:244

Vasiliev, A. A.
Anna Comnena **25**:41

Vellacott, Philip
Aeschylus **11**:207

Venables, Edmund
Basil of Caesaria **35**:19

Critic Index

Verdenius, W. J.
Plato **8**:296

Vergil
Aeneid **9**:312, 329

Vergote, Antoine
St. Benedict of Nursia **29**:37

Versenyi, Laszlo
Hesiod **5**:137
Sappho **3**:455

Very, Jones
Homer **1**:292

Vigfusson, Gudbrand
Hrafnkel's Saga **2**:76

Vinaver, Eugene
Arthurian Legend **10**:81
Chretien de Troyes **10**:180
The Song of Roland **1**:234

Vincent, Patrick R.
Bodel, Jean **28**:192

Vittorini, Domenico
Vita Nuova **18**:346

Vivekananda, Swami
Bhagavad Gita **12**:5

Vlastos, Gregory
Socrates **27**:357

Voltaire, François-Marie Arouet
Aeneid **9**:314
Aristophanes **4**:41
The Book of Job **14**:123
Iliad **1**:288

von Fritz, Kurt
Polybius **17**:160

Vos, Arvin
Aquinas, St. Thomas **33**:51

Vossler, Karl
Inferno **3**:51

Wa, Kathleen Johnson
Lao Tzu **7**:196
Vita Nuova **18**:329

Wadell, Paul J.
Aquinas, St. Thomas **33**:99

Wailes, Stephen L.
Das Nibelungenlied **12**:231

Waithe, Mary Ellen
Hypatia **35**:238

Walbank, F. W.
Polybius **17**:167

Waldock, A. J. A.
Sophocles **2**:368

Waley, Arthur
Confucius **19**:17
Lao Tzu **7**:128

Li Po **2**:137
Murasaki, Lady **1**:421

Walhouse, Moreton J.
Sappho **3**:385

Waliszewski, K.
The Igor Tale **1**:479

Walker, Ian C.
Barbour, John **33**:173

Walker, Janet A.
Izumi, Shikibu **33**:307
Izumi, Shikibu **33**:323

Walker, Roger M.
Razon de Amor **16**:346

Walker, Warren S.
Book of Dede Korkut **8**:98

Wallace, David
Boccaccio, Giovanni **13**:87, 94

Wallace, William
Epicurus **21**:101

Wallace-Hadrill, Andrew
Pliny the Elder **23**:355

Wallacker, Benjamin E.
Po Chu-i **24**:366

Walpole, Horace
Arabian Nights **2**:3

Walsh, George B.
Euripides **23**:191
Hesiod **5**:166

Walsh, P. G.
Livy **11**:342, 350

Walsh, W. E.
Ossian **28**:333

Walshe, M. O'C.
Gottfried von Strassburg **10**:274
Das Nibelungenlied **12**:171
Wolfram von Eschenbach **5**:333

Warburton, William
Apuleius **1**:7

Ward, Benedicta
Bede **20**:102
St. Benedict of Nursia **29**:61

Warmington, B. H.
Seneca, Lucius Annaeus **6**:395

Warton, Joseph
Inferno **3**:6

Watling, E. F.
Seneca, Lucius Annaeus **6**:387

Watson, Burton
Si Shih **15**:391

Watson, Nicholas
Rolle, Richard **21**:388

Webbe, Joseph
Terence **14**:296

Webbe, William
Ovid **7**:290

Webber, Ruth H.
Poem of the Cid **4**:286

Weber, Alfred
Bacon, Roger **14**:20

Webster, T. B. L.
Callimachus **18**:34
Menander **9**:246

Wedin, Michael V.
Science **31**:358

Weigand, Hermann J.
Wolfram von Eschenbach **5**:315, 370

Weil, Simone
Iliad **1**:331

Weiler, Royal W.
Kalidasa **9**:113

Weinberg, Julius R.
Averroes **7**:44
Bacon, Roger **14**:94

Weinberg, S. C.
Layamon **10**:360

Weinbrot, Howard D.
Ossian **28**:368

Weiss, Judith
Havelok **34**:184

Weiss, Paul
The Book of Job **14**:157

Welch, Holmes
Lao Tzu **7**:141
Lieh Tzu **27**:104

Wellek, Rene
Pearl **19**:299

Wenley, R. M.
Socrates **27**:217

West, M. L.
Pindar **12**:333

Westcott, John Howell
Livy **11**:312

Westermann, Claus
The Book of Psalms **4**:428

Westlake, John S.
Anglo-Saxon Chronicle **4**:4

Weston, Jessie L.
Arthurian Legend **10**:28
Chretien de Troyes **10**:133
Gottfried von Strassburg **10**:247
Wolfram von Eschenbach **5**:300

Wetherbee, Winthrop
Romance of the Rose **8**:422

Wethered, H. N.
Pliny the Elder **23**:322

Wheeler, Arthur Leslie
Cattullus **18**:82
Propertius, Sextus **32**:248

Whewell, William
Bacon, Roger **14**:3

Whibley, Charles
Apuleius **1**:15

Whigham, Peter
Catullus **18**:109

Whinfield, E. H.
Khayyam **11**:255
Rumi, Jalal al-Din **20**:338

Whipple, T. K.
Martial **35**:283

Whitehead, Alfred North
Plato **8**:271

Whitelock, Dorothy
Beowulf **1**:101

Whitman, Cedric H.
Aristophanes **4**:133
Euripides **23**:177
Iliad **1**:350
Odyssey **16**:254
Sophocles **2**:362

Wicksteed, Philip H.
Inferno **3**:46

Widdows, P. F.
Phaedrus **25**:380
Lucan **33**:413

Wiersma, S.
Longus **7**:274

Wiesen, David S.
St. Jerome **30**:125

Wiggins, David
Heraclitus **22**:166

Wilbur, James B.
Presocratic philosophy **22**:42

Wilczynski, Jan Z.
Al-Biruni **28**:118

Wilhelm, James J.
Bertran de Born **5**:39

Wilhelmsen, Frederick D.
Cicero, Marcus Tullius **3**:274

Wilkins, Nigel
Bodel, Jean **28**:208

Wilkinson, L. P.
Ovid **7**:329

Williams, Harry F.
Chretien de Troyes **10**:225

Willson, H. B.
Gottfried von Strassburg **10**:278
Hartmann von Aue **15**:148, 165,
175, 196

Wilson, Anita C.
Aesop **24**:63

Wilson, B. W. J. G.
Cicero, Marcus Tullius **3**:281

Wilson, Edmund
Sophocles **2**:341

Wilson, Grace G.
Barbour, John **33**:241

Wilson, H. Schutz
Khayyam **11**:238

Wilson, Harry Langford
Juvenal **8**:23

Wilson, James H.
Cynewulf **23**:49

Wilson, R. M.
Layamon **10**:335

Windelband, Wilhelm
Abelard **11**:3
Augustine, St. **6**:11
Averroes **7**:6

Winkler, John J.
Apuleius **1**:47

Winnington-Ingram, R. P.
Aeschylus **11**:206
Sophocles **2**:415

Winternitz, Moriz
Mahabharata **5**:202

Wiseman, T. P.
Catullus **18**:148

Witte, Karl
Inferno **3**:41

Wittgenstein, Ludwig
Augustine, St. **6**:55

Wittig, Joseph
Cynewulf **23**:66

Wixted, John Timothy
Kokinshu **29**:245

Wolf, Carol Jean
The Dream of the Rood **14**:280

Wolff, Hope Nash
Epic of Gilgamesh **3**:328

Wolfram von Eschenbach
Wolfram von Eschenbach **5**:292,
293

Wolfskeel, Cornelia

St. Catherine **27**:15

Wolpert, Stanley
Mahabharata **5**:281

Wood, Anthony à
Bacon, Roger **14**:3

Woodman, A. J.
Livy **11**:382

Woodruff, F. Winthrop
Bacon, Roger **14**:66

Woodruff, Paul
Plato **8**:364

Woods, Earl R.
William of Ockham **32**:144

Woolf, Rosemary
The Dream of the Rood **14**:230
Rolle, Richard **21**:355

Woolf, Virginia
Aeschylus **11**:126
Murasaki, Lady **1**:418
Sappho **3**:395
Sophocles **2**:326

Wooten, Cecil W.
Demosthenes **13**:189
Hermogenes **6**:202

Woozley, A. D.
Socrates **27**:341

Wordsworth, William
Arabian Nights **2**:5
Sophocles **2**:304

Wrenn, C. L.
Anglo-Saxon Chronicle **4**:13
Beowulf **1**:107
Cædmon **7**:93

Wright, F. A.
Ovid **7**:304
Sappho **3**:396

Wright, Henry Parks
Juvenal **8**:22

Wright, Thomas
Polo, Marco **15**:261
Map, Walter **32**:70

Wyckoff, Dorothy
Albert the Great **16**:54

Yeats, W. B.
Celtic Mythology **26**:22

Yoshikawa, Kojiro
Su Shih **15**:410

Young, Karl
Mystery of Adam **4**:190

Yourcenar, Marguerite
Murasaki, Lady **1**:455

Yousofi, Gholam Hosein

Rumi, Jalal al-Din **20**:373

Youssefi, G. H.
Al-Biruni **28**:154

Yutang, Lin
Confucius **19**:25
Lao Tzu **7**:135

Zacher, Christian K.
Mandeville, Sir John **19**:131

Zaehner, R. C.
Bhagavad Gita **12**:67
Mahabharata **5**:243

Zaenker, Karl A.
Hroswitha of Gandersheim **29**:144

Zahm, John A.
Hypatia **35**:211

Zahniser, A. H. Mathias
Al-Jahiz **25**:271, 276

Zanker, G.
Callimachus **18**:50

Zedler, Beatrice H.
Averroes **7**:22

Zegveld, André
St. Benedict of Nursia **29**:52

Zeitlin, Froma I.
Petronius **34**:363

Zeller, Eduard
Epicurus **21**:97
Presocratic philosophy **22**:25
Socrates **27**:207

Zeydel, Edwin H.
Gottfried von Strassburg **10**:258
Wolfram von Eschenbach **5**:307

Zhirmunsky, Victor
Book of Dede Korkut **8**:96

Zimmer, Heinrich
Arabian Nights **2**:32
Bhagavad Gita **12**:45
Sir Gawain and the Green Knight
2:187

Zweig, Stefan
Cicero, Marcus Tullius **3**:225

ISBN 0-7876 -3257-0